VISUAL C++ 5.0
Developer's Guide

David Bennett, et al.

SAMS
PUBLISHING

201 West 103rd Street
Indianapolis, Indiana 46290

International Standard Book Number: 0-672-31031-7

Library of Congress Catalog Card Number: 96-67201

2000   99   98   97   4   3   2   1

Interpretation of the printing code: the rightmost double-digit number is the year of the book's printing; the rightmost single-digit, the number of the book's printing. For example, a printing code of 97-1 shows that the first printing of the book occurred in 1997.

Composed in AGaramond and MCPdigital by Macmillan Computer Publishing

Printed in the United States of America

President, Sams Publishing	*Richard K. Swadley*
Publishing Manager	*Greg Wiegand*
Director of Marketing	*Kelli S. Spencer*
Product Marketing Managers	*Wendy Gilbride*
	Kim Margolius
Associate Product Marketing Manager	*Jennifer Pock*
Marketing Coordinator	*Linda Beckwith*

Acquisitions Editors
Sherry Prier
Matthew Purcell

Development Editors
Anthony Amico
Fran Hatton

Production Editor
Mary Inderstrodt

Indexer
Erika Millen

Technical Reviewer
Larry Richardson

Editorial Coordinators
Mandie Rowell
Katie Wise

Technical Edit Coordinator
Lynette Quinn

Resource Coordinator
Deborah Frisby

Editorial Assistants
Carol Ackerman
Andi Richter
Rhonda Tinch-Mize

Cover Designer
Alyssa Yesh

Book Designer
Alyssa Yesh

Copy Writer
David Reichwein

Production Team Supervisor
Brad Chinn

Production
Georgiana Briggs
Michael Dietsch
Shawn Ring
Mary Ellen Stephenson

Overview

II General MFC Programming

III   Programming with ActiveX

IV Network Programming with Win32

VI Multimedia, OpenGL, and DirectX

Acknowledgments

I would like to thank Vladi Kelman and Isaac Shpantzer for helping me find the time to work on this book, as well as everyone else at Racotek for their comments, suggestions, and advice—and for putting up with me while I was working on this.

I would also like to send a big thanks to Jim Nord, who not only helped out with several of the chapters in this book, but was also gracious enough to tolerate my clomping around his house at all hours of the night while I was writing this. Hopefully, now that I'm finished writing, he'll actually get to spend an evening alone with his bride-to-be. Thanks for your patience, Molly.

Thanks are also due to all of the folks behind the scenes at Sams—particularly Sherry Prier, for asking me to write this book; Tony Amico, for helping me get started; and Matt Purcell and Greg Wiegand, for all their support.

I'd also like to thank Don Willits of Microsoft for helping out with the bleeding edge of ADO.

Thanks to everyone else, particularly anyone I have left out, who has helped out with this project!

About the Authors

David Bennett currently develops network management software for Racotek, Inc., which provides software and services for wireless mobile data networks. He has been developing desktop software for the last 16 years in industries ranging from healthcare to Las Vegas casinos to the spy business—and has been using Microsoft compilers, APIs, and libraries since the first release of Microsoft C. Along the way, he picked up a B.S. in computer science from Southern Methodist University.

When not stuck behind a keyboard and monitor, David plays rugby for the St. Paul Jazz Pigs, and is still learning to play the guitars he keeps collecting. If you don't run into him on the pitch, in a pub, or in a newsgroup, you might find him on a Quake server near you.

Stephen Makonin currently works as an Information Systems contractor for BC Tel Mobility, using Visual Basic, C, and MS SQL Server (and soon Java). On the side, he programs multimedia applications and games. He has a degree in Business Management and Computer Science. He started programming in Basic when he was 13 years old and progressed to Clipper, Pascal, C, and Assembly. His company has just joined with Sony to become a registered Net Yarose (PlayStation) developer, and he is in the process of working on a game demo with DirectX. Game programming is his main hobby. He also likes tinkering with music. He takes professional voice lessons and enjoys various outdoor activities such as hiking.

Vincent (Vinny) W. Mayfield lives in Niceville, Florida with his faithful yellow Labrador retriever named Gunner. Vinny is a Senior Software Engineer and a Microsoft Certified Professional with more than ten years experience developing software and more than five years developing Windows-based applications with C and C++. He has served in the U.S. Army Reserves and the U.S. Air Force. Vinny is a Senior Software Engineer and Project Manager for BTG, Inc., Delta Research Division, in Niceville, Florida. With BTG, Vincent is developing Microsoft Windows–based applications with Visual C++, MFC, and Oracle. Vincent is a co-author of *ActiveX Programming Unleashed,* Sams Publishing, 1996. He has also done freelance technical consulting with his own company, V Max Technical Solutions as well as technical editing on numerous books for Macmillan Publishing. Vinny is an FAA Commercial Instrument–rated pilot. When not punching holes in the sky or pounding the keyboard, Vinny enjoys spoiling his two nieces Kaitlyn and Mary and his nephew Anthony. In addition, Vinny is a Star Trek fanatic, an aviation enthusiast, a military history buff, and enjoys roughing it in the great outdoors. Vinny hold a B.S. in Mathematics with Minors in Computer Science and Aerospace Science as well as an M.S. in International Relations.

Ted Neustaedter is a software developer in Vancouver, British Columbia, Canada, and works on a contract basis. His expertise is in the areas of Visual C/C++, Visual Basic, OLE/ActiveX, and ODBC. Send e-mail to ted@neumark.com or visit his Web site at http://www.neumark.com.

Mark R. Wrenn is President of SockSoft Corporation (www.socksoft.com), a company specializing in writing software for Windows 95, Windows NT, and the Internet using Visual C++. Mark has more than 15 years of experience as a developer in both the vendor and customer environments. He has led software development teams in the development of both GUI and server software including, most recently, the development of firewall technology for NT. Mark resides in Southern California and is always looking for interesting projects to work on. He can be reached at mrwrenn@socksoft.com.

Tell Us What You Think!

As a reader, you are the most important critic and commentator of our books. We value your opinion and want to know what we're doing right, what we could do better, what areas you'd like to see us publish in, and any other words of wisdom you're willing to pass our way. You can help us make strong books that meet your needs and give you the computer guidance you require.

Do you have access to the World Wide Web? Then check out our site at http://www.mcp.com.

> **NOTE**
>
> If you have a technical question about this book, call the technical support line at 317-581-3833 or send e-mail to support@mcp.com.

As the team leader of the group that created this book, I welcome your comments. You can fax, e-mail, or write me directly to let me know what you did or didn't like about this book—as well as what we can do to make our books stronger. Here's the information:

Fax: 317-581-4669

E-mail: programming_mgr@sams.mcp.com

Mail: Greg Wiegand
         Comments Department
         Sams Publishing
         201 W. 103rd Street
         Indianapolis, IN 46290

Introduction

How To Use This Book

You probably won't want to curl up by the fire and read this cover to cover. (The ending isn't really much of a surprise.) Most readers will read certain sections pertaining to their current interests and refer to the text for reference. We have, however, tried to organize the subjects so that they build on one another. If you are new to Windows programming, you might want to read through Part I and play around with some of the examples before moving on to the more specific topics such as database programming.

What You Need To Use This Book

Although you might have just picked up this book for a little light reading, I have assumed that you will be doing development for Windows 95 or Windows NT 4.0 using Visual C++ 5.0. To build and run the examples on the CD, you will need the following:

> Windows 95 or Windows NT 4.0 (Workstation or Server)
>
> Visual C++ 5.0
>
> A computer to run it on

I know this last item is a bit fuzzy. Windows 95 (and Visual C++) will run on a 25Mhz 486 with 8MB of RAM and 200MB of hard disk space. However, if you are doing real development every day, you will certainly want to upgrade, particularly in RAM and hard disk space.

Windows NT will not run on less than 12MB of RAM, and we recommend at least 32MB for good performance. We would also recommend at least 1G of hard disk space. With just Windows NT, Microsoft Office, Visual C++, and the various SDKs you will use here, a full install including examples and online documentation nearly fills a 950MB partition. Of course, you will most likely not use all of this stuff and can save on disk space, but it is mighty handy to have around.

As far as processor speed goes, my 200Mhz Pentium with 48MB of RAM is nice, but I routinely use a 486/66 with 32MB of RAM that is quite adequate.

Windows NT and Visual C++ also run on non-Intel platforms including DEC Alpha and MIPS machines, which will have different requirements.

Windows 95 Versus Windows NT 4.0

This book talks about developing Applications for Win32, which includes Windows 95 and Windows NT 4.0. With the 4.0 release of Windows NT, the user interface is the same for WinNT and Win95, but there are several important differences in the underlying operating systems.

In general, Windows 95 is a compromise between NT, the industrial-strength operating system, requiring industrial-strength resources and traditional DOS/Windows 3.1, which required less expensive hardware and could be run on almost any machine—but was not a full-featured, multiprocessing, 32-bit operating system. (Heck, Win3.1 isn't really an operating system at all, just a shell above DOS.)

However, Windows 95 is not just a subset of NT; it also includes some elements not found in NT. For starters, unlike Win95, Windows NT does not go out of its way to support 16-bit application compatibility. True, you can run many DOS or 16-bit windows applications on NT, but anything that violates NT security rules just won't go. This includes most DOS and 16-bit Windows games that access hardware directly.

Furthermore, because Windows 95 was marketed more to the home market, it was the operating system that DirectX and the games SDK was first developed for. Most of these components have been moved to NT as well, but there are still some issues that we will discuss when we talk about the DirectX APIs.

The majority of the subjects and APIs discussed in this book will work the same on Win95 and WinNT. I will try to mention any specific differences in the sections dealing with the particular areas that are different.

What's New in Visual C++ 5.0

Visual C++ Version 5.0 has added many new features since the last general release (4.0). These include the following:

General

- Standard C++ library:

    Visual C++ now includes headers and libraries for the ANSI standard C++ extensions, including the Standard Template Library.

- Small block heap manager:

    The C runtime library has changed memory management routines for Win32 to use a more efficient heap manager for small allocations.

■ Win32s no longer supported:

Beginning with 4.2, Win32s is no longer supported by Visual C++.

MFC

■ Internet programming support:

MFC now wraps ActiveX and Win32 Internet (WinInet) technology to simplify Internet programming.

■ New MFC classes and functions:

4.2 added 22 classes and 40 member functions.

■ MFC browse information

A browse information file (MFC.BSC) is included to simplify browsing of the MFC source.

Internet

■ Internet Server API classes:

MFC has added five classes and an AppWizard for the Internet Server API (ISAPI).

■ World Wide Web access:

The Developer Studio now allows direct access to the World Wide Web from within Developer Studio.

ActiveX

■ Wizard changes:

Visual C++ has added several features to the wizards to simplify ActiveX programming.

Database

■ ODBC enhancements:

MFC ODBC classes now support multithreading and bulk row fetching. Transaction support has also been improved.

■ Remote data binding:

Visual C++ includes controls that can bind to local or remote data sources, including ActiveX data sources.

Graphics

■ Open Inventor 3D tools and IVF AppWizard:

Tools from Template Graphics Software, Inc., have been included.

Miscellaneous

- Improved Image Editor:
  The Visual C++ Image Editor can now work with both GIF and JPEG files.
- New examples:
  4.2 added 13 new MFC examples.
- Win32 SDK documentation:
  The Win32 documentation has been updated to include NT 4.0.

Contacting the Main Author

If you have specific questions or comments about the material covered in this book, or problems with the examples included, you may contact me at `bennettd@wavefront.com`. Please keep in mind that I am not Microsoft support. If you have general questions about something you are writing or about how Visual C++ works, please do not e-mail me. You will get much better response for these issues from the various newsgroups and other sources listed in Appendix A, "Additional Resources."

I

Visual C++ 5.0 Environment

1

Visual C++ Environment

by David Bennett

Although Visual C++ is first and foremost a C++ compiler, it also offers a complete development environment made up of many components that work together to simplify the development process. Many of the features of this environment will be familiar to you; after all, some basic features are ones that any integrated development environment is expected to provide. However, many of the features of the development environment are unique to Visual C++ and might seem a bit foreign at first, but you will soon see that these features can significantly improve your productivity.

In this chapter, you will take a tour of all of the components that make up the Visual C++ Environment. You will examine the Developer Studio and the tools it offers to simplify your development tasks, including the Resource editors, Application Wizard, and ClassWizard. You will also take a look at some of the other utilities included with Visual C++ to make your life as a developer a little easier.

For a complete reference on every menu, button, or other widget in the IDE, see the online help. I will try to cover the basics and point out some of the most interesting or useful features of the development environment, but won't be rehashing the whole user's guide.

Developer Studio

Visual C++ 5.0 includes the Microsoft Developer Studio Integrated Development Environment (IDE). This environment is the centerpiece of most any interaction you will have with your C++ projects, including source file creation, resource editing, compiling, linking, debugging, and many other useful features. Developer Studio allows seamless integration of other Microsoft products, including MS Fortran Power Station, MS Visual Test, the MS Development Library, and Visual J++.

In the bad old days, all C files, resource files, help files, and everything else had to be created with one or more editors. Then, each object or resource had to be compiled with its own flavor of compiler, with its own set of switches and options. Then the whole darn thing had to be linked to create an application. Running and debugging an application involved several other steps and utilities. The only truly integrated development environment at that time was DOS DEBUG—of course, only if you were writing in machine language and entering a byte or so at a time.

Several compiler vendors started making integrated development environments, which allowed editing and compiling source in one application or shell, but still required several other functions to be performed outside of the IDE, not to mention the fact that you had to move in and out of the IDE to debug your application. This switching back and forth could quickly consume a big chunk of your development time.

The Developer Studio included with Visual C++ 5.0 allows you to perform everything you need to do throughout the life of your application, without ever leaving the IDE. Developer Studio also includes several features that will make your development tasks much simpler.

When you first start Microsoft Developer Studio, you should see a screen similar to the one in Figure 1.1, although you won't have an open project if this is your first time.

> **NOTE**
>
> Microsoft Developer Studio should be added to your start menu under Programs | Microsoft Visual C++ 5.0—or, if you prefer, create a shortcut to `\Devstudio\SharedIDE\Bin\Msdev.exe`. (Gee, it's nice to finally have a desktop in NT!)

FIGURE 1.1.

Microsoft Developer Studio.

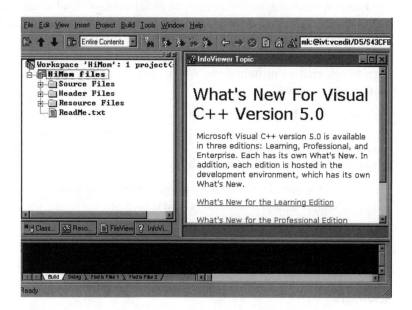

Figure 1.1 shows an example of the windows that you might have open. Unfortunately, production of this book requires standard VGA mode screen shots, so some of the things you see here might appear a bit crowded. If you plan to do much work with Visual C++, you will probably want to use a higher resolution. I find that a 17-inch monitor at 1280×1024 is well worth the cost of the hardware.

> **TIP**
>
> Feel free to try out your own projects in Developer Studio now if you like, but for the rest of this chapter, you might want to install the examples from the CD-ROM and open the HiMom (an MFC version of HelloWorld) example to follow along. You can open an existing workspace by choosing the Open Workspace command from the File

menu. (Note that this is different from the Open command on the File menu.) You can open the HiMom example by opening the file HiMom.dsw, located in the Chapter 1 samples directory on the CD-ROM. Most of the features of Developer Studio are not activated until you have opened a workspace.

View Windows

In addition to the windows for your source files, Developer Studio uses several view windows to present useful information at various stages in project development. When starting a project, you will probably be most interested in the Workspace, InfoViewer Topic, and Output windows, shown in Figure 1.1. Developer Studio also provides separate windows for various debugging information including the Watch, Variables, Registers, Memory, Call Stack, and Disassembly windows.

Each of these windows can be moved around in the workspace in different ways. By default, these windows will dock to an edge of your screen. If you double-click the frame of a docked window, it will undock, and you can freely place it where you like. You can even drag it outside of the Developer Studio window by holding Ctrl while you drag.

However, you might find the docking feature annoying. The window will try to dock when you don't want it to, and it will always float on top of your source windows. You can disable the docking view for each window from the Workspace tab of the Options dialog found on the Tools menu. This will make the view window act just like a regular source code window, which also means you will no longer be able to drag it outside the Developer Studio frame.

Toolbars

You will notice that several different toolbars are used in Developer Studio. Most of these will normally dock at the top of the window, although you may drag the frame of the toolbar anywhere you like. You can attach the toolbar to any edge of the frame or you can just leave it floating around somewhere.

TIP

If you are unsure about what a tool does, hold the mouse pointer over it and a brief description, or tool tip, will pop up, telling you what the tool does.

Many toolbars are not normally displayed. Sometimes these will pop up at appropriate times, such as the Resource toolbar, when you edit resources. At any time, you can select the toolbars you want to be displayed by right-clicking an empty area of Developer Studio (like an unused portion of the menu bar area). You may select the toolbars that are displayed from the Toolbars page of the dialog that is presented by the Customize command on the Tools menu. You may also select which toolbars are displayed by right-clicking in the toolbar area. The New button in the Toolbars dialog will allow you to create your own custom toolbars. To add buttons to a toolbar, go to the Commands tab of the Customize dialog and drag the desired tools from the Commands tab to the new toolbar. You might need to move the Customize dialog out of the way to see the new toolbar.

Project Workspace

Working with the Developer Studio is based on working with Project workspaces. These workspaces represent a particular set of projects, which can represent anything from a single application, to a function library, to an entire suite of applications. Each workspace may include any number of different projects that you want to group into a single workspace so that you can work closely with each separate project at the same time.

The project workspace (.dsw) file is responsible for maintaining all of the information that defines your workspace and the projects that you have included in it. Previously, you might have used make (.mak) files to maintain projects and the processes involved in creating your applications. Developer Studio 5.0 does not create .mak files by default anymore, although you can force Developer Studio to create a makefile based on current project settings by using the Export Makefile command from the Project menu. This is useful if you are using .mak files to automate your builds outside of Developer Studio.

In addition to makefile-type information about your projects, the project workspace file includes information about the settings you have chosen for Developer Studio itself. This means that whenever you open a project workspace, all of the Developer Studio settings that you had when you last worked with this workspace will be restored. All of the windows that you had open before will also be opened and returned to their previous position in the workspace.

You can create a new, empty workspace using the Workspaces tab of the File | New dialog. However, an empty workspace isn't generally of much use. You may create a new workspace whenever you create a new project from the Projects tab of the File | New dialog. This will present you with several different choices, as shown in Figure 1.2.

When you create a new project, Visual C++ will set up default build settings for the type of project you specify here. You may also start up one of the Application Wizards from this dialog. You will see exactly what each of these project types will do for you later in this chapter.

With all of this talk about workspaces, perhaps you would expect that Developer Studio would provide a nice graphical interface to this information. Well, sure enough, it does—the Workspace window.

FIGURE 1.2.
New project dialog.

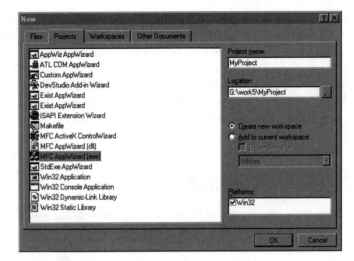

The Workspace Window

When you open a project workspace you should see the Workspace window. If you do not, it was hidden the last time the workspace was open and can be brought to the foreground by selecting the Workspace command from the View menu or simply by pressing Alt-0. This window provides a road map to your projects that allows you to quickly navigate to where you need to go to do the real work of developing your application. You will notice that there are four tabs on the bottom of the window that allow you to view different sorts of information about your projects.

The InfoView gives quick access to the online documentation and has a very intuitive interface. We will leave the InfoView at that and move on to the good stuff, starting with the FileView.

The FileView

You will notice immediately that the FileView will let you view the list of files in your projects, hence the name. What might not be quite so obvious is the fact that it provides a great deal of functionality designed to help you manage your files and projects. Although many workspaces include only a single project, you will see later that you can add any number of projects to a workspace. The FileView will display each project as a different top-level folder that can be expanded just like any other tree control in Windows. The FileView window for the HiMom example is shown in Figure 1.3.

Any files that you create within Developer Studio will be automatically added to your project, so you need to be concerned only with adding files that you have created yourself, outside of Developer Studio. This can include documentation or existing source files that you want to manage as part of your project.

FIGURE 1.3.

*FileView for the
HiMom example.*

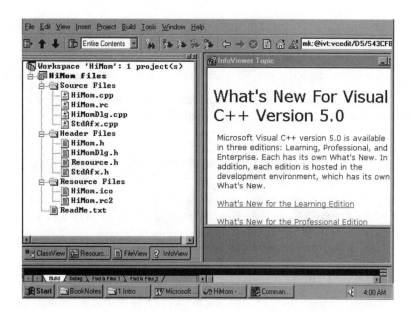

Note that you should not include any of the standard libraries in your project. You should, however, include any libraries that will be built by your project so that the build process can check to see if that library should be rebuilt in order to bring the project up-to-date. Libraries to be included in a project may be specified in the Link tab of the Project Settings dialog (from the Project ¦ Settings menu command).

FileView allows you to drag and drop files to add them to your project or to move or copy them between your projects. If you want to delete a file from your project, simply select the file and press the Delete key. This will not actually delete the file, but will remove it from your project.

FileView will show an icon next to each filename. These icons can give you additional information about the file. For instance, if the icon has a down arrow on it, this file will be used in building the current configuration. In addition, certain add-on products may alter these icons. For example, if you have a source code control system installed, the icon might have a checkmark to denote that you have the file checked out.

You can open a file for editing by double-clicking it. You can also bring up a context menu by right-clicking the file. This gives you several other options, depending on the type of file you selected. Any version of the context menu will allow you to go to the Project Settings dialog by selecting the Settings command.

The context menu will allow you to view a file's Properties dialog, which is different for different file types, but will generally list information about the file, its inputs, outputs, and dependencies. This can be useful in making sure that the files in your project are being put together the way they should.

For source files, the context menu will give you the option to compile that file. Similarly, the context menu for a project will allow you to build the project. You can also use the Set as Active Project command to set it as the default project. For workspaces that contain more than one project, the active project is used whenever you build, execute, or debug.

You may also delete any intermediate files in a project by choosing the Clean command from the project's context menu. This is particularly useful when you see the amount of disk space that even simple projects may take up.

TIP

It is a good idea to delete intermediate files from a project before trying to back it up. Some of the intermediate files can become very large, even for small projects.

The ClassView

As the name suggests, the ClassView displays a tree view of the classes that you have created for your project and allows you to expand the classes to reveal their member functions and variables. The ClassView for the HiMom application is shown in Figure 1.4.

FIGURE 1.4.

ClassView for HiMom project.

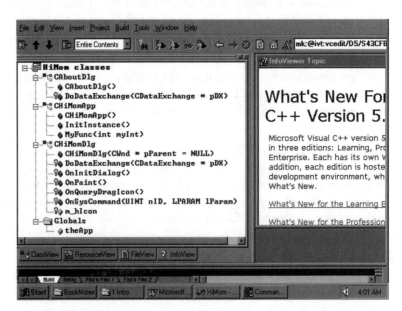

You will notice that each of the class members has one or more icons to the left of it; these give useful information about the member type (data or function) and access class. (Protected members have a key, private members have a padlock, and public members have no access icon.)

You can directly access the source code for your classes by double-clicking the object that you are interested in. Double-clicking a class will immediately open the header file for the class and position the cursor at the start of the class declaration. Double-clicking a member variable will position the cursor on the declaration of the member variable. Double-clicking a member function will take you straight to the function definition, or implementation.

The context menu for a class allows several different choices for you to jump to the more powerful source code browser to examine how a class is used. Choices include direct access to the definitions and references for the class, as well as lists of any base classes and derived classes associated with this class.

The context menu also allows a quick way to add member functions or variables by way of a simple dialog, shown in Figure 1.5.

FIGURE 1.5.
Add Member Function
dialog.

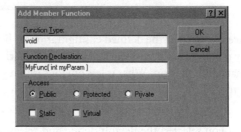

Project Configurations

Visual C++ allows you to work with different build configurations for each project. As long as you are producing the same executable filename (or library), you may select from any number of configurations to determine how the project will be built. Whenever you create a new workspace in Developer Studio, two default configurations will be created for you: one for debug and one for release. The debug configuration will build in many different debugging features that will not be compiled when building release configurations.

You can select a configuration to be the default configuration used for builds from several different places, including the configuration combo box on the Build toolbar, the context menu from FileView, or the Set Active Configuration command from the Build menu. If you want to add or delete configurations, you can do so from the Configurations command from the Build menu.

Project Settings

Each configuration allows you to choose from a wide range of different project settings, appropriately handled by the Project Settings dialog, shown in Figure 1.6. The Project Settings dialog is started from the Settings command of either the Project menu or the FileView context menu.

FIGURE 1.6.
Project Settings dialog.

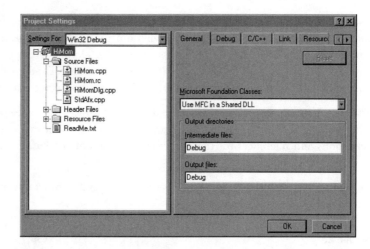

You will notice that each of the defined configurations is listed in the Settings For combo box. It seems fairly obvious that if you selected one configuration, you would be working with the settings for that configuration. What is less obvious is that you can select several configurations at the same time. In this case, you will be presented with the settings that are *common to both projects*.

For example, if you selected the default debug and release configurations, you would not see the Output directories on the General page. This is because each of the configurations has different settings for these fields. If you highlighted a single configuration, you would see where the output will go. If you changed any settings with more than one configuration selected, you would change the settings for *both* projects. This can be very useful, but you should be careful and have only one configuration selected if you only want to modify one configuration or see all of the settings for a configuration—and not just the settings that two configurations have in common.

There are about a gazillion different options available in the Project Settings dialog, so the options are grouped into several different pages, accessed by the tabs at the top. In addition, several pages, such as the C/C++ page shown in Figure 1.7, have drop-down menus in which you can select several different subpages.

It might take a while to find all the various settings, but I think you will find this much easier than trying to keep track of all of the different compiler and linker flags manually. Just remember that you might need to try changing the Category combo box to find the setting you are looking for.

FIGURE 1.7.

Drop-down menu in the C/C++ Project Settings page.

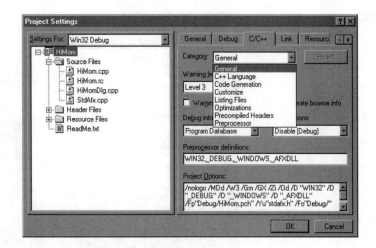

Converting Older Projects

You can use the Open workspace command of the File menu to open project files (or makefiles) from previous versions of Visual C++. When you do this, a warning message will appear suggesting that you save the file to a different name before it performs the conversion. This is generally a good idea if you will still need to use the project from a previous version of Visual C++ (such as when sharing with a group that hasn't upgraded yet), because, once converted, the project file will no longer be usable by older versions of Visual C++.

Working with Multiple Projects

As hinted at earlier, Developer Studio allows you to work with many different projects within the same workspace. This is very handy for working with projects that are closely related. To add a new project to the current workspace, use the File | New command and go to the Project page, shown in Figure 1.8.

To create a new project and add it to the current workspace, simply click the Add to current workspace radio button and create your new project. If you choose to add the new project to the existing workspace, you also have the option of making the new project a dependency of one of the existing projects in the workspace. This is useful for such things as building a library that is in turn used by an application. When you create the library as a dependency, it will be automatically built for you each time you build the application that depends on it. This can help keeping all of the pieces of a project up-to-date.

FIGURE 1.8.
Projects page.

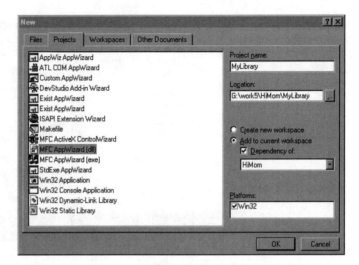

Later, you can modify the dependencies that are set up for a workspace by selecting Dependencies from the Project menu. This will allow you to use the Project Dependencies dialog, shown in Figure 1.9.

FIGURE 1.9.
Project Dependencies dialog.

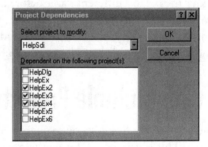

Simply choose one of your projects from the drop-down list at the top and then click any of the other projects that are its dependencies.

You will see each of your projects in the Workspace views, and you may easily switch between projects. If you use multiple projects within a workspace, the Batch Build command on the Build menu will allow you to build any number of your projects at once.

Working with Resources

If you have been developing Windows applications for a while, you are probably familiar with resource scripts. These are files that define all of the resources used by your application, including dialogs, icons, and menus. In the old days, you often had to move back and forth between your source editor and your resource editor, the C compiler, and the resource compiler. Developer Studio makes this much simpler by providing a visual editor for your resources that is fully integrated with the rest of Developer Studio.

The Resource View

In programming for Windows, you will use several different types of resources. Most of these correspond directly to graphics objects such as bitmaps, cursors, and icons, as well as more complicated types such as menus, toolbars, and dialog templates. In addition, you will have a string table and version resource, as well as any custom resources you might define.

In the bad old days, all resources were defined in a text resource script (.rc) file. You had to compile the .rc file with a separate resource compiler and explicitly link your resources to your executable. Visual C++ 5.0 still uses the .rc file, but you will most likely never have to edit it directly. Developer Studio allows you to edit your resources graphically, and will automatically take the necessary steps to compile your resource script and link it to your application.

To help you work with resources, Developer Studio provides the ResourceView, which displays information about the various resources included in each project, grouped by resource type. The ResourceView for the HiMom project is shown in Figure 1.10.

If you created a Windows application with AppWizard, a resource script would automatically be created as part of your new project. However, you can also create a new resource script from the Files tab for the New command on the File menu or open existing resource scripts from the Open command on the File menu. Resource script windows support drag-and-drop, making it quite simple to open an existing resource script from another project and add resources to your current project by just dragging them over.

Like the other Project Workspace views, there is a context menu available by right-clicking in the ResourceView. This allows you to open the selected resource for editing, insert new resources, or import existing resources, among other things. In addition, the context menu gives you access to the Properties page for your resources, as shown in Figure 1.11.

Unlike some properties pages, the resource property pages allow you to change some important aspects of your resource, including the ID and language for the resource. In addition, resources, such as icons and bitmaps that are stored in files outside of the resource script, allow you to specify the filename for the resource here. The Condition field allows you to enter a precompiler symbol that is used to specify that the resource be built into your project only if the given precompiler symbol is defined.

FIGURE 1.10.
The ResourceView.

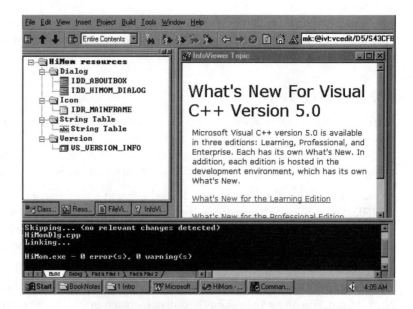

FIGURE 1.11.
Resource Properties dialog.

CAUTION

The context menu will let you open the binary data for any resource. Although this is useful for custom resource types, be very careful with it. It is very simple to accidentally change a byte in a resource and the window will save your changes without prompting. This can easily make your resource unusable.

Importing Resources

If you have already created resources that exist in separate files, you can add these to the resource script for the current project by importing them. You can add a separate image, icon, or cursor file to your current resource script by clicking the Import button in the Insert I Resource dialog. This will allow you to browse for the files containing the resources you want to add to the current project.

Managing Resource IDs

Whenever you create a new resource with the Developer Studio, a resource ID is automatically assigned. This means that the symbol you have entered as the resource ID is defined to be a certain value in a header file. Although you might luck out and never have to deal with resource IDs or resource header files directly, the View menu offers two very useful commands: Resource Symbols and Resource Includes. The Resource Symbols command will produce the dialog shown in Figure 1.12.

FIGURE 1.12.

Resource Symbols dialog.

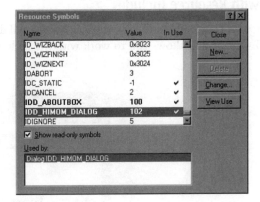

Working with Resource Symbols

The Resource Symbols dialog provides a handy way to work with the symbols that are defined for the currently selected configuration. You will see a list of all of the symbols defined in your project, their values, and whether or not they are currently being used by a resource. If a symbol is in use, the Used by list will show the resources using that symbol. Selecting Show read-only symbols will display predefined Windows symbols in a lighter shade along with your symbols.

You can add new symbols by clicking the New button or change values with the Change button. The View Use button will open a window for directly editing the resource that uses the selected ID. To change the value of a symbol that is in use, use the View Use button to open a window for the resource. If you open the properties dialog for the resource, by right-clicking in the resource and choosing Properties, you can assign a value to the symbol by entering it after the symbol name, like this:

```
IDD_MYDIALOG=111
```

> **TIP**
>
> If you plan to use resource IDs that must be in a consecutive range, as for the
> ON_COMMAND_RANGE macro, it might be easier to define all of the IDs you plan to use
> before creating your resources, because the IDs that are automatically assigned are not
> necessarily consecutive.

Working with Resource Includes

The Resource Includes command from the View menu will display a dialog like that shown in
Figure 1.13. This dialog allows you to work with the include files that define your resource
symbols.

FIGURE 1.13.
Resource Includes
dialog.

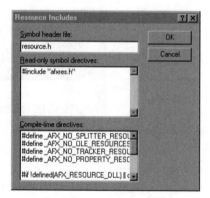

You may change the name of the header file that will contain your resource symbol definitions
here. You may also add any #include or #define directives to the header file. This allows you
to include additional header files, which can help in group projects. Because none of the Developer Studio tools will modify the #included files, these values are much more likely to remain constant.

Resource Templates

You might have noticed that when you create a new resource, the tree list of resource types
available may be expanded, as in Figure 1.14. This provides you with the ability to create resources based on resource templates. This comes in handy whenever you will want to create
many different resources that are similar, and can help standardize the look and feel of your
applications.

You can create resources based on a template by selecting the template and clicking New. If
you just want a plain, blank dialog, select the dialog line before clicking New.

FIGURE 1.14.

Creating resources with resource templates.

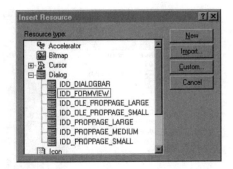

With Developer Studio, you can create your own resource templates by choosing Resource Template from the Files tab of the New dialog displayed by the File | New command. This will open an empty resource script that you can insert resources into. When you are finished, the resource template (.rct) file will be saved in the \Msdev\Templates directory with the other templates. Now, whenever you create a new resource, you will see that your template is shown as one of the choices in the Insert Resource dialog tree. Whenever you create a new resource based on the template, any changes you make to the new resource affect only the new resource and not the template.

Editing Resources

Developer Studio allows you to edit all of your resources with various visual editors that are part of Developer Studio. You can edit any resource by double-clicking it in the ResourceView. In the next few pages, you will be looking at the various resource editors provided by Developer Studio, starting with the Dialog editor, which you will probably be using most often.

Dialog Boxes

In most applications, dialog boxes provide a large portion of the interface between the user and your application. Dialog boxes allow you to provide an interface to the user for certain sets of information as it is needed, without taking up real estate in your main window. Whenever you open a dialog resource, you will get a window similar to the one shown in Figure 1.15.

Adding Controls

If you have just created a new dialog, it's time to make it do something useful. Developer Studio makes this easy. You should notice the controls toolbar floating around your workspace somewhere when you open the dialog. Each of the icons on the toolbar (with the exception of the pointer in the top left) represents a control that you can add to your dialog, including any controls that you have added with Component Gallery.

FIGURE 1.15.

Dialog Box editor.

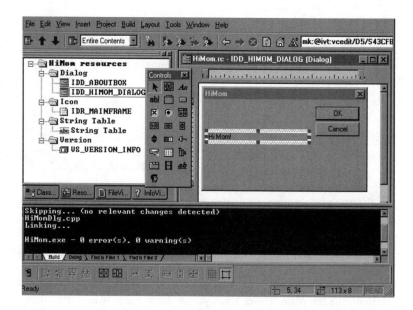

To add a control, select it from the toolbar, click the dialog, and you have a new control. If you are unsure of what some funny picture on the toolbar represents, just hold the mouse pointer over it. Like other toolbars, this will provide tooltip help that will give a short description of the control.

> **NOTE**
>
> The Controls toolbar, like the other toolbars, may be docked or hidden altogether. If you don't see it, try using the Toolbars page of the Tools | Customize dialog to toggle the Controls toolbar on.

When adding a control, it is generally easier to assign its size and location when it is added by dragging a rectangle in your dialog before releasing the mouse to insert the control. However, if you have already inserted a control, you can easily move it by clicking it and dragging a point within the control to the new location. You can easily resize controls by dragging the resize handles (little boxes) on the border of the selected control.

> **NOTE**
>
> You can resize either the normal or drop-down size of a combo box by clicking on its drop-down button to toggle which size is shown.

Control Properties

For most controls, you should change their properties after you have placed them in a dialog. You can edit a control's properties by selecting Properties… from the context menu that you can pull up by right-clicking the control. The Properties dialog looks similar to the one shown in Figure 1.16.

FIGURE 1.16.
Control Properties dialog.

The Properties dialog will be a bit different for each different type of control, but will always allow you to edit the resource ID. Although the ID can be a symbol or a number, you should try to give your resource ID symbol a meaningful name, rather than just a number or the default symbol name. If you want to force your ID to have a certain value, you can specify a value after the resource symbol like this:

```
IDC_MYBUTTON=123
```

For more information about the specifics of the styles and other options on the Properties page, press F1 to bring up context-sensitive help on the current page. You can access the properties of the dialog itself by double-clicking a blank spot in the dialog or its title bar.

Laying Out Your Controls

One of the trickiest parts of designing your dialogs can be getting everything to line up just right where you want it. The dialog editor provides several nifty features for dealing with this in the Layout menu. Many of the options in the Layout menu will not be enabled unless you have a certain type of control selected or have several controls selected.

> **NOTE**
>
> You can select multiple controls by holding the Shift key while clicking on the controls. The dominant control will be the control last selected.

The Size to Content command in the Layout menu (or F7) is particularly useful with static text and button controls. This will make the control just the right size to contain its text, preventing characters from being clipped off or controls that run over your other controls.

> **NOTE**
>
> Most of the commands from the Layout menu are also provided by tools in the Dialog toolbar.

You might notice a blue, shaded line encircling the contents of your dialog box. If you place any controls in the dialog so that they touch this margin line, they will be automatically moved whenever you resize your dialog. Unfortunately, this only works while you are creating your dialog resource and will not help with resizing at runtime. You may create your own guide lines by dragging in either of the ruler bars at the top or left of your dialog. By later adjusting these guides, any controls placed on the guide will be moved with it.

Tab Order

Windows allows you to move from control to control within a dialog by use of the Tab key. This functionality is provided automatically when you create a dialog in Developer Studio, but you might need to do a few things to tweak it to work just the way you want.

To adjust the tab order of your controls, you can choose the Tab Order command from the Layout menu and click the controls in the order that you want them to be tabbed. If you have a complicated dialog and only want to change the tab order of a few controls, you can take a little shortcut by holding the Ctrl key down and selecting the last control that tabs properly before selecting the controls that tab incorrectly. Clicking an empty spot in the dialog, or pressing Enter, will exit the tab order mode.

Testing Your Dialog

You could save your dialog and rebuild the application to test the layout of your dialog, but there is a much simpler method of testing things like tab order. The Layout menu provides the Test command (You can also use Ctrl-T or that little switch on the Dialog toolbar) that will run your dialog for you. This test mode ends whenever you exit the dialog that you are testing.

> **NOTE**
>
> When you choose Save from the File menu or the ResourceView context menu, the whole resource script file is saved, not just the resource you are working on.

Editing Menus

Double-clicking a menu resource in the ResourceView will open a window like the one shown in Figure 1.17 that allows you to edit your menu resource.

FIGURE 1.17.
Menu editor.

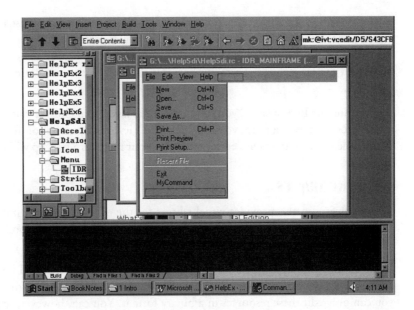

To add a new menu item, double-click in the empty space to the right or bottom of the last menu item. This will open the Menu Item Properties dialog, as shown in Figure 1.18, which lets you enter the menu caption, its associated command ID, and style information. You may freely rearrange your menu items by dragging and dropping.

FIGURE 1.18.
Menu Item Properties dialog.

The Command ID that you enter here will be the command ID that your application will receive when the user selects this menu item.

The Caption is the text that is displayed for the menu item. Placing an ampersand (&) in front of a character will cause that character to become the mnemonic key for that menu item. It is also customary to include text information about accelerators after the caption text, separated by a tab sequence (\t).

The Prompt field is used to enter text that will appear on the status bar as fly-by help when the cursor is on this menu item.

If you choose the Separator style, this will not be a real menu item, but just a separator between menu items. The Checked, Grayed, and Inactive styles determine the initial state of the menu item; these may be changed at runtime. The Help style will cause the menu item to be displayed on the far right of the menu bar, but this convention isn't used as often now as it once was.

By choosing the Pop-up style, you can easily create layers of menus. If you are creating a menu that will be used as a pop-up, you can select the View as Popup option from the right-button context menu to tell the menu editor to display your menu as a pop-up while you are editing it.

Other Resources

Developer Studio also provides visual editors for the other common windows resources, including accelerator tables, bitmaps, icons, cursors, string tables, and toolbars. You may also edit version resources to track various information about the version of your application.

In addition, you may define your own custom resource types that will be bound with your application. Because Developer Studio doesn't "know" how you intend to use these resources, you can only edit these resources in a binary format. You can, however, import existing files into your custom resource.

Application Wizard

It has been rumored that in prehistoric days there was but one piece of code ever written and that all projects since were merely the result of cutting and pasting from other projects. This does seem to have the ring of truth every time I cut and paste the same boilerplate code for Windows applications for each new project. Visual C++ makes this task much simpler by providing the Application Wizard, or AppWizard for short.

What AppWizard Can Do for You

AppWizard is really a collection of different Application Wizards that help to manage different sorts of projects. (I will generally use AppWizard to refer to any of the Application Wizards and will be more specific when discussing one particular AppWizard.) Each of the AppWizards will guide you through the process of creating a new project, prompting for various option selections along the way.

When you have made all of your choices, MFC will create your project for you. For some types of projects, this can be a tremendous time saver. For MFC applications, this means creating all of the source, header, resource, help, and project files necessary to create a skeleton for your application. The project created by the MFC AppWizard (exe) will build without any further modifications and has all of the setup for the application features you selected. This can easily reduce half a day's hunting, cutting, and pasting to just a few seconds.

Starting AppWizard

To use an AppWizard to help you create a new project, use the New command from the File menu. The Projects tab of this dialog, shown in Figure 1.19, will show you a list of all of the available application wizards, including other simple new project types, such as Win32 Application.

FIGURE 1.19.
The New Projects dialog.

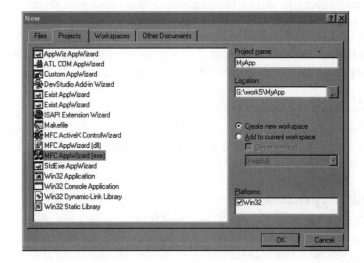

Project Types

The New Projects Workspace gives you the opportunity to create several different types of projects, so let's take a brief look at what Visual C++ will do for you when you choose each project type.

ATL COM AppWizard

This is used to create a new project based on the ActiveX Template Library (ATL). This type of project then allows you to add your own COM objects, using ATL.

Custom AppWizard

This type of project will allow you to create your very own AppWizard, which may then be used to help you create additional projects.

DevStudio Add-In Wizard

This creates a new skeleton project that may be used to add commands to the Developer Studio environment. This project may include the framework required to add a toolbar to Developer Studio, as well as to handle events that occur within Developer Studio.

ISAPI Extension Wizard

This wizard allows you to easily create the framework required to create extensions to Internet Information Server, using the Internet Server API.

Makefile

This project type is used to add a project that works with an external makefile. The project settings will allow you to specify the command line that you want to execute to build this project. By default, this is `NMAKE /f myMake.mak`. If you have existing makefiles that you want to incorporate into a build from Visual C++, without creating one of the other project types to replace your makefile, you should use this project type.

MFC ActiveX ControlWizard

This AppWizard will help you to create the framework for a project that uses the Microsoft Foundation Classes to implement ActiveX controls. We will be looking at how to implement such controls in more detail in Chapter 15, "ActiveX Controls."

MFC AppWizard (DLL)

This will use the MFC AppWizard for DLLs to create a new dynamic link library project for you. The project created implements the code needed to initialize a DLL that uses MFC, but you will need to add functionality to it. We will be looking at DLL projects more closely in Chapter 10, "Dynamic Link Libraries (DLLs)."

MFC AppWizard (EXE)

This will start up the MFC AppWizard to help you create the framework for a full-blown MFC Windows application. We will look at this in more detail in Chapter 2, "MFC Overview," but feel free to try it out if you like. The skeleton application created by AppWizard is a complete application in that it will build and run. You just need to add on the functionality specific to your application.

Win32 Application

The application project type does not use an AppWizard, nor will it create any source files for you. It will, however, create a new project with the default build settings for a Windows application. This type of project is useful for creating a Visual C++ 5.0 project for existing applications that you are moving to VC++ 5.0. You will have to add your existing source files to the new project with the Project | Add to Project | Files dialog.

Win32 Console Application

This project type will create a new project with the build settings appropriate for building console applications. This type of application does not have a Windows graphical interface, but uses a standard command window. You will need to add your own source files. This project type is appropriate for command-line utilities and other applications that do not have a graphical user interface.

Win32 Dynamic Link Library

Like the application project type, you will need to insert your own source files into this project (or create new ones). This option will set up the default project settings for creating a DLL.

Win32 Static Library

This is similar to the Dynamic Link Library option, but the project settings are set to create a standard statically linked library (.lib).

Other Project Types

You might also see additional project types listed. These are custom AppWizards that you have created, or that were provided by a third-party vendor and optionally loaded with Visual C++.

Class Wizard

In developing C++ applications, you will do a lot of work with your own classes. Developer Studio provides you with the Class Wizard to help in organizing your classes and integrating your classes with Windows. ClassWizard may be started from the View menu or by pressing Ctrl-W. The Class Wizard dialog is made up of several different tabs, or pages, each of which allows you to work with different aspects of your classes. We will look at each of these tabs in the following sections.

Message Maps

The Message Maps page allows you to work with assigning message handlers to Windows messages that your application will receive. This is really the heart of programming in the Windows event-driven programming model. The Message Maps tab is shown in Figure 1.20.

We will look at the specifics of using Class Wizard to work with message maps in Chapter 3, "MFC Messages and Commands."

FIGURE 1.20.
Class Wizard—
Message Maps.

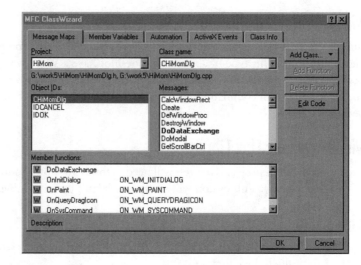

Member Variables

The Member Variables page, shown in Figure 1.21, is used to create member variables of your class that will be used to work with controls in dialogs. Unfortunately, it does not allow you to work with more general sorts of member variables. You will see more on how this page is used in Chapter 5, "Dialogs and Controls."

FIGURE 1.21.
Class Wizard—
Member Variables.

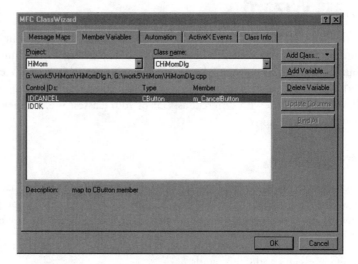

Automation

The Automation tab, shown in Figure 1.22, helps you work with the methods and properties associated with classes that use OLE Automation. We will look at this in more detail in Part III, "Programming with ActiveX."

FIGURE 1.22.

Class Wizard—
Automation.

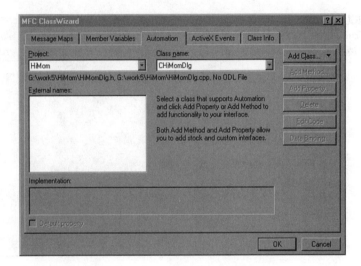

ActiveX Events

The ActiveX Events tab, shown in Figure 1.23, allows you to easily manage the ActiveX events that are supported by your ActiveX classes. We will look at ActiveX events in more detail in Part III of this book.

FIGURE 1.23.

Class Wizard—ActiveX
Events.

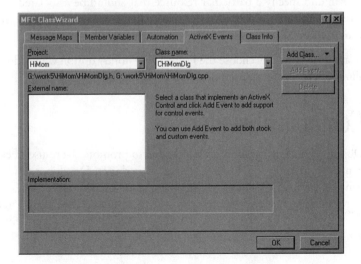

Class Info

The Class Info tab, shown in Figure 1.24, will show you some general information about your classes, including the header and source files in which it is defined, as well as its base class and any resource associated with it.

FIGURE 1.24.

Class Wizard—Class Info.

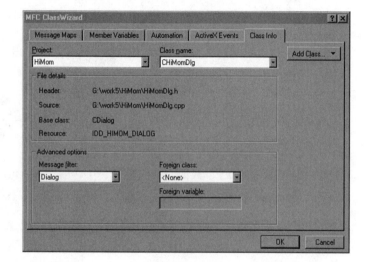

Adding a Class

The Add Class button provides a quick and easy way to create a new class in your project. The New Class dialog, which is presented when you choose New, allows you to choose the name for your new class and the base class that it derives from. You may select the file to create the class in and specify a particular resource that should be associated with the class. If the base class you choose can support OLE automation, you may specify options. The new class can also be automatically added to the Component Gallery.

In addition, you may choose the From a type library option when adding a new class. This will allow you to create classes based on an existing OLE type library.

Component Gallery

Object-oriented programming is intended to promote the re-use of existing software components. To make it even easier to re-use your classes, Developer Studio provides the Component Gallery, which allows you to insert many predefined classes into your project and also provides a handy way to catalog and store your own classes for use in other projects. To start the Component Gallery, as shown in Figure 1.25, choose Components and Controls from the Project | Add to Project menu.

FIGURE 1.25.

*The Component
Gallery.*

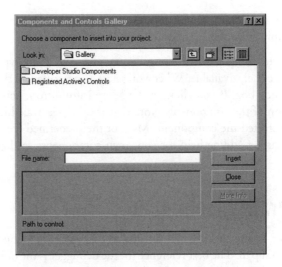

The components included in the gallery are organized in a directory tree structure. When you
first install Visual C++ 5.0, you will see Developer Studio Components, which contains standard Visual C++ components, and Registered ActiveX Controls, which contains any ActiveX
controls registered on your machine as top-level directories. You may also add your own controls in their own directory structures. After you open one of these folders, you will see a list of
available components, as shown in Figure 1.26.

FIGURE 1.26.

*Developer Studio
components.*

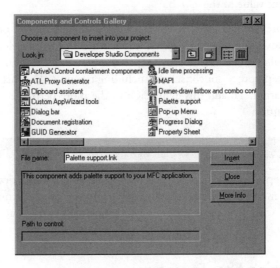

The predefined components in Component Gallery can be used to add a wide variety of
functionality to your applications, ranging from simple controls that can be used in dialogs,
to ActiveX controls that can add some very complex capabilities to your application with a

minimum of effort. Some of the components, such as palette support, add support for functions simply by providing handlers for a few messages.

Many of the components in the gallery might seem a bit cryptic at first glance, but there is a good deal of help available. When you select a component, a short description will appear next in the dialog box. If you click on the More Info button, you will see a much more detailed description of the component. Note that this help is available only if it has been entered by whoever created the component. Most of the predefined components include help, but you might consider adding help for your own components so that others can more easily re-use them.

Integrated Debugger

Developer Studio includes a full-featured debugger for fixing those problems that inevitably manage to slip in. The best reference for the debugger is the online help, and we don't have the space to include it all here, so I will just mention a few things that you may find useful.

Looking at Your Data

When you are debugging, you will be concerned with the values represented by the variables in your program. The simplest way to do this in Developer Studio is to point the mouse at the variable in the source code and wait a second or two. A small tip box will appear that displays the current value of the variable.

For a more detailed view, you can use the right mouse button to produce a Context menu, which allows you to open a quick watch window for the selected variable. The quick watch window allows you to enter any expression you want to evaluate in the expression window. However, preprocessor constants (including resource ID constants) are generally not available for evaluation. To add this expression to the more permanent watch window, click the Add Watch button.

> **TIP**
>
> Developer Studio supports drag-and-drop in many situations. For example, you can highlight a variable and drag it with the right mouse button to the memory window, which will then automatically display the memory for that variable.

Debugging After Exceptions

At some time or another, you will almost definitely find yourself with an application that will trip over an unhandled exception. This will bring up a dialog that will allow you to exit altogether or debug the application. You may actually load the debugger to view the current state of your application at the time of the exception, source code and all, even if you were not running your application from Developer Studio at the time!

Command-Line Tools

Despite all of the whiz-bang tools that Developer Studio offers, let's not forget that the heart of Visual C++ is a C++ compiler, a linker, a library utility, a resource compiler, and a build facility. These can all be accessed from the command line directly. Here are the command-line equivalents for these tools:

`cl.exe`: Compiler

`link.exe`: Linker

`lib.exe`: Library utility

`implib.exe`: Import library utility

`nmake.exe`: Microsoft's make facility

`rc.exe`: Resource compiler

If you need to use these utilities directly from the command line, you will find that all of their command-line arguments and options are detailed in the online help.

Other Tools

In addition to Developer Studio, Visual C++ supplies several external utilities that are added to the program group for Visual C++ when it is installed. Several of these are also available from Developer Studio by way of the Tools menu.

> **TIP**
>
> You can add anything else you like to the Tools menu from the Tools page of the dialog produced by Tools | Customize.

Spy++

Spy++ provides a very detailed view into the goings-on of the Windows operating system. It will allow you to view all processes, threads, and windows on the machine, along with all of the Windows messages that are being sent.

MFC Tracer

This application may be used to enable various levels of debug messages that MFC may send to the Output window of Developer Studio when an application is executing or being debugged.

Register Control

In order to use OLE controls in Win32, the control must be registered with the operating system. Register Control from the Tools menu gives you a convenient method of doing this.

ActiveX Control Test Container

This provides a simple environment that allows you to test your ActiveX controls and how they work when used from a container application.

OLE/COM Object Viewer

This utility provides information about all of the OLE and ActiveX objects that are installed on your system.

Error Lookup

This utility provides a way to easily look up information about the standard error codes that are returned by most Win32 API functions. This might be easier than searching through the various header files used to define errors, although it is a bit slow.

WinDiff

Although WinDiff does not appear in the default Tools menu, it ships with Visual C++ 5.0, in `DevStudio\VC\bin\WinDiff.exe`. WinDiff allows you to compare two files in a convenient Windows app that is much more user-friendly than other compare or diff tools you might have used from the command line.

Help Workshop

Help Workshop is used to help manage your help projects. Although it is not automatically included in the Tools menu, it is included with Visual C++ 5.0. You will see more information about how to use this tool in Chapter 35, "Adding Windows Help."

Summary

As you have seen, the development environment provided for Visual C++ has come a long way from DOS DEBUG. Everything you need to do to develop applications (in most cases, anyway) can be done from within Developer Studio.

In this chapter, you have seen how to use the Developer Studio environment, including the toolbars and dockable view windows and particularly the project workspace window, which allows you to manage the classes, files, and resources in your application, as well as to provide quick access to the online documentation.

You have seen how to create new projects for Visual C++ and the variety of project types and application wizards that are available, as well as how to work with the project settings that affect builds of your application. You have also seen how to create multiple projects in your workspace, including managing dependencies.

In addition, you have seen how Developer Studio provides resource editors for the various Windows resources our projects will use, including dialogs, menus, and other resources.

You have also seen previews of AppWizard and ClassWizard, which is used throughout this book, as well as some of the other tools included with Visual C++.

This chapter has shown you how to get started using the Visual C++ environment, but I obviously haven't shown you everything. I just don't have the time or space. However, with the things have covered here, you should be able to work with applications. If you're curious about what something does, try it! Play around with a few simple projects and get a feel for the environment. When you're done playing, move on to what goes into your applications.

II

General MFC
Programming

2

MFC Overview

by David Bennett

In Chapter 1, "Visual C++ Environment," you looked at the Developer Studio and the tools that it provides to help you develop C++ applications for Windows. Now you will get down to business and look at real application development. To help you with this, the Microsoft Foundation Classes (MFC) provides an application framework, in addition to the general classes and Win32 API wrapper classes that you expect from a Windows class library.

In this chapter, you will

- Develop a complete application with AppWizard
- Examine the application architecture used by MFC
- See how MFC works behind the scenes to make your application run

The Application Framework

The MFC, as the name suggests, provides a set of reusable classes designed to simplify Windows programming. Like any class library, MFC provides classes for certain basic objects, such as strings, files, and collections, that are used in everyday programming. It also provides classes that wrap common Windows APIs and data structures, such as windows, controls, and device contexts. In addition, MFC provides an application framework, including the classes that make up the application architecture hierarchy.

The application framework helps get your application running by providing program initialization, passing Windows messages to the appropriate places, and cleaning it all up when your application exits. The framework also provides a solid foundation for more advanced features, such as ActiveX and document/view processing.

Creating an MFC Application with AppWizard

To kick off your examination of the application framework, you will create the first sample application to illustrate the things that AppWizard can do for you and to provide concrete examples of the MFC application framework.

You will create the HiMom sample included on the CD-ROM, using the AppWizard. In a way, this will be "hello world!" program for MFC, but it also provides much more support for building real applications, so I didn't think HelloWorld would be an appropriate name. (Also, it just so happens that I'd rather say "hi" to my mom than to the rest of the world.) If you would rather use your own application, bear in mind that AppWizard will name many classes and files based on your application name—if your application name is different, the names of your classes and files will be different.

Starting AppWizard

To start a new project with Visual C++, you create a new project workspace. To do this, select the New command from the File menu and choose the Projects tab. This will display the New Project dialog shown in Figure 2.1.

FIGURE 2.1.

The New Project
Workspace dialog box.

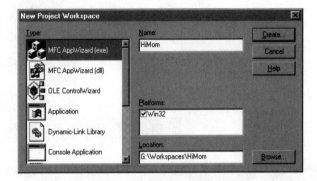

For this example, you use the MFC AppWizard (exe), so make sure it is highlighted in the box on the left. Next, put the name of your project (HiMom) in the project Name box. Be careful to choose a name here that you can live with; AppWizard will use it to create many class names and filenames and may use some awkward abbreviations. You may also need to be careful about using filenames longer than the 8.3 DOS standard. Long filenames are very useful, and Visual C++ and Win32 operating systems have no problem working with them. However, if you have any tools that support only the 8.3 format, it is *much* easier to adjust the filenames now.

If you don't like the location that AppWizard has picked for your project, you can change it now by entering a new path in the Location box or using the Browse button to pick a new spot. You may also choose whether to create the project as part of a brand new workspace, or as part of the current workspace. If you choose to add the new project to the current workspace, you may create the new project as a dependency of an existing project in the current workspace by checking Dependency of: and selecting a dependent project in the drop-down list. When you are satisfied with your choices, click OK to start the AppWizard, which will begin with the dialog shown in Figure 2.2.

This dialog allows you to select the type of application you would like to create. For this example, you will use Multiple documents, which will create an application structure that you may have seen in Word or Excel, in which you may view several documents at the same time. For reasons you can well imagine, your sample application will not provide quite as much functionality as MS Word or Excel, but it will allow multiple documents.

FIGURE 2.2.

MFC App Wizard—step 1.

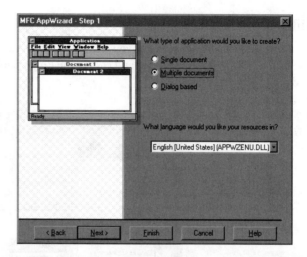

NOTE

In MFC, a document can be any set of data that may be grouped together. Although this can be a word processing document, it can also be a group of settings for an application, such as a terminal session.

Single document applications are similar, but they allow only one open document at a time. You will learn some other differences in Chapter 4, "Frames, Documents, and Views," where you will start to dig into the document/view architecture.

The third choice, Dialog based applications, does not use the document/view architecture at all. These applications are based on a dialog resource. This is useful for small utility applications, but if you plan to implement menus, toolbars, or printing, you should seriously consider using one of the document-based types, because they can implement many of these things for you much easier than you can add these features to dialog-based applications.

For an application type other than multiple documents, the following steps will be slightly different, but I think you will get the picture. If you do have a question about any step, you can press F1 to bring up help on the current page. This applies not only to AppWizard, but to most other areas of Developer Studio as well.

For this example, you will use English as the language of choice for your resources, but if you want, you may choose any other language offered.

By now, you have probably noticed the row of buttons along the bottom of the dialog box. The Back and Next buttons allow you to navigate between the pages of the AppWizard. If you just remembered that you really wanted to change something in a previous step, you can easily go back and change it. When you have entered your selections in a page, click on Next to go to the next step. If you know that you want to use the default settings for the rest of the steps, you could click on Finish to go straight to the end. For the HiMom sample, you could do this now, because you are going to use only the defaults, but let's take a look at the other options available. The Cancel button enables you to exit the AppWizard without creating a new project.

By clicking on the Next button, you can move to the next page, which looks like Figure 2.3.

FIGURE 2.3.

*MFC AppWizard—
step 2.*

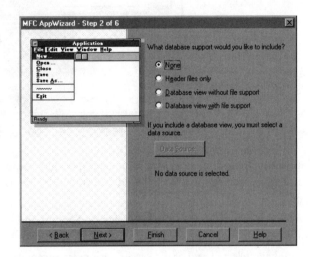

This page allows you to select options for database support in your application. Obviously, if you select None, you will get none (from the AppWizard anyway—you can always add things later, but you have to do it manually). The Header files only option includes the AFXDB.H header file, which includes simple database support, allowing you to create and use recordsets to work with databases.

The two Database view options create a view class for your application based on CRecordView, which gives you a form-based application allowing you to view and update records. The Database view with file support option supports document serialization. If you choose either of these options, you must also choose a data source. You learn about this in much greater detail in Part V, "Database Programming," so let's go ahead to the next page, shown in Figure 2.4.

With this page, you can select options that allow your application to support various levels of object linking and embedding (OLE). Once again, if you select None, that's just what you'll get. You have to add OLE support manually if you change your mind after the application is created. You will explore OLE, COM, and ActiveX in much greater detail in Part III, "Programming with ActiveX," but here's the short version of what the other options mean:

Container support allows your application to contain ActiveX objects.

Mini-server applications can create and manage compound document objects, but they cannot run stand-alone, supporting only embedded objects.

FIGURE 2.4.

*MFC AppWizard—
step 3.*

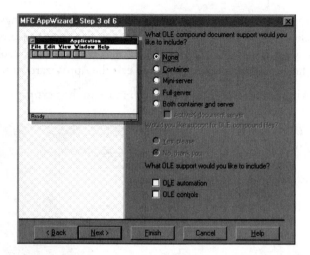

Full-server applications can also create and manage compound document objects, run stand-alone, and support both linked and embedded items.

Select Both container and server if you want your application to be able to place embedded or linked objects into its own documents and be able to create OLE objects for use in container applications.

If you have selected any of the server options, you can also make your application an ActiveX document server.

If you select support for compound files, MFC will serialize your container application's documents using the OLE compound-file format. If you choose "No, thank you," it won't.

You can select Automation to allow automation clients, such as Excel, to access your application.

If you want to include ActiveX controls in your application, such as those provided in the component gallery, select the OLE controls option.

Step 4, shown in Figure 2.5 allows you to select several advanced features that AppWizard can add for you.

Selecting Docking toolbar allows the user to move the toolbar from its default location and dock it to the borders of the window.

The Initial status bar option provides a status bar, including keyboard state indicators and fly-by help for menus and toolbars. This also adds menu commands to hide or display the status bar and toolbar.

The Printing and print preview option tells AppWizard to generate code and menu commands to handle printing tasks automatically.

FIGURE 2.5.

*MFC AppWizard—
step 4.*

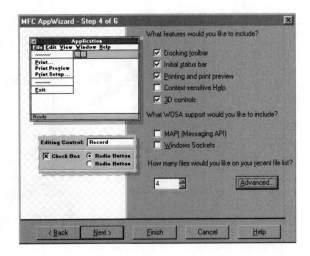

The Context-sensitive Help option generates help files that you can use to give your users help on specific areas of your application. We will be looking at Windows help in Chapter 35, "Adding Windows Help."

If you select 3D controls, all controls in your application will have that nifty chiseled look.

You can include support for the Windows Open Services Architecture (WOSA) by selecting the MAPI (Messaging API) option, which allows your application to integrate with mail systems, or the Windows Sockets option, which enables TCP/IP communications.

The AppWizard automatically implements a most-recently-used file list for you in the File menu. You may set the number of files here to keep in this list.

The Advanced button allows you to select preferences about document types and window styles for your application.

Step 5 allows you to tell AppWizard to include source file comments where it has added things.

This page also gives you the option to use the shared DLL versions of MFC or the statically linked library. If you know that your application will be the only MFC app running at any given time, you may want to use the static libraries, but it is generally better to use the DLL versions, which can be shared by all applications. Using the DLL versions also reduces the disk and memory requirements of your application's executable file.

Step 6, shown in Figure 2.6, shows the classes that AppWizard will create for you.

If you like, you can change the defaults that AppWizard supplies by selecting the class in the top list and editing the fields below. For many of the classes, options will be inactive (grayed). In most of these cases, changing the default doesn't make sense anyway—an application class based on anything other than `CWinApp` just wouldn't work well with MFC.

FIGURE 2.6.

MFC AppWizard—
step 6.

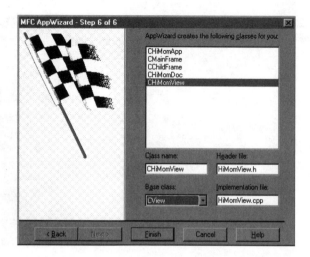

If you don't like the filenames that AppWizard has chosen, you may freely change these (for all but the app class), but you can place only one of the classes in each file.

For MDI applications, you can change only the base class of your view class. You probably will not want to use the base CView class in a real application, but will want to use one of the available derived classes that provide much greater functionality. For more on MFC's view classes, see Chapter 4.

Click Finish here, and you're just about done. AppWizard will display a window like Figure 2.7.

FIGURE 2.7.

The New Project
Information dialog box.

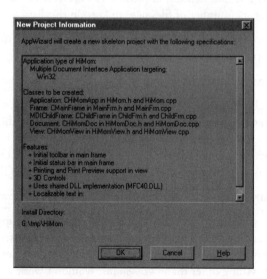

You should review the information presented here to see that it matches the options you selected. If you find that something here doesn't match what you wanted, click on Cancel to go back to step 6. If you are satisfied with your choices, click on OK and let AppWizard do the work for you.

You now have a complete Windows application. You can see this for yourself by choosing the `Build HiMom.exe` command from the Build menu to compile and link, and then choosing the `Execute HiMom` command from the Build menu to run it. You will notice that many cool functions that you expect from a Windows application have already been implemented for you, such as File | New and Print Preview. Now all you have to do is the really good stuff to fit your application.

TIP

AppWizard is extremely useful in creating new projects, but it isn't intended to manage your projects after you have clicked on that last OK. If you find yourself wanting to add functionality to an application midway through development, but forgot to choose a few options in AppWizard when you created it, you can use AppWizard to give you some help. If you create a new project with the AppWizard options you used to create your application and then create another with the options you wish to add (or delete), you can use a utility such as WinDiff to see what the new options have added to each of your source and header files.

Getting to Know Your New Application

Okay, so you clicked a few buttons and got this little app with a bunch of menus that don't do anything. What's it got under the hood? Here, you will look at what AppWizard has created for you and how the application framework that was created provides a solid backbone for your application.

If you're like me, your first instinct may be to open a DOS window and start digging through files. Sure, you can still do this, but it really is easier to use the Project Workspace window— I promise. Remember that you can open any source file, usually to just the right place, by double-clicking on the file or class view of the project workspace.

Classes Created by AppWizard

As you may have already noticed, AppWizard has created a handful of classes for you, based on your application's name. These fall into the basic classes of Application classes, Document classes,

View classes, and Frame classes. Each of these classes is based on one of the classes in the application architecture hierarchy. (You will almost never use the base classes directly, but will derive your own classes from them.) The HiMom example you just created will implement the classes shown in Table 2.1.

Table 2.1. Classes for HiMom.

MFC Base class	Derived class	Filename
CWinApp	CHiMomApp	HiMom.cpp
CDocument	CHiMomDoc	HiMomDoc.cpp
CView	CHiMomView	HiMomView.cpp
CFrameWnd	CMainFrame	MainFrm.cpp
CMDIChildWnd	CChildFrame	ChildFrm.cpp

CDocument, CView, and Frame Classes

The classes that you derive from CDocument are intended to hold the data that your application will work with. Your CDocument class will be responsible for reading and writing data files and will serve as a repository for the information that your CView classes will allow the user to view and manipulate. You may choose not to use these classes and the document/view architecture, but you will see in Chapter 4 that these are very useful in helping you implement many functions common to Windows applications.

Classes based on CMainFrame will implement the main frame for your application. (Kinda makes sense, I suppose.) It is this class that will manage the menus, toolbars, and status bars (even the main window itself) for the main window of your application. Classes derived from CChildFrame are used in MDI applications to manage the child windows created for multiple views. Like the main frame, CChildFrame classes can manage menus, toolbars, status bars, and the window for the children of your main frame. You will look at how the document, view, and frame classes work together in Chapter 4, so let's leave it at that for now and move on to the real heart of your MFC application.

CWinApp

Every true MFC application has a class derived from CWinApp. You can see how AppWizard has done this for you by looking at the following sample from HiMom.h:

```
class CHiMomApp : public CWinApp
{
public:
    CHiMomApp();
```

```
// Overrides
    // ClassWizard generated virtual function overrides
    //{{AFX_VIRTUAL(CHiMomApp)
    public:
    virtual BOOL InitInstance();
    //}}AFX_VIRTUAL
// Implementation
    //{{AFX_MSG(CHiMomApp)
    afx_msg void OnAppAbout();
        // NOTE - the ClassWizard will add and remove member functions here.
        //    DO NOT EDIT what you see in these blocks of generated code !
    //}}AFX_MSG
    DECLARE_MESSAGE_MAP()
};
```

The first line shown here is what gives your application the real power of the MFC application framework. This is where the CHiMom class is derived from CWinApp. Apart from that, you will notice an awful lot of strange comments. These comments give the Class Wizard landmarks to find the pieces of the code that it manipulates.

CAUTION

You should notice the DO NOT EDIT warning in the comments. Although it is possible to change or add some things in these sections, it is not generally a good idea. The changes you make here may confuse ClassWizard to the point that you won't be able to use it to help manage your classes. If you feel you must make changes on ClassWizard's turf, it's best to try out ClassWizard right after you make the changes to see whether things still work. You should also realize that ClassWizard may change the code in these sections. If you ever want to use ClassWizard again, by all means *do not delete these comments!*

Just as your Application class derives from CWinApp, CWinApp itself is derived from a chain of other classes in the application architecture hierarchy, including CWinThread, CCmdTarget, and CObject.

CWinThread

One of the major differences between Windows 3.1 and the Windows NT and Windows 95 operating systems is the use of preemptive multitasking. Although Windows 3.1 supports multiple tasks, only one task could be running at one time, and nobody else could run without the running task giving up the processor. Win32 supports true multitasking through the use of threads, which allow more than one thing to be going on at the same time. True, most processors really execute only one instruction stream at a time, but as far as this chapter is concerned, all threads run at the same time.

When your application first starts, it has one—and only one—thread, known as the *primary thread.* This thread is encapsulated by the CWinApp class that you have derived. This means that a pointer to your CWinApp object is also a pointer to the CWinThread object for the primary thread. Once your application gets going, it can create as many new threads as it wants to manage various tasks.

> **NOTE**
>
> Even though you may not be using more than one thread, the MFC libraries always expect to link with multithreaded runtime libraries. You should select the appropriate multithreaded libraries in the Build Settings under the C/C++ Code Generation options. (This is not the default for new application workspaces that are not created with the MFC AppWizard.)

You learn more about working with threads in Chapter 9, "Multithreading with MFC," but, for now, let's move on to the base class of CWinThread, CCmdTarget.

CCmdTarget

All window classes under MFC, including OLE classes, are derived at some level from CCmdTarget. This class is used as a base class for so many other classes because it allows your class to handle Windows messages.

Windows programs are based on an event-driven model. This means that they run in the traditional sense for only a short time at startup, then spend the rest of their lives waiting around for messages, reacting to them, and waiting again for more messages. These messages can be generated by simply moving the mouse, clicking on a button, or selecting a menu command.

In C programs, these messages were generally handled by large switch blocks involving case statements for each message that your application wanted to process. Because the processing of these messages was often dependent on several other variables, most applications ended up with a massive web of nested switch and if blocks.

To remedy this situation, and to allow you to use the power of C++ freely, MFC has implemented message maps to allow your classes to handle Windows messages in a much cleaner fashion. Any class derived from CCmdTarget may have its own message map, allowing each class to handle the messages it is interested in however it chooses, while leaving other messages to be handled higher in the class hierarchy.

Working with messages is one of the most important things that you will do in Windows programming (so important, that it has its own chapter—Chapter 3, "MFC Messages and Commands"). For now, let's move on to the base class of CCmdTarget, CObject.

CObject

At least as far as MFC is concerned, CObject is the mother of all classes (well, most of them anyway). Almost all the classes in MFC are derived from CObject—with a few notable exceptions, such as CString. Deriving a class from CObject provides several very important features, including serialization, runtime type information, and some very important debugging features.

Serialization

Many features of Windows programming with MFC require the capability of serializing the data in your objects. Perhaps the simplest example of this is saving an object to a file. You need to have a way to convert your object to a series of bytes that can be written to disk and brought back later to restore your object to its previous state.

To implement serialization in your classes, you first derive them, either directly or indirectly, from CObject. Then you can implement the Serialize member function for your class to serialize its data. To see just how to do this, let's start by looking at a few macros MFC provides to help.

The DECLARE_SERIAL and IMPLEMENT_SERIAL Macros

To help implement serialization in your class, MFC provides a pair of macros: DECLARE_SERIAL for use in your class declaration (usually in an .h file) and IMPLEMENT_SERIAL for use in your class implementation (a .cpp file).

The DECLARE_SERIAL macro takes only one parameter: the name of your class. Placing this in your class declaration provides prototypes for the serialization functions and some special handling for the insertion operator. You can see how this is used in the following class declaration:

```
Class CEmployee : public CObject
{
public:
    DECLARE_SERIAL(CEmployee)
    void Serialize(CArchive& ar);
private:
    int        m_EmpNo;
    CString    m_Name;
    float      m_Salary;
};
```

Serialize()

Notice that this example declares a Serialize() function, which takes a reference to a CArchive object, which provides a context for the serialization. The Serialize() function prepares the CArchive object either to read from or write to objects of your class. You must implement the Serialize() function for each class that you intend to serialize.

As mentioned previously, the same `Serialize()` function implements both loading and storing, based on the `CArchive` context. You can use the `CArchive::IsLoading()` or `CArchive::IsStoring()` function to determine the direction of serialization. The implementation for the `CEmployee` class declared earlier might look like this:

```
IMPLEMENT_SERIAL(CEmployee, CObject, 0x200)
void CEmployee::Serialize(CArchive& ar)
{
    // call base class Serialize() first
    CObject::Serialize(ar);
    // then serialize the data for this class
    if(ar.IsLoading())
    {
        ar >> m_EmpNo;
        ar >> m_Name;
        ar >> m_Salary;
    }
    else
    {
        ar << m_EmpNo;
        ar << m_Name;
        ar << m_Salary;
    }
} // end CEmployee::Serialize
```

There are many interesting things that you should notice in this example, beginning with the use of the `IMPLEMENT_SERIAL` macro, which takes three parameters: the class name, the base class it is derived from, and a schema number, which you'll learn about in just a bit.

Next, you should notice that you call the `Serialize` member of the base class. Every implementation of `Serialize()` must call the `Serialize()` function of the base class to allow it to serialize its data first, before you serialize the data for your class.

Serialization Operators

Notice that the serialization is performed by the overloaded insertion and extraction operators. These are predefined for the `CArchive` class for the following data types:

```
BYTE
WORD
DWORD
LONG
double
float
CObject*
```

The insertion and extraction operators are also defined for any class that implements serialization. You can thank the `DECLARE_SERIAL` and `IMPLEMENT_SERIAL` macros for this. If you need to use any other data types, you have to create your own override functions or use macros or type casts to use the supported types.

Serializing Different Versions

Earlier, you learned that the IMPLEMENT_SERIAL macro takes a schema number for its third parameter. This can be any number in the valid range of type UINT, with the exception of -1, which is reserved for use by MFC. The schema number effectively allows you to embed a version number in your serialized data; if the schema number you specify in IMPLEMENT_SERIAL does not match the schema number in the file you are reading, MFC will fail an assert.

If MFC just blows up, how can it support multiple versions? This is where the VERSIONABLE_SCHEMA macro comes in. If you combine your current schema number and the VERSIONABLE_SCHEMA macro by using the OR operator (¦), your Serialize() routine will write your data with the current schema number, but can read any schema. This is handled by use of the CArchive::GetObjectSchema() function, as you will see in the following example. Here, you assume that the previous version of CEmployee did not implement the m_Name member:

```
IMPLEMENT_SERIAL(CEmployee, CObject, VERSIONABLE_SCHEMA¦0x200)
void CEmployee::Serialize(CArchive& ar)
{
    // first, call base class Serialize function
    CObject::Serialize(ar);

    // Now we do our stuff
    if(ar.IsStoring())
    {
        // We are writing our class data,
        //      so we don't care about the schema
        ar << m_EmpNo;
        ar << m_Name;
        ar << m_Salary;
    }
    else
    {
        // we are loading, so check the schema
        UINT nSchema = ar.GetObjectSchema();
        switch(nSchema)
        {
            case 0x100:
                // Old schema, default m_Name
                ar >> m_EmpNo;
                m_Name = ""Dilbert";
                ar >> m_Salary;
                break;
            case 0x200:
                // current version
                ar >> m_EmpNo;
                ar >> m_Name;
                ar >> m_Salary;
                break;
            default:
                // Unknown Version, do nothing
                break;
        } // end switch
    } // end if
} // end CCLient::Serialize()
```

As you can see, you should provide reasonable defaults for data that cannot be retrieved from the archive. On the other hand, you probably should provide some sort of mechanism to report unknown cases to the user, instead of doing nothing, as I did here.

Runtime Type Information

Beginning with version 4.0 of Visual C++, two versions of runtime type information are supported: the ANSI standard C++ typeid() variety and MFC's own, more powerful brand of type identification provided by the CObject class.

If you want to use the ANSI variety of runtime type information (RTTI), you can enable this in the Project Settings dialog by selecting the Enable Run-Time Type Information (RTTI) option on the C++ Language page of the C/C++ tab. This allows you to use the C++ typeid() operator to get the name of the class.

The MFC version of runtime type information provides backward compatibility with MFC apps that predate ANSI RTTI in Microsoft compilers and provides information for efficient serialization and cross-platform compatibility.

Using MFC Runtime Type Information

To use MFC's runtime type information, you can use the DECLARE_DYNAMIC macro, which takes your class name as an argument in your class declaration, and the IMPLEMENT_DYNAMIC macro, which takes your class name and its base class in your implementation. These set up the structures that MFC uses to track type information for your classes.

> **NOTE**
>
> You use only one set of these macros for your CObject class. DECLARE/
> IMPLEMENT_DYNCREATE includes DECLARE/IMPLEMENT_DYNAMIC functionality, and DECLARE/
> IMPLEMENT_SERIAL encompasses both of these.

IsKindOf() **and** RUNTIME_CLASS()

If you have enabled runtime type identification in your classes, you can now verify that any pointer you get is a valid pointer to the class you expect, before your app goes off into the weeds from a faulty pointer. This is done by using the CObject::IsKindOf() function, which takes a pointer to a runtime type information structure. This structure can be provided for constant class types by the RUNTIME_CLASS macro, taking your class name as a parameter. This example demonstrates this a little better:

```
if(pMyPtr->IsKindOf(RUNTIME_CLASS(CEmployee)))
    DoSomething();
else
    DoError();
```

In this example, if CMyPtr points to an object of class CEmployee or any class derived from it, IsKindOf() returns TRUE. If IsKindOf() returns FALSE, you will probably want to report an error.

STATIC_DOWNCAST **and** DYNAMIC_DOWNCAST

In addition to the type information available from CObject, MFC provides macros to validate types when you want to cast a pointer to an object to a pointer to a more specific derived class. You can use STATIC_DOWNCAST to check your casting with code like this:

```
CWnd* pWnd;
pButton = STATIC_DOWNCAST(CButton, pWnd);
```

If you are running a debug build and pWnd is not really a pointer to a CButton class object, MFC will assert; otherwise, the cast is performed as normal. In a nondebug build, STATIC_DOWNCAST will always perform the cast without type checking. If you want to do type checking in release builds, you can use the DYNAMIC_DOWNCAST macro, which works the same way in debug and nondebug builds. If the type check fails, or if the pointer is NULL, DYNAMIC_DOWNCAST will return NULL. It is then up to your application to decide what to do.

ASSERT_KINDOF()

If you want to check that a pointer is of the type you want it to be, you could use a line like the following:

```
ASSERT(pMyPtr->IsKindOf(RUNTIME_CLASS(CEmployee)));
```

This may be a bit cumbersome both to type and to read, so MFC provides a shortcut—the ASSERT_KINDOF macro. The following line behaves exactly the same as the previous ASSERT—it just looks neater:

```
ASSERT_KINDOF(CEmployee, pMyPtr);
```

You can probably guess that the first argument is the desired class type and the second is the pointer in question.

Debugging Support

Because CObject is the base class for almost all other classes in the MFC, it serves as a convenient place to stash a few very important debugging features.

AssertValid()

If you want to be able to verify that an object of your class is valid, you can override the AssertValid() member function of CObject. Like many other debug features, this should only be implemented in builds where _DEBUG is defined. To implement an AssertValid() function for your class, the declaration for your class should look like the following:

```
class CMyClass : public CObject
{
// other stuff for your class
public:
#ifdef _DEBUG
    virtual void AssertValid() const;
#endif
};
```

Now you need to implement your AssertValid() function. This function should perform a quick check that the elements of your class are in order. Your implementation should look something like this:

```
#ifdef _DEBUG
void CEmployee::AssertValid()
{
    // validate the base class
    CObject::AssertValid();
    // validate this class
    ASSERT(m_EmpNo != 0);
} // end CEmployee::AssertValid()
#endif
```

You should perform all your validity tests with the ASSERT macro (and derivatives like ASSERT_KINDOF). You can use AssertValid() in your applications by calling the ASSERT_VALID macro, which takes a pointer to the object to be validated. This macro, like many other debug macros, will not generate any code in nondebug builds, so you won't need to hassle with all those pesky #ifdefs.

The ASSERT Macro

Because I have mentioned asserts several times already, it's about time you look at them in more detail. The ASSERT macro takes any expression that evaluates to a Boolean expression. If this expression is true (nonzero), all is well and the app goes on its merry way. If however, the expression is false (0), a dialog box will appear.

This dialog box gives you three choices. You may choose Abort to stop your app right there; or you can choose Ignore to close the dialog and press on; or you can choose Retry, which enables you to jump right into the debugger at the point that the ASSERT failed, even if you did not start the application in the debugger. From this point, you can easily use the Call Stack window to figure out just where in your code things went amiss.

Remember that the ASSERT macro does not generate any code in nondebug builds. It will not even evaluate the expression. If you want to have the expression evaluated in release builds, you can use the VERIFY macro instead.

Dump()

Another important debugging feature of the CObject class is the Dump() function. This is useful when you want to spit out information about the current state of your class object periodically, or when you have noticed a problem. Once again, this feature should not be implemented in nondebug builds. To use the Dump() function in your classes, you insert code something like this:

```
class CEmployee : public CObject
{
public:
#ifdef _DEBUG
    virtual void Dump(CDumpContext& dc) const;
#endif
    int m_EmpNo;
    CString m_Name;
    // Other class stuff
} // end class CEmployee
```

Your implementation would include code such as this:

```
#ifdef _DEBUG
void CEmployee::Dump(CDumpContext& dc) const
{
    // first, call base class Dump
    CObject::Dump(dc);
    // then dump this class
    dc << "Employee Number: " << m_EmpNo << "\n"
       << "Employee Name: " << m_Name << "\n"
} // end CEmployee::Dump()
#endif
```

> **TIP**
>
> Remember to use newlines or other whitespace to separate your data; it will make your dump much more readable. It is also a good practice to end your output with a newline to ensure your output doesn't get scrambled with the next object to dump.

If you are running your application under the Visual C++ debugger, MFC will set up the dump context passed to Dump() to send its output to the Output window of the debugger.

The insertion operator for the dump context that is used in the examples is defined for the following types:

```
BYTE
WORD
DWORD
int
UINT
LONG
double
float
CObject*
CObject&
void*
LPCTSTR
LPCWSTR
LPCSTR
```

If the type you want to dump isn't supported, you can generally get by with a simple cast. After all, the data is just going to be converted to a string for output.

The TRACE() Macro

In addition to the Dump() function, your application can write to the debug context with the TRACE() macro provided by MFC. The TRACE() macro works much like printf(). It accepts a string that may include placeholders for other variables, using the same % variables that printf() uses, except TRACE() does not support floating-point variables. The TRACE() macros will, however, support Unicode strings.

With the MFC Tracer application (TRACER.EXE), included in the Tools menu of Developer Studio, you can enable or disable several sorts of trace messages provided by MFC's internals, as well as disable tracing altogether.

If you wish to assign MFC's dump context—and the TRACE() and Dump() output that goes with it—to something other than the debugger's Output window, see the documentation for the CDumpContext and Dumpinit.cpp in Msdev\Mfc\Src, which declares CDumpContext afxDump. Unfortunately, the details of doing this are beyond the scope of this book.

Putting It All Together

In this chapter, you have taken a look at the classes in the application architecture hierarchy and have seen many of the features these classes have to offer. Now let's take a look at how MFC brings this all together to get your application off and running.

The first thing that your application will do when it begins executing is initialize all the static and global objects in your application. Perhaps the most important global object that will be created is an instance of your CWinApp class. If you have created your app with AppWizard, this is done for you by code like this from HiMom.cpp in the HiMom sample:

```
/////////////////////////////////////////////////////////////////////////////
// The one and only CHiMomApp object
CHiMomApp theApp;
```

The code created by Visual C++ will call the constructor of your CWinApp class just after creating global variables by loading an initialized data segment and constructing a few other objects that MFC uses internally.

You should be aware that your application is not really running yet when the constructor for your CWinApp (or any other static object) is called. You should avoid doing any serious operations in these constructors, particularly with Windows classes. Simple initialization of your variables (including CString objects) is fine, but you will soon run into trouble if you try to perform operations on other more complicated classes, particularly classes such as CWnd, because the actual window underlying CWnd objects has not been created yet.

WinMain()

Once all the constructors for static objects have run, the runtime library will call MFC's implementation of WinMain(). This function will take care of initializing MFC for you and will then call the InitApplication() and InitInstance() members of your CWinApp class. When these have finished, WinMain() will call the Run() function of your CWinApp class. Normally, this defaults to CWinThread::Run(), which will get the message pump for your application going. At this point, your application will begin to process messages like any good Windows application.

When your application terminates (when a WM_QUIT message is received) MFC will call the ExitInstance() function of your CWinApp class, then the destructors of any static objects, including your CWinApp object. The application then returns control to the operating system and is done.

InitApplication() **and** InitInstance()

The InitApplication() function is really not necessary for Win32 programming, but is a relic from the good (or bad) old days of Win16. In 16-bit windows, two instances of an application could run at the same time, with the InitApplication() code running only when the first instance was started. In Win32, an application that is run twice, it will exist in two totally separate, independent processes. You can place code in InitApplication(), but it is no different than InitInstance() in Win32, except InitApplication() will be called first. If you choose to override the default InitApplication(), you should return TRUE if all is well. If your function returns FALSE, initialization will halt, ending your program.

> **NOTE**
>
> If you are used to doing all your initialization in `WinMain()`, you will find that you can still access the information passed in the parameters to `WinMain()` by way of members of the `CWinApp` class.
>
> The handle to the executing instance of the application, normally passed to `WinMain()` as `hInstance`, is available in `CWinApp::m_hInstance` or by calling `::AfxGetInstanceHandle()`, which can be called from anywhere.
>
> The `hPrevInstance` parameter to `WinMain()` is always `NULL` in Win32 applications, so it is not provided in a member variable.
>
> The `lpszCmdLine` parameter to `WinMain()`, which points to the command-line string, may be found in `CWinApp::m_lpCmdLine`. You will take a closer look at using this in just a bit.
>
> The `nCmdShow` parameter to `WinMain()` is available in the `m_nCmdShow` member. This should be used in your call to `ShowWindow()`.

Your `InitInstance()` function is where all the serious initialization for your app should occur. If you look at the `InitInstance()` function created by AppWizard for the HiMom example shown next, you will notice that it does several very important things. Depending on the options you selected in AppWizard, you may see how AppWizard initializes things such as OLE, Windows sockets, and 3D controls:

```
/////////////////////////////////////////////////////////////////////////
// CHiMomApp initialization
BOOL CHiMomApp::InitInstance()
{
    // Standard initialization
    // If you are not using these features and wish to reduce the size
    //  of your final executable, you should remove from the following
    //  the specific initialization routines you do not need.
#ifdef _AFXDLL
    Enable3dControls();             // Call this when using MFC in a shared DLL
#else
    Enable3dControlsStatic();       // Call this when linking to MFC statically
#endif
    LoadStdProfileSettings();  // Load standard INI file options (including MRU)

    // Register the application's document templates.  Document templates
    //  serve as the connection between documents, frame windows and views.
    CMultiDocTemplate* pDocTemplate;
    pDocTemplate = new CMultiDocTemplate(
        IDR_HIMOMTYPE,
        RUNTIME_CLASS(CHiMomDoc),
        RUNTIME_CLASS(CChildFrame), // custom MDI child frame
        RUNTIME_CLASS(CHiMomView));
    AddDocTemplate(pDocTemplate);
```

```
// create main MDI Frame window
CMainFrame* pMainFrame = new CMainFrame;
if (!pMainFrame->LoadFrame(IDR_MAINFRAME))
    return FALSE;
m_pMainWnd = pMainFrame;

// Parse command line for standard shell commands, DDE, file open
CCommandLineInfo cmdInfo;
ParseCommandLine(cmdInfo);

// Dispatch commands specified on the command line
if (!ProcessShellCommand(cmdInfo))
    return FALSE;
// The main window has been initialized, so show and update it.
pMainFrame->ShowWindow(m_nCmdShow);
pMainFrame->UpdateWindow();
return TRUE;
}

HiMom::InitInstance() from HiMom.cpp
```

LoadStdProfileSettings()

You should also notice a call to LoadStdProfileSettings(). This will load some standard data items, including the files on the Most Recently Used list, from either the application's .ini file or from the Registry. For now, suffice it to say that the Registry allows a hierarchical, secure place to store and retrieve data that was formerly relegated to various .ini files in Win16. Although MFC will default to using .ini files, you should look at Chapter 34, "Developing Complete Applications," for more information on using the Registry to store information about your application that you will want to use the next time your app starts.

Working with the Command Line

In MFC applications, you can handle command-line information in several ways. Traditional C-style argc and argv processing is available by using the __argc and __argv global variables provided. You may also look at the entire command line provided by m_lpCmdLine. Windows applications, however, can support some special command-line options that are best handled with the methods shown next.

As you can see from the previous example, InitInstance() creates a CCommandLineInfo object and passes it to ParseCommandLine(). This function will then call CCommandLineInfo::ParseParam() for each parameter. ParseParam() will modify the CCommandLineInfo structure based on these parameters. In InitInstance(), the resulting CCommandLineInfo object is then passed to ProcessShellCommand(), which is responsible for carrying out any default actions specified in the command line.

The default implementation of ParseParam() will handle the parameters and the actions detailed in Table 2.2.

Table 2.2. Default parameter actions.

Parameter	Action
(No parameter)	Create new document.
`<filename>`	Open specified file.
`/p <filename>`	Print specified file.
`/pt <filename> <printer> <driver> <port>`	Print file to specified printer.
`/dde`	Serve a DDE session.
`/automation`	Start an OLE automation server.
`/embedding`	Prepare to serve an embedded OLE object.

You may use `argc`, `argv` processing along with `ParseCommandLine()` if you want, or you may change the way `ParseCommandLine()` works by creating your own class derived from `CCommandLineInfo` and overriding the `ParseParam()` function.

You may also change your application's behavior by modifying the `CCommandLineInfo` object before you call `ProcessShellCommand()`. For example, if you do not want your application to create a new document by default, you can make sure that the `m_nShellCommand` member of the `CCommandLineInfo` object is not `FileNew` before you pass it to `ProcessShellCommand()`. For more on this, refer to `CCommandLineInfo` in the Visual C++ online documentation.

Creating the Main Window

The last thing that the AppWizard-generated version of `InitInstance` does is call `ShowWindow()` and `UpdateWindow()` to present the main window of your application, which was created earlier in `InitInstance`. Like `InitApplication()`, your `InitInstance()` call should return `FALSE` only if something has gone wrong and you want to bail out of your program right there.

The Message Pump

Now that all the initialization for your program has executed, the `CWinThread::Run()` function will start up the message pump, or message loop, of your application. The message pump will do nothing but wait until it receives a message. At this point, the message is dispatched to a message handler function, provided by your application or by MFC, that will react to the message. The details of message dispatching are covered in the next chapter.

OnIdle()

When I said that the message pump does nothing but wait around between messages, I stretched the truth just a little. When the message pump finds that the message queue is empty, it will call OnIdle(), which may allow you to do some background processing or update the status of your user interface objects, such as disabling toolbars if needed.

The OnIdle() function will be called repeatedly until it returns FALSE, or until a message is received—at which point, the message is dispatched. When OnIdle() returns FALSE, the message pump will sleep until the next message arrives.

If you choose to implement your own OnIdle() function, you should keep in mind that the message queue for your application (or at least this thread) will not be able to process any messages until OnIdle() returns, because this is a non-preemptive method of multitasking. If you want to do preemptive multitasking, see Chapter 9. Also, your implementation of OnIdle() should call the base class implementation, which updates user interface objects and cleans up some internal data structures. With this in mind, the declaration of OnIdle() looks like this:

```
virtual BOOL OnIdle(LONG lCount);
```

The lCount parameter is incremented each time OnIdle() is called and it is set to 0 when new messages are processed.

Summary

In this chapter, you learned how to create an application using AppWizard to save time. You have also looked at the classes that make up the application architecture hierarchy and what they can do for the application. Finally, you saw how MFC uses the application hierarchy to get your application started.

3

MFC Messages and Commands

by David Bennett

Windows programs are based on an event-driven programming model. This means that most of the things your application will do are done in response to various Windows messages. If you have done any Windows programming, you already know this. This chapter will show you how to work with MFC to handle messages with C++ classes. In this chapter, you will learn about

■ Standard Windows commands handled by the MFC

■ How MFC dispatches messages to your application

■ Using ClassWizard to handle messages

■ Implementing your own message maps

Message Categories

Almost everything that your application will do is based on handling Windows messages. These come in three basic varieties: general Windows messages, control notifications, and commands.

The Message IDs for Windows messages are generally prefixed by WM_—for example, WM_PAINT or WM_QUIT. These messages, which are handled by windows and views, can represent a wide range of things that happen in your application. Thankfully, MFC provides default handlers for most of these, as you will see. Note that WM_COMMAND messages receive special handling as either control notifications or commands.

Control notifications are WM_COMMAND messages sent from child windows to their parent window. For example, an edit control will send an EN_CHANGE message to its parent window (usually a dialog box) whenever its content may have changed. Windows messages and control notifications are usually handled by window objects—that is, objects derived from class CWnd.

Commands are WM_COMMAND messages from menus, buttons (including toolbars), and accelerator keys. Command messages may be handled by a wider array of classes, including documents, document templates, windows, views, and the application itself.

Message Handling in MFC

MFC provides a framework for handling windows messages that can be much easier to work with than the web of switches and ifs that are used in traditional Windows programs to control the handling of messages. This is based on the capability of classes derived from CCmdTarget to have their own message maps. MFC uses the message maps of your classes to decide how any given message should be handled, allowing you to take full advantage of the benefits of the C++ language to encapsulate functionality in your classes so that other classes derived from them don't have to reinvent the wheel.

To further expand on reusability, MFC provides default handlers for a wide range of commands used in most Windows applications. Most of the commands that have default handlers are also included in the default menus generated by AppWizard. The following are menu commands that have default handlers in MFC:

File menu commands: New, Open, Close, Save, Save As, Page Setup, Print Setup, Print, Print Preview, Exit, and the most recently used files list

Edit menu commands: Clear, Clear All, Copy, Cut, Find, Paste, Repeat, Replace, Select All, Undo, and Redo

View menu commands: Toolbar and Status Bar

Window menu commands: New, Arrange, Cascade, Tile Horizontal, Tile Vertical, and Split

Help menu commands: Index, Using Help, and About

The menus created by AppWizard generate messages for the standard commands defined in AFXRES.H. For example, the File | New menu item generates a message with the command ID of ID_FILE_NEW. The other standard commands are similarly named, with ID_, the menu name, and the command name.

If you wish to perform one of these standard actions, you can send one of the predefined command messages from anywhere in your application that will be handled by MFC's default handlers. Of course, you can also implement your own handlers for these commands, but you will explore that later. For more information on the default commands, see Technical Note 22 (TN022) in the online help.

Message Dispatching

As mentioned in Chapter 2, "MFC Overview," the Run() function of the CWinThread class provides the message pump for your application. (For now, let's assume there is only one thread in your application. If you want to learn how to use threads to have more than one message pump in your app, see Chapter 9, "Multithreading with MFC.") The only function of the message pump is to wait for messages and then send them where they should go to be handled—this is called dispatching the message.

When the message pump receives a Windows message, it identifies the class that should get first crack at handling the message by consulting an internal structure that maps the handles of existing windows to the class responsible for each window. MFC will then check to see whether this targeted class provides an entry for the message in its message map. If an entry is found, the message is passed to the handler, ending the dispatch process. If an entry for the message is not found, MFC will check the message map of the base class for the targeted class, moving farther up the class hierarchy until an entry is found.

For command messages, the search is quite a bit more complicated. When a command is routed to a class it may allow another class to try to handle it before checking its own message map or routing the command to another command target. In most cases, a command target will route commands in the following order:

1. To the currently active child command target object
2. To itself
3. To other command targets

Table 3.1 lists more specific routing for the usual command target classes. When a class is mentioned in the right side of the table, you should jump to that class on the left side, follow its routing, then go back to where you were to continue the routing.

Table 3.1. Standard command routing.

This object type	*Routes commands in this order*
MDI Main Frame	1. Active `CMDIChildWnd`
	2. This frame window
	3. Application (`CWinApp`)
MDI child frame	1. Active view
	2. This frame window
SDI Main Frame	1. Active view
	2. This frame window
	3. Application (`CWinApp`)
View	1. This view
	2. Document associated with this view
Document	1. This document
	2. Document template associated with this document
Dialog Box	1. This dialog box
	2. Window that owns this dialog
	3. Application (`CWinApp`)

By now, this is as clear as mud, right? The following example will clear things up a bit.

Suppose you add a menu item that will send the ID_MY_COMMAND command message to the MDI main frame of your application:

1. The command is first routed to the main frame, which will check the active child frame first.

2. The child frame will first check the active view, which checks its own message map before routing the command to the associated document.

3. The document will check its own message map before checking the message map of the associated document template.

4. Going back to the child frame's routing, the child frame will check its own message map.

5. Going back to the main frame's routing, the main frame will check its own message map.

6. Ultimately, the message map of the application object is checked, where an entry for your message is found and the appropriate handler is called.

If you find that you must use a different command routing scheme, perhaps to include your own special command target classes, you can do so by overriding the OnCmdMsg() member of CCmdTarget. This may involve overriding OnCmdMsg() for several classes and is beyond the scope of this book; for more information, see Command Routing in the MFC online documentation.

> **NOTE**
>
> MFC speeds up this process by using an internal cache of recent message handler search results, avoiding lengthy searches.

I know this all seems horribly complicated, but it will make much more sense when you work with documents and views in the next chapter. In fact, it will seem much simpler even sooner, when you see how you can use ClassWizard to associate messages with the appropriate handler.

Message Handling with ClassWizard

For most all of your message handling tasks, you will find that ClassWizard can be a great help. ClassWizard allows you to map messages to handlers for all your classes that are derived from CCmdTarget, by using the Message Maps page of ClassWizard. Remember that you can always start ClassWizard from the View menu or by pressing Ctrl+W. Selecting the Message Maps tab will present a dialog box that looks like the one in Figure 3.1.

FIGURE 3.1.
*The ClassWizard
Message Maps page.*

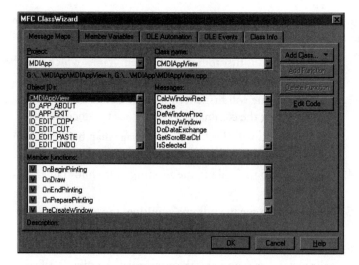

If you have multiple projects in your workspace, you will first need to select the appropriate entry in the Project list. You can then select any of your classes derived from CCmdTarget in the Class name list. This will present you with a list of Object IDs, the messages those objects may receive, and a list of the member functions already implemented in the Member functions list.

The objects listed in the Object ID's list can be of three different types: the classes listed in Class name, menu item objects, and other controls that may send messages to the class you have selected in Class name.

When you select your class name from the top of the Object IDs list, you will see a list of all of the Windows messages that your class is likely to receive, including several functions, such as InitInstance or Create, that aren't really message handlers at all. Nevertheless, ClassWizard will allow you to manage these functions here as well. ClassWizard will display only a certain subset of all available Windows messages, based on the Message filter specified in the Class Info page. This allows you to filter out messages that are not normally handled by certain classes. If you want to handle a message that you don't see listed, try changing the message filter.

TIP

To find out more about a message in the Messages list, highlight the message and press F1 to get help on the specifics of that message and its handler function.

When you select a menu command, such as ID_FILE_OPEN, from the Object IDs list, you will see two entries in the Messages list. To do something when the user selects this command from a menu, select the COMMAND message. The UPDATE_COMMAND_UI message is used to help update the status (checked, grayed, and so forth) of the menu item. You will look at this in greater detail in Chapter 5, "Dialogs and Controls."

The third type of objects listed in the Object IDs list are controls that may send messages to your class. For simple controls such as buttons, you will receive only a limited set of messages, such as BN_CLICKED and BN_DOUBLECLICKED. For more complicated objects, such as edit controls, you will be able to handle many different control notifications.

> **TIP**
>
> If you want your class to handle notifications from a control that is not listed, make sure that the control is highlighted in a resource editor window before you start ClassWizard.

Once you have selected the message that you want to handle, simply click on the Add Function button to create a handler function. ClassWizard will add a declaration for your handler to the declaration of your class and add a message map entry and skeleton handler function to your class implementation.

All you have to do now is add the code to your handler function. You can go straight to your new handler function implementation by double-clicking in the Member functions list or by clicking on the Edit Code button.

Creating Your Own Message Maps

When you create a class with AppWizard or ClassWizard, Visual C++ will produce the code to create a message map for your class. If you create your own CCmdTarget-derived class outside of ClassWizard, you need to create the message map yourself. You should start by adding the following line to the end of your class declaration:

```
DECLARE_MESSAGE_MAP()
```

This macro is defined in AFXWIN.H in the \DevStudio\VC\mfc\include directory. It declares the array that will hold your message map entries and some pointers used to find the message map of the base class. You should be aware, though, that the structures for your class's message map are defined static const. This means that you can have only one message map for all objects of your class, not a different map for each object. This also means that you cannot change a class's message map at runtime, at least not with methods that are discussed here. (It can be done with overrides of PreTranslateMessage() or the functions hidden in the message map itself.)

Next, you add a message map to your class implementation. To see how this is done, let's take a look at the message map implementation created for the CHimMomApp class in HiMom.cpp:

```
/////////////////////////////////////////////////////////////////////////////
// CHiMomApp
BEGIN_MESSAGE_MAP(CHiMomApp, CWinApp)
    //{{AFX_MSG_MAP(CHiMomApp)
```

```
ON_COMMAND(ID_APP_ABOUT, OnAppAbout)
    // NOTE - the ClassWizard will add and remove mapping macros here.
    //    DO NOT EDIT what you see in these blocks of generated code!
//}}AFX_MSG_MAP
// Standard file based document commands
ON_COMMAND(ID_FILE_NEW, CWinApp::OnFileNew)
ON_COMMAND(ID_FILE_OPEN, CWinApp::OnFileOpen)
// Standard print setup command
ON_COMMAND(ID_FILE_PRINT_SETUP, CWinApp::OnFilePrintSetup)
END_MESSAGE_MAP()
```

As you can see in this example, message maps are created by a set of macros, beginning with BEGIN_MESSAGE_MAP() and ending with END_MESSAGE_MAP(). To start the definition of your message map, use the BEGIN_MESSAGE_MAP() macro, which takes the name of your class and the name of its base class as parameters.

The BEGIN_MESSAGE_MAP() macro (defined in AFXWIN.H) actually defines the _messageEntries array, leaving the initializer list open, to be filled by additional macros. If you forget to include the END_MESSAGE_MAP() macro, which closes the initializer list, the compiler will become quite lost, so make sure you end your message map with END_MESSAGE_MAP().

Populating the Message Map

In the previous example, you will see a DO NOT EDIT message from ClassWizard. It is a good idea to avoid editing these sections if you don't have to, but you can make changes here. However, you should be aware that changes to these blocks have the potential to confuse ClassWizard so that you cannot edit your class or must regenerate the .clw file. ClassWizard may just overwrite your new changes. If you make changes to these blocks yourself, try to model your code after other ClassWizard-generated code and check the function of ClassWizard right after making your changes.

That said, you will be populating your message map by using several different macros for different types of messages, including message ranges.

Predefined Windows Message Handlers

For many standard Windows messages, there are predefined message map macros provided in AFXMSG.H. The names for these macros are derived directly from the message ID and they take no parameters. For example, the WM_PAINT message can be mapped by the ON_WM_PAINT() macro. This will map the WM_PAINT message to the OnPaint() function of your class. The other standard Windows messages are implemented in a similar fashion.

Other Windows Messages

For your own user-defined messages, or for Windows commands that do not have a default handler, you can use the generic ON_MESSAGE() macro, which takes the message ID and handler function name:

```
ON_MESSAGE( WM_USER+1, OnMyUserMessage)
```

The handler for these messages would be declared like this:

```
afx_msg LRESULT OnMyUserMessage(WPARAM wParam, LPARAM lParam);
```

Command Messages

For command messages, you will use the ON_COMMAND() macro(), which takes the command ID (which will be in the wParam of the WM_COMMAND message) and the name of the handler function:

```
ON_COMMAND(ID_FILE_NEW, CWinApp::OnFileNew)
```

The handler function will take no parameters and return void:

```
afx_msg void OnFileNew();
```

Control Notifications

Notifications from controls can be mapped by using the ON_CONTROL()() macro, which takes the control ID, the command ID, and the handler function as arguments:

```
ON_CONTROL( BN_CLICKED, IDC_MY_BUTTON, OnMyButtonClicked)
```

The handler for these messages, like command messages, returns void and takes no parameters:

```
afx_msg void OnMyButtonClicked();
```

Command and Control Ranges

There are also macros that will map a handler to messages for a range of commands or controls. This is one of the few areas where you must make your own message map entries, because ClassWizard doesn't handle ranges. Your entries for ranges would look like this:

```
ON_COMMAND_RANGE(ID_MY_FIRST_COMMAND, ID_MY_LAST_COMMAND, myCommandHandler)
ON_CONTROL_RANGE(BN_CLICKED, IDC_FIRST_BUTTON, IDC_LAST_BUTTON, MyButtonHandler)
```

Registered Messages

For message IDs that you have received from the RegisterWindowsMessage() function, you can use ON_REGISTERED_MESSAGE()(), which takes the registered message ID and the handler function. The handler again returns void and takes no parameters.

Other Message Map Macros

AFXMSG.H also defines many other macros designed to map different special cases of messages that you may find useful in creating your own message maps. For example, the ON_CONTROL() example used above can also be written like this:

```
ON_BN_CLICKED(IDC_MYBUTTON, OnMyButtonClicked)
```

This is actually the syntax that ClassWizard uses when it inserts entries like this, but it results in exactly the same entry in the message map as the ON_CONTROL() macro used above. There are also special macros for handling OLE functions and user interface updates that you will learn about later.

Inside the Message Map

The message map macros DECLARE_MESSAGE_MAP, BEGIN_MESSAGE_MAP, and END_MESSAGE_MAP are defined in AFXWIN.H. If you are curious, you can find this file in the \Devstudio\VC\mfc\include directory. In short, DECLARE_MESSAGE_MAP defines functions to return the class's message map (GetMessageMap()), and that of its base class (_GetBaseMessageMap()), as well as an AFX_MSGMAP structure. This structure consists primarily of an array of AFX_MSGMAP_ENTRY structures (_messageEntries[]).

The BEGIN_MESSAGE_MAP() macro implements the GetMessageMap() and _GetBaseMessageMap() functions, then begins initializing the _messageEntries[] array. The initializer list is left without a closing brace, leaving END_MESSAGE_MAP to add an entry that marks the end of the message map and closes the initializer list.

In this code, between BEGIN_MESSAGE_MAP and END_MESSAGE_MAP, you use the message map entry macros, such as ON_COMMAND, which is actually defined like this:

```
#define ON_COMMAND(id, memberFxn) \
    { WM_COMMAND, CN_COMMAND, (WORD)id, (WORD)id, AfxSig_vv, (AFX_PMSG)&memberFxn },
```

The values specified in the message map macros are used to initialize an AFX_MSGMAP_ENTRY, which looks like this:

```
struct AFX_MSGMAP_ENTRY
{
    UINT nMessage;     // windows message
    UINT nCode;        // control code or WM_NOTIFY code
    UINT nID;          // control ID (or 0 for windows messages)
    UINT nLastID;      // used for entries specifying a range of control id's
    UINT nSig;         // signature type (action) or pointer to message #
    AFX_PMSG pfn;      // routine to call (or special value)
};
```

The first four elements are used by MFC to check whether this message map entry applies to the Windows message that is being dispatched. The last two elements specify information about the handler function to be called. pfn is a pointer to the function to call, and nSig is a special signature type, which MFC uses to specify the return type and parameters that will be passed to the function specified by pfn.

The values used for nSig are defined in the AfxSig enum type in Afxmsg_.h. This file also lists the function prototypes that should be used to correspond with each nSig value.

If you are ever unsure of what form a handler function for a given message map macro should take, you can look up the macro—for example, ON_COMMAND—in Afxmsg_.h, see that it uses AfxSig_vv, then find the definition of AfxSig_vv to find that your handler function should return void and take no parameters.

Using ClassWizard to add your handler functions will save you this trouble in most cases; however, there are certain message map entries that ClassWizard does not support, such as ON_COMMAND_RANGE or ON_THREAD_MESSAGE.

Implementing Handler Functions

When you add handler functions with ClassWizard, your handler function will be created for you, with the proper parameters and return type. If you create your message map entries and corresponding handler functions yourself, be very careful to declare your handler function with the parameters and return type that the message map entry expects. Failure to do so will result in a corrupted stack at some point and can cause big headaches.

PreTranslateMessage()

In most cases, the message pump receives messages and dispatches them by way of message maps, as you saw in the previous example. However, if you find that you need to intercept messages prior to the normal dispatch process, MFC offers a way to do this—the PreTranslateMessage() function.

You can override the PreTranslateMessage() member function in any class derived from CWnd, CWinApp, or CWinThread. The function takes a pointer to an MSG structure and returns a BOOL. If PreTranslateMessage() returns TRUE, MFC will assume that you have handled the message. If it returns FALSE, MFC assumes that you have elected not to handle it and will proceed with its normal dispatch process.

Summary

In this chapter, you learned how MFC handles messages, including the default message handlers for common commands. You also looked at how MFC dispatches a message to the appropriate handler function and how to create message maps, both with and without ClassWizard.

4

Frames, Documents, and Views

by David Bennett

At some point, you have undoubtedly used a Windows application that works with documents and views, whether you called them by these names or not. The most common example of this would be almost any Windows-based word processing application. In this chapter, you will explore how you can use MFC to help you create applications such as those, as well as some that are quite different in appearance but have the same underlying structure. In this chapter, you will learn

■ How to use the document/view architecture in MFC

■ How to use the view classes provided by MFC

■ How to add menus, status bars, toolbars, and splitters to your application

The Document/View Architecture

MFC not only provides a set of classes to help you work with document objects, but it provides a complete architecture that ties the various classes together. In this chapter, we will be looking at this architecture and what it can do for your applications. I think you will find the whole of the architecture is much greater than the sum of its parts.

Single Versus Multiple Document Applications

If you have used Windows at all, you should be familiar with applications, such as Microsoft Word, that enable you to work with several different documents within the same application. In Windows terms, this is known as a Multiple Document Interface (MDI). In addition to the support that the Windows SDK provides for MDI, MFC encapsulates MDI in the classes that make up the document/view architecture.

The Single Document Interface (SDI) is similar to MDI, but is designed for simpler applications that work with only one document and one view at any given time. Both MDI and SDI applications can use the document/view architecture provided by MFC in much the same way, except the MDI architecture provides an additional level of functionality to deal with multiple documents and views.

Of course, you are not required to use the document/view architecture in your applications, and you will most likely find situations where you don't even want to have a Windows user interface. You can use MFC in your applications without any GUI interface, or you can base your application on a single dialog. However, if your application fits in the document/view model, you will find that creating your application using either the SDI or MDI flavors of the document/view architecture can greatly simplify your task of adding features that Windows users have come to expect from all good Windows applications.

Document Classes

Although it doesn't take much imagination to see how a document object would apply to a word processing or spreadsheet application, the concept of a document in MFC can also apply to much more. In general terms, a document is any set of data that can logically be grouped. This may include anything from settings for a terminal session to simulation models to information about your favorite records or to just about anything else that you might consider writing to a file. In MFC, document objects are derived from class CDocument. In most cases, your application will somehow present the data in your document to the user. This is done by using views.

View Classes

A view object is just that—a view of the document. This may be either some direct representation of the document object or some other sort of display that is related to the data in your document. For example, your document may store settings for some data acquisition application, and your views will show the data acquired based on those settings. As you might guess, view objects in MFC are derived from class CView. However, you will probably derive your view classes from some of the other classes that MFC provides for you that add functionality to the basic CView class.

Frames

MFC applications that use the document/view architecture use frames to contain the views of the application. In SDI applications, the frame that contains the one and only view will also serve as the main frame, or main window, of your application. In MDI applications, this functionality is split between the main frame, which is the main window for your application, and child frames, which provide a window in which each of your views can run. The frame objects handle the menus, status bars, and toolbars for your application. The frame objects also receive the command messages generated in your views, although you will see later how these can be handled in the view. In SDI applications, frame windows are derived directly from class CFrameWnd, and MDI main frames and child frames derive from CMDIFrameWnd and CMDIChildWnd, respectively.

Document Templates

MFC uses document templates to tie your documents, views, and frames together. As you will see, it is actually the document template that creates new documents and new view windows to display them. Document templates are derived from class CSingleDocTemplate for SDI apps and from class CMultiDocTemplate for MDI apps.

Creating Your Application

The easiest way to create an application that comes prewired to support the document/view architecture is to use the AppWizard to create an application, choosing Single document or Multiple documents in step 1. Although using AppWizard is by no means a requirement for using the document/view architecture, it provides you with premade classes for your documents, views, and frames, as well as initializes your document template. Even if you do not use AppWizard to generate your application, you may find that creating a sample application (which takes about 10 seconds) can provide a useful example of how MFC sets things up for working with documents and views.

In any case, developing an application that uses the document/view architecture will involve creating your document, view, frame, and document template classes. After you have done this, and properly initialized your objects, your documents and views will pretty much take care of themselves.

Creating Your Document Class

Your document class derives from the CDocument class. If you plan to use OLE (which you will explore in Part IV, "Network Programming with Win32"), your documents may derive from COleDocument or COleServerDoc. To start, let's look at the following declaration for a document class created with AppWizard:

```
// MDIAppDoc.h : interface of the CMDIAppDoc class
//
/////////////////////////////////////////////////////////////////////////////
class CMDIAppDoc : public CDocument
{
protected: // create from serialization only
    CMDIAppDoc();
    DECLARE_DYNCREATE(CMDIAppDoc)
// Attributes
public:
// Operations
public:
// Overrides
    // ClassWizard generated virtual function overrides
    //{{AFX_VIRTUAL(CMDIAppDoc)
    public:
    virtual BOOL OnNewDocument();
    virtual void Serialize(CArchive& ar);
    //}}AFX_VIRTUAL
// Implementation
public:
    virtual ~CMDIAppDoc();
#ifdef _DEBUG
    virtual void AssertValid() const;
    virtual void Dump(CDumpContext& dc) const;
#endif
protected:
// Generated message map functions
```

```
protected:
    //{{AFX_MSG(CMDIAppDoc)
        // NOTE - the ClassWizard will add and remove member functions here.
        //    DO NOT EDIT what you see in these blocks of generated code !
    //}}AFX_MSG
    DECLARE_MESSAGE_MAP()
};
/////////////////////////////////////////////////////////////////////////////
```

In this example, AppWizard has declared the document class, derived from CDocument, including the standard constructor and destructor. Notice that the constructor is protected and is not declared virtual. This is done because you will create only new document objects from serialization. It may also seem strange to talk about serialization when you use only the DECLARE_DYNCREATE macro instead of DECLARE_SERIAL. You actually use DECLARE_SERIAL only if you plan to use polymorphic pointers to your object to access serialization functions. This example calls the Serialize() function directly, which is fully supported by DECLARE_DYNCREATE.

In addition, AppWizard has declared overrides for the OnNewDocument() and Serialize() functions, as well as the AssertValid() and Dump() debug functions. The class declaration also declares the message map for the document class.

Document Data

As mentioned previously, your document object will hold the data that is used by your application. When deciding how to structure the data in your document class, you should consider that you will want to support the following operations efficiently:

■ Presenting the data to views
■ Presenting changes in the data to views
■ Storing the data in files
■ Presenting the data in pages for printing

It is a good practice to include your document data as member variables of your document class. This allows you to take full advantage of the serialization features provided by MFC and the predefined operations for File New, Open, Save, Save As, and the most recently used files list. Once you have decided how to represent your data, you implement some of the function overrides discussed in the following sections.

Serialize()

Recall that the Serialize() function of your document class is used to implement several functions involving your document and files. Your serialize implementation should look something like the following:

```
void CMyDocument::Serialize(CArchive& ar)
{
    // call base class Serialize() first
    CDocument::Serialize(ar);
```

```
    // then serialize the data for this class
    if(ar.IsLoading())
    {
        ar >> m_MyDataVariable;
        // load other data members
    }
    else
    {
        ar << m_MyDataVariable;
        // store other data members
    }
    // Serialize your member objects
    m_MyDataObject.Serialize(ar);
    m_MoreDataObject.Serialize(ar);
} // end CMyDocument::Serialize
```

Remember to call the `Serialize()` function of the base class first. You will also notice that the serialize functions for the member objects included in the document class are called. This allows the objects to serialize themselves and is included outside of the `IsLoading()` block, because the `Serialize()` function of these classes will have their own check for `IsLoading()`.

OnNewDocument()

The `OnNewDocument()` function of your document class will be called by the framework whenever the user chooses the New command from the File menu. In MDI applications, a new document object is created, and this function is responsible for initializing it. In SDI applications, the same document object is reused. Your `OnNewDocument()` function is then responsible for reinitializing the document.

> **NOTE**
>
> The constructor for your document object is called only once during the lifetime of SDI Applications. Any reinitialization code will be run only if it is placed in the `OnNewDocument()` function.

If you have created your application with AppWizard, you will see that the default implementation of `OnNewDocument()` simply defers to the `CDocument::OnNewDocument()` function. This function will call the `DeleteContents()` member function of your class to ensure that the document is empty and will reset the dirty flag of your document. If you choose to override `OnNewDocument()`, you should first call the base class function:

```
BOOL CMyDoc::OnNewDocument()
{
    if(!CDocument::OnNewDocument())
        return FALSE;
    // Do any other initialization your document here
    return TRUE;
} // end OnNewDocument()
```

If this function returns FALSE, creation of the new document will be aborted. If an exception is thrown during this operation, the ReportSaveLoadException() function, described later in this section, will be called.

DeleteContents()

The DeleteContents() member of your document class is called by the default implementation of OnNewDocument() to clear out the data in your document without actually deleting the document object. This is particularly necessary for SDI apps, where the same document object is reused. It will also be called just before your document object is destroyed. The default implementation of DeleteContents does nothing, but it can be overridden like this:

```
void CMyDoc::DeleteContents()
{
    // clear data elements
    m_MyCounter = 0;
    // delete dynamic objects created by your document
    delete(m_MyObjectPtr);
} // end DeleteContents()
```

You may also want to call this function to implement something like an Edit | Clear All function to clear your document.

OnOpenDocument()

Whenever the user chooses the File | Open command from a menu, the default handler will call the OnOpenDocument() function of your document object. The default implementation opens the file specified in lpszPathName, calls DeleteContents() to clear out the document object, resets the dirty flag for the document, and then calls the Serialize() function to load the new document from the file. Once again, SDI apps will reuse the same document object, and MDI apps will create a new one. If you need to do any initialization of your document that is not provided by the Serialize() function, you can override OnOpenDocument() like this:

```
BOOL CMyDoc::OnOpenDocument(LPCTSTR lpszPathName)
{
    if(!CDocument::OnOpenDocument())
        return FALSE;
    // Perform any additional initialization for your document here
    return TRUE;
} // end OnOpenDocument
```

If this function returns FALSE, the open document operation will fail.

OnSaveDocument()

When the user selects either the Save or Save As commands from the File menu, the framework will call the OnSaveDocument() function of your document class. For most applications, the default implementation is adequate. It will open the selected file, call the Serialize() function to write your document data to the file, and reset the dirty flag.

OnCloseDocument()

The `OnCloseDocument()` function is called by the framework whenever the user closes a document. The default implementation calls the `DeleteContents()` member of your document, then closes the frame windows for all views associated with this document.

ReportSaveLoadException()

If an exception is thrown while saving or loading your document that is not handled within your code, the framework will call the `ReportSaveLoadException()` function, which will present error messages to the user. This function can also be overridden if you want to do any special messaging. You'll learn more about exceptions in Chapter 7, "General-Purpose Classes."

The Dirty Flag

Users have come to expect that any good Windows app will not let them accidentally do things such as exiting an application without saving their data. To help implement this in your applications, classes derived from `CDocument` provide a dirty flag to keep track of whether the document has changed since it was last saved. The framework checks this flag before closing a document and will automatically prompt the user to save the file.

The dirty flag is automatically cleared when you save or open a document, but it is set for you only when you change an OLE object in your document. Your code is responsible for setting the flag whenever your document changes. This is accomplished by using `SetModifiedFlag()`, which takes a parameter of `TRUE` or `FALSE`. Setting the modified flag to `TRUE`, which is the default parameter, tells the framework that the document contains changes since the last save. You can query the dirty flag in your application by calling the `IsModified()` member of `CDocument`.

There are also several overridable functions of `CDocument` that affect how the framework handles the dirty flag. If you are interested in modifying the default behavior, take a look at `CDocument::CanCloseFrame()` and `CDocument::SaveModified()`.

Accessing Your Document

MFC provides several ways that you will be able to access your document object from within your application. All objects derived from `CView` are associated with a document object when they are created. You can access the document associated with a view by calling `CView::GetDocument()`. In addition, you can access the currently active document from any `CFrameWnd` derivative, including your MDI main frame, by calling `CFrameWnd::GetActiveDocument()`. If you want to find the active document for your application, you can use the `m_pMainWnd` member of your `CWinApp` object like this:

```
pDoc = theApp.m_pMainWnd.GetActiveDocument();
```

Views

Now that you have your application's data set up in documents, you need to be able to present the data to the user. This is done by the view classes, which serve both to present your data to the user and to handle most user input for your data. Remember that you will generally not want to store data in your view—this is what the document is for.

If you want to be able to save settings for your views, you also will want to consider keeping this information in your document. If you want to save settings for your application on a global basis, you should look at loading this data in the InitInstance() function of your application.

The View Classes

MFC provides several different view classes that help you implement different general methods of displaying your data and accepting input from the user. All these classes are based on CView, which provides a great deal of the functionality needed to work with views and their associated documents. However, you will probably not use CView objects directly, because they really don't provide much functionality to manage the display. Instead, your views will most likely be based on the CView derivative classes listed in the next sections.

CScrollView

The CScrollView class, as the name suggests, will add scroll bars to your view. Although you will still have to do your own drawing in the view, it can save you a lot of work by managing window and viewport sizes and managing mapping modes, as well as automatically scrolling when scroll bar messages are received.

Setting Up the Scroll Bars

In order to scroll the display properly in your view, you must tell the scroll view a few things about how to scroll the view. Most importantly, the view must know something about the total size of your document. In most cases, you will want to add a function to your document class that will return the logical size of your document, preferably in units based on the mapping mode that you plan to use for drawing. For more on mapping modes and drawing in general, see Chapter 6, "Drawing and Printing with MFC." For now, you will look at how the view classes can assist your drawing efforts.

To tell the view how to set up its scroll bars, you use the SetScrollSizes() member of the CScrollView class, which takes four parameters. The first parameter is the mapping mode used for the next three parameters. In this section, you use MM_TEXT, which maps one logical unit to one pixel. The second parameter is a SIZE structure that gives the total size of your document.

The third and fourth parameters are also SIZE structures that tell the scroll view how far to scroll when scrolling by pages and by lines, respectively. If you omit the third and fourth parameters, the view will scroll by one-tenth of the total size when the user uses the PgUp or PgDown keys, and by one-tenth of that when the user uses the arrow keys or clicks on the arrows on the scroll bars.

It is generally most convenient to set up your scroll sizes in the OnUpdate() and OnInitialUpdate() functions of your view class, so that the scroll sizes are adjusted any time the underlying document changes. You should also provide a minimum size for your document's view. The following example from the OnUpdate() function will illustrate how to do this:

```
CSize DocSize = GetDocument()->GetMyDocumentSize();
if(DocSize.cx < 100) DocSize.cx = 100;
if(DocSize.cy < 100) DocSize.cy = 100;
SetScrollSizes(MM_TEXT, DocSize);
```

As an alternative to using scroll bars, class CScrollView allows you to scale the view to show the whole document. This is done by using the SetScaleToFitSize() function, which takes one parameter for the total size of the document. If you use this, you do not need to call SetScrollSizes(), although you are free to switch between scale to fit and scroll mode by calling these functions.

Drawing with CScrollView

You will take an in-depth look at drawing in Chapter 6, but I just want to point out a few things about drawing in a scroll view. Your drawing will be done in the OnDraw() member of your view class, but the CScrollView class provides an override to OnPrepareDC() that will set up the device context for your drawing. The overridden OnPrepareDC() function will set the viewport origin in the device context to implement the scroll window. This will work with the mapping mode that you specified in your call to SetScrollSizes(), so you make sure that you use the mapping mode with which you intend to draw. If you need to do anything else in OnPrepareDC(), you are free to override it, but you should call the base class implementation before doing anything else.

In your OnDraw() function, you don't really have to worry about the position of the scroll bars. However, if you are drawing many things that will eventually be clipped, your application is wasting time. You can use the CWnd::GetUpdateRect() function to get the rectangle that needs updating to make your drawing code much more efficient, by only drawing what needs to be drawn.

If you are interested in the current position of the scroll bars, you can get this by using GetScrollPosition() or GetDeviceScrollPosition(), which returns a CPoint object in logical units or device units, respectively.

CFormView **and** CRecordView

Many applications will provide the user with a view similar to what you might see on paper, fill-in-the-blank forms. MFC helps you do this, and much more, with the CFormView class. MFC also provides some specialized derivatives of CFormView to create forms for working with a database. The class provided for ODBC forms is CRecordView; the class for working with DAO is CDaoRecordView. You will look at both of these classes in Part V, "Database Programming."

The user interface for a form view is based on a dialog template, which will be created as a modeless child window of your view window. Therefore, you should make sure that your dialog box does not have a border or a caption. You also need to make sure that the constructor for your view is passed the resource ID of the dialog template that it will be using—it will accept either the integer ID or string name for the resource.

Form view classes created by the wizards will use an initializer list in the implementation of the constructor, like this:

```
MyFormView::MyFormView()
    : CFormView(MyFormView::IDD)
{
    // Constructor code…
```

An enum type, found in the class declaration, is used here to map IDD to the ID of our dialog template.

Control Views

MFC provides several handy view classes that use a Windows control to interface to the user. These include CEditView, CRichEditView, CListView, and CTreeView, which are all derived from the CCtrlView class. You do not use CCtrlView for creating view objects, but it does make a good base class for your own control views. As you might guess, each of the derived classes uses the Windows control with a similar name. CEditView makes use of an Edit control.

Combining the functionality of a control with that of a view in one class presents two different issues specific to control views: how to set style bits for a view and how to handle messages in a control. Both of these are just not normal things to do, but MFC provides solutions, as shown in the next sections.

Setting Control View Styles

Controls are usually created in dialog templates, where the resource editor allows you easy access to the style bits that dictate how the control will work. With control views, you cannot do this. Instead, you must override the PreCreateWindow() member of your view. For example, if you wanted to enable buttons in your tree view, you could do something like this:

```
BOOL CMyTreeView::PreCreateWindow(CREATESTRUCT& cs)
{
```

```
    if(!CTreeView::PreCreateWindow(cs))
        return FALSE;
    cs.style |= TVS_HASBUTTONS;
    return TRUE;
}
```

You should always call the base class version of `PreCreateWindow()` first. This will assign appropriate default values to the CREATESTRUCT and, more importantly, will see to it that MFC loads the appropriate control libraries and registers the correct windows classes.

Handling Control Notifications

Control windows generally send notifications to their parent window to make the application aware of what the user is doing. In the case of control views, this means that the frame actually receives these messages. Because it is desirable to contain all the code to manage your view in the view class, MFC provides the concept of message reflection.

MFC has altered the message routing code somewhat so that control notifications not handled by the parent (in this case the frame) can be reflected to the control window itself. If you use ClassWizard to handle your message maps, you will see an equals sign (=) before messages that may be handled by reflection in your view class.

Choosing to handle these messages results in slightly different macros being added to your message map. For example, ON_CONTROL becomes ON_CONTROL_REFLECT. Several control-oriented Windows messages may also be handled with reflection message map macros. For example, WM_HSCROLL may be handled by ON_WM_HSCROLL_REFLECT(). The different message map macros are required because MFC actually uses different message IDs for reflected messages.

Having said that, there are exceptions. All messages commonly used for owner-drawn controls—WM_DRAWITEM, WM_DELETEITEM, WM_COMPARE_ITEM, and WM_MEASUREITEM—are sent with the original message ID and may be handled as normal, without the _REFLECT macros.

CEditView

If you plan to manipulate simple text in your application, CEditView does just that. It uses an edit control to form the user interface for the view. CEditView does not support different font or color settings though. For those, you use a CRichEditView (discussed in a later section). In addition to wrapping the edit control, CEditView also adds support for the following command messages:

```
    ID_FILE_PRINT
    ID_EDIT_CUT
    ID_EDIT_COPY
    ID_EDIT_PASTE
    ID_EDIT_CLEAR
    ID_EDIT_UNDO
    ID_EDIT_SELECT_ALL
```

```
ID_EDIT_FIND
ID_EDIT_REPLACE
ID_EDIT_REPEAT
```

The catch is that the menu items to generate these commands are not implemented automatically; you must add these yourself. You look at how to add menus later in this chapter.

Working with CEditView Data

The CEditView class deviates from the standard document/view relationship. Because the view encapsulates an edit control, which stores its own data, the data for the edit view is not kept in the document, but in the view itself. Because of this, you must make sure that your application takes great care to synchronize the document and its views (of which you may have several). This can also present a problem when it comes to serializing your document.

To deal with this, it is generally best to call the Serialize function of your CEditView class in the Serialize function of your document. This will write the text length and actual text from your edit control. If you want to generate a readable text file, you can use the CEditView::SerializeRaw() function to omit the length information.

You can access a reference to the CEdit control object itself by using the GetEditControl() member of CEditView. Using this, you can perform any actions normally associated with edit controls, which are covered in Chapter 5, "Dialogs and Controls."

> **TIP**
>
> In Windows NT only, you can call CEdit::GetHandle() to access the actual memory used by the edit control. There is no way to do this in Win95.

Using CRichEditView

If you require greater functionality than CEditView, CRichEditView may just do the trick for you. Like the rich edit control that it is based on, views derived from CRichEditView support the Microsoft Rich Text Format (RTF)—including fonts and colors for your text and allowing the insertion of OLE objects. Because of this, you must include OLE container support in your application.

To support all this functionality, using a rich edit view involves a slightly different architecture than the normal document/view setup. First, your document should derive from CRichEditDoc, rather than plain old CDocument. This is very important, because CRichEditView and CRichEditDoc work very closely together to support your view. CRichEditView will contain the text of the view, and CRichEditDoc will contain any OLE objects.

Because of this relationship, you may have only one view associated with a CRichEditDoc object at any given time. However, this also allows the CRichEditDoc::GetView() call to take you directly to the one and only corresponding view.

To serialize your data, simply call CRichTextDoc::Serialize(). If the m_bRTF member is TRUE, this function will output RTF-formatted text. If m_bRTF is FALSE, the output is just plain text.

> **NOTE**
>
> You must serialize your CRichEditDoc object after all other data, because it reads data until the end-of-file is encountered, rather than a fixed number of bytes.

The CRichEditView class provides almost all the functions provided by the CRichEditControl class, so they are covered with controls in Chapter 5. You may also insert OLE objects into your control with the CreateClientItem() function. This works just like the COleDocument::CreateClientItem() function that is covered in Part IV.

CListView and CTreeView

Although the CListView and CTreeView classes are very useful, there really isn't much to say about them here. They are basically just wrappers for the list and tree controls and work just like other CCtrlView classes.

You will probably want to override the PreCreateWindow() function to adjust the style bits to your preference, as well as call OnInitialUpdate() to add data to the view.

The controls contained in the views can be reached by calling CListView::GetListControl() and CTreeView::GetTreeControl().

That's about it for list and tree views until you get to the controls themselves in Chapter 5.

Document Templates

Document templates provide the framework that MFC uses to bind documents, views, and frames together. In fact, it is the document template that will create new documents and views for your application. Document templates generally come in two flavors: CSingleDocTemplate for SDI apps, and CMultiDocTemplate for MDI apps. You generally won't work with CSingleDocTemplate objects as much as the MDI varieties, so you will mostly be looking at CMultiDocTemplate objects here.

However, many things are similar between the two. They are created with the same parameters and perform many of the same operations. The big difference in their operations stems from the fact that MDI applications may have several child frames in the main frame, whereas SDI apps have only one frame.

Now let's look at how to create a document template. Here is an example of the code from `InitInstance()` generated by AppWizard when you create an MDI app:

```
CMultiDocTemplate* pDocTemplate;
pDocTemplate = new CMultiDocTemplate(
    IDR_MYAPPTYPE,
    RUNTIME_CLASS(CMyAppDoc),
    RUNTIME_CLASS(CChildFrame), // custom MDI child frame
    RUNTIME_CLASS(CMyAppView));
AddDocTemplate(pDocTemplate);
```

First, this declares a pointer to `CMultiDocTemplate` and uses `new` to create a template object on the heap. Template objects should remain in memory for as long as your application exists, even if you do not use the pointers directly after your call to `AddDocTemplate()`.

Second, the constructor is called with four parameters, including a resource ID and class information structures (provided by the `RUNTIME_CLASS` macro) for your document, frame, and view classes.

Finally, `AddDocTemplate()` is called to register the template with MFC. You'll learn more about what this means later, but let's take a closer look at what the parameters to the `CMultiDocTemplate` really mean.

The class information for the document, view, and frame types will be used whenever MFC is told to create a new document or view. If you want to use different combinations of these classes in your application, you should create a separate template for each combination.

The resource ID parameter is really many different parameters in one. In the project that AppWizard will generate, you will notice that both an icon and a menu are created with this ID. When a new frame window is created, it will be associated with this icon and menu. You will see the icon in the main frame if you minimize a view window. The menu will be attached to the main frame.

This allows you to have different menus and icons for different document or view types. If you have defined multiple document templates, you can use the same resource ID for each template or use a different ID for each template. If you do specify a new resource ID, but do not define a new menu with this resource ID, the main menu will remain the same as the last active view.

In addition, the resource ID passed to the `CMultiDocTemplate` constructor is also the ID of a string resource, which can be edited in the string table editor. This string rolls seven different parameters into one, each separated by a newline symbol (\n). From within your application, you can use the `CDocTemplate::GetDocString()` function to access the individual elements. This function takes a `CString` reference, which will hold the returned string, and an index, which is defined by an enum type in `CDocTemplate`. The enum values and their meanings are shown in Table 4.1.

Table 4.1. Resource string parameters.

Enum value	Purpose
windowTitle	Name that appears in the application's title bar.
docName	Root for the default filename. MFC will append 1,2,3... to this when new documents are created.
FileNewName	Name of this document type. If several document types are defined, this is the name that will be presented to users when they create a new document. If this is blank, it is not available to users.
FilterName	Description of file type and wildcard filter—for example, Dave's files (*.dav)
filterExt	Extension for files of this type. This should have no asterisk (*), but should have a period (.)—for example, (.dav)
regFileTypeId	Internal document type used for registration with Windows.
RegFileTypeName	Registry document type used by OLE. This will be exposed to the user.

Unfortunately, there is no function provided to set these values; you must enter them in the string table editor in the order listed, separated by newlines (\n). This also means that you cannot change these parameters at runtime. The string resource created by AppWizard contains the strings entered in the Advanced settings in step 4. The last two parameters are used by OLE and will be discussed later.

Once you have created the document template and called AddDocTemplate(), your application is set up to use the default functionality the MFC provides for creating new documents and views. At this point, you don't really need to do anything else but let MFC do its thing. However, there are some other things that you may find useful at some time.

Creating a Different View for a Document

If your application has a document open and you would like to open a different sort of view to it, you can do so by calling the CreateNewFrame() member of a document template that relates the document type to a new view class. The CreateNewFrame() function takes a pointer to the existing document object and an optional pointer to an existing frame window. If you use CreateNewFrame(), you should be sure to call CDocTemplate::InitialUpdateFrame() to initialize the window. This function takes a pointer to the new frame and a pointer to the existing document. You can see an example of this in the MDISamp example application.

CDocument::OnChangedViewList()

Whenever a new view is attached to a document, the framework will call the document's OnChangedViewList() function. You can override this function in your application if you need to do anything special when a view is added or deleted from the document's view list. The default implementation of OnChangedViewList() will close the document if no views remain in the document's view list.

UpdateAllViews()

When the data in your document changes, you will generally want to update all the views attached to the document. This can be done by using the UpdateAllViews() function of your document object. UpdateAllViews() takes a pointer to the view that generated the change as its first parameter. This function will run through the document's list of views, calling the OnUpdate() function of each view, with the exception of the view that generated the change. If you want to update all the views, specify NULL as the first parameter to UpdateAllViews().

Optionally, you can also pass a long and/or a pointer to a CObject to UpdateAllViews(). These are passed on to the view's OnUpdate() function and can be defined to be anything that you want. Generally, you will want to use these if you can somehow optimize your update routines, based on the changes that were made.

Accessing Views from Your Document

Occasionally, you may want to search through the list of views associated with a document in order to do something with them. If UpdateAllViews() doesn't meet your needs, MFC provides an alternative. Here is an example:

```
void CMyDocument::UpdateSomeViews()
{
    POSITION pos = GetFirstViewPosition();
    while(pos != NULL)
    {
        CView* pView = GetNextView(pos);
        if(myCondition) pView->OnUpdate(NULL, 0, NULL);
    }
} // end UpdateSomeViews()
```

This example declares a POSITION object used to walk through the list of views. You will explore lists in Chapter 7; for now it's enough to know that pos will be NULL when the end of the list is reached. The call to GetFirstViewPosition() sets up the list of views for browsing with the GetNextView() call. You can then do whatever you want with the view pointer that is returned. You should, however, note that I used the generic CView pointer in this example. In the real world, you could cast the return value of GetNextView() to your view type, although you will need to be careful with this if you support multiple view types for the document.

Working with Frames

Up to this point, you have learned that frames will contain your view windows, but really haven't looked at what else they can do. They can do quite a lot for your application. As you will see, frame windows provide the ability to use status bars, toolbars, and splitters. This applies to frame windows in general, regardless of whether you are using the document/view architecture, although how this fits with the document/view framework is mentioned where appropriate.

Status Bars

Many Windows applications provide useful information about the current state of the application in a status bar at the bottom of the application Window. Here, you will see how you can add this functionality to your own applications.

First, you need an object derived from the CStatusBar class. If you have created an MDI or SDI app in AppWizard, you should notice that m_wndStatusBar has already been added as a member of your main frame class. This is a good place to put the status bar object, because it needs to be around as long as the frame window is and should go away when the frame does. Your declaration should look something like this:

```
CStatusBar m_wndStatusBar;
```

Now that you have a CStatusBar object, creating the status bar window is a snap. You simply call the Create() function of CStatusBar, as in this example from the CMainFrame::OnCreate() implementation created by AppWizard:

```
if (!m_wndStatusBar.Create(this) ||
        !m_wndStatusBar.SetIndicators(indicators,
          sizeof(indicators)/sizeof(UINT)))
{
    TRACE0("Failed to create status bar\n");
    return -1;      // fail to create
}
```

The Create() function of CStatusBar takes a parent window parameter. Because Create() is called in the OnCreate() member of the frame, this is this. If the call to Create() is successful, SetIndicators() is called to load the text that will be used in the indicators on the right side of the status bar. This takes a pointer to an array of IDs (UINTs) and the number of elements in the array. The indicators array used in the example is defined like this:

```
static UINT indicators[] =
{
    ID_SEPARATOR,              // status line indicator
    ID_INDICATOR_CAPS,
    ID_INDICATOR_NUM,
    ID_INDICATOR_SCRL,
};
```

Each of the values in this array is the resource ID of a string resource that contains the text to be placed in the indicator box when it is toggled on. The first value, ID_SEPARATOR, is a special case. This is used to indicate that you want to use the first pane of the status bar for text, namely the fly-by help strings that you define when creating menu items and toolbars.

Customizing the Status Bar

You can customize the status bar to display whatever information you want. To do this, begin by adding an entry in the indicators array that is passed to SetIndicators(). If you use 0 for the resource ID, no string will be found, and MFC will create an empty pane with which you can work.

You will most likely now want to size the pane to fit the data you intend to put into it. To do this, you first get some information about the current state of the status bar, then change the areas that you care about and update the status bar with the new settings:

```
m_wndStatusBar.GetPaneInfo(1, nID, nStyle, cxWidth);
m_wndStatusBar.SetPaneInfo(1, nID, nStyle, 50);
```

In this example, the first parameter is the index (0-based) of the pane. In this example, a pane is added between the text area and the three indicators used by default. In addition, nID returns the resource ID of a string resource holding the text for the pane, nStyle returns the style bit settings of the pane, and CxWidth returns the width of the pane. You can modify any or all of these before calling SetPaneInfo(). In this case, you simply set the width to a size that is close to what you want. You can now add whatever text you would like by using the following:

```
m_wndStatusBar.SetPaneText(1, "Hello");
```

In a real application, taking a guess at the size you want is probably not the best method. You may want to do something like the following example to set the size to exactly what you will need:

```
m_wndStatusBar.GetPaneInfo(1, nID, nStyle, nWidth);
pDC = m_wndStatusBar.GetDC();
pDC->SelectObject(m_wndStatusBar.GetFont());
pDC->DrawText(_T("Hello"), -1, myRect, DT_CALCRECT);
m_wndStatusBar.ReleaseDC(pDC);
m_wndStatusBar.SetPaneInfo(1, nID, nStyle, myRect.Width());
```

This example uses several device context functions that you will learn about in Chapter 6.

Adding a Toolbar

Chapter 1, "Visual C++ Environment," discusses how to create a toolbar resource. Now you will see how to make it go. First, you need an object derived from class CToolBar. If you asked for it, AppWizard has already created one for you (as well as the rest of the code you will see here); if not, you need only add the following line to the declaration of your main frame class:

```
CToolBar m_wndToolBar;
```

The toolbar window is created by code like this from `CMainFrame::OnCreate()`:

```
if (!m_wndToolBar.Create(this) ||
    !m_wndToolBar.LoadToolBar(IDR_MAINFRAME))
{
    TRACE0("Failed to create toolbar\n");
    return -1;      // fail to create
}
```

The call to `LoadToolBar()` takes the resource ID of a toolbar resource that you created in the resource editor (or that AppWizard created for you).

The `Create()` call can also take a DWORD with additional style information for the toolbar. This defaults to WS_CHILD|WS_VISIBLE|CBRS_TOP. You may add any of the styles listed in Table 4.2 to affect how your toolbar works.

Table 4.2. Toolbar styles.

Style	Effect
CBRS_TOP	Position toolbar at top of window.
CBRS_BOTTOM	Position toolbar at bottom of window.
CBRS_NOALIGN	Control bar is not repositioned when parent is resized.
CBRS_TOOLTIPS	Enable tool tips.
CBRS_SIZE_DYNAMIC	Make control bar sizeable.
CBRS_SIZE_FIXED	Make control bar a fixed size.
CBRS_FLOATING	Create a floating toolbar.
CBRS_FLYBY	Show fly-by help in the status bar.
CBRS_HIDE_INPLACE	Toolbar is not displayed.
CBRS_BORDER_TOP	Create a border for the toolbar on top.
CBRS_BORDER_LEFT	Create a border for the toolbar on left.
CBRS_BORDER_RIGHT	Create a border for the toolbar on right.
CBRS_BORDER_BOTTOM	Create a border for the toolbar on bottom.

You can also modify these settings later with `SetBarStyle()`. This can be particularly useful if you want to add a particular feature, such as tool tips or fly-by help, as in this example, generated by AppWizard:

```
m_wndToolBar.SetBarStyle(m_wndToolBar.GetBarStyle() |
    CBRS_TOOLTIPS | CBRS_FLYBY | CBRS_DYNAMIC);
```

You should notice that neither tool tips nor fly-by help is included in the defaults for `Create()`. The strings for fly-by help and tool tips are defined in a string resource with the same ID as the command generated by the button—fly-by text first, separated by a newline (\n):

```
"Recall last transaction\nRecall"
```

In addition, you can work with the styles of individual buttons with `SetButtonStyle()` and `GetButtonStyle()`, which use the styles in Table 4.3.

Table 4.3. Toolbar button styles.

Style	Effect
TBBS_CHECKED	The button is down (checked).
TBBS_INDETERMINATE	The button state is undetermined.
TBBS_DISABLED	The button is disabled.
TBBS_PRESSED	The button is currently pressed.
TBBS_CHECKBOX	The button will be a toggle.

Floating and Docking Toolbars

If you desire a floating toolbar, this can be accomplished with the `CFrameWnd::FloatControlBar()` function, which requires a pointer to the toolbar, and a `CPoint` that dictates where the toolbar will float. In this example, the toolbar will float in the top-left corner:

```
FloatControlBar( &m_wndToolBar, CPoint(0,0));
```

Optionally, you can specify one of the alignment styles (listed under Docking Flags) as a third parameter, to dictate the orientation of the toolbar.

If you wish to dock your toolbar to the edges of the frame, you can use something like the following example generated by AppWizard:

```
m_wndToolBar.EnableDocking(CBRS_ALIGN_ANY);
EnableDocking(CBRS_ALIGN_ANY);
DockControlBar(&m_wndToolBar);
```

Note that you must call `EnableDocking()` for both the toolbar and the frame window. You can enable docking only on certain edges of the frame by using a combination of the following docking flags:

```
CBRS_ALIGN_ANY
CBRS_ALIGN_TOP
CBRS_ALIGN_BOTTOM
CBRS_ALIGN_LEFT
CBRS_ALIGN_RIGHT
```

The toolbar will dock only to those edges that are enabled for both the toolbar and the frame.

The `DockControlBar()` call tells the toolbar to dock itself. By default, the toolbar will try to dock to the top, left, bottom, and right sides of the frame, in that order. You can specify one of the following as a second parameter to dictate where the toolbar will dock:

```
AFX_IDW_DOCKBAR_TOP
AFX_IDW_DOCKBAR_BOTTOM
AFX_IDW_DOCKBAR_LEFT
AFX_IDW_DOCKBAR_RIGHT
```

More on Working with Menus

In your Windows application, menus will undoubtedly make up a substantial part of your user interface. You looked at how to create menu resources in Chapter 1, and have seen how document templates can be used to assign a menu to a frame window in this chapter. Here, you will see how to update the user interface for your menus, implement pop-up menus, and create menus dynamically.

Updating the User Interface

MFC provides a mechanism for automatically updating the status of the command-generating controls of your user interface—namely, menus and toolbar buttons. This is done by implementing handlers for the UPDATE_COMMAND_UI message, which can be done from ClassWizard when you select a command object. Alternatively, you could add ON_COMMAND_UPDATE_UI macros to your message map by hand:

```
ON_UPDATE_COMMAND_UI(ID_APP_EXIT, OnUpdateAppExit)
```

You then implement a handler function. Here, I have decided that I may want to disable the File | Exit command, so I have created a handler for the UPDATE_COMMAND_UI message:

```
void CMainFrame::OnUpdateAppExit(CCmdUI* pCmdUI)
{
    if(m_bTrapUser)
        pCmdUI->Enable(FALSE);
}
```

The handler is passed a pointer to a CCmdUI object, which should be used for updating the interface item. This will update both the menu item and toolbar button for the given command.

Pop-Up Menus

You may have seen several different applications that use pop-up menus. It has become increasingly popular for applications to create pop-up menus when the user clicks on the right mouse button, like the context menus found throughout Visual C++.

You can actually add context menu support by simply adding the PopUpMenu component from the component gallery. However, let's look at how you can do this yourself. To create your own pop-up menu, you should first create a menu resource in the resource editor, although you will learn how to create menus in your code in just a bit. When you are creating a pop-up menu in the menu editor, the caption at the top of your menu will not actually be displayed, so use any placeholder you like.

Next, you declare a CMenu object and load it with the resource you created:

```
CMenu myPopupMenu;
myPopupMenu.LoadMenu(IDR_MYPOPUPMENU);
```

Note that you will probably want to do this a bit differently in your application. That is, you may want to declare your CMenu object in your frame class declaration or create it on the heap with the new operator. Now, you allow the user to use the pop-up menu. This is best done by creating a handler for the WM_CONTEXTMENU message with ClassWizard. Then, when you want to display your pop-up menu, you should add something like this:

```
void CMainFrame::OnContextMenu(CWnd* pWnd, CPoint point)
{
    POINT curPos;
    GetCursorPos(&curPos);
    CMenu* pSubMenu = myPopupMenu.GetSubMenu(0);
    pSubMenu->TrackPopupMenu(TPM_LEFTALIGN | TPM_LEFTBUTTON,
                        curPos.x, curPos.y, this);
}
```

Here, you use GetSubMenu() to reach the first submenu that contains your pop-up. You then call TrackPopupMenu() to present the menu to the user. This call accepts a few styles—in this case, dictating that the menu's left edge is aligned with the position you give in the second and third parameters, and that the menu will respond to the left mouse button. The last parameter is a pointer to the parent window; here, it is the main frame.

Once you have called TrackPopupMenu(), it will handle itself until the user chooses a command from the menu or dismisses it. Commands from pop-up menus can be handled just like any other menu command.

Creating Menus Dynamically

If you want to create the menu used in the previous example within your code, this is actually quite simple. First declare your CMenu object as in the example. Then call CMenu::CreatePopupMenu() to get a valid Windows menu and add your menu items to it with CMenu::AppendMenu():

```
m_MyMenu.CreatePopupMenu();
m_MyMenu.AppendMenu(MF_ENABLED, ID_FILE_NEW, _T("&New File"));
m_MyMenu.AppendMenu(MF_ENABLED, ID_FILE_CLOSE, _T("&Close File"));
```

You may also use the InsertMenu() function to place menu items anywhere in the menu. You can also dynamically modify the menu for any window by first getting a pointer to the window's CMenu object with a call to CWnd::GetMenu();.

One advantage of creating your own menus this way is that you no longer have to monkey around with submenus to create the pop-up. In the previous example, you could then replace the call to TrackPopupMenu() with something like this:

```
m_MyMenu.TrackPopupMenu(TPM_LEFTALIGN ¦ TPM_LEFTBUTTON,
                        curPos.x, curPos.y, this);
```

Adding Splitters to Your Application

You have probably seen several applications that provide the capability of splitting the view window into two (or more) different views of the same object. This functionality is supported by MFC, and can actually be added by AppWizard or by inserting the Split Bars component from the component gallery. Let's take a look at just how this works.

First, there are two different types of splitters available: static and dynamic. If you want to set up your application to have a predefined number of windows in its view, and do not want the user to be able to define new splits at runtime, you would use static splitters. If you want to give the user the ability to split your views at runtime, you use dynamic splitters.

MFC's implementation of splitters, or split bars, is based around the CSplitterWnd class. Objects of this class are designed to reside in the frame windows that will hold your views. In SDI apps, this is the main frame; in MDI apps, it is the MDI child frame. You need to add a declaration to your frame class to include a CSplitterWnd object:

```
CSplitterWnd m_wndSplitter;
```

This is used for both the static and dynamic flavors of splitters. For now, let's look at how to implement dynamic splitters.

Dynamic Splitters

You need to override the OnCreateClient() function of your frame class. OnCreateClient() is called from OnCreate() when your application creates the view that will live in the frame. Your implementation should look something like this example, generated by inserting the Split Bars component:

```
BOOL CChildFrame::OnCreateClient(LPCREATESTRUCT lpcs, CCreateContext* pContext)
{
    // CG: The following block was added by the Split Bars component.
    {
        if (!m_wndSplitter.Create(this,
                                  2, 2,
                                  CSize(10, 10),
                                  pContext))
```

```
    {
        TRACE0("Failed to create split bar ");
        return FALSE;    // failed to create
    }
    return TRUE;
    }
}
```

Here, you see that the `CSplitterWnd::Create()` function is called. The `Create()` function takes several parameters, beginning with the parent window, which will be the frame. The next two parameters dictate the maximum number of rows and columns that may be created. In the current implementation, this is limited to 2. If you need more, you have to use static splitters. The next parameter is a `SIZE` structure specifying the minimum size allowed for a pane.

> **NOTE**
>
> In most cases in MFC, you can use classes such as `CSize` in place of their corresponding structures, such as `SIZE`. To be sure of the acceptable parameter types for a function, see the online help.

The last parameter used in the example is a pointer to a `CCreateContext` object. In most cases, this is simply the pointer that is passed to the `OnCreateClient()` function. Optionally, you can also specify styles and a child window ID in the `Create()` function. At this point, your application is all set to go. `OnCreateClient()` will be called when the child frame needs to create a view, which will then call `Create()` for the `CSplitterWnd` object. The object will then create the actual view, based on your document templates.

Creating Different Views

If you wish to create a different type of view in the new pane when the user splits the window, you can do so, but you first have to create your own class based on `CSplitterWnd`. In your new class, you have to provide an override for the `CreateView()` function:

```
BOOL CMySplitterWnd::CreateView(int row, int col,
        CRuntimeClass* pViewClass, SIZE sizeInit,
        CCreateContext* pContext)
{
    if(column == 0)
    {
    return CSplitterWnd::CreateView(row, col, pViewClass, sizeInit, pContext);
    }
    else
    {
    return CSplitterWnd::CreateView(row, col, RUNTIME_CLASS(CRightView), sizeInit,
    pContext);
    }
} // end CreateView()
```

In this example, you create a view of type CRightView in any panes that are not in column 0 (the leftmost column). You can also create a view based on a new document in a similar fashion, although you have to create your own CCreateContext object to pass to the CreateView() function. In this object, you can pass a different document template for the new view.

Static Splitters

Working with static splitters is similar to working with dynamic splitters, but there are some important differences. First, you should call CSplitterWnd::CreateStatic() instead of Create(). You also need to create the views yourself—if you don't, your app will crash. To do this, call CSplitterWnd::CreateView() for each pane that you have defined, as in the following example:

```
BOOL CChildFrame::OnCreateClient(LPCREATESTRUCT lpcs, CCreateContext* pContext)
{
    int nCol;

    if (!m_wndSplitter.CreateStatic(this, 1, 3))
    {
        TRACE0("Failed to create split bar ");
        return FALSE;     // failed to create
    }
    for(nCol=0; nCol < 3; nCol++)
    {
        if(!m_wndSplitter.CreateView(0, nCol,
            RUNTIME_CLASS(CMyView),
            CSize(50, 100), pContext))
        {
            TRACE0("Failed to create view ");
            return FALSE;
        }
        return TRUE;
    } // end for
} // end OnCreateClient()
```

This example defines three panes, arranged horizontally, that all use the same view class and document. If you want to use a different view class or document, you can change this as with the previous example of dynamic splitters.

Adding Drag-and-Drop to Your Application

Many applications in Windows allow the user to work with files graphically by dragging them from a drag-and-drop file source, such as Explorer, to the window for an application that can accept them. This function can be implemented in two ways. The first is with OLE (more about it in Part IV). The second method uses Windows messages to support drag-and-drop.

Enabling Drag-and-Drop

To enable drag-and-drop in a window of your application, you use the CWnd:: DragAcceptFiles()call to enable the receipt of WM_DROPFILES messages. The single parameter for CWnd::DragAcceptFiles() is a BOOL. You can omit this, because it defaults to TRUE, or you can call it with FALSE to disable drag-and-drop.

This can be called from any object derived from CWnd, once its window is created. In this example, you will put a call in the OnCreate() function of the main frame class, after the window is created by the call to CMDIFrameWnd::OnCreate(). This allows the application to accept files that are dropped anywhere in its main window.

Handling WM_DROPFILES Messages

Next, you implement a handler for the WM_DROPFILES message and add an entry to the message map. This is best done with ClassWizard, which creates a default handler for you. The default handler defers to CMDIFrameWnd::OnDropFiles(), which tries to open a new document/view pair for the files that were dragged.

If you wish to do something more specific with the dropped files, you can implement your handler for OnDropFiles() something like this:

```
void CMainFrame::OnDropFiles(HDROP hDropInfo)
{
    UINT i;
    UINT nFiles = ::DragQueryFile(hDropInfo, (UINT) -1, NULL, 0);
    for (i = 0; i < nFiles; i++)
    {
        TCHAR szFileName[_MAX_PATH];
        ::DragQueryFile(hDropInfo, i, szFileName, _MAX_PATH);

        ProcessMyFile(szFileName);
    } // end for
    ::DragFinish(hDropInfo);
} // end OnDropFiles()
```

In this example, you can see that you call DragQueryFile() with a second parameter of -1 (0xFFFFFFFF), which returns the number of files that were dropped. You then use this value to loop through all the files, again using DragQueryInfo() to return the full pathname of the file. Once you have the filename, you can do with it as you please; just make sure that you call DragFinish() to clean up when you are finished. If you don't do this, your application will leak a bit of memory each time you handle dropped files.

Summary

In this chapter, we have taken a look at the document/view architecture that is used in MFC, and how you can use it to easily create very powerful applications. This architecture also helps to ensure that your applications have a similar look and feel, as users will expect from Windows applications.

We also took a look at the various view classes that MFC provides, as well as how to implement several other nifty features, like menus, toolbars, and splitters.

I think that you will agree that using the MFC classes and the document/view architecture is a much better way to start off your applications than programming all of these features from scratch.

5

Dialogs and Controls

by David Bennett

For most Windows applications, dialogs will provide the user interface for many of your application's functionalities. Dialogs can be as simple as a single text message displayed to the user with AfxMessageBox(), or more complicated, like a file open dialog. You can even use a dialog to form the main window of your application. In this chapter, you will see how to

- Use your own dialogs
- Use controls in your dialog
- Use the Windows common dialogs
- Create property sheets, wizards, and dialog bars

Using Your Dialogs

In Chapter 1, "Visual C++ Environment," you learned about creating dialog templates in the resource editor. You will look at this more closely when you explore the controls that you can add to your dialog; for now, let's look at how to work with dialogs in your code.

Dialogs in MFC begin with a CDialog object. The CDialog class derives from the CWnd class, which gives it the functionality of a window, and the CCmdTarget class, which allows the dialog to have its own message map for handling messages. In most cases, you will want to derive a class from CDialog rather than using CDialog itself. Deriving your own class for each dialog allows you to use MFC to work with your controls and exchange data between your dialog and your application much easier than you can using only the Win32 API.

First, let's look at a simple dialog class. You may have noticed that AppWizard will create a class for your About box—nearly the simplest dialog. True, creating a class for the About box, as it is implemented, is a bit of overkill. In fact, if you simply created the template for the dialog, the only code needed to present it could go something like this:

```
CDialog myAboutBox(IDD_ABOUTBOX);
myAboutBox.DoModal();
```

This example brings us to the first thing you do to implement your dialog—create an object derived from CDialog. In this example, creating the CDialog object also associates the dialog template that you (or AppWizard) created in the resource editor to an instance of your CDialog class.

Constructing Dialog Objects

The first way to assign a dialog template to your class, as shown in the previous example, is to pass the resource ID of the dialog template to the constructor of CDialog. Because you will generally be deriving your own classes, this can also be done in the implementation of your class's constructor:

```
CAboutDlg::CAboutDlg() : CDialog(IDD_ABOUTBOX)
```

or, as AppWizard does it:

```
CAboutDlg::CAboutDlg() : CDialog(CAboutDlg::IDD)
```

The second example does exactly the same thing, but AppWizard has defined an enum type that will translate CAboutDlg::IDD to IDD_ABOUTBOX.

Presenting the Dialog

At some point in your application, you will want to present the dialog to the user. Before you do this, decide whether you want your dialog to be modal or modeless. Creating a modal dialog causes your application to wait until the user is finished with the dialog, whereas a modeless dialog is an independent window that can hang around for as long as it likes while your application does its thing.

Presenting a modal dialog is simple; you call the DoModal() function of your dialog object:

```
int nDlgReturn = myDialog.DoModal();
```

This presents the dialog to users and waits until they are finished with it. For most dialogs, the user will finish with the dialog by clicking on the OK or Cancel button, which brings us to the return value of DoModal().

If your dialog uses the default OK or Cancel button, DoModal() will return either IDOK or IDCANCEL. In general, you accept any changes made in a dialog box only when DoModal() returns IDOK. Users expect that they can always press Cancel to back out of a dialog without changing anything. Of course, the implementation of your dialog may return any value you choose to call EndDialog() with—but more on this later.

Modeless Dialogs

If you want to leave your dialog active while your application is doing other things, you create a modeless dialog. This is often useful for things such as application settings that the user may be changing often, or for the Find and Replace dialog you will see later. However, modeless dialogs present a few unique challenges to you as a developer.

Most importantly, your application cannot wait for the user to dismiss a modeless dialog before dealing with the data. This means that you have to implement mechanisms to update your application's data from within the dialog while it is active. You may also need to work out how to update your dialog when certain information changes elsewhere in your application.

You need to make certain that the CDialog object is around throughout the life of the dialog window. To do this, you may want to consider making your dialog objects members of your main frame or application class. Alternatively, you may choose to create the pointers as members and create the dialog objects with the new operator.

Modeless dialogs are also created differently from modal dialogs. First, you call the CDialog constructor with no parameters, because you will attach a dialog template to the dialog object when you create the actual window. This should look something like this:

```
CDialog m_ModelessDlg;
m_ModelessDlg.Create(IDD_MYDIALOG, NULL);
```

The call to Create() tells the dialog to use the dialog template with the ID IDD_MYDIALOG. The second parameter gives the parent window for the dialog. In this case, you specify NULL, which creates the dialog as a child of the main window.

When it is time to delete your modeless dialog, you should use the DestroyWindow() function:

```
m_ModelessDlg.DestroyWindow();
```

If you provide the user with a way to close the modeless dialog from within the dialog (that is, a Close button), you should call DestroyWindow() in its handler to destroy the window. However, the dialog object is still lurking around in memory somewhere.

You have to decide how you want to handle the deletion of the object in your application. It may be useful to keep the object around so that you can access its data members, even after the dialog window is destroyed. In this case, you should make sure to clean up when you are finished with the dialog object, perhaps in CWinApp::ExitInstance().

If you prefer to assign a dialog template at runtime, you can also use CDialog::CreateIndirect() or CDialog::InitModalIndirect(). These involve more than the methods you have explored so far, but if you have used the Windows API versions of these, you will find that the CDialog versions are quite similar.

Creating Dialog Classes with ClassWizard

Now that you have seen how to create dialog objects and present their windows to the user, let's take a step back and see how to create a class for your dialog.

You learned how to create your dialog templates in Chapter 1. Once the template is created, you build a class around it. This is most easily done with ClassWizard.

You may choose to import a class from a file, select an existing class in your project, or create a new class. Choosing to create a new class will produce the dialog shown in Figure 5.1.

FIGURE 5.1.

The Create New Class dialog box.

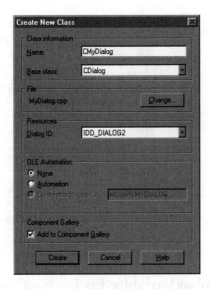

Here, you can choose a name and base class for your class. In most cases, your class will derive directly from `CDialog`. There are two exceptions: if you derive your own class from one of the standard Windows dialog classes (which you learn about shortly) or if you have developed your own class from `CDialog` that you wish to use as the base class for the dialogs in your application.

ClassWizard will assign filenames for the declaration and implementation of your class, based on the name of your class. If you want to change the filenames, click the Change button. This also allows you to add the declaration and implementation of your class to an existing file, which can be handy if you create several small dialog classes.

You can also choose to add the new class automatically to the Component Gallery for easy reuse in other applications. You learn about the OLE options available in Part III, "Programming with ActiveX," so for now let's choose `None`.

Once you decide on the options you like, clicking on Create will create the new class for you and return you to ClassWizard. From the Message Maps page, shown in Figure 5.2, you can add handlers for the notifications generated by each of the controls in your dialog. As you will soon see, each control may be capable to send many different notifications.

Alternatively, you can add your own message map entries and handler functions, as you saw in Chapter 3, "MFC Messages and Commands."

FIGURE 5.2.
*The Class Wizard
Message Maps page.*

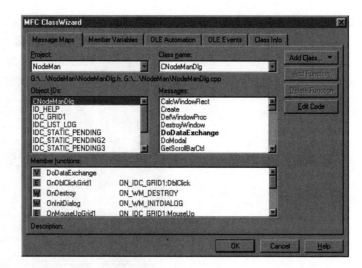

Adding Member Variables for Dialog Controls

ClassWizard is also very useful in adding member variables to your class to handle the data and controls in your dialog. This is done with the Member Variables page shown in Figure 5.3.

FIGURE 5.3.
*The ClassWizard
Member Variables
page.*

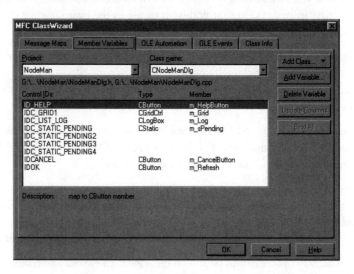

From here, you can add member variables to represent the controls in your dialog by selecting the control ID and clicking on Add Variable to get the Add Member Variable dialog box shown in Figure 5.4.

FIGURE 5.4.

The Add Member Variable dialog box.

Here, you may choose the name for your new member variable. ClassWizard will add m_ to the dialog box automatically, but you don't need to use it if you don't want to. However, it is a good habit to get into for naming your member variables.

Next, you will notice the Category list. For many controls, you can choose to create a member variable to represent either the control itself or the data held in the control. Control variables may be used to manipulate the control in the dialog, and value variables will automatically create a member variable to be used in dialog data exchange (DDX). As you will see later in this chapter, this provides a very powerful mechanism for initializing the controls in your dialog and returning the data when the dialog is dismissed.

For some controls, such as buttons, you cannot create value variables, because these controls don't really represent a data value; they just provide a source for messages to your dialog.

In the Variable type field, you can choose a class or data type for your variable. ClassWizard will present a list of appropriate choices, based on the type of control you have selected. For example, if you are adding a value variable for an edit control, you can choose from several different data types here. Be certain to choose the type of data you will want to work with in your application code, because ClassWizard will allow you to add only one value variable for each control.

For control variables, you will see a list of classes designed to handle the type of control you have selected. For example, if you are adding a control variable for an edit control, you can choose the CEdit class as the type for your control variable. You also can choose any classes that you have included in your project that derive from CEdit. This is useful if you want to create a special class to add functionality to the standard controls.

Using Controls in Your Dialogs

Recall that the control member variables created by ClassWizard allow you to use almost all the functions associated with a control in your dialog by way of a member variable in your dialog. For example, if you had an edit control in your dialog and have created a CEdit member variable to represent it, you could set the text in the edit box like this:

```
m_myEditBox.SetWindowText("Hello");
```

There are also many other functions available in MFC's control classes, some of which you will see in the sections about specific controls later in this chapter. For a full list of available member functions, see the online documentation.

If you don't want to create member variables to represent your controls, you can get a pointer to the CWnd object for a control in a dialog by using the GetDlgItem() function of your CDialog object:

```
CEdit* pNameBox;
pNameBox = (CEdit *) m_myDialog.GetDlgItem(IDC_MYNAME);
```

Note that you are free to cast the return pointer to whatever type you want. You may then use this pointer to operate on your control:

```
pNameBox->SetWindowText("Hello");
```

Of course, the SetWindowText() function is really a member of CWnd, so you could use a CWnd pointer here and avoid the cast, but you can call all the functions of the CEdit class if you use the CEdit pointer.

Note that the Windows objects that you are familiar with from coding to the C API are still there if you need to work with them directly rather than going through the MFC Classes. If you have done much programming with the regular C Windows API, you are familiar with the GetDlgItem() function. You can also still use the global function ::GetDlgItem() or an overridden CWnd::GetDlgItem() to work with the actual window handles for your controls. In addition, every CWnd object has an m_hWnd member that holds the actual handle to its window.

Windows Control Classes

Up to this point, you have learned how you can work with the controls in your dialog, but really haven't seen much about what you can really make your controls do for you. It's time to fix that. Here, you look at the classes that MFC provides for working with the Windows controls that you use in your dialogs. These classes provide a way for your C++ applications to deal with Windows controls as C++ objects.

For each control class, you will look at some of its styles that affect how the control works, the methods that allow you to work with the control, and the notification messages that the control will send back to your application when the user manipulates the control.

The styles for your control can be set in several different ways, starting with the properties dialog for the control when you are creating the dialog template in the Developer Studio. If you are creating controls without using dialog templates, the styles are specified in the call to `CWnd::Create()`. These may be changed at runtime by calls to `CWnd::ModifyStyle()`.

The control methods specified allow you to affect the appearance and functions of the control, as well as manipulate the control's data.

The control notifications are Windows messages that are sent to the parent of the control. In most cases, this is a dialog. You add handlers for some or all of these notifications with ClassWizard or by adding your own message map entries, as you did in Chapter 4, "Frames, Documents, and Views."

CEdit

In the examples so far, you have used edit controls, so let's look at them first. MFC uses the `CEdit` class to allow you to use C++ constructs to work with the functionality of an edit control.

CEdit Styles

There are many styles that affect how an edit control works, but perhaps the most important is the `ES_MULTILINE` style.

Setting the `ES_MULTILINE` style will make your edit control a multiline edit control. Without this style, the user will be able to enter only a single line of text.

If you have specified `ES_MULTILINE`, you may also use `ES_AUTOVSCROLL` to scroll the edit control automatically if the user tries to enter a new line at the end of the edit control. If you do not specify `ES_AUTOVSCROLL`, Windows will not allow entering lines past the bottom of the control.

`ES_WANTRETURN` will allow the user to use the Enter key to add a carriage return in a multiline edit control. Without this, the Enter key will trigger the default pushbutton. This does not affect single-line edit controls.

`ES_READONLY` prevents the user from changing the text.

`ES_AUTOHSCROLL` will automatically scroll the display if the user tries to enter text past the end of the edit control.

You can use the `ES_CENTER`, `ES_LEFT`, and `ES_RIGHT` styles to align the control's text.

`ES_LOWERCASE` and `ES_UPPERCASE` will automatically adjust user input to the desired case.

`ES_NOHIDESEL` will cause the control to keep the selected text in the edit control highlighted when the control loses focus. Without this, the selection is unhighlighted when the control loses the input focus.

ES_OEMCONVERT will convert entered text from ANSI to the OEM character set and back to ANSI, to ensure that the AnsiToOEM() function will work properly. This is most useful in working with filenames.

ES_PASSWORD causes the edit control to display all characters entered as an asterisk (*) to hide the real text. You can specify an alternative character with SetPassWordChar().

CEdit Methods

The CEdit class provides many methods for manipulating the edit control. You will explore several of the more common functions here, although you may need to consult the online documentation for other things you may want to do.

To work with the text in an edit control, you can use the CWnd::SetWindowText() and CWnd::GetWindowText() functions.

The LimitText() function allows you to set the maximum length that the edit control will accept.

The SetSel() and GetSel() members allow you to work with the character positions of the current selection in the edit control. ReplaceSel replaces the current selection with the text you pass it. You can use Clear() to remove any current selection.

The CEdit class supports the Cut(), Copy(), and Paste() members to work with the current selection and the clipboard.

The Undo() member will undo the last editing change to the text. You can use the CanUndo() member to determine whether the last change can be undone.

The GetModify() method tells you whether the text in the edit control has been modified. You can set or clear the modification flag with SetModify().

For multiline edit controls, you can also use the following methods:

> The GetLineCount() function returns the number of lines in a multiline edit control.
> The GetLine() function returns the text for a single line.

You may work directly with the memory that a multiline edit control uses by manipulating the local handles with GetHandle() and SetHandle().

Edit Control Notifications

The following notifications can be handled with an entry in the message map—for example, ON_EN_CHANGE handles the EN_CHANGE message.

EN_CHANGE is sent when the user may have changed the text.

EN_UPDATE is also sent when the user may have altered the text, but before it is changed on the display.

EN_ERRSPACE is sent if the edit control cannot allocate enough memory for an operation.

EN_HSCROLL and EN_VSCROLL are sent when the user has clicked on the appropriate scroll bar, before the screen is updated.

EN_KILLFOCUS is sent when the input focus shifts to another control.

EN_MAXTEXT is sent when inserting more than the maximum amount of text is attempted, either by insertion programmatically or by user input.

EN_SETFOCUS is sent when the control first receives the input focus.

Static Controls

Windows provides several different varieties of static controls. These are generally used as labels for your other controls or just to enhance the appearance of the dialog. This class of control includes static text and group boxes, which usually just add a fancy border around a group of controls, but it may also contain a bitmap or icon.

By default, the Developer Studio will assign static controls with the ID of IDC_STATIC, which is convenient, because you won't need to access most of these at runtime. However, if you do need to work with a static control at runtime, make sure that you assign it a unique ID.

You can assign control variables to static controls with ClassWizard or get a pointer to the object with GetDlgItem(), as you learned earlier.

If you simply want to change the text of a static control, you can do this with CWnd::SetWindowText(). If you want to selectively display or hide a static control, you can do so with the CWnd::ShowWindow() call, using SW_HIDE or SW_SHOWNA as a parameter.

For more complicated operations on static controls, you will want to work through an instance of the CStatic class. This will allow you to work with images displayed by the static control by using the GetBitmap() and SetBitmap() members to work with HBITMAP types, or GetIcon() and SetIcon() to work with HICON types, or GetEnhMetaFile() and SetEnhMetaFile() to work with HENHMETAFILE types.

Although static controls do not generally accept input, they will generate BN_CLICKED or BN_DOUBLECLICKED notifications if you set the SS_NOTIFY style.

Button Controls

Windows supports several different types of buttons, including simple pushbuttons, check boxes, and radio buttons. MFC uses the CButton class to support each of these, depending on the styles selected for the button. CButton is also the base class for CBitmapButton, which allows you to assign a separate bitmap for its up, down, focused, and disabled states.

All buttons may send the BN_CLICKED or BN_DOUBLECLICKED notifications, which may be handled with the ON_BN_CLICKED and ON_BN_DOUBLECLICKED message map macros.

The CButton::SetButtonStyle() function allows you to set the style of a button at runtime, and the CButton::GetButtonStyle() returns the current style of a button. In most cases, you do not need to use these, but the following sections mention a few cases that apply to the different classes of buttons.

Pushbuttons

When you add a control to a dialog template using the button from the toolbar, or when you create your own button control with the BS_PUSHBUTTON style, you are creating a pushbutton. This is the simplest of the button classes, and perhaps the most used. The OK and Cancel buttons that you see in most dialogs are of this type.

In most applications, you do not have to work directly with the button control. Instead, you just add handlers for the command message that it sends to its parent window, usually a dialog. By default, the CButton class provides a handler for the OK and Cancel buttons that will close the dialog and return IDOK or IDCANCEL.

The one thing that you would be most likely to tweak with a pushbutton is setting the BS_DEFPUSHBUTTON style (using the Styles page of the control's Properties dialog) so that this button will send its command message when the user types the Enter key in the dialog.

The other instance in which you would deal with your pushbutton objects directly is implementing owner-draw buttons, where your application is responsible for all the rendering tasks for the button.

Radio Buttons

For those of you who have CD players and digital tuners in your car stereo, the name for this class of buttons may seem a bit odd. The name stems from the old radios that had mechanical station presets. Whenever you pushed in one of the buttons, the button that was previously pushed in would pop back out. This is precisely how radio buttons work. You may select one, and only one, choice from a group of radio buttons. This is generally used in cases where the user has a handful of different mutually exclusive options from which to choose. Radio buttons are added to a dialog with the radio button tool in Developer Studio. If you are creating your controls at runtime, these buttons will have the BS_AUTORADIOBUTTON style set.

When you create a dialog with radio buttons, you will most likely want to group them. By default, all radio buttons you add to a dialog are in the same group. If you wish to use several different groups of radio buttons, this presents a problem. To divide your radio buttons into groups, you should first make sure that the buttons you want to include in a group are listed consecutively in the tab order. Next, you enable the WS_GROUP style (the Group check box in the properties dialog) for the first button of each group.

To initialize the settings of your radio buttons, you use CButton::SetCheck(). You may also query the current state of a button by using CButton::GetCheck(). Because of this, you may want to declare control member variables for your radio buttons.

Once you have your radio buttons grouped, and have initialized them if you want to have a default selection, Windows will handle the group for you, making sure that only the last button selected *is* selected. Additionally, MFC will allow you to query the state of an entire group of radio buttons with DDX_Radio(), which is covered later in this chapter.

Check Boxes

The third class of buttons supported by CButton is check boxes. These are used to present options to the user that can be toggled on and off and are generally independent of any other selections. Check boxes have the BS_CHECKBOX style set and may be added to dialog templates by using the check box tool.

To set the state of your check boxes, use the CButton::SetCheck() function. If you pass 0 to this function, the box will not be checked; if you pass 1, the box will be checked. Additionally, if you have added the BS_3STATE style to your check box, you may pass a 2, which displays the check box in its indeterminate state. You can use the CButton::GetCheck() function to query the current state of your check boxes.

List Box Controls

List box controls present a list of text items for the user to view and/or select. MFC support for list boxes is provided by the CListBox class. To use a list box in your dialog, use the list box tool to insert a list box into your dialog template, and use ClassWizard to create a control variable for the list box.

Alternatively, you can construct your own CListBox object and call Create() to create the Windows list box control and attach it to the CListBox object.

There are many styles associated with list box controls. These may be set when you add the list box control to a dialog template, when you call Create(), or by calling CWnd::ModifyStyle() after the control is created.

List Box Styles

For starters, you will want to specify LBS_NOTIFY if you intend to handle messages from the list box. If you do not specify this style, the list box will not send messages.

LBS_SORT causes strings in the list box to be sorted alphabetically.

You can use the LBS_USETABSTOPS style to tell the list box to enable the expansion of tab characters in the strings listed.

The LBS_MULTIPLESEL style allows the user to select more than one item by using the Ctrl key.

For the entire list of styles, see the online documentation. There are many other styles related to format, scrolling, and special processing that you may be interested in.

List Box Methods

The first thing you will probably want to do with your list box is add strings to it. This can be done with the AddString() method, which takes a pointer to a string. This adds the string to the list box according to the sort style you have specified. To insert a string in a particular spot, you can use InsertString(), which takes an integer index and a string pointer. If you want to add the string to the last position, you can pass -1 for the index.

You may automatically scroll the list so that a certain position appears at the top of the list box by calling SetTopIndex(). This does not affect the sort order of the list box; it just scrolls it.

To remove items from your list box, you can call DeleteItem() to delete a single item, or you can call ResetContent() to clear the whole list box.

To get the total number of items in a list box, you can call GetCount().

To retrieve the text for a given entry, you can call GetText().

If you have selected the LBS_USETABSTOPS style, you can use the SetTabStops() function to specify tab spacing in the list.

If the user has selected something from the list, you can call GetCurSel() to return the index of the item that is selected. If, however, you have set the LBS_MULTIPLESEL style, you call GetSelCount() to find out how many items are selected and then call GetSelItems() to return an array of integer indexes.

A list box also allows you to associate a DWORD value with each entry. This can be any data you like, including pointers. To work with this data, you can call the SetItemData() and GetItemData() methods. If you plan to store pointers in the data, you may want to use SetItemDataPtr() and GetItemDataPtr(). These functions work with LPVOID pointers, so you can avoid many casts and compiler warnings.

List Box Notifications

List boxes that have the LBS_NOTIFY style set send a LBN_SELCHANGE notification when the user changes the selection.

A list box also sends an LBN_DBLCLK notification if the user double-clicks on a selection. This is generally used in Windows applications to select an item and trigger the default pushbutton action. You will probably want to do the same in your applications.

Combo Boxes

Combo boxes share a great deal of functionality with list boxes. Actually a combo box is a list box with an edit control attached. The edit control is displayed to the user. The list attached to it may be displayed in different ways, depending on the style bits.

Combo Box Styles

The CBS_DROPDOWN style has a list that drops down when the user clicks on the drop-down button. This also allows the user to type in a selection.

The CBS_DROPDOWNLIST style is similar, but the user will not be able to enter items not in the drop-down list.

The CBS_SIMPLE style specifies that the list will not drop down at all—it is always visible. The user may also enter a selection with the keyboard.

Combo Box Methods

Combo boxes support most of the methods available for list boxes in working with the list and most of the methods available for single-line edit boxes for the edit box. For information on these, see the previous sections.

Combo Box Notifications

Combo boxes send a CBN_DROPDOWN notification when the user drops down the list.

Combo boxes also send notifications similar to those used by list boxes and edit controls. These include CBN_DBLCLK, CBN_EDITCHANGE, CBN_EDITUPDATE, CBN_SELCHANGE, CBN_SETFOCUS, and CBN_KILLFOCUS.

Dialog Data Exchange

To help you initialize the data in your dialogs and return the data to your application, MFC implements dialog data exchange (DDX). This takes advantage of the fact that your CDialog objects are created before the actual window is created and are still around when the dialog window has gone away. DDX automates the process of loading your dialog object's data into the dialog window and retrieving the data from the dialog when it closes. This process can also include some validation.

Dialog data exchange is done in the DoDataExchange() function of your dialog class, which is called by the UpdateData() function. Your application may call UpdateData() at any time, with TRUE to save and validate the data from your controls or FALSE to update the controls with member data. The default CDialog::OnInitDialog() and CDialog::OnOK() functions will call UpdateData() for you.

If you have used ClassWizard to add member variables for your controls to your dialog class, this will be handled for you. You may also specify some range or length validation parameters in ClassWizard.

The code generated by ClassWizard will look something like this:

```
void CMyDlg::DoDataExchange(CDataExchange* pDX)
{
    CDialog::DoDataExchange(pDX);
    //{{AFX_DATA_MAP(CMyDlg)
    DDX_Control(pDX, IDC_CHECK1, m_Check1);
    DDX_Check(pDX, IDC_CHECK1, m_Option1);
    DDX_CBString(pDX, IDC_COMBO1, m_ComboText);
    DDV_MaxChars(pDX, m_ComboText, 12);
    DDX_Text(pDX, IDC_EDIT1, m_EditText);
    DDX_Text(pDX, IDC_EDIT2, m_EditInt);
    DDV_MinMaxInt(pDX, m_EditInt, 1, 10);
    DDX_Text(pDX, IDC_EDIT3, m_EditFloat);
    DDV_MinMaxFloat(pDX, m_EditFloat, 1.3f, 4.7f);
    DDX_Radio(pDX, IDC_RADIO1, m_RadioSelection);
    //}}AFX_DATA_MAP
}
```

This example shows only a few of the many DDX functions available. For a list of all the predefined functions for dialog data exchange, search for DDX in the online help. Note that the name of the function generally indicates the type of control with which it will exchange data. If you don't happen to find a function listed that suits your needs, you can create your own DDX functions.

Creating Your Own DDX Functions

Each of the standard DDX functions takes three arguments: a pointer to a CDataExchange object, the resource ID of a control, and a reference to a variable.

The CDataExchange class provides two member variables: The m_bSaveAndValidate flag will be TRUE if the data exchange is moving from the controls to the member variables and FALSE if moving data from the member variables to the controls. The m_pDlgWnd member points to the CWnd object (usually a dialog) with which the exchange is working.

The CDataExchange class also provides a few functions that you will use in your DDX function. These include PrepareCtrl() and PrepareEditCtrl(), which prepare a dialog control for data exchange, and the Fail() function, which you can use to throw an exception if something is wrong in your data exchange or validation function.

The following example shows how this is used:

```
void AFXAPI DDX_MyData(CDataExchange* pDX, int nIDC, int& nValue)
{
    HWND hWndCtrl = pDX->PrepareEditCtrl(nIDC);
    if(pDX->m_bSaveAndValidate)
    {
        if(!GetMyData(hWndCtrl, nValue)
        {
            AfxMessageBox("Unable to get value");
            pDX->Fail();
        }
    }
```

```
    else
    {
        SetMyData(hWndCtrl, nValue);
    }
} // end DDX_MyData
```

In this example, you first call `PrepareEditCtrl()` to set up the control for data exchange. This returns the handle for the control specified by `nID`. If you are not working with an edit control, you should call `PrepareCtrl()`. You then check to see whether you are loading or storing the data and call the appropriate functions to work with the custom data. If you run into problems, you call `Fail()` to halt the data exchange and return quietly to the dialog. You need to notify the user in some way that the exchange failed—hence, the `AfxMessageBox()` call.

For additional examples of DDX functions, see `DLGDATA.C` in DevStudio\VC\mfc\src. This file implements all the standard MFC DDX routines, including the `DDX_TextWithFormat()` routine, which will parse data for you, using a simplified version of `sscanf()`.

Data Validation

In the previous example of `DoDataExchange()`, you will also notice several dialog data validation (DDV) functions. These are used to validate the length or range of the data before it is copied back to your member variables. Although your DDX calls may be placed in any order, you must call the DDV function for a control immediately after the DDX call for that control. You can implement your own DDV functions in a similar fashion. If you do this, keep in mind that data validation should occur only when the data is being stored; thus, you should check the `m_bSaveAndValidate` flag before doing anything. Your function should also provide a meaningful message to the user before calling `Fail()` if something doesn't pass the validation.

The DDV functions provided by MFC don't check to see whether a control is hidden or disabled. If you do not want to validate the value of a control in some conditions, you can place `if` blocks around DDV calls in your `DoDataExchange()` function; make sure that they are outside of ClassWizard's `AFX_DATA_MAP` blocks, or ClassWizard will get quite lost.

TIP

You are not really limited to member data items in your DDX functions, you can actually use something like this:

```
DDX_Text(pDX, IDC_MYFIELD, pDoc->m_nMyInt);
```

which enables you to exchange data directly with your document or other more permanent locations. However, be careful with this solution, because the data will be updated even if the validation fails. You may also have to go out of your way to update the document, its views, and/or the dirty flag.

Windows Common Dialogs

There are several common functions that seem to appear in almost every Windows application, including file selection, printing and page setup, find and replace, and color and font selection. To help with these functions, the Windows operating systems provide the common dialogs. MFC in turn provides classes to help you use the common dialogs. Starting with NT 4.0, the same set of dialogs may be used on NT as on Windows 95.

Each of the common dialog classes is based on CCommonDialog, which derives from CDialog. This means that you can use the common dialogs just like any other dialog in your application. In addition, you can derive your own classes from the common dialog classes to suit the needs of your application.

CFileDialog

The most common of the common dialogs is the File dialog. This is used by applications to open new files or to select files for "save as" or any other function your application needs. If you need to do anything with files, you should look at a way to use the CFileDialog class. Even if you have to derive your own class from it, it sure beats having to do the whole thing yourself.

To use the CFileDialog class in your application, you first need to call the constructor, which takes several parameters. The first is a flag that, if TRUE, will create a File Open dialog, or if FALSE, will create a File Save As dialog.

The second parameter allows you to specify a default extension to be added if the user does not specify an extension. By default, this is NULL.

The third parameter specifies the initial filename to appear in the dialog. This also defaults to NULL, which will not display an initial filename.

The fourth parameter gives flags that will be set in the m_ofn.Flags member. Setting various flags here can customize the behavior of the dialog. The available flags are detailed in the online documentation under OPENFILENAME.

The fifth parameter allows you to specify filters to select the files that will appear in the file list. This string is composed of filter descriptions and their file extensions, separated by (¦). The string ends with (¦¦) and a null character. For example, if you wanted to work with C or C++ files, your string might look like this:

```
char szFilter[] = "C Files (*.c)¦*.xlc¦C++ Files (*.cpp)¦*.cpp¦¦";
```

The sixth parameter is a pointer to the dialog's parent or owner window.

Once you have constructed the CFileDialog object, you can initialize it by modifying the m_ofn member, which is an OPENFILENAME structure, before calling the DoModal() function to display the dialog.

> **NOTE**
>
> If you wish to allow multiple selections in the file dialog, you need to specify the
> `OFN_ALLOWMULTISELECT` flag in `m_ofn.Flags`. You also need to replace `m_ofn.lpstrFile`
> with a pointer to a buffer you have allocated, and set `m_ofn.nMaxFile` to the size of the
> buffer, before calling `DoModal()`.

If the `DoModal()` returns `IDOK`, you can use member functions such as `CFileDialog::GetPathName()`
to get the name of the file the user has selected. You may also access the `m_ofn` member directly.

CPrintDialog

The MFC `CPrintDialog` class provides access to the Windows common dialogs for print and
print setup, which allows the user to specify printer specific options. This automatically handles
options specific to the printers that are installed on the user's system.

As with other common dialog classes, you must call the constructor for `CPrintDialog` before
calling `DoModal()`. The constructor takes a Boolean parameter to indicate the type of dialog. If
this is `TRUE`, the Print Setup dialog is shown. If it is `FALSE`, the normal Print dialog is shown,
which will provide access to the Print Setup dialog by way of the Print Setup button.

The second, optional, parameter specifies the flags to be used in the `m_pd.Flags` member. The
`m_pd` member is a `PRINTDLG` structure that you can modify to select several options about the
behavior of the dialog. You may also specify a third parameter for the parent of the dialog.

If `DoModal()` returns `IDOK`, you can use members of `CPrintDialog`, such as `GetPrinterDC()`, to
retrieve the device context for the selected printer, or `GetFromPage()` and `GetToPage()` to get
the page numbers the user has chosen to print. You will learn more about how to use this information in the next chapter.

> **TIP**
>
> You can use the `CPrintDialog::GetDefaults()` member to get information about the
> default printer without displaying the dialog to the user. This will fill in the `m_pd`
> member with information about the default printer.

CPageSetupDialog

In addition to the Print and Print Setup dialogs, Windows 95 and Windows NT add the Page
Setup dialog, which is intended to replace the Print Setup dialog. MFC supports the Page Setup
dialog with the `CPageSetupDialog` class.

Once again, you must call the constructor before calling DoModal() to present the dialog to the user. The constructor allows you to specify flags to be placed in the m_psd member of type PAGESETUPDLG. These flags can be used to enable or disable options such as margins and orientation in the dialog.

If DoModal() returns IDOK, you can use the member functions of CPageSetupDialog to get information about the current printer and page setup. You can also access the m_psd member directly. Of most interest, you can use the CreatePrinterDC() function to create a device context for the current setup.

CColorDialog

Windows provides a common dialog allowing the user to select colors. Conveniently, MFC also provides the CColorDialog class to help you use it. The constructor for CColorDialog takes a COLORREF structure, allowing you to specify an initial color selection, as well as a flags parameter, used to fill in the m_cc.Flags member.

These flags, as well as the rest of the m_cc structure, are defined in the online help for the CHOOSECOLOR structure. For instance, you may specify the CC_FULLOPEN or CC_PREVENTFULLOPEN to present the custom color section of the dialog or prevent the user from choosing custom colors.

Once you have called DoModal() to present the dialog, and it has returned IDOK, you can use CColorDialog::GetColor() to return a COLORREF structure for the color selected.

CFontDialog

MFC provides the CFontDialog class to help you work with the Windows font selection dialog. This presents the user with the list of fonts currently installed on the system.

The constructor for CFontDialog takes an LPLOGFONT parameter to specify an initial font setting, as well as a flag's parameter used to initialize the m_cf CHOOSEFONT structure's flags. Optionally, you may specify a device context for the printer to select fonts from and a pointer to the parent window of the dialog.

The dialog is presented by calling DoModal(), which returns IDOK if the user closed the dialog with the OK button. At this point, you can use CFontDialog::GetCurrentFont() to return a pointer to a LOGFONT structure detailing the user's selection.

CFindAndReplace

Windows also provides a standard Find and Replace dialog, which MFC wraps nicely in the CFindAndReplace class. Although this dialog will not actually perform the find or replace functions for you, it does help by providing the standard interface dialog that users expect.

The Find and Replace dialog is also different from the other common dialogs mentioned so far, because it is intended to be used as a modeless dialog. Therefore, you will want to use the new operator to create a new CFindAndReplace object on the stack. The constructor takes no parameters.

Instead of passing parameters to the constructor, you can modify the m_fr structure (of type FINDREPLACE) to initialize the dialog before calling Create() to present the dialog to the user.

The Create() function is also used to pass some initialization information to the dialog. The first parameter, if set to TRUE, will create a simple Find dialog, or a Find and Replace dialog if set to FALSE. You may also specify the string to find the default replace string, the flags, and the parent window. The default flags specify FR_DOWN to search down the document.

Because this is a modeless dialog, it is also a bit trickier to tie in to your application. To use the Find and Replace dialog, you define a handler for a registered message ID that you have received from the ::RegisterWindowMessage() function. To implement all this, you should have code that looks something like the following in your class declaration:

```
class CMyFrameWnd : public CFrameWnd
{
protected:
    afx_msg LONG OnMyFindReplace(WPARAM wparam, LPARAM lparam);
    // The rest of your class declaration
    DECLARE_MESSAGE_MAP()
};
```

You then create a registered message ID:

```
static UINT WM_FINDREPLACE = ::RegisterWindowMessage(FINDMSGSTRING);
```

The message map entry then looks like this:

```
BEGIN_MESSAGE_MAP( CMyFrameWnd, CFrameWnd )
    // Your other message map entries
    ON_REGISTERED_MESSAGE( WM_FINDREPLACE, OnMyFindReplace )
END_MESSAGE_MAP
```

Now you have to code your handler function to do the actual find or replace operation. Your handler can make use of several different CFindReplaceDialog member functions to retrieve information from the dialog. Your handler may look something like this:

```
afx_msg LONG CMyFrameWnd::OnMyFindReplace(WPARAM wparam, LPARAM lparam);
{
    if(IsTerminating)
    {
        // The dialog is closing, you may want to record this somewhere.
        return TRUE;
    }

    if(pFindDlg->FindNext())
    {
        // User clicked Find Next button
        FindMyString(pFindDlg->GetFindString());
```

```
    }
    if(pFindDlg->ReplaceAll())
    {
        // User clicked Replace All button
        ReplaceAllMyStrings(pFindDlg->GetFindString, pFindDlg
->GetReplaceString);
    }
} // end OnMyFindReplace
```

This is just a simple example. You will want to be a bit more concerned with the results of things such as MatchCase() and SearchDown() in a real implementation.

OLE Common Dialogs

MFC also provides many classes based on COLEDialog to handle dialogs specific to OLE implementations. These include those shown in Table 5.1.

Table 5.1. OLE common dialog classes.

Dialog class	*Function*
COLEInsertDialog	Displays the Insert Object dialog box, used to insert new linked or embedded objects
COLEPasteSpecialDialog	Displays the Paste Special dialog box, used for implementing Edit | Paste Special
COLELinksDialog	Displays the Edit Links dialog box, used to modify information about linked items
COLEChangeIconDialog	Displays the Change Icon dialog box, used to change the icon for an OLE object
COLEConvertDialog	Displays the Convert dialog box, used to convert an OLE object to a new type
COLEPropertiesDialog	Displays the Windows common OLE properties dialog, used to change settings for OLE documents
COLEUpdateDialog	Displays the Update dialog box, used to update all links in a document
COLEChangeSourceDialog	Displays the Change Source dialog box, used to change the source or destination of a link
COLEBusyDialog	Displays the Server Busy and Server Not Responding dialog boxes, for handling calls to busy applications

Because any discussion of these dialogs is swamped in OLE terms and architecture, the dialogs are not discussed here. Suffice it to say that they work in much the same way as the other common modal dialogs discussed in this chapter.

Creating Property Sheets

Windows 95 and Windows NT support the use of property sheets to allow you to present several different pages of options, using tab controls to allow the user to switch between pages. Visual C++ uses this in many places, including the project settings and many properties dialogs. You can use MFC to create your own property sheets for use in your applications. This is becoming part of the standard look and feel of Windows, and your users will expect it.

Property sheets in MFC are actually made up of several different pages based on the CPropertyPage class. The pages are then incorporated in one sheet, supported by CPropertySheet.

Building Property Pages

Property pages are actually dialogs, although they are handled a little bit differently in a property sheet. To create property pages, you create a dialog template for each page. (True, you could create the dialogs in your code with separate Create() calls for each control, but why bother? I figure if you're reading this, you are enough of a masochist without my help, so I'll try to keep this simple.)

When you are designing the dialog templates for your property pages, you should keep in mind how they will appear in the property sheet. This means that you should try to keep all your pages the same size and try to align the first control in each page so that the user doesn't have to reorient to each new page while tabbing through them. To help with this, you can use one of the three dialog templates available when you insert a new dialog resource. You can get to these by expanding the dialog tree in the New Resource dialog. This will help keep all your pages the same size.

In addition, there are a few other things to do when setting up the dialog templates. Your template should have the Child style and a thin border. You should enable a title bar, but be aware that the caption will be used for the tab of the page—try to keep this short. You also should have the template be disabled by default—the property sheet will enable the appropriate page when it is time. If you use the templates intended for property pages, these settings will be set up for you.

Your property pages should not include OK or Cancel buttons; these will be provided by the property sheet.

Next you create a class for each page, based on CPropertyPage. This is best done with ClassWizard, which will automatically notice that you have added new dialog template resources and prompt you to create a new class.

TIP

When ClassWizard enables you to edit the filename for the class, you can change this so that all your pages are in the same file. This can make keeping track of them a bit easier.

Creating the Property Sheet

Now that all the building blocks are laid out, you can put them together into one sheet. To do this, start by creating a class for your sheet, based on CPropertySheet. It's convenient to place this in the same file as your pages, just to keep things together.

Next you create an instance of your sheet class in the frame that will contain the property sheet by calling its constructor, which will look something like this:

```
CMySheetClass m_MySheet(_T("My Options"), this, 1);
```

The constructor takes either the resource ID of an entry in the string table or a string pointer to the caption of the property sheet as its first parameter.

NOTE

The _T macro creates a Unicode string, which is essential for proper localization. If the symbol _UNICODE is defined, this will generate a Unicode string, which can support character sets that use more than one byte per character. If _UNICODE is not defined, _T will generate a plain C-style string.

The other parameters are for the parent window of the sheet and an index to the page that will be active when the sheet is shown.

If you are creating an array of different sheets, you call the constructor with no parameters, then call Construct() for each array element. This takes the same arguments as the constructor.

Next you construct an object for each of your property page classes. It makes sense in most cases to include the pages as members of the sheet; you can then call their constructors in the constructor of the sheet. Make sure that you add these to both versions of the constructor.

> **TIP**
>
> As for any classes defined in separate files, make sure that you include the headers for your property page classes in any file where you use them. This really helps cut down on compile errors.

Once the page objects are created, you call `AddPage()` for each page, something like this (this also fits well into the constructor for the sheet):

```
m_MySheet.AddPage(&m_PageOne);
```

At this point, the property sheet is good to go. You can present it to the user as you would any other dialog. That is, you can call either `DoModal()` to create a modal property sheet or `Create()` to create a modeless property sheet.

I could add more detail here, but it would get a bit lengthy for this spot. Once the property sheet is up and running, you can use its member functions to work with the pages. The `SetActivePage()` member allows you to select the page the user sees, and `GetActivePage()` returns the active page object. There are also several other functions for working with pages, the number of pages, and their indexes.

Dialog Data Exchange with Property Pages

Like all objects derived from `CDialog`, each property page will have its own `DoDataExchange()` function. The `DoDataExchange()` function is called by way of `OnUpdate()` each time the user changes pages.

If you want to do any special validation before the user is allowed to switch pages, you can override the `OnKillActive()` member for your pages. This function is called before `DoDataExchange()`, whenever the user tabs to a new page or clicks on the OK button. If `OnKillActive()` returns `FALSE`, the user is not allowed to change pages. By default, this does not give the user any reason why the change was disallowed, so make sure to spit out a message of some sort.

On the other side of the page change, `OnSetActive()` is called for a page before it is activated. If you override this function, make sure to call the base class implementation, which will set up the page and call `UpdateData()`. This in turn calls `DoDataExchange()`.

Adding an Apply Button

If you are using a modal property page, you will probably just wait until the user has clicked on OK, whereby `DoModal()` returns `IDOK`, before copying any data into more permanent areas of your application. However, you may want to provide the user with a way to implement changes now, particularly in the case of modeless property sheets.

You may be thinking to yourself that the Apply button in the lower-right of the property sheet would be mighty handy for this, if you could just find a way to make it active. You can activate the Apply button by calling `SetModified()` from within any of the pages. You can call this in handlers in your page class, for instance, in response to EN_CHANGE messages from edit controls.

Once you have called `SetModified()`, the Apply button will remain active until the user clicks on it, even when the user changes pages. The default handler for the Apply button will call the `OnKillActive()` and `DoDataExchange()` functions for the visible page and set the modified flag to FALSE for each page. It then calls `OnOK()`, without closing the dialog.

In your `OnOK()` function, you have several options concerning how to update your application. It is generally a good practice to send a windows message back to the main window, which it will then use to update its data. You can do this with the following code:

```
void CMyPage1::OnOK()
{
    CWnd* pMainWnd = AfxGetApp()->m_pMainWnd;
    pMain->SendMessage(WM_USER, 0, 0);
    SetModified(FALSE);
} // end OnOK
```

This will send a message to the main window and wait until it is handled before returning. The main window should then add an appropriate handler function to fetch the data and a message map entry:

```
ON_MESSAGE_MAP(WM_USER, FetchSheetData)
```

Creating Your Own Wizards

Wizards seem to be popping up in just about everything Microsoft makes these days. Although "revolutionary wizard technology" is a little hard to swallow as the renaissance of the computer world, wizards are very handy little gadgets. You can use them to guide the user through a series of steps involved in performing a task, such as creating a new file, or even a new project, the way AppWizard does. Note that ClassWizard just shares the buzzword; it doesn't really work like the wizards that you will create here, which present a series of steps.

Apart from all the hype and marketing propaganda, creating your own wizards is really quite simple. MFC wizards are simply property sheets with a few extra widgets added. In fact, all you have to do to make a wizard is create a property sheet as shown previously and add a call to `CPropertySheet::SetWizardMode()` between adding all the property pages and calling `DoModal()`. Just add a line like this after your calls to `AddPage()`:

```
m_MyWizSheet.SetWizardMode();
```

And, Presto! You've got a new wizard.

By calling `SetWizardMode()`, you tell the property sheet to implement the Next (or Finish for the last page), Back, and Cancel buttons instead of creating a tabbed dialog.

To finish your wizard, you probably will want to tweak a few things. Most notably, you will want to enable the Finish button at some point. By default, only the Back, Next, and Cancel buttons are displayed. These will allow the user to move between the pages, calling the OnSetActive() and OnKillActive() functions as a normal property sheet would when the user changes pages.

To change the function and appearance of the wizard buttons, you call CPropertySheet::SetWizardButtons(), which takes a combination (bitwise-OR) of several flags. This parameter may specify the PSWIZB_BACK and PSWIZB_NEXT to enable the Back and Next buttons, PSWIZB_FINISH to enable the Finish button, or PSWIZB_DISABLEDFINISH to add a disabled Finish button. Note that you can only call SetWizardButtons() after you have called DoModal().

There is one catch, however. You can have either a Next button or a Finish button, but not both. If you specify both flags, the Finish button will be displayed. (Yeah, AppWizard has both a Next and a Finish button, but then again I suppose a bit more work went into AppWizard than this example.)

There is also one more catch. The SetWizardButtons() function is a member of CPropertySheet, although you will probably want to call it from within the OnSetActive() function of a class derived from CPropertyPage. The following example shows how to deal with this, using GetParent() to set up the Finish button:

```
BOOL CLastStepPage::OnSetActive()
{
    CPropertySheet* pParent = (CPropertySheet *) GetParent();
    pParent->SetWizardButtons(PSWIZB_BACK ¦ PSWIZB_FINISH);
    pParent->SetFinishText("Make Gizmo");
    return CPropertyPage::OnSetActive();
} // end OnSetActive()
```

This example also uses the SetFinishText() function to change the text for the Finish button. Note that the button settings will not change when the user changes pages unless you change them. Thus, you should add an OnSetActive() override to each page to set up the buttons appropriately. Otherwise, the example above will not allow users to return to the last page if they ever clicked on Back.

Finally, when users dismiss the wizard by clicking on the Finish button, DoModal() will return ID_WIZFINISH instead of the usual IDOK. The Cancel button will still return IDCANCEL.

Dialog Bars

You may have noticed that many applications include gadgets such as combo boxes in their toolbars, rather than just buttons. You can add this sort of functionality to your applications with another special sort of dialog known as a dialog bar. By using a dialog bar, you can add any sort of control you like to the toolbar. The user can also use the Tab key to move between controls in the dialog bar.

To create a dialog bar, start with a dialog template. It is generally best to use the IDD_DIALOGBAR template provided by expanding the Dialog tree in the dialog presented by the Insert ¦ Resource command. Your dialog template should have the Child style and no other options selected. In particular, the Visible style should not be set. As long as you stick to these few rules, you can add any controls you like to the dialog bar template.

MFC supports dialog bars with the CDialogBar class, which is derived from CControlBar. In most cases, you do not need to derive your own class for a dialog bar, because the control notifications will be sent to the parent, usually the main frame, that should handle them. Thus, you use the base CDialogBar class. The constructor for CDialogBar takes no parameters.

To create the actual window for the dialog bar, call CDialogBar::Create(). You pass a pointer to the parent window, a resource ID of the dialog template to be used, the dialog bar style flags, and a control ID for the dialog bar. The style flags are used to pass alignment styles, like other control bars. These include CBRS_TOP, CBRS_BOTTOM, CBRS_LEFT, and CBRS_RIGHT, as well as CBRS_NOALIGN, which will keep the dialog bar in its current position when the frame is resized.

Once you have called Create(), you need not do anything else with the dialog bar but handle the control notifications that it sends to the frame. You may also wish to add ON_UPDATE_COMMAND_UI handlers for any of the controls in your dialog bar that you wish to disable or otherwise alter at runtime.

Summary

In this chapter, you took a look at dialogs and the things you can do with them in your applications. You learned how to create both modal and modeless dialogs and present them to the user. You have also seen how to work with the controls in your dialog and use Dialog Data Exchange and Dialog Data Validation to simplify the task of fetching data from your dialogs.

6

Drawing and Printing with MFC

by David Bennett

Although it is possible to avoid having to deal with your own drawing in an application, there are many situations in which you will want to have your application handle its own rendering for controls or views. In Windows programs, this is done using the GDI functions included in the Windows API. MFC provides a framework that makes it easier to handle drawing in C++, although if you are familiar with the Windows Graphics Device Interface (GDI), the change is fairly cosmetic.

In this chapter, you will learn how to

■ Paint your own windows

■ Use MFC to work with GDI objects

■ Do your own printing

■ Implement Print Preview

Painting Your Window

If you need to do your own drawing, you will generally do this in one of two places. The first of these is the OnDraw() function of your view class, which will be called by the framework to display your document to the user. The second is in a handler for the WM_PAINT message, which is generally handled by CWnd::OnPaint(). The WM_PAINT message is sent whenever something has occurred that requires you to redraw a portion of your window, or when you explicitly request it.

The rendering that you will do is based upon a device context (DC). The DC contains information about the device that is to be drawn to and various objects, such as pens and fonts, that are currently selected to draw in that device context.

The CDC Class

In MFC, device contexts are encapsulated in the CDC class, which also incorporates most of the common GDI calls. Actually, the CDC class incorporates two device contexts: m_hDC, used for output, and m_hAttribDC, used for attribute queries. In most cases, however, you can do all you need to do with CDC member functions and won't need to worry about working with the data members directly. The Windows API GDI functions take a device context handle, and the CDC member functions use the device context contained in the CDC object.

In addition to the basic CDC class, MFC provides a few other classes derived from CDC that are useful for particular situations:

The CPaintDC class is intended for use in OnPaint() handler functions. CPaintDC will call BeginPaint() on construction and EndPaint() on destruction.

The CClientDC class provides a device context for the client area of a window. This can be used for drawing immediate responses to mouse events.

The CWindowDC class provides a device context for the entire window, including both the client and nonclient areas.

The CMetaFileDC provides a device context for Windows metafiles, which allows you to record a series of drawing commands to be replayed later. The member functions of CMetaFileDC are recorded in a metafile.

GDI Wrapper Classes

In this chapter, you will use a few standard structures. In the C API world, these are the POINT, SIZE, and RECT structures. MFC provides classes that wrap these structures, in addition to providing member functions for working with these objects. The MFC classes may be used interchangeably with the GDI structures in most calls.

> **NOTE**
>
> For any function that takes a POINT, SIZE, or RECT structure, you can substitute a CPoint, CSize, or CRect object. These classes are actually derived from the corresponding structures, so they have the same data structure.

CPoint

The CPoint class is equivalent to the POINT structure, which contains two data items, x and y, to denote a particular point. In addition, the CPoint class provides overridden equality and inequality operators (== and !=) that may be used to compare a CPoint to another point. You can add (or subtract) a CPoint to either a point or a size with the +, +=, -, and -= operators. The Offset() function also allows you to add a value to the members of a CPoint.

CSize

MFC provides the CSize class to encapsulate the SIZE structure. This provides the cx and cy members, used to denote a rectangular area's size. The CSize class does not provide an Offset() function, but does support the ==, !=, +, -, +=, and -= operators. Just remember that the left operand must be a CSize, but the right operand may be a SIZE or a CSize.

CRect

The CRect class is used to work with RECT structures, which incorporate the top, left, bottom, and right members to define a rectangular area. You can use the TopLeft(), BottomRight(), or CenterPoint() functions to return a CPoint representing the appropriate coordinates.

Many other functions require that the CRect be normalized in order to be used properly. That is, the top and left coordinates must be less than the bottom and right coordinates. The Normalize() function will swap coordinates accordingly.

CRect provides Width() and Height() functions to return the width and height of the rectangle, as well as the IsRectEmpty() function used to test whether the rectangle has a width and height of 0. In addition, the Size() function returns a CSize denoting the size of the rectangle.

CRect overloads the following operators to work on CRect: =, ==, !=, +, -, +=, and -=. In addition, the & and &= operators can be used to compute the intersection of a CRect and a rectangle, whereas the ¦ and ¦= operators can be used to find a union.

The PtInRect() function can be used to test whether a CRect contains a given point.

There are also several other CRect functions detailed in the online help.

Mapping Modes

The coordinates used in drawing functions are dependent on the mapping mode currently used in a device context. Different mapping modes use different values for the logical units used, as well as different orientations for the coordinate system. The different mapping modes are detailed in Table 6.1, which lists the direction of positive x and y coordinates, as well as the value of the logical units.

Table 6.1. Mapping modes.

Mapping mode	+X	+Y	Logical unit
MM_TEXT	Right	Down	1 device pixel
MM_HIENGLISH	Right	Up	0.001 inch
MM_LOENGLISH	Right	Up	0.01 inch
MM_HIMETRIC	Right	Up	0.01 millimeter
MM_LOMETRIC	Right	Up	0.1 millimeter
MM_TWIPS	Right	Up	1 twip (1/20 of a point, or 1/1440 of an inch)

In addition, Windows provides two additional mapping modes, which allow an arbitrary logical unit value. MM_ISOTROPIC will use equal X and Y units, preserving a 1:1 aspect ratio; the MM_ANISOTROPIC mode allows independent X and Y units. These settings are generally used to scale a drawing to fit the current size of a window exactly.

To work with the mapping mode of a CDC object, you can use the GetMapMode() and SetMapMode() functions.

> **NOTE**
>
> Although both Windows NT and Windows 95 support 32-bit values for coordinate parameters, Win95 works with only 16-bit coordinates internally.

Working with GDI Objects

A Windows device context uses several types of objects to affect the output of your drawing. These include pens, fonts, bitmaps, brushes, and palettes. Before making drawing calls, you associate the object you want to use with the device context. MFC provides classes derived from CGdiObject to work with these objects. To see how this works, let's look at the CPen class, which encapsulates Windows pen objects.

CPen

MFC uses the CPen class to help you work with GDI pen objects. Pen objects are associated with a device context for use in drawing lines. The current pen object determines the width, color, and pattern of lines drawn with it.

To use a CPen object, you must first create it. The MFC for GDI objects allows you to do this in one of two ways. First, you can create the object and initialize it with the constructor. This process is known as one-stage construction. For example, you can create a new pen with the following code, which creates a pen for drawing a dashed black line five units wide:

```
CPen myPen(PS_DOT, 5, RGB(0,0,0));
```

The second technique is known as two-stage construction and entails constructing the object, then calling an initialization function to initialize the object. Two-stage construction allows much greater flexibility in error handling in the event the initialization fails. The code looks like this:

```
CPen myPen;
if(myPen.CreatePen( PS_DASH, 5, RGB(0,0,0)))
    DoSomethingWithPen();
else
    ReportPenError();
```

The arguments for either the constructor or CreatePen() include a style for the lines drawn, the width of the lines, and their color. The styles can include PS_SOLID, PS_DASH, PS_DOT, PS_DASHDOT, and PS_DASHDOTDOT. The color is passed as a COLORREF, which can be generated with the RGB() macro. This will create a COLORREF based on the red, green, and blue components of a color.

There are also versions of the constructor and CreatePen() which allow you to create geometric or cosmetic pens, allowing greater flexibility in pen styles.

Once you have created a CPen object, you select it into the device context before it may be used. In general, you will want to save the current pen, select your new pen, use it, and return the old pen to the device context. This is shown in the following example:

```
CPen myPen;
if (myPen.CreatePen(PS_SOLID, 1, RGB(0,0,0)))
{
    // Save old pen and select new pen
    CPen* pOldPen = pDC->SelectObject(&myPen);
    //Do Drawing with LineTo(), etc.
    // replace old pen
    pDC->SelectObject( pOldPen );
}
else
{
    ReportErrorToUser();
}
```

The SelectObject() call is used similarly to select other objects, such as fonts, brushes, and palettes.

CFont

MFC uses the CFont class to encapsulate a Windows font, as well as providing member functions to manipulate that font. To work with fonts in MFC, you first create an instance of CFont. Because the constructor takes no parameters, this is trivial.

Next, you initialize the logical font represented by the CFont object. Windows will convert your logical font to a physical font appropriate for the display device when you select the font into the device context.

If you have allowed the user to choose a font from a CFontDialog, you can pass the pointer returned from CFontDialog::GetCurrentFont() to the CFont::CreateFontIndirect() function. This is by far the simplest way to initialize a CFont object.

If you want to select a font within your application, you can use EnumFontFamilies() to retrieve the fonts available for a given device context. CFont::CreatePointFont() can be used to initialize the CFont based on a typeface name and point size.

You can also use CFont::CreateFont() to initialize the CFont object. This will allow you to specify many parameters of the logical font you wish to create.

To use a font in your drawing, you save the current font selected in the device context, select your new font into the device context, do your text output, and select the old font back into the device context. You can do this with CDC::SelectObject(), as you saw for CPen objects.

CBrush

The GDI brush object is encapsulated in the MFC CBrush class. Brushes determine the color and pattern that are used to fill in regions, such as in the CDC::Polygon(), CDC::PaintRect(), or `CDC::PaintRgn()` function. Brushes generally come in four different flavors: solid paints in one solid color, hatched paints a crosshatched pattern, patterned paints from a user-defined bitmap, and null paints nothing.

The null brush is useful in situations where you do not want to paint a region that is normally filled. For example, you use a null brush to draw the outline of a rectangle with `CDC::Rectangle()`, leaving the background intact. (Actually, the null brush is a Windows stock object, which is covered later in this section.)

If you want to create a brush other than a null brush, you can create the `CBrush` object with no parameters, then call `CreateSolidBrush()`, `CreateHatchBrush()`, or `CreatePatternBrush()`. These calls allow you to select the color and pattern information used to initialize the brush. There are also constructors provided that take the same parameters, allowing you to construct the brush in one step.

The brush is then used by selecting it into the current device context, remembering to save and restore the old brush, as you saw in the `CPen` example.

CPalette

Windows color palette objects are used to map the colors that an application wants to use to the colors actually available on a display device. Even when your display is configured to display 256 colors, these 256 colors are chosen from a much wider assortment. The display device's palette assigns real colors to the 256 slots available in the palette.

Normally, Windows will handle the palette for you, adding entries for the colors normally used by Windows and filling in entries to match the colors specified in your application. Windows will approximate these colors if it needs to. If you are developing an application that deals with images, the exact colors used in the palette may be of great interest to you. In this case, you create your own palette.

Palette objects are created with a constructor taking no parameters. `CPalette::CreatePalette()` is then called to initialize the palette. This call takes a pointer to a `LOGPALETTE` structure, which holds an array of `PALETTEENTRY` structures. Each entry holds information about the red, green, and blue components of each color, as well as some other information on how the entry will be used.

You can get a range of palette entries from the logical palette with `GetPaletteEntries()`. You can then modify them to suit your needs before sending them back to the palette with `SetPaletteEntries()`.

You can then select the palette into the device context with `SelectObject()`. Be sure to save the old palette and restore it when you are finished. In addition, you can tell Windows to modify the system palette immediately with `AnimatePalette()`.

Be careful when changing palettes, because the system palette is used by all applications. If you delete a color used by another application, this may drastically change the appearance of applications in the background (particularly wallpaper bitmaps).

CBitmap

Windows uses bitmaps to represent a rectangular image, which can be used to display pictures in a window. These may range from simple pictures, such as custom buttons, to large photographic images. CBitmap objects are created by creating a CBitmap instance and initializing it with the data for the bitmap.

The easiest way to initialize a bitmap is to use LoadBitmap() with a resource ID to read the data from a bitmap resource attached to your application. In addition, you can use LoadOEMBitmap() to load a predefined Windows bitmap for many common display elements. There are also several other initialization functions that you can use to create bitmaps that are appropriate for a specified device context.

Once the bitmap is initialized, you can select it into a device context. However, you generally will not be selecting a bitmap directly into the CDC for your output. Instead, you select the bitmap into a compatible device context so that you can then display it in the actual display context with the BitBlt() function. This whole process looks something like this:

```
void CMoLessDlg::OnPaint()
{
    CPaintDC dc(this); // device context for painting

    CBitmap bmMyImage;
    bmMyImage.LoadBitmap(IDB_BITMAP1);
    CDC dcCompatible;
    dcCompatible.CreateCompatibleDC(&dc);
    dcCompatible.SelectObject(&bmMyImage);
    BITMAP bmInfo;
    bmMyBits.GetObject(sizeof(bmInfo), &bmInfo);
    dc.BitBlt(150,100, bmInfo.bmWidth,
        bmInfo.bmHeight,
        &dcCompatible, 0, 0, SRCCOPY);

}
```

In this example, you can see that you create a compatible device context to load the bitmap. You then use GetObject() to fill in a temporary BITMAP object, which is used to get the dimensions of the bitmap.

All the real drawing is done with the BitBlt() function. The first four parameters specify the location and size of the bitmap to be drawn. The next three parameters specify the source device context and an offset into the bitmap from which to start rendering.

This example uses SRCCOPY for the final, raster operation parameter, which will simply copy the bitmap to the desired location. However, there are many other possible operations that can, in turn, perform operations to combine the bitmap with the existing display, show the bitmap through the pattern specified in a brush, or invert the bitmap.

If you want to be able to edit a bitmap in your application, you can use the CreateBitmapIndirect() function to initialize the bitmap from a BITMAP structure, which specifies all the information about a bitmap other than the actual bits involved. You can then use SetBitmapBits() and GetBitmapBits() to work with the image data.

CRgn

Windows uses regions for painting an area with the current brush and for clipping, which allows you to trim the area that is actually rendered. This is useful for making sure that your drawing stays within certain bounds or does not overwrite existing information in the display.

In MFC, you can create a region by creating an instance of CRgn and calling one of its create functions. You can use the CreateRectRgn(), CreateEllipticRgn(), or CreatePolygonRgn() function to initialize a region based on simple shapes, or the CreatePolyPolygonRgn() or CreateFromPath() function to specify a much more complex region.

After you have created a few regions, you can combine them to form new regions with CombineRgn(). This call takes the address of the two regions to combine and a parameter specifying how to combine them. This specifies the values shown in Table 6.2.

Table 6.2. Region combine modes.

Mode	Operation performed
RGN_COPY	Creates a copy of the first region
RGN_AND	Finds the intersection of the two regions
RGN_OR	Finds the union of both regions
RGN_DIFF	Finds the areas of the first region that are not included in the second
RGN_XOR	Combines both regions, removing overlapping areas

The region you have created can then be used in calls such as FillRgn() or PaintRgn() to paint a region or SelectClipRgn() to set the clipping region. For more on this, see the section titled "Clipping," later in this chapter.

Stock Objects

There are many basic objects that you will undoubtedly use over and over if you do much work with your own drawing. To help, Windows provides a collection of stock objects that may be selected into a device context with the SelectStockObject() function. This can save you the trouble of creating your own objects.

The `SelectStockObject()` function takes only one parameter, which specifies the stock object to be selected. Table 6.3 lists the Windows stock objects available.

Table 6.3. Stock objects.

Stock object	Description
NULL_PEN	Null pen
BLACK_PEN	Black pen
WHITE_PEN	White pen
NULL_BRUSH	Null brush
BLACK_BRUSH	Solid black brush
WHITE_BRUSH	Solid white brush
GRAY_BRUSH	Solid gray brush
DKGRAY_BRUSH	Solid dark gray brush
LTGRAY_BRUSH	Solid light gray brush
HOLLOW_BRUSH	Hollow brush (like null brush, will not fill in polygons)
ANSI_FIXED_FONT	Fixed ANSI system font
ANSI_VAR_FONT	Variable ANSI system font
OEM_FIXED_FONT	OEM-dependent fixed font
SYSTEM_FONT	System font used for menus, dialog box controls, and other text
SYSTEM_FIXED_FONT	Fixed-width system font used prior to Windows 3.0 (the newer SYSTEM_FONT is proportional)
DEFAULT_PALETTE	Default color palette containing the 20 static colors in the system palette used by Windows

Drawing with CDC

Now that you've explored a bit of background, let's see how to use the CDC member functions to do some drawing. There are actually a gazillion different member functions provided in CDC, but you will examine only a few of them here. If you think it would be handy to have a particular function, chances are CDC already supports it—check the online documentation.

Drawing Lines

One of the simplest elements that you can draw is a line, so let's start there. CDC provides many different functions to draw lines, ranging from simple straight lines to multiple Bézier spline curves.

The line drawing functions all draw lines with the currently selected pen. You will look at changing pens in the next section, so for now let's use whichever pen is currently selected.

Each of the line drawing functions will begin drawing from the current position for the device context, as will several other functions. To set the current position, use the `MoveTo()` function, which will move the pen without drawing anything. You can retrieve the current position with `GetCurrentPosition()`.

Simple straight lines can be drawn with the `LineTo()` function, which will draw a line from the current position to the specified point with the selected pen. This will move the current position to the new point. The following example shows how you can draw an X in the current window:

```
CDC* pDC = GetDC();
CRect clientRect;
GetClientRect(&clientRect);
pDC->MoveTo(clientRect.TopLeft());
pDC->LineTo(clientRect.BottomRight());
pDC->MoveTo(clientRect.right, clientRect.top);
pDC->LineTo(clientRect.left, clientRect.bottom);
```

In this example, you use `GetDC()` to return the device context for the current `CWnd`. (This is assuming that the drawing is taking place in a member function of a `CWnd`-based class.) The `GetClientRect()` function is used to get the coordinates bounding the client area of the window, where you will be drawing.

You then use `MoveTo()` and `LineTo()` to draw an X. You can see that both the `MoveTo()` and `LineTo()` functions will accept either a point parameter or separate x and y coordinates.

In addition to drawing straight lines with `LineTo()`, you can draw arcs with `Arc()`, `ArcTo()`, and `AngleArc()`. Because an arc between two points can have two orientations, the `GetArcDirection()` and `SetArcDirection()` functions are provided to let you work with the current direction used to draw arcs.

For more control over the kind of curves you can draw, you can use the `PolyBezierTo()` function to render one or more cubic Bézier splines. This function takes an array of points and an integer, which specifies the number of splines to be drawn. For each spline, there will be three points in the array of points passed. The first two are control points of the spline drawn from the current position to the third point. The `PolyBezier()` function is similar, only it does not deal with the current location.

Drawing Polygons

The `CDC` class also provides functions for drawing simple polygons, such as rectangles and ellipses, by way of the `Rectangle()` and `Ellipse()` functions. In addition, you can draw any polygon you like with the `Polygon()` function, or a set of several polygons with `PolyPolygon()`.

Polygons are automatically filled, using the current brush. To draw just the outline of the polygon, you can select a null brush into the device context.

If you are drawing complex polygons, you may want to look at the `SetPolyFillMode()` function, which allows you to specify the algorithm used to fill in the polygon.

Drawing Text

To output simple text to a device context, you can use the `TextOut()` function, which will render a specified string at the x and y coordinates specified, using the current font for the device context. You can also use `TextOut()` to render text at the current position by using `SetTextAlign()` with the flags set to `TA_UPDATECP`. This will cause `TextOut()` to ignore the x and y parameters, placing the text at the current position.

In addition, the `CDC` class provides many other functions allowing you to choose different options for the location and formatting of text drawn to the device context.

Clipping

You can assign a clipping region to a device context, which will prevent any drawing outside of the region from being rendered. This is useful to contain your drawing to a region within a window, such as for setting margins or preserving a region of a window that you do not want to overwrite.

You can set the clipping region with `SelectClipRgn()`, which takes a region parameter. You will explore region objects later in this chapter. For now, suffice it to say that a region can include any combination of rectangles and regions defined by straight lines and splines.

Once you have established the clipping region, you can use the `PtVisible()` function to determine whether a given point lies within the clipping region. In addition, you can use `RectVisible()` to determine whether any part of a given rectangle lies within the clipping region. These can be very helpful in optimizing your drawing routines, if you check to see whether something will be rendered before wasting your time drawing something that will only be clipped away.

`CDC` also provides many other functions for working with clipping regions. See the online documentation for a complete reference.

Other Cool Drawing Stuff

The subject of drawing your own windows could easily make up an entire book on its own. Although we can't cover everything here, the previous sections give you enough information to get started on basic drawing. In addition, let's look at a few other little tidbits that you may find useful.

Trackers

In many applications, you may wish to allow the user to manipulate objects directly in your display window, particularly if you will be working with OLE objects. MFC provides the CRectTracker class to help you with this. This class can be used to generate borders around an object in your window that may be several different styles, including borders that include resize handles or a hatched pattern over the entire object.

SetWorldTransform()

If you are creating applications for Windows NT, you can use the Windows API ::SetWorldTransform() function to translate between the logical or world coordinate system and the page space for a specified device context. This can be used to scale, rotate, shear, or translate your graphics output.

> **NOTE**
>
> SetWorldTransform() is not supported on Windows 95.

To use this function, you specify a transformation matrix that combines the matrices used to perform the desired transformation operations. I won't go into the linear algebra required to work with these, but the online documentation does cover some of this.

Printing

In Windows programming, sending output to a printer is the same as sending output to the display. You just work with a different device context for each output device. However, the MFC framework handles printing tasks differently than drawing your views or dialogs.

If you use AppWizard to create an application, simple printing will be handled for you, unless you disable the default Print and Print Preview support option in step 4. The framework will take care of presenting the Print dialog and creating a device context for the printer.

By default, the framework then calls the OnDraw() function of your view with a device context for the printer. However, there are occasions where this is not sufficient, such as when you want to print something other than the displayed view, or if your application needs to be more device-specific in its printing routines, such as dealing with different paper sizes or orientation.

The Printing Process

When the user selects the Print command from a menu, the framework handles the ID_FILE_PRINT command with its default handler—the OnFilePrint() member of the view class.

Of course, you could create your own handler for this, but why bother? The framework provides mechanisms to customize printing to meet your needs, while also doing several things for you.

`CView::OnFilePrint()` will start the printing process and loop through the actual printing of each page. Many of the steps in this process involve virtual functions that may be overridden to meet the specific needs of your application.

OnPreparePrinting()

To start with, `OnFilePrint()` will call the `OnPreparePrinting()` function of your view class. The default implementation of this function will call `DoPreparePrinting()` to display the Print dialog and create the device context to be used for printing.

One of the most common reasons for overriding `OnPrepare()` printing is to specify the length of the document to be printed. Your document should provide a function to compute the number of pages on which it will be printed. You can then use this value to modify the `CPrintInfo` structure before calling `CView::DoPreparePrinting()`.

The `CPrintInfo` structure is used throughout the printing process to hold information about the print job, as you will see when you get to the functions that will be using this information. For your `OnPreparePrinting()` override, you will be most interested in the `SetMinPage()` and `SetMaxPage()` functions, which you can use to specify the pages included in the document. You may also set the `m_bDirect` flag to `TRUE` to prevent the display of the Print dialog box when you call `DoPreparePrinting()`. If you bypass the normal Print dialog, you should use `SetToPage()` and `SetFromPage()` to set up the to and from pages that the Print dialog normally sets.

The `CPrintInfo` structure also includes the `m_bPreview` flag that indicates whether the document is being shown in Print Preview or actually sent to a printer. Your code should check this flag if you plan to perform different processing for Print and Print Preview. You will look at Print Preview more closely later.

The following example shows a greatly simplified version of `OnPreparePrinting()`. Here, you assume that the document has a member specifying the number of lines it contains and that each page will hold 55 lines:

```
BOOL CMyView::OnPreparePrinting(CPrintInfo* pInfo)
{
    CMyDoc* pDoc = GetDocument();
    pInfo->SetMaxPage(pDoc->m_nLines / 55);
    return DoPreparePrinting(pInfo);
} // end OnPreparePrinting()
```

After `OnPreparePrinting()` is called, `OnFilePrint()` will create a device context for the selected printer and will call the `OnBeginPrinting()` function of your view class.

OnBeginPrinting()

The `OnBeginPrinting()` function is provided to allow you to do any further initialization required before the framework begins looping through pages. This function is passed a pointer to the printing device context and a pointer to the `CPrintInfo` structure. If you will be creating GDI objects that will be used in printing many different pages, this is a good place to do so.

The Printing Loop

`OnFilePrint()` then calls `CDC::StartDoc()` to start a print job on the device context, before it begins looping through individual pages. For each page to be printed, `OnFilePrint()` will call `CView::OnPrepareDC()`, `CDC::StartPage()`, `CView::OnPaint()`, and `CDC::EndPage()` before starting the next page with `OnPrepareDC()`.

OnPrepareDC()

The `OnPrepareDC()` member of your view class may be overridden to provide any per page initialization you may need to do with the device context. This is a handy place to set up the mapping mode for the DC or to create any fonts required for this page. You may also want to change the viewport origin here if you plan to use the `OnDraw()` function to print.

In addition, if you have not specified a fixed length for the document, this function should check for the end of the document. You can signal the end of printing by setting the `m_bContinuePrinting` member of the `CPrintInfo` structure to `FALSE`.

If you need to send any special escape codes to the printer for each page, you may do so here with the `CDC::Escape()` function.

NOTE

The same `OnPrepareDC()` function is called before both the `OnDraw()` function for screen display and the `OnPrint()` function for printing. Due to this, you should be certain to call the base class version of `OnPrepareDC()` before doing anything else. You should also check the return of `CDC::IsPrinting()` before doing anything specific to printing.

`OnFilePrint()` then calls `CDC::StartPage()` to start printing a new page. This notifies the device driver that data for a new page is on its way. `OnFilePrint()` then calls the `OnPrint()` member of your view class.

OnPrint()

The OnPrint() member of your view class is passed pointers to the device context and the CPrintInfo structure, and is responsible for doing the real work of drawing a page.

However, you may not need to implement this function at all. The default implementation of OnPrint() will simply defer printing to the OnDraw() member of your view, passing the printer DC instead of the usual display DC. If your printed output is similar to the displayed output, this can save a lot of work. The CDC::IsPrinting() member may be useful in your OnDraw() implementation to decide whether to perform certain processing intended only for real printer output.

OnFilePrint() will then call CDC::EndPage() and start printing the next page with OnPrepareDC() unless the last page specified in the CPrintInfo structure has been printed or the m_bContinuePrinting member of CPrintInfo has been set to FALSE. If the printing loop is finished, OnFilePrint() will clean up by calling CDC::EndDoc() to end the print job before calling the OnEndPrinting() member of the view class.

OnEndPrinting()

The OnEndPrinting() member of your view class should be overridden to free any GDI resources that were allocated in the OnBeginPrinting() function. Be certain to call the base class implementation so that MFC will clean up its own resources created in the printing process.

Print Preview

Windows users have come to expect that applications will allow them to preview an application's printed output before it is actually committed to paper. This is generally done with the Print Preview command from the File menu. As it turns out, AppWizard will automatically add an entry to the File menu that sends the ID_FILE_PRINT_PREVIEW command. MFC also provides a default handler for this command—OnPrintPreview().

OnPrintPreview()

In general, OnPrintPreview() works just like OnFilePrint(), calling the same OnBeginPrinting(), OnPrepareDC(), and OnPrint() functions and looping through pages. The exception is that OnPrintPreview() will set the m_bPreview flag in the CPrintInfo structure, and the device context that is created will be a CPreviewDC instead of a regular CDC.

Because of the greater interaction with the user, the framework handles Print Preview differently. For starters, OnPrintPreview() will not present the Print dialog. Nor does the whole process run in a continuous loop for each page. Instead, the functions normally called in the page loop are called in response to the user's use of the Next Page and Previous Page buttons.

OnEndPrintPreview()

When the Print Preview window is closed, the framework will call OnEndPrintPreview(). The default implementation of this function calls OnEndPrinting(), which should handle all the cleanup that you need to do. However, if you find that you need to do anything special when you are finished previewing, you can do so by overriding OnEndPrintPreview(); just be sure to call the base class implementation in your override.

Summary

In this chapter, you have seen how to use the classes that MFC provides to work with the Windows Graphical Device Interface. You also learned how the drawing process can be used within the MFC framework to perform printer output and Print Preview.

7

General-Purpose Classes

by David Bennett

MFC provides a very wide range of functionality, much of which you have already seen in the previous chapters. In this chapter, you will explore a hodgepodge of things that don't quite fit in the previous chapters, or were only mentioned in passing. In this chapter, you will see

- How to use some of MFC's general-purpose classes
- How to work with files in MFC
- How to create your own collection classes
- How to use MFC exception handling

CString

Traditional C-style, null-terminated strings and the wide array of functions used to work with them don't always fit very well into an object-oriented programming model. C-style strings also provide approximately one gazillion ways to shoot yourself in the foot. To support strings in C++, and to help save your feet, MFC provides the CString class, which also provides many functions and operators for simplified string handling.

The CString class can also be used independently of the rest of the MFC framework, because it is not derived from the CObject class. However, CString does define its own serialization operators (>>, <<) that are normally associated with CObject derivatives.

CString **and C Strings**

Although the CString class is intended to replace the old C-style strings, this does not mean that you have to abandon all the libraries you have developed to take character pointers for strings. MFC allows you to use the LPCTSTR operator to get at pointers to the null-terminated string contained in CString objects. Conversely, MFC also provides a CString constructor that accepts a character pointer, allowing you to substitute character pointers for CStrings in function calls.

> **NOTE**
>
> If you pass a CString to a variable argument function, such as printf(), make sure to explicitly cast it using LPCTSTR.

The one catch is that the LPCTSTR operator returns a const char*. This means that you will not be able to modify the string passed to a function with the LPCTSTR operator. If you need to pass a non-const char* pointer, you must use the GetBuffer() member of CString. This will return a non-const LPTSTR pointer, which will allow you to modify the data. GetBuffer() also takes a parameter to specify the minimum size of the buffer returned. This can be used to ensure that the buffer kept in the CString is sufficient for the data that you want to place in it.

If you use `GetBuffer()`, you must then call `ReleaseBuffer()` when you are finished with the pointer. This allows the `CString` to regroup and adjust its internal structures if necessary. Mostly, this means that the `CString` must figure out the new length of the string. You can pass the new length in the `ReleaseBuffer()` call, or you can pass `-1` in `ReleaseBuffer()` to have the `CString` figure its own length. In this case, the buffer must be null-terminated, because the `CString` will simply call `strlen()` to get its new length.

CString and Unicode

In some cases, the characters in a `CString` aren't really `char`s at all. This is because the `CString` class is designed to support Unicode strings, which use a 16-bit data type to support character sets with more than 256 symbols.

If the symbol `_UNICODE` is defined in your application, the `TCHAR` type that `CString` works with is defined to be type `wchar_t`, which takes up 16 bits. All length functions then return values based on 1 character = 2 bytes.

If `_UNICODE` is not defined, `TCHAR` is defined as `char`. However, `CString` will still support multibyte character sets (MBCS), provided your application interprets MBCS lead and trail bytes on its own—all length computations are based on 8-bit characters.

You can define a Unicode string literal with the `_T` macro:

```
SetWindowText(_T"Hi Mom");
```

This will actually create an array of type `TCHAR`, which will be adjusted at compile-time to work with the appropriate type based on whether `_UNICODE` is defined. If there is any chance that your application will someday need to support Unicode, defining all your string literals this way is a good habit.

CString Memory Allocation Issues

When you pass a `CString` object to a function, you are actually passing a copy of the object by value, rather than just a pointer to it. If MFC actually made a copy of the whole array each time a `CString` was passed to a function, it is not hard to see that a performance problem might arise.

To remedy this, the copy constructor of the `CString` class will create a new `CString` that points to the same buffer as the original `CString` and increments a reference count for the original object. As the copied `CString`s are destroyed, the reference count is decremented. The original object is destroyed only when the reference count reaches `0`. In addition, a `CString` will allocate a new buffer and copy the original data before any modifying actions actually take place.

If you want to disable the reference counting mechanism for a `CString`, you can call `LockBuffer()` to set the reference count to `-1`. This will ensure that the `CString` object will always have its own buffer, which no other CString object will use, even when the CString is copied. You can undo this with UnlockBuffer().

You may free up any additional memory allocated by a CString that is not currently holding string data with FreeExtra().

Creating CString Objects

There are several ways to assign and retrieve the value of a CString. First, let's take a look at creating a CString and assigning it a value. The following example shows a few ways you can call the CString constructor:

```
CString strUnicode(_T("Unicode String"));
CString strAsciiZ("Non-Unicode String");
CString strCopy = strAsciiZ;
CString strExp = strUnicode + strAsciiZ;
CString strOne('W');
CString strRepeat('K', 9000);
CString strRes((LPCSTR)ID_FILE_NEW);
CString strNull('\0');
CString strEmpty;
```

Each of these lines represents a valid call to the CString constructor. Of particular interest is the constructor used for strRes, which will create a CString initialized with a value from a string resource—in this case ID_FILE_NEW. The resulting string will have the value Create a new document. You can also initialize a CString with a single character repeated a given number of times, as in the constructor for strRepeat, which will create a string of Ks even longer than Nolan Ryan's.

CString Expressions

The CString class overloads many common operators to work with CString objects. For starters, you can assign a value to a CString with the assignment operator (=). This will accept both CString and char* arguments:

```
CString strOne;
CString strTwo;
strOne = "String One";
strTwo = strOne;
```

In addition, you can also use the plus sign (+) to concatenate two strings, provided one of the arguments is a CString, and += to add to a string, providing that the left operand is a CString:

```
CString strThree;
strThree = strOne + strTwo;
strThree = strOne + "C style string";
strThree = "C style string" + strTwo;
strThree = _T("Unicode string") + strTwo;
strThree += "String Three";
```

Working with Individual Characters

You can access individual TCHAR elements in a CString with the GetAt() and SetAt() functions. In addition, you can use the [] operator in place of the GetAt() function. Unfortunately, you cannot also use this notation to modify characters in a CString. Note also that you cannot use SetAt() to add characters beyond the length of the CString or to insert the null character ('\0'). The following shows a few ways these functions can be used:

```
CString strTmp = "Hi Mom ";
TCHAR myChar;
myChar = strTmp.GetAt(0);
myChar = strTmp[0];
myChar.SetAt(6, '!');
```

Remember that syntax like this is not allowed:

```
myChar[6] = '!'; // Not Allowed
```

Comparing CString Values

The CString class provides several means of comparing strings that are both simpler to use and provide more functionality than strcmp(), although the Compare() function is quite similar, as shown in the following:

```
CString str1 = "AAA";
CString str2 = "BBB";
if(!str1.Compare(str2))
    DoStringsEqual();
if(str1.Compare(str2) < 0)
    DoStr1LessThanStr2();
if(str1.Compare(str2) > 0)
    DoStr1GreaterThanStr2();
```

Like strcmp(), Compare() will perform a case-sensitive comparison. Using this example as an illustration, the Compare() function will return 0 if the strings are equal, < 0 if str1 is less than str2, and > 0 if str1 is greater than str2.

Using Compare() in many situations can be awkward or confusing. I'm not sure how many times I've had to look up the return values to be certain which string was actually greater. To simplify comparisons, the CString class implements the ==, !=, >, <, >=, and <= operators. These will work as long as one of the operators is a CString, as shown in the following:

```
CString str1 = _T("AAA");
CString str2 = _T("BBB");
TCHAR* str3 = _T("CCC");
if((str1 == str2) ||
    (str1 <= str3) ||
    ("DDD" >= str2))
    DoWhatever();
```

In addition, you can use the CompareNoCase() function to do a case-insensitive comparison. This works just like the Compare() function otherwise.

Formatting a `CString`

The `CString` class also provides a member function to format a string that will be stored in the `CString`. This is the appropriately named `Format()` function. It accepts a format string and a variable argument list, just like the `printf()` family. In addition, in place of a format string, you may specify the resource ID of a string resource that contains the format string.

There is one thing to beware of with the `Format()` function, however. It works only with values that fit into a 128-byte buffer. If you need to `Format()` larger buffers, you should call `GetBuffer()` to allocate a larger buffer first:

```
CString strBig;
strBig.GetBuffer(1024);
strBig.Format("%d - %s", myInt, strSomeBigString);
```

Note that because you don't change the contents of the buffer that was returned by `GetBuffer()`, you don't need to call `ReleaseBuffer()` to reset the `CString`'s size. You also need not worry about the size of a `CString`—it will support up to `INT_MAX` characters. If you need more than 2,147,483,647 characters, you'll just have to live without `CString`.

Other `CString` Functions

In addition to the functions already mentioned, the `CString` class supports many other functions. Most of the standard string functions that you are already familiar with are available in various `CString` member functions. These include functions to find substrings, trim whitespace, or convert case.

You will not find functions corresponding to functions such as `sscanf()` or `strtok()`. If you want to use these functions (or any others not implemented as member functions that may modify the string) you have to use `GetBuffer()` to get a pointer to work with, use your standard string functions on it, and then call `ReleaseBuffer()`.

When Not to Use `CStrings`

The `CString` class is useful for simplifying many string operations and for supporting Unicode. Use of `CString` can also help prevent many common programming errors that are easily introduced in working with plain character arrays. However, there is a cost associated with this functionality. First, `CString` objects are passed by value. Second, temporary `CString` objects must often be created in `CString` expressions. Both of these can result in significant amounts of data moving around that don't really have to. For this reason, you should probably avoid `CString` types where this overhead will significantly affect the performance of your application.

Don't let this scare you away from the `CString` class; it is very appropriate for most general string applications, particularly as they relate to output presented to the user. Any performance difference that you might notice by using `CString` (you probably won't notice any) will easily be outweighed by the reduced development, debugging, and maintenance time for your applications.

You may want to combine the best of both worlds by storing your strings as CString, then getting the buffer with GetBuffer() to do your intensive processing before calling ReleaseBuffer() to return the buffer to the CString's control.

CTime and CTimeSpan

The MFC supplies the CTime and CTimeSpan classes to allow your applications to work with time values in your C++ applications. Between these two classes, most of the functionality of the ANSI time functions (those usually found in time.h) are implemented.

The CTime class encapsulates the time_t data type used in the C runtime libraries. This stores absolute times in seconds since January 1, 1970 in four bytes. This allows the representation of times from January 1, 1970 to January 18, 2038. If you need to represent a wider range of dates, see the section on the COleDateTime class later in this chapter.

Constructing a CTime Object

If you are planning to initialize a CTime to the current time, you will probably use the constructor with no parameters and then call GetCurrentTime() (more on this later). This constructor can also be used to create arrays of CTime objects.

You can construct a CTime based on another CTime or by passing a time_t structure, which CTime uses internally, to the constructor.

You may also initialize a CTime by passing the Win32 SYSTEMTIME or FILETIME structures, as well as the DOS time and date words. These constructors also take an optional parameter to indicate whether daylight savings time is in effect. By default, this parameter is -1, which tells MFC to automatically compute whether standard time or daylight savings time is in effect. Additionally, you may construct a CTime by specifying individual parameters for the year, month, day, hour, minute, and second.

CTime and Time Zones

Internally, the CTime class, and the time_t type it is based on, represent universal time coordinated (UTC) or Greenwich Mean Time (GMT). Most CTime functions, including the constructors, will perform the necessary conversions from UTC to local time, including daylight savings time, for you, based on the TZ environment variable. If this is not set when your program initializes, the runtime libraries will look to Windows for information about the time zone, as set in Control Panel.

GetCurrentTime()

You can assign the value of a CTime object to the current time by using the GetCurrentTime() function:

```
CTime tCurTime;
tCurTime = CTime::GetCurrentTime()
```

Note that this is a static function, requiring that you use the assignment operator rather than . or ->. You also must use CTime:: to qualify the function, distinguishing it from the Win32 API call ::GetCurrentTime().

Formatting the Time

You can create a formatted CString from a CTime object by using CTime::Format(). This function takes a pointer to a string specifying the format of the output with text and substitution variables specified with the percent sign (%). Any plain text in the format string will appear in the output string, and any of the substitution variables shown in Table 7.1 will be replaced with information from CTime.

Table 7.1. CTime format variables.

Format variable	Description
%a	Abbreviated day of week (Mon., Tue., and so forth)
%A	Full day of week (Monday, Tuesday, and so forth)
%b	Abbreviated month (Jan, Feb, and so forth)
%B	Full month (January, February, and so forth)
%c	Complete date and time for this locale (depends on settings in control panel)
%d	Day of month as decimal number
%H	Hour in 24-hour format (00 through 23)
%I	Hour in 12-hour format (01 through 12)
%j	Day of year (001 through 366)
%m	Month as decimal number (01 through 12)
%M	Minute as decimal number (00 through 59)
%p	AM/PM indicator, based on locale
%S	Second as decimal number (00 through 59)
%U	Week of year as decimal number (00 through 51); Sunday is first day of week

Format variable	Description
%w	Weekday as decimal number (0 through 6); Sunday is 0
%W	Week of year as decimal number (00 through 51); Monday is first day of week
%x	Date representation for current locale
%X	Time representation for current locale
%y	Year without century (96, 04, and so forth)
%Y	Year with century (1996, 2004, and so forth)
%z	Time zone name or abbreviation, lowercase (blank if time zone is unknown)
%Z	Time zone name or abbreviation, uppercase (blank if time zone is unknown)
%%	Percentage sign

Extracting Time Values

You can extract individual components of the time from a CTime by using the GetYear(), GetMonth(), GetDay(), GetHour(), GetMinute(), GetSecond(), and GetDayOfWeek() functions. In addition, you can extract a time_t structure with GetTime(), or a tm structure with GetLocalTm() or GetGmtTm().

CTime Math

Several different operators are defined for use with CTime objects. First, you can use the assignment operator (=) to assign a value to a CTime from either another CTime or a time_t structure.

You may also compare two CTime objects with the ==, !=, <, >, <=, and >= operators.

You may also subtract a CTime from another CTime. This results in a CTimeSpan object, which MFC uses to represent relative times. You can then add or subtract a CTimeSpan from a CTime with +, -, +=, or -=.

CTimeSpan

You may construct a CTimeSpan object based on another CTimeSpan, a time_t structure, or explicit days, hours, minutes, and seconds specified in the constructor.

You may extract the components of a CTimeSpan with the GetDays(), GetHours(), GetTotalHours(), GetMinutes(), GetTotalMinutes(), GetSeconds(), and GetTotalSeconds() member functions. CTime also provides a Format() function very similar to CTime::Format().

CTimeSpan also supports the ==, !=, <, >, <=, and >= operators for comparing two CTimeSpan objects, as well as +, -, +=, and -= to add or subtract another CTimeSpan.

COleDateTime and COleDateTimeSpan

If your application needs to deal with a wider range of time values than that provided by the CTime class, COleDateTime may be just what you need. The COleDateTime class encapsulates the DATE type used by OLE. This type represents the time in seconds from midnight, December 30, 1899 to December 31, 9999. By convention, a time of 0:00 (midnight) is used in date-only values, and a date of 0 (December 30, 1899) is used in time-only values.

As you might guess from the name, COleDateTime is an OLE class, which will require your application to include afxdisp.h. This will include additional MFC components to support OLE and will make your application dependent on a few more system DLLs. If you are already using OLE, this doesn't add anything new, but if you are not already using OLE and are concerned about system resources, you may want to use your own alternative to the COleDateTime class.

The rest of the COleDateTime class, and its partner COleDateTimeSpan class, are very similar to the CTime and CTimeSpan classes, providing essentially the same operator and member function support.

The MFC File Classes

Eventually, your application will most likely need to work with files outside the document serialization discussed in the context of the document/view architecture. Here, you take a look at the various file classes provided by MFC to help with this.

The MFC file classes are all derived from CFile, which you can also use directly to provide unbuffered binary input and output services. You may also use the CFile member functions on any of the MFC file classes. The CInternetFile, CGopherFile, and CHttpFile classes, which you will learn about in Part V, "Database Programming," are derived from CStdioFile.

To support buffered stream files, MFC provides the CStdioFile class, which can deal with files in either binary or text mode. Text mode provides special processing for carriage return-linefeed pairs, whereas binary mode leaves the data as-is.

The MFC CMemFile class is used to support memory files, and the CSharedFile derived from it can be used to support shared memory files.

> **NOTE**
>
> The `CSharedFile` class may not be used to share memory between processes in Win32. To learn how to share memory between processes, see Chapter 8, "Memory Management."

MFC also provides the `CSocketFile` class, which you will explore in Chapter 16, "Windows Sockets," and the `COleStreamFile` class and a few derivatives. The latter are discussed in Part IV, "Network Programming with Win32," where you will take a closer look at OLE.

Opening a File

You can open a file by passing its pathname to the constructor for `CFile`. You must also specify a set of open flags, which is created by combining the following flags with the bitwise-OR operator (¦):

- `CFile::modeCreate` is used to create a new file. If you do not specify `CFile::modeNoTruncate`, the file will be truncated to 0 length.
- `CFile::modeRead`, `CFile::modeReadWrite`, and `CFile::modeWrite` are used to specify the read/write mode for the file.
- `CFile::modeNoInherit` prevents child processes from inheriting the file.

`CFile::shareDenyNone`, `CFile::shareDenyRead`, `CFile::shareDenyWrite`, and `CFile::shareExclusive` are used to open the file with a given share mode. `shareDenyNone` will allow other processes to access the file, and `shareExclusive` will not allow any other processes to access the file. `shareDenyRead` and `shareDenyWrite` disallow reading or writing by other processes. If the file has already been opened by a process that conflicts with these settings, creation will fail, throwing a `CFileException`.

In derived classes, such as `CStdioFile`, you may also specify `CFile::typeText` or `CFile::typeBinary` to enable or disable special processing for carriage return-linefeed pairs.

You must specify one access permission and one share option; the other flags are optional.

In addition, you may also construct an empty `CFile` object by constructing it with no parameters; then call `CFile::Open()` to open the file. `Open()` takes file path and flags parameters as the constructor does, but it also allows you to specify the exception that will be thrown if the open fails. More on file exceptions later in this chapter.

Reading and Writing with `CFile`

You can read or write a specified number of bytes by using `CFile::Read()` or `CFile::Write()`. Both of these begin at the current file position, which is set to the beginning of the file when it is opened.

To adjust the current position, you can use the `SeekToBegin()` or `SeekToEnd()` members, or the more general `CFile::Seek()` function. `Seek()` allows you to specify an offset for the new position, based on the second parameter. If `CFile::begin` is specified, the new position will be the specified number of bytes from the beginning of the file. If `CFile::Current` is specified, the current position will be moved the specified number of bytes forward from the current position. If `CFile::end` is specified, the current position will be set to the specified number of bytes from the end of the file. The offset may be negative, to allow seeking back into the file, or positive, to seek past the end of the file.

Reading and Writing with `CStdioFile`

For CStdioFiles, you may also use the `CStdioFile::ReadLine()` or `CstdioFile::WriteLine()` member functions, which will read or write an entire line at a time.

If you have specified `CFile::typeText` when the file was opened, these functions will provide some special processing for you. When writing, a newline character in the string to be written will be converted to a carriage return-linefeed pair in the file. When reading, carriage return-linefeed pairs are returned as a single newline character if you use the `LPTSTR` version of `ReadString()`. If you are using the version of `ReadString()` that returns a `CString`, the newline character is omitted.

`CFile::Flush()` can be called to ensure that all buffers are written to the file.

Getting Information About a File

Once you have opened a file, you can use `CFile::GetStatus()` to retrieve information about the file, including the time and date of its creation, last modification, and last read access, as well as its size and attributes.

MFC also provides a static version of `GetStatus()` that can be used on a file without opening it. This function will provide the information mentioned above, as well as filling in the complete pathname for the file.

The `GetLength()` and `SetLength()` functions can be used to manipulate the length of the file, and the `GetPosition()` function will return the value of the current position in the file.

You can also get additional information about the file from the `GetFileName()`, `GetFileTitle()`, and `GetFilePath()` functions.

You can also use several other static functions to work with files without opening them. `SetStatus()` can be used to set the file status, `Rename()` can be used to rename a file, and `Remove()` can be used to delete a file.

Closing Files

When you are finished with a file, you should call CFile::Close(). If you do not call Close(), it will be called automatically when the CFile object is destroyed. Note that deleting a CFile object does not delete the actual file.

CMemFile

The CMemFile class is used to create files in memory. The file is opened when you create it, so you will not need to call Open(). There are, however, some optional parameters to the CMemFile constructor that are of interest. The first version of the constructor allows you to specify the number of bytes that the file will allocate each time it needs to grow. This defaults to 1024 bytes.

You can then call Attach() whether you want to assign a particular buffer to the memory file.

Alternatively, you can assign a buffer to a memory file with a second version of the constructor, which takes a byte pointer to the buffer, its size, and the number of bytes to allocate when new memory is needed.

The Detach() function will effectively close the memory file and return a pointer to the data buffer with which your application can then work.

By default, the CMemFile class uses the malloc(), realloc(), memcpy(), and free() functions of the runtime library. If you want to use different routines, you may derive your own class from CMemFile, overriding the Alloc(), Free(), Realloc(), MemCpy(), and GrowFile() virtual member functions.

CSharedFile

The CSharedFile class is identical to the CMemFile class, other than the fact that it works with handles allocated with GlobalAlloc(), rather than pointers allocated with malloc(). This class does not allow you to share memory between processes in Win32. To learn how you can share memory between processes, see Chapter 8.

CArchive

The CArchive class is designed to store binary streams of data. This is most commonly used for object serialization, which is generally set up by the MFC framework. However, you may want to work more directly with the CArchive class in special serialization functions or in working with Windows Sockets.

When you create a CArchive object, you must pass a pointer to a CFile object and specify a mode for the archive, which will be either CArchive::load or CArchive::store. Each CArchive must be associated with a CFile, which you must create first. The access mode specified for the file must also be compatible with the mode selected for the archive. Furthermore, each file can have only one archive associated with it.

The CArchive class supports many operations that are very similar to CFile, such as Read(), Write(), WriteString(), and ReadString().

In addition, the CArchive class supports many other operations specific to the serialization process.

MFC Collections

It is very common for applications to keep collections of objects around. In C programs, this was often a simple array or a linked list of some sort. MFC provides classes for handling these structures in C++. Actually, MFC provides two sorts of collection classes: collection classes based on templates, which are more flexible but perhaps a bit more complicated, and the non-template original MFC collection classes released in MFC 1.0. Both sets of classes implement lists, arrays, and maps.

A list structure is just that—an ordered list of elements, providing for insertion of new elements at any point, as well as forward or backward traversal of the list.

An array structure is similar to standard C arrays, allowing the insertion and manipulation of elements based on an index. The MFC array classes are also able to grow dynamically as more space is required.

A map structure is a collection of objects that may be accessed with a key. This provides faster access to items by using a hashing technique to map keys to the corresponding values.

MFC NonTemplate Collections

In addition to the template list classes, which you will look at soon, MFC provides three predefined classes to implement doubly linked lists. CPtrList is provided to handle lists of void pointers, CStringList keeps a list of CString objects, and CObList stores a list of pointers to objects derived from CObject.

To support array classes, MFC provides many predefined array classes. CByteArray, CWordArray, CDWordArray, and CUIntArray keep arrays of the simple data types they are named for. In addition, the CPtrArray class keeps an array of null pointers, the CStringArray class maintains an array of CString objects, and the CObArray class works with an array of CObject pointers.

The classes that MFC supports for maps are named based on the mapping function they perform. For example, a map that stores pointer values based on a WORD key performs a WORD to pointer mapping and is supported by the `CMapWordToPtr` class. MFC provides the following predefined map classes: `CMapPtrToWord`, `CMapPtrToPtr`, `CMapStringToOb`, `CMapStringToPtr`, `CMapStringToString`, `CMapWordToOb`, and `CMapWordToPtr`.

When using these classes, be aware that, for the most part, they are not type-safe. For instance, a `CPtrList` works with `void` pointers, allowing you to do just about whatever you like with them—including things you shouldn't do, such as trying to display a float as a string. To allow you to create truly type-safe collection classes, as well as to provide greater opportunities for customization, MFC has provided the template-based collection classes.

MFC Template-Based Collection Classes

The template classes that MFC provides allow you to create type-safe collections that contain objects of any type, including your own types. The MFC template-based collection classes come in two flavors: the simple array, list, and map classes; and arrays, lists, and maps of typed pointers.

The simple classes include the `CArray`, `CList`, and `CMap` template classes. These allow you to create collections of simple C++ types, C++ structures and classes, and other types that you define.

The pointer collection template classes include `CTypedPtrArray`, `CTypedPtrList`, and `CTypedPtrMap`. To use these classes, you will actually be deriving from one of the nontemplate collection classes. The template then provides the casting and type checking necessary to create a type-safe collection. If you are migrating from previous versions of MFC, using these classes is a step in the right direction. However, if you are creating applications from scratch, you should use the `CArray`, `CList`, and `CMap` template classes discussed here.

> **NOTE**
>
> To use these classes, you need to include `AFXTEMPL.H` in your application.

Declaring Simple Collection Classes

To declare a collection object based on the simple collection template classes, you need to specify the type of data you will be storing in the collection. Actually, you specify the type used for storing a value and the type used in function arguments. Generally, the argument type is a reference to the type stored in the collection, as you can see in the following declarations:

```
CArray<int, int> myArray;

CList<CPlayer, CPlayer&> myTeamList;
```

The first example declares an array of ints, where function arguments will pass int by value. The second example declares a list of CPlayer objects, where function arguments will use a reference to a CPlayer.

NOTE

The template classes make use of the copy constructors and assignment operators of your class. If you need to do anything special in these, make sure that these are properly defined.

Declaring map collections is similar, but takes four arguments, because you may have different types for the key and value data. Declaring a map looks something like this:

```
CMap< int, int, CPlayer, CPlayer& > myJerseyList;
```

This example declares a map that will map jersey numbers (ints) to CPlayer objects. Because the key values are ints, it is fine to pass them by value; however, you will want to use a reference to the more complicated CPlayer structure.

Working with Arrays

At this point, the three collection classes start to behave differently, so let's look at them separately. Note also that when I talk about arrays in this section, I am talking about objects derived from the CArray template class and not standard C++ arrays.

When an array is first declared, it is empty. If you know approximately how big your array will be, it is best to tell the array about your plans now so that it won't have to be reallocating memory as you add objects. This is done with the SetSize() member. You can then add objects in several different ways:

```
CArray<CPlayer, CPlayer&> myTeam;
myTeam.SetSize(10);
myTeam.Add(Player1);
myTeam[1] = Player2;
myTeam.SetAt(2, Player3);
myTeam.InsertAt(2, Player4);
```

This example creates a CArray of CPlayer objects. You then call SetSize() to pre-initialize the array, allocating most of the memory that you plan to use. The SetSize() function will also call the default constructor for CPlayer to initialize the values in the array.

You then add four items to the array, using the Add() member, with the [] and = operators, and with the SetAt() and InsertAt() functions. In the example, Player4 is inserted at index 2, resulting in Player3 being shifted to the next location.

Note that Add() will append the new entry to the end of the array. In this example, Player1 will be added as the eleventh object in the array (index 10).

Similarly, to access the data in your CArray, you can use the GetAt() function and the [] operator:

```
CString strName1 = myTeam[0].m_Name;
CString strName2 = myTeam.GetAt(1).m_Name;
```

The GetSize() and GetUpperBound() functions can be used to monitor the size or largest valid index of your array. These are essentially the same, but GetUpperBound() will always return one less, due to the fact that array indexes are zero-based.

When it's time to remove items from the array, you can use RemoveAt() to remove a specific entry. This shifts any elements beyond the removed element up. The RemoveAll() function can be used to remove all elements from the array. In addition, the FreeExtra() function can be used to tidy up by freeing any unused memory above the current upper-bound.

Template-Based Collection Class Helper Functions

The collection classes that you create with CArray, CList, and CMap use helper functions to perform many of the operations involving the objects in your collections. The helper functions used include ConstructElements(), DestructElements(), CopyElements(), CompareElements(), DumpElements(), SerializeElements(), and HashKey(). If the elements in your collections contain other classes, or if they manage their own memory, you will want to write your own implementations of the helper functions for the classes you will be using in collections.

Note that these helper functions are global functions and do not belong to any specific class. This also means that you need to implement them only once for each data type you will be using.

ConstructElements()

The ConstructElements() helper function is called whenever a template-based collection needs to add a new element to the collection. The default implementation simply allocates the required memory and initializes it with zeros. It does not call any constructors of objects.

The ConstructElements() function takes two parameters. The first is a pointer to the first element that needs to be initialized. The second is the number of elements to initialize. Here is a simple example of this:

```
void ConstructElements(CPlayer* pElement, int nCount)
{
    int nIndex;
    for(nIndex = 0; nIndex < nCount; nIndex++, pElement++)
        pElement->CPlayer::CPlayer();
} // end ConstructElements
```

Although the syntax used to call the `CPlayer` constructor may seem a bit foreign, this will take the blank slate allocated by MFC and create a `CPlayer` on it.

If you are keeping a collection of pointers, MFC will allocate only the memory required for the pointer. Your `ConstructElements()` helper should then allocate a new object and initialize the pointer in the collection to point to the new object. If you were maintaining a collection of `CPlayer` pointers, the `ConstructElements()` function would look something like this:

```
void ConstructElements(CPlayer** pElement, int nCount)
{
    int nIndex;
    for(nIndex = 0; nIndex < nCount; nIndex++, pElement++)
        *pElement = new CPlayer;
} // end ConstructElements
```

DestructElements()

The collection templates call `DestructElements()` whenever an element is destroyed. The default implementation does nothing. You should definitely provide your own implementation for this if you allocated your own memory in `ConstructElements()`.

Like `ConstructElements()`, `DestructElements()` takes a pointer to the first element to be destroyed and a count of elements to destroy. For your `CPlayer` class, this would look something like this:

```
void DestructElements(CPlayer* pElement, int nCount)
{
    int nIndex;
    for(nIndex = 0; nIndex < nCount; nIndex++, pElement++)
        pElement->CPlayer::~CPlayer();
} // end DestructElements
```

Again, `DestructElements()` will be a little different if your collection contains pointers to objects, rather than the actual objects. This will look like the following:

```
void DestructElements(CPlayer** pElement, int nCount)
{
    int nIndex;
    for(nIndex = 0; nIndex < nCount; nIndex++, pElement++)
        delete *pElement;
} // end DestructElements
```

CopyElements()

The `CopyElements()` helper function is called by `CArray::Append()` and `CArray::Copy()` when MFC needs to copy a number of elements from one array to another. The default implementation uses `memcpy()` to move the raw data. If simply moving the individual bits of your class is not sufficient, you will need to implement `CopyElements()` for your class. The following example assumes that you have defined an assignment operator appropriate for your class:

```
void CopyElements(CPlayer* pDest, const CPlayer* pSrc, int nCount)
{
    while (nCount-- > 0)
        *pDest++ = *pSrc++;
} // end CopyElements
```

Once again, if your collection keeps pointers rather than the actual objects, you deal with the objects a bit differently.

CompareElements()

The CompareElements() helper function is called by CList::Find(), CMap::Lookup(), and CMap::operator []. If your collection will contain anything other than simple data types (int, char, and so forth), you either implement the comparison operator for your class or override the CompareElements() function to do the comparison. This function returns a BOOL, because the collections don't care about the relative values of two elements. For collections that keep complete objects in them, your override would look something like this:

```
BOOL CompareElements(const CPlayer* pElement1, const CPlayer* pElement2);
{
    return ((*pElement1) == (*pElement2))
} // end CompareElements
```

This example is trivial, provided you have already implemented the comparison operator for your class. If not, you need to figure out how to compare objects of your class and perform that here.

If you are using collections to handle pointers to your objects, you override this function, because the default will simply compare the two pointers, which will most likely not be equal, even if the objects they point to are.

DumpElements()

The DumpElements() function is called by the collection in debug builds whenever unreleased memory is detected. The default implementation does nothing, so overriding this simple function can prove very useful in debugging your helper functions.

The first parameter to DumpElements() is a reference to a dump context; the second and third parameters are the pointer to the first element to dump and the number of elements to dump.

Assuming you have already implemented a dump function for your class, it looks like this:

```
#ifdef _DEBUG
void DumpElements(const CDumpContext& dc, CPlayer* pElement, int nCount)
{
    int nIndex;
    for(nIndex = 0; nIndex < nCount; nIndex++, pElement++)
        pElement->Dump(dc);
} // end DumpElements
#endif
```

SerializeElements()

The collection templates will call `SerializeElements()` to serialize the objects in the collection. The default implementation simply does a bitwise copy. Once again, you see parameters for the first element and a count of elements, as well as a reference to the `CArchive` used for serialization. If your elements are derived from `CObject`, you can use the `Serialize()` function of your element class:

```
void SerializeElements(CArchive& ar, CPlayer* pElement, int nCount)
{
    int nIndex;
    for(nIndex = 0; nIndex < nCount; nIndex++, pElement++)
        pElement->Serialize(ar);
} // end SerializeElements
```

If your element class is not derived from `CObject`, it is easiest to implement a `Serialize()` function similar to `CObject`'s.

HashKey()

The `HashKey()` function is used only by the `CMap` template class, but because you are looking at helper functions, this seems a good place to discuss it. This function is used to generate a hash key to divide the keys to your collection into bins. If you desire a specific hash key scheme, you should override this function.

`HashKey()` takes one argument of the type you have specified for the key arguments and returns a `UINT` hash key value.

Working with CList

Like `CArray` collections, `CList` collections are born empty, although you can specify a block size parameter in the constructor. This is an `int` value that tells MFC to allocate memory in units of the specified number of entries.

Adding Elements

Next, you are likely to want to start adding items. You can do this with the `AddHead()` and `AddTail()` functions, which will add a new element to the head or tail of the list.

In addition, you may insert an element before or after a given position in the list, with the `InsertBefore()` or `InsertAfter()` member functions. These functions take a `POSITION` as the first parameter, as well as the element to be inserted.

The `POSITION` type is used by MFC's list and map collections to denote a particular spot in the collection. You can retrieve a valid `POSITION` in a list either by iteration through the elements of the list or by searching for a particular value.

Iteration

Applications will often find it necessary to traverse through the elements of a list. This process is known as iteration. To start a traversal of the list, you begin at either the start or end of the list. The GetHeadPosition() or GetTailPosition() functions will return a POSITION for the first or last elements.

To retrieve the first element, you can then pass the POSITION to the GetNext() function, which will return the element at the current position, and set the POSITION you passed to the POSITION value for the next element in the list. You can proceed in this manner until the last element in the list is retrieved, after which the POSITION variable will be set to NULL. To traverse the list backwards, the GetPrev() function works similarly.

To get or set an element at the current position, without changing the POSITION value, you can use the GetAt() or SetAt() functions.

Searching a List

The CList template class provides the FindIndex() function, which returns a POSITION value for an element of the list corresponding to the index you pass it. This is a zero-based index, much like you might use for normal arrays. In addition, you can use the Find() function to return a POSITION value for an element that is equivalent to the value passed to Find. You may also specify a POSITION to start searching after.

> **NOTE**
>
> Most documentation states that the Find() function compares only pointers. If your list contains pointer types, this is true. However, if you are including class objects in the list, the equivalency operator (==) defined for the class is used.

Removing Elements from a List

Before attempting to remove an element from a list, you should be certain that the list is not empty. You can test this with the IsEmpty() or GetCount() functions.

Then, if you need to remove items from a list, you can use the RemoveHead() or RemoveTail() functions to remove the first or last elements on the list, or the RemoveAt() function to remove an element at a specified POSITION. In addition, the RemoveAll() function will remove all elements from the list.

Working with Maps

The CMap collection template class allows you to create a collection of values that can be accessed directly by a corresponding key value. Remember that the declaration of a CMap object requires four parameters, rather than the two that are required for CArray or CList.

A map collection is also different from an array or list. You cannot just start throwing values into it with something like the Add() function. Instead, each value that you add to the map must be added with its key value. This is done with the SetAt() function. Note that the SetAt() function will replace an element already in the map if a matching key is found. The [] operator may be used to substitute for SetAt().

To retrieve an element from the map by its key value, you can use the Lookup() function, which takes a key value and a reference to the object retrieved. Lookup() returns TRUE if an element matching the key is found; otherwise, it returns FALSE. Although you can use the [] operator in place of SetAt(), you cannot use [] as a substitute for Lookup(), due to the possibility that a value may not be found.

In addition, you may traverse the map using a POSITION value. To get a starting POSITION value, call GetStartPosition(). You may then start retrieving elements with the GetNextAssoc() function, which moves the POSITION to the next element.

> **NOTE**
>
> Traversing the map using GetNextAssoc() does not return elements in any particular order. The order is indeterminate.

To remove an element based on its key, you can call the RemoveKey() function. Alternatively, you may call the RemoveAll() function to clear the entire map. The IsEmpty() and GetCount() functions are also provided to find the number of elements in the map.

Fine-Tuning Your Map

In many cases, you will want to be certain that the hashing used by your map collection is as efficient as possible so that the lookups and insertions are performed quickly. To optimize this, you should first consider implementing your own HashKey() helper function, described earlier. You can also use GetHashTableSize() to see the number of entries in the hash table, and InitHashTable() to initialize and set the number of entries in the hash table. This should be done before adding elements to the map collection.

Exception Handling

In many cases, it is very useful, if not absolutely necessary, to be able to provide exception handling to your application. This can also make your code much neater by providing a syntax that centralizes the code to handle common errors, avoiding error-prone nests of `if` blocks, based on function return codes. At the very least, you can help cut down on functions that use 101 different levels of indentation.

Current versions of the Visual C++ compiler (starting with 3.0) support the ANSI standard C++ exception handling mechanisms, which you see here. There are, however, several ways that Visual C++ can be used to support exception handling, which are provided only to support applications developed with previous versions of C and C++ compilers or previous versions of MFC.

These outdated methods include the older MFC-specific implementation, which used macros such as TRY and CATCH to implement exception handling, and the old C `setjmp()` and `longjmp()` functions. Although these methods are still supported in Visual C++ 5.0, you should definitely try to use the standard C++ exception handling mechanisms that you will look at here. In addition, you will see how to trap Win32 system-level exceptions.

In fact, MFC now implements the TRY-CATCH macro mechanism by using the ANSI `try` and `catch` keywords within the macros, so you might as well use the ANSI C++ syntax directly. This will also make your code much more portable, and it provides much better cleanup when an exception is thrown.

To enable the code to properly destroy objects left on the frame when an exception is thrown, you need to specify the /CX compiler switch or set Enable exception handling in your Project Settings | C/C++ | C++ Language page. If you do not specify this option, the compiler will warn you when it encounters a `try` block.

Using C++ Exception Handling

In C++, the `try` and `catch` keywords are used around a block of code for which you want to handle exceptions. In the `catch` statement, you can specify the sort of exception to handle. You may also specify several different `catch` blocks to handle different types of exceptions. The following example will help illustrate this:

```
try
{
    // do stuff
}
catch( CMyException tmpExcept )
{
    // do error message
}
catch ( char* str )
```

```
{
    // do error message
}
catch (...)
{
    // catch any remaining exceptions
}
// Contine with your processing
```

If an exception is thrown within the try block, control will jump to the end of the try block and begin searching the catch blocks for a handler for the exception.

If a catch block is declared that matches the type of the exception thrown, the code in the catch block is executed, and execution resumes after the catch block.

If no catch block is found that matches the type of the exception, the application will unwind the call stack, searching for exception handlers at progressively higher levels until an appropriate handler is found.

If no exception is thrown, the catch blocks are not executed.

NOTE

The C++ exception handling model is nonresumable. Once an exception is thrown, control will not return to the try block.

The variable declared in the catch statement may be of any type that you may wish to throw. It may be a simple type, such as an int or char*, or any other type or class you define. However, MFC provides the CException class and several derivatives expressly designed to be used in throw and catch statements. In addition, you may specify ... as the exception type handled in a catch block, which will handle any type of exception. This may be used only in the last catch block for a given try block.

Throwing Exceptions

If at any point in your application you detect a condition that should cause your application to exit a try block and invoke an exception handler, you can throw your own exceptions with the throw statement. The throw statement uses syntax similar to that of the return statement, allowing you to throw any particular variable (or assignment-expression) that you like. Just remember that the type should match the type specified in a catch block somewhere.

> **NOTE**
>
> If you are throwing a pointer to any object, the object should be declared outside the `try` block, because objects declared inside the `try` block are destroyed before the handlers are called.

MFC Exception Classes

To simplify exception handling, MFC provides the `CException` class. The exceptions thrown by MFC classes are derived from the `CException` class. The MFC documentation will indicate the exceptions that may be thrown by a function, as in this example from `CFile::Cfile()`:

```
CFile( LPCTSTR lpszFileName, UINT nOpenFlags );

    throw( CFileException );
```

As in this example, most MFC functions do not actually throw a `CException`, but rather an exception class derived from it. Because the exceptions are derived from `CException`, you may handle any MFC exception by catching a `CException` pointer:

```
try
{
    CFile("MyFile", CFile::modeReadWrite | CFile::ShareDenyNone);
}
catch(CException* pMyException)
{
myException->ReportError();
char myErrString[100];
myException->GetErrorMessage(myErrString, sizeof(myErrString));
// Do whatever with myErrString
}
```

This example also shows the usage for the two member functions of `CException`. These functions may also be called for any of the exception classes discussed here.

`GetErrorMessage()` can be used to fill a buffer with an appropriate error message for the exception. `ReportError()` can be used to display the error message in a message box. `ReportError()` also allows you to specify any additional message-box styles and a resource ID for a string to be displayed if the exception does not provide one. By default, if the exception does not provide a message string, `ReportError()` will display `No error message is available`.

Note that you must handle a pointer to the exception class, because MFC will throw a pointer rather than the exception itself. If you want to throw one of the MFC exception classes, you will also need to throw the pointer, because the compiler won't find a copy constructor for `CException`.

CMemoryException

The CMemoryException is thrown in out-of-memory conditions. Specifically, this exception may be generated by the new operator when memory allocation fails. Because the MFC classes use the new operator, any MFC function that may allocate memory may also throw a CMemoryException.

If your application bypasses the new operator, by using malloc() or some other call to allocate memory, you should throw a pointer to a CMemoryException when the allocation fails. This is most easily done with ::AfxThrowMemoryException().

CNotSupportedException

MFC implements a few functions that are not supported. When you attempt to call unsupported functions, a CNotSupportedException is thrown. You may also find it handy to use this class in your own functions that, for one reason or another, are unsupported. You can throw an unsupported exception by calling ::AfxThrowUnsupportedException().

In general, CNotSupportedExceptions are thrown only when your application code is doing something it shouldn't. If you see these, you should probably look at just what your application is doing to generate them.

CFileException

The member functions of CFile, and its derived classes, may throw CFileExceptions when an error occurs. Additional information about the cause of the error is included in the CFileException class.

The m_cause member of CFileException holds a value representing the cause of the exception. The values for m_cause are defined in an enumerated type in CFileException and include the values shown in Table 7.2.

Table 7.2. CFileException::m_cause values.

m_cause	Description
CFileException::none	No error occurred.
CFileException::generic	An unidentified error occurred; check m_lOsError.
CFileException::fileNotFound	File not found.
CFileException::badPath	All or part of a path is invalid.
CFileException::tooManyOpenFiles	Insufficient file open buffers or handles.
CFileException::accessDenied	The file permissions do not allow this access.

m_cause	Description
CFileException::invalidFile	Using an invalid handle was attempted.
CFileException::removeCurrentDir	Removing current directory disallowed.
CFileException::directoryFull	No more directory entries exist.
CFileException::badSeek	An error occurred trying to set the file pointer.
CFileException::hardIO	A hardware error occurred.
CFileException::sharingViolation	A shared region was locked or SHARE.EXE was not loaded.
CFileException::lockViolation	Locking attempted for an already locked region.
CFileException::diskFull	The disk is full.
CFileException::endOfFile	An attempt to read beyond end-of-file was made.

In addition to m_cause, CFileException provides the m_lOsError member that will reflect operating system-dependent error codes and the m_strFileName member, which contains the name of the file with which the exception was generated. The class also provides functions to map error codes to m_cause values. OsErrorToException() will return one of the enumerated types corresponding to an operating system error, such as the error codes defined in Stdlib.h. and ErrnoToException() will return a cause code from a runtime library error, as defined in Errno.h.

Throwing a CFileException

Although you could construct your own CFileException and throw a pointer to it, it is generally easier to use one of the two functions provided by CFileException to throw the exception for you.

ThrowOsError() will throw a CFileException with m_cause set to a value appropriate to the error. If the error code is unknown, m_cause will be set to CFileException::generic.

The ThrowErrno() function can be used to throw an exception based on your favorite error code from Errno.h. This will also initialize m_cause to an appropriate value.

These functions are both declared static, so you don't even need to bother with creating a CFileException object.

As with the other MFC exception classes, you may also call ::AfxThrowFileException() which allows you to specify the cause, OS error, and filename for the exception.

CArchiveException

`CArchiveExceptions` may be thrown by serialization operations gone bad. This class also includes the `m_cause` member, which will have one of the enumerated values shown in Table 7.3.

Table 7.3. `CArchiveException m_cause` values.

m_cause	Description
CArchiveException::none	No error occurred.
CArchiveException::generic	Unidentified error.
CArchiveException::readOnly	Attempted to write to an archive opened for loading.
CArchiveException::endOfFile	End-of-file reached while reading an object.
CArchiveException::writeOnly	Attempted to read from an archive opened for storing.
CArchiveException::badIndex	Invalid file format.
CArchiveException::badClass	Attempted to read an object into an object of the wrong type.
CArchiveException::badSchema	Attempted to read an object with a different schema number.

If you find that you want to throw an archive exception in your application, you can call `::AfxThrowArchiveException()` and specify one of the causes and an archive name to be included in the exception.

CResourceException

A `CResourceException` is generated when Windows has trouble finding or allocating a requested resource. These are most often thrown when trying to create objects that load resources such as dialog templates or bitmaps, or when trying to allocate GDI resources.

If your application needs to throw a `CResourceException`, you can call `::AfxThrowResourceException()`.

COleException

A `COleException` can be thrown by OLE operations that run into some sort of difficulty. This class includes the `m_sc` member that contains an OLE status code indicating the reason for the exception. You'll learn more about these in Part IV.

You may generate a COleException by calling ::AfxThrowOleException() and passing it a value for m_sc.

If you want to throw an exception from within an OLE automation function, you should look at ::AfxThrowOleDispatchException().

CUserException

The CUserException class is usually thrown in response to invalid or unacceptable user behavior. For example, MFC uses CUserException whenever data validation fails during dialog data exchange. This is a somewhat benign exception, due to the fact that MFC implements handlers for CUserException that do nothing other than exiting your try block.

If you wish to throw a CUserException, you should somehow notify the user of the problem (usually done with ::AfxMessageBox()) before calling ::AfxThrowUserException().

CDBException

A CDBException may be thrown by MFC's Open Database Connectivity (ODBC) objects (which is covered in Part V, "Database Programming"). This class includes: the m_nRetCode member, containing an ODBC RETCODE return code; the m_strError member, containing a string describing the error; and the m_strStateNativeOrigin member, containing a formatted string that includes the SQLSTATE, the native error code, and information on the origin of the error. Your application may throw a CDBException by calling ::AfxThrowDBException().

CDaoException

The MFC classes that support database operations with Data Access Objects (DAO) may throw CDaoExceptions. You will take a closer look at the DAO classes and the errors they generate in Part V, so I'll keep it brief here.

CDaoException provides: the m_scode member, which holds an OLE SCODE value describing the error; the m_nAfxDaoError member, which gives information about a specific component that caused the exception; and the m_pErrorInfo member, which points to a CDaoErrorInfo object.

DAO exceptions can include more than one error, particularly if you are using an ODBC data source with DAO. To handle this, you can call GetErrorCount() to find the number of errors in the exception. You can then call GetErrorInfo() with the index of each error. This will update the m_pErrorInfo member to point at the CDaoErrorInfo object for that particular error.

You can throw a CDaoException with ::AfxThrowDaoException().

CInternetException

CInternetExceptions are thrown by the MFC Internet classes. You will look at the specifics of Internet exceptions in Chapter 22, "The WinInet API," so here's the condensed version: The CInternetException class includes the m_dwError member, containing an error value, including system error codes from Winerror.h and error values from Wininet.h. The m_dwContext member provides a context value associated with the internet operation that caused the exception.

There is not an Afx function to throw CInternetExceptions.

Win32 System Exceptions

For most of your exception handling needs, the standard C++ try and catch syntax, together with the MFC exception classes, should be more than adequate. However, if you need to trap system errors that occur at the system level, you use a slightly different mechanism.

As you will see in the following example, the syntax for handling Win32 system traps is similar to the C++ syntax, except try is replaced with __try and catch is replaced with __except:

```
float fResult;
__try
{
    fResult = x/y;
}
__except(GetExceptionCode() == EXCEPTION_FLT_DIVIDE_BY_ZERO)
{
    TRACE("Caught divide by zero.\n");
}
```

The code in the __try block is executed like the try block in standard C++ until a system trap occurs. When an exception is raised, the except block is used to determine how to handle the exception.

This example uses the GetExceptionCode() function, which returns a value specifying the exception that occurred. These values are defined in Winbase.h and are in the following list (in addition, you include Winnt.h and Excpt.h to use this exception handling mechanism):

```
EXCEPTION_INT_DIVIDE_BY_ZERO
EXCEPTION_INT_OVERFLOW
EXCEPTION_FLT_DENORMAL_OPERAND
EXCEPTION_FLT_DIVIDE_BY_ZERO
EXCEPTION_FLT_INEXACT_RESULT
EXCEPTION_FLT_INVALID_OPERATION
EXCEPTION_FLT_OVERFLOW
EXCEPTION_FLT_UNDERFLOW
EXCEPTION_FLT_STACK_CHECK
```

```
EXCEPTION_ACCESS_VIOLATION
EXCEPTION_GUARD_PAGE
EXCEPTION_STACK_OVERFLOW
EXCEPTION_DATA_TYPE_MISALIGNMENT
EXCEPTION_ARRAY_BOUNDS_EXCEEDED
EXCEPTION_PRIV_INSTRUCTION
EXCEPTION_ILLEGAL_INSTRUCTION
EXCEPTION_INVALID_DISPOSITION
EXCEPTION_INVALID_HANDLE
EXCEPTION_IN_PAGE_ERROR
EXCEPTION_BREAKPOINT
EXCEPTION_SINGLE_STEP
EXCEPTION_NONCONTINUABLE_EXCEPTION
```

Actually, the expression used in the __except statement is a bit misleading. By definition, the expression in an __except statement should evaluate to one of three values: EXCEPTION_ EXECUTE_HANDLER (1), EXCEPTION_CONTINUE_SEARCH (0), or EXCEPTION_CONTINUE_EXECUTION (-1).

EXCEPTION_EXECUTE_HANDLER

Because the equivalence operator (==) returns 1 if its operands are equal, the expression used in the previous example evaluates to EXCEPTION_EXECUTE_HANDLER when the generated exception matches the exception you want to handle. In this case, the handler is executed, and the __try block is abandoned.

EXCEPTION_CONTINUE_SEARCH

If the expression evaluates to 0 (as when the operands of == are not equal), the search for an appropriate handler continues to the next __except block and on up the stack.

EXCEPTION_CONTINUE_EXECUTION

If the expression evaluates to -1, the code attempts to press on from the point of the exception. In some cases, the exception is fatal, and choosing EXCEPTION_CONTINUE_EXECUTION will result in a new trap of type EXCEPTION_NONCONTINUABLE_EXCEPTION.

The Catch

Visual C++ will not allow you to use Win32 System trap handling in the same function with standard C++ exception handling. If you need to mix the two, you use a separate function for trapping system traps, which can then be called from within your try block.

You should also be aware that the individual system traps will behave differently on the different hardware platforms supported by Windows NT.

Summary

In this chapter, you looked at some of the general-purpose classes provided by the Microsoft Foundation Classes, including the CFile class and its derivatives, which are used for file operations, and the MFC collection template classes, which can be used to work with common collections of objects. You have also learned how Visual C++ implements exception handling, including MFC's exception classes, and Win32 system traps.

8

Memory Management

by David Bennett

The Win32 operating systems greatly simplify your task of dealing with memory, although they may require you to handle some things a bit differently from 16-bit environments. In this chapter, you will look at

■ The Win32 memory model
■ Memory allocation
■ Virtual memory
■ Shared memory

The Win32 Memory Model

Windows NT and Windows 95 make up the Win32 family of Microsoft operating systems. Win32 is a catchy title for marketing, but it also happens to be truly descriptive of the operating systems—that is, they use 32 bits. Although this may not seem like an earth-shattering advance, it makes a world of difference when you compare Win32 to 16-bit operating systems such as DOS or Win3.1 (if you even want to call Win3.1 an operating system).

When I say that WinNT and Win95 are 32-bit operating systems, I mean that they use 32-bit variables internally. Specifically, they support 32-bit pointers to memory, which take advantage of the 32-bit registers supported on Intel platforms, starting with the 80386 family of processors and other hardware platforms supported by Windows NT.

Way back when, developers were glad to have the segmented memory scheme supported on Intel's 8088—this allowed access to a whole megabyte of memory (or, 640KB under DOS). Compared to the previous architectures that allowed access to only 64KB, this really was something. However, as applications have risen to the task of consuming all resources available to them (just try running Word 6 in 1MB or less), this architecture has created countless headaches for developers.

First, you had to deal with `near` and `far` pointers: one for dealing with data within 64KB segments, and one for code and data farther away. This was particularly troublesome when you consider that there were 65,536 different possible values for a `far` pointer to one memory location, due to the overlapping segment and data registers.

Furthermore, to overcome the 1MB limit imposed by this architecture, and the 640KB DOS limit, several different (and incompatible) schemes were developed, including the oh-so-difficult-to-keep-straight extended memory (EMS) and expanded memory (XMS). Each of these required developers to jump through different sets of hoops to use memory above the 1MB or 640KB boundaries.

Before I go into any more horror stories (like how I actually worked with paper-tape programs once or how I built my own supercomputer out of raw sand and duct tape), let's look at the solution.

Win32 Memory Address Spaces

Under the Win32 operating systems, each process has access to its own flat address space of 4GB (2^{32}=4,294,967,296). No more segments, no more selectors, no more near and far pointers, no more near and far function calls, no more memory models. (Personally, I thought I had reached nirvana in the 32-bit flat memory model. That is, of course, until the vast number of new APIs available prompted me to write this book.)

Notice that each process has its own separate 4GB logical address space. Win32 allows each process to access its own memory, separate from other processes, with its own 32-bit logical address space. The operating system will convert this to a physical memory address for you, as well as handle virtual memory, as you will see.

Separate address spaces keep your processes insulated from other processes that have gone bad. If one application goes bonkers and starts spewing data through its memory space, other processes are much safer than they were in DOS, where all processes shared the same physical memory space.

This presents some difficulties if you are used to passing pointers between tasks. A given logical address (pointer value) in one process will not reference the same location in physical memory as an identical pointer value in another process. Win32 provides mechanisms for using shared memory, however, as you will see in a moment.

Win32 Reserved Addresses

Although I said that each process can access 4GB, some of this is reserved by the operating system, preventing your process from accessing these areas directly. Both WinNT and Win95 reserve the upper half of the 4GB space for their own use, leaving the lower 2GB available to your application. This should be sufficient for your application for at least a few years.

Windows 95 also reserves the lower 4MB of the address space to support compatibility with 16-bit DOS and Windows applications. Microsoft refers to this area as the Compatibility Arena in its documentation. Windows NT on the other hand, does not reserve this area.

The upper 2GB space is further divided by Windows 95 into the shared arena (between 2GB and 3GB) used for memory-mapped files, shared memory, and some 16-bit items; and the reserved system arena (between 3GB and 4GB) used to hold the privileged portions of the operating system's code.

Virtual Memory

There aren't many machines with 4GB of physical memory lying around, so Win32 makes use of virtual memory. Although a process can use the whole 4GB address range available to it, most don't. Windows maps the logical addresses used by your application to physical storage addresses as needed.

Note that I said *storage* addresses, rather than *memory* addresses. Windows makes use of a swapfile to store additional virtual memory above and beyond the RAM in the machine. Memory blocks that are not currently in use may be written out to disk, and new blocks of memory may be read in from disk as needed. Swapping to disk is much slower than simply having a gazillion bytes of RAM, but it effectively enables a process to use as much virtual memory as you have free disk space. I think you will agree that it is also much nicer to slow down a bit rather than just say, "Out of Memory—Buy more and try again."

All this is handled for you by the operating system, so you don't really have to worry about it. However, Windows does allow you to work with virtual memory directly, as you will see later in this chapter.

What a Difference 16 Bits Makes

Before you move on to memory management in Win32, it is appropriate to look at a few of the things that are different in 32-bit Windows, in comparison to the 16-bit Windows world. As you can probably guess, most of these issues have something to do with the change to 32-bit registers and pointers.

4-Byte Integers

To the great relief of those who have to port UNIX apps to Windows, variables of type int are now a full 4 bytes long. Intel processors (386 and up), use 4-byte values internally (as do the other NT platforms), so Windows now supports this as well. On hardware that supports 32-bit registers, it is actually faster in many cases to use 32-bit values.

If your application does anything that is dependent on int values being only 16 bits, you will need to make a few changes. However, the Windows WORD and DWORD types are still 16 and 32 bits, respectively, and will port nicely from previous versions of Windows.

Of Lands _near and _far

In Win32, all memory pointers are created equal—there is no such animal as a near or short pointer. All pointers reference one logical memory address, without regard to current segment register values. There is also no longer a need to do special processing for data that crosses segment boundaries. As such, the _near, _far, and _huge type modifiers no longer have any meaning and need not be used. However, if you have these in your applications, or just can't break the habit, the compiler will ignore them.

This also applies to the Windows-defined pointer types. For instance, LPSTR is the same as PSTR in Win32, although both types are defined to allow compatibility with previous versions. If you may need to port your application back to Win3.1, you should try to use the appropriate pointer type (LPSTR or PSTR, or similar types), even though the distinction will not affect your Win32 builds. You will also notice that the interfaces defined for Windows functions will use the types (near or far) appropriate for corresponding Win16 functions (if any).

Memory Models

In Win32, there is only one memory model. You will no longer need to choose from (or supply libraries for) the plethora of different memory models supported by DOS. (Everybody say Hallelujah!)

In addition, you will not need to use different runtime library functions for different memory models, nor will you need to supply libraries for different memory models. If your code uses model-specific calls, such as _fmalloc or _nmalloc, these are #defined to the appropriate function (malloc()) for you in WindowsX.h.

Windows Messages

In Win32, the format of many Windows messages has changed to deal with 32-bit handles and the fact that wParam is now 32 bits. For example, the WM_COMMAND message in 16-bit Windows puts the id in wParam and the hwnd and cmd in lParam. The Win32 version puts the id and cmd in wParam, and the hwnd takes the entire lParam.

It is possible to deal with these differences with #ifdefs, although it is much neater to use the message crackers provided in Windowsx.h, which allows you to use the message cracker macro to call a single handler function for the message.

If you will never need to support 16-bit windows, the message crackers need not be used. In fact, because Visual C++ 4.2 and above do not support 16-bit development (not even Win32s), the version of Windowsx.h included with VC++ 5.0 does not bother to define the message cracker variants for Win16. The macros are, however, defined for Win32 to provide compatibility.

Address Calculations

It should be obvious that if you do your own address calculations based on the segmented memory scheme, or use your own routines to poke at the segment registers, your code will have to change to support the flat memory space.

You also should be aware that memory allocated is not guaranteed to start on a segment boundary. Thus, any routines that set only the LOWORD of a pointer will no longer work.

Physical Memory Access

The Win32 operating systems don't generally allow your application to work with physical memory directly. Accordingly, API functions such as AllocSelector() and FreeSelector() are no longer available. In most cases, working with physical memory directly is not necessary; however, if you are writing device drivers or other such beasts, you can use the Win32 Device Driver Kit (DDK) to get at physical memory.

Simple Memory Allocation

This section introduces some of the simple memory allocation functions that are used in everyday programs. The simple allocation operations that you will look at can be divided into two basic categories: stack frame allocation and heap allocation.

Allocation on the Stack Frame

Stack frame allocation is actually so simple it doesn't even necessarily involve a function call. Memory allocated on the stack frame includes variables that are declared local to a function. These are allocated memory on the application's stack, which grows and shrinks as functions are called and returned. To illustrate this, the following function declares a few local variables that are allocated on the stack frame:

```
void MyFunction()
{
    int myInt;
    char myArray[20];
    myStructType myStruct;
    CMyClass myObject(3);

    {
        int myNestedInt = 7;
        cout << "My Nested Int: " << myNestedInt;
    }
    // myNestedInt no longer in scope
} // end MyFunction()
```

Here, you allocate an int, an array of chars, a structure, and a class object. The compiler will automatically allocate space on the stack frame for these variables and will automatically reclaim the memory when the variables go out of scope. In most cases, this happens when the function returns; although, as you see with myNestedInt, variables that are declared in nested brackets go out of scope and are deallocated when the nested bracket block ends.

Variables allocated in this manner are often called automatic variables, because the compiler allocates and deallocates the memory automatically. In addition, the constructors for automatic class variables are called when the memory for the object is allocated, and the destructors are called before the memory is deallocated.

Allocating variables in this manner is very convenient, because you don't have to worry about deallocating the memory or calling the destructors for objects—the compiler takes care of all of this. However, space available on the stack may be limited. To avoid filling up the stack, as well as to provide memory that outlives the scope of a particular function, you use heap allocation.

Heap Allocation

Heap allocation is performed when you use functions, such as new or malloc(), that are traditionally associated with dynamic data structures. Memory allocated in this way is allocated on the application's heap, which is global to the process. Unlike frame allocation, the amount of memory that may be allocated on the heap is limited only by the amount of virtual memory available on the system.

Memory allocated on the heap is persistent through the life of the process until it is deallocated by your application. The compiler will not deallocate any memory allocated on the heap for you (that is, until the process ends, at which point all memory associated with it is deallocated).

The following example shows how you can use new and malloc() to allocate memory on the heap, as well as how to deallocate the memory with delete and free:

```
// Allocating memory on the heap
int* pMyInt = new int;
char* pMyArray = new char[20];
myStructType* pMyStruct = new myStructType;
CMyClass* pMyObject = new CMyClass(3);
BYTE* myBuffer = malloc(MY_BUFFER_SIZE);

// Do stuff with your new memory

// De-allocate memory on the heap
delete pMyInt;
delete pMyArray;
delete pMyStruct;
delete pMyObject;
free(myBuffer);
```

Note that new will call the constructor for any class objects allocated, whereas malloc() simply allocates a block of memory.

When memory is allocated on the heap with new or malloc(), the operating system will keep track of the amount of memory allocated, so you will not need to worry about passing the size to delete or free. The system will deallocate the entire memory block pointed at by the value passed to delete or free.

Debug new and delete

The runtime libraries provided with Visual C++ support versions of new and delete that are enhanced to better support debugging. In debug builds, the new and delete operators will put markers in the heap that are used to detect memory leaks. If you have allocated memory and have not deallocated it when your program exits from a debugging session, the output window will display warnings about the memory that remains deallocated, or is "leaked."

In addition, you can receive more detailed information about memory leaks, including the line number and source module name of the allocation that caused the leak, by inserting the following lines in your application modules:

```
#ifdef _DEBUG
#define new DEBUG_NEW
#endif
```

Note that release builds do not implement support for memory leak detection. The release versions of new and delete are built for speed rather than debug analysis.

> **CAUTION**
>
> You should not mix the use of the new/delete operators and the malloc/realloc/free functions on the same block of memory. For example, using free to delete a memory block that was allocated with new can result in corrupted memory, particularly in debug builds.

Resizing Memory Blocks

For blocks of memory allocated with malloc(), you can resize the block of memory allocated in the event your application finds that it requires a larger chunk of memory. This is done with the realloc() function:

```
char* ptr = malloc(100); // Allocate original block of memory

// Do stuff...

ptr = realloc(ptr, 50); // Resize memory block

// Do more stuff...

free(ptr); // free memory
```

The call to realloc() will effectively add 50 bytes to the buffer originally allocated with malloc(), although the value of the pointer assigned to ptr may be different from the value originally returned by malloc(). Any data in the memory block before the realloc() call will remain in the memory block, even if it is moved.

Heap Functions

In addition to the default heap used by your application, you can allocate your own private heaps with HeapCreate(). This can be useful in situations where you want to preallocate all the memory your application will use before proceeding.

Once you have created a private heap with HeapCreate(), you can use the HeapAlloc(), HeapReAlloc(), and HeapFree() functions much like the malloc(), realloc(), and free() functions to work with memory blocks in your private heap. In addition, you can retrieve the allocated size of a memory block with the HeapSize() function.

To ensure that only one thread can access a given heap, you can use the HeapLock() function to prevent other threads from accessing the heap until HeapUnlock() is called.

To get a list of all the heap handles used by a process, you can use the GetProcessHeaps() call or the GetProcessHeap() call to get the default heap used for the process for its stack, global, and automatic variables, as well as memory allocated with new and malloc().

The `HeapWalk()` function will return a list of all memory blocks allocated on a heap. You can check to see that all the control structures in a heap are valid with `HeapValidate()`.

The `HeapCompact()` function will attempt simple defragmentation of the heap, although this will not be able to defragment badly fragmented heaps. You can destroy a heap with the `DestroyHeap()` function.

Windows Allocation Functions

The Windows `GlobalAlloc()` and `LocalAlloc()` family of functions are also supported, although the standard `new` or `malloc()` functions should generally be used. In Win32, there is no distinction between global and local memory, so `GlobalAlloc()` and `LocalAlloc()` are essentially the same.

> **CAUTION**
>
> In Win32, `GlobalAlloc()` can no longer be used to allocate memory to be shared between processes. To do this, you must use memory-mapped files.

In general, you should use the Windows allocation functions only where you need to use a handle to memory rather than a pointer, as in clipboard functions—unless, of course, you need to provide compatibility with 16-bit Windows.

GlobalMemoryStatus()

The `GlobalMemoryStatus()` function may be used to retrieve information about available physical and virtual memory. This function takes a pointer to a `MEMORYSTATUS` structure. Before calling `GlobalMemoryStatus()`, you should set the `dwLength` field of the `MEMORYSTATUS` structure to the length of the buffer (almost always `sizeof(MEMORYSTATUS)`). The call to `GlobalMemoryStatus()` will then fill in the rest of the structure with information about the percent of memory in use and the total and available amounts of physical, page file, and virtual memory.

Virtual Memory

The Win32 API allows your application to directly manipulate pages of virtual memory. This can be particularly useful in cases where you wish to reserve a large block of contiguous addresses, even though most of that space is never actually committed to physical storage.

In Win32, pages of virtual memory can be in four different states. A committed page is assigned to physical storage, whether in memory or in the swap file. Committed pages may also be locked, which will force them to stay in physical memory until unlocked. Reserved pages involve a reserved block of addresses, but are not assigned to any storage; free pages are unused altogether.

The VirtualAlloc() function may be used to allocate a range of addresses, starting at a specified logical address. Additional parameters to VirtualAlloc() allow you to specify access protection flags and to specify whether the memory will only be reserved or will also be committed to physical storage.

You may also call VirtualAlloc() again to commit pages of virtual memory previously reserved.

In addition, you can specify the PAGE_GUARD flag in the access protection flags to specify a guard page. If an attempt is made to access a guard page, a STATUS_GUARD_PAGE exception is raised, and the PAGE_GUARD flag is removed from that page.

In addition, you may force memory blocks to remain in physical memory (RAM) with GlobalLock(). This should be used carefully, because it will prevent Windows from managing this memory until GlobalUnlock() is called. If one process locks large chunks of memory, other processes may end up thrashing about trying to make do with whatever RAM is left.

The VirtualProtect() function allows you to alter the access protection flags for a block of memory; VirtualQuery() will return information about memory pages. If you need to access pages in other processes, you can do so with the VirtualProtectEx() and VirtualQueryEx() functions.

Memory Exceptions

If your application attempts to access a page that is not yet committed, an exception will be generated. You can handle these exceptions with the mechanisms discussed in Chapter 7, "General-Purpose Classes." With the virtual memory functions shown previously, you can implement your own virtual memory processing scheme to deal with the when and how of dealing with page faults.

Shared Memory

With the advent of separate memory spaces for processes, processes cannot simply allocate a block of memory with GlobalAlloc() and pass it to another process to share memory. When another process looks at a pointer allocated by another process, it just points off into some random location. However, Win32 does support mechanisms to share memory-mapped files between processes. Here, you will look at a method to do this with memory-mapped files.

> **NOTE**
>
> Visual C++ also supports Dynamic Data Exchange (DDE) and provides the DDEML library to help manage your DDE conversations. However, DDE was really intended to meet the needs of 16-bit Windows applications. It won't be discussed any further in this text, although the online documentation does cover the DDEML library.

Memory-Mapped Files

The virtual memory system in Win32 provides the capability of mapping pages of memory to pages in the paging file, or swapfile. Your applications can extend this capability by mapping memory to any file you like, including the system paging file itself. File-mapping can be used to provide faster and simpler file access, as well as to provide for shared memory.

To map a file to memory, you first use the CreateFileMapping() function, which takes a handle to a file that has already been opened with CreateFile(). For most shared memory applications, you can set this handle to 0xFFFFFFFF, which is used to indicate the system paging file. By using this special handle, you do not need to use CreateFile(), although you also won't have a disk file copy of the memory when you are done.

The second parameter to CreateFileMapping() is a pointer to a SECURITY_ATTRIBUTES structure, which may specify whether the returned handle can be inherited by child processes. In addition, a security descriptor pointer is included in the SECURITY_ATTRIBUTES. This is used by WinNT only to support its security mechanisms.

The third parameter allows you to specify the access protection for the block of memory. This value may include PAGE_READONLY, PAGE_READWRITE, or PAGE_WRITECOPY, which provides copy on write access to the committed pages. This means that when a process maps this memory and writes to it, it will get its own copy of the modified data, rather than actually writing to the shared space. In addition, you can combine several other flags to specify additional section attributes. These will allow you to disallow caching of the memory or to reserve the memory without committing it, as you saw in the virtual memory section.

Additional parameters allow you to specify the maximum size of the memory block. If the size of the memory block is larger than the file specified in the first parameter, the file will be enlarged.

The final parameter specifies a name for the memory-mapping object. This name can be used by other processes in a call to CreateFileMapping() or OpenFileMapping() to access the same file-mapping.

Once a memory-mapping object has been created with CreateFileMapping(), you call MapViewOfFile() to map a view of the file into the address space of a process. This function takes a handle returned by CreateFileMapping() or OpenFileMapping() and allows you to specify an access mode and number of bytes to map, as well as an offset into the file-mapping object. In addition, the MapViewOfFileEx() allows you to specify a suggested address at which to begin the mapping.

To see all this in action, let's look at the following example, which creates two simple console apps. The server (see Listing 8.1) writes a string to shared memory and waits until something longer is written. The client (see Listing 8.2) then reads the shared memory, writes a new string to it, and exits. True, this is a bit silly, but it does show how memory-mapped files work without a lot of other monkey business.

To run the following sample code, open two command prompts, starting the server in one and then starting the client in the other.

Listing 8.1. Memory-mapped file server.

```
#include <iostream.h>
#include <windows.h>
#include <stdio.h>

void main()
{
    HANDLE hMapping;
    LPSTR   lpData;

    // Create mapping, or open existing mapping
    hMapping = CreateFileMapping((HANDLE)0xFFFFFFFF,
        NULL, PAGE_READWRITE, 0, 0x0100, "MYSHARE");
    if(hMapping == NULL)
    {
        // error occurred
        cout << "CreateFileMapping() failed.";
        exit(1);
    }

    lpData = (LPSTR)MapViewOfFile(hMapping, FILE_MAP_ALL_ACCESS,
        0,0,0);
    if(lpData == NULL)
    {
        // error occurred
        cout << "MapViewOfFile() failed.";
        exit(1);
    }

    sprintf(lpData, "Server Data String");

    while(strlen(lpData) < 20)
        Sleep(1000);

    cout << "Received: " << lpData << endl;

    UnmapViewOfFile(lpData);
}
```

Listing 8.2. Memory-mapped file client.

```
#include <iostream.h>
#include <windows.h>
#include <stdio.h>

void main()
{
    HANDLE hMapping;
    LPSTR   lpData;
```

```
// Create mapping, or open existing mapping
hMapping = CreateFileMapping((HANDLE)0xFFFFFFFF,
    NULL, PAGE_READWRITE, 0, 0x0100, "MYSHARE");
if(hMapping == NULL)
{
    // error occurred
    cout << "CreateFileMapping() failed.";
    exit(1);
}

lpData = (LPSTR)MapViewOfFile(hMapping, FILE_MAP_ALL_ACCESS,
    0,0,0);
if(lpData == NULL)
{
    // error occurred
    cout << "MapViewOfFile() failed.";
    exit(1);
}

cout << "Server Data: " << lpData << endl;

sprintf(lpData, "My client data string that is longer than 20");

UnmapViewOfFile(lpData);
}
```

Note that you call UnmapViewOfFile() when you are finished with the mapped view. This releases the mapped memory and performs a lazy write of the data to the file that was mapped (unless it was the swapfile, as it is here). If you want to write data to the disk immediately, you can use FlushViewOfFile() to write the mapped memory to the file.

Summary

In this chapter, you learned how Visual C++ can be used to manage memory under Win32. You also saw how Win32 implements a separate flat memory space for each process.

You took a look at how simple allocation functions such as new and malloc() work under Win32, and also explored the debug functions of new. You learned how to work with private heaps, using HeapCreate() and its related functions.

You saw how Win32 works with virtual memory and how your applications can use calls such as VirtualAlloc() to allocate and work with virtual memory directly.

Finally, you learned how your applications can use memory-mapped files to speed up file access and to share memory with other processes.

9

Multithreading with MFC

by David Bennett

The Win32 operating systems support multiple processes, which are given their own memory address space, as you saw in Chapter 8, "Memory Management." In addition, Win32 supports multiple threads within a process. When any application (or process) starts, it has one primary thread. The application may then start up additional threads, which execute independently. All threads share the one memory space of the process in which they are created.

In this chapter, you will see how you can create your own multithreaded applications with MFC, including the following:

- How to enable multithreading in your applications
- How to create worker threads for background processing
- How to create user-interface threads
- How to synchronize your threads

Using Multiple Threads in Your Application

If you have created an MFC application with AppWizard, your application is already set up to handle multiple threads. If not, you have to be certain to link with the multithreaded libraries, which can be set up in the C/C++ ¦ Code Generation page of the Project Settings dialog box. This is generally a good thing to do anyway, because there are few situations where your application will require the single-threaded libraries; you also need to use the multithreaded varieties if you plan to use MFC.

MFC Objects and Threads

When an application has multiple threads, the order in which they are executed is random. Because of this, special care must be taken to ensure that two different threads are not working with certain objects at the same time. You will see how to do this later; for now, keep in mind that the MFC classes may be used by more than one thread at a time, but individual objects may not be used by multiple threads simultaneously. For example, two threads can work with their own CString objects at the same time, but if two threads access the same CString, the results are unpredictable at best.

If you will be using MFC objects in your threads, you must create the thread by using a CWinThread object, as you will see here. Threads that are created without using a CWinThread object will not properly initialize the internal variables that MFC needs to work with multiple threads. For example, if you create a thread directly with _beginthreadex(), the resulting thread will not be able to use MFC objects or other MFC functions.

In addition, although threads share the same memory space, they do not share the same structures that MFC uses to map C++ objects to Windows handles. In general, this means that a thread may access only MFC objects created in that thread. There are, however, ways around this that you will look at later.

Types of Threads

MFC implements two types of threads. Although both types use the same underlying Win32 API thread mechanisms and both make use of CWinThread, they are different in the way that MFC adds functionality to the thread.

If you are interested in creating a thread that simply goes off on its own and does something, such as background calculations, without interfacing with the user, you use what MFC calls a worker thread. These threads are based on CWinThread, but you do not need to explicitly create a CWinThread object, because the AfxBeginThread() call will create one for you.

If, on the other hand, you want to create a thread that will deal with parts of a user interface, you create a user-interface thread. MFC will add a message pump to these threads, providing a message loop that is separate from the main message loop of your application's CWinApp object. Actually, CWinApp is itself a prime example of a user-interface thread, because it is derived from CWinThread. Just as MFC derives CWinApp from CWinThread, you create your own class derived from CWinThread to implement user-interface threads.

Working with Worker Threads

Worker threads are handy for any time you want to do something such as calculations or background printing. They are also useful in cases where you need to wait on an event to occur, such as receiving data from another application, without forcing the user to wait. Let's face it—most users are not known for their patience.

Creating a worker thread is relatively simple; the hard part comes later, when you need to make sure that your thread plays well with others—but more on that later. To get a worker thread up and running, you implement a function that will be run in the thread, then create the thread with AfxBeginThread(). Although you may choose to create your own CWinThread-based class, this is not necessary for worker threads.

Starting the Thread

An MFC thread, whether a worker or user-interface thread, is started with a call to AfxBeginThread(). This function is overloaded to handle the creation of the two flavors of threads, but for now, let's look at the variety used to create worker threads. Here is the prototype for this function:

```
CWinThread* AfxBeginThread( AFX_THREADPROC pfnThreadProc,
        LPVOID pParam, int nPriority = THREAD_PRIORITY_NORMAL,
        UINT nStackSize = 0, DWORD dwCreateFlags = 0,
        LPSECURITY_ATTRIBUTES lpSecurityAttrs = NULL );
```

The first parameter is a pointer to the function that will be run inside the thread. As you will soon see, this function can take a single parameter, which is passed as the second parameter. Generally, this is a pointer to a data structure of some sort.

Each thread also may have its own priority. This parameter may be set to any of the values accepted by `SetThreadPriority()`, which is discussed later.

Because each thread executes independently, it must have its own stack to keep track of function calls and the like. The size of the stack may be specified in the call to `AfxBeginThread()`.

In most cases, you will probably want your thread to start doing its thing right off the bat. However, you may specify the `CREATE_SUSPENDED` flag in the `dwCreateFlags` parameter to create a thread that is suspended upon creation. This thread will not begin executing until `ResumeThread()` is called.

Optionally, you may also specify a `SECURITY_ATTRIBUTES` structure to specify security parameters to be used with the thread.

`AfxBeginThread()` returns a pointer to the newly created `CWinThread` object. You squirrel this away somewhere so that you can work with the member functions of `CWinThread` later.

When you call `AfxBeginThread()`, it will create a new `CWinThread` object for you and call its `CreateThread()` member function. At this point, unless you have specified `CREATE_SUSPENDED`, your new thread will start executing the function you specified, and the thread that called `AfxBeginThread()` will go on its merry way.

The new thread will continue to execute the function specified until that function returns, or until you call `AfxEndThread()` from within the thread. The thread will also terminate if the process it is running in terminates.

Implementing a Thread Function

The sole purpose in life for a worker bee is to make honey. The sole purpose in life for a worker thread is to run its thread function, or controlling function, as it is called in Microsoft's documentation. In general, when the thread starts, this function starts. When the function dies, the thread dies.

First, your thread function should have a prototype that looks like this:

```
UINT MyThreadProc(LPVOID pParam);
```

All thread functions take a single 32-bit argument. Although you could pass a single value here, such as an `int`, it is generally more useful to pass a pointer to a structure or other object that can hold more information. This structure may also be used to return information to the rest of your application.

For example, the following simple thread function could be used to encrypt a string:

```
UINT MyThreadProc(LPVOID pParam)
{
    if(pParam == NULL)
        AfxEndThread(MY_NULL_POINTER_ERROR);
    char *pStr = (char *)pParam;
```

```
    while(*pStr)
        *pStr++ ^= 0xA5;

    return 0;
}
```

This function could be used in a thread created like this:

```
AfxBeginThread(MyThreadProc, pMySecretString);
```

Once the thread is created, it will start executing until it either discovers that the pointer passed to it is null, or it finishes with the string. In either case, whether the function calls AfxEndThread() or simply returns, the function stops executing, its stack and other resources are deallocated, and the CWinThread object is deleted.

Accessing a Thread's Return Code

The exit code specified when the function returns or calls AfxEndThread() may be accessed by other threads in your application with a call to ::GetExitCodeThread(), which takes a handle to the thread and a pointer to a DWORD that will receive the exit code. The handle to the thread is contained in the m_hThread member of CWinThread, so it should be no problem to pass this to ::GetExitCodeThread(), right?

Well, there's a catch: By default, the CWinThread object is deleted as soon as the function returns or calls AfxEndThread(). You can get around this in one of two ways.

First, you can set the m_bAutoDelete member of CWinThread to FALSE, which prevents MFC from deleting the object automatically. You can then access the m_hThread member after the thread terminates. However, you are now responsible for deleting the CWinThread object.

Alternatively, you can use ::DuplicateHandle() to create a copy of the m_hThread member once the thread is created. However, you must be certain that you copy the handle before the thread terminates. The only way to be absolutely certain of this is to specify CREATE_SUSPENDED when the thread is created, copy the handle, then call ResumeThread() to start the thread. As you can see, this gets to be a bit involved; thus, it is generally preferable to change the m_bAutoDelete member.

The exit code value that is returned by GetExitCodeThread() will contain STILL_ACTIVE if the thread is still running, or, if the thread has terminated, the return code that the thread passed when it returned or called AfxEndThread(). Note that STILL_ACTIVE is defined as 0x103 (259 decimal), so avoid using this as a return code from your thread.

User-Interface Threads

User-interface threads are similar to worker threads, because they use the same mechanisms provided by the operating system to manage the new thread. However, user-interface threads provide additional functionality from MFC that allows you to use them to handle user-interface objects, such as dialog boxes or windows. To use this functionality, you will have to do a bit more work than you did with worker threads, but this is still much simpler than using the Win32 API directly to set up a new thread to handle windows messages.

Creating the Thread

To create a user-interface thread, you will use a slightly different version of the `AfxBeginThread()` function. The version used to create user-interface threads takes a pointer to a `CRuntimeClass` object for your thread class. MFC will create this for you with the `RUNTIME_CLASS` macro:

```
AfxBeginThread(RUNTIME_CLASS(CMyThread));
```

If you want to keep track of the MFC object for your thread, use this:

```
(CMyThread*) pMyThread = (CMyThread*) AfxBeginThread(RUNTIME_CLASS(CMyThread));
```

Keeping a pointer to the MFC thread object will allow you to access the member data and functions of your thread class from other threads.

Additionally, you may specify a priority, stack size, and security attributes, as well as the `CREATE_SUSPENDED` flag for the new thread in the call to `AfxBeginThread()`.

Creating a Thread Class

As mentioned earlier, you derive your own class from `CWinThread` in order to create an MFC user-interface thread. The class you derive from `CWinThread` must include its own override for `InitInstance()`, but you may choose whether to override several other functions or use the defaults provided by `CWinThread`. You also need to make sure that you use the `DECLARE_DYNCREATE` and `IMPLEMENT_DYNCREATE` macros in the declaration and implementation of your thread class.

Initializing New Threads

Whenever a new thread is created from your thread class by calling `AfxBeginThread()`, MFC will call the `InitInstance()` function of your thread class. This is the one function that you must override in your thread class. In general, you will want to do any initialization of your thread here, as well as allocate any dynamic memory you know you will need.

However, all that your `InitInstance()` function really must do is return `TRUE` so that MFC knows the initialization succeeded and that it should proceed. If something goes wrong in `InitInstance()`, such as memory allocation failures, it should return `FALSE`. In this case, execution of the thread stops and the thread is destroyed.

If this thread is designed to handle a window, this is a good place to create the window. You should then set the `m_pMainWnd` member of `CWinThread` to a pointer to the window you have created, which will allow the message dispatch system of `CWinThread` to manage messages from this window exclusively.

> **NOTE**
>
> If you create an MFC window object in a thread, that MFC object cannot be used in another thread, but the handle to the underlying window can. If you wish to work with the window in another thread using an MFC object, the second thread should create a new MFC object; then call `Attach()` to attach the new object to the window handle passed from the first thread.

If you have allocated memory in your `InitInstance()` function, or done anything else in the thread that needs cleaning up, you should also override the `ExitInstance()` member of `CWinThread` in your thread class. This is called whenever your thread terminates, including cases where `InitInstance()` returns `FALSE`.

In addition, you can override the `OnIdle()` member to perform tasks when the message queue is empty, as you saw in Chapter 3, "MFC Messages and Commands." Your thread class can also override `ProcessWndProcException()`, which is called to handle exceptions that have not been handled elsewhere. The default implementation will handle exceptions caused by only the `WM_CREATE` or `WM_PAINT` messages.

Handling Messages in Threads

The default implementation of `CWinThread::Run()` will provide a message pump for your new thread. You can override this function to do anything else you would like your thread to do, although most user-interface threads won't do this.

In addition, you may override the `PreTranslateMessage()` function if you want to intercept messages before the message pump dispatches them, although most messages can be handled in the message map.

Your thread class may implement a message map just as for any other class derived from `CCmdTarget`, as you saw in Chapter 3. However, you may also use a special message map macro, `ON_THREAD_MESSAGE`, to handle messages that are sent directly to the thread rather than to a given window. You can send messages directly to a thread with `CWinThread::PostThreadMessage()`, as shown here:

```
pMyThread->PostThreadMessage(WM_USER+1, myWParam, myLParam);
```

This is similar to the `::PostThreadMessage()` API call, which takes an additional parameter—the thread identifier.

Note that the first parameter specifies the message to post. This example uses `WM_USER+1`, which gives a valid user-defined message ID. To then handle the message you posted, the message map for your thread would look something like this:

```
BEGIN_MESSAGE_MAP(CMyThread, CWinThread)
    //{{AFX_MSG_MAP(CMyThread)
```

```
    // NOTE - the ClassWizard will add and remove mapping macros here.
    //}}AFX_MSG_MAP
    ON_THREAD_MESSAGE(WM_USER+1, HandleThreadMessage)
END_MESSAGE_MAP()
```

This will result in messages sent directly to your thread, which have command ID WM_USER+1, to be handled by the HandleThreadMessage() member of your thread class. The handler for your thread message looks like this:

```
afx_msg void CMyThread::HandleThreadMessage(WPARAM wParam, LPARAM lParam)
{
    PostQuitMessage(MY_THREAD_RECEIVED_END_MESSAGE);
}
```

In this case, you decide to use the WM_USER+1 message to tell the thread to exit, although you may choose to implement more elaborate handlers that make use of the wParam and lParam values that are passed from PostThreadMessage().

Terminating Threads

A thread can terminate in several different ways. Normally, a thread will end when the thread function it is running returns. For worker threads, this is pretty straightforward. However, for user-interface threads, you generally don't deal with the thread function directly.

The Run() member of CWinThread is actually the thread function, which, by default, MFC uses to implement a message pump for the thread. This function will exit upon receiving a WM_QUIT message, which a thread may send to itself with a call to PostQuitMessage(), as in the previous example.

Additionally, if your user-interface thread manages an MFC window, as set in the m_pMainWnd member, MFC will call PostQuitMessage() for you when the main window is destroyed. In either case, user-interface threads will call ExitInstance() before actually terminating.

The Win32 API provides the TerminateThread() function, but using this method can have some very dire consequences. Unlike the previous methods of terminating threads gracefully, TerminateThread() stops the thread dead in its tracks, without any provisions for cleaning up allocated memory. More importantly, the thread that is terminated in this way may be interrupted in the middle of several different transactions (such as device driver communications or heap management) that will leave the system in an indeterminate state. In Windows 95, this equates to almost certain doom for the whole system, whereas Windows NT should be able to at least save the rest of the processes. In either OS, the offending process is a goner.

If you need to terminate a thread from outside that thread, try to use some form of communications to tell the thread to terminate itself gracefully. The messages used in the previous example work well for this, although you could also use some global flag or one of the synchronization objects, which are covered later.

Thread Local Storage

In some cases, you use several different threads running the same thread function. For instance, you may be developing a DLL that handles connections to outside processes, and you want to create a new thread for each connection. Although you should still be careful to use the proper synchronization objects to protect global resources, the Win32 API also provides a mechanism to provide storage that is local to a thread.

This is generally necessary only if you are developing libraries that may be called by multiple threads that each require their own dynamic storage. For the threads created here, you could easily allocate memory within a thread and store the pointer in a variable local to the thread function of a worker thread or a member of your CWinThread class. Because threads have their own stack, variables local to the thread function are thread-local. Likewise, an instance of CWinThread has its own set of data members that are thread-local.

Allocating a TLS Index

To use thread-local storage (TLS), you must first allocate a TLS index with a call to TlsAlloc(). This function takes no parameters and will return a DWORD, which is the new TLS index. This index can then be used by any threads in the process in a call to TlsSetValue() or TlsGetValue() to access an LPVOID pointer that is local to that thread. When all threads are finished with a given TLS index, it may be deallocated with TlsFree().

Using Thread-Local Storage

This may all seem a bit confusing, so let's look at a more concrete example. Suppose you are creating a DLL that requires some of its own dynamic memory. Let's also allow the calling process to call the same functions with different threads to work with different connections.

When a process first attaches to the DLL, TlsAlloc() is called to allocate an index that you will use to store the connection data pointers for each thread. The index is stored somewhere where it can be accessed by the functions that need it (that is, globally).

When each thread attaches to the DLL, your DLL code will allocate a block of memory to hold data for this connection. You can then use the TLS index that you stored earlier in a call to TlsSetValue() to save a pointer to the new data.

Whenever a thread needs to access the connection data, it should first call TlsGetValue() with the TLS index you stored. This will return the pointer that was saved with TlsSetValue() for this thread. The pointer can then be used freely.

When a process detaches from the DLL, you should call TlsFree() to free the TLS index.

If you find that you require more than one pointer to thread-local storage, simply allocate a second index with TlsAlloc(). All systems are guaranteed to support at least 64 TLS indexes per process, although you can use the TLS_MINIMUM_AVAILABLE constant to see the actual minimum.

Thread Synchronization

Many developers, when they first learn how to create multiple threads in an application, have a tendency to go overboard and try to use a separate thread for everything an application does. This is not generally a good practice. Not only is it more work to create all those threads, but the effort involved in making sure that they all cooperate may easily increase exponentially with the number of threads.

I don't mean to scare you away from using threads. They are extremely useful—even necessary—in many situations. However, creating a multithreaded application that works correctly is not a trivial task. Very careful consideration must be given to how your threads will communicate with each other and how they will keep from stomping on each other's data.

You must keep in mind that threads in Win32 may (and will) be preempted by the operating system. That is, any thread may be stopped right where it is and another thread allowed to run for a while. Thus, it is safest to assume that all threads are running simultaneously. Even though only one thread at a time actually is using a CPU, there is no way to know when or where a thread will be preempted, or what other threads will do before the original thread resumes execution. On machines with multiple processors, this is not just a safe assumption—several threads actually are running at the same time.

Potential Pitfalls

For an example of how problems can occur, let's suppose that you have a linked list that uses pointers to dynamically allocated memory. Let's also suppose you have thread A that adds items to the list and thread B that deletes items from a list. If thread B is in the middle of deleting an item from the list when it is preempted, then thread A tries to add an item, thread A is likely to run into an item that is only half-deleted, perhaps involving pointers off into the boonies.

It is not hard to see that this can cause real problems. This sort of problem is, however, much more difficult to debug, because the problems are dependent on the timing of when threads are preempted. Dealing with bugs that cannot be duplicated makes ditch-digging suddenly seem like a much more viable career option.

A similar, but perhaps less obvious, problem can arise even with simple data types. Let's say one of your threads used code such as this:

```
if(nCount == 0)
    nCount++;
```

It is quite possible, if not inevitable, that the thread will be interrupted between testing nCount and incrementing it. This provides a window of opportunity for other threads to modify nCount, perhaps setting it to something other than 0. However, when the thread containing this code resumes, it will increment nCount anyway.

It is certainly much more enjoyable to spend the time to design your applications to avoid these problems than it is to try to find the cause of one of these "gotchas" after you have 100,000 lines of code running at sites around the world.

Now that you've seen just how multithreaded applications can go astray, let's see how you can use MFC's thread synchronization mechanisms to help your threads play well with others.

CCriticalSection

In places where you know that your threads will be dealing with things that only one thread at a time should be accessing, you can use critical sections to ensure that only one thread can access certain pieces of code at the same time.

To use MFC's critical sections, you first need to create a CCriticalSection object. Because the constructor takes no arguments, this is trivial.

Next, before a thread in your application needs to enter a critical section of the code, it should call the Lock() member of your CCriticalSection object. If no other threads have the critical section locked, Lock() will lock the critical section and return, allowing the calling thread to continue into the critical section and manipulate data as it sees fit. If a second thread tries to lock the same critical section object, the Lock() call will block until the critical section is available. This occurs when the first thread calls Unlock(), allowing other threads to access the critical section.

> **NOTE**
>
> The Lock() function will accept a timeout parameter, but it is simply ignored.

This provides a simple, lightweight mechanism to limit access to critical sections in your code; however, it does have its limitations.

First, use of the critical section object is purely voluntary on the part of the developer. If you don't use the critical section properly, it won't do anything to protect your data. It is your responsibility to correctly and consistently use critical sections to control access to all data that might potentially be corrupted by simultaneous access by multiple threads. You will have to be responsible for calling Lock() before each bit of code that might cause problems. You will also need to make certain to call Unlock() when you are finished working with the sensitive data; otherwise, the other processes will wait forever on the Lock() call.

Second, CCriticalSection objects are valid only within a process; they cannot be used to protect memory or other resources shared between processes. For this, you will need to use one of the beefier classes, such as CMutex.

CMutex

The MFC CMutex class is similar to CCriticalSection in that it can be used to provide mutually exclusive access to certain sections of your code. Like critical sections, CMutex objects will work to protect your data only if you use them, although they can be used between different processes. Only one thread may own a given mutex at a given time; all others will block on a call to Lock() until the owning thread releases ownership.

First, you create a CMutex object. The prototype for its constructor looks like this:

```
CMutex( BOOL bInitiallyOwn = FALSE,
    LPCTSTR lpszName = NULL,
    LPSECURITY_ATTRIBUTES lpsaAttribute = NULL );
```

The first parameter allows you to specify the ownership of the mutex when it is created. It is often useful to declare a mutex object as a member of a class representing data that needs to be protected from simultaneous access by multiple threads. In cases like this, you can initialize the mutex and lock it while the protected data is initialized; then you can unlock the mutex when it is safe for other threads to start accessing the data.

In addition, you may specify a name for your mutex. This is not necessary if the mutex will be used in only one process, but it is the only way you will be able to share a mutex between processes.

Under Windows NT, the security attributes for the mutex may be specified in the last parameter. Windows 95 simply ignores this parameter.

The Lock() and Unlock() functions are used in much the same way as the calls used for critical sections, except that Lock() allows you to specify a timeout value. If the mutex is unavailable when Lock() is called, the call will block for the specified number of milliseconds, waiting for the mutex to become available, at which time Lock() returns TRUE. If the timeout time elapses before the mutex becomes available, Lock() will return FALSE, and your code should react accordingly.

To share a mutex between two processes, you should create a CMutex object in each process, making certain to use the same name in the call to the constructor. The first thread to call the constructor will actually create the operating system mutex, as well as the CMutex object.

The next thread to call CMutex() will create a CMutex object corresponding to the mutex object that was already created with the same name. If the bInitallyOwn parameter is set to TRUE, the call to CMutex() will not return until the mutex becomes available. You can take advantage of this to create a CMutex only at the time you are ready to wait on it, although you will not be able to specify a timeout value using this method.

CSemaphore

Semaphore objects are similar to mutexes, except instead of providing access to a single thread, they may be created to allow access to only a limited number of threads simultaneously. Semaphores are based on a counter that they keep. When a thread is granted access to the semaphore, this count is decremented. If the count is 0, threads requesting access will have to wait until a thread releases the semaphore, thereby incrementing the semaphore count.

The prototype of the constructor for CSemaphore objects looks like this:

```
CSemaphore( LONG lInitialCount = 1,
    LONG lMaxCount = 1,
    LPCTSTR pstrName = NULL,
    LPSECURITY_ATTRIBUTES lpsaAttributes = NULL );
```

The pstrName and lpsaAttributes parameters work just as they did in CMutex, but you have not seen the first two parameters before. These are used to specify an initial value for the semaphore's counter, as well as a maximum value for the counter. The default values of 1 and 1 will create a semaphore that is essentially the same as a mutex, because only one thread may be granted access to the semaphore at any one time. You will need to modify these parameters when the semaphore is created to allow more than one thread to have access to the semaphore.

The Lock() and Unlock() functions of CSemaphore work the same as those for CMutex, except that CSemaphore may allow a fixed number of concurrent accesses and CMutex allows only one.

CEvent

Although the previous synchronization objects provide a method of protecting various resources or sections of your code, your program will occasionally want to wait for some event to occur, rather than waiting for a resource to become available. This is useful in waiting to receive packets from a network or waiting for a thread to signal that it has completed some task.

To allow you to signal events, Win32 provides the aptly named event object, which MFC encapsulates in the CEvent class. An event object is always in one of two states: signaled or unsignaled (or, set or reset). It is common to create an event object in its unsignaled state, then set it to signaled when an event occurs.

Creation of a CEvent object begins with a call to its constructor:

```
CEvent( BOOL bInitiallyOwn = FALSE,
    BOOL bManualReset = FALSE,
    LPCTSTR lpszName = NULL,
    LPSECURITY_ATTRIBUTES lpsaAttribute = NULL );
```

This is very similar to the constructor for the other CSyncObject-derived objects you have seen so far. These include a name for the object, which may be used by other processes, and a pointer to a security attributes structure. Although an event is not really owned by any one thread, as a mutex is, the bInitiallyOwn parameter allows you to set the initial value of the event. If this is FALSE, the event is initially unsignaled; if TRUE, the event is set to signaled on creation.

The bManualReset parameter is a bit more interesting, because it dictates how the event object will behave. In general, if this parameter is TRUE, the event must be reset manually by your code after it is signaled. If the parameter is FALSE, the event object will reset itself. You will see how this works a bit more clearly when you see how to manipulate the event.

Like other CSyncObjects, you can wait on an event with the Lock() member, which allows you to specify a timeout value. If the wait times out, Lock() returns FALSE. If the event is signaled before the timeout, Lock() returns TRUE.

Signaling an Event

As mentioned previously, an event can be signaled when it is first created, but this is not normally done. To signal an event, you can call SetEvent().

If bManualReset for the event is FALSE, this will allow only one thread that is waiting on the event to proceed (by returning TRUE from the thread's call to Lock()). The event is then reset before any other threads will return from Lock(). If no threads are waiting on the event when SetEvent() is called, the event will remain signaled until one thread is given a lock on it. The event is then set to unsignalled automatically.

If, on the other hand, bManualReset is TRUE, all threads that are waiting on the event will be allowed to continue (Lock() will return TRUE). The event is not reset automatically, so any subsequent calls to Lock() for the event will not have to wait, but will return TRUE. To manually reset the event, you can call ResetEvent(), thus making any further calls to Lock() for the event wait until it is signaled again.

In addition, the PulseEvent() member of CEvent may be used to signal an event. If bManualReset is TRUE, all threads that are currently waiting for the event will acquire a lock and the event is automatically reset.

If bManualReset is FALSE, one waiting thread will be able to acquire a lock before the event is reset. Note that if no threads are currently waiting on the event, the event is reset immediately. Unlike SetEvent(), PulseEvent() will not keep the event signalled until one thread acquires the lock.

CSingleLock

MFC provides classes that can "simplify" access to the synchronization objects discussed previously. These include CMultipleLock, which allows threads to wait for combinations of objects (as you will see next), and CSingleLock, which can be used to work with single synchronization objects.

In most cases, you will not really need to use CSingleLock, despite the Microsoft documentation that says you must. The Lock() and Unlock() functions will work just like the Lock() and Unlock() calls in the underlying CSyncObjects.

The difference is that CSingleLock can provide the IsLocked() function, which can tell you whether your thread will be able to acquire a lock without actually locking the object. Keep in mind that the state of a sync object may change between a call to IsLocked() and the actual Lock() call.

Microsoft also justifies the CSingleLock class as an excuse to be sloppy in your coding habits. If a CSingleLock object falls out of scope and is destroyed, the destructor will call Unlock() for you.

As you can probably guess, I am not sold on the CSingleLock class. It provides very little useful functionality for the extra code it requires and just muddles your source code. On the other hand, the CMultiLock class is extremely useful, if not essential, in writing complex multithreaded applications.

CMultiLock

In complex multithreaded applications, you will often need to acquire several different shared resources to perform an operation, or you may want to wait for one of several different events to be signaled. With what you have seen so far in this chapter, you can do such things in your applications, but it isn't easy.

To help you work with multiple synchronization objects, MFC provides the CMultipleLock class, which can greatly simplify operations, such as waiting for several different resources or a set of different events. The prototype for the CMultiLock constructor shows that it accepts an array of CSyncObject pointers and the size of the array:

```
CMultiLock( CSyncObject* ppObjects[ ], DWORD dwCount, BOOL bInitialLock = FALSE );
```

In addition, you may specify bInitialLock to acquire a lock on the objects specified in the ppObjects array when the CMultiLock is created. However, you will probably want to hold off on any locking until later, when Lock() allows some other special capabilities.

CMultiLock::Lock()

Although you may be interested in using the IsLocked() member to query the status of an individual object handled with the CMultiLock, the real purpose for CMultiLock is its Lock() function, as shown in this prototype:

```
DWORD Lock( DWORD dwTimeOut = INFINITE, BOOL bWaitForAll = TRUE, DWORD dwWakeMask =
0 );
```

The timeout parameter should seem familiar by now. Like the other Lock() calls you have seen, this can be used to specify a maximum time to wait for a lock (in milliseconds). The special value of INFINITE can be used to wait until you shut down the machine to install the latest greatest Win32 OS.

If the bWaitForAll parameter is TRUE, Lock() will not return successfully until all the objects handled in the CMultiLock are available. This is useful for situations where you need to lock several resources at one time, and it can go a long way toward preventing deadlocks. If this bWaitForAll is FALSE, Lock() will return whenever any one object is locked. This is handy for waiting for several different events, where you want to wait for any one to occur, but don't expect all of them.

In addition to the sync objects specified in the constructor for the CMultiLock, the Lock() function can use the dwWakeMask parameter to specify several Windows messages that will cause Lock() to return.

Although your thread will not receive any messages while it is blocked in a call to Lock(), MFC will check the messages that have been sent to your thread, to see whether the Lock() should return.

The flags that you may specify in dwWakeMask are listed in Table 9.1.

Table 9.1. dwWakeMask flags.

Flag	*Message type that will interrupt* Lock()
QS_ALLINPUT	Any message at all
QS_HOTKEY	A WM_HOTKEY message
QS_INPUT	A user input message (either QS_KEY or QS_MOUSE)
QS_KEY	A keyboard message; includes WM_KEYUP, WM_KEYDOWN, WM_SYSKEYUP, and WM_SYSKEYDOWN
QS_MOUSE	Any mouse movement or button message, such as WM_MOUSEMOVE, WM_LBUTTONDOWN, WM_RBUTTONUP, and so forth
QS_MOUSEBUTTON	A mouse button message, such as WM_LBUTTONDOWN, WM_RBUTTONUP, and so forth
QS_MOUSEMOVE	A WM_MOUSEMOVE message
QS_PAINT	WM_PAINT or related messages, such as WM_NCPAINT
QS_POSTMESSAGE	Any posted message not included in the preceding categories
QS_SENDMESSAGE	Any message sent by another thread or application
QS_TIMER	A WM_TIMER message
QS_ALLEVENTS	Any message, other than those covered by QS_SENDMESSAGE

Okay, so Lock() can return for 101 different reasons, but how do you know what caused the return?

CMultiLock::Lock() **Return Values**

To see what caused Lock() to stop waiting, you look at the DWORD that Lock() returns.

If Lock() returns a value between WAIT_OBJECT_0 and WAIT_OBJECT_0 + (dwCount -1), one of the sync objects specified has been locked. You can get the index by subtracting WAIT_OBJECT_0 from the return value. Of course, this is if bWaitForAll is FALSE. If bWaitForAll is TRUE, a value in this range signifies that all the requested sync objects have been locked.

If Lock() returns WAIT_OBJECT_0 + dwCount, a message specified in dwWakeMask is available on the message queue. (Note that the dwCount I use here refers to the number of objects specified in the CMultiLock constructor.)

If Lock() returns a value between WAIT_ABANDONED_0 and WAIT_ABANDONED_0 + (dwCount - 1), one of the objects has been abandoned. This occurs when a process that owns the thread that owns a sync object has died without first releasing the sync object. If bWaitForAll is TRUE, you will receive this return value, but not until all other objects specified in the CMultiLock are locked or abandoned.

Finally, if Lock() returns WAIT_TIMEOUT, you can probably guess that the timeout time has expired.

Cleaning Up

When you are finished with the sync objects that you have locked, you should call Unlock() to unlock all objects used by the CMultiLock. Although this will be called for you when the CMultiLock is destroyed, it is a good practice to call it explicitly, as soon as you are finished with the resources protected by sync objects.

Creating a New Process

In some very large applications, you may wish to create new processes, which include their own memory space and are independent of the process that created them. To do this, you can use CreateProcess().

In short, CreateProcess() takes a filename for an executable file that will be run in the new process. However, CreateProcess() also takes 27 other parameters, either directly or indirectly. Because this is seldom used by the majority of Win32 applications, you won't look at the details of CreateProcess() here. However, if you do need to do this, you will be relieved to know that most of the parameters to CreateProcess() have reasonable default values.

Summary

In this chapter, you have looked at a lot of the nuts and bolts that are used to construct a multithreaded application in MFC. It is now up to you, the developer, to ensure that your application uses these tools and your application uses threads properly, including proper thread synchronization.

You have seen how to set up your application to use threads, as well as how to create worker threads to do background processing without holding up other threads in your application.

You have also explored how to create user-interface threads that can manage windows independently, as well as the details of creating a class to be used to initialize your user-interface thread and handle messages that it receives.

In addition, you have learned how threads can use their own thread-local storage, as well as how to synchronize your threads to share common resources or use events to notify your threads when interesting things happen.

10

Dynamic Link Libraries (DLLs)

by David Bennett

Since the dawn of time (or thereabouts), Windows operating systems have used dynamic link libraries (DLLs) to support commonly used functions. Descendants of Windows, including Windows NT and Windows 95 as well as OS/2, also depend on DLLs to provide a large segment of their functionality.

In this chapter, you look at several different aspects of using and creating DLLs. Here, you will see how to

■ Statically link to DLLs

■ Load DLLs dynamically

■ Create your own DLLs

■ Create MFC extension DLLs

Using Dynamic Link Libraries

For Windows applications, it is virtually impossible to create an application that does not use DLLs. All the Win32 API and countless other functions of the Win32 operating systems are contained in DLLs, although you may not have been aware that the examples shown so far use DLLs at all.

In general, DLLs are just collections of functions in a library. However, unlike their static cousins (.lib files), DLLs are not linked directly into executable files by the linker. Instead, only reference information is included in the executable file. The bulk of the library code is then loaded at runtime. This allows different processes to share libraries in memory, thus cutting down on the memory required to run different applications that share many of the same libraries, as well as keeping the size of EXEs manageable.

However, if your library will be used by a single application, it might be more efficient to create a simple, static link library. Of course, if your functions are to be used in only one program, you might as well simply compile the source into your one application.

In most cases, your project will link to DLLs statically, or implicitly, at link-time. The operating system then manages the process of loading the DLL for you at runtime. However, you can also explicitly or dynamically load DLLs at runtime, as you will see later in this chapter.

Import Libraries

When statically linking to a DLL, you will specify a .lib file in the linker options, either on the command line or in the Link page of Developer Studio's project settings. However, the .lib file that you link to is not your average static library. The .lib files that are used to implicitly link to DLLs are known as import libraries. They do not contain the real meat of the code contained in the library, but only references to each function exported by a DLL file, which has all the good stuff in it. In general, this results in the import libraries being much smaller than the DLL files. You will look at just how these files are created later in this chapter; for now, let's look at some of the other issues involved in linking to DLLs implicitly.

Calling Conventions

In the examples that you have looked at so far, you haven't had to worry about the different calling conventions that may be used to handle parameter passing and calls to functions. That is because the libraries and headers provided in Visual C++ have taken care of this for you. However, if you will be using your own libraries, or those from third parties, you will need to pay attention to this. (These calling convention details apply to plain old static libraries as well.)

If this were a perfect world, you wouldn't have to worry about calling conventions for libraries—they would all be the same. However, this is not a perfect world and a great deal of large-scale development is dependent on some sort of non-C++ library.

By default, Visual C++ will use the C++ calling convention. This means that parameters will be placed on the stack from right to left, the caller is responsible for removing parameters from the stack when the call returns, and function names are mangled (or decorated, depending on your political correctness).

Name mangling allows the linker to differentiate between overloaded functions—that is, functions with the same name but different argument lists. However, if you look for a mangled function name in an old C library, you won't find it.

Although the rest of the C calling convention is identical, C libraries do not mangle the names of their functions, other than prepending an underscore (_) to the name.

If you plan to use a C library in your C++ application, you will need to declare all the functions from the C library as extern "C", like this:

```
extern "C" int MyOldCFunction(int myParm);
```

Declarations for library functions are usually done in a header supplied with the library, although most C libraries do not ship with a header designed for C++ use. In this case, you add the extern "C" modifier to each of the functions in a copy of the header you will make for use with C++. This can be quite a chore, so I generally use a shortcut: You can apply the extern "C" modifier to an entire block of code—namely, the #include that brings in the old C header file. Thus, instead of the drudgery of modifying each function in a header, you can do something like this:

```
extern "C" {
#include "MyCLib.h"
}
```

> **TIP**
>
> If you run into unresolved external errors when linking, the linker will include the function name that it is looking for at the end of the error message. If this name includes strange characters (generated by C++ name mangling), other than a preceding underscore (which is used in standard C linkages), the extern "C" modifier is not being used.

In programs for older versions of Windows, the PASCAL calling convention was also used for Windows API calls. In newer programs, you should use the WINAPI modifier, which maps to _stdcall. Although this is not really a standard C or C++ calling convention, it is the one used by Windows API calls. However, this is generally all taken care of for you in the standard Windows headers.

Loading the DLL

When your application starts, it will try to find all the DLL files that have been implicitly linked to the application and map them into the process's memory space. To find DLL files, the operating system will look in the following places:

1. The directory from which the EXE was run
2. The current directory for the process
3. The Windows system directory
4. The Windows directory
5. The directories in the PATH environment variable

> **NOTE**
>
> For Windows NT, the Windows system directory in number 3 includes both the 32-bit Windows system directory (usually SYSTEM32), which is searched first, and the 16-bit Windows system directory (SYSTEM).

If the DLL is not found, your application will display a dialog box, showing the user the DLL that was not found and the path that was searched. The process then quietly shuts down.

If the proper DLL is found, it is then mapped into the process's memory space, where it will remain until the process terminates. Your application can now call the functions contained in the DLL without any further ado. If you want to dynamically load and unload DLLs, you use the methods discussed next.

> **NOTE**
>
> Unlike Win3.1, global memory in a DLL is not truly global—each process gets its own copy. Sharing memory between processes is discussed in Chapter 8, "Memory Management."

Loading DLLs Dynamically

Occasionally, it is useful to allow your application a bit more control over the loading of DLLs than normal, implicit linking will allow. For instance, you may wish to specify which DLL the user can use, or require the user to select options that affect which DLL is to be used. The dynamic, or explicit, loading process allows you to decide which DLLs will be loaded. This allows you to use several different DLLs that provide the same functions, but work differently. For example, if you develop a transport-independent communications module, your application could decide at runtime whether to load the DLL for TCP/IP or NetBIOS.

::LoadLibrary()

The first thing you do to load a DLL dynamically is to map the DLL module into the memory of your process. This is done with the ::LoadLibrary() call, which takes a single parameter— the name of the module to load. Your code should look something like this:

```
HMODULE hMyDll;
hMyDll = LoadLibrary("MyLib");
if(hMyDll == NULL)
    // Could not load DLL, handle the error…
```

Windows will assume a default file extension of .dll if you don't specify an extension. In the example, Windows will look for MyLib.dll. If you specify a path in the filename, only that specific path is used to find the file; otherwise, Windows will search for the file in the same way that it searches for implicitly linked DLLs (as shown previously), starting with the directory the process's EXE loaded from and continuing on through to the PATH.

Once Windows locates the file, it will compare the full path of the file found to the full path of DLLs already loaded in that process. If there is a match, the handle for that library is returned, rather than having another copy loaded.

> **NOTE**
>
> LoadLibrary() may also be used to load executable files into memory. The handle to the executable module can then be used in calls to FindResource() or LoadResource().

If the file is found and the DLL is loaded successfully, LoadLibrary() returns a handle to the module. Hang on to this handle; you will be using it shortly. If an error occurs, LoadLibrary() will return NULL.

> **NOTE**
>
> If the specified file is not found, Windows will normally display a dialog to the user, stating that the file was not found. However, if you are using MFC, it makes a call to ::SetErrorMode(), instructing Windows to simply return errors to the application, rather than notifying the user before functions such as LoadLibrary() return. This allows your applications to deal with errors as they see fit. If you are not using MFC, you can call SetErrorMode() yourself.

::GetProcAddress()

Provided the DLL has been loaded properly, you will next need to find the addresses for the individual functions before you can use them. This can be done by calling ::GetProcAddress() with the handle returned by LoadLibrary() and the name of the function. This name should be the name of the function as it is exported from the DLL, as shown here:

```
HMODULE hMyDll;
UINT (*pfnMyFunc)(char* strMyName);

hMyDll = ::LoadLibrary("MyLib");
ASSERT(hMyDll != NULL);
pfnMyFunc = (UINT (*)(char*))::GetProcAddress(hMyDll, "MyFunc");
ASSERT(pfnMyFunc != NULL);

UINT nRc = (*pfnMyFunc)("Dave");
```

Alternatively, you may also reference the function by the ordinal number it is exported with:

```
pfnMyFunc = (UINT (*)(char*)) ::GetProcAddress(hMyDll, MAKEINTRESOURCE(42));
```

If the function is not found, GetProcAddress() returns NULL. If the function is found, this will return a generic pointer to a function. It is up to your application to make sure that the pointer you use is defined to point to a function with the same parameter list and return value as the function loaded from the DLL. In the previous example, MyFunc takes a char pointer and returns a UINT. If there is a mismatch in parameter lists, your stack will become corrupted when you make calls through the pointer. This will almost certainly kill your process.

FreeLibrary()

When your application is finished with a particular DLL, it may be unloaded from your process with a call to ::FreeLibrary().

Loading MFC Extension DLLs

If you are loading an MFC extension DLL, you should use `AfxLoadLibrary()` and `AfxFreeLibrary()` instead of `LoadLibrary()` and `FreeLibrary()`. These functions are almost identical to the Win32 API calls, but they will ensure that the MFC structures initialized by an extension DLL are not corrupted by multiple threads. You will see more about MFC extension DLLs later in this chapter.

Resource DLLs

You can also use dynamic loading to load a resource DLL, which MFC will then use to load the default resources for the application. To do this, you first make a call to `LoadLibrary()` to map the DLL into memory; then you call `AfxSetResourceHandle()` to let the framework know that it should get resources from the newly loaded DLL, rather than those linked with the process's executable file. This can be useful if you need to use different sets of resources, as in localization for different languages.

Creating Your Own DLLs

Now that you have seen how DLLs can be used in your application, let's look at how you can create your own. If you are developing real applications, you will most likely want to try to put functions common to more than one process into DLLs so that Windows can more efficiently manage the memory used.

The easiest way to get started with building a DLL project is to use AppWizard to create a new project for you. For simple DLLs, such as the ones you will see in this chapter, you should use the DLL project type. This will create a new project for you, with all the necessary project settings for building a DLL. You will then have to add your own source files to the project manually.

If you plan to use higher level MFC functionality, such as documents and views, or are creating an OLE automation server, the MFC AppWizard (`.dll`) project type will do some extra work for you. This project type will add the appropriate references to the MFC libraries and add source files to declare and implement a `CWinApp`-derived application object for your DLL.

> **TIP**
>
> It is often handy to first create a top-level project for a tester for your DLL and then create the DLL project as a subproject. This way, you can build the tester, and the DLL will be automatically built if necessary.

DllMain()

Most DLLs are simply a collection of loosely related functions that are exported for other applications to use. In addition to the exported functions that are used, every DLL includes a DllMain() function, which is used to initialize the DLL, as well as to clean up when the DLL is unloaded. This function replaces the LibMain and WEP functions used in previous versions of Windows. A sample skeleton for your DllMain() function may look something like this:

```
BOOL    WINAPI    DllMain (HANDLE hInst,
                           DWORD dwReason,
                           LPVOID lpReserved)
{
    switch (dwReason)
    {
        case DLL_PROCESS_ATTACH:
            // Do per-process initialization
            break;
        case DLL_THREAD_ATTACH:
            // Do per-thread initialization.
            break;
        case DLL_THREAD_DETACH:
            // Clean up any per-thread structures.
            break;
        case DLL_PROCESS_DETACH:
            // Clean up any per-process structures.
            break;
    } // end switch

    if(bAllWentWell)
        return TRUE;
    else
        return FALSE;
} // end DllMain()
```

Your DllMain() function may be called at several different times. The dwReason parameter will tell you why DllMain() was called, from one of the following values:

When a process first loads the DLL, DllMain() is called with a dwReason of DLL_PROCESS_ATTACH. Whenever this process then creates a new thread, DllMain() is called with DLL_THREAD_ATTACH. (This is not done for the first thread, because it will call with DLL_PROCESS_ATTACH.)

When the process is finished with the DLL, this function is called with dwReason of DLL_PROCESS_DETACH. When a thread of the process (other than the first thread) is destroyed, dwReason will be DLL_THREAD_DETACH.

Based on the value of dwReason, you should do any per-process or per-thread initialization and cleanup that your DLL requires, as shown in the previous example. In general, per-process initialization deals with setting up any resources that are shared by multiple threads, such as loading shared files or initializing libraries. Per-thread initialization should be used for setting up things that are unique to the thread, such as initializing thread local storage.

Your DLL may include resources that are separate from those in the calling application. If the functions in your DLL will be working with resources from the DLL, you will certainly want to save the `hInst` handle somewhere safe. This handle will be used in calls to load resources from the DLL.

The `lpReserved` pointer is reserved for use by Windows, so your application shouldn't muck with it. However, you may test the value of the pointer. If the DLL has been loaded dynamically, this will be `NULL`; static loads will pass a non-`NULL` pointer.

If all goes well in your `DllMain()`, it should return `TRUE`. If something goes wrong, you can return `FALSE` to abort the operation.

> **NOTE**
>
> If your code does not supply its own `DllMain()`, the compiler will add its own default version, which simply returns `TRUE`.

Exporting Functions from Your DLL

In order for applications to be able to use the functions in your DLL, each function must have an entry in the DLL's exports table. To get the compiler to add an entry to the exports table for a function, you have two options.

You may export functions in your DLL by using the `__declspec(dllexport)` modifier in front of all your function declarations. MFC also provides several macros that evaluate to `__declspec(dllexport)`, including `AFX_CLASS_EXPORT`, `AFX_DATA_EXPORT`, and `AFX_API_EXPORT`. In the current version of Visual C++, these are all the same, but they are provided to support future enhancements that may require different handling.

The `__declspec` method is not used as often as the second method, which involves module definition (`.def`) files and gives you more control of the export process.

Module Definition Files

The syntax of `.def` files in Visual C++ is pretty straightforward, particularly because most of the more complicated options used in earlier versions of Windows no longer apply under Win32. As you can see in the following simple example, the `.def` file gives a name and description for the library, then a list of the functions to be exported:

```
LIBRARY     "MYDLL"
DESCRIPTION 'MYDLL Example Dynamic Link Library'
```

```
EXPORTS
    MyInitialize
    MyCreate
    MyConnect        @3   NONAME
    MySend           @4
    MyReceive        @5
    MyDisconnect
```

You can specify an ordinal number to a function by adding it to the exports line for the function with an @. This ordinal can then be used in calls to GetProcAddress(). Actually, the compiler will assign ordinals to all exports, but the way this is done is somewhat unpredictable if you do not specify ordinals explicitly.

In addition, you will notice the NONAME option in the example. This tells the compiler not to include the name of the function in the export table of the DLL. In some cases, this can save a lot of space in the DLL file. Applications that use an import library to link to the DLL implicitly will not notice a difference, because implicit linking uses only ordinal numbers internally. However, applications that load the DLL dynamically will need to pass the ordinal number, rather than the function name, to GetProcAddress().

Exporting Classes

Creating a .def file to export even simple classes from your DLL can be a bit tricky. You will have to explicitly export every function that may be used by an outside application, including functions that you have not defined yourself.

If you take a look at the map file generated by code that implements a class, you may be surprised to see some of the functions listed there. These will include things such as implicit constructors and destructors or the functions that MFC declares in macros such as DECLARE_MESSAGE_MAP, as well as the functions that you implement yourself.

Although you can export each of these functions yourself, there is an easier way. If you use the AFX_CLASS_EXPORT modifier macro in the declaration of your class, the compiler will take care of exporting all necessary functions to allow applications to use the class contained in the DLL.

DLL Memory Issues

Unlike static libraries, which effectively become part of an application's code, dynamic link libraries in pre-Win32 versions of Windows handled memory a bit differently. Under Win16, DLL memory was kept outside a task's address space and provided the ability to share memory between tasks with the global memory in a shared DLL.

In Win32, the DLL's memory is mapped into memory space of the loading process. Each process gets its own copy of the "global" memory for the DLL, which is reinitialized when a new process loads the DLL. This means that the DLL cannot be used to share memory between processes in the same way that Win16 allows.

However, you can pull a few tricks with the DLL's data segment that will allow you to create a single section of memory that is shared for all processes that use the DLL.

Suppose you have an array of ints that you want to be used by all processes that loaded the DLL. This could be done with the following code:

```
#pragma data_seg(".myseg")
int sharedInts[10];
// Other shared variables
#pragma data_seg()
#pragma comment(lib, "msvcrt" "-section:.myseg,rws");
```

All variables declared between the data_seg pragmas will be allocated in the segment named .myseg. The comment pragma is not just a comment in the traditional sense; rather it tells the C runtime library to mark your new section as readable, writable, and shared.

Building the DLL

If you have created a project with AppWizard, and properly updated the .def file for your DLL, it should be all set to go. However, if you are creating your own make files, or otherwise building without AppWizard projects, you should specify the /DLL option to the linker. This will cause the linker to generate a DLL rather than a stand-alone executable.

> **NOTE**
>
> If you are using a .def file with the LIBRARY line in it, you do not need to explicitly declare the /DLL option to the linker.

If you are using MFC, there are also some special options that concern how your DLL will use MFC libraries. These are covered in the next section on MFC DLLs.

DLLs and MFC

You are by no means forced to use MFC in your DLLs, but there are several very important issues involved with using MFC in your DLL.

There are two levels at which your DLL can work with the MFC framework. The first of these levels is the regular MFC DLL, which can use MFC but may not pass pointers to MFC objects between the DLL and the application. The second level of MFC support is implemented in an MFC extension DLL. This class of DLL requires some extra work to set up, but will allow you to freely pass pointers to MFC objects between the DLL and the application.

Regular MFC DLLs

Regular MFC DLLs allow you to use MFC in your DLL, but they do not require that the calling application also use MFC. In regular DLLs, you can use MFC in any way you see fit, including deriving your own MFC-derived classes in the DLL and exporting them for use in applications.

However, a regular DLL cannot exchange pointers to MFC-derived classes with the application.

If you need to exchange pointers to MFC objects or classes derived from MFC classes, across the application-DLL boundary, you use the extension DLL shown in the next section.

The regular DLL replaces the USRDLL architecture used in previous implementations of MFC. (A regular DLL that links to MFC statically works the same as the obsolete USRDLL-type DLL.) The regular DLL is the architecture of choice for DLLs that will be used by other programming environments, such as Visual Basic or PowerBuilder.

To create a regular MFC DLL with AppWizard, create a new project with the MFC AppWizard (.dll) and choose one of the Regular DLL options in step 1 of 1. You may choose to link to the MFC libraries either statically or dynamically. If you want to change how your DLL links to MFC, you can do so with the combo box in the General page of the project settings dialog.

In previous versions of MFC, USRDLLs required special versions of the static MFC libraries. This is no longer true, so go ahead and use the standard MFC static libs. In addition, the USRDLL architecture would not allow you to link with the dynamic MFC libraries. This is not true of the regular DLL type—you are free to use the dynamic libraries for MFC.

Managing MFC State Information

Each module in an MFC process keeps its own state information. This means that your DLL will have different state information than the calling application. Because of this, any functions that you export that will be called directly by the application's code must tell MFC which state information to use. Before calling any MFC routines in your regular MFC DLL that uses the dynamic MFC libraries, you use the following line at the beginning of your exported functions:

```
AFX_MANAGE_STATE(AfxGetStaticModuleState());
```

This will set the correct state information for the duration of the function in which it is called.

MFC Extension DLLs

MFC allows you to create DLLs that will appear to applications as if they were just that— extensions to MFC, rather than a separate collection of functions. This sort of DLL can be used to create your own MFC-derived classes for applications to use.

To enable your DLL to freely pass pointers to MFC objects between the application and your DLL, you need to create an MFC extension DLL. These DLLs must link to the dynamic MFC libraries, as must any application that will use your MFC extension DLL. In older versions of MFC, this type of DLL was called an AFXDLL.

To create a new MFC extension DLL, it is easiest to start with the MFC AppWizard (.dll) and choose the MFC Extension DLL option in step 1. This will create the new project for you and set up all the proper project settings to create an MFC extension DLL. In addition, it will supply you with a DllMain() for your DLL that does some special processing required to initialize an extension DLL. You should also notice that this type of DLL does not and should not have a CWinApp derived object declared in it.

Initializing Extension DLLs

MFC extension DLLs require some special initialization to fit into the MFC framework. To see how this works, let's look at the DllMain() that is created by AppWizard for you:

```
static AFX_EXTENSION_MODULE MyExtDLL = { NULL, NULL };

extern "C" int APIENTRY
DllMain(HINSTANCE hInstance, DWORD dwReason, LPVOID lpReserved)
{
    if (dwReason == DLL_PROCESS_ATTACH)
    {
        TRACE0("MYEXT.DLL Initializing!\n");

        // Extension DLL one-time initialization
        AfxInitExtensionModule(MyExtDLL, hInstance);

        // Insert this DLL into the resource chain
        new CDynLinkLibrary(MyExtDLL);
    }
    else if (dwReason == DLL_PROCESS_DETACH)
    {
        TRACE0("MYEXT.DLL Terminating!\n");
    }
    return 1;    // ok
}
```

The most important part of this function is the call to AfxInitExtenstionModule(), which initializes your DLL to properly work in the MFC framework. It takes a handle to the DLL's instance, which is passed into DllMain(), and an AFX_EXTENSION_MODULE structure, which will hold information about your DLL for MFC's use.

You will not have to explicitly initialize your AFX_EXTENSION_MODULE structure, but you will need to make sure you declare one. The constructor for CDynLinkLibrary will initialize it for you. You must create a CDynLinkLibrary in your DLL—its constructor will initialize the AFX_EXTENSION_MODULE structure and add your DLL to the list of DLLs that MFC can work with.

Dynamic Loading of MFC Extension DLLs

Beginning with MFC 4.0, the framework supports dynamic loading and unloading of MFC DLLs, including your extensions. To make this work properly for your DLL, you should add a call to AfxTermExtensionModule() in your DllMain() when a process detaches. This function should be passed the AFX_EXTENSION_MODULE that was used earlier in the example. This functionality can be added by adding the following code to the DllMain() shown previously:

```
if(dwReason == DLL_PROCESS_DETACH)
{
    AfxTermExtensionModule(MyExtDll);
}
```

In addition, remember that your new DLL is now an extension DLL and should be dynamically loaded with the AfxLoadLibrary() and AfxFreeLibrary() calls rather than LoadLibrary() and FreeLibrary().

Exports from an Extension DLL

You need to export any functions or classes that you intend for applications to be able to access from your DLL. Although you could add all the mangled names to your DEF file manually, you can use modifiers for your class and function declarations provided by MFC for exporting from extension DLLs. These include AFX_EXT_CLASS and AFX_EXT_API, as shown here:

```
class AFX_EXT_CLASS CMyClass : public CObject
{
// Your class declaration
}

void AFX_EXT_API MyFunc();
```

Debugging DLLs

Debugging DLLs can be a bit different from debugging regular executables. This is mostly due to the fact that a DLL does not run on its own, but rather must be called by another application.

I mentioned briefly that it is convenient to create a project for a test application, then create a subproject of the test app for your DLL. This is a handy way to keep the projects in sync. To debug your DLL, you will need to add it to the Additional DLLs list in the Debug page of the test application's project settings. (If the DLL is not in the path, you should specify the complete pathname.) Then when you debug the test app, you can step into the DLL or set breakpoints or whatever you normally would do in the debugger.

Occasionally, you may find yourself developing a DLL that is called by another program for which you don't have access to a debug version or source code. To allow you to debug DLLs in these situations, you can specify an executable in the Executable for debug session box on the Debug page of the project settings for your DLL project. Then, when you choose Debug from the Build menu, this application will start up, although any breakpoints you set in the DLL will stop execution and allow you to use the debugger normally within your DLL.

Dumpbin.exe

If you are ever curious about the internals of an executable image, such as an EXE or DLL file, you may find the Dumpbin.exe tool to be quite useful. It is found in the \Msdev\Bin directory if it's not already in your path. Although this utility has several different options, allowing you to dump just about anything about an image that you would ever care to know, the most interesting options for DLLs are the /IMPORT and /EXPORT flags. /IMPORT will show you all the functions that the image will need to import and the files in which it expects to find them. On the other hand, the /EXPORT options will show you all the functions exported by an image and their ordinals.

Summary

In this chapter, you took a look at dynamic link libraries, how they are used, and how they can be created.

You saw how applications can link with import libraries to implicitly link to DLLs, as well as how to manage dynamic loading of DLLs at runtime with LoadLibrary() and GetProcAddress().

You also explored how to create your own DLLs, including how to create the projects, export functions with DEF files or __declspec(dllexport), and initialize them in DllMain().

In addition, you learned how to create MFC extension DLLs that can work directly within the framework of MFC, including the specifics of initializing and loading extension DLLs.

III

Programming with ActiveX

11

Overview of ActiveX

by Vincent W. Mayfield

Welcome to the exciting new world of ActiveX programming! But is ActiveX really new? Well, yes and no. You have probably heard a lot of media hype about ActiveX controls, VBScript, ActiveX documents, and other ActiveX themes. Through all the marketing fluff you are probably left wondering: What can ActiveX can do for me? More importantly, what are the foundations of ActiveX? What technologies does ActiveX include and how can I incorporate them in my applications using Visual C++ and MFC? These are some of the same questions I found myself asking when I returned from the Software Development 96 Conference in March 1996.

During a lecture I attended, someone suggested that ActiveX was nothing more than Internet-aware OLE controls. I started asking questions, and someone else informed me that ActiveX is nothing more than a sly marketing attempt to sell OLE under a different name. I was left perplexed and confused, because no one could give me a definitive answer about the internals and framework of ActiveX or even an explicit definition of what ActiveX is. I decided to find out for myself.

I found that ActiveX is composed of a group of technologies or components to develop and implement applications for the Internet. I soon understood why no one could give me a clear definition. At the core of these technologies is OLE. ActiveX is an extension of OLE technologies across the Internet, but is more than that; it also comprises a series of Internet and multimedia services that can be used to create rich Internet applications. To understand ActiveX, you first must understand OLE, so that's where this chapter's exploration of ActiveX begins.

Visual C++ has supported OLE since version 1.0 and MFC version 2.0. ActiveX support has been rather recent, with Visual C++ 4.1 and MFC 4.1. The support for ActiveX and OLE programming contained in Visual C++ and MFC versions 4.1, 4.2, and 4.2b has been modest, but full support was not available until Visual C++ and MFC 5.0. As you go through this chapter, you will explore the Visual C++ and MFC support for OLE and ActiveX programming. You will not be writing any code, however. The purpose of this chapter is to give you the foundation and fundamentals for Chapters 12–15. In this chapter, you first examine each component technology that makes up OLE. This will give you the foundation necessary to successfully design and build applications that use OLE and ActiveX technologies. Next, this chapter will dive into the ActiveX technologies, explaining how the OLE technologies relate to ActiveX and are an extension of OLE across the Internet. Lastly, you will investigate the new technologies in ActiveX and see what they can do for you. Keep in mind during your reading that OLE, ActiveX, and Internet programming are not easily mastered. The key to the deployment of these technologies in your applications is a thorough understanding of their concepts.

OLE History in a Nutshell

In 1991, Microsoft introduced a new specification called OLE 1.0. The acronym stood for *object linking and embedding*. OLE 1.0 was basically a way of handling compound documents. A *compound document* is a way of storing data in multiple formats—such as text, graphics, video, and sound—in a single document. At the time, *object-oriented* was the new programming buzzword, and the OLE 1.0 specification was a move to a more object-oriented paradigm. Furthermore, OLE 1.0 was an effort to move toward a more document-centric approach, instead of an applications-centric approach. Unfortunately, OLE 1.0 was coldly received by software developers. Very few independent software vendors (ISVs) and corporations raced to embrace OLE 1.0 and OLE-enabled applications. This reluctance to deploy OLE 1.0 in applications was due mainly to the fact that OLE 1.0 was very complex and had a steep learning curve. OLE 1.0 had to be coded using a very complex C API, which embodied programming concepts germane to OLE. These new concepts were foreign to most developers.

Fortunately, Microsoft continued to strive to improve OLE. In 1993, Microsoft released the OLE 2.0 specification, which encompassed more than just compound documents; it sported an entire architecture of object-based services that could be extended, customized, and enhanced. The foundation of this services architecture was the Component Object Model (COM). The services available through this architecture are

- COM
- Clipboard
- Drag-and-drop
- Embedding
- In-place activation
- Linking
- Monikers (persistent naming)
- OLE automation
- OLE controls
- OLE documents
- Structured storage
- Uniform Data Transfer (UDT)

From a programmatic view, OLE 2.0 is a series of services built on top of each other, as shown in Figure 11.1. These services form an architecture of interdependent building blocks built on the COM foundation.

The release of OLE 2.0 had such an impact on standard ways of computing that it received two prestigious industry awards: a Technical Excellence award from *PC Magazine* and the MVP award for software innovation from *PC/Computing*. Adding to the OLE 2.0 success was a new and improved programming interface. Developers could now move to OLE-enabled applications much more easily. The OLE 2.0 services incorporate many of the principles embodied in object-oriented programming: encapsulation, polymorphism, and an object-based architecture. Further adding to the success of OLE 2.0 was the release in February 1993 of Visual C++ 1.0 with the Microsoft Foundation Class (MFC) Library Version 2.0. MFC had wrapped the OLE API in a C++ class library, thus making it much easier for programmers to use the OLE services architecture.

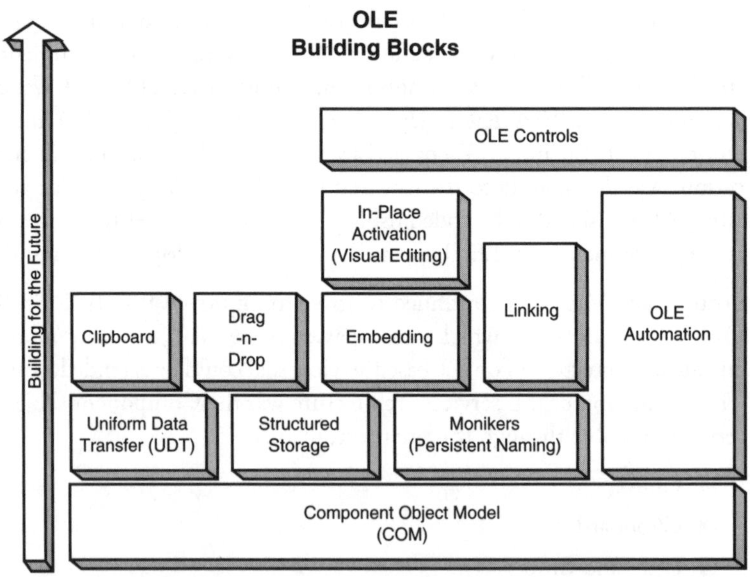

FIGURE 11.1.

The foundation of OLE is COM, with each successive service built on the technologies of the others.

OLE Building Blocks

Building for the Future

OLE Controls

In-Place Activation (Visual Editing)

Clipboard	Drag -n- Drop	Embedding	Linking	OLE Automation

Uniform Data Transfer (UDT)	Structured Storage	Monikers (Persistent Naming)

Component Object Model (COM)

NOTE

Don't let the ease of use of the MFC Library fool you. OLE programming is very difficult to master. However, I recommend that fledgling OLE and ActiveX programmers use MFC. MFC provides a framework to get you up and programming very quickly. Trying to program at the API level initially can lead to frustration and discouragement. If you do not know OLE, my advice is to learn the services, concepts, and standards using Visual C++ 5.0 and MFC, and then go back and understand the low-level C API. Understanding the services, their interfaces, and when to use them is the main key to OLE and ActiveX programming.

Today, OLE is no longer the acronym for object linking and embedding. That term is now obsolete. Microsoft refers to it as simply OLE, pronounced "O-lay." Notice that there is no version number attached to OLE any more. Because OLE is an extensible architecture, it can be enhanced and extended without changing its basic foundation. A testimonial to this capability is OLE controls. OLE controls were not part of the original release of OLE. They were not added to the available OLE services until almost a year after the original release. In fact, objects created with OLE 1.0 still work and interact with modern OLE applications. However, their functionality is limited to the original 1.0 specification, so there is no need for versions. From here on, this chapter will refer to OLE, unless specifically outlining a feature of OLE 1.0 or 2.0.

OLE from the Eyes of the End User

Although many software engineers forget it, the end user is the main reason for our existence as software developers. Because the end user is the main reason software is developed, this section will view OLE from the user's eyes. This will help you grasp the benefits and the available services of OLE and ActiveX. The end user's view is simple, less technical, and very understandable. I firmly believe that users decide in the first 10 minutes of using an application whether they like it. This sets the stage for all further experiences using that application. Therefore, an application's intuitiveness, appearance, ease of use, capability of performing work or entertainment, and performance are of paramount importance.

> **NOTE**
>
> Always keep in mind that the "devil-spawned end user," as the cartoon character Dilbert by Scott Adams would say, is the main reason for our existence as software engineers. The best software engineers never forget this and always tackle every programming endeavor with the end user in mind.

Microsoft, and Apple before it, knew that a large portion of the software had to have a human-to-machine interface. This is why Windows and the Macintosh each has a standard interface—not only from a user's perspective, but also from a programmer's perspective.

Users interact with OLE in three ways:

- OLE documents
- OLE automation
- OLE controls

Even though these are the ways that the end user sees OLE, all the other OLE services are part of these three in some way. For example, COM is a part of all three; linking and embedding are part of OLE documents.

As a computer professional, I am sure you have seen or worked with Microsoft Word or Excel. Microsoft Word is the classic example of an OLE document. This chapter is not going to outline the functionality of Word, but merely point out the features of OLE. However, do not be deceived; OLE documents are not always classic word processors. It is easy to think so because of the word *documents*. Think of an OLE document as a piece of Velcro. You have two pieces: the hook side (the document) and the pile side (the document container).

The first feature of OLE documents is a common user model. This simply means that the user interface (UI) features used to access OLE documents are similar from application to application. The common user model features document-centricity and takes advantage of OLE's integrated data capabilities.

NOTE

OLE user-interface–design guidelines are well documented in *The Windows Interface Guidelines for Software Design,* Microsoft Press, 1995.

One of these integrated data capabilities is called *linking and embedding*. Data objects of different types, created from other applications, can be embedded or linked into an application's OLE document. This enables the user to manipulate the object in the host application without returning to the creating application. The object is simply edited in place, hence the term *in-place editing*. The user interface is modified in the host application with menus, toolbars, and context menus from the application that created the object.

In Figure 11.2, take note of the two kinds of data—text and an embedded Visio drawing. Note also the toolbars and menu.

FIGURE 11.2.

A Microsoft Word document with embedded text and graphics.

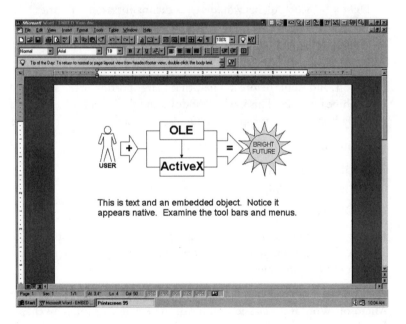

If you double-click the Visio drawing, the Word application changes, and new user interface objects are added to Word from Visio (see Figure 11.3). Notice that the Word user interface performs a metamorphosis and now has the Visio toolbars, floating dialog boxes, and menu items, as well as the Visio drawing and rulers. The user can then edit this drawing object without switching applications. In addition, these objects can be dragged and dropped between and within applications.

FIGURE 11.3.

A Microsoft Word document with the Visio drawing activated for in-place editing.

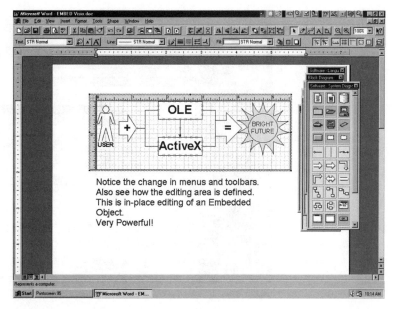

These features are implemented in the same way from application to application. Thus, there is a smaller learning curve for users when they get new applications, because the applications function similarly and have a common user model.

The next level of visibility to the user is OLE automation. OLE automation enables the user to access and modify objects through properties and methods, using a high-level language such as Visual Basic for Applications (VBA), VBScript, or JavaScript. This enables the user to customize objects and the interactivity between objects to perform operations the way the user defines. Microsoft Excel spreadsheets are the classic OLE automation objects. The user can create Excel spreadsheets that update a Microsoft Graph object or update information in a Microsoft Access or Borland Paradox database. The greatest part of OLE automation is that you do not have to be a programmer to take advantage of it. One example of this is demonstrated through VBA. Microsoft has made VBA easy to learn using a Macro Recorder (see Figure 11.4), which records your keystrokes in VB code, and an "object browser," which you use to paste the proper code where you need it. Anyone can learn to use it.

In addition to VBA, VBScript and JavaScript are available. Microsoft has been very kind to us and provided us with the ActiveX Control Pad for free. The ActiveX Control Pad (see Figure 11.5) is an easy way for nonprogrammers to embed ActiveX controls. These are OLE automation objects in Web pages, as you will see later, and you can programmatically manipulate them with VBScript or JavaScript. An example of this might be having a Calendar ActiveX control change the month when the user types in a new month.

FIGURE 11.4.
Microsoft Excel with the Macro Recorder invoked.

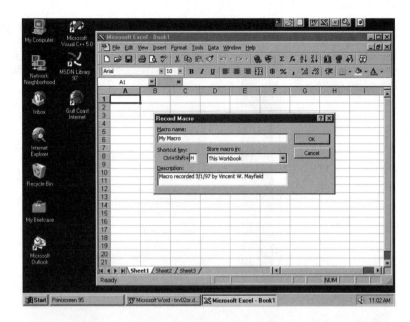

FIGURE 11.5.
The ActiveX Control Pad with VBScript editor.

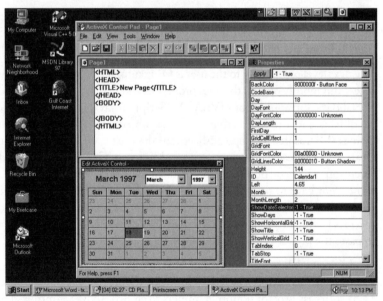

This leads us to OLE controls. OLE controls are the last area of OLE visibility to the end user. They are self-contained, reusable components that can be embedded in applications. To users, they are nothing more than a control that takes their input and passes it to the application that contains it. However, some OLE controls are static in nature, such as a picture control. OLE controls are also OLE automation objects that can have properties set at both compile time and runtime, and OLE controls also have methods that can perform certain operations. The difference between OLE controls and OLE automation objects is that OLE controls are self-contained objects.

They provide two-way communication between the control and the container. OLE controls have an even more special capability beyond simple OLE automation: They can respond and initiate events.

An example of a property might be the date value or the background color in the Microsoft Access Calendar control shown in Figure 11.6. A method might be a function that changes the date value or the background color. To clarify an event, the Calendar OLE control might have an event fired, when the user clicks a day, that lets the container know that a day has been clicked. These properties, methods, and events make OLE controls powerful. They give the programmer and the end user a cornucopia of functionality, as shown in Figure 11.6.

FIGURE 11.6.

Properties, methods, and events of the Microsoft Access Calendar control during development in the Visual C++ Developer Studio.

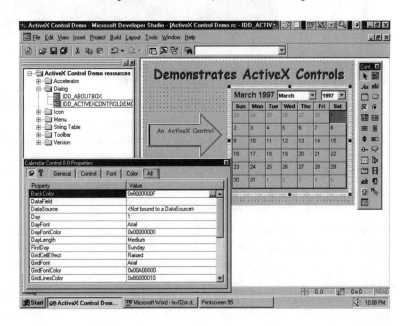

In future sections, you will discover that OLE controls have been extended to ActiveX controls that can be used across the Internet. These components have a very profound impact in the area of application development (see Figure 11.7), because they are prebuilt. From the end user's perspective, they provide increased functionality and lower software costs.

FIGURE 11.7.

Two OLE controls are embedded in an application. These controls come with Visual C++.

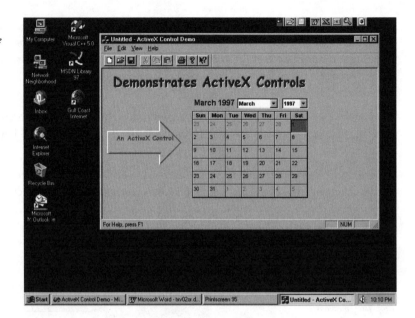

OLE from a Programmer's View

This section presents the OLE services from a programmatic view. For each service, you will be given a description of the technology and a programmer's view of the interfaces to these OLE services. In addition, you will learn the MFC classes that support each OLE service. Pay particular attention to understanding what each service does and where it fits into the architecture. The explanations highlight the interfaces to these objects and some key properties and methods where appropriate. Some of these services will be discussed in detail in later chapters as they pertain to and integrate into ActiveX.

Notice these are the same technologies the end user sees. However, the end user's view is a visual one, and the programmer's view is of a menagerie of interfaces that must be mastered to provide the slick visual representation the end user sees. These sections are intended to give you an overview of the OLE architecture and ActiveX. The specifics of implementation are left for later chapters. You are going to see, though, that Visual C++ and MFC do a lot of the work for you. The MFC implementation of OLE is a kinder, gentler implementation.

As discussed earlier, these services form building blocks on which each element in the architecture builds, as shown in Figure 11.8.

This architecture starts with the foundation, the Component Object Model.

FIGURE 11.8.

A programmatic view of OLE.

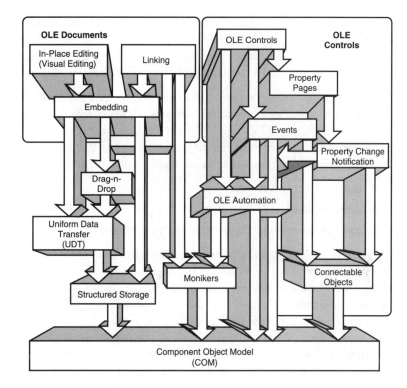

Component Object Model (COM)

When Microsoft designed OLE, it did so with object-oriented programming in mind. COM objects are much like instantiated C++ classes or an Ada package. In fact, COM was designed with C++ programmers in mind. It supports encapsulation, polymorphism, and reusability. However, COM was also designed to be compatible at the binary level and therefore has differences from a C++ object. As a programmer, you are aware that compiled programming languages such as C, C++, Pascal, and Ada are machine-dependent. As a binary object, a COM object concerns itself with how it interfaces with other objects. When not used in the environment of its creator, an interface is exposed that can be seen in the non-native environment. It can be seen because it is a binary object and therefore is not machine-dependent. This does not require the host environment or an interacting object to know anything about the COM object. When the object is created in the womb of its mother application, COM does not concern itself with how that object interacts within it. This interaction is between the mother application and the child object. When the object interacts with the rest of the world, however, COM is concerned about how to interface with that object. It is important to note that COM is not a programming language; it is a binary standard that enables software components to interact with each other as objects. COM is not specific to any particular programming language. COM can work with any language that can support the binary layout of a COM object. It is a programming model to facilitate the programmability of this standard.

COM objects consist of two types of items: *properties* and *methods.* Properties are the data members, and methods are member functions. COM objects have a common interface. No matter what they do, COM objects all have to implement the IUnknown interface. This interface is the main interface for all others and is the base class from which all other COM interfaces are derived. The IUnknown interface has the following member functions:

- ULONG AddRef(void)
- ULONG Release(void)
- HRESULT QueryInterface(REFIID id, void **ipv)

Each object implements a *vtable.* A vtable is nothing more than an array of pointers to member functions implemented in the object (see Figure 11.9). This vtable is shared between all the instances of the object also maintaining the private data of each object. A client application evokes an instance of the interface and gets a pointer to a pointer that points to the vtable. Each time a new interface to the object is instantiated, the reference count of objects is incremented with AddRef(). Conversely, each time a reference is destroyed, the reference counter is decremented with Release(). Once the reference count is zero, the object can be destroyed. In order to see what interfaces an object supports, you can use QueryInterface().

FIGURE 11.9.

This interface maps into a vtable.

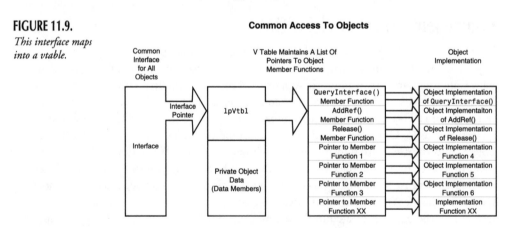

COM interfaces are never directly accessed. They are always accessed through a pointer. The QueryInterface(REFIID id, void **ipv) function takes a reference id and a void pointer. Notice the double indirection on the pointer: **ipv. The id is a 128-bit unique ID that identifies the interface you are retrieving. The ipv pointer is where the pointer to the interface you are trying to retrieve is stored. Consider this code fragment:

```
IAnyInterface* pAny = NULL;
if (pUnknown->QueryInterface(IID_IAnyInterface, (void**)&pAny) == NOERROR)
{
    pAny->DoAnyObjectWork();
    pAny->Release();
}
```

pUnknown is an interface pointer to the object's IUnknown. DoAnyObjectWork() is the member function you want to use to perform some work. You access that function through the pointer to that object's interface pAny.

Visual C++ and MFC encapsulate this IUnknown implementation through the use of *interface maps,* which are much the same as the message maps used to map the windows messages. It is a much easier implementation to understand. Visual C++ and MFC encapsulate much of the work involved in this through the wizards implemented in Visual C++ and the OLE classes implemented in the MFC Class Library. You will learn more about the Visual C++ and MFC implementations in Chapters 12–15.

So far, you have covered a general overview of COM. A more in-depth overview is necessary to really grasp COM. In fact, an entire chapter could be devoted to the subject. If you are interested in further reading, Appendix A, "Additional Resources," provides excellent references to help you further study this topic.

Structured Storage

Unfortunately, most platforms today have different file systems, making sharing data a very difficult task. In addition, these file systems arose during the mainframe days when only a single application was able to update and in some cases access that data at any one time. COM is built with interoperability and integration between applications on dissimilar platforms in mind. In order to accomplish this, COM needs to have multiple applications write data to the same file on the underlying file system. OLE Structured Storage addresses this need.

Structured Storage is a file system within a file. Think of it as a hierarchical tree of storages and streams. Within this tree, each node has only one parent, but each node may have from zero to many children. Think of it as like the Windows 95 Explorer. The folders are the storage nodes, and the files are the streams. Structured Storage provides an organization chart of data within a file, as seen in Figure 11.10. In addition, this organization of data is not limited to files, but includes memory and databases.

Stream objects contain data. This data can be either native data or data from other outside objects. Storage objects are compatible at the binary level; thus, in theory, they are compatible across OLE-compliant platforms. However, you know that there are minute differences between the various platforms. Notice in Figure 11.10 the tree of the Structured Storage object. The definition of the tree is dependent on how the object's creator defined the storage of the object.

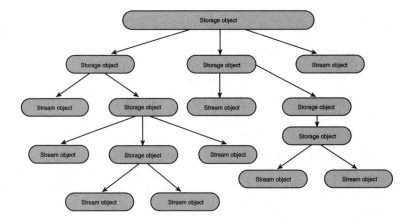

FIGURE 11.10.
Structured Storage is a hierarchical tree of storages and streams.

Structured Storage objects are manipulated using the following OLE interfaces:

■ IPersistStorage

■ IStorage

■ IStream

IStorage, as the name implies, manipulates storage objects and IStream manipulates streams. Rarely would you want to manipulate stream or storage objects individually. More than likely, you would want to manipulate the Persistent Storage object with the IPersistStorage. *Persistent Storage* is data that will continue to exist even after an object is destroyed—for example, if you want to allow the user to define the color of an object such as a text label, you would persistently store that object's foreground and background colors. The next time the object was created you could read in from Persistent Storage the colors previously chosen by the end user. You then could apply those attributes to the object and thus maintain the user's preferences. IPersistStorage enables you to do this by performing the following operations:

■ IsDirty

■ InitNew

■ Load

■ Save

■ SaveCompleted

■ HandsOffStorage

A great way to see what Structured Storage looks like is with a utility that comes with Visual C++ 5.x called Df View. Df View is in the \MSDEV\BIN directory of Visual C++. Df View enables you to look at a compound file also known as an OLE document. OLE documents implement Structured Storage. Figure 11.11 shows an example of Df View. (This is the Word document with an embedded Visio drawing object, shown in Figure 11.2.)

FIGURE 11.11.

Df View shows the hierarchical tree of a Structured Storage object.

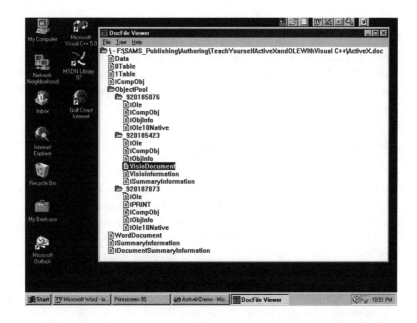

If you double-click a stream object, you can see its binary contents (see Figure 11.12).

FIGURE 11.12.

The binary contents of a stream object.

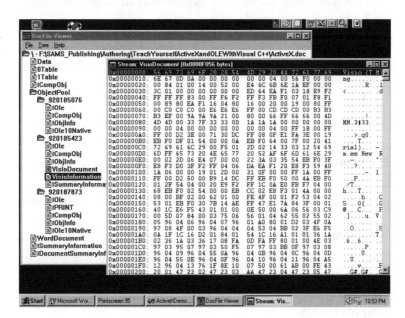

MFC provides an encapsulation of `IPersistStorage` and `IStorage` through an easy-to-use class called `COleDocument`. In addition, to aid in the manipulation of storages and streams, MFC provides `COleStreamFile`. OLE documents and their extension ActiveX documents will be covered in Chapter 12, "ActiveX Documents." It is important to note that compound documents in MFC are not only OLE documents and ActiveX documents, but any file type that represents the Structured Storage of data.

Monikers (Persistent Naming)

Monikers are a way of referencing a piece of data or object in an object-based system such as OLE. When an object is linked, a moniker is stored that knows how to get to that native data. For example, if you link a sound file into a Word document, the WAV file is not stored natively in that document. A moniker is created that can intelligently find the WAV file object. Think of a moniker as a map to where X marks the spot.

To use a moniker to locate and bind to an object, you must use the `IMoniker` interface and call `IMoniker::BindToObject`. By using the intelligent persistent name of that object, the `IMoniker` interface negotiates the location of that object and returns a pointer to the interface of that object's type. The moniker itself then dies. Think of it as similar to de-referencing a pointer in C or C++ to locate a piece of data. Remember that monikers are persistent. `IMoniker` is derived from `IPersistStream`, and thus it can serialize itself into a stream. This gives it persistence. There are five basic types of monikers:

- File monikers
- Item monikers
- Anti-monikers
- Pointer monikers
- Composite monikers

File Monikers

File monikers store a filename persistently. In binding the text filename to the file object, a pointer to the file object interface is returned so that you can manipulate that file object.

Item Monikers

Item monikers point to a specific place inside a file, such as a paragraph or a portion of an embedded video.

Anti-Monikers

Anti-monikers delete the last moniker in a series or chain of monikers, as in a composite moniker.

Pointer Monikers

Pointer monikers simply point to other monikers, wrapping them in a chain. However, it should be noted that pointer monikers are not persistent.

Composite Monikers

A composite moniker is an ordered collection of monikers. At the root of a composite moniker is a file moniker that references the document pathname. It then holds a series of item monikers. Composite monikers are used when you need to have a collection of monikers within a single object.

MFC Encapsulation of Monikers

In the previous section on Structured Storage, you learned that MFC has a class called COleStreamFile. The purpose of this class is to encapsulate the functionality of IStream to provide access to the streams of data in a compound file. Derived from COleStreamFile is CMonikerFile. CMonikerFile is a class that encapsulates the functionality of monikers provided in the IMoniker interface. This class gives the capability to gain access to IStreams named by IMoniker. It is important to note that this class does not encapsulate the entire IMoniker interface. It provides the capability to work with the streams of a compound file. So, if you wish to bind to storage or an object, you have to implement the IMoniker interface directly. This means you will not be able to use MFC directly to implement all the moniker types stated previously.

Uniform Data Transfer (UDT)

Through OLE, you can use Structured Storage to store your objects and monikers to find your objects, but there has to be a mechanism to move this data from the place it is stored (linked or embedded) to where you can output it to the client for manipulation. Uniform Data Transfer (UDT) does this and also notifies the data object and the client of changes in the data. UDT provides this service through the IDataObject interface and is used primarily in three areas:

- Clipboard
- OLE drag-and-drop
- Linking and embedding

Clipboard

The system Clipboard is a system-level service used for interprocess communications. Because it is a system-level service, all applications have access to it. OLE can use the Clipboard to do UDT of objects between processes. With an IDataObject pointer, you can use the function OleSetClipboard() to take a cut or copied object and expose this object to all processes through the Clipboard. Likewise, when you want to paste data from the Clipboard, you can use your

IDataObject pointer to use the OleGetClipboard() function. This is a very powerful mechanism because it maintains the integrity of the object as a whole, enabling you to move complex object data types between applications.

Visual C++ and MFC provide access to the Clipboard through the use of member functions in the classes CWnd and COleClientItem.

Drag-and-Drop

Drag-and-drop is a method by which the user can select and move objects within an application and between applications. UDT is used to perform drag-and-drop actions. On the selection of the object, the source application packages the object and uses an IDataObject pointer to call DoDragDrop(). The source uses the IDropSource interface, which yields a pointer to its implementation. This pointer is passed to DoDragDrop(). The source controls the mouse cursors and handles the object in case of a cancellation.

Once the user brings the dragged object to its new client location or target, the client application evokes the IDropTarget interface. With the pointer to the IDropTarget, the client application tracks the object in relation to itself with the functions available in the IDropTarget interface. One function called IDropTarget::Drop() is called when the object is dropped on the target. Drop() passes the IDataObject pointer of the source to the target. Now that the client has the IDataObject pointer, it is free to manipulate the object.

OLE drag-and-drop will be discussed in detail as it is implemented in Visual C++ and MFC in Chapters 12, "ActiveX Documents"; 13, "ActiveX Containers"; and 14, "ActiveX Servers." Drag-and-drop support is encapsulated in the following MFC classes:

- COleDropSource
- COleDropTarget
- COleClientItem
- COleServerItem
- COleDataSource

Embedding and Linking

A *linked* object is an object that is not stored within an OLE document, but rather outside the document. In the document, a moniker is stored that references the linked object. This OLE function uses UDT to move the data from the data object source to the container application so that the data can be rendered as appropriate. Linked objects are manipulated through the IOleLink interface. By linking an object instead of embedding it, you cut down on the size of the compound file. In addition, you expose the linked object so that multiple people can use it.

An *embedded* object is an object that is stored, through the OLE Structured Storage mechanism, as native data within an OLE document. Although this increases the size of the compound file, it provides a single file object that can contain multiple data types.

OLE Documents

OLE documents are nothing more than compound files that use Structured Storage to hold the objects that make up the document. These objects can be native data, or they can, through the use of monikers, link to data outside the document. In addition, an OLE document can contain objects created by other processes, embedded as if they were natively a part of the document. OLE documents are handled through interfaces just like any other OLE object. As you can see, OLE documents are a conglomeration of several OLE services. Here are some of the interfaces used to implement OLE document interfaces:

- `IOleItemContainer`
- `IPersistFile`
- `IClassFactory`
- `IOleInPlaceActiveFrame`
- `IOleInPlaceUIObject`
- `IOleInPlaceSite`

`COleDocument` encapsulates the functionality of OLE documents and ActiveX documents in MFC. However, it is important to note that there are a series of classes in MFC that are used together to provide this functionality. You will explore these classes in detail in later chapters.

In-Place Activation

OLE documents support *in-place activation,* or what is commonly referred to as "visual editing." This enables you to edit embedded objects in a container application as if they were native. When you activate visual editing in the container, the user interface of the container morphs to support selected user-interface functions of the server application that created the object. There are a whole series of interfaces that enable you to implement and support in-place activation. These interfaces all begin with `IOleInPlace`. Here are some of the interfaces you can use to implement and support in-place activation:

- `IOleInPlaceObject`
- `IOleInPlaceActiveObject`
- `IOleInPlaceSite`
- `IOleInPlaceActiveFrame`
- `IOleInPlaceUIObject`
- `IOleInPlaceSite`

OLE Automation

OLE automation allows you to manipulate the properties and methods of an application from within another application through the use of high-level macro languages and scripting languages such as VBScript and JavaScript. This enables you to customize objects and provide interoperability between applications.

In the world of OLE automation, there are OLE Automation Components and OLE automation controllers. An OLE Automation Component is a service that is exposed by an application for use by another. Microsoft Excel is a good example of this, because it exposes services that can create and manipulate worksheets, cells, and rows.

Services that are available through an OLE Automation Component are stored in a type library. A type library is stored in a binary file with a TLB extension. Object Description Language is used to define the services of an OLE Automation Component. Object Description Language instructions are stored in a file with the extension ODL. The ODL file is compiled into a type library. In Visual C++ 5.*x*, there is a nice utility that reads type libraries and graphically displays the services provided by OLE Automation Components.

The utility in Visual C++ is called OLE/COM Viewer application. Figure 11.13 shows the OLE/COM Viewer, which can be used to view OLE and COM objects graphically.

> **NOTE**
>
> The OLE/COM Viewer Application in Visual C++ is located in the \MSDEV\BIN\ directory; the filename is OLEVIEW.EXE. The OLE/COM Viewer is also available from Microsoft at the following Internet URL:
> http://www.microsoft.com/oledev/olecom/oleview.htm.

Notice that the Type Library Viewer screen shows the disassembled type library in Object Description Language (see Figure 11.14). It also displays the constants, properties, methods, and interfaces to the Automation Component.

OLE automation clients are applications that use the services provided by OLE automation controllers. OLE automation clients work through an interface called IDispatch. This dispatch interface exposes the available services to the controller application.

OLE Controls

As discussed previously, OLE controls are self-contained reuseable components that can be embedded in applications. OLE controls are also OLE automation objects that can have properties set at both compile time and runtime, and OLE controls also have methods that can perform certain operations. The difference between OLE controls and OLE automation objects is that OLE controls are self-contained objects.

FIGURE 11.13.

The OLE/COM Viewer that comes with Visual C++ 5.x.

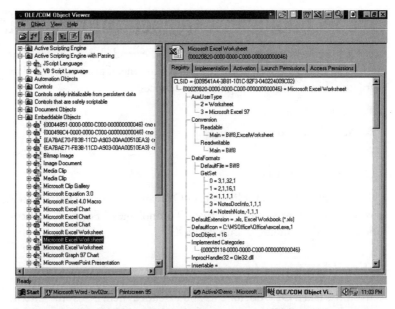

FIGURE 11.14.

The OLE/COM Viewer's function Type Library Viewer.

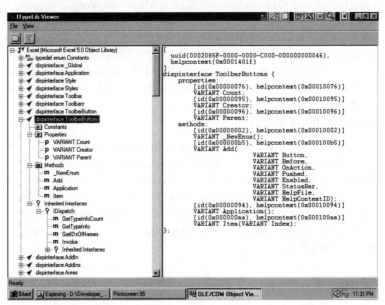

OLE controls provide two-way communication between the control and the container. These components have a very profound impact in the area of application development. These reusable self-contained pockets of functionality are discussed in detail in Chapter 15.

OLE Technologies Extended Through ActiveX

ActiveX has taken the OLE technologies and extended them beyond the bounds of the local machine to enterprise-wide networks and the Internet. Specifically, OLE technologies have been aggrandized into the following ActiveX services:

■ ActiveX documents

■ ActiveX controls

■ COM

■ Internet monikers

This is not the total effect. Elements of OLE are also present in the new ActiveX technologies, as you will see in the section, "ActiveX Technologies." For now, let's concentrate on the evolution of OLE technologies into ActiveX.

ActiveX Documents

ActiveX has taken OLE documents and extended them across the Internet. This technology is a way for existing OLE documents, such as Microsoft Word, Microsoft Project, and Microsoft PowerPoint, to be activated by a Web browser and brought up through a viewer. Thus, you can have compound files with various data that can contain linked and embedded objects being accessed across the World Wide Web (WWW). Using the ActiveX hyperlinks technology, you can extend OLE documents across the Web. ActiveX hyperlinks are discussed in the next section. In addition, ActiveX documents are discussed in depth in Chapter 12.

Asynchronous Storage

The capability to bring ActiveX documents across the WWW gives rise to another ActiveX technology, asynchronous storage. Basically, this extends Structured Storage across the Web, allowing for the storage to happen asynchronously. Obviously, with the slow bandwidth of the Internet, if you allowed a storage operation to happen synchronously, nothing else could happen on the client or server until the transfer of data to or from Persistent Storage took place. Using ActiveX hyperlinks and the technology of asynchronous monikers, asynchronous storage is accomplished.

ActiveX Controls

ActiveX controls are simply OLE controls or OCXs that have been extended to the Internet environment. Microsoft has now replaced the term *OLE control* with *ActiveX control*. Remember, OLE is an extendible architecture; therefore, these reusable components cannot be embedded only in a Web page, but also in a non–Internet-enabled application. ActiveX controls are covered in depth in Chapter 15.

ActiveX controls can be created in a variety of languages, including C, C++, Java, and, according to Microsoft, the next release of Visual Basic. They can also be manipulated though VBScript or JavaScript, so you do not even have to be a programmer to use them.

ActiveX controls are great components, because you have a virtual plethora of little pockets of prefabricated functionality you can take advantage of. The possibilities for ActiveX controls are endless. Currently, ActiveX controls range from a Calendar control to a Picture control, which enables you to display static pictures.

COM is at the base of the ActiveX control technology. ActiveX controls are built on a series of OLE services, with COM as the base. The following list depicts the technologies that are encompassed in the ActiveX control:

- Component object model
- Connectable objects
- Uniform Data Transfer (UDT)
- OLE documents
- Property pages
- Persistent storage
- OLE automation

ActiveX Control: COM

Like the OLE controls previously discussed, ActiveX controls are COM objects. They are in-process OLE automation servers activated from the inside out. Like every other COM object, they expose the IUnknown so that container applications can access their properties and methods through the pointers returned by the interface.

ActiveX Control: Connectable Objects

ActiveX controls support two-way communication from the control to the client application. This method of communication is called *connectable objects*. It enables the control to notify the client of events or invoke a method or event. It also enables the client to communicate directly with the control.

ActiveX Control: Uniform Data Transfer

Controls can be dragged and dropped within their client application if that functionality is enabled in the client application.

ActiveX Control: Compound Documents

In the beginning of this chapter, you saw how an object from another application could be embedded in a host application. In addition, that object could be activated in-place for visual editing. Likewise, OLE controls are built on the concept of OLE documents and can be activated in-place.

ActiveX Control: Property Pages

ActiveX controls have property pages, like their predecessor OLE controls, that expose their properties and methods to the user. From the property pages, the properties can be set.

ActiveX Control: OLE Automation

ActiveX controls are automation servers. Their properties and methods can be set at compile time through the use of property pages, and at runtime through VBScript and JavaScript.

ActiveX Control: Persistent Storage

COM objects can use Persistent Storage in a variety of ways. ActiveX controls use Persistent Storage to store their state. This enables the control to be initialized to the state it was when you last used it.

COM

As you learned previously, COM is a binary standard for objects. Basically, COM operates the way it did before ActiveX, except that COM has been extended so that you can exchange and use objects across the Internet. This has given rise to Distributed COM.

Distributed COM (DCOM)

Distributed COM, also known as DCOM and formerly known as Network OLE, is the basic extension of binary COM objects across LANs, WANs, and the Internet. Now you can instantiate and bind objects across a network.

Internet Monikers

With the advent of ActiveX and the extension of COM across the net, monikers were also extended and incorporated into this architecture. This gave rise to two new types of monikers:

■ URL monikers
■ Asynchronous monikers

URL Monikers

A *URL* is a *uniform resource locator,* used for Web-based addressing of objects. As you learned earlier, monikers are an intelligent naming system, so that by using the IMoniker interface to an moniker object and the intelligent name, you can locate the object. This capability was simply extended to include URLs because of the capability of passing objects across the Net from DCOM.

Asynchronous Monikers

Previously, monikers carried out their binding to the object synchronously. Nothing could happen until the binding was complete. On the high latency, slow-link communications network of the Internet, holding up operations while binding is accomplished is unacceptable. With asynchronous monikers, the interfaces to the object negotiate the transmission of the binding process to perform it asynchronously. Right now, URL monikers are the only implementation of asynchronous monikers.

ActiveX Technologies

ActiveX brings to the table some new technologies not necessarily related to OLE. However, these technologies facilitate the creation of interactive applications for the World Wide Web. These items are

■ ActiveX hyperlinks
■ ActiveX conferencing
■ ActiveX server extensions
■ Code signing
■ HTML extensions
■ ActiveMovie

ActiveX Hyperlinks

ActiveX hyperlinks basically allow in-place activation from HTML files of non-HTML–based documents. Using an ActiveX document container, you can access Microsoft Word, Microsoft Excel, Microsoft PowerPoint, Visio, and CorelDRAW! documents from a hypertext link in an HTML document.

ActiveX Conferencing

The ActiveX conferencing services are a suite of technologies that enable real-time, multiparty, multimedia communication over the Internet. This is much like video teleconferencing except you can do it on a PC. Just think what this does for programmers; we could all work at home and telecommute. This is a programmable interface opening up endless possibilities for innovation.

ActiveX Server Extensions

ActiveX server extensions, formerly known as the ISAPI Internet Server API, are used to give functionality to Internet servers. Previously, this could only be done using common gateway interface (GCI) code. ActiveX server extensions provide an alternative means of achieving this functionality. Usually, server extensions are implemented using a dynamic link library (DLL) and provide some functionality not provided by the HTTP server, such as connecting to a database.

ActiveX Scripts

ActiveX scripts bring OLE automation to the Internet. Automation controllers can now access Automation Component Services across the Internet with DCOM and ActiveX support for scripting. You can use a variety of scripting languages, such as VBScript, JavaScript, Perl, Visual Basic for Applications, Lisp, and Scheme.

Code Signing

Code signing is a new technology that enables electronic signatures for code. This provides security from tampering of interactive applications across the Net. Basically, the application vendors will provide a digital signature for their code that compiles with the code signing specification. On the client side, when an application or component is downloaded from the Net, it calls a Win32 API function called `WinVerifyTrust()`. This function checks the digital signature and verifies it.

HTML Extensions

Hypertext Markup Language (HTML) is the language for all Web-based document production. In order to support ActiveX controls and ActiveX scripts, extensions had to be made to the HTML language. In addition, Web browsers had to be modified to accommodate the new language extensions. Now you can add ActiveX controls to Web pages using the HTML `<OBJECT>` tag.

ActiveMovie

ActiveMovie is a new technology to replace the old Media Control Interface and Video for Windows. ActiveMovie is an audio- and video-streaming framework. With ActiveMovie, you will be able to play back MPEG, AVI, and Apple QuickTime movies.

Summary

This chapter discusses OLE, ActiveX, and the component architecture that makes up OLE. Because OLE is an object-oriented architecture founded on the COM, it is an extendible services architecture. Each OLE component is a building block for the rest of the technologies. Microsoft has extended this architecture to ActiveX to facilitate the creation of Internet-enabled applications. ActiveX builds on OLE and COM and adds new technologies of its own. ActiveX controls are Internet-aware controls that are nothing more than an extension of the OLE control architecture; they make it easy to extend the use of reusable components on the Internet.

12

ActiveX Documents

by Mark R. Wrenn

ActiveX documents are COM software components that present data and information to the user. ActiveX documents allow the user to view data in a variety of ways, perhaps as a graph, a spreadsheet, or text, depending on the purpose of the application. An ActiveX document cannot work alone, but always requires an environment in which to work. The environment is called an ActiveX container. Together, through an agreed-upon set of rules, the ActiveX container and ActiveX document work as one, and give the user the appearance of a single, homogeneous application.

If you look at an ActiveX document running inside an ActiveX container, you can visually identify each component. The ActiveX document occupies the client area of the container and negotiates with the container for menu and toolbar space. The ActiveX container is the frame that surrounds the client area. It shares its menu space and toolbar space with the document. Together, they appear as a single application—but in fact, they are separate pieces of software that work together cooperatively. The only reason they work together is because each follows a well-documented set of rules or COM interfaces. COM is the foundation of all of the OLE and ActiveX technologies. This chapter requires at least an architectural understanding of COM and will look at some of the COM interfaces involved in writing an ActiveX document, but certainly not all of the COM interfaces available. It is well worth your time to review COM and understand it. This chapter will help clarify and solidify your understanding of how ActiveX documents work.

In addition to exploring the COM interfaces required to create an ActiveX document, this chapter examines what has changed between OLE compound documents and ActiveX documents, what MFC classes have been added, and how the Active Template Library can be used to build an ActiveX document. In passing, this chapter mentions ActiveX containers. For more information about ActiveX containers, refer to Chapter 13, "ActiveX Containers."

Just What Is an ActiveX Document?

You might have heard quite a bit of commotion about ActiveX. Some say that ActiveX is nothing more than another name for OLE. Some say that ActiveX is the name for a new set of Internet technologies. The truth lies in a combination of the two. ActiveX is really an evolution of the Microsoft OLE strategy. It includes some new COM interfaces working together with existing OLE COM interfaces. It also includes some new technologies, such as ActiveX server extensions, ActiveX Server Pages, and ActiveVRML.

ActiveX documents fall into the first category—an evolution of OLE interfaces to support the needs of the Internet. In particular, ActiveX documents are OLE embedded documents with the addition of four new COM interfaces: `IOleDocument`, `IOleDocumentView`, `IOleCommandTarget`, and `IPrint`. These new interfaces allow for a significant difference between OLE embedded documents and ActiveX documents: ActiveX documents occupy the entire client area of an ActiveX container, whereas OLE embedded documents occupy a small, well-defined area. This was added so that users browsing the Web with a tool such as the Internet Explorer could click a hyperlink on a Web page and link directly to a Microsoft Word document, Microsoft Excel spreadsheet, or another application. To the user, it appears as though the application data is just another Web page with perhaps more menu items and toolbars. This provides the user with a positive and rich Internet experience.

ActiveX documents first appeared with the release of Microsoft Office 95. Microsoft Office Binder is an ActiveX container, and Microsoft Word and the other Office applications are ActiveX documents. In fact, it is quite interesting to notice the following in the Visual C++ header DOCOBJ.H:

```
#define IMsoDocument            IOleDocument
#define IMsoView                IOleDocumentView
```

Clearly, the IOleDocument and IOleDocumentView interfaces began life as Microsoft Office (Mso) interfaces. It should also be noted that ActiveX documents were originally referred to as DocObjects. You will notice API calls and interfaces that reference this name—for example, the new MFC class CDocObjectServer.

Let's look a little more closely at the four new COM interfaces:

■ IOleDocument is one of the new required interfaces. It allows the container to determine various attributes about the document, to enumerate the views that are supported, and to create specific views.

■ IOleDocumentView is another required new interface. It is the interface that the container uses to communicate with the view. Each view must support this interface in addition to existing OLE interfaces such as IOleInPlaceObject and IOleInPlaceActiveObject.

■ IOleCommandTarget is an optional interface. It allows the container to route commands, that it doesn't handle, to the document. The container also exposes this interface and allows the document to route commands to the container.

■ IPrint is an optional interface. It allows the container to print the contents of the document and to specify to the document what to print and how to print it. This interface works in conjunction with IContinueCallback that the container exposes. IContinueCallback allows the document to inform the container on printing status and allows the container to cancel the printing that is in progress.

What Is New in MFC?

There are two new MFC classes that encapsulate the new ActiveX document interfaces. They are CDocObjectServer and CDocObjectServerItem. CDocObjectServer supports the IOleDocument, IOleDocumentView, IOleCommandTarget, and IPrint interfaces. It is similar to what COleDocument does and replaces this class when you want to support ActiveX documents. CDocObjectServerItem supports OLE server verbs required for ActiveX documents. It derives from `COleServerItem` and overrides `OnHide`, `OnOpen`, and `OnShow` to implement ActiveX document support. It replaces `COleServerItem` when you want to support ActiveX documents.

Some Details about ActiveX Documents

ActiveX documents are the next step in the OLE evolution. They are built upon the foundation of OLE linked and embedded servers. In fact, an ActiveX document can choose to behave like an OLE linked or embedded document if the implementer chooses. Microsoft Word is a good example of this behavior. If you start Microsoft Excel, choose Insert Object, and insert Word into the spreadsheet, it will behave like an embedded document server, as shown in Figure 12.1.

FIGURE 12.1.

Microsoft Word as an embedded document inside Microsoft Excel.

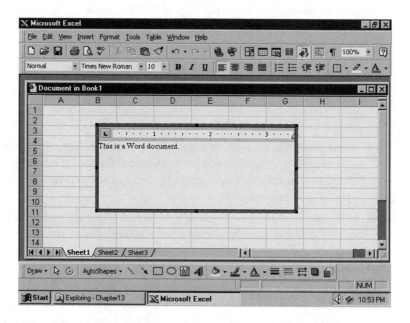

If you start Microsoft Binder and add a Word document to the Binder container, it will behave like an ActiveX document. To determine whether a container supports the ActiveX document specification, it can be queried for support of the `IOleDocumentSite` interface. If the container supports this interface, the Document server can behave like an ActiveX document; otherwise, it should behave like an OLE linked or embedded document.

Because ActiveX documents have an OLE heritage, this chapter will spend some time discussing what it means to be an OLE linked or embedded Document server. OLE Document servers can be thought about in two ways: as in-process servers or local servers and as mini-servers or full servers. These are two separate issues to think about and can be combined as follows: An in-process server can be a mini-server (usually) or a full server (with some care). A local server can be a mini-server (not very often) or a full server (usually). Each of these issues is discussed below.

An in-process server is essentially a DLL. It means that the OLE Document server runs in the same address space as the container. Calls to the various OLE COM interfaces are no different than any other function calls within the container application. There is no additional overhead when you call the OLE Document server. For this reason, in-process servers are the most efficient and perform the best.

A local server is essentially an EXE. In this case, the OLE Document server runs in another address space. Calls to the various OLE COM interfaces require special handling, called *marshalling*. Marshalling is the name for taking all the parameters to an OLE call, flattening them out, sending them over the process boundary, reassembling them on the other side, and calling the OLE interface in the servers address space. As you might imagine, this can be a rather tricky exercise. If you are passing a LONG as a parameter, it is fairly simple to move the data to another process. However, if you are moving a FOOBAR* to another address space, how do you move the data successfully so that the OLE server in another address space can reference it? Fortunately, most of this is handled automatically by OLE. OLE uses the IDL definitions to figure out how to marshall arguments—and, in fact, creates the necessary code to do all the work. The downside to this is that it is more expensive to make OLE calls using this technique as a result of all the marshalling that takes place.

A mini-server is an OLE Document server that only supports embedding. It can not be run stand-alone, and depends on the container for its user interface and storage capabilities. A mini-server is typically implemented as an in-process server. Although there is no reason to create a mini-server as an EXE, because it is not meant to run stand-alone, it is certainly possible to do so.

A full server is an OLE Document server that supports linking and embedding, and can be run as a stand-alone application. A full server is typically implemented as a local server. It is possible to write a full server as a DLL, but this would require another shell to load the DLL in stand-alone mode.

ActiveX documents are typically full servers. It is recommended that they run as stand-alone applications as well as ActiveX Document servers. If you create a new MFC OLE application, you will notice that on the page OLE support is specified you can add ActiveX document support only if the application is a full server, as shown in Figure 12.2. It is possible to write an ActiveX Document server as an in-process server.

FIGURE 12.2.

MFC AppWizard dialog for creating an ActiveX document.

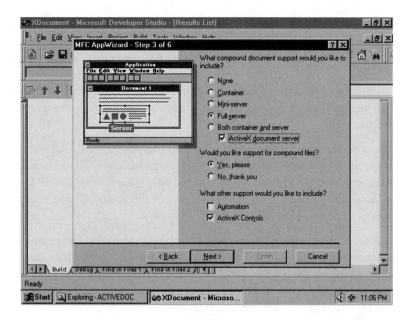

OLE Document servers support linking, embedding, and in-place activation. Not all servers have to support these features. ActiveX documents are both embedded and always in-place active. They do not support linking; so this chapter won't spend any time discussing OLE linking issues.

An embedded OLE document lives within a part of a container and often exists with native container data, as well as other embedded documents. It can be activated by double-clicking or selecting Open from a context menu. OLE 1 specified that when an embedded document was opened that the native application would start and the user could edit the document using the native tool. Figure 12.3 illustrates an embedded document opened in its own native application.

OLE 2 specified that it was also possible to open the embedded document right within the context of the container. This is called in-place activation. ActiveX documents are always in-place active. In addition, they are the only embedded document in the container, and they occupy the entire client area.

OLE and ActiveX Document servers also have to support menu merging. When an OLE document is in-place active, it is given the opportunity to merge any menus that it has with the container's menu. This merging of menus is well-defined. OLE containers own and manage the File, Container, and Window menus. OLE documents own and manage the Edit, Object, and Help menus. ActiveX documents must do some additional Help menu merging.

FIGURE 12.3.

Microsoft Word opened from Excel as a separate application.

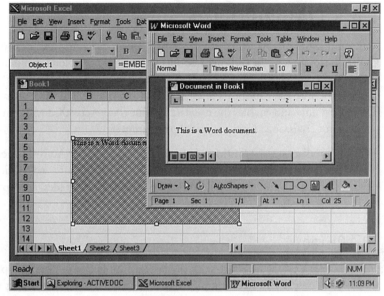

Drag-and-drop is optionally supported by OLE Document servers. OLE drag-and-drop works through the use of the IDataObject, IDropSource, and IDropTarget. IDropSource and IDropTarget are used to track mouse movements and show appropriate user feedback. Ultimately, the target of a drop operation obtains the IDataObject pointer from the IDropTarget interface, and using Uniform Data Transfer can obtain and manipulate the data through the IDataObject methods. The OLE Clipboard is also manipulated through the IDataObject methods.

OLE provides a means by which data from an OLE Document server can be saved with data from the container and other OLE Document servers into a single file. This technology is called *structured storage.* Through the use of the IPersistStorage, IStorage, and IStream interfaces, servers can store their data into a section of a single file. Structured storage makes a single file behave as if it were a file system, complete with hierarchical directories.

New to ActiveX documents is the concept of *programmatic printing.* With the OLE document architecture, it was up to the container to print out its own data. A container can contain several embedded documents, none of which knows anything about the environment in which it is displayed—much less about other embedded documents that are also in the same container environment. So, it would be impossible for an embedded document to control any aspect of printing. Only the container knows enough to control the printing. ActiveX documents change this. Because the document occupies the entire client area, it knows about all the data and can have full control over how the data is printed. ActiveX documents and containers do this through the use of the new IPrint and IContinueCallback interfaces.

The COM Interfaces

ActiveX documents, like their predecessor OLE documents, are built on the foundation of COM. Through a set of well-defined interfaces, it is possible to build an ActiveX document that can operate within any ActiveX container, without knowing anything more about the container than that it supports a set of COM interfaces. This architecture allows for a great deal of flexibility and enables the user to combine these ActiveX document components in ways perhaps not envisioned by the original programmers.

This section discusses 10 COM interfaces that make up the ActiveX document specification. Six of these interfaces are part of the original OLE document specification. Four of them are new to ActiveX. Two of the new ActiveX COM interfaces are optional: `IPrint` and `IOleCommandTarget`.

IOleObject

`IOleObject` is a COM interface with the largest number of methods. It provides the main interface for a container to communicate with an embedded object and is required if an object wants to support embedding. Table 12.1 describes the `IOleObject` interfaces.

Table 12.1. `IOleObject` interfaces.

Interface name	Description
`IUnknown` methods	
QueryInterface	Discovers required interfaces
AddRef	Adds a reference count to the object
Release	Decrements the reference count for the object and eventually deletes the object
`IOleObject` methods	
SetClientSite	Provides a pointer to the container's client site object
GetClientSite	Obtains the pointer to the container's client site object
SetHostNames	Provides the names of the container application and container document
Close	Changes the state of the object from running to loaded
SetMoniker	Allows the container to tell the object about its moniker

Interface name	Description
GetMoniker	Obtains the object's moniker
InitFromData	Allows the object to initialize itself from an IDataObject interface
GetClipboardData	Obtains a current copy of the object in the form of an IDataObject interface
DoVerb	Requests an object to perform one of its actions
EnumVerbs	Enumerates the actions that an object supports
Update	Updates linked objects
IsUpToDate	Requests the object to check if it is up-to-date
GetUserClassID	Returns the object's CLSID
GetUserType	Returns the object's displayable name
SetExtent	Allows the container to tell the object how much display space it has
GetExtent	Obtains the size of the object's display area
Advise	Creates a connection between the container and the document
Unadvise	Removes the connection between the container and the document
EnumAdvise	Enumerates the Advise connections
GetMiscStatus	Returns the status of the object
SetColorScheme	Tells the object what color scheme to use

IDataObject

IDataObject is the means by which data is transferred between OLE objects. This technology is called Uniform Data Transfer. With IDataObject, data can be transferred using a particular format over a specific storage medium. It is also possible to advise others of changed data. Table 12.2 describes the IDataObject interfaces.

Table 12.2. IDataObject interfaces.

Interface name	Description
IUnknown *methods*	
QueryInterface	Discovers required interfaces
AddRef	Adds a reference count to the object
Release	Decrements the reference count for the object and eventually deletes the object
IDataObject *methods*	
GetData	Causes the source data object to render its data as described in a FORMATETC structure and transfers it through the STGMEDIUM structure
GetDataHere	Similar to GetData except that it uses the storage structure allocated by the caller
QueryGetData	Asks the source data object if it is capable of rendering its data as described in the FORMATETC structure
GetCanonicalFormatEtc	Returns a canonical FORMATETC based on an input FORMATETC
SetData	Sets the data of the object according to the FORMATETC and STGMEDIUM structures
EnumFormatEtc	Allows the caller to enumerate the data formats supported by the object
DAdvise	Allows the caller to be notified when data changes
DUnadvise	Removes a notification of data change
EnumDAdvise	Allows the caller to enumerate the advisory connection that has been set up

IPersistStorage

IPersistStorage provides a means for a container to pass a storage interface to an embedded object. The IPersistStorage interface makes use of structured storage and allows object data to be stored in its own area within the structured storage. Table 12.3 describes the IPersistStorage interfaces.

Table 12.3. IPersistStorage interfaces.

Interface name	Description
IUnknown *methods*	
QueryInterface	Discovers required interfaces
AddRef	Adds a reference count to the object
Release	Decrements the reference count for the object and eventually deletes the object
IPersist *method*	
GetClassID	Returns the CLSID
IPersistStorage *methods*	
IsDirty	Allows the caller to determine whether the object has changed since it was last saved
InitNew	Initializes a new storage object and provides it with an IStorage interface
Load	Loads an object from storage
Save	Saves an object to storage
SaveCompleted	Notifies the object that it can write to its storage
HandsOffStorage	Notifies the object to release all storage objects

IPersistFile

IPersistFile provides an interface that allows the object to store itself on the file system rather than in a structured storage object. Table 12.4 describes the IPersistFile interfaces.

Table 12.4. IPersistFile interfaces.

Interface name	Description
IUnknown *methods*	
QueryInterface	Discovers required interfaces
AddRef	Adds a reference count to the object
Release	Decrements the reference count for the object and eventually deletes the object

continues

Table 12.4. continued

Interface name	Description
IPersist method	
GetClassID	Returns the CLSID
IPersistFile methods	
IsDirty	Allows the caller to determine whether the object has changed since it was last saved
Load	Loads an object from the specified file
Save	Saves the object to the specified file
SaveCompleted	Tells the object that the container has finished saving its data
GetCurFile	Obtains the name of the current file

IOleDocument

IOleDocument is one of the new COM interfaces that supports ActiveX documents. It allows the container to discover what kind of views are supported by the document and to obtain pointers to those view interfaces. Table 12.5 describes the IOleDocument interfaces.

Table 12.5. IOleDocument interfaces.

Interface name	Description
IUnknown methods	
QueryInterface	Discovers required interfaces
AddRef	Adds a reference count to the object
Release	Decrements the reference count for the object and eventually deletes the object
IOleDocument methods	
CreateView	Allows the container to request a view object from the document
GetDocMiscStatus	Returns miscellaneous status information about the document
EnumViews	Enumerates views that are supported by the document

IOleInPlaceObject

`IOleInPlaceObject` allows a container to activate and deactivate an in-place active object. It also allows the container the opportunity to set the viewable area of the embedded object. Table 12.6 describes the `IOleInPlaceObject` interfaces.

Table 12.6. `IOleInPlaceObject` interfaces.

Interface name	Description
`IUnknown` *methods*	
QueryInterface	Discovers required interfaces
AddRef	Adds a reference count to the object
Release	Decrements the reference count for the object and eventually deletes the object
`IOleWindow` *methods*	
GetWindow	Obtains a window handle
ContextSensitiveHelp	Determines whether context-sensitive help should be enabled
`IOleInPlaceObject` *methods*	
InPlaceDeactivate	Deactivates an in-place active object
UIDeactivate	Deactivates and removes the user interface of the active object
SetObjectRects	Indicates how much of the object is visible
ReactivateAndUndo	Reactivates the previously deactivated object

IOleInPlaceActiveObject

`IOleInPlaceActiveObject` provides a means for the embedded object to communicate with the container's frame and the container's document window. Table 12.7 describes the `IOleInPlaceActiveObject` interfaces.

Table 12.7. `IOleInPlaceActiveObject` interfaces.

Interface name	Description
`IUnknown` *methods*	
QueryInterface	Discovers required interfaces
AddRef	Adds a reference count to the object

continues

Table 12.7. continued

Interface name	Description
Release	Decrements the reference count for the object and eventually deletes the object
	IOleWindow *methods*
GetWindow	Obtains a window handle
ContextSensitiveHelp	Determines whether context-sensitive help should be enabled
	IOleInPlaceActiveObject *methods*
TranslateAccelerator	Processes accelerator keys
OnFrameWindowActivate	Notifies the object when the container's top-level frame is activated
OnDocWindowActivate	Notifies the object when the container's document window is activated
ResizeBorder	Tells the object that it needs to resize its border space
EnableModeless	Enables or disables modeless dialog boxes

IOleDocumentView

IOleDocumentView is another new COM interface that supports ActiveX documents. It provides the means for a container to communicate with each of the active document views. Table 12.8 describes the IOleDocumentView interfaces.

Table 12.8. IOleDocumentView interfaces.

Interface name	Description
	IUnknown *methods*
QueryInterface	Discovers required interfaces
AddRef	Adds a reference count to the object
Release	Decrements the reference count for the object and eventually deletes the object
	IOleDocumentView *methods*
SetInPlaceSite	Gives the document a pointer to the container's view site
GetInPlaceSite	Gets the pointer to the document's view site

Interface name	Description
GetDocument	Gets the IUnknown pointer of the document
SetRect	Sets the rectangular coordinates of the view port
GetRect	Gets the rectangular coordinates of the view port
SetRectComplex	Sets the rectangular coordinates of the view port, scroll bars, and size box
Show	Asks the view to activate or deactivate itself
UIActivate	Asks the view to activate or deactivate its user interface
Open	Asks the view to open up in a separate window
Close	Asks the view to close itself
SaveViewState	Asks the view to save its state
ApplyViewState	Asks the view to initialize itself to a previously saved state
Clone	Asks the view to create a duplicate of itself

IPrint

IPrint is another new (and optional) ActiveX document COM interface. It allows the container to communicate printing information to the document. Table 12.9 describes the IPrint interface.

Table 12.9. IPrint interfaces.

Interface name	Description
	IUnknown *methods*
QueryInterface	Discovers required interfaces
AddRef	Adds a reference count to the object
Release	Decrements the reference count for the object and eventually deletes the object
	IPrint *methods*
SetInitialPageNum	Sets the page number of the first page

continues

Table 12.9. continued

Interface name	Description
GetPageInfo	Gets the page number of the first page and the total number of pages
Print	Asks the document to print itself

IOleCommandTarget

IOleCommandTarget is another new (and optional) ActiveX document COM interface. It provides a way for the container to pass on commands that it doesn't handle to the document. The reverse is also true; it provides a way for the document to pass on commands to the container. Table 12.10 describes the IOleCommandTarget interfaces.

Table 12.10. IOleCommandTarget interfaces.

Interface name	Description
IUnknown methods	
QueryInterface	Discovers required interfaces
AddRef	Adds a reference count to the object
Release	Decrements the reference count for the object and eventually deletes the object
IOleCommandTarget methods	
QueryStatus	Asks the object for status of one or more commands
Exec	Asks the object to execute a command

The Active Template Library

The Active Template Library (ATL) is a recent addition to the Visual C++ product. It came about primarily as a result of the explosive growth of the Internet and the Microsoft ActiveX strategy. The Microsoft ActiveX strategy is to create dynamic Web pages through the use of various ActiveX controls. In order for these controls to make sense in today's 28.8Kbit Internet market, the controls have to be small and compact so that they can be downloaded from Web servers quickly. To build these controls with MFC is certainly possible, but MFC applications are characteristically large and require large support DLLs. Another alternative to MFC was needed that could create smaller controls, without the need for support DLLs. The Active Template Library is the alternative that Microsoft has provided.

ATL and MFC differ in their approaches. Both libraries rely on C++ capabilities, but that is where their similarities end. MFC is build upon the concept of a class hierarchy. Most of the MFC classes derive from other classes, which eventually derive from CObject. This allows classes to inherit a lot of behaviors from their ancestors. As an example, consider the CButton class. It implements a handful of new methods but inherits a tremendous amount of behavior from the CWnd class. CWnd, in turn, inherits from CCmdTarget, which, inherits from CObject. A strategy like this has a few interesting characteristics:

■ The class hierarchy tends to get deep and therefore requires a lot of study to grasp.

■ Application behavior is accomplished by inheriting from certain classes and overriding methods. This creates a white box effect and again requires a lot of study to understand how to integrate changes into any new derived classes.

■ After the learning curve has been overcome, it is possible to quickly implement applications because so much behavior can be inherited.

> **NOTE**
>
> *White box* is an object-oriented design term that means you are able to see, and many times are required to see, the details of method implementations of classes that you inherit from. For example, if you wanted to override the Add() methods of a linked list class, you would most likely have to know how the linked list class implemented its internal structures in order for you to override the Add() method.
>
> *Black box* is just the opposite. The classes you use are completely opaque to you. You don't know how they are implemented and are able to manipulate the class only through its well-defined interfaces. COM interfaces fall into this category. COM exposes interfaces only and does not expose any internal implementation details.

ATL takes a different approach. It is based on the concept of a template. A template is a way of capturing an algorithm in the form of a pattern. For example, if you had a mathematical formula such as x + y + z that you wanted to implement for integers and for floating-point numbers, you could create two classes:

```
class HighTechInteger
{
public:
    HighTechInteger();
    ~HighTechInteger();
    integer Calculate( int x, int y, int z ) { return( x+y+z ); }
};
```

```
class HighTechFloat
{
public:
   HighTechFloat();
   ~HighTechFloat();
   float Calculate( float x, float y, float z ) { return( x+y+z ); }
};
```

Notice how both implementations have identical algorithms for their `Calculate` methods. Given these classes, however, you could never use the `HighTechInteger` class to handle floating-point numbers. You must maintain two separate classes. This creates opportunities for bugs to be introduced if both classes are not kept in sync. The alternative is to create a template:

```
template <Type> class HighTech
{
public:
   HighTech();
   ~HighTech();
   Type Calculate( Type x, Type y, Type z ) { return( x+y+z ); }
};

HighTech<int>   htInteger;
HighTech<float> htFloat;
```

Notice how this unifies the source code base and increases code reliability since the algorithm is only implemented once.

Another feature of C++ that ATL makes use of is multiple inheritance. C++ allows one class to inherit from several parent classes. Grady Booch, in his book *Object Oriented Design with Applications*, describes special, lightweight classes that are designed for multiple inheritance as *mixin* classes. C++ multiple inheritance can be used in many ways, but classes designed for the mixin approach are typically thin, focused, and easily reusable. Let's consider a mixin scenario:

```
class subtractMixin
{
public:
   int Sub( int x, int y );
};

class MyCoolClass : public CoolBaseClass
{
public:
   int Add( int x, int y );
};

class MyFriendsClass : public CoolBaseClass

{

public:

   int Mult( int x, int y );

}
```

Suppose that the `subtractMixin` class was a useful, reusable algorithm that could be used in a variety of situations—it could be mixed in with many different classes. One way to implement this kind of feature would be as a separate class that could be inherited from to obtain the desired behavior. This class would be considered a mixin class. Mixin classes do not necessarily provide usefulness by themselves, but are useful as additive behaviors. Now suppose you wanted your MyCoolClass to have the capability to subtract as well as add. You could define another method in the MyCoolClass class or just inherit the behavior from subtractMixin:

```
class MyCoolClass : public CoolBaseClass, public subtractMixin
{
public:
    int Add( int x, int y );
};
```

In addition, you could add subtract behavior to MyFriendsClass or any other class by inheriting from subtractMixin. However, it is not very useful to create an instance of subtractMixin by itself. Classes such as subtractMixin are called *mixin classes,* and provide an interesting and useful alternative to deep-class hierarchies.

ATL makes use of both the template concept and the mixin concept. Because many of the COM interfaces are small and clean, they lend themselves to being used as mixin classes. The ATL strategy has these characteristics:

■ There is no large class hierarchy to learn, but there are a number of mixin classes to learn.

■ Application behavior is accomplished by inheriting from the required number of mixin classes. This approach tends to be more *black box,* although not necessarily.

■ It takes more effort to implement the application. Unlike MFC applications that inherit a great deal of behavior, ATL applications inherit only the necessities and must implement the rest manually.

■ ATL applications are smaller than MFC applications as a result of shallow class hierarchies.

ATL Classes Required for ActiveX Document Support

The following provides an overview of some of the ATL classes that you will see in the ACTIVEDOC sample program:

CComObjectRoot

CComObjectRoot is a typedef of CComObjectRootEx. All ATL classes must inherit from this class. This class provides support for all the IUnknown interfaces and maintains the COM object's reference counts. It also determines whether the object will support single or multiple threading.

CComCoClass

CComCoClass is used to obtain CLSID and error information, and determines the default class factory. All classes that must be visible externally should inherit from this class.

CComControl

CComControl provides a number of useful functions for implementing ActiveX controls.

IDispatchImpl

IDispatchImpl provides an implementation of IDispatch.

IProvideClassInfo2Impl

IProvideClassInfo2Impl provides type library information.

IPersistStreamInitImpl

IPersistStreamInitImpl provides a means of storing application data on a single storage stream.

IPersistStorageImpl

IPersistStorageImpl provides a means of asking the object to save and load itself from a storage object.

IQuickActivateImpl

IQuickActivateImpl provides a means for a container to ask for all the interfaces that an object supports all at once.

IOleControlImpl

IOleControlImpl provides an implementation of IOleControl.

IOleObjectImpl

IOleObjectImpl provides an implementation of IOleObject.

IOleInPlaceActiveObjectImpl

IOleInPlaceActiveObjectImpl provides an implementation of IOleInPlaceActiveObject.

IViewObjectExImpl

IViewObjectExImpl provides implementations of IViewObject, IViewObject2, and IViewObjectEx.

IOleInPlaceObjectWindowlessImpl

IOleInPlaceObjectWindowlessImpl provides an implementation of IOleInPlaceObject and IOleInPlaceObjectWindowless.

IDataObjectImpl

IDataObjectImpl provides an implementation of IDataObject.

ISupportErrorInfo

ISupportErrorInfo defines a means by which the application can return error information to the container.

The ACTIVEDOC Program

Let's look at some code to understand how ATL can be used to create an ActiveX document. We will be looking at a sample program called ACTIVEDOC found on the Microsoft Visual C++ 5.0 CD. It can be located in the \DEVSTUDIO\Vc\Samples\Atl\ACTIVEDOC directory. We will focus in on specific areas of this sample code to see how an ATL application is built.

This example builds an in-process ActiveX document around the RichEdit control. The majority of the code is actually in the RichEdit control. The ACTIVEDOC program wraps an ActiveX Document layer around the control and provides a unique opportunity to focus on ATL issues, without being distracted by all the other issues that an application normally would have to worry about. In particular, we will look closely at the declaration of the CActiveDoc class and will notice how COM support is easily added through the mixin concept. We will also look at how support for the new IOleDocument and IOleDocumentView COM interfaces is added. When this example is built, it can be run inside Microsoft Binder or Microsoft Internet Explorer. Figure 12.4 illustrates the ACTIVEDOC program inside Microsoft Binder.

FIGURE 12.4.

The ACTIVEDOC program inside Microsoft Binder.

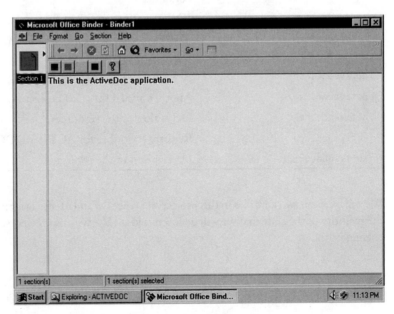

There are 19 files found in the ACTIVEDOC subdirectory. Table 12.11 briefly describes these files.

Table 12.11. Files found in the ACTIVEDOC directory.

Filename	Description
toolbar.bmp	Bitmap used for the (guess what?) toolbar.
activedoc.mak	The Visual C++ make file.
activectl.cpp	Some implementation code for CActiveDoc.
activedoc.cpp	Contains all the DLL entry points.
stdafx.cpp	Contains the precompiled headers.
activedoc.def	DEF table for the DLL exports.
activectl.h	Defines the CActiveDoc interfaces and most of the implementation.
menu.h	Defines the CMenu class and its implementation. This class is used to negotiate menus with the container.
oledocument.h	Defines two new template classes: IOleDocumentImpl and IOleDocumentViewImpl.
resource.h	Standard VC++ resource defines.
stdafx.h	Precompiled header file.
toolbar.h	Defines the CToolbar class and its implementation. This class is used to negotiate toolbars with the container.
activedoc.idl	IDL source for the ActiveDoc class.
activedoc.htm	Web page that demonstrates this ActiveX document used with Internet Explorer.
activedoc.dsp	A Visual C++ 5.0 project file.
activedoc.dsw	Another Visual C++ 5.0 project file.
activedoc.rc	Definition of the resources.
activedoc.rgs	Registry script file for ACTIVEDOC.
activedoc.txt	Description of the project.

We will focus on two keys files in this project: activectl.h and oledocument.h. These files contain the majority of the code that we will be interested in. We will also review some other files as we encounter them.

activectl.h

This file contains the definition of the CActiveDoc class and most of the implementation code. CActiveDoc is the class that implements all the support for ActiveX documents. As we step through this header, we will discuss the important features of the CActiveDoc class.

The following code is from the beginning of activectl.h and shows the include files required by CActiveDoc. The first file, resource.h, is the standard header file that is generated by Visual C++ when dialogs or other resources are added to the project. It contains all the defines necessary for these resources. OleDocument.h is the header file that defines and implements two new classes: IOleDocumentImpl and IOleDocumentViewImpl. We will look more closely at this file later. Menu.h and toolbar.h provide definitions for CMenu and CToolbar. RichEdit.h is the standard header file that describes the RichEdit control.

```
// ActiveCtl.h : Declaration of the CActiveDoc class

#include "resource.h"      // main symbols
#include "OleDocument.h"
#include "Menu.h"
#include "ToolBar.h"
#include <RichEdit.h>
```

Next is the definition of the CActiveDoc class interface. Let's look at the inheritance that the class uses. Notice, as mentioned above, that CActiveDoc is defined through multiple inheritance, or mixins. If you wanted to add or remove functionality from CActiveDoc, you would add or remove a class from which it inherits. Most of the classes that CActiveDoc inherits from are in fact OLE interfaces. Other required classes that CActiveDoc inherits from are CComObjectRoot and CComCoClass. Both of these classes are required. Finally, CActiveDoc inherits from two new classes: IOleDocumentImpl and IOleDocumentViewImpl. These new classes are not part of the ATL library but are defined in the oledocument.h file.

For your information, CLSID_CActiveDoc is the unique OLE identifier for CActiveDoc. It is defined in activedoc.h. IID_IActiveDoc is the unique COM interface identifier for ActiveDoc. It is also defined in activedoc.h. Most of the implementation templates, those that have the Impl at the end of their name, use CActiveDoc as the parameter to the template. This provides a connection between the template classes and the ActiveX document class that you are building. This declaration of CActiveDoc indicates that CActiveDoc supports all the COM interfaces listed in the inheritance list.

```
/////////////////////////////////////////////////////////////////////////
// CActiveDoc
class CActiveDoc :
    public CComObjectRoot,
    public CComCoClass<CActiveDoc, &CLSID_CActiveDoc>,
    public CComControl<CActiveDoc>,
    public IDispatchImpl<IActiveDoc, &IID_IActiveDoc, &LIBID_ACTIVEDOCLib>,
    public IProvideClassInfo2Impl<&CLSID_CActiveDoc, NULL, &LIBID_ACTIVEDOCLib>,
    public IPersistStreamInitImpl<CActiveDoc>,
    public IPersistStorageImpl<CActiveDoc>,
    public IQuickActivateImpl<CActiveDoc>,
    public IOleControlImpl<CActiveDoc>,
```

```
    public IOleObjectImpl<CActiveDoc>,
    public IOleInPlaceActiveObjectImpl<CActiveDoc>,
    public IViewObjectExImpl<CActiveDoc>,
    public IOleInPlaceObjectWindowlessImpl<CActiveDoc>,
    public IDataObjectImpl<CActiveDoc>,
    public ISupportErrorInfo,
    public IOleDocumentImpl<CActiveDoc>,
    public IOleDocumentViewImpl<CActiveDoc>,
    public CMenu<CActiveDoc>,
    public CToolbar<CActiveDoc>
```

Take a look at the next section of the CActiveDoc declaration and implementation:

```
{
public:
    CActiveDoc() : m_wndRTF(_T("RichEdit"), this, 1)
    {
        m_wndRTF.m_hWnd = NULL;
        m_bWindowOnly = TRUE;
    }
```

The class declaration begins with the constructor CActiveDoc(), a part of which is an initialization of m_wndRTF. If you look at the very end of the class declaration, you will notice that m_wndRTF is declared as CContainedWindow. CContainedWindow allows you to either superclass or subclass an existing control. In addition, it connects the existing control to the class that contains it. In our example, CActiveDoc is being declared as a superclass of a RichEdit control. m_wndRTF will provide the connection between the RichEdit control and CActiveDoc. All the message handling for the control will be routed through the CActiveDoc class message maps.

In the next section we encounter the DECLARE_REGISTRY_RESOURCEID macro:

```
DECLARE_REGISTRY_RESOURCEID(IDR_ActiveDoc)
```

This macro is defined as follows in atlcom.h:

```
#define DECLARE_REGISTRY_RESOURCEID(x)\
static HRESULT WINAPI UpdateRegistry(BOOL bRegister)\
{\
return _Module.UpdateRegistryFromResource(x, bRegister);\
}
```

This macro declares a static method called UpdateRegistry. The purpose of this method is to either add or remove the required Registry entries for the ActiveX document. The ATL Object Wizard automatically generates an RGS, or Registry script file. The Registry script file is a specially encoded file that describes, in Backus-Nauer form, the required Registry entries to operate the ActiveX document. The RGS file for this project is as follows:

```
HKCR
{
    ActiveDoc.ActiveDoc.1 = s 'ActiveDoc Class'
    {
        CLSID = s '{93901785-436B-11D0-B965-000000000000}'
    }
    ActiveDoc.ActiveDoc = s 'ActiveDoc Class'
    {
```

```
        CurVer = s 'ActiveDoc.ActiveDoc.1'
    }
    NoRemove CLSID
    {
        ForceRemove {93901785-436B-11D0-B965-000000000000} = s 'ActiveDoc Class'
        {
            ProgID = s 'ActiveDoc.ActiveDoc.1'
            VersionIndependentProgID = s 'ActiveDoc.ActiveDoc'
            InprocServer32 = s '%MODULE%'
            {
                val ThreadingModel = s 'Apartment'
            }
            ForceRemove 'Control'
            'DocObject' = s '8'
            ForceRemove 'Programmable'
            ForceRemove 'Insertable'
            ForceRemove 'ToolboxBitmap32' = s '%MODULE%, 1'
            'MiscStatus' = s '0'
            {
                '1' = s '131473'
            }
            'TypeLib' = s '{93901783-436B-11D0-B965-000000000000}'
            'Version' = s '1.0'
        }
    }
}
```

I won't discuss the syntax of the RGS file in this chapter, but you might recognize some famil-iar text that is part of this file. For example, the name of the ActiveX document is ActiveDoc Class. You can see what its CLSID is. Notice the familiar Registry keywords such as ProgID, InprocServer32, and Insertable. Fortunately, you don't have to write any code to read this file. There is a special routine that is included as part of the ATL library that knows how to read this file and make the appropriate Registry entries. This special routine will be invoked when UpdateRegistry is eventually called.

Following the DECLARE_REGISTRY_RESOURCEID macro are a number of macros enclosed by BEGIN_COM_MAP and END_COM_MAP.

```
BEGIN_COM_MAP(CActiveDoc)


    COM_INTERFACE_ENTRY(IActiveDoc)
    COM_INTERFACE_ENTRY(IDispatch)
    COM_INTERFACE_ENTRY_IMPL(IViewObjectEx)
    COM_INTERFACE_ENTRY_IMPL_IID(IID_IViewObject2, IViewObjectEx)
    COM_INTERFACE_ENTRY_IMPL_IID(IID_IViewObject, IViewObjectEx)
    COM_INTERFACE_ENTRY_IMPL(IOleInPlaceObjectWindowless)
    COM_INTERFACE_ENTRY_IMPL_IID(IID_IOleInPlaceObject,
IOleInPlaceObjectWindowless)
    COM_INTERFACE_ENTRY_IMPL_IID(IID_IOleWindow, IOleInPlaceObjectWindowless)
    COM_INTERFACE_ENTRY_IMPL(IOleInPlaceActiveObject)
    COM_INTERFACE_ENTRY_IMPL(IOleControl)
    COM_INTERFACE_ENTRY_IMPL(IOleObject)
    COM_INTERFACE_ENTRY_IMPL(IQuickActivate)
    COM_INTERFACE_ENTRY_IMPL(IPersistStorage)
    COM_INTERFACE_ENTRY_IMPL(IPersistStreamInit)
    COM_INTERFACE_ENTRY_IMPL(IDataObject)
```

```
        COM_INTERFACE_ENTRY_IMPL(IOleDocument)
        COM_INTERFACE_ENTRY_IMPL(IOleDocumentView)
        COM_INTERFACE_ENTRY(IProvideClassInfo)
        COM_INTERFACE_ENTRY(IProvideClassInfo2)
        COM_INTERFACE_ENTRY(ISupportErrorInfo)
    END_COM_MAP()
```

These macros create a COM interface map that is similar to the message maps used in MFC. They create a way for the `QueryInterface` call to determine whether this COM object supports a specific COM interface, and they provide a mapping to the classes that implement the specified interface. The macros used in the COM interface map can be found in `atlcom.h` and are defined as follows:

```
#define COM_INTERFACE_ENTRY(x)\
    {&IID_##x, \
    offsetofclass(x, _ComMapClass), \
    _ATL_SIMPLEMAPENTRY},

#define COM_INTERFACE_ENTRY_IID(iid, x)\
    {&iid,\
    offsetofclass(x, _ComMapClass),\
    _ATL_SIMPLEMAPENTRY},

#define COM_INTERFACE_ENTRY_IMPL(x)\
    COM_INTERFACE_ENTRY_IID(IID_##x, x##Impl<_ComMapClass>)

#define COM_INTERFACE_ENTRY_IMPL_IID(iid, x)\
    COM_INTERFACE_ENTRY_IID(iid, x##Impl<_ComMapClass>)
```

These macros provide two ways of mapping an interface ID (IID) to a class method. `COM_INTERFACE_ENTRY` generates the IID for you by concatenating the string `IID_` with the parameter that you supply. `COM_INTERFACE_ENTRY_IID` allows you to specify the IID yourself. `COM_INTERFACE_ENTRY_IMPL` and `COM_INTERFACE_ENTRY_IMPL_IID` are similar but map to templatized versions of interfaces.

The next section of `activectl.h` contains the macros `BEGIN_PROPERTY_MAP` and `END_PROPERTY_MAP`. These macros are used to define properties for ActiveX controls and will not be discussed at this time.

```
BEGIN_PROPERTY_MAP(CActiveDoc)
    // PROP_ENTRY("Description", dispid, clsid)
END_PROPERTY_MAP()
```

Next is a section that begins with `BEGIN_MSG_MAP` and `END_MSG_MAP`:

```
BEGIN_MSG_MAP(CActiveDoc)
    MESSAGE_HANDLER(WM_PAINT, OnPaint)
    MESSAGE_HANDLER(WM_GETDLGCODE, OnGetDlgCode)
    MESSAGE_HANDLER(WM_SETFOCUS, OnSetFocus)
    MESSAGE_HANDLER(WM_KILLFOCUS, OnKillFocus)
    MESSAGE_HANDLER(WM_CREATE, OnCreate)
    MESSAGE_HANDLER(WM_DESTROY, OnDestroy)
    MESSAGE_HANDLER(WM_ERASEBKGND, OnEraseBackgnd)
    COMMAND_RANGE_HANDLER(ID_BLACK, ID_BLUE, OnColorChange)
    COMMAND_ID_HANDLER(ID_HELP_ABOUT, OnHelpAbout)
    NOTIFY_CODE_HANDLER(TTN_NEEDTEXT, OnToolbarNeedText)
```

```
    ALT_MSG_MAP(1)
//      MESSAGE_HANDLER(WM_CHAR, OnChar)
//      END_MSG_MAP()
END_MSG_MAP()
```

These macros are very similar to the message maps that are found in MFC. They create a mapping between a Windows message and a method that supports the message.

Next are some macros that define the toolbar that is part of this ActiveX document:

```
BEGIN_TOOLBAR_MAP(CActiveDoc)
    TOOLBAR_BUTTON(ID_BLACK)
    TOOLBAR_BUTTON(ID_RED)
    TOOLBAR_BUTTON(ID_GREEN)
    TOOLBAR_BUTTON(ID_BLUE)
    TOOLBAR_SEPARATOR()
    TOOLBAR_BUTTON(ID_HELP_ABOUT)
END_TOOLBAR_MAP()
```

As official-looking as these macros are, they are not part of ATL. The definition of these macros can be found in toolbar.h, as follows:

```
#define BEGIN_TOOLBAR_MAP(x) public: \
    const static int* _GetToolbarEntries(int& nButtons) { \
    static const int _entries[] = {
#define TOOLBAR_BUTTON(x) x,
#define TOOLBAR_SEPARATOR()      ID_SEP,
#define END_TOOLBAR_MAP() }; nButtons = sizeof(_entries)/sizeof(int); return
_entries; }
```

These macros create an array of toolbar IDs and a method called GetToolbarEntries, which will return the number of buttons and a pointer to the entry array.

The rest of activectl.h deals with the implementation of specific COM methods. As you peruse this code, you will notice that each COM method uses the STDMETHOD macro. This macro is used to describe the standard calling conventions that all COM interfaces must follow. STDMETHOD is defined as follows where STDMETHODCALLTYPE is defined as _stdcall.

```
#define STDMETHOD(method) virtual HRESULT STDMETHODCALLTYPE method
```

The rest of activectl.h provides an inline implementation of the code. Only five inherited methods are overridden: IOleInPlaceActiveObjectImpl::OnDocWindowActive, IPersistStorageImpl::IsDirty, IPersistStreamInitImp::Save, IPersistStreamInitImp::Load, and IOleInPlaceObjectWindowlessImpl::SetObjectRects. I will not discuss the details of these methods. However, note that because only five methods have been overridden, the rest of the COM support was inherited as-is from the ATL base classes.

To summarize, there are a number of pieces of code in activectl.h that provide the framework for ActiveX document support. First, the CActiveDoc class inherits from a number of required COM interface classes. Second, the Registry must be configured with correct entries so that ActiveX containers will know how to load and run the ActiveX document. Third, the ActiveX document interfaces have to be exposed through the QueryInterface method. Much of this is done by using the various `COM_INTERFACE` macros to map an interface with an implementation of the interface. Again, many of these interfaces are inherited from base classes. Fourth, methods that require changing or enhancing have to be overridden.

oledocument.h

This file contains a templatized form of the definitions and implementations of the `IOleDocument` and `IOleDocumentView` COM interfaces. Support for these interfaces is not provided as part of the ATL library. You could use this header file in your own application to provide support for the `IOleDocument` and `IOleDocumentView` interfaces. However, the implementation of these interfaces supports only one view object. If your project requires more than one view, you will need to enhance these classes.

`IOleDocumentImpl` implements the `IOleDocument` methods `CreateView`, `GetDocMiscStatus`, and `EnumViews`.

```
#include <docobj.h>

/////////////////////////////////////////////////////////////////////////////
// IOleDocumentImpl
template <class T>
class ATL_NO_VTABLE IOleDocumentImpl
{
public:
    // IUnknown
    //
    STDMETHOD(QueryInterface)(REFIID riid, void ** ppvObject) = 0;
    _ATL_DEBUG_ADDREF_RELEASE_IMPL(IOleControlImpl)

    // IOleDocument methods
    //
    STDMETHOD(CreateView)(IOleInPlaceSite *pIPSite, IStream *pstm, DWORD /*
    dwReserved */,
        IOleDocumentView **ppView)
    {
        ATLTRACE(_T("IOleDocument::CreateView\n"));
        T* pT = static_cast<T*>(this);

        if (ppView == NULL)
            return E_POINTER;

        // If we've already created a view then we can't create another as we
        // currently only support the ability to create one view
        if (pT->m_spInPlaceSite != NULL)
            return E_FAIL;

        IOleDocumentView* pView;
        pT->_InternalQueryInterface(IID_IOleDocumentView, (void**)&pView);
        // If we support IOleDocument we should support IOleDocumentView
        _ASSERTE(pView != NULL);
```

```
        // If they've given us a site then use it
        if (pIPSite != NULL)
            pView->SetInPlaceSite(pIPSite);

        // If they have given us an IStream pointer then use it to initialize the
            view
        if (pstm != NULL)
        {
            pView->ApplyViewState(pstm);
        }

        // Return the view
        *ppView = pView;

        return S_OK;
    }
    STDMETHOD(GetDocMiscStatus)(DWORD *pdwStatus)
    {
        ATLTRACE(_T("IOleDocument::GetDocMiscStatus\n"));
        *pdwStatus = DOCMISC_NOFILESUPPORT;
        return S_OK;
    }
    STDMETHOD(EnumViews)(IEnumOleDocumentViews** /*ppEnum*/, IOleDocumentView
    **ppView)
    {
        ATLTRACE(_T("IOleDocument::EnumViews\n"));
        T* pT = static_cast<T*>(this);

        if (ppView == NULL)
            return E_POINTER;

        // We only support one view
        pT->_InternalQueryInterface(IID_IOleDocumentView, (void**)ppView);
        return S_OK;
    }
};
```

Notice that the preceding implementation of EnumViews has only one pointer to a view interface: ppView. As a result, this implementation of IOleDocument supports only one instance of a view. It is certainly possible to support more than one—but to do this, you will have to extend these template classes.

Besides doing some error checking, CreateView does two basic things: It accepts an IOleInPlaceSite pointer if one is provided, and it returns a pointer to its only view. To obtain the view interface pointer, it calls its own InternalQueryInterface routine.

GetDocMiscStatus is called by the container to determine what kind of support is provided by the object. This implementation of IOleDocument returns DOCMISC_NOFILESUPPORT. This tells the container that this object does not support reading and writing to files. Other possible status values are shown in Table 12.12.

Table 12.12. DOCMISC **status values.**

Name	*Description*
DOCMISC_CANCREATEMULTIPLEVIEWS	This object can support more than one view.
DOCMISC_SUPPORTCOMPLEXRECTANGLES	This object can support complex rectangles and requires the object to support IOleDocumentView::SetRectComplex.
DOCMISC_CANTOPENEDIT	This object supports activation in a separate window.
DOCMISC_NOFILESUPPORT	This object does not support reading and writing to a file.

Because this object supports only one view, EnumViews returns a pointer to its IOleDocumentView interface.

IOleDocumentViewImpl implements the IOleDocumentView methods: SetInPlaceSite, GetInPlaceSite, GetDocument, SetRect, GetRect, SetRectComplex, Show, UIActivate, Open, CloseView, SaveViewState, ApplyViewState, and Clone.

SetRectComplex, Open, SaveViewState, ApplyViewState, and Clone are not implemented by this version of the IOleDocumentView interface. The rest of the methods are fairly straightforward, with the exception of ActiveXDocActive, which is a helper method of this class that does most of the work of activating the ActiveX document. The tasks that ActiveXDocActive performs are the standard sequence of events that any ActiveX document must follow in order to activate itself inside an ActiveX container. Let's look more closely at this method.

The first item this method takes care of is to make sure that the ActiveX document is in-place active:

```
if (!pT->m_bInPlaceActive)
{
    BOOL bNoRedraw = FALSE;
    hr = pT->m_spInPlaceSite->CanInPlaceActivate();
    if (FAILED(hr))
        return hr;
    pT->m_spInPlaceSite->OnInPlaceActivate();
}
pT->m_bInPlaceActive = TRUE;
```

Next, this method obtains the location of the in-place active window inside the container. It ensures that the ActiveX document window is visible, creating itself (if necessary), and remembers the rectangles by calling the SetObjectRects method.

```
if (pT->m_spInPlaceSite->GetWindow(&hwndParent) == S_OK)
{
    pT->m_spInPlaceSite->GetWindowContext(&spInPlaceFrame,
        &spInPlaceUIWindow, &rcPos, &rcClip, &frameInfo);
```

```
    if (!pT->m_bWndLess)
    {
        if (pT->m_hWnd)
        {
            ::ShowWindow(pT->m_hWnd, SW_SHOW);
            pT->SetFocus();
        }
        else
            pT->m_hWnd = pT->Create(hwndParent, rcPos);
    }
    pT->SetObjectRects(&rcPos, &rcClip);
}
```

After making itself visible, the method goes on to make itself UIActive by calling the IOleInPlaceSite's OnUIActivate() method. After that, it synchronizes the IOleInPlaceFrame and IOleInPlaceUIWindow interfaces by calling their SetActiveObject() and SetBorderSpace() methods.

```
CComPtr<IOleInPlaceActiveObject> spActiveObject;
QueryInterface(IID_IOleInPlaceActiveObject, (void**)&spActiveObject);

// Gone active by now, take care of UIACTIVATE
if (pT->DoesVerbUIActivate(iVerb))
{
    if (!pT->m_bUIActive)
    {
        pT->m_bUIActive = TRUE;
        hr = pT->m_spInPlaceSite->OnUIActivate();
        if (FAILED(hr))
            return hr;

        pT->SetControlFocus(TRUE);
        // set ourselves up in the host.
        //
        if (spActiveObject)
        {
            if (spInPlaceFrame)
                spInPlaceFrame->SetActiveObject(spActiveObject, NULL);
            if (spInPlaceUIWindow)
                spInPlaceUIWindow->SetActiveObject(spActiveObject, NULL);
        }
        if (spInPlaceFrame)
            spInPlaceFrame->SetBorderSpace(NULL);
        if (spInPlaceUIWindow)
            spInPlaceUIWindow->SetBorderSpace(NULL);
    }
}
```

Finally, the method merges its own menus with the container's menus and tells the container to position the ActiveX document so that it is viewable to the user by calling the ShowObject() method of the IOleClientSite interface.

```
// Merge the menus
pT->InPlaceMenuCreate(spInPlaceFrame);
pT->m_spClientSite->ShowObject();
return S_OK;
```

In summary, `activectl.h` and `oledocument.h` provide most of the support for ActiveX documents. The `CActiveDoc` class inherits most of its behavior, whereas `oledocument.h` was written specifically for the ACTIVEDOC sample from scratch and provides support for `IOleDocument` and `IOleDocumentView`. When you write your own ActiveX document using the ATL library, you will need to implement code that is very similar to the `CActiveDoc` class. You might also want to borrow and enhance the `IOleDocument` and `IOleDocumentView` support that is found in `oledocument.h`.

activedoc.htm

The final file I will discuss is `activedoc.htm`. This file deserves an honorary mention even though it is very straightforward. It is an HTML file that allows an ActiveX document to be viewed inside Internet Explorer. If you have Internet Explorer installed on your machine and you double-click this file, you will see the window shown in Figure 12.5.

FIGURE 12.5.

The sample ACTIVEDOC program inside Internet Explorer.

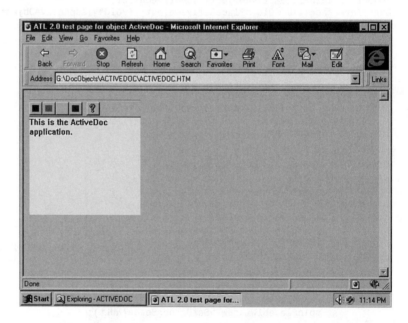

This HTML file demonstrates how you can implement a very lightweight ActiveX document object and include it in your Web pages. The key to activating the ActiveX document object is the OBJECT HTML keyword. Using the CLSID supplied as part of this keyword, Internet Explorer can look up the object in the Registry. Having found the object in the Registry, Internet Explorer can discover that the object supports the ActiveX document interface and interact with it as an ActiveX container.

```
<HTML>
<HEAD>
<TITLE>ATL 2.0 test page for object ActiveDoc</TITLE>
</HEAD>
<BODY>
<OBJECT ID="ActiveDoc" <
 CLASSID="CLSID:93901785-436B-11D0-B965-000000000000">
>
</OBJECT>
</BODY>
</HTML>
```

Summary

This chapter has begun to explore ActiveX documents. ActiveX documents owe much to their OLE document heritage. They share many of the same COM interfaces and add a few new ones of their own.

There are a number of ways to implement an ActiveX document. You could use native COM APIs and do most of the work yourself. You could use MFC. This, in fact, is the easiest tool to use. However, MFC applications tend to be large and for that reason are not suited to downloading over the Internet. Finally, you could use the recent ATL library as you saw in the Microsoft sample program ACTIVEDOC. ATL allows you to build smaller executables but does require a little more work on the part of the programmer.

13

ActiveX Containers

by Mark R. Wrenn

ActiveX containers are the environment through which the end user controls and manipulates the appearance of data. Containers, through their menus, provide a means for the user to view data differently, change data formats, insert new data, and so on. Containers also allow the user to change the viewable size of the data by manipulating the frame and adding toolbars and other "decorations" to the window frame.

This control and manipulation of the data does not usually take place unilaterally on the part of the container. Typically, it requires an interaction between the container and the data. The architecture for this interaction was developed by Microsoft; it is called the ActiveX Container Specification when referring to the container, and the ActiveX Document Specification when referring to the data.

This chapter specifically explores the ActiveX container side of the interaction, although it will be impossible to ignore the ActiveX document side. This chapter examines what has changed between OLE containers and ActiveX containers, what COM interfaces have to be supported, and how to use MFC classes to easily create ActiveX containers. More details about the ActiveX Document Specification can be found in Chapter 12, "ActiveX Documents."

Just What Is an ActiveX Container?

What an exciting industry to work in! Just when you think you have it all figured out, it seems as though everything changes. It wasn't that long ago when Microsoft was all jazzed about compound documents—the ability for the user to combine graphics, text, and data in one document. Now, with ActiveX, it appears as though this has all gone away and everything is suddenly the Internet! Not to worry. Everything you know about OLE technology still applies; it has just been extended to cover new opportunities. As this chapter unfolds, you will see how existing OLE container support has been enhanced with new COM interfaces and how MFC classes have been extended to support them. If you're new to COM, OLE, and ActiveX, you're in the right place. You'll find all the information you need to understand how ActiveX containers work.

So what is an ActiveX container? The short answer is that an ActiveX container is an OLE container with some new COM interfaces—in particular, `IOleCommandTarget`, `IOleDocumentSite`, and `IContinueCallback`. These new interfaces have been added to support corresponding new interfaces in ActiveX documents. These interfaces first appeared in the Microsoft Office Binder application. Binder, as well as Internet Explorer, is an ActiveX container. ActiveX documents differ from OLE embedded documents in that they occupy the entire client area of the container and control much more of the menu. To the user, the ActiveX container appears to be the native application frame window. If you create a new Binder document and insert a Word document, an Excel spreadsheet, or a PowerPoint presentation, you'll notice that as you click each component of the binder, the user interface changes, and the menus and toolbars appear as they would in the native application. This capability of the container to take on the appearance of any native application is what ActiveX containers are all about. They allow the Binder application to bind together several applications into one *binder,* which allows Internet Explorer to download and display any ActiveX document data from a Web server.

Let's explore these new interfaces further. The IOleCommandTarget COM interface allows menu commands or other actions to be routed from the ActiveX document to the ActiveX container. A corresponding IOleCommandTarget interface is defined for the ActiveX document. This corresponding interface allows the container to route menu commands and other actions to the document, allowing a bidirectional communication of commands to flow cooperatively between container and document. The effect to the user is that the container and document behave as a unified application. The user is unable to tell which piece of software supplies support for which menu item. Supporting the IOleCommandTarget interface is optional.

> **NOTE**
>
> With all the various COM interfaces, it is easy to get confused about what each interface is for. Remember that a COM server supplies an interface for someone else to use. It is a means of manipulating the COM server. For example, the container exposes the IOleCommandTarget interface so that other software can route menu commands and the like to the container.

The IOleDocumentSite COM interface provides one method: ActivateMe, which allows the document to ask the container to activate it as a full ActiveX document instead of an OLE in-place, embedded object.

The IContinueCallback COM interface is used to provide printing support. It is used in conjunction with the IPrint COM interface that the ActiveX document exposes. This interface is used by the document to provide progress information to the container and to allow the container the opportunity to cancel the printing operation.

What's New in MFC?

There is no support in MFC for these new COM interfaces. However, it is relatively straightforward to add support for these interfaces using the MFC COM interface macros. We will look at how to do this when we generate and examine the XContainer program.

Some Details About ActiveX Containers

ActiveX containers have a rich history. Their roots go back to the first release of OLE, when OLE meant object linking and embedding. The original intent of OLE 1 was to allow the user to view different types of data in a single interface. Before, OLE 1 applications were strictly monolithic. If you wanted to write a document, you would use a word processor. If you wanted to edit financial data, you would use a spreadsheet. OLE 1 changed that and allowed the user to view documents, spreadsheets, and charts side by side in a single application. Admittedly, this was a little awkward because to edit a piece of data, you had to double-click the data and bring up a separate application to change it. But it was an improvement.

OLE 2 came along and added, in particular, the concept of in-place activation. This meant that the user could double-click a piece of data and, instead of launching a completely separate document, could edit the data inside of the hosting application. This was a great step forward, but still a little awkward. First, you had to double-click the data to activate it. This was counter-intuitive; users were familiar with single-clicking something when they wanted to focus on it. Yet, despite this awkwardness, it was better than OLE 1.

ActiveX documents add yet another layer to OLE 2. Instead of appearing inside another document, ActiveX documents occupy the entire client area of the container. It appears as though the container is the native application. This concept is very useful, particularly when you think of the Internet. A container application that can adapt itself to any document it receives is a powerful tool. This is exactly what browsing the Web is all about: exploring lots of different things and downloading lots of different documents into your browser. Internet Explorer is an example of an ActiveX container that does just that.

Figure 13.1 illustrates the OLE architecture. Notice how the upper layers in the architecture depend, to some degree, on the lower layers. This diagram is like a historical summary of how OLE has changed. Each time the OLE specification changes, another building block is added to the existing foundation.

Now, let's break out the various parts of the OLE architecture and examine them.

Structured Storage

Structured storage is a very interesting concept. It came about as a result of the implementation of compound documents. Not only should the user be able to view and edit dissimilar data within the same application, but he should also be able to save all the changes to the same file. This requirement drove the need for structured storage.

Structured storage is similar to a file system. Data is stored in storage objects that in turn can be stored in other storage objects. Storage streams that contain the real data can be stored in storage objects. This is analogous to files that reside in directories that reside in other directories.

This capability to segregate portions of one file into hierarchical partitions is very useful for documents that contain other embedded objects. Each object can be assigned its own storage area inside the file, and the embedded object can put anything it wants in its own storage area. Figure 13.2 illustrates the hierarchical nature of structured storage.

FIGURE 13.1.
OLE architecture.

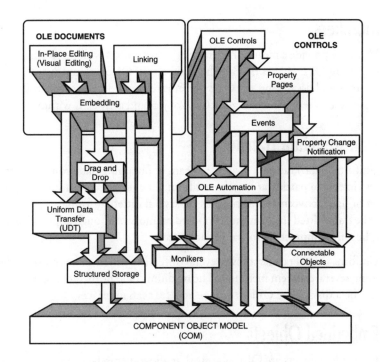

FIGURE 13.2.
Hierarchical structured storage.

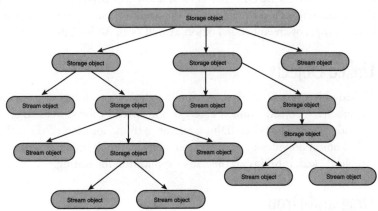

Monikers

Monikers provide a means of referencing other objects without storing the object itself. They are intelligent OLE objects that are the backbone of OLE linking. When a user links an object into a compound document, the OLE object is referenced by a moniker. By activating a moniker, it is possible to retrieve the original OLE object and activate it within the compound document.

Uniform Data Transfer

Uniform Data Transfer provides a means of obtaining data from another object without being restricted to a particular transfer medium. The standard Windows Clipboard allows the transfer of data between applications using several different formats, but each of these formats has to be transmitted through the Clipboard memory. Although appropriate for some kinds of data, it becomes impractical for large data sets.

Uniform Data Transfer allows several different formats to be transferred between applications using several different mediums. The medium could be memory, as with the Clipboard. It could also be a disk or the OLE IStorage and IStream interfaces.

Embedded Objects

Embedded objects are OLE objects that allow themselves to be embedded inside a container. Embedded objects store their data in the structured storage of the container. Microsoft Word is an example of an embedded object as well as an ActiveX document.

Linked Objects

Linked objects are OLE objects that allow themselves to be linked inside a container. Unlike an embedded object, a linked object is not stored in the structured storage of the container. Instead, a linked object contains a reference to the location of the real object. Typically, the linked object provides an iconic representation of itself inside the container. When this icon is double-clicked, it brings up the native application for editing.

Drag-and-Drop

OLE drag-and-drop provides a way by which different applications can move data between themselves. Without OLE drag-and-drop, each application would have to define its own protocol from transferring data between itself and another application. OLE drag-and-drop, in combination with Uniform Data Transfer, provides a more system-wide protocol for exchanging data using the mouse.

In-Place Activation

In-place activation is a key feature of OLE 2. It allows documents to be edited inside the container's client area without launching the native application. This feature is also called *visual editing*. Typically, an object that is in-place activated has some kind of hashed border around it. This indicates to the user that the highlighted object is currently being worked on. Figure 13.3 shows Microsoft Word as an in-place, activated object.

FIGURE 13.3.

Microsoft Word as an in-place, activated object inside Excel.

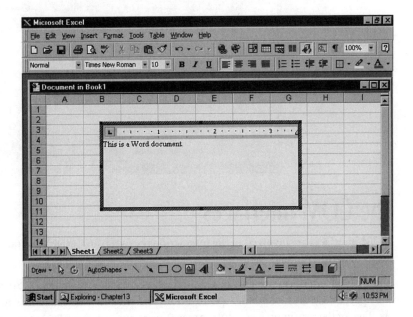

ActiveX Documents

ActiveX documents are in many ways just like in-place, activated documents. The exception is that when an ActiveX document is placed in an ActiveX container, it takes up the entire client area of the container. Gone are the hash marks that identify an in-place, activated object. The ActiveX document does not have to be double-clicked to be activated. It comes up active and appears to be a native application. Figure 13.4 shows Microsoft Word as an ActiveX document. Notice how the ActiveX container appears very similar to the native Microsoft Word application.

FIGURE 13.4.

Microsoft Word as an ActiveX document inside Microsoft Binder, an ActiveX container.

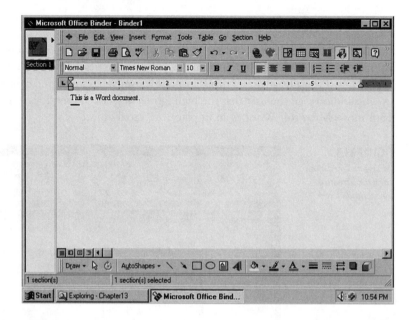

The COM Interfaces

COM interfaces are involved in the interactions between an ActiveX container and an ActiveX document.

Nine COM interfaces are part of the ActiveX container specification. Six of these interfaces were part of the OLE container specification, and the other three are new to ActiveX containers. Two of the new interfaces—IOleCommandTarget and IContinueCallback—are optional. Table 13.1 lists the COM interfaces with the corresponding MFC classes that implement the interface.

Table 13.1. COM interfaces used by containers.

COM interface	Type	MFC class
IOleInPlaceFrame	OLE 2	COleControlContainer
IOleCommandTarget	New, optional	None
IOleInPlaceUIWindow	OLE 2	COleControlContainer
IOleContainer	OLE 2	COleControlContainer
IOleClientSite	OLE 2	COleClientItem
IAdviseSink	OLE 2	COleClientItem
IOleDocumentSite	New, required	None

COM interface	Type	MFC class
IOleInPlaceSite	OLE 2	COleClientItem
IContinueCallback	New, optional	None

These interfaces will now be discussed in more detail.

IOleInPlaceFrame

IOleInPlaceFrame is a COM interface derived from three other COM interfaces: IOleInPlaceUIWindow, IOleWindow, and IUnknown. It controls the top-level frame window of the container. With this interface, it is possible to add and remove items from the composite menu, set status text, manage modeless dialog boxes, and translate accelerator keys. Each of the interfaces that IOleInPlaceFrame derives from contributes required methods. Table 13.2 describes the interfaces.

Table 13.2. IOleInPlaceFrame interfaces.

Interface name	Description
	IUnknown *methods*
QueryInterface	Discovers required interfaces
AddRef	Adds a reference count to the object
Release	Decrements the reference count for the object and eventually deletes the object
	IOleWindow *methods*
GetWindow	Gets the window handle to the frame, the document, the parent, or the in-place object
ContextSensitiveHelp	Gives the container the opportunity to handle context-sensitive help
	IOleInPlaceUIWindow *methods*
GetBorder	Returns the rectangle where ActiveX documents can put their toolbars and other controls
RequestBorderSpace	Used to ask the container for space for toolbars and other controls
SetBorderSpace	Tells the container to allocate the space for toolbars and other controls
SetActiveObject	Called by the ActiveX document to create a link between itself and the ActiveX container

continues

Table 13.2. continued

Interface name	Description
	IOleInPlaceFrame *methods*
InsertMenus	Allows the container to insert its menu items into the shared menu
SetMenu	Allows the ActiveX document to install the merged container/document menu
RemoveMenus	Allows the container to remove its menu items
SetStatusText	Displays status text in the static area
EnableModeless	Enables or disables modeless dialogs at the frame level
TranslateAccelerator	Translates accelerator keystrokes intended for the container

IOleCommandTarget

IOleCommandTarget allows client and server to dispatch commands to each other. With the ActiveX container, it allows the ActiveX document to route commands that it generates to the container. Table 13.3 describes the interfaces.

Table 13.3. IOleCommandTarget interfaces.

Interface name	Description
	IUnknown *methods*
QueryInterface	Discovers required interfaces
AddRef	Adds a reference count to the object
Release	Decrements the reference count for the object and eventually deletes the object
	IOleCommandTarget *methods*
QueryStatus	Asks the object whether it supports a particular type of command
Exec	Executes the requested command

IOleInPlaceUIWindow

IOleInPlaceUIWindow allows ActiveX documents to negotiate border space in the frame window. The interface manages the allocation of border space and the interaction between the document and the frame. IOleInPlaceUIWindow derives from IOleWindow. Table 13.4 describes the interfaces.

Table 13.4. IOleInPlaceUIWindow interfaces.

Interface name	Description
IUnknown *interfaces*	
QueryInterface	Discovers required interfaces
AddRef	Adds a reference count to the object
Release	Decrements the reference count for the object and eventually deletes the object
IOleWindow *interfaces*	
GetWindow	Gets the window handle to the frame, the document, the parent, or the in-place object
ContextSensitiveHelp	Gives the container the opportunity to handle context-sensitive help
IOleInPlaceUIWindow *methods*	
GetBorder	Returns the rectangle where ActiveX documents can put their toolbars and other controls
RequestBorderSpace	Used to ask the container for space for toolbars and other controls
SetBorderSpace	Tells the container to allocate the space for toolbars and other controls
SetActiveObject	Called by the ActiveX document to create a link between itself and the ActiveX container

IOleContainer

IOleContainer is used to query objects in a compound document or to lock the container in the running state. This interface is useful only when the container supports linked objects and requires both the container and the document to implement it. Table 13.5 describes the interfaces.

Table 13.5. I0leContainer interfaces.

Interface name	Description
IUnknown interfaces	
QueryInterface	Discovers required interfaces
AddRef	Adds a reference count to the object
Release	Decrements the reference count for the object and eventually deletes the object
IParseDisplayName method	
ParseDisplayName	Parses a display name into something usable by a moniker
I0leContainer methods	
EnumObjects	Enumerates objects in the container
LockContainer	Keeps the container locked in running mode until it is explicitly released

I0leClientSite

I0leClientSite provides the means by which an ActiveX document obtains information about its container environment. It can determine information about its display area as well as other user interface information from the container. Table 13.6 describes the interfaces.

Table 13.6. I0leClientSite interfaces.

Interface name	Description
IUnknown interfaces	
QueryInterface	Discovers required interfaces
AddRef	Adds a reference count to the object
Release	Decrements the reference count for the object and eventually deletes the object
I0leClientSite methods	
SaveObject	Saves the ActiveX document associated with this site
GetMoniker	Provides a way of creating a moniker to access the embedded ActiveX document
GetContainer	Returns a pointer to the container's I0leContainer interface

Interface name	Description
ShowObject	Positions the ActiveX document so that it is visible to the user; makes sure the container itself is visible to the user
OnShowWindow	Notifies the container when an object is about to become visible or invisible; does not apply to ActiveX documents or other in-place, activated objects
RequestNewObjectLayout	Asks the container to provide more or less space for displaying the ActiveX document

IAdviseSink

IAdviseSink provides a way for an ActiveX document to notify its container when its data or state changes. Table 13.7 describes the interfaces.

Table 13.7. IAdviseSink interfaces.

Interface name	Description
IUnknown *interfaces*	
QueryInterface	Discovers required interfaces
AddRef	Adds a reference count to the object
Release	Decrements the reference count for the object and eventually deletes the object
IAdviseSink *methods*	
OnDataChange	Called when the data has changed
OnViewChange	Called when the view has changed
OnRename	Called when the name has changed
OnSave	Called when the ActiveX document has been saved to disk
OnClose	Called when the ActiveX document has been closed

IOleDocumentSite

IOleDocumentSite allows an ActiveX document to bypass the normal activation sequence for an in-place object and activate directly as a document object. Table 13.8 describes the interfaces.

Table 13.8. IOleDocumentSite interfaces.

Interface name	Description
	IUnknown *interfaces*
QueryInterface	Discovers required interfaces
AddRef	Adds a reference count to the object
Release	Decrements the reference count for the object and eventually deletes the object
	IOleDocumentSite *method*
ActivateMe	Actives the ActiveX document as a document object instead of an in-place object

IOleInPlaceSite

IOleInPlaceSite works in conjunction with IOleDocumentSite. For each view that an ActiveX document instantiates, an IOleInPlaceSite object must exist. IOleDocumentSite manages one or more IOleInPlaceSite objects. This interface provides methods that manage the ActiveX document. Table 13.9 describes the interfaces.

Table 13.9. IOleInPlaceSite interfaces.

Interface name	Description
	IUnknown *interfaces*
QueryInterface	Discovers required interfaces
AddRef	Adds a reference count to the object
Release	Decrements the reference count for the object and eventually deletes the object
	IOleWindow *methods*
GetWindow	Gets the window handle to the frame, the document, the parent, or the in-place object
ContextSensitiveHelp	Gives the container the opportunity to handle context-sensitive help
	IOleInPlaceSite *methods*
CanInPlaceActivate	Gives the object permission to in-place activate
OnInPlaceActivate	Notifies the container that the ActiveX document is about to in-place activate

Interface name	Description
OnUIActivate	Called when the ActiveX document is about to in-place activate and replace the menu with a composite menu
GetWindowContext	Provides window hierarchy information
Scroll	Tells the container how to scroll the object
OnUIDeactivate	Tells the container that the ActiveX document is going away and that the container should restore its user interface.
OnInPlaceDeactivate	Tells the container that the ActiveX document is no longer in-place active
DiscardUndoState	Tells the container to discard its undo state
DeactivateAndUndo	Tells the container to end the in-place, active session and return to its undo state
OnPosRectChange	Used by the ActiveX document to tell the container that its size has changed

IContinueCallback

IContinueCallback provides a mechanism by which the ActiveX document can ask the container if it should continue an interruptible process. This is used in conjunction with the ActiveX document's IPrint interface. Table 13.10 describes the interfaces.

Table 13.10. IContinueCallback interfaces.

Interface name	Description
	IUnknown *interfaces*
QueryInterface	Discovers required interfaces
AddRef	Adds a reference count to the object
Release	Decrements the reference count for the object and eventually deletes the object
	IContinueCallback *methods*
FContinue	Used by printing tasks to determine if printing should continue
FContinuePrinting	Used by the printing tasks to determine if the task should continue; also provides some progress information

More information about these COM interfaces can be found in the Visual C++ help. It is worth the time to read the descriptions of the interfaces in the help system. It provides a good background to the world of COM, OLE, and ActiveX. Another interesting exercise is to grep through the MFC source code to see where Microsoft has implemented these and other COM interfaces in the MFC Class Library. The MFC source code is usually located under the DevStudio\Vc\Mfc directory.

Building an ActiveX Container

There are several ways to build an ActiveX container. The most educational way is to use the native COM interfaces. Building a container this way would take longer, but would greatly increase your understanding of the intricacies of COM. We will not build a container this way in this chapter. If you are interested in trying this, read through the appropriate sections of *Inside OLE,* by Kraig Brockschmidt.

Another way to build an ActiveX container is to make use of the new ATL template library. This library is an alternative approach to using the MFC class library. These libraries are fundamentally different from each other. ATL is based on the idea of a template. Templates are ways of implementing code without knowing what kind of data is being worked with. For example, suppose you had a class that added two integers and another class that added two floating-point numbers. The code for both of these classes would be remarkably similar, perhaps something like c = a + b. The only difference between the two implementations is the type of data used in the calculation. This is the perfect situation for a template class. The code for the template looks the same c = a + b, but the types of a, b, and c are not resolved until the template class is declared in the code. If you are interested in learning more about templates, take a closer look at some of the MFC collection classes, the Standard Template Library, or the ATL. The key benefit to this approach is the small size of programs built with ATL.

MFC is based on the idea of a hierarchical class library. Programmers are encouraged to build layers of classes that can inherit behaviors from their parent classes. This approach tends to make it very easy to implement functionality because, in most cases, you can just inherit it. However, hierarchical classes tend to grow large, both in terms of the size of programs generated and the number of classes to learn and understand. The programming language SmallTalk is built on the idea of inheriting functionality and overriding the behaviors you want to change. The key characteristics of a SmallTalk project is that it takes a new person a long time to learn the SmallTalk hierarchy. But someone who knows SmallTalk can implement new functionality quickly. SmallTalk programs also tend to be large. MFC programs share these characteristics.

For the purpose of this chapter, we will use MFC to build a container program. We do this because we can inherit a great deal of ActiveX container behavior without writing any code. In addition, since containers are not usually downloaded through the Internet, the size of the resulting container program is not as critical as it is for other kinds of ActiveX programs.

The XContainer Program

We will now build a simple ActiveX container called XContainer. We'll step through the Visual C++ AppWizard and review the results. The AppWizard automatically generates much of the code that is needed for a container. The AppWizard does not directly support the new ActiveX container interfaces, however; we will have to add those manually.

Generating XContainer

We will now step through the Visual C++ AppWizard to generate a basic OLE container. To create a new project, select New from the File menu. Figure 13.5 illustrates the dialog that you should see. For the XContainer project, we will use the MFC EXE AppWizard. Fill in the edit boxes as indicated and click OK.

FIGURE 13.5.

Creating a new project with Visual C++.

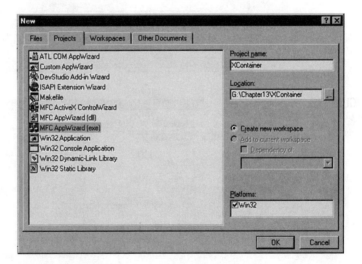

Figure 13.6 illustrates the next dialog you should see. This dialog asks you what kind of application to create. The three basic types are SDI (Single Document Interface), MDI (Multiple Document Interface), and dialog-based. For the purposes of the XContainer program, choose Single document. Click Next to continue.

Figure 13.7 illustrates the next dialog you should see. This dialog allows you to specify the type of automatic database support that will be added to the application. Because we will not be using a database, select None and click Next to continue.

Figure 13.8 illustrates the next dialog you should see. This is where you tell the AppWizard that you want it to generate container support. We will not be supporting ActiveX controls in this example, so you can deselect that option. Click Next to continue.

FIGURE 13.6.

Selecting a single-document application.

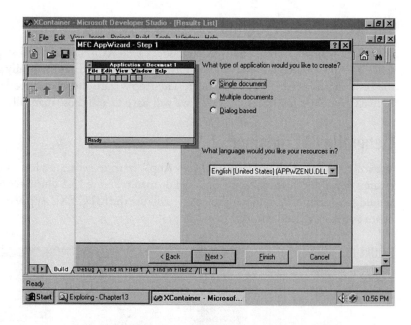

FIGURE 13.7.

Selecting database support.

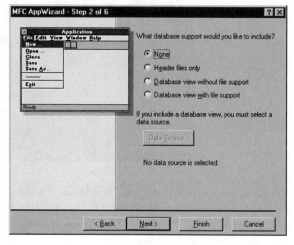

FIGURE 13.8.

Selecting compound document support.

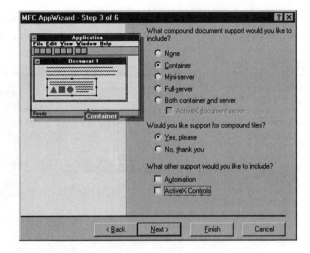

Figure 13.9 illustrates the next dialog you should see. This dialog is for selecting miscellaneous user interface support. Leave the defaults and click Next to continue.

Figure 13.10 illustrates the next dialog you should see. This dialog is for selecting source code comments and MFC library support. Leave the defaults. Source comments are always useful, and making use of MFC in a shared DLL is more efficient than statically linking the MFC library with your application.

FIGURE 13.9.

Selecting additional miscellaneous features.

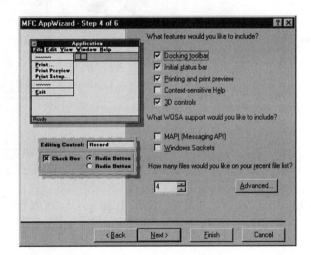

Figure 13.11 illustrates the next dialog that you should see. This is a summary of the MFC classes that the AppWizard will generate for you. Click Finish to continue.

FIGURE 13.10.

Selecting source code comments and MFC support.

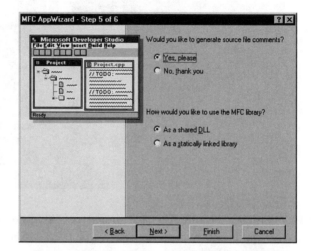

FIGURE 13.11.

The MFC Class review screen appears next.

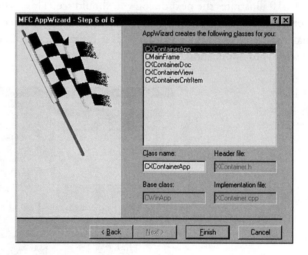

Figure 13.12 illustrates the last AppWizard dialog. Click OK to generate the XContainer code.

FIGURE 13.12.
The final AppWizard screen.

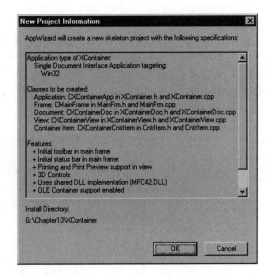

Reviewing the Code

Let's take a look at the files that AppWizard has generated. Table 13.11 contains the list of filenames.

Table 13.11. Generated files and their descriptions.

CPP/header name	Purpose
StdAfx	Precompiled header support.
CntrItem	These files contain a class called `CXContainerCntrItem`. This class is derived from `COleClientItem` and supplies most of the OLE support for the container. We will modify these files to add ActiveX container support.
MainFrm	These files contain the class derived from `CFrameWnd`.
XContainer	These files contain the class derived from `CWinApp`.
XContainerDoc	These files contain the class derived from `COleDocument`.
XContainerView	These files contain the class derived from `CView`.

At this point, compile the XContainer application and run it. Without writing any code, we have a basic OLE container. Click the Edit menu and choose the Insert Object menu item. This will pop up a dialog and ask you to choose an OLE object type to insert into the container. If you have Microsoft Word, select it. Otherwise, choose some other OLE object. Figure 13.13 shows what the first iteration of XContainer looks like with Microsoft Word inserted into the container.

FIGURE 13.13.

The first iteration of XContainer with Microsoft Word.

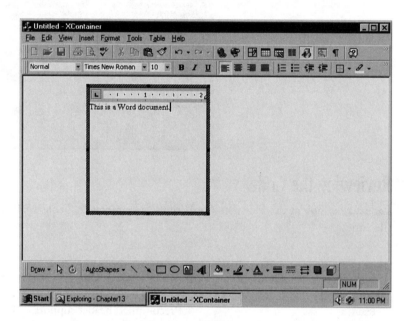

Amazing, isn't it? All we did was click buttons, and voilà! An OLE container! Notice that the Word menus and toolbars have merged with XContainer, and Word does not fill the entire container client area. Also, there is a funny hashed border around the area where Word was placed. These are all characteristics of an embedded document.

AppWizard generates a great deal of code for us. If we were to implement complete support for linked and embedded objects, we would have to add support for the following issues:

- Correctly sizing the embedded object
- Hit testing and selection
- Object activation
- Resizing and moving
- Deleting embedded objects
- Copying and pasting
- Menu merging

Interestingly enough, because an ActiveX document occupies the full client area, many of these issues are not applicable. If you want to learn more about these issues, search for an article titled "Creating an OLE Container" in the Visual C++ help file. It is part of the OLE Container Tutorial. In the XContainer example, we will focus on the new interfaces that need to be implemented to support ActiveX documents in the container.

Adding the New Interfaces

We will now concentrate on adding the new ActiveX COM interface: IOleDocumentSite. The CntrItem.h and CntrItem.cpp files will need to be modified to accomplish this. Listing 13.1 shows the CntrItem.h file.

Listing 13.1. The CntrItem.h file.

```
// CntrItem.h : interface of the CXContainerCntrItem class
//

#if !defined(AFX_CNTRITEM_H__979CFC0E_DFC1_11D0_9845_0000C0E888CF__INCLUDED_)
#define AFX_CNTRITEM_H__979CFC0E_DFC1_11D0_9845_0000C0E888CF__INCLUDED_

#if _MSC_VER >= 1000
#pragma once
#endif // _MSC_VER >= 1000

class CXContainerDoc;
class CXContainerView;

class CXContainerCntrItem : public COleClientItem
{
    DECLARE_SERIAL(CXContainerCntrItem)

// Constructors
public:
    CXContainerCntrItem(CXContainerDoc* pContainer = NULL);
        // Note: pContainer is allowed to be NULL to enable IMPLEMENT_SERIALIZE.
        //  IMPLEMENT_SERIALIZE requires the class have a constructor with
        //  zero arguments.  Normally, OLE items are constructed with a
        //  non-NULL document pointer.

// Attributes
public:
    CXContainerDoc* GetDocument()
        { return (CXContainerDoc*)COleClientItem::GetDocument(); }
    CXContainerView* GetActiveView()
        { return (CXContainerView*)COleClientItem::GetActiveView(); }

    // ClassWizard generated virtual function overrides
    //{{AFX_VIRTUAL(CXContainerCntrItem)
    public:
    virtual void OnChange(OLE_NOTIFICATION wNotification, DWORD dwParam);
    virtual void OnActivate();
```

continues

Listing 13.1. continued

```
    protected:
    virtual void OnGetItemPosition(CRect& rPosition);
    virtual void OnDeactivateUI(BOOL bUndoable);
    virtual BOOL OnChangeItemPosition(const CRect& rectPos);
    //}}AFX_VIRTUAL

// Implementation
public:
    ~CXContainerCntrItem();
#ifdef _DEBUG
    virtual void AssertValid() const;
    virtual void Dump(CDumpContext& dc) const;
#endif
    virtual void Serialize(CArchive& ar);

public:

    IOleDocumentView *m_pDSView;

    BEGIN_INTERFACE_PART(OleDocumentSite, IOleDocumentSite)
        INIT_INTERFACE_PART(CXContainerCntrItem, OleDocumentSite)
        STDMETHOD(ActivateMe)(LPOLEDOCUMENTVIEW);
    END_INTERFACE_PART(OleDocumentSite)

    DECLARE_INTERFACE_MAP()
};

/////////////////////////////////////////////////////////////////////

//{{AFX_INSERT_LOCATION}}
// Microsoft Developer Studio will insert additional declarations immediately
before the previous line.

#endif // !defined(AFX_CNTRITEM_H__979CFC0E_DFC1_11D0_9845_0000C0E888CF__INCLUDED_)
```

This is essentially the file that was generated by the AppWizard with the addition of some MFC macros. These macros are the way that MFC implements COM interfaces. Table 13.12 itemizes these macros.

Table 13.12. MFC macros to implement a COM interface.

Macro name	*Description*
BEGIN_INTERFACE_PART	This macro takes two parameters. The first is the name of a class that the macro will declare. Actually, MFC will prepend an x at the beginning of the name that you supply—in our case, XOleDocumentSite. The second parameter is the COM interface that this generated class will

Macro name	Description
	inherit from. The macro will also declare an instance of this class by prepending m_x in front of the name—in our case, m_xOleDocumentSite.
INIT_INTERFACE_PART	This macro takes two parameters. The first is the name of the class in which the COM interface will live. In our case, the COM interface is inside CXContainerCntrItem. The second parameter is the name of the generated class specified in BEGIN_INTERFACE_PART. These two parameters tell MFC how to connect the classes together.
STDMETHOD	This macro specifies the calling conventions of the COM method and the method name—in our case, ActivateMe. ActivateMe takes one parameter, a pointer to the ActiveX document's IOleDocumentView object.
END_INTERFACE_PART	This macro completes the set and takes one parameter, the name of the generated class.
DECLARE_INTERFACE_MAP	This macro places the actual map in the class for MFC to reference at runtime.

It should be noted that BEGIN_INTERFACE_PART automatically generates the three IUnknown methods for the class XOleDocumentSite: AddRef, Release, and QueryInterface.

Listing 13.2 shows the CntrItem.cpp file.

Listing 13.2. The CntrItem.cpp file.

```
// CntrItem.cpp : implementation of the CXContainerCntrItem class
//

#include "stdafx.h"
#include "XContainer.h"

#include "XContainerDoc.h"
#include "XContainerView.h"
#include "CntrItem.h"

#ifdef _DEBUG
#define new DEBUG_NEW
#undef THIS_FILE
static char THIS_FILE[] = __FILE__;
#endif
```

continues

Listing 13.2. continued

```
//////////////////////////////////////////////////////////////////////////
// CXContainerCntrItem implementation

IMPLEMENT_SERIAL(CXContainerCntrItem, COleClientItem, 0)

CXContainerCntrItem::CXContainerCntrItem(CXContainerDoc* pContainer)
    : COleClientItem(pContainer)
{
    // TODO: add one-time construction code here
    m_pDSView = NULL;
}

CXContainerCntrItem::~CXContainerCntrItem()
{
    // TODO: add cleanup code here
    if( m_pDSView != NULL )
    {
        m_pDSView->Release();
    }
}

void CXContainerCntrItem::OnChange(OLE_NOTIFICATION nCode, DWORD dwParam)
{
    ASSERT_VALID(this);

    COleClientItem::OnChange(nCode, dwParam);

    // When an item is being edited (either in-place or fully open)
    //   it sends OnChange notifications for changes in the state of the
    //   item or visual appearance of its content.

    // TODO: invalidate the item by calling UpdateAllViews
    //   (with hints appropriate to your application)

    GetDocument()->UpdateAllViews(NULL);
        // for now just update ALL views/no hints
}

BOOL CXContainerCntrItem::OnChangeItemPosition(const CRect& rectPos)
{
    ASSERT_VALID(this);

    // During in-place activation CXContainerCntrItem::OnChangeItemPosition
    //   is called by the server to change the position of the in-place
    //   window.  Usually, this is a result of the data in the server
    //   document changing such that the extent has changed or as a result
    //   of in-place resizing.
    //
    // The default here is to call the base class, which will call
    //   COleClientItem::SetItemRects to move the item
    //   to the new position.

    if (!COleClientItem::OnChangeItemPosition(rectPos))
        return FALSE;

    // TODO: update any cache you may have of the item's rectangle/extent
```

```
        return TRUE;
}

void CXContainerCntrItem::OnGetItemPosition(CRect& rPosition)
{
    ASSERT_VALID(this);

    // During in-place activation, CXContainerCntrItem::OnGetItemPosition
    //  will be called to determine the location of this item.  The default
    //  implementation created from AppWizard simply returns a hard-coded
    //  rectangle.  Usually, this rectangle would reflect the current
    //  position of the item relative to the view used for activation.
    //  You can obtain the view by calling CXContainerCntrItem::GetActiveView.

    // TODO: return correct rectangle (in pixels) in rPosition

    rPosition.SetRect(10, 10, 210, 210);
}

void CXContainerCntrItem::OnActivate()
{
    // Allow only one inplace activate item per frame
    CXContainerView* pView = GetActiveView();
    ASSERT_VALID(pView);
    COleClientItem* pItem = GetDocument()->GetInPlaceActiveItem(pView);
    if (pItem != NULL && pItem != this)
        pItem->Close();

    COleClientItem::OnActivate();
}

void CXContainerCntrItem::OnDeactivateUI(BOOL bUndoable)
{
    COleClientItem::OnDeactivateUI(bUndoable);

    // Hide the object if it is not an outside-in object
    DWORD dwMisc = 0;
    m_lpObject->GetMiscStatus(GetDrawAspect(), &dwMisc);
    if (dwMisc & OLEMISC_INSIDEOUT)
        DoVerb(OLEIVERB_HIDE, NULL);
}

void CXContainerCntrItem::Serialize(CArchive& ar)
{
    ASSERT_VALID(this);

    // Call base class first to read in COleClientItem data.
    // Since this sets up the m_pDocument pointer returned from
    //  CXContainerCntrItem::GetDocument, it is a good idea to call
    //  the base class Serialize first.
    COleClientItem::Serialize(ar);

    // now store/retrieve data specific to CXContainerCntrItem
    if (ar.IsStoring())
    {
        // TODO: add storing code here
```

continues

Listing 13.2. continued

```
    }
    else
    {
        // TODO: add loading code here
    }
}

/////////////////////////////////////////////////////////////////////////////
// CXContainerCntrItem diagnostics

#ifdef _DEBUG
void CXContainerCntrItem::AssertValid() const
{
    COleClientItem::AssertValid();
}

void CXContainerCntrItem::Dump(CDumpContext& dc) const
{
    COleClientItem::Dump(dc);
}
#endif

/////////////////////////////////////////////////////////////////////////////

//-------------------------------------------------------------------------
// This code adds support for the IOleDocumentSite interface.  This is the
// only additional COM interface required to create an ActiveX Container.
//-------------------------------------------------------------------------

BEGIN_INTERFACE_MAP(CXContainerCntrItem, COleClientItem)
    INTERFACE_PART(CXContainerCntrItem, IID_IOleDocumentSite, OleDocumentSite)
END_INTERFACE_MAP()

//-------------------------------------------------------------------------
// Three standard IUnknown implementations
//-------------------------------------------------------------------------

STDMETHODIMP_(ULONG) CXContainerCntrItem::XOleDocumentSite::AddRef()
{
    METHOD_PROLOGUE_EX( CXContainerCntrItem, OleDocumentSite )
    return pThis->ExternalAddRef();
}

STDMETHODIMP_(ULONG) CXContainerCntrItem::XOleDocumentSite::Release()
{
    METHOD_PROLOGUE_EX( CXContainerCntrItem, OleDocumentSite )
    return pThis->ExternalRelease();
}

STDMETHODIMP CXContainerCntrItem::XOleDocumentSite::QueryInterface( REFIID iid,
➥LPVOID* ppvObj )
{
    METHOD_PROLOGUE_EX( CXContainerCntrItem, OleDocumentSite )
    return pThis->ExternalQueryInterface( &iid, ppvObj );
}
```

```
//-------------------------------------------------------------------------
// The ActivateMe implementation
//-------------------------------------------------------------------------

STDMETHODIMP CXContainerCntrItem::XOleDocumentSite::ActivateMe(
➥LPOLEDOCUMENTVIEW pDocView )
{
    RECT            rect;
    IOleDocument*   pDoc;
    IOleInPlaceSite* pIOleInPlaceSite;

    METHOD_PROLOGUE_EX(CXContainerCntrItem, OleDocumentSite)

    //---------------------------------------------------------------------
    // Obtain the interface to our IOleInPlaceSite.  We need to give this
    // interface to the ActiveX Document's view.
    //---------------------------------------------------------------------
    pThis->InternalQueryInterface( &IID_IOleInPlaceSite, (void **)
➥&pIOleInPlaceSite );

    if( pDocView == NULL )
    {
        //-----------------------------------------------------------------
        // If the ActiveX Document did not supply us with a view then we
        // need to create a default one.  m_lpObject points to the ActiveX
        // Document's IOleObject interface.  We ask it for the IOleDocument
        // interface.
        //-----------------------------------------------------------------
        if( FAILED( pThis->m_lpObject->QueryInterface( IID_IOleDocument, (void
➥**)&pDoc ) ) )
            return E_FAIL;

        //-----------------------------------------------------------------
        // Ask the IOleDocument interface to create a view for us.  Pass our
        // IOleInPlaceSite interface to the ActiveX Document's view.
        //-----------------------------------------------------------------
        if( FAILED( pDoc->CreateView( pIOleInPlaceSite, NULL, 0, &pDocView ) ) )
            return E_OUTOFMEMORY;

        // This is required since CreateView incremented a reference to our
        // IOleDocument object.
        pDoc->Release();
    } else {
        //-----------------------------------------------------------------
        // The caller has passed us a view interface.  Make sure it has the
        // correct client site.
        //-----------------------------------------------------------------
        pDocView->SetInPlaceSite( pIOleInPlaceSite );

        //-----------------------------------------------------------------
        // Since we will hang on to this interface, increment the reference
        // count.
        //-----------------------------------------------------------------
        pDocView->AddRef();
    }

    pThis->m_pDSView = pDocView;
```

continues

Listing 13.2. continued

```
//-------------------------------------------------------------------
// Negotiate toolbars and menus with the view.
//-------------------------------------------------------------------
pDocView->UIActivate(TRUE);

//-------------------------------------------------------------------
// Now that we have toolbars, etc. filling our client area, let's find
// out what is left for our ActiveX Document view.
//-------------------------------------------------------------------
pThis->GetActiveView()->GetClientRect( &rect );
pDocView->SetRect( &rect );

//-------------------------------------------------------------------
// Show the view to the world!
//-------------------------------------------------------------------
pDocView->Show( TRUE );
return NOERROR;
}
```

This, essentially, is the file that was generated by AppWizard. Some additions have been made to implement the macros that we added to the header file.

The new code starts with the BEGIN_INTERFACE_MAP macro. Table 13.13 itemizes the implementation macros.

Table 13.13. MFC macros for implementing COM interfaces.

Macro name	*Description*
BEGIN_INTERFACE_MAP	This macro takes two parameters. The first parameter is the name of the class that contains the implementation of the COM interface. The second parameter is the name of the MFC base class for the first parameter.
INTERFACE_PART	This macro takes three parameters. The first parameter is the name of the class that contains the implementation of the COM interface. The second parameter is the unique identifier for the COM interface. This identifier starts with IID_, by convention. The third parameter is the name of the generated class. This name needs to match the name in the header file.
END_INTERFACE_MAP	This macro finishes the declaration.

The BEGIN_INTERFACE_PART macro in the header file automatically declares the three IUnknown methods. An implementation of these methods is required here. Notice that the name of the method is CXContainerCntrItem::XOleDocumentSite::AddRef. This kind of syntax indicates that the XOleDocumentSite class is actually declared within the context of the CXContainerCntrItem class. Therefore, in order to reference the AddRef method, you need to tell the compiler that you are declaring the AddRef method, which is part of XOleDocumentSite, which is part of CXContainerCntrItem.

Each COM method must begin with a METHOD_PROLOGUE_EX macro. As the macro name implies, it generates the appropriate prologue code before continuing with the rest of the code.

The most interesting implementation is the ActivateMe method. This method is called by the ActiveX document to tell the container that it should bypass the normal embedded object activation and bring up the document in the full client area. This method takes a pointer to the ActiveX document's IOleDocumentView object.

This method needs to create a connection between the container's IOleInPlaceSite interface and the document's IOleDocumentView interface. Next, it needs to tell the document to set up its menus and toolbars. The container tells the document how big the client area is and finally tells the document to show itself.

That's it! Figure 13.14 shows what XContainer looks like after support has been added for the IOleDocumentSite interface.

FIGURE 13.14.

XContainer as a full ActiveX container.

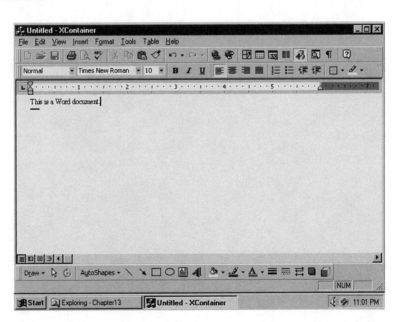

It is also possible to implement the IOleCommandTarget and IContinueCallback COM interfaces in the same manner. However, these interfaces are not required for ActiveX containers.

Summary

This chapter begins to explore the world of ActiveX containers. ActiveX represents Microsoft's continuing evolution of the OLE and COM technologies. It is a credit to the COM architecture that the OLE technologies can effectively change over time without becoming obsolete.

This chapter reviews portions of the OLE and COM architectures that are relevant to ActiveX container technology. Although the MFC classes have not yet changed to support the new ActiveX container COM interfaces, it is relatively easy to add the required support.

Other methods are available to implement ActiveX containers, in addition to using MFC. Containers could be implemented using the native COM interfaces or with the more recent ATL template library. Using MFC is completely appropriate in this case, though, because containers don't have the same constraints put on them as do other Internet-oriented COM objects.

14

ActiveX Servers

by Ted Neustaedter

In this chapter, you'll get an in-depth look at the different types of ActiveX servers, including embeddable servers and automation servers. Included are three distinct examples, which I spent quite a bit of time working on to give you a good understanding of the concepts I'm going to discuss.

After finishing this chapter, you should have a clear understanding of the purpose of each type of ActiveX server as well as a good base for building your own. Hopefully, some of you might even decide to enhance and extend the OpenGL server example I've included.

For those of you looking for some tips and tricks, check out the GLServer example. This little gem is embeddable and returns a bitmap to the container through the metafile device context.

ActiveX Servers Introduction

This chapter discusses the three types of ActiveX servers.

First is the *full server*—not that great a term because it might lead you to believe that it is a fully functional ActiveX server. In fact, it's not. Rather, a full server means that the server is both an ActiveX server and a fully functioning application. For example, in Microsoft Word you can run the application (as I am doing while writing these words), create a document or brochure, and then save the contents to a .DOC file. Or, you can open an application such as WordPad and actually include content that you've created using Microsoft Word.

The second type of server is the opposite of a full server and is also poorly named. It's called a *mini-server*. What this really means is that the server can be used only to include content into another application. As an example, Microsoft Word comes with a whole myriad of applets that can help you produce professional-looking documents. One of these is called Microsoft WordArt. If you attempt to run the WordArt program, you'll get a message telling you that the application can be run only when launched from inside another application.

Now we'll veer off in a totally different direction and talk about the third type of server. This is where things get a bit confusing for some folks. The third type of server—*automation*—doesn't act or appear to be anything like the full server or mini-server. In fact, you can't include content in an application with it. Instead, this type of server exposes special objects, methods, and properties to enable you to tell it what to do. For example, suppose I wanted to take a mail-merge document that I created in Microsoft Word and merge it with a mailing list stored in a Microsoft Access database. Sure, I could open up Microsoft Word and select the mail-merge menu item (along with about half a dozen other steps) and manually achieve my goal. Or, I could write an application in Visual Basic (or any other language that supports automation) and remotely control Microsoft Word. That way, for instance, the program could be set up in such a way that it runs every day at 4:00 a.m., unattended.

There are two flavors of automation servers: in-process and out-of-process servers.

In a nutshell, an in-process server is created from a class stored in a DLL, which is loaded and runs in the same process space as the application that created it. All instances share the same code; however, each has its own independent data area.

An out-of-process server runs in its own address space. This type of server is built as an EXE application (such as for Microsoft Word and Excel) and can either manage multiple instances or launch a new copy of the EXE each time a server object is created.

Okay, I know, it's a lot to grasp right now. Don't worry though, because by the time you get through this chapter I'm sure you'll have a much better grasp of how these different types of servers work. And believe me, with the direction the industry is moving, the most important of these three types of servers will undoubtedly be the ActiveX automation servers.

Three-Tier Development Using Server Components

Traditionally, when we refer to the term *client/server,* we are talking about an application that runs on a PC and connects to a database running on a server somewhere. This is fine for small-to medium-sized businesses with anywhere from 5 to 50 users. However, it really becomes a hassle when you've got 500 or more users. Every time a fix is made to an existing application, you need to distribute the new application to every desktop and ensure it gets properly installed. This process is both time consuming and costly as far as ensuring software and component compatibility on all desktops.

What about Internet and intranet applications? These need to be browser-based applications, but if you attempt to furnish thousands of users with simple CGI scripts, you end up spending a lot of time making sure that you're not getting deadlocks on files or databases.

> **NOTE**
>
> So, how do we handle large numbers of users? The term *scalability* is used to refer to the process of increasing the number of users from one user to hundreds of thousands of users.

To date, Microsoft has been pushing OLE and ActiveX technologies (which are really synonymous terms), including something called remote automation. Basically, *remote automation* permits an application running on PC 1 to connect to and create automation objects on PC 2. What is most significant about this is not the fact that you can now do distributed development without requiring in-depth knowledge of TCP/IP or NetBEUI, but rather that you're getting a glimpse of the world of three-tier development using Microsoft products.

The big problem with remote automation is that it doesn't have any security, it doesn't have a server to manage resources or database connections, and it was never designed to be used with the Internet or intranets.

Microsoft later released distributed COM (DCOM), which improves on the distributed aspect of COM objects, including support for Internet and intranet applications, but doesn't really address security issues or resources.

So, Microsoft announced the availability of the Microsoft Transaction Server (MTS). Not only does it address all of the problems mentioned earlier, it also supports transaction processing. Basically, you can now design ActiveX automation servers as small, simple components that don't need to know anything about the outside world.

Let's look at an example of how MTS could be useful. Given a bank account number, you could build two automation servers: one that performs a debit and a second that performs a credit. Now, all you need to do is tell MTS about these two components (ingrain that word *components* into your brain) by installing them on the server that is running MTS instead of on the client workstation.

You now need to do little more than write a small applet that attaches to the MTS server, starts a transaction, calls the debit component, calls the credit component, and completes the transaction. It is now MTS's responsibility to commit the processing steps these two components performed. If either one fails, MTS will automatically roll back the transaction.

I know this seems weird. I had quite a bit of trouble understanding it myself when I was first introduced to the idea. MTS performs a series of component-based transactions. We're used to doing this at the SQL level, which isn't required anymore. MTS is smart enough to provide a complete transaction handler using something called MSDTC.

That's all I'm going to say about MTS. I just wanted to give you something to think about. After all, this is a chapter on ActiveX servers. Watch carefully—in the next couple of years you're going to see a lot more of MTS.

The point is, we're moving away from the client/server (two-tier) way of thinking. Instead, we're moving to a three-tiered model, wherein the client application is very thin (commonly called a thin client), because it has only minimal functionality to call these automation servers and display results for the user (which can be done by a thin-client application or through a Web browser). The second tier is where the bulk of the work is done. It's an application server with hundreds, even thousands, of these tiny components installed. The third tier is the database tier.

MFC Versus Active Template Libraries

Before we get into the meat and potatoes of actually coding some of these servers, it's important to understand at least a few of the reasons why Microsoft has released a set of templates for developing ActiveX components (which includes automation servers, full and mini-servers, containers, and controls).

MFC is a great class hierarchy, but it can get somewhat bulky at times. This is especially true when you're creating small ActiveX components that you want to display on your Web site.

It's a real annoyance spending 20 minutes downloading support DLLs that don't need to be there. If you decide to statically link an MFC control or component, the end result is a very large DLL, EXE, or OCX.

So, after much debate, it was decided that a newer, leaner API (which really isn't the correct term for it, but I like to call it that) was released with Microsoft Visual C++ 4.2 and called the Active Template Libraries (ATL).

Now, for those of you who have ever done any programming with standard templates, you'll appreciate the beauty of this API (there I go again). It's a great solution for creating tight DLL or EXE components because it doesn't make use of MFC at all (unless you specially include it).

The drawbacks to ATL are there aren't a lot of people out there who can answer questions about it, and there aren't a lot of examples to help you along the way. A friend of mine is trying to implement licensing using ATL and has found it quite difficult and confusing. Also, you can't use the Class Wizard to develop your application, so you're on your own. Luckily, though, you do get an ATL COM Wizard and a couple dialogs for adding classes, methods, and properties.

It's up to you to decide which way to go, but I strongly recommend that you at least consider ATL because it has many good points—such as the ease involved in creating your automation servers.

Designing an MFC Mini-Server

To demonstrate the building of an embeddable server, we will be implementing a fairly simple server but with a slight twist. Most books I've read about ActiveX servers choose to embed silly phrases like *HELLO WORLD* and such. I decided to approach things a little differently. Instead, we'll design a simple OpenGL-embedding server that embeds a three-dimensional, square-shaped object into the container.

AppWizard: Step-by-Step

Begin by selecting File | New from the Developer Studio menu and taking a quick peek at the list of projects you can create. (See Figure 14.1.)

Of particular interest to us are the three types of projects we're going to build:

- ATL COM Wizard
- MFC AppWizard (DLL)
- MFC AppWizard (EXE)

The first project will be an ActiveX mini-server, which we will build as an EXE application. To begin, choose MFC AppWizard (EXE) and, in the Project Name: edit box, type GLServer.

FIGURE 14.1.

*List of Project
AppWizards.*

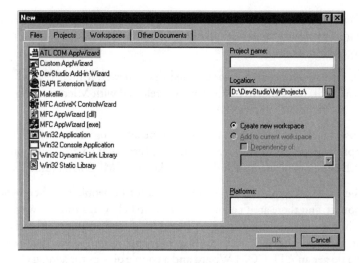

Step 1 of 6

Figure 14.2 shows the first step in creating a mini-server. For our example, we'll create an SDI application.

FIGURE 14.2.

*AppWizard: Step 1
of 6.*

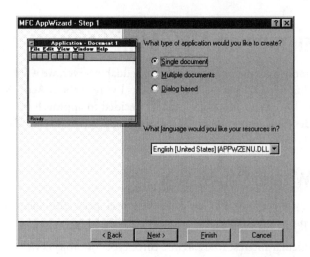

Step 2 of 6

Here, we have the option of including database support, but we'll simply choose None for our example.

Step 3 of 6

Now things get a little more interesting. Figure 14.3 shows the required parameters. You won't require automation, because you'll tackle that in the MFCAuto example later.

You might be wondering about compound files. Basically, they give you the ability to update separate sections of the document when sending visual representation of your data back to the container. GLServer will always repaint the entire window, so you don't really need this support—but leave it set to Yes anyway.

You also don't need support for ActiveX controls. On the other hand, this could be desirable for a full server to enhance the appearance of the application and provide more functionality to the user.

FIGURE 14.3.

AppWizard: Step 3 of 6.

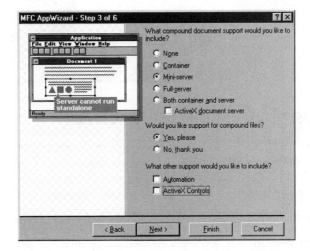

Step 4 of 6

The only thing to change here is to uncheck the Printing and Print Preview option. Because a mini-server needs to support printing itself, this is usually left up to the container application.

Step 5 of 6

Don't change any options in step 5. It is better to use MFC in a DLL rather than to statically link the libraries, because it makes the application much larger and wastes disk space.

Step 6 of 6

You've reached the final step in the wizard. Notice that there are a couple of new classes that you might or might not have seen before (see Figure 14.4), specifically CInPlaceFrame and CGLServerSrvrItem. These new classes are required to provide functionality for the server.

Also, note the base class for CGLServerDoc; it's no longer CDocument but rather COleServerDoc (which is a subclass of CDocument).

FIGURE 14.4.

AppWizard:
Step 6 of 6.

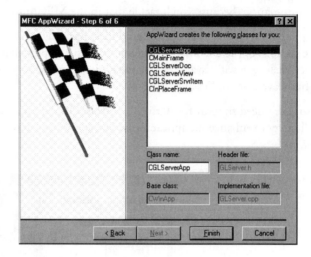

A Closer Look at the GLServer Classes

Now let's open up the GLServer project in the workspace window and take a closer look at the classes AppWizard generated.

CGLServerApp

Notice that in the declaration section for CGLServerApp a few things are slightly different.

A special constant is now being used for multiple inclusion detection. It includes the name of the server along with its unique CLSID.

More important, notice the addition of a new variable. (See Listing 14.1.)

Listing 14.1. The new data member for CGLServerApp.

```
// Implementation
 COleTemplateServer m_server;
```

This is probably the most important object that your project will create. This object is the basis for in-place editing/activation (which will be explained in detail in the section "CInPlaceFrame") and provides the functionality used by full servers, mini-servers, and automation servers.

Now let's take a look at the implementation of the CGLServerApp class.

Listing 14.2 looks at the CLSID, or ClassID. When the class is registered with the Windows 95/NT registry, the value is used to uniquely identify this class from other COM classes.

Listing 14.2. The CLSID source for this application.

```
// {739C0987-D609-11D0-967C-444553540000}
static const CLSID clsid =
{ 0x739c0987, 0xd609, 0x11d0, { 0x96, 0x7c, 0x44, 0x45, 0x53, 0x54, 0x0, 0x0 } };
```

The InitInstance() method shown in Listing 14.3 is really the only new method so far. The first thing to note is that we call AfxOleInit() to initialize the OLE libraries.

The document template is the same as before except that the CGLServerDoc class is now derived from COleServerDoc instead of CDocument.

Notice the call to SetServerInfo(), which lets the framework know what type of activation is available when the user requests to edit the data. Our server will provide in-place activation.

Lastly, notice that we check to see if we are in embedding mode, and if so we call RegisterAll(), which actually creates the object that the container will use. Notice also that we do not support stand-alone execution. (Remember, this is a mini-server that must be embedded into a container application.) If the user attempts to start the application stand-alone, a message box explains that the application must be launched by inserting an object into a container.

Listing 14.3. The source code for CGLServerApp::InitInstance.

```
BOOL CGLServerApp::InitInstance()
{
 // Initialize OLE libraries
 if (!AfxOleInit())
 {
  AfxMessageBox(IDP_OLE_INIT_FAILED);
  return FALSE;
 }
```

continues

Listing 14.3. continued

```
// Standard initialization
// If you are not using these features and wish to reduce the size
//  of your final executable, you should remove from the following
//  the specific initialization routines you do not need.

#ifdef _AFXDLL
 Enable3dControls();      // Call this when using MFC in a shared DLL
#else
 Enable3dControlsStatic();      // Call this when linking to MFC statically
#endif

 // Change the registry key under which our settings are stored.
 // You should modify this string to be something appropriate
 // such as the name of your company or organization.
 SetRegistryKey(_T("Local AppWizard-Generated Applications"));

 LoadStdProfileSettings();  // Load standard INI file options (including MRU)

 // Register the application's document templates.  Document templates
 //  serve as the connection between documents, frame windows and views.

 CSingleDocTemplate* pDocTemplate;
 pDocTemplate = new CSingleDocTemplate(
  IDR_MAINFRAME,
  RUNTIME_CLASS(CGLServerDoc),
  RUNTIME_CLASS(CMainFrame),        // main SDI frame window
  RUNTIME_CLASS(CGLServerView));
 pDocTemplate->SetServerInfo(
  IDR_SRVR_EMBEDDED, IDR_SRVR_INPLACE,
  RUNTIME_CLASS(CInPlaceFrame));
 AddDocTemplate(pDocTemplate);

 // Connect the COleTemplateServer to the document template.
 //  The COleTemplateServer creates new documents on behalf
 //  of requesting OLE containers by using information
 //  specified in the document template.
 m_server.ConnectTemplate(clsid, pDocTemplate, TRUE);

 // Note: SDI applications register server objects only if /Embedding
 //  or /Automation is present on the command line.

 // Parse command line for standard shell commands, DDE, file open
 CCommandLineInfo cmdInfo;
 ParseCommandLine(cmdInfo);

 // Check to see if launched as OLE server
 if (cmdInfo.m_bRunEmbedded || cmdInfo.m_bRunAutomated)
 {
 // Register all OLE server (factories) as running.  This enables the
 //  OLE libraries to create objects from other applications.
 COleTemplateServer::RegisterAll();
```

```
// Application was run with /Embedding or /Automation.  Don't show the
//  main window in this case.
return TRUE;
}


// When a server application is launched stand-alone, it is a good idea
//  to update the system registry in case it has been damaged.
m_server.UpdateRegistry(OAT_INPLACE_SERVER);

// When a mini-server is run stand-alone the registry is updated and the
//  user is instructed to use the Insert Object dialog in a container
//  to use the server.  Mini-servers do not have stand-alone user interfaces.
AfxMessageBox(IDP_USE_INSERT_OBJECT);
return FALSE;
}
```

CGLServerDoc

The `COleServerDoc` document class is the heart of the embeddable server and is ready to roll without any modifications. (You'll want to add some customization to make it useful.)

Although not necessary for our particular application, to enable compound files for storage and data display, we simply call the `EnableCompoundFile()` method during the construction of this document.

Listing 14.4. The `CGLServerDoc` constructor.

```
CGLServerDoc::CGLServerDoc()
{
// Use OLE compound files
EnableCompoundFile();

// TODO: add one-time construction code here
}
```

The `OnGetEmbeddedItem()` notification is called by the class factory to create a new `CGLServerSrvrItem` item. (See Listing 14.5.)

Also listed is the `Serialize()` method, which can be enhanced to automatically serialize data to the container's persistent storage, as required, to save the state of this server.

For example, if your server has special options that were configured, such as font size and color, you could easily add serialization code so that this information gets saved to persistent storage when the user selects Save As in the container application. The data is then serialized with the container's data, not in a separate file, so that when the container is opened in a future editing session and the server is invoked, it can serialize its data and continue where it left off.

Listing 14.5. Source code for `OnGetEmbeddedItem()` and `Serialize()`.

```
/////////////////////////////////////////////////////////////////////////////
// CGLServerDoc server implementation

COleServerItem* CGLServerDoc::OnGetEmbeddedItem()
{
 // OnGetEmbeddedItem is called by the framework to get the  COleServerItem
 //  that is associated with the document.  It is only called when necessary.

 CGLServerSrvrItem* pItem = new CGLServerSrvrItem(this);
 ASSERT_VALID(pItem);
 return pItem;
}


/////////////////////////////////////////////////////////////////////////////
// CGLServerDoc serialization
void CGLServerDoc::Serialize(CArchive& ar)
{
 if (ar.IsStoring())
 {
  // TODO: add storing code here
 }
 else
 {
  // TODO: add loading code here
 }
}
```

CGLServerSrvrItem

When a `GLServer` item is embedded into a container (such as WordPad or MS Word), a new instance of `CGLServerSrvrItem` is created and passed to the container. The `OnGetExtent()` method is called by the container to determine the size of the object being embedded. The default implementation created by the AppWizard uses a hard coded `3000 x 3000 HIMETRIC` unit extent. (See Listing 14.6.)

Listing 14.6. The `OnGetExtent()` implementation code.

```
BOOL CGLServerSrvrItem::OnGetExtent(DVASPECT dwDrawAspect, CSize& rSize)
{
 // Most applications, like this one, only handle drawing the content
 //  aspect of the item.  If you wish to support other aspects, such
 //  as DVASPECT_THUMBNAIL (by overriding OnDrawEx), then this
 //  implementation of OnGetExtent should be modified to handle the
 //  additional aspect(s).

 if (dwDrawAspect != DVASPECT_CONTENT)
  return COleServerItem::OnGetExtent(dwDrawAspect, rSize);

 // CGLServerSrvrItem::OnGetExtent is called to get the extent in
 //  HIMETRIC units of the entire item.  The default implementation
 //  here simply returns a hard-coded number of units.
```

```
CGLServerDoc* pDoc = GetDocument();
ASSERT_VALID(pDoc);

// TODO: replace this arbitrary size

rSize = CSize(3000, 3000);    // 3000 x 3000 HIMETRIC units

return TRUE;
}
```

GLServer will also paint into a special device context, provided by the container, called a *metafile device context* (which can contain any GDI objects, including bitmaps and brushes) when the container calls the nonfiction OnDraw(), as shown in Listing 14.7.

The container uses this metafile representation to display the item when the server is not active. This way, the container doesn't need to start the GLServer application in order to see this embedded data. The GLServer application will not be loaded unless the user specifically requests it.

By default, the AppWizard does not provide any painting; so, if you build this project as is, the embedded object will not contain any data whatsoever.

Listing 14.7. The OnDraw() implementation code.

```
BOOL CGLServerSrvrItem::OnDraw(CDC* pDC, CSize& rSize)
{
 // Remove this if you use rSize
 UNREFERENCED_PARAMETER(rSize);

 CGLServerDoc* pDoc = GetDocument();
 ASSERT_VALID(pDoc);

 // TODO: set mapping mode and extent
 //  (The extent is usually the same as the size returned from OnGetExtent)
 pDC->SetMapMode(MM_ANISOTROPIC);
 pDC->SetWindowOrg(0,0);
 pDC->SetWindowExt(3000, 3000);

 // TODO: add drawing code here.  Optionally, fill in the HIMETRIC extent.
 //  All drawing takes place in the metafile device context (pDC).

 return TRUE;
}
```

When the container wants to store a document with a GLServer-embedded item, it will call Serialize() to save any modifications. The basic implementation simply calls the CGLServerDoc's default implementation of Serialize(). (See Listing 14.8.) The data is not serialized to a file, but to a persistent storage object provided by the container.

There are some cases in which calling the default implementation isn't the correct way to handle storage. For example, suppose that you didn't want to save the data to the container's storage but would rather store it to a separate file and link that file to the container. Microsoft Word has this option. Instead of saving a picture inside the document, you can optionally link to a separate file, thus saving document storage and retrieval time.

Listing 14.8. The Serialize() implementation code.

```
void CGLServerSrvrItem::Serialize(CArchive& ar)
{
 // CGLServerSrvrItem::Serialize will be called by the framework if
 //   the item is copied to the clipboard.  This can happen automatically
 //   through the OLE callback OnGetClipboardData.  A good default for
 //   the embedded item is simply to delegate to the document's Serialize
 //   function.  If you support links, then you will want to serialize
 //   just a portion of the document.

 if (!IsLinkedItem())
 {
  CGLServerDoc* pDoc = GetDocument();
  ASSERT_VALID(pDoc);
  pDoc->Serialize(ar);
 }
}
```

CInPlaceFrame

This class requires a little bit more explanation than the others did. First, let me explain the term in-place activation. Basically, *in-place activation* means that when the user invokes an embedded server by double-clicking the object in the container, instead of bringing up a separate window for editing the server data, the server actually uses the container's window. Figures 14.5 and 14.6 provide examples of in-place activation.

In Figure 14.5 is a WordPad application with an embedded bitmap in it. Currently, the WordPad application is active, allowing you to change the WordPad text.

By double-clicking the bitmap image (remember this is an embedded Paintbrush bitmap), the Paintbrush program is activated in-place. This means that it takes over the client area of the WordPad application. Notice that the toolbars on the top have disappeared and have been replaced by the Paintbrush toolbar on the left side. Not visible here is the fact that the menus have also changed.

Remember, though, that in-place activation is not the only way to edit embedded objects. You can also use out-of-place activation if you embed an icon representation of the image instead of the image itself. This is done either when you first insert the object by choosing the Display as Icon checkbox or by right-clicking the object inside of WordPad, selecting Object Properties, changing to the View tab, and selecting the Display as Icon radio button. This is illustrated in Figure 14.7.

FIGURE 14.5.

WordPad with an embedded bitmap.

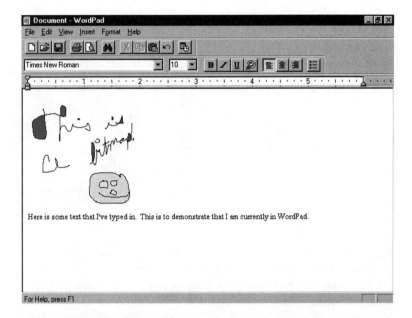

FIGURE 14.6.

Paintbrush in-place activation inside of WordPad.

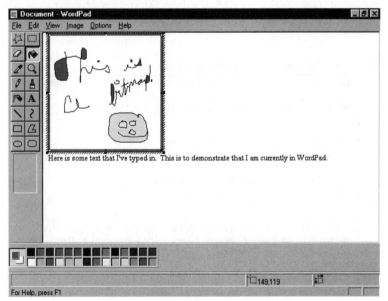

FIGURE 14.7.

*Setting the server item
to out-of-place
activation inside of
WordPad.*

If you look carefully at the in-place activation session (refer to Figure 14.6), you'll notice a funny rectangle around the object with sizers around the edges. This is called the *resizer bar*. You can use this to resize the embedded object during in-place activation. Listing 14.9 includes the default implementation for this resizer bar.

Drag-and-drop support is registered, although the default implementation does nothing. (See Listing 14.9.)

Listing 14.9. The OnCreate() member function.

```
int CInPlaceFrame::OnCreate(LPCREATESTRUCT lpCreateStruct)
{
 if (COleIPFrameWnd::OnCreate(lpCreateStruct) == -1)
  return -1;

 // CResizeBar implements in-place resizing.
 if (!m_wndResizeBar.Create(this))
 {
  TRACE0("Failed to create resize bar\n");
  return -1;      // fail to create
 }

 // By default, it is a good idea to register a drop-target that does
 //  nothing with your frame window.  This prevents drops from
 //  "falling through" to a container that supports drag-drop.
 m_dropTarget.Register(this);

 return 0;
}
```

The AppWizard generates a toolbar that will appear during in-place activation and will temporarily replace the container's toolbars. Listing 14.10 shows the code used to register the toolbars. Although this is an embedded toolbar, it can still have all the properties of a regular toolbar, including the dockable characteristic.

Listing 14.10. The `OnCreateControlBars()` member function.

```
// OnCreateControlBars is called by the framework to create control bars on the
//  container application's windows.  pWndFrame is the top level frame window of
//  the container and is always non-NULL.  pWndDoc is the doc level frame window
//  and will be NULL when the container is an SDI application.  A server
//  application can place MFC control bars on either window.
BOOL CInPlaceFrame::OnCreateControlBars(CFrameWnd* pWndFrame, CFrameWnd* pWndDoc)
{
 // Remove this if you use pWndDoc
 UNREFERENCED_PARAMETER(pWndDoc);

 // Set owner to this window, so messages are delivered to correct app
 m_wndToolBar.SetOwner(this);

 // Create toolbar on client's frame window
 if (!m_wndToolBar.Create(pWndFrame) ||
  !m_wndToolBar.LoadToolBar(IDR_SRVR_INPLACE))
 {
  TRACE0("Failed to create toolbar\n");
  return FALSE;
 }

 // TODO: Remove this if you don't want tool tips or a resizeable toolbar
 m_wndToolBar.SetBarStyle(m_wndToolBar.GetBarStyle() |
  CBRS_TOOLTIPS | CBRS_FLYBY | CBRS_SIZE_DYNAMIC);

 // TODO: Delete these three lines if you don't want the toolbar to
 //   be dockable
 m_wndToolBar.EnableDocking(CBRS_ALIGN_ANY);
 pWndFrame->EnableDocking(CBRS_ALIGN_ANY);
 pWndFrame->DockControlBar(&m_wndToolBar);

 return TRUE;
}
```

CGLServerView

Last but not least is the View class. The only real difference is the addition of a special notification to cancel the embedded session. This is required for keyboard processing only (such as the use of the Esc key), because the mouse handler goes to the container instead of the server (by clicking outside of the embedded server area).

Listing 14.11. The `OnCancelEditSrvr()` member function.

```
/////////////////////////////////////////////////////////////////////////////
// OLE Server support

// The following command handler provides the standard keyboard
//  user interface to cancel an in-place editing session.  Here,
//  the server (not the container) causes the deactivation.
void CGLServerView::OnCancelEditSrvr()
{
 GetDocument()->OnDeactivateUI(FALSE);
}
```

Combining Container and Server Menus During Activation

As you might have noticed in Figures 14.6 and 14.7, when you start in-place activation, the server's menus were combined with the container's menus.

You won't be modifying this functionality in the example, but I want to give you an understanding of just how these two menus are combined.

Both the container and the server provide partial menus. When the server is activated, the two sets of menus are merged together to form the new in-place activation menus. (See Figure 14.8.) The container menus can be merged with this menu before Edit, between View and Help (the two separator bars help to determine this), or after Help.

FIGURE 14.8.

The GLServer *in-place activation partial menus.*

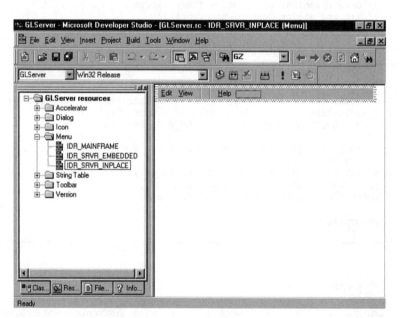

Testing out the GLServer Skeleton

Before adding customization, try compiling the GLServer example the way it is right now and use WordPad to embed it. It won't do much, but you should be able to embed the server and see an empty window inside of the sizer bar (as in Figure 14.9). To register this example, you'll have to run the application. You should get a message from GLServer telling you that the application can only be run from a container. Just click OK. Your GLServer is now registered, and you can insert it into WordPad.

FIGURE 14.9.

The GLServer *skeleton.*

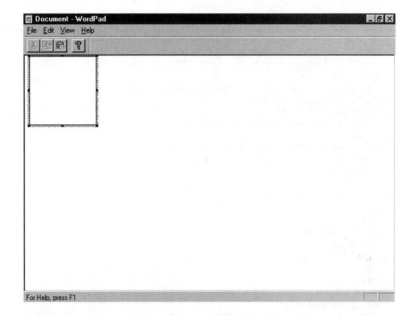

Adding Customization to the GLServer Skeleton

Now let's start adding some customized methods, data members, and so on, and make this server sing.

Customizing CGLServerDoc

Our document class will hold the methods and data members used for this example. Therefore, most of the code that actually draws the OpenGL shape will be stored in this class, and rightly so. Change the CGLServerDoc declaration, as indicated by the bold text shown in Listing 14.12.

Listing 14.12. Modifications to the CGLServerDoc class.

```
class CGLServerDoc : public COleServerDoc
{
public:
 // private member vars

protected: // create from serialization only
 CGLServerDoc();
 DECLARE_DYNCREATE(CGLServerDoc)

// Attributes
public:
 CGLServerSrvrItem* GetEmbeddedItem()
  { return (CGLServerSrvrItem*)COleServerDoc::GetEmbeddedItem(); }
```

continues

Listing 14.12. continued

```
// Operations
public:

// Overrides
 // ClassWizard generated virtual function overrides
 //{{AFX_VIRTUAL(CGLServerDoc)
 protected:
 virtual COleServerItem* OnGetEmbeddedItem();
 public:
 virtual BOOL OnNewDocument();
 virtual void Serialize(CArchive& ar);
 //}}AFX_VIRTUAL

// Implementation
//member vars
private:
 float m_fRadius;
 HGLRC m_hrc;
 LOGPALETTE *m_pPalette;

public:
 CDC *m_pMemoryDC;
 RECT m_rcViewRect;
 CBitmap *m_pOldBitmap, *m_pBitmap;
 HPALETTE m_hPalette, m_hOldPalette;

 void GLDraw(CDC* pDC, RECT *pRect);
 virtual ~CGLServerDoc();

 void CreateGLContext(HDC hdc, RECT& rc);
 BOOL SetGLPixels(HDC hdc);
 unsigned char GetPaletteIndex(int nIndex, UINT nBits, UINT nShift);
 void CreateGLPalette(HDC hdc);

#ifdef _DEBUG
 virtual void AssertValid() const;
 virtual void Dump(CDumpContext& dc) const;
#endif

protected:

// Generated message map functions
protected:
 //{{AFX_MSG(CGLServerDoc)
  // NOTE - the ClassWizard will add and remove member functions here.
  //    DO NOT EDIT what you see in these blocks of generated code !
 //}}AFX_MSG
 DECLARE_MESSAGE_MAP()

};
```

Now, change the CGLServerDoc implementation as shown in Listing 14.13.

Listing 14.13. Modifications to the `CGLServerDoc` implementation.

```cpp
// GLServerDoc.cpp : implementation of the CGLServerDoc class
//

#include "stdafx.h"
#include "gl\glaux.h"

#include "GLServer.h"

#include "GLServerDoc.h"
#include "SrvrItem.h"

#ifdef _DEBUG
#define new DEBUG_NEW
#undef THIS_FILE
static char THIS_FILE[] = __FILE__;
#endif

unsigned char cShift1[2] = { 0, 255 };
unsigned char cShift3[4] = { 0, 0x55, 0xaa, 0xff };
unsigned char cShift7[8] = { 0, 0111 >> 1, 0222 >> 1, 0333 >> 1,
        0444 >> 1, 0555 >> 1, 0666 >> 1, 0377 };
static int nPalColors[13] = { 0, 3, 24, 27, 64, 67, 88, 173,
        181, 236, 247, 164, 91 };
static PALETTEENTRY defPalette[20] =
{
 { 0,    0,    0,    0 }, { 0x80,0,   0,    0 }, { 0,    0x80,0,   0 },
 { 0x80,0x80,0,     0 }, { 0,    0,    0x80, 0 }, { 0x80,0,   0x80, 0 },
 { 0,    0x80,0x80, 0 }, { 0xC0,0xC0,0xC0, 0 }, { 192, 220, 192,  0 },
 { 166, 202, 240,   0 }, { 255, 251, 240,  0 }, { 160, 160, 164,  0 },
 { 0x80,0x80,0x80, 0 }, { 0xFF,0,   0,    0 }, { 0,    0xFF,0,   0 },
 { 0xFF,0xFF,0,     0 }, { 0,    0,    0xFF, 0 }, { 0xFF,0,   0xFF, 0 },
 { 0,    0xFF,0xFF, 0 }, { 0xFF,0xFF,0xFF, 0 }
};

/////////////////////////////////////////////////////////////////////////////
// CGLServerDoc

IMPLEMENT_DYNCREATE(CGLServerDoc, COleServerDoc)

BEGIN_MESSAGE_MAP(CGLServerDoc, COleServerDoc)
 //{{AFX_MSG_MAP(CGLServerDoc)
  // NOTE - the ClassWizard will add and remove mapping macros here.
  //    DO NOT EDIT what you see in these blocks of generated code!
 //}}AFX_MSG_MAP
END_MESSAGE_MAP()

/////////////////////////////////////////////////////////////////////////////
// CGLServerDoc construction/destruction

CGLServerDoc::CGLServerDoc()
{
 // Use OLE compound files
 EnableCompoundFile();
```

continues

Listing 14.13. continued

```
// set defaults
m_pPalette = NULL;
m_hPalette, m_hOldPalette = NULL;
m_hrc = NULL;
m_pMemoryDC = NULL;
m_pBitmap = m_pOldBitmap = NULL;
}

CGLServerDoc::~CGLServerDoc()
{
}

BOOL CGLServerDoc::OnNewDocument()
{
 if (!COleServerDoc::OnNewDocument())
  return FALSE;

 // TODO: add reinitialization code here
 // (SDI documents will reuse this document)

 return TRUE;
}

/////////////////////////////////////////////////////////////////////////
// CGLServerDoc server implementation

COleServerItem* CGLServerDoc::OnGetEmbeddedItem()
{
 // OnGetEmbeddedItem is called by the framework to get the COleServerItem
 //  that is associated with the document.  It is only called when necessary.

 CGLServerSrvrItem* pItem = new CGLServerSrvrItem(this);
 ASSERT_VALID(pItem);
 return pItem;
}

/////////////////////////////////////////////////////////////////////////
// CGLServerDoc serialization

void CGLServerDoc::Serialize(CArchive& ar)
{
 if (ar.IsStoring())
 {
  // TODO: add storing code here
 }
 else
 {
  // TODO: add loading code here
 }
}

/////////////////////////////////////////////////////////////////////////
// CGLServerDoc diagnostics
```

```
#ifdef _DEBUG
void CGLServerDoc::AssertValid() const
{
 COleServerDoc::AssertValid();
}

void CGLServerDoc::Dump(CDumpContext& dc) const
{
 COleServerDoc::Dump(dc);
}
#endif //_DEBUG

/////////////////////////////////////////////////////////////////////////////
// CGLServerDoc commands

void CGLServerDoc::GLDraw(CDC *pDC, RECT *pRect)
{
 // setup
 HDC hdc = pDC->GetSafeHdc();
 CreateGLContext(hdc, *pRect);

 // clear buffers and colors
    glClearColor(0.0f, 0.0f, 0.0f, 10.0f);
    glClear(GL_COLOR_BUFFER_BIT | GL_DEPTH_BUFFER_BIT);

 // push matrix
    glPushMatrix();

 // setup geometric rotation senario
    glTranslatef(0.0f, 0.0f, -m_fRadius);

 // FRONTSIDE
 // draw a side
 glBegin(GL_QUAD_STRIP);
  glColor3f(1.0f, 0.0f, 0.0f); glVertex3f(-1.25f,  0.0f, -0.5f);
  glColor3f(0.5f, 0.0f, 0.0f); glVertex3f(-1.25f, -1.0f, -0.5f);
  glColor3f(1.0f, 0.0f, 0.0f); glVertex3f(-0.75f,  0.0f, -0.5f);
  glColor3f(0.5f, 0.0f, 0.0f); glVertex3f(-0.75f, -1.0f, -0.5f);
 glEnd();

 // draw a side
 glBegin(GL_QUAD_STRIP);
  glColor3f(0.0f, 0.5f, 0.0f); glVertex3f(-0.75f,  0.0f, -0.5f);
  glColor3f(0.0f, 1.0f, 0.0f); glVertex3f(-0.75f, -1.0f, -0.5f);
  glColor3f(0.0f, 0.5f, 0.0f); glVertex3f(-0.25f,  0.5f,  0.0f);
  glColor3f(0.0f, 1.0f, 0.0f); glVertex3f(-0.25f, -0.5f,  0.0f);
 glEnd();

 // draw a side
 glBegin(GL_QUAD_STRIP);
  glColor3f(0.0f, 0.5f, 1.0f); glVertex3f(-0.25f,  0.5f,  0.0f);
  glColor3f(0.0f, 1.0f, 0.5f); glVertex3f(-0.25f, -0.5f,  0.0f);
  glColor3f(0.0f, 0.5f, 1.0f); glVertex3f( 0.25f,  0.5f,  0.0f);
  glColor3f(0.0f, 1.0f, 0.5f); glVertex3f( 0.25f, -0.5f,  0.0f);
 glEnd();
```

continues

Listing 14.13. continued

```
// draw a side
glBegin(GL_QUAD_STRIP);
 glColor3f(0.0f, 0.5f, 0.0f); glVertex3f( 0.25f,  0.5f,  0.0f);
 glColor3f(0.0f, 1.0f, 0.0f); glVertex3f( 0.25f, -0.5f,  0.0f);
 glColor3f(0.0f, 0.5f, 0.0f); glVertex3f( 0.75f,  0.0f, -0.5f);
 glColor3f(0.0f, 1.0f, 0.0f); glVertex3f( 0.75f, -1.0f, -0.5f);
glEnd();

// draw a side
glBegin(GL_QUAD_STRIP);
 glColor3f(0.5f, 0.0f, 0.0f); glVertex3f( 0.75f,  0.0f, -0.5f);
 glColor3f(1.0f, 0.0f, 0.0f); glVertex3f( 0.75f, -1.0f, -0.5f);
 glColor3f(0.5f, 0.0f, 0.0f); glVertex3f( 1.25f,  0.0f, -0.5f);
 glColor3f(1.0f, 0.0f, 0.0f); glVertex3f( 1.25f, -1.0f, -0.5f);
glEnd();

// BACKSIDE
// draw a side
glBegin(GL_QUAD_STRIP);
 glColor3f(0.5f, 1.0f, 0.0f); glVertex3f(-1.25f,  0.0f, -0.5f);
 glColor3f(1.0f, 0.5f, 0.0f); glVertex3f(-1.25f, -1.0f, -0.5f);
 glColor3f(0.5f, 1.0f, 0.0f); glVertex3f(-0.50f,  1.0f,  0.5f);
 glColor3f(1.0f, 0.5f, 0.0f); glVertex3f(-0.50f,  0.0f,  0.5f);
glEnd();

// draw a side
glBegin(GL_QUAD_STRIP);
 glColor3f(0.5f, 0.0f, 1.0f); glVertex3f(-0.50f,  1.0f,  0.5f);
 glColor3f(1.0f, 0.0f, 0.5f); glVertex3f(-0.50f,  0.0f,  0.5f);
 glColor3f(0.5f, 0.0f, 1.0f); glVertex3f( 0.50f,  1.0f,  0.5f);
 glColor3f(1.0f, 0.0f, 0.5f); glVertex3f( 0.50f,  0.0f,  0.5f);
glEnd();

// draw a side
glBegin(GL_QUAD_STRIP);
 glColor3f(0.5f, 1.0f, 0.0f); glVertex3f( 1.25f,  0.0f, -0.5f);
 glColor3f(1.0f, 0.5f, 0.0f); glVertex3f( 1.25f, -1.0f, -0.5f);
 glColor3f(0.5f, 1.0f, 0.0f); glVertex3f( 0.50f,  1.0f,  0.5f);
 glColor3f(1.0f, 0.5f, 0.0f); glVertex3f( 0.50f,  0.0f,  0.5f);
glEnd();

// TOPFACE
glBegin(GL_QUAD_STRIP);
 glColor3f(0.0f, 0.0f, 0.5f); glVertex3f(-1.25f,  0.0f, -0.5f);
 glColor3f(0.0f, 0.0f, 1.0f); glVertex3f(-0.75f,  0.0f, -0.5f);
 glColor3f(0.0f, 0.0f, 0.5f); glVertex3f(-0.50f,  1.0f,  0.5f);
 glColor3f(0.0f, 0.0f, 1.0f); glVertex3f(-0.25f,  0.5f,  0.0f);
 glColor3f(0.0f, 0.0f, 0.5f); glVertex3f( 0.50f,  1.0f,  0.5f);
 glColor3f(0.0f, 0.0f, 1.0f); glVertex3f( 0.25f,  0.5f,  0.0f);
 glColor3f(0.0f, 0.0f, 0.5f); glVertex3f( 1.25f,  0.0f, -0.5f);
 glColor3f(0.0f, 0.0f, 1.0f); glVertex3f( 0.75f,  0.0f, -0.5f);
glEnd();

// BOTTOMFACE
glBegin(GL_QUAD_STRIP);
 glColor3f(0.0f, 0.0f, 0.5f); glVertex3f(-1.25f, -1.0f, -0.5f);
 glColor3f(0.0f, 0.0f, 1.0f); glVertex3f(-0.75f, -1.0f, -0.5f);
```

```
        glColor3f(0.0f, 0.0f, 0.5f); glVertex3f(-0.50f,  0.0f,  0.5f);
        glColor3f(0.0f, 0.0f, 1.0f); glVertex3f(-0.25f, -0.5f,  0.0f);
        glColor3f(0.0f, 0.0f, 0.5f); glVertex3f( 0.50f,  0.0f,  0.5f);
        glColor3f(0.0f, 0.0f, 1.0f); glVertex3f( 0.25f, -0.5f,  0.0f);
        glColor3f(0.0f, 0.0f, 0.5f); glVertex3f( 1.25f, -1.0f, -0.5f);
        glColor3f(0.0f, 0.0f, 1.0f); glVertex3f( 0.75f, -1.0f, -0.5f);
    glEnd();


    glPopMatrix();

// all done drawing, finish up and swap buffers
    glFinish();
    SwapBuffers(wglGetCurrentDC());
SetBkMode(hdc, TRANSPARENT);

// cleanup
    ::wglMakeCurrent(NULL,  NULL);

// delete GL context
    if (m_hrc)
{
        ::wglDeleteContext(m_hrc);
  m_hrc = NULL;
 }
}


void CGLServerDoc::CreateGLContext(HDC hdc, RECT& rc)
{
    PIXELFORMATDESCRIPTOR pfdPixels;

// setup the pixel format
    if (SetGLPixels(hdc) == FALSE)
{
        return;
 }

// create our GL palette
    CreateGLPalette(hdc);

// realize palette
::SelectPalette(hdc, m_hPalette, FALSE);
::RealizePalette(hdc);

// setup pixel format
::DescribePixelFormat(hdc, ::GetPixelFormat(hdc), sizeof(pfdPixels), &pfdPixels);

// create gl context
    m_hrc = wglCreateContext(hdc);
    wglMakeCurrent(hdc, m_hrc);
    glClearDepth(10.0f);
    glEnable(GL_DEPTH_TEST);
    glMatrixMode(GL_PROJECTION);
    glLoadIdentity();
```

continues

Listing 14.13. continued

```
// check for divide by zero
if (rc.bottom != 0)
    gluPerspective(30.0f, (GLfloat)rc.right/rc.bottom, 3.0f, 20.0f);
else
    gluPerspective(30.0f, 1.0f, 3.0f, 20.0f);

    glMatrixMode(GL_MODELVIEW);
m_fRadius = 3.0f + 3.0f / 2.0f;
}

BOOL CGLServerDoc::SetGLPixels(HDC hdc)
{
    int nPixFmt;
    static PIXELFORMATDESCRIPTOR pfdPixels =
    {
        sizeof(PIXELFORMATDESCRIPTOR), 1,
  PFD_DOUBLEBUFFER | PFD_DRAW_TO_WINDOW | PFD_SUPPORT_OPENGL,
        PFD_TYPE_RGBA, 24, 0, 0, 0, 0, 0, 0, 0, 0, 0, 0, 0, 0, 0,
        32, 0, 0, PFD_MAIN_PLANE, 0, 0, 0, 0
    };

    if ((nPixFmt = ChoosePixelFormat(hdc, &pfdPixels)) == 0)
    {
        _ASSERTE(FALSE);
        return FALSE;
    }

    if (SetPixelFormat(hdc, nPixFmt, &pfdPixels) == FALSE)
    {
        _ASSERTE(FALSE);
        return FALSE;
    }

    return TRUE;
}

unsigned char CGLServerDoc::GetPaletteIndex(int nIndex, UINT nBits, UINT nShift)
{
    if (nBits == 1)
  return cShift1[(unsigned char) (nIndex >> nShift) & 0x1];

 else if (nBits == 2)
  return cShift3[(unsigned char) (nIndex >> nShift) & 0x3];

 else if (nBits == 3)
  return cShift7[(unsigned char) (nIndex >> nShift) & 0x7];

 else
  return 0;
}

void CGLServerDoc::CreateGLPalette(HDC hdc)
{
    PIXELFORMATDESCRIPTOR pfdPixels;
    int nPixelFormat, nCounter;
```

```
// only do first time in
if (m_pPalette)
 return;

// calculate pixel format
    nPixelFormat = ::GetPixelFormat(hdc);
    ::DescribePixelFormat(hdc, nPixelFormat, sizeof(pfdPixels), &pfdPixels);

// change palette if necessary
    if (pfdPixels.dwFlags & PFD_NEED_PALETTE)
    {
        nPixelFormat = 1 << pfdPixels.cColorBits;
        m_pPalette = (PLOGPALETTE) new char[sizeof(LOGPALETTE) +
    nPixelFormat * sizeof(PALETTEENTRY)];

        _ASSERTE(m_pPalette != NULL);

        m_pPalette->palVersion = 0x300;
        m_pPalette->palNumEntries = nPixelFormat;

// loop through pixel set and set palette colors
        for (nCounter=0; nCounter < nPixelFormat; nCounter++)
        {
            m_pPalette->palPalEntry[nCounter].peRed = GetPaletteIndex(
        nCounter, pfdPixels.cRedBits, pfdPixels.cRedShift);
            m_pPalette->palPalEntry[nCounter].peGreen = GetPaletteIndex(
        nCounter, pfdPixels.cGreenBits, pfdPixels.cGreenShift);
            m_pPalette->palPalEntry[nCounter].peBlue = GetPaletteIndex(
        nCounter, pfdPixels.cBlueBits, pfdPixels.cBlueShift);
            m_pPalette->palPalEntry[nCounter].peFlags = 0;
        }

        if ((pfdPixels.cColorBits == 8) &&
            (pfdPixels.cRedBits   == 3) && (pfdPixels.cRedShift   == 0) &&
            (pfdPixels.cGreenBits == 3) && (pfdPixels.cGreenShift == 3) &&
            (pfdPixels.cBlueBits  == 2) && (pfdPixels.cBlueShift  == 6))
        {
    for (nCounter = 1 ; nCounter <= 12 ; nCounter++)
                m_pPalette->palPalEntry[nPalColors[nCounter]] =
defPalette[nCounter];
        }

// create GL paletter
m_hPalette = ::CreatePalette((LPLOGPALETTE)m_pPalette);

// realize palette
        ::SelectPalette(hdc, m_hPalette, FALSE);
        ::RealizePalette(hdc);
    }
}
```

I know a lot of additions are here, but trust me, the result is worth the effort—especially if you decide to add your own enhancements later (such as choice of shapes, colors, lighting, textures, and so on), but I'll leave that to your imagination.

I'm not going to spend a lot of time explaining how OpenGL works, but I will tell you that the only method you will need to call is the GLDraw() method. Pass it a device context to draw in and a rectangle for the size.

> **NOTE**
>
> OpenGL can only draw to overlapped child windows, so don't try passing it a metafile device context or a memory device context. The call to SetPixelFormat() will always return FALSE.

Customizing CGLServerView

During in-place activation, you'll want the shape to appear in the view window that the server creates; therefore, you'll need to override the OnDraw() method of the view class. Please add the changes shown in Listing 14.14 to your code.

Because OpenGL can draw only to an overlapped window, I've fooled the system a little bit here. After calling the GLDraw() method with the view window's HDC, I copied its contents (using the palette that GLDraw() created) into a memory device context (in the CGLServerSrvrItem::OnDraw() method). That way, the server item will be able to copy the image to the metafile device context.

Notice the call to UpdateAllItems(). This tells the document to inform all server items that they need to redraw themselves. (A call to CGLServerSrvrItem::OnDraw() is made.)

To ensure that you always have the correct window size, each time you perform a draw, delete the previous memory DC and bitmap, and re-create the bitmap based upon the new window size.

It's really important to remember to *realize the palette* (the process of selecting the palette into the device context) into the memory DC; otherwise, you'll get an ugly-looking shape.

Listing 14.14. Modifications to the CGLServerView implementation.

```
void CGLServerView::OnDraw(CDC* pDC)
{
 CGLServerDoc* pDoc = GetDocument();
 ASSERT_VALID(pDoc);

 // check if memory DC is there, if so, copy contents to it
 if (pDoc->m_pMemoryDC != NULL)
 {
   // restore old palette and bitmap
   ::SelectPalette(pDoc->m_pMemoryDC->GetSafeHdc(), pDoc->m_hOldPalette, FALSE);
   pDoc->m_pMemoryDC->SelectObject(pDoc->m_pOldBitmap);
```

```
  // cleanup previous device context stuff
  pDoc->m_pMemoryDC->DeleteDC();
  delete pDoc->m_pBitmap;
  delete pDoc->m_pMemoryDC;
}

// Get the window size
GetClientRect(&pDoc->m_rcViewRect);

// prepare memorydc and bitmap
pDoc->m_pMemoryDC = new CDC();
pDoc->m_pBitmap = new CBitmap();

// create a compatible dc and bitmap
pDoc->m_pMemoryDC->CreateCompatibleDC(pDC);
pDoc->m_pBitmap->CreateCompatibleBitmap(pDC,
  pDoc->m_rcViewRect.right, pDoc->m_rcViewRect.bottom);
pDoc->m_pOldBitmap = pDoc->m_pMemoryDC->SelectObject(pDoc->m_pBitmap);

// draw the shape(s)
pDoc->GLDraw(pDC, &pDoc->m_rcViewRect);

// realize palette into memory dc
pDoc->m_hOldPalette = ::SelectPalette(pDoc->m_pMemoryDC->GetSafeHdc(),
             pDoc->m_hPalette, FALSE);
::RealizePalette(pDoc->m_pMemoryDC->GetSafeHdc());

// BitBlt to metafile dc
pDoc->m_pMemoryDC->BitBlt(0, 0, pDoc->m_rcViewRect.right,
  pDoc->m_rcViewRect.bottom, pDC, 0, 0, SRCCOPY);

// update the server item as well
pDoc->UpdateAllItems(NULL);
}
```

Customizing `CGLServerSrvrItem`

As I stated earlier, the `OnDraw()` for this class draws to a metafile device context that the container uses to display the server data when the server is not activated.

Use the memory DC created in the `CGLServerView` class and copy it to the metafile DC. Here we'll also need to realize the palette.

Listing 14.15 shows contains the required modifications to `OnDraw()`.

Listing 14.15. Modifications to the `CGLServerSrvrItem` implementation.

```
BOOL CGLServerSrvrItem::OnDraw(CDC* pDC, CSize& rSize)
{
 CGLServerDoc* pDoc = GetDocument();
 ASSERT_VALID(pDoc);
```

continues

Listing 14.15. continued

```
// TODO: set mapping mode and extent
//   (The extent is usually the same as the size returned from OnGetExtent)
pDC->SetMapMode(MM_ANISOTROPIC);
pDC->SetWindowOrg(0,0);
pDC->SetWindowExt(3000, 3000);

// calculate drawing rectangle
CRect rect;
rect.TopLeft() = pDC->GetWindowOrg();
rect.BottomRight() = rect.TopLeft() + pDC->GetWindowExt();

// BitBlt memory DC to metafile DC
if (pDoc->m_pMemoryDC != NULL)
{
 // realize palette into memory dc
 HPALETTE hOldPalette = ::SelectPalette(pDC->GetSafeHdc(),
         pDoc->m_hPalette, FALSE);
 ::RealizePalette(pDC->GetSafeHdc());

 // BitBlt to metafile dc
 if (pDC->StretchBlt(rect.left, rect.top,
    rect.right - rect.left,
    rect.bottom - rect.top,
    pDoc->m_pMemoryDC, 0, 0,
    pDoc->m_rcViewRect.right,
    pDoc->m_rcViewRect.bottom, SRCCOPY) == FALSE)
 {
  return FALSE;
 }

 // restore old palette
 ::SelectPalette(pDC->GetSafeHdc(), hOldPalette, FALSE);
}

return TRUE;
}
```

Testing the GLServer Example

Compile the GLServer example and embed it into WordPad as before. You should see a 3D, square-shaped object inside of the sizer bar (as in Figure 14.10). Now click the container, and the exact same image should be inside of the container as a metafile bitmap.

FIGURE 14.10.
The GLServer
example in action.

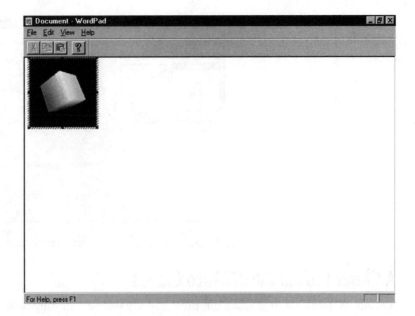

Designing an MFC Automation Server

This section shows you how to create your own automation server with MFC. You'll use the AppWizard and ClassWizard to quickly and easily create the necessary class and methods for the demonstration.

The example is an in-process DLL server that will expose a class called SimpleMFC. You'll create four methods—Add, Subtract, Multiply, and Divide—to see how a server works. The first three methods accept two long numbers and return a long (the result of the calculation). The fourth method will also accept two long values, but will instead return a double precision number.

Using the AppWizard

Select File | New from the Developer Studio menu, choose MFC AppWizard (DLL), and in the Project Name: edit box, type MFCAuto.

AppWizard will present a single-step process to create the server. Select the Automation checkbox and press Finish. (See Figure 14.11.)

FIGURE 14.11.
Step 1 of 1.

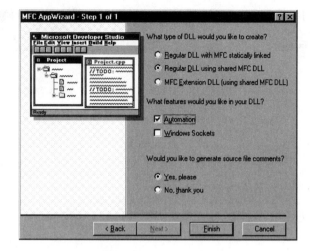

A Closer Look at the MFCAuto Classes

The AppWizard used to generate this project is very simple. The only code it generated is the required CLSID (because you chose the Automation checkbox) and the registration of the DLL in the InitInstance() method, as shown in Listing 14.16.

Listing 14.16. Registration code for the automation server.

```
BOOL CMFCAutoApp::InitInstance()
{
 // Register all OLE server (factories) as running.  This enables the
 //  OLE libraries to create objects from other applications.
 COleObjectFactory::RegisterAll();

 return TRUE;
}
```

Adding Customization to the MFCAuto Sample Skeleton

In order to make the server usable, you'll need to create a class derived from CCmdTarget. This is the root automation class provided by MFC.

Now do the following:

1. Within the workspace window, select the MFCAuto project, right-click, and select New Class.

2. In the Name: text box, type CSimpleMFC.

3. From the Base Class: combo box, select CCmdTarget.

4. For Automation type select Createable by type ID: and make sure that the text in the text box says MFCAuto.SimpleMFC.

The values for the new class are shown in Figure 14.12.

FIGURE 14.12.
Adding the
CSimpleMFC *class.*

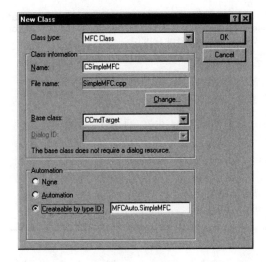

Notice the addition of a new entry in the workspace window. The ISimpleMFC node is actually a COM interface that has been created for you, along with an ODL (object definition language) file. This will be used to create a type library to expose a SimpleMFC class to other applications. To see this ODL file (shown in Listing 14.17), double-click the ISimpleMFC node. Included in this file is the UUID for the class. After we finish coding this example, it will also include our user-defined methods Add, Subtract, Multiply, and Divide.

Listing 14.17. The object definition language (ODL) for MFCAuto.

```
// MFCAuto.odl : type library source for MFCAuto.dll

// This file will be processed by the MIDL compiler to produce the
// type library (MFCAuto.tlb).

[ uuid(761B3A7D-D545-11D0-967C-444553540000), version(1.0) ]
library MFCAuto
{
 importlib("stdole32.tlb");

 //  Primary dispatch interface for CSimpleMFC

 [ uuid(761B3A8A-D545-11D0-967C-444553540000) ]
 dispinterface ISimpleMFC
 {
  properties:
   // NOTE - ClassWizard will maintain property information here.
   //    Use extreme caution when editing this section.
   //{{AFX_ODL_PROP(CSimpleMFC)
   //}}AFX_ODL_PROP
```

continues

Listing 14.17. continued

```
methods:
  // NOTE - ClassWizard will maintain method information here.
  //    Use extreme caution when editing this section.
  //{{AFX_ODL_METHOD(CSimpleMFC)
//}}AFX_ODL_METHOD

};

//  Class information for CSimpleMFC

[ uuid(761B3A8B-D545-11D0-967C-444553540000) ]
coclass SimpleMFC
{
 [default] dispinterface ISimpleMFC;
};

//{{AFX_APPEND_ODL}}
//}}AFX_APPEND_ODL}}
};
```

The CSimpleMFC class that was generated is fairly simple; however, note the OnFinalRelease() method generated as a result of choosing Automation support. As the code documentation states, this notification is called when the last instance of this class is deleted. You can optionally implement this code to perform special cleanup.

Listing 14.18. The OnFinalRelease() notification.

```
void CSimpleMFC::OnFinalRelease()
{
 // When the last reference for an automation object is released
 // OnFinalRelease is called.  The base class will automatically
 // deletes the object.  Add additional cleanup required for your
 // object before calling the base class.

 CCmdTarget::OnFinalRelease();
}
```

Adding Methods to the MFCAuto Example

Listing 14.19 shows the prototypes for the four methods you will be adding. This will come in handy in just a moment.

Listing 14.19. CSimpleMFC instance method prototypes.

```
long Add(long First, long Second);
long Subtract(long First, long Second);
long Multiply(long First, long Second);
double Divide(long First, long Second);
```

Now, add these prototypes as follows:

1. Open ClassWizard by selecting View | ClassWizard.
2. Select the Automation tab from the MFC ClassWizard dialog, and in the Class Name: combo box select `CSimpleMFC`.
3. Select Add Method.
4. In the External Name: text box, type `Add`.
5. In the Return type: combo box, choose `long`.
6. Add the first and second methods in the Parameter List: list box, using `long` as the type for each.

Repeat these steps for each of the four methods and select `Double` as the Return type: for the `Divide` method. You can use Figure 14.13 as a guideline.

FIGURE 14.13.
Using ClassWizard to add methods to `MFCAuto`.

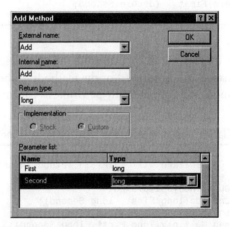

> **NOTE**
>
> The `MFCAuto` example does not use any properties—but as you might have already guessed, if you need to add one or more properties, you can add them with ClassWizard under the Automation tab by using Add Property.

Now change the implementation code for these methods, as shown in Listing 14.20.

Listing 14.20. Implementing the `CSimpleMFC` instance methods.

```
///////////////////////////////////////////////////////////////////////////
// CSimpleMFC message handlers
```

continues

Listing 14.20. continued

```
long CSimpleMFC::Add(long First, long Second)
{
 return First + Second;
}

long CSimpleMFC::Subtract(long First, long Second)
{
 return First - Second;
}

long CSimpleMFC::Multiply(long First, long Second)
{
 return First * Second;
}

double CSimpleMFC::Divide(long First, long Second)
{
 return (double)First / (double)Second;
}
```

Take another look at the declaration for the CSimpleMFC class, shown in Listing 14.21. ClassWizard has added prototypes for the methods to the ODL file. When this class is registered, the methods will automatically be visible as part of the SimpleMFC COM class.

Listing 14.21. ClassWizard changes to the ODL file for new methods.

```
  methods:
  // NOTE - ClassWizard will maintain method information here.
  //    Use extreme caution when editing this section.
  //{{AFX_ODL_METHOD(CSimpleMFC)
  [id(1)] long Add(long First, long Second);
  [id(2)] long Subtract(long First, long Second);
  [id(3)] long Multiply(long First, long Second);
  [id(4)] double Divide(long First, long Second);
  //}}AFX_ODL_METHOD
```

Testing the MFCAuto Example

Compile the server example and then choose Tools | Register Control, which will register this automation server with the operating system. You can test the example using any application that can create automation servers.

For the test, I've included an application called AutoTest.EXE, written in Visual Basic 5.0, that can be used to call the server. This test application drives both the MFCAuto example discussed here and the ATLAuto example discussed later in this chapter. See Listing 14.22 for the source code.

Listing 14.22. The Visual Basic application to test MFCAuto.DLL.

```
Private Sub Command1_Click(Index As Integer)
    Dim xOBJ As Object
    Dim lItem1 As Long, lItem2 As Long

    ' perform MFCAuto Out-of-Process Tests
    If Index >= 0 And Index <= 3 Then
        ' Use late binding to create SimpleMFC Object
        Set xOBJ = CreateObject("MFCAuto.SimpleMFC")
    Else
        ' Use late binding to create SimpleATL Object
        Set xOBJ = CreateObject("SimpleATL.SimpleATL.1")
    End If

    ' convert values
    lItem1 = CLng(Text1(Index).Text)
    lItem2 = CLng(Text2(Index).Text)

    ' determine action
    Select Case Index
        Case 0, 4:  Text3(Index).Text = CStr(xOBJ.Add(lItem1, lItem2))
        Case 1, 5:  Text3(Index).Text = CStr(xOBJ.Subtract(lItem1, lItem2))
        Case 2, 6:  Text3(Index).Text = CStr(xOBJ.Multiply(lItem1, lItem2))
        Case 3, 7:  Text3(Index).Text = CStr(xOBJ.Divide(lItem1, lItem2))
    End Select

    ' kill object
    Set xOBJ = Nothing
End Sub
```

AutoTest.EXE is shown in Figure 14.14. Use three control arrays in this example, one for each of the columns. The first number in each calculation is a called Text1, the second number is Text2, and the result is Text3. I wrote this driver using late binding so that you can see that we are creating the object using the name MFCAuto.SimpleMFC. The object could also be created using the CLSID, or you can optionally use the References option in Visual Basic to include the class (an example of using early binding).

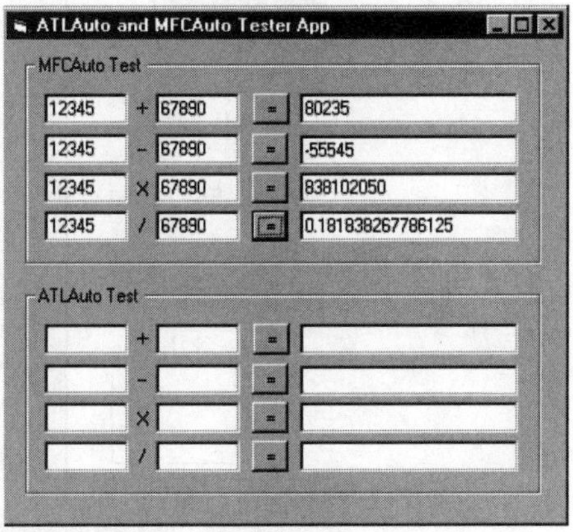

FIGURE 14.14.

The AutoTest application.

Designing an Automation Server Using the Active Template Libraries

In this section, I show you how to create your own automation server using the newer and more compact Active Template Libraries. This demonstration will show you that reduced size is the main reason why ATL is preferable to MFC, but there is the price of ease of development. Simple applications are fairly straightforward; it's the complicated ones that pose the bigger problem.

As with the MFCAuto server, this example is an in-process DLL server that exposes a class called SimpleATL. Once again, you'll create four methods—Add, Subtract, Multiply, and Divide—to see how the server works. The same prototypes will be used as were used in the previous example. See Listing 14.23 for a quick reminder of what they looked like.

Listing 14.23. CSimpleATL instance method prototypes.

```
long Add(long First, long Second);
long Subtract(long First, long Second);
long Multiply(long First, long Second);
double Divide(long First, long Second);
```

Using the ATL COM AppWizard

Select File | New from the Developer Studio menu, choose ATL COM AppWizard, and in the Project Name: edit box, type ATLAuto.

As before, AppWizard will present you with a single-step process to create the server. Use the default settings, as shown in Figure 14.15, and select Finish.

FIGURE 14.15.

Step 1 of 1.

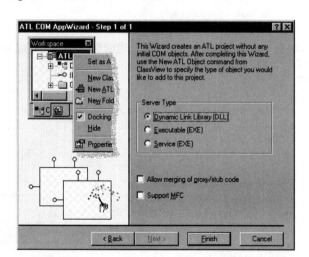

This AppWizard does even less than did the MFC AppWizard (DLL). No classes have been created, only the globals required for the DLL. You'll need to do the rest.

Adding Customization to the ATLAuto Example

Simply put, you'll have to do all the work here. ClassWizard will not be able to help, so you're on your own. Let's proceed as follows:

1. Select the project inside of the workspace window and click the right mouse button.
2. Choose New ATL Object.
3. Select Simple Object from the ATL Object Wizard dialog box (see Figure 14.16) and click Next.
4. In the ATL Object Wizard Properties dialog box, in the Short Name: text box, type SimpleATL and click OK.

FIGURE 14.16.
The ATL Object Wizard dialog.

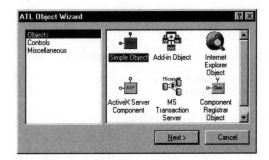

You now have two new nodes under ATLAuto in the workspace window. The first node is CSimpleATL, which is a class derived from several different interfaces (shown in Listing 14.24).

Listing 14.24. The CSimpleATL declaration.

```
class ATL_NO_VTABLE CSimpleATL :
 public CComObjectRootEx<CComSingleThreadModel>,
 public CComCoClass<CSimpleATL, &CLSID_SimpleATL>,
 public IDispatchImpl<ISimpleATL, &IID_ISimpleATL, &LIBID_ATLAUTOLib>
{
public:
 CSimpleATL()
 {
 }

DECLARE_REGISTRY_RESOURCEID(IDR_SIMPLEATL)

BEGIN_COM_MAP(CSimpleATL)
 COM_INTERFACE_ENTRY(ISimpleATL)
 COM_INTERFACE_ENTRY(IDispatch)
END_COM_MAP()
```

continues

Listing 14.24. continued

```
// ISimpleATL
public:
};
```

The second node is the `ISimpleATL` interface itself, which is derived from `IDispatch`. The ATL Object Wizard automatically generates an Interface Definition Language (IDL) file for this project. (See Listing 14.25.) This file is also used to produce the type library for one or more COM interfaces.

Listing 14.25. The IDL (Interface Definition Language) file `ATLAuto`.

```
// This file will be processed by the MIDL tool to
// produce the type library (ATLAuto.tlb) and marshalling code.

import "oaidl.idl";
import "ocidl.idl";

  [
   object,
   uuid(0BA6438E-D52B-11D0-967C-444553540000),
   dual,
   helpstring("ISimpleATL Interface"),
   pointer_default(unique)
  ]
  interface ISimpleATL : IDispatch
  {
};
  [
   uuid(0BA64381-D52B-11D0-967C-444553540000),
   version(1.0),
   helpstring("ATLAuto 1.0 Type Library")
  ]
library ATLAUTOLib
{
 importlib("stdole32.tlb");
 importlib("stdole2.tlb");

  [
   uuid(0BA6438F-D52B-11D0-967C-444553540000),
   helpstring("SimpleATL Class")
  ]
  coclass SimpleATL
  {
   [default] interface ISimpleATL;
  };
};
```

If you haven't already done so, open the `CSimpleATL` class. You will notice that the `ISimpleATL` interface is listed as one of its subnodes. This is an indication that the `CSimpleATL` class implements at least the `ISimpleATL` interface, if not any methods or properties of this interface.

Next, add methods to this interface. To do this, follow the procedures listed here:

1. Select the ISimpleATL node and click the right mouse button.
2. Select Add Method.
3. For the Method Name: text box, type the name of the method name (Add, Subtract, Multiply, or Divide).
4. For Add, Subtract, and Multiply in the Parameters: text box, type [in]long First, long Second,[out,retval]long *pVal.
5. For Divide in the Parameters: text box, type [in] long First, long Second,[out, retval] double *pVal. (See Figure 14.17.)

FIGURE 14.17.

Adding a method to the ISimpleATL *interface.*

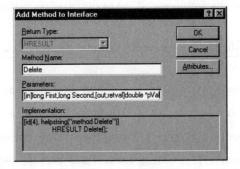

Before I give you the implementations code, let me explain the parameters. ATL implementations must return an HRESULT for all methods and properties—thus, the need for a strange new parameter format. As you might have guessed, the [in] notation means that the parameters following it are input parameters; the [out] notation means that the parameters are output parameters (such as setting the value of a passed string or number); and the [out, retval] notation means that the parameter following (only one is permitted here) is a return value.

Thus, a method called Add defined as

```
[in] long First, long Second, [out, retval] long *pVal
```

means that the prototype must look like

```
HRESULT Add(long First, long Second, long *pVal)
```

and the type library will expose a prototype as follows:

```
long Add(long First, long Second)
```

Let's take a look at the method portion of the IDL file now and see what it produced. (See Listing 14.26.)

Listing 14.26. The modified Method section of the IDL file for ATLAuto.

```
interface ISimpleATL : IDispatch
{
  [id(1), helpstring("method Add")] HRESULT Add([in] long First, long Second,
[out,retval] long *pVal);
  [id(2), helpstring("method Subtract")] HRESULT Subtract([in] long First, long
Second, [out,retval] long *pVal);
  [id(3), helpstring("method Multiply")] HRESULT Multiply([in] long First, long
Second, [out,retval] long *pVal);
  [id(4), helpstring("method Divide")] HRESULT Divide([in] long First, long Second,
[out, retval] double *pVal);
};
```

Take a peek at the prototypes added to the CSimpleATL class. (See Listing 14.27.)

Listing 14.27. The modified Method section of the CSimpleATL class.

```
// ISimpleATL
public:
 STDMETHOD(Divide)(/*[in]*/ long First, long Second, /*[out,retval]*/ double
*pVal);
 STDMETHOD(Multiply)(/*[in]*/ long First, long Second, /*[out,retval]*/ long
*pVal);
 STDMETHOD(Subtract)(/*[in]*/ long First, long Second, /*[out,retval]*/ long
*pVal);
 STDMETHOD(Add)(/*[in]*/ long First, long Second, /*[out,retval]*/ long *pVal);
```

> **NOTE**
>
> There is a big difference between adding methods to the interface and simply adding methods to the class. Methods added to the class will not automatically be exposed to external applications; they require a special macro called STDMETHOD() to expose them. By using the Object Wizard, this is done automatically and the methods will be exposed to external applications.

Finally, add the implementation code for the methods, as shown in Listing 14.28.

Listing 14.28. The method implementations for CSimpleATL.

```
STDMETHODIMP CSimpleATL::Add(long First, long Second, long * pVal)
{
 *pVal = First + Second;
 return S_OK;
}
```

```
STDMETHODIMP CSimpleATL::Subtract(long First, long Second, long * pVal)
{
 *pVal = First - Second;
 return S_OK;
}

STDMETHODIMP CSimpleATL::Multiply(long First, long Second, long * pVal)
{
 *pVal = First * Second;
 return S_OK;
}

STDMETHODIMP CSimpleATL::Divide(long First, long Second, double * pVal)
{
 *pVal = (double)First / (double)Second;
 return S_OK;
}
```

Testing the ATLAuto Example

As before, compile the server example and then choose Tools | Register Control, which will register this automation server with the operating system. Remember, you can test the example by using any application that can create automation servers.

As mentioned earlier, the test I've included is the application AutoTest.EXE, written in Visual Basic 5.0 that can be used to call the server. Now that both servers are created, you can run the tests side by side because both the MFCAuto and ATLAuto examples can be tested using this tool. Refer to Listing 14.22 for the source code.

Summary

There are so many more things that I would like to be able to tell you about automation servers and so many more examples I would like to give you, but unfortunately, there is a limit to the size that this chapter can be. Therefore, let's quickly recap what you've learned in this chapter and move on.

ActiveX servers come in three flavors:

- A full server is an EXE that can run as both an application and an embedded server. (Optional support can be added for both automation and ActiveX controls.)
- The mini-server is an EXE that can be run in embedded mode only. (Optional support can be added for both automation and ActiveX controls.)
- The automation server (EXE or DLL) might or might not have an interface, and exposes classes with methods and properties to allow an external application to control it.

The embedded server can run in-place or out-of-place, depending on its implementation and eventual use. It can support Persistent Storage by serializing data to either the container's storage or a separate file. The server provides a mechanism to display its data in activation (by directly painting the server's view) and while inactive by providing the container with a metafile representation of its data.

The automation server can run in-process (meaning it runs in the same process space as the application that created it) or out-of-process (meaning it runs in its own process space). It can be designed using either the Microsoft Foundation Classes (MFC) or, if size is an issue, the Active Template Libraries (ATL) provide a tighter, less cluttered alternative.

15

ActiveX Controls

by Vincent W. Mayfield

This chapter covers ActiveX and OLE controls. OLE controls, also called OLE control extensions, are commonly referred to as OCXs. OLE controls are known as OCXs for their file extension, and also as ActiveX controls, which are OLE controls extended for use in Internet applications. A developer can create ActiveX controls for use in Internet applications, and those controls can be utilized in non-Internet applications. ActiveX controls are a superset of OLE controls. Therefore, throughout this chapter, the terms OLE control, OCX, and ActiveX control are used somewhat interchangeably. (See Figure 15.1.)

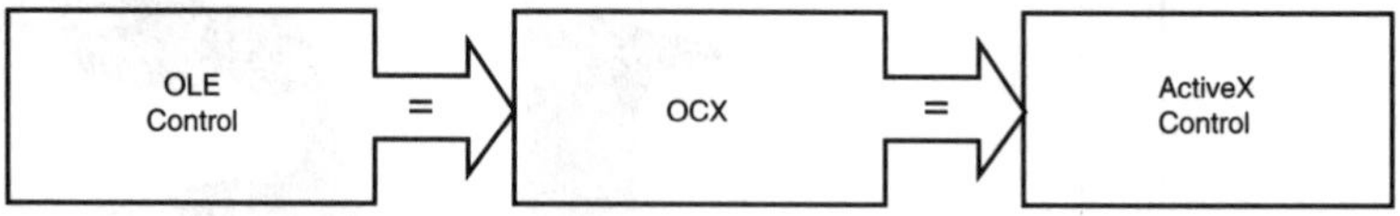

FIGURE 15.1.
OLE controls, OCXs, and ActiveX controls are terms that refer to similar entities that refer to the same thing.

If a control is an OLE control, it is not necessarily an ActiveX control. Conversely, if a control is an ActiveX control, it is an OLE control. There are some distinct things that make a control an ActiveX control. Not to overtrivialize things, but for all intents and purposes, OLE controls and ActiveX controls are the same except for some minor differences. I don't want you to feel that ActiveX controls are some entirely new thing, as the marketing types would have us believe. This chapter highlights those differences. With Visual C++ 4.2, OLE controls were first called ActiveX controls. Let's take a look at the origins of the OLE control.

A Short History

The term *control*, or *custom control*, has been around since Windows 3.0, when it was first defined. In fact, a custom control was nothing more than a dynamic link library (DLL) that exported a defined set of functions. Unlike a DLL, a custom control can manipulate properties and handle the firing of events in response to user or programmatic input.

The Visual Basic development environment had caught on in the development community. Custom controls were necessary because developers found they needed better ways to express the user interface of their applications. Many times there was simply no way to perform a complex operation in Visual Basic and reflect it in a meaningful way to the end user. As a result, the custom control came to be. Initially these custom controls were DLLs written in the C programming language. Unfortunately, or fortunately depending on your perspective, these C DLLs had no way of allowing Visual Basic to query the control for information on the properties and methods supported by the control. This made custom controls difficult to use in the Visual Basic development environment. There was great difficulty exporting the functions of the custom control to Visual Basic.

In 1991, Microsoft unveiled the VBX. The VBX stood for Visual Basic Extension. The idea was that these little reusable software components could be embedded in their container applications. To everyone's surprise, VBXs took off like wildfire. Companies cropped up all over the place developing these little reusable software components. VBXs were able to provide a wide range of functionality, from a simple text label to a complex multimedia or communications control. VBXs were written in C and C++, and provided a wide variety of capabilities that could not have been done in a Visual Basic application otherwise. VBXs became extremely popular.

Because VBXs had become popular, demand for them grew within the developer market. Soon, developers wanted them for 32-bit applications and even on non-Intel platforms such as the DEC Alpha, RISC, PowerPC, and the MIPS. Developers wanted to extend VBXs by using Visual Basic for Applications to connect VBXs with applications such as Access, PowerPoint, Excel, Project, and Word.

Unfortunately, VBXs were severely restricted. They were built on a 16-bit architecture that is not designed as an open interface. They were primarily designed to accommodate the Visual Basic environment. This made VBXs almost impossible to port to a 32-bit environment.

In 1993, OLE 2.0 was released. With the release of OLE 2.0, Microsoft extended the OLE architecture to include OLE controls. OLE controls, unlike their predecessors, the VBX and the custom control, are founded on a binary standard, called the Component Object Model (COM). In addition, OLE controls support both a 16- and 32-bit architecture.

> **NOTE**
>
> Kraig Brockschmidt wrote what is sometimes considered the bible for all OLE programmers. The book is *Inside OLE,* published by Microsoft Press. The original title of the book was *Inside OLE 2.0,* but as you discovered in Chapter 12, "ActiveX Documents," OLE is an ostensibly virtual standard building on each layer. Therefore, in the second edition, the 2.0 was dropped. This book is an excellent reference. *Inside OLE* thoroughly explores the OLE standard from the API level. Negligent is the OLE programmer who has not thoroughly read *Inside OLE.*

Instead of creating an extended architecture for VBXs, Microsoft decided to develop the OCX to offer the benefits of a component architecture to a wider variety of development environments and development tools. (See Figure 15.2.) COM and OLE are open architectures, giving them a wider variety of input from the industry. Like their predecessor the VBX, OLE controls are also known by their file extension; OCXs, likewise, have taken the market by storm.

FIGURE 15.2.

*The progression of
development of the
OLE and ActiveX
control.*

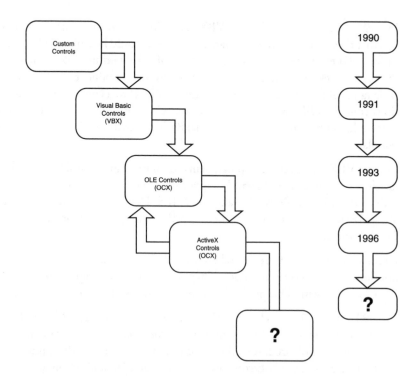

From 1993 to 1995, OLE controls have flourished. Many Independent Software Vendors (ISVs) converted their VBXs to OLE controls, and in some cases maintained three versions: VBX, 16-bit OCX, and 32-bit OCX. The makers of Visual C++ and MFC created the OLE control Developer's Kit, and even incorporated it into Visual C++ 2.0 and 1.5, further adding to the success of OLE custom control.

Between 1995 and 1996, the Internet took the world like a blitzkrieg, causing Internet mania. Everyone had to become Web-enabled. Companies found themselves making Web sites because they saw the Internet as the great advertisement media for the year 2000 and beyond. In 1997, this trend has continued. Unfortunately, in previous years the Internet had been a relatively static environment. This is due in part to the Internet's roots with the big-iron diehards who grew up with the IBM mainframes, VAXs, and UNIX boxes (the "dummy terminal" era). However, PC computers have become household devices for almost everyone. Users have become accustomed to graphical interaction with their machines, thanks to the Macintosh, Microsoft Windows, and X Window/Motiff. In addition, thanks to Sun Microsystems and their invention of the Java programming language and the Java applet, the Internet is no longer a static environment. The days of static Web pages have changed. Now Web pages have exploded to life with multimedia, sound, and dynamic interaction.

Microsoft, realizing the potential and the hype surrounding the Internet explosion, decided they needed to get with the program and take on a role of leadership in this emerging environment.

Microsoft boldly announced it was going to "activate" the Internet in 1996 with ActiveX technologies (a little late, but better late than never). Thus, from these ActiveX technologies, the ActiveX controls were born. ActiveX controls were nothing really new, just an extension of their mother, the OLE control. ActiveX controls are simply OLE controls implemented to be smarter and are enhanced to be utilized across the Internet.

What Is an ActiveX/OLE Control?

Now that you know a little of the history behind an OLE control, this section explores just what an OLE control is. An OLE control is an embeddable Component Object Model object that is implemented as an in-process server dynamic link library (DLL). It supports in-place activation as an inside-out object.

NOTE

The title of the book *OLE Controls Inside Out,* by Adam Denning, Microsoft Press, is a play on words because OLE controls are activated from the inside out. This book is also an excellent reference.

As an OLE in-proc object, an OLE control is loaded into the address space of its container. As you are probably aware, every Win32 process has a 4GB address space.

NOTE

A Win32 process is a running instance of an application loaded into memory.

The lower 2GB is where the application is loaded, and the upper 2GB is where the system is loaded. An OLE control is loaded in the lower 2GB with the application. Therefore, they share the same resources with the application; hence the term in-process.

An OLE control is also a server. Why is it a server? Well, it provides two-way communication between the "container application" and the control. It can also respond to user-initiated events, such as mouse movements, keyboard input, and programmatic scripting input—and it can pass that input to the container application for action.

OLE controls are also in-place activated. This means that they can be placed in the active state by the user or the container and edited or manipulated. This is a functionality OLE controls inherit from OLE documents. Like a DLL, the OLE control is a library of functions. In fact, an OLE control can be considered a "super DLL." More than just a super DLL, an OLE control is a detached object that can fire and respond to events, process messages, has unique properties, and possesses multithreaded capabilities. OLE controls are also known as OCXs because of their file extension, but they are actually DLLs. OCXs can contain several controls. Unlike DLLs, OCXs respond to user input and support two-way communication or notification between themselves and their container.

An OLE control can have its own data set and can act as an OLE automation component because you can manipulate its properties and methods. OLE controls can be both 16- and 32-bit as well as Unicode. OLE controls, like OLE automation objects, can have properties set at both compile time and runtime, and OLE controls have methods that can perform certain operations. The difference between OLE controls and OLE automation objects is that they are self-contained objects. OLE controls provide two-way communication between the control and the container, whereas OLE automation objects do not. In addition, OLE controls do not need a user interface. As such they can provide hidden services such as a timer, communications, or mail.

OLE controls cannot stand alone; they must be embedded in an OLE container. OLE controls provide prepackaged components of functionality that are reusable and customizable. OLE controls are at the top of the OLE architecture. Thus, they are built on several OLE technologies. In addition, OLE controls can be used in a wide variety of development tools, such as Delphi, Visual C++, Borland C++, Gupta, Visual Basic, Oracle Developer 2000, and PowerBuilder. OLE controls can also be used in a variety of non-programming environments, such as Microsoft Word, Microsoft Excel, Lotus, HTML, and Internet Explorer. OLE controls are very powerful, reusable components.

ActiveX/OLE Control Architecture

The beauty of OLE controls is that they are programmable and reusable. They expose themselves to the outside world and can be utilized in a variety of programming and non-programming environments. An OLE control is like an OLE compound document, but it is extended by using OLE automation through the IDispatch interface to support properties and methods. What makes OLE controls unique are events. OLE controls have three sets of attributes that are exposed to the outside world:

- Properties
- Methods
- Events

Properties

Properties are named attributes or characteristics of an OLE control. These properties can be set or queried. Some examples of properties are color, font, and number.

Usually, OLE controls provide access to their properties through property sheets. *Property sheets* are separate OLE automation entities. This feature is not limited to design/compile time, but can be displayed at runtime to allow the user to manipulate the control's properties, events, or methods. Property sheets are user-interface components that are basically tabbed dialogs. OLE automation provides the mechanism by which controls communicate with their property sheets.

OLE controls have what are called *stock properties*. These are properties common to all OLE controls. MFC allows you to take advantage of these stock properties because they are already built in. Table 15.1 lists all of the stock properties supported by MFC.

Table 15.1. Stock properties for ActiveX and OLE controls supported by MFC, and their methods.

Stock property	Get/set stock methods	Purpose
Appearance	`void SetAppearance (short sApear) short GetAppearance( )`	Allows you to set the appearance of an ActiveX control to either flat or 3D.
BackColor	`OLE_COLOR GetBackColor ( ) void SetBackColor (OLE_COLOR dwBkColor)`	Allows you to set the background colors of the control.
BorderStyle	`short GetBorderStyle ( ) void SetBorderStyle(short sBorderStyle)`	Allows you to set the border style of the control to normal or none.
Caption	`BSTR GetText( ) void SetText(LPCTSTR pszText)`	Allows you to set the caption of the ActiveX control.
Enabled	`BOOL GetEnabled( ) void SetEnabled(BOOL bEnabled)`	Allows you to enable or disable the control.
Font	`LPFONTDISP GetFont( ) void SetFont (LPFONTDISP pFontDisp)`	Allows you to set the font properties used by the control.
ForeColor	`OLE_COLOR GetForeColor( ) void SetForeColor (OLE_COLOR dwForeColor)`	Allows you to set the fore colors of the control.
hWnd	`OLE_HANDLE GetHwnd( )`	Holds the control's window handle.

continues

Table 15.1. continued

Stock property	Get/set stock methods	Purpose
ReadyState	long GetReadyState( )	Allows you to get or set the ready state of the control with the following values:
		READYSTATE_UNINITIALIZED
		READYSTATE_LOADING
		READYSTATE_LOADED
		READYSTATE_INTERACTIVE
		READYSTATE_COMPLETE
Text	const CString& InternalGetText( )	Allows you to get and set the control's text. (This property is the same as Caption, except it is called Text.)

You can include the stock properties in your OLE controls by using the Class Wizard. Select the View | Class Wizard menu item or press Ctrl+W. After Class Wizard is displayed, as in Figure 15.3, select the Automation tab.

FIGURE 15.3.

Using the Class Wizard to invoke stock properties.

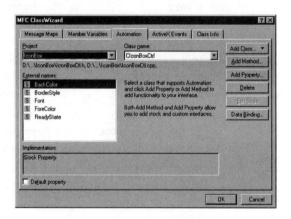

Select the Add Property button to invoke the Add Property dialog. If you use the External name combo box, you can select which stock properties you want your control to have. (See Figure 15.4.)

FIGURE 15.4.

You can select stock properties to support using the External name combo box.

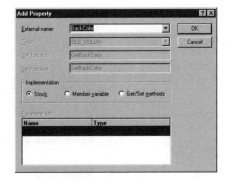

MFC and Visual C++ 5.0 also provide stock property sheets to add to our user interface for user setting stock properties. These are general (see Figure 15.5), color (see Figure 15.6), font (see Figure 15.7), and picture properties (see Figure 15.8).

NOTE

Although general, font, and color are stock properties, the picture properties are not. Microsoft developers added an additional property page for our use: the picture properties. The picture properties allow you to use metafiles, bitmaps, and so on in the OLE control. Microsoft even implemented for methods for the picture properties. However, Microsoft did not do a property page for the general properties. You will have to create this page yourself.

FIGURE 15.5.

A property sheet with some of the general stock properties.

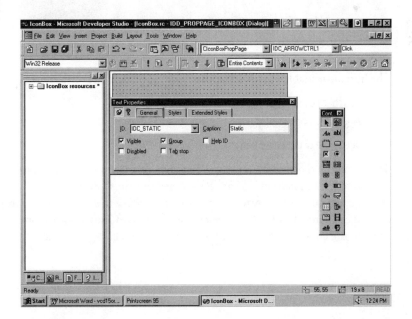

FIGURE 15.6.

A property sheet with the font stock properties.

FIGURE 15.7.

A property sheet with the color stock properties.

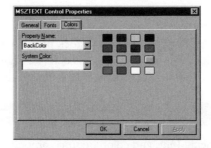

FIGURE 15.8.

A property sheet with the various picture properties.

The human-readable class IDs for these property pages are as follows:

■ `CLSID_CColorPropPage`

■ `CLSID_CFontPropPage`

■ `CLSID_CPicturePropPage`

When you use the Visual C++ App Wizard to generate an ActiveX control, it generates a class derived from `COleControl`. In that class's `.cpp` file, the App Wizard puts support in for a property page to allow your control to have a user interface to set the control properties. This property page is derived from `COlePropertyPage`, and MFC has a macro for declaring the property pages in the control. Listing 15.1 shows the macros `BEGIN_PROPPAGEIDS` and `END_PROPPAGEIDS`.

Listing 15.1. The use of the BEGIN_PROPPAGEIDS and END_PROPPAGEIDS to declare the ColePropertyPage for your control.

```
1: BEGIN_PROPPAGEIDS( CMySampleCtrl, 1 )
2:    PROPPAGEID( CMyPropPage::guid )
3: END_PROPPAGEIDS(CSampleCtrl)
```

Notice on line 2 that PROPPAGEID gets passed the globally unique identifier, or GUID (pro-nounced goo-id like Druid), and also a class ID, called a CLSID, of the property page. The GUID for the property page is declared in the .cpp of the class created by App Wizard and derived from ColePropertyPage.

Now, if you wanted to implement the stock property pages that MFC provides, you will have to pass the CLSID of the stock property pages, as shown in the previous bulleted list. This is demonstrated in Listing 15.2.

Listing 15.2. Adding in declarations for the stock font property page, color property page, and the picture property page.

```
1: BEGIN_PROPPAGEIDS( CMySampleCtrl, 4 )
2:    PROPPAGEID( CMyPropPage::guid )
3:    PROPPAGEID( CLSID_CfontPropPage )
4:    PROPPAGEID( CLSID_CcolorPropPage )
5:    PROPPAGEID( CLSID_CPicturePropPage )
6: END_PROPPAGEIDS(CSampleCtrl)
```

Notice in line 1 of Listing 15.2 that the second parameter is now 4. This second parameter represents the number of property pages.

WARNING

Don't forget to increment the number of property pages when you add them. It will compile fine; but when you go to use the ActiveX control, it will cause an assertion failure in the debug mode. When you use the control in the release mode, it will show only the number of pages set in the second parameter of the BEGIN_PROPPAGEIDS macro.

OLE controls also have persistent properties. These properties are stored in the container and set at design or compile time. Controls also have the capability to save persistent information about their properties at runtime, and thus, in effect, can save their state. This means that the controls can load their persistent properties at initial load time.

Events

Events are notifications triggered by the control in response to some external action on the control. Usually, this is input by the user, such as a mouse click or keyboard input. That event is then communicated to the control's container by the control. This is done through a communications mechanism known as Lightweight Remote Procedure Call (LRPC). LRPCs are the scaled-down little brothers of the Remote Procedure Call (RPC).

RPCs are an interprocess communications mechanism used to provide two-way communications between applications. This can be on the same computer or between computers across a network. RPC is the mechanism that Network OLE, also known as Distributed COM (DCOM), uses to exchange objects across process and computer boundaries. RPC is much more than just a communications method. It allows a function in a process on one computer to evoke a function in a process on another computer. This can even be done on computers across an enterprise-wide network or the Internet.

Lightweight Remote Procedure Calls, unlike their big brother RPCs, are only for communications between processes or within processes on a single computer. LRPCs are the mechanism by which an OLE control dispatches, through the IDispatch interface, control notifications to the container, and the reverse, from the container to the control. This communication is based on posting messages or events to window handles to transfer data between processes. It is also known as *marshaling*.

The Microsoft Foundation Classes provide support for several stock events. These events are listed in Table 15.2.

Table 15.2. The stock events supported in MFC and Visual C++ and their event map entries.

Stock events	*Functions*	*Event map entry*
Click	void FireClick( )	EVENT_STOCK_CLICK( )
DblClick	void FireDblClick( )	EVENT_STOCK_DBLCLICK( )
Error	void FireError(SCODE scode, LPCSTR lpszDescription, UINT nHelpID = 0)	EVENT_STOCK_ERROR( )
KeyDown	void FireKeyDown(short nChar, short nShiftState)	EVENT_STOCK_KEYDOWN( )
KeyPress	void FireKeyPress(short* pnChar)	EVENT_STOCK_KEYPRESS( )
KeyUp	void FireKeyUp(short nChar, short nShiftState)	EVENT_STOCK_KEYUP( )

Stock events	Functions	Event map entry
MouseDown	void FireMouseDown(short nButton, short nShiftState, float x, float y)	EVENT_STOCK_MOUSEDOWN( )
MouseMove	void FireMouseMove(short nButton, short nShiftState, float x, float y)	EVENT_STOCK_MOUSEMOVE( )
MouseUp	void FireMouseUp(short nButton, short nShiftState, float x, float y)	EVENT_STOCK_MOUSEUP( )

I think you will find that handling events is very easy. One of the great things about the folks at Microsoft who developed Visual C++ and MFC is that they have been extremely developer-oriented. They set up a system to handle events very similar to the message maps. They have what is called an *event map*. The event map has two macros to define the beginning and the end of the event map, as shown in Listing 15.3 in lines 1 and 5, respectively. Notice in line 3 the stock event for the mouse move event, as shown in Table 15.2.

Listing 15.3. The event map of an ActiveX/OLE control.

```
1: BEGIN_EVENT_MAP(CMySampleCtrl, COleControl)
2: //{{AFX_EVENT_MAP(CMySampleCtrl)
3:     EVENT_STOCK_MOUSEMOVE( )
4: //}}AFX_EVENT_MAP
5: END_EVENT_MAP()
```

The Visual C++ Class Wizard handles putting the event map entries in for you. You can put them in by hand, but I don't recommend it. Let the tool do it for you; there is less chance for error.

To add a stock or custom event, select the View | Class Wizard menu item or press Ctrl+W. After Class Wizard is displayed, as in Figure 15.9, select the ActiveX Events tab.

Then press the Add Event button, which will bring up the Add Event dialog. If you use the External name combo box, you can select which stock events you want to utilize in your control. (See Figure 15.10.)

FIGURE 15.9.

Using the Class Wizard to invoke stock events.

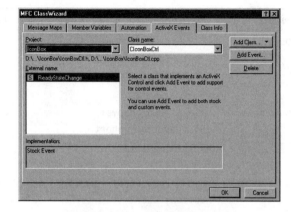

FIGURE 15.10.

You can select stock events to support using the External name combo box.

Methods

Methods are functions performed by the control to access the control's functionality. This allows some external source the capability to manipulate the appearance, behavior, or properties of the control. These are actions such as `GetColor`, `SetColor`, `CutToClipBoard`, `PasteFromClipboard`, and so on. Methods are inherited from OLE automation. A method is the interface that an application or a programmer can set or receive values from an OLE control.

Methods are a lot like member functions in C++. They provide accessor functions that provide and grant access to an OLE control's properties and data. An OLE control's properties are like a C++ class's member variable. Like properties, methods are both stock and custom. Stock methods provide access to stock properties, such as color, font, and picture. Likewise, custom methods provide access to custom properties. With methods, you can change a control's appearance or initialize it with a value. Using VBScript, Visual Basic for Applications, JavaScript, Visual Basic, or Visual C++, you can program a link between it and another application or control the program itself. It is through methods that the control communicates with its container and the container communicates with the control.

Like events, MFC provides two stock methods and handles the dispatch of all methods (custom and stock), much like the message map and event map. Again, it has two macros that define the beginning and end of the dispatch map. These macros are BEGIN_DISPATCH_MAP and END_DISPATCH_MAP, and can be seen in lines 1 and 5 of Listing 15.4.

Listing 15.4. The dispatch map that maps the methods handled by an ActiveX/OLE control.

```
1: BEGIN_DISPATCH_MAP(CMySampleCtrl, COleControl)
2:     //{{AFX_DISPATCH_MAP(CSampleCtrl)
3:     DISP_STOCKPROP_REFRESH( )
4:     //}}AFX_DISPATCH_MAP
5: END_DISPATCH_MAP()
```

Notice also line 3 of Listing 15.4. It has the DISP_STOCKPROP_REFRESH stock method. This is one of two stock methods supported by MFC. The other is DISP_STOCKPROP_DOCLICK. These methods are also known as the DoClick and Refresh methods. The DoClick method fires a click event to the container. The Refresh method is used by the container to force the update of the control's appearance.

It is important to note that the IDispatch interface handles the dispatching of messages to the control, and likewise to the container. The main function offered by IDispatch is the Invoke method. IDispatch provides a level of indirection so you cannot directly call the methods of a control. IDispatch::Invoke does the invoking for you. The IDispatch interface handles control notifications to the container, and the reverse, from the container to the control. This communication is based on posting messages or events to window handles to transfer data between processes. It is also known as marshaling.

To create custom methods or add stock methods to your control in Visual C++ by using the Class Wizard, select the View | Class Wizard menu item or press Ctrl+W. After Class Wizard is displayed, as in Figure 15.11, select the Automation tab.

FIGURE 15.11.

Using the Class Wizard to invoke stock or custom methods.

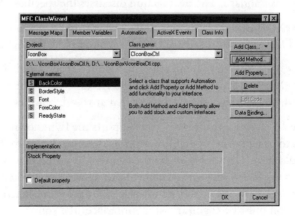

Press the Add Method button, which will invoke the Add Method dialog. If you use the External name combo box, you can select which stock methods you want your control to have, as in Figure 15.12, or you can create a new method by typing its name in the External name combo box.

FIGURE 15.12.

You can select stock methods to support using the External name combo box or create a new method.

OLE Control Interfaces

Like all other COM objects, OLE controls are manipulated through interfaces. In the original OLE control and OLE container specification, OLE controls were required to support certain interfaces, whether or not they needed or utilized them. This left some controls bloated with code and overhead that they did not need.

Currently, the only interface a control is required to implement is the IUnknown. This is mentioned so that you realize a new standard has been published. In December of 1995, Microsoft published the OLE controls and OLE Container Guidelines Version 2.0. This was an extension of Version 1.1. With the advent of ActiveX controls, the standard was changed to the 1996 standard for ActiveX controls and ActiveX containers, and is again an extension to the previous standard. The next section discusses the specifics of an ActiveX control.

An ActiveX/OLE control exposes interfaces. Likewise, a container exposes interfaces to the OLE control. OLE controls and ActiveX/OLE containers link through interfaces. (See Figure 15.13.)

There are approximately 26 interfaces for OLE controls and their containers. The next section on ActiveX controls discusses the new interfaces. This is not considered an all-inclusive list, because there are a few other interfaces that are used, but these represent the main interfaces.

In Table 15.3, notice that each object supports the IUnknown. This is now the only interface required to be supported by an OLE control. However, if you implemented only the IUnknown, you would have a control that did pretty much nothing. The idea is to implement only the interfaces needed to support the control. In Figure 15.14, you can see how an OLE control's interfaces relate to the container interfaces. In addition, when you write the code for your control, you must be cognizant of the interfaces the control supports, and you must also be cognizant that not all OLE containers support all interfaces. In order to be compatible with as many containers as possible, you must check for the support of your interfaces by the container and degrade your control's functionality gracefully in the event an interface is not supported. This can be likened to error checking—except that you still want your control to function, but with degraded capability or through an alternative interface.

FIGURE 15.13.

OLE controls and their containers communicate through interfaces using LRPCs.

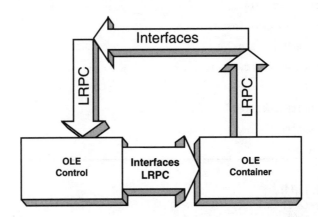

The most important interfaces are IOleControl and IDispatch. IDispatch is the mechanism through which OLE controls communicate. IOleControl encapsulates the basic functionality of an OLE control. Table 15.3 shows the COM interfaces an OLE control or an OLE container can support in order to facilitate the operations between them. With MFC, most of the interfaces are hidden from you. You will utilize them, but you cannot realize it. You can always explicitly use an interface if you want, but MFC has encapsulated most of them to make them easier for you to use.

Table 15.3. COM interfaces for facilitating operations between controls and containers.

OLE control	Control site	Client site	Container
IClassFactory2	IOleControlSite	IOleClientSite	IOleInPlaceUIWindow
IOleObject	IUnknown	IOleInPlaceSite	IOleInPlaceFrame
IDataObject	IAdviseSink	IUnknown	
IViewObject	IDispatch		
IPersistStorage	IUnknown		
IOleInPlaceActiveObject			
IOleCache			
IPersistStreamInit			

continues

Table 15.3. continued

OLE control	Control site	Client site	Container
IOleControl			
IConnectionPointContainer			
IConnectionPoint			
IProvideClassInfo			
IProperNotifySink			
ISpecifyPropertyPages			
IPerPropertyBrowsing			
ISimpleFrameSite			
IDispatch			
IUnknown			

FIGURE 15.14.

How the OLE control interfaces relate to the OLE container interfaces.

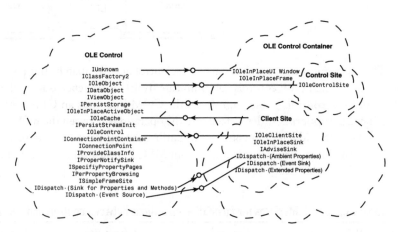

The important thing to remember is that the interfaces a control supports define that control. However, you should implement only the interfaces your control requires to function. This idea will become more apparent in the following section on ActiveX controls.

ActiveX Controls

An ActiveX control is a superset of an OLE control that has been extended for the Internet environment. This does not mean that ActiveX controls can be utilized only in the Internet environment; quite the contrary, they can be utilized in any container that can support their interfaces. ActiveX controls must still be embedded in a container application. When an end user encounters a page with an ActiveX control, that control is downloaded to the client machine if it is not already there and used; this is, of course, provided that the user's browser supports ActiveX controls. The two most prevalent browsers that support ActiveX controls are Microsoft Internet Explorer and Netscape, with the help of the Ncompass plug-in.

The major difference between the OLE control and the "superset" ActiveX control is that the standard is different. In the new standard, an ActiveX control must support at least the IUnknown interface and must be self-registering. It is a simple COM object. The control must have more interfaces than just IUnknown, or it would have no functionality. The idea is that the control support only the interfaces it needs, so it can be as lightweight as possible. In contrast, in the previous standard an OLE control was required to support a whole armada of COM interfaces, whether the control needed them or not. This made the controls bloated with code that was not utilized or needed. In the world of Internet development, code bloat is unacceptable.

It is important to note that there has emerged a type of ActiveX control, written specifically by the author to be used in Internet Web pages. There is nothing special about it except the interfaces it supports. It is sometimes called Internet ActiveX control, and it cannot function in a non-Internet environment.

Supporting the IUnknown

The minimum interface for an ActiveX control to support is the IUnknown. As discussed in Chapter 11, "Overview of ActiveX," the IUnknown is an interface that supports three methods: QueryInterface, AddRef, and Release.

All COM interfaces are inherited either directly or indirectly from the IUnknown; hence, all other interfaces have these three functions also. With a pointer to the IUnknown, a client can get a pointer to other interfaces the object supports through QueryInterface. In short, an object can use QueryInterface to find out the capabilities of another object. If the object supports the interface, it returns a pointer to the interface. Listing 15.5 demonstrates the use of the pointer to a control's IUnknown interface to QueryInterface to find out the class information using MFC.

Listing 15.5. The use of the pointer to a control's IUnknown interface and then utilizing QueryInterface to get the class information.

```
1:  // Function to get a pointer to a control's IUnknown and use
2:  // QueryInterface to see if it supports the interface.
3:  int MyClass::DoControlWork()
4:  {
5:      LPUNKNOWN lpUnknown;
6:      LPPPROVIDECLASSINFO lpClassInfo;
7:
8:      lpUnknown = GetControlUnknown();
9:
```

continues

Listing 15.5. continued

```
10:      if(lpUnknown == NULL)
11:      {
12:            // return my error code to let me know IUnknown was NULL
13:            return ERROR_CODE_IUNKNOWN_NULL;
16:      }
15:      else
16:      {
17:            if(SUCCEEDED(lpUnknown->QueryInterface(IID_IProvideClassInfo,
18:                                          (void**) &lpClassInfo)))
19:            {
20:                  // QueryInterface Returned a Succeeded so this
21:                  // Interface is Supported
22:                  // {
23:                  //         Perform some function with lpClassInfo such
24:                  // as getting the class info and examining the class attributes
25:                  // {
26:
27:                  lpClassInfo->Release();
28:            }
29:            else
30:            {
31:                  // Control Does Not Support Interface
32:                  return ERROR_INTERFACE_NOT_SUPPORTED;
33:            }
34:      }
35:      return SUCCESSFUL;
36: }
```

In addition, the object can manage its own lifetime through the AddRef and Release functions. If an object obtains a pointer to an object, AddRef is called, incrementing the object's reference count. After an object no longer needs the pointer to the interface, Release is called, decrementing the object's reference count. After the reference count reaches zero, an object can safely destroy itself.

Although the IUnknown is a necessary implementation, you should also take a look at the other interfaces an ActiveX control can implement. Table 15.4 shows the potential COM interfaces an ActiveX control can support.

In addition, the control can implement its own custom interfaces. By implementing only the interfaces it needs, the ActiveX control can be as lean as possible. The previous OLE control standard required that in order to be compliant with the standard, the control had to implement certain interfaces. With ActiveX controls, this is no longer the case. You are only required to implement IUnknown.

Table 15.4. The potential COM interfaces for an ActiveX control.

Interface	*Purpose*
IOleObject	Principal mechanism by which a control communicates with its container.

Interface	*Purpose*
IOleInPlaceObject	Means by which activation and deactivation of an object are managed.
IOleInPlaceActiveObject	Provides communications between an in-place active object and the outermost windows of the container.
IOleControl	Allows support for keyboard mnemonics, properties, and events.
IDataObject	Allows for the transfer of data and the communication of changes in the data.
IViewObject	Allows the object to display itself.
IViewObject2	An extension of the IViewObject interface. It allows you to find the size of the object in a given view.
IDispatch	An interface that can call virtually any other COM interface. It is used in OLE automation to evoke late binding to properties and methods of COM objects.
IConnectionPoint Container	Supports connection points for connectable objects.
IProvideClassInfo	Encapsulates a single method by which you get all of the information about an object's co-class entry in its type library.
IProvideClassInfo2	An extension to the IProvideClassInfo that provides quick access to an object's IID for its event set.
ISpecifyPropertyPages	An interface that denotes an object as supporting property pages.
IPerPropertyBrowsing	Supports methods to get access to the information in the property pages supported by an object.
IPersistStream	Provides methods for loading and storing simple streams.
IPersistStreamInit	Designed as a replacement for IPersistStream. Adds an initialization method, InitNew.
IPersistMemory	Allows the method to access a fixed-sized memory block for an IPersistStream object.
IPersistStorage	Supports the manipulation of storage objects to include loading, saving, and exchanging.
IPersistMoniker	An interface to expose to asynchronous objects the capability to manipulate the way they bind data to the object.

continues

Table 15.4. continued

Interface	Purpose
`IPersistPropertyBag`	Allows the storage of persistent properties.
`IOleCache`	An interface to control access to the cache inside an object.
`IOleCache2`	Allows the selective update of an object's cache.
`IExternalConnection`	Allows the tracking of external locking on an embedded object.
`IRunnableObject`	Enables a container to control its executable objects.

A Control Must Be Self-Registering

In order for an ActiveX control or any other COM object to be utilized, it must be registered in the System Registry. The System Registry is a database of configuration information divided into a hierarchical tree. This tree consists of three levels of information: hives, keys, and values. The System Registry is a centralized place where you can go to find out information about an object. (See Figure 15.15.)

> **NOTE**
>
> The System Registry in Windows 95 can be viewed through a program called `regedit.exe`. This program can be found in the `\WINDOWS` directory of Windows 95 and the `\WINNT\SYSTEM32` directory in Windows NT 4.0. If you are using Windows NT 3.51, the System Registry can be viewed with a program called `regedt32.exe`, which is found in the same directory as specified for Windows NT 4.0.

If the control is not registered in the registry, it is unknown and therefore unusable by the system. If you're not in the registry, the rest of the system does not know you're there.

Thus, it is a requirement for ActiveX controls to be self-registering. This means an ActiveX control must implement and export the functions `DllRegisterServer` and `DllUnregisterServer`. In addition, it is a requirement for ActiveX controls to register all of the standard registry entries for automation servers and embeddable objects. Listing 15.6 demonstrates the use of `DllRegisterServer` to support self-registration of the control using MFC. Visual C++'s App Wizard generates this code for you.

FIGURE 15.15.

The Windows 95 System Registry as seen through the Regedit program.

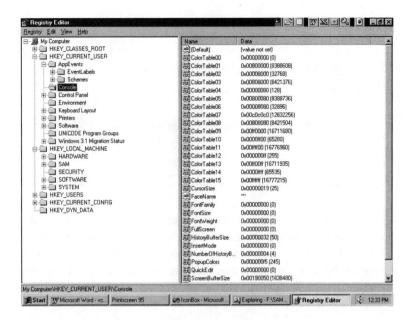

Listing 15.6. Using the `DllRegisterServer` to support self-registration of the control.

```
1:  /////////////////////////////////////////////////////////
2:  // DllRegisterServer - Adds entries to the system registry
3:
4:  STDAPI DllRegisterServer(void)
5:  {
6:      AFX_MANAGE_STATE(_afxModuleAddrThis);
7:
8:      if (!AfxOleRegisterTypeLib(AfxGetInstanceHandle(), _tlid))
9:          return ResultFromScode(SELFREG_E_TYPELIB);
10:
11:     if (!COleObjectFactoryEx::UpdateRegistryAll(TRUE))
12:         return ResultFromScode(SELFREG_E_CLASS);
13:
14:     return NOERROR;
15: }
```

Listing 15.7 demonstrates the use of `DllUnregisterServer` to support self-unregistration of a control using MFC. Visual C++'s Control Wizard generates this code for you.

Listing 15.7. Using `DllUnregisterServer` to support self-unregistration of a control.

```
1:  /////////////////////////////////////////////////////////
2:  // DllUnregisterServer - Removes entries from the
     ➥system registry
3:
```

continues

Listing 15.7. continued

```
4:  STDAPI DllUnregisterServer(void)
5:  {
6:      AFX_MANAGE_STATE(_afxModuleAddrThis);
7:
8:      if (!AfxOleUnregisterTypeLib(_tlid))
9:          return ResultFromScode(SELFREG_E_TYPELIB);
10:
11:     if (!COleObjectFactoryEx::UpdateRegistryAll(FALSE))
12:         return ResultFromScode(SELFREG_E_CLASS);
13:
14:     return NOERROR;
16:  }
```

Listings 15.6 and 15.7 show you how to support registration and unregistration, and Listing 15.8 shows you how to register your control and its capabilities. Notice in line 15 of Listing 15.8 the variable dwMyControlOleMisc. It contains the status bits of your control. This is very important because it contains the capabilities of your control. These capabilities can be looked up in the System Registry to find out what capabilities your control contains, without instantiating the object.

Listing 15.8. How to register your control and your control's capabilities in MFC.

```
1:  ///////////////////////////////////////////////////////////////
2:  // CMyCtrl::CMyCtrlFactory::UpdateRegistry -
3:  // Adds or removes system registry entries for CMyCtrl
4:  BOOL CMyCtrl::CMyCtrlFactory::UpdateRegistry(BOOL bRegister)
5:  {
6:      if (bRegister)
7:          return AfxOleRegisterControlClass(
8:              AfxGetInstanceHandle(),
9:              m_clsid,         // Records the Object's CLSID
10:             m_lpszProgID,    // Records a Unique Program ID for MyControl
11:             IDS_MYCONTROL,   // Records a Human Readable Name of MyControl
12:             IDB_MYCONTROL,   // Records the Bitmap to Represent MyControl
13:             TRUE,            // Records that MyControl can be insertable
14:                              // in a Container's Insert Object Dialog
15:             dwMyControlOleMisc, // Records the Status bits of MyControl
16:             tlid,            // Records the Unique ID of the MyControls
17:                              // Control Class
18:             wVerMajor,       // Records the Major Version of MyControl
19:             wVerMinor);      // Records the Minor Version of MyControl
20:     else
21:         return AfxOleUnregisterClass(m_clsid, m_lpszProgID);
22:  }
```

The possible status bits that can be set for a control are shown in Table 15.5. These bits identify the capabilities of the control.

Table 15.5. The OLE misc status bits symbolic constants and what they mean to controls and objects.

Symbolic constant	Meaning
OLEMISC_RECOMPOSEONRESIZE	Identifies an object that upon resizing by the container will rescale its presentation data.
OLEMISC_ONLYICONIC	Identifies an object that only exists in the iconic state.
OLEMISC_INSERTNOTREPLACE	Identifies an object that initializes itself from the currently selected container data.
OLEMISC_STATIC	Identifies that an object is static and contains no native data, only presentation data.
OLEMISC_CANTLINKINSIDE	Identifies items such as OLE 1.0 objects, static objects, and links. These are objects that cannot be linked source objects. In addition, when the object is bound, it cannot run another object.
OLEMISC_CANLINKBYOLE1	Identifies that an object can be linked by the containers that conform to the OLE 1.0 specification.
OLEMISC_ISLINKOBJECT	Identifies that an object is a linked object. This is only important for OLE 1.0 objects.
OLEMISC_INSIDEOUT	Identifies that an object can be in-place activated without the need for toolbars or menus.
OLEMISC_ACTIVATEWHENVISIBLE	Identifies that an object can only be activated in the visible state. The OLEMISC_INSIDEOUT flag must also be set.
OLEMISC_RENDERINGISDEVICEINDEPENDENT	Identifies that the object's presentation data will remain the same, regardless of the target container.

continues

Table 15.5. continued

Symbolic constant	Meaning
OLEMISC_INVISIBLEATRUNTIME	Identifies controls that are invisible at runtime, such as Internet Explorer's Timer control or Internet Explorer's PreLoader control.
OLEMISC_ALWAYSRUN	Tells a control that a control should be set in the running state even when not visible.
OLEMISC_ACTSLIKEBUTTON	Identifies controls that can act like buttons.
OLEMISC_ACTSLIKELABEL	Identifies controls that can change the label provided by the container.
OLEMISC_NOUIACTIVATE	Identifies whether a control supports user-interface activation.
OLEMISC_ALIGNABLE	Identifies that a control can be aligned with other controls for containers that support control alignment.
OLEMISC_SIMPLEFRAME	Identifies that the control supports the ISimpleFrameSite interface.
OLEMISC_SETCLIENTSITEFIRST	In the new OLE container specification, this flag identifies controls that support the SetClientSide function being called after the control is created but before it is displayed.
OLEMISC_IMEMODE	In the Double Byte Character Set versions of Windows, identifies that the control supports the Input Method Editor Mode, for internationalized controls.

These miscellaneous status bits are especially important when used in conjunction with component categories as an accurate picture of what your control can or cannot do. This picture of what the control can do can be obtained from the System Registry.

Component Categories

Previously, in order to be registered on the system, an OLE control was registered through entries in the registry with the `Control` keyword. To your benefit, controls can be utilized for multiple purposes. Therefore, a way was needed to identify a control's functionality as opposed to just listing the interfaces it supports. This is where component categories come in.

Component categories are a way of describing what a control does. They provide a better method for containers to find out what a control does without creating it and having to query for its methods using an `IUnknown` pointer and `QueryInterface`. Creating a control object involves a lot of overhead. A container would not want to create a control if the container itself does not support the functionality the control requires.

Component categories are not specific to ActiveX but are an extension of the OLE architecture. Each component category has its own GUID and a human-readable name stored in a well-known place in the System Registry. When a control registers itself, it does so using its component category ID. In addition, it registers the component categories it supports and the component categories it requires its container to support.

For backward compatibility, the control should also register itself with the `Control` keyword for containers that do not support the new component categories. The control should also register the key `ToolBoxBitmap32`. This key identifies the module name and resource ID for a 16×15 bitmap. `ToolBoxBitmap32` provides a bitmap to use for the face of a toolbar or toolbox button in the container application. If a control can be inserted in a compound document, it should also register the Insertable key.

Component categories can be mixed and matched depending on their type. Microsoft maintains a list of component categories. Any categories that are new should be submitted to Microsoft for inclusion in the list. This promotes interoperability. The following component categories have been identified:

- Simple Frame Site Containment
- Simple Data Binding
- Advanced Data Binding
- Visual Basic Private Interfaces
- Internet-Aware Controls
- Windowless Controls

This list is not all-inclusive.

Simple Frame Site Containment

A Simple Frame Site Container control contains other controls—for example, a 3D group box that contains a group of check boxes. The GUID for this component category is `CATID - {157083E0-2368-11cf-87B9-00AA006C8166} CATID_SimpleFrameControl`. In order to support a

Simple Frame Site Container, the OLE container application must implement the ISimpleFrameSite interface and the control must have its status bit set to OLEMISC_SIMPLEFRAME.

Simple Data Binding

A control or container that supports Simple Data Binding supports the IPropertyNotifySink interface. Data binding is how controls affiliate their persistent properties and how containers exchange property changes from their user interface to the control's persistent properties. This allows the persistent storage of their properties, and at runtime binds the data to the control synchronizing property changes between the control and the container. The GUID for this component category is CATID - {157083E1-2368-11cf-87B9-00AA006C8166} CATID_PropertyNotifyControl.

> **NOTE**
>
> Although a control that supports Simple Data Binding is meant to provide binding to a data source, such binding should not be required for the functionality of the control. Even though a lot of the functionality of the control is lost, the control should degrade gracefully and still be able to function, although potentially limited, independent of any data binding.

Advanced Data Binding

Advanced Data Binding is similar to Simple Data Binding except it supports more advanced binding techniques, such as asynchronous binding and Visual Basic Data Binding. The GUID for this component category is CATID - {157083E2-2368-11cf-87B9-00AA006C8166} CATID_VBDataBound.

Visual Basic Private Interfaces

These component categories are for components that specifically support the Visual Basic environment. Controls or containers that use these categories can support alternative methods. This is in case a container encounters a control, or a control encounters a container that does not support the Visual Basic Private Interfaces categories. The GUID for this component category is CATID - {02496840-3AC4-11cf-87B9-00AA006C8166} CATID_VBFormat, if the container implements the IBVFormat interface for data formatting to specifically integrate with Visual Basic, or CATID - {02496841-3AC4-11cf-87B9-00AA006C8166} CATID_VBGetControl if the container implements IVBGetControl so that controls can enumerate other controls on a Visual Basic form.

Internet-Aware Controls

Internet-aware controls implement one or more persistent interfaces to support operation across the Internet. All of these categories provide persistent storage operations. The following are GUIDs for components that fall into this category:

■ CATID - {0de86a50-2baa-11cf-a229-00aa003d7352} CATID_RequiresDataPathHost

■ CATID - {0de86a51-2baa-11cf-a229-00aa003d7352} CATID_PersistsToMoniker

■ CATID - {0de86a52-2baa-11cf-a229-00aa003d7352} CATID_PersistsToStorage

■ CATID - {0de86a53-2baa-11cf-a229-00aa003d7352} CATID_PersistsToStreamInit

■ CATID - {0de86a54-2baa-11cf-a229-00aa003d7352} CATID_PersistsToStream

■ CATID - {0de86a55-2baa-11cf-a229-00aa003d7352} CATID_PersistsToMemory

■ CATID - {0de86a56-2baa-11cf-a229-00aa003d7352} CATID_PersistsToFile

■ CATID - {0de86a57-2baa-11cf-a229-00aa003d7352} CATID_PersistsToPropertyBag

The `RequiresDataPathHost` category means that the object requires the container to support the `IBindHost` interface because the object requires the capability to save data to one or more paths.

All of the rest of the categories listed are mutually exclusive. They are used when an object only supports a single persistence method. If a container does not support a persistence method that a control supports, the container should not allow itself to create controls of that type.

Windowless Controls

Windowless controls are controls that do not implement their own window and rely on the use of their container's window to draw themselves. These types of controls are non-rectangular controls such as arrow buttons, gauges, and other items modeled after real-world objects. In addition, this includes transparent controls. The GUID for this component category is `CATID - {1D06B600-3AE3-11cf-87B9-00AA006C8166}` `CATID_WindowlessObject`.

Component Categories and Interoperability

Components that do not support a category should degrade gracefully. In the case where a control or container is unable to support an interface, the control should either clearly document that a particular interface is required for the proper operation of the component or at runtime notify the user of the component's degraded capability.

By using self-registration, components can be self-contained, which is necessary for Internet operations. By using `DllRegisterServer` and `DllUnregisterServer` and the component category's API functions to register itself and the component categories it supports, a control can further its interoperability in a variety of environments.

Code Signing

In the Internet environment, users must download the components to their local machine and utilize them. This is an extreme hazard to the local machine by allowing the implementation of this foreign code.

This is where a new security measure called *code signing* comes in. Browsers typically warn the user that they are downloading a potentially unsafe object; however, the browser does not physically check the code for authenticity to ensure it has not been tampered with nor does it verify its source.

Microsoft has implemented *authenticode,* which embodies the Crypto API. This allows developers to digitally sign their code so that it can be checked and verified at runtime. This function is built into the browser and displays a certificate of authenticity (see Figure 15.16) if the control is verified.

FIGURE 15.16.

The certificate the user is shown at runtime after the code has been authenticated.

Currently, the code-signing specification and the certification process are being reviewed by the World Wide Web Consortium (W3), and the current specifications are subject to change. Internet Explorer and all Microsoft controls naturally support code signing and authenticode, but as of yet Netscape does not. Netscape has gone to W3 with a proposal on extending its own digital certificate standard. In the spirit of cooperation, Netscape eventually will support the code-signing specification, or at a minimum Microsoft will embrace both standards.

Code signing works with DLLs, EXEs, CABs, and OCXs. When a developer creates these items, he attains a digital certificate from an independent certification authority. He then runs a one-way hash on the code and produces a digest that has a fixed length. Next, the developer encrypts the digest using a private key. This combination of an encrypted digest coupled with the developer's certificate and credentials is a signature block unique for the item and the developer. This signature block is embedded into the executable program.

Here's the way code signing works on the client machine. When a user downloads a control, for example, from the Internet, the browser application such as Internet Explorer or Netscape calls a Win32 API function called `WinVerifyTrust`.

> **NOTE**
>
> At present, Netscape does not currently support code signing.

`WinVerifyTrust` then reads the signature block. With the signature block, the `WinVerifyTrust` can authenticate the certificate and decrypt the digest using the developer's public key. Using the public key, the function then rehashes the code with the hash function stored in the signature block and creates a second digest. This digest is then compared with the original. If they do not match, this indicates tampering and the user is warned. (See Figure 15.17.) On the contrary, if the digest had matched, instead of the warning in Figure 15.17, the user would have gotten the certificate of authenticity, shown in Figure 15.16.

FIGURE 15.17.

The warning the user is shown at runtime to tell him of a potential danger because the code cannot be authenticated.

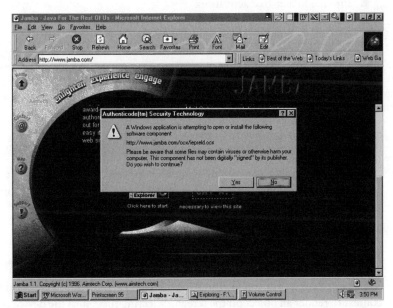

Despite code signing, the user is in control and can choose to heed or ignore the warning. If the hashes check out, the browser displays a certificate.

The code-signing mechanism provides some security for end users and developers alike. It is a deterrent to malicious tampering with executable code for the intent of information warfare such as viruses, and it is also a deterrent for those who can pirate the code developed by others.

Please be aware again that this is a proposed standard and has not yet been officially accepted, although there is nothing I can see at this time that can compete with it. It is safe to say that no matter what, Microsoft will continue to support and refine it. The bottom line is you will need to continue to monitor the standard.

Performance Considerations

ActiveX controls are designed to work across the Internet. As such, they are Internet-aware. Unfortunately, the Internet is low bandwidth and highly subject to server latency. This means that ActiveX controls must be lean and mean, or to put it more plainly, highly optimized. Because ActiveX controls implement only the interfaces they need, they are already partially optimized. ActiveX controls are optimized to perform specific tasks. However, there are several things you can do to help optimize your controls.

■ Optimize control drawing.

■ Don't always activate when visible.

■ Provide flicker-free activation.

■ Provide windowless activation.

■ Optimize persistence and initialization.

■ Use windowless controls.

■ Use a device context that is unclipped.

■ While inactive, provide mouse interaction.

> **TIP**
>
> These performance considerations and optimizing techniques apply to OLE controls as well as ActiveX controls. You may have already developed OLE controls to the old standard, but you can still apply most of these principles to them.

Optimize Control Drawing

When you draw items, you have to select items such as pens, brushes, and fonts into the device context to render an object on the screen. Selecting these into the device context requires time, and is a waste of resources when the container has multiple controls that are selecting and de-selecting the same resources every time they paint. The container can support optimized drawing. This means that the container handles the restoration of the original objects after all the items have been drawn. IViewObject::Draw supports optimized drawing by using the DVASPECTINFOFLAG flags set in the DVASPECTINFO structure. You must use this to determine if your container supports optimized drawing when implementing API functions. MFC encapsulates this check for you in the `COleControl::IsOptimizedDraw` function. You can then optimize how you draw your code by storing your GDI objects as member variables instead of local variables. This prevents them from being destroyed when the drawing function finishes. Then, if the container supports optimized drawing, you do not need to select the objects back because the container has taken care of this for you.

Don't Always Activate When Visible

If your control has a window, it might not need to be activated when visible. Creating a window is a control's single biggest operation and therefore should not be done until it is absolutely necessary. Therefore, if there is no reason for your control to be activated when visible, you will need to turn off the `OLEMISC_ACTIVATEWHENVISIBLE` miscellaneous status bit.

Provide Flicker-Free Activation

When your control has a window, it must sometimes make the transition from the active to the inactive state. A visual flicker occurs when the control redraws from the active to the inactive state. Two methods—drawing off-screen and copying to the screen in one big chunk, and drawing front to back—can eliminate flicker. The `IViewObjectEx` API function provides the necessary functions to use either method or a combination of both. With MFC the implementation is much simpler; simply do what is shown in Listing 15.9.

Listing 15.9. How to set the `noFlickerActive` flag in MFC.

```
1:  DWORD CMyControl::GetControlFlags()
2:  {
3:      return COleControl::GetControlFlags() ¦ noFlickerActivate;
4:  }
```

Optimizing Persistence and Initialization

Optimizing persistence and initialization means basically one thing: Keep your code as lean as possible. Because of the cheapness of hard drive space and memory, some programmers have gotten lazy in the creation of this code, and allowed it to become bloated and slow. With Internet applications, this is a death sentence. Most people access the Internet with 14.4 modems. A megabyte of data takes almost nine minutes on a 14.4 modem. Users will get impatient if they have to wait long periods of time. What can you do? You can do several things.

First of all, make sure you do not leave any non-utilized blocks of code or variables. You should also take any debugging or testing blocks out of your code. For example, you have written your code so a message box displays when you reach a certain segment of code. Take it out! It will only add to your code size. However, if you delimit your debugging blocks of code using the preprocessor `#ifdef _DEBUG` and `#endif`, you will not have to worry about the code being included in the release builds, because the debugging blocks of code will be left out of the compile.

Second, today's compilers have optimizing options on them. In the past, these optimizing compilers were not very efficient and sometimes introduced bugs in an application that had already been tested. However, compilers have gotten much better. Use them! Let the compiler do some of the work for you. You might have to tweak and play with the optimizations to find the best combination of options.

> **WARNING**
>
> Make sure you perform your compiler optimizations before you send your code to testing. However, any time you touch the code, it should go back through testing. Therefore, if you have to tweak the compiler optimizations after it has been through testing, make sure you send it back through testing! This can help prevent you from discovering a bug after release.

You should also turn off the incremental linking option on your compiler when you do a release build. Incremental linking can add serious bloat to your code.

> **NOTE**
>
> For an excellent article on keeping your code small, see "Removing Fatty Deposits from Your Applications Using 32-bit Liposuction Tools," by Matt Pietrek, in *Microsoft Systems Journal*, October 1996, Vol 11, No 10. Pietrek has many useful suggestions and even provides a nice tool to assist you.

The last thing you should take into account is utilizing asynchronous operations to perform initialization and persistence operations. Asynchronous downloading gives the user the illusion that things are occurring faster than they are. In addition, you might want to give the user other visual cues that progress is being made, such as a progress indicator or a message box. However, you will have to weigh the performance issues associated with their addition.

Use Windowless Controls

You should consider making your control a windowless control if appropriate. Creating a window is a control's single biggest operation, taking almost two-thirds of its creation time. This is a lot of unnecessary overhead for the control. Most of the time, a control does not need a window and can utilize its container's window and allow the container to take on the overhead of maintaining that window. This will allow you to model your controls after real-world objects, such as gauges, knobs, and other non-rectangular items.

By using the API function `IOleInPlaceSiteEx::OnInPlaceActivateEx` and setting the `ACTIVATE_WINDOWLESS` flag, you can have your control placed in the windowless mode. Listing 15.10 demonstrates how you can do this with MFC.

Listing 15.10. How to set the windowless flag in MFC.

```
1:   DWORD CMyControl::GetControlFlags()
2:   {
3:       return COleControl::GetControlFlags() ¦ windowlessActivate;
4:   }
```

In addition, a whole series of API functions allows you to manipulate windowless controls. MFC has encapsulated many of these functions for you also. The books online in Visual C++ have a complete reference for these functions. The Win32 API references also have API level functions.

Use a Device Context that Is Unclipped

If you have a window and you are sure your control does not draw outside of that window, you can disable the clipping in your drawing of the control. You can yield a small performance gain by not clipping the device context. With MFC, you can do what is shown in Listing 15.11 to remove the `clipPaintDC` flag.

Listing 15.11. How to set the `clipPaintDC` flag in MFC.

```
1:   DWORD CMyControl::GetControlFlags()
2:   {
3:       return COleControl::GetControlFlags() & ~clipPaintDC;
4:   }
```

NOTE

The `clipPaintDC` flag has no effect if you have set your control to be a windowless control.

With the API functions in the ActiveX SDK, you can implement the `IViewObject`, `IViewObject2`, and `IViewObjectEx` interfaces to optimize your drawing code so you do not clip the device context.

While Inactive, Provide Mouse Interaction

You can set your control to inactive because it does not always need to be activated when visible. You might still want your control to process mouse messages such as `WM_MOUSEMOVE` and `WM_SETCURSOR`. You will need to implement the `IPointerInactive` interface in order to process the mouse messages. If you are using MFC, you need only implement the following function as the framework handles the rest for you. In Listing 15.12, you can see how to set the mouse pointer as inactive.

Listing 15.12. How you set the pointer inactive flag in MFC.

```
1:   DWORD CMyControl::GetControlFlags()
2:   {
3:        return COleControl::GetControlFlages() ¦ pointerInactivate;
4:   }
```

However, you will need to override the OLEMISC_ACTIVATEWHENVISIBLE miscellaneous status bit with OLEMISC_IGNOREACTIVATEWHENVISIBLE. This is because OLEMISC_ACTIVATEWHENVISIBLE forces the control to always be activated when visible. You have to do this to prevent the flag from taking effect for containers that do not support the IPointerInactive interface.

Reinventing the Wheel

In today's software development environment, software engineers are not only designers and programmers, but increasingly, software engineers are taking on the role of component integrators. End users demand that their software be developed quickly, be rich in features, and integrate with the rest of the software they use. With the advent of OLE, CORBA, and OpenDoc, you now have hundreds of thousands of reusable components and objects to choose from. There is an abundance of dynamic link libraries, controls, automation components, and document objects at your fingertips. ActiveX/OLE controls especially provide an off-the-shelf, self-contained reusable package of functionality, created by someone else. OLE controls provide functionality of all types such as multimedia, communications, user-interface components, report writing, and computational. (See Figure 15.18.)

FIGURE 15.18.

Some of the numerous OLE/ActiveX controls available.

This is functionality that you do not have to create. The major key to component integration is to be able to integrate all of the components with a custom application so that they work in single harmonious union, as if they were native to the application.

However, before you embark on creating this application, you should take care not to "reinvent the wheel." OLE/ActiveX controls, the Component Object Model, and the object-oriented paradigm present a unique opportunity for you to truly have code reuse. In order to achieve this nirvana of code reuse, you should evaluate what components are already out there. Likewise, before you decide to write your own OLE controls, you should take a look at what is already out there and see if you can utilize what is already available, as opposed to reinventing the wheel.

When you choose to utilize off-the-shelf components, there are a few things you should consider. You should ask the following questions:

1. How long has the manufacturer been in business?
2. Do they supply the source code with the component? The source code would come in handy if the manufacturer went out of business or had a bug in their component that they were not going to fix.
3. What are the licensing fees and distribution costs?
4. Is the control Web-enabled?
5. What kind of support and money-back guarantee do they provide?
6. What tools will the component be supported in?
7. What kind of documentation, such as programmer's manuals, help files, and installation guides, does the control come with?

These questions can save you a lot of heartache later. Integration of these off-the-shelf components is sometimes tricky. Make sure you thoroughly research the components you choose. To find some of these available off the shelf components, look in some of the computer industry trade magazines.

Visual C++ ActiveX Controls

Visual C++ 5.0 comes with a plethora of ActiveX controls. Therefore, before you take the time to create your own control, take a look around and see what is available. Take a look at all of the ActiveX controls available to you from the Components and Controls Gallery in Visual C++. First go to the Project | Add to Project | Components and Controls menu item and invoke the Components and Controls Gallery dialog box, as shown in Figure 15.19. Then click the Registered ActiveX Controls folder. Take a look at all of the ActiveX controls available, as shown in Figure 15.20.

FIGURE 15.19.

The Components and Controls Gallery dialog box.

FIGURE 15.20.

The list of registered ActiveX controls in the Components and Controls Gallery dialog box.

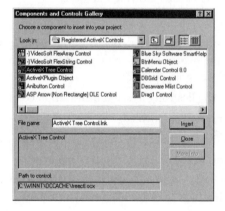

Internet Explorer Stock Controls

So that you do not go out and reinvent the wheel, it is important to note that there are several controls that come stock with Internet Explorer. You can utilize these controls in your Web pages and in your application development efforts. These controls provide a variety of functionality. The following ActiveX controls come with Internet Explorer:

■ Animated button

■ Chart

■ Gradient

■ Label

■ Marquee

■ Menu

■ Popup menu

■ Popup window

■ Stock ticker

- PreLoader
- Timer
- View tracker

> **NOTE**
>
> A demo of the functionality of each of these controls is available on the Microsoft World Wide Web site at the following Internet URL:
>
> `http://www.microsoft.com/activex/gallery/default.htm`.
>
> In addition, a number of other third-party vendors have their controls demonstrated at the same Microsoft WWW site.

Testing an ActiveX/OLE Control

In order to ensure your ActiveX control works properly, you should test it in as many environments as possible. As a minimum, you should test your ActiveX/OLE controls in the following environments:

- A Web page
- The ActiveX control container
- Visual C++
- Any other development environments

Displaying a Control in a Web Page

In order to "activate the Internet" with ActiveX controls, as the Microsoft marketing folks are fond of saying, you have to have a way of embedding those ActiveX controls in an HTML file.

The World Wide Web Consortium (W3C) controls the HTML standard. The current HTML standard is version 3.2. Like most standards, it is continually updated and modified as technology progresses. As the standard progresses, the controlling agency tries to ensure backward compatibility so that any HTML browser that does not yet support the newest standard will degrade gracefully and allow the HTML to be viewed.

> **NOTE**
>
> The current World Wide Web Consortium (W3C) HTML standard is available at the following Internet URL:
>
> `http://www.w3.org/pub/WWW/`

The <OBJECT> HTML tag is used to allow the insertion of dynamic content in the Web page such as ActiveX controls. The tag is just a way of identifying such dynamic elements. It is up to the browser to parse the HTML tags and perform the appropriate action based on the meaning of the tag. In Listing 15.13, you can see the HTML syntax for the <OBJECT> tag. This syntax comes directly from the World Wide Web Consortium (W3C), which controls the HTML standard. In this case, it is HTML standard version 3.2.

Listing 15.13. The HTML syntax for the <OBJECT> tag.

```
 1:  <OBJECT
 2:      ALIGN= alignment type
 3:      BORDER= number
 4:      CLASSID= universal resource locator
 5:      CODEBASE= universal resource locator
 6:      CODETYPE= codetype
 7:      DATA= universal resource locator
 8:      DECLARE
 9:      HEIGHT= number
10:      HSPACE= value
11:      NAME= universal resource locator
12:       SHAPES
13:       STANDBY= message
14:       TYPE= type
15:       USEMAP= universal resource locator
16:       VSPACE= number
17:       WIDTH= number
18:  </OBJECT>
```

By utilizing the <OBJECT> tag, you can insert an object such as an image, document, applet, or control into the HTML document.

Table 15.6 shows the acceptable range of values to be utilized by the parameters of the <OBJECT> tag.

Table 15.6. The values for the parameters of the <OBJECT> tag.

Parameter	*Values*
ALIGN= *alignment type*	Sets the alignment for the object. The alignment type is one of the following values: BASELINE, LEFT, MIDDLE, CENTER, RIGHT, TEXTMIDDLE, TEXTTOP, and TEXTBOTTOM.
BORDER= *number*	Specifies the width of the border if the object is defined to be a hyperlink.

Parameter	*Values*
CLASSID= *universal resource locator*	Identifies the object implementation. The syntax of the universal resource locator depends on the object type. For example, for registered ActiveX controls, the syntax is CLSID:class-identifier.
CODEBASE= *universal resource locator*	Identifies the codebase for the object. The syntax of the universal resource locator depends on the object.
CODETYPE= *codetype*	Specifies the Internet media type for code.
DATA= *universal resource locator*	Identifies data for the object. The syntax of the universal resource locator depends on the object.
DECLARE	Declares the object without instantiating it. Use this when creating cross-references to the object later in the document or when using the object as a parameter in another object.
HEIGHT= *number*	Specifies the height for the object.
HSPACE= *number*	Specifies the horizontal gutter. This is the extra, empty space between the object and any text or images to the left or right of the object.
NAME= *universal resource locator*	Sets the name of the object when submitted as part of a form.
SHAPES	Specifies that the object has shaped and shared hyperlinks.
STANDBY= *message*	Sets a message to be displayed while an object is loaded.
TYPE= *type*	Specifies the Internet media type for data.
USEMAP= *universal resource locator*	Specifies the image map to use with the object.
VSPACE= *number*	Specifies a vertical gutter. This is the extra white space between the object and any text or images above or below the object.
WIDTH= *number*	Specifies the width for the object.

In Listing 15.14, you can see HTML document source code with an embedded ActiveX object in it. In addition, note the <PARAM NAME= VALUE> tag. This tag was utilized to set any properties your ActiveX control can have.

Listing 15.14. The HTML page with an embedded <OBJECT> tag showing an ActiveX ActiveMovie control embedded in the page.

```
1:   <HTML>
2:   <HEAD>
3:   <TITLE>AN EMMBEDDED ActiveX Control</TITLE>
4:   </HEAD>
5:   <BODY>
6:
7:   <p align=center><font size=6><em><strong><u>An EMMBEDDED ActiveX Control
     </u></strong></em></font></p>
8:   <OBJECT>
9:   ID="ActiveMovie1"
10:  WIDTH=347
11:  HEIGHT=324
12:  ALIGN=center
13:  CLASSID="CLSID:05589FA1-C356-11CE-BF01-00AA0055595A"
14:  CODEBASE="http://www.microsoft.com/ie/download/activex/amovie.ocx#
     Version=4,70,0,1086"
15:     <PARAM NAME="_ExtentX" VALUE="9155">
16:     <PARAM NAME="_ExtentY" VALUE="8573">
17:     <PARAM NAME="MovieWindowSize" VALUE="2">
18:     <PARAM NAME="MovieWindowWidth" VALUE="342">
19:     <PARAM NAME="MovieWindowHeight" VALUE="243">
20:     <PARAM NAME="FileName" VALUE="E:\vinman\dstuds.avi">
21:     <PARAM NAME="Auto Start" VALUE="TRUE">
22:  </OBJECT>
23:
24:  </BODY>
25:  </HTML>
```

When a browser such as Internet Explorer encounters this page, it begins to parse the HTML source code. When it finds <OBJECT> in line 8, it realizes it has encountered a dynamic object. The browser then takes lines 10–12—the WIDTH, HEIGHT, and ALIGN attributes, which in this case are 347, 324, and CENTER, respectively—and sets up a placeholder for the object on the rendered page. It then takes the ID "ActiveMovie1" in line 9, and the CLASSID "CLSID:05589FA1-C356-11CE-BF01-00AA0055595A" in line 13 and checks to see if this control has been registered before in the registry. If the control object has never been registered, it then uses the CODEBASE attribute to locate the OCX on the server machine and proceeds to download the object into the \WindowsIN95\OcaCAccheCHE directory. The browser then registers AMOVIE.OCX by calling DllRegisterServer to register the control on the local machine. Now with the control properly registered, the browser can get the CLSID for the object from the registry. In order to utilize the control, it passes the CLSID to CoCreateInstance to create the object, and this returns the pointer to the control's IUnknown. It can utilize this pointer and the property information in lines 15–22 to actually render the object on the page.

FIGURE 15.21.

The HTML document as it appears in Internet Explorer with the ActiveX ActiveMovie control embedded in it.

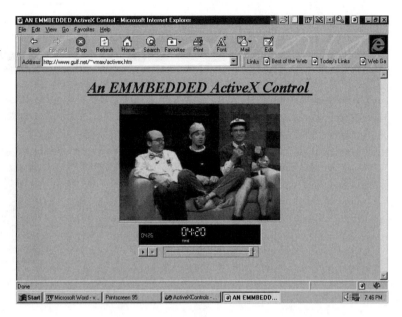

Now you can see that embedding controls to enhance a Web page with dynamic content is fairly easy. It is important that you, as an ActiveX control designer, understand how they are rendered.

ActiveX Control Pad

The ActiveX Control Pad provides a method of generating the HTML code, discussed earlier, to embed ActiveX and other dynamic objects into HTML source. (See Figure 15.22.) This is a free tool provided by Microsoft to aid in the production of Internet-enabled applications.

> **NOTE**
>
> You can download the ActiveX Control Pad from Microsoft at the following Internet URL:
>
> `http://www.microsoft.com/workshop/author/cpad`

This tool can be used to quickly embed your control in a page so you can test its functionality. The ActiveX Control Pad can be a great timesaver, freeing you from having to remember how to write HTML source code. It will even allow you to test your ability to utilize VBScript (see Figure 15.23) to do OLE automation with your code.

FIGURE 15.22.

The ActiveX Control Pad with the Active-Movie control properties being edited.

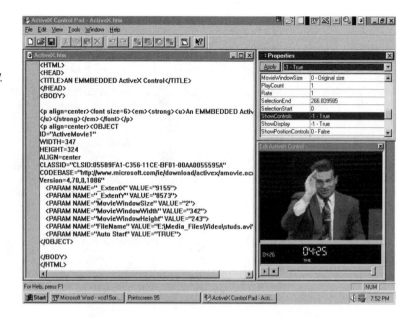

FIGURE 15.23.

The ActiveX Script Wizard helps you create scripts to further "activate" your controls.

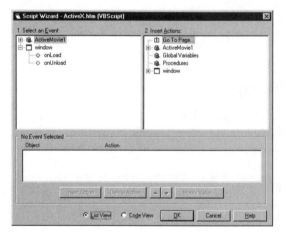

In addition, the ActiveX Control Pad comes with a suite of ActiveX controls for you to utilize in the development of your Web pages and your OLE-enabled applications. Some of these controls are the same controls that come with Internet Explorer; however, there are a few new ones to add to your bag of OLE controls. These controls will be discussed in Chapter 13, "ActiveX Containers."

ActiveX/OLE Control Test Container

The ActiveX Control Container is provided with Visual C++ to allow you to fully test your ActiveX control. The ActiveX Control Test Container allows you to test your control's registration, events, properties, and methods. To invoke the ActiveX Control Test Container, select the Tools | ActiveX Control Test Container menu. After you do this, you should see the ActiveX Control Test Container, as shown in Figure 15.24.

FIGURE 15.24.

The ActiveX Control Test Container is a tool that helps you test your controls.

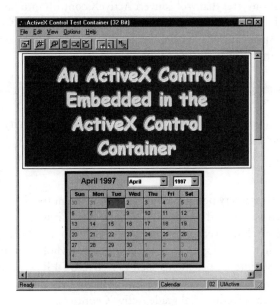

In addition to ActiveX Control Test Container, you might want to consider using Rational Software's Visual Test. Formerly, this was Microsoft Visual Test.

ActiveX/OLE Controls in Development Tools

One last way to test your ActiveX /OLE controls is with your development tools: Visual C++, Borland C++, Visual Basic, Delphi, PowerBuilder, Access, and almost any other mainstream Windows or Internet development suites. Become familiar with these development tools and ensure that they work in all environments. In addition, most of these tools come with ActiveX controls. So, use and take advantage of the components provided for you. This will make your job much easier and make your users much happier.

Methods of Creating ActiveX/OLE Controls

Currently, there are three ways of creating ActiveX controls with Visual C++:

- ■ Visual C++ and Microsoft Foundation Classes (MFC)
- ■ ActiveX Template Library (ATL)
- ■ ActiveX Developer's Kit (BaseCtl Framework)

The traditionally used programming languages for creating OLE controls are C++ and C. Recently, Microsoft released a compiled version of Visual Basic, called Visual Basic 5.0 Control Creation Edition, that can create OLE controls. It has been rumored that Microsoft is also creating a converter that will convert ActiveX controls into Java applets. Those of you who are Borland Delphi Pascal programmers can now create ActiveX controls with a third-party add-on from Apiary Inc., called OCX Expert. This Delphi add-on takes VCLs created in Delphi and converts them to 32-bit ActiveX controls.

NOTE

Information on OCX Expert can be obtained from Apiary Inc. at the following Internet URL:

`http://www.apiary.com/`

Visual Basic is a very popular language/development tool because it is easy to learn and utilize. It has even been called a quasi-4GL. Many times, it is chosen for development endeavors for these reasons. However, in my opinion Visual C++ and MFC provide much more power and flexibility in the development of applications as a whole, but most importantly in the development of user interface elements such as ActiveX/OLE controls. Even if Microsoft develops a compiled version of Visual Basic, it is unlikely that it will give you the control you need to develop serious commercial grade ActiveX controls.

Developers are often almost fanatically religious about their development tools. As a software engineer, you should be concerned with the right tool to fit the job. I highly recommend Visual C++ and Microsoft Foundation Class. Programming in C++ is now much easier with class libraries such as MFC and Integrated Development Environments such as Visual C++. Some even consider it a fourth generation language (4GL), but theoreticians can argue that point. Nevertheless, it is a very powerful tool.

This book covers OCXs created with Visual C++ and MFC. I will mention the other two ways to create ActiveX controls with Visual C++, but the primary emphasis and the example will be with Visual C++ and MFC. First, I'll touch on the other two ways to create a control with Visual C++.

ActiveX Template Library (ATL)

Because of the low bandwith and high potential for server latency, ActiveX controls need to be light and fast. Some developers have complained that MFC-based controls come with the overhead of the MFC runtime dynamic link libraries. In answer to their pleas, the Visual C++ Development team created the ActiveX Template Library. The ActiveX Template Library is a set of template-based C++ classes used to create small, fast COM objects. These classes eliminate the need for any external DLLs or any C runtime library code.

In fact, the ATL will produce an in-process server that is less than 5KB. Compared to the 22KB control plus the 1.4M MFC DLL, that is a significant decrease in size. However, this reduction in size comes with an increased complexity and an increase in the required work to create an ActiveX control. The ATL does provide all the COM connections for you, and a Visual C++ Wizard called the ATL COM AppWizard, to guide you in setting up the framework for your control. Previously you had to get the ATL COM AppWizard separately, but it now comes with Visual C++ 5.0.

The ATL not only allows you to build controls, but it also has support for you to build the following COM objects:

■ In-process servers

■ Local servers

■ Service servers

■ Remote servers that use the Distributed Component Object Model or remote automation

■ COM thread models including single threading, apartment-model threading, and free threading

■ Aggregatable servers

■ Various interface types including custom COM interfaces, dual interfaces, and IDispatch interfaces

■ Enumerations

■ Connection points

■ OLE-error mechanisms

Because the ActiveX Template Library provides C++ templates, you have a lot of flexibility when customizing a COM object. As such, you utilize the classes by instantiating an instance of the provided class from the template and use it as the basis for your class. This differs from the traditional method of deriving your control's classes from the classes in MFC. This is the distinction between a class library and a template library.

The code in the ATL is highly optimized for the task of creating light, fast COM objects. It still has a lot of the flexibility of the MFC way, and like the MFC way of creating the controls, it keeps you from having to write a lot of low-level COM code. It requires a thorough understanding of OLE, COM, and their interfaces.

You need to copy these files into the root of your Visual C++ C:\MSDEV directory. Run each file, and each will self-install. Make sure you follow the instructions and register the register.dll in the \BIN directory, with regserv32.exe and multcast.dll in the \TEMPLATE directory. If you fail to do so, the ATL will not compile properly, nor will the ATL Wizard work properly.

The ATL COM AppWizard

One of the nicest features the developers of the ActiveX Template Library included is a Visual C++ Wizard, which performs some of the more mundane tasks of creating a framework for a COM object, such as a control. This leaves you the task of making your control perform the functionality you want it to have, as opposed to re-creating abilities all ActiveX controls need. The ATL COM AppWizard is the mechanism to create that framework. It will get you up and running quickly, although not as quickly as Visual C++ ActiveX Control Wizard and MFC.

The next few paragraphs go over the selections in the ATL COM AppWizard to create a basic control. You will need to first launch Visual C++. After you have Visual C++ up and running, select File from the menu and then New from the popup menu. You will then see the New dialog box, as shown in Figure 15.25.

Select the Project Property tab. From the list control, select the ATL COM AppWizard. You need to give your control a title and a location. In this case, call it `ATLLT Simple Control` and accept the default location. Then press the Create button.

You are now looking at the first page of the ATL COM AppWizard. (See Figure 15.25.) Here, the ATL COM AppWizard asks you a series of questions about what kind of COM object you want to create:

- ■ What server type would you like to create? DLL? EXE? Service?
- ■ Do you want to allow the merging of proxy/stub code?
- ■ Do you want support for MFC?

FIGURE 15.25.

Step 1 of the ATL COM AppWizard in Visual C++.

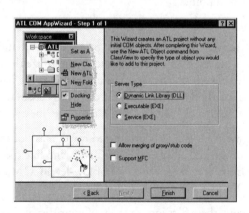

At the top of the Wizard is a group of radio buttons. You need to select the type of server you want the ATL COM AppWizard to create. Your options are an in-process server (DLL), local (EXE), or a service (EXE). When creating a service, you are required to use script-based registration. In addition, when creating a service or executable, you are unable to use MFC or allow merging of proxy/stub code. You will need to choose DLL, because you are creating a control and thus an in-process server.

When marshaling interfaces are required, select the Allow merging of proxy/stub code check box. This option places the proxy and stub code generated by the MIDL compiler in the same DLL as the server. Even though the wizard does some of the work for you, note that in order to merge the proxy/stub code into the DLL, the wizard adds the file `dlldatax.c` to your project. You need to make sure that precompiled headers are turned off for this file, and you need to add `MERGE_PROXYSTUB` to the defines for the project. In this case, don't select this option.

Why the Support MFC check box was included is unclear. The main purpose of using the ATL is to get away from the overhead of MFC. You could have just used the OLE Control Wizard with MFC and saved yourself a lot of time and effort in the first place. However, if for some reason you want to utilize the MFC Class Library, check this option. It will give you access to the MFC Class Library functions. But for this example, don't select this option.

You must then choose the Finish button. You will see the New Project Information dialog displayed, as shown in Figure 15.26.

FIGURE 15.26.
The New Project Information dialog of the ATL COM AppWizard in Visual C++.

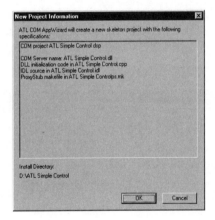

When you click the OK or Finish button of the New Project Information dialog, the ATL COM AppWizard will create a basic COM object for you and implement all the features you selected in it. This control need only be compiled and it is up and running. You now have the framework to start customizing this control.

ActiveX Developer's Kit (BaseCtl Framework)

The ActiveX Software Developer's Kit provides another way to produce ActiveX controls. This is by far the most difficult way to create a control. Microsoft provides it as a "bare bones" method of creating a control. This is not for the faint of heart and requires extensive knowledge of OLE, COM, and the OLE control interfaces. Only minimal functionality is provided in the code base. You will have to hand code all your messaging, which is, at best, a daunting task. The only reason to use this method is to try to create the lightest and fastest control possible; however, the time and complexity involved in creating a control with this method might not be worth the performance gains. This method is not recommended unless you absolutely have to use it. The ActiveX Template Library and Microsoft Foundation Class methods are much easier to implement and much more flexible. Creating and testing a control is no easy task; there are a lot of factors involved. Why not use the tools available to make your job easier? Some diehard, low-level C programmers or assembly language programmers might want to dive into this low-level approach head first, but make sure you are prepared. It would take a whole chapter to even begin addressing this method of creating a control. The next section covers how to get the Framework and set it up, but it is up to you to examine the samples that come with the SDK and explore the quagmire that awaits you in using this method. I highly discourage you from using this method unless it is absolutely necessary.

Getting the BaseCtl Framework

To get the BaseCtl Framework, you will need to get the ActiveX Software Developer's Kit. An updated version of the ActiveX SDK was released the same time Internet Explorer 3.0 was released. The new ActiveX SDK was updated to include the new technology and features of Internet Explorer 3.0.

> **NOTE**
>
> The most current ActiveX SDK is available from Microsoft, at no charge, at the following Internet URL:
> `http://www.microsoft.com/intdev/sdk/`
> or you can get it from the Microsoft Developer's Network Level II subscription.

In addition, you will need to obtain the Win32 Software Developer's Kit. The ActiveX SDK requires the August 1996 or later version of the Win32 SDK. The required Win32 SDK components come with Visual C++ 5.0.

> **NOTE**
>
> The most current Win32 SDK is available from Microsoft through an MSDN Library Professional Subscription Level II. Microsoft Sales can be reached at 1-800-426-9400.

If you have Visual C++, your Win32 environment is already set for you.

Setting Up the BaseCtl Framework

The BaseCtl Framework comes on the ActiveX SDK. After the ActiveX SDK installed, the BaseCtl Framework is in C:\INetSdk\Samples\BaseCtl\Framework (assuming that you installed it on your C: drive). You will have to compile the BaseCtl Framework libraries before you can create a control, or compile any of the examples that come with the ActiveX SDK.

To compile the BaseCtl Framework in Visual C, follow these instructions.

1. Click the Options menu item in the Tools popup menu.
2. Click the Directories tab in the Options dialog box.
3. Add the full path to the installed components:

   INetSDK\Include to the includes directories.

   INetSDK\Lib to the library directories.

   INetSDK\Bin to the executable files directories.

   These paths must be moved to the top of the search paths.
4. Create a project file and make files:

   Click the New menu item on the File popup menu.

   From the New dialog box, select Project Workspace and click the OK button.

   Type the name of the project in the New Project Workspace dialog.

   Select what type of application you are building. If you are building an ActiveX control, choose Dynamic Link Library. If you are going to build the BaseCtl Framework Libraries, choose Static Library.

   Type the path to the sample or library. You can use the Browse button if you are unsure.

   Click the Create button.

   Click the Files into Project menu item on the Insert popup menu.

   Select all the *.CPP, *.C, *.DEF, and *.RC files in the directory, including any ODL files, and click the Add button.

   Click the Settings menu item on the Build popup menu.

   Select the Link tab.

   Add the libraries needed to compile the application.

   If the sample you are building does not use MFC, you will need to turn off MFC support in the Project Settings dialog.
5. You can now build the project in Visual C++.

After you have compiled the debug and release versions of the BaseCtrl Framework, you can start creating your control. You might want to use one of the sample controls as a template—but if you do that, you might want to just use MFC or the ATL.

Creating an ActiveX/OLE Control with Visual C++ and MFC

Visual C++ and MFC comes in three flavors: 16-bit, Win32s/32-bit, and 32-bit. Visual C++ 1.52c and MFC 2.53 are for 16-bit developers. Visual C++ 4.2 and MFC 4.2 are for 32-bit developers. For those of you who still desire Win32's development platform for the development of 32-bit applications to run under 16-bit Windows, there are Visual C++ 4.1 and MFC 4.1. The newer versions of Visual C++ will no longer support Win32s. This section concentrates on the 32-bit environment and does not cover Win32s or 16-bit development. Building 16-bit OLE controls is possible with Visual C++ 1.52c, but 16-bit development is rapidly being left behind. In addition, the latter about 16-bit development being left behind can be said of the Win32s world as well.

Obtaining the ActiveX SDK

First, you need to get the ActiveX Software Developer's Kit. An updated version of the ActiveX SDK was released at the same time Internet Explorer 3.0 was released. The new ActiveX SDK was updated to include the new technology and features of Internet Explorer 3.0.

NOTE

The most current ActiveX SDK is available from Microsoft, at no charge, at the following URL:

`http://www.microsoft.com/intdev/sdk/`

CAUTION

The ActiveX SDK is intended to run only on Windows 95 and Windows NT 4.0 machines running the release version of Internet Explorer 3.0.

The ActiveX SDK file obtained from the Microsoft WWW site is a self-extracting archive. In addition, if you subscribe to Level II or higher of the Microsoft Developer's Network Library, the most recent ActiveX SDK should be included in future releases of MSDN.

The Microsoft Developer's Network is a subscription for four levels of information and products. It contains, depending on what level you subscribe to, all the Software Developer's Kits, the knowledge bases, documentation for all of Microsoft's developer products, how-to articles, samples, bug lists and workarounds, the operating systems, specifications, device-driver kits, and the latest-breaking developer news. It is issued in CD format (see Figure 15.16) and is released and updated quarterly. The Level II subscription alone comes with over 35 CDs, packed full of development information that is updated quarterly. The MSDN Library CD directly integrates with the Visual C++ IDE.

Using the Right Version of Visual C++ and MFC

Visual C++ comes as a yearly subscription, or you can purchase the single release professional version. The professional version is version 4.0. With the subscription, you get the updates throughout the year. Right now, that is version 4.2. You can only get 4.2 through the subscription. You can still create OLE controls with version 4.0, but to get the enhancements to create ActiveX controls you must have version 4.2. In addition, Microsoft recently released Visual C++ Enterprise Edition 4.2. The Enterprise edition of Visual C++ includes additional database tools such as an SQL debugger and visual database views. The Enterprise Edition 4.2 or greater can be utilized to develop ActiveX controls.

As previously mentioned, a new version of the ActiveX SDK was released in September 1996. The Visual C++ development team at Microsoft has also released a patch for Visual C++ 4.2 and MFC 4.2 to allow developers to utilize the new features to create ActiveX applications. This patch will be included in the next subscription release of Visual C++ and MFC 4.3. The patch is called Visual C++ Patch 4.2b. You will need to download this patch and incorporate it with Visual C++ 4.2 in order to create ActiveX controls.

WARNING

The Visual C++ 4.2b release is only for use on Visual C++ and MFC versions 4.2. Do not apply this patch to any other version of Visual C++, or your software and operating system will not operate properly.

> **NOTE**
>
> The Visual C++ 4.2b release patch is available from Microsoft, at the following Internet URL:
>
> ```
> http://www.microsoft.com/visualc/v42/v42tech/v42b/vc42b.htm
> ```

The patch is a self-extracting archive. After you get the patch and extract it, make sure you follow the directions in the readme file. (If you are reading this, Visual C++ and MFC 4.3 have been released. If you have them loaded, you need not apply the patch.)

Lastly, I need to mention that Microsoft has sadly discontinued the Visual C++ subscription. They are now on version 5.0, and Visual C++ comes in the Basic, Professional, and Enterprise Editions. I included the above to help those that may have an earlier release of Visual C++.

Using Visual C++ and MFC for ActiveX and OLE Controls

Previously, OLE controls had to have certain interfaces implemented whether they needed them or not. This meant that controls were larger than they needed to be. This is fine if you are utilizing them on a local machine, but with ActiveX controls that need to be downloaded and installed across the low-bandwidth, high-latency Internet, any excess baggage is less efficient in achieving this end. In order to get Web Masters to utilize your controls to activate their Web pages, your ActiveX controls need to be lean, mean, and efficient downloading machines.

Visual C++ comes with a Control Wizard to help you create controls. It is one of the fastest ways to create a control. In fact, if you are a newcomer to creating controls, it is the best way to learn. Why? Because it creates a framework for you. You can be up and running very quickly. However, there are a few drawbacks you need to be aware of.

In order to utilize a control created with Visual C++ and based on MFC, the MFC dynamic link library (DLL) must reside on the client machine. This file is about 1.2MB and must be downloaded to the client machine. However, this must only occur the first time, if the MFC DLL does not reside on the client machine already. So, you take a small performance hit the first time your control is used. Furthermore, it should also be noted that MFC-based controls tend to be fatter than the controls created by the other two methods.

You will need to weigh the options carefully, considering performance, programmer skill, time-table, and environment. This is not to say that MFC-based controls are not suitable for use in the ActiveX environment, but simply to make you aware of the factors associated with choosing this method. If you are building controls for an intranet that is high-bandwidth and potentially low-latency, the size of the control and the associated DLL are not a major factor. Speed of development, less complexity, and rich features can be more important. In fact, a basic OCX created with the OLE Control Wizard is only 23KB. 23KB, even on the sluggish Internet, is not extremely large, especially in comparison to some of the large graphic files and AVI files embedded in Web pages. The name of the game is optimization and asynchronous download-ing. These topics will be discussed in Chapter 8, "Memory Management."

Help is on the way. The Visual C++/MFC team at Microsoft realizes that performance is very important in the Internet environment. They are feverishly working to make ActiveX controls created with Visual C++ and MFC leaner and meaner, as well as working the download of the MFC DLL issue. Visual C++ and MFC can be the best way to create controls, but you will have to weigh each situation accordingly.

MFC Encapsulation of ActiveX and OLE Controls

MFC encapsulates the OLE control functionality in a class called COleControl (see Figure 15.27). COleControl is derived from CWnd and, in turn, from CCmdTarget and CObject.

FIGURE 15.27.
The class hierarchy for COleControl.

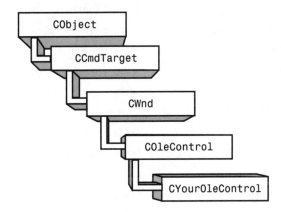

COleControl is the base class from which you derive to create any OLE control you want. What's nice is that your control inherits all the functionality of the base class COleControl. (See Table 15.5.) You can then customize the control to the capabilities you want to include in it. As you know, an OLE control is nothing more than a COM object. With MFC, the complexities of dealing with the COM interfaces are abstracted into an easy-to-use class. In addition, MFC provides a framework for your control so you can worry about the details of what you want your control to do instead of re-creating functionality that all controls have to contain in order to work.

Table 15.5. The member functions of COleControl that are encapsulated by the Microsoft Foundation Classes.

Function	Function
COleControl	ControlInfoChanged
RecreateControlWindow	GetClientSite
InitializeIIDs	GetExtendedControl
EnableSimpleFrame	LockInPlaceActive

continues

Table 15.5. continued

Function	Function
SetInitialSize	TransformCoords
PreModalDialog	IsModified
PostModalDialog	SetModifiedFlag
ExchangeExtent	ExchangeStockProps
GetClientRect	OnGetPredefinedValue
ExchangeVersion	IsConvertingVBX
SetModifiedFlag	WillAmbientsBeValidDuringLoad
DoSuperclassPaint	InvalidateControl
IsOptimizedDraw	SelectFontObject
SelectStockFont	OnMapPropertyToPage
TranslateColor	GetNotSupported
SetNotPermitted	SetNotSupported
ThrowError	GetReadyState
AmbientBackColor	InternalSetReadyState
AmbientDisplayName	Load
AmbientForeColor	DisplayError
AmbientFont	DoPropExchange
AmbientLocaleID	GetClassID
AmbientScaleUnits	GetMessageString
AmbientShowGrabHandles	IsSubclassedControl
AmbientShowHatching	OnClick
AmbientTextAlign	OnDoVerb
AmbientUIDead	OnDraw
AmbientUserMode	OnDrawMetafile
GetAmbientProperty	OnEdit
FireClick	OnEnumVerbs
FireDblClick	OnEventAdvise
FireError	OnKeyDownEvent
FireEvent	OnKeyPressEvent
FireKeyDown	OnKeyUpEvent
FireKeyPress	OnProperties
FireKeyUp	OnResetState

Function	Function
FireMouseDown	OnAppearanceChanged
FireMouseMove	OnBackColorChanged
FireMouseUp	OnBorderStyleChanged
FireReadyStateChange	OnEnabledChanged
DoClick	OnFontChanged
Refresh	OnForeColorChanged
GetAppearance	OnTextChanged
SetAppearance	OnAmbientPropertyChange
GetBackColor	OnFreezeEvents
SetBackColor	OnGetControlInfo
GetBorderStyle	OnMnemonic
SetBorderStyle	OnRenderData
GetEnabled	OnRenderFileData
SetEnabled	OnRenderGlobalData
GetForeColor	OnSetClientSite
SetForeColor	OnSetData
GetFont	OnSetExtent
GetFontTextMetrics	OnSetObjectRects
GetStockTextMetrics	OnGetColorSet
InternalGetFont	SetFont
SelectStockFont	GetHwnd
GetText	InternalGetText
SetText	OnGetInPlaceMenu
GetControlSize	OnHideToolBars
SetControlSize	OnShowToolBars
GetRectInContainer	OnGetDisplayString
SetRectInContainer	OnGetPredefinedStrings
BoundPropertyChanged	BoundPropertyRequestEdit

You are probably wondering why all of these member functions are listed here for you. The purpose is to emphasize the amount of work already done for you by the Microsoft Foundation Classes. In the COleControl class are 128 member functions. So, when you derive your control from COleControl, your control inherits the capability to utilize those predefined functions.

In addition, MFC itself provides a whole range of capability already created for you when you utilize it. It also includes a functionality to do messaging and automated data exchange.

With MFC version 4.2, Microsoft added some new classes to MFC to facilitate the creation of ActiveX controls. These new classes add to MFC's impressive range of functionality. These five new classes are listed in Table 15.6.

Table 15.6. The new classes added to Microsoft Foundation Classes version 4.2 to support ActiveX controls.

Function	Definition
CMonikerFile	When this class is instantiated as an object, it encapsulates a stream of data named by an IMoniker interface object. It allows you to have access and manipulate that data stream pointed to by an IMoniker object.
CAsyncMonikerFile	Works much the same as a CMonikerFile except it allows asynchronous access to the IStream object pointed to by the IMoniker object.
CDataPathProperty	This class encapsulates the implementation of OLE Control Properties so they can be implemented asynchronously.
COleCmdUI	This class encapsulates the process by which MFC updates the user interface.
COleSafeArray	This class encapsulates the function of an array of arbitrary type and size.

In addition to the new classes in MFC, Microsoft also enhanced COleControl to simplify the creation of ActiveX controls. These functions add to the already impressive armada of capabilities encapsulated in COleControl. Table 15.7 lists the 31 new member functions added to COleControl.

Table 15.7. The member functions of COleControl that have been added to support ActiveX controls.

Function	Function
ClientToParent	GetWindowlessDropTarget
GetCapture	ClipCaretRect
GetControlFlags	GetClientOffset
GetDC	GetClientRect
InvalidateRgn	GetFocus
GetActivationPolicy	OnGetNaturalExtent

Function	*Function*
OnGetViewExtent	ReleaseCapture
OnInactiveMouseMove	ResetVersion
OnQueryHitRect	SerializeStockProps
SetFocus	OnGetViewRect
OnGetViewStatus	OnInactiveSetCursor
OnQueryHitPoint	OnWindowlessMessage
ReleaseDC	ParentToClient
ResetStockProps	ScrollWindow
SerializeVersion	SerializeExtent
SetCapture	

The OLE Control Wizard

The beauty of Visual C++ and MFC is that they perform the mundane task of creating the framework for your control, leaving you the task of making your control perform the functionality you want it to create. At the center of this is the AppWizard, which houses the OLE Control Wizard. Visual C++ 4.2, with the 4.2b patch, has augmented the OLE Control Wizard to specifically support ActiveX controls. In this section, you examine each feature of the Control Wizard and create your first ActiveX MFC control.

You will need to first launch Visual C++. After you have Visual C++ up and running, select File from the menu and then New from the popup menu. You will then see the New dialog box, as shown in Figure 15.28.

FIGURE 15.28.

The New dialog box in Visual C++.

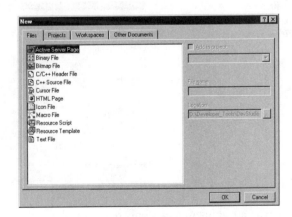

Select Project Workspace. This yields the New Projects Workspaces dialog box. (See Figure 15.29.) At the New Projects dialog box, you need to select the OLE Control Wizard from the list box on the left, and you need to give your control a title and a location. In this case, call it simple control and accept the default location.

FIGURE 15.29.

The New project information dialog box in Visual C++.

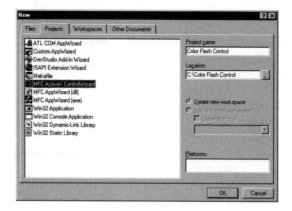

You are now looking at the first page of the OLE Control Wizard. (See Figure 15.30.) Here, the OLE Control Wizard asks you a series of questions about what you would like in your control:

■ How many controls do you want in the project?

■ Do you want a runtime license for your controls?

■ Would you like the wizard to document your controls with source file comments?

■ Would you like a help file generated for your control?

FIGURE 15.30.

Step 1 of the OLE Control Wizard in Visual C++.

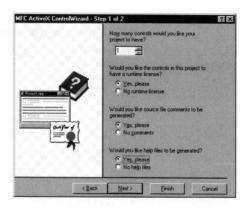

In this case, you are going to create only one control, so select one control for this project. As you have already learned, one OCX can contain several controls.

Also, select the choice for the Control Wizard to include licensing support for this control. In addition, ask the Control Wizard to document the code it is going to write for you in the control framework with comments.

Lastly, ask the Control Wizard to generate a basic help file, so you can provide online help for the Webmasters and programmers who will be utilizing this control. It is extremely important that this control be well-documented. Then select the Next button and go to page 2 of the OLE Control Wizard. (See Figure 15.31.)

FIGURE 15.31.
Step 2 of the OLE Control Wizard in Visual C++.

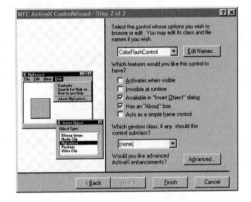

Step 2 of the OLE Control Wizard presents you with more options for this OLE control.

- Editing the names of the classes for your control.
- Which features do you want in your control?

    Activates when visible?

    Invisible at runtime?

    Available in Insert Dialog dialog?

    Has an About box?

    Acts as a simple frame control?

- Would you like the Wizard to create your control as a subclass to an existing control?
- Would you like advanced ActiveX enhancements for your control?

The OLE Control Wizard enables you to control the naming of each of the controls in your project to include the class names, source filenames, and property sheet names (see Figure 15.30). If you press the Edit Names button (see Figure 15.31), you will get the Edit Names dialog, as shown in Figure 15.32. It does provide a default naming convention, and in this case, you will accept the defaults provided by the Control Wizard.

Next are questions regarding which features you want to have in this control. You need to keep in mind the previously discussed section on optimizations. Does the control need to be active when visible, or is it invisible at runtime like a timer control or a communications control? This control will need to be active and visible. You want this control to be available in the Insert Object dialog, so choose this option. No doubt you are proud of the controls you create, so you can include an About dialog box to post your name or your company's name. Lastly, do you want this control to be a simple frame control and support the `ISimpleFrameSite` interface? This is so the control can act as a frame for other controls. For this example's purposes, you will not choose this option.

FIGURE 15.32.
The Edit Names dialog in step 2 of the OLE Control Wizard in Visual C++.

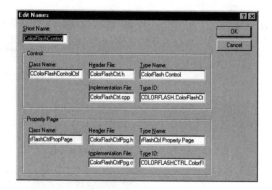

You now need to take a look and select the advanced options that support ActiveX enhancements. Click the Advanced button and go to the Advanced ActiveX controls Features dialog, as depicted in Figure 15.33.

FIGURE 15.33.
The Advanced dialog of step 2 of the OLE Control Wizard in Visual C++.

From the Advanced ActiveX controls Features dialog, you can choose one of six options. Keep in mind the previous information you have covered on these options:

- Windowless activation
- Unclipped device context
- Flicker-free activation
- Mouse pointer notification when inactive
- Optimized drawing code
- Loads properties asynchronously

Choose all but Windowless activation, and click the OK button. Then you need to select the Finish button. Here, you will get a summary of the features that the OLE Control Wizard will create for you in the New Project Information dialog. (See Figure 15.34.)

FIGURE 15.34.

The New Project Information dialog of the OLE Control Wizard in Visual C++.

When you click the OK button of the New Project Information dialog, the OLE Control Wizard will create a basic control for you and implement all the features you selected in it. This control needs only to be compiled before it is up and running. The OLE Control Wizard even added an ellipse in this control's drawing code so it will have something to display. You now have the framework to start customizing this control. The nice thing is that most of that functionality is already encapsulated in MFC. To assist you in this endeavor, Visual C++ provides you with the Class Wizard. The sky is the limit on what types of creations are possible now that you have the framework built for you.

Summary

This chapter discusses the ActiveX control, which is a superset of the OLE control. OLE controls are nothing more than COM objects, and ActiveX controls are a leaner and meaner implementation of the OLE control to facilitate its use on the Internet. ActiveX/OLE controls allow you to use prepackaged components of functionality to aid you in creating useful Windows-based applications.

IV

Network Programming with Win32

16

Windows Sockets

by David Bennett

If you have done network programming in UNIX, you are probably familiar with the implementation of sockets in the Berkeley Software Distribution (BSD) version 4.3 of UNIX. The Windows Sockets (WinSock) API is based on the BSD version of sockets, but it also provides extensions specific to Windows. In addition, WinSock 2.0 can support many network protocols, including TCP/IP, DECNet, and Novell's IPX/SPX.

In this chapter, you will look at the following implementations of Windows Sockets:

- Windows Sockets 1.1
- MFC WinSock Classes
- Windows Sockets 2.0

Windows Sockets, or WinSock, is a part of Microsoft's Windows Open Systems Architecture (WOSA), which specifies interfaces that you can develop client applications with, as well as interfaces that vendors use to develop service providers to implement the Windows Sockets for specific networks.

The Windows Sockets specification is an interface specification that is supported by several vendors, each of which provides its own DLL to work with its transport stack. In version 1.1 of WinSock, each vendor supplied a WSOCK32.DLL (or WINSOCK.DLL for 16-bit environments) that implements the WinSock API, although this version is limited to TCP/IP protocols.

For version 2 of WinSock, the Windows operating systems provide the API in a single WS2_32.DLL, which may then make use of several vendor-supplied transport and name space providers to work with different network protocols. The WS2_32.DLL supports both the WinSock 1.1 functions and many additional functions that have been added with the WinSock 2 specification.

When Should I Use Sockets?

In general, sockets are most useful in situations where you are developing applications on both sides of the communication. For example, where you are developing both a client and a server for a particular application, you can use sockets to exchange your own data structures, or packets, to communicate between your applications. In many cases where you are writing only the client, you may want to consider one of the higher-level Internet interfaces that you will look at in Chapter 22, "The WinInet API."

What Is a Socket?

A socket is an abstraction for a communication endpoint—it provides a mechanism to send and receive data. In Windows sockets, these come in two flavors: datagram sockets and stream sockets.

Datagram Sockets

Datagram sockets provide unreliable, connectionless communication of packets. In this case, "unreliable" means that delivery of a packet is not guaranteed, nor are packets guaranteed to arrive in the order sent. In fact, the same datagram packet may be delivered more than once. For TCP/IP implementations of WinSock, datagram sockets use the User Datagram Protocol (UDP), although WinSock 2 also supports other protocols.

In many cases, such as communicating between two processes on the same machine or between two machines on a lightly loaded LAN, you may not see packets that are not delivered, arrive out of order, or are duplicated. However, your application should be able to deal with these possibilities.

If you are writing applications to communicate over more complicated networks, such as the Internet, you will certainly encounter the unreliable nature of datagram sockets. If your application does not deal with these cases appropriately, your app will break. Nonetheless, datagram sockets are useful in situations where you want to send packet- or record-based data. Datagram sockets also provide the ability to send broadcast packets to more than one destination address.

Stream Sockets

If you need to be certain that the data you send will arrive—in order and unduplicated—you will want to use stream sockets, which provide a reliable connection-based transport. As the name implies, *stream sockets* provide a stream of data, rather than individual datagrams, or packets. For TCP/IP implementations of WinSock, stream sockets use the Transmission Control Protocol (TCP). Stream sockets are most useful in situations where you are sending large amounts of data or where you want to ensure that all data arrives in order and unduplicated. In addition, your applications will be notified if the connection closes.

Using the WinSock API

In this section, you look at how to use version 1.1 of the Windows Sockets API, although you also will explore some of the differences between version 1 and 2 of the WinSock APIs. For the most part, however, WinSock 2 adds new functions to the WinSock 1.1 functions. You will look at these new functions in the section on WinSock 2 later in this chapter.

Many of the functions used in the WinSock API are identical to the Berkeley sockets implementation in UNIX. However, there are some differences—mostly in the form of additional functions provided specifically in WinSock implementations of sockets that allow for asynchronous event handling in a Windows environment.

For starters, the WinSock API is different because it must be initialized before it can be used. This is done with the WSAStartup() function, which allows you to negotiate a version of the

WinSock specification that your application may use, as well as returning other information about the specific implementation of WinSock that you are using.

Initializing WinSock

The first parameter to WSAStartup() is a WORD value that specifies the highest version of the WinSock spec that your application wishes to use, with the major version in the low-order byte and the minor version in the high-order byte.

As of January 1996, the most widely used version of WinSock is 1.1, although WinNT 4.0 supports WinSock 2 and a version of WS2_32.DLL is in beta test for Win95, allowing the use of the WinSock API with network protocols other than the TCP/IP suite.

The second parameter specifies a pointer to a WSADATA structure. When you call WSAStartup() with code something like this:

```
#include <winsock.h>
// For WinSock 2, include winsock2.h

WSADATA WSAData;
int nRc = WSAStartup(0x0101, &WSAData);
if(nRc)
{
    // An error occurred in WinSock initialization
    return;
}
if(WSAData.wVersion != 0x0101)
{
    // Version supported is insufficient
    // Report error to user, clean up, and return
    WSACleanup();
    return;
}
```

WSAStartup() will return WSASYSNOTREADY if the WinSock DLL or the underlying network subsystem is not properly initialized or just not found. In addition, this function allows your application to negotiate a version of the WinSock spec to be used. In general, you should specify the highest version of WinSock that you would like to use in the call to WSAStartup(). If this version is lower than any version that the DLL supports, WSAStartup() will return WSAVERNOTSUPPORTED.

If the version you request is higher than (or equal to) a version that the DLL supports, the wVersion field of WSAData will contain the version that your application should use, and the wHighVersion field will contain the highest version supported by the DLL.

If the version returned in wVersion field is unacceptable to your application, you should call WSACleanup() and either abort your application or search for a different wsock32.dll to try— of course, you will need to dynamically load the new DLL, as you saw in Chapter 10, "Dynamic Link Libraries (DLLs)," to call WSAStartup() from it.

In addition to version information, several other interesting tidbits are returned in the WSADATA structure, including strings that give information about the specific vendor implementation of WinSock, the maximum number of sockets available to a process, and the maximum datagram size that may be sent.

Creating a Socket

The socket() function is used to create a socket to be used in communications. This function takes three parameters, including an address format, the type of socket, and a protocol to use. For WinSock version 1.1, most calls to socket() will look like one of the following:

```
// To create a datagram socket
SOCKET myUDPSock = socket(AF_INET, SOCK_DGRAM, IPPROTO_UDP);

// To create a stream socket
SOCKET myTCPSock = socket(AF_INET, SOCK_STREAM, IPPROTO_TCP);
```

The first parameter specifies that you will be using Internet addresses with this socket, and the other two arguments specify the type of socket you want to create and the protocol to use for the socket. The previous examples create a datagram socket using UDP and a stream socket using TCP. These are the two most common socket types used for TCP/IP networking, although several other protocols may be supported by the WinSock implementation you are using.

TIP

If the third parameter to socket() is 0, an appropriate protocol will be selected for you based on the address family and socket type. This is the recommended method of selecting a protocol.

If the call to socket() is successful, it will return a new socket descriptor. If it fails, socket() will return 0, and you will need to call WSAGetLastError() to get more specific information about the error that occurred.

Working with Datagram Sockets

For most applications of datagram sockets, your apps will use a sequence of events such as those shown in Figure 16.1 to communicate between a client and a server application.

First, both client and server create a datagram socket, as you saw previously. Next, the server calls bind() to assign a well-known port to a socket. This well-known port is generally specified when developing your applications so that both client and server will use the same port to refer to the server socket. Once the server has bound its socket to the well-known port, the client can use sendto() to send to the server. Both client and server can use sendto() and recvfrom() to pass packets around until they are finished, at which point closesocket() is called to close the socket. Now let's take a closer look at how each of these steps works, starting with binding an address to a socket.

FIGURE 16.1.

Datagram socket usage.

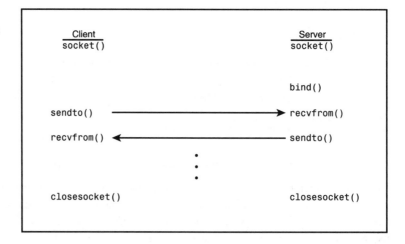

bind()

A call to bind() is passed the socket descriptor and a pointer to an address structure, as well as the length of that structure. The socket descriptor is simply the value returned by a previous call to socket(), but the address structure can be a bit stickier. This structure may (and usually will) be different for each type of network protocol used, although for now you will look at just TCP/IP addresses.

The sockaddr_in structure is used to specify an IP address in a call to bind():

```
struct sockaddr_in {
        short   sin_family;
        u_short sin_port;
        struct  in_addr sin_addr;
        char    sin_zero[8];
};
```

For IP addresses, the sin_family field will always be AF_INET. The sin_port field specifies the port that will be assigned to the socket, and the sin_addr field gives the host address for the socket; the sin_zero field is simply filler.

Port Numbers

In most cases, simply sending packets to a given machine's address, such as 192.9.200.93, is not sufficient to specify for which process on the machine (or even which segment of a process) the packet is intended. The port number allows you to be more specific. Your application may use any port number from 1 to 65,535 to bind a socket, although these numbers are usually divided into the following ranges:

Port 0. Not used. If you pass a 0 for the port number, an unused port between 1,024 and 5,000 will be selected for you.

Port 1-255. Reserved for well-known services, such as FTP, telnet, finger, and so forth.

Port 256-1,023. Reserved for other general-purpose services, such as routing functions.

Port 1,024-4,999. Used for arbitrary client ports. Your client sockets will generally use a port in this range.

Port 5,000-65,535. Used for user-defined server ports. Your server sockets should use a port number from this range if a client will need to know about the server's port ahead of time.

IP Addresses

The `sin_addr` field of a `sockaddr_in` holds the actual IP host address in an `in_addr` structure, defined in `winsock.h` (or `winsock2.h` for version 2). It looks something like this:

```
struct in_addr {
        union {
                struct { u_char s_b1,s_b2,s_b3,s_b4; } S_un_b;
                struct { u_short s_w1,s_w2; } S_un_w;
                u_long S_addr;
        } S_un;
#define s_addr  S_un.S_addr
};
```

In short, the `in_addr` structure is 4 bytes, each representing one of the numbers generally found in the dotted notation of an IP address. For example, the IP address 1.2.3.4 would end up as 0x04030201. The different members of the union allow you to work with the data in the format most convenient to your application.

In most cases, you can specify the `s_addr` field as `INADDR_ANY` in calls to `bind()`. This will allow the socket to send or receive from any IP address that is assigned to the local machine. In most cases, each machine has only one IP address, although a machine may have several network cards, each supporting its own IP address. If you want your socket to work with only one of these addresses, you must specify the actual address. The `inet_addr()` function is often useful for this, because it will take an ASCII string specifying the dotted decimal notation of an IP address (such as 192.9.200.93) and will return a `u_long` suitable for assignment to `s_addr`. In addition, the `inet_ntoa()` function will perform the opposite conversion, taking a `u_long` and returning an ASCII string.

Name and Address Functions

To help out with finding an address and port for your call to `bind()`, WinSock also offers several helper functions, which allow you to retrieve host names, addresses, and ports.

The gethostname() function can be used to return a string containing the host name of the local machine. Depending on the implementation of WinSock that you are using, this may be a simple host name, such as keymaster, or a fully qualified domain name, such as keymaster.racotek.com.

To find the address of any host based on its name, you can use the gethostbyname() function, which takes a string holding the host name and will look up the address for that name. This may be a simple lookup in the host's file local to the machine or may involve sending requests across the network to a name server, depending on how your network is configured. gethostbyname() returns a hostent structure, which contains a list of all addresses found for a given host name, as well as some other information concerning the address type and aliases for the host name.

In addition, you can retrieve a host's name (and the rest of the fields in the hostent structure), based on an IP address with the gethostbyaddr() function.

To find the port number associated with a given service, such as FTP or telnet, you can use the getservbyname() function to return a servent structure, which includes the port number of the service. Most implementations of WinSock will return this information from the services file on the local machine. You can also retrieve information about a service from its port number using the getservbyport() function.

In addition, the getprotobyname() and getprotobynumber() functions can return a protoent structure, returning information about a given protocol, based on the name or number of the protocol.

Asynchronous Lookup Functions

In cases where these functions send requests to a name server over a network, the function may block for an indeterminate period of time. To enable your application to do other things while waiting for a response, the WinSock API provides the following functions: WSAAsyncGetHostByName(), WSAAsyncGetHostByAddr(), WSAGetServByName(), WSAAsyncGetServByPort(), WSAAsyncGetProtoByName(), and WSAAsyncGetProtoByNumber().

These functions allow you to specify a Windows message that will be sent to a window handle that you specify when the call completes. Generally, you will specify a user-defined message for the notification. This message can be handled with a message map entry such as the one below, which uses the message ID WM_USER+1:

```
ON_COMMAND(WM_USER+1, OnAsyncLookup)
```

The prototype for the handler function looks like this:

```
LONG OnAsyncLookup(WPARAM wParam, LPARAM lParam);
```

This handler function can extract the error code and buffer length from the lParam by using the WSAGETASYNCERROR() and WSAGETASYNCBUFLEN() macros. In addition, the wParam will contain the asynchronous task handle that was returned by the original WSAAsync... call.

If you want to cancel one of these asynchronous requests before it completes, you can call WSACancelAsyncRequest(), passing the handle of the request returned by the original WSAAsync call.

Creating a Server Socket

Now that you have explored how to bind an address to a socket, let's take a look at just how this is used. The following example shows how to create a socket with a well-known port of 5150:

```
SOCKET sServSock;
sockaddr_in addr;
int nSockErr;
sServSock = socket(AF_INET, SOCK_DGRAM, IPPROTO_UDP);
addr.sin_family = AF_INET;
addr.sin_port = htons(5150);
addr.sin_addr.s_addr = htonl(INADDR_ANY);
if(bind(sServSock, (LPSOCKADDR)&addr, sizeof(addr)) == SOCKET_ERROR)
{
    nSockErr = WSAGetLastError();
    // Handle error
}
```

Ten Little Endians

You should notice that in the previous example, we have used the htons() and htonl() functions, rather than simply assigning a constant to the sin_port and sin_addr fields of our address. These functions are used to convert the byte order of the port and address parameters.

Unfortunately, not all CPUs are created equally. Different processors use different byte-ordering schemes in their internal representations of numbers, often referred to as *big-endian* or *little-endian*. Because networks are often used to connect heterogeneous computers, many parameters in sockets programming, such as the port and address here, must be converted to a common network byte order before they are passed to WinSock, and must also be converted back to the native host byte order when returned from WinSock calls.

To simplify these conversions, WinSock provides four basic functions. For converting from native host to network format, you can use htons() for short (16-bit) values and htonl() for long (32-bit) values. To convert back from network to host formats, the ntohs() and ntohl() functions work with short and long values, respectively.

For most operations with the MFC classes that you will see later in this chapter, you will not need to worry about explicitly converting to and from network byte order—MFC will do it for you where needed.

Receiving Data on a Datagram Socket

Once you have created a socket in your server application and bound it to a specific address and port, you are ready to receive data from client applications. This is done with the recvfrom() function. The prototype for recvfrom() looks like this:

```
int recvfrom (SOCKET s, char FAR * buf, int len, int flags,
              struct sockaddr FAR *from, int FAR * fromlen);
```

The first parameter is the socket descriptor returned from socket(), followed by a pointer to the buffer to receive the new datagram and the length of the buffer. The flags parameter can specify MSG_PEEK to peek at the data, filling the buffer, but leaving datagram in the input queue. The last two parameters are used to return the address of the socket that sent the datagram. This address can then be used to send a reply to the sender.

recvfrom() will return the number of bytes received if a datagram is successfully read. If an error occurs, recvfrom() will return SOCKET_ERROR, and you should call WSAGetLastError() to find the specific error code.

> **NOTE**
>
> If the size of the buffer passed to recvfrom() is too small to receive the entire datagram, the buffer is filled with the data that will fit, and the rest of the datagram falls into the bit bucket and is lost. In this case, recvfrom() returns SOCKET_ERROR, and WSAGetLastError() returns WSAEMSGSIZE.

Sending Data on a Datagram Socket

Sending a datagram is accomplished with the sendto() function:

```
int sendto (SOCKET s, const char FAR *buf, int len, int flags,
            const struct sockaddr FAR *to, int tolen);
```

Once again, the first parameter gives the socket descriptor, followed by a pointer of the buffer to send and the length of the data. The last two parameters are used to specify an address structure that refers to the destination socket's address and port.

If sendto() completes successfully, it will return the number of bytes actually sent, which may be different than the value passed in len. If an error occurs, sendto() returns SOCKET_ERROR, and you should call WSAGetLastError() for a specific error code.

If you attempt to send a datagram that is larger than the maximum datagram size supported by the implementation of WinSock, the error returned will be WSAEMSGSIZE. The maximum allowable datagram size is returned by the WSAStartup() call.

Using Stream Sockets

Due to the fact that stream sockets use connection-based protocols, they are used a bit differently, because you must first establish the connection, then read data from the stream, rather than one datagram or record at a time. The general usage for stream sockets is shown in Figure 16.2.

FIGURE 16.2.

Stream socket usage.

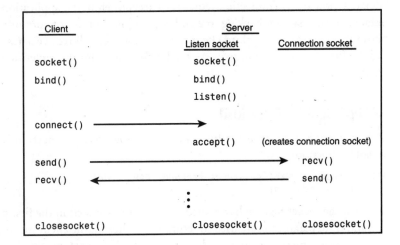

Stream Sockets and the Server

Like datagram sockets, stream sockets for server processes are created with a call to socket() and must have an address assigned to them with bind(), like this:

```
SOCKET sServSock;
sockaddr_in addr;
int nSockErr;
sServSock = socket(AF_INET, SOCK_STREAM, 0);
addr.sin_family = AF_INET;
addr.sin_port = htons(5050);
addr.sin_addr.s_addr = htonl(INADDR_ANY);
if(bind(sServSock, (LPSOCKADDR)&addr, sizeof(addr)) == SOCKET_ERROR)
{
    nSockErr = WSAGetLastError();
    // Handle error
}
```

The only difference between this example and the example we saw for datagram sockets is that the socket() call is passed SOCK_STREAM instead of SOCK_DGRAM. In addition, the protocol was passed as 0—WinSock will pick the transport based on the address family and socket type.

Listening for Connections

Now that you have created the socket and bound it to an address, you need to have a way to establish a connection to a client. To do this, you use the `listen()` function:

```
int listen(SOCKET s, int backlog);
```

This tells socket s to begin listening for client connection requests. The backlog parameter tells WinSock how many connection requests to accept before the application accepts them. For instance, if you have set backlog to 2 and your application is not currently accepting connections for some reason, the third client to try to connect will receive a WSAECONNREFUSED error, and the first two connection requests will be queued up for the server to process when it gets around to it.

Accepting a Connection

Once the socket is set to listen for connections, the actual connection is accepted with the `accept()` function:

```
SOCKET accept (SOCKET s, struct sockaddr FAR* addr,
    int FAR* addrlen);
```

As usual, the socket that we have called `listen()` on is passed in the first parameter. The second and third parameters are used to return the address of the client socket that is connecting. The `sockaddr` structure is used just like you saw in the `bind()` or `recvfrom()` functions.

If the connection is successfully accepted, `accept()` will return the descriptor for a brand new socket that will be used to handle the new connection. If there is an error, `accept()` returns INVALID_SOCKET, and you need to call `WSAGetLastError()` to retrieve more detailed information about the error.

The original socket will continue to listen for new connection requests, which may then be accepted with additional calls to `accept()`. Each connection accepted will have its own socket created, which is returned by `accept()`. To see this in action, look at the following example:

```
SOCKET sServSock;
sockaddr_in addr;
int nSockErr;
int nNumConns = 0;
SOCKET sConns[5];
sockaddr ConnAddrs[5];
int nAddrLen = sizeof(sockaddr);

// Create the socket
sServSock = socket(AF_INET, SOCK_STREAM, 0);

// Assign a well-known port to the socket
addr.sin_family = AF_INET;
addr.sin_port = htons(5050);
addr.sin_addr.s_addr = htonl(INADDR_ANY);
if(bind(sServSock, (LPSOCKADDR)&addr, sizeof(addr)) == SOCKET_ERROR)
{
```

```
    nSockErr = WSAGetLastError();
    // Handle error… Do not continue
}
// Listen for client connection requests
if(listen(sServSock, 2) == SOCKET_ERROR)
{
    nSockErr = WSAGetLastError();
    // Handle error… Do not continue
}
while(nNumConns < 5)
{
    // Accept Connection
    sConns[nNumConns] = accept(sServSock, ConnAddrs[nNumConns], &nAddrLen);
    if(sConns[nNumConns] == INVALID_SOCKET)
    {
        nSockErr = WSAGetLastError();
        // handle error
    }
    else
    {
        // New socket has been connected successfully
        StartNewHandlerThread(sConns[nNumConns]);
        nNumConns++;
    }
} // end while
```

This example will create a server socket, bind an address to it, and wait for client connection requests. It will then accept up to five different connections, saving the socket descriptor and corresponding address in an array and calling a function to start a new thread to handle each new connection.

Requesting a Connection

In order for the server to receive connection requests, someone must first request a connection. Your client applications will do this by using the connect() function:

```
int connect (SOCKET s, const struct sockaddr FAR* name,
    int namelen);
```

The sockaddr and namelen parameters are used to specify the address and port to which you wish to connect. The sockaddr structure passed to connect should be identical to that passed to the bind() call on the server. This is where you will use the well-known port assignments that you gave to your server sockets. To see how this works, take a look at the following example, which creates the client socket, binds it to a default address, and connects to the server:

```
SOCKET sClntSock;
sockaddr_in_addr;
sockaddr_in ServerAddr;
int nSockErr;

// Create the socket
sClntSock = socket(AF_INET, SOCK_STREAM, 0);
```

```
// Assign an address to the socket
addr.sin_family = AF_INET;
addr.sin_port = 0;      // WinSock will assign a port
addr.sin_addr.s_addr = htonl(INADDR_ANY);
if(bind(sClntSock, (LPSOCKADDR)&addr, sizeof(addr)) == SOCKET_ERROR)
{
    nSockErr = WSAGetLastError();
    // Handle error - You should not continue
}
// Connect to Server
ServerAddr.sin_family = AF_INET;
ServerAddr.sin_port = htons(5050);
ServerAddr.sin_addr.s_addr = inet_addr("192.9.200.93");
if(connect(sClntSock, ServerAddr, sizeof(ServerAddr)) == SOCKET_ERROR)
{
    nSockErr = WSAGetLastError();
    // Handle error - You should not continue
}
```

Sending and Receiving with Stream Sockets

Once a connection has been made between a client socket and a server socket, data can be sent with the send() call:

```
int send (SOCKET s, const char FAR * buf,
       int len, int flags);
```

send() takes a pointer to the data to be sent and the length of the data, as well as a flags parameter, that may specify MSG_DONTROUTE to tell WinSock not to use routing information in sending the data, or MSG_OOB to send out-of-band data.

Note that the length of data sent in a single send() call cannot exceed the maximum packet size of the underlying network. If you attempt to send more than this, send() will fail, and WSAGetLastError() will return WSAEMSGSIZE.

To receive data from a stream socket, the recv() function is used. Here is the prototype for recv():

```
int recv (SOCKET s, char FAR* buf, int len, int flags);
```

The buf and len parameters specify the buffer that will receive the data and its length. The flags parameter may be set to MSG_OOB to receive out-of-band data or MSG_PEEK, which will fill the buffer with received data, but will also leave that data on the input queue.

If there is data in the input queue for the socket, recv() will return the number of bytes read, which will be the number of bytes available in the input queue, up to the size specified in len. If the connection has closed gracefully, recv() will return 0; if the connection has closed ungracefully, SOCKET_ERROR is returned and WSAGetLastError() will give the specific error.

Out-of-Band Data

The send() and recv() functions allow you to work with out-of-band data. This is generally used for data that should take priority over the regular data stream and can be processed separately.

Waiting for Events

By default, a socket is set to block on I/O operations when it is created with socket(). This means that a recvfrom() call will halt the execution of the thread until a datagram is received. In many cases, you will want your application to continue doing other things, such as responding to user input, while it is waiting for data. One way to do this is to take advantage of the multithreading capabilities of Win32 by creating a separate worker thread for each socket and using blocking calls. However, WinSock also provides two other methods of receiving data asynchronously, by using the BSD style select() function, and by using the WinSock-specific WSAAsyncSelect() function.

Using select()

In UNIX implementations of BSD sockets, you could use the ioctl() function to modify the behavior of file descriptors. Because WinSock sockets are not really file descriptors, you need to use the ioctlsocket() function, which works similarly. You can use ioctlsocket() to set a socket to non-blocking mode with code such as this:

```
ioctlsocket(s, FIONBIO, 1);
```

Once a socket is in non-blocking mode, any call that cannot be completed immediately will return an error, and WSAGetLastError() will return WSAEWOULDBLOCK.

The select() function allows your application to check the status of a set of sockets or block while waiting for an event to occur. One of the most common usages of select() is to specify all the sockets on which you want to wait for data. Whenever data is received by a socket, select() will return, specifying which sockets have data waiting in their input queue. You can then call recvfrom() to retrieve the data.

Using WSAAsyncSelect()

Although the select() method shown previously might be easiest to use if you are porting an application from UNIX, WinSock provides an alternative that is better suited to Windows programming. The WSAAsyncSelect() function allows you to specify a Windows message to be sent to your application when certain events occur. The prototype for WSAAsyncSelect() looks like this:

```
int WSAAsyncSelect (SOCKET s, HWND hWnd,
                unsigned int wMsg, long lEvent);
```

hWnd specifies the handle of the window to which the message specified in wMsg will be sent. In general, wMsg specifies a user-defined message (WM_USER+n). The last parameter, lEvent, specifies the events that will cause WinSock to send the message. This value is generated by combining the following flags with the bitwise-OR operator (¦):

FD_READ   Data is waiting to be read.

FD_WRITE   Socket is ready for writing.

FD_OOB   Out-of-band data is waiting to be read.

FD_ACCEPT An incoming connection is waiting to be accepted.

FD_CONNECT Connection of socket has completed.

FD_CLOSE   Connection has closed.

For example, to be notified when a socket receives data or when the connection closes, you could use something like this:

```
WSAAsyncSelect(mySocket, hMyWnd, WM_USER+1, FD_READ ¦ FD_CLOSE);
```

WSAAsyncSelect() will automatically place the socket in non-blocking mode, so you will not need to call ioctlsocket() to do so.

Note that only the most recent call to WSAAsyncSelect() is used by WinSock. This means that you cannot request to receive a different Windows message for different events on the same socket. You must specify all events that you are interested in, then figure out which event has occurred in the handler for the message, as shown in this example:

```
LONG OnSocketEvent(WPARAM wParam, LPARAM lParam)
{
    char myBuffer[100];
    sockaddr fromAddr;
    if(WSAGETSELECTERROR(lParam))
    {
        // An error occurred
        return 0L;
    }
    switch (WSAGETSELECTEVENT(lParam))
    {
        case FD_READ:
            // data has been received, read it.
            // wParam is the descriptor for the socket that
            // generated the message.
            recvfrom(wParam, myBuffer, sizeof(myBuffer), 0,
                    &fromAddr, sizeof(fromAddr));
            // Do stuff with the datagram…
            break;
        default:
            // some other event occurred,
            // here we just ignore it.
            break;
    } // end switch
} // end OnSocketEvent()
```

If you are using MFC, the message map entry for this handler will look like this:

```
ON_COMMAND(WM_USER+1, OnSocketEvent)
```

Closing a Socket

When you are finished with a socket, you should close it with the `closesocket()` function, shown below:

```
int closesocket(SOCKET s);
```

This function takes a single parameter for the socket to close, but its behavior is also determined by the option settings for the socket, as set with `setsockopt()`. You can get the current settings for a socket with `getsockopt()`. The settings that affect the `closesocket()` function are the `SO_LINGER` and `SO_DONTLINGER` options.

If the `SO_DONTLINGER` option is set to `TRUE`, `closesocket()` will return immediately, but WinSock will continue to try to send all remaining data before closing the socket. This is generally called a graceful shutdown.

If `SO_LINGER` is enabled and the timeout is nonzero, WinSock will also perform a graceful shutdown, attempting to send any data in its buffers, but the `closesocket()` function will not return until all data is sent or the timeout value expires.

If `SO_LINGER` is enabled with a timeout value of zero, the socket is shut down immediately, and any unsent data still in its buffers will be lost.

MFC and the WinSock API

The Microsoft Foundation Classes provide two different classes for working with sockets in your applications. The first, `CAsyncSocket`, provides a lower-level interface that corresponds almost directly to the C API calls shown above. The `CSocket` class, derived from `CAsyncSocket`, provides a higher level of abstraction for dealing with socket communications. `CSocket` also allows you to pass C++ objects between MFC applications with the use of a `CArchive` object associated with the `CSocket`.

To initialize sockets under MFC, you should use the `AfxSocketInit()` function. This call will initialize MFC's internal structures for sockets, as well as calling `WSAStartup()`. The `WSADATA` structure passed to `AfxSocketInit()` is the same as that used in `WSAStartup()` and will return the same values.

> **NOTE**
>
> MFC version 4.21, which ships with VC++ 5.0, supports only WinSock 1.1, so the version of WinSock requested is set to 1.1 in the call to `WSAStartup()`.

Creating a CAsyncSocket

Like many other MFC objects, creation of a socket involves two steps: creating the CAsyncSocket object by calling its constructor, then creating the underlying socket by calling Create(). The constructor for CAsyncSocket does not take any parameters, because it simply constructs a new, blank socket object. The call to Create() does the actual work of creating the underlying socket.

The Create() function takes several parameters, as shown in its prototype:

```
BOOL Create( UINT nSocketPort = 0,
            int nSocketType = SOCK_STREAM,
            long lEvent = FD_READ | FD_WRITE | FD_OOB | FD_ACCEPT | FD_CONNECT |
            FD_CLOSE,
            LPCTSTR lpszSocketAddress = NULL );
```

The first parameter specifies a port number to assign to the socket. By default, this is 0, which tells Windows to assign a port number as it sees fit. In many cases, particularly in "server" applications, you will want to explicitly assign a "well-known" port number to the socket. This is called a well-known port because you allocate a constant port number when you are developing your applications. Client applications can then use this port to connect to the server, as you will see soon.

The nSocketType parameter specifies whether the new socket will be a stream socket (SOCK_STREAM) or a datagram socket (SOCK_DGRAM).

The lEvent parameter specifies the events that will generate notifications to the application. By default, all events will generate notifications.

The last parameter allows you to specify a network address to which the socket will be bound. By default, this is 0, indicating that the socket will be bound to the address of the local machine. However, you may specify a different address for the socket. For IP implementations of WinSock, this would be a string containing the desired IP address—192.9.200.93, for example. In addition, the CAsyncSocket class will handle host name resolution for you, so you may also specify addresses such as ftp.racotek.com.

If you need to know the address that WinSock has assigned to a socket, you can use the GetSockName() member function.

Error Handling with CAsyncSocket

Most member functions of CAsyncSocket will return TRUE if the call completed successfully and FALSE if an error occurs. When a call returns FALSE, CAsyncSocket::GetLastError() will return a more specific error code.

Socket Options and CAsyncSocket

The SetSockOpt() and GetSockOpt() functions may be used to work with the socket options for a CAsyncSocket. These work just like the setsockopt() and getsockopt() functions you saw earlier, except that you will not need to pass the socket descriptor, because these are member functions of the CAsyncSocket class. In addition, the IOCtl() member function can be used to set socket options such as blocking mode. This function is similar to the ioctlsocket() function in the WinSock C API discussed earlier.

Sending and Receiving Datagrams

For CAsyncSockets that you have created of type SOCK_DGRAM, the SendTo() and ReceiveFrom() member functions provide functionality identical to the sendto() and recvfrom() functions in the WinSock C API. These may be used to send a datagram to a specific address without the overhead of establishing a connection or to receive a datagram and its source address from another application.

Connecting to a Server

Stream sockets in client applications can connect to a server by using the Connect() method, which takes two sets of parameters:

```
BOOL Connect( LPCTSTR lpszHostAddress, UINT nHostPort );
BOOL Connect( const SOCKADDR* lpSockAddr, int nSockAddrLen );
```

The first version of Connect() allows you to specify a host address as an ASCII string, such as 192.9.200.93 or ftp.racotek.com, as well as the port number. The second version takes a SOCKADDR structure, as used in the C API version of connect().

connect() will return TRUE if the call is successful, or FALSE if an error occurs, at which point you can call GetLastError() to retrieve more specific error information. By default, CAsyncSockets use the notification callbacks for asynchronous events. In this case, if the Connect() call does not complete immediately, it will return FALSE, and a subsequent call to GetLastError() will return WSAEWOULDBLOCK. The OnConnect() message handler function is then called when the Connect() call has completed, whether successfully or unsuccessfully.

The OnConnect() message handler may be overridden in classes that you derive from CAsyncSocket. Here is its prototype:

```
virtual void OnConnect( int nErrorCode );
```

If nErrorCode is 0, the connection completed successfully, and the socket is ready to begin sending and receiving data. If an error occurred in the connection, nErrorCode will contain a more specific error code.

Accepting Connections to a Server

Once you have created a server stream socket by calling its constructor and Create(), you can tell it to start listening for connection requests with the Listen() member of CAsyncSocket. This function takes a backlog parameter that tells WinSock how many connection requests to hold in the queue before they either are accepted or WinSock begins returning WSAECONNREFUSED to clients trying to connect. By default, this value is set to 5, which should be sufficient for most applications.

To accept a client's connection request, the Accept() method is used. Here is the prototype for Accept():

```
virtual BOOL Accept( CAsyncSocket& rConnectedSocket,
             SOCKADDR* lpSockAddr = NULL, int* lpSockAddrLen = NULL );
```

The first parameter is a reference to a new socket that will handle the new connection. This should be a reference to a socket that you have already created by calling its constructor, but you should not call Create() on the new CAsyncSocket. In addition, you may specify a pointer to a SOCKADDR structure and its length, which will be filled with the address of the client socket, as you saw in the C API accept() function.

The Accept() function is generally called from the OnAccept() member function, which you can override in classes you derive from CAsyncSocket. OnAccept() is called when the CAsyncSocket has received connection requests in its queue. This way, Accept() will not need to block, waiting for connection requests. The OnAccept() function is passed one parameter, specifying an error code. If this is 0, all is well and you should be able to call Accept() successfully.

Sending and Receiving Stream Data

Data is sent on a stream socket with the Send() member of CAsyncSocket. Like its counterpart in the WinSock C API, Send() takes a pointer to a buffer and the length of the data to be sent. Optionally, you may specify a flags parameter of MSG_DONTROUTE to send data without routing or MSG_OOB to send out-of-band data.

The OnSend() notification function, if implemented, is called by the framework when a socket's buffers are free and another send is possible. However, this notification is generally used only in applications where you are sending large amounts of data—the default implementation in CAsyncSocket does nothing.

On the other hand, the OnReceive() notification function is often overridden in classes derived from CAsyncSocket. This function is called when the socket has received data, which will be held in the socket's buffers until your application reads it with a call to the Receive() member of CAsyncSocket.

CAsyncSocket::Receive() takes a pointer to a buffer and its size, as well as an optional flags parameter, which may specify either MSG_PEEK to read the new data (but leave it in the queue so that it can be read by subsequent calls to Receive()) or MSG_OOB to receive out-of-band data.

Receive() will read as much data as is currently available in the socket's input queue, up to the length of the buffer passed. If the connection has closed gracefully, Receive() will return 0; if the connection has closed less than gracefully, Receive() will return SOCKET_ERROR, and an error code of WSACONNRESET will be returned from GetLastError(). Similarly, any other error will cause Receive() to return SOCKET_ERROR with the specific error returned by GetLastError().

Closing a Socket

When you are finished with a CAsyncSocket, you may call its Close() member to release the system resources associated with the socket. Note that Close() is called by the destructor of CAsyncSocket when the object is deleted or goes out of scope. The behavior of the Close() function is dependent on the SO_LINGER and SO_DONT_LINGER options of the socket, as you saw in the close() function of the WinSock C API.

Additionally, you may use the ShutDown() member of CAsyncSocket to disable sends, receives, or both for a given CAsyncSocket. This is generally done only when a socket is on its way down, because it cannot be reused. You must still call Close() to actually release the system resources associated with the socket.

Using CSocket

MFC's CSocket class, derived from CAsyncSocket, provides a higher-level interface to the WinSock API. It uses the CSocketFile and CArchive classes to simplify input and output with sockets. The CSocket class will also handle blocking calls for you, while still processing Windows messages, as you will see soon.

Creating a CSocket

To create a new CSocket object, you need to first construct a blank CSocket by calling its constructor, which takes no parameters, then calling Create():

```
BOOL Create( UINT nSocketPort = 0, int nSocketType = SOCK_STREAM,
        LPCTSTR lpszSocketAddress = NULL );
```

For client sockets, the default parameters are usually sufficient, although for server sockets, you will generally want to specify a port number for the socket. Although you can use the CSocket class to work with SOCK_DGRAM sockets, the default type, SOCK_STREAM, must be used if you intend to use CArchive objects with the socket. In special cases, such as where your server machine has several different addresses, you may wish to specify a specific address for the socket. The default value of NULL specifies that INADDR_ANY will be used when the socket is created.

Making Connections

The CSocket class uses the Connect(), Listen(), and Accept() functions of the CAsyncSocket base class to establish connections between client and server sockets. For more on these, see CAsyncSocket above. The one major exception is that CSocket objects will never call OnConnect(). Instead, the call to Connect() will block until the connection is successfully established or an error occurs. The thread that calls Connect() will, however, be able to process Windows messages while Connect() is blocking.

Sending and Receiving Data

Once a CSocket is created (and connected, if you are using a stream socket) you can use the SendTo()/ReceiveFrom() and Send()/Receive() calls to send and receive data as you would with a CAsyncSocket object. The one exception to this is that CSocket objects will never call the OnSend() notification function. Instead, any calls to Send() will simply block until all the data is sent. Although the CAsyncSocket calls are available to CSocket object, the real benefit of using CSocket is that it allows you to use CArchives to work with socket data.

Using CArchive with CSocket

The greatest benefit of using the CSocket class is that it allows you to pass data between CArchive objects on both sides of the connection. However, this also implies that you must have an MFC application on each side of the connection so that both sides will know how to deal with the data used by CArchive for serialization.

Creating a CSocketFile

In previous chapters, you used CArchive objects in conjunction with files. This is also the case with using CArchives with sockets, but you need to use a special sort of file based on the CSocketFile class. To create a CSocketFile, simply call its constructor, passing a pointer to a CSocket that has already been connected, as shown in the following:

```
CSocket mySocket;
CSocketFile* pMyFile;
CArchive* pArchiveIn;
CArchive* pArchiveOut;
mySocket.Create();
mySocket.Connect("MyServerHost", 5150);
pMyFile = new CSocketFile(&mySocket, TRUE);
// Create separate archives for input and output
pArchiveIn = new CArchive(pMyFile, CArchive::load);
pArchiveOut = new CArchive(pMyFile, CArchive::store);
```

This example also demonstrates how to create CArchive objects that may be used to read and write data from the socket. Note that you create separate CArchive objects for input and output, although you need not create both if your socket will be dealing only with data in one direction.

Sending and Receiving with CArchive

Once you have created a CArchive associated with a connected CSocket, you can use the insertion (<<) and extraction (>>) operators to read or write to the archive, just as you would in normal serialization operations. However, you must keep in mind that a single CArchive can be used only to move data in one direction. If you need to send and receive data, you need two separate CArchive objects: one created with load for receiving and one created with store for sending.

When you have written all the data to the archive that you wish to send, you must call CArchive::Flush() to flush the archive's buffers. The call to Flush() is what will actually send the data over the network. Without this call, the other end of the connection may well wait forever to receive data.

Cleaning Up

When you are finished with a CSocket, you can call the CAsyncSocket::Close() function to release the resources associated with the socket, including its buffers. In addition, you may wish to call CAsyncSocket::Shutdown() to disable reading or writing to the socket while in the process of shutting down communications.

You should also destroy the CArchive, CSocketFile, and CSocket objects when you are done with them. You also could just let them go out of scope, at which point the destructors are called automatically.

Windows Sockets 2

Windows Sockets version 2 supports most of the functionality of WinSock 1.1, but adds several features that greatly enhance the functionality of the WinSock API.

Most importantly, WinSock 2 supports protocols other than the TCP/IP family and provides support for additional network functionality, such as Quality of Service (QOS) and multipoint sessions, as well as supporting the different name spaces that may be used with different networks.

WinSock 2 also introduces the use of overlapped I/O with sockets functions, at least on Windows NT. Additionally, WinSock 2 supports scatter/gather I/O, allowing you to pass multiple send and receive buffers in a single function. WinSock 2 also supports socket groups, sharing sockets between processes, and enhanced connection setup and shutdown functionality.

> **NOTE**
>
> For the most part, the WinSock 1 API is preserved in WinSock 2, other than the fact that pseudo-blocking is not implemented. Thus, the `WSACancelBlockingCall()`, `WSAIsBlocking()`, `WSASetBlockingHook()`, and `WSAUnhookBlockingHook()` functions are not supported. These were intended to provide asynchronous functionality to Win3.1 applications. For the Win32 operating systems, which implement preemptive multitasking and provide more sophisticated synchronization mechanisms, these functions are not necessary.

New Functions for WinSock 2

The WinSock 2 API consists primarily of new functions, although several options have been added to functions from the WinSock 1.1 API. Specifically, new options are available to the `getsockopt()` and `setsockopt()` functions, and new operations are available to the `ioctlsocket()` function. You will look at some of these new features in the following sections.

The new functions added for version 2 of the WinSock API are shown in Table 16.1.

Table 16.1. WinSock API version 2 additions.

Function	Description
Socket Functions	
WSASocket()	Extended version of socket(), allows multiple protocols, overlapped I/O, and socket groups
WSAIoctl()	Extended version of ioctlsocket(), allows overlapped I/O
WSADuplicateSocket()	Allows socket sharing between processes
WSAJoinLeaf()	Used in creating multipoint sessions
Protocol Functions	
WSAEnumProtocols()	Retrieves information about available protocols
Connection Functions	
WSAConnect()	Extended version of connect(), allows for QOS and exchange of connect data
WSAAccept()	Extended version of accept(), allows conditional acceptance, exchanging connect data, and socket groups

Function	*Description*
WSASendDisconnect()	Starts shutdown of a socket; allows sending disconnect data
WSARecvDisconnect()	Shuts down reception on a socket; allows for receipt of disconnect data
Data Functions	
WSASendTo()	Extended version of sendto(), allows overlapped I/O and scatter/gather I/O
WSARecvFrom()	Extended version of recvfrom(), allows overlapped I/O and scatter/gather I/O
WSASend()	Extended version of send(), allows overlapped I/O and scatter/gather I/O
WSARecv()	Extended version of recv(), allows overlapped I/O and scatter/gather I/O
Asynchronous Support Functions	
WSAWaitForMultipleEvents()	Used to wait for a combination of events (same as WaitForMultipleEvents())
WSAEventSelect()	Associates network events with an event object
WSAEnumNetworkEvents()	Retrieves information about network events that have occurred on a socket
WSAGetOverlappedResult()	Returns completion information for overlapped operations (same as GetOverlappedResult())
Event Functions	
WSACreateEvent()	Creates an event object (same as CreateEvent())
WSACloseEvent()	Closes an event object (same as CloseEvent())
WSASetEvent()	Sets an event object (same as SetEvent())
WSAResetEvent()	Resets an event object (same as ResetEvent())
Quality of Service Functions	
WSAGetQOSByName()	Retrieves QOS parameters for well-known services

continues

Table 16.1. continued

Function	Description
	Byte Order Conversion Functions
WSAHtonl()	Extended version of htonl()
WSAHtons()	Extended version of htons()
WSANtohl()	Extended version of ntohl()
WSANtohs()	Extended version of ntohs()

Using Multiple Protocols

One of the most important new features of WinSock 2 is support for protocols other than TCP/IP. Your application should first find out which protocols are available, using WSAEnumProtocols(). You can then choose one of the available protocols in creating a new socket with WSASocket().

Listing Available Protocols

The WSAEnumProtocols() function, shown below, is used to discover which protocols are available to the application:

```
int WSAEnumProtocols (LPINT lpiProtocols, LPWSAPROTOCOL_INFO lpProtocolBuffer,
    ILPDWORD lpdwBufferLength);
```

In most cases, lpiProtocols will be NULL, although you may specify a null-terminated array of protocol values (such as IPPROTO_TCP) to narrow the set of WSAPROTOCOL_INFO structures returned in the array at lpProtocolBuffer.

If WSAEnumProtocols() is successful, it will return the number of WSAPROTOCOL_INFO records returned; otherwise, it will return SOCKET_ERROR and you should call WSAGetLastError() to retrieve a specific error code.

The following is the WSAPROTOCOL_INFO structure:

```
typedef struct _WSAPROTOCOL_INFOA {
    DWORD dwServiceFlags1;
    DWORD dwServiceFlags2;
    DWORD dwServiceFlags3;
    DWORD dwServiceFlags4;
    DWORD dwProviderFlags;
    GUID ProviderId;
    DWORD dwCatalogEntryId;
    WSAPROTOCOLCHAIN ProtocolChain;
    int iVersion;
    int iAddressFamily;
    int iMaxSockAddr;
    int iMinSockAddr;
    int iSocketType;
```

```
    int iProtocol;
    int iProtocolMaxOffset;
    int iNetworkByteOrder;
    int iSecurityScheme;
    DWORD dwMessageSize;
    DWORD dwProviderReserved;
    CHAR    szProtocol[WSAPROTOCOL_LEN+1];
} WSAPROTOCOL_INFOA, FAR * LPWSAPROTOCOL_INFOA;
```

Note that there are actually two different versions of this structure: The WSAPROTOCOL_INFOW structure is used for applications that use Unicode, and the szProtocol array is of type WCHAR.

Although we don't have the space to cover each of the elements in this structure, they are documented in the online help. Note that the iAddressFamily, iSocketType, and iProtocol fields will contain values suitable for the address family, socket type, and protocol parameters for WSASocket().

WSASocket()

WinSock 2 provides an extended version of the socket() function for creating sockets with advanced features. Although the socket() function is still supported in WinSock 2, you must use WSASocket() in order to use protocols other than TCP/IP, overlapped I/O, socket groups, or multipoint sessions. The following is the prototype for WSASocket():

```
SOCKET WSASocket (int af, int type, int protocol,
    LPWSAPROTOCOL_INFO lpProtocolInfo, GROUP g, DWORD dwFlags);
```

The af, type, and protocol parameters are the same as those passed to socket(), although a wider range of values is supported, allowing protocols other than the TCP/IP family.

Values for af can include AF_INET for IP addressing, AF_IPX for IPX addressing, or AF_NETBIOS for NetBIOS addressing, as well as many others. The af values supported are dependent on the transport providers installed, so the list of acceptable values is constantly changing. For more information on address family values, see the documentation for the transport stack you are using or refer to winsock2.h.

WSASocket() also may support many different socket types, although most implementations will use SOCK_DGRAM or SOCK_STREAM, as used in socket().

As an alternative, you can pass a pointer to a WSAPROTOCOL_INFO structure in lpProtocolInfo and specify a value of FROM_PROTOCOL_INFO for any of the first three parameters. In this case, the appropriate values from the WSAPROTOCOL_INFO structure will be used.

You can specify a value of WSA_FLAG_OVERLAPPED in the dwFlags parameter to create a socket that will support overlapped I/O operations.

The g parameter can be used to work with socket groups, as you will see later. There are also several other flags that may be specified to work with multipoint sessions, as you will see in just a bit.

Multiprotocol Name Resolution

The WinSock 2 API offers functions to provide enhanced name resolution, allowing the use of multiple name space providers to support the different addressing schemes that may be used for different network protocols.

The functions that you will look at in this section are intended to replace the lookup functions from WinSock 1, such as gethostbyname() or WSAAsyncGetHostByName(), although these functions are still supported by ws2_32.dll. The inet_addr() and inet_ntoa() functions are also superseded by the WinSock 2 WSAAddressToString() and WSAStringToAddress() functions.

Listing Available Name Space Providers

The WSAEnumNameSpaceProviders() function will return an array of WSANAMESPACE_INFO structures containing information about the name space providers available on the local machine. Here is its prototype:

```
INT WSAAPI WSAEnumNameSpaceProviders (LPDWORD lpdwBufferLength,
    LPWSANAMESPACE_INFO lpnspBuffer);
```

Upon successful completion, this function will return the number of WSANAMESPACE_INFO structures copied to lpnspBuffer; otherwise, as in cases where the buffer is not large enough, this will return SOCKET_ERROR, and GetLastError() will provide a specific error code.

The following is the WSANAMESPACE_INFO structure:

```
typedef struct _WSANAMESPACE_INFOA {
    GUID            NSProviderId;
    DWORD           dwNameSpace;
    BOOL            fActive;
    DWORD           dwVersion;
    LPSTR           lpszIdentifier;
} WSANAMESPACE_INFOA, *PWSANAMESPACE_INFOA, *LPWSANAMESPACE_INFOA;
```

Note that there are two versions of this structure; the other version uses a Unicode string for lpszIdentifier.

Looking Up an Address

The name space functions provided by WinSock 2 can support a wide variety of name space providers for different addressing schemes. The functions that you will look at here provide flexibility to work with these different schemes that is not present in the lookup functions provided by WinSock 1.

To perform a general query of a name space, or several name spaces, you will use the WSALookupServiceBegin() function, which allows you to specify a starting point for a search and returns a handle to be used in subsequent calls to WSALookupServiceNext(), which will return the actual results of the query. You can continue calling WSALookupServiceNext() until no more entries are found, then close the lookup handle with a call to WSALookupServiceEnd().

You can convert an ASCII string containing a readable version of an address into a SOCKADDR structure by using the WSAStringToAddress() function, which is intended to replace the inet_addr() function. You can also convert a SOCKADDR into a readable string with the WSAAddressToString() function, which is intended to replace inet_ntoa().

Overlapped and Scatter/Gather I/O

WinSock 2 allows your application to use standard Windows NT overlapped I/O mechanisms in working with various asynchronous calls, although, like other overlapped operations, this is not supported on Windows 95. WinSock 2 also provides for scatter/gather I/O, which allows you to specify multiple send and receive buffers in a single call.

To use overlapped I/O with sockets, you must create the socket with WSASocket(), rather than socket(), and you must specify the WSA_FLAG_OVERLAPPED flag when creating the socket.

Once you have created a socket that has overlapped operations enabled, you can specify either a pointer to a WSAOVERLAPPED structure, which can specify an event object to signal when the operation is complete, or a pointer to a completion routine that will be called upon completion of calls such as WSASend(), WSASendTo(), WSARecv(), WSARecvFrom(), and WSAIoctl().

You can perform a blocking wait for events, like those specified in a WSAOVERLAPPED structure with WSAWaitForMultipleEvents(), which maps to the Win32 API WaitForMultipleEvents() function.

Alternatively, you could poll for overlapped operation completion with WSAGetOverlappedResult(), which maps to the Win32 API GetOverlappedResult() function.

In working with event objects, you can use either the WinSock 2 functions WSACreateEvent(), WSACloseEvent(), WSASetEvent(), and WSACloseEvent(), or you can use the standard Win32 API functions, with the same names (without the WSA) that perform the same functions.

WinSock 2 also provides the new WSAEventSelect() function, which is similar to WSAAsyncSelect() but will signal an event rather than sending a windows message when the specified events occur. In responding to events triggered by WSAEventSelect(), you can also use the new WSAEnumNetworkEvents() function to retrieve the events that have occurred on a socket. The WSAEventSelect() and WSAEnumNetworkEvents() functions are most useful in applications that do not have a Windows message loop, such as services.

Quality of Service

Many of the network transports that WinSock 2 can support provide guaranteed quality of service (QOS). The new WSAConnect() function allows you to specify quality of service flow specifications for both sending and receiving data over the new connection. You can also use the new WSAIoctl() function to change the QOS parameters for a socket at any time.

You can initialize the QOS structures used in WSAConnect() or WSAIoctl() with values appropriate to a particular well-known service or media type by using WSAGetQOSByName().

WinSock 2 also provides the ability to create socket groups, which can share quality of service information and relative socket priorities. The WSASocket() and WSAAccept() functions allow for creating a socket that is assigned to a group. The getsocketopt() and setsocketopt() functions can be used to retrieve the group id for a socket by using the SO_GROUP_ID option, or to get or set the priority by using the SO_GROUP_PRIORITY option.

Multipoint Sockets

The WinSock 2 API also allows you to take advantage of the multipoint or multicast capabilities of various networking protocols. You can create sockets as nodes in a multipoint session by specifying additional flags when creating the socket with WSASocket(). In many cases, you can also add a node to a multipoint session with the WSAJoinLeaf() function. The WSAIoctl() function is also used to set several multipoint options for a socket.

Shared Sockets

With WinSock 2, you can share sockets between processes by calling the WSADuplicateSocket() function, which will return a special WSAPROTOCOL_INFO structure. This structure can then be passed to another process, using a separate IPC mechanism, where it can be passed to the WSASocket() function, which will create a new descriptor for the underlying socket.

Extended Connection Operations

WinSock 2 provides enhanced features for establishing and shutting down connections. You can conditionally accept connections and send data along with the connection request, as well as when shutting down the connection.

You can implement conditional acceptance of a connection by providing a condition function to the WSAAccept() function. The condition function can decide whether to accept the connection, based on information about the connect request that is passed to it. This function can also be used to assign the new socket to a socket group.

The WSAConnect() function allows you to send a block of data along with the connection request. This data is then passed to the condition function provided to WSAAccept() on the server side.

In addition, The WSASendDisconnect() function can be used to send a final block of data, along with the shutdown request for a socket. This data can be read on the other end of the connection by the WSARecvDisconnect() function.

Protocol-Specific Extensions

In previous versions of WinSock, vendors could supply additional functionality by adding functions to `winsock.dll` and exporting them for applications to use. However, in WinSock 2, the API is supported by a single DLL, `WS2_32.DLL`. Thus, vendors cannot simply add functions to the WinSock DLL. For WinSock 2, vendor-supplied extensions are implemented, using the `WSAIoctl()` function. The details of particular extensions will be provided by the individual service provider vendors.

Summary

In this chapter, you took a look at the Windows Sockets API. You learned how it is implemented for both version 1.1, which supports only TCP/IP protocols, and version 2, which supports many additional network protocols within the Windows Open Systems Architecture (WOSA).

You also explored how to use the WinSock C API functions, such as `socket()` to create both datagram and stream sockets, as well as the `connect()`, `listen()`, and `accept()` functions to manage connections between stream sockets. You saw how to send and receive data with the `sendto()` and `recvfrom()` calls for datagram sockets and the `send()` and `recv()` functions for stream sockets.

You also learned how to use the lookup functions provided by the WinSock API to look up information about host addresses, port number assignments to services, and available protocols, as well as how to use the Windows extensions that implement these functions asynchronously.

You looked at the MFC `CAsyncSocket` class, which provides a low-level mapping of the WinSock C API functions in a single class for ease of use with C++. You also learned how to use MFC's `CSocket` class, which provides a higher-level interface, allowing your applications to use `CArchive` objects to send and receive data over a network by way of serialization.

Finally, you took a brief look at the WinSock 2 API that adds support for multiple networks and other additional features, including multiple name space providers, overlapped and scatter/gather I/O, quality of service, shared sockets, and enhanced connection setup and shutdown functionality.

17

Pipes and Mailslots

by David Bennett

In addition to Windows sockets, there are several different interfaces provided by Visual C++ for interprocess communications (IPC), which may also by used for communicating between processes over a network. In this chapter, you will take a look at pipes, both named and anonymous, and mailslots to communicate between processes.

Anonymous pipes are used to send data in one direction between a child process and its parent or between two different child processes. Anonymous pipes enable your application to use a file-like interface to send data between processes, although they can only be used locally—to use pipes over a network, you must use named pipes.

Named pipes can be used for two-way communications between a server process and one or more client processes. Like anonymous pipes, named pipes use a file-like interface, but they may also be used to communicate over a network.

Mailslots are used to provide one-way communications to a computer across the network. In addition, mailslots can be used to broadcast messages to groups of computers on the network. Pipes are used to send a stream of data; mailslots send individual datagrams, or messages. Delivery of mailslot datagrams is not guaranteed, nor is delivery confirmed. If you need to know that your data was received, you need to use pipes.

Anonymous Pipes

As mentioned, anonymous pipes are generally used for communications between a parent process and a child process or between two child processes. Typically, anonymous pipes are used to redirect the standard input, standard output, or standard error for a process, as you will see. Because anonymous pipes are anonymous—that is, they do not have a name that may be used by other processes—they are generally not used for unrelated processes. For processes that are not related, or for processes that wish to communicate over a network, see named pipes in the next section.

Creating an Anonymous Pipe

An anonymous pipe is created with the CreatePipe() function:

```
BOOL CreatePipe(PHANDLE hReadPipe, PHANDLE hWritePipe,
    LPSECURITY_ATTRIBUTES lpPipeAttributes, DWORD nSize);
```

The first two parameters specify pointers to the read and write handles for the pipe, which are filled in by the call to CreatePipe(). Note that the read handle can be used only for read operations, and the write handle can be used only for write operations. The nSize parameter allows you to pass a suggested size for the buffer assigned to the pipe, although Windows may assign a different actual size to the buffer. If you specify an nSize parameter of 0, the default buffer size is used. In Windows NT, you may also specify the security attributes for the pipe, although Windows 95 ignores this parameter. CreatePipe() will return TRUE if successful or FALSE if an error occurs—at which point you can call GetLastError() to retrieve a specific error code.

Inherited Handles

Once you have created an anonymous pipe with CreatePipe(), you can use the pipe to communicate within the creating process—for instance, between threads. However, to use the pipe to communicate between processes, any processes other than the creating process must inherit the handles to the pipe before they may use them.

To allow a child process to inherit a handle to the pipe, the handle must first be inheritable. This can be specified by setting the bInheritHandle member of the LPSECURITY_ATTRIBUTES structure to TRUE before calling CreatePipe(). In addition, you can use the DuplicateHandle() function to create a copy of the read or write handles with different inheritability options.

Assuming that the handles are inheritable, passing a value of TRUE for the bInheritHandles parameter of CreateProcess() will allow the new child process to use the read and write handles of the anonymous pipe.

However, just because a process has inherited a handle, does not mean that it knows the value of that handle. When a process inherits a handle, the Windows internal tables contain information about the handle and the object to which it refers—in this case, a pipe. To pass the actual value of the handle to a new process, you must use some other IPC mechanism, such as shared memory or named pipes.

Redirecting Standard Input and Output with Pipes

It may seem redundant to use anonymous pipes—if you have to use another IPC mechanism to send the handle, why not just use that mechanism to do all your communications?

There is a way to use anonymous pipes for redirecting the standard input, standard output, and standard error files of a child process without having to use an alternate IPC mechanism. When a process creates a child process, the child will inherit the standard input, standard output, and standard error handles of its parent. You can set the standard handles of the parent process with a call to SetStdHandle() before creating the new process. The new process can be set to use an anonymous pipe for its standard input, output, or error streams.

Writing to a Pipe

To write to a pipe, you can use the WriteFile() function of the Win32 API, which is used for normal file I/O operations:

```
BOOL WriteFile(HANDLE hFile, LPCVOID lpBuffer, DWORD nNumberOfBytesToWrite,
    LPDWORD lpNumberOfBytesWritten, LPOVERLAPPED lpOverlapped);
```

The hFile parameter should be the write handle for a pipe returned from CreatePipe().

Although WriteFile() is the same function that can be used to write to disk files, it will work differently when used with pipes. First, overlapped I/O is not supported for use with anonymous pipes—the lpOverlapped parameter is ignored. Second, WriteFile() will not return until an error occurs or all the data passed to it is written to the pipe. If the pipe's buffer is full, a call to WriteFile() will not return until some of the data in the buffer is read, making room for the data to be written.

In addition to WriteFile(), if you have assigned a pipe's write handle to the standard output or standard error, any functions that write to these "files"—such as using the insertion operator (<<) with cout, cerr, or printf()—will send their data to the pipe. Note, however, that the runtime library may not immediately write the output from functions such as printf()—several calls may be buffered until the buffer fills. If you wish to send output from functions such as this to the pipe immediately, you can insert the flush or endl manipulators if you are using cout and insertion, or call _flushall() to tell the runtime library to flush all of its buffers immediately.

Reading from a Pipe

Reading from a pipe is done with the ReadFile() function:

```
BOOL ReadFile(HANDLE hFile, LPVOID lpBuffer, DWORD nNumberOfBytesToRead,
    LPDWORD lpNumberOfBytesRead, LPOVERLAPPED lpOverlapped);
```

The hFile parameter should be the read handle returned by a call to CreatePipe().

Once again, overlapped I/O is not supported for pipes. A call to ReadFile() for a pipe also will return when any write operation to the pipe completes, regardless of the number of bytes that were requested. That is, if you request to read 100 bytes in a call to ReadFile() and another process writes 10 bytes to the file, ReadFile() returns immediately, and the lpNumberOfBytesRead parameter is used to reflect the actual number of bytes read. In addition, ReadFile() will return FALSE if an error occurs. ReadFile() will also return FALSE if all write handles to the pipe are closed—in this case, GetLastError() will return ERROR_BROKEN_PIPE.

In addition, if you have assigned a pipe handle to a process's standard input, any functions that normally read from standard input, such as the extraction from the cin stream or a C runtime function such as getchar(), will read data from the pipe rather than from the keyboard.

Using an Anonymous Pipe for Standard Output

To see how this works, let's look at the example in Listing 17.1, which creates a child process (logger.exe, shown in Listing 17.2) that will send its standard output to an anonymous pipe. The parent process then reads from the pipe until the child process closes the write handle to the pipe.

Listing 17.1. A parent process creating a child process.

```
#include <stdio.h>
#include <Windows.h>
main()
{
```

```
        STARTUPINFO myStartup;
        PROCESS_INFORMATION myInfo;
        HANDLE hRead, hWrite, hTmp;
        BOOL bReturn;
        char readBuf[100];
        DWORD bytesRead = 0;

        // Create Anonymous Pipe
        if(CreatePipe(&hRead, &hWrite, NULL, 0))
            printf("Pipe Created OK\n");
        else
            printf("Pipe Creation Error: %d\n", GetLastError());

        // Get current std out for this process
        hTmp = GetStdHandle(STD_OUTPUT_HANDLE);

        // Set standard out to the pipe
        SetStdHandle(STD_OUTPUT_HANDLE, hWrite);

        // Create child process
        // Use this process's startup info for the child
        GetStartupInfo(&myStartup);
        bReturn = CreateProcess(".\\logger\\debug\\logger.exe",
                        NULL, NULL, NULL, TRUE,
                        CREATE_NEW_CONSOLE,
                        NULL, NULL, &myStartup, &myInfo);

        // Restore this standard output of this process
        SetStdHandle(STD_OUTPUT_HANDLE, hTmp);
        if (bReturn)
            printf("Create Process OK\n");
        else
            printf("CreateProcess error: %u \n", GetLastError());

        // Close handle so that ReadFile() will return
        // when child process closes pipe.
        // This will not close the pipe,
        // since the child still holds a copy of hWrite.
        CloseHandle(hWrite);
        // Read until pipe is closed
        while(ReadFile(hRead, readBuf, 100, &bytesRead, NULL))
        {
            readBuf[bytesRead] = '\0';
            printf("Read %d bytes from pipe [%s]", bytesRead, readBuf);
        }
        if(GetLastError() == ERROR_BROKEN_PIPE)
            printf("Pipe Closed by child process\n");
        else
            printf("Read Error: %d\n", GetLastError());
        return 1;
} // end main
```

In this example, you set the standard output of the current (parent) process to use your anonymous pipe, then create the child process, which will inherit the standard output of the parent process. You then restore the standard output of the parent process to its original value. The parent then reads data from the pipe until an error occurs or until all handles to the write end of the pipe are closed.

The child process created in Listing 17.1 simply spits out some text to both standard output, which will go to the pipe, and standard error, which will go to the child process console window. The .endl manipulator will cause each line to be immediately written to the pipe. The child process then goes away quietly. Its source is shown in Listing 17.2.

Listing 17.2. A child process sending output to an anonymous pipe.

```
#include <stdio.h>
#include <iostream.h>
main()
{
    int i;
    // Send some output to standard out and standard error
    for(i=0; i<10; i++)
    {
        printf("Logging %d\n", i);
        cout << "Output Line: " << i << endl;
        cerr << "Error Line: " << i << endl;
    }
    return 1;
}
```

Named Pipes

Named pipes provide an interface for interprocess communications similar to that of anonymous pipes, although named pipes are much easier to share between unrelated processes. Named pipes are more flexible to use for the following reasons:

- They can be used over a network.
- They can be referenced by name.
- They support connections to more than one client.
- They support two-way communications over the pipe.
- They support asyncronous, overlapped I/O.

To use a named pipe, a server process creates an initial instance of the pipe. The server process will then listen for connection requests to an instance of the pipe. Each connection requires a separate instance of the pipe to be created. Each client application then has a connection to a single instance of the pipe—the data streams between instances of a pipe are not shared. Each instance has its own buffers.

> **NOTE**
>
> Windows 95 supports only named pipe clients. Only Windows NT currently supports the server end of named pipes.

Sending and receiving data on a named pipe is then accomplished with ReadFile(), WriteFile(), ReadFileEx(), and WriteFileEx().

Creating a Named Pipe

Before a pipe may be used, it must first be created by the server process. Once the pipe is created, other processes may connect to the pipe using its name. A new named pipe is created with the CreateNamedPipe() function:

```
HANDLE CreateNamedPipe(
    LPCTSTR lpName,
    DWORD dwOpenMode,
    DWORD dwPipeMode,
    DWORD nMaxInstances,
    DWORD nOutBufferSize,
    DWORD nInBufferSize,
    DWORD nDefaultTimeOut,
    LPSECURITY_ATTRIBUTES lpSecurityAttributes);
```

The first parameter gives the name of the pipe, according to the universal naming convention (UNC), which allows you to specify the network name of a machine and the name of the pipe. The value passed in lpName should be a pointer to a null-terminated string of the following format:

\\.**pipe***pipename*

The *pipename* portion may be any name you choose (other than backslashes), but the first part of the pipe name should be as shown in the example. You can create a pipe only on the local machine, as specified by the period. Note that pipe names are not case-sensitive.

The dwOpenMode parameter contains information about how the new pipe will behave. One of the following access mode flags must be specified:

> PIPE_ACCESS_DUPLEX allows data transmission in both directions.
>
> PIPE_ACCESS_INBOUND allows data to flow only to the server. The server can read from the pipe, and the clients can only write data.
>
> PIPE_ACCESS_OUTBOUND allows data to be transmitted only from the server (which can only write) to the clients (which can only read).

In addition, you may combine additional parameters with a logical OR (¦), including FILE_FLAG_WRITE_THROUGH, which will cause write operations on the pipe to block until the data has been successfully transmitted to the other side of the connection, or FILE_FLAG_OVERLAPPED, which allows you to use overlapped I/O operations with the pipe. You may also specify additional flags to control the security access mode of the pipe.

The dwPipeMode parameter specifies the type, read mode, and wait mode of the pipe. The type of the pipe is either PIPE_TYPE_BYTE (the default), which creates a pipe dealing with a continuous stream of bytes, or PIPE_TYPE_MESSAGE, which creates a pipe that handles separate messages.

The read mode of the pipe may be set to PIPE_READMODE_BYTE (the default), where the continuous byte stream is read, or PIPE_READMODE_MESSAGE, which allows reads to work with messages. Note that message read mode can be used only with pipes of type PIPE_TYPE_MESSAGE.

By default, named pipes are in a blocking mode, which may be specified by PIPE_WAIT. To set the pipe to non-blocking mode, you may specify PIPE_NOWAIT.

The nMaxInstances parameter specifies the maximum number of instances of the pipe that may be created. If you want to allow as many instances as system resources will allow, you can specify PIPE_UNLIMITED_INSTANCES.

nOutBufferSize and nInBufferSize specify the sizes of the input and output buffers used with the pipe.

Additionally, you may specify a default timeout value for the pipe and its security attributes, although security is implemented only in Windows NT.

If CreateNamedPipe() fails, it will return INVALID_HANDLE_VALUE, and a call to GetLastError() will return a more specific error code. If the pipe is successfully created, CreateNamedPipe() will return the handle to the server end of the pipe.

Creating Additional Instances

In order to use a named pipe to accept connections from multiple clients, a separate instance of the pipe must be created for each connection. Each instance is created with a new call to CreateNamedPipe(), specifying the same name as the original call to CreateNamedPipe().

When CreateNamedPipe() is called to create a new instance of a pipe that has already been created, the same pipe access (duplex, inbound, or outbound), pipe type (byte or message), instance count, and timeout value must be used. However, other parameters, such as the read or wait modes, may be different for each instance.

Listening for Connections

Once the pipe is created, the server process must listen for connection requests with the ConnectNamedPipe() function, which takes the pipe handle returned from CreateNamedPipe() and a pointer to an OVERLAPPED structure, as shown in the following:

```
BOOL ConnectNamedPipe(HANDLE hNamedPipe,
    LPOVERLAPPED lpOverlapped);
```

ConnectNamedPipe() waits for a connection request from a client and then sets up the connection for the pipe instance specified in the first parameter. However, the manner in which the waiting is performed may be different, depending on the wait mode of the pipe and whether or not overlapped I/O is used.

By default, named pipes are created in blocking mode, although you may create a non-blocking pipe by passing PIPE_NOWAIT to CreateNamedPipe() or by calling SetNamedPipeHandleState(), which may also be used to change the read mode and buffering attributes of a named pipe.

If lpOverlapped is not NULL, overlapped I/O will be used, regardless of the mode of the pipe. If lpOverlapped is NULL, ConnectNamedPipe() will block for a blocking pipe or will be non-blocking for a non-blocking pipe.

CAUTION

If the pipe is created with FILE_FLAG_OVERLAPPED, you must specify a valid OVERLAPPED structure. If you do not, ConnectNamedPipe() may report completion incorrectly.

Non-Blocking

If the pipe is set to non-blocking mode, ConnectNamedPipe() will return immediately. If the pipe is available to accept a new connection, ConnectNamedPipe() returns TRUE; if the pipe has already been connected, it will return FALSE, and a call to GetLastError() will return ERROR_PIPE_CONNECTED. Only after the call to ConnectNamedPipe() that results in ERROR_PIPE_CONNECTED is the connection ready to send and receive data.

NOTE

Non-blocking, or polling, is generally supported only to provide compatibility with Microsoft LAN Manager 2.0. In most cases, you will want to use blocking mode named pipes.

Blocking

If the pipe is set to blocking, which is the default, the behavior of ConnectNamedPipe() depends on whether you specify a non-NULL value in the lpOverlapped parameter. Note that if you create the pipe with the FILE_FLAG_OVERLAPPED option, you must specify a pointer to a valid OVERLAPPED structure.

If lpOverlapped is NULL, ConnectNamedPipe() will block until a connection is established or an error occurs. If a connection is successfully established after the call is made, ConnectNamedPipe() will return TRUE, and the connection is ready to go.

In addition, a connection may have actually been established prior to the call to ConnectNamedPipe(), in which case the function returns FALSE, and a call to GetLastError() will return ERROR_PIPE_CONNECTED. In this case, the connection formed is just as valid as if ConnectNamedPipe() returned TRUE, although if ConnectNamedPipe() returns FALSE and any other value is returned by GetLastError(), an error has occurred and the pipe has not been connected.

Overlapped I/O

Many of the operations used with named pipes—or with regular files—can support overlapped I/O. This allows a given function to return immediately while time-consuming operations continue in the background. Your process may then be notified asynchronously when the function has completed. The ConnectNamedPipe(), ReadFile(), ReadFileEx(), WriteFile(), WriteFileEx(), and TransactNamedPipe() functions can support overlapped I/O.

> **NOTE**
>
> Overlapped I/O is not supported on Windows 95.

The OVERLAPPED structure

For every call that uses overlapped I/O, a pointer to an OVERLAPPED structure must be passed:

```
typedef struct _OVERLAPPED {
    DWORD   Internal;
    DWORD   InternalHigh;
    DWORD   Offset;
    DWORD   OffsetHigh;
    HANDLE hEvent;
} OVERLAPPED;
```

The first two members of the structure are reserved for operating system use, and the next two fields are used to specify a file offset when working with real files. These fields are ignored for functions using named pipes. The hEvent is the one field of real interest in named pipe functions, because it specifies a handle for an event that will be set when the operation completes.

When you call ConnectNamedPipe() using overlapped I/O, the function will return FALSE. If a connection was established before the call to ConnectNamedPipe(), GetLastError() will return ERROR_PIPE_CONNECTED and the pipe is ready to use. If the system is waiting for the call to complete asynchronously, GetLastError() will return ERROR_IO_PENDING. Any other return value indicates that a real error has occurred.

In the case where ERROR_IO_PENDING is returned, you can wait for the event to be set with any of the wait functions, such as WaitForSingleObject(), WaitForMultipleObjects(), or SleepEx().

To find the result of an overlapped operation, you can call GetOverlappedResult() with the handle of the pipe (or file) operated on and a pointer to the OVERLAPPED structure used for the operation. In addition, you may request that the GetOverlappedResult() function wait for the operation to complete—in this case, you will not need to use one of the wait functions listed previously.

If GetOverlappedResult() returns TRUE, the operation was successful. In the event of an error, GetOverlappedResult() will return FALSE, and GetLastError() will give more specifics.

Once the pipe is connected, you can use GetNamedPipeHandleState() to retrieve information about this instance of the pipe, including the pipe state, the number of current instances of the pipe, buffering settings, and the user name associated with the client process.

Connecting to a Named Pipe

To connect a client application to an instance of a named pipe, your application should first call WaitNamedPipe() to wait for an instance of the named pipe to be available for connecting. WaitNamedPipe() takes the name of the pipe to wait for and a timeout value, in milliseconds. You may specify a timeout value of NMPWAIT_WAIT_FOREVER to wait forever or NMPWAIT_USE_DEFAULT_WAIT to use the default timeout value that the server process used in calling CreateNamedPipe().

If an instance of the pipe becomes available before the timeout expires, CreateNamedPipe() will return TRUE; otherwise, it will return FALSE, and GetLastError() can be used to return a more specific error message. Note that WaitNamedPipe() will return FALSE with a GetLastError() return of ERROR_FILE_NOT_FOUND if the server process has not yet called CreateNamedPipe() to create the pipe.

Once an instance of the pipe is available for connecting, you can call CreateFile() to open a file handle to be used with the new connection to the pipe. Here is the prototype for CreateFile():

```
HANDLE CreateFile( LPCTSTR lpFileName,DWORD dwDesiredAccess,
          DWORD dwShareMode, LPSECURITY_ATTRIBUTES lpSecurityAttributes,
   DWORD dwCreationDistribution, DWORD dwFlagsAndAttributes,
   HANDLE hTemplateFile );
```

The *lpFileName* parameter should point to the universal name for the pipe, including the host name, with the following:

```
\\Gozer\pipe\mypipe.
```

Keep in mind that in C or C++ code, you need to precede each backslash in the string with an additional backslash, because the backslash is used for escape sequences.

For connecting to a named pipe, the dwCreationDistribution parameter should always be OPEN_EXISTING. The dwFlagsAndAttributes parameter allows you to specify many different option flags, most of which are intended to be used only with disk files. Of interest in working with pipes are FILE_FLAG_WRITE_THROUGH, which will cause WriteFile() calls to this pipe to block until the data is successfully transmitted, and FILE_FLAG_OVERLAPPED, which will allow this connection to use overlapped I/O.

If the connection is successfully established, CreateFile() will return TRUE; otherwise, it will return FALSE, and you should call GetLastError() to retrieve a more specific error code.

Writing to a Named Pipe

Once the connection is established, writing to a named pipe is done with the WriteFile() function:

```
BOOL WriteFile(HANDLE hFile, LPCVOID lpBuffer,
    DWORD nNumberOfBytesToWrite, LPDWORD lpNumberOfBytesWritten,
    LPOVERLAPPED lpOverlapped );
```

The hFile parameter is the handle returned from either CreateFile() or ConnectNamedPipe(), depending on whether your application is the client or server for the named pipe. The data to be sent is specified by lpBuffer and nNumberOfBytesToWrite, and the value pointed to by lpNumberOfBytesWritten will be updated to reflect the actual number of bytes written. In cases where the data to be sent on a non-blocking, byte-mode pipe is bigger than the pipe's buffers, the actual number of bytes sent may be less than the number of bytes requested to send.

In addition, you may specify a pointer to an OVERLAPPED structure to use overlapped I/O so that you are notified asynchronously (by waiting for the event in the OVERLAPPED structure) when the write operation is complete.

If WriteFile() completes successfully, it will return TRUE; otherwise, it returns FALSE, and you should call GetLastError() for more info. If you specified FILE_FLAG_WRITE_THROUGH in CreateFile() or CreateNamedPipe(), WriteFile() will block until the data is actually sent across the network, although it does not have to be read by the remote process.

In addition, WriteFileEx() may be used to perform write operations using overlapped I/O:

```
BOOL WriteFileEx(HANDLE hFile, LPCVOID lpBuffer,
    DWORD nNumberOfBytesToWrite, LPOVERLAPPED lpOverlapped,
    LPOVERLAPPED_COMPLETION_ROUTINE lpCompletionRoutine );
```

When you use this function, the event in the overlapped structure is ignored. Instead of signaling the event, WriteFileEx() will call the function passed in lpCompletionRoutine when the operation completes. The prototype for this completion function should look like this:

```
VOID WINAPI WriteCompletion(DWORD dwErr, DWORD cbWritten,
    LPOVERLAPPED lpOverlapped);
```

dwErr will contain any error that occurred, and cbWritten will contain the number of bytes actually written. In addition, lpOverlap will contain a pointer to the OVERLAPPED structure passed to WriteFileEx().

Reading from a Named Pipe

To read from a named pipe, you can call ReadFile() once the pipe has been successfully connected with CreateFile() or ConnectNamedPipe():

```
BOOL ReadFile(HANDLE hFile, LPVOID lpBuffer,
    DWORD nNumberOfBytesToRead, LPDWORD lpNumberOfBytesRead,
    LPOVERLAPPED lpOverlapped);
```

This function takes the handle returned by `CreateFile()` or `ConnectNamedPipe()`, a pointer to the buffer to receive the data, and the number of bytes to read. You may also specify a pointer to an `OVERLAPPED` structure if you want to use overlapped I/O to wait for the read to complete.

If `ReadFile()` completes successfully, it will return `TRUE`; otherwise, it returns `FALSE` and you should call `GetLastError()` for more info. Upon successful reads, the value pointed to by `lpNumberOfBytesRead` is updated to reflect the actual number of bytes read.

> **NOTE**
>
> `ReadFile()` will return when a write operation completes on the write end of the pipe, or the number of bytes requested is read, or an error occurs.

In addition, you may use `ReadFileEx()` to perform read operations using overlapped I/O:

```
BOOL ReadFileEx(HANDLE hFile, LPVOID lpBuffer,
    DWORD nNumberOfBytesToRead, LPOVERLAPPED lpOverlapped,
    LPOVERLAPPED_COMPLETION_ROUTINE lpCompletionRoutine);
```

When you use `ReadFileEx()`, the event specified in the `OVERLAPPED` structure is not signaled. Instead, the function passed in `lpCompletionRoutine` is called. This function should look like this:

```
VOID WINAPI ReadComplete(DWORD dwErr, DWORD cbBytesRead,
    LPOVERLAPPED lpOverlapped);
```

If an error occurred, the error code will be passed in `dwErr`, and `cbBytesRead` will contain the actual number of bytes read. `lpOverlapped` will contain the pointer to an `OVERLAPPED` structure passed to `ReadFileEx()`.

If you want to look at the data in a pipe's buffer without removing it from the input queue, you can use the `PeekNamedPipe()` function, which will read a portion of the data in the buffer and return other information about the data remaining in the buffer.

Transactions with Named Pipes

In addition to the `ReadFile()` and `WriteFile()` functions, the Windows API provides two additional calls that can simplify common operations for named pipes. In many cases, a client will want to send a request to a server and read a response. For message-type pipes set to message-type read mode, the `TransactNamedPipe()` function will do this for you in a single API call:

```
BOOL TransactNamedPipe(HANDLE hNamedPipe, LPVOID lpInBuffer,
    DWORD nInBufferSize, LPVOID lpOutBuffer,
    DWORD nOutBufferSize, LPDWORD lpBytesRead,
    LPOVERLAPPED lpOverlapped);
```

This function takes parameters for the pipe handle (write and read buffers) and a pointer to the number of bytes actually read. In addition, you may use overlapped I/O to specify an event to be signaled when the operation completes. `TransactNamedPipe()` may be used on either the client or server side of the connection, but it is most often used on the client end.

In addition, your client applications may use the `CallNamedPipe()` function to connect to a given named pipe, send a message, and receive a message—all in one API call, which incorporates the functionality of the `CreateFile()`, `TransactNamedPipe()`, and `CloseHandle()` functions. Here is the prototype for `CallNamedPipe()`:

```
BOOL CallNamedPipe(LPCTSTR lpNamedPipeName, LPVOID lpInBuffer,
    DWORD nInBufferSize, LPVOID lpOutBuffer, DWORD nOutBufferSize,
    LPDWORD lpBytesRead, DWORD nTimeOut);
```

The parameters are similar to those for `TransactNamedPipe()`, with the exception that you specify the name of the pipe rather than a handle, because the call to `CreateFile()` is handled for you. `CallNamedPipe()` also does not support overlapped I/O.

Closing a Pipe

When you are finished with a pipe, you should call `CloseHandle()` to close the instance of the pipe. In addition, you may want to call `FlushFileBuffers()` to ensure that any data remaining in the pipe's buffers is sent before the connection is closed.

On the server side, you may also call `DisconnectNamedPipe()` to forcibly disconnect the client. The handle for this instance of the pipe may then be used to accept a new connection with `ConnectNamedPipe()`.

Mailslots

Mailslots provide a mechanism for one-way communications between processes over a network. Mailslots differ from named pipes, because they may be used to broadcast messages to a group of different machines within the same domain. Mailslots are also different because they use unreliable communications. That is, data sent to a mailslot is not guaranteed to arrive, nor is the sender notified if the data did not successfully arrive.

> **CAUTION**
>
> You should use mailslots only for sending information that is of interest, but that isn't critical. For example, you might use mailslots to broadcast status updates for a process to various users every five minutes. If one of the user's displays doesn't get updated occasionally, this might be okay. However, this would be quite unacceptable if you were sending something like accounting transactions.

Any process that creates a mailslot for receiving data is known as a mailslot server. Even though the process that creates the mailslot may be a client application receiving data from a server application, the process that creates the mailslot is the server for that mailslot. Note that each machine on a network may act as a server for a given mailslot, although only the process that creates the mailslot (or a process that otherwise gains access to the mailslot handle, that is, through inheritance) can read data from the mailslot.

Any process that knows the name of the mailslot may send data to it. Processes that send data to mailslots are known as *mailslot clients*.

Creating a Mailslot

To create a mailslot that may be used to receive messages, your application will use the CreateMailSlot() function:

```
HANDLE CreateMailslot(LPCTSTR lpName, DWORD nMaxMessageSize,
    DWORD lReadTimeout, LPSECURITY_ATTRIBUTES lpSecurityAttributes);
```

The first parameter is a pointer to an ASCII string containing the name of the mailslot to create. Mailslots are created only on the local machine, so the full UNC name that should be specified here should look something like this:

```
\\.\mailslot\[path]name
```

Note that, unlike named pipes, names for mailslots support a pseudo-directory structure. You may specify a path in the name of the mailslot to help organize the mailslots on a system.

CreateMailslot() also accepts parameters for the maximum message size and a timeout time for read operations, as well as an optional security structure. You may specify a timeout value of MAILSLOT_WAIT_FOREVER to have read operations for the mailslot block until a message is received, without timing out.

If CreateMailslot() completes successfully, it will return a handle to the new mailslot. If an error occurs, it will return INVALID_HANDLE_VALUE, and GetLastError() can be used to retrieve additional information about the cause of the error.

To create a typical mailslot, your code would look something like this:

```
hSlot = CreateMailslot("\\\\.\\mailslot\\MySlots\\MsgSlot",
                       300,
                       MAILSLOT_WAIT_FOREVER,
                       NULL);
if(hSlot == INVALID_HANDLE_VALUE)
{
    printf("CreateMailslot error: %d \n", GetLastError());
    exit(0);
}
```

If you wish to change the read timeout value after the mailslot is created, you can use SetMailslotInfo() to do so. In addition, GetMailslotInfo() may be used to retrieve information about the mailslot, including its maximum message size, the size of the next message in its queue, the number of messages in the queue, and the read timeout value.

Reading from a Mailslot

To read a message from a mailslot, you can use the ReadFile() function, which will return whenever a new mailslot message is received, regardless of the number of bytes to read specified.

In addition, the GetMailslotInfo() function can be used to find out the number of messages waiting in the mailslot and the size of the next message.

Writing to a Mailslot

In order to write a message to a mailslot, you must use CreateFile() to open a handle to the mailslot and then use WriteFile() to send a message before calling CloseHandle() to close the handle to the mailslot.

When calling CreateFile(), you must specify the name of the mailslot to which to send. The name you specify may allow you to broadcast to mailslots with the same name on all the machines in a domain.

To specify a mailslot on this machine:

`\\.\mailslot\`*`[path]`*`name`

To specify a mailslot on a specific remote machine:

`\\RemoteMachineName\mailslot\`*`[path]`*`name`

To broadcast to a mailslot on all machines in a domain:

`\\DomainName\mailslot\`*`[path]`*`name`

To broadcast to a mailslot on all machines in the top-level domain:

`\\*\mailslot\`*`[path]`*`name`

In addition, your call to CreateFile() should specify a mode of GENERIC_WRITE, a sharing mode of FILE_SHARE_READ, and a creation mode of OPEN_EXISTING.

Once CreateFile() completes successfully, you can use the handle it returns in calls to WriteFile() to send messages to the mailslot.

Closing a Mailslot

When you are finished using a mailslot, you should call CloseHandle() to release the system resources used by the mailslot. All handles belonging to a process are automatically closed when a process exits. When all handles to a mailslot are closed, the mailslot is destroyed, and any data in its buffers is lost.

Summary

In this chapter, you took a look at several of the mechanisms that the Win32 API provides for interprocess communication, including anonymous pipes, named pipes, and mailslots.

You learned how to create anonymous pipes with `CreatePipe()`, as well as how to use `ReadFile()` and `WriteFile()` to read and write with pipes. You also saw how to assign a pipe to the standard input, standard output, or standard error streams for a child process by using `SetStdHandle()` before creating the child process.

You looked at named pipes, which may be used to communicate between processes over a network. You also saw how to create a named pipe with `CreateNamedPipe()` and wait for clients to connect with `ConnectNamedPipe()`, including how to use overlapped I/O to perform time-consuming operations asynchronously. On the client side, you learned how to connect to a named pipe with `WaitNamedPipe()` and `CreateFile()`, as well as how to use `ReadFile()`, `WriteFile()`, `ReadFileEx()`, and `WriteFileEx()` to send and receive data.

The third IPC mechanism you explored was the mailslot, which may be used to send datagrams to a process over a network or even broadcast messages to all machines on a given domain. You saw how to create mailslots with `CreateMailslot()`, as well as how to connect to an existing mailslot with `CreateFile()`. You learned how to use `ReadFile()` and `WriteFile()` to send and receive data with a mailslot.

18

Remote Procedure Calls (RPCs)

by David Bennett

Many applications today are intended to run on a network, using either a client-server model or a more general distributed computing model. This sort of architecture allows you to share resources among computers on the network. For instance, a single machine may act as a centralized database server for many clients. Additionally, servers on the network may be used for other CPU or memory-intensive operations that could not be performed in a reasonable time on a standard desktop client machine.

To enable you to develop distributed applications relatively simply, Microsoft supports the Remote Procedure Call (RPC) model for distributed computing. The RPC standard was originally developed as part of the Open Software Foundation (OSF) Distributed Computing Environment (DCE) specification. The Microsoft implementation of RPC, as you will see in this chapter, is compatible with other DCE implementations of RPC, such as on UNIX servers. The Microsoft RPC API is also similar to that found in native DCE environments, with certain additions to enable some Windows-specific functionality.

How RPC Works

In general, RPC allows your client applications to make function calls just as they normally would, with the exception that the RPC runtime libraries pass the call to an RPC server somewhere on the network. When the server is finished, it passes the data back to the client, and the original function call returns—just as if it were a local function call.

Although there are many ways that you could implement distributed computing, the RPC library provides a lot of functionality to help you with this. The RPC runtime can handle all the conversions, such as byte-order, necessary to send data (even pointers) across a network to whatever sort of machine is there to receive it. The RPC library also provides functionality that can automatically locate a server for a given function on the network and manage the connections between client and server.

Figure 18.1 shows how this all fits together to perform a remote procedure call. The client application calls a stub for the remote procedure, which may look just like a local function call. The stub then converts the function's arguments into a standard network data representation (NDR) and calls the RPC runtime library to pass the request to the remote server. The RPC runtime on the server side receives the request and calls a server stub function, which translates the data into the proper format for the local machine and calls the server function, which does the real work of the function. When this function returns, the return value and any other output parameters then follow a similar path back to the original calling process.

Designing with RPC

Remote procedure calls can be very useful in many situations, although they do introduce some overhead. For starters, passing parameters in RPC can involve extra processing to convert to and from network representation. In addition, additional memory allocations may be required to handle the input or output parameters. As with any network communications, there also is a certain latency involved with every message sent over the network.

FIGURE 18.1.
Remote procedure calls.

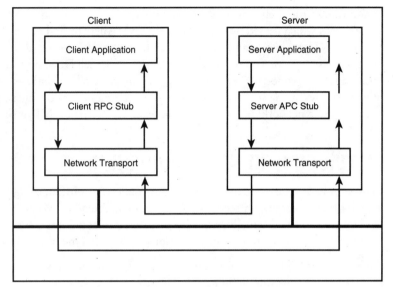

In general terms, you want to minimize the number of individual calls. For example, if you need to perform a calculation on each element of a large array, you should design your RPC calls so that each call can work on a whole row (or all rows) of the array, rather than making a separate RPC call for each element. By using a few calls that do a lot, rather than many calls that do very little, you cut down on the significance of the overhead induced by using RPC.

Components of an RPC Application

To use RPC between a client and a server, you will obviously need to develop a client and a server process, although there are some other components that go into developing the client and server sides of the process.

To start with, any RPC call uses an interface that is defined in a file of *interface definition language* (IDL). The IDL file is then processed with Microsoft's IDL (MIDL) compiler, which will generate header files that define the client and server stubs that are used to implement the RPC.

The client application uses the RPC function stub generated by the MIDL compiler. The client application is also linked with the RPC runtime libraries, which are called by the stub function to implement the call over the network. The RPC runtimes, in turn, use one of a set of DLLs to implement the specific network protocol that is to be used.

The server application also includes a header file generated by the MIDL compiler specifically for the server side of things. The server also links with RPC runtime libraries, although a server application uses some additional functions to register itself as a server for a particular interface and begin listening for requests for that interface.

In addition to the client and server processes, a third process may also be involved. This is a *name service,* which is used by the client to discover where to find servers for a given interface. Windows NT provides a name service called the Microsoft Locator, although you may also use other name services on your network, such as the DCE Cell Directory Service (CDS) available through DCE's name-service daemon (nsid). Unfortunately, Windows 95 does not currently provide its own name service, so if you wish to use name service functionality, you must be connected to a network that provides a name service, either on NT or some other system.

Developing an RPC Application

In most cases, it is easiest to first develop your application without using RPC. Simply develop your application locally, with each function that you intend to execute remotely defined in its own separate C file. (Actually, there is no reason you could not use C++, but the functions used in RPC should be stand-alone functions, rather than members of a class.)

Once you have the functionality of your application ironed out, you can add RPC functionality to it. This begins with defining the interface.

Defining an Interface

To define an interface for the remote functions of your application, let's create an interface definition language file, which uses a syntax very similar to C. However, there are some C types that are not allowed in IDL, as well as some extra constructs that are used to specify various attributes of the functions and parameters that are used in remote calls.

Throughout this chapter, you will look at a simple example of RPC, using a function that uses RPC to compute the factorial of a number in an RPC server. The interface for this function is defined in RpcFact.idl:

```
[
    uuid (C16F6562-520D-11D0-B338-444553540000),
    version(1.0),
    endpoint("ncalrpc:[myFactorial]")
]
interface rpcfactorial
{
    long RpcFactorial([in] long nVal);
}
```

The first part of this file, defined in brackets, is the interface header. The header defines a *universally unique identifier,* or UUID, which may be used by servers to register the interface so that clients may locate this particular interface. In addition, you may specify a version, because you may, in fact, have several different versions of an RPC interface active on the same network at the same time. The last element of the header specifies an endpoint for the interface.

This gives the type of network protocol that will be used and an address and port that are used to receive requests for this interface.

The body of the interface declares the functions that are implemented as part of this interface. In this case, there is only one function, which takes a `long` parameter and returns a `long`. In addition, you specify that the parameter is used only as an input to the function. This helps the stub functions minimize the processing that must be done to pass arguments back and forth to the server. You will take a closer look at different types of parameters soon. For now, let's look at the header elements more closely.

Universally Unique IDs

The UUID specified in the interface header is composed of five groups of numbers that should uniquely identify this interface to the world. These values are sometimes referred to as *globally unique identifiers,* or GUIDs.

Although I suppose you could make up some number for this value, there is a better way. Microsoft provides a utility to generate UUIDs for you. You can access this from the command line using the `uuidgen` utility, which can generate any number of UUIDs for you. It will also output these in several different convenient formats for you. For instance, the following command line will generate a template for an IDL file, including the new UUID that was generated:

```
uuidgen -i -oMyFunc.idl
```

The UUID that is generated is based on a random number, as well as information about the local machine and the current time. This combination provides a pretty good chance that this ID will be unique.

In addition, you may generate a new UUID without ever leaving Developer Studio. If you "insert" the GUID generator component from the Component Gallery, you can generate a new ID. This component does not actually add any code to your application, it simply generates a new ID and prompts you for the format to copy to the clipboard. You can then insert this text into your IDL file from any application that supports cut-and-paste. Unfortunately, the current version of the GUID generator does not support the IDL skeleton format. The registry format lends itself best to insertion into your IDL file.

Endpoints

The endpoint for an interface may be specified in many different ways, depending on the protocol to be used. The current version of the Microsoft RPC libraries supports the protocols shown in Table 18.1 for endpoints (note that many of these are supported only on NT platforms).

Table 18.1. Supported endpoint protocols.

IDL string	Protocol	Restrictions
ncacn_ip_tcp	TCP	
ncadg_ip_udp	UDP	NT only
ncacn_np	Named pipes	Client-only for 95
ncacn_nb_tcp	NetBIOS over TCP	NT only
ncacn_nb_ipx	NetBIOS over IPX	NT only
ncacn_nb_nb	NetBIOS over NetBEUI	
ncadg_ipx	Datagram IPX	NT only
ncacn_spx	SPX	
ncacn_at_dsp	AppleTalk DSP	Server-only on NT
ncacn_vns_spp	Vines SPP	NT only
ncalrpc	Local procedure call	

Because each of these protocols uses a different format for network names or addresses, the rest of the endpoint specification is dependent on the protocol used. For example, a TCP endpoint specifies an IP address and port, whereas a named pipe or local procedure call endpoint specifies a name, as shown in the following:

```
endpoint("ncacn_ip_tcp:192.9.200.93[5150]")
endpoint("ncalrpc:[myFactorial]")
endpoint("ncacn_np:\\MyServer[\\pipe\\MyPipeName]")
```

Interface Body

The body section of the interface description file specifies the functions that make up this interface. In general, these are very similar to standard C declarations of the functions. However, IDL supports only a subset of the base types supported by C. Most notably, the types int and void * are not supported. This is due to the fact that IDL is strongly typed, as is necessary to be able to pass parameters to heterogeneous computers over the network.

In addition, you can use the import directive in your IDL file to include C header files. This directive is similar to the #include directive in C, although import will cause the MIDL compiler to ignore any function prototypes in the imported file.

For more on the types of parameters supported and how they are handled by RPC, see the section titled "Parameter Passing in RPCs" later in this chapter.

IDL Attributes

Each parameter listed in an interface definition, as well as the interface itself, may have several different attributes associated with it. These attributes generally appear in brackets, as in the previous example, where [in] specifies that the nVal parameter is used as input only.

The most common sort of attribute deals with the direction of parameters as input or output of a function. This can be in, out or both (specified as [in,out]). In addition, there are many other sorts of attributes that may be specified. You will look at some of these later in this chapter as they apply to the sections where they are used.

The Application Configuration File (ACF)

In addition to the IDL file, you may use an *application configuration file* (ACF) to specify options that are local to the application—that is, options that do not affect how the RPC is processed over the network. Our example uses the very simple ACF file shown here:

```
[
    auto_handle
]
interface rpcfactorial
{
}
```

Use of an ACF file is optional. You may choose to incorporate the attributes of the ACF file into the IDL file, although the two files allow you to separate aspects of the interface that deal with over-the-wire issues and issues that are local to one machine.

In general, the header in the ACF file will contain one of the following attributes: auto_handle, implicit_handle, or explicit_handle. These attributes deal with how the client stubs handle binding of requests for this interface. You will see more on this later.

You may also specify the code or nocode attributes for a function or for the entire interface. These options specify whether the MIDL compiler will generate stub code for a given function or interface.

Using the MIDL Compiler

The MIDL compiler takes your IDL and ACF files and compiles them to generate several different C files. In most RPC applications, the MIDL compiler will output a header file that provides the C function declarations for the functions specified in the IDL file, as well as C files that implement the client and server functions. For this factorial example, the header file generated is RpcFact.h, and RpcFact_c.c and RpcFact_s.c implement the client and server stubs, respectively. The MIDL compiler may also be used in conjunction with other interfaces apart from RPC, such as distributed COM interfaces. In these cases, the MIDL compiler will generate additional output files.

The MIDL compiler can be executed from the command line, or you can add it to a custom build step for your Visual C++ project. To compile the IDL for this example, you use the following command line:

```
midl.exe /c_ext /ms_ext /app_config RpcFact.idl
```

The options in this line tell the MIDL compiler to use Microsoft extensions to C and IDL. The /app_config option tells the compiler to allow options normally found in an ACF file to appear in the IDL file, although the compiler will automatically look for an ACF file with the same name as the IDL file and compile it as needed. For more information on the many other options available to the MIDL compiler, try calling midl.exe with the /? option or see the online documentation. In most cases, the command line shown previously should be adequate.

The MIDL Compiler and Visual C++

You can also specify that Visual C++ use the MIDL compiler in a custom build step when building your Visual C++ projects. To do this, start by creating an IDL file and inserting it into your project. You can then specify a custom build step for the IDL file by opening the Project | Settings dialog, selecting the IDL file from an expanded view of the project on the left, and tabbing to the Custom Build page. Make sure that you have only the IDL file selected on the left, or you will change the way your whole build works.

On the Custom Build page, you should enter a command line such as the following:

```
midl.exe /e_ext /ms_ext /app_config $(InputPath)
```

You should also add the files generated by this step to the Output files list. For this example, these include RpcFact.h, RpcFact_s.c, and RpcFact_c.c. If you are using different names, your files will be named similarly.

It is also convenient to add the C files for the client and server stubs to the appropriate client and server projects. This will tell Visual C++ to compile the stubs as it would any other source file and link the generated object to your application automatically.

Developing the RPC Server

Once you have an interface defined, you need to create a process that will respond to requests for that interface, performing the requested operations and returning any results to the client. The process that does this is the RPC server.

Base Functions

The meat of any RPC operation is performed in the base function. This consists simply of what the function would be if it were a simple local function call. The base function for our example is found in RpcFact.c, as shown in the following:

```
#include <windows.h>
#include "RpcFact.h"
long RpcFactorial(long nVal)
{
    long nResult = 1;
    for(;nVal > 0; nVal--)
        nResult *= nVal;
    return (nResult);
}
```

You will notice that there is nothing special about this function that gives away the fact that it will be used for RPC, other than that the RpcFact.h file that is included is generated by the MIDL compiler and includes a few extra declarations.

As I mentioned earlier, it is generally easier to develop your server functions as plain local function first, then convert them to use RPC. As long as you keep the code for your server functions in separate files, this is relatively simple.

The RPC Server Body

The real work of making your functions available to RPC is done in the RPC server body. The code in the body is responsible for setting up the bindings for the RPC interfaces, registering them with the name service, and listening for RPC requests. This may seem like a lot of work, although I think that you will find that most of it is boilerplate that can be simply cut and pasted from server to server.

Protocol Sequences

One of the first things that the RPC server process is responsible for is declaring which protocol sequences it will use for accepting RPC requests. The protocols that are supported are specified by the strings you use in endpoint definitions in IDL, such as ncacn_ip_tcp or ncacn_np.

The RPC library provides several functions that you may use to specify the protocol sequence that your server will use. These functions also tell the library how to define the specific endpoint that the server will use to support an interface. To select a single protocol to use to receive RPC requests, you use one of the following functions, all beginning with RpcServerUseProtseq:

RpcServerUseProtseqEp() specifies a single protocol sequence and allows you to explicitly define the endpoint at runtime.

RpcServerUseProtseqIf() specifies a single protocol sequence, using the endpoint that was specified in the IDL file for the given interface.

RpcServerUseProtseq() also registers a single protocol sequence, but it tells the RPC runtime to assign an unused endpoint dynamically at runtime.

In addition, the following functions allow you to use all available protocols to support an interface:

RpcServerUseAllProtseqs()registers all available protocol sequences using dynamic endpoints.

RpcServerUseAllProtseqsIf()registers all available protocol sequences, using the endpoints specified in the IDL for the interface.

In this example, let's use RpcServerUseAllProtseqsIf() to register all available protocols, using the endpoints specified in the IDL file:

```
if(lRetVal = RpcServerUseAllProtseqsIf(1, rpcfactorial_v1_0_s_ifspec, NULL))
{
    cout << "Error in RpcServerUseAllProtseqsIf: " << lRetVal << endl;
    return(1);
}
```

The second parameter value is defined in RpcFact.h, which is generated by the MIDL compiler for you. This value is used to uniquely define the interface.

Registering the Interface

The next thing that the server will do is register the interfaces it supports. This adds an entry to an internal registry table used by the RPC runtime libraries to map the UUID in incoming RPC requests to the actual function that will implement the function. In most cases, you will need only a single implementation for each function, although it is possible to specify multiple implementations for the same function.

Registering an interface is done with the RpcServerRegisterIf() function. You may also use the RpcServerRegisterIfEx() function, which allows you to specify an auto-listen interface or to specify a callback function to use for security.

Our example uses RpcServerRegisterIf() to register a single implementation for the interface, as specified in the IDL file:

```
if(RpcServerRegisterIf(rpcfactorial_v1_0_s_ifspec, NULL, NULL))
{
    cout << "Error in RpcServerRegisterIf" << endl;
    return(1);
}
```

Exporting Bindings to the Name Service

The next step for your server to take is to export the binding for your interface to the name service. This will allow client applications to locate your server when it needs to make requests for this interface. However, if you plan to use only clients that connect to a predefined well-known endpoint for your interface, you do not need to register your interface with the name service.

To do this, you first get a list of the bindings that have been created to support this interface. The bindings are created for you when you call any of the RpcServerUse functions to choose protocol sequences to support the interface. RpcServerInqBindings() will return a binding vector structure, containing information about the bindings that the RPC library has generated.

This binding vector is then passed as one of the parameters to RpcNsBindingExport(), which will register the bindings with the name service.

Our example uses RpcServerInqBindings() to return the bindings that have been created and passes this to RpcNsBindingExport() to register the bindings with the name service:

```
if(RpcServerInqBindings(&bindVector))
{
    cout << "Error in RpcServerInqBindings" << endl;
    return(1);
}
if(RpcNsBindingExport(RPC_C_NS_SYNTAX_DEFAULT,
    (UCHAR *) "/.:/autorpc",
    rpcfactorial_v1_0_s_ifspec, bindVector, NULL))
{
    cout << "Error in RpcNsBindingExport" << endl;
    return(1);
}
```

Listening for Requests

Once you have selected a protocol sequence, registered the interface, and exported its bindings to the name service, you can use RpcServerListen() to notify the runtime library that your server is ready to start accepting client requests for the interfaces it supports. Here is the prototype for RpcServerListen():

```
RPC_STATUS RPC_ENTRY RpcServerListen(unsigned int  MinimumCallThreads,
    unsigned int  MaxCalls, unsigned int  DontWait);
```

RpcServerListen() allows you to specify the minimum number of threads that the server will use to service client requests and the maximum number of calls (or requests) that may be processed simultaneously. (Note that the specified maximum is only a suggestion, and not an absolute limit.) Allowing the server to process more than one request at a time can greatly increase the performance of the server, but you must make sure that your functions will work properly if they run in two threads at the same time. (For more on this, see Chapter 9, "Multithreading with MFC.")

The last parameter allows you to specify whether the call to RpcServerListen() will return immediately. If DontWait is FALSE, the call to RpcServerListen() will start up the server and process requests, returning only when RpcMgmtStopServerListening() is called from another thread of the server, from within an RPC handler, or from a client.

If DontWait is TRUE, RpcServerListen() will return as soon as it has done the setup necessary to start listening. The thread that called RpcServerListen() is then free to do whatever else it wants while RPC requests are being handled.

If you want to wait until RpcMgmtStopServerListening() is called, you can do so with the RpcMgmtWaitServerListen() function.

The complete body for the server used in the RpcFact sample is shown in Listing 18.1.

Listing 18.1. The RpcFact_s.c server program.

```c
#include <Windows.h>
#include <iostream.h>
#include <rpc.h>
#include "RpcFact.h"
#include "memstub.h"
main()
{
    RPC_BINDING_VECTOR *bindVector;
    RPC_STATUS lRetVal;
    if(lRetVal = RpcServerUseAllProtseqsIf(1, rpcfactorial_v1_0_s_ifspec, NULL))
    {
        cout << "Error in RpcServerUseAllProtseqsIf: " << lRetVal << endl;
        return(1);
    }
    if(RpcServerRegisterIf(rpcfactorial_v1_0_s_ifspec, NULL, NULL))
    {
        cout << "Error in RpcServerRegisterIf" << endl;
        return(1);
    }
    if(RpcServerInqBindings(&bindVector))
    {
        cout << "Error in RpcServerInqBindings" << endl;
        return(1);
    }
    if(RpcNsBindingExport(RPC_C_NS_SYNTAX_DEFAULT,
        (UCHAR *) "/.:/autorpc",
        rpcfactorial_v1_0_s_ifspec, bindVector, NULL))
    {
        cout << "Error in RpcNsBindingExport" << endl;
        return(1);
    }

    cout << "Calling RpcServerListen" << endl;
    if(RpcServerListen(1, 5, FALSE))
    {
        cout << "Error in RpcServerListen" << endl;
        return (0);
    }
    return(0);
} // end main
```

NOTE

The preceding example includes the file memstub.h, which implements memory allocation for RPC functions. For more on this see the section titled "Memory Allocation."

Building the Server

When building the server, you need to make sure to link with the OBJ file created when the server stubs are compiled. For this example, RpcFact_s.c compiles to RpcFact_s.obj. In addition, you need to link with the RPC runtime libraries rpcns4.lib and rpcrt4.lib. These are actually import libraries, which refer your server application to the RPC DLLs at runtime.

The RPC Client

Now that you have an RPC server up and running, let's take a look at what goes into developing an RPC client. One of the main goals of the RPC specification is to make client RPC calls as simple as possible—and it does just that. The following source code implements a simple client application for the factorial RPC server that you created earlier:

```
#include <windows.h>
#include <iostream.h>
#include <rpc.h>
#include <stdlib.h>
#include "..\RpcFact.h"
#include "..\memstub.h"
main()
{
    long nVal;
    cout << "calling rpcfact" << endl;
    nVal = RpcFactorial( 5);
    cout << "RpcFact returns: " << nVal << endl;
    return(0);
}
```

> **NOTE**
>
> In the preceding example, RpcFact.h and memstub.h are included from the parent directory. This is done to share these common files with the server project in the above directory.

As you can see, the call to RpcFactorial() looks just like any other local function call, even though the function is actually executed on a remote machine by way of an RPC server. The only things that you really need to do with the client application is make sure that you include the header file generated by the MIDL compiler (RpcFact.h, in this case) and that you link with the client stub object (RpcFact_c.obj from RpcFact_c.c) and the RPC runtime libraries (rpcns4.lib and rpcrt4.lib).

Of course, this example is the simplest case. It uses automatic dynamic binding to locate a server for the interface and does not implement any exception handling. You explore different ways of binding to a server and exception handling later on in this chapter, but for now, take a closer look at how the RPC mechanism works with passing parameters.

Parameter Passing in RPCs

In the previous example, you used parameters of type long. However, you can freely use any of the base types shown in Table 18.2, including structures and unions made up of the base types.

Table 18.2. RPC parameter base types.

Base type	Description
byte	8 bits
char	Maps to unsigned char in C
small	8-bit integer
short	16-bit integer
long	32-bit integer
hyper	64-bit integer
float	32-bit floating-point number
double	64-bit floating-point number
boolean	8-bit Boolean value
wchar_t	16-bit value, used for Unicode
handle_t	Used for binding handles

Actually, the Microsoft implementation also supports the int type for 32-bit platforms, but this should be avoided. The void * type is also supported, but only as it is used in the specialized case of context handles, as you will see later.

It is also a good idea to explicitly define your char variables as signed or unsigned. This will help avoid conflicts between applications for different machines.

Arrays and Strings

Arrays pose their own particular problems when you send them across a network. First of all, you must be able to specify the number of elements in the array. Secondly, you may be able to optimize performance by sending only a portion of the array that is relevant to the current function. The following example shows the IDL for a function that has the size of an array and the array itself passed to it:

```
long myArrayFunc([in] long lSize, [in, size_is(lSize)] long myArray[]);
```

IDL also allows you to use the first_is, last_is, length_is, and max_is keywords to work with arrays.

Additionally, you can use the string attribute for arrays of type char, wchar_t, or byte. This tells the RPC runtime to handle the array as a null-terminated string—the runtime then computes the length of the string to pass.

Unions

You can use unions in the parameters that you pass to and from RPC functions; however, you need to use some special IDL constructs, including the switch_type and switch_is keywords. Because unions may be of different types and sizes, the additional IDL tells the RPC library how to determine what data is actually contained in the union so that it can pack the data in the union into a network message. For more on the specifics of using unions with RPC, see the online documentation.

Pointers

The idea of passing a pointer in a remote procedure call to a different computer may seem a bit strange to you—and it should. If you simply passed a pointer off to another computer, it would be meaningless in the remote machine's address space. This is why the void * type is not allowed in RPC.

However, you can pass non-void pointers as parameters to RPC functions, although this does not result in just passing the value of the pointer. The RPC mechanism implements pointer emulation. This is capable of passing both a pointer and the memory that it points to, doing the remote processing, and returning the memory to its original spot on the client. Because the only way to pass parameters by reference in C is to pass a pointer, it is very useful to be able to pass pointers in RPC.

In the most general case, all the memory involved must be passed to the function, manipulated, then passed back. This could get to be a rather costly operation. To help optimize this interaction, IDL provides for the definition of three types of pointers, as specified by the ref, unique, or ptr attributes, that may be used to describe individual parameters, structure members, or function return types.

■ *Full pointers,* specified by the ptr attribute, are the most flexible sort of pointer, but they are also the least efficient, because they do not allow the stubs to make any assumptions in dealing with them.

■ *Unique pointers,* specified by the unique attribute, tell the stubs to assume that no other pointer involved in the RPC can point to the same memory as this pointer.

■ *Reference pointers,* specified by the ref attribute, are the most restrictive type of pointer used by IDL—and also the most efficient. A reference pointer has the same restrictions as unique pointers, as well as a few others: A ref pointer cannot be NULL, it must always point to valid memory, and the value of the reference pointer cannot change. Reference pointers should be used anytime you are passing a simple parameter by reference.

You can specify a default pointer type to use by using the `pointer_default` attribute in your IDL file. This pointer type will be used for all pointers that do not specify an explicit pointer type attribute.

Memory Allocation

For full and unique pointers, the server can modify the value of any pointers passed to it. This includes assigning a newly allocated memory address to the pointer. When this occurs, the contents of the new memory are passed back to the client, which then allocates new memory and copies the data returned from the server.

When the stubs need to allocate or deallocate memory in these cases, they rely on a pair of helper functions called `midl_user_allocate()` and `midl_user_free()`. In general, these should be simple wrappers for the C++ `new` and `delete` operators or the C `malloc()` and `free()` functions. In the RpcFact example that we have been using in this chapter, these functions are implemented in the `memstub.h` file:

```
void __RPC_FAR * __RPC_API midl_user_allocate(size_t len)
{
    return(new(unsigned char [len]));
}
void __RPC_API midl_user_free(void __RPC_FAR * ptr)
{
    delete(ptr);
}
```

It is also permissible for an RPC call to set the value of a full or unique pointer to `NULL`, even if it previously referenced data. The client application may then be left with a block of memory that is allocated but no longer has a pointer to it, causing a phenomenon called *memory orphaning*, which generally results in a memory leak. If your application will be dealing with pointers in this manner, you need to find ways of handling this.

Binding to an RPC Server

Before any remote calls can be processed, the client must create a binding handle, which is a data structure that contains information about a logical connection between the client and an RPC server. The binding handle is similar to a file handle; you cannot manipulate it directly, but will create it with calls to the RPC runtime library and will use it in making your remote calls.

There are two different methods that your client application can bind to a server. The first is *automatic binding,* where the client stubs will handle all the binding chores for you, as you saw in the previous example.

In addition, you may bind to a server manually. Although this requires a bit more work in your client code, *manual binding* is more efficient than automatic binding, which actually creates a new binding for each RPC call made. Manual binding also allows you to use a context handle, which may be used to maintain state information about the client on the RPC server. This is not available with automatic binding.

Automatic Binding

Automatic binding is often the most convenient way of binding when your application does not care which specific server handles the RPC and when you do not need to maintain any state information between the client and the server. This method of binding does not require any special code in your client apps to deal with binding handles—the client stubs will do it all for you.

To use automatic binding, you simply need to specify the `auto_handle` attribute in the ACF file that is fed into the MIDL compiler, as in this example:

```
[auto_handle]
interface rpcfactorial
{
}
```

The `auto_handle` attribute is used by default if no other handle attribute is specified or if you omit the ACF file altogether.

The possible downside of auto binding is that it requires a name service to be accessible to the client somewhere on the network. If you are using NT, the Microsoft Locator can provide this for you, although if you are running a network of only Windows 95 (or Win3.1), you may want to look at manual binding. In addition, your RPC server must export the interfaces it supports to the name service with `RpcNsBindingExport()`, as you saw earlier.

Manual Binding

Binding your client to an RPC server manually requires more work on the client side, but it also allows you to take advantage of some of the features of RPC that are not available by using auto handles. Manual binding is also more efficient than automatic binding, particularly if you will be making many RPC calls.

The handles used in binding to an RPC server come in three different flavors: *primitive handles, user-defined handles,* and *context handles.* For the time being, you will look at primitive handles, although you will learn about the other types later. Primitive handles are defined as type `handle_t` in both the IDL file for an interface and in the client code.

A binding handle can also be used in your RPCs in two different ways. In *explicit binding,* you create a binding handle that is passed as an argument to each RPC call that will use that binding handle. The alternative is *implicit binding,* where the binding handle is not passed as an argument.

Creating a Binding Handle

In cases where you are using a well-known port or name for the endpoint of an interface, you can create a binding handle directly from the code in your client application. However, in most cases, it is best to get the binding handle from the name service, as we will see in the next section.

To create a binding handle "from scratch," let's use the `RpcBindingFromStringBinding()` function. This function creates a binding handle from a string binding, which is an ASCII string containing the object (or interface) UUID, the protocol sequence, the server's network address, the endpoint, and any endpoint options. An example string binding might look like this:

```
E2BC6204-53BF-11D0-B338-444553540000@ncacn_ip_tcp:192.9.200.93[5150]
```

Working with a string like this can obviously be a bit unwieldy at times, so the RPC library provides the `RpcStringBindingCompose()` function, which takes parameters for the individual elements of the string binding. Using this, you could create the previous string binding with a call code like this:

```
RPC_STATUS status;
char * pszUuid = "E2BC6204-53BF-11D0-B338-444553540000";
char * pszProtSeq = "ncacn_ip_tcp";
char * pszNetAddr = "192.9.200.93";
char * pszEndpoint = "5150";
char * pszOptions = NULL;
char pszStringBind[256];
status = RpcStringBindingCompose(pszUuid, pszProtSeq, pszNetAddr,
          pszEndpoint, pszOptions, &pszStringBind);
```

In addition, you can use the `RpcBindingToStringBinding()` function to generate a binding string from a binding handle that has already been created.

To create the binding handle, your client will include code something like this:

```
handle_t hBinding;
status = RpcBindingFromStringBinding(pszStringBind, &hBinding);
if(status != RPC_S_OK)
    // An error occurred creating the handle
```

If the binding handle is created successfully—that is, if `RpcBindingFromStringBinding()` returns `RPC_S_OK`—the binding handle is ready to use in making RPC calls. When you are finished with the binding handle, you should call `RpcBindingFree()` to release it.

Retrieving a Binding Handle from the Name Service

In most cases, the preferred method of obtaining a binding handle is to retrieve it from the name service. This eliminates the need for the client to worry about the specific endpoint used for an interface or finding a server that supports it.

To retrieve entries from the name service, you will begin with a call to `RpcNsBindingImportBegin()` to initialize an import context, which is then used by `RpcNsBindingImportNext()` to retrieve an individual entry.

Your client application can create the import context and get the first binding handle that matches with code that looks something like this:

```
RPC_STATUS status;
RPC_NS_HANDLE hImportContext;
RPC_BINDING_HANDLE hBinding;
status = RpcNsBindingImportBegin(RPC_C_NS_SYNTAX_DEFAULT,
NULL, rpcfactorial_v1_0_s_ifspec, NULL, &hImportContext);
status = RpcNsBindingImportNext(hImportContext, &hBinding);
```

If the call to RpcNsBindingImportNext() is successful, the binding handle that is returned can be used for RPCs. If for some reason this entry is unacceptable, you can call RpcNsBinding ImportNext() again to retrieve additional matching entries. When no more entries are found, RpcNsBindingImportNext() will return RPC_S_NO_MORE_BINDINGS.

When you have found a binding handle that is acceptable for your client, you should call RpcNsBindingImportDone() to release the import context:

```
status = RpcNsBindingImportDone(hImportContext);
```

> **TIP**
>
> A binding handle that is returned from the name service may not always point to an RPC server that is currently up and running. You may want to try a remote call using the binding handle before you release the import context. This way, if you find that the server is not up, you can try a new binding.

In addition to the import method, you can use the RpcNsBindingLookup family of functions. These functions work similarly to those mentioned previously, but allow you to work with a list, or vector, of available entries, rather than one at a time. These functions include RpcNsBindingLookupBegin(), RpcNsBindingLookupNext(), and RpcBindingLookupDone(). You also need to use RpcNsBindingSelect() to retrieve a handle from the list of available bindings.

When you are finished with the binding handle, you should call RpcBindingFree() to release it.

Implicit Binding

In implicit binding, the binding handle is stored in a global variable that is declared in the client stub output from the MIDL compiler. The client application will bind the implicit handle once, before any RPC calls are made, then each call will use that handle implicitly.

To use implicit binding, you need to specify an implicit handle in the ACF file that is fed to the MIDL compiler to generate the client stub code. An ACF file that does this would look like the following:

```
[
    implicit_handle(handle_t hFactBind)
]
```

```
interface rpcfactorial
{
}
```

This generates a global variable (`hFactBind`) of type `handle_t`. Your client application must initialize this handle, using one of the binding methods shown previously, before any RPCs can be made using this interface.

Explicit Binding

You may also bind to a server explicitly for each RPC call that is made. This allows your client application to distribute processing around the network by sending the same RPC call to different servers simultaneously. To use explicit binding, each RPC function must have a binding handle passed to it as a parameter.

You can specify that a function use explicit binding in the IDL file that defines the interface. This is done by specifying a binding handle as the first parameter passed to the function. (In the Microsoft implementation, this does not necessarily have to be the first parameter, but DCE implementations do require this, so it's a good idea.) Here is an IDL file that specifies explicit binding:

```
[
    uuid (C16F6562-520D-11D0-B338-444553540000),
    version(1.0)
]
interface rpcfactorial
{
    long RpcFactorial([in] handle_t hl,
                      [in] long nVal);
}
```

A client application that wants to call RPCs using explicit binding must first create a binding handle, as you saw previously, and pass it to each RPC that is to be called with that binding.

User-Defined Handles

In cases where your client application wants to associate some other data along with a particular binding, you may find it useful to use a user-defined binding handle.

To use a user-defined binding handle, you must first define your user-defined handle in the IDL file for the interface. The following IDL file gives an example of this:

```
[
    uuid (C16F6562-520D-11D0-B338-444553540000),
    version(1.0)
]
interface rpcfactorial
{
typedef struct {
    unsigned char * pszBindingString;
    unsigned char MyData[32];
```

```
} MY_DATA_TYPE;
typedef [handle] MY_DATA_TYPE * MY_HANDLE_TYPE;

    long RpcFactorial([in] MY_HANDLE_TYPE h1,
                      [in] long nVal);
}
```

This example defines a data structure that can be passed as the first parameter to calls to `RpcFactorial()`. However, sooner or later, all RPC calls need to get a primitive binding handle from somewhere in order to connect to the server. For user-defined handles, the primitive handle comes from one of two helper functions that you must implement in order to use user-defined handles.

For each user-defined handle type that you will use, you must implement a bind function and an unbind function. The specific function names are based on the name of the handle type you define in the IDL file. The prototype for the bind function to be used with the previous IDL file looks like this:

```
RPC_BINDING_HANDLE __RPC_USER MY_HANDLE_TYPE_bind(MY_HANDLE_TYPE mhl);
```

This function should return a valid binding handle based on the data in your handle type. This may include importing a handle from the name service, looking up an entry in your own internal tables, or any other way you feel like finding a binding handle.

The second helper function is called after each RPC call completes. It is passed the original user-defined handle that you passed to the RPC, as well as the primitive handle that was returned by the bind function and used for the RPC. This function can be used to clean up anything that was done in the bind function for this particular call. The prototype for the unbind function looks like this:

```
void __RPC_USER MY_HANDLE_TYPE_unbind(MY_HANDLE_TYPE mhl, RPC_BINDING_HANDLE hl);
```

Context Handles

In cases where you want to allow the RPC server to maintain context information about a particular client application, you can use context handles. These are often useful for maintaining state information or large amounts of data between individual RPC calls. In addition to pointing to the context information, the context handle will also serve as a binding handle.

To use a context handle, you must first define it in the IDL file for the interface. The context handle will also appear as a parameter to the functions that will use it. Here is an excerpt of an IDL file that uses a context handle:

```
typedef [context_handle] void * PCONTEXT_HANDLE_TYPE;
typedef [ref] PCONTEXT_HANDLE_TYPE * PPCONTEXT_HANDLE_TYPE;
long RemoteInit([out] PPCONTEXT_HANDLE_TYPE pphContext,
    [in] long lMyInitParameter);
long RemoteDoStuff([in] PPCONTEXT_HANDLE_TYPE pphContext,
    [in] long lMyOtherParameter);
long RemoteDone([in] PPCONTEXT_HANDLE_TYPE pphContext);
```

The server should create a new context for a client when the client calls a function such as in this RemoteInit() example. To do this, it will generally allocate a new structure to contain whatever context information you will need and then return a pointer, or similar index, to this structure to the client.

The context handle is opaque to the client application—it can use the handle only in subsequent calls to RPC functions on that server and cannot touch the data directly. Actually, the data resides only on the server. Because of this, it is fine for the server to use a pointer into its own memory space as the actual value of the context handle that is returned to the client.

The context handle can also serve as a binding handle, as you might use in explicit binding. However, the context handle cannot be used for binding until it is initialized by the RPC call that initializes it. This means that calls to functions like the RemoteInit() example use an alternate binding handle. If you do not provide one explicitly, an auto handle will be used.

If you are dynamically allocating memory in your context information, you want to be able to clean up on the server side in the event that the client application terminates the connection before the context is freed. You can add this to your server by adding a context rundown routine, which is named based on the typedef name that you used in the IDL file for the context handle. For the context handle in the previous example, the prototype for this function would look like this:

```
void __RPC_USER PCONTEXT_HANDLE_TYPE_rundown (PCONTEXT_HANDLE_TYPE hContext);
```

It is also possible that the RPC server goes away while the client has a context handle open. In this case, the client will want to reset its context information. This can be done with the RpcSsDestroyClientContext() function, which will clean up the memory allocated on the client side to manage the context handle.

Exception Handling for RPCs

Although the code for an RPC client may be deceptively simple, considering the work it does in binding to remote servers and handling the details of parameter passing over a network, the complexity of the underlying RPC mechanisms can produce many different errors that you would never see in plain old local function calls.

Due to this, you should pay special attention to exception handling in your applications that will be using RPC. Any exceptions that occur in the server application, including its stubs and the RPC runtime library, will be propagated back to the client application.

To help in handling these exceptions, the Microsoft implementation of RPC provides the macros listed below. Note that in Win32 implementations, these macros map directly to the __try, __except, and __finally family of exception handling constructs provided in Visual C++. If you are developing only for Win32, it is best to use the __try syntax directly, although the following macros can be used for compatibility with MS-DOS and Win3.1 systems:

```
RpcTryFinally
RpcFinally
RpcEndFinally
RpcTryExcept
RpcExcept
RpcEndExcept
RpcExceptionCode
RpcAbnormalTermination
```

Summary

In this chapter, you learned how the OSF standard for Remote Procedure Calls (RPC) is implemented by Microsoft for Visual C++ and how it can be used to develop applications. You saw how to develop client and server applications that use RPC to distribute processing over a network of potentially heterogeneous computers.

You also explored how to define the interfaces that are used in RPC, including IDL syntax to define the functions of an interface and the ways in which various types of parameters are specified in IDL files, which are then compiled by the MIDL compiler to generate stub functions that help hide much of the processing involved in RPCs.

You took a look at how to implement an RPC server to service requests for RPCs from clients, including how to implement the RPC functions and export them to a name service, which clients can use to locate appropriate RPC servers.

This chapter also discussed how to implement an RPC client, including the use of automatic binding, implicit binding, and explicit binding, as well as how to create binding handles manually or retrieve them from a name service. You learned how to use user-defined handles and context handles.

This chapter should serve as a good starting point in your development of distributed systems using RPC, although there are also many other features of the RPC environment that are beyond the scope of this text. For more information on the RPC environment, refer to the online documentation for the Win32 SDK.

19

Messaging API (MAPI)

by David Bennett

It seems that almost everyone is using some type of electronic mail these days. In fact, many people are using several e-mail systems, including mainframe-based systems, mail systems on a LAN, Internet mail, and messaging environments such as Lotus Notes, Microsoft Exchange, or Novell's GroupWise.

In the past, trying to use all these systems together could be quite difficult, particularly if you are developing applications that interact with several different messaging systems. To help you develop applications that work with different messaging systems, or just to add simple e-mail capabilities to your apps, Microsoft supports the Messaging API, or MAPI.

The MAPI standard allows you to work with a wide variety of messaging systems by using a single API, instead of a different programming interface for each messaging system. MAPI can also be used to work with messaging systems other than traditional e-mail—fax and voice mail, for example.

In this chapter, you will take a look at MAPI and what it can do for you. You will explore simple uses of MAPI, such as adding the ability to send e-mail to your apps, as well as examine the features of MAPI that allow you to develop your own messaging applications.

MAPI Architecture

The standard for the messaging API is a part of Microsoft's Windows Open Systems Architecture, or WOSA. MAPI provides a specification that details how both client applications and messaging service providers can interact with each other through a centralized messaging subsystem, using common API calls.

The components of the MAPI architecture can be grouped into two basic categories: client applications and service providers. *Client applications* are used to provide interaction with the user, and *service providers* are used to provide a wide range of different services that client applications may use by way of the messaging API.

Client Applications

Client applications that use MAPI fall into three basic categories: messaging-aware, messaging-enabled, and messaging-based applications.

Messaging-aware applications are generally intended to perform some other primary task, such as word processing or spreadsheet tasks, but implement some basic messaging features, such as the ability to send a document over e-mail from within the application.

On the other hand, a *messaging-enabled application* requires the use of a messaging system and is intended primarily to perform several different sorts of messaging operations.

The *messaging-based application* requires access to a wide range of messaging operations, including addressing, storage, and transport services. This sort of application is designed to work without the user having to be concerned with the underlying messaging system, such as group scheduling applications.

Service Providers

Service providers are used to implement the underlying services that a client application can access through the messaging API. The three main types of service providers are message store providers, address book providers, and transport providers.

Message store providers are a sort of warehouse for messages. They are used to hold messages in a hierarchical structure, usually contained in persistent storage of some sort, such as a disk file. Message store providers are also responsible for implementing the interfaces that client applications and other service providers can use to work with the messages held in the message store. The Win32 operating systems supply their own message store provider, known as Personal Folders.

Address book providers maintain a list of addresses used for sending messages. The address book provider is also responsible for implementing the interfaces that other applications use to gain access to the addresses held in the address book. The Win32 operating systems supply their own address book implementation, called the Personal Address Book (PAB).

Transport providers are responsible for the transmission of messages between systems. This includes any work that must be done to establish remote connections and send and receive messages in the appropriate formats, using the appropriate protocols. Transport providers are also responsible for receiving messages from remote systems, converting their format as needed, and storing them in the local message store.

The MAPI service providers that are available on a given system are determined by the MAPI profiles for that system. As you will see soon, the MAPI profile tells the messaging subsystem which of the service provider DLLs to load.

The MAPI Spooler

The MAPI spooler is a separate process within the messaging subsystem, which also includes the various messaging APIs. The MAPI spooler is responsible for accepting messages to be sent from a message store and forwarding them to a transport provider. Conversely, it is responsible for receiving messages from remote messaging systems by way of a transport provider and passing them on to a message store.

The MAPI spooler also implements store-and-forward functionality, where it will hold messages until the messaging system that they are intended for becomes available. Some message store-and-transport providers may, however, bypass the MAPI spooler.

The MAPI spooler is also responsible for coordinating the efforts of the various service providers on a system. It is the spooler that will load the DLLs that implement the individual service providers.

Information about the service providers that are currently enabled on the local machine is kept in the registry under the following key:

`HKEY_CURRENT_USER\Software\Microsoft\Windows Messaging Subsystem\Profiles`

These profiles are not formatted to be read or modified directly with the registry editor—entries are generally added when you install new service providers. You also can edit these entries by using the Microsoft Exchange client (Outlook in Office 97), by selecting the Services command from its Tools menu.

The MAPI APIs

The messaging API is not really a single API—it is a family of related APIs. The MAPI specification provides interfaces for both client applications and service providers in several forms, including simple MAPI, common messaging calls (CMC) API, extended MAPI, and OLE messaging.

Simple MAPI includes a set of C APIs used to work with messaging. It includes functions that allow your application to establish a MAPI session, send and receive messages, and shut down the MAPI session. For most messaging-aware applications that perform basic messaging operations, simple MAPI should be sufficient.

Common messaging calls (CMC) API is similar to simple MAPI, although it uses a different set of functions. CMC is an implementation of the X.400 API Association (XAPIA) specification for common messaging calls, which is intended to provide a platform-independent API for working with messaging. For new applications, you should consider using CMC rather than simple MAPI, due to its greater standardization and portability, as well as some additional functionality. However, if you must use simple MAPI, you will find that it works very much like CMC and is documented in the online help.

Extended MAPI provides a greater degree of control over the components of a messaging system than simple MAPI allows. Extended MAPI is based on Microsoft's Common Object Model (COM) specification and uses an object-oriented approach to the interface. Extended MAPI should be used in message-based applications that require more direct interaction with the message store, address book, and transport providers.

The OLE messaging API is primarily intended for higher-level application development environments, such as Visual Basic. MAPI OLE messaging provides greater functionality than simple MAPI, but it is not as full-featured as extended MAPI.

Availability of MAPI Interfaces

In addition to the service providers that are available on a machine, the registry also holds information about which of the APIs are currently available. For Windows NT, the APIs that are currently available on the local machine will have entries in the registry under the following key:

`HKEY_LOCAL_MACHINE\SOFTWARE\Microsoft\Windows Messaging Subsystem`

For Windows 95, these settings are included in the [Mail] section of win.ini, which is in your Windows directory.

Here are the individual entries for each API:

Simple MAPI	`MAPI=1`
Extended MAPI	`MAPIX=1`
CMC	`CMC=1`
OLE Messaging	`OLEMessaging=1`

If an entry for a given API is 1, the API can be used by your application. If the entry is 0 or does not exist, the given API has not been installed on the local machine.

In addition, the version of the messaging API installed is given in the MAPIXVER entry.

MAPI Support in MFC

The Microsoft Foundation Classes provide a simple mechanism to allow your application to send its documents to other users, using MAPI. This is implemented in two CDocument member functions—OnFileSendMail() and OnUpdateFileSendMail(). OnFileSendMail() serializes the document's data and includes it as an attachment in a new mail message. It then invokes the user interface of the user's default messaging system to add addressing and text to the mail message. This is the only MAPI functionality that is directly encapsulated in MFC, although you can use any of the APIs we have discussed in this chapter from within an MFC application.

Adding MAPI Support

There are several ways that you can go about adding MFC CDocument MAPI support to your application. You can add MAPI support to new applications with an option in AppWizard, or you can add the MAPI component from the component gallery, although it is often easiest to add MFC MAPI support by hand.

With AppWizard

If you are creating a new project, the easiest method is to choose the MAPI (Messaging API) option from the MFC AppWizard. This will add a Send command to your application's File menu and will add the appropriate message map entries for the CDocument MAPI functions. Of course, the message map is added only for the CDocument-derived class that AppWizard creates for you—if you add new document classes, you need to add the appropriate message map entries manually.

With the MAPI Component

If you have already created your project, you can add similar functionality by adding the MAPI component to your project with Project | Add to Project | Components and Controls | Developer Studio Components. When you add the MAPI component to your project, you will be prompted for which document class to add MAPI support to—if you want to add support for several document classes, you need to add the component once for each document class.

Adding the MAPI component will also add some "temporary" code to the InitInstance() member of your CWinApp class. This code attempts to add a Send command to your File menu, although you should add the menu item yourself and delete the code that the MAPI component inserts.

By Hand

In many cases, using the MAPI component may actually be more work than just adding the appropriate code by hand, so let's take a look at just how to do this. This should also explain more about just what the AppWizard has done when you choose to add MAPI support. You can manually add MAPI send support to your MFC apps with the following steps:

1. Add a menu item for the Send command. The menu item should have an ID of ID_FILE_SEND_MAIL. (You can use whatever ID you like, but this is the standard command ID.) By convention, the Send item is generally found on the File menu, although you may choose to place it elsewhere.

2. Add entries to your message map. For each of your CDocument classes, you should add the following message map entries:

```
ON_COMMAND(ID_FILE_SEND_MAIL, OnFileSendMail)
ON_UPDATE_COMMAND_UI(ID_FILE_SEND_MAIL, OnUpdateFileSendMail)
```

You might be tempted to add these with ClassWizard, but it is easier to add these by hand, because you will not be adding an implementation for these handlers. The framework will locate the handlers from within the CDocument class. If you add the message maps with ClassWizard, you have to delete the implementations that it generates for the two handler functions.

The OnFileSendMail() handler will check to see whether a message service is available, then serialize your document and add it as an attachment to a new mail message. The user interface for the messaging system is then invoked to allow the user to add addresses and such.

The OnUpdateFileSendMail() handler is used to update the state of the Send menu item, depending on whether a messaging service is available.

3. Build your app and start sending documents!

Common Messaging Calls

The common messaging calls (CMC) API provides a simple way to quickly add messaging capabilities to your client applications, without having to be concerned with the complexity of the underlying messaging system. By using CMC, your application can support a wide range of different messaging systems, including those supported by MAPI on Microsoft systems, as well as other messaging systems supported on platforms like UNIX.

The CMC API allows your application to work with a simplified model of the messaging system. From a CMC application's point of view, the messaging system consists of a directory, a submission queue, and a receiving mailbox. This same virtual architecture is found in Microsoft's implementation of CMC, which uses MAPI in its internal implementation, as well as other implementations of CMC, which do not use MAPI.

Most of the definitions and function prototypes that you will need for writing CMC applications are included in xcmc.h. The implementation of the CMC API is found in MAPI32.DLL, although the CMC functions are not currently exported by the MAPI32.LIB import library. You need to dynamically load MAPI32.DLL with a call to LoadLibrary(), then find the address of each function with a call to GetProcAddress(), as you saw in Chapter 10, "Dynamic Link Libraries (DLLs)." Make sure that the function pointers you use are defined to take the proper parameter list and return the correct type for the actual CMC calls. If these are off by a byte or two, your app will most likely go down in flames with a corrupt stack.

Starting a Session

All the messaging operations that you will perform in CMC are done within the context of a messaging session. The CMC session is established by a call to cmc_logon(), which will verify the user account with the message service, set up the settings for the session, and return a session handle that will be used in future CMC calls.

The cmc_logon() function takes many different parameters, including the message service to use, user name and password, the character set to use, a handle for the parent of any dialogs created by cmc_logon(), the version of CMC to use, and option flags:

```
CMC_return_code cmc_logon (CMC_string service, CMC_string user,
    CMC_string password, CMC_object_identifier character_set,
    CMC_ui_id ui_id, CMC_uint16 caller_CMC_version,
    CMC_flags logon_flags, CMC_session_id FAR * session,
    CMC_extension FAR * logon_extensions);
```

You will learn the usage of the logon_extensions parameter later in this section when you look at using CMC extensions.

You may also use cmc_query_configuration() to get information about the current setup of CMC, including the default user and messages service, user logon requirements, and many other things.

When you are finished with a session, you should close the session with a call to cmc_logoff().

If you successfully opened a CMC session with cmc_logon(), you can get an extended MAPI session handle by calling scMAPIFromCMC(). This allows you to use the same session for CMC calls and extended MAPI calls, which, in turn, allows you to use CMC calls for basic messaging operations and extended MAPI calls for advanced functions not available via the CMC API.

Listing 19.1 shows how you can load the MAPI32.DLL library, get the function addresses for the CMC functions, use cmc_query_configuration() to determine whether the CMC implementation provides a dialog box, and initialize a session with cmc_logon().

Listing 19.1. Initialization functions for CMC.

```
#include "xcmc.h"
HMODULE hMAPILib;
CMC_return_code cmcStatus;
CMC_session_id cmcSession;
CString tmpStr;
CMC_boolean bUiAvail;

// Define function pointers
typedef CMC_return_code (FAR PASCAL *LPFNCMCLOGON)(CMC_string,
          CMC_string, CMC_string, CMC_enum, CMC_ui_id,
          CMC_uint16, CMC_flags, CMC_session_id FAR *,
          CMC_extension FAR *);
LPFNCMCLOGON lpfncmc_logon;
typedef CMC_return_code (FAR PASCAL *LPFNCMCQUERYCONF)(
          CMC_session_id, CMC_enum, CMC_buffer,
          CMC_extension FAR *);
LPFNCMCQUERYCONF lpfncmc_query_configuration;

// Load DLL
hMAPILib = LoadLibrary("MAPI32.DLL");
// Get function addresses
lpfncmc_logon = (LPFNCMCLOGON)GetProcAddress(hMAPILib, "cmc_logon");
lpfncmc_query_configuration = (LPFNCMCQUERYCONF)GetProcAddress(hMAPILib,
                                       "cmc_query_configuration");

// Check configuration of default logon
cmcStatus = (*lpfncmc_query_configuration)(
          0,                       // Query default settings
          CMC_CONFIG_UI_AVAIL,     // Logon UI available?
          &bUiAvail,               // Return buffer
          NULL);                   // No extensions
if(cmcStatus != CMC_SUCCESS)
{
    // Handle error…
}
else
    if(bUiAvail)
        printf("Logon UI is available");

// Create new session using defaults
```

```
cmcStatus = (*lpfncmc_logon)(NULL, NULL, NULL,
                NULL, 0, CMC_VERSION,
                CMC_LOGON_UI_ALLOWED | CMC_ERROR_UI_ALLOWED,
                &cmcSession, NULL);
if(cmcStatus != CMC_SUCCESS)
{
    // Handle error…
}
```

Sending Messages with CMC

The CMC API provides two functions for sending messages. The first, cmc_send_documents(), provides a simple method for sending messages. The more general cmc_send() is a bit more involved, but provides greater flexibility.

cmc_send_documents()

The function cmc_send_documents() includes all the functionality that you will need to send a message. It even creates a session for you, if you have not already done so with cmc_logon(). The following is the prototype for cmc_send_documents():

```
CMC_return_code cmc_send_documents ( CMC_string recipient_addresses,
    CMC_string subject, CMC_string text_note, CMC_flags send_doc_flags,
    CMC_string file_paths, CMC_string file_names, CMC_string delimiter,
    CMC_ui_id ui_id );
```

This function allows you to pass simple ASCII strings for most of the parameters. For the recipient_addresses, file_paths, and file_names strings, you may specify multiple values in the same string, separated by the delimiter character passed in delimiter. The recipient addresses can be either a specific address, such as bobjones@somewhere.com, or a recipient's name as it appears in the address book or other name service, such as Bob Jones.

In addition to specifying all the parameters for a new message, you can use a dialog provided by the messaging system by specifying CMC_SEND_UI_REQUESTED in the send_doc_flags parameter. This will allow the user to use a general-purpose new message dialog to select addressees and enter the text of the message, as well as attach files. If you use this UI option, any values that you specify for the message will appear as default values in the dialog. If you are using a UI from the service provider, you can specify a handle for the parent of the send dialog in ui_id, although specifying 0 is usually sufficient.

Your app can provide general message send functionality by calling cmc_send_documents() using the message service's UI:

```
cmcStatus = (*lpfncmc_send_documents)(NULL, NULL, NULL,
                CMC_SEND_UI_REQUESTED | CMC_LOGON_UI_ALLOWED |
CMC_ERROR_UI_ALLOWED,
                NULL, NULL, NULL, 0);
```

This example also makes use of the CMC_LOGON_UI_ALLOWED and CMC_ERROR_UI_ALLOWED flags, which will allow the message service to handle any logon or error handling tasks with its own UI, if it provides a UI for these tasks.

A user interface may not be provided by all service providers, although the message service provided with Win32 provides a full-featured send UI.

A call to cmc_send_documents() that does not use the UI might look something like this:

```
cmcStatus = (*lpfncmc_send_documents)("to:Bob Jones, cc:Jim Smith",
              "Very Important Subject",
              "It's time for lunch. Where to?",
              0,
              "C:\\tmp\\menu1.txt,C:\\tmp\\menu2.txt",
              "Chico's Menu, Q's Menu",
              ",",
              0);
```

cmc_send()

For greater control of the messages sent from within your application, you can use the cmc_send() function:

```
CMC_return_code cmc_send ( CMC_session_id session, CMC_message FAR * message,
    CMC_flags send_flags, CMC_ui_id ui_id, CMC_extension FAR * send_extensions);
```

In addition to the session, flags, ui_id, and extensions, this function takes the address of a CMC_message structure to specify the message that will be sent. This structure contains information about the message, including its contents, recipients, and any attachments:

```
typedef struct {
    CMC_message_reference FAR   *message_reference;
    CMC_string                  message_type;
    CMC_string                  subject;
    CMC_time                    time_sent;
    CMC_string                  text_note;
    CMC_recipient FAR           *recipients;
    CMC_attachment FAR          *attachments;
    CMC_flags                   message_flags;
    CMC_extension FAR           *message_extensions;
} CMC_message;
```

The CMC_message structure includes pointers to an array of CMC_recipient structures for the addressees and an array of CMC_attachment structures to indicate any file attachments. When filling in each of these variable-length arrays, you must specify CMC_RECIP_LAST_ELEMENT in the recip_flags field of the last CMC_recipient structure, or CMC_ATT_LAST_ELEMENT in the attach_flags element of the last CMC_attachment structure.

As with cmc_send_documents(), you can allow the user to use the send dialog provided by the messaging service by specifying CMC_SEND_UI_REQUESTED in the send_flags.

Listing 19.2 shows how you can initialize a CMC_message structure and use cmc_send() to send it.

Listing 19.2. Initializing and sending a CMC message.

```
CMC_message Msg;
CMC_recipient RecipIn;
CMC_attachment myAtt[2];
CMC_time tTime;
HMODULE hMAPILib;
LPFNCMCSEND lpfncmc_send;

// Load DLL
hMAPILib = LoadLibrary("MAPI32.DLL");

// Get function addresses
lpfncmc_send = (LPFNCMCSEND)GetProcAddress(hMAPILib, "cmc_send");

RecipIn.name = "Bob Jones";
RecipIn.name_type = CMC_TYPE_INDIVIDUAL;
RecipIn.address = NULL;
RecipIn.role = CMC_ROLE_TO;
RecipIn.recip_flags = CMC_RECIP_LAST_ELEMENT;
RecipIn.recip_extensions = NULL;

myAtt[0].attach_title = "Attached.txt";
myAtt[0].attach_type = NULL;
myAtt[0].attach_filename = "C:\\tmp\\menu1.txt";
myAtt[0].attach_flags = 0;
myAtt[0].attach_extensions = NULL;

myAtt[1].attach_title = "NextAtt.txt";
myAtt[1].attach_type = NULL;
myAtt[1].attach_filename = "C:\\tmp\\menu2.txt";
myAtt[1].attach_flags = CMC_ATT_LAST_ELEMENT;
myAtt[1].attach_extensions = NULL;

Msg.message_reference = NULL;
Msg.message_type = NULL;
Msg.subject = "Message Subject";
Msg.time_sent = tTime;
Msg.text_note = "This is the message text";
Msg.recipients = &RecipIn;
Msg.attachments = myAtt;
Msg.message_flags = 0; // CMC_MSG_LAST_ATTACHMENT

cmcStatus = (*lpfncmc_send)(0, &Msg, 0, 0, NULL);
if(cmcStatus != CMC_SUCCESS)
{
    tmpStr.Format("Error in cmc_send: %d", cmcStatus);
    AfxMessageBox(tmpStr);
}
```

Address Resolution with CMC

When addressing a message from within your application, you can always fill in the
CMC_recipient array explicitly, as in the previous example, or you can use the cmc_look_up()
function to help:

```
CMC_return_code cmc_look_up (CMC_session_id session, CMC_recipient FAR *
recipient_in,
    CMC_flags look_up_flags, CMC_ui_id ui_id, CMC_uint32 FAR * count,
    CMC_recipient FAR * FAR * recipient_out, CMC_extension FAR *
look_up_extensions);
```

The operation of cmc_look_up() is determined by the options specified in look_up_ flags. In most cases, you will want to use cmc_look_up() in one of the following ways:

■ You can use the message service's UI to allow the user to generate a list of recipients by specifying the CMC_LOOKUP_ADDRESSING_UI flag. In this case, you can pass a NULL value for recipient_in or use it to pass default addresses to the dialog. An array of CMC_recipient structures reflecting the user's choices is returned in recipient_out.

■ You can present the message service's dialog for managing the details about a recipient by specifying the CMC_LOOKUP_DETAILS_UI flag. In this case, you must provide a valid CMC_recipient structure that resolves to a single address book entry.

■ You can resolve the identity of the current user by passing CMC_LOOKUP_RESOLVE_IDENTITY flag. A CMC_recipient structure for the current user will be returned via recipient_out.

■ You can resolve a possibly ambiguous address by specifying CMC_LOOKUP_RESOLVE_PREFIX_SEARCH. This will return an array containing CMC_recipient structures for each entry name that begins with the prefix passed in the name in recipient_in. Some address book implementations may allow you to use wildcards in the prefix. If you specify the CMC_LOOKUP_RESOLVE_PREFIX_SEARCH flag, you may also specify CMC_LOOKUP_RESOLVE_UI to present the user with a dialog to resolve ambiguous addresses.

NOTE

In many cases, the CMC libraries will allocate memory for data that is returned by way of a pointer, as in the recipient_out parameter of cmc_look_up(). When you are finished using the data that is returned, you should free the memory with a call to cmc_free(). The memory allocated by the CMC library may not be in a single block of memory, so you must use cmc_free(), rather than Win32 API calls such as free().

Listing 19.3 shows how you can use cmc_lookup() to check for an ambiguous address. If the address passed in is ambiguous, it will present a dialog to the user to choose a single address.

Listing 19.3. Checking for an ambiguous address.

```
CMC_return_code cmcStatus;
CMC_recipient RecipIn;
CMC_recipient *pRecipOut;
CMC_uint32 nCount;

RecipIn.name = strName;
RecipIn.name_type = CMC_TYPE_INDIVIDUAL;
```

```
RecipIn.address = NULL;
RecipIn.role = CMC_ROLE_TO;
RecipIn.recip_flags = CMC_RECIP_LAST_ELEMENT;
RecipIn.recip_extensions = NULL;

cmcStatus = (*lpfncmc_look_up)(cmcSession, &RecipIn,
                CMC_LOOKUP_RESOLVE_PREFIX_SEARCH | CMC_LOOKUP_RESOLVE_UI |
                CMC_ERROR_UI_ALLOWED | CMC_LOGON_UI_ALLOWED,
                0, &nCount, &pRecipOut, NULL);

// Do something with the data at pRecipOut…

// Free memory allocated by CMC
cmcStatus = (*lpfncmc_free)(pRecipOut);
```

Receiving Messages with CMC

The common messaging calls provide three functions for working with messages in a user's inbox. The cmc_list() function is used to retrieve a list of message summaries, and cmc_read() is used to retrieve entire messages. In addition, the cmc_act_on() function allows you to manipulate messages—for instance, to delete them.

Listing Messages

To retrieve a list of messages in a user's inbox based on certain selection criteria, you can use the cmc_list() function:

```
CMC_return_code cmc_list (CMC_session_id session, CMC_string message_type,
    CMC_flags list_flags, CMC_message_reference * seed,
    CMC_uint32 FAR * count, CMC_ui_id ui_id,
    CMC_message_summary FAR * FAR * result,
    CMC_extension FAR * list_extensions);
```

The message_type parameter may be used to select a particular type of message to list. This can be NULL to retrieve all message types.

The CMC_message_reference pointed to by seed is used to tell the address service to start searching after the message referenced in seed.

You may specify a maximum number of records to retrieve in the variable to which count points. Upon return, this will contain the actual number of records returned. If you specify the CMC_LIST_COUNT_ONLY flag, only the count is updated. Otherwise, cmc_list() will return an array of CMC_message_summary structures for messages found. Here is the structure:

```
typedef struct {
    CMC_message_reference    *message_reference;
    CMC_string      message_type;
    CMC_string      subject;
    CMC_time        time_sent;
    CMC_uint32      byte_length;
    CMC_recipient      *originator;
```

```
    CMC_flags       summary_flags;
    CMC_extension       *message_summary_extensions;
} CMC_message_summary;
```

Additionally, you can specify flag values of either CMC_LIST_MSG_REFS_ONLY to fill in only the message reference information in the returned array, or CMC_LIST_UNREAD_ONLY to list only unread messages.

Listing 19.4 will get a listing of all messages available in the inbox and display the subject for each.

Listing 19.4. Obtaining and displaying the subject for messages in the inbox.

```
CMC_uint32 nCount = 0;
CMC_message_summary *pMsgSumList;
CMC_message_summary *pMsgSum;
CMC_return_code cmcStatus;

cmcStatus = (*lpfncmc_list)(cmcSession, NULL, 0, NULL,
                &nCount, 0, &pMsgSumList, NULL);
pMsgSum = pMsgSumList;
while(!(pMsgSum->summary_flags & CMC_SUM_LAST_ELEMENT))
{
    cout << pMsgSum->subject << endl;
    pMsgSum++;
}
```

Reading Messages

To retrieve the contents of a message, you can use the cmc_read() function:

```
CMC_return_code cmc_read ( CMC_session_id session,
    CMC_message_reference * message_reference, CMC_flags read_flags,
    CMC_message FAR * FAR * message, CMC_ui_id ui_id,
    CMC_extension FAR * read_extensions);
```

The message_reference parameter may contain a valid CMC_message_reference, such as that returned in the message_reference field of the CMC_message_summary structures returned by cmc_list(), or it can be NULL, in which case the first message in the mailbox is read. You can also specify that cmc_read() read the first unread message by specifying CMC_READ_FIRST_UNREAD_MESSAGE in read_flags.

By default, a message that is returned by cmc_read() is marked as read in the mailbox. You can disable this behavior by passing the CMC_DO_NOT_MARK_AS_READ flag.

Upon successful completion, cmc_read() returns CMC_SUCCESS, and the pointer pointed to by the message is updated to point to a CMC_message structure, which cmc_read() has allocated memory for and filled in with the information for the message read. When you are finished with the CMC_message structure, you should call cmc_free() to release the memory allocated by cmc_read().

The body of the message text is generally contained in the text_note field of the CMC_message, although if the message_flags field includes CMC_MSG_TEXT_NOTE_AS_FILE, the message text will appear in the first attachment file.

Information about any attachments to the message is contained in the array of CMC_attachment structures accessed through the attachments field of the CMC_message structure. The last attachment will have CMC_ATT_LAST_ELEMENT set in the attach_flags. When you read a message with cmc_read(), any attached files are stored as temporary disk files. The name for the temporary file for an attachment is stored in the attach_filename field. You can use any of the Win32 file I/O operations to work with these files.

Manipulating Messages

To perform operations on a message in the mailbox, (other than reading) you can use the cmc_act_on() function:

```
CMC_return_code FAR PASCAL cmc_act_on( CMC_session_id session,
    CMC_message_reference FAR *message_reference,
    CMC_enum operation, CMC_flags act_on_flags,
    CMC_ui_id ui_id, CMC_extension FAR *act_on_extensions);
```

The message_reference parameter points to a valid CMC_reference structure. Generally, this is returned in the message_reference field of a CMC_message_summary from a call to cmc_list(), or the message_reference field of a CMC_message from a call to cmc_read().

The operation parameter specifies the operation to be performed on the message. Currently, the only operation supported by the base CMC API is CMC_ACT_ON_DELETE, which deletes the message. There are, however, additional operations which may be specified in extensions to cmc_act_on(), in which case the operation parameter should be set to CMC_ACT_ON_EXTENDED.

If the call to cmc_act_on() completes successfully, it will return CMC_SUCCESS. For more on other possible error codes, see the online documentation.

CMC Data Extensions

The CMC API provides a way for your application to access functionality that is not provided by the base specification of the CMC API by allowing you to pass CMC_extension structures to the CMC calls. These extensions can be used to add parameters to functions, as well as to provide a mechanism for returning additional data.

Each of the defined extensions belongs to a set of extensions. Both the individual extensions and the set as a whole are assigned unique identifiers by the X.400 API Association. For example, the MAPI SDK currently supports two different extension sets: the common extension set and a set of Microsoft-specific extensions.

Supported Extensions

The *common extension set,* identified by the constant CMC_XS_COM, provides a set of extensions that are available in most messaging systems. These extensions are defined in xcmcext.h. The common extensions are listed in Table 19.1.

Table 19.1. Common messaging system extensions.

Extension	Description
CMC_X_COM_ATTACH_CHARPOS	Allows the placement of icons for attachments within the message text
CMC_X_COM_CAN_SEND_RECIP	Checks whether the message service is ready to send to a particular recipient
CMC_X_COM_CONFIG_DATA	Used to return additional configuration information from cmc_query_configuration()
CMC_X_COM_PRIORITY	Used to assign message priorities
CMC_X_COM_RECIP_ID	Used to associate unique recipient IDs to resolved addresses
CMC_X_COM_SAVE_MESSAGE	Used to save a message to the receive folder (inbox)
CMC_X_COM_SENT_MESSAGE	Used to create a CMC_message structure for a message sent with cmc_send(); this can be used to return information selected by the user with the message service's UI
CMC_X_COM_SUPPORT_EXT	Used to query for which extensions are supported
CMC_X_COM_TIME_RECEIVED	Used to receive the time that a message was delivered

The set of Microsoft-specific extensions is identified by the CMC_XS_MS constant. These interfaces, listed in Table 19.2, are defined in xcmcmsxt.h.

Table 19.2. Microsoft-specific messaging system extensions.

Microsoft extension	Description
CMC_X_MS_ADDRESS_UI	Used to modify the caption and recipient box label in the address book dialog box
CMC_X_MS_ATTACH_DATA	Used to attach OLE objects or embedded messages
CMC_X_MS_FUNCTION_FLAGS	Used to pass additional flags to alter certain behaviors of the cmc_look_up(), cmc_list(), or cmc_read() functions
CMC_X_MS_MESSAGE_DATA	Used to provide additional information about a message; currently, used only to determine whether notification of receipt is requested
CMC_X_MS_SESSION_FLAGS	Used to pass additional flags to cmc_logon() and cmc_logoff()

Determining Extension Support

Before using any of the CMC extensions in your application, you should check to see whether they are implemented for the message service that you are using. You can do this by using the `CMC_X_COM_SUPPORT_EXT` extension in a call to `cmc_query_configuration()`. The following example shows how you can check to see whether the common extensions are supported:

```
#include <xcmc.h>
#include <xcmcext.h>

// Load MAPI32.DLL and get Function pointers…
CMC_boolean bUiAvail;
CMC_return_code cmcStatus;
CMC_extension QueryExt;
CMC_X_COM_support QuerySup[1];

QuerySup[0].item_code  =  CMC_XS_COM;
QuerySup[0].flags      =  0;
QueryExt.item_code        =  CMC_X_COM_SUPPORT_EXT;
QueryExt.item_data        =  1;
QueryExt.item_reference   =  QuerySup;
QueryExt.extension_flags  =  CMC_EXT_LAST_ELEMENT;

cmcStatus = (*lpfncmc_query_configuration)(
             0,                       // Query default settings
             CMC_CONFIG_UI_AVAIL,  // Logon UI available?
             &bUiAvail,               // Return buffer
             &QueryExt);              // No extensions
if(cmcStatus != CMC_SUCCESS)
    cerr << "cmc_logon error: " << cmcStatus << endl;
if (QuerySup[0].flags & CMC_X_COM_NOT_SUPPORTED)
    cerr << "Common Extensions Not Supported" << endl;
```

Using CMC Extensions

Once you have verified that the message service supports an extension, you can use the extension by first creating a `CMC_extension` structure and filling in its fields with data appropriate to the particular extension. This `CMC_extension` structure is then passed to the CMC call. Additional data may then be returned in the `CMC_extension` structure. This may involve data that had memory allocated by the CMC call, in which case you should be certain to call `cmc_free()` to release the memory when you are finished with it.

Simple MAPI

The simple messaging API provides a set of basic functions that you can use to add messaging capabilities to your applications. However, in most cases, new applications that require basic messaging capabilities should use the newer common messaging calls, which provide greater cross-platform compatibility. If your application will need greater access to the internal workings of a messaging system, you should look at the extended MAPI.

Unfortunately, there is not space in this book to discuss the simple MAPI in detail here. You will find that it is generally very similar to the CMC API.

Simple MAPI includes the functions shown in Table 19.3.

Table 19.3. Simple MAPI functions.

Function	Purpose
MAPILogon()	Starts a new messaging session
MAPILogoff()	Ends a session
MAPIAddress()	Addresses a message
MAPIResolveName()	Presents a dialog for resolving ambiguous names
MAPIDetails()	Displays the details dialog for a recipient
MAPISendDocuments()	Provides a dialog box to send a message
MAPISendMail()	Sends a message
MAPIFindNext()	Finds messages of a specified type
MAPIReadMail()	Reads a message
MAPISaveMail()	Saves a message
MAPIDeleteMail()	Deletes a message
MAPIFreeBuffer()	Frees memory allocated by MAPI calls

Extended MAPI

Extended MAPI provides a much broader range of features than simple MAPI or CMC, allowing applications to work more intimately with the various service providers. However, it also requires a bit more work on your part to implement.

Extended MAPI provides an extensive object-oriented programming interface based on the OLE COM. Extended MAPI defines a set of objects that consist of collections of properties, methods, and event notifications. These objects are used to represent things such as sessions, messages, folders, attachments, message stores, address books and mail users, and many others. MAPI objects are accessed by using various MAPI interfaces, which are derived from the standard OLE interfaces, such as IUnknown.

Extended MAPI allows your applications to implement and use MAPI forms, which can provide a user interface and a forms server for working with special types of messages that you can define for your own applications.

You can also use extended MAPI to create extensions to the Microsoft Exchange client to add custom functionality or custom interfaces to the Exchange client.

Extended MAPI can also be used to implement the various providers used in the messaging system, including your own address books, message stores, and transport providers.

A complete discussion of extended MAPI is a bit beyond the scope of this book, but it is fairly well documented in the online help included with Visual C++.

OLE Messaging Library

The Microsoft OLE messaging library provides a set of objects that can be used to add messaging functionality to your applications. Although you can use the OLE messaging library from C++ applications, it is intended primarily for use in Visual Basic or Visual Basic for Applications (VBA). To use the OLE messaging library in your C++ applications, you need to deal with several OLE automation issues, which are beyond the scope of this chapter.

In short, I wouldn't recommend using the OLE messaging library for C++ applications in most cases. It is generally easier to use the CMC API to implement the functions supported by the OLE messaging library.

Summary

In this chapter, you have taken a look at the Messaging API, which provides several sets of APIs to work with messaging in the Windows Open Systems Architecture (WOSA).

You saw how the MAPI architecture is laid out, consisting of various address book, message store, and transport service providers, all tied together with the Win32 messaging subsystem, which provides the various APIs for client applications.

You explored the features of MFC that support the addition of simple message send functionality to your applications by using the `OnFileSendMail()` and `OnUpdateFileSendMail()` members of the `CDocument` class, including how to add these features with AppWizard or the MAPI component.

You also learned how to use the CMC API, including how to begin a session with `cmc_logon()`, send messages with either `cmc_send_documents()` or `cmc_send()`, look up destination addresses with `cmc_look_up()`, read messages with `cmc_list()` and `cmc_read()`, and delete messages with `cmc_act_on()`. You also saw how to work with extensions to the CMC API.

Finally, you took a brief look at the other APIs that make up the Messaging APIs, including simple MAPI, extended MAPI, and the OLE messaging library.

20

Telephony API (TAPI)

by David Bennett

In this chapter, you will take a look at Microsoft's telephony API, which allows you to add telephony capabilities to your applications, whether you just want to dial a number for the user or write a full-blown call center application.

The telephony API provides the ability to work with simple voice and data calls, as well as a wide variety of different features, including conference calls, call waiting, fax, voice mail, and caller ID.

TAPI is a part of the Windows Open Systems Architecture (WOSA), which presents a common API that applications can use to access a wide variety of different telephony hardware. The interface to the hardware is provided by various service providers, which register with TAPI. Your application can then make calls to TAPI, which will be passed on to the appropriate service provider.

In this chapter, you look at TAPI version 2.0, which is included in Windows NT 4.0 and should be released for Windows 95 about the time you get this book.

However, most of the concepts in this chapter also apply to previous versions of TAPI.

The Telephony APIs

Windows telephony actually supports two different APIs. The first is called *assisted telephony* and provides only the most basic functionality, allowing your application to dial a call. On the other hand, the *full telephony* API can support just about anything you might want to do with anything, such as a telephone.

TAPI is also divided into three different service levels: basic telephony, supplemental telephony, and extended telephony.

Basic telephony is the heart of any application that uses TAPI. It supports basic functionality for single-line telephones (and modems) and can be used to handle basic inbound or outbound calls.

Supplemental telephony provides additional functionality, including support for multiline phones, display phones, conference calls, hold, park, and transfer, among other things. However, not all service providers support supplemental telephony.

Extended telephony provides a means of accessing any additional functionality that may be supported by a service provider. Although the actual features that may be implemented by a given service provider are not defined, the interface to these extended features is.

The telephony API is intended to deal only with the *telephony* issues with which your application deals. To manipulate the content of a call, you need to use one of the other Win32 APIs, such as the Comm API for data communications or the wave audio or Media Control Interface (MCI) APIs to work with audio on a call.

Telephony Devices and TAPI

The telephony API provides an abstraction of a basic phone line. This may correspond to a physical line for Plain Old Telephone Service (POTS), or it may represent more complex systems, such as PBX, T1, switched 56, or multichannel ISDN connections. The details of implementing the actual connection are left up to the individual service providers.

TAPI also abstracts phone devices, which correspond to the desktop telephone, and provide a microphone, a speaker, and perhaps various display capabilities. A phone device may be a desktop phone attached to the computer or it may even be the PC itself, provided it is equipped with the proper hardware.

TAPI can be used with a wide variety of different telephony hardware in any number of different configurations, ranging from a simple modem attached to a PC, to complex multiline telephony cards that control a whole office full of telephones. TAPI provides a consistent interface to telephony functions, regardless of the underlying physical configuration.

Assisted Telephony

The easiest way to add simple dialing capabilities to your applications is by using assisted telephony, which allows you to dial a voice call with a single function. However, assisted telephony handles only the dialing of the call; additional APIs, such as the Win32 Comm API, must be used to transfer data over this call.

In general, assisted telephony is intended to be used in applications that provide dialing capabilities as an additional feature, rather than applications that are used primarily for telephony.

Actually, two different executables are used in dialing a call with assisted telephony. The first is your client application, which will call `tapiRequestMakeCall()`. This function sends a request to TAPI32.DLL, which then forwards the request to an assisted telephony server that will perform the actual dialing.

An assisted telephony server is any process that calls `lineRegisterRequestRecipient()` to register itself with the telephony system. The Win32 operating systems provide dialer.exe that acts as an assisted telephony server, although this is provided only with WinNT 4.0, Win95 OSR2, or later versions.

Assisted telephony is not intended to be used in the same application with the rest of the telephony API. If you need more than simple dialing capabilities, skip to the next section on full TAPI.

Placing a Call

To dial a voice call using assisted telephony, you can use the `tapiRequestMakeCall()` function:

```
LONG tapiRequestMakeCall(LPCSTR lpszDestAddress, LPCSTR lpszAppName,
    LPCSTR lpszCalledParty, LPCSTR lpszComment);
```

`lpszDestAddress` points to a string containing the address to dial. This string can contain a destination address in either dialable address format or canonical address format. Both of these formats are basically an ASCII string containing an address or a phone number, such as 555-1234, although both also support special control characters and other information. The canonical address format differs from the dialable address format in that the canonical address is intended to be universal—it may contain additional information, such as a country code. TAPI provides functions to help in manipulating address strings, as you will see later.

Optionally, you may also specify ASCII strings for the name of your application, the name of the called party, or an additional comment string. Depending on the assisted telephony server you are using, these parameters may or may not be used. Dialer.exe will display the destination address string while dialing.

When you call `tapiRequestMakeCall()`, the telephony system will try to find a telephony server that is currently running to service the request. If none is found, it will launch the highest-priority server that can be found.

Retrieving Location Information

The only other function that is provided for assisted telephony is `tapiGetLocationInfo()`:

```
LONG tapiGetLocationInfo(LPCSTR lpszCountryCode, LPCSTR lpszCityCode );
```

This will return null-terminated strings for the country code and city (area) code that are currently configured for the local machine.

Basic Telephony

In this section, you look at the basic functions of the full telephony API. These functions are supported by all TAPI service providers (although some options may not be). Basic telephony provides functions that use line devices to work with basic calls using a simple single line.

To work with additional features, such as multiline phones, you need to use the functions provided by the supplemental telephony API.

Initializing TAPI

Before using any of the other functions of TAPI, you must first initialize a TAPI session with a call to `lineInitializeEx()`:

```
LONG lineInitializeEx(LPHLINEAPP lphLineApp, HINSTANCE hInstance,
    LINECALLBACK lpfnCallback, LPCSTR lpszFriendlyAppName,
    LPDWORD lpdwNumDevs, LPDWORD lpdwAPIVersion,
    LPLINEINITIALIZEEXPARAMS lpLineInitializeExParams);
```

A TAPI session handle will be returned at `lphLineApp`. This session handle will be required for most of the other TAPI functions that you will look at in this chapter.

The `hInstance` parameter may be used to pass the instance handle of your application or DLL, or you can pass `NULL` to use the module handle for the root executable of your process.

The `lpfnCallback` parameter is used to pass the address of a callback function to use when completing asynchronous calls using the hidden window method. If you are using event handle or completion port methods to handle asynchronous calls, this should be `NULL`. You will look at the different asynchronous event methods later.

You can pass a readable ASCII string for the name of your application in `lpszFriendlyAppName`. This string may be used to display the name of the application that originated a call or first accepted a call.

`lineInitializeEx()` also returns the number of lines supported at `lpdwNumDevs` and the highest version of TAPI that is supported at `lpdwAPIVersion`.

The `lpLineInitializeExParams` parameter points to a `LPLINEINITIALIZEEXPARAMS` structure, which is used to pass additional options for the TAPI session. This structure is shown in the following:

```
typedef struct lineinitializeexparams_tag {
    DWORD   dwTotalSize;
    DWORD   dwNeededSize;
    DWORD   dwUsedSize;
    DWORD   dwOptions;

  union
  {
    HANDLE  hEvent;
    HANDLE  hCompletionPort;
  } Handles;
    DWORD   dwCompletionKey;
} LINEINITIALIZEEXPARAMS, FAR *LPLINEINITIALIZEEXPARAMS;
```

In most cases, you can set all three of the size fields to `sizeof(LINEINITIALIZEEXPARAMS)`.

The other fields in this structure are used to pass parameters associated with how this session will handle asynchronous events, so let's look at the options provided by TAPI for handling asynchronous event notification.

Asynchronous TAPI Functions

Unlike some of the other APIs that you have seen so far, all the functions in the telephony API are either synchronous or asynchronous. The synchronous functions, such as lineInitializeEx(), will always do what they have to do and return when the operation is complete. Similarly, the asynchronous functions, which are generally used to perform operations that may take an indeterminate amount of time, will always return immediately, and the final results of the operation are returned by one of the three asynchronous notification methods provided by TAPI: hidden window callback functions, events, or completion queues.

TAPI uses these different notification mechanisms to alert your application that TAPI has a new message to send to your application. There are many different messages that may be sent by TAPI, as you will see when you look at some of the functions that complete asynchronously, starting with lineMakeCall(). In many cases, a given TAPI function may generate many different messages, used to report on the status of an operation.

Hidden Window Callbacks

The hidden window mechanism allows you to assign a callback function to your TAPI session. This callback function is called whenever TAPI needs to send a message back to your application. The catch is that TAPI processes the calling of the callback function by creating a hidden window when you call lineInitializeEx(). TAPI then sends messages to this window, which is handled by a TAPI function that will call your app's callback function.

> **NOTE**
>
> The hidden window method requires that your application have a message loop, and that message processing is allowed to occur in order to receive TAPI messages.

To use the hidden window callback method, you must specify a value of LINIINITIALIZEEXOPTION_USEHIDDENWINDOW in the dwOptions field of the LINEINITIALIZEEXPARAMS structure. You must also pass the address of your callback function in the call to lineInitializeEx(). The prototype for your callback function should look like this:

```
VOID FAR PASCAL myTapiCallback(DWORD hDevice, DWORD dwMsg,
    DWORD dwCallbackInstance, DWORD dwParam1,
    DWORD dwParam2, DWORD dwParam3);
```

This function will be called whenever TAPI needs to send a message to your application. The parameters passed to the callback are used to give information about the message sent. hDevice will receive the handle of the device that generated the callback. In most of the cases that you will see here, this is a handle returned by lineOpen(). In addition, dwCallbackInstance will receive a user-defined context value, as set in the lineOpen() call, which you will see shortly.

The type of message is determined by the value passed in dwMsg, and the last three parameters will return data specific to that message. You can take a closer look at some of the messages that can be received throughout this chapter.

The Event Handle Method

The second asynchronous notification method supported by TAPI uses an event handle. When you call lineInitializeEx() with the dwOption field of the LINEINITIALIZEEXPARAMS structure set to LINEINITIALIZEEXOPTION_USEEVENT, an event handle will be returned in the hEvent field of the Handles union in that structure. You can then use the Win32 API functions, such as WaitForSingleObject() or WaitForMultipleObjects(), to wait on this event. TAPI will set the event whenever it has a new message to send to your application.

When the event is signaled, your application should call lineGetMessage() to retrieve the message sent by TAPI. You could also forgo waiting for the event and simply call lineGetMessage(), because this will block until a new message is received. Here is the prototype for lineGetMessage():

```
LONG lineGetMessage(HLINEAPP hLineApp,
    LPLINEMESSAGE lpMessage, DWORD dwTimeout);
```

The hLineApp parameter should be passed the session handle returned by lineInitializeEx(). dwTimeout can be used to specify a timeout value, in milliseconds, to wait for a message to arrive. The message that is received will be written to a LINEMESSAGE structure at lpMessage. Here is the structure:

```
typedef struct linemessage_tag {
    DWORD   hDevice;
    DWORD   dwMessageID;
    DWORD   dwCallbackInstance;
    DWORD   dwParam1;
    DWORD   dwParam2;
    DWORD   dwParam3;
} LINEMESSAGE, FAR *LPLINEMESSAGE;
```

The hDevice and dwCallbackInstance fields, like those you saw for the hidden window callback, are used to identify the device handle that generated the message and the callback instance assigned to the line with lineOpen(). The other fields give information specific to the particular message type, which is determined by the value of dwMessageID.

The Completion Port Method

The third method of asynchronous event notification used by TAPI uses the completion port mechanism that WinNT supports for use with asynchronous calls like file I/O. In short, a completion port provides a queue of messages that are generated by TAPI and can be received by your application.

To use completion ports with TAPI, you must first create the completion port with a call to CreateIoCompletionPort(). The handle to this port must then be passed in the hCompletionPort field of the LINEINITIALIZEEXPARAMS structure passed to lineInitializeEx(). The dwCompletionKey field can be set to a value you choose to associate with messages generated by the TAPI session. You must also set dwOption to LINEINITIALIZEEXOPTION_USECOMPLETIONPORT, provided your fingers don't fall off typing it.

To receive new messages from the completion port, your application should call GetQueuedCompletionStatus(), which will block for a specified period, waiting for a new message. When one is received, a pointer to a LINEMESSAGE structure is returned at the address passed to GetQueuedCompletionStatus() in lpOverlapped.

You saw how the LINEMESSAGE structure is laid out—although, with the completion port method, because TAPI allocates dynamic memory to pass the structure, you must use LocalFree() to deallocate the memory when you are done with it. You should also close the handle to the completion port when your application is done using TAPI.

For now, you have seen how to set up the three different completion methods and how they allow you to retrieve messages from TAPI. You look at the messages that can be received soon, but for now, let's get back to setting up to use TAPI, after the call to lineInitializeEx().

> **NOTE**
>
> When you are finished with your TAPI session, you should close it with a call to lineShutdown().

The next group of functions that you will look at deals with a single line, rather than the TAPI session as a whole. This allows different lines, which may be supported by different service providers, to support different versions of TAPI, as well as different line capabilities. Most of these functions will use a device ID to identify a given line. This is an index value, ranging from 0 to one less than the number of lines returned by lineInitializeEx().

Negotiating API Versions

Obviously, there are differences between the different versions of the telephony API. However, a service provider may support several different versions of TAPI. Furthermore, TAPI may provide access to lines from different providers; therefore, each line may support a different version of TAPI.

To help your application find out what version of TAPI is supported for a particular line, and thus which version your application should use, you can use the lineNegotiateAPIVersion():

```
LONG lineNegotiateAPIVersion(HLINEAPP hLineApp, DWORD dwDeviceID,
    DWORD dwAPILowVersion, DWORD dwAPIHighVersion,
    LPDWORD lpdwAPIVersion, LPLINEEXTENSIONID lpExtensionID);
```

This function will attempt to find the highest version of TAPI that your application and the line provider have in common.

The dwDeviceID parameter is an index for the line in question. This can be a value from 0 to one less than the number of lines returned in lineInitializeEx().

You should specify the highest version of TAPI that your app will support in dwAPIHighVersion, with the major revision in the high-order word and the minor revision in the low-order word. For TAPI 2.0 apps, this should be 0x00020000. Similarly, you should specify the lowest version of TAPI that your application can adapt to in dwAPILowVersion.

If a compatible version is found, lineNegotiateAPIVersion() will return 0, and the version that should be used is returned at lpdwAPIVersion. If no matching version can be found, this will return LINEERR_INCOMPATIBLEAPIVERSION.

If you are using any particular extensions specific to a service provider, you should also negotiate the version of the extensions with a call to lineNegotiateExtVersion().

Device Capabilities

Before using a specific line in your applications, you should also check to make sure that the line in question will support the operations for which you want to use it. However, you will also see in the next section how you can specify the capabilities that your app requires when attempting to open a line.

To retrieve information about a device's capabilities, you can use the lineGetDevCaps():

```
LONG lineGetDevCaps(HLINEAPP hLineApp, DWORD dwDeviceID,
    DWORD dwAPIVersion, DWORD dwExtVersion,
    LPLINEDEVCAPS lpLineDevCaps);
```

This function takes the TAPI session handle in hLineApp, the API version from lineNegotiateAPIVersion() in dwAPIVersion, and any extension version in dwExtVersion. The index of the device to query is passed in dwDeviceID.

Upon completion, this function will return a LINEDEVCAPS structure at lpLineDevCaps. This structure contains many different fields concerning the capabilities of a given line:

```
typedef struct linedevcaps_tag {
    DWORD   dwTotalSize;
    DWORD   dwNeededSize;
    DWORD   dwUsedSize;
    DWORD   dwProviderInfoSize;
    DWORD   dwProviderInfoOffset;
    DWORD   dwSwitchInfoSize;
    DWORD   dwSwitchInfoOffset;
    DWORD   dwPermanentLineID;
    DWORD   dwLineNameSize;
    DWORD   dwLineNameOffset;
    DWORD   dwStringFormat;
    DWORD   dwAddressModes;
    DWORD   dwNumAddresses;
    DWORD   dwBearerModes;
    DWORD   dwMaxRate;
    DWORD   dwMediaModes;
    DWORD   dwGenerateToneModes;
    DWORD   dwGenerateToneMaxNumFreq;
    DWORD   dwGenerateDigitModes;
```

```
        DWORD    dwMonitorToneMaxNumFreq;
        DWORD    dwMonitorToneMaxNumEntries;
        DWORD    dwMonitorDigitModes;
        DWORD    dwGatherDigitsMinTimeout;
        DWORD    dwGatherDigitsMaxTimeout;
        DWORD    dwMedCtlDigitMaxListSize;
        DWORD    dwMedCtlMediaMaxListSize;
        DWORD    dwMedCtlToneMaxListSize;
        DWORD    dwMedCtlCallStateMaxListSize;
        DWORD    dwDevCapFlags;
        DWORD    dwMaxNumActiveCalls;
        DWORD    dwAnswerMode;
        DWORD    dwRingModes;
        DWORD    dwLineStates;
        DWORD    dwUUIAcceptSize;
        DWORD    dwUUIAnswerSize;
        DWORD    dwUUIMakeCallSize;
        DWORD    dwUUIDropSize;
        DWORD    dwUUISendUserUserInfoSize;
        DWORD    dwUUICallInfoSize;
  LINEDIALPARAMS    MinDialParams;
  LINEDIALPARAMS    MaxDialParams;
  LINEDIALPARAMS    DefaultDialParams;
        DWORD    dwNumTerminals;
        DWORD    dwTerminalCapsSize;
        DWORD    dwTerminalCapsOffset;
        DWORD    dwTerminalTextEntrySize;
        DWORD    dwTerminalTextSize;
        DWORD    dwTerminalTextOffset;
        DWORD    dwDevSpecificSize;
        DWORD    dwDevSpecificOffset;
        DWORD    dwLineFeatures;
        DWORD    dwSettableDevStatus;
        DWORD    dwDeviceClassesSize;
        DWORD    dwDeviceClassesOffset;
} LINEDEVCAPS, FAR *LPLINEDEVCAPS;
```

Note that this structure can be of a variable size. Many of the pieces of information contained in the structure are passed with size and offset fields. The offset points to the address of the data from the start of the LINEDEVCAPS structure—the length of the data block is passed in the size parameter.

Before calling lineGetDevCaps(), you should fill the dwTotalSize field with the total size of your buffer. If this size is insufficient, lineGetDevCaps() will return LINEERR_STRUCTURETOOSMALL, and the required size will be passed back in the dwNeededSize field of the LINEDEVCAPS structure. You can then allocate a larger buffer and try again.

For more information on the specific fields of this structure, see the online documentation.

Placing Outbound Calls

Placing a call with the telephony API requires several steps:

1. Initialize a TAPI session with lineInitializeEx().

2. Negotiate an API version with `lineNegotiateAPIVersion()`.

3. Check the capabilities of the line with `lineGetDevCaps()`.

4. Open a line with `lineOpen()`.

5. Place the call with `lineMakeCall()`.

Opening a Line

To open a line device, you will be using the `lineOpen()` function, which returns a line device handle that will be used in subsequent TAPI calls to manage the line. You can use `lineOpen()` to open either a specific line, by its device ID or index, or you can request that TAPI attempt to find a line that meets the requirements specified by your application. The prototype for `lineOpen()` is shown in the following:

```
LONG lineOpen(HLINEAPP hLineApp, DWORD dwDeviceID, LPHLINE lphLine,
    DWORD dwAPIVersion, DWORD dwExtVersion, DWORD dwCallbackInstance,
    DWORD dwPrivileges, DWORD dwMediaModes, LPLINECALLPARAMS const lpCallParams);
```

You can open a specific line by passing its index in `dwDeviceID`. Alternatively, you can pass the constant `LINEMAPPER` in the `dwDeviceID` parameter. This tells `lineOpen()` to try to open a line with the characteristics that you specify in the `LINECALLPARAMS` structure passed in `lpCallParams`. You can retrieve the actual ID of the device that was opened with a call to `lineGetID()`.

The value passed in `dwPrivileges` determines what access you have to the line device. If you plan to make only outbound calls, this can be `LINECALLPRIVILEGE_NONE`, or you may specify `LINECALLPRIVILEGE_MONITOR` if you only want to monitor inbound and outbound calls. If your application needs to have ownership of inbound calls, you should specify `LINECALLPRIVILEGE_OWNER`. There are also several additional values that you may use for other, more specific, situations.

For the purposes of `lineOpen()`, only the first few fields of the `LINECALLPARAMS` structure (up to `dwAddressMode`) are used, allowing you to specify a desired bearer mode, data rate, media mode, address mode, or other options.

If the line is opened successfully, `lineOpen()` returns 0, and a handle for the line device will be returned at `lphLine`. This handle can then be used for TAPI operations on the line. If an error occurs, `lineOpen()` will return a non-zero error code. You will find most of the TAPI error codes in `tapi.h`.

Line Status Messages

Once you have opened a line device, your application may receive `LINE_LINEDEVSTATE` messages whenever the state of the line changes. You can select which line states will generate messages for your application with a call to `lineSetStatusMessages()`. You can also see which line state messages are currently enabled by calling `lineGetStatusMessages()`. You will look at how to handle these messages soon. You can also query the current state of a line at any time with a call to `lineGetLineDevStatus()`.

Making a Call

To place an outbound call on a line that you have opened with `lineOpen()`, you can use the `lineMakeCall()` function:

```
LONG lineMakeCall(HLINE hLine, LPHCALL lphCall, LPCSTR lpszDestAddress,
    DWORD dwCountryCode, LPLINECALLPARAMS const lpCallParams);
```

When calling `lineMakeCall()`, the `hLine` parameter should be a handle returned by `lineOpen()` and `lpszDestAddress` should point to a null-terminated dialable address, such as 555-1234. You can also specify the country code in `dwCountryCode` if you need to use a value other than the default for your system.

You can also specify many different options for the call setup by filling in a `LINECALLPARAMS` structure at `lpCallParams`.

`lineMakeCall()` is the first function that you will look at that completes asynchronously. When `lineMakeCall()` is called, it will attempt to start making the call. If an error occurs, the function will return a negative error code. If the call setup is successfully started, `lineMakeCall()` will return a positive request ID and a handle to the new call will be returned at `lphCall`, although this handle is not valid until `lineMakeCall()` completes, as indicated by a `LINE_REPLY` message.

If additional dialing is required for a call, you can use the `lineDial()` function. This is useful in situations where you need to dial additional numbers with an existing call, as in setting up a consultation call before forwarding an existing call.

In the next section, you will see how to handle TAPI messages, such as `LINE_REPLY`, that are sent to your application as a result of asynchronous functions, such as `lineMakeCall()`.

Receiving TAPI Messages

Earlier in this chapter, you saw how to set up your application for one of the three asynchronous notification mechanisms, including hidden window callbacks, event notifications, and completion ports. In this section, you take a look at how to handle the TAPI messages sent to your application. For the sake of example, you will look at a callback function for the hidden window method, although the other notification methods will use similar handling for TAPI messages.

As you saw earlier, using the hidden window method for event notification requires a callback function with the following prototype:

```
VOID FAR PASCAL myTapiCallback(DWORD hDevice, DWORD dwMsg,
    DWORD dwCallbackInstance, DWORD dwParam1,
    DWORD dwParam2, DWORD dwParam3);
```

In most cases, the first thing that your callback function will do is open a `switch` block, based on the value passed in `dwMsg`, which tells you what type of message was received. This can include any of the following messages:

LINE_ADDRESSSTATE is sent when the status of an address, on a line the application currently has open, changes.

LINE_AGENTSPECIFIC is sent when an ACD agent on an open line changes status.

LINE_AGENTSTATUS is sent when an ACD agent on an open line changes status.

LINE_APPNEWCALL is sent when TAPI has spontaneously created a new call handle for you, other than the direct result of TAPI calls.

LINE_CALLINFO is sent when the call information for a call changes.

LINE_CALLSTATE is sent when the status of a call changes; it is also sent to notify the app of incoming calls.

LINE_CLOSE is sent whenever a line is forcibly closed.

LINE_CREATE is sent to an application whenever a new line device is created.

LINE_DEVSPECIFIC is sent to notify the application of device-specific information about a line, address, or call.

LINE_DEVSPECIFICFEATURE is sent to notify the application of device-specific information about a line, address, or call.

LINE_GATHERDIGITS is sent in response to lineGatherDigits() when the request terminates or is canceled.

LINE_GENERATE is sent when a tone- or digit-generation request completes or is canceled.

LINE_LINEDEVSTATE is sent when the state of a line device changes.

LINE_MONITORDIGITS is sent in response to lineMonitorDigits() when the operation completes or is canceled.

LINE_MONITORMEDIA is sent when a call's media mode changes.

LINE_MONITOR_TONE is sent in response to lineMonitorTones() when a tone is received.

LINE_PROXYREQUEST is sent to deliver requests to a registered proxy function handler.

LINE_REMOVE is sent when a line device is removed from the system.

LINE_REPLY is sent to report completion information for asynchronous calls.

LINE_REQUEST is sent when a request from another application is received.

Messages Generated by lineMakeCall()

When you attempt to place a call with lineMakeCall(), TAPI may send several messages to your application. These include a LINE_REPLY message when lineMakeCall() completes and several different LINE_CALLSTATE messages, which are sent as the call enters different states.

LINE_REPLY

For the LINE_REPLY message, the request ID returned by the original lineMakeCall() call is passed in dwParam1, and the completion status of the operation is passed in dwParam2. If this value is 0, the operation was successful; otherwise, a negative error code is returned.

LINE_CALLSTATE

For the LINE_CALLSTATE message, the handle of the call is passed in dwDevice and the new state of the call is passed in dwParam1. The call state can be any of the following values:

LINECALLSTATE_IDLE—There is no call.

LINECALLSTATE_OFFERING—A new call is being offered to the application.

LINECALLSTATE_ACCEPTED—An offered call has been accepted by an application.

LINECALLSTATE_DIALTONE—The line is receiving a dial tone.

LINECALLSTATE_DIALING—The line is dialing.

LINECALLSTATE_RINGBACK—The other end of a connection is ringing.

LINECALLSTATE_BUSY—The line is receiving a busy tone.

LINECALLSTATE_SPECIALINFO—The network is sending special information.

LINECALLSTATE_CONNECTED—A connection has been made.

LINECALLSTATE_PROCEEDING—The call is proceeding, dialing is complete.

LINECALLSTATE_ONHOLD—The call is on hold.

LINECALLSTATE_CONFERENCED—The call is part of a conference call.

LINECALLSTATE_ONHOLDPENDCONF—The call is on hold while a conference is being set up.

LINECALLSTATE_ONHOLDPENTRANSFER—The call is on hold.

LINECALLSTATE_DISCONNECTED—The call has been disconnected by the other party.

LINECALLSTATE_UNKNOWN—The call state is not known.

Depending on the state of the call, additional state information may be passed in dwParam2. This can include specifics about the type of busy signal, type of connection, type of dial tone, type of disconnect, or other special information.

dwParam3 may also provide additional information when your application's privileges to a call change. Normally, this is 0, but it may be LINECALLPRIVILEGE_MONITOR or LINECALLPRIVILEGE_OWNER when the privileges change.

At any time, you can check the current status of a call with the lineGetCallStatus() function, which will return the call state as well as other information, such as the privileges and features of a call.

Ending a Call

When ending a call, there are several steps that undo successive layers of call and line setup:

1. The call is disconnected with `lineDrop()`.
2. Then the call handle may be deallocated with `lineDeallocateCall()`.
3. If you are finished with the line, you should close the line device with a call to `lineClose()`.

Dropping a Call

The `lineDrop()` function is used to disconnect, or drop, a call:

```
LONG lineDrop(HCALL hCall, LPCSTR lpsUserUserInfo, DWORD dwSize);
```

This function will initiate the disconnection of the call handle passed in `hCall`, although the actual disconnect operation will complete asynchronously. Your application will be notified when the call is finished disconnecting, with a `LINE_CALLSTATE` message. In most cases, when the call is dropped, the call state will transition to `LINECALLSTATE_IDLE`.

Similarly, if a call is disconnected by the remote side, you will receive a `LINE_CALLSTATE` message reflecting the disconnection with a call state of `LINECALLSTATE_IDLE`. In this case, you will not need to call `lineDrop()`, but should deallocate the call handle with `lineDeallocateCall()`.

For networks that support it, you can send a user-to-user information string, passed in `lpsUserUserInfo`, of size `dwSize`, when disconnecting.

Deallocating a Call Handle

When you are finished with a call handle (after the call has finished disconnecting) you can deallocate it with a call to `lineDeallocateCall()`:

```
LONG lineDeallocateCall(HCALL hCall);
```

This function will complete synchronously. Once it is called, the call handle is invalid and should not be used in any subsequent TAPI calls.

Closing a Line

If you are finished with a line, you should close it so that it will be available to other TAPI applications. This is done with a call to `lineClose()`:

```
LONG lineClose(HLINE hLine);
```

`lineClose()` will complete synchronously. Once it is called, you should not use the line handle in any further TAPI calls. If you need a new line, you should open a new line device handle with `lineOpen()`.

Once again, if you are finished with TAPI altogether, you should close the TAPI session with a call to lineShutdown().

Receiving Inbound Calls

To allow your application to receive inbound calls with TAPI, you must initialize a TAPI session with lineInitialize() and open a line device with lineOpen(), as you saw earlier. This will allow your application to begin receiving asynchronous messages from TAPI.

You can also set the number of rings that must occur before a call is answered with lineSetNumRings(). You can also query the current setting with lineGetNumRings().

Receiving New Calls

When an incoming call is detected on a line that you have opened with lineOpen(), TAPI will send a LINE_CALLSTATE message to your application with a call state of LINECALLSTATE_OFFERING. This message will also contain a handle for the new call in dwDevice and the privileges that your application has for the new call in dwParam3.

In addition, you can retrieve a list of all new calls for a line with a call to lineGetNewCalls(). This is particularly useful to retrieve the handles for any calls that already exist when you open a line.

You can also retrieve additional information about a call with the lineGetCallInfo() and lineGetCallStatus() functions. In addition, if the call is part of a conference call, you can retrieve the handles to the other calls that make up the conference with the lineGetConfRelatedCalls() function.

Answering a Call

If your application has LINECALLPRIVILEGE_OWNER privileges for the new call, you can answer the call with the lineAnswer() function. Your application can also change the privileges it has for a call with the lineSetCallPrivilege() function. The prototype for lineAnswer() is the following:

```
LONG lineAnswer(HCALL hCall, LPCSTR lpsUserUserInfo, DWORD dwSize);
```

When calling lineAnswer(), the hCall parameter should receive the handle for the new call, as received in the LINE_CALLSTATE message. The lpsUserUserInfo and dwSize parameters may be used to send data to the remote party on networks that support this feature.

If an error occurs in lineAnswer(), it will return a negative error code; otherwise, it will return a positive request ID. The answer operation will complete asynchronously with a LINE_REPLY message with the request ID returned by lineAnswer(). If this message has a dwParam2 value of 0, the operation completed successfully; otherwise, dwParam2 will contain the error code.

Answering a call with `lineAnswer()` will also generally result in generating a new `LINE_CALLSTATE` message for the new call, with a call state of `LINECALLSTATE_CONNECTED`.

Once the new call is answered, your application can call other TAPI functions with the call handle, just as you saw for outbound calls. The new inbound call can also be closed with `lineDrop()`, as you saw earlier.

The call can be handed off to any other application that has opened the line device that the call was received on. This is done with the `lineHandoff()` function.

Media Stream Devices

In order to use other Win32 APIs—such as the comm, wave, or MCI APIs—to work with the media stream on a given TAPI device, you must first retrieve a handle for a media stream device that is appropriate for that API. This is done with the `lineGetId()` function:

```
LONG lineGetID(HLINE hLine, WORD dwAddressID, HCALL hCall,
    DWORD dwSelect, LPVARSTRING lpDeviceID, LPCSTR lpszDeviceClass);
```

To open a media stream device on a given line, you should pass the line device handle (from `lineOpen()`) in `hLine`. Alternatively, you can specify a call handle in `hCall` or an address ID in `dwAddressID`. The parameter that is used is determined by the `dwSelect` parameter, which may have the following values:

```
LINECALLSELECT_LINE
LINECALLSELECT_ADDRESS
LINECALLSELECT_CALL
```

The type of media stream device opened is determined by an ASCII string passed by `lpszDeviceClass`. This can be one of the following values, as well as other strings which may be defined by a given service provider:

> `comm`—A communications port
> `comm/datamodem`—A modem on a communications port
> `comm/datamodem/portname`—Name of device to which a modem is attached
> `wave/in`—A wave audio device for input
> `wave/out`—A wave audio device for output
> `midi/in`—A MIDI device for input
> `midi/out`—A MIDI device for output
> `tapi/line`—A line device
> `tapi/phone`—A phone device
> `ndis`—An NDIS network device
> `tapi/terminal`—A terminal device

The requested device ID is returned in a `VARSTRING` structure at `lpDeviceID`. In many cases, an appropriate handle is returned inside the `VARSTRING`, although the variable size mechanism allows for larger identifiers. The identifier can then be extracted from the VARSTRING structure and be used in calls to the appropriate API.

For many devices, you can present a configuration dialog to the user with a call to lineConfigDialog(). The settings that the user chooses can then be retrieved with a call to lineGetDevConfig(). The data structure returned is not intended to be used directly by your application, although the settings can be restored at a later time with a call to lineSetDevConfig().

Additionally, many service providers can provide your application with an icon representing a given device with the lineGetIcon() function.

Working with TAPI Addresses

TAPI provides several functions to help in manipulating the addresses used in telephony. The lineTranslateAddress() function can be used to convert between canonical and dialable address formats, and lineTranslateAddress() can be used to set the current location information to use for address translation. To retrieve the available address translation capabilities, you can use the lineGetTranslateCaps() function.

For some locations, your application will want to maintain a toll list. This can be manipulated with the lineSetTollList() function.

Some line devices can support multiple addresses. You can get the capabilities and status of a given address with lineGetAddressCaps() and lineGetAddressStatus(). Both of these functions take an address ID, which can be retrieved with a call to lineGetAddressID().

Registering as an Assisted TAPI Service Provider

You saw earlier how assisted telephony makes use of a service provider to handle calls to tapiRequestMakeCall(). You can register your own application as a provider for assisted telephony by calling lineRegisterRequestRecipient(). This will make your application eligible to receive LINE_REQUEST messages from TAPI.

When your application receives a LINE_REQUEST message, TAPI has one or more requests pending for your application. You can retrieve the individual requests with the lineGetRequest() function. Your application can then execute the request.

Supplemental Telephony

In addition to the basic telephony API that you saw above, there are many other functions provided in the supplemental telephony subset of TAPI. These functions can all be used in conjunction with the basic telephony API to provide additional features, such as working with digits and tones, advanced call features, and working with phone devices. Note, however, that telephony service providers are not obligated to support these functions. The following sections summarize the functions available in supplemental telephony.

Additional Line Device Functions

The following functions can be used to provide supplemental functionality with line devices. For more on the specifics of each of these functions, see the online help.

Digit and Tone Functions

lineMonitorDigits() monitors the digits on a call, one at a time.

lineGatherDigits() collects a group of digits on a call.

lineGenerateDigits() generates a series of digits on a call.

lineMonitorTones() monitors the tones on a call.

lineGenerateTone() generates a tone on a call.

Advanced Call Handling

lineAccept() accepts a call and notifies both caller and called party.

lineRedirect() redirects an offered inbound call to another address.

lineSecureCall() prevents interference, such as call waiting, on a call.

lineCompleteCall() places a call completion request.

lineUncompleteCall() cancels a call completion request.

lineHold() places a call on hold.

lineUnhold() takes a call off of hold.

lineSetupTransfer() sets up a call for transfer to another address.

lineCompleteTransfer() transfers a call (can also be used for three-way conferences).

lineBlindTransfer() transfers a call.

lineSwapHold() swaps the active call with a call on hold.

lineSetupConference() prepares for the addition of a party to a conference.

linePrepareAddToConference() prepares to add a call to a conference.

lineAddToConference() adds a call to a conference.

lineRemoveFromConference() removes a call from a conference.

lineGetConfRelatedCalls() retrieves handles for calls in a conference.

linePark() parks a call.

lineUnpark() retrieves a parked call.

lineForward() enables or disables call forwarding.

linePickup() picks up a call for another address.

Agent Functions

lineAgentSpecific() allows access to proprietary functions of the agent handler.

lineGetAgentActivityList() retrieves a list of activities an agent performs.

lineGetAgentCaps() retrieves the agent capabilities of a line device.

lineGetAgentGroupList() lists agent groups.

lineGetAgentStatus() obtains agent status for an address.

lineSetAgentActivity() sets the agent activity code for an address.

lineSetAgentGroup() sets the agent groups for an agent on an address.

lineSetAgentState() sets the agent state for an address.

Proxy Functions

lineProxyMessage() generates TAPI messages for proxy requests.

lineProxyResponse() indicates completion of a proxy request.

Miscellaneous

lineSetCallQualityOfService() sets the quality of service for a call.

lineSetCallData() sets the call data of a LINECALLINFO structure.

lineSetCallTreatment() sets the sounds presented to a user when a call is on hold or unanswered.

lineSetLineDevStatus() sets the line device status.

lineSendUserUserInfo() sends user-to-user information.

lineSetTerminal() specifies a terminal device for monitoring events.

lineSetCallParams() changes the parameters for a call.

lineMonitorMedia() enables or disables media mode notifications for a call.

lineSetMediaControl() sets up a media stream for media control.

lineSetMediaMode() sets the media mode for a call.

Phone Devices

The following functions provide support for phone devices:

phoneInitializeEx() initializes the use of TAPI phone functions.

phoneShutdown() shuts down the use of TAPI phone functions.

phoneNegotiateAPIVersion() negotiates a version of the phone functions.

phoneOpen() opens a phone device.

phoneClose() closes a phone device.

phoneSetRing() rings a phone device.

phoneGetRing() retrieves the ring mode of a phone device.

Phone Settings and Status

phoneGetDevCaps() retrieves capabilities of a phone device.

phoneGetID() returns a device ID for a device class associated with a phone device.

phoneGetIcon() retrieves an icon for the phone device.

phoneConfigDialog() provides a dialog for configuring the phone device.

phoneSetStatusMessages() sets the status messages that a phone device will send.

phoneGetStatusMessages() retrieves the set of status messages enabled for a phone device.

phoneGetStatus() retrieves the status of a phone device.

phoneSetHookSwitch() sets the hookswitch mode of the hookswitch devices for a phone device.

phoneGetHookSwitch() retrieves the mode of a hookswitch device.

phoneSetVolume() sets the speaker volume for a hookswitch device.

phoneGetVolume() retrieves the current volume.

phoneSetGain() sets the gain for a hookswitch device's microphone.

phoneGetGain() retrieves the current gain.

Display

phoneSetDisplay() sends information to the display of a phone device.

phoneGetDisplay() retrieves information from a phone device display.

phoneSetButtonInfo() sets information associated with a phone device button.

phoneGetButtonInfo() retrieves information associated with a phone device button.

phoneSetLamp() sets the lighting mode for a lamp on a phone device.

phoneGetLamp() retrieves the current lighting mode for a lamp.

phoneSetData() sends information to a phone device's data area.

phoneGetData() retrieves information from a phone device's data area.

Extended Telephony

The functions provided in the extended telephony subset of the telephony API do not implement specific features, but provide a common interface to features that may be implemented by various service providers. Extended telephony consists of the following functions:

`lineNegotiateExtVersion()` negotiates an extension version for a line device.

`lineDevSpecific()` provides a device-specific escape function.

`lineDevSpecificFeature()` provides a device-specific escape function, allowing switch features to be sent to the switch.

`phoneNegotiateExtVersion()` negotiates an extension version for a phone device.

`phoneDevSpecific()` provides access to access-extended features of a phone device.

Summary

In this chapter, you explored Microsoft's telephony API, which provides a single, consistent interface that can support a wide range of telephony devices.

You saw how your applications can add simple phone dialing capabilities by using the `tapiRequestMakeCall()` function provided with assisted telephony.

You also looked at how your applications can use the basic telephony functions of full TAPI, including how to initialize TAPI, negotiate TAPI versions, and open line devices. You also saw how TAPI implements asynchronous event handling by sending TAPI messages.

In addition, you learned how your applications can use TAPI to initiate outbound calls, as well as accepting new inbound calls. You explored how you can use TAPI in conjunction with other Win32 APIs that can be used to manipulate the media stream, by retrieving a handle to a media stream device with the `lineGetID()` function.

You also took a brief look at the additional capabilities of the telephony API provided by the supplemental telephony and extended telephony subsets of the telephony API.

21

Cryptography API (CAPI)

by David Bennett

The use of public networks, such as the Internet, is increasing faster than ever. Applications are using these networks to send an ever-growing variety of data, including many things that are not meant to be seen by the general public. One way that your applications can safely send sensitive data over public networks, which are inherently non-secure, is to encrypt it before it is sent, then decrypt it on the other end. This way, you can keep your private data private and still be able to take advantage of the benefits of public networks like the Internet.

To help you secure your data, Microsoft provides the Cryptography API, or CryptoAPI, which provides a simple method for you to use a variety of cryptography services in your applications, without having to worry about the underlying algorithms.

> **NOTE**
>
> The CryptoAPI first appears in Windows 95 in the OEM Service Release 2 (OSR2). Earlier versions do not support the CryptoAPI.

Cryptography 101

Before you dig into the details of working with the CryptoAPI, let's take a quick look at how cryptography is used and define a few of the terms that will be used throughout the rest of the chapter.

Encrypting Data

The most common use of cryptography is for encrypting data, which makes it unreadable to someone intercepting your network transmissions or rummaging through your files. Encryption uses an encryption algorithm, or cipher, to take your *plaintext,* or unencrypted message, and transform it into *ciphertext*—an encrypted format that can be read only by those possessing the key to unlock the cipher.

There are many algorithms used for encryption, each with its own advantages and disadvantages. Some are very simple to implement, like the secret decoder ring you find in breakfast cereal, but are also simple for others to break. Other algorithms are more complicated to implement and require a good deal more processing time, but provide greater security.

In the past, many applications implemented only very basic encryption—such as an exclusive-OR applied to a file—because more complicated algorithms were too difficult to code by hand. In many cases, this resulted in "encrypted" data that was quite simple for others to access. With the CryptoAPI, you can easily add some very sophisticated encryption algorithms to your applications with a minimum of effort on your part.

Of course, any encryption algorithm can be broken—it's just a question of the effort involved to break it. Modern algorithms simply make it very difficult to break the code—it's theoretically possible, but it may take 1,000 years of processing. At this point, those who have a vested interest in getting their hands on your data will probably find it easier to just bribe one of the users for the passwords.

Digital Signatures

In addition to encrypting data, cryptography can be used to verify that a given document, or any other data, came from a given source and that it has not been tampered with along the way. This is done by using digital signatures. A *digital signature* is created by a combination of a user's private key, known only to that user, and the data that is to be signed. This way, when a piece of data is received, the recipient may verify that the signature is authentic by using the public key, which may be freely distributed without compromising security.

Session Keys

Many encryption methods implement symmetric encryption that makes use of a session key. In these algorithms, the same key is used to both encrypt and decrypt a piece of data. These algorithms are generally much faster than public key algorithms, but they also require that you find a way to securely transmit the session key to the receiving party.

Public and Private Keys

In addition to encryption methods that use a single session key for both encryption and decryption, there are other methods that use a pair of keys—one that is public and one that is private. The private key should be available only to the owner of the key pair, but the public key can be freely distributed. If one of the keys in the pair is used for encryption, the other must be used for decryption.

For example, to send encrypted data to a user, you can encrypt the data using that user's public key. The recipient must then use a private key to decrypt the data.

On the other hand, a user can create a digital signature, which is known only to that user, with his private key. Anyone else that has that user's public key can then verify the signature.

In most cases, public/private key algorithms are used only for small pieces of data, because the algorithms used with them require a great deal of processing time. For example, public/private key algorithms are often used to encrypt a session key, which is then sent along with the bulk of the data encrypted with that session key.

Cipher Types

There are two basic types of encryption algorithms, or ciphers, supported in the CryptoAPI: stream ciphers and block ciphers. Each type may include many different algorithms.

Stream Ciphers

Stream ciphers work on a stream of data. For each bit of plaintext, a bit of ciphertext is created. Stream ciphers are generally faster than block ciphers, although they may not be quite as secure.

The Microsoft RSA Base Provider, included with Win32 operating systems, implements the RC4 stream cipher.

Block Ciphers

Block ciphers work with an entire block of data (usually around 64 bits) at a time. These algorithms are generally quite a bit slower than stream ciphers, although they are generally more secure.

Because block ciphers require a full block to do their work, they will make use of padding to round out the data to be encrypted to a multiple of the block size.

The only block cipher implemented by the Microsoft RSA Base Provider is the RC2 block cipher, which uses a block size of 64.

Block Cipher Modes

Block ciphers also generally support a variety of different cipher modes:

- The *Electronic Codebook (ECB)* mode is used to encrypt each block independently of the rest of the encrypted data.
- The *Cipher Block Chaining (CBC)* mode encrypts blocks so that each block is dependent on other parts of the message. Each block of plaintext is XORed with the previous block of plaintext before it is encrypted. The first block of data is XORed with an initialization vector before it is encrypted. For the CryptoAPI, this is the default if you do not specify another mode explicitly.
- *Cipher Feedback (CFB)* mode allows you to use a block cipher to encrypt small pieces of plaintext at a time. This can be useful if you want to encrypt data from a stream, such as keyboard input, as it arrives, although CFB mode is generally much slower than other modes.
- *Output Feedback (OFB)* mode is similar to CFB, but it uses a different algorithm internally.

CryptoAPI Architecture

Your application can access cryptography functions via the CryptoAPI, which is implemented as part of the Win32 operating systems. The operating system in turn interfaces with various

Cryptographic Service Providers (CSPs) by way of the cryptographic service provider interface (CryptoSPI) to implement the actual functionality.

Each CSP can provide different functionality, including different algorithms for generating keys or encrypting data. Some CSPs may even allow you to work with special hardware for cryptography. All the while, your application is insulated from this by being able to use a single, consistent API, regardless of the CSP being used. Currently, Win32 provides the Microsoft RSA Base Provider with the operating system; other CSPs are available from third parties.

Key Containers

Each CSP also manages its own key containers, which serve as a storehouse for all the persistent keys generated by the CSP for each user. In general, all the actual keys used by a CSP are kept within the service provider—the client application accesses these keys only through opaque handles, thus keeping the actual key values safely tucked away in the CSP.

Most of the CSPs maintain two pairs of public/private keys for each user. The *key exchange pair* is generally used to encrypt session keys so that they can be safely stored or exchanged with other users. The *digital signature key pair* is generally used to create digital signatures.

CryptoAPI Configuration

When you install a new CSP, the setup program for that provider should update the system to reflect the installation of the new provider. The configuration information for the CryptoAPI is stored in several locations in the Registry, including the following keys:

```
HKEY_LOCAL_MACHINE\SOFTWARE\Microsoft\Cryptography\Defaults
HKEY_CURRENT_USER\Software\Microsoft\Cryptography\Providers
```

> **NOTE**
>
> These entries should not be edited directly.

The entries under HKEY_LOCAL_MACHINE are updated whenever a new Cryptographic Service Provider is installed.

However, entries in HKEY_CURRENT_USER are not added automatically when a CSP is installed. The entries under this key are used to determine which CSP should be the default provider for each provider type. These entries can be added with calls to CryptSetProvider().

In addition, the HKEY_CURRENT_USER Registry settings for cryptography may be used by CSPs to store information about the user's key containers. The Microsoft RSA Base Provider that ships with Win32 uses the Registry in this way.

For certain CSPs (including the Microsoft RSA Base Provider), each user that is to use the CryptoAPI must have a key container created before the user can attach to the service provider. The Win32 operating systems do not currently provide a utility to do this, although you will see how you can use CryptAcquireContext() to create key containers.

Connecting to a Service Provider

Before using the CryptoAPI functions, you must first connect to a cryptographic service provider. You do this with the CryptAcquireContext() function, which will attempt to find an appropriate CSP and return a handle to it that will be used in later CryptoAPI calls. The CSP may also provide its own user interface to prompt the user for a password before granting access. Here is the prototype for CryptAcquireContext():

```
BOOL CRYPTFUNC CryptAcquireContext(HCRYPTPROV *phProv, LPCTSTR pszContainer,
    LPCTSTR pszProvider, DWORD dwProvType, DWORD dwFlags);
```

CryptAcquireContext() tries to find a CSP based on the name of the CSP, specified in pszProvider, and the desired type of provider, specified in dwProvType. You may pass a NULL pointer for pszProvider to use the default provider for a given CSP type, as specified in the Registry. Your application can set the default CSP for a given provider type with a call to CryptSetProvider().

The value of dwProvType can be one of several predefined provider types, including PROV_RSA_FULL, which is the type for the Microsoft RSA Base Provider that comes with Win32 systems.

In addition, new CSPs may define their own type. In this case, you need to consult the documentation for the specific service provider. If you are developing your own service provider, you should be sure to tell client application developers about the type that should be used for your provider.

CryptAcquireContext() also tries to locate a specific key container within the service provider, as specified in pszContainer. You may specify a value of NULL for pszContainer, in which case the CSP will use a default key container, usually with the same name as the current user. Note, however, that this container must already exist if you do not specify the CRYPT_NEWKEYSET flag.

The dwFlags parameter is generally set to 0, although you may specify one of the following flags to modify the behavior of the call to CryptAcquireContext():

CRYPT_VERIFY_CONTEXT. This flag is used for clients that need only to be able to verify digital signatures. The application will not have access to the private keys stored in the CSP. Because this usage does not require access to private keys, this flag can be used to bypass any password-prompting user interface that the CSP might use.

CRYPT_NEWKEYSET. This flag can be used to create a new key container with the name in pszContainer. This flag is generally not used by user applications, although you may wish to use it in a second call to CryptAcquireContext() if the first fails with an error of NTE_BAD_KEYSET, indicating that the key container could not be found.

CRYPT_DELETEKEYSET. This will cause the CSP to delete the key container specified in pszContainer. When you use this flag, the handle returned through phProv is not set to a valid context, so it should not be used in subsequent CryptoAPI calls—not even CryptReleaseContext(). In most cases, this flag is reserved for use by administrative applications.

If an error occurs, CryptAcquireContext() will return FALSE, and GetLastError() should be called to get the specific error code. If a suitable service provider is found, CryptAcquireContext() will return TRUE, and the handle pointed at by phProv can be used for additional CryptoAPI calls.

When you are finished with the session, you should call CryptReleaseContext() to release the session. In addition, you should first call CryptDestroyKey() and CryptDestroyHash() to clean up any keys or hashes that were created, before closing the session with CryptReleaseContext().

Provider Parameters

Once you have obtained a valid provider handle from CryptAcquireContext(), you can retrieve additional information about the selected provider by using the CryptGetProvParam() function. This call allows you to find information such as the name and version of the provider, the key container name, and the available key containers, as well as specifics about the algorithms and implementation used by the provider.

You may also use CryptSetProvParam() to set various parameters used by the CSP, although the only parameter currently supported is PP_CLIENT_HWND, which may be used to specify a window handle for the CSP to use when interacting directly with the user—for instance, when verifying user identity when CryptAcquireContext() is called. Note that not all CSPs will interact directly with the user.

Working with Keys

Keys are involved in most cryptographic operations that you will be performing, including encryption, decryption, and digital signature operations. Before you move on to these operations, let's first take a look at how your application can work with keys in the CryptoAPI. It is important to make sure that these keys (other than public keys) remain secret, because anyone who has the key may decrypt encrypted data or forge digital signatures.

Creating a Key

Both session keys and public/private key pairs can be created with a call to CryptGenKey():

```
BOOL CRYPTFUNC CryptGenKey(HCRYPTPROV hProv, ALG_ID Algid,
    DWORD dwFlags, HCRYPTKEY *phKey);
```

The hProv parameter holds the handle that was generated by CryptAcquireContext().

To generate a session key, the Algid parameter specifies the encryption algorithm for which you want to create a key. Depending on the CSP you use, this may have several different values, although the RSA Base Provider that ships with Win32 allows CALG_RC2 and CALG_RC4 to create keys for the RC2 block cipher and the RC4 stream cipher.

You can also generate a new public/private key pair with CryptGenKey(). If you specify an Algid of AT_KEYEXCHANGE, the CSP will generate a new key exchange pair that is held in the CSP. You may also generate a new digital signature key pair by specifying AT_SIGNATURE.

The dwFlags parameter is used to specify a combination of several options for the new key. You must specify the CRYPT_EXPORTABLE option to create a key that may later be exported from the CSP. In most cases, you need to specify CRYPT_EXPORTABLE when creating session keys.

The CRYPT_CREATE_SALT option can be specified to tell the CSP to generate a random salt value. If you do not specify this option, the key will be created with a salt value of 0.

You may also specify the CRYPT_USER_PROTECTED option, which tells the CSP to somehow notify the user when certain operations are performed with this key. The implementation of this option is left up to the individual CSP. The Microsoft RSA Base Provider does not implement this.

If an error occurs, CryptGenKey() returns FALSE and you should call GetLastError() for a specific error code. If all goes well, CryptGenKey() will return TRUE, and the handle pointed to by phKey is updated to contain a handle to the new key.

Note that in most cases, you will deal with the handle to the key and not the key itself. If you need access to the actual key, you must explicitly export it from the CSP with a call to CryptExportKey().

When you finish using a particular key, you should clean up by calling CryptDestroyKey().

Deriving a Key from a Password

Although CryptGenKey() generates a purely random key value, you can also generate a session key derived from a password or other base data by using CryptDeriveKey(). This function cannot, however, be used to generate public/private key pairs. Here is the prototype for CryptDeriveKey():

```
BOOL CRYPTFUNC CryptDeriveKey( HCRYPTPROV hProv,
    ALG_ID Algid, HCRYPTHASH hBaseData,
    DWORD dwFlags, HCRYPTKEY *phKey);
```

This function is quite similar to the CryptGenKey() function, except that it creates only session keys and it takes an additional hBaseData parameter.

hBaseData is a handle to a hash object that has been created with CryptCreateHash(). You can then add data to the hash object with CryptHashData(). You will look more closely at how these functions work later in this chapter in the discussion about creating digital signatures, but the following example shows how you can create a key from a password:

```
#define _WIN32_WINNT 0x0400
#include <windows.h>
#include <wincrypt.h>
HCRYPTPROV hProv = 0;
HCRYPTHASH hPwdHash;
HCRYPTKEY hPwdKey;
char szPassword[] = "Open Sesame";
DWORD dwLength;

// Connect to a Service Provider
if(!CryptAcquireContext( &hProv, NULL, NULL, PROV_RSA_FULL, 0))
{
    printf("Error in CryptAcquireContext: 0x%x\n", GetLastError());
    // Do not continue from here
}

// Create an empty hash object
if(!CryptCreateHash(hProv, CALG_MD5, 0, 0, &hPwdHash))
    printf("Error in CryptCreateHash: 0x%x\n", GetLastError());

// Compute hash value
if(!CryptHashData(hPwdHash, (BYTE *)szPassword, strlen(szPassword), 0))
    printf("Error in CryptHashData: 0x%x\n", GetLastError());

// Create key from password hash
if(!CryptDeriveKey(hProv, CALG_RC2, hPwdHash, CRYPT_EXPORTABLE, &hPwdKey))
    printf("Error in CryptDeriveKey: 0x%x\n", GetLastError());

// Use the hPwdKey key handle for something...

// Clean up
if(hPwdHash) CryptDestroyHash(hPwdHash);
if(hPwdKey) CryptDestroyKey(hPwdKey);
if(hProv) CryptReleaseContext(hProv, 0);
```

Key Parameters

Once a key is created, you can manipulate various parameters associated with the key with `CryptGetKeyParam()` and `CryptSetKeyParam()`. These functions allow you to access things such as the algorithm used to create the key, including the cipher block length, salt value, initialization vector, padding mode, and cipher mode, as well as the permissions for the key, which dictates the operations that may be performed with the key.

Exchanging Keys

In the CryptoAPI architecture, all keys are generally kept in a key container within the CSP. This provides a safe way to store your keys where they are not accessible to others. However, it also means that you must do some additional work in order to export the key from the CSP.

There are two general cases where you will want to export a key from the safety of the CSP's key container.

The first case is when you want to save a session key for later use. Because the CSP does not store session keys in persistent storage, your application will store a session key itself if it will be needed later on (for example, when you want to read your files next week). If you do not store the session key, you will find that the CryptoAPI can do a very good job of hiding your data from you as well as from the bad guys.

The second case where keys must be exported is where you need to be able to send a session key to other users, so that they may decrypt data that you have encrypted with the session key.

In both cases, you will first need to export the key from the CSP. This will give you a key blob, or special (usually encrypted) data structure that you can then store away or send to another user. When you are ready to use the key for decryption or signature validation, you must import the key from the key blob back into the CSP, where its handle can then be used for calls such as `CryptDecrypt()`.

> **CAUTION**
>
> It is generally a good idea to implement some method of exporting and backing up your public/private key pairs. If your local machine should run into something such as a hard drive failure, your key pairs may otherwise be lost—and so may any data encrypted with them.

Exporting a Key

To export a key from the CSP, you must use the `CryptExportKey()` function:

```
BOOL CRYPTFUNC CryptExportKey( HCRYPTKEY hKey, HCRYPTKEY hExpKey,
    DWORD dwBlobType, DWORD dwFlags, BYTE *pbData, DWORD *pdwDataLen);
```

You should notice that this function takes the handles to two different keys. The first (`hKey`) is the handle to the key that you want to export; the second (`hExpKey`) is a handle to a key that will be used to encrypt the key blob that is exported.

In general, when you are exporting a session key, `hExpKey` should be a handle for the recipient's public key (even if the recipient is the current user). You can retrieve a handle to a user's public key by calling `CryptGetUserKey()`.

When you are exporting a private key, `hExpKey` should specify a session key used to encrypt the private key. If you are exporting a public key, there is no need to encrypt the key blob, so `hExpKey` should be `0`.

The dwBlobType parameter specifies the type of key blob that is to be created. For exporting session keys, you should use SIMPLEBLOB; PUBLICKEYBLOB and PRIVATEKEYBLOB should be used when exporting public and private keys, respectively.

The last two parameters are used to refer to the buffer that will receive the key blob and its length. When CryptExportKey() returns, the value pointed at by pdwDataLen will reflect the actual size of the key blob exported. You should make sure to save the actual size of the key blob, because this will be needed when you import the key blob back into a CSP.

Note that key blobs may be fairly large (up to 256 bytes for session keys, or up to 5,000 bytes for private key blobs). To find out how much space is required for the key blob, you can call CryptExportKey() with pbData of NULL. This will update the value pointed at by pdwDataLen to reflect the size of the buffer required.

CryptExportKey() will return TRUE if successful or FALSE if an error occurs, in which case you should call GetLastError() for a more detailed error.

Note that if the buffer length is not big enough to hold the blob, CryptExportKey() will fail and GetLastError() will return ERROR_MORE_DATA. The value at pdwDataLen will be updated to reflect the required size for the key blob.

The following example shows how you can generate a session key and export it, using your own public exchange key:

```
HCRYPTPROV hCsp;
HCRYPTKEY hSessionKey;
HCRYPTKEY hMyPublicKey;
DWORD dwKeyBlobLen;
typedef unsigned char byte;
byte bKeyBlob[256];

if(!CryptGenKey(hCsp, CALG_RC4, CRYPT_EXPORTABLE,
        &hSessionKey))
{
    tmpStr.Format("Error in CryptGenKey: 0x%x",
        GetLastError());
    AfxMessageBox(tmpStr);
}
if(!CryptGetUserKey(hCsp, AT_KEYEXCHANGE, &hMyPublicKey))
{
    tmpStr.Format("Error in CryptGetUserKey: 0x%x",
        GetLastError());
    AfxMessageBox(tmpStr);
}
dwKeyBlobLen = sizeof(bKeyBlob);
if(!CryptExportKey(hSessionKey, hMyPublicKey, SIMPLEBLOB, 0, bKeyBlob,
                        &dwKeyBlobLen))
{
    tmpStr.Format("Error in CryptExportKey: 0x%x",
        GetLastError());
    AfxMessageBox(tmpStr);
}
```

```
// Save the key blob or send it to someone else

// Clean up
if(hSessionKey) CryptDestroyKey(hSessionKey);
if(hMyPublicKey) CryptDestroyKey(hMyPublicKey);
if(hCsp) CryptReleaseContext(hCsp, 0);
```

Importing a Key

When you have retrieved a key blob from a disk file or from another user, you import the key blob back into a CSP before you can use the key in other CryptoAPI operations. This is done with the CryptImportKey() function:

```
BOOL CRYPTFUNC CryptImportKey( HCRYPTPROV hProv, BYTE *pbData,
    DWORD dwDataLen, HCRYPTKEY hImpKey, DWORD dwFlags, HCRYPTKEY *phKey);
```

CryptImportKey() takes a pointer (pbData) to the key blob that was generated at some time by CryptExportKey() and the length of the key blob (dwDataLen), as well as the handle of the key that should be used to decrypt the key blob.

If the key blob was encrypted with a session key, hImpKey should be a handle for that session key; if the key blob was created with a key exchange public or private key, or if the key blob is not encrypted at all, hImpKey should be 0.

If an error occurs, CryptImportKey() returns FALSE, and GetLastError() can be used for more detail. If the key blob is successfully imported, CryptImportKey() returns TRUE, and the handle at phKey is updated to refer to the newly imported key.

Encrypting Data

Now that you have seen how to work with the various keys that may be used, let's take a look at how to put the keys to work encrypting data. This is done with the CryptEncrypt() function:

```
BOOL CRYPTFUNC CryptEncrypt(HCRYPTKEY hKey, HCRYPTHASH hHash,
    BOOL Final, BYTE *pbData, DWORD *pdwDataLen, DWORD dwBufLen );
```

The hKey parameter is a handle to the key that will be used for the encryption. In fact, the type of encryption to be used is determined by the type of the key. This handle is created by calls to CryptGenKey(), CryptDeriveKey(), or CryptImportKey().

All encryption of data in the CryptoAPI, regardless of the CSP, is done using a symmetric algorithm. Public/private key algorithms are reserved for use on smaller bits of data, such as key blobs and signatures.

The pbData and pdwDataLen parameters are used to specify the data that is to be encrypted. Note that the encrypted data is written back over the plaintext data at pbData. Because of this, CryptEncrypt() must also know the maximum size of the buffer, as passed in dwBufLen.

In addition, you may determine the buffer size that is required to hold the encrypted data by making a call CryptEncrypt(), with pbData set to NULL and pdwDataLen pointing to the length of the data to encrypt. The size of the buffer required will be returned at pdwDataLen. This way, you can ensure that your buffer is big enough to contain the encrypted data.

If an error occurs, CryptEncrypt() returns FALSE and GetLastError() should be called for more information. If the encryption succeeds, CryptEncrypt() returns TRUE, the encrypted data is copied to pbData, and the length of the encrypted data is returned at pdwDataLen.

Note that some algorithms may require more space for the encrypted data than for the original plaintext.

The following example shows how you can use the CryptoAPI to encrypt a simple string:

```
typedef unsigned char byte;
byte bSecret[100] = "This is my great big secret…";
HCRYPTPROV hCsp;
HCRYPTKEY hSessionKey;
DWORD dwSecretLen;
CString tmpStr;

// Generate a session key
if(!CryptGenKey(hCsp, CALG_RC4, CRYPT_EXPORTABLE,
    &hSessionKey))
{
    tmpStr.Format("Error in CryptGenKey: 0x%x",
        GetLastError());
    AfxMessageBox(tmpStr);
}
// Encrypt the data in bSecret
// The encrypted data is copied back into bSecret
dwSecretLen = strlen((char *)bSecret) + 1;
if(!CryptEncrypt(hSessionKey, 0, TRUE, 0, bSecret,
    &dwSecretLen, sizeof(bSecret)))
{
    tmpStr.Format("Error in CryptEncrypt: 0x%x",
        GetLastError());
    AfxMessageBox(tmpStr);
}
```

Encrypting Multiple Blocks of Data

If you need to encrypt a large amount of data, it may be convenient to encrypt it in several different sections—this is essential if you are encrypting files that are too big to fit into memory all at once.

You can use CryptEncrypt() to encrypt a piece of data in blocks by making multiple calls to CryptEncrypt(), setting the Final parameter to FALSE for all but the last block, then setting Final to TRUE for the last block.

If you are using a block cipher—that is, if the key used is a block cipher key—the size of each block that you encrypt should be a multiple of the block size used by the cipher. You can find the block size used by a key by using CryptGetKeyParam() to return the KP_BLOCKLEN parameter. On the last block (when Final is TRUE), CryptEncrypt() will add any padding necessary to make the last block come out to a multiple of the cipher block size.

You must also be sure to call CryptEncrypt() with TRUE for other key types, because this tells the CSP to reset its internal structures, such as the feedback register for chaining mode or the state of a stream cipher, for the next encryption operation. If you are encrypting all your data in one call to CryptEncrypt(), you should always pass Final as TRUE.

Hashing While Encrypting

As you will see later, it is necessary to create a hash object before creating a digital signature for a piece of data. To help simplify your code and make processing more efficient, you can use CryptEncrypt() to update the data contained in a hash object while you are encrypting the data.

To do this, you should first create the hash with CryptCreateHash(). You can then specify the handle of the hash object in the hHash parameter of CryptEncrypt(). When you are finished with the encryption, this hash can then be used in calls such as CryptSignHash().

Decrypting Data

Obviously, being able to encrypt your data isn't much use if you cannot somehow decrypt it at some later time. This can be done with the CryptDecrypt() function—provided you have access to the proper key for the encryption. The prototype for CryptDecrypt() looks like this:

```
BOOL CRYPTFUNC CryptDecrypt(HCRYPTKEY hKey, HCRYPTHASH hHash,
    BOOL Final, DWORD dwFlags, BYTE *pbData, DWORD *pdwDataLen);
```

The handle for the key to be used for decrypting the data is specified in hKey. Remember that this is not the key itself, but a handle used by the CSP. This handle is returned by calls such as CryptGenKey(), CryptDeriveKey(), or CryptImportKey().

The pbData and pdwDataLen parameters are used to specify the location and size of the data to be decrypted. They also point to the locations where the decrypted data and its size will be written.

As with CryptEncrypt(), you can use multiple calls to CryptDecrypt() to decrypt a large piece of data in smaller sections. Just remember to specify Final as TRUE only for the last block. If you are using a block cipher, make sure that the block size you use is a multiple of the cipher's block size.

Note that in some cases, the data that is encrypted may include additional padding that was not present in the original plaintext.

You may also fill in a hash object while decrypting by specifying a handle to a valid hash object, created with CryptCreateHash(), in the hHash parameter.

Digital Signatures

Digital signatures are useful for verifying that a piece of data really is from whom it says it is, and that it has not been tampered with at any point along the way. The actual signature is a small data structure (usually less than 256 bytes) that can be sent along with the signed data.

The first step in creating a digital signature involves creating a hash value for the data to be signed. This hash value is a small piece of data (usually 128 or 160 bytes) that is generated from the data to be signed. The hash value can be thought of as something similar to a checksum or CRC value.

The digital signature is then created by encrypting the hash value with a user's private key. Using the private key ensures that no one may forge the signature without knowing the private key.

The signature is then verified by creating a hash of the received data and comparing it to the hash value that results from decrypting the signature, using the public key of the user that signed the data.

As you will see, the CryptoAPI simplifies this process for you by relieving you of the chores involved in working with the encryption or hashing algorithms directly.

Creating a Signature

The first step in creating the digital signature is creating a hash value that will be signed. To do this, you first create a hash object, which specifies how the hash will be created; you then compute the hash value, based on the data to be signed.

To create a new hash object, you use the CryptCreateHash() function:

```
BOOL CRYPTFUNC CryptCreateHash( HCRYPTPROV hProv, ALG_ID Algid,
    HCRYPTKEY hKey, DWORD dwFlags, HCRYPTHASH *phHash);
```

This will create a new hash object, based on the CSP (hProv), the algorithms to be used (Algid), and a hash key (hKey), which may be required in keyed hashes, such as the MAC algorithm.

If the hash is successfully created, CryptCreateHash() returns TRUE and the new hash handle is returned through phHash; otherwise, GetLastError() should be called for a specific error code.

The algorithms supported for use with a hash object depend on the individual CSP, although the Microsoft RSA Base Provider supports the following values of Algid:

CALG_MAC	Message Authentication Code (requires a key)
CALG_MD2	MD2
CALG_MD5	MD5
CALG_SHA	US DSA Secure Hash Algorithm

When you are finished with a hash object, you should destroy it with a call to CryptDestroyHash().

Computing the Hash Value

Once you have created a valid hash object, its value must be set, based on the data to be signed. This is done with CryptHashData() or CryptSessionKey(), if you are creating a hash for a session key. In addition, you may create the hash value in a call to CryptEncrypt() or CryptDecrypt(), as you saw earlier.

To create a hash value for a stream of data, you can use the CryptHashData() function:

```
BOOL CRYPTFUNC CryptHashData(HCRYPTHASH hHash, BYTE *pbData,
    DWORD dwDataLen, DWORD dwFlags);
```

This function takes a handle to a hash object created with CryptCreateHash(), a pointer to the data to compute a hash value for, and its length, as well as a set of flags. Note that the Microsoft Base Provider does not use any of the flag values.

CryptHashData() can be called several times to compute a hash value for large pieces of data one block at a time.

Additionally, you can use the CryptHashSessionKey() function to compute a hash value for a session key:

```
BOOL CRYPTFUNC CryptHashSessionKey( HCRYPTHASH hHash,
    HCRYPTKEY hKey, DWORD dwFlags);
```

CryptHashSessionKey() takes a handle for a hash object created with CryptCreateHash() and a handle to the key that is to have a hash value created for it. The dwFlags parameter is ignored in current implementations.

Working with Hash Parameters

You can access various parameters of a hash object—including the algorithm used, the size of the hash value, and the hash value itself—with a call to CryptGetHashParam().

You can also use CryptSetHashParam() to set the parameters for a hash object. This may be used to set the actual hash value, although this is generally not recommended.

Signing the Hash

Once you have created a hash value based on the data to be signed, you can call CryptSignHash() to sign the hash. This process essentially encrypts the hash object using the current user's private key. The following is the prototype for CryptSignHash():

```
BOOL CRYPTFUNC CryptSignHash( HCRYPTHASH hHash, DWORD dwKeySpec,
    LPCTSTR sDescription, DWORD dwFlags, BYTE *pbSignature,
    DWORD *pdwSigLen);
```

The hHash parameter specifies a handle to the hash object that is to be signed. You can specify which of the user's private keys is used to create the signature by setting the dwKeySpec parameter to AT_KEYEXCHANGE or AT_SIGNATURE.

The sDescription parameter is used to pass a description of the data that is being signed. This string is added to the hash before the signature is created. When the signature is verified, the same description string must be supplied by the verifying application.

You specify the location where the new signature will be created in pbSignature and the length of this buffer in pdwSigLen. When the signature is created, its actual length is returned through pdwSigLen.

The signature that is created can then be sent to other users or saved to disk for later verification.

The following example shows how you can create a signature for a piece of data:

```
typedef unsigned char byte;
HCRYPTHASH hSigHash;
CString tmpStr;
DWORD dwSigLen;
byte bSecret[4096];  // Your secret data here
byte bSignature[256];
char szDesc[] = "My Secret Data";

// Create new hash object
if(!CryptCreateHash(hCsp, CALG_MD5, 0, 0, &hSigHash))
{
    tmpStr.Format("Error in CryptCreateHash: 0x%x\n", GetLastError());
    AfxMessageBox(tmpStr);
}
// Compute hash value for data in bSecret buffer
if(!CryptHashData(hSigHash, bSecret, sizeof(bSecret), 0))
{
    tmpStr.Format("Error in CryptHashData: 0x%x\n", GetLastError());
    AfxMessageBox(tmpStr);
}
// Create signature
dwSigLen = sizeof(bSignature);
if(!CryptSignHash(hSigHash, AT_SIGNATURE, szDesc, 0, bSignature, &dwSigLen))
{
    tmpStr.Format("Error in CryptSignHash: 0x%x\n", GetLastError());
    AfxMessageBox(tmpStr);
}
else
    // You may now use the signature at bSignature
```

Authenticating a Signature

To verify a signature for a piece of data, you must first create a new hash object with CryptCreateHash() and compute a hash value for the data with CryptHashData(), CryptHashSessionKey(), CryptEncrypt(), or CryptDecrypt().

The handle to this new hash value, as well as the signature, description string, and handle to the key pair used to create the signature, is then passed to the CryptVerifySignature() function:

```
BOOL CRYPTFUNC CryptVerifySignature(HCRYPTHASH hHash, BYTE *pbSignature,
    DWORD dwSigLen, HCRYPTKEY hPubKey, LPCTSTR sDescription, DWORD dwFlags);
```

The following example shows how you can verify a signature in your applications:

```
HCRYPTKEY hMyPublicSigKey;
CString tmpStr
HCRYPTHASH hVerifyHash;
char szDesc[] = "My Secret Data";
// Get my public signature key
if(!CryptGetUserKey(hCsp, AT_SIGNATURE, &hMyPublicSigKey))
{
    tmpStr.Format("Error in CryptGetUserKey: 0x%x",
        GetLastError());
    AfxMessageBox(tmpStr);
}
// Create new hash object
if(!CryptCreateHash(hCsp, CALG_MD5, 0, 0, &hVerifyHash))
{
    tmpStr.Format("Error in CryptImportKey: 0x%x", GetLastError());
    AfxMessageBox(tmpStr);
}
// compute hash value for data in bSecret buffer
if(!CryptHashData(hVerifyHash, bSecret, sizeof(bSecret), 0))
{
    tmpStr.Format("Error in CryptImportKey: 0x%x", GetLastError());
    AfxMessageBox(tmpStr);
}
// Verify signature contained in bSignature buffer
if(!CryptVerifySignature(hVerifyHash, bSignature, dwSigLen, hMyPublicSigKey,
  szDesc, 0))
{
    if(GetLastError() == NTE_BAD_SIGNATURE)
        AfxMessageBox("Signature Verification Failed");
    else
    {
        tmpStr.Format("Error in CryptVerifytSignature: 0x%x", GetLastError());
        AfxMessageBox(tmpStr);
    }
}
```

Summary

In this chapter, you learned how to use the CryptoAPI to add greater security to the data that your application sends over a network or saves to disk.

You saw how the CryptoAPI architecture supports many Cryptographic Service Providers and how your application can establish a session with a CSP by calling CryptAcquireContext().

You took a look at how your application can use the CryptEncrypt() and CryptDecrypt() functions to encrypt and decrypt data, as well as how to work with the keys used for encryption, including the CryptGenKey() and CryptDeriveKey() functions.

You also explored how to exchange keys between users by exporting them from a CSP with `CryptExportKey()`, sending them somewhere else, and importing them back into a CSP with `CryptImportKey()`.

You learned how to use the CryptoAPI to create a digital signature for a piece of data by using `CryptCreateHash()` and `CryptHashData()` to generate a hash object that can be signed with a call to `CryptSignHash()`. You also saw how to verify the signature with `CryptVerifySignature()`.

22

The WinInet API

by David Bennett

Visual C++ 5.0 includes the Windows Internet Extensions API, known as WinInet. This includes both a set of C functions and an MFC class hierarchy that allows your applications to add connectivity to Internet servers without having to worry about the specifics of the underlying protocols, such as File Transfer Protocol (FTP), Hypertext Transfer Protocol (HTTP), or Gopher.

The WinInet APIs allow you to connect to Internet servers, search for files, and retrieve files. You can also send files to the server or even open a file in place on the server. For many operations, you can use synchronous, blocking calls, or you may use the asynchronous completion mechanisms provided by WinInet.

Using the WinInet C API

Before you get into the meat of the WinInet C API, let's take a look at some of the basic concepts that will be used throughout the WinInet functions, such as the handle hierarchy with which the API functions work. You will also look at how the WinInet functions handle error codes and buffer passing, as well as how asynchronous operations are implemented, before moving on to the specific functions of the WinInet API used for FTP, HTTP, and Gopher communications.

Handles

Most of the WinInet functions make use of a special sort of handle, HINTERNET. This handle type is used to represent Internet sessions, individual connections, and the results of various open or find calls.

These handles are similar to the file handles used in other Win32 functions, although they are not interchangeable with base Win32 handles. For example, you cannot use an HINTERNET handle in calls such as ReadFile(), and you cannot use a handle returned from CreateFile() in calls to InternetReadFile().

One difference between the HINTERNET handles and other Win32 handles is the fact that Internet handles are arranged in a tree hierarchy. The session handle returned by InternetOpen() is the root of the tree, and connection handles returned from InternetConnect() branch from that root. The handles to individual files and search results then make up the leaves of the tree.

Handles can inherit attributes, such as the asynchronous mode settings, from the handle from which they were derived. You can also take advantage of the hierarchy to close the handles for a whole branch of the tree in a single call to InternetCloseHandle()—if you close an Internet handle, any handles descended from it will also be closed.

Each HINTERNET handle can have many different options associated with it, depending on the specific type of handle. These options can be accessed with the InternetQueryOption() and InternetSetOption() functions. These can be used to access information such as the specific type of handle, timeout settings, callback and context values, buffer sizes, and many other settings.

Error Handling

The functions that make up the WinInet API handle errors the same way that the general Win32 functions do. The return value of the function will tell whether the call was successful or not—functions that return a BOOL return FALSE when an error occurs, and functions that return an HINTERNET return NULL when an error occurs or a valid handle if the function succeeded.

In the event that a function fails, more specific error information is available by way of a call to GetLastError(). In addition, if GetLastError() returns ERROR_INTERNET_EXTENDED_ERROR, more information about failed operations with FTP or Gopher servers can be retrieved with a call to InternetGetLastResponseInfo().

For HTTP operations, you can also use the InternetErrorDlg() function to display a dialog box that explains errors to the user and allows the user to select several choices on how to handle the error.

Passing Buffer Parameters

Many of the WinInet API functions return variable length strings by way of a pointer (lpszBuffer) and the buffer length (lpdwBufferLength). In the event that the buffer size passed is too small to hold the returned string (or the pointer is NULL), the function will fail and GetLastError() will return ERROR_INSUFFICIENT_BUFFER. The value at lpdwBufferLength will, however, be updated to reflect the total space needed, including the NUL terminator. You can use this value to allocate a new buffer and repeat the call. Note that when the call completes successfully, the value at lpdwBufferLength does not include the NULL terminator in its count.

Asynchronous I/O

By default, the WinInet API functions operate synchronously. This is convenient when you want to create a separate thread for each operation. However, in cases where you don't want a separate thread for each call, it is useful to handle request completion asynchronously, particularly for operations that may take an indeterminate amount of time to complete.

To enable asynchronous operation, you set the INTERNET_FLAG_ASYNC flag in a call to InternetOpen(). Any calls made on the returned session handle, or any handles derived from it, may then complete asynchronously. In addition, you must specify a callback function and a nonzero context value in order for a call to complete asynchronously.

A callback function is attached to a handle with a call to InternetSetStatusCallback(). This callback function may then be inherited by any handle derived from the handle passed to InternetSetStatusCallback(). The callback function is called by both synchronous and asynchronous functions to report the status of an operation. You will look at the callback function in more detail later.

A context value may be passed to many of the WinInet functions. This may be used to identify the operation that has generated a call to the callback function. If you specify a context value of 0 to any function, it will operate synchronously, even if the INTERNET_FLAG_ASYNC flag is set.

When calling functions that may complete asynchronously, you should always check the return value, because it is possible that the operation will complete immediately. If an operation will complete asynchronously, the original function call will "fail" and GetLastError() will return ERROR_IO_PENDING, which simply signifies that the operation will call the callback function when it completes.

General Internet Functions

There are many functions in the WinInet API that are used for any sort of Internet connection, such as beginning a session, enabling asynchronous I/O, or manipulating URLs. Here, you will take a look at these general functions before moving on to the protocol-specific elements of the WinInet API.

Beginning a WinInet Session

Before using most of the WinInet functions, you must first open a new session with a call to InternetOpen(), which will initialize the WinInet library and return a session handle that will be the root of the handle hierarchy for the rest of your operations within that session. The following is the prototype for InternetOpen():

```
HINTERNET InternetOpen(LPCTSTR lpszAgent, DWORD dwAccessType,
    LPCTSTR lpszProxyName, LPCTSTR lpszProxyBypass, DWORD dwFlags);
```

InternetOpen() allows you to specify how this session will make use of a proxy server. The dwAccessType parameter may specify INTERNET_OPEN_TYPE_DIRECT to resolve all addresses locally, INTERNET_OPEN_TYPE_PROXY to send requests to the proxy server, or INTERNET_OPEN_TYPE_PRECONFIG to retrieve proxy configuration information from the registry. In cases where you are using a proxy server, its name is passed in lpszProxyName, although this can be NULL to read proxy information from the registry.

You can also specify a list of addresses that will be resolved locally in the lpszProxyBypass string. Requests for any address contained in this string will not be forwarded to the proxy server, but will be resolved locally.

You may specify the INTERNET_FLAG_OFFLINE flag in dwFlags to specify that all download requests for this session be handled by the persistent cache—if a requested file is not in the cache, operations to access it will fail.

You may also specify the INTERNET_FLAG_ASYNC flag to enable asynchronous operations for this session handle, as well as any handles derived from it.

Whenever you are finished with a session, you should close the session handle with a call to InternetCloseHandle(). This will also close any handles that have been derived from the session handle.

Setting Handle Options

If there are certain options that you want to use for all the Internet handles that you will be using in this session, it is easiest to set the options on the session handle. Any handles that are derived from the session handle, such as connection handles created by `InternetConnect()`, will inherit the options from the session handle. In addition, you could set options for a connection handle, which will be inherited by any handles derived from that connection handle. Note however, that only new handles derived from the modified handle will inherit the new settings. Handles that have already been created will maintain their current settings.

Specific option settings for an Internet handle are set with a call to the `InternetSetOption()` function:

```
BOOL InternetSetOption(HINTERNET hInternet, DWORD dwOption,
    LPVOID lpBuffer, DWORD dwBufferLength);
```

The handle to be modified is passed in `hInternet`. The buffer passed by `lpBuffer`, and its length passed in `dwBufferLength`, are used to pass in data for the specific option that is to be set. The option to set is specified by the value of `dwOption`, and can be one of the following values:

`INTERNET_OPTION_CALLBACK` is the address of the callback function for this handle.

`INTERNET_OPTION_CONTEXT_VALUE` is the context value to be used with this handle.

`INTERNET_OPTION_CONNECT_TIMEOUT` is the timeout value, in milliseconds, for connection requests.

`INTERNET_OPTION_CONNECT_RETRIES` is the number of times to retry a connection request.

`INTERNET_OPTION_CONNECT_BACKOFF` is the delay value, in milliseconds, to wait between connection retries.

`INTERNET_OPTION_CONTROL_RECEIVE_TIMEOUT` is the timeout value, in milliseconds, for receiving control information for FTP sessions.

`INTERNET_OPTION_CONTROL_SEND_TIMEOUT` is the timeout value, in milliseconds, for sending control information for FTP.

`INTERNET_OPTION_DATA_SEND_TIMEOUT` is the timeout value, in milliseconds, for sending data.

`INTERNET_OPTION_DATA_RECEIVE_TIMEOUT` is the timeout value, in milliseconds, for receiving data.

`INTERNET_OPTION_ASYNC_PRIORITY` is the priority for an asynchronous download (not currently implemented).

`INTERNET_OPTION_REFRESH` allows options for this handle to be reloaded from the Registry.

`INTERNET_OPTION_PROXY` is proxy information for this handle or for global proxy information if `hInternet` is NULL. `lpBuffer` should point to an `INTERNET_PROXY_INFO` structure.

INTERNET_OPTION_USER_AGENT is the user agent string to use for HTTP requests.

INTERNET_OPTION_USERNAME is the user name for handles created with InternetConnect().

INTERNET_OPTION_PASSWORD is the password for handles created with InternetConnect().

INTERNET_OPTION_READ_BUFFER_SIZE is the size, in bytes, of the buffer for reading data.

INTERNET_OPTION_WRITE_BUFFER_SIZE is the size, in bytes, of the buffer for writing data.

You can also set the options for a handle with the InternetSetOptionEx() function, which takes an additional dwFlags parameter. The flags may be set to ISO_GLOBAL to modify the settings globally or ISO_REGISTRY to modify the settings in the registry.

Querying Handle Options

You can query the current settings for a handle's options with the InternetQueryOption() function:

```
BOOL InternetQueryOption(HINTERNET hInternet, DWORD dwOption,
    LPVOID lpBuffer, LPDWORD lpdwBufferLength);
```

This function works much like InternetSetOption() and allows you to query all the options listed previously. In addition, you can query several additional values that are not set with InternetSetOption():

INTERNET_OPTION_HANDLE_TYPE returns one of the following constants, indicating the type of handle:

```
INTERNET_HANDLE_TYPE_INTERNET
INTERNET_HANDLE_TYPE_CONNECT_FTP
INTERNET_HANDLE_TYPE_CONNECT_HTTP
INTERNET_HANDLE_TYPE_CONNECT_GOPHER
INTERNET_HANDLE_TYPE_FTP_FIND
INTERNET_HANDLE_TYPE_FTP_FIND_HTML
INTERNET_HANDLE_TYPE_FTP_FILE
INTERNET_HANDLE_TYPE_FTP_FILE_HTML
INTERNET_HANDLE_TYPE_GOPHER_FIND
INTERNET_HANDLE_TYPE_GOPHER_FIND_HTML
INTERNET_HANDLE_TYPE_GOPHER_FILE
INTERNET_HANDLE_TYPE_GOPHER_FILE_HTML
INTERNET_HANDLE_TYPE_HTTP_REQUEST
```

INTERNET_OPTION_PARENT_HANDLE returns the handle from which this handle was derived.

`INTERNET_OPTION_KEEP_CONNECTION` returns one of the following constants, indicating this handle's use of persistent connections:

```
INTERNET_KEEP_ALIVE_UNKNOWN
INTERNET_KEEP_ALIVE_ENABLED
INTERNET_KEEP_ALIVE_DISABLED
```

`INTERNET_OPTION_REQUEST_FLAGS` returns flags concerning the current download. Currently, only a request flag value of `INTERNET_REQFLAG_FROM_CACHE` is supported, indicating that the request is being satisfied from the cache.

`INTERNET_OPTION_EXTENDED_ERROR` returns the actual WinSock error code from the last error.

`INTERNET_OPTION_SECURITY_CERTIFICATE_STRUCT` returns an `INTERNET_CERTIFICATE_INFO` structure containing the certificate for SSL/PCT servers.

`INTERNET_OPTION_SECURITY_CERTIFICATE` returns a formatted string containing the certificate for an SSL/PCT server.

`INTERNET_OPTION_SECURITY_KEY_BITNESS` returns the size of the encryption key in bits.

`INTERNET_OPTION_OFFLINE_MODE` is not yet implemented.

`INTERNET_OPTION_CACHE_STREAM_HANDLE` returns the file handle used for writing cached data.

`INTERNET_OPTION_ASYNC` is not yet implemented.

`INTERNET_OPTION_SECURITY_FLAGS` returns a combination of the following security flags:

```
SECURITY_FLAG_128BIT
SECURITY_FLAG_40BIT
SECURITY_FLAG_56BIT
SECURITY_FLAG_IETFSSL4
SECURITY_FLAG_IGNORE_CERT_CN_INVALID
SECURITY_FLAG_IGNORE_CERT_DATE_INVALID
SECURITY_FLAG_IGNORE_REDIRECT_TO_HTTP
SECURITY_FLAG_IGNORE_REDIRECT_TO_HTTPS
SECURITY_FLAG_NORMALBITNESS
SECURITY_FLAG_PCT
SECURITY_FLAG_PCT4
SECURITY_FLAG_SECURE
SECURITY_FLAG_SSL
SECURITY_FLAG_SSL3
SECURITY_FLAG_UNKNOWNBIT
```

`INTERNET_OPTION_DATAFILE_NAME` returns the filename for the file backing a download.

`INTERNET_OPTION_URL` returns the URL of a download.

`INTERNET_OPTION_REFRESH` returns TRUE if the handle's settings may be reloaded from the Registry.

INTERNET_OPTION_VERSION returns an INTERNET_VERSION_INFO structure containing the version of WinInet.dll.

Verifying Internet Connectivity

If your application is capable of operating with or without an Internet connection, you may want to use the InternetAttemptConnect() function, which will attempt to connect to the Internet. If this returns ERROR_SUCCESS, the connection was successful and your application should be able to access information on the Internet. If any other error is returned, the connection could not be established and your application should respond appropriately, perhaps operating in an offline mode.

Connecting to a Server

For most cases, in order to communicate with an FTP, HTTP, or Gopher server, you must first establish a connection, although you will see that InternetOpenUrl() does not require you to create a session explicitly before retrieving files. Establishing a connection is done with the InternetConnect() function, which will return a handle (HINTERNET) for the connection. The new connection handle is derived from a session handle created by InternetOpen() and will inherit the attributes of the session handle, like the asynchronous mode.

For the FTP protocol, InternetConnect() establishes a genuine connection to the server, although for protocols such as Gopher and HTTP, the actual connection is not established until a specific request is made. The connection represented by the handle returned by InternetConnect() is a sort of "virtual connection" and can be used to store configuration information for the connection.

The prototype for InternetConnect() is the following:

```
HINTERNET InternetConnect(HINTERNET hInternetSession, LPCTSTR lpszServerName,
    INTERNET_PORT nServerPort, LPCTSTR lpszUsername, LPCTSTR lpszPassword,
    DWORD dwService, DWORD dwFlags, DWORD dwContext);
```

The handle passed in hInternetSession comes from a call to InternetOpen(), and the lpszServerName and nServerPort parameters refer to the desired server. You can specify a value of INTERNET_INVALID_PORT_NUMBER to use the default port for the requested service, or you may use one of the following constants:

```
INTERNET_DEFAULT_FTP_PORT
INTERNET_DEFAULT_GOPHER_PORT
INTERNET_DEFAULT_HTTP_PORT
INTERNET_DEFAULT_HTTPS_PORT
```

The optional lpszUsername and lpszPassword parameters may be required to connect to servers that require a login.

The dwService parameter specifies the service to which to connect. This can be one of the following constants:

```
INTERNET_SERVICE_FTP
INTERNET_SERVICE_HTTP
INTERNET_SERVICE_GOPHER
```

The dwFlags parameter is used to specify options for the service. Currently, only the INTERNET_CONNECT_FLAG_PASSIVE flag is implemented, which specifies the use of passive mode for FTP connections.

If an error occurs in InternetConnect(), it will return NULL, and you can call GetLastError() or InternetGetLastResponseInfo() for more detail on the error. If the connection is success-fully established, InternetConnect() will return a valid connection handle, which can be used in the protocol-specific functions that you will explore soon.

Adding a Callback Function

InternetConnect(), like many other functions that you will look at in this chapter, can be used asynchronously. To do this, the INTERNET_FLAG_ASYNC flag must have been set when the session handle was created by InternetOpen(). You also must assign a context value and have a call-back function assigned to the handle. A callback function is attached to a handle with the InternetSetStatusCallback() function:

```
INTERNET_STATUS_CALLBACK InternetSetStatusCallback(
    HINTERNET hInternet, INTERNET_STATUS_CALLBACK lpfnInternetCallback);
```

The hInternet parameter specifies the handle that will use the callback function specified in lpfnInternetCallback. Any handles that are derived from this handle—after the callback is attached—will also use this callback function.

The callback function specified in lpfnInternetCallback should have the following prototype:

```
void CALLBACK myCallback(HINTERNET hInternet, DWORD dwContext,
            DWORD dwInternetStatus, LPVOID lpvStatusInformation,
            DWORD dwStatusInformationLength);
```

When the callback function is called to report the status of an asynchronous operation, the hInternet and dwContext parameters give the Internet handle and context value used in the operation, and the reason for calling the function is given in dwInternetStatus. The data re-turned through lpvStatusInformation (of length dwStatusInformationLength) is dependent on the reason for the callback, given in dwInternetStatus. The following are possible values for dwInternetStatus:

INTERNET_STATUS_RESOLVING_NAME, the name being resolved, is contained in lpvStatusInformation.

INTERNET_STATUS_NAME_RESOLVED, the name contained in lpvStatusInformation, was successfully resolved.

INTERNET_STATUS_CONNECTING_TO_SERVER indicates connecting to the server specified by the SOCKADDR structure at lpvStatusInformation.

INTERNET_STATUS_CONNECTED_TO_SERVER indicates that the connection to the server at the address specified in the SOCKADDR structure at lpvStatusInformation was successful.

INTERNET_STATUS_SENDING_REQUEST indicates sending a request to the server. lpvStatusInformation will be NULL.

INTERNET_STATUS_REQUEST_SENT indicates that the request was successfully sent. lpvStatusInformation points to a DWORD holding the number of bytes sent.

INTERNET_STATUS_RECEIVING_RESPONSE indicates waiting to receive a response. lpvStatusInformation will be NULL.

INTERNET_STATUS_RESPONSE_RECEIVED indicates a response was successfully received. lpvStatuInformation points to a DWORD holding the number of bytes received.

INTERNET_STATUS_REDIRECT indicates that an HTTP request is about to be redirected to a new URL. lpvStatusInformation points to the new URL string.

INTERNET_STATUS_CLOSING_CONNECTION indicates that the connection to the server is closing. lpvStatusInformation will be NULL.

INTERNET_STATUS_CONNECTION_CLOSED indicates the connection closed successfully. lpvStatusInformation will be NULL.

INTERNET_STATUS_HANDLE_CREATED indicates that a new handle has been created by InternetConnect(). This occurs before the connection is established.

INTERNET_STATUS_HANDLE_CLOSING indicates that the handle in hInternet has been closed.

INTERNET_STATUS_REQUEST_COMPLETE indicates that an asynchronous operation has completed. lpvStatusInformation points to an INTERNET_ASYNC_RESULT structure containing the dwResult and dwError fields. dwResult will contain the value that was returned from the operation, and dwError will contain the error code for the operation.

In many cases, your application may be concerned only with handling the completion of asynchronous operations, specified by a call to the callback function with a value of INTERNET_STATUS_REQUEST_COMPLETE passed in dwInternetStatus, although some operations may generate many other calls to the callback function. For example, a call to InternetConnect() may generate a dozen or so different calls to the callback function. Because your callback may be called many times, you should try to minimize the operations performed within the callback. Spending excessive time in the callback, like displaying a dialog box, may cause some operations to timeout before the callback returns.

Working with URLs

The WinInet API provides several functions that can be useful in simplifying the processing of URLs. You can parse a URL into its various components with InternetCrackUrl(), and InternetCreateUrl() can be used to create a URL string from the individual components. The InternetCanonicalizeUrl() function can be used to convert a URL to canonical form, as well as convert any unsafe characters into escape sequences. You can also merge a base URL and a relative URL into a single URL string with InternetCombineUrl().

Basic File Operations

For many WinInet functions, you need to explicitly establish a connection (using `InternetConnect()`) before using the protocol-specific functions. However, the WinInet API does provide a simple method for retrieving data from an FTP, HTTP, or Gopher server, in a somewhat generic manner using the `InternetOpenUrl()` function:

```
HINTERNET InternetOpenUrl(HINTERNET hInternetSession,
    LPCTSTR lpszUrl, LPCTSTR lpszHeaders, DWORD dwHeadersLength,
    DWORD dwFlags, DWORD dwContext);
```

Each call to `InternetOpenUrl()` will establish its own connection, so you do not need to create one explicitly with a call to `InternetConnect()`. You do, however, need to pass a valid session handle, returned from `InternetOpen()` in `hInternetSession`.

`InternetOpenUrl()` will return an Internet handle for the file requested by the URL string passed by `lpszUrl`. If this completes successfully, you can use this handle in calls to functions such as `InternetReadFile()`, as you will see shortly.

For HTTP requests, you can specify a pointer to an additional header string in the `lpszHeaders`. The length of this string should be passed in `dwHeadersLength`, although you can pass a length of -1 if the headers string is null-terminated—`InternetOpenUrl()` will then figure out the length of the headers string.

The following are option flags that may be included in `dwFlags`:

> `INTERNET_FLAG_RELOAD` reloads the file from the network, even if it is cached locally.

> `INTERNET_FLAG_DONT_CACHE` means do not cache the data.

> `INTERNET_FLAG_RAW_DATA` returns raw data (`FIND_DATA` structures). Otherwise, directories will be returned in HTML formatting.

> `INTERNET_FLAG_SECURE` requests use of secure sockets layer or PCT for HTTP requests.

> `INTERNET_FLAG_EXISTING_CONNECT` attempts to use an existing connection if possible.

Querying Data Availability

If `InternetOpenUrl()` completes successfully, it returns an Internet file handle. You can check to see how much data is available for this file handle by calling `InternetQueryDataAvailable()`, which can also be used with the file handles returned by the protocol-specific functions that you will see later.

The `InternetQueryDataAvailable()` function takes an Internet file handle and a pointer to a `DWORD` where the number of bytes available will be written. Currently, the `dwFlags` and `dwContext` parameters must be 0:

```
BOOL InternetQueryDataAvailable(HINTERNET hFile,
    LPDWORD lpdwNumberOfBytesAvailable,
    DWORD dwFlags, DWORD dwContext);
```

`InternetQueryDataAvailable()` will return the amount of data that can be read immediately by a call to `InternetReadFile()`. If the end-of-file has not been reached and there is not any data immediately available for reading, this function will block until data is available.

Reading Data

You can read data from a file handle with `InternetReadFile()`. This can be used for handles returned from `InternetOpenUrl()`, as well as handles returned from protocol-specific functions such as `FtpOpenFile()`, `GopherOpenFile()`, or `HttpOpenRequest()`. The following is the prototype for `InternetReadFile()`:

```
BOOL InternetReadFile(HINTERNET hFile, LPVOID lpBuffer,
    DWORD dwNumberOfBytesToRead, LPDWORD lpNumberOfBytesRead);
```

`InternetReadFile()` will attempt to read the number of bytes specified in `dwNumberOfBytesToRead` into the buffer at `lpBuffer`. Upon completion, the `DWORD` at `lpNumberOfBytesRead` will contain the number of bytes actually read. If there is not enough data currently available to satisfy the request, it will block until enough data is received. The only time that the actual number of bytes requested will be less than the number requested is when the end-of-file has been reached.

Moving the File Pointer

You can move the file pointer for calls to `InternetReadFile()` by calling the `InternetSetFilePointer()` function:

```
BOOL InternetSetFilePointer(HINTERNET hFile, LONG lDistanceToMove,
    PVOID pReserved, DWORD dwMoveMethod, DWORD dwContext);
```

The file handle passed in `hFile` can be any file handle returned from calls such as `InternetOpenUrl()` or `FtpOpenFile()`, with the exception that caching must be enabled for the handle—that is, it must not have been created with the `INTERNET_FLAG_DONT_CACHE` or `INTERNET_FLAG_NO_CACHE_WRITE` options.

The `lDistanceToMove` parameter specifies the number of bytes to move the file pointer from a location specified by `dwMoveMethod`, which can have the following values:

  `FILE_BEGIN` moves from the beginning of the file.
  `FILE_CURRENT` moves from the current position.
  `FILE_END` moves from the end-of-file.

Positive values of `lDistanceToMove` move forward in the file, and negative values move backward.

Currently, `pReserved` and `dwContext` must be 0. This operation will always complete synchronously, although subsequent calls to `InternetReadFile()` may complete asynchronously.

Writing to Internet Files

For Internet file handles that have been opened with `InternetOpenUrl()`, as well as other functions such as `FtpOpenFile()`, you can write data to a file with the `InternetWriteFile()` function:

```
BOOL InternetWriteFile(HINTERNET hFile, LPCVOID lpBuffer,
    DWORD dwNumberOfBytesToWrite, LPDWORD lpdwNumberOfBytesWritten);
```

This function will write the number of bytes in `dwNumberOfBytesToWrite` from `lpBuffer` to the file specified by `hFile`. On completion, the `DWORD` at `lpdwNumberOfBytesWritten` will contain the actual number of bytes written.

Note that the transfer may not be completed until you call `InternetCloseHandle()` to close the file handle and flush its buffers.

FTP Client Functions

The following functions are provided by the WinInet API to work with connections to an FTP server. The connection handle (`hFtpSession`) used in these calls is obtained by a call to `InternetConnect()`, as you saw earlier.

The Current Directory

You can retrieve the current directory for an FTP connection by calling `FtpGetCurrentDirectory()`:

```
BOOL FtpGetCurrentDirectory(HINTERNET hFtpSession,
    LPCTSTR lpszCurrentDirectory, LPDWORD lpdwCurrentDirectory);
```

The `lpdwCurrentDirectory` parameter should point to a `DWORD` containing the size of the buffer at `lpszCurrentDirectory`, which will receive a null-terminated ASCII string containing the absolute path to the current directory. A buffer of size `MAX_PATH` is sufficient for all pathnames.

You can set the current directory for an FTP connection with the `FtpSetCurrentDirectory()` function:

```
BOOL FtpSetCurrentDirectory(HINTERNET hFtpSession,
    LPCTSTR lpszDirectory);
```

`lpszDirectory` points to a null-terminated ASCII string containing either an absolute or relative path to the new current directory.

TIP

For the `Ftp` functions listed in this section, you can use either forward (`/`) or backward (`\`) slashes in your path strings. `FtpSetCurrentDirectory()` will translate these to the appropriate character for the server.

Creating and Removing Directories

You can create a new directory on the FTP server with the `FtpCreateDirectory()` function:

```
BOOL FtpCreateDirectory(HINTERNET hFtpSession,
    LPCTSTR lpszDirectory);
```

You can specify either an absolute path or a path relative to the current directory in the null-terminated string passed by `lpszDirectory`.

You can remove a directory from the FTP server with the `FtpRemoveDirectory()` function:

```
BOOL FtpRemoveDirectory(HINTERNET hFtpSession,
    LPCTSTR lpszDirectory);
```

`lpszDirectory` points to a null-terminated string containing either an absolute path or a path relative to the current directory for the directory to be removed.

Finding Files

You can begin a search for a file or a general listing of files on an FTP server with the `FtpFindFirstFile()` function:

```
HINTERNET FtpFindFirstFile(HINTERNET hFtpSession, LPCTSTR lpszSearchFile,
    LPWIN32_FIND_DATA lpFindFileData, DWORD dwFlags, DWORD dwContext);
```

You can specify a valid directory or filename in the null-terminated string at `lpszSearchFile`. Additionally, you may specify a NULL or empty string to begin retrieving a listing of files in the current directory.

Information about the first file found is returned in a WIN32_FIND_DATA structure at `lpFindFileData`.

To retrieve information on additional files found, you can call `InternetFindNextFile()`:

```
BOOL InternetFindNextFile(HINTERNET hFind, LPVOID lpvFindData);
```

The `hFind` parameter gives the find handle returned by `FtpFindFirstFile()`, and a WIN32_FIND_DATA structure is returned via `lpvFindData` with information on the next file in the listing.

If no more matching files are found, `InternetFindNextFile()` returns FALSE, and a call to `GetLastError()` will return ERROR_NO_MORE_FILES.

The nature of the FTP protocol dictates that only one find handle be open at any given time for any particular FTP connection handle. Thus, you must call `InternetCloseHandle()` to close one find handle before starting a new search. You also cannot begin a search with `FtpFindFirstFile()` while a file handle returned by `FtpOpenFile()` is open.

Retrieving a File

You can copy files from the FTP server to a local drive with the `FtpGetFile()` function:

```
BOOL FtpGetFile(HINTERNET hFtpSession, LPCSTR lpszRemoteFile,
    LPCSTR lpszNewFile, BOOL fFailIfExists,
    DWORD dwFlagsAndAttributes, DWORD dwFlags,
    DWORD dwContext);
```

Null-terminated strings containing the source and destination filenames are passed in `lpszRemoteFile` and `lpszNewFile`. You can specify a value of `TRUE` for `fFailIfExists` to cancel the operation if a local file with the name passed in `lpszNewFile` already exists.

The `dwFlagsAndAttributes` parameter contains flags for the file attributes of the new file. These can be any of the file attribute flags used with the Win32 `CreateFile()` function.

The `dwFlags` parameter may contain the flags listed next, which control the transfer mode, as well as several others that control caching operation:

> `FTP_TRANSFER_TYPE_ASCII` performs an ASCII transfer, converting control and formatting information to local formats, such as replacing newlines with carriage-return, linefeed pairs.

> `FTP_TRANSFER_TYPE_BINARY` transfers the file in binary mode; no changes are made to the data. This is the default.

Sending a File

You can copy a file from a local drive to the FTP server with the `FtpPutFile()` function:

```
BOOL FtpPutFile(HINTERNET hFtpSession, LPCSTR lpszLocalFile,
    LPCTSTR lpszNewRemoteFile, DWORD dwFlags, DWORD dwContext);
```

`lpszLocalFile` and `lpszNewRemoteFile` point to null-terminated strings containing the local and remote filenames, respectively. The `dwFlags` parameter may specify one of the transfer type constants used in `FtpGetFile()`.

Opening a File on the FTP Server

The WinInet API allows you to access a file in place on the FTP server, which can be useful when you want to read or write data using memory buffers rather than a local file. You can also have more control of the progress of a file transfer by handling the read or write operations manually. You can open a file for reading or writing in-place on the FTP server with a call to `FtpOpenFile()`:

```
HINTERNET FtpOpenFile(HINTERNET hFtpSession, LPCSTR lpszFileName,
    DWORD fdwAccess, DWORD dwFlags, DWORD dwContext);
```

The `hFtpSession` parameter should be a handle returned by `InternetConnect()`. The name of the file is passed in `lpszFileName()`.

To open the file for reading, you should specify GENERIC_READ in fdwAccess. For writing, fdwAccess should be set to GENERIC_WRITE. You cannot use both for a given handle.

The dwFlags parameter can be used to specify the transfer mode for the file by using either FTP_FLAG_TRANSFER_ASCII or FTP_FLAG_TRANSFER_BINARY. In addition, you may specify other flags that dictate how caching will be used with this file.

FtpOpenFile() returns a handle to the file on the server, which can be used in calls such as InternetReadFile() or InternetWriteFile().

When you are finished with this handle, you should call InternetCloseHandle() to release the handle. This is particularly important, because the FTP protocol allows only one file transfer at a time for a given connection. Because of this, most other FTP functions that you call while a file handle is open will fail with an error code of ERROR_FTP_TRANSFER_IN_PROGRESS.

Other FTP File Operations

You can delete a file on the FTP server with FtpDeleteFile():

```
BOOL FtpDeleteFile(HINTERNET hFtpSession, LPCTSTR lpszFileName);
```

You can also rename files on the FTP server with FtpRenameFile():

```
BOOL FtpRenameFile(HINTERNET hFtpSession,
    LPCTSTR lpszExisting, LPCTSTR lpszNew);
```

HTTP Client Functions

As you saw earlier, you can use InternetOpenUrl() to make simple HTTP requests to retrieve files; however, for more complicated operations, you need to use the HTTP-specific functions that you will look at here. These functions require an HINTERNET parameter, which is a connection handle returned from InternetConnect().

In this section, you will see how to use the WinInet HTTP functions to create a request, send it to the server, and retrieve the results. You will also look at some special functions used to work with cookies and the persistent cache.

HTTP Requests

There are several steps involved in sending an HTTP request and retrieving its results. To start with, a new request is created with HttpOpenRequest(). You can then modify the headers for the request with HttpAddRequestHeaders() before sending the request to the server with HttpSendRequest().

Creating an HTTP Request

A new HTTP request is created by calling the HttpOpenRequest():

```
HINTERNET HttpOpenRequest(HINTERNET hHttpSession, LPCTSTR lpszVerb,
    LPCTSTR lpszObjectName, LPCTSTR lpszVersion,
    LPCTSTR lpszReferer, LPCTSTR FAR * lpszAcceptTypes,
    DWORD dwFlags, DWORD dwContext);
```

The handle passed in hHttpSession is returned by a call to InternetConnect().

The two most important elements of an HTTP request are the object to act on, passed in lpszObjectName, and the verb to use, passed in lpszVerb, which specifies the action the server should perform on the object.

The string containing the object name, which is passed by lpszObjectName, will generally contain a filename to retrieve.

The lpszVerb parameter points to a string containing the verb to use for the request. You can specify a NULL pointer here to use the GET default verb, or you may pass a pointer to a string for the following verbs:

> GET retrieves data.
> HEAD retrieves server response headers.
> POST sends information for the server to act on.
> PUT sends information for the server to store.
> DELETE removes a resource from the server.
> LINK establishes a link between URLs.

If you are using a version of HTTP other than 1.0, you may specify that version in a string at lpszVersion. If this value is NULL, the default of HTTP/1.0 will be used.

The lpszAcceptTypes parameter is used to specify the type of information that the client application will accept. lpszAcceptTypes is a pointer to a null-terminated array of pointers to strings containing data types that will be accepted, such as image/jpeg or audio/*. If lpszAcceptTypes is NULL, the request will use text/* to accept only text files.

You may also choose to specify the URL of a referring page in lpszReferer, a context value for asynchronous I/O in dwContext, or other options for the call in dwFlags. HttpOpenRequest() accepts the same flags that you saw for InternetOpenUrl() earlier.

Upon successful completion, HttpOpenRequest() returns an HINTERNET handle for the request. This handle is then passed to calls such as HttpAddRequestHeaders(), HttpSendRequest(), and HttpQueryInfo().

Request Headers

HTTP requests can have a variety of different headers attached to them to clarify just how a particular request is to be satisfied. The WinInet HttpAddRequestHeaders() function can be used to add headers, as well as modify or remove existing headers:

```
BOOL HttpAddRequestHeaders(HINTERNET hHttpRequest, LPCTSTR lpszHeaders,
    DWORD dwHeadersLength, DWORD dwModifiers);
```

The operation performed by HttpAddRequestHeaders() is specified by the value passed in dwModifiers, which can have a combination of the following values:

HTTP_ADDREQ_FLAG_REPLACE replaces an existing header. If the new header value is empty, this removes an existing header.

HTTP_ADDREQ_FLAG_ADD, when used with _REPLACE, adds the header if it does not already exist.

HTTP_ADDREQ_FLAG_ADD_IF_NEW adds a header only if it does not already exist.

HTTP_ADDREQ_FLAG_COALESCE combines headers with the same name into a single header.

HTTP_ADDREQ_FLAG_COALESCE_WITH_COMMA uses a comma to combine headers with the same name.

HTTP_ADDREQ_FLAG_COALESCE_WITH_SEMICOLON uses a semicolon to combine headers of the same name.

The headers to be added are passed in lpszHeaders, which points to a string containing individual headers, separated by a CR/LF pair. The length of this string is passed in dwHeadersLength, which may be -1L if the lpszHeaders string is null-terminated.

Sending an HTTP Request

An HTTP request, as specified by an HINTERNET created by HttpOpenRequest(), is sent to the server with a call to HttpSendRequest():

```
BOOL HttpSendRequest(HINTERNET hHttpRequest, LPCTSTR lpszHeaders,
    DWORD dwHeadersLength, LPVOID lpOptional, DWORD dwOptionalLength);
```

HttpSendRequest() allows you to specify any additional headers to send with the request in lpszHeaders, with the length of the string in dwHeadersLength.

You can also specify any additional data to be sent immediately after the request headers by passing a pointer to the data in lpOptional and its length in dwOptionalLength. This is normally used only with the POST or PUT operations, which send data to the server.

HttpSendRequest() will send the request to the server and read the status code and response headers from the server. You can access the information in the response headers with HttpQueryInfo(). The body of any data returned can be read with the InternetReadFile() function.

Handling HttpSendRequest() Errors

If HttpSendRequest() completes successfully, it will return TRUE; otherwise, it will return FALSE and you should call GetLastError() to retrieve the specific error code. In addition, the WinInet API provides a special function for dealing with errors in HttpSendRequest(): InternetErrorDlg(). It can also be used to detect errors in the response headers that do not result in failure of the

`HttpSendRequest()` call. It will present a dialog box to the user, detailing the error and requesting input about how to handle the error.

The prototype for `InternetErrorDlg()` is the following:

```
DWORD InternetErrorDlg(HWND hWnd, HINTERNET hInternet,
    DWORD dwError, DWORD dwFlags, LPVOID *lppvData);
```

The hWnd parameter gives the parent of the dialog box to be created, and the handle in hInternet is the handle of the HTTP request, as returned from `HttpOpenRequest()` and used in the `HttpSendRequest()` call.

The dwError parameter specifies the error that should be handled by the dialog box. This can have the following values:

> ERROR_INTERNET_HTTP_TO_HTTPS_ON_REDIR notifies the user of a zone crossing between non-secure and secure sites.
>
> ERROR_INTERNET_INCORRECT_PASSWORD displays a dialog prompting for username and password.
>
> ERROR_INTERNET_INVALID_CA notifies the user that a certificate for an SSL site was not found.
>
> ERROR_INTERNET_POST_IS_NON_SECURE displays a warning about posting data on a non-secure connection.
>
> ERROR_INTERNET_SEC_CERT_CN_INVALID displays the certificate with an invalid common name and allows the user to select a certificate to respond to a server request.
>
> ERROR_INTERNET_SEC_CERT_DATE_INVALID notifies the user of an expired SSL certificate.

The dwFlags parameter specifies what action the function will take in handling an error. The following values are supported:

> FLAGS_ERROR_UI_FLAGS_CHANGE_OPTIONS indicates that the user's choices from the dialog box may result in changes to the options of the request handle passed in hInternet.
>
> FLAGS_ERROR_UI_FLAGS_GENERATE_DATA indicates that the function will query the handle in hInternet for any needed information.
>
> FLAGS_ERROR_UI_FILTER_FOR_ERRORS indicates that the response headers received from the server will be scanned for errors.

The function of the lppvData parameter has not yet been defined, so a value of NULL should be passed.

Retrieving Response Information

Information that the server sends back to a client application in the response headers can be accessed by using the `HttpQueryInfo()` function:

```
BOOL HttpQueryInfo(HINTERNET hHttpRequest, DWORD dwInfoLevel,
    LPVOID lpvBuffer, LPDWORD lpdwBufferLength, LPDWORD lpdwIndex);
```

The `hHttpRequest` parameter should be a handle returned from `HttpOpenRequest()`.

The `dwInfoLevel` parameter is used to specify what information to return and how to return it. This value is formed by combining one of these indexes with one of the flags in the next list:

```
HTTP_QUERY_MIME_VERSION
HTTP_QUERY_CONTENT_TYPE
HTTP_QUERY_CONTENT_TRANSFER_ENCODING
HTTP_QUERY_CONTENT_ID
HTTP_QUERY_CONTENT_DESCRIPTION
HTTP_QUERY_CONTENT_LENGTH
HTTP_QUERY_ALLOW
HTTP_QUERY_PUBLIC
HTTP_QUERY_DATE
HTTP_QUERY_EXPIRES
HTTP_QUERY_LAST_MODIFIED
HTTP_QUERY_MESSAGE_ID
HTTP_QUERY_URI
HTTP_QUERY_DERIVED_FROM
HTTP_QUERY_LANGUAGE
HTTP_QUERY_COST
HTTP_QUERY_WWW_LINK
HTTP_QUERY_PRAGMA
HTTP_QUERY_VERSION
HTTP_QUERY_STATUS_CODE
HTTP_QUERY_STATUS_TEXT
HTTP_QUERY_RAW_HEADERS
HTTP_QUERY_RAW_HEADERS_CRLF
HTTP_QUERY_REQUEST_METHOD
```

The indexes listed can be combined with one of the following flags, which specify how the requested data will be returned:

`HTTP_QUERY_FLAG_NUMBER` indicates that the requested data will be returned as a DWORD.

`HTTP_QUERY_CUSTOM` allows you to specify a custom header to search for in `lpvBuffer`. If the header is found, its value is returned in `lpvBuffer`.

`HTTP_QUERY_FLAG_COALESCE` indicates that headers of the same name will be combined in the returned data.

`HTTP_QUERY_FLAG_REQUEST_HEADERS` is used to query the headers used for the request, rather than the response headers.

`HTTP_QUERY_FLAG_SYSTEMTIME` can be used to return date and time values as SYSTEMTIME structures rather than as strings.

The information that is returned will be written at `lpvBuffer`, and its length will be written at `lpdwBufferLength`.

The `lpdwIndex` parameter is used to return information on multiple headers with the same name. On calling `HttpQueryInfo()`, you can specify the 0-based index of the header to retrieve in the DWORD at `lpdwIndex`. Upon return, the value at `lpdwIndex` will be set to the index of the next matching header, or `ERROR_HTTP_HEADER_NOT_FOUND` if no more matching headers are found.

Getting Your Hands in the Cookie Jar

Many Internet applications make use of *cookies,* which can be used to store bits of data on the local machine that are associated with a particular URL. In most cases, cookies are used to maintain state information for HTTP sessions. Cookies are stored in the `windows\cookies` directory on Win95 or `winnt\cookies` directory on WinNT.

You can add a new cookie to the local system with the `InternetSetCookie()` function:

```
BOOL InternetSetCookie(LPCSTR lpszUrlName,
    LPCSTR lpszCookieName, LPCSTR lpszCookieData);
```

This function takes pointers to three null-terminated strings: `lpszUrlName` points to the URL with which to associate the cookie, `lpszCookieName` points to the name of the cookie, and `lpszCookieData` points to the string that will be saved for the new cookie.

> **NOTE**
>
> Because no `HINTERNET`s are involved, the cookie functions do not require that you call `InternetOpen()` before using them.

You can retrieve data stored in a cookie for a given URL or its parent URLs, by calling `InternetGetCookie()`:

```
BOOL InternetGetCookie(LPCSTR lpszUrlName, LPCSTR lpszCookieName,
    LPSTR lpszCookieData, LPDWORD  lpdwSize);
```

This function tries to find a cookie named in `lpszCookieName` that is associated with the URL in `lpszUrlName` or its parent URLs and will return any data found at `lpszCookieData` and its length at `lpdwSize`.

Working with the Cache

Many of the WinInet functions that you have looked at so far in this chapter can make use of the persistent cache to store received data to disk, depending on certain flags. This allows applications such as browsers to be able to retrieve frequently accessed data more efficiently than having to download it each time.

The WinInet API provides the following functions, which allow you to work with the cache more directly from within your applications:

`CreateUrlCacheEntry()` creates an entry in the cache.

`GetUrlCacheEntryInfo()` retrieves information about a cache entry.

`SetUrlCacheEntryInfo()` sets information in a cache entry.

`CommitUrlCacheEntry()` saves data to the cache.

`DeleteUrlCacheEntry()` deletes a file from the cache.

`RetrieveUrlCacheEntryFile()` retrieves cache data as a file.

`UnlockUrlCacheEntryFile()` unlocks a cache file locked with `RetrieveUrlCacheEntryFile()`.

`RetrieveUrlCacheEntryStream()` opens a stream for data from the cache.

`ReadUrlCacheEntryStream()` reads cached data from a stream opened with `RetrieveUrlCacheEntryStream()`.

`UnlockUrlCacheEntryStream()` releases a stream locked by `RetreiveUrlCacheEntryStream()`.

`FindFirstUrlCacheEntry()` begins a search of cache entries.

`FindNextUrlCacheEntry()` retrieves individual cache entries.

`FindCloseUrlCache()` closes a search handle created by `FindFirstUrlCacheEntry()`.

Gopher Client Functions

The WinInet API also provides functions that can be used by your client applications to retrieve information from Gopher servers. The Gopher protocol was developed at the University of Minnesota to provide an ASCII-based system for browsing a series of menus to locate various resources on a network.

The WinInet Gopher functions require the use of a Gopher connection handle that was created with a call to `InternetConnect()`.

To access objects on a Gopher server, a special ASCII string known as a Gopher locator is used. This string is similar to the URL strings used in HTTP requests. You can create a locator string with a call to `GopherCreateLocator()`. You can also retrieve specific information about a locator string with the `GopherGetLocatorType()` function.

To find Gopher resources on a server, you can start a query with `GopherFindFirstFile()` and retrieve individual entries with the `InternetFindNext()` function, as you saw earlier for FTP connections.

You can request information from the server about a Gopher object with a call to `GopherGetAttributes()`. To retrieve a file from the server, you can use `GopherOpenFile()` to open a file handle, which can then be used in calls to `InternetReadFile()`.

MFC WinInet Classes

In addition to the Win32 Internet Extension C API that you saw previously, MFC provides the WinInet classes that encapsulate this functionality into a set of classes that you can use to easily add Internet functionality to your C++ applications.

These classes add some additional functionality to the WinInet C API, including buffered I/O, default parameters, exception handling, and automatic cleanup of handles and connections.

Figure 22.1 shows the relationship of the classes that make up the MFC WinInet classes.

FIGURE 22.1.
MFC WinInet classes.

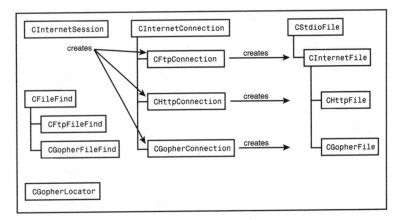

CInternetSession

Any application that is going to use the WinInet classes will first need to have a `CInternetSession` object. This object is used to create and initialize an Internet session and may be used to handle a connection to a proxy server. Often, if your application will maintain an Internet session for the duration of the application, it is most convenient to make your `CInternetSession` object a member of your `CWinApp` object.

Connection Classes

For many Internet operations, you will also need to open a connection to a server. MFC uses the `CInternetConnection` class to represent a connection to a server, as well as a class derived from `CInternetConnection` for each specific protocol. These include `CFtpConnection`, `CGopherConnection`, and `CHttpConnection`. These objects are created by member functions of `CInternetSession`.

File Classes

To help your application work with the files used in various Internet protocols, MFC provides several new Internet file classes derived from `CInternetFile`. These include `CInternetFile` itself for FTP files, `CHttpFile` for HTTP files, and `CGopherFile` for Gopher files. As you will see, these objects are returned from `CInternetSession::OpenURL()` or the protocol-specific functions `CFtpConnection::OpenFile()`, `CGopherConnection::OpenFile()`, or `CHttpConnection::OpenRequest()`.

CInternetException

Many of the member functions for the WinInet classes may throw an exception in the event of errors. In most cases, a `CInternetException` is thrown. For more on handling these exceptions, see Chapter 7, "General-Purpose Classes." In your applications, you can generate a `CInternetException` with a call to `::AfxThrowInternetException()`.

Using CInternetSession

The CInternetSession class provides a context for all the other operations that will be performed using the WinInet classes. In this section, you take a look at how to create a CInternetSession and how it can be used to perform simple file retrieval. You also see how the WinInet classes allow you to handle asynchronous operations.

Creating a Session

To establish an Internet session in MFC, you need only construct a new CInternetSession object—although you may want to derive your own class from CInternetSession, as you will see in the discussion about asynchronous I/O. The constructor for CInternetSession takes a fair number of parameters, although you will notice that all these have reasonable default values provided. The following is the constructor for CInternetSession:

```
CInternetSession( LPCTSTR pstrAgent = NULL, DWORD dwContext = 1,
    DWORD dwAccessType = PRE_CONFIG_INTERNET_ACCESS,
    LPCTSTR pstrProxyName = NULL, LPCTSTR pstrProxyBypass = NULL,
    DWORD dwFlags = 0 );
```

The pstrAgent parameter can be used to specify the name of your application, which may be used, in turn, to identify your application to servers for certain protocols. By default, this is NULL—in which case, MFC will get the application name with a call to AfxGetAppName().

dwContext specifies a context value that will be used for asynchronous operations on this CInternetSession and any objects that are created by it.

The dwAccessType parameter is used to tell MFC how to connect to the network. You can use INTERNET_OPEN_TYPE_DIRECT to connect directly, or INTERNET_OPEN_TYPE_PROXY to connect through a proxy server. The default, INTERNET_OPEN_TYPE_PRECONFIG, will access the network as configured in the registry.

If you are using proxy access, you will also need to specify the name of the proxy server in pstrProxyName. In addition, you may specify a list of server addresses that should be accessed directly, without using the proxy server, in pstrProxyBypass.

The dwFlags parameter allows you to specify several options for how your Internet session will behave. You can specify INTERNET_FLAG_DONT_CACHE to tell the framework not to cache data, or you may specify INTERNET_FLAG_OFFLINE to tell the framework to access only data that is currently in the cache—attempts to access data not in the cache will return an error. In addition, you may specify the INTERNET_FLAG_ASYNC flag to enable asynchronous operations for the session.

Retrieving a File

Once an Internet session is established, you can begin retrieving files with calls to CInternetSession::OpenURL(). Note that you do not need to establish a connection explicitly before using this function; it will create its own session if necessary.

`OpenURL()` makes use of the `InternetOpenURL()` Win32 API function and has the same limitations: You can only retrieve data, and you cannot manipulate data on the server. For operations requiring this sort of interaction, you need to open a connection, as you will see later.

`OpenURL()` takes a URL string and returns a pointer to an object of a type appropriate for the file specified in the URL. Table 22.1 lists the types of URL currently supported, with the type of pointer that is returned by `OpenURL()`.

Table 22.1. URL types and associated file classes.

URL type	`OpenURL()` *return type*
`http:\\`	`CHttpFile*`
`ftp://`	`CFtpFile*`
`gopher:\\`	`CGopherFile*`
`file://`	`CStdioFile*`

Note that the `CStdioFile` object may be used just like any other `CStdioFile`, as you saw in Chapter 7.

The following is the prototype for `CInternetSession::OpenURL()`:

```
CStdioFile* OpenURL( LPCTSTR pstrURL, DWORD dwContext = 1, DWORD dwFlags = 0,
    LPCTSTR pstrHeaders = NULL, DWORD dwHeadersLength = 0 );
```

The first parameter, pstrURL, points to the URL string for the file to retrieve. The dwContext parameter is used for asynchronous operations, as you will see soon.

`OpenURL()` also supports several flags, as passed in dwFlags, that can be used to alter the behavior of `OpenURL()`. `INTERNET_FLAG_RELOAD` will force the framework to reload the file from the network, even if it is found in the cache. `INTERNET_FLAG_DONT_CACHE` can be specified to prevent the framework from saving the file in the cache.

The `INTERNET_OPEN_FLAG_USE_EXISTING_CONNECT` flag tells the framework to try to use an existing connection to retrieve the file, rather than opening a new connection for each call to `OpenURL()`.

For FTP applications, you can also specify `INTERNET_FLAG_PASSIVE` to use passive FTP semantics.

Applications requesting files using HTTP may specify the `INTERNET_FLAG_SECURE` flag to use secure transactions, either with Secure Sockets Layer (SSL) or PCT. In addition, HTTP requests may include additional RFC822, MIME, or HTTP headers, as specified with pstrHeaders and dwHeadersLength.

The following example shows how an application can create an Internet session and use `OpenURL()` to retrieve a file using HTTP:

```
#include <AfxInet.h>
    // Create Session Object
    CInternetSession mySession;
```

```
CHttpFile *pHttpFile;
CString tmpStr;
char inBuf[10000];
UINT nBytesRead;
try
{
    // Open HTTP file
    pHttpFile =(CHttpFile *) mySession.OpenURL("http://www.racotek.com");
}
catch (CInternetException)
{
    AfxMessageBox("Received Exception from OpenURL()");
    // Handle exception
}
if(pHttpFile == NULL)
    AfxMessageBox("Error in OpenURL");
else
{
    // Read from file
    nBytesRead = pFile->Read(inBuf, sizeof(inBuf));
    tmpStr.Format("Read %d bytes", nBytesRead);
    AfxMessageBox(tmpStr);
}
```

Note that, although this example shows how you can handle the CInternetException that may be thrown by OpenURL(), it doesn't do any real error handling. In addition, your application will probably want to use a more robust and efficient buffer mechanism than the simple large array I have used here.

OpenURL() can be used in a similar fashion for other protocols, such as Gopher, FTP, or local files. Just make sure to use the appropriate file object (CGopherFile, CInternetFile, or CStdioFile).

If you are unsure of the type of service for an HINTERNET, you can use CInternetSession::ServiceTypeFromHandle() to determine whether the handle is to be used with FTP, HTTP, Gopher, or local files.

Establishing a Connection

For applications that need to perform more interactive operations with a server, you need to establish a connection. In MFC, a connection is represented by a class derived from CInternetConnection, including CFtpConnection, CHttpConnection, and CGopherConnection. You can create a new connection object by calling one of the get-connection methods of class CInternetSession. These include GetFtpConnection(), GetHttpConnection(), and GetGopherConnection(). You will see examples of each of these in the next sections.

Asynchronous Operations with CInternetSession

The MFC WinInet classes allow you to take advantage of the asynchronous mechanism that the WinInet C API provides for monitoring the status of operations in progress. The callback function that you saw earlier in the C API is implemented as an overridable member function of CInternetSession. Thus, if you want to use the WinInet classes asynchronously, you must first derive your own class from `CInternetSession`, overriding the `OnStatusCallback()` member function. Here is the prototype for this callback function:

```
virtual void OnStatusCallback( DWORD dwContext, DWORD dwInternetStatus,
    LPVOID lpvStatusInformation, DWORD dwStatusInformationLength);
```

When this function is called, it will receive the context value for the operation that generated the call in `dwContext`. For some functions, such as `CInternetSession::GetFtpConnection()`, this is the context value that was passed to the object's constructor; other functions, such as `CInternetSession::OpenURL()`, allow you to specify a context value for that operation.

The reason that the callback function was called is passed in `dwInternetStatus`, and additional information may be supplied in `lpvStatusInformation` and `dwStatusInformationLength`. The value of `dwInternetStatus` and the information passed in `lpvStatusInformation` is the same as that returned by the C API callback function that you saw earlier.

In order to use asynchronous operations with an object of your new `CInternetSession` class, you must pass a value of `INTERNET_FLAG_ASYNC` in the `dwFlags` parameter of the constructor for your new class. In addition, you must specify a non-zero context value for the operations that you want to complete asynchronously.

> **NOTE**
>
> As of January 1997, many of the MFC WinInet methods *require* a non-zero context value, implying that they cannot be used in a synchronous manner. In many cases, a context value of `0` (or `NULL`) will cause an `ASSERT` or will cause the function to fail.

The last step in enabling asynchronous operations is a call to `CInternetSession::EnableStatusCallback()`, which takes a single `BOOL` parameter. If this is `TRUE` (the default), the callback function will be enabled. You can disable asynchronous operation by calling `EnableStatusCallback()` with a parameter of `FALSE`.

Once asynchronous operation is enabled, any calls that are made with a non-zero context value may complete asynchronously—the function will return "failure" (`FALSE` or `NULL`), and a subsequent call to `GetLastError()` will return `ERROR_IO_PENDING`. Various events in the processing of the request will then generate calls to `OnStatusCallback()`. When the operation is complete, `OnStatusCallback()` will be called with a status of `INTERNET_STATUS_REQUEST_COMPLETE`.

Other `CInternetSession` Members

The `CInternetSession` class encapsulates the session handle used earlier in the WinInet C API. As with the session handle, you can manipulate various options for the `CInternetSession` with the `QueryOption()` and `SetOption()` member functions, which are very similar to the C API functions `::InternetQueryOption()` and `::InternetSetOption()`.

The `GetContext()` member of `CInternetSession` can be used to retrieve the context value that was assigned to the session.

`CInternetSession::Close()` should be called when you are finished with a session.

You can also retrieve the actual `HINTERNET` handle for the session by using the `HINTERNET` operator provided by the `CInternetSession` class.

Working with FTP

To establish an FTP connection, you can use `CInternetSession::GetFtpSession()`, which will return a pointer to a new `CFtpConnection` object. `GetFtpSession()` allows you to specify the server and port to connect to, the user name and password to use, and a flag for active or passive mode. However, you can use the default for many of these parameters.

Once you have established the FTP connection, most of the operations that your application will need to perform are accessed by way of the member functions of `CFtpConnection`. When you are finished with the connection, you should call `CFtpConnection::Close()` to close the connection.

FTP Directories

`CFtpConnection` allows you to work with the current directory on the FTP server by way of its `GetCurrentDirectory()` and `SetCurrentDirectory()` member functions. In addition, you can retrieve the current server directory as a URL by calling `CFtpConnection::GetCurrentDirectoryAsURL()`.

You can also create a directory on the server with `CFtpConnection::CreateDirectory()` or remove a directory with `CFtpConnectionRemoveDirectory()`.

Finding Files

To help locate files on an FTP server, MFC provides the `CFtpFileFind` class, which is derived from `CFileFind`. To create a new `CFtpFileFind` object, you must first create a valid `CFtpConnection`. The constructor for `CFtpFileFind` then takes a pointer to the `CFtpConnection` and an optional context value.

Once you have created the `CFtpFileFind` object, you can use its member functions to search for files. To begin a search, you can call `CFtpFileFind::FindFile()`, which takes parameters for the filename to find and a set of flags. The flags may be used to specify how the find is to operate. For example, you may specify `INTERNET_FLAG_RELOAD` to force the find to get the most current data from the server, rather than using cached data. You may specify a `NULL` pointer to the filename (the default) to browse all files in the current directory.

To find the next file that matches the search string, you can use `CFtpFileFind::FindNextFile()`. For example, if you specified a `NULL` pointer to the filename in `FindFile()`, you can walk through the whole directory by making calls to `FindNextFile()` until it returns `FALSE`. If you have read the entire directory, a call to `GetLastError()` will return `ERROR_NO_MORE_FILES`; other return values indicate a more substantial error.

After a successful call to `FindFile()` or `FindNextFile()`, you can call `CFtpFileFind::GetFileURL()` to return a `CString` that contains the URL for the found file.

In addition, you can use the member functions of `CFindFile`, from which `CFtpFindFile` is derived, to get information about the current file. `CFindFile` implements methods such as `GetLength()` and `GetFileName()` to retrieve information about the file, as well as many others that can be used to retrieve information about a file's attributes.

FTP Files

You can copy a file from the FTP server to the local machine with the `CFtpConnection::GetFile()`. This function allows you to specify the local and remote filenames, as well as several other parameters to specify the attributes of the new file, what to do if this file already exists, a context value for asynchronous I/O, and the transfer mode. Fortunately, the default transfer mode is `FTP_TRANSFER_TYPE_BINARY`, rather than the default for many command-line FTP utilities; thus, you have to work harder if you want to mangle your .exe files by adding carriage returns.

Similarly, the `CFtpConnection::PutFile()` method allows you to transfer a file from the local machine to the server. However, `PutFile()` allows you to specify only the two filenames: transfer mode and context value. The attributes of the new file are left up to the FTP server.

You can also open a file in place on the server using the `CFtpConnection::OpenFile()` method, which will return a pointer to a `CInternetFile` object. You may then use the `CInternetFile::Read()` or `CInternetFile::Write()` methods to read from or write to the file.

`OpenFile()` is useful for instances where your application wants to create a file on the server from data in memory rather than from a local disk file, or when you want to read a file directly into memory rather than into a disk file. `OpenFile()` may also be useful in cases where you want to be able to control the progress of a file transfer more closely—for example, to display the status to the user.

`CFtpConnection` also provides the `Remove()` method for removing files from the FTP server and the `Rename()` method for renaming files on the server.

Working with HTTP

In this section, you will explore the MFC WinInet classes that are used for working with HTTP, starting with the `CHttpConnection` class and including the `CHttpFile` class.

HTTP Connections

MFC provides the `CHttpConnection` class to represent connections to an HTTP server. A new connection is established by calling `CInternetSession::GetHttpConnection()`, which allows you to specify the server and port to connect to, as well as a user name and password. In many cases, you need only specify the server name—the defaults for the other parameters are usually sufficient. The following is the prototype for GetHttpConnection():

```
CHttpConnection* GetHttpConnection( LPCTSTR pstrServer,
    INTERNET_PORT nPort = INTERNET_INVALID_PORT_NUMBER,
    LPCTSTR pstrUserName = NULL, LPCTSTR pstrPassword = NULL );
```

HTTP Files

To work with files from an HTTP server, you will be working with CHttpFile objects. As you saw earlier, you can create a CHttpFile object with CInternetSession::OpenURL(), although here you will see how you can implement greater functionality by creating a CHttpFile object from a connection that you have explicitly created with a call to CHttpConnection::OpenRequest(). You will also take a look at the various member functions of CHttpFile that can be used to build requests, send them to the server, and retrieve their results.

Creating a New CHttpFile

Once you have created a CHttpConnection with CInternetSession::GetHttpConnection(), you can create a CHttpFile from this connection by calling CHttpConnection::OpenRequest():

```
CHttpFile* OpenRequest( LPCTSTR pstrVerb, LPCTSTR pstrObjectName,
    LPCTSTR pstrReferer = NULL, DWORD dwContext = 1,
    LPCTSTR* pstrAcceptTypes = NULL, LPCTSTR pstrVersion = NULL,
    DWORD dwFlags = INTERNET_FLAG_EXISTING_CONNECT );
```

The pstrVerb parameter specifies the verb to use for the request. If this pointer is NULL, GET is used. In addition, you may specify the verb as an int, using one of the following constants:

```
HTTP_VERB_POST
HTTP_VERB_GET
HTTP_VERB_HEAD
HTTP_VERB_PUT
HTTP_VERB_LINK
HTTP_VERB_DELETE
HTTP_VERB_UNLINK
```

pstrObjectName points to a string containing the target object of the specified verb. In most cases, this is a filename, executable module, or search specifier. You can parse the object name, as well as several other elements from a URL, with ::AfxParseURL().

The additional parameters allow you to specify the referring page, the type of data to accept, the version of HTTP to use, a context value, and a set of flags, which give options for things such as cache usage.

Adding HTTP Headers

You can add additional headers to the request contained in the CHttpFile by calling CHttpFile::AddRequestHeader(), which allows you to specify a header string as either a CString or a C string and its length, and a set of option flags for the header operation. You saw the possible flag values in the discussion of the ::HttpAddRequestHeaders() function.

Sending the Request

Once you have added all the desired headers to the request, it is forwarded to the server with a call to `CHttpFile::SendRequest()`, which allows you to specify additional headers to send (as a `CString` or character array), as well as any optional data that will be sent for operations such as `POST` or `PUT`.

Once the request has been sent successfully, you can call `CHttpFile::QueryInfoStatusCode()` to return the status of the request by updating a `DWORD` at an address you pass. The status may have many different specific values, but these are grouped into the following ranges:

```
200-299 Success
300-399 Information
400-499 Request Error
500-599 Server Error
```

If the request has completed successfully, you can read the data returned from the server by using the `Read()` method of `CHttpFile`.

Working with Gopher

In this section, you will look at the MFC WinInet classes that are used to work with Gopher servers, including `CGopherConnection`, `CGopherLocator`, `CGopherFileFind`, and `CGopherFile`.

Gopher Connections

A connection to a Gopher server is represented by the `CGopherConnection` class. You create a new `CGopherConnection` by calling `CInternetSession::GetGopherConnection()`:

```
CGopherConnection* GetGopherConnection( LPCTSTR pstrServer,
    LPCTSTR pstrUserName = NULL, LPCTSTR pstrPassword = NULL,
    INTERNET_PORT nPort = INTERNET_INVALID_PORT_NUMBER);
```

This function is passed the name of the Gopher server and optional user name and password strings. You can also specify a port on the Gopher server if the server uses a port other than the default.

Gopher Locators

Like the URLs used for locating HTTP files, the Gopher protocol uses locator strings to access files. In the MFC WinInet classes, the locator string is encapsulated by objects of class `CGopherLocator`, which are created by calls to `CGopherConnection::CreateLocator()`. This allows you to create a `CGopherLocator` from the individual components of the locator string or from a complete locator string. The locator object can then be used in calls to `CGopherFileFind::FindFile()` and `CGopherConnection::OpenFile()`.

Finding Gopher Files

The MFC WinInet classes include the `CGopherFileFind` class to help you find files on a Gopher server. Unlike many of the other WinInet classes, a new `CGopherFileFind` object is not created by a member function of `CInternetSession` or a connection class; however, you must pass a pointer to a valid `CGopherConnection` object in the constructor for `CGopherFileFind`:

```
CGopherFileFind( CGopherConnection* pConnection, DWORD dwContext = 1 );
```

To begin a search of a Gopher server, you use the `CGopherFileFind::FindFile()` function, which allows you to begin a search for a particular filename string. There are two versions of `FindFile()`. The first allows a reference to a `CGopherLocator` parameter, which will receive the results of the first file found. The second version requires that you use `CGopherFileFind::GetLocator()` to retrieve the results.

Regardless of which version of `FindFile()` you used to begin the query, you can retrieve additional results by calling `CGopherFileFind::FindNextFile()` to find the next file and `CGopherFileFind::GetLocator()` to retrieve the locator for the found file. When no more files are found, `FindNextFile()` will return `FALSE` and `GetLastError()` will return `ERROR_NO_MORE_FILES`.

Working with Gopher Files

To retrieve data from a Gopher server, you use the `CGopherFile` class. `CGopherFile` objects are created by a call to `CGopherConnection::OpenFile()`, which takes a reference to a `CGopherLocator` as a parameter. The `CGopherLocator`, which specifies the file to open, is returned by `CGopherConnection::CreateLocator()` or `CGopherFileFind::GetLocator()`.

If `CGopherConnection::OpenFile()` completes successfully, you can use the returned `CGopherFile` to read the data in the file by calling `CGopherFile::Read()`. You can also use the other member functions of `CInternetFile` (the base class for `CGopherFile`) to work with the file, although the Gopher protocol does not allow you to write data to the server.

Summary

In this chapter, you explored how to use both the WinInet C API and the MFC WinInet classes to add Internet functionality to your applications, without having to know the details of the underlying protocols, such as FTP, HTTP, or Gopher.

You saw how the WinInet C API uses a hierarchy of special handles of type `HINTERNET` to manage Internet sessions, connections, and files, as well as the functions used to work with these handles, such as `InternetOpen()`, `InternetConnect()`, and `InternetOpenUrl()`. You also took a look at the MFC WinInet class hierarchy, including `CInternetSession`, `CInternetConnection`, and `CInternetFile`, as well as the protocol-specific classes derived from them, such as `CFtpConnection` and `CHttpFile`.

23

The Internet Server API (ISAPI)

by David Bennett

In this chapter, you will look at the Internet Server API, which can be used to create your own custom enhancements to ISAPI-compliant HTTP servers, such as the one included with Microsoft's Internet Information Server. You look at both the C APIs that are included in ISAPI and the MFC classes that are provided to encapsulate these functions.

ISAPI allows you to create two sorts of extensions to a Web server. The first is called an Internet Server Extension Application, or ISA. You will see how to implement a DLL that can be called by the Web server on behalf of a client to provide custom functionality, similar to Common Gateway Interface (CGI) scripts. However, ISAs, which are loaded as DLLs into the server's memory address space, are more efficient than CGI scripts, which are separate executables that must be started each time a request is made for the script.

The second sort of extension that you can create is an ISAPI filter, which can be called by the Web server to assist in handling various events in the processing of an HTTP request, ranging from the reading and writing of raw data to the output of log file entries. ISAPI filters can be used to add any number of different sorts of functionality to a Web server, including custom authentication, compression, encryption, or logging schemes.

In this chapter, you will explore version 2.0 of ISAPI, which is included with Visual C++ 5.0.

Developing a Server Extension Application

To get things started, let's look at how to create an Internet Server Extension Application (ISA), which is not really a standalone application, but a DLL that can be loaded by the Web server to process requests more efficiently than CGI scripts. You will see the entry points that your DLL must export in order to be an ISA, as well as how your extensions communicate with the client and the server.

To install an ISA on your server, you need only copy the ISA DLL to a directory that is accessible by the HTTP server. The functions of this extension can then be accessed by a client with a request something like this:

```
http::/scripts/myISA.dll?SendList?param1=3
```

ISA Entry Points

The DLLs that you develop with ISAPI will interact with the HTTP server by way of three entry points that your DLL exports. The first of these, GetExtensionVersion(), is called by the server when it first loads the extension DLL, and it is used to report the version of ISAPI supported by the ISA. You may also choose to implement and export a TerminateExtension()

function, which will be called before the extension DLL is unloaded, although this is not required. The final entry point that you must implement is `HttpExtensionProc()`, which will be called by the server to process requests to the ISA.

> **NOTE**
>
> Because the Web server supports concurrent threads, your ISA functions may be called by several different threads at the same time. Make sure that your ISA is thread-safe by using the mechanisms you learned in Chapter 9, "Multithreading with MFC."

GetExtensionVersion()

Your extension DLL must export a `GetExtensionVersion()` function. This will be called by the server when it first loads your DLL, and it is intended to be used to report version information about your DLL to the server; however, you may also choose to do any other initialization that your DLL requires in this function.

Other than any initialization specific to your extension, the code for `GetExtensionVersion()` is fairly generic. You can pass a description of your ISA and the version of ISAPI that it supports back to the server. Most implementations will look something like this:

```
BOOL WINAPI GetExtensionVersion( HSE_VERSION_INFO *pVer)
{
    pVer->dwExtensionVersion = MAKELONG( HSE_VERSION_MINOR, HSE_VERSION_MAJOR);
    strncpy(pVer->lpszExtensionDesc, "A Description of Your ISA Here",
            HSE_MAX_EXT_DLL_NAME_LEN);
    return TRUE;
}
```

If something goes wrong in any additional initialization that you perform in `GetExtensionVersion()`, you can return `FALSE`, which will abort the loading of your extension.

> **NOTE**
>
> Your ISA is like any other DLL in that you can specify an entry point to be called when loading the DLL. You can also use this entry point (usually `DllMain()`) to perform any necessary initialization for your ISA.

TerminateExtension()

Your ISA may also export an implementation of the `TerminateExtension()` function, although this is not required. This function is called whenever the server wants to unload the extension

DLL and may be useful for cleaning up any dynamic structures or extra threads that you started in GetExtensionVersion(). Here is the prototype for TerminateExtension():

```
BOOL WINAPI TerminateExtension(DWORD dwFlags);
```

The dwFlags parameter will receive one of two values: When dwFlags is HSE_TERM_ADVISORY_UNLOAD, the server would like to unload your DLL to tidy up a bit. If you don't want to let the server unload your DLL, you can return FALSE. Otherwise, returning TRUE will allow the server to unload the DLL. On the other hand, if dwFlags is HSE_TERM_MUST_UNLOAD, your DLL is about to be unloaded whether you like it or not, so if you need to clean up, you had better do it now.

HttpExtensionProc()

In most cases, the bulk of the code for your ISA will be in the HttpExtensionProc() function, which is called by the server for each request to the ISA. The following is the prototype for this function:

```
DWORD HttpExtensionProc(LPEXTENSION_CONTROL_BLOCK *lpEcb);
```

At first glance, the prototype for HttpExtensionProc() looks quite simple, although the EXTENSION_CONTROL_BLOCK (ECB) structure is a bit complicated—it provides many different fields that are passed into your DLL, as well as several different fields that are returned to the server.

In addition, the ECB contains pointers to several different utility functions, provided by the server, that your DLL can use in processing the request. It is these functions that allow your ISA to receive additional information from the client and send information back to the client.

You will be looking at the ECB in greater detail in just a bit, but for now, let's take a look at a simple example to see how the basics of the HttpExtensionProc() entry point work. The following implementation will return a very simple HTML page to the client for any requests made to the ISA:

```
#include <httpext.h>
#include <stdio.h>
#include <wininet.h>
DWORD WINAPI HttpExtensionProc( EXTENSION_CONTROL_BLOCK *pECB)
{
    BOOL bRc;
    char strStatus[100] = "200 OK";
    DWORD dwMsgLen;
    DWORD dwError;
    char retBuf[1000];

    sprintf(retBuf, "<FONT COLOR=BLUE SIZE=4>Hi Mom!</FONT>\r\n");
    // Send HTTP headers back to the client
    bRc = pECB->ServerSupportFunction( pECB->ConnID,
                             HSE_REQ_SEND_RESPONSE_HEADER,
                             strStatus,
                             NULL,
                             (LPDWORD) "Content-Type: text/html\r\n\r\n");
```

```
    if(!bRc)
    {
        // An error occurred
        dwError = GetLastError();
        pECB->dwHttpStatusCode = HTTP_STATUS_SERVER_ERROR;
        return(HSE_STATUS_ERROR);
    }

    // Send response data to client
    dwMsgLen = strlen(retBuf);
    bRc = pECB->WriteClient(pECB->ConnID, retBuf, &dwMsgLen, HSE_IO_SYNC);
    if(bRc == FALSE)
    {
        dwError = GetLastError();
        // Do something with the error code...
        pECB->dwHttpStatusCode = HTTP_STATUS_SERVER_ERROR;
        return(HSE_STATUS_ERROR);
    }

    return(HSE_STATUS_SUCCESS);
} // end HttpExtensionProc
```

NOTE

Your ISA files should include httpext.h, although you will not need to link with any special libraries—all the ISAPI-specific functions that you will use are passed via pointers from the Web server.

In this example, you use two of the callback functions provided by the Web server via pointers in the ECB. You use ServerSupportFunction() to send the HTTP headers for the response to the client, then use WriteClient() to send the body of an HTML page that is returned to the client. You will look at both of these functions in greater detail later in this chapter.

The return values for HttpExtensionProc() are used to tell the server about the status of the request and whether or not it can free up its resources for the session:

HSE_STATUS_SUCCESS—The operation completed successfully, and the server can free up any resources for the session.

HSE_STATUS_ERROR—An error occurred in processing. The server can close the connection and free its resources.

HSE_STATUS_PENDING—The ISA has queued the request and will notify the server when it is finished processing.

HSE_STATUS_SUCCESS_AND_KEEP_CONN—The operation has completed successfully, but the server should keep the connection open, provided it supports persistent connections.

You can also specify additional information about the status of a request handled by your ISA by setting the value of the dwHttpStatusCode field of the ECB to one of the following values (defined in WinInet.h) before returning from HttpExtensionProc():

HTTP_STATUS_BAD_REQUEST

HTTP_STATUS_AUTH_REQUIRED

HTTP_STATUS_FORBIDDEN

HTTP_STATUS_NOT_FOUND

HTTP_STATUS_SERVER_ERROR

HTTP_STATUS_NOT_IMPLEMENTED

The Extension Control Block

The HTTP server passes requests to your extension DLL by passing a pointer to an EXTENSION_CONTROL_BLOCK structure, which contains information about the request to your ISA. This structure also allows you to pass certain information back to the server, as well as providing pointers to a set of helper functions that can be used to communicate with the client. Here is the structure:

```
typedef struct _EXTENSION_CONTROL_BLOCK {
    DWORD       cbSize;
    DWORD       dwVersion;
    HCONN       ConnID;
    DWORD       dwHttpStatusCode;
    CHAR        lpszLogData[HSE_LOG_BUFFER_LEN];
    LPSTR       lpszMethod;
    LPSTR       lpszQueryString;
    LPSTR       lpszPathInfo;
    LPSTR       lpszPathTranslated;
    DWORD       cbTotalBytes;
    DWORD       cbAvailable;
    LPBYTE      lpbData;
    LPSTR       lpszContentType;
    BOOL (WINAPI * GetServerVariable) ( HCONN       hConn,
                                        LPSTR       lpszVariableName,
                                        LPVOID      lpvBuffer,
                                        LPDWORD     lpdwSize );
    BOOL (WINAPI * WriteClient)  ( HCONN       ConnID,
                                   LPVOID      Buffer,
                                   LPDWORD     lpdwBytes,
                                   DWORD       dwReserved );
    BOOL (WINAPI * ReadClient)  ( HCONN       ConnID,
                                  LPVOID      lpvBuffer,
                                  LPDWORD     lpdwSize );
    BOOL (WINAPI * ServerSupportFunction)( HCONN       hConn,
                                           DWORD       dwHSERRequest,
                                           LPVOID      lpvBuffer,
                                           LPDWORD     lpdwSize,
                                           LPDWORD     lpdwDataType );
} EXTENSION_CONTROL_BLOCK, *LPEXTENSION_CONTROL_BLOCK;
```

General Request Parameters

The first group of fields in the extension control block is used to send information about the request from the server. The cbSize field is used to give the total size of the structure, and dwVersion will hold the version of ISAPI that is being used. In addition, the server will pass a value in connID that can be used to identify the connection to the client making the request. connID should not be modified by your DLL, but will be used in calls to the helper functions, as you will soon see.

Query Information

The extension control block also passes pointers to four null-terminated strings that give information specific to the client request. The string at lpszMethod gives the HTTP method that was requested, such as GET or PUT. Any additional information passed for a query is provided in lpszQueryString. If a path was specified in the client request, it will be passed via lpszPathInfo. In addition, the HTTP server will translate the path to a directory on the local server, which is passed in lpszPathTranslated.

GetServerVariable()

Many other variables are available from the server via the GetServerVariable() function pointer passed in the ECB. Here is the prototype for GetServerVariable():

```
BOOL (WINAPI * GetServerVariable) ( HCONN hConn,
                                    LPSTR lpszVariableName,
                                    LPVOID lpvBuffer,
                                    LPDWORD lpdwSize );
```

This function takes the connection ID (as passed in the ConnID field of the ECB) and one of the following constants used to select a value to retrieve (several of these values are also available directly from the ECB):

AUTH_TYPE—Type of authentication being used (for example, basic). If this is empty, no authentication is used.

CONTENT_LENGTH—Number of bytes expected from the client.

CONTENT_TYPE—Content type of the information received in a POST request.

PATH_INFO—Additional path information passed by the client, from the URL, after the ISA name, but before the query string.

PATH_TRANSLATED—Path information after translation by the server.

QUERY_STRING—The query string, information after the ? in the request URL.

REMOTE_ADDR—IP address of the client.

REMOTE_HOST—Host name of the client.

REMOTE_USER—Username of the client. This is empty if the user is anonymous.

UNMAPPED_REMOTE_USER—Username before any ISAPI filters map the request to an NT user account.

REQUEST_METHOD—The HTTP request method, or verb.

SCRIPT_NAME—The name of the script being executed (the name of your ISA).

SERVER_NAME—The server's host name or IP address.

SERVER_PORT—The TCP port the request was received on.

SERVER_PORT_SECURE—A string containing 0 or 1. If the request is on a secure port, this will be 1.

SERVER_PROTOCOL—The HTTP version of the protocol being used (for example, HTTP/1.0).

SERVER_SOFTWARE—The name and version of the Web server software.

HTTP_ACCEPT—HTTP accept headers (for example, text/html, image/*).

URL—Base portion of the URL.

ALL_HTTP—Any additional HTTP headers that have not been parsed into other variables returned above.

If the call to GetServerVariable() is successful, it will return TRUE and the requested data will be copied to lpvBuffer, with the length returned at lpdwSizeofBuffer. If the buffer passed in lpdwSizeofBuffer is too small for the returned value, the function will return FALSE, and a subsequent call to GetLastError() will return ERROR_INSUFFICIENT_BUFFER. The following example shows the use of GetServerVariable() to retrieve the server name:

```
lSize = sizeof(strServerName);
bRc = pECB->GetServerVariable(pECB->ConnID, "SERVER_NAME",
          strServerName, &lSize);

if(!bRc)
    dwError = GetLastError();
```

Additional Request Data

A client request may include a block of data. If additional data is sent, the total amount of data sent will be passed to HttpExtensionProc() in the cbTotalBytes field. The first block of the actual data is also passed to your DLL in a buffer at lpbData. The length of the data available at lpbData is passed in the cbAvailable field of the extension control block.

If more data has been sent by the client, that is, if cbTotalBytes is greater than cbAvailable, the rest of the data may be retrieved from the client by using the ReadClient() callback function, which is accessed via a pointer passed in the ECB. Here is the prototype for ReadClient():

```
BOOL (WINAPI * ReadClient)  ( HCONN      ConnID,
                              LPVOID     lpvBuffer,
                              LPDWORD    lpdwSize );
```

When calling `ReadClient()`, you should pass the connection ID (from the ECB `ConnID` field) in `hConn`, a pointer to your receive buffer in `lpvBuffer`, and a pointer to the size of your buffer in `lpdwSize`. If the data is read successfully, `ReadClient()` will return `TRUE`, the data will be copied to `lpvBuffer`, and the actual size of the data read will be returned at `lpdwSize`. If an error occurs, `ReadClient()` will return `FALSE`, and you should call `GetLastError()` for a specific error code.

ServerSupportFunction()

The next callback function that you will look at, `ServerSupportFunction()`, gives your ISA access to many different functions that the server can perform for you, ranging from sending HTTP headers, to setting up asynchronous I/O, to transmitting files. Here is the prototype for `ServerSupportFunction()`:

```
BOOL (WINAPI * ServerSupportFunction)( HCONN hConn, DWORD dwHSERequest,
    LPVOID lpvBuffer, LPDWORD lpdwSize, LPDWORD lpdwDataType);
```

The `hConn` parameter should be passed the connection ID from the `ConnID` field of the ECB. The actual function that is performed by `ServerSupportFunction()` and how the remaining parameters are used is determined by the value of `dwHSERequest`, which can have one of the values in the following sections.

HSE_REQ_SEND_URL_REDIRECT_RESP

A URL redirect (302) message is sent to the client. You should pass the new URL string in `lpvBuffer`, and its size should be passed in `lpdwSize`.

HSE_REQ_SEND_URL

`HSE_REQ_SEND_URL` sends data to the client, based on a URL that specifies data local to the server. The null-terminated URL string is passed by `lpvBuffer`, and a pointer to its length should be passed in `lpdwSize`.

HSE_REQ_SEND_RESPONSE_HEADER

`HSE_REQ_SEND_RESPONSE_HEADER` sends an HTTP server response to the client. `lpvBuffer` should point to an HTTP status string—for example, `200 OK`. You may also append additional HTTP headers to the response by passing a pointer to a null-terminated string in the `lpdwDataType` parameter.

HSE_REQ_MAP_URL_TO_PATH

`HSE_REQ_MAP_URL_TO_PATH` translates a logical path to a physical path on the server. The logical path is passed in a buffer at `lpvBuffer`, and a pointer to the length of the buffer is passed in `lpdwSize`. Upon return, the translated path is written at `lpvBuffer`, and the `DWORD` at `lpdwSize` is updated to hold the size of the string returned.

HSE_REQ_DONE_WITH_SESSION

HSE_REQ_DONE_WITH_SESSION is used to tell the server when the ISA is finished with a session. You will look at how this is used when you look at asynchronous operations.

HSE_REQ_IO_COMPLETION

HSE_REQ_IO_COMPLETION sets up a callback function for the completion of asynchronous operations. You will look at this in more detail in just a bit.

HSE_REQ_TRANSMIT_FILE

HSE_REQ_TRANSMIT_FILE tells the server to transmit a file to the client. lpvBuffer points to a HSE_TF_INFO structure. (See the section "Sending Files" later in this chapter.)

HSE_REQ_GET_SSPI_INFO

HSE_REQ_GET_SSPI_INFO retrieves information about a secure connection. lpvBuffer receives the context handle, and *lpdwDataType receives the credential handle.

WriteClient()

The WriteClient() function pointer provided in the ECB is used to send a block of data to the client that made the request to your ISA. In many cases, this will be HTML data, although it could be any other data you wish to send to the client. The following is the prototype for WriteClient():

```
BOOL WriteClient( HCONN ConnID, LPVOID Buffer,
    LPDWORD lpdwBytes, DWORD dwReserved);
```

You should pass the value from the ConnID field of the ECB for the ConnID parameter. The value passed in Buffer should point to your data, and lpdwBytes should point to a DWORD with the length of the data to send. The dwReserved field can be used to specify how the call should complete. If dwReserved is HSE_IO_SYNC, the call will complete synchronously, blocking until it is finished. If dwReserved is set to HSE_IO_ASYNC, the call will return immediately, and the operation will complete asynchronously. You will look at asynchronous operations in the next section.

If WriteClient() completes successfully, it will return TRUE and the DWORD at lpdwBytes will be updated to reflect the actual number of bytes sent. If an error occurs, WriteClient() will return FALSE, and you should call GetLastError() for a specific error code. The example below shows how you can send data (in this case a null-terminated string of HTML) to the client:

```
// Send response data to client
dwMsgLen = strlen(retBuf);
bRc = pECB->WriteClient(pECB->ConnID, retBuf, &dwMsgLen, HSE_IO_SYNC);
```

```
if(bRc == FALSE)
{
    dwError = GetLastError();
    // Do something with the error code...
    pECB->dwHttpStatusCode = HTTP_STATUS_SERVER_ERROR;
    return(HSE_STATUS_ERROR);
}
```

Sending Files

In addition to the WriteClient() callback function, you can also send a file to the client by calling ServerSupportFunction(), with dwHSERequest set to HSE_REQ_TRANSMIT_FILE. This will use the WinSock TransmitFile() function to send a file more quickly than WriteClient().

> **NOTE**
>
> You can also send a file to the client by calling ServerSupportFunction() with HSE_REQ_SEND_URL, provided the server can access the file by a URL.

When calling ServerSupportFunction(), you should set dwHSERequest to HSE_REQ_TRANSMIT_FILE, and lpvBuffer should point to an HSE_TF_INFO structure, shown in the following:

```
typedef struct _HSE_TF_INFO  {
    PFN_HSE_IO_COMPLETION   pfnHseIO;
    PVOID   pContext;
    HANDLE hFile;
    LPCSTR pszStatusCode;
    DWORD   BytesToWrite;
    DWORD   Offset;
    PVOID   pHead;
    DWORD   HeadLength;
    PVOID   pTail;
    DWORD   TailLength;
    DWORD   dwFlags;
} HSE_TF_INFO, * LPHSE_TF_INFO;
```

The pfnHseIO and pContext fields are used to pass a callback function and context value to be used when the operation completes. If these values are not specified, the values set by a call to ServerSupportFunction(), using HSE_REQ_IO_COMPLETION, will be used. However, if values are passed in the pfnHseIO and pContext fields, these will override those set using HSE_REQ_IO_COMPLETION for the duration of this operation. You will see exactly how these are used in the next section.

> **NOTE**
>
> The HSE_REQ_TRANSMIT_FILE operation always completes asynchronously.

The file handle passed in `hFile` must have been previously opened with `CreateFile()`, using the `FILE_FLAG_SEQUENTIAL_SCAN` and `FILE_FLAG_OVERLAPPED` flags.

You should specify the number of bytes to send in the `BytesToWrite` field (0 will send the whole file) and may also specify a beginning offset from the start of the file in Offset.

Optionally, you can have the server attach HTTP headers to your file by specifying the `HSE_IO_SEND_HEADER` flag in the `dwFlags` field. This will build an HTTP header for the status code string specified in the `pszStatusCode` field—for example, `200 OK`. If you use this option, you should not also use the `HSE_REQ_SEND_HEADERS` operation of `ServerSupportFunction()` to send headers.

You can also specify additional data blocks to be sent before and after the data from the file by setting `pHead` and `pTail` to point to appropriate buffers and specifying the lengths of the data in `HeadLength` and `TailLength`.

You may also include `HSE_IO_DISCONNECT_AFTER_SEND` in the `dwFlags` field, which tells the server to disconnect the client connection when the file transfer is complete. If you do not specify this flag, you need to notify the server when you are finished with the session by calling `ServerSupportFunction()` with `HSE_REQ_DONE_WITH_SESSION`.

Asynchronous Operations

ISAPI supports asynchronous completion for the `WriteClient()` function and the `HSE_REQ_TRANSMIT_FILE` operation provided by `ServerSupportFunction ()`. Both of these functions can complete asynchronously by calling a callback function that you specify by calling `ServerSupportFunction()` for the `HSE_REQ_IO_COMPLETION` operation. This allows you to specify a callback function in the `lpvBuffer` parameter and a context value in `lpdwDataType` to be used in subsequent asynchronous operations. The code to set up a callback function would look something like this:

```
BOOL bRc;
bRc = pECB->ServerSupportFunction(pECB->ConnID,HSE_REQ_IO_COMPLETION,
                                  MyCompletionFunc, NULL, (DWORD *)0x123);
```

> **NOTE**
>
> If you call `ServerSupportFunction()` using `HSE_REQ_IO_COMPLETION` and different values for the callback function and context values, the previous values will be replaced.

Your ISA can now begin asynchronous operations with either the `WriteClient()` function or `ServerSupportFunction()`, with a `dwHSERequest` value of `HSE_REQ_TRANSMIT_FILE`.

NOTE

You can have only one asynchronous operation pending for each session.

Once you have initiated an asynchronous operation from within your `HttpExtensionProc ()` callback, you can return a status of `HSE_STATUS_PENDING` from your `HttpExtensionProc()` function. When the operation completes, you should call `ServerSupportFunction()` with `dwHSERequest` of `HSE_DONE_WITH_SESSION` to notify the server that you are finished with the session.

The I/O Completion Callback

The callback function that is installed with the previous code should have the following prototype:

```
VOID WINAPI MyIoCompletionFunc(EXTENSION_CONTROL_BLOCK * pECB,
    PVOID pContext, DWORD cbIO, DWORD dwError );
```

Whenever an asynchronous operation completes, the server will make a call to the callback function that is installed. The server will pass a pointer to the ECB (`pECB`) for the session that started the I/O operation, the context value (`pContext`) that was passed with `HSE_REQ_IO_COMPLETION` (or the `HSE_TF_INFO` structure), the number of bytes transferred (`cbIO`), and an error code (`dwError`).

Your callback function can then do any additional processing that is necessary. You can also initiate an additional asynchronous operation. When you are finished with all the processing for the session, you should call `ServerSupportFunction()` with a `dwHSERequest` value of `HSE_DONE_WITH_SESSION` so that the server can close the connection and free the resources it has allocated for the session.

The following example shows a callback function that simply tells the server that you are finished with a session when the asynchronous operation completes:

```
VOID WINAPI MyCompletionFunc(EXTENSION_CONTROL_BLOCK *pECB,
                          PVOID pContext, DWORD cbIO, DWORD dwError)
{
    pECB->ServerSupportFunction(pECB->ConnID, HSE_REQ_DONE_WITH_SESSION,
                             NULL, NULL, NULL);
} // end MyCompletionFunc
```

Writing to the Server Log

Your ISA can send data to the server's log file by writing a string to the buffer pointed to by the `lpszLogData` field of the ECB. `lpszLogData` points to a buffer of size `HSE_LOG_BUFFER_LEN`. If you write a null-terminated string to this buffer, the string will be written to the server's log file when you return from HttpExtensionProc(). The following example shows how you can use this to append your own string to the entry the server writes to the log for a request:

```
// Add Entry to Log File
strcpy(pECB->lpszLogData, "My Additional Log Text.");
```

Exception Handling in ISAs

ISAPI extension DLLs gain a significant performance advantage over CGI scripts, because they are part of the Web server's process and do not require additional process startup time. However, this also introduces the potential for additional problems. In many cases, if your ISA produces a GPF, or crashes for some other reason, the whole server will crash.

Because of this, you should be careful to handle any exceptions that may arise from your ISA. You should enclose any potentially risky code with the __try/__except mechanism that you learned in Chapter 7, "General-Purpose Classes." It's not a bad idea to enclose the entire body of each of your callback functions in a __try block. This way, problems that arise in your ISA will not affect the rest of the Web server.

The same precautions should also be taken for ISAPI filter DLLs that you will look at later.

Debugging Your ISA

Your Internet server extension can be debugged just like any other DLL, as you saw in Chapter 10, "Dynamic Link Libraries (DLLs)." However, some extra setup is required to run the Web server as a standalone executable for debugging, rather than as a service.

> **NOTE**
>
> This section discusses specifically the Microsoft HTTP server, shipped with the MS Internet Information Server (IIS), although other servers that support ISAPI should behave similarly.

First of all, you need to have access to a server for debugging—trying to do debugging on a production server usually doesn't go over very well.

Secondly, you need to stop all three of the IIS services. Even though you will be using only the HTTP service, you must also stop the Gopher and FTP services. This can be done from the Services applet in Control Panel, or with the Internet Service Manager that was installed with IIS.

Next, you need to specify the executable for the debug session in the debug settings for your ISA project. This should be the full path to the IIS server, which is generally something like this:

```
c:\winnt\system32\inetsrv\inetinfo.exe
```

You must also specify the following in the program arguments:

```
-e W3Svc
```

Now, when you start debugging your ISA project, the Internet information server will be started up, and any breakpoints that you have set up for your ISA will halt execution and allow you to debug the code in your ISA DLL.

> **NOTE**
>
> These steps for debugging an ISAPI extension application also apply to debugging ISAPI filters, which you will see later in this chapter.

Converting from CGI to ISAPI

If you have existing CGI scripts that you wish to convert to ISAPI extension DLLs, you can use the following basic steps.

First of all, you convert your CGI executable into an ISA DLL. For the most part, the `main()` function of your CGI executable can simply be pasted into the `HttpExtensionProc()` of the ISA project, with the additional changes listed later. You also need to add a `GetExtensionVersion()` entry point.

Extension DLLs must be thread-safe, whereas CGI scripts generally do not need to be. You should make sure that any critical sections or shared data are properly protected.

CGI scripts receive data from the client by reading from `stdin`. In an ISA, this should be changed to read data from the `lpbData` buffer passed in the ECB and by using the `ReadClient()` function.

Various information from the server is passed to CGI scripts through environment variables, which are read with `getenv()`. For an ISA, you should replace these calls with calls to `GetServerVariable()`.

CGI scripts send data back to the client by writing to `stdout`. In most cases, this should be replaced with calls to `WriteClient()` in ISA applications, although there are some special cases.

When sending completion status, instead of writing `Status: NNN ...` to `stdout`, you should use the `HSE_REQ_SEND_RESPONSE_HEADER` operation of `ServerSupportFunction()` or `WriteClient()`.

Also, when sending a redirect response, instead of writing either the `Location:` or `URI:` header to `stdout`, you should use `ServerSupportFunction()` with the `HSE_REQ_SEND_URL` operation for local URLs, or the `HSE_REQ_SEND_URL_REDIRECT_RESP` operation for remote (or unknown) URLs.

ISAPI Filters

In addition to the ISAPI server extensions that you have already seen, ISAPI also allows you to create extension DLLs that act as filters, processing various HTTP events either before or after the server has processed a request. These filters can be used to provide your own custom authentication, encryption, compression, or logging functions, as well as many other filtering operations.

Installing a Filter

For the Microsoft Internet Information Server (IIS), the filters that are used are specified in the registry under the following value:

HKEY_LOCAL_MACHINE\System\CurrentControlSet\Services\W3Svc\Parameters\Filter DLLs

This value is a comma-separated list of the filters that will currently be used by the server. The filters are processed in order of their priority, as you will see. In the event of a tie in priority, the filters will be processed in the order they are listed in the registry.

> **NOTE**
>
> When adding or removing filters from the list, be careful not to disturb the existing entries.

ISAPI Filter Architecture

Like the extension DLLs that you saw earlier, ISAPI filters are DLLs that are loaded into the Web server's process. Filter DLLs communicate with the server by way of a pair of entry points that are exported by the filter DLL.

The first of these entry points is GetFilterVersion(), which is called when your filter DLL is loaded, allowing your filter to report its supported version and register for the events that it wishes to handle.

When an event that your filter has registered for occurs, the second entry point, HttpFilterProc(), will be called. This function should perform its processing on the event before passing control back to the server. At this point, your filter may decide whether the event should also be handled by other filters in the current filter chain.

GetFilterVersion()

When the Web server loads a filter DLL, it will call the `GetFilterVersion()` function that is exported by your DLL. This function should have the following prototype:

```
BOOL WINAPI GetFilterVersion( PHTTP_FILTER_VERSION pVer);
```

The single parameter is a pointer to an `HTTP_FILTER_VERSION` structure, which looks like this:

```
typedef struct _HTTP_FILTER_VERSION
{
    [in] DWORD      dwServerFilterVersion;
    [out] DWORD     dwFilterVersion;
    [out] CHAR      lpszFilterDesc[SF_MAX_FILTER_DESC_LEN+1];
    DWORD       dwFlags;
} HTTP_FILTER_VERSION, *PHTTP_FILTER_VERSION;
```

When `GetFilterVersion()` is called, the server will pass its version in the `dwServerFilterVersion` field. You should pass the version that your filter is using back to the server in the `dwFilterVersion` field. For the current version of ISAPI, you can use the `HTTP_FILTER_REVISION` constant. You can also write a short ASCII string description of your filter in the buffer passed at `lpszFilterDesc`.

The real meat of this function is what you return in the `dwFlags` parameter. This value includes a combination (bitwise-OR) of the following flags, which specify which events your filter is interested in processing:

`SF_NOTIFY_READ_RAW_DATA` allows the filter to process incoming data from the client, including headers.

`SF_NOTIFY_SEND_RAW_DATA` allows the filter to process data that is being sent back to the client.

`SF_NOTIFY_PREPROC_HEADERS` allows the filter to access the HTTP headers after they have been preprocessed by the server.

`SF_NOTIFY_AUTHENTICATION` allows the filter to be involved in the user authentication process.

`SF_NOTIFY_URL_MAP` allows the filter to participate in the mapping of a URL to a physical path.

`SF_NOTIFY_LOG` allows the filter to be involved in the process of writing to the server log.

`SF_NOTIFY_END_OF_NET_SESSION` tells the filter when the server is closing a session with a client.

`SF_NOTIFY_ACCESS_DENIED` allows the server to process `401 Access Denied` responses before they are sent to the client.

The following flags should also be included to specify whether you are interested in events on only secure or nonsecure connections, or both:

SF_NOTIFY_SECURE_PORT—The filter will receive notifications only for events on secure ports.

SF_NOTIFY_NONSECURE_PORT—The filter will receive notifications only for events on nonsecure ports.

The last set of flags that can be included in the dwFlags field is used to set the priority of your filter in relation to the other filters present on the system:

SF_NOTIFY_ORDER_DEFAULT—The filter will have the default priority. This should be used for most filters.

SF_NOTIFY_ORDER_LOW—The filter will be processed at a lower priority. This is useful for filters that don't care when they are notified—for instance, for logging events.

SF_NOTIFY_ORDER_MEDIUM—The filter will have a medium priority.

SF_NOTIFY_ORDER_HIGH—The filter will have a high priority, receiving notifications before filters of lower priority.

TIP

When requesting notifications, you should request only those that you need to process. Requesting additional notifications that are not necessary can affect the performance of the server.

You may also include any additional initialization code for your filter in the GetFilterVersion() function (or you could also implement a DllMain()). If all goes well, and your filter has initialized properly, you should return TRUE from GetFilterVersion(). If you return FALSE, the filter will not be loaded.

HttpFilterProc()

Once your filter is loaded and has registered for the notifications that it wants to receive, the server will make a call to your HttpFilterProc() whenever one of the requested events occurs.

NOTE

If an event is handled by another filter with a higher priority, your filter will not be notified if the higher-priority filter chooses not to pass the event on down the filter chain.

In this section, you will take a quick look at the basics of implementing HttpFilterProc(). In the following sections, you will take a closer look at more of the specifics of certain operations.

The prototype for your HttpFilterProc() should look something like this:

```
DWORD WINAPI HttpFilterProc(PHTTP_FILTER_CONTEXT pfc,
    DWORD notificationType, VOID *pvNotification);
```

Your filter is passed an HTTP_FILTER_CONTEXT structure via pfc. This structure provides information about the request, as well as pointers to several utility functions, as you will see in just a bit. The type of event that generated the notification is passed in notificationType. This may include any of the SF_NOTIFY_... values that were used in the GetFilterVersion() call. The value of notificationType also determines how the pvNotification pointer is used. You will look at the specifics of handling each notification type in the following sections.

Your implementation of HttpFilterProc() should perform a switch on the value passed in notificationType, doing whatever processing is necessary, and should then return one of the following values:

SF_STATUS_REQ_FINISHED—The filter has satisfied the client's request, and the server should tear down the connection.

SF_STATUS_REQ_FINISHED_KEEP_CONN—The filter has satisfied the client's request, but the server should keep the connection open.

SF_STATUS_REQ_NEXT_NOTIFICATION—The next filter in the chain should be allowed to process the event.

SF_STATUS_REQ_HANDLED_NOTIFICATION—This filter has handled the event, and no other filters should be notified.

SF_STATUS_REQ_ERROR—An error has occurred. The server will call GetLastError() and forward the error to the client.

SF_STATUS_REQ_READ_NEXT—This should be returned only when filtering on the SF_NOTIFY_READ_RAW_DATA event for stream filters that are negotiating session parameters.

The following example shows the complete implementation of a simple filter, which simply adds a bit of graffiti to the Web server's log file:

```
#include <windows.h>
#include <stdio.h>
#include <httpfilt.h>
BOOL WINAPI GetFilterVersion( PHTTP_FILTER_VERSION pVer)
{
    pVer->dwFilterVersion = HTTP_FILTER_REVISION;
    strcpy(pVer->lpszFilterDesc, "My Sample Extension");
    pVer->dwFlags =
        SF_NOTIFY_SECURE_PORT |        // Notify for both port types
        SF_NOTIFY_NONSECURE_PORT |
        SF_NOTIFY_LOG |                // Notify when writing log
        SF_NOTIFY_ORDER_LOW;           // Filter at low priority
    return TRUE;
```

```
}
DWORD WINAPI HttpFilterProc( PHTTP_FILTER_CONTEXT pfc,
                             DWORD notificationType,
                             VOID *pvNotification)
{
    PHTTP_FILTER_LOG pLog;
    char *pBuf;

    switch(notificationType)
    {
        case SF_NOTIFY_LOG:
            // This is the only case we are interested in
            // We will modify the server name to show we were here
            pLog = (PHTTP_FILTER_LOG) pvNotification;
            // Allocate new memory for the new string
            // The server will deallocate this when the request ends
            pBuf = (char *) pfc->AllocMem(pfc, 100, 0);
            // Write to our new string
            sprintf(pBuf, "Server: [%s] Logged with MyFilt",
                        pLog->pszServerName);

            // Replace the server name pointer
            pLog->pszServerName = pBuf;

            break;
        default:
            // We should not receive any other notifications
            // Since we only registered for SF_NOTIFY_LOG
            break;
    }
    // Tell the server to call the next filter
    return(SF_STATUS_REQ_NEXT_NOTIFICATION);
} // end HttpExtensionProc
```

Although this filter may not be horribly practical, it does show the basic structure of a filter, including the processing for the SF_NOTIFY_LOG notification and the use of the AllocMem() function, which you will learn about later.

The HTTP_FILTER_CONTEXT Structure

Much of the interaction between your filter and the Web server is done through the HTTP_FILTER_CONTEXT structure that is passed in the call to HttpFilterProc():

```
typedef struct _HTTP_FILTER_CONTEXT
{
    DWORD     cbSize;
    DWORD     Revision;
    PVOID     ServerContext;
    DWORD     ulReserved;
    BOOL      fIsSecurePort;
    PVOID     pFilterContext;
BOOL    (WINAPI * GetServerVariable) (
    struct _HTTP_FILTER_CONTEXT *     pfc,
    LPSTR      lpszVariableName,
    LPVOID     lpvBuffer,
    LPDWORD    lpdwSize);
```

```
BOOL    (WINAPI * AddResponseHeaders) (
    struct _HTTP_FILTER_CONTEXT *    pfc,
    LPSTR    lpszHeaders,
    DWORD    dwReserved);
BOOL    (WINAPI * WriteClient) (
    struct _HTTP_FILTER_CONTEXT *    pfc,
    LPVOID    Buffer,
    LPDWORD   lpdwBytes,
    DWORD     dwReserved);
VOID *    (WINAPI * AllocMem) (
    struct _HTTP_FILTER_CONTEXT *    pfc,
    DWORD    cbSize,
    DWORD    dwReserved);
BOOL    (WINAPI * ServerSupportFunction) (
    struct _HTTP_FILTER_CONTEXT *    pfc,
    enum SF_REQ_TYPE    sfReq,
    PVOID    pData,
    DWORD    ul1,
    DWORD    ul2);
} HTTP_FILTER_CONTEXT, *PHTTP_FILTER_CONTEXT;
```

The cbSize field gives the size of this structure, and the Revision field gives the version of ISAPI being used. The ServerContext and ulReserved fields are reserved for use by the Web server— keep yer grubbies off. If the notification is for a secure connection, fIsSecurePort will be TRUE; otherwise, it will be FALSE.

If your filter wants to store any context information for this request, you can assign a context value (usually a pointer to a structure) to the pFilterContext field. If you store a value here, it will also be given to subsequent notifications that your filter receives in processing this request.

If you do allocate memory to store data for a request, you should free the memory when the SF_NOTIFY_END_OF_NET_SESSION notification is received (or whenever you know that you are finished with the data). You should also look at the AllocMem() function later in this section.

The remainder of the HTTP_FILTER_CONTEXT structure includes pointers to various utility functions that the server provides to your filter.

GetServerVariable()

The GetServerVariable() function pointer passed to your filter DLL is not quite the same as the GetServerVariable() function that you saw for ISAPI extensions. This version takes a pointer to the HTTP_FILTER_CONTEXT structure, which is passed into your HttpFilterProc() function, instead of an HCONN. However, the variables that are available via this function and the way it uses the other parameters are the same as the GetServerVariable() function you saw earlier in this chapter.

AddResponseHeaders()

The AddResponseHeaders() function pointer passed in to HttpFilterProc() can be used to attach additional HTTP headers to the response sent to the client. Here is the prototype for AddResponseHeaders():

```
BOOL (WINAPI * AddResponseHeaders) (PHTTP_FILTER_CONTEXT pfc,
    LPSTR lpszHeaders, DWORD dwReserved);
```

This function takes a pointer to the filter context (*pfc*), which is passed to your HttpFilterProc() function, and a pointer to a null-terminated string containing the additional HTTP headers. dwReserved is reserved for future expansion.

WriteClient()

Like the WriteClient() callback that you saw for ISAPI applications, this function allows you to send data directly to the client. The following is the prototype for WriteClient():

```
BOOL (WINAPI * WriteClient) (PHTTP_FILTER_CONTEXT pfc,
    LPVOID buffer, LPDWORD lpdwBytes, DWORD dwReserved);
```

When calling WriteClient(), you should pass the pointer to the filter context (as passed to your HttpFilterProc() function) in *pfc*, a pointer to the data to send in *buffer*, and a pointer to the length of the data in *lpdwBytes*. The *dwReserved* parameter is not currently used.

> **NOTE**
>
> The WriteClient() function provided for ISAPI filters does not currently support asynchronous I/O.

AllocMem()

If your filter needs to allocate memory when working with a request, you may find the AllocMem() function handy. This will allocate a block of memory that is automatically deallocated when the server is done with a request and tears down the connection. The prototype for AllocMem() is this:

```
VOID * (WINAPI * AllocMem) (PHTTP_FILTER_CONTEXT pfc,
    DWORD cbSize, DWORD dwReserved);
```

Once again, *pfc* takes the pointer to the filter context, as passed to HttpFilterProc(), and *dwReserved* is not currently used. Upon successful completion, AllocMem() will return a pointer to a new block of memory of the size specified in cbSize.

ServerSupportFunction()

Like the ServerSupportFunction() that you saw for ISAPI applications, this function provides a variety of different utility functions to your filter. The following is the prototype for ServerSupportFunction():

```
BOOL (WINAPI * ServerSupportFunction) (struct _HTTP_FILTER_CONTEXT *pfc,
    enum SF_REQ_TYPE sfReq, PVOID pData, DWORD ul1, DWORD ul2);
```

The operation performed is determined by the value of *sfReq*, which may have one of the following values:

SF_REQ_SEND_RESPONSE_HEADER

This option sends a complete HTTP response header to the client. You may choose to specify a status string—for example, 401 Access Denied—in a string pointed to by pData. You may also specify additional headers, such as the content type, to append in a string pointed to by *ul1*. This string should include a terminating carriage-return/linefeed (\r\n).

SF_REQ_ADD_HEADERS_ON_DENIAL

This option allows you to specify additional headers that will be sent to the client in the event the server denies the HTTP request. The additional headers are passed in a string pointed to by pData. This string should include a terminating cr-lf (\r\n).

SF_REQ_SET_NEXT_READ_SIZE

For raw data filters that return SF_STATUS_READ_NEXT from HttpFilterProc(), this option can be used to specify the number of bytes to read in the next read. The number of bytes to read is passed in *ul1*.

SF_REQ_SET_PROXY_INFO

This option can be used to specify that a request is a proxy request. *ul1* should be set to 1.

SF_REQ_GET_CONNID

This option returns the connection ID that is passed to ISAPI applications for this request. You can use this value to coordinate operations between your ISAPI applications and filters. pData should point to a DWORD that will receive the connection ID.

> **TIP**
>
> If you are developing an ISAPI filter that works closely with an ISAPI extension application, you can include both sets of entry points in the same DLL.

Handling Filter Notifications

In this section, you will look at the different notifications that can be received by an ISAPI filter and the data that is passed with each type of notification.

SF_NOTIFY_READ_RAW_DATA

This notification is sent to your filter whenever the server is receiving raw data from the client. The pvNotification parameter of HttpFilterProc() will point to an HTTP_FILTER_RAW_DATA structure:

```
typedef struct _HTTP_FILTER_RAW_DATA
{
    PVOID          pvInData;
    DWORD          cbInData;
    DWORD          cbInBuffer;
    DWORD          dwReserved;
} HTTP_FILTER_RAW_DATA, *PHTTP_FILTER_RAW_DATA;
```

The `pvInData` field points to a buffer containing the raw data, and the length of the data is passed in the `cbInData` field. This will include both HTTP headers and additional data. The total size of this buffer is passed in `cbInBuffer`.

SF_NOTIFY_SEND_RAW_DATA

This notification is sent to your filter when the server is sending data back to the client. The `pvNotification` parameter of `HttpFilterProc()` will point to an `HTTP_FILTER_RAW_DATA` structure, as you saw previously, which refers to the outgoing data.

SF_NOTIFY_PREPROC_HEADERS

This notification is sent to your filter when a request is received from a client. The `pvNotification` parameter of `HttpFilterProc()` will point to an `HTTP_FILTER_PREPROC_HEADERS` structure, which includes pointers to utility functions that can be used to manipulate the headers for a request. These utility functions are discussed in the following sections.

GetHeader()

The first of these functions is `GetHeader()`:

```
BOOL (WINAPI * GetHeader) (PHTTP_FILTER_CONTEXT pfc,
    LPSTR lpszName, LPVOID lpvBuffer, LPDWORD lpdwSize);
```

This function allows you to retrieve the header with the name you specify in a string at `lpszName`. This name should include the trailing colon—for example, `Content-Type:`. You may also specify the special values of `method`, `url`, or `version` to retrieve portions of the HTTP request line.

If a header is found for the name passed in `lpszName`, it will be returned in a buffer at `lpvBuffer`.

SetHeader()

The second of the utility functions is `SetHeader()`, which can be used to change the value of a header or even delete an existing header:

```
BOOL (WINAPI * SetHeader) (PHTTP_FILTER_CONTEXT pfc,
    LPSTR lpszName, LPSTR lpszValue);
```

This function allows you to specify a new value for the header named in the string at `lpszName`. The new value for the header is passed in a string at `lpszValue`. If this string is empty, the specified header will be deleted.

AddHeader()

The third utility function, AddHeader(), can be used to add additional headers:

```
BOOL (WINAPI * SetHeader) (PHTTP_FILTER_CONTEXT pfc,
    LPSTR lpszName, LPSTR lpszValue);
```

The name of the new header is specified in a string at lpszName, and the value of the new header is passed in a string at lpszValue.

SF_NOTIFY_AUTHENTICATION

This notification is sent to your filter when the server is about to authenticate a user making a request. The pvNotification parameter of HttpFilterProc () will point to an HTTP_FILTER_AUTHENT structure:

```
typedef struct _HTTP_FILTER_AUTHENT
{
    CHAR * pszUser;
    DWORD  cbUserBuff;
    CHAR * pszPassword;
    DWORD  cbPasswordBuff;
} HTTP_FILTER_AUTHENT, *PHTTP_FILTER_AUTHENT;
```

This structure contains pointers to the username (pszUser) and password (pszPassword) for the user being authenticated. If the user is anonymous, these strings will be empty. The cbUserBuff and cbPasswordBuff fields give the total size of the buffers holding the username and password. Your filter can change the contents of these buffers, provided they are not over-flowed. These buffers will be at least SF_MAX_USERNAME and SF_MAX_PASSWORD bytes long, respectively.

SF_NOTIFY_URL_MAP

This notification is sent when the server is attempting to map a URL to a physical path. The lpvNotification parameter of HttpFilterProc() will point to an HTTP_FILTER_URL_MAP structure:

```
typedef struct _HTTP_FILTER_URL_MAP
{
    const CHAR * pszURL;
    CHAR *       pszPhysicalPath;
    DWORD        cbPathBuff;
} HTTP_FILTER_URL_MAP, *PHTTP_FILTER_URL_MAP;
```

The requested URL is passed in the string at pszURL, and the physical path that it is being mapped to is given at pszPhysicalPath. Your filter may change the string at pszPhysicalPath, provided you do not go over the size of the buffer given in cbPathBuf.

SF_NOTIFY_LOG

This notification is passed to your filter when the server is about to write an entry to its log file. The lpvNotification parameter of HttpFilterProc() is passed a pointer to an HTTP_FILTER_LOG structure:

```
typedef struct _HTTP_FILTER_LOG
{
    const CHAR * pszClientHostName;
    const CHAR * pszClientUserName;
    const CHAR * pszServerName;
    const CHAR * pszOperation;
    const CHAR * pszTarget;
    const CHAR * pszParameters;
    DWORD   dwHttpStatus;
    DWORD   dwWin32Status;
} HTTP_FILTER_LOG, *PHTTP_FILTER_LOG;
```

The pointers in this structure refer to the client's host name, username, and server name, as well as the operation, target, and parameters for the HTTP request. In addition, dwHttpStatus holds the HTTP status of the request, and dwWin32Status holds any Win32 error code.

You cannot modify the contents of the strings passed by the HTTP_FILTER_LOG structure, although you can replace the values of the pointers. If you change the pointer values, you should assign them to new buffers that are allocated with the AllocMem() function provided by the HTTP_FILTER_CONTEXT structure so that the memory can be properly released when the session is closed.

SF_NOTIFY_END_OF_NET_SESSION

This notification is sent to your filter when the server is disconnecting a session. There is no specific data associated with this notification, although it is a good place to clean up any information you have stored about a request in progress.

SF_NOTIFY_ACCESS_DENIED

When a request has been denied by the server, your filter will receive this notification. The lpvNotification parameter of HttpFilterProc() will be passed a pointer to an HTTP_FILTER_ACCESS_DENIED structure:

```
typedef struct _HTTP_FILTER_ACCESS_DENIED
{
    const CHAR * pszURL;
    const CHAR * pszPhysicalPath;
    DWORD        dwReason;
} HTTP_FILTER_ACCESS_DENIED, *PHTTP_FILTER_ACCESS_DENIED;
```

This structure includes the requested URL at pszURL and the physical path it was mapped to at pszPhysicalPath. The dwReason field contains a bitmap that specifies why the request was denied. This can include the following values:

SF_DENIED_LOGON—Logon failed.

SF_DENIED_RESOURCE—The Access Control List (ACL) for the resource did not allow the operation.

SF_DENIED_FILTER—An ISAPI filter denied the request.

SF_DENIED_APPLICATION—An ISAPI application or a CGI script denied the request.

SF_DENIED_BY_CONFIG—This flag may be included with the others if the server's configuration did not allow the request.

ISAPI Support in MFC

Visual C++ 5.0 also provides support for ISAPI extension applications and filters using MFC classes which encapsulate the ISAPI you have seen earlier in this chapter. The classes provided by MFC to work with ISAPI include the following:

CHttpServer—Base class for deriving your ISAs

CHttpServerContext—Encapsulates the context for each client request

CHtmlStream—Class for managing HTML responses

CHttpFilter—Base class for deriving ISAPI filters

CHttpFilterContext—Wrapper for the HTTP_FILTER_CONTEXT structure

In addition, MFC defines a set of macros that enables you to define a parse map to map requests to your ISA for specific functions in your implementation. Visual C++ also provides an Application Wizard for creating ISAs and ISAPI filters that use the MFC ISAPI classes.

Creating ISAPI DLLs with AppWizard

Visual C++ 5.0 provides an Application Wizard that can be used to generate the skeleton of an ISAPI filter or ISA. In fact, it can be used to create both a filter and an ISA in the same DLL project. To use the ISAPI AppWizard, select the File|New command and choose the ISAPI Extension Wizard from the Projects page. You will also need to select a name and location for your new project.

The first step in the ISAPI Extension Wizard allows you to choose whether you wish to create a filter object or a server extension object (ISA). This dialog also allows you to choose names for your classes and descriptions for your filter or ISA, as well as to decide whether to use MFC as a DLL or as a statically linked library.

If you are only creating a server extension, you can click on Finish to see a short summary of the project that the wizard will create for you. Just click OK in this dialog, and the wizard will create the skeleton of a server extension for you.

If you are creating a filter object, clicking on Next will present a second dialog that allows you to set up the priority for your filter and the types of connection and specific notifications that it is interested in handling. These options correspond directly to the flags that are returned in the GetFilterVersion() function that you saw earlier.

> **NOTE**
>
> The ISAPI Extension Wizard will allow you to create both a filter and a server extension in the same DLL project. This can be quite useful if your filter and ISA will interact with each other directly.

Once you have created the framework for your DLL with the ISAPI Extension Wizard, you are ready to start adapting the MFC classes that it creates to suit the needs of your specific implementation. In the following sections, you will look at each of the classes that MFC provides to help in working with ISAPI.

CHttpServer

An MFC ISA will have one—and only one—object derived from CHttpServer. This class encapsulates both the GetExtensionVersion() and HttpExtensionProc() entry points that you saw earlier. In addition, it provides several other methods that can simplify the processing of client requests, and the CHttpServer class allows you to create CHtmlStream objects that can be used for building responses.

Your ISA should create one instance of your class derived from CHttpServer. You can specify a delimiter character used to separate command parameters in requests for your ISA, although the default (&) should generally be used.

CHttpServer::GetExtensionVersion()

The CHttpServer class provides a member function that is identical to the GetExtensionVersion() function you saw earlier, which reports version information back to the server when the ISA is first loaded. This function can also be used to perform initialization of your ISA.

CHttpServer::HttpExtensionProc()

The CHttpServer class also implements a member function that is exported as the HttpExtensionProc() that you saw earlier. This function is called once for each client request that is received. The default implementation of this function will create a new CHttpServerContext object for the request, parse the request, call the CHttpServer::InitInstance() member function, and call CHttpServer::CallFunction() to use a parse map to route the client request to a function in your ISA. It will also use the

`CHttpServer::OnParseError()` function to generate HTML responses to handle various errors that may occur.

InitInstance()

The `InitInstance()` member of `CHttpServer` is called by the default implementation of `CHttpServer::HttpExtensionProc()` each time a new request is received. You can override this function in your class derived from `CHttpServer` to perform any initialization for each request. Any initialization that should be performed only once, when the DLL is first loaded, should not appear in `InitInstance()`, but should be placed somewhere else—in the `GetExtensionVersion()` member function, for example.

CallFunction()

The `CallFunction()` member of `CHttpServer` is called by the default implementation of `CHttpServer::HttpExtensionProc()` to map the command in the client request URL to a specific function in your ISA. The default implementation of this function uses a parse map (similar to message maps) to choose the appropriate function to call, based on command information from the ECB structure. If you want to perform your own custom mapping of commands to implementation functions, you can override this function—in which case, you will not need to implement a parse map.

Parse Maps

MFC provides a set of macros for defining a parse map in your ISA. The parse map is a structure, similar to MFC message maps, that is used by the `CallFunction()` method to map a client request to a function that will handle the request. You should define one—and only one—parse map in each of your MFC ISA DLLs.

A parse map begins with the `BEGIN_PARSE_MAP` macro, which takes parameters for the class defining the map and its base class (usually `CHttpServer`), and ends with the `END_PARSE_MAP` macro, which takes the name of the class defining the map.

Between the begin and end macros, you can add entries for specific commands with the `ON_PARSE_COMMAND` macro, which takes parameters for the name of a member function, the class name that the member function belongs to, and a list of constants representing the parameters to be passed to the handler function. The following are the constants used to represent the available argument types:

ITS_PSTR—A pointer to a string

ITS_I2—A 2-byte integer (short)

ITS_I4—A 4-byte integer (long)

ITS_R4—A float

ITS_R8—A double

ITS_EMPTY—Handler takes no additional arguments (the third parameter to ON_PARSE_COMMAND cannot be blank, so this acts as a placeholder)

To illustrate how this works, let's take a look at an example parse map, which will map the command myFunc1 to CMyIsa::myFunc1() and myFunc2 to CMyIsa::myFunc2():

```
BEGIN_PARSE_MAP(CMyIsa, CHttpServer)
    ON_PARSE_COMMAND(myFunc1, CMyIsa, ITS_I2 ITS_PSTR)
    ON_PARSE_COMMAND_PARAMS("param1 param2=default")
    ON_PARSE_COMMAND(myFunc2, CMyIsa, ITS_I4)
    ON_PARSE_COMMAND_PARAMS("myIndex=123")
    DEFAULT_PARSE_COMMAND(myFunc1, CMyIsa)
END_PARSE_MAP(CMyIsa)
```

> **TIP**
>
> In mapping client request commands to handler functions, the command string passed by the client must match the name of the handler function. For example, if the client requests the DoSomething command, this will map to CMyIsa::DoSomething(). If you wish to map commands to functions with names other than the command string, you can do so, but you need to add your own entries to the parse map, without using the ON_PARSE_COMMAND macro. Or, you could override the CallFunction() method altogether. For hints on how to do this, see afxisapi.h for the definition of ON_PARSE_COMMAND.

The ON_PARSE_COMMAND_PARAMS macro, used in the example, is used to specify the names of the parameters for the command in the ON_PARSE_COMMAND immediately preceding it. This macro is also used to assign default values to the parameters—if a default value is not assigned in the parse map, the client must supply a value or the call will fail. In the example, when the client requests the myFunc1 command, it must specify a parameter named param1. If the client does not specify a param2 parameter, it will default to an empty string.

The example also shows the usage for the DEFAULT_PARSE_COMMAND macro, which specifies a handler function (and its class) for cases where the client does not include a command in the request.

Handler Functions

The handler functions specified in the `ON_PARSE_COMMAND` macros should be members of your `CHttpServer`-derived class. They should all return void and take a pointer to a `CHttpServerContext` object as their first parameter. They should also take additional parameters, as specified in the `ON_PARSE_COMMAND` macro.

For example, for the following parse map entry:

```
ON_PARSE_COMMAND(foo, CMyIsa, ITS_I4 ITS_PSTR)
```

the prototype for the handler function should look like this:

```
void CMyIsa::foo(CHttpServerContext* pCtxt, int nParam1, LPTSTR pszParam2);
```

OnParseError()

The `OnParseError()` member of `CHttpServer` is called by MFC to create an HTML response for the client, based on a set of error codes. If you wish to generate your own custom error messages, you can override this member function.

ConstructStream()

MFC will call the `ConstructStream()` method of `CHttpServer` to create a new `CHtmlStream` object. If you wish to modify the default behavior, you can override this function.

StartContent()

This function can be used to insert the `<Body>` and `<HTML>` tags into an HTML stream to be returned to the client.

EndContent()

This function can be used to insert the `</Body>` and `</HTML>` tags into an HTML stream to be returned to the client.

WriteTitle()

This function will insert the title string returned by `GetTitle()` (surrounded by `<Title>` and `</Title>`) into an HTML string to be returned to the client.

GetTitle()

This function is called by MFC to retrieve a title to add to the HTML page to be returned to the client. You can override this function to supply a title other than the default.

AddHeader()

You can call this function to add additional headers to the HTML stream to be returned to the client.

CHttpServerContext

The default implementation of CHttpServer::HttpExtensionProc() will create a new CHttpServerContext object each time it is called to process a new client request. This class encapsulates the ECB structure that you saw earlier, which is available directly via the m_pECB member. The m_pStream member also provides direct access to the CHtmlStream object that will be returned to the client.

This class implements member functions that correspond directly to the GetServerVariable(), ReadClient(), WriteClient(), and ServerSupportFunction() functions that are passed in the ECB, as you saw earlier.

In addition, CHttpServerContext overloads the insertion operator (<<) to write data to the CHtmlStream object associated with the CHttpServerContext object.

CHtmlStream

The CHtmlStream class provides an abstraction for writing HTML data into a temporary memory file before it is sent back to the client. CHtmlStream objects are created by the default implementation of CHttpServer::ConstructStream(), which is called by the default implementation of CHttpServer::CallFunction() to create a new HTML stream to associate with the CHttpServerContext object for a client request. CallFunction() also calls CHtmlStream::InitStream(), which you may override, to initialize the new stream.

You can retrieve the size of the stream file by calling the GetStreamSize() method or by accessing the m_nStreamSize member directly.

CHtmlStream provides the Write() method to allow you to write data to the stream, as well as to allow an overload of the insertion operator (<<) that performs the same function.

There are also several other members of CHtmlStream that can be used to more closely control the memory used by the stream. Many of these functions can be overridden in classes you derive from CHtmlStream if you are interested in changing the way CHtmlStream deals with memory.

CHttpFilter

MFC provides the CHttpFilter class to encapsulate the functionality required for implementing an ISAPI filter. It will export GetFilterVersion() and HttpFilterProc() entry points, which call CHttpFilter member functions of the same name. For each MFC ISAPI filter, one—and only one—CHttpFilter object should be created. As you will see in just a bit, multiple CHttpFilterContext objects will be created by the CHttpFilter—one for each notification that is received.

CHttpFilter::GetFilterVersion() corresponds directly to the GetFilterVersion() function that you saw earlier. You should override this function in your class derived from CHttpFilter to specify the priority of your filter and the events it wants to process.

You may also override CHttpFilter::HttpFilterProc() to implement your event handlers, although the default implementation will create a new CHttpFilterContext object for you and call one of the other member functions of CHttpFilter, which you can override to handle each specific event. Here are the member functions that are called, with the events that generate calls to them:

SF_NOTIFY_READ_RAW_DATA	OnReadRawData()
SF_NOTIFY_SEND_RAW_DATA	OnSendRawData()
SF_NOTIFY_PREPROC_HEADERS	OnPreprocHeaders()
SF_NOTIFY_AUTHENTICATION	OnAuthentication()
SF_NOTIFY_URL_MAP	OnUrlMap()
SF_NOTIFY_LOG	OnLog()
SF_NOTIFY_END_OF_NET_SESSION	OnEndOfNetSession()

The implementation of these functions is very similar to the handling for the event notifications that you saw earlier.

CHttpFilterContext

A new CHttpFilterContext object is created by MFC whenever a new notification is received. This object provides your filter with information about the notification and also provides mechanisms for your filter to communicate with the server, as well as the client making the request. This class encapsulates the HTTP_FILTER_CONTEXT structure that you saw earlier. This structure can be directly accessed via the m_pFC member of CHttpFilterContext.

The CHttpFilterContext class provides member functions that correspond directly to the GetServerVariable(), AddResponseHeaders(), WriteClient(), ServerSupportFunction(), and AllocMem() functions that you saw earlier, during the discussion of the C version of ISAPI for creating filters.

The Internet Service Manager API

So far in this chapter, you have learned about how ISAPI allows you to add extension applications and filters to the HTTP server. However, the Internet Server API also provides an interface, known as the Internet Service Manager API (ISMAPI). This allows you to create your own Internet servers that can be managed with the Internet Service Manager application, which is used to start, stop, or pause Internet services on the local machine or across the network.

ISMAPI allows you to create a configuration DLL for your new Internet service. The Internet service manager can then be configured to load your configuration DLL to allow the user to control your Internet service from within the Internet service manager. ISMAPI defines the entry points that your configuration DLL should export, allowing the user to discover servers on the network, change the state of your service, configure a server, and get information about servers and services on the network. For more on the Internet Service Manager API, see the online documentation.

Summary

In this chapter, you have seen how the Internet Server API (ISAPI) can be used to create both Internet Server Extension Applications (ISAs) and ISAPI filters, which can be used to add functionality to ISAPI-compliant HTTP servers like that supplied with Microsoft's Internet Information Server.

You saw how to create an ISA extension DLL, which can process requests made directly by a client, and the entry points that are exported by an ISA DLL, including `GetExtensionVersion()`, `TerminateExtension()`, and `HttpExtensionProc()`—the real workhorse function of an ISA.

You took a look at the information provided to your ISA by the server in the `EXTENSION_CONTROL_BLOCK` structure, which also provides pointers to utility functions such as `GetServerVariable()`, `WriteClient()`, `ReadClient()`, and `ServerSupportFunction()`.

Next, you saw how to create an ISAPI filter DLL, which can be used to perform special processing for many different events while handling an HTTP request. You saw how the `GetFilterVersion()` and `HttpFilterProc()` functions can be implemented and exported for use by the Web server, as well as the `HTTP_FILTER_CONTEXT` structure, which is used to pass information about a request and to provide utility functions for your filter, including `GetServerVariable()`, `AddResponseHeaders()`, `WriteClient()`, `AllocMem()`, and `ServerSupportFunction()`.

In addition, you took a look at the MFC classes that are provided to encapsulate ISAPI, including the `CHttpServer`, `CHttpServerContext`, and `CHtmlStream` classes that are used to create ISAs using parse maps, as well as the `CHttpFilter` and `CHttpFilterContext` classes, which can be used to implement ISAPI filters. You also saw how to use the ISAPI Extension Wizard to create a framework for applications using these MFC classes.

V

Database Programming

24

Database Overview

by David Bennett

If you are writing real applications for Windows, you will almost certainly need to make use of a database at some time. This might be a simple database, such as the Jet Engine used by Microsoft Access, or it might be a much more complex distributed or multitiered database server system, such as Oracle. Whatever sort of database you are using, from simple local text files to corporate mainframe systems, Visual C++ includes interfaces that allow you to work with the database from your C++ applications. The next few chapters look at these interfaces in greater detail. This chapter gives an overview of the database interfaces available with Visual C++ 5, including each of the following:

- Open Database Connectivity (ODBC) 3.0
- The MFC ODBC classes
- OLE DB
- ActiveX Data Objects (ADO)

In addition, because all the interfaces that this chapter discusses use Structured Query Language (SQL) as the primary command and query language for working with the databases, you will also take a look at the basics of SQL.

ODBC 3.0

The Open Database Connectivity, or ODBC, API is perhaps the most widely used database interface for windows applications today. ODBC provides a standard interface to a wide range of different sorts of data sources, ranging from simple text files to full-blown database server systems. Of course, if you are using a more primitive data source, such as simple ASCII files or Excel spreadsheet files, you will not be able to take advantage of some of the more advanced features supported by a richer database server, such as Oracle or Informix. Nevertheless, the ODBC interface provides the tools to allow you to take advantage of these features.

Furthermore, ODBC makes the access to these features available in a common API, which can greatly simplify your application development if you plan to support a number of different databases. Instead of having to add special code for the proprietary interface used for each database, you need to code for the ODBC API. Special ODBC drivers provide any necessary translation between the ODBC API and the proprietary interface used to actually communicate with the database.

You should note, however, that there are many features that can differ significantly from one ODBC driver to another. Thus, although ODBC takes a big step in the right direction toward standard database access, you might find that you will need to add some code to your applications that must do things a bit differently for different database types.

Chapter 25, "Open Database Connectivity (ODBC)," takes a look at the latest version of ODBC, ODBC 3.0. The ODBC 3.0 C API is best suited for C or C++ applications that want to have fairly direct control of a complete set of features on a wide number of different databases. If you are building MFC applications, it might be simpler to use the MFC database classes, although these generalized classes do not give you as much control of your database interactions as ODBC does. In fact, you might often need to use some native ODBC calls in conjunction with the MFC database classes to perform some types of operations.

MFC's Database Classes

The Microsoft Foundation Classes provide a set of classes that encapsulate the ODBC API and make it a bit simpler to use in C++ applications. However, this simplicity comes with the cost of giving up a bit of the finer control provided by using the ODBC API directly. The Microsoft Foundation Classes also provide a set of classes that encapsulate the Data Access Objects (DAO) interface. The DAO classes are quite similar to the ODBC classes but also have some fairly significant differences.

Of the database interfaces discussed in this book, the MFC database classes are one of the simplest to use, particularly if you are performing only some of the more common simple database operations. The MFC classes also provide some very simple mechanisms for integrating your data into graphical applications, as you will see in Chapter 26, "MFC Database Classes."

OLE DB

OLE DB is Microsoft's new database interface based on the Common Object Model (COM). This interface provides a great deal of flexibility, allowing you to access a wide range of different types of data sources, including just about any sort of data that can be represented in a tabular form, from Excel spreadsheets to special data acquisition hardware. OLE DB also provides the mechanisms that allow you to create OLE DB data source providers to meet the needs of your particular application.

However, the flexibility and range of features included in OLE DB are not free. The interface can be a bit complicated to use, and you will certainly write a good deal more code to work directly with the OLE DB interface. For most user applications, it is easier to use ActiveX Data Objects, which provide a simpler interface to OLE DB data sources, without sacrificing a great deal of flexibility.

ActiveX Data Objects (ADO)

The very latest addition to Microsoft's family of database interfaces is ActiveX Data Objects, or ADO, which specifies a set of COM objects used to work with data from various data sources. Microsoft provides an implementation of ADO objects that use the OLE DB interface, although you might also choose to use other implementations of ADO objects, which may provide the same simple interface to access other sorts of data. You might even want to implement your own ADO provider.

ADO is intended to replace the Data Access Objects (DAO) and Remote Data Objects (RDO) that you might be familiar with. ADO provides a more general interface to a wider array of data sources, whether they are on the local machine or distributed around your network.

Because the objects used in ADO are COM objects, they are easily used from a wide range of programming environments, including Visual Basic (VB), Visual Basic for Applications (VBA), VBScript, and JavaScript, as well as Visual C++. Although it is a bit more complicated to use ADO objects in C++, the new VC++ 5.0 compiler support for COM objects makes it almost as easy to use ADO in C++ as it is in Visual Basic, without all of the overhead.

Structured Query Language

Once upon a time, every database system had its own sort of programming interface and every time you wanted to look at data in a different way, you had to submit change requests to the department that hacked out the rather complicated code to change your queries. To make it easier for knowledgeable users to come up with their own ad hoc queries, Structured Query Language, or SQL, was developed. This allowed users to use a common language to easily define their own queries to retrieve or modify data in a way that was best suited to their needs at the time. Nevertheless, although SQL is a relatively simple language, it is powerful enough to perform almost any operations you would need to do with a database. Thus, it has become the most common language used for programming database applications, as well as for end-user, ad hoc queries, and is supported by a wide range of different database systems.

All the database interfaces in the next four chapters allow you to use SQL within the framework of the database interface, so let's take a quick look at the basics of the SQL language. This section looks at a generic version of the SQL grammar, which can be used with ODBC and the other interfaces we will be working with. The grammar used by ODBC is based on the ANSI SQL-92 standard.

Note that almost every database provides its own dialect of SQL that can use slightly different syntax or support a slightly different set of features, so the grammar that you see here might not work with the query tools provided by your favorite database. However, the ODBC driver for a particular database will provide any necessary translation from the generic SQL to the specific dialect required by your database.

The following sections look at the three basic groups of SQL statements. Data Definition Language (DDL) is used to set up the structure of the database, and Data Control Language (DCL) is used to work with user permissions for certain objects. Lastly, but most importantly, Data Manipulation Language (DML) is used to do everything else, including adding and modifying data as well as performing queries. These languages are all a part of SQL and are not really separate languages, although most applications will use only statements from one of the three available groups.

Data Definition Language

Data Definition Language is the portion of SQL used for defining the structure of the database and creating objects within the database. DDL uses the following three different SQL verbs to work with objects in the database:

CREATE: Creates a new object

ALTER: Modifies an existing object

DROP: Removes an object

The verbs listed here are used to work with several types of objects in the database, including tables, indexes, and views. Each of these object types uses a different syntax for the verbs, so we will look at one object type at a time.

Tables

Tables are the most commonly used object in relational databases. They hold the actual data in tables, consisting of rows (records) and columns (fields). In many user applications, the tables that you will be using will have already been created for you, whereas other situations will require that you create your own tables.

SQL Data Types

Tables are constructed of columns that contain several types of data, so, before moving on to the specifics of creating a table, let's look at the available data types for columns.

The SQL data types that we will look at here are grouped according to ODBC SQL conformance levels, although most implementations do not adhere strictly to the conformance-level specifications. Most drivers will support all the minimum conformance level, but you should check your system's documentation to see whether any others are supported.

The following types are supported by at the minimum conformance level:

CHAR(n): A fixed-length character string of n characters

VARCHAR(n): A variable length character string with a maximum length of n

LONG VARCHAR: A variable length character string with no specified maximum length

The following data types are defined in the core conformance level:

DECIMAL(p,s) or NUMERIC(p,s): These are equivalent and define a floating-point value with a precision of p decimal places and a scale of s places to the right of the decimal point.

SMALLINT: A 2-byte integer.

INTEGER: A 4-byte integer.

REAL: A 4-byte, floating-point value.

FLOAT or DOUBLE PRECISION: These are equivalent types that specify an 8-byte, floating-point value.

In addition, the extended conformance level specifies the following types, although support for these can vary widely between different databases:

BIT: A single bit

TINYINT: A 1-byte integer

BIGINT: An 8-byte integer

BINARY(*n*): A fixed-length binary field of *n* bytes

VARBINARY(*n*): A variable-length binary field with a maximum length of *n* bytes

LONG VARBINARY: A variable-length binary field with no specified maximum length

DATE: A date value

TIME: A time value

TIMESTAMP: A value containing both time and date

Creating a Table

Creating a table is done with a CREATE TABLE statement, which has the general syntax:

```
CREATE TABLE table-name ({column-name data-type},…)
```

Basically, you will need to specify the name of the new table, as well as the name and data type for each of its columns. The following statement gives an example that is perhaps a bit clearer:

```
CREATE TABLE Employee (
    EmpId       INTEGER,
    EmpName     VARCHAR(50),
    Salary      NUMERIC(6,2),
    Dept        CHAR(10) )
```

This will create a new table named Employee. This table will have four columns of various different data types. Unfortunately, almost every database supports a different set of data types, so the exact list of types available to you depends on the database that you are using.

You can further qualify the columns of a table by adding additional modifiers after the column's data type. The most common qualifier is NOT NULL, which is used to specify a column for which a value must be specified. If you attempt to add a new row (or change an existing row) that does not include a value for these columns, the database will return an error. For example, if you wanted to ensure that all rows include an employee ID and name, you could specify the table like this:

```
CREATE TABLE Employee (
    EmpId       INTEGER        NOT NULL,
    EmpName     VARCHAR(50)    NOT NULL,
    Salary      NUMERIC(6,2),
    Dept        CHAR(10) )
```

You can also specify that a certain value for a column appears only once in the table by using the UNIQUE modifier, as shown in the following example, which makes sure that duplicate employee IDs are not added to the table.

```
CREATE TABLE Employee (
    EmpId       INTEGER        NOT NULL,
    EmpName     VARCHAR(50)    NOT NULL,
    Salary      NUMERIC(6,2),
    Dept        CHAR(10) )
```

You can also specify default values for a column, which will be used in any new rows for which explicit values are not specified. This is done by adding the DEFAULT modifier:

```
CREATE TABLE Employee (
    EmpId       INTEGER        NOT NULL,
    EmpName     VARCHAR(50)    NOT NULL,
    Salary      NUMERIC(6,2),
    Dept        CHAR(10)       DEFAULT 'Staff')
```

The table in the preceding example will assign a value of 'Staff' for any new rows that do not give a value for the Dept column.

Several other column modifiers can be supported by any particular database. Such additional modifiers give you the ability to specify a primary key or to specify referential integrity constraints, which can be used to ensure that the data in the database cannot be corrupted by user applications.

Dropping a Table

To remove a table from the database, use the DROP TABLE command:

```
DROP TABLE table-name
```

This deletes all the data from the table and then removes the framework for the table itself. You will see how to simply remove all the data from the table with DELETE, in the section titled "DELETE statements" later in this chapter.

You can qualify the drop operation by specifying the CASCADE or RESTRICT keywords. Specifying CASCADE will remove the table as well as any views or integrity constraints that reference the table, as shown here:

```
DROP TABLE Employee CASCADE
```

The RESTRICT modifier will not allow the dropping of the table if it is referenced in any views or referential constraints, as shown here:

```
DROP TABLE Employee RESTRICT
```

Altering an Existing Table

Occasionally, you might want to modify the structure of a table after it has been created and data has been added to it. Alteration of existing tables is not supported by all databases, although the ability to add columns is more widely supported than the ability to remove existing columns.

To add a column, you would execute a statement of the following form:

```
ALTER TABLE table-name ADD COLUMN column-name data-type
```

For the Employee table created previously, you might want to add a column for the employee's phone extension. This could be done with a statement like this:

```
ALTER TABLE Employee ADD COLUMN Extension INTEGER
```

When a new column is added, it will be given a value of NULL in existing rows. You will not be able to specify default values or other constraints when adding new columns.

If you later decided that you didn't really want to keep the extension in the Employee table, you could remove that column with a statement like this:

```
ALTER TABLE Employee DROP COLUMN Extension
```

As shown earlier with tables, a database might let you qualify the dropping of a column with the CASCADE or RESTRICT keywords. If you include the CASCADE modifier, any views or constraints that reference the dropped column will also be dropped, as in the following example:

```
ALTER TABLE Employee DROP COLUMN Extension CASCADE
```

Using the RESTRICT modifier will prevent the dropping of the column if it is referenced in views or referential constraints.

Indexes

Indexes are database objects used to more efficiently access the rows in a table. The index keeps track of the rows in the table based on the values of a certain column or set of columns. Indexes can drastically improve your database performance for certain types of lookup operations, provided the index is created properly to deal with the sorts of queries that are most commonly used. However, you should be aware that there can be a good amount of overhead associated with maintaining an index. If you go around creating a gazillion different indexes on a table, you will find that your performance will suffer.

Indexes are created with a CREATE INDEX statement, which has the following general syntax:

```
CREATE [UNIQUE] INDEX index-name
    ON table-name (column-name(s)) [ASC,DESC]
```

The UNIQUE modifier tells the database to ensure that the value of the index is unique; the database will not allow the addition of rows with a duplicate value for the column or columns used in the index. For example, you could create an index on the Employee table that makes it more efficient to look up rows by employee ID, with the following statement:

```
CREATE UNIQUE INDEX MyEmpIdIndex ON Employee (EmpId)
```

The preceding statement will also ensure that the database will not allow the insertion of rows with duplicate employee IDs.

In the preceding example, we used a single column for the index, although you can also use a combination of several columns. For example, you can create an index on the name and department of an employee with a statement like this:

```
CREATE INDEX MyNameDeptIndex ON Employee (EmpName, Dept)
```

Some databases will also allow you to specify the direction of the index. You can create the index in an ascending order by adding the ASC modifier or in a descending order by adding the DESC modifier.

It is not possible to modify an index, although you should never need to do this; you can simply drop the index and create a new one, without losing any data. An index is dropped with a statement like the following:

```
DROP INDEX index-name
```

Views

Views are best thought of as a sort of virtual table. To user applications, a view looks just like a table and is used in exactly the same way. However, a view does not store its own data; it only references the data held in tables. In general, views are used to present the data held in tables to the user in different ways, which are more convenient for the user.

You can use views to present subsets of the columns in a table, or several tables, that are specific to a particular sort of common query. This allows the user to see a table that makes sense to them, although your database can be structured differently for performance or integrity reasons.

You can use views to implement security. For example, you could use a view to provide users access to a certain subset of the columns in a table, while other columns in the table remain secured.

You can also use views to provide logical data independence, which can isolate your applications from changes that might be made in the actual tables of a database. If you change a table in the database, you can simply adjust the view to handle the new table, and you do not need to go back and change every application that has been written.

Views are created with CREATE VIEW statements, like the following example, which creates a rather useless view that simply exposes all the columns of a table:

```
CREATE VIEW MyView AS SELECT * FROM MyTable
```

Basically, you give the view a name and add a SELECT statement that specifies the data that will make up the view. You can also name the columns of your view, as in the following example, which exposes a portion of the Employee table:

```
CREATE VIEW MyView (Id, Name) AS SELECT (EmpId, EmpName) FROM Employee
```

You can also create views that use much more complex select statements, including joins that combine several different tables into a single view. However, because this chapter hasn't yet discussed more complicated SELECT statements, we will leave our discussion of views here.

You cannot modify existing views, although you can always simply drop the view and create it anew, without losing any data. A view is dropped from the database with a statement like the following:

```
DROP VIEW view-name
```

Data Control Language

If you are writing applications to work with local database files, such as Microsoft Access, you will probably not be overly concerned with the security of individual objects within your database. Even if you were, most desktop databases do not support this level of security. However, if you are using larger database server systems, security of individual objects within the database should be a concern. Data Control Language is the segment of the SQL language that allows you to work with user privileges for objects in the database.

Granting Privileges

The SQL language allows you to grant certain privileges on a particular object to a set of users. The privileges that can be granted are listed here:

SELECT: Allows the user to query data.

INSERT: Allows the user to add new rows.

DELETE: Allows the user to delete rows.

UPDATE: Allows the user to modify existing rows.

REFERENCES: This privilege is required if a user will be modifying a table that has referential integrity constraints that refer to columns in another table. The user must have the REFERENCES privilege on the columns used in the constraint.

Privileges for a certain object are granted with a GRANT statement, such as the following:

```
GRANT SELECT ON Employee TO PUBLIC
```

The preceding example makes use of the PUBLIC keyword to grant the SELECT privilege on the Employee table to all users. You can also grant several privileges to several users in a single statement, as shown in the following code line. You cannot, however, grant privileges to multiple objects in the same statement.

```
GRANT SELECT, INSERT ON Employee TO Bob, Doug
```

For the UPDATE and REFERENCES privileges, you can grant access to specific columns, as in the following example, which allows Bob and Doug to update only the Salary and Dept columns.

```
GRANT UPDATE (Salary, Dept) ON Employee TO Bob, Doug
```

Revoking Privileges

You can revoke privileges for database objects by using REVOKE statements, which use similar syntax as the GRANT statements shown earlier in this chapter. For example, if you had used the following statement to grant privileges:

```
GRANT SELECT ON Royalties TO Ed, Alex, Michal, Dave
```

you could revoke a user's privileges to the Royalties table with a statement like this:

```
REVOKE SELECT ON Royalties FROM Dave
```

You can also add CASCADE or RESTRICT modifiers to your REVOKE statements. If you want to revoke a user's privileges for a certain table, it would also make sense to revoke the user's privileges on any views that require access to that table. The CASCADE modifier will do this for you. On the other hand, the RESTRICT modifier will prevent you from revoking a privilege that is required according to other privileges the user has been granted.

Data Manipulation Language

In the previous sections, you looked at the parts of SQL used to set up your databases. Now you get to the juicy bits where you actually get your hands on the data and look at the real meat of SQL known as Data Manipulation Language, or DML, which consists of the following basic types of statements:

- SELECT
- INSERT
- DELETE
- UPDATE

You can probably guess what each of these statements does, but let's look at the specifics of each of them in the following sections.

SELECT Statements

The SELECT statement is the true heart and soul of SQL. Every time you want to retrieve data from the database, you will use SELECT. The basic syntax of a SELECT statement is fairly simple, although there are many additional clauses that can be included, as you will see in just a bit. In its most simple form, the SELECT looks like this:

```
SELECT select-list FROM table-name
```

The select-list can take on several different forms. Perhaps the simplest, and also the most common, is *, which will select all columns from the selected table, as in the following example, which will retrieve all the columns in MyTable for each of the rows in the table.

```
SELECT * FROM MyTable
```

You can also select certain fields from the table by specifying the fields, as in the following example:

```
SELECT EmpId, EmpName FROM MyTable
```

In addition, you can specify constant literals in the select-list. This is rarely needed in C++ applications but is very common in report generation utilities, where constant text is added for formatting purposes. For example, the following statement will return '_ _ _ _' as if it were the value of another column:

```
SELECT EmpId, '_ _ _ _', EmpName FROM MyTable
```

This could be useful in presenting the results to the user, although your C++ applications will usually find better ways of formatting data for the user.

The WHERE Clause

In the examples you have seen so far, we have retrieved all the rows in a table. You can limit the set of rows that is returned by using a WHERE clause. WHERE clauses can contain a wide range of different conditional expressions that are used to choose which rows to return. The simplest of these expressions involve the following comparison operators: <, >, <=, >=, =, or <>. For example, the following statement retrieves all rows for which the employee ID is 123:

```
SELECT * FROM Employee WHERE EmpId = 123
```

You can also combine several conditions by using AND and OR, as in the following examples:

```
SELECT * FROM Employee WHERE Salary > 50000 AND Salary < 60000
```

```
SELECT * FROM Employee WHERE Dept = 'MIS' OR Dept = 'Sales'
```

In addition, you can use the NOT operator to negate a condition, as in the following example, which selects all rows for employees who are not in Human Resources:

```
SELECT * FROM Employee WHERE NOT Dept = 'HR'
```

This simple example is equivalent to the following statement that uses the inequality operator:

```
SELECT * FROM Employee WHERE Dept <> 'HR'
```

Expressions

In place of individual column names, you can also use numerical expressions involving multiple columns combined with the following arithmetic operators: +, -, /, *. Expressions can be used in the select-list, as in the following example:

```
SELECT PartNum, PartCost + ExtraCost FROM Parts
```

The WHERE clause can also include expressions, as in the following example:

```
SELECT PartNum FROM Parts WHERE (ExtraCost / PartCost) > .25
```

The LIKE Predicate

In addition to the comparison operators, SQL offers a special comparison operator for character strings. The LIKE predicate allows you to select rows based on a string that matches a certain pattern. In the matching pattern, you can include any normal characters, as well as the special characters % and _. You can attempt to match any string of characters of any length with % or any single character with _. For example, to select any rows that contain Database in the Title field, you can use a query like the following:

```
SELECT ChapterNum FROM Chapters WHERE Title LIKE '%Database%'
```

You could also search for titles that have ata starting at the second character position with the following statement:

```
SELECT ChapterNum FROM Chapters WHERE Title LIKE '_ata%'
```

The IN Predicate

You can also use the IN predicate to simplify some of your WHERE clauses that are used to select rows with a value that belongs to a certain set of values. For example, look at the following query:

```
SELECT EmpNum FROM Employee
    WHERE Dept = 'MIS' OR Dept = 'HR' OR Dept = 'Sales'
```

This could be simplified by using the IN predicate, as in the following query:

```
SELECT EmpNum FROM Employee WHERE Dept IN ('MIS', 'HR', 'Sales')
```

You can negate the IN predicate, as in the following example, which selects all employees that are not in the listed departments:

```
SELECT EmpNum FROM Employee WHERE Dept IN ('MIS', 'HR', 'Sales')
```

> **NOTE**
>
> The IN predicate is specified in the core conformance level and is not supported by all drivers.

The BETWEEN Predicate

In many cases, you will need to select rows based on column values that fall into a certain range. For example, you could execute a query like the following:

```
SELECT EmpNum FROM Employee WHERE Salary > 20000 AND Salary < 30000
```

This query could be simplified by using the BETWEEN predicate, as in the following example:

```
SELECT EmpNum FROM Employee WHERE Salary BETWEEN 20000 AND 30000
```

Like the other comparison operators, you can apply BETWEEN to non-numeric columns, as in the following example:

```
SELECT EmpNum FROM Employee WHERE Name BETWEEN 'Andersen' AND 'Baker'
```

You can also negate the BETWEEN predicate by adding the NOT modifier to select rows that do not fall into the given range.

> **NOTE**
>
> The BETWEEN predicate is defined in the core conformance level and is not supported by all drivers.

The DISTINCT Keyword

In many cases, you will want to find all the possible values for a particular column found in a set of rows. You can do this by using the DISTINCT keyword, which will eliminate duplicate entries in the returned result set, as in the following example, which will return one row for each of the department codes found in the Employee table:

```
SELECT DISTINCT Dept FROM Employee
```

Without the DISTINCT keyword, you would receive a row for each entry in the Employee table, rather than just a list of the individual values used in the Dept column.

The ORDER BY Clause

By default, the rows returned by a query are presented in an arbitrary order. If you want to have the rows returned in any specified order, you will need to use an ORDER BY clause, which allows you to specify one or more columns to use in sorting the rows returned. For each column, you can also specify the ASC or DESC modifiers to specify an ascending or descending order for sorting on that column.

The following example will return rows sorted by employee ID in ascending order:

```
SELECT EmpId FROM Employee ORDER BY EmpId ASC
```

If you specify more than one column in the ORDER BY clause, the rows will first be sorted by the first column; then, rows with equal values for the first column will be further sorted by the second column. For example, the following statement will sort rows by ascending order of Salary, with rows of equal salary sorted in descending order by EmpId:

```
SELECT EmpId, Salary FROM Employee ORDER BY Salary ASC, EmpId DESC
```

Aggregation

In many cases, you will want to compute values based on all the rows returned in the result set, such as the total for a column in all the returned rows. These sorts of computations can be done with the aggregate functions shown here:

AVG: Mean average of the column values

COUNT: Number of rows returned

MAX: Maximum value for the column in the result set

MIN: Minimum value for the column in the result set

SUM: Total of all values for this column in the result set

Perhaps the most common use of aggregation is to retrieve the number of rows returned by a given query, as in the following example, which returns the number of rows in the Employee table:

```
SELECT COUNT(*) FROM Employee
```

If you use COUNT(*), all of the rows in the query will be counted. However, if you specify a column name, only rows for which the column value is non-null will be counted. For example, if the Dept column was NULL in one or more rows, the following query would return only the number of rows containing a value for Dept:

```
SELECT COUNT(Dept) FROM Employee
```

You can also use the DISTINCT keyword in conjunction with the aggregate functions, as in the following query, which returns the number of different department codes that are used:

```
SELECT COUNT(DISTINCT Dept) FROM Employee
```

In many cases, you will want to use aggregate functions on certain groups of rows in the result set. This can easily be done by adding a GROUP BY clause, which can specify the column used to group the rows that are included in aggregate computations. The following example will generate a list of department codes, followed by the total of the salaries for each department:

```
SELECT Dept, SUM(Salary) FROM Employee GROUP BY Dept
```

Earlier, you saw how the WHERE clause is used to filter the rows that are returned in a query. In a similar fashion, you can restrict the rows returned using aggregation by adding a HAVING clause, as in the following example, which will return only salary totals for departments that have a total salary of less than $200,000:

```
SELECT Dept, SUM(Salary) FROM Employee
    GROUP BY Dept
    HAVING SUM(Salary) < 200000
```

In more complicated queries, it can be a bit confusing to see how various WHERE and HAVING clauses work with each other to produce the end result. When working with aggregation, keep in mind that processing is done in the following order:

1. All rows that meet the WHERE clause are selected.

2. Aggregate values are computed.

3. The rows resulting from aggregation are filtered by the HAVING clause.

ODBC SQL Literal Values

In some of the previous examples, you have seen the use of simple literal, or constant, values in the SQL statements. For numeric values, whether integral or floating-point, you need to use only the decimal representation. For strings, you simply enclose the string in single quotes.

> **TIP**
>
> Be sure to use single, rather than double, quotes around your literals in the SQL statements you use in your C++ code. The compiler will quickly get confused if you don't.

You can use NULL as a literal when setting a column to a NULL value.

Now, here's the part where literals get interesting—specifying values for dates and times. It seems that almost every database system has an entirely different, and thus non-portable, way of specifying literals for these data types. To help with this, the flavor of SQL used by ODBC provides a portable syntax for specifying these values.

For date literals, use either of the following formats:

```
{ d 'yyyy-mm-dd' }
```

```
--(* VENDOR(Microsoft), PRODUCT(ODBC) d 'yyyy-mm-dd' *)--
```

Similarly, for time literals, use either of the following formats:

```
{ t 'hh:mm:ss' }
```

```
--(* VENDOR(Microsoft), PRODUCT(ODBC) t 'hh:mm:ss' *)--
```

Use the following formats for representing timestamp values:

```
{ ts 'yyyy-mm-dd hh:mm:ss' }
```

```
--(* VENDOR(Microsoft), PRODUCT(ODBC) ts 'yyyy-mm-dd hh:mm:ss' *)--
```

> **NOTE**
>
> You are free to use the native syntax supported by your particular database, although this may cause difficulties if you move to a new database.

SQL Functions

The SQL used by ODBC also specifies many different functions that can be used in your queries, either in the select-list or in the WHERE clause. Functions can also be allowed in an ORDER BY clause, depending on your driver. You can divide these functions into five groups, including string functions, numeric functions, time and date functions, system functions, and data type conversion functions.

When calling functions in SQL, the ODBC grammar specifies one of the following notations:

```
{fn function-name}
```

or

```
--(* VENDOR(Microsoft), PRODUCT(ODBC) fn functionName *)--
```

In addition, most drivers will support a native SQL version of these functions. Thus, if you wanted to select a list of employee names and the length of their names, you could use any one of the following queries:

```
SELECT Name, {fn LENGTH(Name)} FROM Employee

SELECT Name, --(* VENDOR(Microsoft),PRODUCT(ODBC) fn LENGTH(Name)*)-- FROM Employee

SELECT Name, LENGTH(Name) FROM Employee
```

String Functions

The functions defined in ODBC SQL for working with strings include the following:

ASCII (string_exp): Returns the ASCII value of the first character in the string.

BIT_LENGTH(string_exp): Returns the length of the string in bits.

CHAR(code): Returns the character with the ASCII value passed in code.

CHAR_LENGTH(string_exp): Returns the length of the string in characters.

CHARACTER_LENGTH(string_exp): Same as CHAR_LENGTH().

CONCAT(string_exp1, string_exp2): Returns the result of appending string_exp2 to string_exp1.

DIFFERENCE(string_exp1, string_exp2): Returns an integer value that contains the difference in the SOUNDEX values of the two string expressions.

INSERT(string_exp1, start, length, string_exp2): Returns string_exp1 with length characters from string_exp1 deleted, beginning at start, and the contents of string_exp2 inserted at start.

LCASE(string_exp): Returns string_exp converted to all lowercase.

LEFT(string_exp, count): Returns the leftmost count characters of string_exp.

LENGTH(string_exp): Returns the length of string_exp in characters, minus any trailing blanks.

LOCATE(string_exp1, string_exp2 [, start]): Returns the starting position of the first occurrence of string_exp1 within string_exp2. Optionally, you can specify a start value to begin searching in string_exp2 at character number start.

LTRIM(string_exp): Returns string_exp with any leading blanks removed.

OCTET_LENGTH(string_exp): Returns the length in bytes.

POSITION(string_exp1 IN string_exp2): Returns the position of string_exp1 in string_exp2.

REPEAT(string_exp, count): Returns a string consisting of string_exp repeated count times.

REPLACE(string_exp1, string_exp2, string_exp3): Returns a string generated by finding occurrences of string_exp2 within string_exp1 and replacing them with string_exp3.

RIGHT(string_exp, count): Returns the rightmost count characters in string_exp.

RTRIM(string_exp): Returns string_exp with any trailing blanks removed.

SOUNDEX(string_exp): Returns a character string that represents the sound of string_exp. The type of value returned is datasource-specific.

SPACE(count): Returns a string made up of count spaces.

SUBSTRING(string_exp, start, length): Returns a string made up of length characters taken from string_exp, starting at start.

UCASE(string_exp): Returns string_exp converted to all uppercase.

Numeric Functions

The ODBC SQL specification also includes the following numeric functions:

ABS(numeric_exp): Returns the absolute value of numeric_exp.

ACOS(float_exp): Returns the arccosine of float_exp in radians.

ASIN(float_exp): Returns the arcsine of float_exp in radians.

ATAN(float_exp): Returns the arctangent of float_exp in radians.

ATAN2(float_exp1, float_exp2): Returns the arctangent of the x and y coordinates given in float_exp1 and float_exp2, in radians.

CEILING(numeric_exp): Returns the smallest integer greater than or equal to numeric_exp.

COS(float_exp): Returns the cosine of float_exp, where float_exp gives an angle in radians.

COT(float_exp): Returns the cotangent of float_exp, where float_exp gives an angle in radians.

DEGREES(numeric_exp): Returns the angle given in radians in numeric_exp to degrees.

EXP(float_exp): Returns the exponential value of float_exp.

FLOOR(numeric_exp): Returns the largest integer less than or equal to numeric_exp.

LOG(float_exp): Returns the natural logarithm of float_exp.

LOG10(float_exp): Returns the base-10 logarithm of float_exp.

MOD(integer_exp1, integer_exp2): Returns the modulus (remainder) of integer_exp1 divided by integer_exp2.

PI(): Returns the constant pi.

POWER(numeric_exp, integer_exp): Returns numeric_exp to the power of integer_exp.

RADIANS(numeric_exp): Returns the angle given in degrees in numeric_exp to radians.

RAND([integer_exp]): Returns a random, floating-point value. Optionally, you may specify a seed value in integer_exp.

ROUND(numeric_exp, integer_exp): Returns the value of numeric expression rounded to integer_exp places to the right of the decimal point. You can specify negative values of integer_exp to round to a certain number of decimal places to the left of the decimal point.

SIGN(numeric_exp): Returns -1 if numeric_exp is less than 0, 1 if it is greater than 0, or 0 if numeric_exp is equal to 0.

SQRT(float_exp): Returns the square root of float_exp.

TAN(float_exp): Returns the tangent of the angle given in radians in float_exp.

TRUNCATE(numeric_exp, integer_exp): Returns numeric_exp truncated to integer_exp places to the right of the decimal point. You can specify a negative value of integer_exp to truncate to integer_exp places to the left of the decimal.

Time and Date Functions

The following functions are provided to help you work with times and dates in various formats:

CURRENT_DATE(): Returns the current date.

CURRENT_TIME([time-precision]): Returns the current local time. You may specify a precision value, in seconds in time-precision.

CURRENT_TIMESTAMP([timestamp-precision]): Returns the current time and date in a timestamp format. You may specify a precision, in seconds, in timestamp-precision.

CURDATE(): Returns the current date.

CURTIME(): Returns the current time.

DAYNAME(date_exp): Returns a character string containing the day of the week for date_exp in the data source's local language.

DAYOFMONTH(date_exp): Returns the number of the day of the month for the date in date_exp.

DAYOFWEEK(date_exp): Returns the day of the week as an integer in the range 1-7, with 1 being Sunday.

DAYOFYEAR(date_exp): Returns the day of the year in the range 1-366.

EXTRACT(extract-field FROM extract-source): This is used to extract certain fields from the date or time in extract_source. You can specify one of the following for extract-field:

    YEAR

    MONTH

    DAY

    HOUR

    MINUTE

    SECOND

HOUR(time_exp): Returns the hour from time_exp in the range 0-23.

MINUTE(time_exp): Returns the minute from time_exp in the range 0–59.

MONTH(time_exp): Returns the month from time_exp in the range 1–12.

MONTHNAME(date_exp): Returns the name of the month in date_exp.

NOW(): Returns a timestamp for the current time and date.

QUARTER(date_exp): Returns the quarter for date_exp, in the range 1–4. 1 denotes the quarter from January 1 to March 31.

SECOND(time_exp): Returns the second from time_exp in the range 0–59.

TIMESTAMPADD(interval, integer_exp, timestamp_exp): Returns a timestamp created by adding integer_exp time units to the timestamp in timestamp_exp. The type of units is specified by interval and can be one of the following:

```
SQL_TSI_FRAC_SECOND
SQL_TSI_SECOND
SQL_TSI_MINUTE
SQL_TSI_HOUR
SQL_TSI_DAY
SQL_TSI_WEEK
SQL_TSI_MONTH
SQL_TSI_QUARTER
SQL_TSI_YEAR
```

TIMESTAMPDIFF(interval, timestamp_exp1, timestamp_exp2): Returns the number of time units generated by subtracting timestamp_exp2 from timestamp_exp1. The units used are specified by interval, which can be one of the values listed previously for TIMESTAMPADD().

WEEK(date_exp): Returns the week of the year for date_exp in the range 1–53.

YEAR(date_exp): Returns the year from date_exp.

System Functions

The following functions are supported in the ODBC version of SQL. These are used to provide a variety of functions related to some of the constructs used in ODBC.

DATABASE(): Returns the name of the database being used by the current connection.

IFNULL(exp, value): If exp is a NULL value, IFNULL() will return value. Otherwise, exp is returned.

USER(): Returns the database username being used with the current connection.

Data Type Conversion

The ODBC SQL dialect allows you to explicitly convert the value of a column or expression to a different type by using the CONVERT() function, shown here:

```
CONVERT(value_exp, data_type)
```

value_exp is the column name or expression to convert, and data_type is used to specify the new type. Possible values for data_type include the following values:

```
SQL_BINARY
SQL_CHAR
SQL_DECIMAL
SQL_DOUBLE
SQL_FLOAT
SQL_INTEGER
SQL_LONGVARCHAR
SQL_NUMERIC
SQL_REAL
SQL_SMALLINT
SQL_TYPE_DATE
SQL_TYPE_TIME
SQL_TYPE_TIMESTAMP
SQL_VARCHAR
```

You can also specify many more values in data_type, as shown in the online ODBC Programmer's Guide.

NOTE

The ODBC Programmer's Guide is in `DevStudio\SharedIDE\help\ODBC.HLP`. This contains many things that you will not find in the Developer Studio HTML help.

For example, if you wanted to select a date field as a character string, you might use a query something like the following:

```
SELECT EmpNum, {fn CONVERT(HireDate, SQL_CHAR)}
    FROM Employee
    WHERE {fn CONVERT(HireDate, SQL_CHAR)} LIKE '%Jan%'
```

Joins

One of the more important operations performed with relational databases is the *join*, which returns rows of data that are gathered from two or more different tables that are joined in the processing of the query. Joins are even more important if you are working with databases that are thoroughly normalized.

NOTE

Normalization is a process that, more or less, involves structuring the database in order to give it certain properties and ensuring that certain types of operations are performed successfully. To go into any more depth, we would need to talk about more general database theory than we have space for here. If you want to read more about normalization, relations, and the umpteenth normal form, consult a general relational database text.

To perform a join, select columns from more than one table. For example, assume that you have a Parts table that lists information about parts, including a description, and a separate Prices table that lists pricing information for the parts. The following query would perform a join on these two tables:

```
SELECT Description, Price FROM Parts, Prices
```

However, you might be surprised at the results. The preceding example will return the Cartesian product of the two tables, which is a fancy name for all of the possible combinations of the rows in the Parts table and the rows in the Prices table. In most cases, this is not a useful result.

To narrow the set of returned rows to something more useful, you will need to add a WHERE clause. One of the most common cases is when you have a common identifier in both tables. For example, if both the Prices and Parts tables included a PartNum column, you could generate rows that match a part's description to its price with the following query:

```
SELECT Description, Price FROM Parts, Prices
    WHERE Parts.PartNum = Prices.PartNum
```

NOTE

You will notice that in the preceding WHERE clause, we used Parts.PartNum and Prices.PartNum instead of just PartNum. This is often necessary in joins to distinguish the PartNum column of one table from the column of the same name in another table, although it is not necessary if ambiguous column names are not involved. You can also resolve ambiguity of column names in the select-list with the same syntax.

Correlation Names

To help simplify some of your queries, SQL allows you to use correlation names, which can reduce the verbosity of your queries and are necessary for some more complicated queries that you will see later. For example, if you had the following query:

```
SELECT MyFirstTable.Name, MyFirstTable.Num, MySecondTable.Date,
    MySecondTable.Time FROM MyFirstTable, MySecondTable
    WHERE MyFirstTable.Id = MySecondTable.Id
```

it could be simplified by using the correlation names f, for MyFirstTable, and s, for MySecondTable, as in the following:

```
SELECT f.Name, f.Num, s.Date, s.Time
    FROM MyFirstTable f, MySecondTable s,
    WHERE f.Id = s.Id
```

In this case, the use of correlation names does not affect the meaning of the query in any way; it merely simplifies the notation. However, in more complicated queries, you might find yourself selecting from the same table more than once, as when using subqueries. In these cases, correlation names are essential for specifying exactly which table you are using.

Outer Joins

The syntax for joins you have seen so far performs an inner join, which might not generate the full Cartesian product of the joined tables. For example, if you created a join with the following query:

```
SELECT * FROM Employee, Department
    WHERE Employee.DeptNum = Department.DeptNum
```

the database would process this statement by collecting all the rows present in the Employee table, matching those with the rows in the Department table. This result does not include results for which no corresponding entry exists in the Employee table. It also will not return any rows for which a matching entry is not found in the Department table. To create a query that will return rows that do not include a matching row in one of the tables, you will need to use an outer join.

For example, suppose you wanted to select rows for each employee, including those who have not been assigned to a department yet. You can do so by using an outer join like the following:

```
SELECT * FROM
    {oj Employee LEFT OUTER JOIN Department ON
        Employee.DeptNum = Department.DeptNum}
```

In the preceding example, we used a LEFT OUTER JOIN, which ensures that all rows of the left table (Employee) will be represented in the result set. You could also use a RIGHT OUTER JOIN to ensure that all rows in the right table are represented, or a FULL OUTER JOIN, which ensures that all rows from both tables are represented, whether or not a matching row appears in the other table.

Subqueries

In the WHERE clause examples that we have seen so far, we have done comparisons on literal values or comparing two columns, or Boolean combinations of these. However, it is also possible to retrieve information used in a WHERE clause by executing another query, known as a *subquery*.

The first case in which a subquery could be used is with an EXISTS (or NOT EXISTS) predicate. Suppose you wanted to select a list of departments that had no employees assigned to them. You could do so with the following query:

```
SELECT DeptName FROM Department
    WHERE DeptNum NOT EXISTS (SELECT * FROM Employee)
```

This will return the name of all departments, for which the department number is not found in any of the records in the Employee table.

You could also select a list of departments that have at least one particularly well-paid employee with a query like the following:

```
SELECT DeptName FROM Department d
    WHERE EXISTS
        (SELECT * FROM Employee e
        WHERE e.Salary > 100000 AND d.DeptNum = e.DeptNum)
```

The second case in which subqueries are useful is when using the IN or NOT IN predicates. For example, you could return a list of all the departments that currently have personnel assigned to them by using a query like the following:

```
SELECT DeptName FROM Department
    WHERE DeptNum IN (SELECT DeptNum FROM Employee)
```

The third case in which subqueries are often used involve comparisons that use the ANY or ALL keywords. For example, if you kept separate tables for employees and executives, and wanted to select a list of executives that were paid more than all the regular employees (taken individually, not totalled), you could use the following query:

```
SELECT Ex.Name FROM Executives Ex
    WHERE Ex.Salary > ALL
        (SELECT Emp.Salary FROM Employee Emp)
```

Similarly, you could use the ANY modifier to select a list of executives for which at least one regular employee was better paid with the following query:

```
SELECT Ex.Name FROM Executives Ex
    WHERE Ex.Salary < ANY
        (SELECT Emp.Salary FROM Employee Emp)
```

Union Queries

SQL allows you to generate a single result set from two independent queries by combining them with the UNION keyword. By default, duplicate rows are removed from the result set, although you can disable this by using UNION ALL instead of UNION. Also, you may choose to sort the end result by specifying an ORDER BY clause, which must come after the last query in the union.

For example, you could generate a list of employees in the MIS and Sales departments with the following query:

```
SELECT * FROM Employee WHERE Dept = 'MIS'
UNION
SELECT * FROM Employee WHERE Dept = 'SALES'
```

Of course, there are several other ways that you could more efficiently generate the same results as the above query, but this shows a simple example of how UNION works.

INSERT Statements

So, now that you have seen how to get rows out of a database in umpteen different ways, how do you get them in there in the first place? This is where the appropriately named INSERT statement comes in. The basic syntax for an INSERT statement looks like this:

```
INSERT INTO table-name [(column-list)]
    VALUES (value-list)
```

If you are adding values for each of the columns, omit the column-list and simply assign values for each of the columns, in the order they appear in the table, such as in the following example:

```
INSERT INTO Employee
    VALUES (123, 'Bob Jones', 35000, 'MIS')
```

If you plan to specify only the values for certain columns, you must include a list of the columns that you are assigning values to. The values must then be listed in the order of the columns in the column list. This is useful for cases in which the table is set up with default values for a column or when you want to leave a column NULL. The following example will add a new employee record, leaving the Salary NULL:

```
INSERT INTO Employee ( EmpId, EmpName, Dept )
    VALUES ( 123, 'Joe Bob Griffin', 'Sales' )
```

In addition, instead of using the VALUES clause used previously, you could insert rows based on the values returned by a SELECT statement. For example, if your company spun off its MIS department to an outsourcing firm, you could add new records in the FormerEmployee table with a statement like the following:

```
INSERT INTO FormerEmployee (EmpId, EmpName, Reason)
    SELECT EmpId, EmpName, 'Outsourced' FROM Employees
    WHERE Dept = 'MIS'
```

DELETE Statements

Now that you've added all sorts of rows to a table, how do you get rid of them? This is where the DELETE statement comes in. The basic DELETE statement is very simple; you can only delete entire rows, so there is no need to specify individual columns. The basic DELETE statement looks like this:

```
DELETE FROM Employee
```

However, this simple statement is very powerful. It will delete *all* the rows from the Employee table. In most cases, you will want to add a WHERE clause, which can take any of the forms you saw previously, with SELECT statements. For example, you could delete a specific row from the Employee table like this:

```
DELETE FROM Employee WHERE EmpId = 456
```

UPDATE Statements

The UPDATE statement allows you to modify the values for existing rows in the database. For example, you could give all employees a $100 raise with the following statement:

```
UPDATE Employee SET Salary = Salary + 100
```

You can limit the rows affected by the update by adding a WHERE clause, as shown earlier. For example, you could effect a new minimum salary with the following statement:

```
UPDATE Employee SET Salary = 21000 WHERE Salary < 21000
```

Of course, you could also use UPDATE to update more than one column at a time or even set a column to NULL. For instance, in the following example, suppose Mary was getting married, changing her name, and taking an extended honeymoon. We could change the name, set her department to NULL, and change her current status in one fell swoop with the following statement:

```
UPDATE Employee
    SET EmpName = 'Mary Jones', Dept = NULL, Status = 'On Leave'
    WHERE EmpNum = 324
```

Calling Procedures

Many database systems allow you to use SQL to call procedures provided by the system or defined by the user. These are often used to make your applications more efficient by executing stored procedures on the server without involving network traffic, or slower client processing, in certain operations. To call a procedure, use either of the following statement formats:

```
{ call myProcedure }
```

```
--(* VENDOR(Microsoft), PRODUCT(ODBC) call myProcudure *)--
```

In most cases, calling procedures involves a return value and/or one or more input or output parameters. We will be looking at how each of the specific database interfaces handles parameters in each of the following chapters, although each of them allows you to specify placeholders for parameters by adding a question mark (?) where the parameters will go, as in the following example:

```
{call ?=PromoteEmployee(?, 'Manager', ?) }
```

The preceding example provides for three parameters: the return value of the procedure and two additional input parameters.

Summary

This chapter took a brief look at the database interfaces used with Visual C++ 5.0. This should give you an idea of which of the following chapters will be most useful for you in developing your particular applications.

You also took a look at Structured Query Language, or SQL, which is the language used to interact with the database in each of the interfaces discussed in the next few chapters.

If you are new to databases, or relational databases in particular, I highly recommend reading through a general text on relational databases before diving in and developing full-scale applications.

Now, on to the nuts and bolts of database programming with Visual C++.

25

Open Database Connectivity (ODBC)

by David Bennett

The Open Database Connectivity (ODBC) library is provided with Visual C++ to allow your applications to connect to a wide variety of different databases. It provides a common programming interface for accessing databases ranging from simple ASCII files to much more complex mainframe databases. ODBC uses Structured Query Language (SQL) to access all the data sources it supports, including data sources such as text files, which are not traditionally accessed with SQL.

In addition to Windows platforms, the ODBC library is also being implemented on various other platforms, including UNIX, so the ODBC API can be a valuable tool for producing platform-independent applications. ODBC also standardizes the SQL grammar that is used by your applications—if the data source you are using uses a different dialect of SQL for its native operations, ODBC will perform the necessary translation for you. This can be a great help in developing database-independent applications.

However, this does not mean that just because you use ODBC your apps will work anywhere. Developing truly platform-independent applications can require a great deal of additional development work, not to mention testing.

In this chapter, you will explore ODBC Version 3.0, which ships with Visual C++ 5.0. Version 3 has changed many of the names of functions and data types that were found in version 2 of ODBC, although the structure of the API is basically the same. Many of the changes found in ODBC 3.0 were made to ensure that the Microsoft ODBC API conforms with the Call-Level Interface (CLI) specifications from X/Open and ISO/IEC for database APIs.

> **NOTE**
>
> The ODBC documentation in the Visual C++ 5.0 Infoviewer is for version 2.5 only. However, the following Windows Help files for ODBC 3.0 are installed in the `DevStudio\SharedIDE\Help` directory:
>
> `ODBC.HLP`—*ODBC 3.0 Programmer's Reference*
> `SDKGUIDE.HLP`—*ODBC 3.0 SDK Guide*
> `ODBCJET.HLP`—*ODBC Microsoft Desktop Database Drivers Help*
> `ODBCJTNW.HLP`—*ODBC Desktop Database Drivers, What's New*
>
> These help files can be viewed with `WinHlp32.exe`. You can add these help files to the Tools menu of Developer Studio by adding an entry using the Tools | Customize menu command and selecting the Tools page to insert an entry with a command of `WinHlp32.exe` and the full path to the help file in the arguments box.

ODBC Architecture

ODBC applications can use the ODBC API to access data from a variety of different data sources. Each of the different data source types is supported by an ODBC driver specific to that type of data source—it is the driver that implements the meat of the ODBC API functions and performs the actual communication with the database.

The ODBC environment helps you manage connections to different data sources by providing the driver manager, which is implemented in `ODBC32.dll`. Your application need only link to the driver manager, which handles the ODBC API calls and passes them off to the appropriate driver. The driver manager also provides certain translations, such as converting between ODBC versions 3.*x* and 2.*x* if the application and driver support different versions. Both the interface between your application and the driver manager, and the interface between the driver manager and individual drivers use the same ODBC API.

The driver manager will load the appropriate driver when your app tries to connect to a data source of that type, so you don't need to worry about keeping track of separate driver DLLs for each data source type.

Figure 25.1 illustrates how the various components of the ODBC environment work together to provide flexible database access for your applications.

FIGURE 25.1.
ODBC architecture.

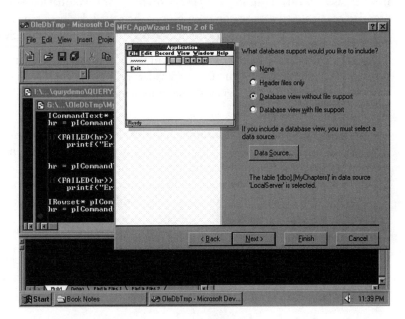

The figure illustrates how your application can use the ODBC API to access a variety of different data sources by linking to a single library—the driver manager.

ODBC Drivers

ODBC allows your applications to access different databases by using different drivers for each database. You can use ODBC to access any database for which a driver is supplied. Visual C++

5.0 provides drivers for the following databases, although many other drivers are available either from Microsoft or from other database vendors:

- Oracle
- SQL Server
- Microsoft Access
- Microsoft FoxPro
- Microsoft Excel
- dBASE
- Paradox
- Text Files

In some cases, the database driver itself will manipulate the data, as is the case with text file drivers. This sort of driver is known as a *single-tier driver*.

In other cases, you may be using *multiple-tier drivers*, in which the database driver uses a database's proprietary client software to communicate to the actual database server. This is most often the case with traditional RDBMS systems, such as Oracle, Informix, or SQL Server.

Each of these drivers supports slightly different levels of functionality. Obviously, an RDBMS such as SQL Server or Oracle can support a wider variety of operations than plain old text files. Likewise, the drivers for these types of data sources support more of the functionality provided by ODBC.

In general, each ODBC driver conforms to one of three levels of conformance: the Core API level and extension levels 1 and 2. However, many drivers may not implement some functions of their claimed conformance level, and most will implement several higher-level functions. In general, you should plan to test your application with each of the drivers that it may use, because there may be many subtle (or not so subtle) differences between drivers.

Core API Conformance

Core API conformance provides a minimum of ODBC functionality, including connecting to a database, executing SQL statements, and accessing the results of a query. This level also includes limited capabilities for cataloging a database and retrieving error information.

Extension Level 1 Conformance

Extension level 1 includes additional features, giving your applications more complete access to the schema of a database, supporting transactions and stored procedures, and supporting scrollable cursors.

Extension Level 2 Conformance

Extension level 2 provides additional features that are generally found only in complete client/server database implementations, such as more detailed access to the data dictionary, bookmark support, access to special columns, and additional optimization capabilities.

SQL Grammar Conformance

ODBC drivers must support a standard minimum SQL grammar. However, each driver may support a different set of extensions to this minimum standard. ODBC defines conformance levels based on the SQL-92 Entry, Intermediate, and Full levels, as well as the FIPS 127-2 Transitional level. In many cases, as you will see later in this chapter, advanced functionality can be provided via escape sequences, which are standardized in the ODBC API—the driver will translate these as needed for a particular data source.

ODBC Driver Manager

The ODBC Driver Manager provides several very useful features to your application. First, as you saw earlier, the driver manager takes care of loading individual drivers as needed (when your application tries to connect to a data source). It also maintains a table of the functions in that driver, based on the connection handle, so that any subsequent ODBC API calls you make are routed to the correct driver. The driver manager also provides several functions that are not provided by drivers, allowing your application to see which drivers and data sources are available on the local system. In addition, the driver manager will do some preliminary error checking on many calls before passing them off to the appropriate driver.

Data Sources

In ODBC, a data source is just that—a source of data. It can be an individual file used in desktop database applications, such as MS Access or FoxPro, or it can be a full-blown Relational Database Management System (RDBMS), such as Informix, Oracle, or SQL Server. The concept of a data source allows all the nitty-gritty details of a connection to be hidden from the user, who only selects a data source from a list of data source names and does not worry about network addresses or specific file locations. Data sources are made available on the local machine by using the ODBC Data Source Administrator, or they may be added programmatically.

ODBC Data Source Administrator

Your ODBC application connects to an ODBC data source, rather than directly to any particular database. The ODBC data sources available to applications on the local machine are configured with the ODBC Data Source Administrator application, which can be found in the Control Panel, by clicking on the icon labeled 32-bit ODBC. This will bring up the tabbed dialog shown in Figure 25.2.

FIGURE 25.2.
ODBC Data Source Administrator.

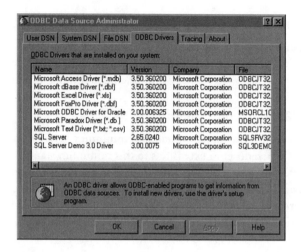

The ODBC Drivers tab lists the drivers that are currently installed on the local machine. The data sources that are configured are shown on the User DSN, System DSN, and File DSN tabs.

The User DSN page lists data sources that are configured on the local machine for the current user, and data sources that can be used by any user on the local machine are shown on the System DSN tab. The File DSN tab lists file data sources, which store all the information needed to make a connection in a .DSN file and may be accessed by any user on any machine that has access to the file (and has the appropriate drivers installed).

In addition, the Tracing tab allows you to specify log file tracing options for ODBC, and the About tab gives information about the current version of ODBC components installed on the local machine.

Adding a Data Source

Before using an ODBC application, you must add the data sources that it will be using. You can add a data source to any of the DSN tabs by clicking on the Add button, which will present you with a dialog to choose the driver to use. Depending on the sort of database driver you choose, you will be presented with additional dialogs prompting for things such as the database name, server address, or other default settings for this data source.

ODBC Installation and Setup Programming

In addition to the utilities such as the Data Source Administrator, the ODBC SDK provides functions that you can use in your own installation and configuration utilities. This goes beyond the scope of this chapter, but is documented in the *ODBC 3.0 Programmer's Reference.*

ODBC API Basics

Before you get into the various functions provided by the ODBC API, let's look at a few key concepts used throughout the API. In this section, you will look at allocating various handles that are used by ODBC, data types used in ODBC, and how ODBC passes error information to your application.

ODBC Handles

The ODBC API introduces new handle types that are used to reference information about your app's ODBC environment, specific database connections, SQL statements, and descriptors. In ODBC 3.0, each of these handle types are allocated with a single function—SQLAllocHandle()—and freed with a single function—SQLFreeHandle().

The SQLAllocHandle() function allocates the internal structures for the various handle types:

```
SQLRETURN SQLAllocHandle(SQL_SMALLINT HandleType, SQLHANDLE InputHandle,
    SQLHANDLE * OutputHandlePtr);
```

> **NOTE**
>
> In ODBC 3.0, this function replaces the ODBC 2.*x* SQLAllocEnv(), SQLAllocConnect(), and SQLAllocStmt() functions, although these are still supported by the driver manager, which maps them to SQLAllocHandle().

The HandleType parameter can be one of the following values:

```
SQL_HANDLE_ENV
SQL_HANDLE_DBC
SQL_HANDLE_STMT
SQL_HANDLE_DESC
```

These values determine which sort of handle is being allocated. You will look at specific examples of allocating each type when you learn about allocating environment, connection, statement, and descriptor handles.

The InputHandle specifies the handle from which the new handle is derived. For example, a connection handle is allocated based on an environment handle. An environment handle, however, is not derived from another handle, so InputHandle should be set to SQL_NULL_HANDLE.

The OutputHandlePtr should point to the new handle that is to be allocated.

If the new handle is successfully allocated, SQlAllocHandle()will return SQL_SUCCESS; otherwise, it will return SQL_ERROR. You will look at how to handle ODBC errors in just a bit.

When you are finished with a particular ODBC handle in your application, you should free the structures associated with the handle by calling `SQLFreeHandle()`, which takes the type of handle to free and the actual handle that is to be freed.

> **NOTE**
>
> `SQLFreeHandle()` replaces the ODBC 2.*x* functions `SQLFreeEnv()`, `SQLFreeConnect()`, and `SQLFreeStmt()`. The driver manager will map these calls to `SQLFreeHandle()`.

ODBC Data Types

ODBC defines many different standard data types that are used in ODBC applications. There are C data types, which are used in your application code, and SQL data types, which are used to describe the type of data that is used within a data source. Many of the ODBC calls that move data from the application to the data source, or vice versa, can automatically perform conversion between many of these types.

Some of the most common C data types defined in ODBC are listed in Table 25.1, although there are many others described in the *ODBC 3.0 Programmer's Reference*. The C type identifier is a constant used to represent the type, the ODBC typedef gives the type you should use in declaring this type of variable, and the C type shows what the preprocessor will resolve this to.

Table 25.1. ODBC C data types.

C type identifier	ODBC C typedef	C type
SQL_C_CHAR	SQLCHAR *	unsigned char *
SQL_C_SSHORT	SQLSMALLINT	short int
SQL_C_USHORT	SQLUSMALLINT	unsigned short int
SQL_C_SLONG	SQLINTEGER	long int
SQL_C_ULONG	SQLUINTEGER	unsigned long int
SQL_C_FLOAT	SQLREAL	float
SQL_C_DOUBLE	SQLDOUBLE	double
SQL_C_BIT	SQLCHAR	unsigned char
SQL_C_STINYINT	SQLSCHAR	signed char
SQL_C_UTINYINT	SQLCHAR	unsigned char
SQL_C_SBIGINT	SQLBIGINT	_int64
SQL_C_UBIGINT	SQLUBIGINT	unsigned _int64
SQL_C_BINARY	SQLCHAR *	unsigned char *
SQL_C_VARBOOKMARK	SQLCHAR *	unsigned char *

ODBC uses SQL data types to describe the data types that are stored in the database. Table 25.2 shows some of the more common types, listing the constant SQL type identifier that is used in your apps and a sample SQL definition for the type. For a complete listing, see the *ODBC 3.0 Programmer's Reference*.

Table 25.2. ODBC SQL data types.

SQL type identifier	Sample SQL definition
SQL_CHAR	CHAR(n)
SQL_VARCHAR	VARCHAR(n)
SQL_LONGVARCHAR	LONG VARCHAR
SQL_DECIMAL	DECIMAL(p,s)
SQL_NUMERIC	NUMERIC(p,s)
SQL_SMALLINT	SMALLINT
SQL_INTEGER	INTEGER
SQL_REAL	REAL
SQL_FLOAT	FLOAT(p)
SQL_DOUBLE	DOUBLE PRECISION
SQL_BIT	BIT
TINYINT	TINYINT
SQL_BIGINT	BIGINT
SQL_BINARY	BINARY(n)
SQL_VARBINARY	VARBINARY(n)
SQL_LONGVARBINARY	LONG VARBINARY
SQL_TYPE_DATE	DATE
SQL_TYPE_TIME	TIME(p)

ODBC Diagnostics

The ODBC API provides two levels of diagnostic information about calls to the API. At the first level, each function returns a SQLRETURN value, which will contain a small set of values indicating the general success or failure of an operation. At the second level, each function call also generates at least one diagnostic record. These diagnostic records give specific information about any errors that occurred or other information about the operation.

SQLRETURN Values

All the ODBC functions return a SQLRETURN (signed short) value, which will receive a value indicating the success or failure of a function. If a call is completed successfully, it will return either SQL_SUCCESS or SQL_SUCCESS_WITH_INFO, which is used to notify your application that additional information about the operation can be retrieved by calling SQLGetDiagRec(). SQL_SUCCESS_WITH_INFO is often used to pass warning messages to your application. These diagnostic records are useful both for debugging your application and for deciding how to handle certain situations at runtime.

> **TIP**
>
> Because there are two success codes, you should be careful not to simply check for a SQLRETURN value of SQL_SUCCESS.

Currently, all error return codes are defined to be less than 0, although there are some other positive return codes that do not necessarily indicate successful completion. These include SQL_NO_DATA (called SQL_NO_DATA_FOUND in ODBC 2.*x*), which is returned when an operation completes successfully, but there is no data to be had; SQL_STILL_EXECUTING, which is used with asynchronous operations; and SQL_NEED_DATA, which is used to indicate that the function needs additional data to complete.

In most cases, if an error occurs in an ODBC function, it will return SQL_ERROR (or SQL_INVALID_HANDLE if things are really wrong).

Diagnostic Records

Each of the ODBC API functions can generate a set of diagnostic records that reflect information about the performance of the operation. These diagnostic records are stored in the structures associated with the ODBC handle that generated the error. For instance, if an error occurs when calling SQLExecDirect(), the statement handle that was used will contain the diagnostic records, whereas errors in something like SQLConnect() will be stored in the connection handle that was used.

The diagnostic records generated by a function can be accessed from the handle until another call is made that uses that handle.

All ODBC calls will return at least a header record and may contain many additional status records. These records consist of a predefined set of fields, as well as others that may be defined by the particular driver you are using.

SQLGetDiagField()

You can retrieve the value of a particular field from a diagnostic record by using the SQLGetDiagField() function:

```
SQLRETURN SQLGetDiagField(SQLSMALLINT HandleType, SQLHANDLE Handle,
    SQLSMALLINT RecNumber, SQLSMALLINT DiagIdentifier, SQLPOINTER DiagInfoPtr,
    SQLSMALLINT BufferLength, SQLSMALLINT * StringLengthPtr);
```

> **NOTE**
>
> In ODBC 3.0, SQLGetDiagField() and SQLGetDiagRec() replace SQLError().

The Handle and HandleType parameters are used to specify the handle to retrieve records from and its type.

The RecNumber field is used to specify the record to retrieve. To retrieve information from the header record, this should be set to 0. You can retrieve the total number of additional status records available for a handle by retrieving the SQL_DIAG_NUMBER field from record 0.

The DiagIdentifier parameter specifies which field to return. This may be one of the fields that are predefined in the ODBC API or any additional fields that may be added by specific drivers. The following are some of the most common fields (note that the header record and status records contain different fields):

Header Record Fields

SQL_DIAG_NUMBER—Number of status records available

SQL_DIAG_RETURN_CODE—The return code for the previous function call

Status Record Fields

SQL_DIAG_SQLSTATE—A five-character SQLSTATE code (see SQLSTATEs)

SQL_DIAG_MESSAGE_TEXT—A plaintext message about the error or warning

SQL_DIAG_NATIVE—The native error code from the driver or data source

SQL_DIAG_COLUMN_NUMBER—The column (if any) associated with this record

SQL_DIAG_ROW_NUMBER—The row (if any) associated with this record

For details on the other fields available in diagnostic records, see the online documentation for SQLGetDiagField().

The information for the requested field is returned in the buffer at DiagInfoPtr, and the length of the data is returned at StringLengthPtr.

SQLSTATES

There are a great number of possible values for SQLSTATE codes that can be returned in the SQL_DIAG_SQLSTATE field, many of which may have a variety of different meanings, depending on the driver you are using. Because of this, you should be careful in how you use the SQLSTATE codes in your programming logic if you intend to use a variety of drivers.

However, in most cases, the following SQLSTATEs can be safely used in your programming logic, because they are generally implemented in the same way in most drivers and can be useful in controlling program flow:

01004—Data truncated
01S02—Option value changed
HY008—Operation canceled
HYC00—Optional feature not implemented
HYT00—Timeout expired

For a complete listing of possible SQLSTATEs, see Appendix A of the *ODBC 3.0 Programmer's Reference*, included in the online documentation. In addition, the SQLSTATEs that can be returned for each function are listed in the online documentation for that function.

SQLGetDiagRec()

In addition to the SQLGetDiagRec() function shown previously, ODBC 3.0 provides the SQLGetDiagRec() function, which will retrieve some of the most commonly used fields from a status record in one fell swoop. This function will return the SQLSTATE, the native error code, and the diagnostic message text that is contained in status records. However, to access the header record, you must use SQLGetDiagField().

Creating an ODBC Application

In this section, you will be looking at how to create an ODBC application using the ODBC API directly. In the next chapter, you will see how you can use the MFC database classes and AppWizard to help you create database applications.

Most ODBC applications will perform the following basic steps:

1. Allocate the ODBC environment.
2. Allocate a connection handle.
3. Connect to a data source.
4. Execute SQL statements.
5. Retrieve query results.
6. Disconnect from the data source.
7. Free the ODBC environment.

You will learn each of these steps in the next sections, starting with the allocation of the ODBC environment.

> **NOTE**
>
> When creating an application that uses the ODBC C API, you include `<sqlext.h>` (which will also include `sql.h`) and link to `ODBC32.LIB`.

Allocating the ODBC Environment

Before using any other ODBC functions, you must first allocate the ODBC environment, which initializes some of the internal structures used by ODBC. To do this, you must first allocate a variable of type `SQLHENV`, which will serve as a handle to your ODBC environment. This handle is then initialized with the `SQLAllocHandle()` function that you saw previously.

To allocate the ODBC environment, `HandleType` should be set to `SQL_HANDLE_ENV`, and `OutputHandlePtr` should point to the environment handle to be allocated. `InputHandle` should be set to `SQL_NULL_HANDLE`, because the environment is not derived from another handle. You will see an example of this when you look at `SQLConnect()` later.

You should only allocate one environment for an application. The same environment can, however, be used for multiple threads and multiple data source connections.

When you are finished with ODBC in your application, you should free the ODBC environment with a call to `SQLFreeHandle()`, passing a `HandleType` of `SQL_HANDLE_ENV` and the environment handle you have allocated.

Setting Your Application's ODBC Version

The ODBC driver manager is designed to support version 2.*x* drivers and applications, as well as newer ODBC 3.0 components. Depending on the version of ODBC that your application is using, certain functions will behave differently. This requires that your application specify which version of the ODBC API it is using before you go on to allocate connection handles.

Setting the version of ODBC that your application is using is done by calling `SQLSetEnvAttr()` to set the `SQL_ATTR_ODBC_VERSION` environment attribute to `SQL_OV_ODBC3`. You can see an example of this when you connect to a data source.

Allocating a Connection Handle

Next, you allocate a connection handle for each data source that you intend to use. This is also done with the `SQLAllocHandle()` function that you saw previously—`HandleType` is set to `SQL_HANDLE_DBC`, and you should pass the previously allocated environment handle in

InputHandle. A pointer to the connection handle to be allocated should be passed in OutputHandlePtr.

Once you have allocated a connection handle, you can attach the returned connection handle to a data source with the SQLConnect... functions that you will see next.

When you are finished with a connection, you should free the connection with a call to SQLFreeHandle().

Connection Options

The ODBC API allows you to set many different options associated with a connection handle by calling SQLSetConnectAttr():

```
SQLRETURN SQLSetConnectAttr(SQLHDBC ConnectionHandle, SQLINTEGER Attribute,
    SQLPOINTER ValuePtr, SQLINTEGER StringLength);
```

You should pass a previously allocated SQLHDBC in ConnectionHandle, although, depending on the attribute set, it does not need to be connected to a data source yet. The value passed in Attribute determines the option to be set and may include the values listed next, as well as others that may be defined later. You will look at several of these options in more detail later in this chapter:

SQL_ATTR_ACCESS_MODE sets read-only mode.

SQL_ATTR_ASYNC_ENABLE enables asynchronous operations.

SQL_ATTR_AUTO_IPD enables automatic population of the IPD after a call to SQLPrepare().

SQL_ATTR_AUTOCOMMIT sets auto-commit mode for transaction processing.

SQL_ATTR_CURRENT_CATALOG sets the catalog (also called database or qualifier) for the current connection. This is generally something like a specific database name.

SQL_ATTR_LOGIN_TIMEOUT sets the timeout value for establishing a connection to a data source.

SQL_ATTR_CONNECTION_TIMEOUT sets the timeout value for operations on a connection, other than login or query execution.

SQL_ATTR_METADATA determines how string arguments are used in catalog functions.

SQL_ATTR_ODBC_CURSORS specifies the type of cursor support that is used.

SQL_ATTR_PACKET_SIZE sets the size of the network packets used.

SQL_ATTR_QUIET_MODE disables dialogs from the driver or sets the parent window for any dialogs.

SQL_ATTR_TRACE enables tracing for the driver manager.

SQL_ATTR_TRACEFILE sets the name of the trace file.

SQL_ATTR_TRANSLATE_LIB sets the name of a DLL to use for translation between a driver and a data source.

SQL_ATTR_TRANSLATE_OPTION sets an option value specific to the translation DLL being used.

SQL_ATTR_TXN_ISOLATION sets the level of transaction isolation in use.

The ValuePtr and StringLength parameters should contain information specific to the option being set.

You can retrieve the current settings for any of these options with a call to SQLGetConnectAttr().

Connecting to a Datasource

Once you allocate a connection handle with SQLAllocConnect(), you must connect the handle to a data source before you can start operating on that data source. ODBC provides three functions that can be used for this. SQLConnect() provides the most direct method of connecting from your code, and SQLDriverConnect() presents a dialog to the user to choose a data source. The third connect function, SQLBrowseConnect(), can be used to browse available data sources, while prompting for any additional information that may be required.

SQLConnect()

The first of the connection functions that you will look at is SQLConnect(). This function provides you with the most direct programmatic control of the connection, although if you want to allow the user to choose data sources at runtime, you need to code all the user interface for selecting data sources yourself. That said, let's look at how it works. The prototype for SQLConnect() is shown in the following:

```
SQLRETURN SQLConnect(SQLHDBC ConnectionHandle, SQLCHAR* ServerName,
    SQLSMALLINT NameLength1, SQLCHAR* UserName, SQLSMALLINT NameLength2,
    SQLCHAR* Authentication, SQLSMALLINT NameLength3);
```

When calling SQLConnect(), ConnectionHandle should be a connection handle that has been allocated with SQLAllocConnection(). The remaining parameters are used to pass strings for the data source name (ServerName), user ID (UserName), and password (Authentication). For many data sources, such as text files, that are on the local machine, you do not need to specify a user ID or password, and you can pass NULL pointers for UserName and Authentication.

> **NOTE**
>
> All string parameters that are passed as inputs to ODBC functions will consist of a pointer to the string and a separate parameter for its length, which is used to support languages that require this. For C/C++ applications, you should pass a pointer to a null-terminated string and set the length parameter to SQL_NTS (Null-Terminated String).

When you call SQLConnect() or one of the other connect functions, the ODBC driver manager will load the requested driver if it is not already loaded and will connect to the requested data source. If an error occurs, SQLConnect() will return SQL_ERROR (or SQL_INVALID_HANDLE), and you should call SQLGetDiagRec() to retrieve specific information about the error(s).

The following example shows how you can use SQLConnect() to connect to a data source named "MyData". It also shows the use of SQLGetDiagRec() for retrieving error information:

```
#include <sqlext.h>
SQLRETURN sr;
char szDSN[] = "MyData";
char szUID[] = "sa";
char szAuthStr[] = "";

// Allocate Environment
sr = SQLAllocHandle(SQL_HANDLE_ENV, SQL_NULL_HANDLE, &hOdbcEnv);
if(sr != SQL_SUCCESS)
    TRACE("Error in Allocating Environment.\n");
// Set the App's ODBC Version
sr = SQLSetEnvAttr(hOdbcEnv, SQL_ATTR_ODBC_VERSION,
        (SQLPOINTER)SQL_OV_ODBC3, SQL_IS_INTEGER);
if(sr != SQL_SUCCESS)
    TRACE("Error in Setting ODBC Version.\n");

// Allocate Connection
sr = SQLAllocHandle(SQL_HANDLE_DBC, hOdbcEnv, &hDbConn);
if(sr != SQL_SUCCESS)
    TRACE("Error in Allocating Connection.\n");
// Set Connect Timeout
sr = SQLSetConnectAttr(hDbConn, SQL_ATTR_LOGIN_TIMEOUT, (void*)5, 0);
if(sr != SQL_SUCCESS)
    TRACE("Error in Setting Login Timeout.\n");
// Connect to Data Source
sr = SQLConnect(hDbConn, (UCHAR *)szDSN, SQL_NTS,
                    (UCHAR *)szUID, SQL_NTS,
                    (UCHAR *) szAuthStr, SQL_NTS);

// Get Error Info or warnings for SQL_SUCCESS_WITH_INFO
if(sr != SQL_SUCCESS)
{
    SQLCHAR SqlState[6];
    SQLINTEGER NativeError;
    SQLCHAR ErrMsg[SQL_MAX_MESSAGE_LENGTH];
    int i = 1;
    TRACE("Error in SQLConnect(): %d.\n", sr);
```

```
      while(SQLGetDiagRec(SQL_HANDLE_DBC, hDbConn, i, SqlState,
                          &NativeError, ErrMsg, sizeof(ErrMsg), NULL)
                     != SQL_NO_DATA)
         TRACE("Diag: %d, SQLSTATE: %s NativeError: %d ErrMsg: %s\n",
               i++, SqlState, NativeError, ErrMsg);
}
else
    TRACE("Connected OK\n");
// Work with the Database...
// Disconnect
sr = SQLDisconnect(hDbConn);
// Free Handles
if(hDbConn != SQL_NULL_HANDLE)
    SQLFreeHandle(SQL_HANDLE_DBC, hDbConn);
if(hOdbcEnv != SQL_NULL_HANDLE)
    SQLFreeHandle(SQL_HANDLE_ENV, hOdbcEnv);
```

SQLDataSources()

You will see in just a bit that the SQLDriverConnect() function will present a dialog to users, allowing them to select a data source from those available. However, if you wish to code your own browsing function, you can retrieve the available data sources by calling SQLDataSources():

```
SQLRETURN SQLDataSources(SQLHENV EnvironmentHandle, SQLUSMALLINT Direction,
    SQLCHAR * ServerName, SQLSMALLINT BufferLength1, SQLSMALLINT * NameLength1Ptr,
    SQLCHAR * Description, SQLSMALLINT BufferLength2, SQLSMALLINT *
NameLength2Ptr);
```

To list all the available data sources, you should call SQLDataSources() with Direction set to SQL_FETCH_FIRST. This will return the data source name in the buffer at ServerName and its description at Description. In most cases, you can set the NameLength1 and NameLength2 parameters to NULL, because you usually don't need to receive the length of the null-terminated strings that are returned.

To retrieve the name and description for the remaining data sources, you should call SQLDataSources(), with fDirection set to SQL_FETCH_NEXT, until it returns SQL_NO_DATA_FOUND, which indicates that all entries have been read:

```
UWORD fDirection = SQL_FETCH_FIRST;
SQLRETURN retcode;
SQLCHAR szDSN[SQL_MAX_DSN_LENGTH+1];
SQLCHAR szDescription[100];
while(retcode == SQL_SUCCESS)
    {
        retcode = SQLDataSources(henv, fDirection,
                      (UCHAR *)szDSN, sizeof(szDSN), NULL,
                      (UCHAR *)szDescription, sizeof(szDescription), NULL);
        fDirection = SQL_FETCH_NEXT;
        if(retcode != SQL_SUCCESS)
            TRACE("SQLDataSources returns: %d", retcode);
        else
            TRACE("DSN: [%s](%d) Desc: [%s](%d)",
                  szDSN, swLen, szDescription, swLen2);
    } // end while
```

SQLDriverConnect()

The next of the connect functions that you will look at is SQLDriverConnect(), which can present a dialog to the user for selecting a data source. SQLDriverConnect() can also be used to pass additional connection parameters that are not supported by the SQLConnect() function. Here is the prototype for SQLDriverConnect():

```
SQLRETURN SQLDriverConnect(SQLHDBC ConnectionHandle, SQLHWND WindowHandle,
    SQLCHAR * InConnectionString, SQLSMALLINT StringLength1,
    SQLCHAR * OutConnectionString, SQLSMALLINT BufferLength,
    SQLSMALLINT * StringLength2Ptr, SQLUSMALLINT DriverCompletion);
```

ConnectionHandle should be passed a connection handle that was previously allocated with SQLAllocHandle(), and WindowHandle may be passed the window handle for the parent of any dialog boxes that may be created.

The InConnectionString parameter points to a connection string that is passed into SQLDriverConnect(), consisting of a series of attribute keywords and their values. For example, to connect to a data source named SalesData for user JohnDoe with a password of JaneDoe, you might pass a string like the following:

```
"DSN=SalesData;UID=JohnDoe;PWD=JaneDoe"
```

The DSN, UID, and PWD attribute keywords are defined by ODBC, although individual drivers may support many additional keywords.

The value that you pass for DriverCompletion determines whether a dialog is presented to the user for selecting a data source. If you set DriverCompletion to SQL_DRIVER_NOPROMPT, no dialog will be presented. If InConnectionString includes incorrect or insufficient information, SQLDriverConnect() will return SQL_ERROR.

On the other hand, if you specify SQL_DRIVER_PROMPT, a dialog will always be presented to the user—the attributes passed in InConnectionString are used only as initial values in the dialog.

If you specify SQL_DRIVER_COMPLETE or SQL_DRIVER_COMPLETE_REQUIRED, a dialog is presented to the user only if the attributes passed in InConnectionString are insufficient to connect to a data source. If you have specified SQL_DRIVER_COMPLETE_REQUIRED, only the controls for required information will be enabled in the dialog.

When a connection to a data source is established, SQLDriverConnect() will return the actual connection string that was used in OutConnectionString. This can be used to determine the options that the user has selected from a dialog.

SQLBrowseConnect()

The last of the connection functions is SQLBrowseConnect(), which provides an iterative method for your application to browse available data sources. Note that this function does not provide the user interface for browsing, as SQLDriverConnect() does. SQLBrowseConnect() is generally available only for client/server database systems and is not usually supported for local databases, such as MS Access. Here is the prototype for SQLBrowseConnect():

```
SQLRETURN SQLBrowseConnect(SQLHDBC ConnectionHandle, SQLCHAR * InConnectionString,
    SQLSMALLINT StringLength1, SQLCHAR * OutConnectionString,
    SQLSMALLINT BufferLength, SQLSMALLINT * StringLength2Ptr);
```

When calling SQLBrowseConnect(), you should first pass in a connection string in InConnectionString similar to that used in SQLDriverConnect(). If the information in this string is sufficient to connect to a data source, SQLBrowseConnect() will return SQL_SUCCESS or SQL_SUCCESS_WITH_INFO, and your connection is all set to go.

If additional information is required, SQLBrowseConnect() will return SQL_NEED_DATA. More specific information on the data required is returned in OutConnectionString, which will receive a string similar to the string passed in InConnectionString, although it will also list additional attributes that must be specified.

In general, attributes that must be specified are of the following format: *KEYWORD:PROMPT=?;*, where *KEYWORD* is an attribute name, such as UID, and *PROMPT* is a string suitable for prompting the user. (You do not need to use the prompt string when building InConnectionString.) In addition, some attributes returned in OutConnectionString will present a list of possible choices in the following format: *KEYWORD:PROMPT={CHOICE1, CHOICE2, CHOICE3};*.

For example, if you call SQLBrowseConnect() with InConnectionString of DSN=MyRDBMS, it may return SQL_NEED_DATA with OutConnectionString receiving DSN=MyRDBMS;UID:User Name=?;DATABASE:Database={EmpDB, InventoryDB, AccountsDB}.

You should then be able to call SQLBrowseConnect() again with InConnectionString of DSN=MyRDBMS;UID=JohnDoe;DATABASE=EmpDB. If all goes well, SQLBrowseConnect() will return SQL_SUCCESS or SQL_SUCCESS_WITH_INFO and your connection is ready for executing SQL statements against the data source.

Retrieving Connection Information

In addition to the connection options, you can access a wide range of information about the ODBC driver and data source associated with an SQLHDBC by using the SQLGetInfo() function:

```
SQLRETURN SQLGetInfo( SQLHDBC ConnectionHandle, SQLUSMALLINT InfoType,
    SQLPOINTER InfoValuePtr, SQLSMALLINT BufferLength, SQLSMALLINT *
StringLengthPtr);
```

When calling SQLGetInfo(), ConnectionHandle should be a connection handle that was previously attached to a data source. The InfoType parameter is used to specify which piece of information is to be retrieved. For more on the specific values supported, see the online documentation for SQLGetInfo(). For now, let's say that just about anything you might want to know about a driver or a data source is available via this function, including information on conformance levels, support for various functions, and data types supported.

Depending on the value you pass for InfoType, the data returned at InfoValuePtr may take several different formats, including null-terminated strings, 16-bit integers, or 32-bit values. You should set BufferLength to the maximum size of the buffer at InfoValuePtr. On return, the value at StringLengthPtr will contain the actual length of the data returned.

Disconnecting a Session

Regardless of which of these connect functions you use to establish a connection, you should disconnect from the data source when you are finished with it by calling SQLDisconnect(). If you do not intend to reuse the connection handle, you should also deallocate the connection handle with a call to SQLFreeHandle().

Executing SQL Statements

Once you have successfully connected to a data source, it is time to get down to the real work of manipulating the data. This is done by executing Structured Query Language statements against the connected data source. For more on the syntax of SQL, see Chapter 24, "Database Overview."

In the following sections, you will look at how statement handles are used to execute SQL against a data source, including the use of SQLExecDirect() for direct executions, and the SQLPrepare() and SQLExecute() functions, which can be used to prepare a SQL statement in a separate step, which can then be executed multiple times.

Statement Handles

Before executing a statement, you must allocate a statement handle, which provides a data structure for ODBC to keep track of the SQL statement to be executed and the results it will return. Allocating a statement is done with the SQLAllocHandle() function you saw earlier—HandleType should be set to SQL_HANDLE_STMT, InputHandle should receive a previously allocated connection handle, and OutputHandle should point to a new handle of type SQLHSTMT that will be initialized. You can see an example of this in the next section where you see how to use the statement handle and SQLExecDirect() to execute SQL statements.

The SQLSetStmtAttr() and SQLGetStmtAttr() functions allow you to set and retrieve options for a statement handle in the same way that SQLSetConnectAttr() and SQLGetConnectAttr() work with options for connection handles. You will look at some of the specific options for statements later in this chapter.

When you are finished with a statement handle, you should deallocate it by calling SQLFreeHandle(), with HandleType set to SQL_HANDLE_STMT.

SQLExecDirect()

As the name suggests, `SQLExecDirect()` is the most direct method of executing an SQL statement against the data source. For statements that will be executed only once, this is also the fastest method of submitting SQL statements. The following is the prototype for `SQLExecDirect()`:

```
SQLRETURN SQLExecDirect(SQLHSTMT StatementHandle, SQLCHAR* StatementText,
    SQLINTEGER TextLength);
```

This function simply takes a null-terminated string containing an SQL statement (`StatementText`) and executes it on the data source connected to the statement handle in `StatementHandle`. (Remember that, for C/C++ applications, length parameters like `TextLength` should be set to `SQL_NTS`.)

If `SQLExecDirect()` returns `SQL_SUCCESS`, the statement was successfully executed against the data source. In some cases, where the statement was successful, but something abnormal occurred, it will return `SQL_SUCCESS_WITH_INFO`. In this case, or if `SQLExecDirect()` returns `SQL_ERROR`, you can retrieve additional information by calling `SQLGetDiagRec()`.

The following example shows the use of `SQLExecDirect()` to perform a simple `INSERT`:

```
SQLHSTMT hstmt;
SQLCHAR MySqlText[200] =
    "INSERT INTO MyTable VALUES (123, 'John Doe')";

// Allocate new Statement Handle,
// based on previous connection
sr = SQLAllocHandle(SQL_HANDLE_STMT, hDbConn, &hstmt);
if(sr != SQL_SUCCESS)
    TRACE("Error Allocating Handle: %d\n", sr);
sr = SQLExecDirect(hstmt, MySqlText, SQL_NTS);
if(sr != SQL_SUCCESS)
    TRACE("Error on INSERT: %d\n", sr);
```

Prepared SQL Statements

In addition to the `SQLExecDirect()` method that you saw above, ODBC also allows you to prepare SQL statements in a separate step before executing them. This can be a much more efficient way to do things if you will be executing the same statement many times. You parse the SQL only once and can then execute the statement many different times, without the parsing overhead. This technique is particularly useful when combined with statement parameters, which you will see later.

The `SQLPrepare()` function is used to prepare an SQL statement for execution:

```
SQLRETURN SQLPrepare(SQLHSTMT StatementHandle, SQLCHAR * StatementText,
    SQLINTEGER TextLength);
```

This function takes a `StatementHandle` previously allocated with `AllocHandle()` and a pointer to a null-terminated string that contains the `StatementText`. Remember that in C/C++ apps, you should pass `SQL_NTS` for parameters like `TextLength`.

When a statement is prepared, the ODBC standard SQL grammar that is passed to `SQLPrepare()` is translated to the native SQL dialect for the data source. You can retrieve this native translation by calling `SQLNativeSql()`.

SQLExecute()

Once the statement is prepared by `SQLPrepare()`, you can execute the statement by calling `SQLExecute()` with the statement handle that was passed to `SQLPrepare()`.

Although you can gain some performance advantages by preparing static SQL statements that will be executed several times, prepared statements are most useful when you use parameters with them, as you will see in the next section. You will also take a look at an example after you look at parameters.

Working with Parameters

So far, you have seen how to execute SQL statements based on a relatively static string. You have also seen how to use `SQLPrepare()` to create an SQL statement that can be executed many different times—but often, you don't want to execute exactly the same statement many times. It would be convenient if you could use the same general statement many times, with different values each time. Well, it turns out that ODBC lets you do just this by allowing the use of parameters in your SQL statements.

For example, you could use `SQLPrepare()` to prepare an SQL statement like one of the following examples:

```
"SELECT * FROM Employees WHERE empNo = ?;"
"{? = call GetEmpNo(?, ?)}"
```

The question marks (?) in these statements serve as placeholders, or markers, for statement parameters. Parameters can be used to pass values into an SQL statement, as in the preceding `SELECT` example. They may also be used to return output values, such as in the procedure call example. A value can be assigned to the parameter at runtime by binding a variable to the parameter with `SQLBindParameter()`.

SQLBindParameter()

The `SQLBindParameter()` function allows you to bind a buffer in memory to a given parameter marker, before the statement is executed. Its prototype is shown here:

```
SQLRETURN SQLBindParameter(SQLHSTMT StatementHandle, SQLUSMALLINT ParameterNumber,
    SQLSMALLINT InputOutputType, SQLSMALLINT ValueType, SQLSMALLINT ParameterType,
    SQLUINTEGER ColumnSize, SQLSMALLINT DecimalDigits, SQLPOINTER
```

```
ParameterValuePtr,
    SQLINTEGER BufferLength, SQLINTEGER * StrLen_or_IndPtr);
```

The `StatementHandle` parameter refers to the statement handle that you are using to execute the SQL statement.

The parameters in an SQL statement are numbered from left to right, starting with 1. You can call `SQLBindParameter()` for each parameter, with the appropriate value for `ParameterNumber`.

The `InputOutputType` parameter specifies how the parameter is used. For SQL statements that do not call procedures, such as `SELECT` or `INSERT` statements, this will be `SQL_PARAM_INPUT`. For procedure parameters, you can also use parameters of type `SQL_PARAM_OUTPUT` and `SQL_PARAM_INPUT_OUTPUT`.

The `ValueType` parameter is used to specify the C type of the variable that is being bound— `SQL_C_SLONG`—and the `ParameterType` argument specifies the SQL type only of the parameter— `SQL_INTEGER`. These parameters specify how ODBC will perform any conversion of the data. For more on ODBC data types, see the earlier section on ODBC data types.

The `ColumnSize` and `DecimalDigits` parameters are used to specify the size of the SQL parameter and its precision. These parameters are used only for certain values of `ParameterType` where they are applicable.

The `ParameterValuePtr` parameter points to the buffer in your application that holds the value to be substituted in the SQL statement, and `BufferLength` is used to pass the length of the buffer for binary or character parameters.

The buffer at `StrLen_or_IndPtr` is used to specify information about the data passed in `ParameterValuePtr`. The value in this buffer can have one of the following values:

- The length of the parameter at `ParameterValuePtr`.
- `SQL_NTS`—The buffer holds a null-terminated string.
- `SQL_NULL_DATA`—The buffer holds a `NULL` value.
- `SQL_DEFAULT_PARAM`—A procedure should use a default parameter value.
- `SQL_LEN_DATA_AT_EXEC`—Used to pass parameter data with `SQLPutData()`.

For output parameters, this buffer will also receive one of these values after the statement is executed.

The following example shows how you can prepare a statement and execute it several times with different parameter values:

```
SQLRETURN sr;
SQLHSTMT hstmt;
SQLCHAR MySqlText[200] =
    "INSERT INTO MyTable VALUES (?, ?)";
unsigned long Param1;
SQLINTEGER Len1;
```

```
char Param2[20];
SQLINTEGER Len2;

// Allocate a new statement handle
sr = SQLAllocHandle(SQL_HANDLE_STMT, hDbConn, &hstmt);
// Prepare statement
sr = SQLPrepare(hstmt, MySqlText, SQL_NTS);

// Bind Parameters
sr = SQLBindParameter(hstmt, 1, SQL_PARAM_INPUT, SQL_C_ULONG ,
            SQL_INTEGER, 0, 0, &Param1, sizeof(Param1), &Len1);
sr = SQLBindParameter(hstmt, 2, SQL_PARAM_INPUT, SQL_C_CHAR,
            SQL_CHAR, 0, 0, Param2, sizeof(Param2), &Len2);

// Use statement to insert multiple rows
for(int i=1;i<6;i++)
{
    Param1 = i + 100;
    sprintf(Param2, "%d", Param1);
    Len1 = sizeof(Param1);
    Len2 = SQL_NTS;
    // Execute statement with parameters
    sr = SQLExecute(hstmt);
}
```

Parameter Arrays

In the previous example, you passed one set of parameter values for each call to SQLExecute().
Although this can add some efficiency to your code, you can gain even more in terms of both
network overhead and data source execution time by passing an entire array of parameters to a
single SQLExecute() call. Unfortunately, like many other advanced features of ODBC, this may
not be supported by all drivers.

To pass arrays of parameters, you set the SQL_ATTR_PARAMSET_SIZE statement attribute to the
length of your parameter array(s). You should also set the SQL_ATTR_PARAM_STATUS_PTR attribute
to point to an array to receive the status for the result of each set of parameters.

Row-Wise Binding

In the previous example, you used column-wise binding to bind a separate buffer for each parameter, although you can also simplify your code somewhat by binding parameters by row.
This allows you to define a structure that will hold all your parameters for a statement. You can
then pass an array of these structures when calling SQLExecute().

To use row-wise binding, you set the SQL_ATTR_PARAM_BIND_TYPE statement attribute to the size
of the structure you have defined to hold the parameters. You will then bind each parameter
individually, binding to the address of the corresponding structure field for the first element of
the array. This is very similar to the row-wise binding that you will see for column data later in
this chapter.

Passing Parameter Data at Execution Time

Earlier, when you explored SQLBindParameter(), you saw that you could pass a value of SQL_DATA_AT_EXEC in the indicator array specified by StrLen_or_IndPtr. This allows you to pass data for lengthy parameters at the time the statement is executed. This can be useful for values that are too long to store in conventional parameter buffers.

To pass parameter data at execution time, you bind the desired parameters with the SQL_DATA_AT_EXEC flag set in the indicator array, then call SQLExecute(), which will return SQL_NEED_DATA if data is required for parameters.

You will then call SQLParamData() to retrieve information about the required parameter data. If parameter data is required, SQLParamData() will return SQL_NEED_DATA, and the parameter number that is required will be returned in the buffer at ValuePtrPtr.

> **NOTE**
>
> ODBC drivers are not required to ask for required parameter data in any particular order, so don't assume they will be requested in numerical order.

You can then call SQLPutData() to pass the data for the parameter. This may be called several times to pass long data values.

You then should call SQLParamData() again to see whether any additional parameter data is required. Once all required data has been sent, SQLParamData() will execute the statement and return SQL_SUCCESS or SQL_SUCCESS_WITH_INFO, provided the statement executed without error.

Parameter Information

In cases where your application code does not know ahead of time about the parameters required for a particular SQL statement, you can use the SQLNumParams() function to retrieve the number of parameters required and can then call SQLDescribeParam() to retrieve specifics about each parameter.

Working with Result Sets

Okay, so you can send SQL to the database with SQLExecDirect() or SQLExecute(), but how do you get your hands on the data the SQL returns? In this section, you will look at how to work with the data (called the result set) returned by calls like SQLExecDirect().

The result set returned by a query is like a temporary table—it includes rows of columns. Rows are retrieved from the result set using cursors, which come in several different flavors. The default cursor used in ODBC is a forward-only cursor, which allows you to access the rows in the result set only one row at a time. Furthermore, if you want to back up in the result set, you close the cursor and start over at the first row. You look at the forward-only cursor first, because it is supported in all drivers. You look at other cursor types, which can be used to access more than one row at a time, later on in this chapter.

In most cases, the best way to retrieve data from a result set is to bind the columns of the result set to specific memory locations ahead of time. Then, when you call SQLFetch(), the data for each column is copied into the memory location that you have bound for that column. You will also see how you can use SQLGetData() to retrieve one column at a time from the current row, after it has been fetched.

Binding Columns

There are two ways to access the data from individual rows of a result set. The first involves binding a column to a location in memory with SQLBindCol() before calling SQLFetch(), at which point the data from the row will be copied into the assigned locations. The second method, which you will see in just a bit, involves calling SQLGetData() to copy a column's data into a memory location after the call to SQLFetch().

SQLBindCol()

To assign the memory location that a column's data should be copied to when a row is fetched, you use the SQLBindCol() function:

```
SQLRETURN SQLBindCol( SQLHSTMT StatementHandle, SQLUSMALLINT ColumnNumber,
    SQLSMALLINT TargetType, SQLPOINTER TargetValuePtr, SQLINTEGER BufferLength,
    SQLINTEGER * StrLen_or_IndPtr);
```

The StatementHandle parameter should be the statement handle on which you are performing SQLExecDirect() and SQLFetch().

The ColumnNumber parameter specifies the number of the column to bind, starting with 1 and numbering left to right (column 0 is used for retrieving bookmarks, as you will see later).

The TargetType parameter is used to specify the desired C data type (for example, SQL_C_CHAR) that the data will be returned as. You saw the available data types in the beginning of this chapter.

When SQLFetch() is called to fetch the next row in the result set, ODBC will attempt to convert the data for each bound column from SQL format to the type specified by the TargetType parameter of SQLBindCol(). This may include some rather elaborate conversions, such as converting a numeric value into an ASCII string or converting character strings into various numeric formats.

If errors occur in the conversion process, or if certain events such as data truncation occur, SQLFetch() will return SQL_ERROR or SQL_SUCCESS_WITH_INFO, and the specific conversion errors (or warnings) can be retrieved with SQLGetDiagRec().

Remember that SQLGetDiagRec() should be called repeatedly until it returns SQL_NO_DATA_FOUND. This allows you to retrieve multiple errors for the same call to SQLFetch().

The TargetValuePtr parameter is a pointer to the location in memory where you want ODBC to place the data, and BufferLength should be passed the maximum size of this data buffer. (For strings, you should include space for the null terminator.)

The memory location at StrLen_or_IndPtr will receive the length of the actual data returned for the bound column each time SQLFetch() is called. In the event a column's data is NULL, this value will be set to SQL_NULL_DATA.

SQLFetch()

To access each row of the result set, including the first row, you call the SQLFetch() function:

```
SQLRETURN SQLFetch(SQLHSTMT StatementHandle);
```

This function simply makes the next row in the result set the current row. It will also copy the data from any bound columns into the memory locations assigned with SQLBindCol(). When there are no more rows available, a call to SQLFetch() will return SQL_NO_DATA_FOUND.

The best method of getting the number of rows in a result set is simply scrolling through the rows with SQLFetch() until no more are found. You can retrieve the count of rows in a result set with SQLRowCount(), but this is not supported in all drivers.

The following example shows the use of SQLExecDirect(), SQLBindCol(), and SQLFetch() to retrieve a single row of data:

```
SQLRETURN sr;
SQLHSTMT hstmt;
SQLCHAR mySql[] = "SELECT Num, Title, Pages FROM MyChapters";
// Column Date Variables
SQLINTEGER Lengths[4];
unsigned long Num;
SQLCHAR Title[50];
unsigned long Pages;
// Allocate Statement Handle
sr = SQLAllocHandle(SQL_HANDLE_STMT, hDbConn, &hstmt);

// Execute SQL statement
sr = SQLExecDirect(hstmt, (UCHAR*)"Select * from MyChapters", SQL_NTS);

// Bind each column
sr = SQLBindCol(hstmt, 1, SQL_C_ULONG, &Num,
            sizeof(Num), &Lengths[1]);
sr = SQLBindCol(hstmt, 2, SQL_C_CHAR, Title,
            sizeof(Title), &Lengths[2]);
```

```
sr = SQLBindCol(hstmt, 3, SQL_C_ULONG, &Pages,
            sizeof(Pages), &Lengths[3]);
// Fetch the first row
sr = SQLFetch(hstmt);
TRACE("Num: %d Title: [%s] Pages: %d\n", Num, Title, Pages);
```

Multiple Result Sets

It is possible for a single call to `SQLExecute()` to generate several different result sets, as is the case when you execute a batch of SQL statements or call a procedure that returns multiple result sets. Once you are finished with the current result set, you can call `SQLMoreResults()` to move on to the next result set. Generally, you will then want to rebind columns and fetch rows from the new result set with `SQLFetch()`.

Closing the Cursor

When you call a function that creates a result set, such as `SQLExecute()`, a cursor is opened for you. When you are finished working with a result set, you should close the cursor that was used to fetch the data by calling `SQLCloseCursor()`.

Reusing Statement Handles

You could allocate a separate statement handle for every SQL statement that your application will execute, although it is often neater (and saves overhead) if you can reuse your statement handles for multiple operations.

Before you can use a statement handle for a new operation, you should first free the parameter and result set bindings that were used for the previous operation by calling `SQLFreeStmt()`, with the `SQL_UNBIND` option to free any column bindings and the `SQL_RESET_PARAMS` option to free any parameter bindings. You can then use the statement handle for a new operation, as if it were newly allocated. However, you should make sure that the statement attributes are correct for the new operation.

SQLGetData()

ODBC also offers an alternative to using `SQLBindCol()` to bind columns to memory locations before calling `SQLFetch()`. You can call `SQLGetData()` to retrieve a single column's data, after the current row has been selected with `SQLFetch()`. This function provides the same sort of data conversion that is set up with `SQLBindCol()`.

In most cases, your application should either bind all columns or retrieve all columns with `SQLGetData()`. Depending on the driver you are using, there may be some rather strict limitations on support for mixing bound columns and `SQLGetData()`. For instance, many drivers do not allow you to call `SQLGetData()` for bound columns, and any columns that you intend to use `SQLGetData()` on must come after the last bound column.

Here is the prototype for SQLGetData():

```
SQLRETURN SQLGetData( SQLHSTMT StatementHandle, SQLUSMALLINT ColumnNumber,
    SQLSMALLINT TargetType, SQLPOINTER TargetValuePtr,
    SQLINTEGER BufferLength, SQLINTEGER * StrLen_or_IndPtr);
```

The parameters used for SQLGetData() are identical to those used for SQLBindCol(). The only difference is when the actual data transfer takes place. When using SQLBindCol(), the data is transferred each time you call SQLFetch(), whereas SQLGetData() is a one-time affair, retrieving the data from a row after it is selected with SQLFetch().

For columns that contain large character-, binary-, or driver-specific data, you can use multiple calls to SQLGetData() to retrieve the information. On the first call to SQLGetData(), ODBC will move up to BufferLength bytes into the buffer at TargetValuePtr. If there is still more data to retrieve, the call to SQLGetData() will return SQL_SUCCESS_WITH_INFO, and a subsequent call to SQLGetDiagRec() will show a SQLSTATE of 01004 (data truncated). You can then make additional calls to SQLGetData() with the same column number to retrieve additional blocks of the data in the column. When all the data has been retrieved, SQLGetData() will return SQL_SUCCESS.

In addition, you can use SQLGetData() to retrieve information from result sets that may have a variable number of columns. In this case, you may find the functions in the next section useful in determining information about the columns in the result set.

Column Information

Although it is generally a good idea for your database application to know what sort of data it will be retrieving ahead of time, you may find cases, such as a general database browser app, where the application does not know which columns will be returned in a result set at compile time. You can retrieve the number of columns in a result set by calling SQLNumResultCols() and can get specific information about each column with SQLDescribeCol() and SQLColAttribute().

SQLDescribeCol()

Once you know how many columns there are, you can call SQLDescribeCol() for each column:

```
SQLRETURN SQLDescribeCol(SQLHSTMT StatementHandle, SQLSMALLINT ColumnNumber,
    SQLCHAR * ColumnName, SQLSMALLINT BufferLength, SQLSMALLINT * NameLengthPtr,
    SQLSMALLINT * DataTypePtr, SQLUINTEGER * ColumnSizePtr,
    SQLSMALLINT * DecimalDigitsPtr, SQLSMALLINT * NullablePtr);
```

This will return the column name at ColumnName and the length of this string at NameLengthPtr. The length of the buffer at ColumnName should be passed in BufferLength.

The SQL data type of the column is returned at DataTypePtr. This value will be one of the constants, such as SQL_CHAR, that you saw in the earlier section on ODBC data types.

The precision and scale of the column are returned at `ColumnSizePtr` and `DecimalDigitsPtr`, respectively.

The value returned at `NullablePtr` indicates whether the column allows NULL values. This will be one of the following values:

`SQL_NO_NULLS`—NULL values are not allowed.

`SQL_NULLABLE`—NULL values are allowed.

`SQL_NULLABLE_UNKNOWN` indicates the driver cannot determine whether NULL values are allowed.

SQLColAttribute()

You can also retrieve various attributes of a result set column by calling `SQLColAttribute()`, which allows you to get at information such as the format, case-sensitivity, display size, owner, or precision, or to update permission of a column.

Retrieving More Than One Row at a Time

Earlier in this chapter, you saw how to access a result set one row at a time by calling `SQLFetch()` to access each row. You can also fetch a group of rows, or rowset, at a time by using the `SQLFetchScroll()` function instead of `SQLFetch()`. This is done by using cursors. In this section, you will be looking at block cursors, which allow you to retrieve groups of rows at a time, as well as scrollable cursors, which allow additional navigation within the result set. (In most cases, a scrollable cursor is a block cursor with additional functionality.)

Earlier, when you were retrieving one row at a time, you were also using a cursor, but it was a special single-row, forward-only case of a nonscrollable block cursor.

Block Cursors

Earlier in this chapter, you saw how to retrieve a single row at a time. As you might guess, this is generally not the most efficient way to retrieve large amounts of data—in addition to the overhead of a greater number of function calls, there can be a great deal more network overhead involved in requesting rows individually. To make your apps more efficient, you can use a block cursor, which retrieves a block of rows, or rowset, in a single request. You will see how to use block cursors soon.

Scrollable Cursors

With block cursors and forward-only cursors, you must close the cursor and start again from the top to return to a row in a previous rowset. Scrollable cursors allow your application to more easily navigate in any direction in a rowset. However, this additional functionality can introduce some significant additional overhead. In general, if you simply need to retrieve all the data in a rowset for report generation, block cursors are best. If you need to provide more flexible scrolling ability, such as in interactive applications, go ahead and use scrollable cursors.

The ODBC Cursor Library

For database drivers that do not support cursors, the ODBC SDK provides a cursor library (ODBCCR32.DLL) that implements block, static cursors and positioned updates and deletes. The cursor library sits between the application and the driver that actually connects to the data source. The cursor library may be distributed with your applications and is enabled by setting the SQL_ATTR_ODBC_CURSORS attribute on a connection before connecting to the data source.

Using Block Cursors

Using block cursors to retrieve data from a result set is similar to retrieving one row at a time, although there are a few extra things you must do. To use block cursors, have your application do the following:

1. Set the number of rows to be retrieved in each rowset.
2. Bind columns to memory locations.
3. Call SQLFetchScroll() to retrieve each rowset.

> **NOTE**
>
> In ODBC 3.0, SQLFetchScroll() replaces SQLExtendedFetch(). In addition, SQLFetch() has been enhanced to support block cursors.

Setting the Size of a Rowset

Call SQLSetStmtOption() to set the SQL_ATTR_ROW_ARRAY_SIZE option to the number of rows you want to receive in a rowset. By setting this attribute to a value greater than one, you tell ODBC to use a block cursor.

Binding Columns for a Rowset

If you are using SQLFetchScroll() to retrieve more than one row at a time, you can set up column-wise binding, as you saw with SQLFetch(), or you can use row-wise binding, which binds rows to a structure holding all the columns.

Column-Wise Binding

By default, a statement handle is set to use column-wise binding, as you saw earlier. The one difference when binding columns for use with block cursors is that instead of defining a single variable to receive data for a single row and column, the buffer pointer you specify in SQLBindCol() should point to an array of buffers that is long enough to receive a whole rowset worth of data for that column.

Row-Wise Binding

In addition, it is often useful to bind a rowset to memory in a row-wise fashion when using block cursors. This presents the data to your application as a single array of a structure that contains all the columns of the rowset, rather than a separate array for each column. Row-wise binding may also provide greater efficiency, depending on the driver you are using.

To implement row-wise binding, you must do the following:

1. Define a structure to hold a single row's data.

   This structure should have a field for each column to be bound, as well as an SDWORD field for the length of each column.

2. Allocate an array of this structure.

   The allocated array should contain as many elements as the size of your rowset. You should also include an additional element if your application will append new rows of data or search for key values.

3. Enable row-wise binding for the statement handle.

   This is done by calling SQLSetStmtAttr() with Attribute set to SQL_ATTR_ROW_BIND_TYPE and ValuePtr set to the size of the structure you have defined to receive the data.

4. Call SQLBindCol() for each column to be bound.

   When calling SQLBindCol(), the TargetValuePtr parameter should point to the data field corresponding to the column in the first element of the array, and StrLen_or_IndPtr should point to the corresponding size field in the first element of the array.

The following code shows how you can use row-wise binding:

```
// This structure is used to retrieve row data
struct rowTag {
    unsigned long Num;
    SDWORD NumLen;
    SQLCHAR Title[50];
    SDWORD TitleLen;
    unsigned long Pages;
    SDWORD PagesLen;
} myRows[10];
// Execute the SQL statement
```

```
sr = SQLExecDirect(hstmt,
        (UCHAR*)"SELECT Num, Title, Pages FROM MyChapters", SQL_NTS);
// Set the number of rows to retrieve
sr = SQLSetStmtAttr(hstmt, SQL_ATTR_ROW_ARRAY_SIZE, (void *) 5,
SQL_IS_INTEGER);

// Set the size of the structure for each row.
sr = SQLSetStmtAttr(hstmt, SQL_ATTR_ROW_BIND_TYPE,
        (void *) sizeof(myRows[0]), SQL_IS_INTEGER);

// Bind each column
sr = SQLBindCol(hstmt, 1, SQL_C_ULONG, &myRows[0].Num,
        sizeof(myRows[0].Num), &myRows[0].NumLen);
sr = SQLBindCol(hstmt, 2, SQL_C_CHAR, myRows[0].Title,
        sizeof(myRows[0].Title), &myRows[0].TitleLen);
sr = SQLBindCol(hstmt, 3, SQL_C_ULONG, &myRows[0].Pages,
        sizeof(myRows[0].Pages), &myRows[0].PagesLen);
// Fetch the first set of rows
sr = SQLFetch(hstmt);
```

Calling `SQLFetch()` for Block Cursors

Once you have your bindings set up, and have set the desired length for the rowset, you can start retrieving rowsets by calling the `SQLFetch()` function, as you saw previously. The difference is that if you have specified a rowset size of greater than one, more than one row will be retrieved.

> **NOTE**
>
> In ODBC 2.x, you had to use `SQLExtendedFetch()` to retrieve more than one row.

Row Status Information

In ODBC 2.x, the `SQLExtendedFetch()` function took additional parameters for returning an array of row status values and a count of rows returned. In ODBC 3.0, you can specify a location that will receive the number of rows retrieved by `SQLFetchScroll()` by setting the `SQL_ATTR_ROWS_FETCHED_PTR` statement attribute to point to the location to receive the number of rows.

In addition, you can specify a value of the `SQL_ATTR_ROW_STATUS_PTR` statement attribute to point to an array of `SQLUSMALLINT`s that will receive one of the following values for each row in the rowset. These values reflect the state of the row since it was last retrieved from the data source:

`SQL_ROW_SUCCESS`—The row is unchanged.

`SQL_ROW_SUCCESS_WITH_INFO`—The row was fetched successfully, but generated a warning that can be retrieved with `SQLGetDiagRec()`.

`SQL_ROW_UPDATED`—The row has been updated.

SQL_ROW_DELETED—The row has been deleted.

SQL_ROW_ADDED—The row has been added.

SQL_ROW_ERROR—The row could not be retrieved due to error.

SQL_ROW_NOROW—No row was retrieved for this position in the rowset.

Block Cursors and Single-Row Functions

If you are using a block cursor, you take an extra step before using functions such as SQLGetData() that operate on a single current row. You set the current row pointer by calling SQLSetPos() with the SQL_POSITION option.

Using Scrollable Cursors

In addition to the block cursor operations that you saw previously, many drivers support scrollable cursors, which allow you to use SQLFetchScroll() to move freely around in the result set, without having to start over at the beginning.

When you fetch a new rowset with a scrollable cursor, the new rowset may also include changes that have been made to the result set since it was first selected from the data source. ODBC provides four different types of scrollable cursors—each can detect different changes in the result set:

- *Static cursors* are the simplest, because they do not reflect any changes to the result set once it has been retrieved from the data source.
- *Dynamic cursors*, on the other hand, reflect all changes to the result set, including any changes that may be made by other users of the database.
- *Keyset-driven cursors* generally detect any changes to the values of the rows that were initially selected in the result set, although they may not detect any new rows that are added or any changes to the ordering of the rows in the result set. This type of cursor builds a keyset containing the key for each row in the result set. This is used to determine whether any of the rows in the result set have changed.
- *Mixed cursors* are a combination of keyset-driven and dynamic cursors. They generally will detect only changes to the values for the rows within the current keyset, but will detect any changes when you fetch a rowset outside of the current keyset.

In any case, changes to the result set are detected only when a new rowset is fetched with a call to SQLFetchScroll(). Furthermore, the detection of changes may also be affected by the current transaction isolation level, which you will look at when you talk about transactions.

Cursor Support

The following items returned by SQLGetInfo() give information about the level of cursor support provided by the current driver:

SQL_CURSOR_SENSITIVITY indicates whether a cursor can detect changes made outside of this cursor—for example, by other users.

SQL_SCROLL_OPTIONS indicates only the types of cursors supported (forward-only, static, keyset-driven, dynamic, or mixed).

SQL_DYNAMIC_CURSOR_ATTRIBUTES1, SQL_FORWARD_ONLY_CURSOR_ATTRIBUTES1, SQL_KEYSET_CURSOR_ATTRIBUTES1, and SQL_STATIC_CURSOR_ATTRIBUTES1 return a bitmap of the fetch-type values that may be used in SQLFetchScroll() for the given cursor type.

SQL_KEYSET_CURSOR_ATTRIBUTES2 and SQL_STATIC_CURSOR_ATTRIBUTES2 indicate whether the cursor can detect its own updates, deletes, and inserts.

Setting the Cursor Type

Before executing a statement that returns a result set, you can set the type of cursor that will be used by setting the SQL_ATTR_CURSOR_TYPE statement attribute. In addition, for keyset-driven and mixed cursors, you can set the size of the keyset used by setting the SQL_ATTR_KEYSET_SIZE statement attribute. By default, this attribute is set to 0, in which case the keyset size will be set to the size of the entire result set. To use a mixed cursor, you can specify a value for the keyset size that is smaller than the size of the result set.

As an alternative to setting the SQL_ATTR_CURSOR_TYPE attribute explicitly, you can allow ODBC to select a cursor type based on the values you set for the SQL_ATTR_CONCURRENCY, SQL_ATTR_CURSOR_SCROLLABLE, or SQL_ATTR_CURSOR_SENSITIVITY attributes. Any time you make a change to one of these four attributes, the other three settings may be changed by the driver to reflect the currently selected cursor type.

Calling SQLFetchScroll()

To retrieve a new rowset from the result set using a scrollable cursor, you should use the SQLFetchScroll() function, which allows you to move to random locations within the result set. The following is the prototype for SQLFetchScroll():

```
SQLRETURN SQLFetchScroll(SQLHSTMT StatementHandle, SQLSMALLINT FetchOrientation,
    SQLINTEGER FetchOffset);
```

The FetchOrientation parameter specifies how to move through the result set to find the next rowset to retrieve. This may be set to one of these values:

SQL_FETCH_FIRST retrieves the first rowset in the result set.

SQL_FETCH_NEXT retrieves the next rowset in the result set. (If the cursor is positioned before the first row, this is equivalent to SQL_FETCH_FIRST.)

SQL_FETCH_LAST retrieves the last rowset in the result set.

SQL_FETCH_PRIOR retrieves the previous rowset in the result set.

SQL_FETCH_ABSOLUTE retrieves the rowset starting with the row specified in FetchOffset. You can specify a negative value for FetchOffset to retrieve the rowset, starting with the row a given number of rows from the end of the result set.

SQL_FETCH_RELATIVE retrieves the rowset beginning with the row FetchOffset rows from the start of the current rowset. This may include negative values to move backwards.

SQL_FETCH_BOOKMARK retrieves the rowset beginning with the row specified by a bookmark value passed in FetchOffset.

Other than the ability to move at will through the result set, this function works just like SQLFetch()—the rowset that is retrieved will be moved into memory locations, as specified in SQLBindCol() calls.

Using Bookmarks

Many ODBC drivers support the use of bookmarks to directly access a given row in a result set, as you saw in SQLFetchScroll() with the SQL_FETCH_BOOKMARK option.

You can determine what level of support the current driver offers for bookmarks by calling SQLGetInfo() with the SQL_BOOKMARK_PERSISTENCE option.

To use bookmarks, you should use SQLSetStmtAttr() to set the SQL_ATTR_USE_BOOKMARK attribute to SQL_UB_VARIABLE before executing the SQL statement that generates the result set.

ODBC 3.0 uses only variable-length bookmarks, which will be of different sizes for different drivers. Once you have retrieved a result set with bookmarks enabled, you can call SQLColAttribute() for the SQL_DESC_OCTET_LENGTH field for column 0 to find the length needed to hold a bookmark.

You can retrieve the bookmark for a given row by either binding column 0 of the result set or using SQLGetData() to retrieve column 0 from a row. These bookmarks can then be used in subsequent calls such as SQLFetchScroll(). Bookmarks are also used to perform updates, deletions, and fetches by bookmark with the SQLBulkOperations() function, which you will see later.

Inserting, Updating, and Deleting Rows

To insert, update, or delete rows from a data source, you can always simply execute SQL statements to manipulate the rows. This must be supported by all ODBC drivers, and is the best way to perform updates or deletes if you simply want to change a set of rows. However, if you are writing an app that provides more flexible user interaction with the data, this may get to be complicated.

To help simplify applications that involve dynamic user interaction with the data, ODBC allows you to update and delete rows, based on a result set that you have already retrieved. However, these positioned updates or deletions are not supported by all drivers.

In addition, you can perform bulk operations with the SQLBulkOperations() function, which can be used to insert new rows or perform updates, deletions, and fetches based on bookmarks. You will look at this function shortly.

Positioned Updates and Deletions

First of all, you can retrieve a particular result set by executing an SQL query that uses the FOR UPDATE OF clause:

```
SELECT Col1, Col2 FROM myTable FOR UPDATE OF Col1, Col2;
```

This will retrieve the desired rows and tell the data source that you may be altering the data in these rows.

> **NOTE**
>
> To use positioned updates or deletions, you must set the cursor concurrency type of the cursor used in this statement, because the default is read-only. (See the "Cursor Concurrency Types" section later in this chapter.)

You also name the cursor that is used for this result set by calling SQLSetCursorName(). All cursors have a name, but if you don't name it explicitly, it will be assigned a fairly unwieldy name generated by the driver. You can retrieve the current cursor name by calling SQLGetCursorName().

Next, you call SQLFetch() or SQLFetchScroll() to find the row on which you want to operate. You then make the row you want to modify the current row by calling SQLSetPos() with the SQL_POSITION option.

Next, you use a second statement handle to execute an UPDATE or DELETE statement that uses the WHERE CURRENT OF clause, as in the following examples:

```
"UPDATE MyTable SET MyCol = 123 WHERE CURRENT OF myCursorName"
"DELETE FROM MyTable WHERE CURRENT OF myCursorName"
```

where myCursorName is the name that you assigned to the cursor used to retrieve the initial result set. This will perform the update on the current row, as you specified with SQLSetPos().

For updating columns with long data fields, you can use the SQLPutData() function, which can be used to add data one piece at a time, much like the SQLGetData() function.

Updating and Deleting Rows with SQLSetPos()

In addition, some drivers will allow you to update or delete rows directly with the SQLSetPos() function, instead of involving a second SQL statement.

> **NOTE**
>
> When using SQLSetPos() for updates or deletions, you must set the SQL_ATTR_CONCURRENCY statement attribute to something other than the default setting of SQL_CONCUR_READ_ONLY.

To delete a row with SQLSetPos(), you simply execute an SQL statement that retrieves the row you want to delete, call SQLFetchScroll() to retrieve a rowset that contains the desired row, then call SQLSetPos() for the desired row with the Operation parameter set to SQL_DELETE.

For updating rows with SQLSetPos(), the process is very similar, but adds a few steps. First, you retrieve a result set by executing an SQL query and call SQLFetchScroll() to select a rowset that contains the row to be updated. You also bind memory locations for the column data and associated length/indicator buffers for each column, using SQLBindCol().

Next, you simply modify the data in the bound data buffers to reflect the changes you want to make. The value in the length/indicator buffer should be set to the length of the new value, or SQL_NTS for null-terminated string values. For columns that are to be set to NULL, you should set the length/indicator value to SQL_NULL_DATA. In addition, you can specify a length/indicator value of SQL_COLUMN_IGNORE for columns that are to remain unchanged.

Then, you call SQLSetPos() with an operation of SQL_UPDATE and the number of the row (the index within the current rowset). The following example helps illustrate this:

```
SQLRETURN sr;
SQLHSTMT hstmt;

struct rowTag {
    unsigned long Num;
    SDWORD NumLen;
    SQLCHAR Title[50];
    SDWORD TitleLen;
    unsigned long Pages;
    SDWORD PagesLen;
} myRows[10];

// Allocate new statement handle
sr = SQLAllocHandle(SQL_HANDLE_STMT, hDbConn, &hstmt);
// Set number of rows to fetch
sr = SQLSetStmtAttr(hstmt, SQL_ATTR_ROW_ARRAY_SIZE, (void *) 5, SQL_IS_INTEGER);
// Set size of a row
sr = SQLSetStmtAttr(hstmt, SQL_ATTR_ROW_BIND_TYPE,
            (void *) sizeof(myRows[0]), SQL_IS_INTEGER);
// Set cursor type
```

```
sr = SQLSetStmtAttr(hstmt, SQL_ATTR_CURSOR_TYPE,
            (void*) SQL_CURSOR_DYNAMIC, SQL_IS_UINTEGER);
// Set cursor concurrency
sr = SQLSetStmtAttr(hstmt, SQL_ATTR_CONCURRENCY,
            (void*) SQL_CONCUR_LOCK, SQL_IS_UINTEGER);
// Execute SQL to retrieve a result set
sr = SQLExecDirect(hstmt, (UCHAR*)
        "Select Num, Title, Pages from MyChapters",
        SQL_NTS);

// Bind columns
sr = SQLBindCol(hstmt, 1, SQL_C_ULONG, &myRows[0].Num,
                sizeof(myRows[0].Num), &myRows[0].NumLen);
sr = SQLBindCol(hstmt, 2, SQL_C_CHAR, &myRows[0].Title,
                sizeof(myRows[0].Title), &myRows[0].TitleLen);
sr = SQLBindCol(hstmt, 3, SQL_C_ULONG, &myRows[0].Pages,
                sizeof(myRows[0].Pages), &myRows[0].PagesLen);
// Fetch first rowset
sr = SQLFetch(hstmt);
// Update the second row in the rowset
myRows[2].Num = 222;
myRows[2].NumLen = 0;
sprintf((char*)myRows[2].Title, "Updated Title");
myRows[2].TitleLen = SQL_NTS;
myRows[2].Pages = 22;
myRows[2].PagesLen = 0;
sr = SQLSetPos(hstmt, 2, SQL_UPDATE, SQL_LOCK_NO_CHANGE);
```

SQLBulkOperations()

Beginning with version 3.0, the ODBC API also allows you to perform insertions, updates, deletions, and fetches en masse with the SQLBulkOperations() function:

```
SQLRETURN SQLBulkOperations(SQLHSTMT StatementHandle, SQLUSMALLINT Operation);
```

This function takes the statement handle that you want to operate on and one of the following values for Operation:

```
SQL_ADD
SQL_UPDATE_BY_BOOKMARK
SQL_DELETE_BY_BOOKMARK
SQL_FETCH_BY_BOOKMARK
```

In the next sections, you will see how to use SQLBulkOperations() for each of these operations.

Inserting with SQLBulkOperations()

To insert new rows, you first execute a query that returns a result set for the table you want to add rows to.

Next, you use SQLBindCol() to bind arrays of data to the columns of the result set. You must also set the value of SQL_ATTR_ROW_ARRAY_SIZE to the length of these arrays by calling SQLSetStmtAttr().

You can then call SQLBulkOperations() with an Operation of SQL_ADD to insert new rows, containing the data in the bound columns. If you have set the SQL_ATTR_ARRAY_STATUS_PTR statement attribute, this array will receive the status of the insert operation for each row:

```
SQLRETURN sr;
SQLHSTMT hstmt;
struct rowTag {
    unsigned long Num;
    SDWORD NumLen;
    SQLCHAR Title[50];
    SDWORD TitleLen;
    unsigned long Pages;
    SDWORD PagesLen;
} myRows[10];

sr = SQLAllocHandle(SQL_HANDLE_STMT, hDbConn, &hstmt);
sr = SQLSetStmtAttr(hstmt, SQL_ATTR_CURSOR_TYPE,
            (void*) SQL_CURSOR_DYNAMIC, SQL_IS_UINTEGER);
sr = SQLSetStmtAttr(hstmt, SQL_ATTR_CONCURRENCY,
            (void*) SQL_CONCUR_LOCK, SQL_IS_UINTEGER);
// Execute SQL statement to open cursor
sr = SQLExecDirect(hstmt, (UCHAR*)
        "Select Num, Title, Pages from MyChapters",
        SQL_NTS);

sr = SQLBindCol(hstmt, 1, SQL_C_ULONG, &myRows[0].Num,
            sizeof(myRows[0].Num), &myRows[0].NumLen);
sr = SQLBindCol(hstmt, 2, SQL_C_CHAR, myRows[0].Title,
            sizeof(myRows[0].Title), &myRows[0].TitleLen);
sr = SQLBindCol(hstmt, 3, SQL_C_ULONG, &myRows[0].Pages,
            sizeof(myRows[0].Pages), &myRows[0].PagesLen);
sr = SQLSetStmtAttr(hstmt, SQL_ATTR_ROW_ARRAY_SIZE, (void *) 3, SQL_IS_INTEGER);
sr = SQLSetStmtAttr(hstmt, SQL_ATTR_ROW_BIND_TYPE,
            (void *) sizeof(myRows[0]), SQL_IS_INTEGER);

// Place new row data into bound variables
for(int i=0;i<3;i++) {
    myRows[i].Num = 700 + i;
    myRows[i].NumLen = 0;
    sprintf((char*)myRows[i].Title, "Bulk Chapter %d", i);
    myRows[i].TitleLen = SQL_NTS;
    myRows[i].Pages = 20 + i;
    myRows[i].PagesLen = 0;
}
// Add new rows to the database
sr = SQLBulkOperations(hstmt, SQL_ADD);
```

Updating with SQLBulkOperations()

Except for inserting new rows, the other operations supported by SQLBulkOperations() all use bookmarks to specify the rows that will be manipulated. Thus, you must set the SQL_ATTR_USE_BOOKMARKS statement attribute to SQL_UB_VARIABLE before executing a query that returns the initial result set with which you will be working.

Next, to update rows, you bind the columns you wish to update with `SQLBindCol()`. You should also bind column 0 to an array that will hold bookmarks.

You then fill the bookmark array with the bookmarks for the rows that you wish to update and update the other corresponding bound arrays for the row data. You should also set the `SQL_ATTR_ROW_ARRAY_SIZE` statement attribute to the number of rows (and corresponding bookmark array entries) that you wish to update.

You can then call `SQLBulkOperations()` with an `Operation` of `SQL_UPDATE_BY_BOOKMARK` to update the rows with the data in the bound arrays. If you have set the `SQL_ATTR_ROW_STATUS_PTR` statement attribute, this array will contain the status of each of the updates.

Deleting with `SQLBulkOperations()`

Deleting rows with `SQLBulkOperations()` is very similar to updating rows. You execute a statement that returns an appropriate result set (with bookmarks enabled), bind column 0 to an array that you fill with the bookmarks for rows to be deleted, set the `SQL_ATTR_ROW_ARRAY_SIZE` statement attribute to the number of bookmark entries, and call `SQLBulkOperations()` with an `Operation` of `SQL_DELETE_BY_BOOKMARK`.

Fetching with `SQLBulkOperations()`

Fetching by bookmark is also very similar to the update and delete operations shown above. You should simply bind columns for the data you wish to retrieve, including column 0, which you fill with bookmarks for the rows to fetch.

You then set the number of rows to fetch by setting the `SQL_ATTR_ROW_ARRAY_SIZE` statement attribute and call `SQLBulkOperations()` with `SQL_FETCH_BY_BOOKMARK`.

Asynchronous Operations

Previously, you looked at features of ODBC that are used to support asynchronous operations. Basically, ODBC provides a mechanism that allows you to return from a call, such as `SQLExecute()`, immediately and then occasionally poll to see whether the operation has completed.

This mechanism is provided for single-threaded operating systems, such as Win3.1, and is not appropriate for use in the Win32 environment, which allows you to start a new thread for blocking calls that may take an arbitrary period of time to complete.

Unfortunately, ODBC 3.0 does not provide for true asynchronous operations (overlapped I/O) in the Win32 environment.

Transactions

In many cases, it is necessary to have several different SQL statements operate together as a single transaction—that is, if one of the operations in a transaction fails, none of the other operations should affect the database. For example, if you are processing a sales order, you will want to update both your shipping and your billing tables. If one of these updates fails, and the other is entered into the database, you could easily end up billing for things that were never sent or, worse yet, shipping free stuff. Although creative use of this feature may have some beneficial effects on your short term revenues, it's probably not a good career move.

> **NOTE**
>
> In SQL, to group a set of statements together in a transaction, you could use COMMIT and ROLLBACK statements. However, this is highly discouraged in ODBC, and can in fact leave the driver quite confused about the current state of a transaction. Instead, you should use the SQLEndTrans() function for commits and rollbacks.

ODBC Commit Modes

In ODBC, transactions are handled in one of two different ways, depending on the current commit mode of the connection. The connection can be set to either auto-commit mode (the default) or manual-commit mode. The commit mode for a connection is set by calling SQLSetConnectAttr() for the SQL_ATTR_AUTOCOMMIT option.

Auto-Commit Mode

The default mode for a new connection is auto-commit, which is supported by all drivers. In this mode, each statement operates as a separate transaction, the driver will take care of committing each operation on the database automatically, and you really don't have to worry about transaction processing at all.

If you submit a batch of SQL statements in a single SQLExecute() call, ODBC does not define whether this is treated as a single transaction or whether each statement is a separate transaction. If you want to send a batch as a transaction, use manual-commit mode.

Manual-Commit Mode

In cases where you want to ensure that multiple SQL statements can be performed as a transaction, you should always use manual-commit mode, which requires your application to explicitly end a transaction with a call to SQLEndTrans().

Once again, this is not supported by all drivers. You can check on the current driver's transaction support by calling `SQLGetInfo()` for the `SQL_TXN_CAPABLE` option. In addition, the `SQL_MULTIPLE_ACTIVE_TXN` option will tell you whether you can have multiple transactions pending at the same time.

To make use of multiple active transactions, you must have multiple connections, because only one transaction is ever in progress for each connection.

Your application does not need to explicitly begin a transaction. The driver will begin one automatically when the connection is made, when you switch to manual-commit mode, or when the previous transaction is completed.

You will, however, complete each transaction with a call to `SQLEndTran()`:

```
SQLRETURN SQLEndTran(SQLSMALLINT HandleType, SQLHANDLE Handle,  SQLSMALLINT
CompletionType);
```

In most cases, you will set `HandleType` to `SQL_HANDLE_DBC` and pass the current connection handle in `Handle`. This will end the transaction on the current connection handle. In addition, you may also specify `SQL_HANDLE_ENV` and pass your environment handle. This will end the current transactions for all connections associated with this environment. This does not, however, combine the transactions for all connections into a single atomic operation.

The `CompletionType` parameter specifies how to complete the transaction. If this is set to `SQL_COMMIT`, any changes made in this transaction are written to the database, whereas a value of `SQL_ROLLBACK` will cause any changes made in this transaction to be rolled back, as if they never occurred at all.

> **NOTE**
>
> If you switch back to auto-commit mode from manual-commit mode, the transaction in progress will be committed.

When you end a transaction with `SQLEndTrans()`, different drivers may choose to close any open cursors for the connection, as well as to close the access plans for these cursors. To find the behavior that the current driver supports, you can call `SQLGetInfo()` for the `SQL_CURSOR_COMMIT_BEHAVIOR` and `SQL_CURSOR_ROLLBACK_BEHAVIOR` options.

Transaction Isolation Levels

When you are working with a data source that may have multiple transactions active at one time (from within your application or from other users), you should be concerned with the transaction isolation level, which determines how concurrent transactions may interact with each other. In general, this interaction is described by whichever of the following—generally undesirable—conditions may occur:

■ *Dirty reads* involve an operation that reads data that is not yet committed, and may eventually be rolled back.

■ *Nonrepeatable reads* occur when a transaction reads the same row twice, but may receive different data, because another transaction has changed something.

■ *Phantoms* occur when a row has been changed to match a query, but it was not selected in an initial query.

You set the current transaction isolation level for a connection by calling `SQLSetConnectAttr()` for the `SQL_ATTR_TXN_ISOLATION` option. This can be set to one of the following values:

`SQL_TXN_READ_UNCOMMITTED`—Any of the above inconsistencies may occur.

`SQL_TXT_READ_COMMITTED`—Dirty reads are prevented.

`SQL_TXN_REPEATABLE_READ`—Dirty reads and nonrepeatable reads are prevented.

`SQL_TXN_SERIALIZABLE`—All of the above anomalies are prevented.

Once again, not all ODBC drivers are created equal—you can determine the isolation modes that are supported by calling `SQLGetInfo()` for the `SQL_TXN_ISOLATION_OPTION`. You can also retrieve the default level by using the `SQL_DEFAULT_TXN_ISOLATION` option.

> **NOTE**
>
> Regardless of the transaction isolation level, all transactions will be able to see any changes that have been made from within that transaction.

Although higher isolation levels can prevent some inconsistencies in the data, they may also introduce a greater amount of overhead, thus affecting your application's performance—and that of other apps that use the same data source. When choosing an isolation level to use, you should weigh this performance cost against the potentials for data inconsistency.

Cursor Concurrency Types

It is in the nature of higher isolation levels to limit inconsistencies in the data by limiting the concurrency of the data source—that is, how multiple operations may occur on the data source simultaneously. You can optimize the concurrency of your application's operations by setting the concurrency type of the cursor that is used with a statement handle.

This is done by calling SQLSetStmtAttr() for the SQL_ATTR_CONCURRENCY option, which can have the following values:

SQL_CONCUR_READ_ONLY indicates the cursor is read only.

SQL_CONCUR_LOCK uses the lowest level of locking sufficient to ensure that a row may be updated.

SQL_CONCUR_ROWVER uses optimistic concurrency control, based on row version.

SQL_CONCUR_VALUES uses optimistic concurrency control, using values.

You can determine the available options for the current driver by calling SQLGetInfo() for the SQL_SCROLL_CONCURRENCY option.

The following example shows ODBC transactions in action:

```
SQLRETURN sr;
SQLHSTMT hstmt;

sr = SQLAllocHandle(SQL_HANDLE_STMT, hDbConn, &hstmt);
// Set manual-commit mode for connection
sr = SQLSetConnectAttr(hDbConn, SQL_ATTR_AUTOCOMMIT,
        (void*)SQL_AUTOCOMMIT_OFF , SQL_IS_UINTEGER);
// Execute first statement
sr = SQLExecDirect(hstmt,
            (UCHAR*) "INSERT INTO MyChapters VALUES (41, 'Rollback', 123)",
            SQL_NTS);
// Execute second statment
sr = SQLExecDirect(hstmt,
            (UCHAR*)"INSERT INTO MyChapters VALUES (42, 'Rollback', 321)",
            SQL_NTS);
if(bCommitChanges)
    // Make changes to permanent database
    sr = SQLEndTran(SQL_HANDLE_DBC, hDbConn, SQL_COMMIT);
else
    // Ignore any changes made
    sr = SQLEndTran(SQL_HANDLE_DBC, hDbConn, SQL_ROLLBACK);

// Set commit mode back to auto
sr = SQLSetConnectAttr(hDbConn, SQL_ATTR_AUTOCOMMIT,
        (void*)SQL_AUTOCOMMIT_ON , SQL_IS_UINTEGER);
```

Catalog Functions

In most cases, when you are developing a database application, you should already know about the structure of the database. However, for certain browser-type applications or administrative tools, your app may not know much about the data source until runtime. You can retrieve information about the structure (catalog, schema, and so forth) of a database with the following functions provided by ODBC:

SQLTables() returns information about the tables in a database.

SQLColumns() returns the names of the columns in a table.

SQLSpecialColumns() returns information about the columns that uniquely identify a row, and any columns that are automatically updated when the row is updated (rowids).

SQLPrimaryKeys() returns the columns that make up a table's primary key.

SQLForeignKeys() returns the columns in a table that refer to the primary key of another table, as well as the columns in other tables that refer to this column's primary key.

SQLProcedures() returns a list of procedures available on this data source.

SQLProcedureColumns() returns information about the parameters for a procedure, as well as info about its result set.

SQLTablePrivileges() returns information about the privileges associated with tables in the database.

SQLColumnPrivileges() returns a list of columns and the privileges associated with them for a given table.

SQLStatistics() returns a set of statistics for a table and its associated indexes.

Summary

In this chapter, you took the whirlwind tour of the ODBC 3.0 API, which can be used to provide a standard interface to a wide variety of different data sources, ranging from simple text files to full-featured RDBMSs.

You learned how to set up your ODBC applications, including the use of handles for the ODBC environment, data source connections, and SQL statements, as well as how ODBC reports errors to your application.

You took a look at how to establish a connection to a data source directly using SQLConnect(), or more indirectly by using SQLDriverConnect().

Next, you explored how to execute SQL statements against the data source, using either SQLExecDirect() or SQLPrepare() and SQLExecute() to work with prepared statements. You also saw how to use parameters to make your applications more efficient in executing similar SQL statements.

Then, you saw how to retrieve data from a database by binding program variables to the columns in a result set, both one row at a time and in groups of rows. You also took a look at how different types of cursors can be used.

You learned how to use ODBC to manipulate the data in the data source by adding, updating, and deleting rows, using positioned updates, the `SQLSetPos()` function, and the `SQLBulkOperations()` function. You also took a look at how several statements can be executed as a single operation by using transactions.

In the next chapter, you will explore how MFC has encapsulated the ODBC API, providing a simple C++ interface to ODBC.

26

MFC Database Classes

by David Bennett

The Microsoft Foundation Classes (MFC) comprise several classes that can be used to provide a simpler C++ interface to databases. These are particularly useful in quickly generating applications that present a simple, consistent interface to the user. However, you can also easily integrate the MFC database classes with the full power of the ODBC API.

MFC provides classes for using the ODBC API to interface with ODBC data sources, as well as classes for working with Data Access Objects (DAO) to work with desktop databases. In this chapter, you will look at the ODBC classes specifically, although the DAO classes are very similar. You can find more on the DAO classes in the online documentation.

In this chapter, you explore the three main classes that MFC provides for database access. These include the CDatabase class, which is used to manage a connection to a data source; the CRecordset class, which is used to manage a set of rows returned from the database; and the CRecordView class, which simplifies the display of data from CRecordset objects.

Once you have taken a look at these classes that make up the building blocks of MFC database applications, you will see how you can use AppWizard to help set up an application to use the MFC ODBC classes.

The CDatabase Class

The MFC CDatabase class is used to encapsulate your application's dealings with a connection to the database. This may be a connection to a database server over the network, or it may just be used to keep track of your settings for a desktop database on the local machine. In most cases, the methods associated with CDatabase correspond directly to the functions of the ODBC C API that work with connection handles.

Opening a Database Connection

To create a new CDatabase and connect it to a database, you construct a new CDatabase object and call its OpenEx() member:

```
virtual BOOL OpenEx( LPCTSTR lpszConnectString, DWORD dwOptions = 0 );
```

When calling OpenEx(), you may use lpszConnectString to specify a full connection string:

```
"DSN=MyDataSource;UID=sa;PWD=DontTell"
```

This string specifies the name of the data source to connect to and the user ID and password used to connect to it. In addition, this string may contain additional keyword-value pairs that are supported by the ODBC driver for that data source.

To make things even easier for you, the developer, you can pass a NULL value for lpszConnectString, in which case MFC will allow the user to choose a data source from a dialog. Although this option may be easier for you, keep in mind that the data source selection dialog may not always be the best choice for presenting a simple selection interface to the user.

By default, when you call `OpenEx()`, the database is opened as shared with write access and does not load the cursor library. You can modify the way the database is opened by passing a combination (bitwise-OR) of the following flags in the `dwOptions` parameter:

`CDatabase::openExclusive` is not currently supported.

`CDatabase::openReadOnly` opens with read-only access.

`CDatabase::useCursorLib` loads the ODBC cursor library, which can support static snapshots for drivers that do not support this natively. However, you will not be able to use dynasets if the cursor library is loaded, even if the driver supports them. (You'll learn more about cursors and dynasets later.)

`CDatabase::noOdbcDialog` prevents the display of any connection dialogs.

`CDatabase::forceOdbcDialog` indicates the ODBC connection dialog will always be presented to the user.

If `OpenEx()` successfully connects to the data source, it will return TRUE. It will only return FALSE in the event that the user cancels the connection dialog. If an error occurs in connecting, such as a connection timeout or an invalid password, an exception will be thrown. The following example shows `OpenEx()` in action:

```
CDatabase *pDb;
BOOL bStatus;
// Allocate new CDatabase
pDb = new CDatabase;
// Set login timeout (in seconds);
pDb->SetLoginTimeout(3);
// Open database, catch exceptions
try
{
    bStatus = pDb->OpenEx("DSN=MyDataSource");
    if(bStatus)
        TRACE("DB Opened Successfully\n");
    else
        TRACE("Open Data Source Cancelled\n");
}
catch(CMemoryException *pEx)
{
    pEx->ReportError();
}
catch(CDBException *pEx)
{
    pEx->ReportError();
    TRACE("RetCode: %d strError: [%s] strState: [%s]\n",
        pEx->m_nRetCode, pEx->m_strError,
        pEx->m_strStateNativeOrigin);
}
```

Exception Handling

In the previous example, the errors in the call to `OpenEx()` are handled by an exception handler. The MFC database classes report most errors by throwing exceptions rather than returning error codes. For errors specific to database operations, a CDBException object is thrown, although other exception types, such as CMemoryException, may also be thrown.

When handling an exception, you can simply use the CException::ReportError() function to alert the user to the exception, or you may do more extensive error processing based on the member variables of the CDBException. These include m_nRetCode, which gives the ODBC SQLRETURN value that was generated; m_strError, which holds a string with text describing the error; and m_strStateNativeOrigin, which holds a string containing the SQLSTATE, native error, and error message string, including the ODBC component that generated the error.

Connection Timeouts

Connecting to a database server over a network may take considerably longer than local connections, and any number of things may go wrong along the way. As in the previous example, you can set the length of time that MFC will wait for a connection to be established before giving up and throwing an exception by calling CDatabase::SetLoginTimeout().

You can also set the time that MFC will wait for any other database operations by calling CDatabase::SetQueryTimeout().

Open()

In addition to the OpenEx() member, CDatabase provides the Open() member, shown below, which opens the database in the same way, but uses a slightly different format for the parameters:

```
virtual BOOL Open( LPCTSTR lpszDSN, BOOL bExclusive = FALSE,
          BOOL bReadOnly = FALSE, LPCTSTR lpszConnect = "ODBC;",
          BOOL bUseCursorLib = TRUE );
```

The string in lpszDSN contains the name of the data source, whereas the lpszConnect string contains any other options that you saw for the lpszConnectString parameter of OpenEx(). Note that in calls to Open(), lpszConnect must contain "ODBC";, which is used to allow for future implementation of additional database libraries.

The bExclusive, bReadOnly, and bUseCursorLib parameters allow you to use Boolean values for the same options that were passed in the dwOptions parameter of OpenEx().

Whether you use Open() or OpenEx(), you should close the connection to the data source when you are finished with it by calling CDatabase::Close().

Connection Information

At any time, you can call the IsOpen() member of CDatabase to see whether it is currently connected. In addition, The GetConnect() member of CDatabase will return the connect string that was used to connect to the database, and the GetDatabaseName() member will return just the name of the data source that is being used.

The CDatabase class also provides several member functions that can be used to query the capabilities of the current connection (that is, the operations supported by the ODBC driver). These include CanUpdate(), CanTransact(), GetBookmarkPersistence(), GetCursorCommitBehavior(), and GetCursorRollbackBehavior(). You will look at what the results of each of these functions means later on.

Executing SQL Statements with CDatabase

For general queries that return result sets, it is usually easier to use the CRecordset class, which you will look at next. However, you can execute SQL statements that do not return result sets without using a CRecordset. This is done by calling CDatabase::ExecuteSQL():

```
void ExecuteSQL( LPCSTR lpszSQL );
```

This function simply takes an SQL string passed in lpszSQL and executes it against the current data source. Notice that ExecuteSQL() does not return a value. If something goes wrong—for example, the SQL statement fails—a CDBException will be thrown. Your application needs to catch these in order to determine whether the statement did not execute properly.

OnSetOptions()

When you call ExecuteSQL(), the MFC framework will make a call to the OnSetOptions() member of CDatabase before it sends the SQL statement to the database. This allows the CDatabase object to set up any options that are required before executing SQL statements.

In the default implementation, this function simply sets the SQL_QUERY_TIMEOUT option for the statement handle (that will be used for the operation) to the value that was specified with a call to CDatabase::SetQueryTimeout(). You can add any other options you may need by deriving your own class from CDatabase and overriding the OnSetOptions() member function, which is passed the statement handle that MFC will use to execute the statement.

> **TIP**
>
> The CDatabase class also provides an additional, undocumented, virtual function, which gives your class the opportunity to bind parameters to a statement executed with ExecuteSQL(). To use this function, you derive your own class from CDatabase and override the BindParameters() function:
>
> ```
> void CDatabase::BindParameters(HSTMT hstmt);
> ```
>
> To actually bind parameters, you use the ODBC C API, as shown in the previous chapter. When doing these sorts of things, it is very useful to take a look at the source code for the MFC database classes, included with Visual C++ in DBCORE.CPP.

Transactions with CDatabase

The CDatabase class is also responsible for managing transactions for the database connection. Transactions allow you to execute a series of SQL statements as a single operation—if one of the operations in a transaction fails, the rest of the operations in the transaction can also be undone.

This is most useful when you need to make several different, but related, changes to a database. For instance, if you are entering a sales order, you may want to update both your shipping table and your billing table. If you update one of these and the other update fails, you can expect a few extra customer service calls.

> **NOTE**
>
> Not all ODBC drivers support transactions. You can find out whether the current driver supports transactions by calling CDatabase::CanTransact().

To begin a transaction using the MFC ODBC classes, you should call CDatabase::BeginTrans(). You can then execute the operations that make up the transaction by calling CDatabase::ExecuteSQL() or by using CRecordset objects derived from this CDatabase.

> **CAUTION**
>
> For some ODBC drivers, calling BeginTrans() when CRecordset objects have already been opened can cause problems with Rollback() processing. To avoid difficulties, it is best to call BeginTrans() first, then open the recordsets that will be used for the transaction.

A transaction can end in one of two different ways. If all of the operations were successful and you want to go through with the transaction, you should call CDatabase::CommitTrans(). If an error has occurred, and you want to cancel the transaction, you should call CDatabase::Rollback(), which will "undo" all the operations performed with this CDatabase (and any derived recordsets) since the call to BeginTrans().

This example shows a simple transaction involving two row insertions made by calling ExecuteSQL():

```
try
{
    if(pDb->BeginTrans())
        TRACE("Transaction started\n");
    else
        TRACE("Error in BeginTrans()\n");
```

```
    pDb->ExecuteSQL("INSERT INTO myChapters VALUES (21, 'Chap. 21', 12)");
    pDb->ExecuteSQL("INSERT INTO myChapters VALUES (22, 'Chap. 22', 22)");
    if(pDb->CommitTrans())
        TRACE("Transaction Commited\n");
    else
        TRACE("Error in CommitTrans\n");
}
catch(CDBException *pEx)
{
    pEx->ReportError();
    if(pDb->Rollback())
        TRACE("Transaction Rolled Back\n");
    else
        TRACE("Error in Rollback()\n");
}
```

Effects of Transactions on CRecordsets

Ending a transaction on a CDatabase object can have different effects on the CRecordsets that are created from it, depending on the ODBC driver that you are using. Calling CRecordset::GetCursorCommitBehavior() and CDatabase::RollbackBehavior() will allow you to find out how your driver affects CRecordsets when you call CommitTrans() or Rollback(). Both of these functions will return one of the following values:

SQL_CB_CLOSE—The cursors for any CRecordsets are closed. If you want to use them after completing a transaction, you call CRecordset::Requery().

SQL_CB_DELETE—Any cursors for CRecordsets associated with this CDatabase are deleted. You should call CRecordset::Close() and reopen the CRecordset if you need to use it again.

SQL_CB_PRESERVE—The CRecordsets built from this CDatabase are not affected, and your app can continue to use them in their current state.

Using the ODBC API Directly

For some applications, the MFC database classes may not give you quite enough control over the database interaction. If you need to do anything not directly supported by the MFC classes, you can call the ODBC C API directly. Of course, to call the ODBC API, you need ODBC handles. Well, it just so happens that you can get the ODBC connection handle from the m_hdbc member of CDatabase. You can also get statement handles from the m_hstmt member of the CRecordset class.

You may freely mix ODBC C API calls with use of the MFC database classes in your applications. However, you may want to take a look at the source code for the MFC classes to see how the MFC member functions use the ODBC API.

NOTE

The current version of MFC (4.21) uses version 2.5 of the ODBC API.

The `CRecordset` Class

Although the `CDatabase` class allows you to execute SQL statements against a database, it is the `CRecordset` class that provides the real meat of your application's interaction with the data. `CRecordset` is used to encapsulate queries of the database, as well as to add, update, or delete rows.

You will seldom need to derive your own classes from `CDatabase`, but you will almost never use `CRecordset` objects without deriving your own class, because the `CRecordset` class provides a framework for your own derived classes to use member variables to receive the data from rows returned by the database, as you will see next.

Deriving Classes from `CRecordset`

The main purpose of the `CRecordset` class is to give your applications access to the result set returned by a database query. MFC allows you to derive classes from `CDatabase` that use member variables to work with the data in the result set.

To begin with, you will want to declare a member of your `CRecordset` class for each of the columns that you will be using. These variables will be automatically updated by MFC by using Record Field Exchange (RFX), as you will see soon. Shown below is the definition for a recordset class created by ClassWizard, showing the member variables defined for working with column data:

```
class CMyRecordset : public CRecordset
{
public:
    CMyRecordset(CDatabase* pDatabase = NULL);
    DECLARE_DYNAMIC(CMyRecordset)
// Field/Param Data
    //{{AFX_FIELD(CMyRecordset, CRecordset)
    long      m_Num;
    CString   m_Title;
    long      m_Pages;
    long      m_mykey;
    CString   m_name;
    //}}AFX_FIELD
// Overrides
    // ClassWizard generated virtual function overrides
    //{{AFX_VIRTUAL(CMyRecordset)
    public:
```

```
    virtual CString GetDefaultConnect();    // Default connection string
    virtual CString GetDefaultSQL();    // Default SQL for Recordset
    virtual void DoFieldExchange(CFieldExchange* pFX);  // RFX support
    //}}AFX_VIRTUAL
// Implementation
#ifdef _DEBUG
    virtual void AssertValid() const;
    virtual void Dump(CDumpContext& dc) const;
#endif
};
```

Next, you should add code to the constructor of your class to set the m_nFields member to the number of fields that your class uses. You should also initialize the values of the member variables that you have declared for column data to a suitable default value. The following example shows the constructor created by ClassWizard for the class defined previously:

```
CMyRecordset::CMyRecordset(CDatabase* pdb)
    : CRecordset(pdb)
{
    //{{AFX_FIELD_INIT(CMyRecordset)
    m_Num = 0;
    m_Title = _T("");
    m_Pages = 0;
    m_mykey = 0;
    m_name = _T("");
    m_nFields = 5;
    //}}AFX_FIELD_INIT
    m_nDefaultType = dynaset;
}
```

You will then set up Record Field Exchange for your class. Before retrieving any data, you will also open the CRecordset. You will look at both of these in the next sections.

Record Field Exchange

The MFC framework can move data back and forth between the database and the member variables of your CRecordset by using record field exchange, which works very much like the Dialog Data Exchange mechanism that you saw in Chapter 5, "Dialogs and Controls."

The exchange is set up by implementing the DoFieldExchange() function for your CRecordset class. Like the CDialog::DoDataExchange() function, the bulk of your implementation will use a set of macros that MFC provides for defining Record Field Exchange. Like the DFX_ macros, MFC provides a range of different RFX_ macros for different data types. Table 26.1 shows the available RFX_ macros and the data types for the member variables with which they are used.

Table 26.1. Record field exchange macros.

RFX_ *macro*	*Member variable type*
RFX_Binary()	CByteArray
RFX_Bool()	BOOL
RFX_Byte()	int
RFX_Date()	CTime
RFX_Double()	double
RFX_Int()	int
RFX_Long()	LONG
RFX_LongBinary()	CLongBinary
RFX_Single()	float
RFX_Text()	CString

Each of the macros listed in the table takes three parameters: the CFieldExchange pointer passed to DoFieldExchange(), the name of the database field, and the member variable to hold the data for that field. The following example should help illustrate how these are used:

```
void CMyRecordset::DoFieldExchange(CFieldExchange* pFX)
{
    //{{AFX_FIELD_MAP(CMyRecordset)
    pFX->SetFieldType(CFieldExchange::outputColumn);
    RFX_Long(pFX, _T("[Num]"), m_Num);
    RFX_Text(pFX, _T("[Title]"), m_Title);
    RFX_Long(pFX, _T("[Pages]"), m_Pages);
    RFX_Long(pFX, _T("[mykey]"), m_mykey);
    RFX_Text(pFX, _T("[name]"), m_name);
    //}}AFX_FIELD_MAP
}
```

Once you set up your DoFieldExchange() function, the member variables of your recordset class will be automatically updated to hold the values for the current row when you fetch a new row. The data from the member variables will also be used automatically when you add new records or update existing records, as you will see later.

GetFieldValue()

As an alternative to record field exchange, you can always call CRecordset::GetFieldValue(), which will allow you to retrieve the value of any field in the current row, even if you have not defined a member variable for the column or set up record field exchange. This function can be used to retrieve the value for a column based on either its index or the column name. You can retrieve values as either a CString or a CDBVariant object, which allows you to handle many different types of data using a single data type.

Opening a Recordset

Before you can start working with a recordset, you need to construct a new CRecordset object and then call its Open() member to open the recordset.

The constructor for the CRecordset class takes a pointer to a CDatabase object that will be used for interacting with the database. If you have already created a CDatabase, you can simply pass a pointer to that object.

Alternatively, you can pass NULL in the CRecordset constructor, in which case MFC will construct a new CDatabase object and open it for you, using the connect string returned by CRecordset::GetDefaultConnect(). The default implementation of GetDefaultConnect() simply returns ODBC;. If you use ClassWizard to create your CRecordset class, it will override GetDefaultConnect() for you, based on the data source you select. If you are not using ClassWizard, you will either pass a valid pointer to a CDatabase object in your CRecordset constructor, or provide your own override for GetDefaultConnect().

Next, you open the recordset by calling CRecordset::Open():

```
virtual BOOL Open( UINT nOpenType = AFX_DB_USE_DEFAULT_TYPE,
           LPCTSTR lpszSQL = NULL, DWORD dwOptions = none );
```

Recordset Types

The first parameter of Open() specifies the type of recordset that will be opened. This value affects the type of ODBC cursor used to retrieve the recordset and determines your application's ability to scroll between records in the recordset and the types of changes to the database that will be made available to your application. The nOpenType parameter may have one of the following values:

> CRecordset::dynaset—This type uses a keyset-driven cursor, and allows both forward and backward scrolling. Whenever a new record is fetched, your application will be able to see any changes to the rows that were initially retrieved when the recordset was opened, but you will not see any additional rows that may be added by other applications. The dynaset will also not reflect any changes to the ordering of the rows within the recordset.

> **NOTE**
>
> The dynaset type is not supported by the ODBC cursor library. If you use this type, and your driver supports keyset-driven cursors, make sure that you do not load the cursor library when you create your CDatabase.

> CRecordset::snapshot—This type allows both forward and backward scrolling, but you will not see any changes made by other applications (unless you close and reopen the recordset, or call Requery()).

CRecordset::dynamic—This type uses a dynamic cursor, which allows scrolling in both directions. You will see any changes to the data values, as well as any new records or changes in ordering, each time you fetch a new row from the recordset.

CRecordset::forwardOnly—This type of recordset allows only forward scrolling and will not reflect any changes made to the database.

> **NOTE**
>
> Many ODBC drivers do not support the cursor types required for several of the above recordset types. If you request an unsupported type, Open() will throw an exception.

Defining the Contents of the Recordset

The lpszSQL parameter of CRecordset::Open() defines the data that will be retrieved for the recordset. lpszSQL should be passed a null-terminated string that contains either an SQL SELECT statement or a CALL statement that returns a result set from a procedure. The string passed in lpszSQL may also simply be the name of the table—MFC will interpret this to select all the rows of the table.

In addition, you can pass NULL for lpszSQL, in which case MFC will call CRecordset::GetDefaultSQL(), which should return a string containing the default SQL string for the recordset. If you create your CRecordset class with ClassWizard, it will implement GetDefaultSQL() for you.

In the SQL string passed in lpszSQL or returned from GetDefaultSQL(), you may include WHERE, GROUP BY, and ORDER BY clauses, but you can make your recordset more flexible by placing any WHERE clause in the m_strFilter member of your CRecordset class. Similarly, you can place GROUP BY or ORDER BY clauses in the m_strSort member. By doing this, you can more easily change the filter or sorting for your recordset, without having to change the base SQL string or modifying the return value of GetDefaultSQL().

Recordset Options

The third, and last, parameter of CRecordset::Open() allows you to specify several different options for the recordset. dwOptions is a bitmap that may contain a combination of many different constants. For more on the available options, see the online documentation for CRecordset::Open().

If you want to set any specific options before the recordset retrieves any data, you can also override the OnSetOptions() member of CDatabase. This function is called as part of the default implementation of CRecordset::Open() and sets up several different options on the statement handle that is used to retrieve data.

The following code illustrates how to create a recordset and call Open() to start retrieving data, including some simple exception handling:

```
BOOL bRc;
// Allocate new recordset
CMyRecordset* pRecordset = new CMyRecordset(pDb);
// Open Recordset, catching exceptions
try
{
    // Open recordset with dynamic cursor
    bRc = pRecordset->Open(CRecordset::dynamic,
            "SELECT Num, Title, Pages FROM MyChapters",
            CRecordset::none);
    if(bRc)
        TRACE("Recordset Opened OK\n");
    else
        TRACE("Recordset Not Opened\n");
}
catch(CMemoryException *pEx)
{
    pEx->ReportError();
}
catch(CDBException *pEx)
{
    pEx->ReportError();
    TRACE("RetCode: %d strError: [%s] strState: [%s]\n",
        pEx->m_nRetCode, pEx->m_strError,
        pEx->m_strStateNativeOrigin);
}
```

Additional Information

After calling Open(), you can retrieve the entire SQL string that was used to select records by calling CRecordset::GetSQL(). Also, if you were unsure of the name of the table retrieved, you can get it by calling CRecordset::GetTableName(). In addition, you can get the total number of fields returned by calling CRecordset::GetODBCFieldCount() and can retrieve information about each field by calling CRecordset::GetODBCFieldInfo().

Refreshing the Recordset

If you want to refresh the recordset, you can call CRecordset::Requery(). This will go out and retrieve the data from the database again, including any changes that were made since the recordset was opened. If you are using a static cursor recordset, this is the only way to get at any changes made to the data by other users. Like many other functions, Requery() is not supported by all ODBC drivers—you can call CRecordset::CanRestart() to find whether the current driver supports this.

Closing the Recordset

When you are finished with the recordset, you should call `CRecordset::Close()`. After calling `Close()`, you can call `Open()` if you want to reopen the recordset. This may be necessary if you are using transactions with certain ODBC drivers.

Moving About in the Recordset

The member variables that you defined in your `CRecordset` class to hold column data are only intended to hold one value at a time. To access the data for the rows in the recordset, you move to a specific row in the recordset. The `CRecordset` class provides several methods that make moving around the recordset quite simple, starting with `CRecordset::MoveNext()`.

Moving Forward

`MoveNext()` takes no parameters and simply moves on to the next row in the recordset, updating the member variables of the recordset along the way. Note that calling `Move()` after you have scrolled to the last record will throw an exception. To prevent this, you should call `IsEOF()` to find out whether you are at the end of the recordset before calling `Move()`.

> **NOTE**
>
> The first row is automatically selected when the recordset is opened, so the recordset member variables will reflect the first row, without a call to `MoveNext()`.

The following example shows the use of `MoveNext()` to trace through the rows in the recordset. Note that exception handling has been removed to simplify the example, but your applications should be prepared to catch any exceptions that may be thrown:

```
do
{
    TRACE("Num: %d Title: [%s] Pages: %d\n", pRecordset->m_Num,
        pRecordset->m_Title, pRecordset->m_Pages);
    pRecordset->MoveNext();
}
while(!pRecordset->IsEOF());
```

Scrolling

If your recordset uses a forward-only cursor, you'll have to make do with just the `MoveNext()` function. However, if your driver supports scrolling, you have several other options. (You can check whether the recordset supports scrolling by calling `CRecordset::CanScroll()`.)

The `MoveFirst()` and `MoveLast()` methods will move to the first or last record in the recordset. You can also move to any specific row by calling `SetAbsolutePosition()`, which takes a zero-based index into the recordset.

Additionally, the MovePrev() member will move to the previous row. Calling MovePrev() when you are already at the beginning of the recordset will generate an exception, so it is a good idea to call IsBOF() to check whether you are at the beginning of the recordset before calling MovePrev().

Using Bookmarks

You can also navigate to specific rows in the recordset by using bookmarks, provided your ODBC driver supports it. (You can determine whether this is supported by calling CanBookmark().) The GetBookmark() member can be called to retrieve a bookmark for the current row in the recordset. You can then return to that specific row later by passing the bookmark value to SetBookmark().

CRecordset::Move()

Each of the previous navigation functions is also supported by the more generic Move() function, which can also be used to move a number of rows forward or backward from the current row. Here is the prototype for Move():

```
virtual void Move( long nRows, WORD wFetchType = SQL_FETCH_RELATIVE );
```

The nRows parameter takes the number of rows to move—positive values are used to move forward, and negative values may be used to move backward.

You may omit the wFetchType parameter and simply use the SQL_FETCH_RELATIVE default, or you may specify one of the following values:

SQL_FETCH_RELATIVE—Fetch the row nRows from the current row.

SQL_FETCH_NEXT—Fetch the next row.

SQL_FETCH_PRIOR—Fetch the previous row.

SQL_FETCH_FIRST—Fetch the first row in the recordset.

SQL_FETCH_LAST—Fetch the last row in the recordset.

SQL_FETCH_ABSOLUTE—Fetch the nRowth row in the recordset.

SQL_FETCH_BOOKMARK—Fetch the row specified by a bookmark value passed in nRows.

If an error occurs in the Move() operation, it will throw an exception; otherwise, the current row is set to the new row, and the member variables of the recordset will be updated to hold the data for the new row.

Bulk Row Fetching

Up until now, you have been looking at how to use the CRecordset class to retrieve the data for a single row at a time, which may not always be the most efficient way of doing things. You can often make your applications more efficient and easier to program by fetching a group of rows (rowset) all at once using Bulk Record Field Exchange (Bulk RFX).

> **NOTE**
>
> When using Bulk RFX, many of the CRecordset functions are not supported and will throw exceptions. Most notably, this includes AddNew(), Edit(), Delete(), and Update(). Currently, MFC does not support bulk additions, updates, or deletions.

When using Bulk RFX, the member variables of your recordset class should be pointers to the type of data expected. The following shows the declaration of a recordset class for use with Bulk RFX:

```
class CMyBulkSet : public CRecordset
{
public:
    CMyBulkSet(CDatabase* pDatabase = NULL);
    DECLARE_DYNAMIC(CMyBulkSet)
// Field/Param Data
    long*    m_Num;
    LPSTR    m_Title;
    long*    m_Pages;
// Length buffer pointers
    long* m_NumLen;
    long* m_TitleLen;
    long* m_PagesLen;
// Overrides
    public:
    virtual CString GetDefaultConnect();    // Default connection string
    virtual CString GetDefaultSQL();    // Default SQL for Recordset
    virtual void DoBulkFieldExchange(CFieldExchange* pFX);  // RFX support
// Implementation
#ifdef _DEBUG
    virtual void AssertValid() const;
    virtual void Dump(CDumpContext& dc) const;
#endif
};
```

The constructor for this class should look something like the following:

```
CMyBulkSet::CMyBulkSet(CDatabase* pdb)
    : CRecordset(pdb)
{
    m_Num = NULL;
    m_Title = NULL;
    m_Pages = NULL;

    m_NumLen = NULL;
    m_TitleLen = NULL;
    m_PagesLen = NULL;
    m_nFields = 3;
    m_nDefaultType = dynaset;
}
```

Opening a `CRecordset` for Bulk RFX

To enable bulk row fetching for your `CRecordset`, you specify the `CRecordset::useMultiRowFetch` flag in the options parameter of `CRecordset::Open()`. You will probably also want to specify the number of rows to be retrieved in each rowset by calling `CRecordset::SetRowsetSize()` *before* calling `Open()`—otherwise, a default size of 25 rows is used. You can retrieve the current rowset size by calling `CRecordset::GetRowsetSize()`.

> **NOTE**
>
> Bulk RFX is not supported by Class Wizard. If you want to use Bulk RFX, you add it manually.

The following example shows how to open a recordset for Bulk RFX, for which MFC will allocate data buffers:

```
// Allocate new recordset
CMyBulkSet* pBulkSet = new CMyBulkSet(pDb);
// Open Recordset, catching exceptions
try
{
    // Set Number of rows in rowset
    pBulkSet->SetRowsetSize(5);

    // Open recordset with dynamic cursor
    bRc = pBulkSet->Open(CRecordset::dynamic,
            "SELECT Num, Title, Pages FROM MyChapters",
            CRecordset::useMultiRowFetch);
    if(bRc)
        TRACE("Recordset Opened OK\n");
    else
        TRACE("Recordset Not Opened\n");
}
catch(CMemoryException *pEx)
{
    pEx->ReportError();
}
catch(CDBException *pEx)
{
    pEx->ReportError();
    TRACE("RetCode: %d strError: [%s] strState: [%s]\n",
        pEx->m_nRetCode, pEx->m_strError,
        pEx->m_strStateNativeOrigin);
}
```

Implementing Bulk Record Field Exchange

When fetching rows in bulk, you will use Bulk Record Field Exchange, which is similar to regular RFX, with the exception that it will retrieve up to the number of rows in the rowset and place the data into array members of your recordset. For each column, you will also want to allocate an array of longs that will receive the length of each field returned.

You can manually allocate these arrays, just as you would for RFX column variables as you saw earlier, or you can have MFC allocate the memory for you. If you are allocating your own buffers, you let MFC know by specifying the CRecordset::userAllocMultiRowBuffers option when you call Open() for the recordset. By default, MFC will allocate the memory for you. If you choose to let MFC allocate the arrays, you should declare your member variables as pointers to the appropriate type and initialize them to NULL.

DoBulkFieldExchange()

If you have enabled Bulk RFX, MFC will call the DoBulkFieldExchange() member of your recordset class instead of DoFieldExchange(). You will want to implement this function in your recordset class to move data from the database into the member arrays of your class. The implementation of DoBulkFieldExchange() is very similar to that of DoFieldExchange(), except that you should use the Bulk RFX_ macros. For example, instead of using RFX_Int(), you should use RFX_Int_Bulk(). In addition, some of the bulk functions, such as RFX_Text_Bulk(), take a fifth parameter for the maximum allowable buffer size.

The only difference in the bulk macros is that they take a fourth parameter—the address of an array of longs that will receive the length of each field returned. This array will hold SQL_NULL_DATA for any field that has a NULL value. You should also make sure that the pointer to the column data points to an array of variables, rather than the single variable used in plain RFX.

The following example shows an implementation of DoBulkFieldExchange():

```
void CMyBulkSet::DoBulkFieldExchange(CFieldExchange* pFX)
{
    pFX->SetFieldType(CFieldExchange::outputColumn);
    RFX_Long_Bulk(pFX, _T("[Num]"), &m_Num, &m_NumLen);
    RFX_Text_Bulk(pFX, _T("[Title]"), &m_Title, &m_TitleLen, 50);
    RFX_Long_Bulk(pFX, _T("[Pages]"), &m_Pages, &m_PagesLen);
}
```

Fetching Bulk Records

When you call Open() with the CRecordset::useMultiRowFetch option set, the first rowset will be fetched from the data source and copied into the member variables. To retrieve the next complete rowset, you can call MoveNext(). You may also call Move() to fetch a new rowset; however, you should be aware that the parameter to Move specifies the number of rows to move, not the number of rowset blocks. For example, if your rowset size is 10, Open() will fetch the first 10 rows, a call to MoveNext() will fetch the next 10 (rows 11–20), and a call to Move(5) will fetch rows 6–15.

You can retrieve the number of rows actually fetched in any call to Open(), Move(), or MoveNext() by calling CRecordset::GetRowsFetched(). You can also get the status for an individual row by calling CRecordset::GetRowStatus(), which will tell you things such as whether the row was successfully retrieved or whether an error occurred. This function will also tell you whether the row has been updated, deleted, or added since the last fetch.

In addition, you can refresh the data and status for the current rowset by calling `CRecordset::RefreshRowset()`.

The following example shows how you can use `MoveNext()` to dump the data returned by a recordset using Bulk RFX:

```
do
{
    for(int i=0;i<5;i++)
    {
        if(pBulkSet->GetRowStatus(i+1) == SQL_ROW_SUCCESS)
            TRACE("Num: %d Title: [%s] Pages: %d\n",
                *(pBulkSet->m_Num + i),
                pBulkSet->m_Title + i*50,
                *(pBulkSet->m_Pages + i));
        else
            TRACE("No Row Fetched\n");
    }
    // Get Next rowset
    pBulkSet->MoveNext();
}
while(!pBulkSet->IsEOF());
```

CheckRowsetError()

When you call any of the cursor navigation functions, including `Open()`, `Requery()`, `Move()`, or `MoveNext()`, the MFC framework will call `CRecordset::CheckRowsetError()` to process any errors that may occur. If your application needs to do any special error processing, you can override this function.

Using Single-Row Functions

For functions such as `CRecordset::GetFieldValue()`, which work on a single row, you set the current row within the rowset. This is done with the `SetRowsetCursorPosition()` member of `CRecordset`.

Changing Data in a Recordset

In most cases, if your application is to do any real work, it will eventually modify the data in the database. This may consist of adding new rows to tables, deleting rows, or updating the data in an existing row. Because deleting a row is the simplest of these operations, let's start with that.

Deleting a Row

To delete a row from a data source, you simply open the recordset and call `Move()` or `MoveNext()` until the row you want to delete is the current row; then call `CRecordset::Delete()`. This will remove the current row from the database and set the recordset's member variables to NULL values. You call `Move()` or `MoveNext()` to move to another valid row.

You can check to see whether the current row has been deleted by calling the IsDeleted() member of CRecordset.

Adding a New Row

Before adding a new row, you should be certain that you have not opened the recordset as read-only—you can easily check this by calling CRecordset::CanAppend() to see whether you can add records using this recordset.

Adding a new row involves three separate steps: first, you should call CRecordset::AddNew() to create a new empty row. You will then set the member variables of the recordset to the values you want to place in the new row. Finally, you call CRecordset::Update() to add the new row to the database. The following example illustrates this:

```
if(pRecordset->CanAppend())
{
    pRecordset->AddNew();
    pRecordset->m_Num = 222;
    pRecordset->m_Title = "New MFC Record";
    pRecordset->m_Pages = 321;
    if(pRecordset->Update())
        TRACE("Row Added OK\n");
    else
        TRACE("Row Not Added\n");
} // end if CanAppend()
```

If you are using a dynaset, the new row will appear as the last row in the recordset. However, if you are using a snapshot, you call Requery() to update the recordset to include the new row.

Editing an Existing Row

Like adding a new row, editing an existing row requires three separate steps: first, you call CRecordset::Edit() to begin the update process for the current row. Next, you can change the values of the member variables of the recordset. When you call CRecordset::Update(), these changes are transferred to the database. If you choose not to update the row after you have called Edit(), you can cancel the update by calling CancelUpdate().

> **NOTE**
>
> Before attempting to edit a row, you should check to see whether the recordset allows editing of existing rows by calling CRecordset::CanUpdate().

The following example shows how you can use Edit() and Update() to modify the current existing row in the database:

```
if(pRecordset->CanUpdate())
 {
    pRecordset->Edit();
```

```
    pRecordset->m_Num = 222;
    pRecordset->m_Title = "New MFC Record";
    pRecordset->m_Pages = 21;
    if(pRecordset->Update())
        TRACE("Row Added OK\n");
    else
        TRACE("Row Not Added\n");
} // end if CanAppend()
```

Working with NULL Values

If you want to set a field in the row to a NULL value, you should first check to see whether a NULL value is acceptable for that field by calling IsFieldNullable(). You can then set the field to a NULL value by calling SetFieldNull(). You can also check to see whether a field is currently set to a NULL value by calling IsFieldNull().

Row Locking

When updating rows, you have a choice of how the framework will lock rows that are being updated. Optimistic locking will lock the row only during the processing of the Update() call, and pessimistic locking will lock the row when you call Edit() and will not release it until after you call Update(). You can set the locking mode by calling CRecordset::SetLockingMode() after you have opened the recordset, but before any calls to Edit().

Transactions

Your application may want to make several changes to the database in a single operation, possibly involving more than one recordset. To do this, you call the BeginTrans() member function of the CDatabase that is to be used for the transaction. You can then make changes to the database using recordsets derived from that connection. If all goes well, you can commit the changes to the database by calling the CommitTrans() member of the CDatabase. If something goes wrong and you want to roll back all the previous changes since the last BeginTrans(), you can call CDatabase::Rollback().

> **NOTE**
>
> Not all recordsets will allow transactions—you can check on transaction support by calling CRecordset::CanTransact().

Using Statement Parameters

In many cases, you will want to execute many queries that are very similar, but with a few variable values. For example, suppose you want to derive a CRecordset class that will retrieve a set of employee records that fall within a certain salary range. Instead of deriving a separate class for each range you might want to deal with, you can create one class that makes use of statement parameters to modify the query at runtime.

To use parameters, you can add parameter placeholders to the SQL strings that make up the query for your recordset. Most often, you will parameterize the m_strFilter string, although you may also use parameters in the m_strSort string or in the SQL string passed to Open(). For the salary range example in this chapter, you might want to use a value of m_strFilter such as the following:

```
m_strFilter = "WHERE Salary >= ? AND Salary <= ?";
```

This statement uses two parameters—MFC will substitute real values for the ? in the SQL whenever you call Open() or Requery() for the recordset. To implement the parameters, you add member variables to your recordset class for each parameter and set the m_nParams member of CRecordset to the number of parameters you will be using.

Next, you modify the DoFieldExchange() member of your recordset to move values between your parameter member variables and the SQL statement sent to the database. You add a call to CFieldExchange::SetFieldType() to set the field type to CFieldExchange::param and then add RFX_ macros for each of your parameters. The RFX_ macros for your parameters must appear in the order of the placeholders used in the SQL statement—the parameter name given in the RFX_ macro is not used for parameter matching, so you can choose any arbitrary name you like.

The following example helps illustrate adding parameters to DoFieldExchange():

```
void CMyRecordset::DoFieldExchange(CFieldExchange* pFX)
{
    //{{AFX_FIELD_MAP(CMyRecordset)
    pFX->SetFieldType(CFieldExchange::outputColumn);
    RFX_Long(pFX, _T("[Num]"), m_Num);
    RFX_Text(pFX, _T("[Title]"), m_Title);
    RFX_Long(pFX, _T("[Pages]"), m_Pages);
    RFX_Long(pFX, _T("[mykey]"), m_mykey);
    RFX_Text(pFX, _T("[name]"), m_name);
    //}}AFX_FIELD_MAP
    pFX->SetFieldType(CFieldExchange::param);
    RFX_Text(pFX, "myFirstParam", m_strParamOne);
    RFX_Long(pFX, _"mySecondParam", m_nParamTwo);
}
```

Recordset Error Handling

In most cases, if an error occurs in the ODBC processing associated with a recordset, MFC will throw an exception of type CDBException. Your applications should catch these in order to respond to errors that may occur. For more on exception handling in MFC, see Chapter 7, "General-Purpose Classes."

In addition, you may want to override CRecordset::Check(), which is called by the framework to check the return code from ODBC operations.

The CRecordView Class

The last of the MFC database classes that you will be looking at is CRecordView. This class is basically a form view, with several enhancements that make it easier to display data from a recordset. The CRecordView class allows you to use dialog data exchange to display data directly from the recordset. It also provides default implementations for moving to the first, last, next, or previous records in the recordset.

Creating a CRecordView

Like any other dialog classes, CRecordView uses a dialog template to define the layout of the view window. Thus, you will want to use the resource editor to create a dialog template for your record view before creating the actual class implementation for your view.

Next, you will want to derive a new class from CRecordView for your view. While you can do this manually, it is much easier to do this with ClassWizard. If you start ClassWizard after adding a new dialog template, you will be prompted to create a class for the new resource. You can then select Create a new class to start defining your new view class.

In the New Class dialog, you name your class and set the Base class to CRecordView. You may also choose to add support for OLE automation in this dialog. When you click OK in this dialog, you will receive a dialog prompting for the recordset class to use with this view. You may choose one of your existing recordset classes from the drop-down list, or you may click on New to have ClassWizard guide you through creating a new recordset class for use with this view.

Dialog Data Exchange with CRecordView

The CRecordView class supports a slightly modified version of the dialog data exchange mechanism that you saw in Chapter 5. The difference is that instead of moving data between controls and member variables in the view class, you can move data between the view controls and the column data member variables of the CRecordset associated with the view class.

This is done by using special DDX_Field functions in your implementation of DoDataExchange(). This is also most easily set up using ClassWizard. If you go to the Member Variables tab of ClassWizard for your view class, you can add variables for each of the controls in the view. If you select a control and click Add Variable, you will see the Add Member Variable dialog. You can add variables from the associated CRecordset by using the drop-down list in the Member variable name field. This will automatically add the appropriate code to your DoDataExchange() function—whenever the view is updated, it will display the data from the recordset.

The following example shows the DoDataExchange() function from a simple CRecordView class:

```
void CMfcExView::DoDataExchange(CDataExchange* pDX)
{
    CRecordView::DoDataExchange(pDX);
```

```
//{{AFX_DATA_MAP(CMfcExView)
DDX_FieldText(pDX, IDC_EDIT1, m_pSet->m_ID, m_pSet);
DDX_FieldText(pDX, IDC_EDIT2, m_pSet->m_Title, m_pSet);
DDX_FieldText(pDX, IDC_EDIT3, m_pSet->m_Number, m_pSet);
//}}AFX_DATA_MAP
}
```

OnGetRecordset()

The OnGetRecordset() member of CRecordView is called by the framework to retrieve a pointer to the CRecordset associated with the view. The framework will call OnGetRecordset() on the initial update of the view, as well as on successive updates. The default implementation supplied by ClassWizard will return the pointer stored in CRecordView::m_pSet and will create a new object of the associated recordset class for you if necessary. You can provide your own implementation of this function if you want to add any special processing to the creation of the recordset.

CRecordView::OnMove()

The OnMove() member of CRecordview() provides a handy way to move your view to a new row in the recordset—it will call the Move() member of the associated CRecordset and update the display to show the new row. OnMove() will also automatically update the database if the current row has been modified in the record view.

OnMove() takes only one parameter, specifying where to move. This can be one of the following constants:

```
ID_RECORD_FIRST
ID_RECORD_LAST
ID_RECORD_NEXT
ID_RECORD_PREV
```

When moving around the recordset, you may also find the IsOnFirstRecord() and IsOnLastRecord() members of CRecordView useful. These will return TRUE if the view is currently positioned on the first or last row of the recordset.

Creating Database Applications with AppWizard

Now that you have seen what goes into the framework of MFC's database classes, let's take a look at how AppWizard can help you put the pieces together to turn out an application.

When creating an application with the MFC application AppWizard, step 2 allows you to choose from several different levels of database support for your application.

> **NOTE**
>
> The AppWizard database options are not available for dialog-based applications.

The Header file's only option includes only the header files for the MFC database classes and adds build settings to link with the MFC database libraries, but it will not define any classes for you.

Both of the Database view options create a recordset and record view class for you. You must choose a data source to be used with these classes by clicking on the Data Source button, which will present a dialog allowing you to choose a data source and set the type of recordset to use. You will also be prompted for specific tables, views, and stored procedures in the data source to use for the recordset and record view classes.

The Database view with file support option provides support for document serialization and the File menu options associated with document files, whereas the Database view without file support option does not support serialization and does not add the Open, Close, Save, or Save As commands to the File menu.

Summary

In this chapter, you explored MFC's support for database operations in your applications. You began by examining the basic classes that MFC provides for working with ODBC data sources, including CDatabase, CRecordset, and CRecordView.

You saw how to create a new CDatabase object and use it to connect to an ODBC data source, as well as how to use CDatabase to execute SQL statements against the data source, including transactions.

You also learned how the CRecordset class can be used to provide a simple way to move data from rows in the database back and forth between member variables of the recordset by using Record Field Exchange. You took a look at how to open the recordset using different cursor types and SQL queries using various selection clauses, including parameterized statements. You also explored how to select different rows from the recordset, as well as how to add, delete, and update rows in the recordset.

Next, you saw how the CRecordView class can be used to provide a convenient interface between the user and the data in a recordset, including a special case of dialog data exchange that supports the member variables of an associated recordset.

Last, you learned how to use AppWizard to help you set up the framework for an application that will use the MFC ODBC database classes.

27

Using OLE DB

by David Bennett

This chapter takes a look at one of Microsoft's newest additions to its set of database APIs: OLE DB, which is intended to replace the older Data Access Objects (DAO) and Remote Data Objects (RDO) APIs. OLE DB provides a Common Object Model (COM) interface between data providers and the consumers of that data, which is extremely flexible. However, this flexibility can make things a bit complicated at times. The next chapter looks at Active Data Objects (ADO), which are not quite as flexible, but a bit simpler to work with.

The OLE DB architecture defines three basic classes of applications, although there can be a wide range of different sorts of applications in each class, ranging from the most primitive to the very complex RDBMS systems:

> *Data providers* are applications that own their own data and expose it in a tabular format. Data providers expose the rowset COM interfaces of OLE DB and can range from simple providers that expose a single table of data to more complicated, distributed database systems.

> *Consumers* are applications that use the OLE DB interfaces to manipulate the data stored in a data provider. User applications fall into the consumer class.

> *Service providers* are sort of a combination of data providers and consumers. Service providers do not own their own data, but use the OLE DB consumer interface to access the data stored in data providers. The service provider then makes this data available to consumers by exposing the data provider interfaces. Service providers are often used to provide higher-level services to applications, such as advanced, distributed query processing.

OLE DB Components

The OLE DB interface consists of several classes of COM objects that represent various components of a database application. These include the pieces listed here:

- Enumerators: Used to list available data sources.
- Data Sources: Represent individual data and service providers. These are used to create sessions.
- Sessions: Used to create transactions and commands.
- Transactions: Used to group multiple operations into a single atomic transaction.
- Commands: Used to send text (such as SQL) commands to a data source and return rowsets.
- Rowsets: Used to work with tabular data.
- Errors: Used to retrieve information about errors.

The next sections take a closer look at each of these components and the COM interfaces that each component exposes. Each component must export a set of mandatory OLE DB interfaces and can also implement some, none, or all the optional interfaces.

Data Sources

Data source objects are used to manage a connection to a data source and to create session objects for that data source. A data source object is instantiated with CoCreateInstance() or by binding to a moniker. Data sources must expose the following interfaces:

IDBProperties: Used to set connection parameters and retrieve provider capabilities.

IDBInitialize: Used to connect to a data source.

IDBCreateSession: Used to create session objects for the connection.

Ipersist: Used in storing the data source information in persistent storage.

Optional Interfaces

The following interfaces may also be implemented, depending on the OLE DB provider being used:

IDBDataSourceAdmin: Used to create, destroy, or modify data sources.

IDBInfo: Used to retrieve information about the keywords and literals that are supported by a provider.

IPersistFile: Used to store data source settings in persistent storage.

ISupportErrorInfo: Used for advanced error reporting with OLE DB error objects.

Sessions

Session objects are created by data source objects and provide a context for transactions. They are used to create new transaction, command, and rowset objects.

IGetDataSource: Used to retrieve the data source that created the session.

IOpenRowset: Used to open a rowset, exposing data from the provider.

ISessionProperties: Used to work with the properties of the session.

Optional Interfaces

The following interfaces may also be implemented, depending on the OLE DB provider being used:

IDBCreateCommand: Used to create command objects.

IDBSchemaRowset: Used to retrieve information about the schema of the database.

IIndexDefinition: Used to create or drop indexes from the data provider.

ISupportErrorInfo: Used for advanced error reporting with OLE DB error objects.

`ITableDefinition`: Used to create, drop, or alter tables in the data source.

`Itransaction`: Used to work with transactions.

`ITransactionJoin`: Used to work with distributed transactions.

`ITransactionLocal`: Used to work with local, nondistributed transactions.

`ITransactionObject`: Allows more detailed access to nested transaction objects.

Transaction Objects

Transaction objects are used to manipulate transactions in OLE DB. They can also be used to perform nested transactions—that is, transactions that consist of several different transactions.

`IConnectionPointContainer`: Provides an interface for creating connection points for receiving COM notifications.

`Itransaction`: Used to work with transactions.

Optional Interfaces

The following interfaces may also be implemented, depending on the OLE DB provider being used:

`ISupportErrorInfo`: Used for advanced error reporting with OLE DB error objects.

`ITransactionOptions`: Used to work with transaction options.

`ISupportErrorInfo`: Used for advanced error reporting with OLE DB error objects.

Commands

Command objects are used to send a text command to a data source. For data sources that support SQL, SQL commands are executed with a command object, including both data definition language commands as well as queries that generate rowset objects. For other sorts of data sources that do not support SQL, command objects are used to send other sorts of text commands, as appropriate for the data provider, to the data source. However, providers are not required to support commands. For instance, most simple providers that export tabular information will not support commands.

Command objects must support the following interfaces:

`Iaccessor`: Used to create accessors, which define bindings of command parameters or column data to data buffers.

`IColumnsInfo`: Retrieves information about the columns in a rowset.

`Icommand`: Provides the methods to execute a command.

`ICommandProperties`: Used to set the properties of the command object.

`ICommandText`: Used to set the text of the command that will be sent to the provider.

`IConvertType`: Provides information on the available type conversions.

Optional Interfaces

The following interfaces may also be implemented, depending on the OLE DB provider being used:

IColumnsRowset: Used to provide more detailed information about the columns in a rowset.

ICommandPrepare: Used to prepare commands before execution.

ICommandWithParameters: Used for setting up commands that use variable commands.

ISupportErrorInfo: Used for advanced error reporting with OLE DB error objects.

Rowsets

Rowset objects are used to expose a table of data, arranged in rows and columns, as you might be familiar with from SQL databases. Rowsets can be created by either session or command objects. All rowset objects must expose the following interfaces:

Iaccessor: Used to create accessor objects, which define the bindings of column data to data buffers.

IColumnsInfo: Provides information about the columns returned in a rowset.

IConvertType: Provides information on the available type conversions.

Irowset: Provides the interface for fetching data and managing rows.

IRowsetInfo: Used to work with the properties of a rowset and other rowset information.

Optional Interfaces

The following interfaces may also be implemented, depending on the OLE DB provider being used:

IColumnsRowset: Provides more detailed information about the columns in a rowset.

IConnectionPointContainer: Provides an interface for creating connection points for receiving COM notifications.

IRowsetChange: Used to insert, delete, and update rows in the rowset.

IRowsetIdentity: Used to compare two row handles.

IRowsetLocate: Used to perform scrolling within a rowset.

IRowsetResynch: Used to resynchronize the rowset data to the data source.

IRowsetScroll: Used to perform approximate scrolling within the rowset.

IRowsetUpdate: Used to work with delayed updates.

ISupportErrorInfo: Used for advanced error reporting with OLE DB error objects.

Enumerators

Enumerators are used to search for available data sources and additional enumerators on the system, which can then be searched in a recursive manner. This is accomplished via the ISourcesRowset interface, which can be used to generate a rowset describing the available data sources. The OLE DB SDK includes a root enumerator, which searches the registry for installed data sources and additional enumerators.

IParseDisplayName: Converts a displayable name string to a moniker.

ISourcesRowset: Retrieves the set of available data sources and enumerators.

Optional Interfaces

The following interfaces may also be implemented, depending on the OLE DB provider being used:

IDBInitialize: Initializes the enumerator.

IDBProperties: Used to work with the properties of the enumerator.

ISupportErrorInfo: Used for advanced error reporting with OLE DB error objects.

Errors

Error objects are used to retrieve additional information about errors that are generated by other OLE DB objects. Error objects must expose the following interfaces:

IErrorInfo: Used to retrieve information about an error.

IErrorRecords: Used to add and retrieve records from an error object.

OLE DB Data Consumer Applications

Now that we have taken a brief look at the objects used in data consumer applications, let's see how to put them all together to create an application that uses OLE DB to work with an OLE DB data provider.

Application Structure

Most OLE DB applications that query a data source will have the following basic structure:

Initialize COM environment

Connect to data source

Open a session

Execute a command

Process results

Clean up

Initializing COM

Because OLE DB is a COM interface, you will need to initialize the COM environment before you can use any of the OLE DB objects. This is done with a single call to CoInitialize(), as shown here:

```
HRESULT hr = CoInitialize(NULL);
```

CoInitialize() takes only one parameter, which is currently reserved and must be NULL. When you are finished with all the COM interfaces in your application, you should free the resources used by the COM library by calling CoUninitialize().

In most cases, it is also best to retrieve a pointer to the default OLE task memory allocator with a call to CoGetMalloc(), shown here:

```
HRESULT CoGetMalloc(DWORD dwMemContext, LPMALLOC * ppMalloc);
```

When calling CoGetMalloc(), set dwMemContext to MEMCTX_TASK and pass the address of a pointer to an IMalloc interface. Upon return, this pointer will be set to the default task memory allocator, which is used for allocating or freeing memory for use with COM interfaces. We will look at just how the IMalloc interface is used later on in this chapter.

The following example shows how to initialize the COM environment:

```
HRESULT hr;
IMalloc* g_pIMalloc = NULL;

// Initialize COM environment
hr = CoInitialize(NULL);

// Go ahead and fetch the IMalloc interface for later use
hr = CoGetMalloc(MEMCTX_TASK, &g_pIMalloc);
```

Connecting to a Data Provider

The OLE DB interface is used to work with data sources by way of an OLE DB data or service provider. Thus, you must create and initialize a provider object before proceeding to work with the data it exposes. Initializing a provider consists of three steps:

1. Creating an instance of the provider
2. Setting provider properties
3. Initializing the provider

Creating a Provider Instance

The OLE DB architecture allows for many different sorts of data and service providers. Currently, the most common data provider is MSDASQL, which provides OLE DB access to ODBC data sources. This provider is very useful, because it can take advantage of existing ODBC drivers while development continues on additional native OLE DB providers. MSDASQL also ships with the OLE DB SDK, so we will be using this provider in the examples throughout this chapter.

Creating an instance of the OLE DB provider is done with a call to the COM function CoCreateInstance(), shown here:

```
STDAPI CoCreateInstance( REFCLSID rclsid, LPUNKNOWN pUnkOuter,
    DWORD dwClsContext, REFIID riid, LPVOID * ppv);
```

When calling CoCreateInstance(), pass rclsid the class ID of the OLE DB provider you want to instantiate. For the examples in this chapter, this will be CLSID_MSDASQL. The pUnkOuter parameter is used to create objects as part of an aggregate. For the purposes of this chapter, this will always be NULL. dwClsContext is used to pass the context that the new object will run in. For more on how this parameter is used, see the earlier chapters on ActiveX, OLE, and COM. For our examples, we will be setting dwClsContext to CLSCTX_INPROC_SERVER. The last two parameters, riid and ppv, specify the type of interface to return and a pointer to the interface pointer to be returned. For initializing a data provider, use an IDBInitialize interface, so pass IID_IDBInitialize for riid and the address of an IDBInitialize pointer in ppv. The following example shows CoCreateInstance() in action, as it is used to instantiate the MSDASQL OLE DB ODBC provider:

```
IDBInitialize* pIDBInitialize;

hr = CoCreateInstance(CLSID_MSDASQL, NULL,
                      CLSCTX_INPROC_SERVER,
                      IID_IDBInitialize,
                      (void**)&pIDBInitialize);
if(FAILED(hr))
    TRACE("CoCreateInstance Failed\n");
else
    TRACE("CoCreateInstance Successful\n");
```

NOTE

You can also instantiate a data source from its entry in an enumerator, which can be used to browse available data sources.

Setting Provider Properties

For some providers, you might be able to simply use the default properties of the provider and move right on to initializing the provider. However, in most cases, you will want to specify one or more properties before initializing the provider.

Properties for a data source object are divided into two property sets: The DBPROPSET_DBINIT property set contains properties that can be set before the data source is initialized, and the DBPROPSET_DATASOURCE property set, which contains properties that can be set after the data source is initialized.

The DBPROPSET_DBINIT property set contains the following individual properties:

> DBPROP_INIT_DATASOURCE: Specifies the name of the data source to connect to.
>
> DBPROP_AUTH_USERID: Specifies the user ID that is used to connect to the data source.
>
> DBPROP_AUTH_PASSWORD: Specifies the password to be used when connecting to the data source.
>
> DBPROP_INIT_HWND: Specifies the window handle to be used as a parent of any dialogs that the data source might need to present to the user, prompting for additional information.
>
> DBPROP_INIT_MODE: Specifies the access permissions for the data source. This can be used to set options like read-only mode.
>
> DBPROP_INIT_PROMPT: Specifies whether the user will be prompted for additional initialization information. This can be set to one of the following values:
>
>> DBPROMPT_PROMPT: The provider will always prompt the user for initialization information.
>>
>> DBPROMT_COMPLETE: Will prompt the user only if additional information is required.
>>
>> DBPROMT_COMPLETEREQUIRED: Will prompt the user only if additional information is required, and the user will only be allowed to enter the missing required information.
>>
>> DBPROMPT_NOPROMPT: Does not prompt the user.
>
> DBPROP_INIT_TIMEOUT: Specifies the number of seconds to wait for initialization to complete.
>
> DBPROP_AUTH_CACHE_AUTHINFO: Used to tell the provider whether it is allowed to cache sensitive information, such as passwords.
>
> DBPROP_AUTH_ENCRYPT_PASSWORD: Used to determine whether the password must be encrypted when it is sent to the data source.
>
> DBPROP_AUTH_INTEGRATED: A string used to specify the authentication service that will be used to authenticate the user.

`DBPROP_AUTH_MASK_PASSWORD`: Specifies that the password will be masked when sent to the data source. This provides a weaker form of encryption than `DBPROP_AUTH_ENCRYPT_PASSWORD`.

`DBPROP_AUTH_PERSIST_ENCRYPTED`: Specifies that the data source object will persist authentication information in encrypted form.

`DBPROP_AUTH_PERSIST_SENSITIVE_AUTHINFO`: Allows the data source to persist authentication information.

`DBPROP_INIT_IMPERSONATION_LEVEL`: Specifies the level of impersonation that the server can use when impersonating the client.

`DBPROP_INIT_LCID`: Specifies the preferred locale for text that is returned to the consumer.

`DBPROP_INIT_LOCATION`: Specifies the location (such as server name) of the data source.

`DBPROP_INIT_PROTECTION_LEVEL`: Specifies the level of authentication protection in communications between the client and the server.

`DBPROP_INIT_PROVIDERSTRING`: Used to specify a provider-specific string containing additional connection information.

In addition, you can use the `DBPROPSET_DATASOURCE` property to set the `DBPROP_CURRENTCATALOG` property, which determines which catalog or database is to be used within the data source. For more detail on the acceptable values for the properties listed here, see the OLE DB specification.

The `DBPROP` Structure

In order to set the properties for a data source, you will need to set up an array of `DBPROP` structures containing the values for each property that you want to set within the property set. This structure, which is also used for retrieving current settings, is shown here:

```
typedef struct tagDBPROP {
    DBPROPID      dwPropertyID;
    DBPROPOPTIONS dwOptions;
    DBPROPSTATUS  dwStatus;
    DBID          colid;
    VARIANT       vValue;
} DBPROP;
```

The `dwPropertyID` field should be set to one of the property IDs listed here, such as `DBPROP_INIT_DATASOURCE`. If the `dwOptions` field is set to `DBPROPOPTIONS_SETIFCHEAP`, the provider can only set this property if it is simple to do so. For options that you require the provider to set, you should set `dwOptions` to `DBPROPOPTIONS_REQUIRED`. For certain options, it is possible to set options for individual columns, in which case the `colid` field should be set to the desired column ID. Otherwise, `colid` should be set to `DB_NULLID`, which will set the property for all columns.

The `vValue` field is used to pass the desired value for the property, as specified in a `VARIANT` object. For more on working with `VARIANT` data, see Chapter 12, "ActiveX Documents."

After calling SetProperties(), which you will see in just a bit, you can check the dwStatus field to see whether the provider was able to successfully set the property. If all went well, this will be set to DBPROPSTATUS_OK.

The DBPROPSET Structure

When setting a data source's properties, you will also need to fill in the values in a DBPROPSET structure, which will include a pointer to the array of DBPROP structures you filled in earlier. The DBPROPSET structure is shown here:

```
typedef struct tagDBPROPSET {
    DBPROP * rgProperties;
    ULONG    cProperties;
    GUID     guidPropertySet;
}
```

The rgProperties should point to the beginning of the array of DBPROPSET structures you set up earlier, and the cProperties field should be set to the number of entries in that array. guidPropertySet should contain the GUID that identifies the property set containing the properties to be set, such as DBPROPSET_DBINIT.

Using IDBProperties

The properties for data source objects, shown earlier, as well as enumerator objects, shown later, are set by using the IDBProperties interface. You can retrieve a pointer to the IDBProperties interface of the data source object by calling QueryInterface() on the data source object.

SetProperties()

When setting properties for an object, you will call IDBProperties::SetProperties(), shown here:

```
HRESULT SetProperties (ULONG cPropertySets, DBPROPSET rgPropertySets[]);
```

When you call SetProperties(), rgPropertySets should point to an array of DBPROPSET structures, as shown earlier, and cPropertySets should be passed the number of DBPROPSET structures in this array. If all goes well, SetProperties() will return S_OK; otherwise, it might return several errors, as specified in the OLE DB specification.

The following example shows how to set some of the more common options for a data source object used with MSDASQL:

```
#include "oledb.h"
HRESULT hr;
// Set Properties for the Data Source
DBPROP InitProps[5];
DBPROPSET rgInitPropSet[1];
IDBProperties* pIDBProperties;
char szDBName[100] = "LocalDb30";
WCHAR wszBuf[100];
```

```
IDBInitialize* pIDBInitialize;
hr = CoCreateInstance(CLSID_MSDASQL, NULL,
                      CLSCTX_INPROC_SERVER,
                      IID_IDBInitialize,
                      (void**)&pIDBInitialize);


VariantInit(&InitProps[0].vValue);
InitProps[0].dwOptions = DBPROPOPTIONS_REQUIRED;
InitProps[0].colid = DB_NULLID;
InitProps[0].dwPropertyID = DBPROP_INIT_PROMPT;
InitProps[0].vValue.vt = VT_I2;
InitProps[0].vValue.iVal = DBPROMPT_PROMPT;

VariantInit(&(InitProps[1].vValue));
InitProps[1].dwOptions = DBPROPOPTIONS_REQUIRED;
InitProps[1].colid = DB_NULLID;
InitProps[1].dwPropertyID = DBPROP_INIT_DATASOURCE;
MultiByteToWideChar(CP_ACP, 0, szDBName, -1, wszBuf, 100);
V_VT(&(InitProps[1].vValue)) = VT_BSTR;
V_BSTR(&(InitProps[1].vValue)) = SysAllocString(wszBuf);


rgInitPropSet[0].guidPropertySet = DBPROPSET_DBINIT;
rgInitPropSet[0].cProperties = 2;
rgInitPropSet[0].rgProperties = InitProps;

hr = pIDBInitialize->QueryInterface(IID_IDBProperties,
                                    (void**)&pIDBProperties);

hr = pIDBProperties->SetProperties(1, rgInitPropSet);
```

GetProperties()

The IDBProperties interface also allows you to retrieve the current property settings by calling GetProperties(), shown here:

```
HRESULT GetProperties (ULONG cPropertyIDSets, const DBPROPIDSET rgPropertyIDSets[],
    ULONG * pcPropertySets, DBPROPSET ** prgPropertySets);
```

When you call GetProperties(), rgPropertyIDSets should point to an array of DBPROPIDSET structures, which enumerate the specific properties that you are interested in, and cPropertyIDSets gives the number of DBPROPIDSET structures in the array.

GetProperties() will return a pointer to an array of DBPROPSET structures containing the current settings at prgPropertySets, and the number of structures in this array will be returned at pcPropertySets.

The array of DBPROPSET structures returned by GetProperties() is allocated by the provider. When you are done with this array, you should free the memory by calling IMalloc::Free(), using the IMalloc pointer returned from CoGetMalloc() and passing the pointer returned from GetProperties() at prgPropertySets.

GetPropertyInfo()

`IDBProperties` also supports the `GetPropertyInfo()` function, which allows you to retrieve information about all the properties supported by the provider, including the property set, property ID, data type, applicable object, and read/write permissions for supported properties.

Using IDBInitialize

When you called `CoCreateInstance()` to create an instance of your data provider, you requested a pointer to an `IDBInitialize` interface. Alternatively, you can retrieve a pointer to the `IDBInitialize` interface of the provider by calling `QueryInterface()` on the data source object. The `IDBInitialize` interface supports two functions: `Initialize()` and `Uninitialize()`.

Initialize()

After you have created an instance of the provider, set any necessary parameters, and retrieved an `IDBInitialize` interface from the data source object, you are ready to initialize the data source. Thankfully, this is very simple: Just call `IDBInitialize::Initialize()`, which takes no parameters. If the data source initializes successfully, this will return `S_OK` and your app is all set to go. The following example shows a typical call to `Initialize()`:

```
hr = pIDBInitialize->Initialize();
if(FAILED(hr))
    TRACE("Error in Initialize\n");
else
    TRACE("Initialize OK\n");
```

> **NOTE**
>
> Keep in mind that the examples in the text are somewhat simplified to show the concepts discussed. In the event this were a real application, you would probably want to add more sophisticated error handling. We will look at error processing in more detail at the end of this chapter, in the section titled "Extended OLE DB Error Handling."

IDBInitialize::Uninitialize()

If you wanted to reset the data source object to an uninitialized state, you would do so by calling `IDBInitialize::Uninitialize()`. This is useful for reinitializing the data source object with different parameters.

Creating a Session

In order to work with the data associated with a data source object, you will need to next create a session object. Session objects are used to provide a context for transactions, as well as providing the interfaces to create rowsets and commands, which allow you to work directly with the data. We will be looking at transactions later in this chapter, in the section titled "Transactions," so for now we will focus on simply creating the session.

To create a session, you will first need to obtain a pointer to an `IDBCreateSession` interface. This is done with a call to the `QueryInterface()` member of the data source object. The `IDBCreateSession` interface includes a single function, `CreateSession()`, which, as you might guess, is used to create a new session. The prototype for `CreateSession()` is shown here:

```
HRESULT CreateSession (IUnknown * pUnkOuter, REFIID riid,
                       IUnknown ** ppDBSession);
```

The `pUnkOuter` parameter is used to create the new session as part of an aggregate. If you are not using aggregates, this should be set to `NULL`. The `riid` parameter is used to tell `CreateSession()` what type of interface pointer you would like to have returned at `ppDBSession`. `riid` can specify any of the interfaces supported by session objects. It is generally easiest to specify the interface that you intend to use next, which will most often be `IID_IDBCreateCommand` or `IID_IOpenRowset`. The following example shows how to create a session, retrieving a pointer to an `IDBCreateCommand` interface:

```
/* Create Session */
IDBCreateSession* pIDBCreateSession = NULL;
IDBCreateCommand* pIDBCreateCommand = NULL;
IDBInitialize* pIDBInitialize;

hr = CoCreateInstance(CLSID_MSDASQL, NULL,
                      CLSCTX_INPROC_SERVER,
                      IID_IDBInitialize,
                      (void**)&pIDBInitialize);

// Retrieve a pointer to an IDBCreateSession interface
hr = pIDBInitialize->QueryInterface(IID_IDBCreateSession,
                                    (void**)&pIDBCreateSession);

// Create a session, returning an IDBCreateCommand interface pointer
hr = pIDBCreateSession->CreateSession(NULL, IID_IDBCreateCommand,
                                      (IUnknown**)&pIDBCreateCommand);
if(FAILED(hr))
    TRACE("Error in CreateSession\n");
```

Opening a Rowset

For many OLE DB providers, you can open a rowset object in one of two different ways. The first is by using the `IOpenRowset` interface of the session object you created. `IOpenRowset::OpenRowset()` must be supported by all providers and will return a rowset containing all the rows for the specified table.

The second method of creating a rowset object involves the use of a command object, which allows much greater flexibility in choosing a query to select rows from the database and is the method of choice for accessing SQL providers. The next sections look at both of these methods.

Using IOpenRowset

The most basic method of creating a rowset object is to use `IOpenRowset::OpenRowset()` to open a rowset containing all of the rows of a specified table. Before calling `OpenRowset()`, you must obtain a pointer to the `IOpenRowset` interface of the session object. This can be done with a simple call to `QueryInterface()`.

After you have a pointer to an `IOpenRowset` interface, you can call the `OpenRowset()` method, shown here:

```
HRESULT OpenRowset(IUnknown * pUnkOuter, DBID * pTableID, DBID * pIndexID,
    REFIID riid, ULONG cPropertySets, DBPROPSET rgPropertySets[],
    IUnknown **ppRowset);
```

`OpenRowset()` can be used to open a rowset for either a table or an index, as specified by the `pTableID` and `pIndexID` parameters. To open a rowset for a table, `pTableID` should point to the `DBID` of the table, and `pIndexID` should be set to `NULL`. The `riid` parameter is used to request the type of interface pointer for the new rowset to return at `ppRowset`.

In addition, you can pass additional property settings for the new rowset by passing an array of `DBPROPSET` structures in `rgPropertySets` and passing the number of elements in the array in `cPropertySets`.

If the call to `OpenRowset()` is successful, it will return `S_OK` and you can then use the new rowset object to begin working with the data, as you will see later in this chapter.

Rowset Properties

When calling `OpenRowset()`, you can set any of the properties in the rowset property group. You can also query the current properties of a rowset object by calling `IRowsetInfo::GetProperties()`. The properties that make up the `Rowset` property group are listed here:

> `DBPROP_ABORTPRESERVE`: Determines whether the rowset is preserved after an aborted transaction.
>
> `DBPROP_APPENDONLY`: Used to create a rowset that is used only for appending new rows.
>
> `DBPROP_BLOCKINGSTORAGEOBJECTS`: Determines whether using storage objects will block other rowset methods.
>
> `DBPROP_BOOKMARKS`: Determines whether the rowset supports bookmarks.
>
> `DBPROP_BOOKMARKSKIPPED`: Determines whether bookmarks for inaccessible rows can be passed to `IRowsetLocate::GetRowsAt()`.
>
> `DBPROP_BOOKMARKTYPE`: Specifies the type of bookmark used.

DBPROP_CACHEDEFERRED: Determines whether the consumer will cache column data.

DBPROP_CANFETCHBACKWARDS: Determines whether the rowset can fetch backwards.

DBPROP_CANHOLDROWS: Determines whether the rowset will cache rows or transfer them immediately.

DBPROP_CANSCROLLBACKWARDS: Determines whether the rowset can scroll backwards.

DBPROP_CHANGEINSERTEDROWS: Determines whether the rowset allows updates to newly inserted rows.

DBPROP_COLUMNRESTRICT: Determines whether access rights are determined on a column-by-column basis.

DBPROP_COMMANDTIMEOUT: The number of seconds before a command times out.

DBPROP_COMMITPRESERVE: Determines whether the rowset is preserved after a transaction is committed.

DBPROP_DEFERRED: Determines whether the rowset will fetch the data for a row immediately or defer until an accessor is used on the columns.

DBPROP_DELAYSTORAGEOBJECTS: Determines whether storage objects are used in delayed update mode.

The following properties are set to VARIANT_TRUE if the specified interface is exposed by the rowset:

```
DBPROP_IAccessor
DBPROP_IColumnsInfo
DBPROP_IConnectionPointContainer
DBPROP_ConvertType
DBPROP_IRowset
DBPROP_IRowsetChange
DBPROP_IRowsetIdentify
DBPROP_IRowsetInfo
DBPROP_IRowsetLocate
DBPROP_IRowsetResynch
DBPROP_IRowsetScroll
DBPROP_IRowsetUpdate
DBPROP_ISupportErrorInfo
DBPROP_ILockBytes
DBPROP_ISequentialStream
DBPROP_IStorage
DBPROP_IStream
```

DBPROP_IMMOBILEROWS: Determines whether rows will be reordered as they are inserted or deleted.

DBPROP_LITERALBOOKMARKS: Determines whether bookmarks can be compared literally.

DBPROP_LITERALIDENTITY: Determines whether row handles can be compared literally.

DBPROP_MAXOPENROWS: Gives the maximum number of rows that can be open on the rowset.

DBPROP_MAXPENDINGROWS: The maximum number of rows for which changes can be pending at any given time.

DBPROP_MAXROWS: The maximum number of rows that can be returned in a rowset.

DBPROP_MAYWRITECOLUMN: Determines whether a column is writeable.

DBPROP_MEMORYUSAGE: Gives the percentage of total available virtual memory that can be used by the rowset.

DBPROP_NOTIFICATIONGRANULARITY: Determines at what times notifications are sent.

DBPROP_NOTIFICATIONPHASES: Returns the notification phases that are supported by the provider.

The following properties are used to specify whether the various phases of the notifications are cancelable:

```
DBPROP_NOTIFYCOLUMNSET
DBPROP_NOTIFYROWDELETE
DBPROP_NOTIFYROWFIRSTCHANGE
DBPROP_NOTIFYROWINSERT
DBPROP_NOTIFYROWRESYNCH
DBPROP_NOTIFYROWSETRELEASE
DBPROP_NOTIFYROWSETFETCHPOSITIONCHANGE
DBPROP_NOTIFYROWUNDOCHANGE
DBPROP_NOTIFYROWUNDODELETE
DBPROP_NOTIFYROWUNDOINSERT
DBPROP_NOTIFYROWUPDATE
```

DBPROP_ORDEREDBOOKMARKS: Determines whether bookmarks can be compared to find their relative positions.

DBPROP_OTHERINSERT: Determines whether the rowset can see rows inserted by another application.

DBPROP_OTHERUPDATEDELETE: Determines whether the rowset can see updates or deletes from other applications.

DBPROP_OWNINSERT: Determines whether the rowset can see rows inserted by any consumer of this rowset.

DBPROP_OWNUPDATEDELETE: Determines whether the rowset can see changes made by any consumer of the rowset.

DBPROP_QUICKRESTART: Determines whether IRowset::RestartPosition() is relatively quick to execute.

DBPROP_REENTRANTEVENTS: Determines whether reentrancy is supported in notification callbacks.

DBPROP_REMOVEDELETED: Determines whether handles for deleted rows will be returned when rows are fetched.

DBPROP_REPORTMULTIPLECHANGES: Determines whether the rowset will send notifications for operations that change multiple rows.

DBPROP_RETURNPENDINGINSERTS: Determines whether the rowset can fetch pending insert rows.

DBPROP_ROWRESTRICT: Determines whether access permissions are determined on a row-by-row basis.

DBPROP_ROWTHREADMODEL: Determines the threading model used by the rowset.

DBPROP_SERVERCURSOR: Determines whether the cursor used by the rowset creates an entity on the server.

DBPROP_STRONGIDENTITY: Determines whether the row handles for newly inserted rows can be compared.

DBPROP_TRANSACTEDOBJECT: Determines whether objects created in a column participate in transactions.

DBPROP_UPDATABILITY: Determines which methods of modifying the data are supported.

Executing Commands

OLE DB command objects are used to send text command strings to the provider. The most obvious example of these commands is the SQL statements sent to SQL providers, such as MSDASQL. However, this mechanism is flexible enough to support additional sorts of providers that take their own command syntax.

Creating a Command

New command objects are created by calling IDBCreateCommand::CreateCommand(). In order to call CreateCommand(), you will need to obtain a pointer to the IDBCreateCommand interface of a session object. In many cases, it is easiest to request an IDBCreateCommand interface pointer when calling CreateSession(), although you can also retrieve a pointer to the IDBCreateCommand interface by calling QueryInterface() on the session object.

Once you have a pointer to the IDBCreateCommand interface, creating a new command object requires a simple call to CreateCommand(), shown here:

```
HRESULT CreateCommand( IUnknown* pUnkOuter, REFIID riid, IUnknown ** ppCommand);
```

Like several other functions we have seen so far, the pUnkOuter parameter is used to create the new command as part of an aggregate, while the riid parameter is used to specify the type of interface pointer to return at ppCommand.

Setting the Command Text

OLE DB command objects are used to send text commands to the provider. Thus, you must set the text of the command after it is created, and before executing the command. Setting the text of the command is done with a call to ICommandText::SetCommandText().

First, you will need to obtain a pointer to the ICommandText interface of the command object by calling QueryInterface(), as we have seen earlier. Then, you can call SetCommandText(), shown here:

```
HRESULT SetCommandText (REFGUID rguidDialect, LPCOLESTR pwszCommand);
```

The rguidDialect parameter is used to specify the syntax that is to be used in parsing the command. GUID's for dialects can be defined by individual providers, or they can support DBGUID_DBSQL, which specifies ANSI SQL syntax, and is supported by MSDASQL. The pwszCommand parameter should point to a null-terminated Unicode string containing the command.

You can also retrieve the current text of the command by calling ICommandText::GetCommandText().

Executing the Command

To send the command to the provider, you will need to call ICommand::Execute(), which will execute the command and return a rowset reflecting the results. If you are executing a query, like an SQL SELECT statement, the rowset that is returned will give the results of the query. If you are executing other sorts of commands that do not return results, an empty rowset object will be returned. The prototype for Execute() is shown here:

```
HRESULT Execute (IUnknown * pUnkOuter, REFIID riid, DBPARAMS * pParams,
                 LONG * pcRowsAffected, IUnknown ** ppRowset);
```

The riid parameter specifies the type of interface pointer to return at ppRowset for the rowset that is created by the command. If the command that is being executed updates, deletes, or inserts rows, the number of rows that are affected will be returned at pcRowsAffected. In addition, pParams can be used to pass a pointer to a DBPARAMS structure describing parameter values to be used with the command. We will look at parameters in more detail later in this chapter.

The following example shows how to create a command, set its command text, and execute it:

```
IDBCreateCommand* pIDBCreateCommand = NULL;
ICommand* pICommand = NULL;
ICommandText* pICommandText = NULL;
IRowset* pIComRowset = NULL;
```

```
hr = pSomeSessionInterface->QueryInterface(IID_IDBCreateCommand,
                                (LPVOID*)&pIDBCreateCommand);

hr = pIDBCreateCommand->CreateCommand(NULL, IID_ICommand,
                                (IUnknown**) &pICommand);

hr = pICommand->QueryInterface(IID_ICommandText,
                                (LPVOID*)&pICommandText);

hr = pICommandText->SetCommandText(DBGUID_DBSQL,
                                L"SELECT * FROM MyTable");

hr = pICommand->Execute(NULL, IID_IRowset, NULL, NULL,
                            (IUnknown**)&pIComRowset);
if(FAILED(hr))
    TRACE("Error executing command\n");
```

Preparing Commands

Like other database APIs, OLE DB allows you to prepare statements before executing. This can provide for greater optimization of the operation when the same command is executed repetitively. This is particularly useful when combined with command parameters, as we will see in the next section. To prepare a command, you will need to call `ICommandPrepare::Prepare()`, shown here:

```
HRESULT Prepare (ULONG cExpectedRuns);
```

`Prepare()` should be called after you have set the command text, and before calling `Execute()`. The `cExpectedRuns` parameter can be used to tell the provider how many times you expect to execute the command, which can be useful in determining how to optimize the command. If you cannot estimate the number of times the command will be executed, you can pass `0`, in which case the provider will use a default value.

Using Parameters with Commands

OLE DB allows you to define commands that take parameters, which can be used to simplify your programming efforts, as well as to make your applications more efficient. Using parameters with command requires four basic steps:

1. Create a command with parameter placeholders.
2. Create an accessor describing the binding information for the parameters.
3. Call `ICommandWithParameters::SetParameterInfo()` to set up the parameters for the command.
4. Call `ICommand::Execute()` to execute the command with one or more sets of parameters.

Parameter Placeholders

When creating a command that uses parameters, the text of the command will contain place-holders (?) for the locations that the parameters will be filled in. The following SQL command shows a typical example of an INSERT statement that uses parameters:

```
INSERT INTO MyTable (EmpNo, Name, Salary) VALUES (?,?,?)
```

Accessors

We will be talking more about creating accessors in just a bit, so you might want to skip ahead to read about them. However, the following example will also show how to create an accessor for parameters.

ICommandWithParameters::SetParameterInfo()

To tell a command about the types of parameters that will be used, you will need to get an ICommandWithParameters interface from the command object and call its SetParameterInfo() method, shown here:

```
HRESULT SetParameterInfo (ULONG cParams, const ULONG rgParamOrdinals[],
                          const DBPARAMBINDINFO rgParamBindInfo[]);
```

You should set cParams to the number of parameters that you want to set type information for. For each parameter, add an entry in the rgParamOrdinals array containing the parameter's ordinal. Parameters are numbered left to right, starting with 1.

The array passed in rgParamBindInfo should contain a DBPARAMBINDINFO structure for each of the parameters. This structure is shown here:

```
typedef struct tagDBPARAMBINDINFO {
    LPOLESTR        pwszDataSourceType;
    LPOLESTR        pwszName;
    ULONG           ulParamSize;
    DBPARAMFLAGS    dwFlags;
    BYTE            bPrecision;
    BYTE            bScale;
} DBPARAMBINDINFO;
```

If the provider you are using has its own provider-specific data types, you can specify the provider's data type in pwszDataSourceType.

If the parameter in question has a name, you should enter the name of the parameter in pwszName; otherwise, this should be NULL.

The ulParamSize field should be set to the maximum possible length of a value for this parameter. For fixed-length types, this should be the size of the data type. For type DBTYPE_STR and DBTYPE_BYTES, this is the size in bytes, whereas for type DBTYPE_WSTR, the size is given in characters, which are 2 bytes.

The dwFlags field is used to specify a bitmap of options concerning the parameter. This can be a combination of the following values:

DBPARAMFLAGS_ISINPUT: This should be set for parameters that are used as input to a command.

DBPARAMFLAGS_ISOUTPUT: This is used for parameters that return output from a command.

DBPARAMFLAGS_ISSIGNED: This should be set if the data type for this parameter is signed.

DBPARAMFLAGS_ISNULLABLE: If the parameter can accept NULLs, this should be set.

DBPARAMFLAGS_ISLONG: This flag should be set if the data for the parameter is very long.

For numeric types, you should specify the precision and scale of a parameter's values in the bPrecision and bScale fields.

ICommand::Execute()

When using parameters with a command, you will need to call ICommand::Execute(), as shown earlier. The only difference is that you will need to pass a pointer to a DBPARAMS structure in the pParams parameter. The DBPARAMS structure is shown here:

```
typedef struct tagDBPARAMS {
    void *    pData;
    ULONG     cParamSets;
    HACCESSOR hAccessor;
} DBPARAMS;
```

In the DBPARAMS structure, pass the handle to an accessor that describes the data buffer for the parameters in hAccessor. Then supply a pointer to your data buffer in pData. The cParamSets field should be set to the number of parameter sets that you have provided in the pData buffer. If this is set to 1, only one set of parameter data will be read from pData and the command will be executed once with this set of data. If you specify a value of cParamSets greater than 1 and include multiple parameter sets in pData, the command will be executed once for each set of parameters.

The following example shows how to set up a command that uses parameters and execute it multiple times to insert new rows into a database:

```
// Structure for parameter data
typedef struct tagMyParmsStruct {
    ULONG ulNum;
    char szTitle[100];
    ULONG ulPages;
} MyParmsStruct, *pMyParmsStruct;
MyParmsStruct myParameters[5];

ICommand* pIParmCommand = NULL;
ICommandText* pIParmCommandText = NULL;
ICommandPrepare* pICommandPrepare = NULL;
```

```
IAccessor* pIParmAccessor = NULL;
IRowset* pIParmRowset;
HACCESSOR hParmAccessor = NULL;
ICommandWithParameters* pIParmCommandWithParms = NULL;
ULONG parmOrdinals[3] = {1,2,3};
DBPARAMS myDbParams;

DBBINDING rgParmBind[] =
{
    1, offsetof(MyParmsStruct, ulNum), 0, 0, NULL, NULL,
        NULL, DBPART_VALUE, DBMEMOWNER_CLIENTOWNED,
        DBPARAMIO_INPUT, sizeof(ULONG), 0, DBTYPE_UI4, 0, 0,
    2, offsetof(MyParmsStruct, ulPages), 0, 0, NULL, NULL,
        NULL, DBPART_VALUE, DBMEMOWNER_CLIENTOWNED,
        DBPARAMIO_INPUT, sizeof(ULONG), 0, DBTYPE_UI4, 0, 0,
    3, offsetof(MyParmsStruct, szTitle), 0, 0, NULL, NULL,
        NULL, DBPART_VALUE, DBMEMOWNER_CLIENTOWNED,
        DBPARAMIO_INPUT, 100, 0, DBTYPE_STR, 0, 0
};

DBPARAMBINDINFO parmTypeInfo[] =
{
    L"DBTYPE_I4", L"num", sizeof(ULONG), DBPARAMFLAGS_ISINPUT, 0, 0,
    L"DBTYPE_I4", L"pages", sizeof(ULONG), DBPARAMFLAGS_ISINPUT, 0, 0,
    L"DBTYPE_CHAR", L"title", 100, DBPARAMFLAGS_ISINPUT, 0, 0
};

// Create Command
hr = pIDBCreateCommand->CreateCommand(NULL, IID_ICommand,
                                      (IUnknown**) &pIParmCommand);

hr = pIParmCommand->QueryInterface(IID_ICommandText,
                        (LPVOID*)&pIParmCommandText);

// Set command text with placeholders
hr = pIParmCommandText->SetCommandText(DBGUID_DBSQL,
            L"INSERT INTO MyChapters (Num, Pages, Title) VALUES (?,?,?)");

// Prepare the command
pIParmCommandText->QueryInterface(IID_ICommandPrepare,
                                  (void**)&pICommandPrepare);
hr = pICommandPrepare->Prepare(0);
pICommandPrepare->Release();

// Create Accessor
hr = pIParmCommand->QueryInterface(IID_IAccessor, (LPVOID*)&pIParmAccessor);

hr = pIParmAccessor->CreateAccessor(DBACCESSOR_PARAMETERDATA, 3, rgParmBind,
                        sizeof(rgParmBind[0]), &hParmAccessor, NULL);

// Tell command about parameters
hr = pIParmCommand->QueryInterface(IID_ICommandWithParameters,
                                   (LPVOID*)&pIParmCommandWithParms);

hr = pIParmCommandWithParms->SetParameterInfo(3, parmOrdinals, parmTypeInfo);

myDbParams.pData = myParameters;
myDbParams.cParamSets = 1;
myDbParams.hAccessor = hParmAccessor;
```

```
for(int i=0;i<5;i++)
{
    myParameters[0].ulNum = 101+i;
    sprintf(myParameters[0].szTitle, "My Chapter %d", i);
    myParameters[0].ulPages = 42+i;

    // Execute command, using parameters
    hr = pIParmCommand->Execute(NULL, IID_IRowset, &myDbParams, NULL,
                        (IUnknown**)&pIParmRowset);
}
```

Working with Rowsets

Up to this point, we have seen how to create rowset objects either with `IOpenRowset::OpenRowset()`, or by creating a command object and calling `ICommand::Execute()`. This section shows how you can retrieve the actual data from the rowset by using an accessor, as well as how to retrieve additional information about the data in the rowset.

Retrieving Column Information

After you have created a rowset object, you can use its `IColumnsInfo` interface to retrieve information about the columns in the rowset, including the column IDs, data types, updatability, and other info. To start, you will need a pointer to the `IColumnsInfo` interface of the rowset, which can be obtained by calling `QueryInterface()`.

> **NOTE**
>
> All command objects also expose the `IColumnsInfo` interface, although calling `GetColumnInfo()` before the command is executed can be an expensive operation.

GetColumnInfo()

From the `IColumnsInfo` interface, you can call the `GetColumnInfo()` method to retrieve information about the columns in the rowset. The prototype for `GetColumnInfo()` is shown here:

```
HRESULT GetColumnInfo (ULONG * pcColumns, DBCOLUMNINFO ** prgInfo,
                    OLECHAR ** ppStringsBuffer);
```

`GetColumnInfo()` will return the number of columns included in the rowset at `pcColumns`. In addition, it will return a pointer to an array of `DBCOLUMNINFO` structures—one for each column—at `prgInfo`, and a pointer to a buffer containing all string values associated with the columns (such as column names) will be returned at `ppStringsBuffer`. Both of these buffers are allocated by OLE DB and should be freed with a call to `IMalloc::Free()` when you are finished with them.

DBCOLUMNINFO

When `GetColumnInfo()` is called, a pointer to an array of DBCOLUMNINFO structures is returned at prgInfo. This array will include a DBCOLUMNINFO structure for each column in the rowset, possibly including a bookmark column.

NOTE

Any rowset can return a bookmark column, regardless of whether bookmarks were requested or how the rowset was created. Your applications should be prepared to handle these, even if that means simply ignoring the bookmark column.

The DBCOLUMNINFO structure returned from `GetColumnInfo()` is shown here:

```
typedef struct tagDBCOLUMNINFO {
    LPOLESTR       pwszName;
    ITypeInfo *    pTypeInfo;
    ULONG          iOrdinal;
    DBCOLUMNFLAGS  dwFlags;
    ULONG          ulColumnSize;
    DBTYPE         wType;
    BYTE           bPrecision;
    BYTE           bScale;
    DBID           columnid;
} DBCOLUMNINFO;
```

The pwszName field points to a string containing the column name. The memory for this string is allocated by OLE DB in the block of memory specified by the pointer returned in ppStringsBuffer when `GetColumnInfo()` is called. This way, you can access each of the column names simply by using the pwszName pointer, but you need to call only `IMalloc::Free()` for the one pointer returned in ppStringsBuffer.

In the current release, pTypeInfo is reserved and should always return NULL, whereas the iOrdinal field will return the ordinal for the column. The bookmark column will be column 0, and the others will be numbered in order, starting with 1. The column ID for the column is returned in the columnid field.

The dwFlags field contains a bitmap that describes the characteristics of the column and can contain a combination of the following values:

DBCOLUMNFLAGS_CACHEDEFERRED: This flag is set if the column's data is cached, as determined by setting the DBPROP_CACHEDEFERRED property for the rowset.

DBCOLUMNFLAGS_ISBOOKMARK: Set if the column contains a bookmark.

DBCOLUMNFLAGS_ISFIXEDLENGTH: Set if all values for this column are the same length.

DBCOLUMNFLAGS_ISLONG: Set if the column contains long data, which is best retrieved by using one of the storage interfaces, although you can also retrieve the data with `IRowset::GetData()`.

DBCOLUMNFLAGS_ISNULLABLE: Set if you are allowed to set the column to NULL.

DBCOLUMNFLAGS_ISROWID: Set if the column contains a rowid, which is used only to identify the row and cannot be written to.

DBCOLUMNFLAGS_ISROWVER: Set if this column is only used for a provider-specific versioning scheme.

DBCOLUMNFLAGS_MAYBENULL: Set if the column can return a NULL value. In certain cases, such as with outer joins, this attribute can be different than DBCOLUMNFLAGS_ISNULLABLE.

DBCOLUMNFLAGS_MAYDEFER: Set if the data is not fetched from the data source until it is retrieved with a call to IRowset::GetData(). You can set this attribute by setting the DBPROP_DEFERRED property in the rowset property group.

DBCOLUMNFLAGS_WRITE: Set if the column can be written to by calling IRowsetChange::SetData().

DBCOLUMNFLAGS_WRITEUNKNOWN: Set if it is not known whether the column can be written.

The ulColumnSize field contains maximum length of the column's data. For columns of type DBTYPE_STR or DBTYPE_WSTR, this is given in characters (which are 2 bytes). For columns of type DBTYPE_BYTES, the maximum length is given in bytes. If there is not a maximum length, ulColumnSize will be set to 0xFFFFFFFF.

The wType field gives the type of the column data, and the bPrecision field gives the maximum precision for columns with numeric data types. If the column does not hold a numeric value, bPrecision is set to 0xFFFFFFFF. In addition, the bScale field gives the number of digits to the right of the decimal point.

IColumnsRowset::GetColumnsRowset()

In addition to GetColumnInfo(), you can retrieve more complete information about the columns in a rowset by calling GetColumnsRowset(), using the IColumnsRowset interface of a rowset or command object. GetColumnsRowset() will return a rowset object, which can contain a wide variety of optional information about the columns as well as the information returned by GetColumnInfo(). However, not all providers implement the IColumnsRowset interface.

Working with Accessors

In order to work with the data in a rowset, you will generally want to use accessor objects. *Accessors* are used to tell OLE DB about the structure of your client application's buffers, which are used either to hold column data from a rowset or values for command parameters.

Accessors are created by calling IAccessor::CreateAccessor(), which is exposed by both command objects and rowset objects. If you know about the structure of the rowset that will be returned from a command or if you are using command parameters, you will usually want to create an accessor from the command object before calling Execute(). All rowsets created by calls to Execute() will inherit any accessors that were created for the command object. In cases in which you do not know about the structure of the rowset ahead of time, you can create the accessor from the rowset object after it is created by a call to IOpenRowset::OpenRowset() or ICommand::Execute().

CreateAccessor()

After you have acquired a pointer to the IAccessor interface of a command or rowset object, you create the accessor by calling IAccessor::CreateAccessor(), shown here:

```
HRESULT CreateAccessor (DBACCESSORFLAGS dwAccessorFlags, ULONG cBindings,
    const DBBINDING rgBindings[], ULONG cbRowSize, HACCESSOR * phAccessor,
    DBBINDSTATUS rgStatus[]);
```

The dwAccessorFlags parameter is used to specify a combination of the following options for the accessor:

DBACCESSOR_PASSBYREF: Creates a reference accessor, which contains only pointers to the actual data buffers. For accessors used for parameters, these pointers refer to the application's memory, whereas row accessors contain pointers to the provider's memory. This type of accessor can provide greater efficiency, but it also requires prior knowledge of the provider's buffer layout and is generally used only with tightly coupled consumer/provider pairs. For more on reference accessors, see the OLE DB specification.

DBACCESSOR_ROWDATA: The accessor is used to describe bindings to columns in a rowset.

DBACCESSOR_PARAMETERDATA: The accessor is used to describe the bindings for parameters of a command.

DBACCESSOR_OPTIMIZED: This flag is used to create an optimized accessor, which can provide better performance. All optimized accessors must be created before the first row is fetched.

> **NOTE**
>
> An accessor can be either a rowset accessor or a parameter accessor, or it can even be both.

The cBindings parameter gives the number of bindings contained in the accessor, which is also the number of DBBINDING structures in the array passed in rgBindings.

The DBBINDING **Structure**

A DBBINDING structure is used to describe each binding in an accessor. This structure is shown here:

```
typedef struct tagDBBINDING {
    ULONG        iOrdinal;
    ULONG        obValue;
    ULONG        obLength;
    ULONG        obStatus;
    ITypeInfo *  pTypeInfo;
    DBOBJECT *   pObject;
    DBBINDEXT *  pBindExt;
    DBPART       dwPart;
    DBMEMOWNER   dwMemOwner;
    DBPARAMIO    eParamIO;
    ULONG        cbMaxLen;
    DWORD        dwFlags;
    DBTYPE       wType;
    BYTE         bPrecision;
    BYTE         bScale;
} DBBINDING;
```

The iOrdinal field gives the ordinal of the column (0 for the bookmark column, 1–*n* for other columns) or the parameter (numbered right to left in the command text, starting with 1).

The obValue, obLength, and obStatus fields give the offset into the consumer's buffer for the value, length, and status for a column or parameter. The binding can use any combination of these, as determined by the value passed in the dwPart field of the DBBINDING structure.

The pTypeInfo and pBindExt fields are reserved, and should be set to NULL. In addition, dwFlags is currently reserved and should be set to 0.

The pObject field can be used to access OLE objects by passing a pointer to a DBOBJECT structure, which specifies options for the object and a requested interface. For more on this, see the online documentation.

The dwPart field is used to specify which parts of the buffer are to be bound and can include any combination of the following values:

> DBPART_VALUE: The value of the column/parameter.
>
> DBPART_LENGTH: The length of the column/parameter.
>
> DBPART_STATUS: The status for the column/parameter.

The dwMemOwner field is used to specify who will assume ownership of any memory that must be allocated by the provider. For example, when returning a value with wType of DBTYPE_BYREF | DBTYPE_STR, if dwMemOwner is DBMEMOWNER_CLIENTOWNER, the client will own the memory at the pointer returned and is responsible for freeing it. If dwMemOwner is set to DBMEMOWNER_ PROVIDEROWNED, the provider will free the memory.

The eParamIO field is used to specify the type of bound parameter and is ignored for row accessors. eParamIO can have a combination of the following values:

DBPARAMIO_NOTPARAM: Used for row accessors.

DBPARAMIO_INPUT: Specifies an input parameter.

DBPARAMIO_OUTPUT: Specifies an output parameter.

The cbMaxLen field is used to pass the maximum length of the consumer's buffer for the data value at obValue.

The wType field specifies the data type for the value part of the buffer. This can include a wide range of types defined for OLE DB, as specified by a DBTYPE_ constant. Just a few of the possibilities are listed here:

DBTYPE_NUMERIC: A floating-point value.

DBTYPE_I2: A 2-byte integer.

DBTYPE_I4: A 4-byte integer.

DBTYPE_BOOL: A Boolean value.

DBTYPE_VARIANT: An OLE variant.

DBTYPE_BYTES: An array of bytes.

DBTYPE_STR: An ASCII string.

DBTYPE_WSTR: A Unicode string.

OLE DB will provide type conversion between the type specified in the binding and the actual type of the data stored in the provider. For more on the specifics of this conversion and special cases, see the OLE DB specification.

Lastly, the bPrecision and bScale fields are used to specify the desired precision and scale of NUMERIC and DECIMAL data.

Accessing Data with the Accessor

When you call CreateAccessor(), the handle to the new accessor will be written at phAccessor and an array of DBBINDSTATUS structures passed by rgStatus will be updated to reflect the status of each of the bindings, telling you whether each binding was validated successfully.

After the accessor is created, you can use it to move data between the provider and your consumer application each time you fetch the data for a new row—or, in the case of parameter accessors, each time you execute the command. You will see how to use accessors in fetching the data for a row in the next section, when you look at IRowset::GetData().

When you are done with an accessor, you can clean up the resources it is using by calling IAccessor::ReleaseAccessor() and passing the accessor handle returned by CreateAccessor().

In addition, you can query the bindings that are currently used by an accessor by calling IAccessor::GetBindings().

Fetching Rows

Now that you have seen how to create the rowset and accessor objects, let's get down to business and start fetching data. When a rowset is created, it is positioned at the beginning of the rowset. You can retrieve the first set of rows within the rowset by calling `IRowset::GetNextRows()`, shown here:

```
HRESULT GetNextRows (HCHAPTER hReserved, LONG lRowsOffset, LONG cRows,
                     ULONG * pcRowsObtained, HROW ** prghRows);
```

As you might guess, `hReserved` is currently reserved and can be ignored.

The `lRowsOffset` parameter gives the offset from the current row at which to begin fetching rows. If this value is `0`, successive calls will scroll forward through the recordset, starting with the next row not yet fetched. You can use a positive value of `lRowsOffset` to skip over a number of rows. If the `DBPROP_CANSCROLLBACKWARDS` property for the rowset is set to `VARIANT_TRUE`, you can also use a negative value for `lRowsOffset`, which will back up a number of rows in the rowset and begin fetching forward from there.

`cRows` gives the number of rows to fetch. Positive numbers fetch forward, and a negative value can be used to fetch backwards, provided that the rowset's `DBPROP_CANFETCHBACKWARDS` property is set to `VARIANT_TRUE`. The actual number of rows fetched is returned at `pcRowsObtained`.

If any rows are successfully fetched, the provider will return a pointer to an array of handles to the individual rows fetched at `prghRows`. You can set `*prghRows` to `NULL` to have the provider allocate an array for you (which must be freed with `IMalloc::Free()`), or you can pass a pointer to a buffer you have allocated; just make sure it is big enough for the number of rows being fetched.

At any time, you can reset the current position of the rowset to the beginning by calling `IRowset::RestartPosition()`.

IRowset::GetData()

To get to the data for each row returned by `GetNextRows()`, you will need to make one more function call to `IRowset::GetData()`, shown here:

```
HRESULT GetData (HROW hRow, HACCESSOR hAccessor, void * pData);
```

This function takes a row handle (`hRow`), such as the one returned from `GetNextRows()`, an accessor handle (`hAccessor`), such as the one returned by `CreateAccessor()`, and a pointer to a data buffer (`pData`). This data buffer will be filled with the data for the row, as described in the bindings of the accessor.

The following example shows how to create an accessor and use it to retrieve data from a rowset that was previously created by calling `ICommand::Execute()`:

```
// Structure for Row data
typedef struct tagMyRowStruct {
    ULONG ulNum;
```

```
    char szTitle[100];
    ULONG ulPages;
} MyRowStruct, *pMyRowStruct;

MyRowStruct  myRowData;
ULONG RowCount = 0;
HROW *pRowHandles = NULL;

IAccessor* pIRowAccessor = NULL;
HACCESSOR hRowAccessor = NULL;

DBBINDING rgRowBind[] =
{
    1, offsetof(MyParmsStruct, ulNum), 0, 0, NULL, NULL,
        NULL, DBPART_VALUE, DBMEMOWNER_CLIENTOWNED,
        DBPARAMIO_NOTPARAM, sizeof(ULONG), 0, DBTYPE_UI4, 0, 0,
    2, offsetof(MyParmsStruct, szTitle), 0, 0, NULL, NULL,
        NULL, DBPART_VALUE, DBMEMOWNER_CLIENTOWNED,
        DBPARAMIO_NOTPARAM, 100, 0, DBTYPE_STR, 0, 0,
    3, offsetof(MyParmsStruct, ulPages), 0, 0, NULL, NULL,
        NULL, DBPART_VALUE, DBMEMOWNER_CLIENTOWNED,
        DBPARAMIO_NOTPARAM, sizeof(ULONG), 0, DBTYPE_UI4, 0, 0
};


// Create Accessor
hr = pIComRowset->QueryInterface(IID_IAccessor, (LPVOID*)&pIRowAccessor);

hr = pIRowAccessor->CreateAccessor(DBACCESSOR_ROWDATA, 3, rgRowBind,
                            sizeof(rgRowBind), &hRowAccessor, NULL);

// Fetch row handles for next 10 rows
hr = pIComRowset->GetNextRows(NULL, 0, 10, &RowCount, &pRowHandles);
if(SUCCEEDED(hr))
{
    for(int i=0; (i<RowCount) && (i<10); i++)
    {
        // Fetch Data for each row handle
        hr = pIComRowset->GetData(pRowHandles[i], hRowAccessor, &myRowData);
        if(FAILED(hr))
            TRACE("Error in GetData\n");
        else
        {
            TRACE("Num: %d Title: [%s] Pages: %d\n",
                myRowData.ulNum, myRowData.szTitle, myRowData.ulPages);
        }
    } // end for
}
```

When you are finished with a row or set of rows from the rowset, you should call
IRowset::ReleaseRows() to release the resources for the rows.

Using IRowsetLocate

In addition to the GetNextRows() function, you can use several different functions of the
IRowsetLocate interface to navigate within a rowset by using bookmarks.

By calling `IRowsetLocate::GetRowsByBookmark()`, you can fetch a set of rows that match an array of bookmarks.

You can also begin fetching a set of rows a specified number of rows from a row that matches a bookmark by calling `IRowsetLocate::GetRowsAt()`.

The `IRowsetLocate` interface also exposes the `Compare()` function, which can be used to compare two bookmarks to determine their relative positions in the rowset or to check whether they refer to the same row.

IRowsetScroll

OLE DB also specifies the `IRowsetScroll` interface, which is derived from `IRowsetLocate` and provides functions that are useful for applications that allow the user to scroll through a rowset. Most of the results returned by functions of `IRowsetScroll` are approximations and should only be used where "close enough" is all that your application needs.

The handiest of the functions included in the `IRowsetScroll` interface is `GetRowsAtRatio()`, which allows you to fetch a number of rows that fall somewhere near a certain fractional number of rows in the rowset. For example, you could use `GetRowsAtRatio()` to simply fetch a set of rows that are somewhere around three-fourths of the way into the rowset.

In addition, `IRowsetScroll` exposes the `GetApproximatePosition()` function, which will return an approximate row number for a given row, as specified by its bookmark.

Updating the Data Source

Up to this point, you have seen how to retrieve data from a data source. Now let's take a look at how to make changes to the data in the data source. Often, the simplest way to make changes to the database is just to execute a command that adds new rows or does any other modifying that you are interested in, such as SQL `INSERT`, `DELETE`, or `UPDATE` statements. However, OLE DB also provides several other programmatic mechanisms, as you will see in this section.

IRowsetChange

The first modification mechanism that we will look at is the `IRowsetChange` interface, which can be exposed by rowset objects—although it is not required and thus is not implemented by all providers.

Inserting Rows

For inserting rows, you can use `IRowsetChange::InsertRow()`, shown here:

```
HRESULT InsertRow (HCHAPTER hReserved, HACCESSOR hAccessor,
                   void * pData, HROW * phRow);
```

When calling InsertRow(), you can pass the handle to an accessor that you have previously created to describe the bindings of the row data, in which case the data for the new row is taken from the buffer at pData, as specified by the accessor. If you pass an accessor handle for an accessor with no bindings, a new row will be created with default values. After the new row is created, its handle will be returned at phRow.

> **NOTE**
>
> If the OLE DB provider uses delayed update mode—that is, if it supports the IRowsetUpdate interface—the changes are not transmitted to the database until you call IRowsetUpdate::Update(). We will look at this in more detail in the next section on the IRowsetUpdate interface.

Deleting Rows

The IRowsetChange interface also allows you to delete rows by calling IRowsetChange::DeleteRows(), shown here:

```
HRESULT DeleteRows (HCHAPTER hReserved, ULONG cRows, const HROW rghRows[],
                    DBROWSTATUS rgRowStatus[]);
```

To delete a number of rows, pass the number of rows to delete in cRows and fill the rghRows array with the handles of the rows to delete. When DeleteRows() returns, you can check the result of each deletion by looking at the element of rgRowStatus that corresponds to each row. If this value is DBROWSTATUS_S_OK, the row was successfully deleted.

Updating Rows

For existing rows in a rowset, you can modify the current values by calling IRowsetChange::SetData(), shown here:

```
HRESULT SetData (HROW hRow, HACCESSOR hAccessor, void * pData);
```

When calling SetData(), you should pass the handle of the row to be updated in hRow and the handle of the accessor that describes the data in pData should be passed in hAccessor. SetData() will read the data from pData according to the bindings in the accessor and update the row's data accordingly. Once again, keep in mind that if the rowset supports IRowsetUpdate, the data will not be changed until you call IRowsetUpdate::Update().

IRowsetUpdate **and Delayed Updates**

If a rowset supports the IRowsetUpdate interface, it will always operate in delayed update mode and changes made via the IRowsetChange interface will not be sent to the data source until you call IRowsetUpdate::Update(). For rowsets that do not support IRowsetUpdate, the rowset will always operate in immediate update mode and changes made via the IRowsetChange interface are sent immediately.

The IRowsetUpdate interface provides a simple method of caching changes to the database and sending them to the data source in one batch. This can make your applications more efficient, and can also be used as a simple method of managing transactions, although we will take a look at a more robust transaction mechanism in the section titled "Transactions," later in this chapter.

IRowsetUpdate::Update()

For rowsets that support IRowsetUpdate, you can make changes to the rowset via the IRowsetChange interface. These changes are cached within the rowset until you send them to the data source with a call to IRowsetUpdate::Update(), shown here:

```
HRESULT Update (HCHAPTER hReserved, ULONG cRows, const HROW rghRows[],
    ULONG * pcRows, HROW ** prgRows, DBROWSTATUS** prgRowStatus);
```

When calling Update(), you can pass a value of 0 in cRows to update all pending changes for the rowset. In addition, you can choose to update only certain rows by passing an array of row handles in rghRows and passing the number of entries in this array in cRows.

Upon completion, Update() will return the number of rows for which updates were attempted at pcRows, and will return pointers to an array of row handles at prgRows, and to an array of row statuses at prgRowStatus. These arrays can be used to see which rows were updated, and whether or not the update was successful. If the entry in the row status array is DBROWSTATUS_S_OK, the changes were made successfully.

> **NOTE**
>
> You can retrieve a list of all rows for the rowset that have pending changes by calling IRowsetUpdate::GetPendingRows(). You can also check on the pending change status for a specific set of rows by calling IRowsetUpdate::GetRowStatus().

IRowsetUpdate::Undo()

If the rowset you are using uses delayed updates, you can also choose to undo any pending changes that the rowset is holding on to by calling IRowsetUpdate::Undo(), shown here, instead of Update():

```
HRESULT Undo (HCHAPTER hReserved, ULONG cRows, const HROW rghRows[],
    ULONG * pcRows, HROW ** prgRows, DBROWSTATUS ** prgRowStatus);
```

Undo() allows you to specify rows to undo with the same mechanism you saw above for Update(), although you can always pass a value of 0 for cRows to undo all changes since the last call to Update(). Also, like Update(), Undo() will return arrays of the row handles and statuses of the rows for which changes were undone.

IRowsetUpdate::GetOriginalData()

If you want to compare the current values of a row in the rowset (which can include delayed changes) to the original value of the row data (from when the row was originally fetched or last had changes sent to the data source), you can retrieve the original data by calling `IRowsetUpdate::GetOriginalData()`, which takes a row handle, and an accessor handle, which specifies how the data is to be returned in you buffer.

> **NOTE**
>
> `GetOriginalData()` does not have any effect on any pending changes that can be cached in the rowset.

Transactions

I mentioned earlier, when I first talked about creating session objects, that the session is used for managing transactions. This section discusses how to use a session to manage transactions, which can involve many different operations on many recordsets created by the session. Although you could use the `IRecordsetUpdate` `Update()` and `Undo()` functions to implement some simple transaction processing, it is not as robust as the session method, nor does it allow you to work with multiple recordsets or nest transactions.

Beginning a Transaction

When a session is created, it is in autocommit, or implicit commit, mode. This means that each operation is committed automatically and you do not need to do much with the session object.

To use the session's transaction management capabilities, you will need to begin a transaction, which will place the session in a manual, or explicit, commit mode, where all of the operations that occur between the start and end of the transaction are handled as one operation—that is, either all of the changes are made, or none of the changes is made.

Beginning a transaction is done with a call to `ITransaction::StartTransaction()`. You will need to call `QueryInterface()` on the session object to get a pointer to the `ITransaction` interface, then call `StartTransaction()`, shown here:

```
HRESULT StartTransaction (ISOLEVEL isoLevel, ULONG isoFlags,
    ITransactionOptions * pOtherOptions, ULONG * pulTransactionLevel);
```

The `isoLevel` parameter is used to set the isolation level for the new transaction, which determines the level at which this transaction is isolated from other operations on the database.

Although a low level of isolation can execute more quickly, it also opens the door to one or more of the following difficulties:

Dirty Reads: When a transaction reads data that has been modified by a second transaction, but has not yet been committed. If this second transaction is rolled back, inconsistencies can occur.

Non-repeatable Reads: When a transaction reads a row, which is subsequently changed by another transaction. The first transaction is unable to re-read that data and get the same result.

Phantoms: A transaction reads a set of rows, and a second transaction adds new rows. If the first transaction requeries the database, it will not receive the same set of rows.

isoLevel can be set to one of the following values:

ISOLATIONLEVEL_CHAOS: As the name suggests, this level is susceptible to most isolation difficulties.

ISOLATIONLEVEL_READUNCOMMITTED: Allows a transaction to read the uncommitted data of other transactions. This can allow dirty reads, non-repeatable reads, and phantoms.

ISOLATIONLEVEL_READCOMMITTED: The transaction cannot see the uncommitted data of other transactions. This eliminates the possibility of dirty reads, but the other problems can occur.

ISOLATIONLEVEL_REPEATABLEREAD: The transaction will not see any changes made by other transactions to values that it has read. This eliminates dirty and non-repeatable reads, but can allow phantoms.

ISOLATIONLEVEL_SERIALIZABLE: This forces transactions to be executed as if they were executed serially, rather than concurrently. This eliminates all of the above difficulties.

The isoFlags parameter is not currently used and should be set to 0. The pOtherOptions parameter can be set to NULL or can contain a pointer to a session options object returned by GetOptionsObject().

When the new transaction is created, StartTransaction() will return the nesting level of the new transaction at pulTransactionLevel. You can pass NULL in pulTransaction if you are not concerned with the transaction level.

Committing a Transaction

After you have started a transaction, you are free to perform operations on the data that will be part of the transaction. If all of the operations that make up the transaction are successful and you want to commit the changes to the database, you will need to call ITransaction::Commit().

Although Commit() is a method of the ITransaction interface, you can call it via a pointer to an ITransactionLocal interface, because it is derived from ITransaction.

The prototype for Commit() is shown here:

```
HRESULT Commit(BOOL fRetaining, DWORD grfTC, DWORD grfRM);
```

The fRetaining parameter is used to specify whether the session will remain in manual commit mode after this transaction is committed. If you plan to start a new transaction right away, you can pass TRUE for fRetaining and avoid an additional call to StartTransaction(). If you pass FALSE, the session will revert to autocommit mode.

The grfTC parameter is used to specify when the call to Commit() will return. If this is set to XACTTC_ASYNC, Commit() will return immediately and the commit is completed asynchronously. If this is set to XACTTC_SYNC_PHASEONE or XACTTC_SYNC_PHASETWO, the call to commit will not return until after the first or second phase of the commit protocol is completed.

Currently, the grfRM parameter must be set to 0.

> ### CAUTION
>
> Committing a transaction can invalidate the rowsets that have been created from this session. For rowsets with the DBPROP_COMMITPRESERVE property set to FALSE, the rowset will be invalidated, or zombied, when the transaction is committed. If DBPROP_COMMITPRESERVE is set to TRUE, the rowset will remain unaltered when the transaction is committed.

Aborting a Transaction

If something has gone wrong in the processing of the operations that make up the transaction or if you just change your mind, you can abort the transaction by calling ITransaction::Abort(). This will "undo" all the operations that were performed up to that point, leaving the data source as if the operations never occurred at all.

The prototype for ITransaction::Abort() is shown here:

```
HRESULT Abort( BOID * pboidReason, BOOL fRetaining,
BOOL fAsync);
```

You can pass a pointer to a BOID in pboidReason giving the reason for the abort, or you can just set pboidReason to NULL, thus not giving a reason for the abort.

Like Commit(), if the fRetaining parameter is set to TRUE, the session will remain in manual commit mode after the abort and you will not need to call StartTransaction() to begin a new manual transaction. If you pass FALSE for fRetaining, the session will enter autocommit mode after the call to Abort().

If you pass TRUE for fAsync, the abort operation will complete asynchronously. You can set fAsync to FALSE to force the call to Abort() to block until the abort completes.

> **CAUTION**
>
> Aborting a transaction can also invalidate rowsets in the session, depending on the value of the DBPROP_ABORTPRESERVE property of each rowset.

Using Enumerators

OLE DB provides enumerator objects to allow your application to view a list of all the available data sources, as well as other available enumerators. This provides a recursive, hierarchical mechanism to search through all available data sources and enumerators, in much the same way as the DOS directory structure lets you search through all available files and directories.

This architecture also allows providers to implement their own enumerators, which are able to enumerate the data sources that they know how to handle. For example, if someone were to implement a data provider for accessing a certain type of widget data, that provider might also implement an enumerator that can list all of the available widget data. Due to the hierarchical nature of OLE DB enumerators, the consumer could use the system root enumerator to find the widget enumerator, which can then be used to locate a specific widget.

Instantiating the Root Enumerator

To start searching for a particular data source, you will need a starting point. OLE DB provides this in the form of its root enumerator, provided with the OLE DB SDK, and identified by CLSID_OLEDB_ENUMERATOR. To create an instance of the root enumerator, you should call CoCreateInstance() to create a new object of class CLSID_OLEDB_ENUMERATOR. In almost all cases, it is easiest to request that CoCreateInstance() return a pointer to the ISourcesRowset interface, which you will be using next.

ISourcesRowset::GetSourcesRowset()

After you have created an enumerator, you will probably want to start finding out about the available data sources (and other enumerators) on the system. This is done by retrieving a rowset listing the available sources by calling ISourcesRowset::GetSourcesRowset(), shown here:

```
HRESULT GetSourcesRowset(IUnknown pUnkOuter, REFIID riid, ULONG cPropertySets,
    DBPROPSET rgPropertySets[], IUnknown ** ppSourcesRowset);
```

As in other OLE DB functions that create new objects, the pUnkOuter parameter is used only in creating aggregates, and the riid parameter is used to request the type of interface pointer to return at ppSourcesRowset. Because GetSourcesRowset() creates a rowset object, you will want to request one of the rowset interfaces, such as IRowset or IAccessor. You can set specific options for the new rowset by filling in the rgPropertySets array with DBPROPSET structures and setting cPropertySets to the number of entries added.

You saw earlier in this chapter how to work with rowsets, so we won't spend any more time on that now, but we will take a look at the data that is returned in the read-only rowset generated by `GetSourcesRowset()`. The new rowset will contain the following columns:

`SOURCES_NAME`: The name of the data source or enumerator.

`SOURCES_PARSENAME`: A string that can be passed to `ParseDisplayName()` to obtain a moniker for the data source or enumerator. We will see how to use this later.

`SOURCES_DESCRIPTION`: A brief text description of the data source or enumerator.

`SOURCES_TYPE`: Used to determine the type of this entry. This will be `DBSOURCETYPE_DATASOURCE` for entries describing data sources or `DBSOURCETYPE_ENUMERATOR` for entries describing enumerators.

`SOURCES_ISPARENT`: This field is meaningful only in rows that describe enumerators. If this is set to `VARIANT_TRUE`, the enumerator described in this row contains the enumerator that was used to call `GetSourcesRowset()`. You can use this enumerator to provide the OLE DB equivalent of moving up one directory in the directory tree.

Using the information contained in the rowset generated by `GetSourcesRowset()` you can browse through the list of available data sources and enumerators. After you have located an object that you want to instantiate and use, whether it be a data source or an enumerator, you will need to generate a moniker for the object and call `BindMoniker()`, as you will see next.

Instantiating Objects from the Sources Rowset

The entries in the rowset generated by `GetSourcesRowset()` contain valuable information about available OLE DB objects, but they do not contain the objects themselves, and, without objects, you can't make OLE DB *do* anything. Fortunately, enumerators do allow you to create objects, based on the information contained in the sources rowset.

Instantiating an object from the sources rowset begins with the `SOURCES_PARSENAME` field of the rowset. This string provides the information needed to create the object specified by the rowset entry. This string is converted into a moniker by calling the `ParseDisplayName()` method of the `IParseDisplayName` interface exposed by enumerators. The prototype for `ParseDisplayName()` is shown here:

```
HRESULT ParseDisplayName( IBindCtx *pbc, LPOLESTR pszDisplayName,
    ULONG *pchEaten, IMoniker **ppmkOut);
```

The pbc parameter can be used to pass a bind context for the binding operation. In most cases, you can simply pass `NULL` in pbc. You should pass the value returned in the `SOURCES_PARSENAME` field in the pszDisplayName parameter.

If `ParseDisplayName()` succeeds, it will return a pointer to the `IMoniker` interface of the new moniker at ppmkOut. It will also return the number of characters in the string passed in pszDisplayName that correspond to the new moniker. In most cases, you can ignore this value.

After you have created a moniker for the object by calling `ParseDisplayName()`, you can create the new data source or enumerator object by passing the moniker pointer in a call to `BindMoniker()`, shown here:

```
HRESULT BindMoniker( LPMONIKER pmk, DWORD grfOpt,
    REFIID iidResult, LPVOID FAR *ppvResult);
```

You should pass the moniker pointer returned from `ParseDisplayName()` in pmk and the type of interface pointer you would like to receive in iidResult. grfOpt is reserved and must be 0. If `BindMoniker()` is successful, a new object is created and the requested interface pointer is returned at ppvResult. At this point, you have a fully functional data source or enumerator object that you are free to use.

The following example shows how to use an enumerator to search through the available data sources, find the entry for MSDASQL, and instantiate it from a moniker:

```
IRowset * pIRowset = NULL;
IAccessor* pIAccessor = NULL;
DBBINDING rgBind[3];
ULONG cbRow = 0;
const ULONG SOURCES_CBMAXLEN = 64;
HACCESSOR hAccessor = NULL;
#define MAX_NUM_SOURCES 16
ULONG RowsReturned = 0;
HROW rghRows[MAX_NUM_SOURCES];
HROW* pRows = rghRows;
WCHAR myParseName[DEF_SOURCES_CBMAXLEN];
IDBInitialize* pIDBInitialize;
ULONG chEaten;
IMoniker* pIMoniker = NULL;
IParseDisplayName* pIParseDisplayName;


// Create Enumerator
hr = CoCreateInstance(CLSID_OLEDB_ENUMERATOR, NULL,
                      CLSCTX_INPROC_SERVER,
                      IID_ISourcesRowset,
                      (LPVOID*)&pISrcRowset);

// Generate rowset from the enumerator
hr = pISrcRowset->GetSourcesRowset(NULL, IID_IRowset,
                          0, NULL, (IUnknown**)&pIRowset);

//Create an accessor for the sources rowset
hr = pIRowset->QueryInterface(IID_IAccessor, (LPVOID*)&pIAccessor);

// Set up bindings for CreateAccessor
rgBind[0].iOrdinal = 1; //eid_SOURCES_NAME;
rgBind[0].cbMaxLen = DEF_SOURCES_CBMAXLEN;
rgBind[0].wType = DBTYPE_STR;

rgBind[1].iOrdinal = 2; //eid_SOURCES_PARSENAME;
rgBind[1].cbMaxLen = DEF_SOURCES_CBMAXLEN * sizeof(WCHAR);
rgBind[1].wType = DBTYPE_WSTR;
```

```
rgBind[2].iOrdinal = 4; //eid_SOURCES_TYPE;
rgBind[2].cbMaxLen = sizeof(ULONG);
rgBind[2].wType = DBTYPE_UI4;

for(int i=0;i<3;i++)
{
    rgBind[i].obValue = cbRow;
    rgBind[i].obLength = 0;
    rgBind[i].obStatus = 0;
    rgBind[i].pTypeInfo = NULL;
    rgBind[i].pObject = NULL;
    rgBind[i].pBindExt = NULL;
    rgBind[i].dwPart = DBPART_VALUE; // ¦ DBPART_LENGTH ¦ DBPART_STATUS;
    rgBind[i].dwMemOwner = DBMEMOWNER_CLIENTOWNED;
    rgBind[i].eParamIO = DBPARAMIO_NOTPARAM;
    rgBind[i].dwFlags = 0;
    rgBind[i].bPrecision = 0;
    rgBind[i].bScale = 0;

    cbRow += rgBind[i].cbMaxLen;
}

hr = pIAccessor->CreateAccessor(DBACCESSOR_ROWDATA, 3, rgBind,
                            sizeof(rgBind[0]), &hAccessor, NULL);

// Get Row handles from sources rowset
hr = pIRowset->GetNextRows(NULL, 0, MAX_NUM_SOURCES,
                    &RowsReturned, &pRows);
if(SUCCEEDED(hr))
{
    BYTE* pData = NULL;
    pData = new BYTE[cbRow];

    for(ULONG i=0; (i<RowsReturned) && (i<MAX_NUM_SOURCES); i++)
    {
        memset(pData, 0, cbRow);
        hr = pIRowset->GetData(rghRows[i], hAccessor, pData);
        if(FAILED(hr))
            TRACE("Error in GetData\n");
        else
        {
            TRACE("Name: [%s] ParseName: [%S] Type: %d\n",
                pData + rgBind[0].obValue,
                pData + rgBind[1].obValue,
                *(ULONG *)(pData + rgBind[2].obValue));

            if(!strcmp((const char *)pData+rgBind[0].obValue, "MSDASQL"))
                wcscpy(myParseName, (const WCHAR*)(pData+rgBind[1].obValue));
        } // end else
    } // end for

    delete pData;
}
else
{
    TRACE("Error in GetNextRows\n");
}
```

```
// Instantiate MSDASQL from enumerator info
hr = pISrcRowset->QueryInterface(IID_IParseDisplayName, (void**)
&pIParseDisplayName);

// Create Moniker
hr = pIParseDisplayName->ParseDisplayName(NULL, myParseName, &chEaten, &pIMoniker);

// Instantiate from moniker
hr = BindMoniker(pIMoniker, 0, IID_IDBInitialize, (void**)&pIDBInitialize);
```

Extended OLE DB Error Handling

In addition to the return codes and various status arrays returned by the functions of the OLE DB API, the OLE DB specification defines a set of interfaces for retrieving extended information about errors.

If a provider supports extended error objects for a given object, the object will expose the ISupportErrorInfo interface. You can call the InterfaceSupportsErrorInfo() member of ISupportErrorInfo to determine whether error objects are supported for a given interface.

If error objects are supported for a given interface and the return code for a method of that interface indicates that an error has occurred, you can retrieve a pointer to an IErrorInfo interface by calling the OLE automation function GetErrorInfo().

You can use this pointer to call one of the following methods to retrieve additional information about the first error returned:

GetDescription(): Returns a textual description of the error.

GetGUID(): Returns the GUID of the interface that generated the error.

GetHelpContext(): Returns the help context ID for the error.

GetHelpFile(): Returns the path to the help file containing a description for the error.

GetSource(): Returns the name of the component that generated the error.

However, the methods of IErrorInfo will return only the information about the first error returned, even though many providers can support multiple errors from a single function call. To access the full set of errors returned, you can call QueryInterface() on the IErrorInfo pointer to get a pointer to an IErrorRecords interface.

Using the IErrorRecords interface pointer, you can call GetRecordCount() to retrieve the number of available error records. You can then call IErrorRecords::GetErrorInfo() to retrieve an IErrorInfo interface pointer for each error. You can then use the methods of IErrorInfo shown above to retrieve info about the errors. The following example shows how to retrieve extended error information for multiple errors:

```
// pObjWithErrors is a pointer to the object that generated the error
// and IID_BadIID is the interface ID for the interface that generated
// the error
```

```
IErrorInfo* pErrorInfo;
IErrorInfo* pErrorInfoRec;
IErrorRecords* pErrorRecords;
ISupportErrorInfo* pSupportErrorInfo;
HRESULT hr;
ULONG i;
ULONG ulNumErrorRecs;
char szBuffer [MAXBUFLEN+1];
DWORD MyLocale = 0x409 // Locale for American English
char szTmp[MAXBUFLEN+32];

hr = pObjWithErrors->QueryInterface (IID_ISupportErrorInfo,
                                (void**)&pSupportErrorInfo);

if (SUCCEEDED(hr))
{
    hr = pSupportErrorInfo->InterfaceSupportsErrorInfo(IID_BadIID);
  if (hr ==S_OK)
  // Object supports error objects
  {
    // Retrieve error object
    hr = GetErrorInfo (0,&pErrorInfo);

    //retrieve IErrorRecord pointer
    hr = pErrorInfo->QueryInterface (IID_IErrorRecords,
                        (LPVOID FAR*)&pErrorRecords);

    // Get Count of available error records
    hr = pErrorRecords->GetRecordCount (&ulNumErrorRecs);

    // Dump info for each error
    for (i=0;i<ulNumErrorRecs;i++)
    {
        BSTR bstrDescription = NULL;
        BSTR bstrSource = NULL;
        WCHAR wszSource = NULL;
        WCHAR wszDescription = NULL;

        // Get record for individual error
        hr = pErrorRecords->GetErrorInfo (i,MyLocale,&pErrorInfoRec);

        hr = pErrorInfoRec->GetDescription (&bstrDescription);
        hr = pErrorInfoRec->GetSource (&bstrSourceOfError);

        if (bstrDescription!=NULL )
        {
            WideCharToMultiByte(CP_ACP, 0, bstrDescription, -1,
                szBuffer, MAXBUFLEN+1, NULL, NULL);
            TRACE("Description: %s \n", szBuffer);
            SysFreeString (bstrDescription);
        }
        if (bstrSource!=NULL )
        {
            WideCharToMultiByte(CP_ACP, 0, bstrSource, -1,
                szBuffer, MAXBUFLEN+1, NULL, NULL);
            TRACE("Source: %s \n");
            SysFreeString (bstrSource);
        }
```

```
        // Clean up
        if (pErrorInfoRec)
            pErrorInfoRec->Release();
    } // end for

    if (pErrorInfo)
        pErrorInfo->Release();
    if (pErrorRecords)
        pErrorRecords->Release();
    } // end if S_OK
} // end if SUCCEEDED

if (pSupportErrorInfo)
    pSupportErrorInfo->Release();
```

For SQL providers, you can also retrieve ODBC-specific error information by calling `IErrorRecords::GetCustomErrorObject()` to return a custom error object for each error. These custom error objects support the `ISQLErrorInfo` interface, which can be used to call `GetSQLInfo()` for the error. `GetSQLInfo()` will return the SQLSTATE and native error generated by the provider.

Summary

This chapter takes a look at programming consumer applications in OLE DB, Microsoft's new database API based on the Common Object Model. However, consumer applications are only part of the OLE DB picture. OLE DB also allows you to implement your own data providers, which maintain their own data, or service providers, which gather data from one or more data providers and pass it on to consumer applications.

This chapter also looks at the component objects that make up OLE DB, including data source objects, sessions, commands, transactions, rowsets, and errors—and how to use them in developing a consumer application, using the MSDASQL OLE DB ODBC data provider, provided by Microsoft, which allows you to use OLE DB to access existing ODBC data sources.

As you might have noticed, OLE DB applications can get to be a bit complicated, not to mention verbose. The next chapter looks at Active Data Objects (ADO), which is similar to OLE DB, but provides a simpler interface.

28

Programming with ActiveX Data Objects (ADO)

by David Bennett

This chapter takes a look at ActiveX Data Objects, or ADO, Microsoft's latest object-oriented interface to databases and other similar sources of data. ADO is intended to replace the Data Access Objects (DAO) and Remote Data Objects (RDO) interfaces, providing both a wider array of features, as well as a higher degree of flexibility.

ADO provides a specification for a set of objects that can be used to work with data from many different sorts of applications. ADO is based on the Common Object Model (COM), which provides objects that are available from a wide range of programming languages, including Visual C++, as well as Visual Basic, Visual Basic for Applications (VBA), Visual J++, VBScript, and JavaScript applications. ADO can also be quite useful in server or middle-tier applications, particularly when used with Microsoft's Active Server Pages.

ADO Data Sources

ADO provides only a specification for the various objects used in ADO and does not provide a specific implementation. However, Microsoft does include an ADO implementation to access any available OLE DB data sources, including Microsoft's new Active Directory provider, which exposes an OLE DB interface for working with file systems. This implementation of ADO for OLE DB is known as ADODB.

ADODB can also be used to access the Microsoft OLE DB provider for ODBC (MSDASQL), which will provide access to any available ODBC data sources.

We will be using Microsoft's ADO implementation for OLE DB (ADODB), coupled with MSDASQL to access various ODBC data sources in the examples in this chapter. However, you might find other implementations useful in your applications, as they become available. You might also want to implement your own ADO objects at some point, although this is a bit beyond the scope of this chapter.

ADO Objects

The ADO interface is based on a collection of objects that is considerably simpler to use than the OLE DB objects in the last chapter. Although the structure of the objects in ADO is similar to OLE DB, ADO objects are not as dependent on the object hierarchy. In most cases, you can simply create and use only the objects you need to work with, and not worry about creating many other "parent" objects that you don't really care to do anything with.

The following object classes make up the bulk of the ADO interface:

> `Connection`: Used to represent a connection to a data source, as well as to handle some commands and transactions.
>
> `Command`: Used to work with commands sent to the data source.
>
> `Recordset`: Used to work with a tabular set of data, including fetching and modifying data.

`Field`: Used to represent information about a column in a recordset, including the values for the column, as well as other information.

`Parameter`: Used to pass data to and from commands that are sent to the data source.

`Property`: Used to manipulate specific properties of the other objects used in ADO.

`Error`: Used to retrieve more specific information about errors that may occur.

This chapter will look at each of these objects in greater detail in the next few sections and then takes a look at how to use ADO within applications.

Connection **Objects**

ADO uses `Connection` objects to represent an individual connection to a data source. If you are using ADODB, this will be a connection to an OLE DB data source. Of course, if you are also using MSDASQL, this OLE DB data source might also correspond to an ODBC data source. The connection can be an actual network connection to a database server or a connection to a local database file, such as those used by Microsoft Access.

Any operations performed on a data source require a `Connection` object, although you don't necessarily need to create it yourself. In many cases, you can simply let ADO create a connection used by `Command` or `Recordset` objects. However, you can also perform many operations by using just the `Connection` object. `Connection` objects are also used to create a single connection that is used by several other objects, which can be useful for optimizing your application. `Connection` objects are also used to manage transactions in ADO.

Connection **Properties**

All ADO `Connection` objects have the following properties, although specific implementations offer additional properties:

`Attributes`: Used to describe certain characteristics of the connection. For ADODB, this will contain the current setting for transaction retention.

`CommandTimeout`: Contains the timeout value to be used for executing commands. This value is also used for other `Command` objects using this connection, although the `Command` objects can override this value by setting their own command timeout.

`ConnectionString`: Contains information that is used to connect to the data source. This can include the provider, data source, user, password, and/or filename of the data source.

`ConnectionTimeout`: The timeout value that is used when attempting to establish a connection.

`DefaultDatabase`: The default database, or catalog, that is used within the data source.

`IsolationLevel`: The isolation level that is used with transactions on this connection.

Mode: Indicates the read/write and sharing permissions for the connection.

Provider: Used to specify the provider that will be used. This defaults to MSDASQL.

Version: Specifies the version of the ADO implementation.

Connection objects also contain a Properties collection, which is used to work with certain characteristics of the connection and an Errors collection, which contains information about any errors or warnings generated by an operation on the connection.

Connection **Methods**

All ADO connections will also support the following methods, although additional methods might also be provided:

Open: Used to open a connection to a data source.

Close: Used to close a data source connection and its dependent objects.

Execute: Executes a command against the connected data source. In most cases, this is an SQL query.

BeginTrans: Begins a transaction on the connection.

CommitTrans: Commits the current transaction.

RollbackTrans: Rolls back any changes made in the current transaction.

Command **Objects**

Command objects are used to represent specific commands that will be executed against the data source. Command objects are used to keep track of parameters associated with the command, as well as other settings. You can create a command using an existing connection, or you can have ADO create a new connection for use with the new command.

Command **Properties**

All Command objects will have the following properties:

ActiveConnection: This is used to specify the connection that is to be used with the command. You can set this to an existing Connection object or you can specify a connection string for a new connection to be used with the command.

CommandText: Contains the text of the command, usually an SQL statement.

CommandTimeout: Contains the timeout value that is used for this command.

CommandType: Specifies the type of the command, which can be a text command, such as a complete SQL statement, a table name, or a stored procedure.

Prepared: Specifies whether the command will be prepared prior to the first execution.

`Command` objects also include a `Parameters` collection, which is used to work with values passed between the `Command` object and procedure calls or parameterized commands, as well as a `Properties` collection containing specific characteristics of the command.

Command **Methods**

All `Command` objects will also support the following methods:

`CreateParameter`: Used to create a new parameter object for use with the command.

`Execute`: Executes the command against the data source.

Recordset **Objects**

`Recordset` objects provide for most of your interactions with the data. They are used to contain a set of records returned from the data source. You can open a recordset directly by calling its `Open()` method, or you can generate a recordset by calling `Execute()` on a connection or command object.

The `Recordset` object represents all of the rows returned from the data source, although you might only work with one row at a time—the current row. The data in a row is manipulated by working with the `Field` objects contained in the recordset's `Fields` collection.

Recordset **Properties**

All `Recordset` objects will have the following properties. Most of these can be used to set or retrieve information about the current state of the recordset, and setting others can perform operations, such as scrolling, on the recordset.

`AbsolutePage`: Used to move the current row to the start of a specified page of rows. The number of rows in a page is set in the `PageSize` property.

`AbsolutePosition`: Used to make a row at the specified absolute position the current row.

`ActiveConnection`: Used to specify the connection that is to be used for the recordset. This can reference an existing connection, or you can pass a connection string for a new connection that will be created for this recordset.

`BOF`: This is true if the recordset is currently positioned before the first row.

`EOF`: This is true if the recordset is positioned after the last row.

`Bookmark`: This property contains the bookmark for the current row.

`CacheSize`: Specifies the number of rows of data that will be cached in local memory.

`CursorType`: Specifies the type of cursor that is used with this recordset. The cursor can be a forward-only, keyset, static, or dynamic cursor.

EditMode: Indicates if the current row has been modified since being fetched, or if it is a new row that has not yet been written to the data source.

Filter: Specifies a filter for the rows that will be visible in the recordset. This can specify an SQL where clause, an array of bookmarks, or a constant allowing you to view only pending, affected, or fetched records.

LockType: Specifies the locking mechanism used when the provider opens the rows in the recordset.

MaxRecords: This can be used to specify the maximum number of rows that will be returned in a recordset.

PageCount: Indicates how many pages of rows are present in the recordset, based on the PageSize property.

PageSize: Specifies the number of rows in a page. This is used in conjunction with the PageCount and AbsolutePage properties.

RecordCount: Indicates the number of rows currently in the recordset.

Source: Specifies where the data in the recordset comes from. This can be a command object, SQL statement, stored procedure, or table name.

Status: Indicates the status of the current row after a batch update or other bulk operations.

Recordset Methods

Recordset objects also expose the following methods:

AddNew: Used to create a new row in the recordset.

CancelBatch: Cancels a batch update in progress.

CancelUpdate: Cancels any changes made to the current row.

Clone: Creates a new recordset that is a duplicate of the current recordset.

Close: Closes the recordset.

Delete: Deletes one or more records from the recordset.

GetRows: Used to fetch a block of rows into an array.

Move: Sets the current row of the recordset.

MoveFirst: Makes the first row of the recordset the current row.

MoveLast: Makes the last row of the recordset the current row.

MoveNext: Positions the recordset on the next row.

MovePrevious: Positions the recordset on the previous row.

NextRecordset: Used to move to the next recordset returned by compound queries. This will clear the recordset and return the data for the next recordset generated.

Open: Used to open a recordset directly, rather than as a result of methods from other objects, such as commands or connections.

Requery: Refreshes the data in the recordset by re-executing the query that generated it.

Resync: This will update the data for any rows in the recordset with the most current data from the data source. However, this will not return any new rows, as Requery would.

Supports: Used to determine whether the recordset supports a variety of different operations, including bookmarks, modifying the data, and batch updates, among other things.

Update: Used to submit any changes made to the current row to the data source.

UpdateBatch: Submits any changes made in the current batch update to the data source.

Fields Collections and Field Objects

Recordset objects contain a collection of Field objects used to work with the individual columns of the rowset. Each column that is returned in the rowset will have an associated Field object in this collection. The Field object gives you access to column metadata, such as the column name and data type, as well as the actual value for the column in the current row.

Fields Collection Members

The Fields collection includes a Count property, which gives the number of individual Field objects in the collection, as well as an Item property, which is used to retrieve individual Field objects. In addition, the Fields collection includes a Refresh method, although this has no real effect on the Fields collection.

Field Object Properties

Each of the individual Field objects will have the following properties:

ActualSize: Indicates the actual length of the data for the current row's value.

Attributes: This property contains a group of settings for this column, including its updatability, nullability, and other information.

DefinedSize: Indicates the maximum size allotted for a value of this column.

Name: Indicates the name of the column. You may access individual fields in the collection either by this name or by their ordinal value.

NumericScale: Indicates how many places to the right of the decimal point are used to represent this value.

OriginalValue: This property contains the original value of the column as it was last fetched from the data source, prior to any changes you have made.

Precision: Indicates the maximum number of digits used to represent the value for numerical columns.

Type: This gives the type of data used for values in this column.

UnderlyingValue: This property reflects the current value of the column in the data source. This can differ from the Value and OriginalValue properties due to changes made by other applications since the row was originally fetched.

Value: This property contains a VARIANT holding the current data value for this column of the current row in the recordset.

Field **Object Methods**

Each Field object also will implement the following methods:

AppendChunk: This is used to add portions of long data objects to the data source, allowing you to work with smaller blocks of data than the entire value.

GetChunk: This is used to retrieve large data objects in smaller, more manageable pieces.

Parameter **Objects and the** Parameters **Collection**

Command objects contain a Parameters collection, which contains all of the parameters associated with the command. Each of the individual Parameter objects is used to contain information about a parameter that is passed into the command text at runtime, or returned from a procedure executed in a command. New Parameter objects are created with the CreateParameter() method of a Command object.

Parameters **Collection Members**

The Parameters collection includes a Count property, which gives the number of individual Parameter objects in the collection, as well as an Item property, which is used to retrieve individual Parameter objects. You can add new Parameter objects to the collection with the Append() method, or delete them from the collection with the Delete() method. In addition, the Refresh() method can be used to gather information from the provider about parameters used in procedures or parameterized commands.

Parameter **Object Properties**

Each of the Parameter objects in the Parameters collection of a command will have the following properties, although some properties might not be available for certain providers:

Attributes: This property contains a combination of several bit flags that indicate whether the parameter accepts signed, nullable, and/or long data values.

Direction: Indicates if the parameter is used for input, output, or both.

Name: Contains the name of the parameter.

NumericScale: Used to determine the number of places to the right of the decimal that are used for numeric parameters.

Precision: Indicates the total number of digits used to represent a value for the parameter.

Size: Contains the maximum size of the parameter value in bytes or characters.

Type: Specifies the data type for the parameter's value.

Value: Contains the actual value assigned to the parameter.

Parameter Object Methods

The only method provided by Parameter objects is AppendChunk(), which is used to append data to large text or binary parameter values.

Property Objects and the Properties Collection

Connection, Command, Recordset, and Field objects all include a Properties collection, which is used to hold the individual Property objects associated with the object. Property objects are used to represent individual option settings or other characteristics of an ADO object that are not handled by the built-in properties of the object. Although each of the ADO objects can support different sorts of properties, they are all manipulated by using the standard Property object.

Properties Collection Members

The Properties collection includes the Count property, which gives the number of Property objects in the collection, as well as the Item property, which is used to access individual Property objects in the collection. In addition, the Properties collection supports the Refresh method, which may be used to retrieve information for certain dynamic properties exposed by the provider, although this has no effect for properties that we will see here.

Property Object Properties

A Property object is relatively simple. It does not expose any methods and has only the following properties:

Attributes: This property indicates the characteristics of the property, including whether it is supported, required, or optional. This also includes the read/write permissions for the property.

Name: Contains the name of the property.

Type: Indicates the data type used for values of this property.

Value: Contains the actual value of the property.

Error Objects and the Errors Collection

ADO Connection objects contain an Errors collection, which contains Error objects that give specific information about any errors that might have occurred on the connection for a single operation. In most cases, Error objects are generated only when errors are returned by the database system, not when procedural errors occur in ADO. Any given operation can generate any number of different Error objects, including errors that contain information about warnings that were generated. Whenever a new operation generates an error, the Errors collection is cleared before the errors from the new operation are added.

Errors Collection Members

The Errors collection contains a Count property, which gives the number of Error objects currently in the collection, as well as an Item property, which is used to access the individual Error objects. The Errors collection also supports the Clear() method, which is used to remove any Error objects currently in the collection.

Error Object Properties

Error objects do not expose any methods, but do include the following properties that give additional information about specific errors:

Description: Provides a text description of the error that is suitable for display to the user.

HelpContext: Returns a context ID that can be used to access a specific topic in a Windows help file that is relevant to the error.

HelpFile: Returns a fully qualified path to a Windows help file that can contain help for the specific error.

NativeError: Contains a database-specific Long value that is returned from the provider.

Number: This returns a numeric value that indicates the specific error that occurred.

Source: Returns a string indicating the component that generated the error—for example, ADODB.Connection or SQL Server.

SQLState: Returns a five-character string containing an ANSI standard SQLSTATE value for the specific error.

Using ADO Objects in VC++

ADO is based on the Common Object Model, or COM. This allows ADO objects to be used from a wide range of different programming environments, including things like Visual Basic or VBScript as well as Visual C++. Unfortunately, this also means that almost all of the documentation you might find for ADO shows how to use the ADO objects in Visual Basic. However, the C++ interface to COM objects, although it provides greater flexibility and efficiency, is not as simple to use as the Visual Basic interface.

This section looks at some of the basics of using ADO from C++ applications, before moving on to the specifics of database operations.

Initializing COM

Because ADO is a COM interface, your application will need to initialize the COM environment before doing anything else with ADO. This is done with a call to CoInitialize(). However, it is often useful to be able to use certain ADO functionality, such as object constructors, when initializing static or global ADO objects.

In C++, the constructors for static or global objects are called before any other application code is executed. This presents a bit of a dilemma, although you can easily work around this by adding a declaration like the following to your source file, before any other declarations that use ADO:

```
struct InitOle {
    InitOle()  { ::CoInitialize(NULL); }
    ~InitOle() { ::CoUninitialize();   }
} _init_InitOle_;
```

You will never actually use this structure from within your application, but its constructor will be called upon program initialization, which will automatically call CoInitialize() to initialize the COM environment. This will also unload the COM environment by calling CoUninitialize() when your program exits.

Using #import

If you have used COM interfaces with previous versions of Visual C++, you probably know that COM programming can be considerably more complicated than the Visual Basic documentation for objects might lead one to believe. However, Visual C++ 5.0 goes a long way toward simplifying your C++ COM programming endeavors.

One of the most important features is the new #import preprocessor directive, which can be used to automatically generate C++ classes for the COM interfaces implemented in a COM type library. These classes can greatly simplify the use of the objects in the type library from C++ applications.

The classes created from the type library are implemented in two files that are generated in the output directory of your project. These are a `.tlh` file, which contains definitions for the classes, and a `.tli` file containing the implementation of the classes. These files are automatically included in your project's build when you add the `#import` directive to your source file.

For the examples in this chapter, we have added an `#import` directive to our `stdafx.h` header file, as shown here:

```
#import "D:\\Program Files\\Common Files\\System\\ADO\\MSADO10.DLL" no_namespace
rename("EOF", "ADOEOF")
```

The preceding `#import` directive creates classes from the `MSADO10.DLL` type library, which is installed with ADO, as part of the OLE DB SDK. The path to this library can vary, depending on your installation.

The `no_namespace` option tells the precompiler not to use a separate namespace for the definitions of the new classes. The rename clause is required, because the ADO type library redefines `EOF`, which is already defined in `stdio.h`, `ios.h`, and `streamb.h`, which is included in `afxwin.h`. The rename clause simply renames the `EOF` identifier as `ADOEOF`. Thus, where the ADO documentation shows that we would use `EOF`, we will be using `ADOEOF` instead.

Recordset-Only ADO

In the previous example, we imported from the `MSADO10.DLL` library, which implements the full range of ADO objects. There is also another library that is installed with ADO that implements only recordset objects. This is `MSADOR10.DLL`, which implements the recordset-only version of ADO, also known as ADO/R. This version works exactly the same as full ADO, other than the fact that objects such as connections and commands are not supported. ADO/R is generally most useful for applications that simply display information from a data source.

COM Support Classes

Writing ADO applications, as well as other COM programs, is much easier if you make use of some of the COM support classes that are supported by the VC++ 5.0 compiler. The support classes include the following:

`_com_error`: This class is used in handling exception conditions generated by the type library, or one of the other support classes.

`_com_ptr_t`: This class defines a smart pointer for use with COM interfaces, and is useful in creating and destroying ADO objects.

`_variant_t`: Encapsulates the VARIANT data type and can greatly simplify your application code, because working with VARIANT data directly can be a bit messy.

`_bstr_t`: Encapsulates the BSTR data type. This provides built-in handling of resource allocation and deallocation, as well as other common operations.

For more on the specifics of each of these classes, see the online documentation, although you will see these classes in action in the examples later in this chapter.

Smart Pointers and ADO

The previous section briefly mentioned the _com_ptr_t class. This class is used to implement smart pointers for COM interfaces, and we will be using this class in most of our interactions with ADO objects, although we will not be using the class directly. When you use the #import directive to create C++ classes for ADO, MSAD010.TLH defines several pointer types based on _com_ptr_t, with lines like the following:

```
_COM_SMARTPTR_TYPEDEF(_Connection, __uuidof(_Connection));
```

It's not particularly obvious, but this line defines the type _ConnectionPtr, which is a smart pointer that gives you access to ADO Connection objects. In the following sections, we will look at how these pointer classes may be used.

Creating ADO objects

Creating ADO objects with the classes generated by #import is quite simple. First, you need to declare a smart pointer to the type of ADO object that you want to create. For example, for a connection, you would declare a pointer like this:

```
_ConnectionPtr  pConn;
```

Then, to create an instance of the object, you need to call the CreateInstance() method of the smart pointer class, as in the following examples:

```
hr = pConn.CreateInstance( __uuidof( Connection ) );
hr = pConn.CreateInstance("ADODB.Connection");
```

Each of the preceding examples is equivalent: They make use of an overloaded CreateInstance() function. You may also specify a context value for running executable code in a second parameter. If you don't specify a context, this defaults to CLSCTX_ALL.

> **NOTE**
>
> Note that CreateInstance() is a method of the pointer class and not the object pointed to. Thus it is referenced with . and not ->.

You may also simplify this process by passing a class ID in the constructor of the pointer, as shown here:

```
_ConnectionPtr pConn(__uuidof( Connection ));
```

In the previous examples, the __uuidof() function, provided by the C++ compiler, returns the GUID associated with the Connection object of ADO. For other types of objects, you would pass the object type to __uuidof(). You will see examples of how to create each of the other ADO object types as this chapter gets to them.

The ADO License Key

In the previous example, you saw how to easily create an ADO object. Well, there is a catch. Apparently, the marketing folks in Redmond have decided that you must register a license key for ADO. This is done automatically for you when you install the OLE DB SDK or Active Server Pages. However, the license key most likely will not be installed on machines that you distribute your application to. Because of this, you must pass the license key when creating the first instance of an ADO object in your app.

> **CAUTION**
>
> Your ADO applications will not run on machines that do not have the license key installed unless you pass the ADO license key when your application creates its first instance of an ADO object.

You may freely distribute your applications that use ADO; you just have to do a little extra work to say the magic word, which is the license key gxwaezucfyqpwjgqbcmtsncuhwsnyhiohwxz. I'm sure if you could actually pronounce this, real magic would happen. Unfortunately, I can't, so we will just stick to using it to work with ADO.

The code to create an instance of a connection object while passing the license key looks something like this:

```
HRESULT hr;
BSTR bLicenseKey;
IClassFactory2 *pFactory = NULL;
// Allocate string containing the key
bLicenseKey = SysAllocString( L"gxwaezucfyqpwjgqbcmtsncuhwsnyhiohwxz" );
// Load the code to create an ADO object
hr = CoGetClassObject( __uuidof(Connection),
                       CLSCTX_INPROC_SERVER,
                       NULL,
                       IID_IClassFactory2,
                       reinterpret_cast<void**>(&pFactory) );
// Create an instance using the license key
hr = pFactory->CreateInstanceLic( NULL,
                                  NULL,
                                  __uuidof(IUnknown),
                                  bLicenseKey,
                                  reinterpret_cast<void**> (&pFactory) );
// Construct a _ConnectionPtr
_ConnectionPtr pConn(pFactory);
// You can now use pConn normally.
```

You will need to use the license key and the extra code associated with it only when you create your first ADO object. After that, you can create objects in the simpler way shown previously.

Working with Properties

The classes created by the #import directive make it much simpler to work with the properties of a COM object. In fact, it is almost as simple to use these properties in C++ as it is in VB, which is a whole lot easier than working with the "native" COM interface.

The classes generated by #import allow you to reference the properties of ADO objects as if they were simple data members of the object. For example, you could retrieve the Version property of a Connection object like this:

```
_bstr_t bVersion = m_piConnection->Version;
```

However, you need to be a bit careful with this notation, because the mechanism used to present properties this way depends on overloaded functions that need to know the desired return type. In the example shown previously, you know that a _bstr_t return type is expected.

This is not true of some other cases where you could use a "real" _bstr_t data member. For example, the following code is perfectly legitimate:

```
_bstr_t MyString = L"Trace This";
TRACE("My String: %S\n", MyString);
```

However, when you pass parameters to functions such as TRACE() or printf(), the compiler does not know what data type it should cast the parameters to. This will cause statements like the following to fail:

```
TRACE("Version: %S\n", m_piConnection->Version);
```

You can overcome this by either providing an explicit cast or an intermediate assignment to a variable of the appropriate type, as in the following example:

```
TRACE("Version: %S\n", (_bstr_t) m_piConnection->Version);
```

Unfortunately, the data types that can be used with the ADO class properties and methods are not really documented anywhere (other than this text, of course). To find more information about the specific implementation of these classes, such as the types that can be used for properties, you might need to take a look at the files generated by #import. Most importantly, you will need to look at the .tlh file generated in your project's output directory. You can also consult the examples later on in this chapter.

Calling Methods

The classes generated by #import also make it much simpler to call the methods of ADO objects. The classes provide access to the methods of ADO objects that actually return the values that you would expect, and allow you to avoid the hassle of dealing with the return value as an extra (and of course, undocumented) parameter of the method.

Again, you might need to consult the `.tlh` file that is generated by `#import` to find the exact C++ types that are expected in calls to ADO methods, because these will differ somewhat from the types documented in the Visual Basic documentation provided with ADO.

Releasing ADO Interfaces

When you are finished using any COM interface, you should call `Release()` on the interface in order to free up its resources. Actually, failure to do so often causes GP faults in ADO under Windows 95. However, the smart pointer classes that are created by `#import` will take care of this for you when the smart pointer is destroyed, such as when it goes out of scope, or when your program exits.

You should, however, be careful to call `Release()` for any interfaces that you are using directly, without the smart pointer classes.

Processing ADO Errors

ADO allows you to work with a wide range of different database components, including ADO implementations, OLE DB providers, ODBC drivers, and the database systems themselves. Partly because of this, and partly because ADO is a very new technology and still has a few bugs, errors caused by ADO operations can be reported in several different ways. Errors from particular calls can be reported by way of C++ exceptions, `HRESULT` return values, and/or in the `Errors` collection of a `Connection` object. You should be prepared to handle error information from any and all of these sources, particularly while developing new applications.

ADO C++ Exceptions

Most errors that occur in ADO applications as a result of programming errors, such as bad parameters and such, will generate a C++ exception of some sort. In most cases, an exception of class `_com_error` will be thrown. However, your application should be prepared to handle other sorts of exceptions. For more on general exception handling in C++, see Chapter 7, "General-Purpose Classes."

To handle the exceptions that might be thrown by ADO operations, you should execute your ADO operations within a `try` block and provide a `catch` block for an object of type `_com_error`. This class is used to return errors from the classes that are created by the `#import` directive, as well as the COM support classes. The `_com_error` class encapsulates any `HRESULT` values that might be generated, as well as any `IErrorInfo` object that might be generated by the underlying OLE DB provider.

The `_com_error` class provides several different member functions that can be used to extract information about an error. Among others, these include the following:

> `Error()`: Returns the `HRESULT` associated with an error.
>
> `ErrorMessage()`: Returns a text string describing the `HRESULT` value.

Description(): Retrieves a text string describing the error.

Source(): Returns the name of the component that generated the error.

HelpContext(): Retrieves a Windows help context value that applies to the error.

HelpFile(): Retrieves the path to a Windows help file that applies to the error.

GUID(): Returns the GUID of the COM interface that generated the error.

The following example shows how you can use C++ exception handling to deal with exceptions thrown by ADO. This example uses a simple call to Connection.Close(), which will rarely throw exceptions, but also does not unnecessarily complicate the example.

```
try
{
    hr = pConn->Close();
}
catch(_com_error &ce)
{
    _bstr_t bstrDescription(ce.Description());
    _bstr_t bstrSource(ce.Source());
    TRACE("_com_error exception thrown\n");
    TRACE("HRESULT = 0x%081x\n", ce.Error());
    TRACE("HRESULT description: %s\n", ce.ErrorMessage());
    TRACE("Description: %s\n", (LPCTSTR) bstrDescription);
    TRACE("Source: %s\n", (LPCTSTR) bstrSource);
}
catch(…)  // Handle any other exception types
{
    TRACE("Unknown Exception was thrown.");
}
if(FAILED(hr))
    TRACE("Bad HRESULT Returned: 0x%081x (%d)\n", hr, hr);
```

ADO HRESULT Values

In addition to handling any C++ exceptions that may be thrown, your applications should also check the HRESULT code that is returned from ADO operations, as shown in the previous example. Generally, these codes are defined in winerror.h, but there are also several other header files in which these error codes are defined, depending on the component that generated the error. When developing new applications, you might find yourself searching these header files often to find what the cause of an error is. You should also be aware that these error codes are usually defined in hex, although some header files define HRESULT values in using decimal notation.

TIP

For a compilation of most of the HRESULT codes that can be returned by ADO, see Microsoft knowledge base article Q168354, which condenses the definitions found in several header files. It also lists hex and decimal representations.

The Errors Collection

The last of the error-reporting mechanisms that we will be looking at here is the Errors collection of the ADO Connection object, which can contain multiple Error objects for the last ADO operation on the connection. In most cases, the errors (or warnings) reported in the Errors collection are generated by the database, whereas errors that are generated in other components, such as ADODB, are reported via exception or HRESULT.

> **CAUTION**
>
> For many ADO errors, the Errors collection might not be filled in, so you should be sure to check the other error-reporting mechanisms shown previously.

The Errors collection is contained only in the Connection object, and not in other objects, such as the Recordset. Thus, you will need to check the Errors collection of the Connection object that is being used for a particular operation. You can access the connection for a Command or Recordset object by using its ActiveConnection property.

ADO will clear the Errors collection before each operation, so the errors in the collection refer only to the last operation. You can check on the number of Error objects in the collection by retrieving the Count property. The individual Error objects are then retrieved via the Item property.

The Error object provides several properties that you can use to gather more information about the error, including the following:

Description: Provides a text description of the error that is suitable for display to the user.

NativeError: Contains a database-specific Long value that is returned from the provider.

Number: This returns a numeric value that indicates the specific error that occurred.

Source: Returns a string indicating the component that generated the error—for example, ADODB.Connection or SQL Server.

SQLState: Returns a five-character string containing an ANSI standard SQLSTATE value for the specific error.

HelpContext: Returns a context ID that can be used to access a specific topic in a Windows help file that is relevant to the error.

HelpFile: Returns a fully qualified path to a Windows help file that may contain help for the specific error.

The following example shows some simple debug output based on the Error objects in the Errors collection:

```
ErrorsPtr    pErrors;
ErrorPtr     pError;
```

```
HRESULT     hr = (HRESULT) 0L;
long        nCount;
pErrors = pConn->GetErrors();
nCount = pErrors->GetCount();
for( long i = 0; i < nCount; i++ )
{
    TRACE( "TRACE of ADO Error %d of %d", i+1, nCount );
    // Retrieve individual error object
    hr = pErrors->get_Item((_variant_t) i, &pError );
    // temporary variables to convert property types
    _bstr_t bstrSource      ( pError->GetSource() );
    _bstr_t bstrDescription( pError->GetDescription() );
    _bstr_t bstrHelpFile    ( pError->GetHelpFile() );
    _bstr_t bstrSQLState    ( pError->GetSQLState() );
    TRACE( "\tNumber      \t= %ld", pError->GetNumber());
    TRACE( "\tSource      \t= %s",  (LPCTSTR) bstrSource);
    TRACE( "\tDescription \t= %s",  (LPCTSTR) bstrDescription);
    TRACE( "\tHelpFile    \t= %s",  (LPCTSTR) bstrHelpFile);
    TRACE( "\tHelpContext \t= %ld", pError->GetHelpContext());
    TRACE( "\tSQLState    \t= %s",  (LPCTSTR) bstrSQLState);
    TRACE( "\tHelpContext \t= %ld", pError->GetHelpContext());
    TRACE( "\tNativeError \t= %ld", pError->GetNativeError());
} // end for
```

Opening a Connection

In ADO, it is possible to work with Recordset objects without explicitly creating and opening a Connection object. However, even if you don't work directly with it, a Connection object is created. In addition, you will need to work with Connection objects to handle transactions. You will also need to create your own connection if you want to share a single Connection between multiple Recordset or Command objects.

This chapter will work with the C++ classes created by the compiler when the #import directive is used on the ADO library. This makes creating a new Connection object very simple: You only need to declare a connection pointer and call its CreateInstance() member function, as shown below:

```
_ConnectionPtr pConn;
hr = pConn.CreateInstance("ADODB.Connection");
```

Alternatively, you could use the __uuidof() function in the call to CreateInstance(), or specify a context, as in the following example:

```
hr = pConnCreateInstance(__uuidof(Connection), CLSCTX_INPROC_SERVER);
```

After you have created an instance of a Connection object, you will need to call its Open() method to connect to a data source. Open() takes three parameters: a connection string, a user ID, and a password. The following code shows a simple example of Open():

```
hr = pConn->Open("LocalDb30", "Admin", "");
```

If you look in `msado10.tlh`, you might notice that the `Open()` function takes parameters of type `_bstr_t`. You can pass simple strings, as in the previous example, due to conversions provided by the `_bstr_t` class.

The previous example used a very simple connection string that simply gave the name of the ODBC data source that we want to connect to. In some cases, you might want to use a more complicated connection string, made up of pairs of keywords and values, as in the following example:

```
hr = pConn->Open("Data Source=LocalDb30;Provider=MSDASQL", "Admin", "");
```

ADO will process any of the following keywords. Any other keyword-value pairs are passed on to the provider.

> `Provider`: Used to specify the provider to use.
>
> `Data Source`: Specifies the name of the data source to use.
>
> `User`: Gives the user name to be used with the data source.
>
> `Password`: Gives the user's password.
>
> `File Name`: Gives the name of a provider-specific file holding connection information, such as an ODBC file DSN.

You may also access the connection string by using the `ConnectionString` property of the `Connection` object.

Connection Timeout

By default, ADO will wait 15 seconds for the connection to be established. If your application wants to wait a different amount of time before giving up, you will need to set the `ConnectionTimeout` property of the `Connection` object before calling its `Open()` method. The `ConnectionTimeout` value is given in seconds.

> **NOTE**
>
> The `ConnectionTimeout` property specifies a timeout value for establishing the connection. This should not be confused with the `CommandTimeout` property, which specifies the timeout value for operations on the database after a connection is established.

Connection Access Modes

In many cases, it is useful to restrict your application's access to a data source, such as opening it as read-only. This is done by setting the connection's `Mode` property before calling `Open()`.

You can also read this property to retrieve the connection's mode. The Mode property can have a combination (bitwise OR) of any of the following values:

adModeUnknown: This is returned if the mode cannot be determined.

adModeRead: Read-only.

adModeWrite: Write-only.

adModeReadWrite: Read-write.

adModeShareDenyRead: Prevents others from opening a connection with read privileges.

adModeShareDenyWrite: Prevents others from opening a connection with write privileges.

adModeShareExclusive: Combination of DenyRead and DenyWrite.

adModeShareDenyNone: Prevents others from opening any connection to the data source.

The following example shows how to set a connection timeout and access mode before opening the connection:

```
_ConnectionPtr pConn;
hr = pConn.CreateInstance("ADODB.Connection");
pConn->ConnectionTimeout = 120;
pConn->Mode = adModeRead | adModeShareExclusive;
hr = pConn->Open("LocalDb30", "Admin", "");
```

The Default Database

Some larger data sources, such as Informix, Oracle, and SQL Server, can handle many different databases. In some cases, each SQL statement will need to specify which database it is working with. However, you can simplify things by setting a default database for your SQL statements when you set the DefaultDatabase property of the Connection object. Unless you explicitly use another database, this database will be used for all SQL statements.

Closing the Connection

When you are finished using a Connection object, you should close the connection by calling its Close() method. This will also close all ADO objects that are using this connection, such as Recordset or Command objects. The Close() method takes no parameters, as shown in the following example:

```
pConn->Close();
```

ADO Connection objects also support several other properties and methods, discussed later in the chapter.

Using Recordsets

In ADO, the Recordset object is used for the majority of your interaction with the data in a data source, although you will see that Command objects, as well as Connection objects, can be used to execute SQL commands against the database. In any case, any data that is returned will be returned as part of a Recordset object, which allows you to retrieve row data and scroll through the result set, as well as modifying the data in the database.

Recordset Feature Support

Unfortunately, not all of the features of the Recordset object that this chapter discusses are supported by all providers. You can determine what features are supported on a given recordset by calling its Supports() method. Supports() takes one parameter, which can be one of the following values and will return TRUE if the feature is supported. You can use Supports() to query a recordset's support for the following features:

adAddNew: The AddNew() method is supported.

adApproxPosition: The AbsolutePosition and AbsolutePage properties are supported.

adBookmark: The Bookmark property is supported.

adDelete: The Delete() method is supported.

adHoldRecords: You can retrieve more rows without committing all pending changes to current rows.

adMovePrevious: The MovePrevious() and Move() methods are supported, allowing you to scroll backwards.

adResync: The Resync() method is supported.

adUpdate: The Update() method can be called to update the data source.

adUpdateBatch: Batch update mode and the UpdateBatch() method are supported.

Opening a Recordset

There are several different ways that a Recordset object can be created. You can create a recordset as the result of a command executed with a Command or Connection object or by itself. This section shows how to create a recordset from scratch.

To begin, you will need to declare a smart pointer to a recordset, using the classes that were generated by #import. You will also need to call CreateInstance() on the pointer to create the Recordset object, as shown here:

```
_RecordsetPtr  pRecordset;
hr = pRecordset.CreateInstance("ADODB.Recordset");
```

Open()

You will then need to call the recordset's Open() method, which executes a query against the data source and returns the result set into the recordset. The prototype for _Recordset.Open(), as generated by #import in msado10.tlh, is shown here:

```
HRESULT Open (
    const _variant_t & Source,
    const _variant_t & ActiveConnection,
    enum CursorTypeEnum CursorType,
    enum LockTypeEnum LockType,
    long Options );
```

The Source parameter is used to query the database for the rows that will make up the recordset. In most cases, you will want to simply pass a string containing an SQL query in Source, as shown, although you may also simply pass a table name, which is interpreted as SELECT * FROM table-name. It is also possible to pass a reference to an existing Command object in the Source parameter. The Options parameter is used to tell ADO what sort of value is passed in Source. This can be one of the following constants:

adCmdText: Source is a text command, such as an SQL query.

adCmdTable: Source is a table name.

adCmdStoredProc: Source references a stored procedure.

adCmdUnknown: The type of source is not known. ADO will try to figure out what type of value is used.

The ActiveConnection parameter is used to specify the Connection object that this recordset will use to communicate with the data source. In the previous example, we passed a pointer to the IDispatch interface of a Connection object that we have previously opened. In addition, you can let ADO create a connection for you by passing a connection string in ActiveConnection. This string takes the same format as the connection string that we used to open a Connection object.

If you let ADO create a connection for you in this way, you may access the connection via the recordset's ActiveConnection property. This is necessary when working with transactions or accessing the Errors collection of the connection.

The CursorType parameter is used to specify the type of cursor that will be used to open the recordset. The type of cursor used determines whether your application is able to freely scroll backward and forward through the recordset and also determines what sort of changes made to the database are made visible to the recordset while it is open. CursorType can be set to one of the following values:

adOpenForwardOnly: This is the default value, which specifies a cursor that can only be scrolled forward.

adOpenKeyset: This specifies a keyset-driven cursor, which may be scrolled freely and will detect some types of changes made to the rows contained in the recordset.

adOpenDynamic: This specifies a dynamic cursor, which may be scrolled and will detect all changes made to the data handled by the recordset. However, dynamic cursors can be expensive to use.

adOpenStatic: This uses a static cursor, which may be freely scrolled, but does not reflect any changes made to the data underlying the recordset.

You can query the cursor type used by a recordset by checking its CursorType property. For a more thorough discussion of the issues involved with different cursor types, see Chapter 25, "Open Database Connectivity (ODBC)."

The LockType parameter specifies the type of locking used by the recordset. This will affect how concurrent operations are allowed to affect the database simultaneously. LockType may be passed one of the following values:

adLockReadOnly: The recordset will be read-only.

adLockPessimistic: Locks rows when you begin editing.

adLockOptimistic: Locks rows only when actually sending updates to the database.

adLockBatchOptimistic: Used with batch updates, as you will see later.

You may query the type of locking that is used by a recordset by checking the LockType property of the recordset.

The following example creates and opens a recordset, using an existing connection:

```
RecordsetPtr  pRecordset;
// Create an instance
hr = pRecordset.CreateInstance("ADODB.Recordset");
_variant_t vConn;
vConn = (IDispatch*) pConnection;
hr = pRecordset->Open("SELECT * FROM MyChapters",
                vConn,
                adOpenStatic, adLockOptimistic,
                adCmdText);
```

Limiting the Rows in a Recordset

You may also limit the total number of records that will be returned into a recordset by setting the MaxRecords property of the recordset before calling its Open() method. Furthermore, you may set the number of rows that are cached locally in the recordset (as opposed to kept in a cursor on the database server) by setting the CacheSize property of the recordset to the number of rows that you want to hold locally. Once again, this property should be set before calling Open(). The value of the CacheSize property will not affect how your application code must be written—but, depending on your network environment, can have a substantial effect on your app's overall performance.

Filtering Rows in the Recordset

When opening a recordset, you specified a command or query that generates a set of rows. You can limit the set of rows returned by setting the recordset's `Filter` property. The `Filter` property is basically an extension to the query (or table name, which generates a simple SQL query) given in the `Source` parameter of `Open()`. The string in `Filter` contains a `WHERE` clause used to limit the query contained in the source. Note, however, that the string you add to `Filter` should not contain the actual `WHERE` keyword. The value of the `Filter` property is also limited in that you can use column names that are contained in the recordset only.

You may also set the value of the `Filter` property to one of the following constants, which will limit the contents of the recordset to rows with a certain status:

> `adFilterNone`: Cancels the current value of `Filter` and restores the contents of the recordset to the full result of the original query.
>
> `adFilterPendingRecords`: In batch update mode, this can be used to select only those rows that have changed but not yet been updated in the database.
>
> `adFilterAffectedRecords`: Selects only rows that were affected by the last `Delete()`, `Resync()`, `UpdateBatch()`, or `CancelBatch()` operation.
>
> `adFilterFetchedRecords`: Limits the rows in the recordset to those that are currently contained in the local cache.

You may also set the `Filter` property to an array of bookmark values, which will limit the rows in the recordset to those referenced in the bookmark array.

> **NOTE**
>
> Rows that are excluded by the `Filter` property are still contained in the recordset, but you will not be able to view them until you change the `Filter` property to make them visible again.

Refreshing the Recordset

After you have opened a `Recordset` object, you may call its `Requery()` method to repeat the query and return a new result set. This is useful in situations where you suspect the underlying data in the database might have changed. `Requery()` will toss out all of the rows currently in the recordset and execute the query again, using the current values of the `Source` and `Filter` properties.

Similarly, you may resynchronize the data in the recordset with the data in the data source by calling the `Resync()` method of the recordset. This is different than the `Requery()` method in that only the rows currently in the recordset are updated, rather than executing the whole query again. The prototype for `Requery()` as generated by `#import` is shown here:

```
HRESULT Resync ( enum AffectEnum AffectRecords );
```

You may pass any of the following values in the `AffectRecords` parameter:

> `adAffectCurrent`: Refreshes only the current record.

> `adAffectGroup`: Refreshes only the rows that satisfy the current `Filter` property.

> `adAffectAll`: Refreshes all of the rows contained in the recordset, including those that do not satisfy the current `Filter` setting.

Getting at the Data in the Recordset

Although the ADO `Recordset` object will handle caching of a set of rows to cut down on the number of fetches made against a data source, in general you can access the rows contained in a rowset only one row at a time. However, we will see how to retrieve an array of rows later, when we talk about the `GetRows()` function. For now, we will be retrieving column information by working with the `Field` objects contained in the recordset's `Fields` collection.

To start, you can find the number of fields contained in the collection by checking the `Count` member of the recordset's `Fields` collection.

You can then access individual `Field` objects via the `Item` property of the `Fields` collection. This then gives you access to the other properties of the `Field` object, including the field's name, size, type, and value. It is easiest to see how this works by moving straight to an example, like the following, which will dump the available information for each of the fields of the current row:

```
FieldsPtr pFields;
pFields = pRecordset->Fields;
int lNumFields = pFields->Count;
for(short i=0; i< lNumFields; i++)
{
    FieldPtr pField = pFields->GetItem((_variant_t) i );
    _bstr_t Name = pField->Name;
    _bstr_t Value = pField->Value;
    TRACE("\t %S = %S (type: %d)\n", (LPCTSTR) Name, (LPCTSTR) Value, (short)
    pField->Type);
}
TRACE("\n\n");
```

> **NOTE**
>
> The `Value` properties of `Field` objects are also used for changing data in the database, as you will see later.

Navigating in the Recordset

As mentioned, you can access data only one row at a time by using the `Fields` collection. This section shows how you can move around in the recordset, making a new row the current row. You can move around in the recordset with a variety of different member functions of the `Recordset` object.

Simple Scrolling

The first set of `Recordset` methods for navigating in the recordset is also the simplest: Each of these functions takes no parameters and does just what you would think it does. You can call `MoveFirst()` to make the first row in the recordset the current record. Similarly, you can call `MoveLast()` to make the last row in the recordset the current row. You may also call `MoveNext()` or `MovePrevious()` to move to the next row in the recordset, either forward or backward, respectively.

> **NOTE**
>
> When you first open a recordset, the current row is set to the first row.

When moving through the recordset, you can use the `EOF` property of the recordset to determine whether you have reached the end of the recordset. `EOF` will be set to `TRUE` after you have called `MoveNext()` to scroll past the last row in the recordset. Similarly, if you are scrolling backward, you can use the `BOF` property to determine whether you have attempted to scroll past the beginning of the recordset.

> **NOTE**
>
> Remember that we renamed `EOF` to `ADOEOF` when using `#import` to avoid a conflict. Thus, `EOF` will be replaced with `ADOEOF` in the following examples.

The following example shows how to use `MoveFirst()` and `MoveNext()` to access each of the rows in a recordset:

```
FieldsPtr pFields;
FieldPtr pField;
int lNumFields;
_variant_t vVal;
_variant_t vShow;
hr = pRecordset->MoveFirst();
pFields = pRecordset->Fields;
lNumFields = pFields->Count;
while(!(pRecordset->ADOEOF))
{
```

```
for(short i=0; i<lNumFields; i++)
{
    // TRACE the values of each column
    pField = pFields->GetItem(_variant_t(i));
    vVal = pField->Value;
    hr = VariantChangeType(&vShow, &vVal, 0, VT_BSTR);
    if(hr == S_OK)
        TRACE("\t%S", vShow.bstrVal);
} // end for
TRACE("\n");
hr = pRecordset->MoveNext();
} // end while
```

Move()

The ADO `Recordset` object also provides the `Move()` function, which gives a more flexible function for moving around in the recordset. The prototype for the `Move()` function, as generated by `#import`, is shown herre:

```
HRESULT Move (
    long NumRecords,
    const _variant_t & Start = vtMissing );
```

The `NumRecords` parameter specifies the number of records that the current record pointer will move. If you pass a positive value of `numRecords`, the pointer will move forward. If you pass a negative value, the current row pointer will move backward. If you do not pass a `Start` parameter, the current row pointer will move from the current row. However, you may pass a bookmark value in `Start`. The current row will then be moved `NumRecords` number of rows from the row specified by the bookmark.

If you attempted to move past the last row, `EOF` will be set to `TRUE`. Similarly, `BOF` will be set to `TRUE` if you attempt to move backward past the first row.

Absolute Positioning

ADO `Recordset` objects also allow you to set the current row to an absolute position within the recordset by setting the `AbsolutePosition` property of the recordset to the number of the desired current row. The rows in the recordset are numbered from 1 to the number of rows in the recordset.

> **NOTE**
>
> If you delete records from the recordset or requery or reopen the recordset, the `AbsolutePosition` of a given record can change.

Scrolling by Pages

The ADO Recordset object also allows you to scroll through the recordset by pages. This is very useful in applications in which you are displaying data to the user by pages. To use page scrolling, you will first need to set the PageSize property of the recordset to the number of rows that you would like to see in a page. You can then find the number of pages contained in the recordset by looking at the PageCount property. To set the current row to the first row in a logical page, simply set the AbsolutePage property to the number of the page that you want to position the current row on. Like absolute rows, pages are numbered starting with 1.

Using Bookmarks

If the recordset that you are using supports bookmarks (as indicated by a call to Recordset.Supports()), you can use bookmark values to make a particular row the current row. You can retrieve the bookmark value for the current row by reading the Bookmark property of the recordset. If you save this value somewhere, you can later set the Bookmark property of the recordset to this value to once again make the row indicated by the bookmark the current row.

The GetRows() Method

Up to this point, you have seen how to retrieve data from the recordset by working with one row at a time. However, the Recordset object does allow you to retrieve data into an array that can contain data for a whole group of rows. This can often be used to make your applications more efficient. The prototype for GetRows(), as generated by #import, is shown here:

```
_variant_t GetRows (
    long Rows,
    const _variant_t & Start = vtMissing,
    const _variant_t & Fields = vtMissing );
```

The Rows parameter is used to pass the number of rows that you want to fetch, or it may be set to adGetRowsRest to retrieve all of the remaining rows. The set of rows returned will begin with the current row by default, although you can pass the bookmark for a row to start with in the Start parameter. The Fields parameter may be used to specify which of the columns in the recordset is returned. You may specify a single column to retrieve by passing its ordinal number or its name in Fields. In addition, you may request a set of fields by passing an array of ordinal values or field names in Fields.

GetRows() will return a two-dimensional array of variants. The first array subscript denotes the field, and the second subscript is used to reference a particular row.

The following example uses GetRows() to retrieve all of the row data in the table:

```
LONG lNumRecords;
LONG lIndex[2];
LONG lNumFields;
_variant_t vRowsFetched;
_variant_t vVal;
_variant_t vShow;
```

```
vRowsFetched = m_piRecordset->GetRows(adGetRowsRest);

// Get Number of Rows in Array
SafeArrayGetUBound(vRowsFetched.parray, 2, &lNumRecords);

// Get Number of Columns in Array
SafeArrayGetUBound(vRowsFetched.parray, 1, &lNumFields);
for(lIndex[1]=0; lIndex[1] <= lNumRecords; lIndex[1]++)
{
    for(lIndex[0]=0; lIndex[0] <= lNumFields; lIndex[0]++)
    {
        // Get Field Value
        hr = SafeArrayGetElement(vRowsFetched.parray, &lIndex[0], &vVal);
        // Convert value for display
        hr = VariantChangeType(&vShow, &vVal, 0, VT_BSTR);
        if(hr == S_OK)
            TRACE("\t%S", vShow.bstrVal);
    } // end for lIndex[0]
    TRACE("\n");
} // end for lIndex[1]
TRACE("End of GetRows\n\n");
```

Inserting New Rows

Inserting rows with the ADO `Recordset` object is quite simple, but does involve a few steps. The basic sequence consists of the following:

1. Call `AddNew()`.
2. Update the fields of the current row.
3. Call `Update()`.

Calling `AddNew()` will create a new record and make it the current row of the recordset. You can then use the `Fields` collection of the recordset to fill in the values of the new row.

When you are done making your changes to the new row, you will need to call `Update()` on the recordset to save the changes to the data source. In just a bit, you will see that you can also update column values with `Update()`, but for now, you will be calling `Update()` with no parameters.

TIP

You should call `Update()` for each row that you add, before moving on to another row or calling `AddNew()` again.

```
_RecordsetPtr pRset;
_variant_t vTmp;
FieldsPtr pFields;
FieldPtr  pField;
_variant_t vConn;

// Create new recordset
hr = pRset.CreateInstance("ADODB.Recordset");
```

```
// Use existing connection
vConn = (IDispatch*) m_piConnection;
// Open recordset for a table
hr = pRset->Open("MyChapters",
                 vConn,
                 adOpenStatic, adLockOptimistic,
                 adCmdTable);
// Add Row to Recordset
hr = pRset->AddNew();

// Update fields
pFields = pRset->Fields;
pField = pFields->Item["Num"];
pField->Value = 123L;
pField = pFields->Item["Title"];
pField->Value = "ADO AddNew Chap.";
pField = pFields->Item["Pages"];
pField->Value = 42L;

// Save changes to data source
hr = pRset->Update();
```

If you decide that you do not want to send any changes to the database, you can call `CancelUpdate()` on the recordset, instead of `Update()`. If you were in the process of adding a new row, the new row is never added to the data source.

You may pass two parameters to `AddNew()` to initialize the new row. The first parameter is an array of ordinal values or column names that specify the fields to initialize. The second parameter is an array of the values that correspond to those fields. If you pass values in the `AddNew()` call, the record will be added to the data source immediately, and no call to `Update()` is required.

In general, it is simplest to use the previous method, because you won't have to deal with all of the extra code needed to build the variants that hold the safe arrays for passing to `Update()`.

Updating Rows

Updating rows in an ADO recordset involves basically the same operations as for adding a new row. You simply position the recordset's current row at the row that you want to update, make changes to the `Field` objects for the values that you want to change, and call `Update()` to save the changes to the data source.

However, as mentioned earlier, you may also specify new values for a set of fields when calling `Update()`. The prototype for `Update()`, as generated by #import, is shown here:

```
HRESULT Update (
    const _variant_t & Fields = vtMissing,
    const _variant_t & Values = vtMissing );
```

In the `Fields` parameter, you may pass an array of either field names or their ordinal values. You then pass an array of the new values for those fields in the `Values` parameter. However, it is much easier to modify the current row via the `Fields` collection than it is to build the arrays to pass to `Update()`.

Batch Updates

Some providers allow you to cache any changes made to the recordset locally and send them to the data source in one batch. This is known as *batch update mode*. If batch update mode is not supported, you will always be working in *immediate update mode*. You can determine whether the provider you are using supports batch update mode by calling the Supports() method of the recordset with CursorOptions set to adUpdateBatch.

To send the batch of updates to the data source, you will need to call the UpdateBatch() method of the recordset, shown here:

```
HRESULT UpdateBatch ( enum AffectEnum AffectRecords );
```

The AffectEnum parameter is used to determine which records will be updated in the data source. This may be set to one of the following constants:

adAffectCurrent: Send changes only for the current row.

adAffectGroup: Send changes for all modified records that satisfy the Filter property.

adAffectAll: Send all pending changes to the data source.

If you decide to cancel the whole batch of updates, you may call the recordset's CancelBatch() method, shown here:

```
HRESULT CancelBatch (enum AffectEnum AffectRecords );
```

The call to CancelBatch() takes the same values for AffectEnum as for UpdateBatch().

Deleting Rows

As you might guess, you can delete rows from a recordset by calling the recordset's Delete() method, shown here:

```
HRESULT Delete ( enum AffectEnum AffectRecords );
```

If you pass a value of adAffectCurrent for the AffectEnum parameter, only the current row will be deleted.

You may also pass adAffectGroup, which will delete all rows that satisfy the Filter property.

If the recordset is in immediate update mode, the rows are deleted from the data source immediately. If the recordset is in batch update mode, the rows are not actually deleted from the data source until you call UpdateBatch().

Executing Commands

In ADO, there are two different ways to execute commands. The first is to call the Execute() method of the Connection object. The second method involves Command objects, which can be used for more complex command processing and can use parameterized commands.

Executing Commands with the Connection

You can execute simple commands by using the `Execute()` method of the `Connection` object, shown here:

```
_RecordsetPtr Execute (
    _bstr_t CommandText,
    VARIANT * RecordsAffected,
    long Options );
```

The text of the command, which is generally an SQL command, is passed in the `CommandText` parameter. You may also pass the address of a `VARIANT` in `RecordsAffected`. Upon completion, the long value in the `VARIANT` at `RecordsAffected` will contain the number of rows that were affected by the command. In addition to SQL commands, you may pass a table name or stored procedure in `CommandText`. The `Options` parameter is used to specify the type of command that is passed in `CommandText`. Options may be passed one of the following values:

> `adCmdText`: `CommandText` is a text (usually SQL) command.
>
> `adCmdTable`: `CommandText` is a table name.
>
> `adCmdStoredProc`: `CommandText` is a stored procedure.

For commands that generate a result set, `Execute()` will return a pointer to a recordset, containing the results of the command. You can use this recordset to retrieve the results of the command.

> **NOTE**
>
> Remember that the `CommandTimeout` property of the `Connection` object gives the timeout value that will be used when executing commands.

The following example shows how to execute a simple command using the `Execute()` method of the `Connection` object:

```
_RecordsetPtr pRs;
_variant_t vRowsAffected;
pRs = m_piConnection->Execute(
    "INSERT INTO MyChapters VALUES (1, 'One', 12)",
    &vRowsAffected, adCmdText);
```

Using Command Objects

ADO `Command` objects allow you to have more interaction with commands executed against the data source. To use a `Command` object, you will first need to create an instance of the `Command` object, as shown here:

```
_CommandPtr pCommand;
hr = pCommand.CreateInstance("ADODB.Command");
```

You will then want to set the CommandText property of the command, which will generally contain an SQL command to be executed, although you may pass a table name or a stored procedure. You should also set the CommandType property, which tells ADO what type of command is contained in CommandText.

In addition, you may set the CommandTimeout property of the command to give a timeout value to use for this command. Otherwise, the CommandTimeout property for the connection will be used.

Before executing a command with a Command object, you must also set the ActiveConnection property of the command. You may either set this to a pointer to an existing Connection object or pass a connection string, in which case ADO will open a new connection for you.

To then execute the command, you will need to call the Execute() method of the command, shown here:

```
_RecordsetPtr Execute (
    VARIANT * RecordsAffected,
    VARIANT * Parameters,
    long Options );
```

The value of the Options parameter gives the type of command that is contained in the command's CommandText property. You can pass the address of a VARIANT in RecordsAffected, which will receive a long value giving the number of rows that were affected by the command. We will look at how the Parameters parameter may be used to pass parameters in the next section.

The following example shows how to use a Command object to execute a simple command:

```
_CommandPtr pCommand;
hr = pCommand.CreateInstance("ADODB.Command");

pCommand->ActiveConnection = m_piConnection;

pCommand->CommandTimeout = 5;
pCommand->CommandType = adCmdText;
pCommand->CommandText = "INSERT INTO MyChapters VALUES (?, 'test', 22)";
_variant_t vNull;
vNull.vt = VT_ERROR;
vNull.scode = DISP_E_PARAMNOTFOUND;
pRset = pCommand->Execute(&vRowsAffected, &vNull, adCmdText);
// Do with the Recordset at pRset what you will
pRset = 0;
```

Commands with Parameters

By using the Command object, as opposed to the Connection.Execute() function, you can use parameters with your commands. This is most useful in cases wherein you have the same command that you want to execute several times with slightly different values. To start using parameters, you will first need to add a placeholder for each parameter in the command text string, as in the following example:

```
"INSERT INTO MyChapters VALUES (?, ?, 0)"
```

Creating Parameter **Objects**

You will then need to create a Parameter object to describe each of the parameters that will be used. New Parameter objects are created with the CreateParameter() method of a Command object, shown here:

```
_ParameterPtr CreateParameter (
    _bstr_t Name,
    enum DataTypeEnum Type,
    enum ParameterDirectionEnum Direction,
    long Size,
    const _variant_t & Value = vtMissing );
```

CreateParameter() allows you to name the parameter by passing the Name parameter. You will also need to specify the parameter's Type, Direction, and Size. The Type is given as one of the type constants, such as adBSTR or adInteger. The Direction can be one of the following constant values:

adParamInput: The parameter is an input to the command.

adParamOutput: The parameter is an output parameter of a procedure or function.

adParamInputOutput: The parameter is used for both input and output.

adParamReturnValue: The parameter is the return value of a function or stored procedure.

For variable length data types, you will also need to pass the maximum length for the parameter in Size. In addition, you may pass an initial value for the parameter in Value.

You will then need to append the new Parameter object to the command's Parameters collection. This is done by calling the Append() method of the command's Parameters collection, which takes a pointer to the Parameter object to be added.

Now, to set the value of a particular parameter, you can simply set the Value property of the Parameter object.

Next, you simply call the command's Execute() method, which will use the parameters that have been appended to the command's Parameters collection. Any input parameters will be used in formulating the command that is actually sent to the data source, and any return values or output parameters will be updated with the results of the command.

The following example uses parameters with an INSERT command, to reuse the same command with different values:

```
_CommandPtr pCommand;
_ParameterPtr pParam1;
_ParameterPtr pParam2;
ParametersPtr pParameters;
_RecordsetPtr pRset;
_variant_t vRowsAffected;
_variant_t vNull;
hr = pCommand.CreateInstance("ADODB.Command");
```

```
m_piConnection->IsolationLevel = adXactChaos;
m_piConnection->Attributes &= !adXactCommitRetaining;
pCommand->ActiveConnection = m_piConnection;
pCommand->CommandTimeout = 5;
pCommand->CommandType = adCmdText;
pCommand->CommandText = "INSERT INTO MyChapters VALUES (?, 'test', 22)";
// Create Parameter objects
pParam1 = pCommand->CreateParameter("", adInteger, adParamInput,
          sizeof(_variant_t), 543L);

pParam2 = pCommand->CreateParameter("", adBSTR, adParamInput,
          0, L"Parameter Chap.");
pParameters = pCommand->Parameters;
// Add Parameters to the Parameters collection
hr = pParameters->Append(pParam1);
hr = pParameters->Append(pParam2);

vNull.vt = VT_ERROR;
vNull.scode = DISP_E_PARAMNOTFOUND;
// Execute Command
pRset = pCommand->Execute(&vRowsAffected, &vNull, adCmdText);
pRset = 0;   // This is essential.
// Assign a new value for parameter 1
pParam1->Value = 123L;
// Execute command with new parameter values
pRset = pCommand->Execute(&vRowsAffected, &vNull, adCmdText);
pRset = 0;
}
```

CAUTION

In the current ADODB implementation, you must free the recordset that results from a call to Command.Execute() before calling Execute() again. Setting the pointer to 0, as in the previous example, will cause the smart pointer to free the Recordset object.

For simple input parameters, you can skip some of this work and simply pass an array of parameter values in the Parameters parameter of Command.Execute(). However, this will not work for output or return value parameters. This also involves a good deal of work in setting up the safe arrays, which this chapter doesn't cover.

Transactions

Transactions allow you to perform several different operations on a database that are executed as a single, atomic operation. This is very useful in cases in which you want to update several tables, but only if all of the updates are performed successfully. Transactions can help you avoid the ill effects of partially completed operations if one of the updates should fail.

To begin a transaction on a connection, call its BeginTrans() method, which takes no parameters. You may then perform any changes to the data source that you want to be a part of the transaction.

If all goes well and you want to save all of the changes to the database, you should call the connection's `CommitTrans()` method. If something goes wrong or you just change your mind, you can call `RollbackTrans()`, which will undo any of the changes since the call to `BeginTrans()`.

```
long lTransLevel;
_RecordsetPtr pRs;
_variant_t vRowsAffected;
m_piConnection->IsolationLevel = adXactChaos;
m_piConnection->Attributes &= !adXactCommitRetaining;
m_piConnection->Attributes &= !adXactAbortRetaining;
// Start Transaction
lTransLevel = m_piConnection->BeginTrans();
pRs = m_piConnection->Execute(
    "INSERT INTO MyChapters VALUES (1, 'One', 12)",
    &vRowsAffected, adCmdText);
pRs = m_piConnection->Execute(
    "INSERT INTO MyChapters VALUES (2, 'Two', 13)",
    &vRowsAffected, adCmdText);

if(IsEverythingAOK())
    hr = m_piConnection->CommitTrans();
else
    hr = m_piConnection->RollbackTrans();
```

After you have called `CommitTrans()` or `RollbackTrans()` to end a transaction, ADO might or might not automatically start a new transaction for you. This is controlled by setting the `Attributes` property of the `Connection`. If you include `adXactCommitRetaining` in `Attributes`, a new transaction will be started for you after a call to `CommitTrans()`. Similarly, including `adXactAbortRetaining` will start a new transaction after a call to `RollbackTrans()`.

Summary

This chapter took a look at Microsoft's latest object-oriented database interface: ActiveX Data Objects. ADO provides a common interface that can be used in a wide variety of different programming environments, including Visual C++, Visual Basic, VBScript, and JavaScript. ADO also allows you to access a wide variety of different data sources, including any OLE DB or ODBC data sources.

You have seen the various objects that make up the ADO interface, including connections, recordsets, and commands, as well as several other classes that are used by these objects. You also saw how these objects are used from C++ applications, which is greatly simplified by the new COM support classes provided with Visual C++ 5.0.

You saw how to perform all of the basic database operations with ADO, including connecting to a data source, executing commands, and retrieving the results, as well as some more advanced operations, such as parameterized commands and transactions.

This ends our discussion of the database interfaces that are available to your Visual C++ applications. We will now move on to some other topics that you will find useful in making your applications behave as real Win32 applications should.

VI

Multimedia, OpenGL, and DirectX

29

Multimedia Programming and ActiveMovie 1.0

by Stephen Makonin

Overview of Multimedia and Graphics

Not so long ago, Microsoft's idea of multimedia and graphics was to have about 30 different APIs to do specific areas of multimedia. With DirectX 2, and now DirectX 3, we are seeing a convergence of these APIs into one big API. The advantage of this is that all the multimedia and graphic functionality is there in one place, but it all has a common interface. This means that DirectDraw shares commonalties with DirectSound (such as the `SetCooperativeLevel()` function).

Even now, with the release of ActiveMovie and MPEG-2 player for the Internet, our multimedia and graphical applications no longer need to be confined to a PC. We can create applications that involve numerous people, and express what we want more graphically and with sound. As you can see, the sky (or sometimes the amount of money in your pocket) is the limit.

This chapter and Chapter 30, "DirectX 3.0," show you the basics on how to use the following:

> In this chapter, I show you ActiveMovie 1.0 and how to make a simple movie player. I'll discuss different areas of the ActiveMovie and the movie player itself.
>
> Chapter 30 presents a scaled-down game created with DirectX 3.0. The game will cover all areas of DirectX in a synergistic way. Chapter 30 will also cover DirectDraw, Direct3D, DirectInput, DirectSound, and DirectPlay.
>
> Using fonts will be covered in the DirectX chapter.
>
> MIDI files will also be covered in the DirectX chapter. This is because MIDI files make up one of the areas that has not been incorporated into the DirectSound API.

Terms and Ideas

In this section, I will discuss, at a high level, some terms and ideas that you might need to know before tackling the ActiveMovie and DirectX discussions and examples. So let's get down to business.

GDI

GDI stands for Graphics Device Interface. It is a common interface among graphical APIs that allows them to interact with each other. An example is using TrueType fonts in DirectX. Even though there is no specific set of functions devoted to fonts in DirectX, the GDI interface makes it possible to display any font on any drawing surface.

MCI

MCI, or Media Control Interface, is the old way of playing multimedia files such as WAV, MIDI, or AVI files. The ActiveMovie and DirectSound APIs are Microsoft's new way of playing multimedia files. Although MCI is old, we still need it to play MIDI files; it seems that Microsoft forgot to include a function to play MIDI files in DirectSound.

MMX

With Intel's launch of the new MMX add-on to its Pentium CPU, multimedia has entered into a fresh, crisp, and pristine age—almost like the Renaissance. Not only is there a speed up in performance, but graphics and sound are better quality. This has made many a multimedia and game programmer's mouth water in anticipation. Oh, by the way, if you are trying to find out what MMX stands for, well, I hate to disappoint you, but it is not an acronym.

DVD

The last subject I'll discuss is DVD, or Digital Versatile Disc. This promises to be another revolution in the multimedia industry, opening up a whole new market that will be very lucrative, including such things as movies in which you can choose the ending. Unfortunately, the API for the DVD runs about $5000, which means that it will not be easily available for independent multimedia/game developers like me, unless I take out a loan from the bank!

The next few years will prove to be interesting. Multimedia is becoming more and more accessible, and easier to use. But PCs will always be ahead of the game because of the flexibility and ease with which we can create multimedia applications and games. Many people might not like this statement, but Microsoft has done a lot to give the independent developer tools for expressing ideas. So let us start learning about Microsoft's two newest members of the multimedia family: ActiveMovie and DirectX.

Overview of ActiveMovie

ActiveMovie is an ActiveX SDK that allows you to play movie files on a PC or over the Internet. It replaces the MCI API with more ease and functionality. I will demonstrate how to use ActiveMovie with a sample movie player I created, called Movie Play. So, enjoy the making of a movie player!

I will demonstrate the ease with which you can make an application that plays a movie. When looking at ActiveMovie for the first time, you might think it seems complex and convoluted. You might end up scratching your head and wondering how Microsoft could say that this SDK is simple to use. After you dive into it, however, and take a look at the example I provide, called

Movie Play, you shouldn't have problems creating what you want. Movie Play demonstrates how simple it is to create an application that plays video streams. The framework for this application can be used in other applications that you want to have play movies.

Movie Play Example

To run Movie Play, type the following:

```
MOVPLAY filename
```

where *filename* is the movie file you want to play.

I designed the example so you could associate `*.avi` and `*.mpg` with `movplay.exe`. Thus, when you click the movie file, it is played with Movie Play. Use the Esc key to stop playing the movie file and exit the program. Press F4 to pause and unpause the movie.

The Setup

To set up an active movie, use the following objects:

> `IGraphBuilder`, which is responsible for taking care of the filters and loading the movie file you want to play. Some of the functions that you will use are `RenderFile()`, `QueryInterface()`, and `Release()`.

> `IVideoWindow`, which is used for placing the movie stream in a window, and for movie stream properties such as height and width. Some of the functions that you will use are `put_Owner()`, `GetPosition()`, `SetPosition()`,`put_WindowStyle()`, and `Release()`.

> `IMediaControl`, which is used to run, pause, and stop the movie file that you have loaded. Some of the functions that you will use are `Run()`, `Pause()`, `Stop()`, and `Release()`.

> `IMediaEvent`, which is responsible for telling you what is going on. For instance, `EC_COMPLETE` tells you that the movie file is finished playing. Some of the functions that you will use are `GetEvent()` and `Release()`.

First, create the `IGraphBuilder` object. To do this, use the `CoCreateInstance()` function. Its prototype is shown here:

```
STDAPI CoCreateInstance(REFCLSID rclsid, LPUNKNOWN pUnkOuter, DWORD dwClsContext,
                        REFIID riid, LPVOID * ppv);
```

As you can see, this is standard COM initialization stuff:

```
IGraphBuilder   *GraphBuilder   =NULL;

CoInitialize(NULL);
hres=CoCreateInstance(CLSID_FilterGraph,NULL,CLSCTX_INPROC_SERVER,IID_IGraphBuilder,
                        (void**)&GraphBuilder);
if(FAILED(hres))
{
```

```
    GotErr=1001;
    wsprintf(ErrMessage,"create GraphBuilder");
    return;
}
```

Next, load a movie file into `IGraphBuilder`, where you can render it for display.

To render the movie, use the `RenderFile()`, which has the following prototype:

```
HRESULT RenderFile(LPCWSTR lpwstrFile, LPCWSTR lpwstrPlayList);
```

After converting the multibyte string to a Unicode string, feed it to the `RenderFile()` function for consumption, as shown here:

```
WNDCLASS wc;
wchar_t  *wfilename;

wfilename=(wchar_t*)malloc(strlen(filename)*sizeof(wchar_t));
hres=mbstowcs(wfilename,filename,strlen(filename));
hres=GraphBuilder->RenderFile(wfilename,NULL);
if(FAILED(hres))
{
    GotErr=1002;
    wsprintf(ErrMessage,"open %s",filename);
    return;
}
```

Ask `IGraphBuilder` to give you `IVideoWindow` object. Do this with the `QueryInterface()` function, as shown here:

```
HRESULT QueryInterface(REFIID iid, void ** ppvObject);

IVideoWindow    *VideoWindow    =NULL;

hres=GraphBuilder->QueryInterface(IID_IVideoWindow,(void**)&VideoWindow);
if(FAILED(hres))
{
    GotErr=1003;
    wsprintf(ErrMessage,"create VideoWindow");
    return;
}
```

Now that you have an `IVideoWindow` object, you can get the rectangular size of the movie and resize your window. Assign the `IVideoWindow` to a window by supplying the window's handle:

```
HRESULT put_Owner(OAHWND Owner);

VideoWindow->put_Owner((OAHWND)hWnd);
```

Next, tell IVideoWindow what style you want to use. I have chosen WS_CHILD, WS_CLIPCHILDREN, and WS_CLIPSIBLINGS, so the child window is created and excludes drawing in the area that the child window occupies:

```
HRESULT put_WindowStyle(long WindowStyle);
```

```
VideoWindow->put_WindowStyle(WS_CHILD¦WS_CLIPCHILDREN¦WS_CLIPSIBLINGS);
```

Now, resize your window to the size of the movie. The GetWindowPosition() tells you the rectangular size of the movie. Call SetWindowPos() to resize the window. Then get the coordinates of your window with GetClientRect(), and set the size and position of IVideoWindow with SetWindowPosition(). The last two lines might seem unnecessary, but if you don't call them, IVideoWindow has a tendency to not stay in the center of the window. This sometimes results in the movie being cut off by one of the sides of the window.

```
RECT     rect;
```

```
VideoWindow->GetWindowPosition(&rect.left,&rect.top,&rect.right,&rect.bottom);
```

```
SetWindowPos(hWnd,HWND_TOP,rect.left,rect.top,rect.right,rect.bottom,SWP_SHOWWINDOW);
```

```
GetClientRect(hWnd,&rect);
```

```
VideoWindow->SetWindowPosition(rect.left,rect.top,rect.right,rect.bottom);
```

The prototypes for these functions are

```
HRESULT GetWindowPosition(long *pLeft, long *pTop, long *pWidth, long *pHeight);
```

```
BOOL SetWindowPos(HWND hWnd, HWND hWndInsertAfter, int X, int Y, int cx, int cy,
UINT uFlags);
```

```
BOOL GetClientRect(HWND hWnd, LPRECT lpRect);
```

```
HRESULT SetWindowPosition(long Left, long Top, long Width, long Height );
```

Next, create the IMediaControl and IMediaEvent objects. You will use these later to control and monitor your movie.

```
IMediaControl   *MediaControl   =NULL;
IMediaEvent     *MediaEvent     =NULL;

hres=GraphBuilder->QueryInterface(IID_IMediaControl,(void**)&MediaControl);
if(FAILED(hres))
{
    GotErr=1004;
    wsprintf(ErrMessage,"create MediaControl");
    return;
}

hres=GraphBuilder->QueryInterface(IID_IMediaEvent,(void**)&MediaEvent);
if(FAILED(hres))
{
```

```
    GotErr=1005;
    wsprintf(ErrMessage,"create MediaEvent");
    return;
}
```

Playing a Movie

You have set up all the necessary objects. Here is the main loop, wherein the movie is played:

```
BYTE            ShutDown;
BYTE            Paused;
BYTE            KeyPressed;

MediaControl->Run();

while(!ShutDown)
{
    if(GotErr)
        goto ExitNow;

    if(PeekMessage(&msg,NULL,0,0,PM_NOREMOVE))
    {
        if(!GetMessage(&msg,NULL,0,0))
            return(msg.wParam);
        TranslateMessage(&msg);
        DispatchMessage(&msg);
    }
    else if(Active)
    {
        MediaEvent->GetEvent(&event,&p1,&p2,10);
        if(event==EC_COMPLETE)
            ShutDown=TRUE;

        if(KeyPressed&&!ShutDown)
        {
            if(Paused)
                MediaControl->Pause();
            else
                MediaControl->Run();
            KeyPressed=FALSE;
        }
    }
    else
    {
        WaitMessage();
    }
}

ExitNow:

MediaControl->Stop();
SetWindowPos(hWnd,HWND_TOP,0,0,0,0,SWP_HIDEWINDOW);
DestroyWindow(hWnd);
```

Run() is used to play the movie. Pause() pauses the movie, and Stop() stops the movie. You need to know when the movie has finished so that you can exit the Movie Play application.

The GetEvent() function helps. When it returns the event EC_COMPLETE, you know that the movie is finished playing. The prototype for GetEvent() is

```
HRESULT GetEvent(long * lEventCode, long * lParam1, long * lParam2, long
msTimeout);
```

Cleaning Up

Each object you created has a function called Release(), which will do some cleanup and remove the object from memory. Its prototype is

```
ULONG Release(void);
```

Remember, you used put_Owner() with IVideoWindow to link to your window. You need to call put_Owner() again and feed it a NULL to break the link. If you don't do this, messages will still be sent to the window causing error messages to appear when you try to shut down your application.

```
static void RemoveMoviePlay(void)
{
    if(GraphBuilder!=NULL)
    {
        if(MediaEvent!=NULL)
        {
            MediaEvent->Release();
            MediaEvent=NULL;
        }

        if(MediaControl!=NULL)
        {
            MediaControl->Release();
            MediaControl=NULL;
        }

        if(VideoWindow!=NULL)
        {
            VideoWindow->put_Owner(NULL);
            VideoWindow->Release();
            VideoWindow=NULL;
        }

        GraphBuilder->Release();
        GraphBuilder=NULL;
    }

    CoUninitialize();

    if(GotErr) StartUpFail(hWnd);
}
```

Summary

Wow, wasn't that simple? You are now on your way to understanding the basics of ActiveMovie. Like anything else, after you get into using the API, things begin to make more sense. There are a lot more advanced areas you can get into, such as creating graphic filters, which is how you store the video stream data. For most people, being given an API that plays video streams easily and can also be used on the Internet eases development of multimedia applications considerably. It has been fun, but not as much fun as the next chapter, "DirectX 3.0."

30

DirectX 3.0

by Stephen Makonin

This chapter will show you the basics for using DirectX and discuss its five components. This chapter also shows some neat effects you create with DirectX, and how easy it is to do. The best way to understand DirectX is to learn each component, one at a time. At first, DirectX might seem overwhelming and complex, but Microsoft has done a good job of making the API easy to understand and easy to develop in.

The five components of DirectX are

- DirectDraw
- Direct3D
- DirectInput
- DirectSound
- DirectPlay

So, what does each component do? I'm glad you asked. I thought at this point I would tell you a bit about each of the five components of DirectX.

DirectDraw interfaces with the display hardware, which allows you to do things like set graphics modes, change palette colors, and manipulate 2D graphics.

Direct3D is built on top of DirectDraw and has two sub-APIs: the Retained Mode and the Intermediate Mode. With Direct3D you can easily render and display complex 3D models in real time.

DirectInput enables you to control input devices such as the keyboard, mouse, and joystick. The nice thing about this API is that future input devices can also be controlled without changing its functions.

DirectSound enables you to play digital audio with real-time mixing of sound effects. Unfortunately, there is no MIDI interface so you must use either MCI functions or a third-party library.

DirectPlay gives you the functionality to create multiplayer games and interactive applications. It easily enables you to connect to other people via direct serial connection, modem, IPX, and the Internet.

> **NOTE**
>
> Remember, DirectX 3.0 is not supported by Windows NT yet, but DirectX 2.0 is. It is recommended that you use Windows 95.

When looking at the source code for this demo, you might wonder where the MFC and C++ objects are. Using MFC and objects will only muddy the waters, and you would spend most of your time learning my interface to DirectX instead of actually learning DirectX.

From DOS to DirectX

When I first got into using DirectX, I had just finished some DOS game examples. I remember reading through Microsoft's DirectX manuals and thinking to myself, "How could I program in this API? I have no control over the hardware!". Programming in DOS for years allowed me to control the hardware and do whatever I wanted with it. With DirectX, on the other hand, you must take that leap of faith and trust Microsoft's capability to have an API that performs as well as DOS. It took a while for me to do this; control is a hard thing to give up.

The DirectX API lets you concentrate on the important items, like the storyline and how the player interacts with your game. If you had to write every component that Microsoft's DirectX provides, it would take years for you to produce something tangible. If you are like me, a one-person operation, the API will save you countless headaches. DirectX is nowhere near being perfect and needs to do a lot of growing up before it becomes a well-received, mature product, but you still can do impressive things with it.

The Quest Example

I have provided a graphic demo on the CD-ROM, which I dubbed "The Quest." I made sure that the code is in an easy-to-read form. Although the demo does not really have a point, it allows you to get a chance to see how each component of DirectX works together. This demo is actually a stripped-down version of a bigger project I am currently working on. I will not discuss all the parts of the example because that is out of the scope of the chapter, but if you poke around in it I am sure you find a couple of goodies.

> **NOTE**
>
> The MIDI snippets were written by Joseph Fuoco, a good friend of mine. The graphic tiles were provided by my company. Please do not use the music or the tiles for profitable purposes without my permission. (They are not royalty-free.)

DirectDraw

DirectDraw is the "all you need to create 2D graphics" API. You can do anything from placing a graphics image on the screen to changing the colors of a palette. Just think of DirectDraw as being the API that controls everything you seen on the screen.

In this section I will show you how to

■ Set video modes

■ Use palettes

- Create drawing surfaces
- Use special effects

DirectDraw is a fairly big API and will take about half of this chapter to discuss. So, without further ado, here is DirectDraw.

The Setup

At this point, you might want to load The Quest program and open the DRAW.CPP source file. Find the function called SetupDirectDraw(), which is where we the initialize of all DirectDraw objects. Here is how to initialize the DirectDraw object:

```
LPDIRECTDRAW DDObj=NULL;
if(DirectDrawCreate(NULL,&DDObj,NULL)!=DD_OK)
{
    GotErr=3000;
    wsprintf(ErrMessage,"create DirectDraw object");
    return;
}
```

The DirectDrawCreate() function creates a DirectDraw object that you will use. The LPDIRECTDRAW variable is a pointer to the DirectDraw object you have created. The prototype for DirectDrawCreate() is HRESULT DirectDrawCreate(GUID FAR * lpGUID, LPDIRECTDRAW FAR * lplDD, IUnknown FAR * pUnkOuter).

Setting the Graphics Mode

The Quest example uses 320×200, 256-color graphics mode. Because you have to go into Xmode, you must use the SetCooperativeLevel() to have exclusive, full-screen control of the graphics display. After this function is called, you can call the SetDisplayMode() function. You might notice that you'll pass the 8, for 8-bit color, instead of 256, for 256 colors. Shown here is code that sets up the graphics mode:

```
#define MAX_HEIGHT      200
#define MAX_WIDTH       320
#define PALETTE_BITS      8
if(DDObj-
>SetCooperativeLevel(hWnd,DDSCL_EXCLUSIVE|DDSCL_FULLSCREEN|DDSCL_ALLOWMODEX)!=DD_OK)
{
    wsprintf(ErrMessage,"get exclusive access to video screen");
    GotErr=3001;
    return;
}
if(DDObj->SetDisplayMode(MAX_WIDTH,MAX_HEIGHT,PALETTE_BITS)!=DD_OK)
{
    wsprintf(ErrMessage,"set video mode to
%ix%ix%i",MAX_WIDTH,MAX_HEIGHT,PALETTE_BITS);
    GotErr=3002;
    return;
}
```

The prototypes for `SetCooperativeLevel()` and `SetDisplayMode()` are

```
HRESULT SetCooperativeLevel(HWND hWnd, DWORD dwFlags);
HRESULT SetDisplayMode(DWORD dwWidth, DWORD dwHeight, DWORD dwBPP, DWORD
dwRefreshRate, DWORD dwFlags);
```

Creating Surfaces and Buffers

Next, create the primary surface, a back buffer, and an off-screen buffer. Use the `CreateSurface()` function to create these type of drawing surfaces. The prototype for `CreateSurface()` is

```
HRESULT CreateSurface(LPDDSURFACEDESC lpDDSurfaceDesc, LPDIRECTDRAWSURFACE FAR *
lplpDDSurface,
                      IUnknown FAR * pUnkOuter);
```

The `ddsd` structure tells `CreateSurface()` how to create the surface you want. The `ddsd.dwFlags` variable tells you what parts of the structure you are using; in this case, use the capabilities and back-buffer variables. The `DDSCAPS_PRIMARYSURFACE` constant describes that this surface will be the primary surface. `DDSCAPS_3DDEVICE` is discussed later in the section "Direct3D." `DDSCAPS_FLIP` and `DDSCAPS_COMPLEX` describe the surface as being able to flip what is displayed between the primary surface and the back buffer. The `ddsd.dwBackBufferCount` variable describes the amount of back buffers needed; in this case, one back buffer is needed. Next, use the `GetAttachedSurface()` function to retrieve the pointer to the back buffer that was created. The prototype for `GetAttachedSurface()` is

```
HRESULT GetAttachedSurface(LPDDSCAPS lpDDSCaps, LPDIRECTDRAWSURFACE2 FAR *
lplpDDAttachedSurface);
```

I use the `SetColorKey()` to set the transparency colors for the surface so that when I place a bitmap on the back buffer, it ignores color 255 on the bitmap I want to place. Notice that I do not use `SetColorKey()` for the primary surface. The prototype for `SetColorKey()` is

```
HRESULT SetColorKey(DWORD dwFlags, LPDDCOLORKEY lpDDColorKey);
```

In Xmode, you cannot access the primary surface directly; you must do all your work in the back buffer and then flip the surfaces to display what you did.

Finally, create an off-screen plain, which the `DDSCAPS_OFFSCREENPLAIN` constant describes. The `DDSCAPS_SYSTEMMEMORY` constant, in effect, tells `CreateSurface()` that you want this surface allocated in system memory instead of video memory. You will also notice that I have created a 520×400 surface, which gives the 100-pixel border needed when rendering a 2D scene. Here is the code that shows how to create these surfaces:

```
#define RND_HEIGHT          400
#define RND_WIDTH           520
#define TRASPARENT_COLOR 0xFF
LPDIRECTDRAWSURFACE DDScreen=NULL;
LPDIRECTDRAWSURFACE DDBuffer=NULL;
LPDIRECTDRAWSURFACE DDRender=NULL;
DDSURFACEDESC ddsd;
DDSCAPS       ddscaps;
```

```
ddsd.dwSize=sizeof(ddsd);
ddsd.dwFlags=DDSD_CAPS|DDSD_BACKBUFFERCOUNT;
ddsd.ddsCaps.dwCaps=DDSCAPS_PRIMARYSURFACE|DDSCAPS_3DDEVICE|DDSCAPS_FLIP|DDSCAPS_COMPLEX;
ddsd.dwBackBufferCount=1;
if(DDObj->CreateSurface(&ddsd,&DDScreen,NULL)!=DD_OK)
{
    GotErr=3003;
    wsprintf(ErrMessage,"allocate enough memory");
    return;
}
ddscaps.dwCaps=DDSCAPS_BACKBUFFER;
if(DDScreen->GetAttachedSurface(&ddscaps,&DDBuffer)!=DD_OK)
{
    GotErr=3004;
    wsprintf(ErrMessage,"attach surface");
    return;
}
ddck.dwColorSpaceLowValue=TRASPARENT_COLOR;
ddck.dwColorSpaceHighValue=TRASPARENT_COLOR;
if(DDBuffer->SetColorKey(DDCKEY_SRCBLT,&ddck)!=DD_OK)
{
    GotErr=3009;
    wsprintf(ErrMessage,"set color");
    return;
}
ddsd.dwSize=sizeof(ddsd);
ddsd.dwFlags=DDSD_CAPS|DDSD_HEIGHT|DDSD_WIDTH;
ddsd.ddsCaps.dwCaps=DDSCAPS_OFFSCREENPLAIN|DDSCAPS_SYSTEMMEMORY;
ddsd.dwHeight=RND_HEIGHT;
ddsd.dwWidth=RND_WIDTH;
if(DDObj->CreateSurface(&ddsd,&DDRender,NULL)!=DD_OK)
{
    GotErr=3011;
    wsprintf(ErrMessage,"allocate enough memory");
    return;
}
ddck.dwColorSpaceLowValue=TRASPARENT_COLOR;
ddck.dwColorSpaceHighValue=TRASPARENT_COLOR;
if(DDRender->SetColorKey(DDCKEY_SRCBLT,&ddck)!=DD_OK)
{
    GotErr=3012;
    wsprintf(ErrMessage,"set color");
    return;
}
```

Creating a Palette

After creating the surfaces, you can create the palette object. If you were in 16-bit color or higher mode, you would not have to do this because these types of mode do not require any palette maintenance. Use the `CreatePalette()` to create the palette object. The prototype for `CreatePalette()` is

```
HRESULT CreatePalette(DWORD dwFlags, LPPALETTEENTRY lpColorTable,
                    LPDIRECTDRAWPALETTE FAR * lplpDDPalette, IUnknown FAR *
pUnkOuter);
```

DDPCAPS_8BIT indicates that you want an 8-bit color palette. DDPCAPS_ALLOW256 indicates that you want to use all 256 palette entries. Without this setting, Windows has a tendency to reserve some of the palette entrees for its own use. The ScrPal structure is where all the RGB information for each color is held. The final step is to attach the palette to each of the surfaces using the SetPalette() function. The prototype for SetPalette() is

```
HRESULT SetPalette(LPDIRECTDRAWPALETTE lpDDPalette);
```

By doing it this way, you could actually have a different palette for each surface. Here is how to create the palette object:

```
LPDIRECTDRAWPALETTE DDPalette=NULL;
PALETTEENTRY        ScrPal[MAX_COLORS];
if(DDObj-
>CreatePalette(DDPCAPS_8BIT¦DDPCAPS_ALLOW256,ScrPal,&DDPalette,NULL)!=DD_OK)
{
    GotErr=3005;
    wsprintf(ErrMessage,"create a palette");
    return;
}
DDScreen->SetPalette(DDPalette);
DDBuffer->SetPalette(DDPalette);
DDRender->SetPalette(DDPalette);
```

Loading Game Tiles

When you run The Quest, your character wanders around on a map. To construct the map, I used a series of graphic tiles. I wrote a DOS program that took all my graphic tiles and combined them into one file called TILES.BIN. I then copied the raw data into a surface object for use. It should be pretty straightforward. You might notice that I used the Lock() function so that Windows can give a pointer to the surface. After I finished copying the raw data, I used the Unlock() function so that Windows has control of the memory again. The prototypes for Lock() and Unlock() are

```
HRESULT Lock(LPRECT lpDestRect, LPDDSURFACEDESC lpDDSurfaceDesc, DWORD dwFlags,
HANDLE hEvent);
HRESULT Unlock(LPVOID lpSurfaceData);
```

I repeated this process until all the map tiles were loaded into their respective surfaces. The TILES.NDX file stores the height and width of each map tile, as well as the offset, from the start of the file, at its location. The following code snippet shows the LoadShapesAndIndices() function. It shows how I loaded a file of raw graphic data into an array of surfaces.

```
typedef struct SHAPE_TYPE
{
    LPDIRECTDRAWSURFACE tile;
    byte                height;
    byte                width;
}SHAPE,*SHAPE_PTR;
SHAPE*shapes;
TilesSize=FileSize("GAMEDAT\\TILES.BIN");
if(GotErr)
```

```
{
    GotErr=5003;
    goto CleanUp;
}
TilesPtr=(LPBYTE)LocalAlloc(LPTR,TilesSize);
if(TilesPtr==NULL)
{
    GotErr=1105;
    wsprintf(ErrMessage,"allocate enough memory");
    goto CleanUp;
}
LoadFile("GAMEDAT\\TILES.BIN",TilesPtr);
if(GotErr)
{
    GotErr=5004;
    goto CleanUp;
}
for(i=0;i<max.Tiles;i++)
{
    tile=(TILE*)tiles;
    TilesSize=(dword)(tile->offset2<<16)+tile->offset1;
    shapes[i].height=tile->height;
    shapes[i].width=tile->width;
    ddsd.dwSize=sizeof(ddsd);
    ddsd.dwFlags=DDSD_CAPS|DDSD_HEIGHT|DDSD_WIDTH;
    ddsd.ddsCaps.dwCaps=DDSCAPS_OFFSCREENPLAIN;
    ddsd.dwHeight=shapes[i].height;
    ddsd.dwWidth=shapes[i].width;
    if(DDObj->CreateSurface(&ddsd,&shapes[i].tile,NULL)!=DD_OK)
    {
        GotErr=3006;
        wsprintf(ErrMessage,"allocate enough memory");
        goto CleanUp;
    }
    ddck.dwColorSpaceLowValue=TRANSPARENT_COLOR;
    ddck.dwColorSpaceHighValue=TRANSPARENT_COLOR;
    if(shapes[i].tile->SetColorKey(DDCKEY_SRCBLT,&ddck)!=DD_OK)
    {
        GotErr=3007;
        wsprintf(ErrMessage,"set color");
        goto CleanUp;
    }
    ddsd.dwSize=sizeof(ddsd);
    if(shapes[i].tile->Lock(NULL,&ddsd,0,NULL)!=DD_OK)
    {
        GotErr=3010;
        wsprintf(ErrMessage,"lock surface");
        goto CleanUp;
    }
    srcmem=TilesPtr+TilesSize;
    trgmem=(LPBYTE)ddsd.lpSurface;
    for(j=0;j<shapes[i].height;j++)
    {
        memcpy(trgmem,srcmem,shapes[i].width);
        trgmem+=ddsd.lPitch;
        srcmem+=shapes[i].width;
    }
    shapes[i].tile->Unlock(NULL);
    tiles+=6;
}
```

Using Palettes and Colors

Because you are in 8-bit color, you must take care of the palette. There are a lot of neat things you can do with palettes, such as palette animation and fading. I like using fading, and it is a elementary special effect that all games programmers use. So let us explore the palette.

Loading Palette Files

The palette I used is saved in a file that I then loaded into memory. The LoadPalette() is pretty straightforward; it loads the file into the WorldPal structure for later use.

> **NOTE**
>
> Remember, the RGB indexes range from 0 to 255 in Windows, not 0 to 63 as in DOS.

Listing 30.1 shows how to load the palette file.

Listing 30.1. Loading a palette file.

```
typedef struct COLOR_TYPE
{
    byte red;
    byte green;
    byte blue;
}COLOR,*COLOR_PTR;
typedef struct PALETTE_TYPE
{
    COLOR color[MAX_COLORS];
}PALETTE,*PALETTE_PTR;
PALETTE WorldPal;
void LoadPalette(char*FileName)
{
    LoadFile(FileName,(byte*)&WorldPal);
    if(GotErr)
    {
        GotErr=5000;
        return;
    }
}
```

Setting the Palette

After the palette is loaded, you can set it. The first thing to do is to zero out the transparent color so it is black, like color 0. Next, translate the palette structure into a structure that the palette object can understand. Finally, call the SetEntries() function to activate the palette.

The prototype for SetEntries() is

```
HRESULT SetEntries(DWORD dwFlags, DWORD dwStartingEntry, DWORD dwCount,
LPPALETTEENTRY lpEntries);
```

By setting parameter 2 to 0 and parameter 3 to 265, you are asking the SetEntries() function to activate all 256 colors. The code you use to activate the palette is shown here:

```
#define MAX_COLORS 256
void SetPalette(void)
{
    short i;
    WorldPal.color[TRASPARENT_COLOR].red=0;
    WorldPal.color[TRASPARENT_COLOR].green=0;
    WorldPal.color[TRASPARENT_COLOR].blue=0;
    for(i=0;i<MAX_COLORS;i++)
    {
        ScrPal[i].peRed=WorldPal.color[i].red;
        ScrPal[i].peGreen=WorldPal.color[i].green;
        ScrPal[i].peBlue=WorldPal.color[i].blue;
    }
    ScrPal[TRASPARENT_COLOR].peRed=0;
    ScrPal[TRASPARENT_COLOR].peGreen=0;
    ScrPal[TRASPARENT_COLOR].peBlue=0;
    DDPalette->SetEntries(0,0,MAX_COLORS,ScrPal);
}
```

When loading certain images to the screen, you might want to blank out the palette. You would do this in much the same way you set the palette. First, set all the RGB values in ScrPal to 0. Then use the SetEntries() function to activate the newly created palette. This is demonstrated here:

```
void BlankPalette(void)
{
    short index;
    for(index=0;index<MAX_COLORS;index++)
    {
        ScrPal[index].peRed=0;
        ScrPal[index].peGreen=0;
        ScrPal[index].peBlue=0;
    }
    DDPalette->SetEntries(0,0,MAX_COLORS,ScrPal);
}
```

Fading the Palette

For the fading effect, I use two variables: lighting, which holds the percentage of visibility, and AjustLighting, which flags the palette fading engine to start modifying the palette. For instance, when the variable daytime is set to TRUE, you get 100 percent visibility; when the night-time variable is TRUE, you get only 30 percent visibility. Here is the syntax to use:

```
byte lighting;
word AjustLighting;
void main(void)
{
```

```
    ...
    while()
    {
        if(daytime)
        {
            lighting=100;
            AjustLighting=TRUE;
        }
        elseif(nighttime)
        {
            lighting=30;
            AjustLighting=TRUE;
        }
    ...
    if(AjustLighting) ChangePalette();
    ...
    }
}
```

Now that you have seen the syntax for the palette fading engine, I'll show you how the engine works. The first thing to do is to determine if you just started the fade or if you are in the middle of fading. If you just started, you can calculate how much to increment each RGB value for each color. Next, set the value of AjustLighting to 768, which will be your check value. When AjustLighting becomes FALSE or 0, you have finished adjusting the visibility. Then modify each RGB value.

I use the WaitForVerticalBlank() function so that the *snow effect* does not happen. Vertical blank (vertical retrace) is a period of time in which the video card is not accessing memory to update the screen. At this time, it is best to change palette colors and draw graphics so you get smooth animation. If you try to do any graphics updates while the video card is accessing memory, random dots will appear on the screen while the palette is being adjusted or a graphic is being placed, hence the term snow effect. The prototype for WaitForVerticalBlank() is

```
HRESULT WaitForVerticalBlank(DWORD dwFlags, HANDLE hEvent);
```

Then call SetEntries() to activate the newly created palette. The function that houses the fading engine is shown here:

```
void ChangePalette(void)
{
    static PALETTEENTRY target[MAX_COLORS];
    static byte         NewCalc=TRUE;
    short               i;
    if(NewCalc)
    {
        for(i=0;i<MAX_COLORS;i++)
        {
            target[i].peRed=(byte)((dword)(WorldPal.color[i].red*lighting)/100);
            target[i].peGreen=(byte)((dword)(WorldPal.color[i].green*lighting)/
100);
            target[i].peBlue=(byte)((dword)(WorldPal.color[i].blue*lighting)/100);
        }
        NewCalc=FALSE;
```

```
    }
    AjustLighting=MAX_COLORS*3;
    for(i=0;i<MAX_COLORS;i++)
    {
        if(ScrPal[i].peRed<target[i].peRed)
            ScrPal[i].peRed++;
        else if(ScrPal[i].peRed>target[i].peRed)
            ScrPal[i].peRed--;
        else
            AjustLighting--;
        if(ScrPal[i].peGreen<target[i].peGreen)
            ScrPal[i].peGreen++;
        else if(ScrPal[i].peGreen>target[i].peGreen)
            ScrPal[i].peGreen--;
        else
            AjustLighting--;
        if(ScrPal[i].peBlue<target[i].peBlue)
            ScrPal[i].peBlue++;
        else if(ScrPal[i].peBlue>target[i].peBlue)
            ScrPal[i].peBlue--;
        else
            AjustLighting--;
    }
    DDObj->WaitForVerticalBlank(DDWAITVB_BLOCKBEGIN,NULL);
    DDPalette->SetEntries(0,0,MAX_COLORS,ScrPal);
    if(!AjustLighting)
        NewCalc=TRUE;
}
```

Using Fonts

No special API exists to support fonts. You have to use HDCs (or device context handles) to display fonts. All routines that handle fonts are located in the FONT.CPP source file. Using fonts is quite easy and takes very little effort.

The Setup

To create a font, use the CreateFont() function; as you can see, it needs a lot of parameters. The prototype for CreateFont() is

```
HFONT CreateFont(int nHeight, int nWidth, int nEscapement, int nOrientation, int
fnWeight,
            DWORD fdwItalic, DWORD fdwUnderline, DWORD fdwStrikeOut, DWORD
fdwCharSet,
            DWORD fdwOutputPrecision, DWORD fdwClipPrecision, DWORD
fdwQuality,
            DWORD fdwPitchAndFamily, LPCTSTR lpszFace);
```

This code is an example of how to use the CreateFont() function:

```
HFONT tinyfont;
HFONT smallfont;
HFONT largefont;
void StartupFonts(void)
{
```

```
largefont=CreateFont(28,0,0,0,FW_NORMAL,FALSE,FALSE,FALSE,ANSI_CHARSET,OUT_DEFAULT_PRECIS,
    CLIP_DEFAULT_PRECIS,DEFAULT_QUALITY,VARIABLE_PITCH,"Arial");
if(largefont==NULL)
{
    GotErr=2004;
    wsprintf(ErrMessage,"load Arial Font");
    return;
}
smallfont=CreateFont(14,0,0,0,FW_NORMAL,FALSE,FALSE,FALSE,ANSI_CHARSET,OUT_DEFAULT_PRECIS,
    CLIP_DEFAULT_PRECIS,DEFAULT_QUALITY,VARIABLE_PITCH,"Arial");
if(smallfont==NULL)
{
    GotErr=2005;
    wsprintf(ErrMessage,"load Arial Font");
    return;
}
tinyfont=CreateFont(10,5,0,0,FW_NORMAL,FALSE,FALSE,FALSE,ANSI_CHARSET,OUT_DEFAULT_PRECIS,
    CLIP_DEFAULT_PRECIS,DEFAULT_QUALITY,VARIABLE_PITCH,"Arial");
if(smallfont==NULL)
{
    GotErr=2016;
    wsprintf(ErrMessage,"load Arial Font");
    return;
}
}
```

Setting Font Colors

The SetTextColor() function allows you to set the font with a predefined set of colors. I use the macro RGB() to get a color's number and store it in a COLORREF variable. The prototype for RGB() is

```
COLORREF RGB( BYTE bRed, BYTE bGreen, BYTE bBlue );
```

Here is an example:

```
#define BLUE_FONT          0
#define RED_FONT           1
#define PURPLE_FONT        2
#define BLUE_FONT2         3
#define PURPLE_FONT2       4
#define BRIGHT_FONT        5
COLORREF textcolor;
COLORREF textshadow;
void SetTextColor(short scheme)
{
    switch(scheme)
    {
        case BLUE_FONT:
            textshadow=RGB(51,51,251);
            textcolor=RGB(51,0,135);
            break;
        case RED_FONT:
            textshadow=RGB(123,15,0);
            textcolor=RGB(255,15,0);
            break;
```

```
        case PURPLE_FONT:
            textshadow=RGB(67,19,143);
            textcolor=RGB(123,123,223);
            break;
        case BLUE_FONT2:
            textshadow=RGB(51,0,135);
            textcolor=RGB(51,51,251);
            break;
        case PURPLE_FONT2:
            textshadow=RGB(51,51,251);
            textcolor=RGB(123,123,223);
            break;
        case BRIGHT_FONT:
            textshadow=RGB(67,19,143);
            textcolor=RGB(199,199,243);
            break;
        default:
            return;
    }
}
```

Displaying Your Text

First, use the SetTextColor() function to set the color of your font; then call the PrintText() function. Basically, the PrintText() function needs the text you want displayed, the coordinates, and the font you want to use. Notice that I then use the Flip() function, because the text is actually written to the back buffer. After the text is written, use the Flip() function to display it to the screen. The prototype for Flip() is

```
HRESULT Flip(LPDIRECTDRAWSURFACE2 lpDDSurfaceTargetOverride, DWORD dwFlags);
```

Here is one of the functions that displays text to the screen:

```
#define LARGE_FONT          0
#define SMALL_FONT          1
#define TINY_FONT           2
void LoadMessage(void)
{
    LoadPalette("GAMEDAT\\WORLD.PAL");
    SetPalette();
    SetTextColor(PURPLE_FONT);
    PrintText("Loading, Please Wait...",1,189,SMALL_FONT);
    DDScreen->Flip(NULL,DDFLIP_WAIT);
}
```

In the PrintText() function, the first thing to do is to call the GetDC() function of the surface you want the text to be put into.

> **NOTE**
>
> Remember, you are in XMode and cannot access the primary surface directly. You have to use the back buffer.

Call the SetBkMode() function to set the text background to transparent. Then set the text color with the SetTextColor() function, call the ExtTextOut() function, and feed it the surface's HDC to display the text. Notice that in the PrintText() function I have done this twice, because I want the text I display to have a shadow. Finally, call ReleaseDC() to release the HDC. The prototypes for these functions are

```
HRESULT GetDC(HDC FAR * lphDC);
HRESULT ReleaseDC(HDC hDC);
int SetBkMode(HDC hdc, int iBkMode );
COLORREF SetTextColor(HDC hdc, COLORREF crColor);
BOOL ExtTextOut(HDC hdc, int X, int Y, UINT fuOptions, CONST RECT *lprc, LPCTSTR
lpString,
            UINT cbCount, CONST INT *lpDx );
```

Here is the code showing the font engine:

```
void PrintText(char*text,short x,short y,short size)
{
    HDC    hdc;
    short tx,ty;
    DDBuffer->GetDC(&hdc);
    switch(size)
    {
        case LARGE_FONT:
            SelectObject(hdc,largefont);
            tx=x;
            ty=y-5;
            break;
        case SMALL_FONT:
            SelectObject(hdc,smallfont);
            tx=x+1;
            ty=y-3;
            break;
        case TINY_FONT:
            SelectObject(hdc,tinyfont);
            tx=x;
            ty=y;
            break;
        default:
            return;
    }
    SetBkMode(hdc,TRANSPARENT);
    SetTextColor(hdc,textshadow);
    ExtTextOut(hdc,tx+1,ty+1,0,0,text,strlen(text),0);
    SetTextColor(hdc,textcolor);
    ExtTextOut(hdc,tx,ty,0,0,text,strlen(text),0);
    DDBuffer->ReleaseDC(hdc);
}
```

Cleaning Up

Cleaning up the fonts you create is very simple; just use the DeleteObject() function as shown here:

```
void RemoveFonts(void)
{
```

```
        DeleteObject(tinyfont);
        DeleteObject(smallfont);
        DeleteObject(largefont);
}
```

The prototype for `DeleteObject()` is

```
BOOL DeleteObject(HGDIOBJ hObject);
```

Bitmaps and Special Effects

DirectDraw provides a number of special effect you can use to manipulate bitmaps or images. These special effects are provided to you when you use the `Blt()` function. The `Blt()` function *blits*, or copies, the image on one surface to another. By providing information to any `DDBLTFX` structure you can perform effects like arithmetic stretching, mirroring, and rotating. I will show you how to shrink and enlarge images, using the mirroring effect, and how to clear surfaces. You will notice the `DDBLT_KEYSRC` constant as a parameter in the `Blt()` function; this lets you use the transparent color of the source image. The prototype for `Blt()` is

```
HRESULT Blt(LPRECT lpDestRect, LPDIRECTDRAWSURFACE2 lpDDSrcSurface, LPRECT
lpSrcRect,
            DWORD dwFlags, LPDDBLTFX lpDDBltFx);
```

Shrinking and Enlarging Images

Here are the `VDisplayBox()` and `VPutShape2()` functions:

```
void VDisplayBox(short size,short action)
{
    short sx,sy;
    float i;
    word tx,ty;
    if(action==DISP_BOX)
    {
        tx=(MAX_WIDTH>>1)-(shapes[size].width>>1);
        ty=(MAX_HEIGHT>>1)-(shapes[size].height>>1)-5;
        VPutShape(tx,ty,size);
    }
    else if(action==OPEN_BOX)
    {
        for(i=0.0;i<1.1;i+=(float)0.1)
        {
            sx=(short)(shapes[size].width*i);
            sy=(short)(shapes[size].height*i);
            tx=(MAX_WIDTH>>1)-(sx>>1);
            ty=(MAX_HEIGHT>>1)-(sy>>1)-5;
            RenderView(p.x,p.y,p.dir);
            VPutShape2(tx,ty,sx,sy,size);
            DisplayView();
        }
    }
    else
    {
```

```
        for(i=1.0;i>0.0;i-=(float)0.1)
        {
            sx=(short)(shapes[size].width*i);
            sy=(short)(shapes[size].height*i);
            tx=(MAX_WIDTH>>1)-(sx>>1);
            ty=(MAX_HEIGHT>>1)-(sy>>1)-5;
            RenderView(p.x,p.y,p.dir);
            VPutShape2(tx,ty,sx,sy,size);
            DisplayView();
        }
    }
}
void VPutShape2(short x,short y,word width,word height,short TileNum)
{
    RECT    tiledim;
    RECT    scrspace;
    tiledim.left=0;
    tiledim.top=0;
    tiledim.right=shapes[TileNum].width;
    tiledim.bottom=shapes[TileNum].height;
    scrspace.left=x;
    scrspace.top=y;
    scrspace.right=width+x;
    scrspace.bottom=height+y;
    DDBuffer->Blt(&scrspace,shapes[TileNum].tile,&tiledim,
    DDBLT_KEYSRC,NULL);
}
```

The VDisplayBox() function uses the VPutShape2() function to open a window box, which is used for the main menu of The Quest. When running The Quest, the main menu first opens. Its window enlarges from a pixel in the center of the screen to its original size, And when the main menu closes, its window shrinks from its original size to a pixel in the center of the screen.

So how does VPutShape2() work? All you have to do is use the Blt() function. If you want the image to shrink, give the width and height parameters a value that is smaller than the width and height of the image you want displayed. If you want the image to enlarge, give the width and height parameters a value that is larger than the width and height of the image you want displayed.

Mirroring Images

The next effect I want to show you is one that I use a lot. Mirroring is very useful in cutting down memory consumption. Suppose you wanted to have a box made from tiles. You would have to save each side and each corner, which would mean you would need eight tiles. With mirroring, you need to save only two tiles: one of the corners and one of the sides. Then use the mirroring effect to create the other six tiles at rendering time.

You can use the Blt() function to perform the mirroring effect. Which type of mirroring you want to use depends on the constant placed in ddfx.dwDDFX variable.

Let's take my box example again. Suppose you had a tile with the northwest corner drawn on it. You would do the following to create the other three corners:

To mirror the tile so it has a northeast corner, use the `DDBLTFX_MIRRORLEFTRIGHT` constant.

To mirror the tile so it has a southwest corner, use the `DDBLTFX_MIRRORUPDOWN` constant.

To mirror the tile so it has a southeast corner, use the `DDBLTFX_MIRRORUPDOWN` and the `DDBLTFX_MIRRORLEFTRIGHT` constants.

The following is an example of how to implement the mirroring effect:

```
void VPutChunk(short x,short y,CHUNK_PTR chunks,byte ChunkNum)
{
    RECT    tiledim;
    RECT    scrspace;
    DDBLTFX ddfx;
    word    TileNum;
    if(ChunkNum>0xFB)
        return;
    TileNum=chunks[ChunkNum].SpriteIndex[AnimIndex];
    tiledim.left=0;
    tiledim.top=0;
    tiledim.right=shapes[TileNum].width;
    tiledim.bottom=shapes[TileNum].height;
    if(tiledim.right>30)
        x-=(word)((tiledim.right-30)>>1);
    if(tiledim.bottom>(chunks[ChunkNum].ylen<<4))
        y-=(word)(tiledim.bottom-(chunks[ChunkNum].ylen<<4));
    scrspace.left=x;
    scrspace.top=y;
    scrspace.right=shapes[TileNum].width+x;
    scrspace.bottom=shapes[TileNum].height+y;
    ddfx.dwSize=sizeof(ddfx);
    switch(chunks[ChunkNum].MirrorType)
    {
        case MIRROR_NONE:
            DDRender-
>Blt(&scrspace,shapes[TileNum].tile,&tiledim,DDBLT_KEYSRC,NULL);
            break;
        case MIRROR_HORZ:
            ddfx.dwDDFX=DDBLTFX_MIRRORLEFTRIGHT;
            DDRender-
>Blt(&scrspace,shapes[TileNum].tile,&tiledim,DDBLT_DDFX¦DDBLT_KEYSRC,&ddfx);
            break;
        case MIRROR_VERT:
            ddfx.dwDDFX=DDBLTFX_MIRRORUPDOWN;
            DDRender-
>Blt(&scrspace,shapes[TileNum].tile,&tiledim,DDBLT_DDFX¦DDBLT_KEYSRC,&ddfx);
            break;
        case MIRROR_FULL:
            ddfx.dwDDFX=DDBLTFX_MIRRORLEFTRIGHT¦DDBLTFX_MIRRORUPDOWN;
            DDRender-
>Blt(&scrspace,shapes[TileNum].tile,&tiledim,DDBLT_DDFX¦DDBLT_KEYSRC,&ddfx);
            break;
    }
}
```

Clearing the Screen and Surfaces

Occasionally, you will need to clear the screen to a certain color. The ClearSurface() function clears a specified surface to a specified color. It uses the Blt() function with the fourth parameter having a value of DDBLT_COLORFILL. The Blt() function then looks in the variable dwFillColor for the color you want the surface to be filled with.

The ClearScreen() function clears the screen to a specified color. It works the same way as the ClearSurface() function but uses the Flip() function at the end to display the results to the screen. Here is the code showing how to use the ClearSurface() and ClearScreen() functions.

```
void ClearSurface(LPDIRECTDRAWSURFACE Surface,byte color)
{
    DDBLTFX ddfx;
    ddfx.dwSize=sizeof(ddfx);
    ddfx.dwFillColor=color;
    Surface->Blt(NULL,NULL,NULL,DDBLT_COLORFILL,&ddfx);
}
void ClearScreen(byte color)
{
    DDBLTFX ddfx;
    ddfx.dwSize=sizeof(ddfx);
    ddfx.dwFillColor=color;
    DDBuffer->Blt(NULL,NULL,NULL,DDBLT_COLORFILL,&ddfx);
    DDScreen->Flip(NULL,0);
}
```

Loose Ends

By now you should have a pretty good idea of the steps needed to display images:

1. Blit the image to the back buffer.
2. Flip the back buffer to the primary surface.
3. Watch the image appear on the screen.

Two topics I want to briefly discuss before leaving DirectDraw are

- ■ How to copy the surface of an off-screen plain to the back buffer, with lightning-fast speed
- ■ How to allow for a constant pause, even if you are using a 386 or a Pentium Pro

Off-Screen to Back-Buffer Flipping

The fastest way to copy an off-screen plain to the back buffer for display is to use the BltFast() function of the target surface. rect holds the top-left and bottom-right corners of the area you want to copy. DDBLTFAST_SRCCOLORKEY tells the BltFast() function to use the transparency of the source surface. The prototype for BltFast() is

```
HRESULT BltFast(DWORD dwX, DWORD dwY, LPDIRECTDRAWSURFACE2 lpDDSrcSurface,
                LPRECT lpSrcRect, DWORD dwTrans);
```

The following code demonstrates BltFast() in our make-shift flip:

```
while(1)
{
    ddrval=DDBuffer->BltFast(0,0,DDRender,&rect,DDBLTFAST_SRCCOLORKEY);
    if(ddrval==DD_OK)
    {
        break;
    }
    if(ddrval==DDERR_SURFACELOST)
    {
        ddrval=DDScreen->Restore();
        if(ddrval!=DD_OK)
        {
            break;
        }
    }
    if(ddrval!=DDERR_WASSTILLDRAWING)
    {
        break;
    }
}
```

So, why do we have this big loop? Microsoft says that in some cases the surface might get lost when using the BltFast() function. The only way to bring back the surface is to use the Restore() function and try again. If there is any activity in the back buffer, the BltFast() function will fail. If the return value is equal to DDERR_WASSTILLDRAWING, we can try again and again, until we succeed. The prototype for Restore() is

```
HRESULT Restore();
```

Constant Timing

Trying to time an event just right can be a pain, especially when you take into account that everyone has a computer with different horsepower. Using the WaitForVerticalBlank() function is an easy and effective way of conquering the problem. No matter what machine it is— a 386 or a Pentium Pro—the time between vertical retraces is as constant as the North Star. Here is the code for the time-delay function:

```
void syncdelay(short_count)
{
    short temp;
    for(temp=0;temp<=count;temp++);
    {
        DDObj->WaitForVerticalBlank(DDWAITVB_BLOCKBEGIN,NULL);
    }
}
```

DirectDraw Cleaning Up

Now that you are done with DirectDraw, you can clean it up. All objects have a Release() function that you can use to remove the object. It is a good idea to check for NULL first and then set the object pointer to NULL afterward. The prototype for Release() is

```
ULONG Release();
```

The following code demonstrates how to clean up. Keep in mind the we will talk about the DDZBuffer object in "Direct3D" section.

```
void RemoveDirectDraw(void)
{
    int i;
    if(DDObj!=NULL)
    {
        if(DDPalette!=NULL)
        {
            DDPalette->Release();
            DDPalette=NULL;
        }

        if(DDZBuffer!=NULL)
        {
            DDZBuffer->Release();
            DDZBuffer=NULL;
        }

        if(DDScreen!=NULL)
        {
            DDScreen->Release();
            DDScreen=NULL;
        }
        if(DDRender!=NULL)
        {
            DDRender->Release();
            DDRender=NULL;
        }
        for(i=0;i<max.Tiles;i++)
        {
            if(shapes[i].tile!=NULL)
            {
                shapes[i].tile->Release();
                shapes[i].tile=NULL;
            }
        }
        DDObj->RestoreDisplayMode();
        DDObj->Release();
        DDObj=NULL;
    }
    GlobalFree(shapes);
    GlobalFree(world);
}
```

Direct3D

Now let us get into some 3D programming. Direct3D is the API for this job. Direct3D works closely with DirectDraw to display 3D models and scenes. Direct3D basically does all the calculations needed to do 3D manipulations on your mesh model and then tells DirectDraw what it wants displayed. You could think of Dirct3D as one big calculation API full of complex mathematical formulas.

Direct3D has two component APIs: Retained Mode and Intermediate Mode. So what is the differences between these to sets of APIs?

Retained mode is a set of high-level Direct3D functions. There are functions that allow you to load and save your 3D meshes into .x file format.

Intermediate mode is a set of low-level Direct3D functions. For the purpose of this book, we will not get into any Intermediate Mode code.

The Intermediate Mode Versus OpenGL Debate

Currently, there is a huge debate on whether Intermediate Mode and OpenGL should be separate or if OpenGL will become Intermediate Mode. Microsoft has plans to modify OpenGL to use DirectDraw—not the old, slow graphical user interface (GUI). Eventually, one API will win out over the other. No matter which one it is, it will have the speed of Intermediate Mode and the functionality of OpenGL.

Using 3D Studio

If you take a look in the RAWDAT directory, you will see some 3D Studio files. Basically, I created The Quest's title page with 3D Studio and then used a utility for Microsoft that converted the 3D Studio file into a format that Direct3D can understand, by calling the .x format. By using 3D Studio to do this, I spent minutes to do what would have taken hours (using Intermediate Mode).

> **NOTE**
>
> When creating your 3D Studio file, make sure you create a light source. Also make sure you do not use any texture; you get better results mapping the texture yourself. Also, when converting to the .x format, use the -m option, or your mesh will look very weird when you go to view it.

The Setup

At this point, you might want to open the 3D.CPP source file. Find the function called SetupDirect3DRM(), which is where you initialize all the main Direct3D objects. The following code shows how to initialize the Direct3D Retained Mode object:

```
LPDIRECT3DRM D3DRMObj=NULL;
if(Direct3DRMCreate(&D3DRMObj)!=D3DRM_OK)
{
    GotErr=2006;
    wsprintf(ErrMessage,"create Direct 3D RM object");
    return;
}
```

The prototype for `Direct3DRMCreate()` is

```
HRESULT Direct3DRMCreate(LPDIRECT3DRM FAR * lplpD3DRM);
```

Z Buffers

In order to perform 3D rendering, you must have created a Z buffer and have it attached to the back buffer. Use the `CreateSurface()` function as you did in the DirectDraw section. The `DDSD_ZBUFFERBITDEPTH` constant tells `CreateSurface()` that you want to set the Z buffer depth, which I set to 16 in the `ddsd.dwZBufferBitDepth` variable. The prototype for `AddAttachedSurface()` is

```
HRESULT AddAttachedSurface(LPDIRECTDRAWSURFACE2 lpDDSAttachedSurface);
```

Listing 30.2 shows how to initialize the Z Buffer.

Listing 30.2. Z Buffer initialization.

```
#define MAX_DEPTH   16
LPDIRECTDRAWSURFACE DDZBuffer=NULL;
ddsd.dwSize=sizeof(ddsd);
ddsd.dwFlags=DDSD_CAPS¦DDSD_HEIGHT¦DDSD_WIDTH¦DDSD_ZBUFFERBITDEPTH;
ddsd.ddsCaps.dwCaps=DDSCAPS_ZBUFFER¦DDSCAPS_SYSTEMMEMORY;
ddsd.dwHeight=MAX_HEIGHT;
ddsd.dwWidth=MAX_WIDTH;
ddsd.dwZBufferBitDepth=MAX_DEPTH;
if(DDObj->CreateSurface(&ddsd,&DDZBuffer,NULL)!=DD_OK)
{
    GotErr=3013;
    wsprintf(ErrMessage,"allocate enough memory");
    return;
}
if(DDBuffer->AddAttachedSurface(DDZBuffer)!=DD_OK)
{
    GotErr=3014;
    wsprintf(ErrMessage,"attach surface");
    return;
}
```

Creating a Scene and Device

Use the `CreateFrame()` function to create your *scene*, which is also known as a *parent frame*. Next, use the `CreateDeviceFromSurface()` function to tell Direct3D what surface to do the rendering in. Last, use `SetQuality()` to set the rendering quality. The prototypes for these functions are

```
HRESULT CreateFrame(LPDIRECT3DRMFRAME lpD3DRMFrame, LPDIRECT3DRMFRAME*
lplpD3DRMFrame);
HRESULT CreateDeviceFromSurface(LPGUID lpGUID, LPDIRECTDRAW lpDD,
LPDIRECTDRAWSURFACE lpDDSBack,
                          LPDIRECT3DRMDEVICE * lplpD3DRMDevice);
HRESULT SetQuality (D3DRMRENDERQUALITY rqQuality);
```

The following code demonstrates how to create a scene and a device:

```
LPDIRECT3DRMDEVICE   D3DRMDevice =NULL;
LPDIRECT3DRMFRAME    D3DRMScene  =NULL;
if(D3DRMObj->CreateFrame(NULL,&D3DRMScene)!=D3DRM_OK)
{
    GotErr=2011;
    wsprintf(ErrMessage,"create scene");
    return;
}
if(D3DRMObj->CreateDeviceFromSurface(NULL,DDObj,DDBuffer,&D3DRMDevice)!=D3DRM_OK)
{
    GotErr=2007;
    wsprintf(ErrMessage,"create device");
    return;
}
if(D3DRMDevice->SetQuality(D3DRMRENDER_GOURAUD)!=D3DRM_OK)
{
    GotErr=2008;
    wsprintf(ErrMessage,"set quality");
    return;
}
```

Creating a Scene

What I have done is broken down the Direct3D initialization process into two sections: global initialization, the section you just went though, and scene initialization, which is this section. Global initialization calls functions that all scenes will use, whereas scene initialization is specific to the scene itself.

Loading a Mesh

The first thing to do when creating a scene is to create a mesh builder, using CreateMeshBuilder(), to load the .x file into. Also, set the perspective to TRUE using SetPerspective() so that when you map a texture to the mesh, the mesh builder will correct the perspective of the texture. Then set the rendering quality for this mesh. Lastly, use ScaleMesh(), discussed in the next section, to scale down the mesh. I remember the first time I used Direct3D; I did not use the ScaleMesh() function. When I ran the program I was working on, I did not see anything but a black screen. This was because the mesh was too big to be viewed. The prototypes for these functions are

```
HRESULT CreateMeshBuilder(LPDIRECT3DRMMESHBUILDER* lplpD3DRMMeshBuilder);
HRESULT SetPerspective(BOOL perspective);
HRESULT Load(LPVOID lpvObjSource, LPVOID lpvObjID, D3DRMLOADOPTIONS d3drmLOFlags,
            D3DRMLOADTEXTURECALLBACK d3drmLoadTextureProc, LPVOID lpvArg);
```

The following code demonstrates how to load an .x file into MeshBuilder:

```
LPDIRECT3DRMMESHBUILDER D3DRMMeshBuilder    =NULL;
D3DRMObj->CreateMeshBuilder(&D3DRMMeshBuilder);
D3DRMMeshBuilder->SetPerspective(TRUE);
if(D3DRMMeshBuilder-
>Load("GAMEDAT\\INTRO.X",NULL,D3DRMLOAD_FROMFILE,NULL,NULL)!=D3DRM_OK)
```

```
{
    GotErr=2010;
    wsprintf(ErrMessage,"load GAMEDAT\\INTRO.X");
    return;
}
D3DRMMeshBuilder->SetQuality(D3DRMRENDER_GOURAUD);
ScaleMesh(D3DRMMeshBuilder,D3DVAL(32));
```

Scaling the Mesh

`ScaleMesh()` is a simple function. It allows you to scale your mesh to look bigger or smaller on the screen. `ScaleMesh()` uses `GetBox()` to select the mesh and then scales it with the `Scale()` function. The prototypes for these functions are

```
HRESULT GetBox(D3DRMBOX *lpD3DRMBox);
HRESULT Scale(D3DVALUE sx, D3DVALUE sy, D3DVALUE sz);
```

The following code demonstrates how to scale the size of a mesh:

```
float ScaleMesh(LPDIRECT3DRMMESHBUILDER mesh,D3DVALUE dim)
{
    D3DRMBOX box;
    mesh->GetBox( &box );
    D3DVALUE sizex=box.max.x-box.min.x;
    D3DVALUE sizey=box.max.y-box.min.y;
    D3DVALUE sizez=box.max.z-box.min.z;
    D3DVALUE largedim=D3DVALUE(0);
    if(sizex>largedim)
        largedim=sizex;
    if(sizey>largedim)
        largedim=sizey;
    if(sizez>largedim)
        largedim=sizez;
    D3DVALUE scalefactor=dim/largedim;
    mesh->Scale(scalefactor,scalefactor,scalefactor);
    return scalefactor;
}
```

Loading a Texture

Next, load a texture and map it onto your mesh. The prototypes for these functions are

```
HRESULT LoadTexture(const char * lpFileName, LPDIRECT3DRMTEXTURE*
lplpD3DRMTexture);
HRESULT SetTexture(LPDIRECT3DRMTEXTURE lpD3DRMTexture);
HRESULT CreateWrap(D3DRMWRAPTYPE type, LPDIRECT3DRMFRAME lpRef,
                D3DVALUE ox, D3DVALUE oy, D3DVALUE oz, D3DVALUE dx, D3DVALUE dy,
                D3DVALUE dz, D3DVALUE ux, D3DVALUE uy, D3DVALUE uz, D3DVALUE ou,
                D3DVALUE ov, D3DVALUE su, D3DVALUE sv,
                    LPDIRECT3DRMWRAP* lplpD3DRMWrap);
HRESULT Apply(LPDIRECT3DRMOBJECT lpObject);
```

The following code demonstrates how to load an `.bmp` file as a texture:

```
LPDIRECT3DRMTEXTURE D3DRMTexture;
LPDIRECT3DRMWRAP    D3DRMWrap;
if(D3DRMObj->LoadTexture("GAMEDAT\\INTRO.BMP",&D3DRMTexture)!=D3DRM_OK)
```

```
{
    GotErr=2012;
    wsprintf(ErrMessage,"load GAMEDAT\\INTRO.BMP");
    return;
}
D3DRMMeshBuilder->SetTexture(D3DRMTexture);
D3DRMTexture->Release();
D3DRMTexture=NULL;
D3DRMObj-
>CreateWrap(D3DRMWRAP_SPHERE,D3DRMScene,D3DVAL(0.0),D3DVAL(0.0),D3DVAL(0.0),
D3DVAL(0.0),D3DVAL(0.0),D3DVAL(1.0),D3DVAL(0.0),D3DVAL(1.0),D3DVAL(0.0),D3DVAL(0.0),
    D3DVAL(0.0),D3DVAL(1.0),D3DVAL(1.0),&D3DRMWrap);
D3DRMWrap->Apply(D3DRMMeshBuilder);
D3DRMWrap->Release();
D3DRMWrap=NULL;
```

Lights and View

The prototypes for the functions in this section are

```
HRESULT CreateFrame(LPDIRECT3DRMFRAME lpD3DRMFrame, LPDIRECT3DRMFRAME*
lplpD3DRMFrame);
HRESULT SetPosition(LPDIRECT3DRMFRAME lpRef, D3DVALUE rvX, D3DVALUE rvY, D3DVALUE
rvZ);
HRESULT SetRotation(LPDIRECT3DRMFRAME lpRef, D3DVALUE rvX, D3DVALUE rvY, D3DVALUE
rvZ,
                    D3DVALUE rvTheta);
HRESULT AddVisual(LPDIRECT3DRMVISUAL lpD3DRMVisual);
HRESULT CreateLightRGB(D3DRMLIGHTTYPE ltLightType, D3DVALUE vRed, D3DVALUE vGreen,
                    D3DVALUE vBlue, LPDIRECT3DRMLIGHT* lplpD3DRMLight);
HRESULT SetOrientation(LPDIRECT3DRMFRAME lpRef, D3DVALUE rvDx, D3DVALUE rvDy,
                    D3DVALUE rvDz, D3DVALUE rvUx, D3DVALUE rvUy, D3DVALUE rvUz);
HRESULT AddLight(LPDIRECT3DRMLIGHT lpD3DRMLight);
HRESULT CreateViewport(LPDIRECT3DRMDEVICE lpDev, LPDIRECT3DRMFRAME lpCamera, DWORD
dwXPos,
        DWORD dwYPos, DWORD dwWidth, DWORD dwHeight, LPDIRECT3DRMVIEWPORT*
lplpD3DRMViewport);
```

The first section of code creates a frame to set the mesh in. Use the SetPosition() to place the frame in the scene, which is just like placing an image on a surface but with an extra dimension. To make the frame rotate in the scene (which gives the effect that the mesh is rotating on the screen), use the SetRotation() function. After manipulating what you want the frame to do, add the mesh to your scene in the frame you create. The frame is actually linked to the scene. Because you are done with the frame, you can deallocate it.

In the next section of code, place a directional light (spotlight for those 3D Studio people). First, create the light object with CreateLightRGB(). I like using this function because it allows me to create different colored lights. Again, create your frame. To make the directional light in the upper-left corner of the screen, use SetOrientation() to move the frame position. Think of the frame you create as the point at which you want to place something. Then add directional light to your scene with the AddLight() function.

The last section is the last step. Create a camera and set its position with the SetPosition() function. Then create a view port with CreateViewport() from which to view your scene.

```
LPDIRECT3DRMFRAME    D3DRMCamera =NULL;
LPDIRECT3DRMFRAME    D3DRMLightFrame;
LPDIRECT3DRMLIGHT    D3DRMLight;

D3DRMObj->CreateFrame(D3DRMScene,&D3DRMMeshFrame1);
D3DRMMeshFrame1->SetPosition(D3DRMScene,D3DVAL(0.0),D3DVAL(4.0),D3DVAL(0.0));
D3DRMMeshFrame1-
>SetRotation(D3DRMScene,D3DVAL(0.0),D3DVAL(1.0),D3DVAL(0.0),D3DVAL(0.1));
D3DRMMeshFrame1->AddVisual(D3DRMMeshBuilder);
D3DRMMeshFrame1->Release();
D3DRMMeshFrame1=NULL;
D3DRMObj-
>CreateLightRGB(D3DRMLIGHT_DIRECTIONAL,D3DVAL(1.0),D3DVAL(1.0),D3DVAL(1.0),&D3DRMLight);
D3DRMObj->CreateFrame(D3DRMScene,&D3DRMLightFrame);
D3DRMLightFrame->SetOrientation(D3DRMScene,D3DVAL(0.0),D3DVAL(-1.0),
D3DVAL(1.0),D3DVAL(0.0),
    D3DVAL(1.0),D3DVAL(0.0));
D3DRMLightFrame->AddLight(D3DRMLight);
D3DRMLightFrame->Release();
D3DRMLightFrame=NULL;
D3DRMLight->Release();
D3DRMLight=NULL;
D3DRMObj->CreateFrame(D3DRMScene,&D3DRMCamera);
D3DRMCamera->SetPosition(D3DRMScene,D3DVAL(0.0),D3DVAL(0.0),D3DVAL(-50.0));
D3DRMObj->CreateViewport(D3DRMDevice,D3DRMCamera,0,0,D3DRMDevice->GetWidth(),
D3DRMDevice->GetHeight(),&D3DRMView);
```

Rendering the Scene

Remember the SetRotation() used in the last section to allow your mesh to rotate in a circle? Use Move() to rotate the mesh one unit. Next, use Clear() to clear your view, much like clearing the screen. Finally, use Render() to render your new view. Now that wasn't hard, was it? The prototypes for these functions are

```
HRESULT Move(D3DVALUE delta);
HRESULT Render(LPDIRECT3DRMFRAME lpD3DRMFrame);
HRESULT Update();
```

The following code demonstrates how The Quest's Tile page works:

```
void Render3DTile(void)
{
    ClearSurface(DDBuffer,0);
    D3DRMScene->Move(D3DVAL(1.0));
    D3DRMView->Clear();
    D3DRMView->Render(D3DRMScene);
    D3DRMDevice->Update();

    SetTextColor(PURPLE_FONT2);
    PrintText("P r e s s   [ E S C ]   T o   S t a r t",80,136,SMALL_FONT);
    SetTextColor(BLUE_FONT2);
    if(MapEdit) PrintText("MAP EDIT MODE",117,157,TINY_FONT);
    PrintText("Music Copyright (C) 1996, By Joseph Fuoco",1,181,TINY_FONT);
    PrintText("Tiles Copyright (C) 1996, By Makonin Consulting
Corp.",1,190,TINY_FONT);
    DDScreen->Flip(NULL,DDFLIP_WAIT);
}
```

Direct3D Cleaning Up

Cleaning up in Direct3D is the same as in DirectDraw; use the `Release()` function on each object you create.

DirectInput

DirectInput is an API that controls input devices. DirectInput is designed in such a way that input devices could be added to DirectInput, and you would program them the same way you did your mouse. Currently, DirectInput has support for three input devices: the mouse, keyboard, and joystick. For some reason, Microsoft has decided that the functions for the control of the joystick should be different than those for the mouse and keyboard. The API itself is quite small compared to that of DirectDraw.

I will demonstrate how to program the mouse and the keyboard. I won't discuss how to program for a joystick or gamepad, but I will talk about their functions.

Controlling the Joystick

I'll talk about joysticks and gamepads first. The remaining sections are on the mouse and the keyboard.

Calibrating the Joystick

The joystick API comes with Windows 95, which means that the player probably already has the joystick calibrated and tested. At some point, or as an option in your application/game, you might want the player to re-calibrate the joystick. To do this, call the Control Panel's joystick setup application like this:

```
WinExec("control JOY.CPL",SW_NORMAL);
```

Reading the Joystick

To read the status of a joystick, use the `joyGetPosEx()` function:

```
MMRESULT joyGetPosEx(UINT uJoyID, LPJOYINFOEX pji);
```

Creating a function to read the joystick might look something like this:

```
#define JOYSTICK_CENTRE   0
#define JOYSTICK_LEFT     1
#define JOYSTICK_RIGHT    2
#define JOYSTICK_UP       3
#define JOYSTICK_DOWN     4
byte JoystickHorz;
byte JoystickVert;
byte JoystickB1;
byte JoystickB2;
void UpdateJoystick(void)
```

```
{
    JOYINFOEX jsinfo;
    word      pos;
    jsinfo.dwSize=sizeof(JOYINFOEX);
    jsinfo.dwFlags=JOY_RETURNBUTTONS¦JOY_RETURNX¦JOY_RETURNY;
    joyGetPosEx(0,&jsinfo);
    JoystickB1=(byte)(jsinfo.dwButtons&JOY_BUTTON1);
    JoystickB2=(byte)(jsinfo.dwButtons&JOY_BUTTON2);
    if(jsinfo.dwXpos<16384)
        JoystickHorz=JOYSTIC_LEFT;
    else if(jsinfo.dwXpos>49151)
        JoystickHorz=JOYSTIC_RIGHT;
    else
        JoystickHorz=JOYSTIC_CENTRE;

    if(jsinfo.dwYpos<16384)
        JoystickVert=JOYSTIC_UP;
    else if(jsinfo.dwYpos>49151)
        JoystickVert=JOYSTIC_DOWN;
    else
        JoystickVert=JOYSTIC_CENTRE;
}
```

The Mouse and Keyboard Setup

The first thing to do is to create the DirectInput object with `DirectInputCreate()`. The prototype is

```
HRESULT DirectInputCreate(HINSTANCE hinst, DWORD dwVersion,
LPDIRECTINPUT*lplpDirectInput,
                        LPUNKNOWN punkOuter);

if(DirectInputCreate(nInst,DIRECTINPUT_VERSION,&DI,NULL)!=DI_OK)
{
    GotErr=6000;
    wsprintf(ErrMessage,"create Direct Input Object");
    return;
}
```

Next, call `EnumDevices()` to get all the input devices. Feed it the CALLBACK function, listed here:

```
HRESULT EnumDevices(DWORD dwDevType, LPDIENUMCALLBACK lpCallback, LPVIOD pvRef,
DWORD dwFlags);
if(DI->EnumDevices(0,DIEnumDevicesProc,NULL,DIEDFL_ATTACHEDONLY)!=DI_OK)
{
    GotErr=6010;
    wsprintf(ErrMessage,"fine input devices");
    return;
}

BOOL CALLBACK DIEnumDevicesProc(LPCDIDEVICEINSTANCE lpddi,LPVOID pvRef)
{
    if(GET_DIDEVICE_TYPE(lpddi->dwDevType)==DIDEVTYPE_MOUSE)
    {
        MouseGUID=lpddi->guidProduct;
        MouseFound=TRUE;
    }
    if(GET_DIDEVICE_TYPE(lpddi->dwDevType)==DIDEVTYPE_KEYBOARD)
```

```
        {
            KeyboardGUID=lpddi->guidProduct;
            KeyboardFound = TRUE;
        }
        if(MouseFound && KeyboardFound)
            return DIENUM_STOP;
        else
            return DIENUM_CONTINUE;
    }
```

Basically, the CALLBACK function determines whether these devices exist. If they do, set the global flags (KeyboardFound and MouseFound) and save their GUIDs. Next, use CreateDevice() to create an instance of the device for DirectInput to use. The following code demonstrates this:

```
HRESULT CreateDevice(REFGUID rguid, LPDIRECTINPUTDEVICE*lplpDirectInputDevice,
LPUNKNOWN*pUnkOuter);

if(DI->CreateDevice(KeyboardGUID,&DIKeyboard,NULL)!=DI_OK)
{
    GotErr=6001;
    wsprintf(ErrMessage,"capture keyboard");
    return;
}
if(DI->CreateDevice(MouseGUID,&DIMouse,NULL)!=DI_OK)
{
    GotErr=6002;
    wsprintf(ErrMessage,"capture mouse");
    return;
}
```

The next step is to use SetCooperativeLevel(), which sets how the application/game will share input devices with other applications. As you can see, I use DISCL_NONEXCLUSIVE and DISCL_FOREGROUND, which basically means that my game is greedy and will not let any other application use the mouse and keyboard:

```
HRESULT SetCooperativeLevel(HWND hwnd, DWORD dwFlags);

if(DIKeyboard-
>SetCooperativeLevel(hWnd,DISCL_NONEXCLUSIVE|DISCL_FOREGROUND)!=DI_OK)
{
    GotErr=6003;
    wsprintf(ErrMessage,"capture keyboard");
    return;
}
if(DIMouse->SetCooperativeLevel(hWnd,DISCL_EXCLUSIVE|DISCL_FOREGROUND)!=DI_OK)
{
    GotErr=6004;
    wsprintf(ErrMessage,"capture mouse");
    return;
}
```

This next step is to make DirectInput expandable for future input device. Use the SetDataFormat() to tell DirectInput what data you need from the device.

```
HRESULT SetDataFormat(LPCDIDATAFORMAT lpdf);
```

```
if(DIKeyboard->SetDataFormat(&c_dfDIKeyboard)!=DI_OK)
{
    GotErr=6005;
    wsprintf(ErrMessage,"set device data format");
    return;
}
if(DIMouse->SetDataFormat(&c_dfDIMouse)!=DI_OK)
{
    GotErr=6006;
    wsprintf(ErrMessage,"set device data format");
    return;
}
```

Finally, use Acquire(), which allows DirectInput to grab the device. If my game had set the cooperative level (where other applications could use the devices I use), every time another application used the input device I would have to call Acquire() to get control back.

```
HRESULT Acquire();

if(DIKeyboard->Acquire()!=DI_OK)
{
    GotErr=6008;
    wsprintf(ErrMessage,"acquire keyboard");
    return;
}
KeyboardAcquired=TRUE;
if(DIMouse->Acquire()!=DI_OK)
{
    GotErr=6009;
    wsprintf(ErrMessage,"acquire mouse");
    return;
}
MouseAcquired=TRUE;
```

Windows Messaging Versus DirectInput

At this point you might be asking yourself, "Would it not be easier to use Windows Messaging to do this?" You are right; you could—but it is an issue of control! Using DirectInput allows you to react faster to input devices. However, it is a matter of preference, so I will leave it up to you to choose.

Controlling Input Devices

When I check an input device, I call ()UpdateInputDevices—a function that reads the input devices I acquired. I find that this function is a nice, clean way of updating the input device that can be do anywhere, at any time.

The Keyboard

In The Quest, I use the keyboard to receive a string of data—the prompt to enter in the user's name. I also use the keyboard for meta-commands such as the P key (which pauses the game) or the Esc key (which displays the main menu).

Receiving String Data

The following is a function that gets input from the keyboard and places it in a string of no more than the specified amount:

```c
void GetStr(char*prompt,char*string,short x,short y,int len)
{
    char input;
    int  pos;
    char line[121];
    pos=0;
    string[pos]='\0';
    do
    {
        ASCIIKey=FALSE;
        wsprintf(line,"%s %s%c",prompt,string,'_');
        while(!ASCIIKey)
        {
            RenderViewEdit(p.x,p.y);
            if(WhereInExec==EXEC_EDITMAP)
                EditStatus(p.x,p.y);
            SetTextColor(BRIGHT_FONT);
            PrintText(line,x,y,SMALL_FONT);
            DisplayView();
            UpdateInputDevices();
            if(done)
            {
                done=FALSE;
                string[0]='\0';
                return;
            }
        }
        input=ASCIIKey;
        switch(input)
        {
            case 8:
                if(pos>0)
                {
                    string[pos]='\0';
                    pos--;
                    string[pos]='\0';
                }
                break;
            case 13:
                string[pos]='\0';
                break;
            default:
                if(pos<len)
                {
                    string[pos]=input;
                    pos++;
                    string[pos]='\0';
                }
                break;
        }
    }while(input!=13);
}
```

You will notice that while waiting for the player to press a key, I keep rendering my scene for DirectDraw so that the screen can still be animated. ASCIIKey is a global variable that gets updated by UpdateInputDevices(); it holds the last ASCII character retrieved from the keyboard.

Receiving Meta-Commands

Listing 30.3 shows the part of UpdateInputDevices() that taps keystrokes.

Listing 30.3. Updating input devices.

```
HRESULT GetDeviceState(DWORD cbData, LPVOID lpvData);
byte        KeyboardState[256];
byte        KeyboardDown[256];
HRESULT     dirval;
    if(ReadKeyboard)
    {
        while(1)
        {
            dirval=DIKeyboard->GetDeviceState(256,&KeyboardState);
            if(dirval==DIERR_NOTACQUIRED||dirval==DIERR_INPUTLOST)
                DIKeyboard->Acquire();
            else
                break;
        }

        switch(WhereInExec)
        {
            case EXEC_STATRUP:
                break;
            case EXEC_TITLES:
                if(KeyPressed(DIK_F4))
                    MapEdit=!MapEdit;
                break;
            case EXEC_INTRO:
                break;
            case EXEC_GAMEPLAY:
                if(KeyPressed(DIK_P))
                {
                    GamePause=!GamePause;
                    if(GamePause) PauseBox();
                }
                if(!GamePause)
                {
                    if(KeyPressed(DIK_M))
                    {
                        MusicState=!MusicState;
                        if(MusicState)
                        {
                            StartBackgroundMusic(hWnd,MusicPlaying,TRUE);
                        }
                        else
                        {
                            LastPlayed=MusicPlaying;
                            StopBackgroundMusic();
                            MusicPlaying=LastPlayed;
```

continues

Listing 30.3. continued

```
                    }
                }
            }
            break;
        case EXEC_MKCHAR:
            break;
        case EXEC_ENDING:
            break;
        case EXEC_SHUTDOWN:
            break;
        case EXEC_EDITMAP:
            if(KeyPressed(DIK_UP))
                p.y--;
            else if(KeyPressed(DIK_DOWN))
                p.y++;
            if(p.x<0)
                p.x=(short)(MAP_WIDTH+p.x);
            else if(p.x>MAP_WIDTH-1)
                p.x=(short)(p.x-MAP_WIDTH);
            if(KeyPressed(DIK_LEFT))
                p.x--;
            else if(KeyPressed(DIK_RIGHT))
                p.x++;
            if(p.y<0)
                p.y=(short)(MAP_HEIGHT+p.y);
            else if(p.y>MAP_HEIGHT-1)
                p.y=(short)(p.y-MAP_HEIGHT);
            break;
        case EXEC_MENU:
            break;
    }
    if(KeyPressed(DIK_ESCAPE)&&!GamePause)
        done=TRUE;
    for(i=1;i<256;i++)
    {
        if(KeyPressed((byte)i))
        {
            ASCIIKey=TranslateKey((byte)i);
            break;
        }
    }
}
```

Use GetDeviceState() to get a snapshot of what is happening with the keyboard. At this point you might be asking, "What are all the constants with EXEC_ in front of them?". EXEC_ tells you what part of the game you are in. For instance, whenever the global variable WhereInExec is equal to EXEC_MENU, you know that the player is in the main menu.

The following code shows the KeyPressed() function:

```
byte KeyPressed(byte key)
{
    if(KeyboardState[key]&0x80&&!KeyboardDown[key])
    {
        KeyboardDown[key]=TRUE;
```

```
    }
    else if(!(KeyboardState[key]&0x80)&&KeyboardDown[key])
    {
        KeyboardDown[key]=FALSE;
        return(TRUE);
    }
    return(FALSE);
}
```

If you do not call this function and the player presses P to pause the game, the game will pause and unpause while the player holds the key down. This function stops that from happening and doesn't return TRUE until the player stops pressing the P key.

<blockquote>

NOTE

Remember that GetDeviceState() returns scan codes, not ASCII characters, so I created a function called TranslateKey() that translates the ASCII charters I need.

</blockquote>

The Mouse

In this game, I allow the player to use the mouse to move his character around the game world. The mouse cursor represents an arrow in the direction you want to head. When the player presses the right button of the mouse, his character begins to walk. When the player stops pressing the mouse's right button, his character stops walking.

Trapping a Mouse

Ah yes—how to build the perfect mousetrap! Well, if you haven't already guessed, it is very similar to the keyboard. The code in Listing 30.4 shows how.

Listing 30.4. The mousetrap.

```
if(ShowMouse)
{
    while(1)
    {
        dirval=DIMouse->GetDeviceState(sizeof(MouseState),&MouseState);
        if(dirval==DIERR_NOTACQUIRED||dirval==DIERR_INPUTLOST)
            DIMouse->Acquire();
        else
            break;
    }
    MouseX+=(short)MouseState.lX;
    if(MouseX>MAX_WIDTH-1)
        MouseX=MAX_WIDTH-1;
    if(MouseX<0)
        MouseX=0;
```

continues

Listing 30.4. continued

```
MouseY+=(short)MouseState.lY;
if(MouseY>MAX_HEIGHT-1)
    MouseY=MAX_HEIGHT-1;
if(MouseY<0)
    MouseY=0;
if(MouseState.rgbButtons[0]&0x80)
    MouseLB=TRUE;
else
    MouseLB=FALSE;
if(MouseState.rgbButtons[1]&0x80)
    MouseRB=TRUE;
else
    MouseRB=FALSE;
}
}
```

As you can see, I used `GetDeviceState()` again. After that, I updated for global variables that store the mouse's screen *x* and *y* position, and each button state.

Reacting to the Mouse

If you load `TQ.CPP` and scroll down to the `WinMain()` function, you should find the code for Listing 30.5.

Listing 30.5. Using the mouse.

```
if(MouseRB)
{
    if(TickCount>LastCount+1)
    {
        o.x=p.x;
        o.y=p.y;
        switch(MouseCursor)
        {
            case 1:
                p.x--;
                p.dir=WEST;
                break;
            case 2:
                p.y--;
                p.dir=NORTH;
                break;
            case 3:
                p.x++;
                p.dir=EAST;
                break;
            case 4:
                p.y++;
                p.dir=SOUTH;
                break;
```

```
          }
          if(p.x<0)
               p.x=(short)(MAP_WIDTH+p.x);
          else if(p.x>MAP_WIDTH-1)
               p.x=(short)(p.x-MAP_WIDTH);
          if(p.y<0)
               p.y=(short)(MAP_HEIGHT+p.y);
          else if(p.y>MAP_HEIGHT-1)
               p.y=(short)(p.y-MAP_HEIGHT);
          walking=TRUE;
          if(!CheckWalkable(p.x,p.y,PlayerElev))
          {
               p.x=o.x;
               p.y=o.y;
               walking=FALSE;
          }
          LastCount=TickCount;
     }
}
else
{
     walking=FALSE;
}
DrawView(p.x,p.y,p.dir);
```

When the right button of the mouse is pressed down, the player's character walks in the same direction that the mouse arrow is pointing.

DirectInput Cleaning Up

Cleaning up in DirectInput is the same as in DirectDraw: Use the `Release()` function on each object you create. There is, however, one step that you must do first before you release the input device. Use the `Unacquire()` if the device is acquired:

```
HRESULT Unacquire();

if(MouseAcquired)
{
     DIMouse->Unacquire();
     MouseAcquired=FALSE;
}
if(DIMouse!=NULL) DIMouse->Release();

if(KeyboardAcquired)
{
     DIKeyboard->Unacquire();
     KeyboardAcquired=FALSE;
}
if(DIKeyboard!=NULL) DIKeyboard->Release();
```

DirectSound

DirectSound is all you need to play sound effects. Think of DirectSound as being the API that controls all that you hear. Sound effects add a new dimension to your application/game. If used effectively, sound complements the graphics and creates a better experience. However, there are two fundamental things that are missing for DirectSound:

1. A function that will load a WAV file into a sound buffer
2. An API for playing and controlling MIDI files

Because these two pieces are missing, you have to write your own—or use mine!

This section explores how to set up DirectSound, how to play sound effects, how to clean up DirectSound, and how to play MIDI files.

Setup

The first thing to do is to create a DirectSound object with the `DirectSoundCreate()` function. The following code shows its prototype and an example of the way to call it:

```
HRESULT DirectSoundCreate(GUID FAR * lpGuid, LPDIRECTSOUND * ppDS, IUnknown FAR *
pUnkOuter);

LPDIRECTSOUND  DSObj=NULL;
if(DirectSoundCreate(NULL,&DSObj,NULL)!=DS_OK)
{
    GotErr=8005;
    wsprintf(ErrMessage,"create DirectSound");
    return;
}
```

Next, call the `SetCooperativeLevel()` function to tell how you want DirectSound to play with other applications. In this case, I chose `DSSCL_NORMAL` because Microsoft says so. No, actually, because it works the best for sharing recourses and multitasking.

```
HRESULT SetCooperativeLevel(HWND hwnd, DWORD dwLevel);

if(DSObj->SetCooperativeLevel(hWnd,DSSCL_NORMAL)!=DS_OK)
{
    GotErr=8006;
    wsprintf(ErrMessage,"set cooperative level");
    return;
}
```

After that is done, you can the load your sound effects. I have created a function that loads a WAV file and puts it into a sound buffer. The following is an example on how I would call my `LoadSoundFX()` function:

```
for(i=0;i<MAX_SOUNDFX;i++)
    DSSoundFX[i]=NULL;
LoadSoundFX("GAMEDAT\\GATE.WAV",0);
```

```
if(GotErr) return;
LoadSoundFX("GAMEDAT\\PING.WAV",1);
if(GotErr) return;

LoadSoundFX("GAMEDAT\\STATIC.WAV",2);
if(GotErr) return;
LoadSoundFX("GAMEDAT\\WALK.WAV",3);
if(GotErr) return;
```

So, what is involved in loading the WAV file into a sound buffer? Well, it's quite simple, really. Follow these steps:

1. Load the WAV file in a temporary buffer.
2. Get the pointer to the format information stored in the WAV file.
3. Create a sound buffer with `CreateSoundBuffer()`.
4. Lock the buffer to write the sound data in it.
5. Copy the sound data from the temporary buffer to the sound buffer.
6. Unlock the sound buffer and remove the temporary buffer from memory.

In the DSBUFFERDEC, use DSBCAPS_CTRLDEFAULT and DSBCAPS_STATIC so that you can change things such as the volume and panning, and have a static sound effect that can live in the soundcard's memory. Tell DirectSound the size of the buffer, which is the length of the file minus the length of the file header. The WAV is a pointer that is 20 bytes in from the beginning of the temporary buffer that describes the settings and format of the WAV file.

The prototype for `CreateSoundBuffer()` is listed here:

```
HRESULT CreateSoundBuffer(LPDSBUFFERDESC lpDSBufferDesc, LPLPDIRECTSOUNDBUFFER
lplpDirectSoundBuffer,
                     IUnknown FAR * pUnkOuter);
```

You will notice that when you use `Lock()`, you need to pass two pointer and size variables. This is because all sound buffers are circular buffers—which means that if you have a buffer of size 600 at position 500, you should copy a sound of size 200. The first pointer would equal 500, and its length would be 100. The second pointer would equal 0 and have a length of 100.

Listing 30.7. Loading a WAV file.

```
#define WAV_HDR_SIZE       44
#define MAX_SOUNDFX        4
#define SND_GATE           0
#define SND_PING           1
#define SND_STATIC         2
#define SND_WALK           3
LPDIRECTSOUNDBUFFER DSSoundFX[MAX_SOUNDFX];
void LoadSoundFX(char*filename,int num)
{
```

continues

Listing 30.7. continued

```
DSBUFFERDESC      dsbd;
LPWAVEFORMATEX    wav;
dword             len;
byte              *buf;
byte              *ptr1;
byte              *ptr2;
dword             size1;
dword             size2;

len=FileSize(filename);
buf=(byte*)GlobalAlloc(GPTR,len);
if(buf==NULL)
{
    GotErr=7100;
    wsprintf(ErrMessage,"allocate enough memory");
    return;
}

LoadFile(filename,buf);
if(GotErr)
{
    GotErr=7101;
    return;
}
ptr1=buf+20;
wav=(LPWAVEFORMATEX)(ptr1);
memset(&dsbd,0,sizeof(dsbd));
dsbd.dwSize=sizeof(dsbd);
dsbd.dwFlags=DSBCAPS_CTRLDEFAULT¦DSBCAPS_STATIC;
dsbd.dwBufferBytes=len-WAV_HDR_SIZE;
dsbd.lpwfxFormat=wav;
if(DSObj->CreateSoundBuffer(&dsbd,&DSSoundFX[num],NULL)!=DS_OK)
{
    GotErr=7102;
    wsprintf(ErrMessage,"create sound buffer %i",num);
    return;
}

if(DSSoundFX[num]->Lock(0,len-WAV_HDR_SIZE,&ptr1,&size1,&ptr2,&size2,0)!=DS_OK)
{
    GotErr=7103;
    wsprintf(ErrMessage,"lock memory");
    return;
}
memcpy(ptr1,buf+WAV_HDR_SIZE,size1);
if(size2)
    memcpy(ptr2,buf+size1+WAV_HDR_SIZE,size2);
if(DSSoundFX[num]->Unlock(ptr1,size1,ptr2,size2)!=DS_OK)
{
    GotErr=7104;
    wsprintf(ErrMessage,"unlock memory");
    return;
}

GlobalFree(buf);
}
```

Playing Sound Effects

After setting up your DirectSound objects, the fun stuff begins—playing the special effects! Use the SetCurrentPosition() to set the position to 0; in other words, set the position to the beginning of the sound buffer. Next, use Play() to play what is in the sound buffer. And from the deep bowels of silence should come the sound effect you play.

```
HRESULT SetCurrentPosition(DWORD dwNewPosition);
HRESULT Play(DWORD dwReserved1, DWORD dwReserved2, DWORD dwFlags);
void PlaySoundFX(int num)
{
    DSSoundFX[num]->SetCurrentPosition(0);
    DSSoundFX[num]->Play(0,0,0);
}
```

DirectSound Cleaning Up

Cleaning up in DirectSound is the same as in Direct. Use the Release() function on each object you create:

```
void RemoveDirectSound(void)
{
    int i;
    if(DSObj!=NULL)
    {
        for(i=0;i<MAX_SOUNDFX;i++)
        {
            if(DSSoundFX[i]!=NULL)
            {
                DSSoundFX[i]->Release();
                DSSoundFX[i]=NULL;
            }
        }
        DSObj->Release();
        DSObj=NULL;
    }
}
```

Playing MIDI Music

In order to play MIDI files, you must use the MCI API. I use the mciSendString() function to do this. The prototype for mciSendString() is shown here:

```
MCIERROR mciSendString(LPCTSTR lpszCommand, LPTSTR lpszReturnString, UINT cchReturn,
                       HANDLE hwndCallback);
```

The first thing to do, as part of the startup, is to close any MCI devices that are open. Call mciSendString() as follows:

```
if(mciSendString("close all",NULL,0,0)!=0)
{
```

```
      GotErr=8004;
      wsprintf(ErrMessage,"close all MCI devices");
      return;
}
```

You now have a function that plays the MIDI files. The first step in playing a MIDI file is to close the device you want to use. In this case, the device is called MUSIC:

```
mciSendString("close MUSIC",NULL,0,0);
```

Next, tell MCI to open the MIDI file—and last, tell MCI to start playing it:

```
wsprintf(OpenStatement,"open GAMEDAT\\%s.MID type sequencer alias MUSIC",FileName);
if(mciSendString(OpenStatement,NULL,0,0)!=0)
{
      GotErr=8001;
      wsprintf(ErrMessage,"load file GAMEDAT\\%s.MID",FileName);
      return;
}
mciSendString("play MUSIC from 0 notify",NULL,0,hWnd);
```

If you want the music to loop after it finishes playing, add these lines in the Event procedure:

```
case MM_MCINOTIFY:
      if(wParam==MCI_NOTIFY_SUCCESSFUL&&LoopMusic)
          mciSendString("play MUSIC from 0 notify",NULL,0,hWnd);
```

As part of the cleanup routine, call mciSendString() again to close any devices that are still in use.

DirectPlay

You need to have a network to use the DirectPlay API. This is disappointing, because I do not have a network! So, in this section, I will discuss only conceptual aspects of DirectPlay—and not code, code, code.

DirectPlay allows you to create multiplayer games through the following connections:

- Direct serial connection
- Modem
- IPX network
- TCP/IP (or Internet)

DirectPlay has three layers:

> DirectPlayLobby allows you to connect to a client application, which is the game interface the player uses, and a server application, which keeps control of the situation.

> DirectPlay gives you an interface that simplifies connecting via a service provider. Because this version now supports peer-to-peer communication, sending messages to a specific player is possible.

A service provider provides the protocols in order to communicate with other players. The list of connections listed previously are all service providers.

Things to Consider

There are a number of issues you must consider when developing a multiplayer game, such as data passing, interface, and synchronization.

When you pass data back and forth, it takes precious time because of low bandwidth. You must come up with ways of passing only the data needed, and nothing more. Compressing the data to a smaller size, before sending, also helps. Some special talents of a game programmer are to find ways around limitations and to be resourceful.

Another thing to consider is the interface. How will the players interact with each other? You might want each player to be able to pass messages to each other. Will the players work against each other, work toward a common goal, or both? Low bandwidth is a problem that might limit the kind of interface you want.

One of the most important issues is synchronization between all players. Microsoft provides a function called `WaitForSingleObject()`, which helps matters. Without good synchronization, each player will not see a true picture of what is going on.

Terminology

You will encounter some terminology along your travels through DirectPlay. So, I thought I would take the time to define a few terms:

Data: Information that is associated with a player or a group

Group: A collection of players within a session

Message: A packet of text used so that one player can communicate to another

Player: A person's application within the session

Session: A number of applications that communicate with each other via the service provider

Each of these five terms has a function that monitors and controls what happens in its respective area.

Other Sources

There are many books about DirectPlay that describe, in detail, how to create multiplayer games. Some of these books are

Windows 95 Game Developer's Guide Using the Game SDK
Published by Sams, written by Marrison and Weems

Win32 Game Developer's Guide With DirectX 3.0
Published by Waite Group Press, written by Kolb

DirectDraw Programming
Published by M&T, written by Timmins

Cutting Edge Direct3D Programming
Published by Coriolis Group Books, written by Trujillo

Another good source of information on DirectX is the Internet. Here are some sites you might be interested in:

Multimedia Expo on Microsoft's Web site
`http://www.microsoft.com/DirectX/default.asp`

Directly Exchange Web site
`http://www.dex.fonager.dk/`

Summary

I hope that I have given you a good starting point for mastering the APIs of DirectX. After all that was said and done, I have to admit that DirectX has made my life easier in conquering the many aspects of game programming. It has cut my development time by a third.

As Microsoft adds more and more functionality to DirectX, it will begin to surpass the flexibility of DOS and become the number one multimedia and game development API. I've found DirectX to be easy to understand because its different sections have things in common, which helps speed the learning curve so you can begin programming in a short period of time.

VII

Advanced Win32 Programming

31

Working with the Registry

by David Bennett

Microsoft first introduced the Registry with OLE on Windows 3.1 to hold configuration information for OLE. Since then, the Registry, as implemented in Windows 95 and Windows NT, has grown to encompass a much wider range of information. The Win32 Registry is intended to hold the following sorts of information:

■ Application settings (formerly held in .ini files)

■ Windows configuration (formerly in system.ini or windows.ini)

■ User-specific settings

■ Environment settings (formerly held in environment variables)

■ OLE/COM/ActiveX configuration information

In addition, your applications might find the Registry useful for saving other sorts of information.

Using the Registry to hold this information provides a single source for configuration info, as opposed to the mish-mash of various .ini files that could be scattered around your disk. The Registry also provides a simple mechanism for saving info for the current user or current configuration. The Registry even allows you to manage the Registry on other machines across the network.

In addition, under Windows NT, the Registry can provide a level of security that was unknown with previous configuration storage mechanisms. This prevents a wayward application from corrupting things like system information as well as keeping unauthorized users away from certain things.

If you are used to searching through system.ini to find certain settings, it might take a little while to get used to finding certain things in the Registry—but I think you will find that the hierarchical structure of the Registry makes things much easier to find, after you know where to look.

Registry Keys

The Registry is arranged in a hierarchical tree-like structure. Each node in the tree is called a key. Each key can then contain additional keys, or subkeys, which allow further branching, as well as values, which are used to store actual data.

Key names are made up of simple strings of printable ANSI characters. Key names may not include certain characters, including spaces, backslashes (\), or wildcards (? or *). In addition, key names starting with a period (.) are reserved.

Registry Values

Although Registry keys are used to organize the data in the Registry, the values contained in these keys are used to contain the actual data. Values within a key are identified by their name, which can contain any of the characters allowed for key names. The actual data contained in a value may take several different forms, ranging from a simple integer value to a user-defined binary object. The types of data that may be stored in a value are listed in Table 31.1.

Table 31.1. Registry value data types.

API constant	Description
REG_BINARY	Raw binary data.
REG_DWORD	32-bit integer in local machine format.
REG_DWORD_LITTLE_ENDIAN	32-bit integer in little-endian format. (This is the format used on Intel machines.)
REG_DWORD_BIG_ENDIAN	32-bit integer in big-endian format. (This format is commonly found on other platforms, such as UNIX.)
REG_EXPAND_SZ	A null-terminated string that contains unexpanded environment variables (such as %PATH%).
REG_LINK	A Unicode symbolic link.
REG_MULTI_SZ	An array of null-terminated strings, ending in two null characters.
REG_NONE	No value type.
REG_RESOURCE_LIST	A device-driver resource list.
REG_SZ	A null-terminated string.

The Registry is capable of handling some very large values. However, for any data value that is relatively large (greater than 1–2KB), you should save the data in a separate file and include only a reference to the file (such as the filename and path) in the Registry.

Editing the Registry Manually

Generally, Win32 operating system users should not be required to edit the Registry by hand. Any Registry manipulation should be done by your applications or their setup programs. However, as a developer, it is often useful to be able to get your hands on the Registry settings directly while in the process of developing your applications.

Well, it turns out that Microsoft provides utilities to let you do just that. On Windows 95, the REGEDIT.EXE utility is provided. On Windows NT, you get the REGEDT32.EXE utility. Both of these applications perform essentially the same function, allowing you to browse the Registry and add or change keys and values. A snapshot of the Registry editor is shown in Figure 31.1.

FIGURE 31.1.

The Registry Editor.

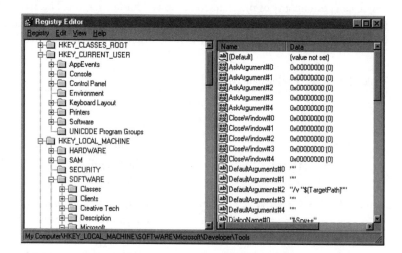

Although both REGEDIT.EXE and REGEDT32.EXE perform the same basic functions, there are several differences. For the most part, REGEDT32.EXE provides additional functions to work with the security features of the NT Registry. In addition, REGEDIT.EXE might display certain data types differently.

Registry Structure

At first glance, the huge amount of information stored in the Registry can be a bit overwhelming. However, the hierarchical nature helps to organize the available information—after you know where to find what you're looking for. In this section, we will be taking a look at the main branches of the Registry tree and some of the more commonly used areas within those keys.

HKEY_LOCAL_MACHINE

Information that concerns the configuration of the local machine, independent of any particular user, is stored in the top-level key HKEY_LOCAL_MACHINE. This configuration information is further organized into several different subkeys, including Config, Enum, hardware, Network, Security, SOFTWARE, and System.

The Config and Enum subkeys are found only on Windows 95. These keys contain information used by Windows 95's plug and play subsystem. Information about the various configurations is stored in `Config`, and the `Enum` subkey contains information about specific devices on the system. In addition, the hardware subkey provides some additional information about the system's hardware. In most cases, your applications will not need to be concerned with these areas.

The `Network` and `Security` subkeys contain information about Microsoft's networking and security subsystems.

The `System` subkey contains a wide range of different information about the current configuration of the Windows system. `System\CurrentControlSet\control` contains information about the general configuration of Windows, and `System\CurrentControlSet\Services` contains information about the configuration of specific services. This includes the full-blown services found on Windows NT, as well as several other subsystems, such as Windows sockets, which are found on both NT and 95.

The `SOFTWARE` subkey is used to contain configuration info for user applications. This is one of the areas that is most likely to be used by your applications. For information that you want to save for your applications that is not specific to any particular user, you should add a subkey under `HKEY_LOCAL_MACHINE\SOFTWARE`.

The standard practice is to add a key under `SOFTWARE` for your company name and then add a key under that for the specific product. You should then use a separate key under this for each version of the specific product. For example, if you have installed the MKS toolkit to satisfy that craving for the vi editor, you would see that the following key is used for holding configuration information:

`HKEY_LOCAL_MACHINE\SOFTWARE\Mortice Kern Systems\Toolkit\4.4b`

In the preceding example, the company name is Mortice Kern Systems, the product is named Toolkit, and the version is 4.4b. Although there are certainly vendors who do not follow this convention, it is a good idea to try to stick to it; it can save you a great deal of trouble later, as your list of installed products grows.

HKEY_CURRENT_CONFIG

Windows 95 uses the `HKEY_CURRENT_CONFIG` key to point to the current configuration entry key (such as `0001`) under `HKEY_LOCAL_MACHINE\Config`. This key is used to store information about the current configuration for things like printers and displays.

This key is not found in the Windows NT Registry.

HKEY_USERS

The `HKEY_USERS` key is used to store information about the configuration or preferences used by individual users. Depending on your setup, you might have many different users listed here or simply the default user profile, which is found under the `.Default` subkey. In most cases, your applications will not access HKEY_USERS directly but will go through HKEY_CURRENT_USER instead.

HKEY_CURRENT_USER

You can think of HKEY_CURRENT_USER as a virtual, *top-level key.* It does not really contain its own top-level tree, but it points to the key under HKEY_USERS for the user who is currently logged on. This provides a convenient way for your applications to store and retrieve settings specific to a particular user. The operating system will handle changing the key that this points to as users come and go.

Under HKEY_CURRENT_USER, you will find a variety of subkeys that hold information about the current user's Windows preferences, default colors, and remote networking addresses.

The most commonly used subkey under HKEY_CURRENT_USER is Software, where your applications should add any information that might change according to the user. Again, any keys that you use under HKEY_CURRENT_USER\Software should be structured by your company name and then individual products. For example, Adobe's Acrobat reader stores user-dependent configuration information in keys under the following key:

HKEY_CURRENT_USER\Software\Adobe\Acrobat

HKEY_CLASSES_ROOT

If you take a look at HKEY_CLASSES_ROOT in the Registry editor, you will see a great many different entries. These are generally one of two different types of entries. The first is an entry for a filename extension, such as .cpp. In most cases, these entries simply provide an unnamed value that names a class definition subkey.

The second type of entry contains a class definition, which is used by the Windows shell and OLE to store information about registered classes. An example of this sort of entry would be HKEY_CLASSES_ROOT\Excel.Chart, which contains information about an Excel spreadsheet class. Each of these entries will have a CLSID subkey that contains an unnamed value holding that class's class ID.

In addition, a sort of cross-referenced list of all of the registered class IDs is contained in HKEY_CLASSES_ROOT\CLSID. These entries contain information that OLE uses to start up servers for each class.

HKEY_DYN_DATA

Windows 95 uses the HKEY_DYN_DATA key to hold a special sort of reference to real-time dynamic data. This includes the current system hardware configuration in the Configuration Manager subkey.

In addition, the `PerfStats` subkey contains references to additional data that is exported by certain components of the system, such as network drivers or other Vxd's. The data in this area is only stored in RAM and is not written to disk. This allows for better performance for values that are frequently, if not constantly, updated.

Although you may view information under `HKEY_DYN_DATA` with the normal Registry API, the dynamic keys under `HKEY_DYN_DATA` are generally manipulated with a special set of API calls. For more on these, see the Microsoft Device Driver Kit (DDK) documentation. However, unless you are writing device drivers and such, your applications should not create keys or write values in this area.

You can view the information found in `HKEY_DYN_DATA` with the system monitor application, found under the Programs | Accessories | System Tools menu of the Windows 95 Start menu.

This key is not supported under Windows NT.

HKEY_PERFORMANCE_DATA

Windows NT also provides a special area of the Registry devoted to real-time data, such as that generated by network drivers or other system components. You may use the regular Registry API to retrieve values from this key, although the data is handled a bit differently.

When you query a value from `HKEY_PERFORMANCE_DATA`, the data is retrieved from special system components designed to respond to these requests. Thus, you cannot add entries for dynamic data with the regular Registry API.

In addition, the data is formatted in some rather complicated structures designed to thoroughly describe the dynamic data that is available.

Working directly with the dynamic data in this key goes a bit beyond the scope of this chapter, but you can find more information in the MSDN documentation under SDK Documentation | Platform SDK | Windows Base Services | General Library | Performance Data Helper.

However, you can easily view the data stored in this key with the NT Performance Monitor application, which will even give you some nifty, real-time graphs.

INI File Mapping

The Registry is intended to replace the `.ini` files that were used to save application configuration information. For all new applications that you are developing for 32-bit Windows, you should use the Registry, although Windows 95 does still support the use of `.ini` files.

However, Windows NT does not maintain certain files like `win.ini` and `system.ini`. To provide compatibility with older applications, Windows NT provides the ability to map `.ini` files to the Registry. You may also take advantage of this ability to map the `.ini` files used by your older applications to the Registry.

This mapping allows older applications to make calls to functions such as `GetProfileString()` and `WriteProfileString()`, which are redirected to work with values in the Registry instead of in `.ini` files.

To set up this mapping, a subkey with the name of the `.ini` file should be added to `HKEY_LOCAL_MACHINE\SOFTWARE\Microsoft\Windows NT\CurrentVersion\IniFileMapping`. You can then add an unnamed value under this key that specifies where in the Registry the information (that was formerly in the `.ini` file) can be found. You may also choose to add separate value entries for each section of the `.ini` file; each entry should contain a string pointing to a separate Registry key for each section.

In the event that no `.ini` file mapping is found, NT will look for a real `.ini` file on the disk.

The Registry API

The Registry is stored in binary files that your applications should not access directly. However, the Win32 API provides a wide range of functions that allow you to work with the Registry. We will be looking at this API in the following sections.

Opening a Key

Before you can do anything else with the Registry, you will need to open a key in the Registry. This will provide you with a handle to the key, which can then be used for other operations. To open a handle to a key, you will use the `RegOpenKeyEx()` function, shown here:

```
LONG RegOpenKeyEx( HKEY hKey, LPCTSTR lpSubKey,
    DWORD ulOptions, REGSAM samDesired, PHKEY phkResult);
```

I know it sounds a bit like the chicken and the egg, but to open a key, you will first need to pass an already open key handle in the `hKey` parameter of `RegOpenKeyEx()`. You can get away with this by using one of the predefined handle values used for the top-level keys of the Registry, as listed here:

```
HKEY_CLASSES_ROOT
HKEY_CURRENT_CONFIG
HKEY_CURRENT_USER
HKEY_LOCAL_MACHINE
HKEY_USERS
HKEY_PERFORMANCE_DATA (NT only)
HKEY_DYN_DATA (95 only)
```

Starting from one of these keys, you can open a subkey by passing its name in `lpSubKey`. You may specify a subkey several levels below the key given in `hKey` by separating key names with a backslash (\), as in the following `lpSubKey` string:

```
"SOFTWARE\\SAMS\\RegEx\\1.0"
```

The ulOptions parameter is currently reserved and must be set to 0. The samDesired parameter is used to specify the access rights that you want to assign to the handle. This can be a combination of the following values:

KEY_ALL_ACCESS: Gives all access.

KEY_CREATE_LINK: You may create symbolic links.

KEY_CREATE_SUB_KEY: Allows creation of subkeys.

KEY_ENUMERATE_SUBKEYS: Allows enumeration of subkeys.

KEY_EXECUTE: Grants read access.

KEY_NOTIFY: Allows change notifications.

KEY_QUERY_VALUE: Allows querying of subkey data.

KEY_READ: Combination of KEY_QUERY_VALUE, KEY_ENUMERATE_SUB_KEYS, and KEY_NOTIFY.

KEY_SET_VALUE: Allows setting subkey data.

KEY_WRITE: Combination of KEY_SET_VALUE and KEY_CREATE_SUB_KEY.

The newly opened key is returned at the address passed in phkResult. If the key is opened successfully, RegOpenKeyEx() will return ERROR_SUCCESS; otherwise, an error from WinError.h is returned.

If you are unsure of the subkey you want to open or if you are writing a browser-type application, you can list the available subkeys by making successive calls to RegEnumKeyEx().

You can also retrieve additional information about a key you have opened by calling RegQueryInfoKey(). This will give you data such as the number of subkeys, the maximum length of subkeys and data values, and the last time the key was written to.

> **NOTE**
>
> The API also includes functions such as RegOpenKey(), RegQueryValue(), and RegSetValue(). These functions are intended only for compatibility with Win3.1. Where they are available, your 32-bit apps should use the Ex (extended) form, like RegOpenKeyEx().

When you are done with the key, you should close it with a call to RegCloseKey(), which takes the key handle as its only parameter.

You will see an example of using RegOpenKeyEx() in the next section.

Reading Data from the Registry

You can read data from the Registry with the RegQueryValueEx() function, shown here:

```
LONG RegQueryValueEx( HKEY hKey, LPTSTR lpValueName,
    LPDWORD lpReserved, LPDWORD lpType,
    LPBYTE lpData, LPDWORD lpcbData );
```

You should pass the handle for the key in hKey and the name of the value to open in lpValueName. lpReserved is—you guessed it—reserved, and must be set to NULL. lpType points to a buffer that will receive the type of the value. This will be one of the type constants shown in Table 31.1, like REG_DWORD. The actual value is returned at lpData, and its length is returned at lpcbData. When calling RegQueryValueEx(), you should pass the maximum length of the data buffer given in lpData in the location at lpcbData.

You can list all of the available values in a key by making repeated calls to RegEnumValueEx(), as shown in the following example, which will open a key and dump the values for all of the values in the key:

```
LONG lRc;
HKEY hReadKey;
DWORD dwDataType;
DWORD dwLength;
char szMessage[100];
DWORD dwMaxUsers;
DWORD dwIndex = 0;
char szValueName[100];
DWORD dwValueLen;
char bData[100];
DWORD dwDataLen;

// Open Key
lRc = RegOpenKeyEx(HKEY_LOCAL_MACHINE,
                "SOFTWARE\\SAMS",
                0,
                KEY_READ,
                &hReadKey);
if(lRc != ERROR_SUCCESS)
    TRACE("Error in RegOpenKeyEx: 0x%x (%d)\n", lRc, lRc);
// Set length of data buffer
dwLength = sizeof(szMessage);
// Query Value
lRc = RegQueryValueEx(hReadKey,
                    "Message",
                    NULL,
                    &dwDataType,
                    (LPBYTE) szMessage,
                    &dwLength);
TRACE("Message: [%s] Type: %d Length: %d\n", szMessage,
        dwDataType, dwLength);

// Set length of data buffer
dwLength = sizeof(dwMaxUsers);
// Query Value
lRc = RegQueryValueEx(hReadKey,
                    "MaxUsers",
                    NULL,
                    &dwDataType,
                    (LPBYTE) &dwMaxUsers,
                    &dwLength);
TRACE("MaxUsers: %d Type: %d Length: %d\n", dwMaxUsers,
        dwDataType, dwLength);
// List all Values in key
```

```
do
{
    dwValueLen = sizeof(szValueName);
    dwDataLen = sizeof(bData);
    lRc = RegEnumValue(hReadKey,
                       dwIndex,
                       szValueName,
                       &dwValueLen,
                       NULL,
                       &dwDataType,
                       (LPBYTE) bData,
                       &dwDataLen);
    if(lRc == ERROR_SUCCESS)
    {
        TRACE("Name: [%s] Type: %d ", szValueName, dwDataType);
        switch(dwDataType)
        {
        case REG_SZ:
            TRACE("Value: [%s]\n", (char*) bData);
            break;
        case REG_DWORD:
            TRACE("Value: %d\n", *((DWORD*) bData));
            break;
        default:
            TRACE("Unhandled Data Type\n");
            break;
        } // end switch
    } // end if
    else
        if(lRc == ERROR_NO_MORE_ITEMS)
            TRACE("No more Values\n");
        else
            TRACE("Error in RegEnumValue()\n");
    dwIndex++;
}
while(lRc == ERROR_SUCCESS);
// Close Key
lRc = RegCloseKey(hReadKey);
if(lRc != ERROR_SUCCESS)
    TRACE("Error in RegCloseKey: 0x%x (%d)\n", lRc, lRc);
```

You can also query a list of different values on a particular call with a single call to
`RegQueryMultipleValues()`. However, in most cases, I prefer to use multiple calls to
`RegQueryValueEx()`, because it keeps code somewhat simpler.

Creating a Key

Of course, before you can work with any keys specific to your application, you will need to
first add those keys to the Registry. This is done with the `RegCreateKeyEx()` function, shown
here:

```
LONG RegCreateKeyEx( HKEY hKey, LPCTSTR lpSubKey, DWORD Reserved,
    LPTSTR lpClass, DWORD dwOptions, REGSAM samDesired,
    LPSECURITY_ATTRIBUTES lpSecurityAttributes,
    PHKEY phkResult, LPDWORD lpdwDisposition );
```

You should pass the handle of the parent key, which has previously been opened, in hKey and the name of the new key to create in lpSubKey. Note that the new key name passed in lpSubKey might include backslashes to navigate to the desired location for the new key, as shown in the example in "Writing to the Registry."

You may pass a string that gives a class name for the new key in lpClass or set lpClass to NULL.

The dwOptions parameter allows you to set one of the following special options for the new key:

REG_OPTION_NON_VOLATILE: Creates a key that is not volatile. The data will be saved in a file and will be restored when the system is restarted.

REG_OPTION_VOLATILE: This will create a volatile key, which is not preserved through system restarts. This sort of key will also not be saved in a call to RegSaveKey(). This value is ignored in Windows 95.

REG_OPTION_BACKUP_RESTORE: Creates the key with all of the privileges needed for the key to be backed up or restored, regardless of the value passed in samDesired. This is not supported in Windows 95.

The samDesired parameter specifies the permissions that will be granted for the new key. This can be one of the values that you saw for the samDesired parameter of RegOpenKeyEx(), like KEY_ALL_ACCESS. In addition, under Windows NT, you can pass a pointer to a SECURITY_ATTRIBUTES structure in lpSecurityAttributes. This can be used to add user-level security to the new key. However, under Windows 95, the lpSecurityAttributes member of the SECURITY_ATTRIBUTES structure is ignored, because the Windows 95 Registry does not support security.

Upon successful completion, the handle for the newly created key is returned at phkResult. In addition, the DWORD at lpdwDisposition will receive a value that indicates if the key was newly created or existed previously and was simply opened. This will receive one of the following values:

REG_CREATED_NEW_KEY: The key did not exist previously and was created.
REG_OPENED_EXISTING_KEY: The key existed previously and was opened.

You will see an example of RegCreateKeyEx() in the next section.

When you are done with the key, you should close it with a call to RegCloseKey().

> **NOTE**
>
> RegCloseKey() will save changes to the key with a lazy write only. If your application requires that the data be written immediately, you will need to call RegFlushKey(), which will not return until all changes are written.

You can also delete a key by calling RegDeleteKey().

Writing to the Registry

Values are written to the Registry with the `RegSetValueEx()` function, shown here:

```
LONG RegSetValueEx( HKEY hKey, LPCTSTR lpValueName, DWORD Reserved,
    DWORD dwType, CONST BYTE *lpData, DWORD cbData );
```

You pass the handle for the key that contains the value in `hKey` and the name of the value to update in `lpValueName`. Once again, `Reserved` is reserved and should be passed `0`. The type of data value to update is passed in `dwType`. This should be one of the constants shown in Table 31.1, such as `REG_DWORD`. You pass the new value by passing a pointer to the data in `lpData` and the length of that data in `cbData`. For string values, be sure to include the null terminator in the byte count.

NOTE

If you are assigning a string value, you should include the NULL terminator in the length passed in `cbData`.

You can delete a value from a particular key in the Registry by calling `RegDeleteValue()`.

The following example shows how to create a new key and add a few configuration values:

```
LONG lRc;
HKEY hNewKey;
DWORD dwDisposition;
char *lpszNewMessage = "Hi Mom!";
DWORD dwNewMaxUsers = 42;
// Create new key
lRc = RegCreateKeyEx(HKEY_LOCAL_MACHINE,        // parent key
                    "SOFTWARE\\SAMS",           // new key name
                    0,                          // reserved
                    NULL,                       // no class
                    REG_OPTION_NON_VOLATILE,    // non-volatile
                    KEY_ALL_ACCESS,             // all permissions
                    NULL,                       // default security
                    &hNewKey,                   // new key handle
                    &dwDisposition);            // Disposition var.
if(lRc != ERROR_SUCCESS)
    TRACE("Error in RegCreateKeyEx: 0x%x (%d)\n", lRc, lRc);
if(dwDisposition == REG_CREATED_NEW_KEY)
    TRACE("New Key Created\n");
if(dwDisposition == REG_OPENED_EXISTING_KEY)
    TRACE("Existing key opened.\n");
// Add Values
lRc = RegSetValueEx(hNewKey,                    // key to add value to
                    "Message",                  // Value name
                    0,                          // reserved
                    REG_SZ,                     // data type
                    (BYTE*)lpszNewMessage,      // data buffer
                    strlen(lpszNewMessage)+1);  // data length
```

```
if(lRc != ERROR_SUCCESS)
    TRACE("Error in RegSetValueEx: 0x%x (%d)\n", lRc, lRc);
lRc = RegSetValueEx(hNewKey,                 // key to add value to
                    "MaxUsers",              // Value name
                    0,                       // reserved
                    REG_DWORD,               // data type
                    (BYTE*)&dwNewMaxUsers,   // data buffer
                    4);                      // data length

if(lRc != ERROR_SUCCESS)
    TRACE("Error in RegSetValueEx: 0x%x (%d)\n", lRc, lRc);
// Flush Key
// Use this only if you need to wait for data to be written
lRc = RegFlushKey(hNewKey);
if(lRc != ERROR_SUCCESS)
    TRACE("Error in RegFlushKey: 0x%x (%d)\n", lRc, lRc);
// Close Key
lRc = RegCloseKey(hNewKey);
if(lRc != ERROR_SUCCESS)
    TRACE("Error in RegCloseKey: 0x%x (%d)\n", lRc, lRc);
```

Registry Security

In Windows NT, you can assign user-level security to individual keys in the Registry. You can set the security for a key when you create it or by calling RegSetKeySecurity(). You can check on the current security settings for a key by calling RegGetKeySecurity().

Security is not available for the Windows 95 Registry.

Saving Registry Keys to a File

You can save the contents of a key, including all of its subkeys and values, to a file with the RegSaveKey() function. Then reload the key from the file with a call to RegLoadKey().Unload a key from the Registry with the RegUnloadKey() function, which removes the key from the Registry but leaves the data in the underlying file untouched.

You can also use the RegRestoreKey() function to replace the current data for a key with data from a new file. However, this function will fail if the key is restored or any of its subkeys are open. If this is the case, use RegReplaceKey() which will replace a specified key with data from a file, although it will not take effect until the next time the system is restarted.

> **NOTE**
>
> The functions in this section might behave quite differently on Windows NT than they do on Windows 95. For more on these functions, see the online documentation.

Remote Registry Access

The Win32 Registry allows you to interact with the Registry on remote computers, provided you have the appropriate privileges. This is done with the RegConnectRegistry() function, shown here:

```
LONG RegConnectRegistry( LPTSTR lpMachineName, HKEY hKey, PHKEY phkResult );
```

When calling RegConnectRegistry(), pass a string containing the remote machine name in lpMachineName and one of the predefined Registry keys (such as HKEY_LOCAL_MACHINE) in hKey. If the connection request is accepted, the handle returned at phkResult can be used like any local Registry key handle—with the exception that it works with the Registry on the remote machine.

> **NOTE**
>
> RegConnectRegistry() does not allow you to access the HKEY_CLASSES_ROOT or HKEY_CURRENT_USER keys.

As with local keys, you should call RegCloseKey() for the key returned by RegConnectRegistry() when you are done with it.

Registry Change Notifications

You can request that Windows set an event whenever the values or attributes of a key are changed. Do this with the RegNotifyChangeKeyValue() function. For more on this, see the online documentation.

Summary

The Registry provides a new alternative to the old .ini files that were used to store configuration information for the Windows system and other applications. The Registry provides a hierarchical organization, as well as security and remote access.

This chapter shows how the Registry is structured and examines some of the more commonly used segments of the key hierarchy.

You have seen how to use the Registry API to open existing keys and retrieve values from them, as well as create your own keys and add new values. You also learned how to connect to the Registry on remote machines.

Although the Registry might seem a bit foreign at first, it is a definite improvement over the .ini files of the past and can help make your applications better. Proper use of the Registry is one of the features of well-behaved Win32 applications. Your customers will expect it.

32

Extending the Windows Shell

by David Bennett

With Windows 95, and later with Windows NT 4.0, the user interface for the operating system has been totally revamped. Gone is the dreaded Program Manager that has been around since Windows 3.1. This new user interface, which is now supported by both Windows 95 and Windows NT, is known as the Windows shell.

The new Windows shell provides a much more flexible and more powerful user interface that can be fully customized by the user. This chapter tells you how to add features to your applications that will allow them to cooperate with the shell, as well as provide features that your users will expect from industrial-strength Win32 applications.

In this chapter, we will see how to do the following:

- Interact with the Win32 taskbar
- Create application toolbars
- Work with long filenames
- Use standard Win32 file operations
- Work with the shell namespace
- Add your own desktop shortcuts

NOTE

Older versions of Windows NT, such as 3.51, do not support the new Windows Shell.

Working with the Taskbar

By now, you have probably noticed the Win32 taskbar. (See Figure 32.1.) This usually appears at the bottom of the desktop, although it can also be configured to hide itself, in which case you will need to move the cursor to the bottom of the screen to make it appear. In addition, you can move the taskbar to one of the sides or the top of the desktop by simply dragging it.

On the left (or top) of the taskbar, you will find the Start button, which brings up the Start menu. This menu allows you to shut down the system, open a recent document, or start one of any number of different applications that have been installed in the Programs menu. We will see how to add a menu entry for your applications in Chapter 35, "Adding Windows Help."

The bulk of the taskbar is filled with icons for applications that are running. This basic functionality is handled for you when your application creates its main window, although you will see how your applications can take advantage of some additional, advanced features of the taskbar buttons.

At the far right (or bottom) of the taskbar, you will find the system tray, or status area. This generally displays the time, as well as application-specific status icons. We will take a look at how to add your own icons to this area in just a bit.

FIGURE 32.1.
Win32 taskbar.

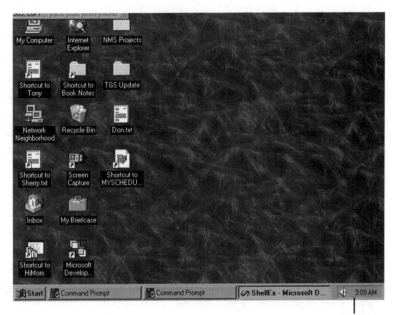

Taskbar

Taskbar Buttons

You have probably already seen that for most applications you start, a button is added to the taskbar for the application. You can use this button to bring the application to the foreground. Technically, this button is added by the operating system whenever an application creates an unowned primary window with the WS_EX_APPWINDOW style set, although you won't see it until ShowWindow() is called to display the window. To make sure that your application will have a taskbar button created for it, you should specify the WS_EX_APPWINDOW-extended style when you call CreateWindowEx(). This is the default for MFC applications, so you probably won't call CreateWindowEx() directly.

TIP

The taskbar button is not added until the main window is created, so if the application you are developing does something like a blocking call that will never return, before the main window is created (such as in calls like CWinApp::InitInstance() or CDialog::OnInitDialog()), you might never see a taskbar button for the application—but it is still there. Under Windows NT, you can use the task manager (available by right-clicking an empty space on the NT taskbar) to kill the process if necessary. Windows 95 does not provide the task manager, but you may kill a wayward process using the process viewer found in \DevStudio\VC\bin\win95\PVIEW95.EXE.

If you want to create an application that does not get a button added to the taskbar, you will need to specify the WS_EX_TOOLWINDOW-extended style when calling CreateWindowEx(). You will also need to make sure that WS_EX_APPWINDOW is not included in the extended styles.

For MFC applications, you do not call CreateWindowEx() directly. For MDI and SDI applications, you can modify the extended styles for your main window in CMainFrame::PreCreateWindow(), as shown here:

```
BOOL CMainFrame::PreCreateWindow(CREATESTRUCT& cs)
{
    BOOL bRetVal;

    bRetVal = CMDIFrameWnd::PreCreateWindow(cs);

    cs.dwExStyle |= WS_EX_TOOLWINDOW;

    cs.dwExStyle &= (~WS_EX_APPWINDOW);

    return bRetVal;
}
```

For dialog-based applications, it is generally easiest to modify the dialog template in your project's .rc file to include the WS_EX_TOOLWINDOW-extended style, as shown here:

```
IDD_SHELLDLG_DIALOG DIALOGEX 0, 0, 185, 93
STYLE DS_MODALFRAME | WS_POPUP | WS_VISIBLE | WS_CAPTION | WS_SYSMENU
EXSTYLE WS_EX_TOOLWINDOW
CAPTION "ShellDlg"
FONT 8, "MS Sans Serif"
BEGIN
    DEFPUSHBUTTON   "OK",IDOK,128,7,50,14
    PUSHBUTTON      "Cancel",IDCANCEL,128,23,50,14
    LTEXT           "TODO: Place dialog controls here.",IDC_STATIC,5,34,113,8
END
```

As an alternative, you can prevent the creation of a taskbar button for your application by creating a hidden window and making it the parent of your application's primary window.

If your application will be processing events while in the background, you can occasionally tell the user that something has happened that would warrant his attention. You can make the taskbar button for your application flash by calling FlashWindow(), even if the main window is hidden or minimized.

The System Tray

In the new Win32 shell, the system tray is the area on the far-right corner (or on the bottom if you are using a vertical taskbar) of the taskbar. This area is also known as the status area or the notification area. (See Figure 32.2.) In most cases, you will see the time displayed in this area, although it might be disabled. You might also see any number of different application-specific icons. This can include icons representing things such as a print job in progress, anti-virus software, sound settings, or the Win95 system agent, to name a few.

By double-clicking one of these icons, you bring up part of the application, such as a dialog to change current settings. You can also right-click the icon in the system tray to access a context menu, which can give you even more options specific to that application.

FIGURE 32.2.

System tray context menu.

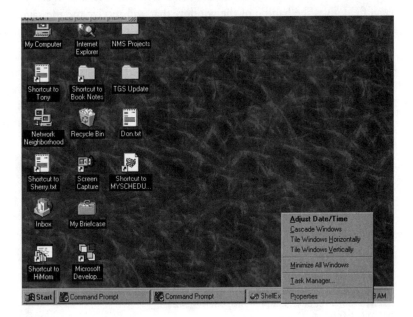

Adding to the System Tray

Your applications can include their own icons in the system tray, and begin receiving Windows messages from them, when you call the Shell_NotifyIcon() function, shown here:

```
WINSHELLAPI BOOL WINAPI Shell_NotifyIcon( DWORD dwMessage, PNOTIFYICONDATA pnid );
```

This function is used to send several different messages that control how your icon in the system tray operates. Shell_NotifyIcon() and other shell functions are defined in shlobj.h. The dwMessage parameter specifies the operation that will be performed. To add a new icon for your application, this should be set to NIM_ADD, although you may also pass NIM_MODIFY to change a current icon or NIM_DELETE to remove an existing icon.

The second parameter to Shell_NotifyIcon() is a pointer to a NOTIFYICONDATA structure, which is used to pass a variety of different information. The ASCII version of this structure is here:

```
typedef struct _NOTIFYICONDATAA {
        DWORD cbSize;
        HWND hWnd;
        UINT uID;
        UINT uFlags;
        UINT uCallbackMessage;
        HICON hIcon;
        CHAR    szTip[64];
} NOTIFYICONDATAA, *PNOTIFYICONDATAA;
```

The cbSize field should always be set to sizeof(NOTIFYICONDATA).

When mouse events occur on the icon in the system tray, such as moving over the icon, clicking, or double-clicking, the icon will send a Windows message back to your application. The hWnd field gives the handle of the window that will receive the message, while uID specifies a value that will be passed back to your application in the wParam of this message.

The uFlags field is used to indicate which of the remaining fields contains valid data. This may be a combination of NIF_ICON, NIF_MESSAGE, or NIF_TIP. To pass a new icon, set uFlags to NIF_ICON and pass a handle to the icon in hIcon. The value passed in uCallbackMessage gives the message ID of the Windows message that will be sent to your application when the user does something with the icon. Lastly, you may pass a short string for tooltip help text for the icon in szTip by setting NIF_TIP in uFlags.

The following example adds a new icon to the system tray:

```
BOOL bRc;
NOTIFYICONDATA niData;
HICON hIcon;

hIcon = AfxGetApp()->LoadIcon(IDI_ICON1);

niData.cbSize = sizeof(NOTIFYICONDATA);
niData.hWnd = m_hWnd;
niData.uID = 123;        // value returned in wParam
niData.uFlags = NIF_ICON | NIF_MESSAGE | NIF_TIP;
niData.uCallbackMessage = WM_USER + 42;
niData.hIcon = hIcon;
sprintf(niData.szTip, "My Status Icon");

bRc = Shell_NotifyIcon(NIM_ADD, &niData);
```

To remove the icon from the system tray, pass the same structure to the Shell_NotifyIcon() function, using NIM_DELETE.

Handling Notifications

When mouse events occur in the icon that was added, a Windows message will be sent to the window handle that we passed in the hWnd field of the NOTIFYICONDATA structure. In this case, the sample code is taken from a dialog application, so the main window for your application will receive a message with a message ID of WM_USER + 42, with the wParam field set to 123. In addition, the lParam in the message will be set to one of the mouse event message IDs, such as WM_LBUTTONDOWN. Now, let's take a look at how to handle these messages.

First, you will need to add a message handler for the message ID that you passed in the call to Shell_NotifyIcon(). In MFC apps, this is most easily done by adding an entry to your message map, as shown here:

```
BEGIN_MESSAGE_MAP(CShellDlgDlg, CDialog)
    //{{AFX_MSG_MAP(CShellDlgDlg)
    ON_WM_SYSCOMMAND()
    ON_WM_PAINT()
```

```
ON_WM_QUERYDRAGICON()
ON_BN_CLICKED(IDC_ADD_TRAY_ICON, OnAddTrayIcon)
ON_BN_CLICKED(IDC_DEL_TRAY_ICON, OnDelTrayIcon)
//}}AFX_MSG_MAP

ON_MESSAGE(WM_USER + 42, OnNotifyMsg)

END_MESSAGE_MAP()
```

You will then need to implement the message handler function. A simple example is shown here:

```
afx_msg LRESULT CShellDlgDlg::OnNotifyMsg(WPARAM wParam, LPARAM lParam)
{

    TRACE("Message Received: wParam: %d lParam: 0x%x", wParam, lParam);

    switch(lParam)
    {
    case WM_MOUSEMOVE:
        TRACE("\tWM_MOUSEMOVE\n");
        break;
    case WM_LBUTTONDOWN:
        TRACE("\tWM_LBUTTONDOWN\n");
        break;
    case WM_LBUTTONUP:
        TRACE("\tWM_LBUTTONUP\n");
        break;
    case WM_LBUTTONDBLCLK:
        TRACE("\tWM_LBUTTONDBLCLK\n");
        break;
    case WM_RBUTTONDOWN:
        TRACE("\tWM_RBUTTONDOWN\n");
        break;
    case WM_RBUTTONUP:
        TRACE("\tWM_RBUTTONUP\n");
        break;
    case WM_RBUTTONDBLCLK:
        TRACE("\tWM_RBUTTONDBLCLK\n");
        break;
    } // end switch
    return 0;
}
```

This example simply provides TRACE output for each of the received messages. You may do whatever you want when handling these messages, although it is standard operating procedure to provide a pop-up context menu when the user right-clicks your icon. You may add a simple context menu by adding code like the following to your message handler:

```
// Handle context menu
if(wParam == 123 && lParam == WM_RBUTTONDOWN)
{
    CMenu ContextMenu;
    CPoint CursorPos;

    // Get cursor position for positioning menu
    GetCursorPos(&CursorPos);

    ContextMenu.CreatePopupMenu();
```

```
// Add some commands to the menu
ContextMenu.AppendMenu(MF_STRING, WM_USER+51, _T("Command 1"));
ContextMenu.AppendMenu(MF_STRING, WM_USER+52, _T("Command 2"));
ContextMenu.AppendMenu(MF_STRING, WM_USER+53, _T("Command 3"));

// This is needed to correctly handle the case
//    where the user clicks outside the menu.
SetForegroundWindow();

// Present the menu
ContextMenu.TrackPopupMenu( TPM_RIGHTALIGN | TPM_RIGHTBUTTON,
    CursorPos.x, CursorPos.y, this, NULL);

} // end handle context menu
```

Application Desktop Toolbars

The Windows shell allows your application to create toolbars directly on the desktop. These are known as *application desktop toolbars,* or *appbars.* If you use Microsoft Office, you have probably seen that it creates an appbar that gives you quick access to the functions of Office from the desktop.

Appbars may be attached to any of the edges of the desktop, or, like other toolbars, may be allowed to float around the desktop. They can even be set to always float on top of other applications.

Appbar Messages

Your applications will interact with the operating system to coordinate appbar functionality. This is done by sending appbar messages with the SHAppBarMessage() function, shown here:

```
WINSHELLAPI UINT APIENTRY SHAppBarMessage( DWORD dwMessage, PAPPBARDATA pData );
```

The type of message to send is specified by the value passed in dwMessage, which may be one of the values listed here:

ABM_ACTIVATE: Sent to tell the OS that the appbar has been activated. You should send this message whenever your appbar receives WM_ACTIVATE messages.

ABM_GETAUTOHIDEBAR: Used to retrieve the handle of the autohide toolbar assigned to a screen edge.

ABM_GETSTATE: Retrieves the current autohide and always-on-top state of the taskbar.

ABM_GETTASKBARPOS: Retrieves the current position of the taskbar.

ABM_NEW: Registers a new appbar with Windows.

ABM_QUERYPOS: Requests a new position for the appbar.

ABM_REMOVE: Deregisters an appbar.

ABM_SETAUTOHIDEBAR: Used to register or deregister an autohide toolbar.

ABM_SETPOS: Used to set the position of an appbar.

ABM_WINDOWPOSCHANGED: Sent to notify Windows when an appbar has moved. You should send this message every time your appbar receives a WM_WINDOWPOSCHANGED message.

We will be looking at the specifics for working with these messages in the section "Handling Appbar Notifications."

The second parameter is a pointer to an APPBARDATA structure, which is used to pass a variety of different information regarding the specifics of operations. This structure is used both for passing requested values, as well as returning information from the operating system. The APPBARDATA structure is shown here:

```
typedef struct _AppBarData {
    DWORD   cbSize;
    HWND    hWnd;
    UINT    uCallbackMessage;
    UINT    uEdge;
    RECT    rc;
    LPARAM  lParam;
} APPBARDATA, *PAPPBARDATA;
```

Many fields in the APPBARDATA are used only with certain messages, so we will look at these fields as we need them. However, you should always set cbSize to sizeof(APPBARDATA) and set hWnd to the handle of the appbar window.

Registering an Appbar

To register your appbar with Windows, you will need to send the ABM_NEW message, using SHAppBarMessage(), as shown previously. In the APPBARDATA structure, you specify how notifications for the appbar will be delivered. The window handle passed in the hWnd field gives the destination window, and the uCallbackMessage field contains the message ID that will be sent for any notifications. This is generally a user-defined message, such as WM_USER+1.

The following example shows how to register our dialog as an appbar with the Windows shell:

```
APPBARDATA abData;

 abData.cbSize = sizeof(APPBARDATA);
 abData.hWnd = m_hWnd;

 abData.uCallbackMessage = WM_USER + 777;

 if(!SHAppBarMessage(ABM_NEW, &abData))
     TRACE("Error in SHAppBArMessage\n");
 else
     TRACE("Appbar registered OK\n");
```

Your appbar is now registered with the shell, and you may begin receiving notifications from the shell. However, the appbar's position has not yet been set. The next section shows how to set the appbar's position.

Positioning the Appbar

Your application will need to position the appbar after registering it. You will also need to re-position the appbar in response to ABN_POSCHANGED notifications. This may be done with code like the following:

```
// For now, use only the top edge
abData.uEdge = ABE_TOP;

// Default to whole screen for now
CRect defRect(0,0,GetSystemMetrics(SM_CXSCREEN),
    GetSystemMetrics(SM_CYSCREEN));

abData.rc = defRect;

SHAppBarMessage(ABM_QUERYPOS, &abData);

// Adjust position of our appbar
switch(abData.uEdge)
{
case ABE_TOP:
    abData.rc.bottom = abData.rc.top + 80;
    break;
case ABE_BOTTOM:
    abData.rc.top = abData.rc.bottom - 80;
    break;
case ABE_LEFT:
    abData.rc.right = abData.rc.left + 400;
    break;
case ABE_RIGHT:
    abData.rc.left = abData.rc.right - 400;
    break;
}

// Notify the shell of the new position
if(!SHAppBarMessage(ABM_SETPOS, &abData))
    TRACE("Error in SHAppBarMessage\n");
else
    TRACE("Appbar positioned OK\n");

// Move the displayed window
MoveWindow(&abData.rc);
```

NOTE

Registering the appbar with the shell simply allows the shell to reserve the space for the appbar and adjust other windows accordingly. Registering does not, however, handle moving your appbar. Thus, you must register any change in your appbar with the shell and actually move the window in separate steps, as shown previously.

Handling Appbar Notifications

After you register your appbar with the Windows shell, you may begin to receive certain notification messages. These will be sent to the window that you specified in the hWnd field of the APPBARDATA structure that you passed when you sent the ABM_NEW message. The ID for all of the notification messages is specified by the uCallbackMessage field passed.

To handle these notifications, you can add a message handler by adding a message map entry like the following, which handles notifications that use a message ID of WM_USER+76:

```
ON_MESSAGE(WM_USER + 76, OnAppbar)
```

In general, the appbar notifications are used only to tell your appbar when it needs to resize to adjust to the changing desktop. The notification code is passed to your handler in the wParam and may be one of the following values:

> ABN_FULLSCREENAPP: This is sent whenever a full-screen application opens or closes. lParam is set to TRUE if an app is opening or FALSE if it is closing. Your appbar should call SetWindowPos() to display itself properly.
>
> ABN_POSCHANGED: This is sent when the desktop taskbar changes its position or size. Your appbar should recompute its size and position.
>
> ABN_STATECHANGE: This is sent when the taskbar's always-on-top or autohide properties change.
>
> ABN_WINDOWARRANGE: This notification is sent once before the desktop cascades or tiles its windows, with lParam set to TRUE. After the cascade or tile, it will be sent again with lParam set to FALSE.

The following shows a skeleton handler for these notifications:

```
afx_msg LRESULT CShellDlgDlg::OnAppbar(WPARAM wParam, LPARAM lParam)
{
    TRACE("Appbar Notification: wParam: %d lParam: %d\n", wParam, lParam);

    switch(wParam)
    {
    case ABN_FULLSCREENAPP:
        TRACE("ABN_FULLSCREENAP: \n");
        break;
    case ABN_POSCHANGED:
        TRACE("ABN_POSCHANGED: \n");
        break;
    case ABN_STATECHANGE:
        TRACE("ABN_STATECHANGE: \n");
        break;
    case ABN_WINDOWARRANGE:
        TRACE("ABN_WINDOWARRANGE: \n");
        break;
    } // end switch lParam
} // end OnAppBar()
```

Autohide Appbars

You may also register your appbar as an autohide appbar. This sort of appbar will appear only when the user moves the mouse to the edge of the desktop with the appbar attached and will hide itself when it is not in use. However, you may only have one autohide appbar on each edge of the desktop.

You can register an autohide appbar by sending the ABM_SETAUTOHIDEBAR message with SHAppBarMessage() instead of the ABM_NEW message. If an autohide appbar is already attached to the requested edge, the function will fail. You can retrieve the window handle of the appbar that is currently attached to a given edge of the desktop by sending the ABM_GETAUTOHIDEBAR message with SHAppBarMessage().

Removing an Appbar

Before you destroy your appbar, you must deregister the appbar with the Windows shell. Failure to do so can leave the desktop in an indeterminate state and will consume valuable screen real estate, as well as possibly rearrange all of the icons on the desktop. Needless to say, your users may not appreciate this.

An appbar is removed by sending the ABM_REMOVE message with SHAppBarMessage(), using the APPBARDATA that specifies the appbar to remove. This can be done with code like the following:

```
APPBARDATA abData;

abData.cbSize = sizeof(APPBARDATA);
abData.hWnd = m_hWnd;

abData.uCallbackMessage = WM_USER + 777;

if(!SHAppBarMessage(ABM_REMOVE, &abData))
    TRACE("Error in SHAppBArMessage\n");
else
    TRACE("Appbar registered OK\n");
```

Long Filenames

This isn't really a shell issue, but this seems like as good a place as any to talk about long filenames. Both Windows NT and Windows 95 support filenames that are no longer limited to eight characters plus a three character extension. Not only can you use longer filenames, but you can also include additional characters, such as spaces or as many periods as your little heart desires.

The fact that Win32 supports long filenames means that your Win32 applications should support them also. This means that you must do some things a bit differently than you did in your old apps that supported the 8.3 format.

To start, you should always use the newer API functions that support long filenames instead of the older API functions that are still available to your applications but do not support long filenames. For example, when creating or opening files, you should always use the `CreateFile()` function instead of the older `OpenFile()`, `_lcreate()`, or `_lopen()` functions.

Also, your applications will need to handle filename variables differently. You can no longer assume that a filename will fit into 12 characters. You should also be prepared to handle filenames with several periods or spaces in them.

In addition, filenames in Win32 might not even name real files on the local machine. The first example of this is the use of Universal Naming Convention (UNC) names to represent files on machines across the network. These filenames take the form of `\\MyServer\MyDir\MyFile`, where the server name is preceded by a double backslash (`\\`) and the next directory represents a share exported by that server. Normal directory paths may then follow. You may use UNC filenames with the newer Win32 functions to work with files across the network without going to the trouble of establishing a connection.

In addition, Win32 filenames can refer to objects in the shell namespace, such as printers and special folders. We will see more on this in "The Shell Namespace."

This might seem like a lot of things to be concerned about in your applications, but Windows can help you out with most of these if you simply use the common file dialogs wherever possible. This not only saves you the trouble of implementing your own user interface for opening or saving files, but also includes all of the processing for long filenames (even the special ones, such as shell namespace items and UNC names).

If you want to get additional information about a particular file, you can use the `SHGetFileInfo()` function to get all sorts of information about a file, including its attributes, display name, executable type, file type, and various icon information. For more details on `SHGetFileInfo()`, see the online help.

Shell File Operations

Undoubtedly, many of your applications will need to perform various file operations, such as copying, moving, deleting, or renaming files. At first glance, this seems like a trivial task. However, as you make your applications more user-friendly and robust, you will find that there are a great many special cases that your application will need to handle. Some of these can include asking the user whether he or she wants to overwrite existing files or create new directories, displaying meaningful error messages, or providing the user with feedback on the ongoing status of an operation and a means to cancel operations in progress.

Well, it just so happens that the Win32 shell can help out greatly with the finer points of implementing file operations, including the special cases listed previously. You can take advantage of the built-in file operations in the Win32 shell by using the `SHFileOperation()` function to perform file copy, move, rename, or delete operations on any number of different files, including wildcard filenames and whole directory trees. The prototype for SHFileOperation() is shown here:

```
WINSHELLAPI int WINAPI SHFileOperation( LPSHFILEOPSTRUCT lpFileOp );
```

SHFileOperation() takes only a single parameter, although the SHFILEOPSTRUCT structure that is passed contains several juicy bits of information, allowing you to customize the way that the shell will handle your file operations. This structure is shown here:

```
typedef struct _SHFILEOPSTRUCT {
    HWND          hwnd;
    UINT          wFunc;
    LPCSTR        pFrom;
    LPCSTR        pTo;
    FILEOP_FLAGS  fFlags;
    BOOL          fAnyOperationsAborted;
    LPVOID        hNameMappings;
    LPCSTR        lpszProgressTitle;
} SHFILEOPSTRUCT, FAR *LPSHFILEOPSTRUCT;
```

The most important member of this structure is the wFunc field, which dictates what operation is to be performed. You may specify one of the following constants:

> FO_COPY: Copies the files specified in pFrom to the new locations given in pTo, leaving the original files in place.
>
> FO_MOVE: Moves the files in pFrom to new locations given in pTo.
>
> FO_RENAME: Renames the files specified in pFrom to the names given in pTo.
>
> FO_DELETE: Deletes the files given in pFrom.

The files that are to be operated on are passed in the strings at pFrom and pTo. These members are actually pointers to a list of strings; each individual filename has a null terminator, and the end of the list is specified with a double null. Even if you only pass a single filename, you will still need to add a double null to the end of the string.

However, if you want to specify a list of different destinations in pTo, you must set the FOF_MULTIDESTFILES flag in fFlags and give a matching destination for each source given in pFrom. If you do not specify FOF_MULTIDESTFILES, the shell assumes that you are passing a single destination directory for all of the source files.

The filenames in pFrom and pTo can refer to either files or directories, and can contain wildcard characters such as ? or *. If you specify wildcards in the pFrom list, the shell will search through subdirectories to find matching filenames, unless you specify the FOF_FILESONLY option in fFlags, which will tell the shell not to deal with subdirectories.

You may also choose to use fully qualified paths or specify relative paths, which are based on the current global drive and directory settings. You may work with the current directory settings using GetCurrentDirectory() and SetCurrentDirectory().

User Confirmations

If you use SHFileOperation() to perform your file operations, the shell can prompt the user for you in certain situations. Any confirmation dialogs that the shell will create for you will use the window handle passed in the hwnd field of the SHFILEOPSTRUCT as a parent window. If you do not want the shell to present any confirmation dialogs to the user, you can include the FOF_NOCONFIRMATION flag in fFlags. If you use this flag, the shell will assume a yes for any confirmations it might have asked for otherwise.

If you specify a directory that does not exist in pTo for move or copy operations, the shell will prompt the user before creating the new directory. This confirmation dialog is shown in Figure 32.3.

FIGURE 32.3.
New directory confirmation.

If you want to disable this confirmation, pass the FOF_NOCONFIRMMKDIR flag.

The shell will also prompt the user for confirmation with a dialog like that shown in Figure 32.4 before overwriting files in a move or copy operation.

FIGURE 32.4.
Overwrite confirmation.

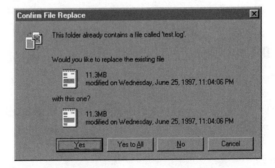

You can have the shell automatically rename the copied files instead of overwrite existing files by passing the FOF_RENAMEONCOLLISION flag. If you set this flag, any files that would overwrite an existing file will be renamed before being copied. For example, MyFile.dat would be renamed to Copy of MyFile.dat if a file with that name already existed in the source directory.

Progress Dialogs

Another valuable feature of SHFileOperation() is its capability to display a progress dialog to the user. This is particularly important if you are working with large files, a long list of files, or network file operations. Most users, myself included, want to be reassured that something useful is still going on and that the application hasn't just wandered off into the weeds somewhere. SHFileOperation() provides a simple, standard way to do this.

By default, for lengthy file operations, the shell will display a dialog box like that shown in Figure 32.5, with the nifty flying papers and the name of the file currently being worked on. However, the shell is smart enough to avoid displaying a progress dialog for operations that are expected to complete in a short period of time.

FIGURE 32.5.
Progress dialog.

You may pass a title for this dialog in the lpszProgressTitle field of the SHFILEOPSTRUCT structure. This dialog also provides a Cancel button. If you do not want to display a Progress dialog, pass the FOF_SILENT flag. In addition, you may request a simple progress dialog, which does not display filenames, by including the FOF_SIMPLEPROGRESS flag.

Operation Success

If an error occurs in SHFileOperation(), it will return a nonzero value. However, just because SHFileOperation() returns 0 does not necessarily mean that things went the way you intended. For example, the user might have chosen not to overwrite a file by aborting the copy. You can determine whether the user canceled an operation by looking at the fAnyOperationsAborted field of the SHFILEOPSTRUCT that is returned. This will be set to TRUE if the user chose to cancel the operation.

In addition, if you were performing a file move or copy to a directory that did not previously exist, and the user chose not to create the new directory in the confirmation dialog, SHFileOperation() will return success (0), even though the files were not actually copied. Thus, unless you have disabled confirmations, you should verify that the files were successfully copied.

The following example shows SHFileOperation() at work:

```
int nRc;

// Remember to escape directory slashes,
//    separate names with a null,
```

```
//   and terminate with an extra null
char strFrom[] = "C:\\ShTest\\test.log\0c:\\ShTest\\test2.log\0";
char strTo[] = "C:\\ShTest2\0";

char strTitle[] = "My Progress Title";

SHFILEOPSTRUCT FileOp;

FileOp.hwnd = m_hWnd;
FileOp.wFunc = FO_COPY;
FileOp.pFrom = strFrom;
FileOp.pTo = strTo;
FileOp.fFlags = FOF_ALLOWUNDO;
FileOp.hNameMappings = NULL;
FileOp.lpszProgressTitle = strTitle;

nRc = SHFileOperation(&FileOp);
if(nRc)
    TRACE("An error occurred: 0x%x (%d)\n", nRc, nRc);
else
    TRACE("SHFileOperation completed OK\n");

if(FileOp.fAnyOperationsAborted)
    TRACE("An Operation was aborted!!!\n");
```

File Mappings

In addition, you may request that `SHFileOperation()` returns a list of the actual filenames that were used in an operation by including the `FOF_WANTMAPPINGHANDLE` flag. Specifying this will cause the shell to return a handle to a filename mapping object in the `hNameMappings` field of the `SHFILEOPTSTRUCT`. This will contain an array of `SHNAMEMAPPING` structures that contains the old path and the new path computed by the shell for each file involved in the operation. You will need to free this array when you are done with it by calling `SHFreeNameMappings()`.

The Shell Namespace

One of the most important changes made to the Win32 shell was the addition of a desktop that contains a hierarchy of folders and other objects that operate independently of the dreaded Program Manager application window. The objects on the desktop can represent several different things. To start, actual files may be represented, as well as folders that represent real file system directories. In addition, you will notice several other special folders, like My Computer or Network Neighborhood, that do not represent actual files or directories in the file system, as well as shortcuts, which refer to an actual file or other object in another location.

All of the objects that are present on the desktop, as well as the objects contained in subfolders of the desktop (including subfolders of subfolders), are contained in what is known as the shell *namespace*. The namespace tracks both objects that represent physical files and other special objects that do not represent physical files. This section shows how your applications can work with the objects contained in the shell namespace.

Getting Started

The shell namespace is arranged in a hierarchical tree structure, much like the file systems used by Win32. Instead of the directory path that you would use to specify a particular file, objects in the namespace are generally identified by a Pointer to an Identifier List, or PIDL.

Each object contained in a particular folder has an identifier that uniquely identifies that object within that particular folder. Thus, to uniquely identify a particular object somewhere in the namespace hierarchy, you will need to use a list of the unique IDs for all objects in the path to the specified object. A PIDL points to just such a list of identifiers. Most of the functions shown here use PIDLs to represent particular objects in the namespace. The shell functions define the ITEMIDLIST type to contain identifier lists, as well as the LPITEMIDLIST type, which points to such a list.

Each object contained in the namespace is actually a COM object that exposes the IShellFolder interface. This interface allows you to work with certain properties of the object, as well as to enumerate any other objects that it contains. The next few sections show how to use this interface.

To start browsing the namespace or to reach any particular object, you will need to retrieve a starting point for your search. The desktop itself is at the root of the entire namespace, so this makes a good place to start. You can retrieve an IShellFolder interface for the desktop with a call to SHGetDesktopFolder(), shown here:

```
WINSHELLAPI HRESULT WINAPI SHGetDesktopFolder( LPSHELLFOLDER *ppshf );
```

This function simply returns a pointer to the IShellFolder interface of the desktop, which is the root of the entire namespace. The next few sections show how to traverse the tree and get information about objects using the IShellFolder interface.

> **NOTE**
>
> To use some of the shell functions from this section, you should use #include shlobj.h.

Traversing the Tree

To traverse the tree, you will need an IShellFolder interface for a starting point, as shown previously. You will also need an identifier for the next object down the hierarchy. There are two different ways you can retrieve such an identifier. The first uses SHGetSpecialFolderLocation() to retrieve certain special identifiers for top-level folders in the desktop. The second way is to scroll through the identifiers contained in a folder by using IShellFolder::EnumObjects().

::SHGetSpecialFolderLocation()

The ::SHGetSpecialFolderLocation() function allows you to retrieve an identifier for one of several different special objects on the top level of the desktop.

```
WINSHELLAPI HRESULT WINAPI SHGetSpecialFolderLocation( HWND hwndOwner,
    int nFolder, LPITEMIDLIST *ppidl    );
```

The window handle passed in hwndOwner is used as the parent of any dialogs, such as error messages, that the shell presents to the user. The nFolder parameter should contain one of the following constants, which specifies which folder you want to retrieve an identifier list for:

CSIDL_BITBUCKET: File system object containing the files in the user's recycle bin.

CSIDL_COMMON_DESKTOP: File system directory that contains the desktop objects common to all users.

CSIDL_COMMON_PROGRAMS: File system directory containing the directories for the Start menu program groups that are common to all users.

CSIDL_COMMON_STARTMENU: File system directory containing the objects in the Start menu for all users.

CSIDL_COMMON_STARTUP: File system directory containing the programs that appear in the Startup folder for all users. (Programs in this folder are started automatically when a user logs in.)

CSIDL_CONTROLS: Virtual folder containing icons for Control Panel applets.

CSIDL_DESKTOP: Virtual folder for the root of the namespace.

CSIDL_DESKTOPDIRECTORY: File system directory containing file objects that appear on the desktop.

CSIDL_DRIVES: Virtual folder containing objects that appear in My Computer, including local storage devices, mapped network drives, printers, and the Control Panel.

CSIDL_FONTS: Virtual folder containing fonts.

CSIDL_NETHOOD: File system directory containing objects appearing in the Network Neighborhood.

CSIDL_NETWORK: Virtual folder containing the root of the network tree, which appears in Network Neighborhood.

CSIDL_PERSONAL: File system directory used for holding personal documents.

CSIDL_PRINTERS: Virtual folder containing installed printers.

CSIDL_PROGRAMS: File system directory containing the user's program group file system directories.

CSIDL_RECENT: File system directory containing the user's recently used documents.

CSIDL_SENDTO: File system directory containing menu items for the Send To menu.

CSIDL_STARTMENU: File system directory containing items on the Start menu.

CSIDL_STARTUP: File system directory containing items in the Startup folder for the individual user.

CSIDL_TEMPLATES: File system directory containing document templates.

If the call to SHGetSpecialFolderLocation() is successful, a pointer to the requested object's identifier list is returned at ppidl. We'll see how to get an IShellFolder interface for the object referenced by this PIDL in the section "Retrieving an IShellFolder Interface."

Enumerating Folder Contents

You can scroll through any or all of the objects contained in a folder by calling the EnumObjects() member of the IShellFolder interface. The prototype for EnumObjects() is shown here:

HRESULT EnumObjects(HWND hwndOwner, DWORD grfFlags, LPENUMIDLIST *ppenumIDList);

The hwndOwner parameter should be passed a window handle used for the parent of any dialogs the call presents to the user. The grfFlags parameter determines what sort of objects are enumerated; this can be a combination of the following flags:

SHCONTF_FOLDERS: Include folders

SHCONTF_NONFOLDERS: Include non-folder objects

SHCONTF_INCLUDEHIDDEN: Include hidden or system objects

Upon completion, EnumObjects() will return a pointer to an IEnumIDList interface that is created at ppenumIDList. This interface provides the methods that are used to scroll through the enumerated objects.

IEnumIDList::Next(), shown here, is used to retrieve a PIDL for one or more of the objects contained in the folder:

HRESULT IEnumIDList::Next(ULONG celt, LPITEMIDLIST *rgelt, ULONG *pceltFetched);

The celt parameter is used to specify the number of PIDLs requested. Upon return, an array of PIDL is returned at rgelt and the actual number of PIDL's returned is passed back at pceltFetched. We'll see how to get an IShellFolder interface based on one of these PIDLs in the section "Retrieving an IShellFolder Interface."

In addition, you can use IEnumIDList::Skip() to skip over a number of PIDLs, or you can use IEnumIDList::Reset() to return to the beginning of the list. You can also use IEnumIDList::Clone() to create a new enumeration object that is identical to the current enumeration object.

Retrieving an IShellFolder Interface

After you have an IShellFolder interface for a given folder in the namespace and a PIDL for one of the objects contained in that folder, you can obtain an IShellFolder interface pointer for the lower-level object by calling IShellFolder::BindToObject(), shown here:

```
HRESULT BindToObject( LPCITEMIDLIST pidl, LPBC pbcReserved,
    REFIID riid, LPVOID *ppvOut );
```

When calling BindToObject(), you should pass a pointer to an ITEMIDLIST that identifies the subfolder, relative to the parent folder. For the time being, pbcReserved is reserved and must be NULL, and riid must be set to IID_IShellFolder. Upon completion, a pointer to the IShellFolder interface of the subfolder is returned at ppvOut.

> **NOTE**
>
> Like any other COM interface, you should call the Release() member of any IShellFolder interface when you are finished with it.

Browsing the Namespace

If you want to allow the user to select an object from the namespace, you can take advantage of the ::SHBrowseForFolder() function, which will present a dialog to the user, based on your initial criteria. When the user has selected an object, a pointer to an ITEMIDLIST identifying the object is returned.

Additional Information

The IShellFolder interface also allows you to retrieve additional information about the objects contained in the folder. In this section, we will see how to get at this information.

GetDisplayNameOf()

You can retrieve a string, suitable for display to the user, that names an object in the folder with a call to IShellFolder::GetDisplayNameOf(), shown here:

```
HRESULT GetDisplayNameOf( LPCITEMIDLIST pidl, DWORD uFlags, LPSTRRET lpName );
```

This function takes a PIDL to the object to retrieve the name of an object in pidl. The uFlags parameter is used to request a particular format for the display name to be returned. This can be one of the following flags:

SHGDN_NORMAL: Default display name, best suited to displaying file objects on their own.

SHGDN_INFOLDER: Display name best suited for displaying file objects in the context of their folder.

SHGDN_FORPARSING: Display name suitable for passing to ParseDisplayName(). This generally gives the full path.

The display name is returned in a STRRET structure at lpName. This structure contains a uType field that determines the format of the returned string and a union of different fields that refer to the returned string. If uType is set to STRRET_CSTR, the string is returned as an array of char's in the cStr member of the STRRET. If uType is set to STRRET_OFFSET, the string is contained in the identifier at pidl, beginning a number of bytes from the start of pidl. The offset is given by the uOffset member of the STRRET. If uType is STRRET_WSTR, the display name is returned as a wide-character string at a location specified by the pOleStr member of the STRRET.

> **NOTE**
>
> The shell can return strings in any of the possible formats: STRRET_CSTR, STRRET _OFFSET, or STRRET_WSTR, so your applications will need to be able to handle all of them.

ParseDisplayName()

You can generate an item identifier for an object, based on its display name, by calling IShellFolder::ParseDisplayName().

> **NOTE**
>
> To use ParseDisplayName(), you must use a display name that was generated with the SHGDN_FORPARSING flag.

::SHGetPathFromIDList()

In addition, you can retrieve a path to a file system object, based on an ID list that identifies the object, relative to the root of the namespace (the desktop). This is done by calling ::SHGetPathFromIDList().

SetNameOf()

You may also rename an object in the namespace by using IShellFolder::SetNameOf(). Changing the name of a file or directory in the file system with SetNameOf() will change the name of the file or directory in the file system.

Retrieving Object Attributes

You can retrieve the attributes of one or more objects in a folder by calling IShellFolder::GetAttributesOf() function, shown here:

```
HRESULT GetAttributesOf( UINT cidl, LPCITEMIDLIST *apidl, ULONG *rgfInOut );
```

You should specify the number of objects to retrieve attributes for in `cidl`, and specify an array containing pointers to an `ITEMIDLIST` for each object involved. A bitmap containing the attributes for the specified objects is returned at `rgfInOut`. If you have specified more than one object, the attributes returned in `rgfInOut` reflect the attributes that the objects have in common.

Cleaning Up

For any of the preceding functions that return a PIDL, the memory for the ID list is allocated using the shell's `IMalloc` interface. Like other memory that is allocated by COM objects, you will need to free this memory when you are done with it. You can retrieve the shell's `IMalloc` interface with a call to `::SHGetMalloc()`. You can then pass the PIDL to `IMalloc::Free()` to free the memory allocated by the shell.

In addition, for any of the preceding functions that return a COM interface pointer, such as an `IShellFolder` or `IEnumIDList` pointer, you will need to call the `Release()` member of the interface to free up the resources allocated for the interface.

The Shell API at Work

The following example shows several of the functions discussed here. This example lists the names of all of the objects in the desktop folder and moves on to create an `IShellFolder` interface for the recent document's folder:

```
HRESULT hr;
LPSHELLFOLDER pDesktop;
LPSHELLFOLDER pRecentFolder;
LPITEMIDLIST pIdl;
LPENUMIDLIST pEnum;
LPITEMIDLIST pEnumPidl[1];
ULONG ulNumPidls;
STRRET srName;
LPMALLOC pMalloc;

// Get the shell's IMalloc interface
hr = SHGetMalloc(&pMalloc);

// Start with the desktop
hr = SHGetDesktopFolder(&pDesktop);

// List objects in desktop folder
hr = pDesktop->EnumObjects(m_hWnd, SHCONTF_FOLDERS |
                                   SHCONTF_NONFOLDERS |
                                   SHCONTF_INCLUDEHIDDEN,
                                   &pEnum);
do
{
    char *pStr;

    // Get PIDL for next object
    hr = pEnum->Next(1, pEnumPidl, &ulNumPidls);
```

```
    if(ulNumPidls)
    {
        // TRACE information for the objects in the desktop
        hr = pDesktop->GetDisplayNameOf(pEnumPidl[0], SHGDN_NORMAL,
                                        &srName );

        // crack STRRET structure
        switch(srName.uType)
        {
        case STRRET_CSTR:
            TRACE("Name (CSTR): %s\n", srName.cStr);
            break;
        case STRRET_OFFSET:
            pStr = ((char*) pEnumPidl[0]) + srName.uOffset;
            TRACE("Name (OFFSET): %s\n", pStr);
            break;
        case STRRET_WSTR:
            TRACE("Name (WSTR): %S\n", srName.pOleStr);
            // Free OLE string
            pMalloc->Free(srName.pOleStr);
            break;
        } // end switch
    } // end if ulNumPidls

} while(ulNumPidls != 0);


// Get an IShellFolder interface for the recent docs folder

// Get a PIDL for the user's recent documents folder
hr = SHGetSpecialFolderLocation(m_hWnd, CSIDL_RECENT, &pIdl );
if (hr != NOERROR)
    TRACE("Error in SHGetSpecialFolderLocation: 0x%x\n", hr);

// Get an IShellFolder interface for recent docs folder
hr = pDesktop->BindToObject(pIdl, NULL,
                            IID_IShellFolder,
                            (void**) &pRecentFolder);

// Do what you will with the folder...

// Clean up
// Free PIDL's
pMalloc->Free(pIdl);
pMalloc->Free(pEnumPidl[1]);

// Release COM interfaces
hr = pDesktop->Release();
hr = pRecentFolder->Release();
hr = pEnum->Release();
hr = pMalloc->Release();
```

Shell Extensions

The Win32 shell also allows you to add a great deal of customization to the user's desktop by implementing your own shell extensions. These extensions can be used to add additional functionality into the desktop and are largely used for supporting shell operations for object types that are not supported by the shell itself. The shell extensions that you supply can provide any of the following types of handlers for dealing with certain operations the user might attempt with the shell:

Context menu handlers: Add additional options to the context menu for an object

Icon handlers: Provide special icons for instance- or class-specific file objects

Data handlers: Provide support for moving additional data formats to the clipboard

Drop handlers: Allow additional file types to act as drop targets

Property sheet handlers: Implement additional property pages to an object's property sheet

Copy hook handlers: Determine whether an object can be copied, moved, renamed, or deleted

Drag-and-drop handlers: Implement an additional context menu for drag-and-drop operations on a particular object

Unfortunately, the actual implementation of the COM interfaces needed to create your own shell extensions goes a bit beyond the scope of this chapter. For more information, see *Shell Extensions* in the online documentation.

Summary

This chapter looks at the new Windows shell that was introduced with Windows 95 and Windows NT 4.0. You have seen how you can use the Win32 shell API to more closely integrate your applications with the Windows shell. Taking advantage of these features can save you an awful lot of coding effort, allowing you to use features that are already done for you. In addition, using the shell API will make your applications look much more like real Win32 applications.

33

Custom AppWizards

by David Bennett

In Part II, "General MFC Programming," you saw how you, as a developer, could use the Application Wizards of Visual C++ to quickly and easily create skeleton applications that were customized according to your selections in a series of steps.

In this chapter, you will see just how easy it can be to create your own custom AppWizards with the Custom AppWizard Application Wizard. You will also see how the parts of your custom AppWizard work together to generate new projects, and how you can further customize your AppWizard by changing templates and modifying the executable code for your AppWizard.

How Do AppWizards Work?

Before we get into the nuts and bolts of creating your own AppWizards, let's step back and take a look at just how AppWizards work in general. Although you have probably used an AppWizard more than once, you might not be aware what's going on behind the scenes to create your new project.

When you start one of the Application Wizards from the Projects tab of the File | New dialog, Developer Studio calls a special DLL to handle the dialogs for each step of the AppWizard. Each AppWizard has its own special DLL that handles these step dialogs. Custom AppWizard DLLs are given the extension .AWX.

When you finish with the AppWizard step dialogs, the AppWizard creates the new project from a set of special template files. These template files include the framework for the source code as well as other things, such as binary resources for your new application. The settings that were chosen in the step dialogs are used in processing the template file to create the new application files, allowing the template to be customized according to the user's selections.

We will be looking at this process and how you can customize it in greater detail in the following sections.

Creating a Custom AppWizard

Creating a new custom AppWizard project involves the following basic steps:

1. Create a new custom AppWizard project with Application Wizard.
2. Modify and/or add new template files to your custom AppWizard project.
3. Create the dialogs for the steps of your AppWizard.
4. Add any other custom modifications to the AppWizard code.
5. Build the custom AppWizard project.
6. Start creating applications with your new AppWizard.

This process allows you to spend as little or as much effort as you want, depending on the level of customization you want to add to your new AppWizard.

Starting a New AppWizard Project

To begin a new project for creating a custom AppWizard, go to the Projects tab of the dialog presented by the File | New menu in Developer Studio.

You will need to assign a project name and a location for the new project. You can also choose to create a new workspace for the project or add the project to an existing workspace. You should then select Custom AppWizard from the list on the left and click OK. This will bring up the custom AppWizard, presenting you with some options for your new AppWizard project.

The dialog for step 1 allows you to choose the name of your AppWizard, as it will appear in the new project dialog, as well as the number of custom steps you want to add.

However, the most important part of this dialog is choosing a starting point for your new AppWizard. You may choose to create your new AppWizard based on an existing project, based on a standard MFC AppWizard, or from scratch, by implementing your own custom steps.

Creating an AppWizard from an Existing Project

The first option you have is to create a new AppWizard from an existing project. This will take an existing project that you have already set up and create an AppWizard project that will generate projects identical to the existing project you selected. The difference is that your project will be given the name you assigned in the new project dialog. This name is also inserted into other appropriate places in the project created by this AppWizard, such as filenames and the names of the classes that are generated.

If you choose this option, you can build your AppWizard project without any further modification, although you might also make additional changes, as you will see later. Building your new AppWizard project as is will create a new AppWizard and automatically add it to the available choices in the new project dialog. You may then use this wizard to create new projects, based on the original project that you used to create your AppWizard.

Creating an AppWizard from a Standard MFC AppWizard

The second option is to create a new custom AppWizard using the Standard MFC AppWizard steps. This allows you to use one of the standard MFC AppWizards as a starting point for your custom AppWizard. This will create a new project for a custom AppWizard that is identical to the standard MFC AppWizard (other than the fact it has a different name in the new project dialog). You can choose to leave the project as is, but you will probably want to customize it a bit, as you will see later.

When you choose to create a custom AppWizard based on the MFC AppWizard, you can also choose to add your own additional custom steps to the wizard. At this point, you should enter the number of custom steps you intend to add. This will create the skeleton for your custom steps for you. We will look at implementing custom steps in the section "Creating Step Dialogs."

If you choose this option, you should click Next to move on to step 2. This dialog allows you to choose to base your new custom AppWizard on either the standard MFC executable AppWizard or the standard MFC DLL AppWizard. You may also select which languages will be supported by your custom AppWizard. This will affect how certain resources are created by your new wizard, as you will see later.

Creating a Custom AppWizard with Your Own Custom Steps

The third option is to create a new custom AppWizard project using your own custom steps. This will create a bare-bones framework for your AppWizard project, but you will need to add all of the meat yourself. We will be looking at how to do this in the next sections.

Components of a Custom AppWizard Project

When you finish with the Custom AppWizard, you will have the basic skeleton of a new AppWizard project created for you. This project consists of two basic types of files: source files for your special AppWizard DLL and template files.

The files found in the Source Files and Header Files folders of the new project are used to create the DLL that is used by the AppWizard to present the step dialogs, and control the creation of a new project. The Help Files folder also contains files for adding help to your new AppWizard.

Template files are used to provide the new AppWizard with the structure of a new application. These include resource templates, as well as text templates, which are both contained in the Template Files folder. The Template Files folder also contains two special template files: `newproj.inf` and `confirm.inf`.

We will be looking at how all of these files work together to create a new AppWizard in the following sections.

Template Files

There are several types of template files that go into creating a new AppWizard. These include the special template files `newproj.inf` and `confirm.inf`, which play a key role in the creation of a new project, as well as text templates and custom resource templates, which make up the building blocks of the new application.

NEWPROJ.INF

The NEWPROJ.INF template file is used by your AppWizard to control how the files of a new project are created from the template files contained in your AppWizard project. This file contains a set of statements that govern how a new project is created, as well as additional directives that can be used for controlling the processing of the file. An example of NEWPROJ.INF that was created by the Custom AppWizard from an existing project is shown here:

```
$$// newproj.inf = template for list of template files
$$//  format is 'sourceResName' \t 'destFileName'
$$//   The source res name may be preceded by any combination
$$//        of '=', '-', '!', '?', ':', '#', and/or '*'
$$//      '=' => the resource is binary
$$//      '-' => the file should not be added to the project
$$//              (all files are added to the project by default)
$$//      '!' => the file should be marked exclude from build
$$//      '?' => the file should be treated as a help file
$$//      ':' => the file should be treated as a resource
$$//      '#' => the file should be treated as a template (implies '!')
$$//      '*' => bypass the custom AppWizard's resources when loading
$$//              if name starts with / => create new subdir

/res

ROOT.CLW     $$root$$.clw
README.TXT   ReadMe.txt
ROOT.H       $$root$$.h
ROOT.CPP     $$root$$.cpp
DIALOG.H     $$root$$Dlg.h
DIALOG.CPP   $$root$$Dlg.cpp
STDAFX.H     StdAfx.h
STDAFX.CPP   StdAfx.cpp
:ROOT.RC2    res\$$root$$.rc2
=:ROOT.ICO   res\$$root$$.ico
RESOURCE.H   resource.h
ROOT.RC      $$root$$.rc
```

Statements in NEWPROJ.INF

The NEWPROJ.INF file shown above includes several different types of statements, including comments, directory creation statements, and file creation statements.

Comments are added to the file by beginning a line with $$//. Any text on the remainder of the line is ignored and is used only for readability. The comment characters must be on the very beginning of the line. However, if you begin a line with one of the other directives, you can add a comment to the end of the line simply by adding // before the comment text.

You can have the AppWizard create a new subdirectory of the new project by simply adding the new directory name to a line in newproj.inf, as in the following line in the above example:

```
/res
```

The remainder of the statements in the previous example are used to create files in the new project, based on the templates contained in your AppWizard project. These statements consist of the name of the source template to be used and the destination for the new file. Take, for example, the following statement:

```
README.TXT   ReadMe.txt
```

This statement will take the template named README.TXT and process it, writing the output to a new file named ReadMe.txt in the new project. You may also use macros in the names of the destination files, as in the following line:

```
ROOT.CPP   $$root$$.cpp
```

This will create a new file, with a name based on the $$root$$ macro, which resolves to the name of the project. We will look at the other macros that are available, and how they are used, in the next section.

You may also add one or more of several modifiers to the beginning of a line containing a file creation statement. These modifiers are listed in the opening comments of the newproj.inf file and are further described in Table 33.1.

Table 33.1. Template name modifiers.

Modifier	Description
=	This causes the template to be copied verbatim, without any processing. This is generally used for binary resources like .ico or .bmp files.
+	Indicates that the file is to be added to the makefile for the project. This is used for source files like .CPP or .ODL files.
*	Tells AppWizard to use a standard AppWizard template, instead of a custom template specific to your custom AppWizard. In most cases, you won't need this flag, because if your AppWizard doesn't find a template in your custom AppWizard directory, it will try to grab a standard template.
-	The file will not be added to the project, although it will be copied to the project directory.
!	The file will be marked to be excluded from the build.
?	The file is handled as a help file and added to the Help Files folder of the new project.
:	The file will be treated as a resource file and added to the Resource Files folder of the new project.
#	The file will be treated as a template and added to the Template Files folder of the new project.

Macros in Template Files

Earlier, you saw a little coverage on the use of macros, such as $$ROOT$$, in template files. Macros are used to represent variable values in your template files. In general, these macros are set based on the user's selections in the AppWizard step dialogs. Macros can have two different types: text macros and Boolean macros. Text macros, such as the ROOT macro, evaluate to text values that can be inserted in your templates. Boolean macros, such as those used in conditionals, simply evaluate to Boolean values.

You may use macros in the destination filenames in newproj.inf, as you saw earlier, by enclosing the macro name in $$, as in the following statement:

```
ROOT.CPP   $$root$$.cpp
```

Similarly, you may also use macro names in any other places in your template text by using the $$ delimiters.

You will also see that macros can be used as parameters to directives, such as conditional directives. However, when macros are used as parameters to directives, they should be used without the $$ delimiters.

There are several standard macros that you can use in your templates. You may also define your own macros, as you will see in the following sections.

Standard Macros

There are many standard macros that can be set by the standard MFC AppWizard, based on the user's selections in the standard MFC AppWizard step dialogs. Some of the more common standard macros are discussed in this section.

The following macros are set according to the user's selections in the New Project dialog:

FULL_DIR_PATH: Gives the full path to the new project's directory.

ROOT: Gives the project name (all uppercase).

root: Gives the project name (all lowercase).

Root: Gives the project name (case as entered).

SAFE_ROOT: Gives the project name, removing any characters that are not allowed in preprocessor or C/C++ symbols.

TARGET_INTEL: Set to TRUE if the Intel platform is targeted. Similar macros are set for other platforms.

VERBOSE: Set to TRUE if the user chooses to generate a ReadMe.txt file and include source file comments.

In addition, many other standard macros are defined if you are using the standard MFC AppWizard steps. For more on these, see the online documentation.

User-Defined Macros

In addition to the standard macros shown previously, your custom AppWizard can define its own macros to reflect user choices from your custom AppWizard step dialogs.

You define your own macros by adding an entry to your AppWizard's dictionary. The dictionary is a mapping of class CMapStringToString that is a member variable of the CCustomappWiz class in your custom AppWizard's DLL code.

Any custom macros that you add to your AppWizard's dictionary may be used in your templates, just like any of the standard macros.

Directives in Template Files

You may also include several different directives in your newproj.inf file, as well as other text template files. These are mostly used to control the processing of the template file, based on the user's selections in the AppWizard steps.

Conditional Directives

You may add conditional directives to your template to selectively include or exclude certain statements. You can use a simple conditional with the $$IF and $$ENDIF directives, as shown here:

```
$$IF(VERBOSE)
readme.txt ReadMe.txt
$$ENDIF
```

In the preceding example, if the VERBOSE macro is set, a ReadMe.txt file will be added to the new project. Otherwise, ReadMe.txt will not be created in the new project. You may also add more complex conditionals using the $$ELIF and $$ELSE directives, as in the following example:

```
$$IF(PROJTYPE_DLL)
dllroot.clw $$root$$.clw
$$ELIF(PROJTYPE_DLG)
dlgroot.clw $$root$$.clw
$$ELSE
root.clw     $$root$$.clw
$$ENDIF //DLG, DLL
```

Loops

You may also repeat a block of statements a certain number of times by using the $$BEGINLOOP directive, which takes a single macro parameter that should indicate the number of times to execute the loop. The end of the loop is indicated with the $$ENDLOOP directive.

$$INCLUDE

You may also include additional template files with the $$INCLUDE directive, which takes a macro parameter that should evaluate to the name of a custom template. The text from this custom template is then read into the current file, much like standard C/C++ #include processing.

The Default Language

You may create custom template files that are language-dependent by appending the three-letter code to the name of the template file, such as TEMPLATE_DEU.RC. You may tell the AppWizard to search for templates for a particular language by using the $$SET_DEFAULT_LANG directive, which specifies a macro that evaluates to a three-letter language code. This value is used when searching for template files from your own custom AppWizard directory or from the standard AppWizard templates.

CONFIRM.INF

When the user completes the step dialogs for an AppWizard, the New Project Information dialog is displayed, prompting for final approval to create the new project. The text that your AppWizard will display in this dialog is described in the CONFIRM.INF template.

This template file can use conditional directives and text macros, as shown previously, to define the text that will be presented. The resulting text should summarize the options that the user selected in the step dialogs. This can also contain additional information about the project to be created, including things such as new classes to be created.

To get a taste of what this file looks like, take a look at the portion of the CONFIRM.INF file shown here:

```
$$// confirm.inf = the text emitted to the confirmation dialog for
$$//    this configuration
$$IF(PROJTYPE_DLL)
$$IF(EXTDLL)
Creating MFC Extension DLL (using a shared copy of MFC) $$Root$$.dll targeting:
$$ELSE //!EXTDLL
$$IF(MFCDLL)
Creating Regular DLL (using a shared copy of MFC) $$Root$$.dll targeting:
$$ELSE //!MFCDLL
Creating Regular DLL (using MFC statically linked) $$Root$$.dll targeting:
$$ENDIF //MFCDLL
$$ENDIF //EXTDLL
$$IF(TARGET_INTEL)
        Win32
$$ELIF(TARGET_MIPS)
        Win32 (MIPS)
$$ELIF(TARGET_ALPHA)
        Win32 (ALPHA)
```

```
$$ENDIF //INTEL&MIPS&ALPHA
$$IF(TARGET_68KMAC)
        Macintosh
$$ENDIF
$$IF(TARGET_POWERMAC)
        Power Macintosh
$$ENDIF

Main source code in: $$Root$$.h and $$Root$$.cpp
$$IF(AUTOMATION ¦¦ SOCKETS)

Features:
$$IF(AUTOMATION)
    + OLE Automation support enabled
$$ENDIF
$$IF(SOCKETS)
    + Windows Sockets Support
$$ENDIF //SOCKETS
$$ENDIF //AUTOMATION ¦¦ SOCKETS
...
```

This is just a snippet of the file created for you if you choose to begin with one of the standard MFC AppWizards. If you are creating your AppWizard project based on an existing project or based on your own custom steps, you will need to start from scratch when creating this template.

Text Templates

Your custom AppWizard uses text templates to provide the basis for creating text files in the new projects that it creates. These are used for any type of text files, including .cpp or .h source code files, as well as other text file types like .rc, .rc2, .odl, .rtf, and even .clw.

It is perfectly acceptable to simply add a regular .cpp file as a template for a .cpp file to create in the new project. However, you might want to add to the customization done by your AppWizard by adding conditional processing or text macros within your text templates. You can use the macros and directives that you saw earlier, in your text templates, as well as in .INF files.

Macros are commonly used in source code comments, as well as the names of include files and new classes that are used, as shown in the following example:

```
// $$root$$Dlg.cpp : implementation file
//

#include "stdafx.h"
#include "$$root$$.h"
#include "$$root$$Dlg.h"
$$IF(VERBOSE)
    // Add your source code comments in these blocks.
$$ENDIF
$$IF(OLE_INIT)
```

```
struct InitOle {
    InitOle()  { ::CoInitialize(NULL); }
    ~InitOle() { ::CoUninitialize();   }
} _init_InitOle_;
$$ENDIF
```

You may edit these template files in Developer Studio by double-clicking the filename in the Template Files folder in the Workspace window.

> **NOTE**
>
> For .rc files, Developer Studio will try to open the file as a resource script that points to existing resource files. However, these resource files will not exist in your AppWizard project, only in the projects that it creates. Thus, you will generally see a warning dialog if you try to open .rc files. You may click the Edit Code button to edit the text of these files.

Binary Resource Templates

Binary resource templates are used by your custom AppWizard in creating new files that do not contain plain text, such as bitmap (.bmp) or icon (.ico) files. These template files are handled a bit differently than text templates, and, because they can be any binary data, they cannot contain the directives or macros that you have seen in other templates.

Although binary resource templates are simple resource files, they are stored in your AppWizard project differently than the resources that are used to build your AppWizard DLL, such as any bitmaps used in your custom step dialogs.

Creating Binary Templates

To add a new binary template to your custom AppWizard project, you will first need to create the file to be used. In most cases, as for icon files, you can simply create a new icon in the Developer Studio's resource editor. After you have created the file that you want to use, you can add it to your project with the following steps:

1. Copy the file to your project's TEMPLATE directory.
2. Choose Resource from the Insert menu.
3. Select the type of the resource and click Import.
4. In the Import Resource dialog, select the file from the TEMPLATE directory, select Custom from the Open As list, and click Import.
5. In the Resource Type dialog, choose TEMPLATE from the Resource Type list and click OK.

Your custom resource template has now been added to your AppWizard project. You may edit most common resource file types from within Developer Studio simply by double-clicking the filename in the Template Files folder of the Workspace window. Of course, if you are using your own types of custom binary files, Developer Studio might not know how to edit these.

Programming Your AppWizard DLL

When you created your custom AppWizard project, files were created in the Source Files and Header Files folders of your AppWizard project and are used to build the DLL for your custom AppWizard. In many cases, you will never need to touch these source files; you might do a great deal of customization simply by editing the template files for your AppWizard. However, if you are creating your own step dialogs or adding your own macros, you will need to make some modifications to this code.

Defining Macros

If you are changing anything in the source for your AppWizard DLL, you will most likely want to add your own macros that can be used in parsing the template files for new projects. This is particularly necessary if you will be creating your own step dialogs, because you will need some way of conveying the user's selections from your dialogs to the template parsing operations.

When you created your custom AppWizard project, the AppWizard created several classes for your project. One of the most important is the class derived from `CCustomAppWiz`, which will be named according to your project name, but will end in `AppWiz`.

To add your own macros, you will need to add entries to the `m_Dictionary` member of the one and only object derived from `CCustomAppWiz`. `m_Dictionary` is a collection of type `CMapStringToString`, which contains mappings from macro name to macro text value. Generally, macros are added to the dictionary in the `OnDismiss()` member of your step dialog classes.

To see how to add macros to the dictionary, look at the following example, which comes from a custom AppWizard project named `MyCust` (thus, the class names will have `MyCust` in them). Your class names will be different. The member variables used in the following code, such as `m_SetOption` and `m_DocTitle`, are values that were retrieved from the user via the step dialog.

```
BOOL CCustom1Dlg::OnDismiss()
{
    if (!UpdateData(TRUE))
        return FALSE;

    else
    {
        if (m_SetOption)
        {
            // Set value of existing macro
            MyCustaw.m_Dictionary["VERBOSE"]="Yes";
```

```
        // Add our own Boolean Macro
        MyCustaw.m_Dictionary["MYOPTION"]="Yes";
    }
    else
    {
        // Remove our option macro
        MyCustaw.m_Dictionary.RemoveKey("MYOPTION");
    }

    // Set one of our text macro values
    MyCustaw.m_Dictionary["MY_DOC_TITLE"]=m_DocTitle;

    return TRUE;
    } // end else
} // end OnDismiss
```

For more on working with collection classes such as CMapStringToString, see Chapter 7, "General-Purpose Classes."

Creating Step Dialogs

If you chose to add a number of your own custom steps when you created your custom AppWizard project, you will notice that a class for each of your dialog steps was created for you. These classes are named something like CCustom1Dlg and are derived from CAppWizStepDlg, which is in turn derived from good ol' CDialog. You should also notice that dialog templates for each of your steps were added to your custom AppWizard project.

You can develop the dialogs for your step dialogs by setting up the dialog templates and adding code to the step dialog classes, just as you would for any other CDialog. The additional thing that you will generally want to do is add code to the OnDismiss() member of your step dialog classes to add macros to the dictionary.

There are other places in the code for your AppWizard DLL in which you might want to add even greater customization, although we cannot cover them all here. For more information, see *Creating Custom AppWizards* in the *Visual C++ User's Guide* in the online help.

Building a Custom AppWizard

When you created your custom AppWizard project with the custom AppWizard, all of the project settings for your project were set to create a new AppWizard. In general, you shouldn't need to modify any of these settings, other than adding template files to the project.

When you build a custom AppWizard project, the code for your custom AppWizard will be compiled to build an AppWizard DLL, which is given the extension of .AWX. This file will also be copied to Developer Studio's template directory, which is found in \DevStudio\SharedIDE\Template. If your project built successfully, you will notice that you may now use the new AppWizard by selecting it from the New Project dialog, just as you would use any other AppWizard.

Debugging a Custom AppWizard

To debug your custom AppWizard project, because it is a DLL you will need to specify the executable to use for debugging, just as you would for any other DLL. This is done by setting the Executable For Debug Session box on the Debug tab of the Build | Settings dialog.

For debugging custom AppWizards, you should specify the executable for Developer Studio itself, which is usually installed to a path similar to this:

```
c:\DevStudio\SharedIDE\bin\MSDEV.EXE
```

After you set this, starting the debugger on your custom AppWizard project will start up a second instance of Developer Studio. You can use the first instance of Developer Studio to set breakpoints in your DLL and perform other debugging tasks. In the second instance of Developer Studio, you will need to create a new project using your custom AppWizard. This will execute your custom AppWizard code, allowing you to debug your code.

Summary

One of the most important features of the Visual C++ 5.0 Developer Studio is the introduction of Application Wizards, which greatly simplifies the task of creating new projects that already include all of the boilerplate skeleton needed for the new project, allowing you to spend more time on the important areas of your projects.

In this chapter, you learned how to extend this feature even further by creating your own AppWizards that can be tailored to create new projects that come with your own custom features preinstalled.

VIII

Finishing Touches

34

Developing Complete Applications

by David Bennett

This chapter looks at several items that go into making complete Windows applications. Basically, a complete Windows application is one that does everything that a Windows user expects it to, including several things that generally get put off until the end of product development, such as install and uninstall utilities for your applications and some more esoteric matters, such as standard user interfaces.

Although I have added this chapter to the tail end of this book, please do not assume that this chapter is any less important than the nuts and bolts of the networking APIs or the foundations of MFC. Often, fine details like this are more important to your customers than that one-of-a-kind, nifty feature you added.

This chapter looks at Microsoft's logo programs, which can certainly help your commercial application sales. The logo guidelines also give you a better idea of how any good Windows application should behave.

This chapter also shows you how to write well-mannered installation routines for your applications, as well as uninstall applications for cleaning up after yourself.

Microsoft Logo Programs

You have probably noticed applications on your local store shelves that feature one or more different Microsoft logos. If you are developing commercial software, you can qualify your products to wear one of several different Microsoft logos on your packaging, advertising, or other marketing propaganda. This section takes a brief look at some of these programs, so that you can at least keep the requirements in mind, whether or not you intend to go through Microsoft for official endorsement.

For the most complete, up-to-date information of Microsoft's logo programs, see the MSDN web site at `http://www.microsoft.com/msdn/isvlogo.htm`. You can also reach the Microsoft logo department by e-mail at `winlogo@microsoft.com` or by voice at (206) 936-8220.

Currently, Microsoft supports the following programs for vendors of Visual C++ applications for Win32:

Designed for BackOffice: This is designed for use with applications that take advantage of Microsoft Back Office.

Designed for Windows NT and Windows 95: This program is intended for commercial applications designed for use on Windows 95 or Windows NT platforms. We will look at the requirements for this program in "Installing Your Applications."

Windows CE: This program allows you to advertise that your applications have been designed for Windows CE and certified by Microsoft.

Microsoft Office 97 Compatible: This program is designed for certifying applications that are integrated with Microsoft Office and have a similar look and feel.

Each of these programs involves certification testing by Microsoft. You will need to contact Microsoft at one of the addresses listed above to arrange this.

In addition, Microsoft supports a program that allows you to use the ActiveX logo for your products. This program does not involve certification testing, although you will need to register with Microsoft and adhere to their license requirements. As far as your ActiveX software is concerned, the only real requirement is that you support the IUnknown interface.

Windows NT and Windows 95 Logo Requirements

Microsoft allows you to join their Windows NT and Windows 95 logo program, which allows your applications, after certification testing, to use the Microsoft logos on your product packaging and literature. Even if you do not choose to join the logo program, it is a good idea to try to follow these guidelines. This will help ensure that your applications behave in the way that your users expect a good application to behave. To qualify for the logo, your applications must meet the following basic requirements:

- Your application must be a 32-bit application. If you develop applications with Visual C++ 5.0 for the Win32 platform, this is taken care of.

- Your applications must run properly on both Windows NT and Windows 95. More and more of the features that were specific to either NT or 95 are being moved to the other OS, so this requirement is becoming easier to meet. However, you will still need to handle any differences between 95 and NT gracefully.

- Your applications must provide a graphical installation utility. This must include registering all components and default installation to the Program Files directory. We will look at installation programming a little later, in "Installing Your Applications."

- Your application must provide an uninstall routine. This should completely remove your application, leaving any system files and shared components intact.

- Your application must provide certain UI features. This includes using system metrics, support for keyboard access to all functions, and support for things such as high-contrast viewing option and accessibility aids.

- Your application must support universal naming conventions (UNCs) and long filenames. If you stick to the Win32 API functions and common file dialogs, most of this is already taken care of.

- All ActiveX controls must be signed. This tells your users that your controls are actually from you, and should be safe to use.

- Applications must support OLE. Your application must be either an OLE container or an OLE server (or both). Your applications must support drag-and-drop.

- Applications that support telephony must use TAPI. For more on the telephony API, see Chapter 20, "Telephony API (TAPI)."

As for the official logo program, there are several additional requirements, as well as some exceptions. You can find the latest requirements in the *Designed for Microsoft Windows NT and Windows 95 Logo Handbook for Software Applications* on Microsoft's Web site.

User Interface Guidelines

One of the most important features of the Windows operating systems is the fact that they help provide a consistent user interface. Even though Windows applications perform a wide range of functionality, the basic interface is the same. All minimize buttons look the same, file commands are found on the File menu, the right mouse button presents a context menu, and so on. This commonality makes applications user-friendly, and is perhaps the biggest reason that sales of Windows and associated applications are what they are today.

However, the Windows APIs are flexible enough that you could write applications that will appear totally alien to your users. In general, redesigning the entire user interface is a bad idea—but hey, if you want to shoot yourself in the foot, it is a free country.

The best way to prepare for developing a consistent Windows application interface is to be a user of Windows applications. The more you use a variety of different well-behaved Windows applications, the more it will seem like second nature to make your applications behave as your users will expect them to. Yes, you do want your applications to stand out from the crowd, but this is best done by adding functionality, rather than forcing your customers to learn new ways of doing simple, standard operations, like finding the Help menu.

If you want some more specific guidelines about how your Windows user interface should be designed, you might want to look at *The Windows Interface: An Application Design Guide* from Microsoft Press. However, no amount of GUI design documentation will substitute for just taking a step back and putting yourself in the shoes of your users.

If you stick to using the prepackaged features of the Windows API, such as the common dialogs and the shell API functions, your applications will already be well on their way to behaving like good Windows applications. In addition, if you use the Microsoft Foundation Classes and the Application Wizard to create your applications, all the basics of a standard Windows user interface will be laid out for you.

Installing Your Applications

Okay, so now that you have developed the world's greatest application, you need to make sure that it is also easy for the user to install. I think you will agree that everyone has something better to do than install software, particularly when you consider the flood of new products, new revisions, and bug fixes that seem to pour into the market every day. I know you don't like having to spend a lot of time and effort to install applications, so let's make sure that your users don't have to.

To help you write installation utilities for your applications, Visual C++ 5.0 includes a free SDK edition of InstallShield. Visual C++ also allows you to use the Setup SDK if you prefer to roll your own installation utilities. We will look at both of these tools in the next section, but first, let's take an overall look at what needs to be done to properly install your applications.

Setup Guidelines

Regardless of how you implement your install routines, all good installation programs for Windows applications should have certain common characteristics. This helps the users install your application in a way that they are familiar with, even if they have never used your application before.

To start, all applications should have a graphical user interface for the installation. This is generally a separate application named SETUP.EXE. Every application should have its own SETUP.EXE, allowing the user to easily find your installation routine on your distribution diskettes or CD-ROM. In addition, the Add/Remove Programs applet in the Control Panel will search for a file named SETUP.EXE on a floppy or CD-ROM drive, allowing the user to easily access your setup utility.

Your setup application should present the user with a series of dialogs that are used to retrieve information about how the user wants to install your application. Some of this information might be unique to your particular application, although most good installations will provide some common options.

The user should be allowed to decide how much of your application to install. This is particularly important for large application suites, such as Visual C++ itself, for example. Most commonly, setup utilities allow the following configuration options:

Typical: This should be the default. It should install all of the most commonly used components.

Minimum: This installs only the bare minimum to the user's hard disk. For CD-ROM applications, this can include the option to run from the CD, writing only certain configuration files to the hard disk.

Custom: This option should allow more advanced users to pick and choose which segments of your application actually get installed.

Full: This should install all of the application components to the user's hard drive. Of course, for some CD-based applications, it might not be practical to install several CDs' worth of data to the user's disk.

Silent: The silent installation option allows users to run your setup utility without requiring any interaction with the user. This is extremely useful for installing the same application on multiple machines or across a network.

Your setup utility should be able to automatically detect certain things about the user's environment that might affect your application. For example, if your application is dependent on certain hardware, your setup utility should check for its presence. In addition, if your application needs to be installed differently for different Win32 platforms, your setup utility should be able to detect the target platform and react accordingly.

> **NOTE**
>
> Your setup routine should be able to detect any previous installations of your application. Your setup application should also be able to handle upgrading an existing installation.

In addition, your setup utility should be able to calculate the amount of disk space that your new installation will take, as well as the amount of free space available on the user's disk. If there is not enough free space for your install, you should notify the user. However, you should also allow the user to continue installing despite this warning.

Copying Your Files

One of the most important functions of your install utility is to copy your application's files from the distribution media to the user's hard drive. Although this seems like a relatively straightforward task, there are several important issues that this section looks at.

Destination Directories

Before copying your files onto the user's hard drive, you will need to figure out where to put them. Unless you have a very good reason for placing certain files in a fixed location, you should allow the user to choose the directories that your application will be installed to. Many users, myself included, prefer to keep operating system components and application components on separate disk drives, and nothing is more irritating than having a setup utility throw a wrench in your plans.

That said, it is good practice to provide certain default choices for where your application files should go. Unless the user chooses otherwise, the files for your application should be placed in their own directory in the Program Files folder. For example, your application's executable and any supporting files should be added to a directory like the following:

```
\Program Files\My Application
```

Similarly, any files that can be shared between more than one of your applications, such as supporting DLLs for a suite of applications, should be installed to the following directory:

```
\Program Files\Common Files\System
```

Note that the root of the above directories is unspecified. This is because the Program Files directory is not always in the same place. However, you can find the current location of the Program Files directory in the `ProgramFilesDir` value in the following Registry key:

`HKEY_LOCAL_MACHINE\SOFTWARE\Microsoft\Windows\CurrentVersion`

You can also find the location of the Common Files directory under the same key, in the `CommonFilesDir` value.

Any files shared on a system-wide basis should be installed to the System directory under the system's root directory. You can find the location of the system root directory by consulting the `SystemRoot` value in the above Registry key. Remember that the path to the system root is different for NT and 95, and may also be changed by the user.

Do not install any files that are not intended to be shared system-wide in the System directory. Files such as the MFC runtime libraries belong here, but application-specific files most definitely do not. The System directory is cluttered enough the way it is; let's not add to it if we don't have to.

> **NOTE**
>
> Your setup utility should provide the user with a status indicator of some sort, to see how the installation is progressing, and how much longer the installation will take. You should also allow the user to gracefully cancel an installation in progress.

Prompting for New Media

In some cases, your application will require more than one disk (either floppy or CD) for distribution. This means that you will need to prompt the user to insert the next disk at some point. Any prompting for new media that you do should be sure to get the user's attention (a beep works well for this) and should also be absolutely clear about which disk should be inserted next. Make sure that your prompts match the actual labels on your distribution media. In addition, your installation should make every effort to ensure that each disk needs to be inserted once.

Overwriting Files

Before your installation goes off and overwrites any existing files, you should check to see that the version of the file you are installing is newer than the file currently on the hard disk. You should alert the user of any version discrepancies and allow him to choose whether or not to overwrite a file. This is particularly important for any shared components; your application should not install older versions of any files that will break other previously installed applications. You should use the `GetFileVersionInfo()` function to check on file versions; simply checking file dates might not always be sufficient.

Usage Counts

For any shared files that you install, you should increment the usage count for that file. Usage counts are kept in the Registry under HKEY_LOCAL_MACHINE\SOFTWARE\Microsoft\Windows\CurrentVersion\SharedDLLs. This key consists of values that are named with the full path to the shared file in question and contains the number of installed applications that use the file. If an entry does not already exist for your shared file, you should add one.

Replacing Files in Use

Occasionally, your setup routine might need to replace a file that is currently in use and cannot be overwritten. Usually, these are DLLs that are in use by the operating system. To update these files, you will need to copy the new file to a different name. You can then add an entry to the Wininit.ini file, which will update the DLL the next time the OS restarts, before any DLLs are loaded.

The Wininit.ini file should be placed in the system root directory and should include a [rename] section. Entries in this section are in the following format:

```
DestinationFileName=SourceFileName
```

To delete a file, you can add a line like the following:

```
NUL=FileNameToDelete
```

This is useful for cleaning up the temporary files you copied in the first place.

Adding Registry Entries

For Win32 vapplications, you should not add any setup information to files such as config.sys, autoexec.bat, or system.ini. All these things are now handled in the Registry. This section looks at the types of entries that your setup program may add.

Application Configuration Information

Any configuration information that is specific to your application should be added to the Registry. For any settings that are specific to a particular user, you should add values to a key for your application under HKEY_CURRENT_USER\SOFTWARE\YourCompany\YourApp.

For any configuration that is not specific to an individual user, you should add values to the following key:

```
HKEY_LOCAL_MACHINE\SOFTWARE\YourCompany\YourApp\YourVersion
```

Setting the Application Path

Back in the bad old days, any executable file that you wanted to use had to be in a directory that appeared in the PATH environment variable. In Win32, this is no longer the case. Win32 allows you to assign a search path for executable files on a per application basis. This is done by adding a Registry entry under the following key:

```
HKEY_LOCAL_MACHINE\SOFTWARE\Microsoft\Windows\CurrentVersion\AppPaths\YourApp.Exe
```

The name of this key should match the name of your executable file. You should add a Path value to this key, containing a list of directories to search, separated by semicolons (;). You should also include a Default value in this key that contains the absolute path to the executable for your application. This is used to locate your application when the user types your executable name, without a path, in the program Run dialog.

New File Types

If your application introduces any new file types, you might want to add Registry entries that control the shell's handling of the new file type, including a context menu for the new type of file. A context menu is presented to the user whenever he clicks the right mouse button on an icon for a file.

Despite the advent of long filenames, file extensions are still used to determine the type of a file. Thus, you should include an entry for the extension of your new file type that points to a more descriptive type for your files. For example, you might add the following entry:

```
HKEY_CLASSES_ROOT\.abc = alphafile
```

You should then add a key for your file type, with a default value giving a short text description of the file type, as in the following:

```
HKEY_CLASSES_ROOT\alphafile = Alphabet File
```

You may also assign an icon to be used for displaying files of this type on the desktop by adding an entry such as the following:

```
HKEY_CLASSES_ROOT\alphafile\DefaultIcon =
        c:\Windows\Program Files\My Alpha App\Alphabet.exe,0
```

In addition, you can add menu items to the context menu for your file type by adding entries like the following:

```
HKEY_CLASSES_ROOT\alphafile\shell\open\command = Alphabet.EXE %1
```

```
HKEY_CLASSES_ROOT\alphafile\shell\print\command = Alphabet.EXE /p %1
```

```
HKEY_CLASSES_ROOT\alphafile\shell\printto\command = Alphabet.EXE /p %1
```

These entries are for standard context menu choices. `Open` is used to open a file, and `print` is used to print the file from the shell. The `printto` entry does not really appear on the context menu, but is used for handling the case where your file type is dropped on a printer object.

You may add any additional command entries that you like. Simply set the value to a valid command line, including the executable to use to handle the command, as well as any command-line arguments that you wish to pass. The special characters (`%1`) will evaluate to the name of the file.

For many applications, you will need to enclose the filename placeholder in quotes in order to handle long filenames with spaces, as in the following example:

```
HKEY_CLASSES_ROOT\alphafile\shell\vi\command = vi.EXE /p "%1"
```

Using AutoPlay

If your application is distributed on CD-ROM, Windows 95 and Windows NT 4.0 allow you to automatically start up your installation program when the CD is inserted. This feature is known as AutoPlay. Setting up your CD for AutoPlay is very easy: Simply add a file called `autorun.inf` to the root directory of your CD. (Why Microsoft chose AutoPlay as the product name and autorun as the filename, I don't know.) The `autorun.inf` file tells the OS what executable to run automatically. You may also specify an icon, as in the following complete `autorun.inf` file:

```
[autorun]
open=setup.exe
icon=MySetup.ico
```

InstallShield

Visual C++ 5.0 includes a special SDK Edition of InstallShield, which provides a simple, graphical interface for creating full-featured setup routines. This is the easiest way to develop install and uninstall utilities for your applications. If you use InstallShield, your setup routine will also automatically meet most of the guidelines for setup applications discussed previously.

> **NOTE**
>
> InstallShield can be installed using the Visual C++ setup program, although it is installed using a separate menu item on the first install screen.

InstallShield allows you to use a simple Project Wizard to get your setup program project up and running in a hurry. You can also easily add features to your setup, including custom dialogs, multiple configuration options, Registry updates, and an addition of your application to the Start menu. For more on using InstallShield, see the online help available in InstallShield application.

For installing larger or more complicated applications, you might want to purchase the Professional Edition of InstallShield. This version will enable you to use languages other than English, create 16-bit installations, generate self-extracting setup utilities, use command-line build utilities, work with greater numbers of components and file groups, and many other things. In addition, the Professional Edition entitles you to technical support from InstallShield Software, Inc.

The Setup API

In addition to the InstallShield package distributed with Visual C++ 5.0, the Win32 API includes support for a set of functions that you may use to help when writing your own installation routines from scratch. This is known as the Setup API.

About the .inf File

The setup API makes use of .inf files that describe various aspects of your installation. The .inf file consists of several different sections, each detailing a specific sort of operation, including copying files, adding Registry entries, adding to the event log, and even installing services. Details about .inf files may be found in the online help.

Setup API Functions

The Setup API uses several different functions to carry out installation, based on the information in the .inf file. The API includes routines to retrieve information directly from the .inf file, as well as some helper routines that may be used for presenting a common user interface for such things as prompting the user for a new disk. However, you will need to implement the majority of the user interface for your setup routine yourself.

The Setup API also provides functions to work with file queues. These allow you to queue up any file operations that your setup routine will perform, based on the user's choices in your setup application's dialogs. When the user has approved all of the selections that he has made, you can then start executing all of the queued operations.

Uninstallation

Any good Windows application should include an uninstallation utility that will remove any trace of your application, should the user decide to clean house. If you have used InstallShield to generate your setup program, it can also automatically generate an uninstall routine for you. If you choose to implement your setup from scratch, you will need to maintain a log of all of the files that you have installed, so that they may be removed at a later time.

Your uninstall routine should also remove any related entries in the user's environment, including Registry entries, Start menu entries, and shortcuts for your application. However, your uninstall should leave any documents created by your application in place, unless the user chooses to explicitly remove them. If you have used InstallShield to create your uninstall, this will also be handled for you.

Add/Remove Programs

To give the user a simple way of finding your uninstall routine, you can add an entry for your uninstall to the Registry, which will cause your application's uninstall to show up in the Add/Remove Programs applet from the Control Panel.

To set this up, you will need to add Registry entries to the following key:

```
HKEY_LOCAL_MACHINE\Software\Microsoft\Windows\CurrentVersion\Uninstall\YourAppName
```

To this key, you should add a `DisplayName` value that gives a string naming your application, as it will appear in the Add/Remove Programs applet. You should also add an `UninstallString` value, which gives the full path to your uninstall application, including any necessary command-line parameters.

Summary

The first thing that your users are likely to see in your application is your installation routine. Windows users have come to expect certain common features from installation applications, such as a graphical user interface, user-selectable configurations, and the addition of Registry entries for your application configuration. Although setup utilities for your applications might be one of the last things you create when developing a project, they are nevertheless very important. If your users can't set up your application, they will never see the rest of your application.

35

Adding Windows Help

by David Bennett

Perhaps one of the most important features of a user-friendly Windows application is a good help system. This is especially important when you consider how many people never take the time to read a manual before diving right in to your application. In a way, this is a good sign; if your application interface is similar to other applications, users will feel right at home. However, eventually, users will want a bit more information about what a particular widget does or how to create a certain type of gizmo.

This is where online help comes in handy. If properly implemented, your help system can quickly and easily tell the user what he wants to know. Fortunately, Windows has standardized the user interface to Windows help. In this chapter, you will see how to implement Windows help in your applications, including how to add context-sensitive help to give your users the easiest access to relevant help topics.

WinHelp Basics

Microsoft has already done most of the work for you when it comes implementing help for your application. They have taken care of handling all of the user-interface framework that is presented to the user. You need to add the specific content for your project, and add code to your application to start up the Windows help facility. You will see how to implement your own help later in this chapter, but let's start with the basics of how Windows help works.

Windows help is handled by a separate program named WinHelp.exe, or WinHelp for short. This program presents the standard help dialog to the user, displaying the contents of your help project, as shown in Figure 35.1.

FIGURE 35.1.
WinHelp dialog.

You can quickly try this out yourself by entering a command line like the following:

```
WinHelp MyHelp.hlp
```

By default, the WinHelp dialog provides three tabs, although you may add your own custom tabs if you like. The Contents tab will display the table of contents for your help file, as shown in Figure 35.1.

The Index tab will display a list of the topics contained in your help file, and allows the user to search the list to find the subject he is interested in, as in Figure 35.2.

FIGURE 35.2.
WinHelp Index tab.

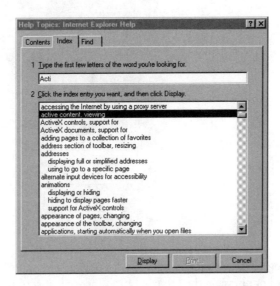

In addition, WinHelp allows the user to do a full-text search through the help file by using the Find tab. However, before the user can access the Find tab, the user will see the Find Setup Wizard dialog as shown in Figure 35.3.

FIGURE 35.3.
Find Setup Wizard.

This dialog allows the user to specify how WinHelp should create the database file (.FTS) that is used to help perform the full-text search. For large help files, like those used with Developer Studio, building this database can take several minutes.

After the database has been created, the user is presented with the Find tab, as shown in Figure 35.4.

FIGURE 35.4.
WinHelp Find tab.

This dialog allows the user to search the list of words contained in the help file, or begin typing a key word or phrase in the top edit box. Whenever a word or phrase is selected, the user will see the list of topics containing that word in the bottom list box. Double-clicking one of these topics or clicking the Display button will bring up the help text for the selected topic.

Most users of Windows applications are familiar with how to use this interface to retrieve the help information that they want. All you have to do is make sure that your help file contains this information and that it is structured to allow easy access. Now let's take a look at how to implement your own help projects.

Help Options in AppWizard

When creating applications with AppWizard, you might have already noticed that the AppWizard gives you the option to automatically add context-sensitive help to your applications. This option is available for any application that you create with the MFC AppWizard, whether it is a dialog-based, single document or a multiple-document application. If you choose to add context-sensitive help, the AppWizard will set up the basic framework that you will need to add effective help to your application, including some basic help information on the standard menu items.

For a document-based application, selecting the context-sensitive help option will create a Help Topics menu item to the Help menu, which would otherwise only contain the About menu choice. The Help Topics command is set up for you to open the contents page of your help file. Strictly speaking, this is not context-sensitive help, but if you don't select the context-sensitive help option in AppWizard, only the About box will be created for you.

For real context-sensitive help, your new application will include support for the Shift-F1 keystroke, which will put the application in help mode. The user can then click any particular control to see help text for the particular button, edit box, and so on. In addition, the default toolbar will contain a Context Help button, which has the same effect as typing Shift-F1. You will see just how the code generated by the AppWizard implements these features later on in this chapter.

If you have chosen the context-sensitive help option for a dialog-based application, a Help button will be added to your application that will pull up the index for your help file. However, true context-sensitive help is not implemented for you, so Shift-F1 will not be functional in your project.

Help Project Components

If you have chosen to create a project with AppWizard, using context-sensitive help, you will notice that quite a few new files have been added to your project directory. Most of these will reside in the hlp subdirectory of your project. You can view these files from developer studio by opening the Help Files folder in the FileView tab of the Workspace window. (The help project file (.hpj) is shown in the Source Files folder.)

Depending on your particular application, the help project will consist of one or more of the following sorts of files:

.rtf files: These are specially formatted rich-text format (RTF) files that make up the body of your help text, including additional information like hyperlinks.

.bmp files: Bitmap files may be added to your help project. These are added as illustrations in the help text to represent particular items in the user interface. The projects created by AppWizard will include a bitmap for each of the toolbar buttons on the standard toolbar.

.cnt file: Each help project will contain a single file that holds the information used to present a table of contents for the help file.

.hpj file: The help project file is used to control how all of the individual components of your help project are put together to build the .hlp file that is used by your application.

MakeHelp.bat: To help with building your help project, AppWizard creates a batch file named MakeHelp.bat that will handle the task of building your help project. This batch file is called when your application project is built.

.hm files: In addition, if you have built your project, you will notice one or more help map files. These files are used to map resource identifiers to the help context values that are used in working with the .hlp file. These are generated by the help map utility, makehm.exe, which is called from within MakeHelp.bat.

The next few sections discuss each of these file types in more detail.

Authoring Help Topics

The actual text of all of your help topics is created in .rtf files. Rich-text format allows you to create files that use only the ASCII character set, but can also include additional formatting information, as well as special information about links.

For some reason, Microsoft has never felt that it needed to include the capability to edit .rtf files from within Developer Studio. Microsoft's recommendation is to use an additional editor, such as Microsoft Word, which can save files in an RTF format. However, because .rtf files only use the standard ASCII character set, you may use any plain ASCII editor to work with the .rtf files, although the files are much more difficult to work with in plain ASCII.

> **TIP**
>
> Actually, if you are developing full-scale help files, I *highly* recommend that you use a third-party tool to help. I use RoboHelp, by Blue Sky Software, and have been very happy with it. RoboHelp, and other available tools (both free and commercial), can make the creation of help files much, much easier on you.

For example, see Figure 35.5 for the simple .rtf file as shown in Microsoft Word.

The same file would look like the one in Figure 35.6 in a native ASCII text editor, such as NotePad.

> **TIP**
>
> When using an RTF editor, such as Word, you should display all hidden text and footnotes, because these have special meaning when creating help files. In Word, you can turn on hidden text in the Tools | Options | View dialog. You can display footnote text with the View | Footnotes menu command.

FIGURE 35.5.

RTF in Microsoft Word.

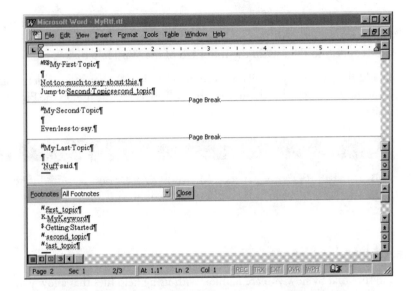

FIGURE 35.6.

RTF in NotePad.

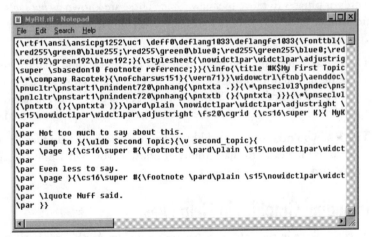

Creating Help Topics

Individual topics in your .rtf files are separated by a hard page break. These are used to separate the RTF text into the individual pages that will be displayed by WinHelp. In addition, each topic may contain several special footnotes.

To start with, most of your topics should include a footnote using the special character (#), which is used to assign a context name to the topic. This context name given in the footnote text is used for referencing this topic as the destination of a hypertext link or directly from your application.

Secondly, you might want to add a footnote using the special character (κ). The text for this footnote lists keywords that may be used in searches to find this particular topic. These keywords appear to the user in the Index tab of the WinHelp dialog.

In addition, you may specify a footnote with the ($) character, which assigns a topic name. Topic names assigned with this footnote will appear to the user in the Find tab of the WinHelp dialog.

Adding Hot Spots

I'm sure that by now you are familiar with using help files that allow you to click certain keywords or phrases to move to a new topic. These are known as *hot spots,* or hypertext links. To implement these hot spots in your help files, you will need to add a few special things to your .rtf file.

The displayed text that you want to make a hot spot should be formatted with double underlining. Immediately following the double .rtf underlined text, add a context name, which should be formatted as hidden text. This hidden text gives the context name for a topic somewhere in your help file. Remember that the context name for a topic is assigned using the # footnote.

This is all you need to do to add hypertext links to your help files. However, you might also want to use tables to format groups of links, as you will see in the .rtf files-generated by AppWizard.

Including Graphics in Help Files

As you will see in the .rtf files that are created by AppWizard, you can also add graphics to your help files. You can include bitmap files anywhere in your help file by adding a directive to your .rtf file in the location where you intend to display the bitmap. The format of the directive looks like this:

```
{bmc MyPic.bmp}
```

The directive is enclosed in curly braces and uses the bmc command to indicate that the filename of a bitmap file will follow.

NOTE

When compiling a help project that includes bitmaps, you will need to make sure that the .bmp files are in the bitmap file path, as specified in the BMROOT setting in the [OPTIONS] section of the .hpj file.

Managing Help Projects

As mentioned, Microsoft does not provide any integrated tools for developing your own .rtf files that go into a help project. However, Visual C++ 5.0 does include a tool that is very useful for managing all of the other tasks involved in developing help projects. This tool is the Help Workshop.

You won't find the Help Workshop in any of the menus in Developer Studio, although you can add it to your Tools menu as you saw in Chapter 1, "Visual C++ Environment." The executable for Help Workshop is found in ...\vc\bin\hcw.exe under whichever directory you have installed Developer Studio.

Help Workshop allows you to do many different things associated with help project development, including the following:

Create and edit help project (.hpj) files

Edit contents (.cnt) files

Compile your help project

Test your help project

The next few sections cover each of these items.

Help Project Files

The help project (.hpj) file controls how the various pieces of your help project are assembled to create the .hlp file that is actually used by your applications. This file contains several sections, similar to those that you might have seen in .ini files. You may edit the .hpj file for your project with any text editor or you may edit it from within the Help Workshop, as shown in Figure 35.7.

Help project files contain the following sections:

[OPTIONS]: This section contains several different option settings that affect how the help project is built, including the title of the project, the context name for the contents page, and the directories that are searched for component files.

[FILES]: This section lists all of the .rtf files that are to be used in creating the help file.

[ALIAS]: This section maps numeric constants to context names, which are used for context-sensitive help.

[MAP]: This section contains the mappings that assign numeric values to the context constants, in much the same way that #define is used in C/C++ files. In most cases, this section simply #include's one or more .hm files that contain the actual mappings.

FIGURE 35.7.

Help Project Files in Help Workshop.

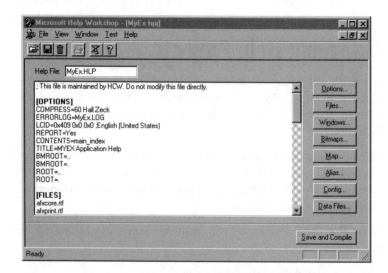

You may edit the help project file directly, using a text editor, although it is generally easier to use Help Workshop, which provides a nice graphical interface for filling in all of the relevant settings, including additional help on what each of the settings means. For example, a portion of the dialog for setting project options is shown in Figure 35.8.

FIGURE 35.8.

Help Workshop Options settings.

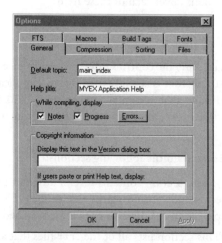

Contents Files

The contents (.cnt) file specifies the help page that will be displayed to the user when he or she chooses the Contents tab of WinHelp. Once again, you can edit the .cnt file directly with a text editor, although it is easier to use the graphical interface provided by Help Workshop. To do this, simply open your .cnt file in Help Workshop, which will present a dialog like the one shown in Figure 35.9.

FIGURE 35.9.
Editing contents files.

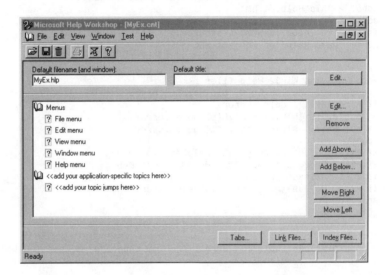

This dialog allows you to use the buttons on the left to edit or remove existing entries, as well as to add new entries to your table of contents.

Compiling Help Projects

Before your applications can make use of your help projects, all the components previously discussed must be compiled to create a single Windows help file, which is given a .hlp extension. You may compile your help project from within Help Workshop by selecting the Compile command from the File menu. This is useful for when you are developing your help project.

However, if you created your application with AppWizard, you will notice that a batch file named MakeHelp.bat has been added to your project directory. This file is called whenever you build your Visual C++ project and is responsible for creating the help file for your project. An example of MakeHelp.bat is shown here:

```
@echo off
REM -- First make map file from Microsoft Visual C++ generated resource.h
echo // MAKEHELP.BAT generated Help Map file.  Used by HELPSDI.HPJ.
>"hlp\HelpSdi.hm"
echo. >>"hlp\HelpSdi.hm"
echo // Commands (ID_* and IDM_*) >>"hlp\HelpSdi.hm"
```

```
makehm ID_,HID_,0x10000 IDM_,HIDM_,0x10000 resource.h >>"hlp\HelpSdi.hm"
echo. >>"hlp\HelpSdi.hm"
echo // Prompts (IDP_*) >>"hlp\HelpSdi.hm"
makehm IDP_,HIDP_,0x30000 resource.h >>"hlp\HelpSdi.hm"
echo. >>"hlp\HelpSdi.hm"
echo // Resources (IDR_*) >>"hlp\HelpSdi.hm"
makehm IDR_,HIDR_,0x20000 resource.h >>"hlp\HelpSdi.hm"
echo. >>"hlp\HelpSdi.hm"
echo // Dialogs (IDD_*) >>"hlp\HelpSdi.hm"
makehm IDD_,HIDD_,0x20000 resource.h >>"hlp\HelpSdi.hm"
echo. >>"hlp\HelpSdi.hm"
echo // Frame Controls (IDW_*) >>"hlp\HelpSdi.hm"
makehm IDW_,HIDW_,0x50000 resource.h >>"hlp\HelpSdi.hm"
REM -- Make help for Project HELPSDI


echo Building Win32 Help files
start /wait hcw /C /E /M "hlp\HelpSdi.hpj"
if errorlevel 1 goto :Error
if not exist "hlp\HelpSdi.hlp" goto :Error
if not exist "hlp\HelpSdi.cnt" goto :Error
echo.
if exist Debug\nul copy "hlp\HelpSdi.hlp" Debug
if exist Debug\nul copy "hlp\HelpSdi.cnt" Debug
if exist Release\nul copy "hlp\HelpSdi.hlp" Release
if exist Release\nul copy "hlp\HelpSdi.cnt" Release
echo.
goto :done

:Error
echo hlp\HelpSdi.hpj(1) : error: Problem encountered creating help file

:done
echo.
```

The first half of `MakeHelp.bat` is devoted to generating the help mapping (`.hm`) file that is used to associate help contexts with the resource identifiers used within your C++ project. You will look at help mapping files and the `makehm` utility in more detail later.

The most important part of `MakeHelp.bat` is the line that actually compiles your help project. This is done by calling `hcw.exe`, as in the following line:

```
start /wait hcw /C /E /M "hlp\HelpSdi.hpj"
```

The `/C` switch tells `hcw` to compile the help project file that is specified, and the `/E` switch tells `hcw` to exit when it finishes. The `/M` option is used to minimize the window for `hcw` so that it is out of the way while it is compiling.

TIP

When compiling your help project from the command line or from within Developer Studio, you see only very basic error messages, like the one shown here:

```
hlp\HelpSdi.hpj(1) : error: Problem encountered creating help file
```

Obviously, this doesn't give you much help on what went wrong. You can see more detailed error messages if you try to compile the help project from within the Help Workshop GUI.

If your help project compiles successfully, you will be the proud owner of a bouncing baby help file with a .hlp extension. The remainder of MakeHelp.bat simply copies this file (and your contents file) to the appropriate target directories. Make sure that you distribute these files with your application.

Testing Help Projects

The next section shows how to call on the Windows help system from your applications. However, it is often useful to make sure that your help file is behaving as expected before you integrate it with your application.

Help Workshop can be a great help when you test your help file, and you don't need to change the source code in your application and rebuild each time.

From the Test menu of Help Workshop, you can test the contents file for your help project, send a macro to WinHelp, or use a graphical interface to make calls to the WinHelp API directly. In addition, you can close all of the help windows that are left hanging around with a single menu command.

Calling WinHelp from Your Applications

Now that you have created a working help file, you need to be able to access the help file from within your application. This is done by using the ::WinHelp() function, although you will also take a look at some of the MFC functions that simplify calling ::WinHelp().

::WinHelp()

The Win32 API provides access to many different features of the WinHelp system via a single function call, ::WinHelp(). The prototype for ::WinHelp() is shown here:

```
BOOL WinHelp( HWND hWndMain, LPCTSTR lpszHelp,
              UINT uCommand, DWORD dwData );
```

The hWndMain parameter should be passed a handle of the window that is requesting help, and the lpszHelp parameter should contain the path to the help file that is to be used.

The uCommand parameter is used to specify the operation that will be performed, and dwData is used in different ways depending on the value of uCommand. Some of the most commonly used values of uCommand are shown here:

HELP_FINDER: Displays the Help Topics dialog box, containing the table of contents for the help file.

HELP_HELPONHELP: Displays help information on using WinHelp. The file winhlp32.hlp must be available for this.

HELP_CONTEXT: Displays a topic identified by a context ID that appears in the [MAP] section of the .hpj file. dwData should contain the context ID.

HELP_CONTEXTPOPUP: This is similar to HELP_CONTEXT, but the help topic is displayed as a pop-up window. dwData should contain the context ID.

HELP_QUIT: This tells WinHelp to close all WinHelp windows. dwData is ignored.

For more on additional commands for use with ::WinHelp(), see the online help in Developer Studio.

Using Help with MFC

The Microsoft Foundation Classes provide easy access to the WinHelp system, particularly if you have created your application with AppWizard.

CWinApp::WinHelp()

The CWinApp class supports a WinHelp() method that can simplify the process of displaying help. The prototype for CWinApp::WinHelp() is shown here:

```
virtual void WinHelp( DWORD dwData, UINT nCmd = HELP_CONTEXT );
```

Basically, this function simply wraps the Win32 API ::WinHelp() function, although MFC will keep track of the window handle and help file path for you. The values of dwData and nCmd should be the same as the values of dwData and uCommand shown previously for ::WinHelp().

MFC Help Handlers

If you have created your MFC application with AppWizard and selected the context-sensitive help option, you will notice that several handlers have been added to the message map for your applications. These are used to handle the messages that are generated by the commands on the Help menu that AppWizard generates. An example of these message map entries is shown here:

```
ON_COMMAND(ID_HELP_FINDER, CFrameWnd::OnHelpFinder)
ON_COMMAND(ID_HELP, CFrameWnd::OnHelp)
ON_COMMAND(ID_CONTEXT_HELP, CFrameWnd::OnContextHelp)
ON_COMMAND(ID_DEFAULT_HELP, CFrameWnd::OnHelpFinder)
```

The `ID_HELP_FINDER` message is sent by the Help Topics command on the Help menu. The handler function, `OnHelpFinder()`, simply calls `CWinApp::WinHelp()`, as shown here:

```
AfxGetApp()->WinHelp(0L, HELP_FINDER);
```

The `ID_HELP` message is sent when the user presses F1. The `OnHelp()` function will attempt to display a help topic that is relevant to the current window. If none is found, the default help topic will be displayed.

The `ID_CONTEXT_HELP` message is sent when the user enters help mode by pressing shift-F1 or clicks the help mode tool. The `OnContextHelp()` handler places the application in help mode. Once in help mode, user input is handled differently. MFC will try to display help for any controls clicked, rather than send the command message for the control.

When no help topics are found for a particular context, the `ID_DEFAULT_HELP` message is sent. MFC handles this by displaying the table of contents for the help file.

In addition, the `CWinApp` class supports the `OnHelpUsing()` method, which will display help on using the WinHelp interface. You can easily add support for this to your application by adding a menu item with the ID of `ID_HELP_USING` and adding the following message map entry:

```
ON_COMMAND( ID_HELP_USING, OnHelpUsing )
```

In most cases, it is easiest to use the predefined command IDs for requesting help and simply use the message map entries to call the appropriate handlers in the `CWinApp` class. However, you might want to call `CWinApp::WinHelp()` directly from your application in some cases.

Adding Context-Sensitive Help

You can make your applications much more user-friendly by presenting help for a particular dialog or menu command that the user has selected when he presses F1. This is much easier to use than searching through the whole help file for the information.

Using the MFC help framework, adding context-sensitive help is rather simple. To show how to do this, we will add a new menu command to an application and add context-sensitive help for it.

You will need to add the menu to your application, adding a command handler for it as you normally would. For the sake of our example, assume that the new command is given the ID of `ID_MY_COMMAND`.

Next, you will need to add a help topic for this command, as shown earlier. For this example, make sure to use the (#) footnote to assign a context name of `my_command`.

Now, you will need to add an entry to the `[ALIAS]` section of the project's `.hpj` file, like the following:

```
HID_MY_COMMAND = my_command
```

Now when you build your application, Developer Studio will call on MakeHelp.bat. One of the first things that this batch file will do is call on the makehm utility to map help context IDs for the resource ID's that are used in your application. This mapping is written to a .hm file, which would contain a line like the following:

```
HID_MYCOMMAND                          0x18003
```

This .hm file is included in the [MAP] section of the help project (.hpj) file. This mapping, when combined with the entry in the [ALIAS] section, will tell WinHelp to bring up the my_command help topic whenever the user highlights the new menu command and presses F1.

Summary

One of the most important attributes of a good Windows application is ease of use. Adding online help to your application certainly goes a long way toward making your application easier to use.

In this chapter, you have seen how the Windows help system can provide your users easy access to the information that they will need when using your application.

You saw how to author your own rich-text format help topic files, and how these are compiled along with help project, contents, and help mapping files to create a Windows help file (.hlp) that can be used with your applications.

You also saw how to call upon the services of WinHelp from your application, both with and without the aid of the Microsoft Foundation Classes.

IX

Appendix

A

Additional Resources

by Vincent W. Mayfield

As you probably know, the documentation provided with Visual C++ is superb, and the Info-Viewer in Visual C++ provides fingertip access to a wealth of information. One of the great things about Visual C++ and MFC is the plethora of resources available to you as a programmer from Microsoft and third-party sources. This chapter provides you with a wealth of sources of information to aid you in your development activities. Remember, knowledge is power. That power can help you develop killer professional, commercial-grade applications.

Visual C++ Resources

As you go out into the cutthroat world of applications development and create your own Visual C++ applications, you should be armed to the teeth with the knowledge of the multitude of available sources of information that can assist you in your programming endeavors. Chances are that the problem you are having or your area of inquiry has been explored by another programmer. Why reinvent the wheel? Visual C++, MFC, and Microsoft Windows programming in general have an abundance of resources, such as Software Developer's Kits, magazines, Internet sites, books, and—most importantly—the Microsoft Developer's Network (MSDN) Library subscription.

Microsoft Developer's Network

The MSDN is one of the greatest assets in my set of development tools. Many times it has saved me countless hours of development time and frustration. I cannot imagine doing without it.

What is this great tool? How can you get it? MSDN is a subscription available from Microsoft or an approved reseller.

> **NOTE**
>
> Microsoft Developer's Network subscription information can be obtained by calling Microsoft at 800-759-5474; you can obtain information online at the following Internet URL:
>
> `http://www.microsoft.com/msdn/`

There are four levels of subscription:

- Library
- Professional
- Enterprise
- Universal

The subscription is for one year and is updated every quarter. Each of these levels has a cornucopia of goodies to aid you in the development process. The Library subscription is the basic level; the top level is the Universal subscription. At each level, you get the previous level's items. The following sections explain the components of each level.

Library Subscription

The MSDN Library is the centerpiece of all levels. The MSDN Library is a CD that is updated quarterly. This CD contains more than 1.5GB of developer product documentation, technical articles from Microsoft and other third-party sources, more than 1,800 reusable code samples, and the Developer Knowledge Base. This is more than 150,000 pages of essential information on programming for Windows. Each quarter, this information is enhanced and updated with the latest in Windows programming information. The MSDN Library is encapsulated in Microsoft's InfoViewer (see Figure A.1).

FIGURE A.1.
The Microsoft Developer's Network Library.

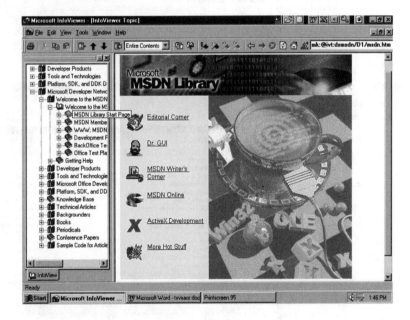

The InfoViewer contains the capability of doing a full text search on a string that you define (see Figure A.2).

As you can see, the results are displayed in a separate window, identifying all the places where the item you searched for resides (see Figure A.3). If you double-click on the item in the returned window, the article is displayed in the output window, as in Figure A.4.

FIGURE A.2.

The Query dialog box in the MSDN Library.

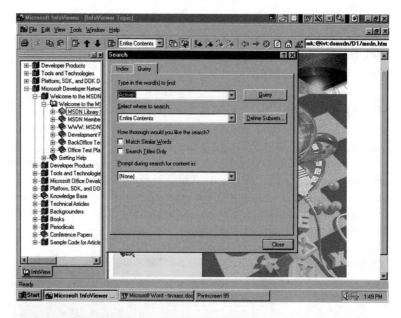

FIGURE A.3.

The results of the search for the string.

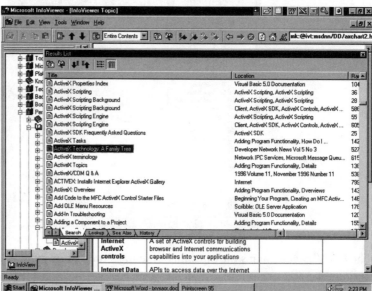

You can type in notes and put bookmarks on the articles you use frequently, but one of the nicest features is that the MSDN Library integrates into the Visual C++ Developer Studio (see Figure A.5). You don't even have to leave your development environment to use the MSDN Library.

FIGURE A.4.

An article displayed in the output window.

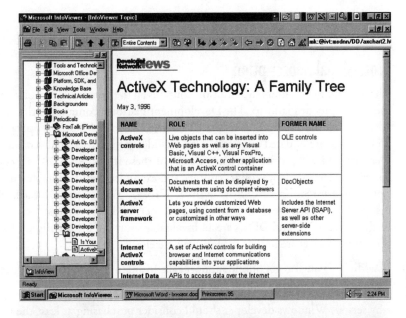

FIGURE A.5.

The Microsoft Developer's Network Library integrated with the Visual C++ Developer Studio.

In addition, with an MSDN subscription you also get a subscription to *The Developer Network News*, which is published every two months. It contains up-to-the-minute information on the hottest Microsoft technology. Articles consist of information on developing software for the Windows family of operating systems from the people who make the operating system.

As a member of MSDN, you get a 20 percent discount on all Microsoft Press books—and several of the hottest books are on the MSDN Library CD.

Professional Subscription

The MSDN Professional subscription contains all the benefits of the Library subscription plus the Development Platform. The Development Platform contains all the Software Developer's Kits (SDKs), the Device Driver Kits (DDKs), and all the Microsoft operating systems on over 35 CDs that are updated quarterly. This includes the international versions and, as an MSDN member, you will receive the beta releases of these items. An SDK is a companion CD that contains a development toolkit, samples and examples, redistributables, and API documentation. There are SDKs for ODBC, MAPI, WIN32, TAPI, DirectX, BackOffice, and OLE, to name a few. DDKs are similar kits for developers of device drivers, such as printers and video cards. These SDKs and DDKs are an invaluable source of information. Most of the SDKs and their components are not available anywhere else.

In addition, you also get phone support calls to aid in the setup of the Development Platform or the MSDN Library.

Any serious Windows developer should consider purchasing at least the MSDN Professional subscription. Now that I have it I do not know how I ever got along without it.

Enterprise Subscription

With the Enterprise subscription of MSDN you get all the benefits of the Professional and Library subscriptions plus the BackOffice Test Platform. The BackOffice Test Platform is a set of CDs with the latest released versions of the server components of Microsoft BackOffice:

- Windows NT Server
- Microsoft SQL Server
- Microsoft SNA Server
- Microsoft Systems Management Server
- Microsoft Exchange Server

With your MSDN Enterprise subscription, you get five simultaneous license connections for each of the products on the BackOffice Test Platform. You will get beta and interim releases of the BackOffice products before they reach the stores. This gives you the edge you need to stay on the tip of the spear.

In addition, you get four phone support incidents, which can be used to aid in the setup of your BackOffice server products or to answer your tough development questions. This puts the Microsoft engineers at your service.

Universal Subscription

As an MSDN Universal subscriber, you receive all the benefits of the Enterprise subscription, plus a one-year subscription to the following development tools:

- Microsoft Visual Basic Enterprise Edition
- Visual SourceSafe
- Visual C++ Enterprise Edition
- Visual FoxPro Professional Edition
- Microsoft Project
- Microsoft Office Professional
- Microsoft Access Developer's Kit
- Visual J++ Enterprise Edition

Hardcopy Visual C++ Documentation

Some developers prefer hardcopy documentation. You can order printed copies of Visual C++ documentation from Microsoft Press.

> **NOTE**
>
> Microsoft Press can be reached at 800-MSPRESS; you can visit the online bookstore at the following Internet URL:
>
> `http://www.microsoft.com/mspress/`

All the hardcopy references are available from the Books Online resource that comes with your Visual C++ CD-ROM (see Figure A.6). These books are viewable with the InfoViewer and are capable of a full text search. If you prefer the hardcopy editions, they are titled as follows:

- *Language Reference*
- *Run-Time Library Reference*
- *Visual C++ User's Guide*
- *Programming with the Microsoft Foundation Class Library*
- *Microsoft Foundation Class Library Reference, Part I*
- *Microsoft Foundation Class Library Reference, Part II*

FIGURE A.6.

The Books Online and InfoViewer in Visual C++.

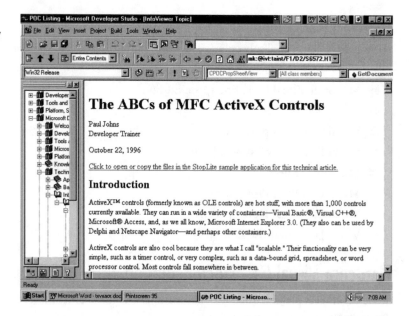

Magazines and Journals

You can go broke with all the magazine subscriptions available in dealing with computers and computer programming. The following are some of the really good magazines for developers. All these magazines are excellent, but I have found *Microsoft Systems Journal* and *Windows Tech Journal* to be especially helpful.

Microsoft Systems Journal
Miller Freeman
P.O. 56621
Boulder, CO 80322-6621
800-666-1084

Windows Tech Journal
Oakley Publishing Company
P.O. Box 70167
Eugene, OR 97401
800-234-0386

Visual C++ Professional
Oakley Publishing Company
P.O. Box 70167
Eugene, OR 97401
800-234-0386

Inside Microsoft Visual C++
The Cobb Group
9420 Bunsen Parkway
Suite 300
Louisville, KY 40220
800-223-8720

Visual C++ Developer
Pinnacle Publishing
18000 72nd Avenue South
Suite 217
Kent, WA 98032
800-788-1900
Internet: http://www.pinpub.com

NT Developer
Oakley Publishing Company
P.O. Box 70167
Eugene, OR 97401
800-234-0386

Windows Developer's Journal
Miller Freeman
P.O. 56565
Boulder, CO 80322-6565
800-365-1425
Internet: http://www.wdj.com

C/C++ Users Journal
Miller Freeman
P.O. 52582
Boulder, CO 80322-2582
800-365-1364
Internet: http://www.cuj.com

Software Development
Miller Freeman
P.O. Box 1126
Skokie, IL 60076-8126
415-905-2200
Internet: http://www.sdmagazine.com

Dr. Dobb's Journal
Miller Freeman
P.O. 56188
Boulder, CO 80322-6188
800-456-1215
Internet: `http://www.ddj.com`

Conferences

There are several excellent developers' conferences. Until March 1996, I had never been to a development conference. I was able to talk my boss into going—and taking me and two of my developers—to Software Development 96 in San Francisco at the Moscone Center. My boss was so impressed, she has championed the effort to send many more of my company's developers and managers next year.

I garnered so much information, it took me months to assimilate it all. I got training from renowned industry professional trainers such as Richard Hale Shaw and Bruce Eckel. I actually got to meet Jeff Prosise (Microsoft engineer and columnist for MSJ), Charles Petzold (father of Microsoft Windows), Jim McCarthy (former senior developer and project manager of Visual C++), and Bjarne Stoustrup (inventor of C++). There were product demos, seminars, and freebies galore.

I highly recommend that you attend one of the professional developers' conferences. Although I have been only to SD 96, several of my friends have recommended the following:

COMDEX
`http://www.comdex.com`

Software Development Conference
`http://www.mfi.com/sdconfs`

VBIT
`http://www.windx.com`

Visual C++ Developers Conference
`http://www.vcdj.com`

The information and experience you receive are well worth the time and investment to attend. I was excited and motivated when I was able to meet and talk with my peers in the industry, as well as the leaders and legends. Take the time to attend. If your boss won't pay for it, get the boss to go with you. You won't be sorry!

Software

There are a lot of third-party add-ons and programs to enhance and integrate with your application. In addition, there are several multimedia CD-ROM titles that may be of use to you in enhancing your software development skills. Here are a few of them:

ActiveX Software Developer's Kit
The ActiveX SDK is a toolkit for developers, to aid in the development of applications that leverage the ActiveX technologies. It contains all the API documentation, specifications, and re-distributables. In addition, it contains sample source code and examples. The most current ActiveX SDK is available from Microsoft, at no charge, at the following Internet URL: `http://www.microsoft.com/intdev/sdk/`.

ActiveX Template Library
The ActiveX Template Library is a Visual C++ App Wizard add-on that allows you to create light, fast COM objects. It comes with Visual C++ 5.0, or it is available free from Microsoft at the following Internet URL: `http://www.microsoft.com/visualc/v42/atl/default.htm`.

Mastering Internet Development
This is a multimedia training application from Microsoft Press. This CD-ROM contains a well–laid-out tutorial on Internet development and is part of the Microsoft Certified Professional curriculum. Microsoft Press can be reached at 800-MSPRESS, or you can visit the online bookstore at the following Internet URL: `http://www.microsoft.com/mspress/`.

Mastering Microsoft Visual C++ 5.0
This is a multimedia training application from Microsoft Press. This CD-ROM contains a well–laid-out tutorial on Visual C++ and is part of the Microsoft Certified Professional curriculum. Microsoft Press can be reached at 800-MSPRESS, or you can visit the online bookstore at the following Internet URL: `http://www.microsoft.com/mspress`.

Crystal Reports
Crystal Reports is report writer software. The standard edition comes with Visual C++ Professional. The Crystal Reports Professional has many more features, including an intuitive interface and an easy-to-use report designer. It has support for almost every database known to the modern programmer. It also integrates into Microsoft Developer Studio. For more information, contact Seagate Software at the following Internet URL: `http://www.img.seagatesoftware.com/`.

Microsoft Visual SourceSafe
Visual SourceSafe provides source code and distributable control. It tracks your changes and keeps track of who made them. It is an invaluable tool to be used in

software configuration management. Visual SourceSafe comes with the Enterprise Edition of Visual C++. However, it can be purchased separately if you have only the standard or professional editions. The nice thing about Visual SourceSafe is that it integrates with the Visual C++ IDE. If you try to edit a file without having checked it out, it prompts you to do so. It is available from Microsoft, and you can get information on Visual SourceSafe at the following Internet URL: `http://www.microsoft.com/ssafe/`.

Microsoft Visual Test

Visual Test is a great tool to automate the testing of your software. It integrates with all of Microsoft's development tools and also integrates with Nu Mega Bounds Checker. Microsoft recently sold Visual Test to Rational Software. Information on Visual Test can be obtained at Rational Corporations Home Page at the following Internet URL: `http://www.rational.com/vtest/`.

Nu-Mega Bounds Checker

Nu-Mega Bounds Checker is a must for Visual C++ developers. It is a tool to help you detect and eliminate those pesky memory leaks. It also has the capability of spying into DLLs and the low-level operating system calls. I once used it to find out that an ODBC Driver (not my software) was causing my memory leak. It is an excellent enhanced debugger. Information on Nu-Mega can be obtained at the following Internet URL: `http://www.numega.com`.

InstallShield

For all your installation needs, InstallShield is the tool. A scaled-down SDK version comes with Visual C++; however, I highly recommend that you purchase the Professional version. Most major software vendors use InstallShield, and users have become accustomed to the InstallShield setup interface. It is very easy to use. Information on InstallShield can be found at InstallShield Corporation's Home Page at the following Internet URL: `http://www.installshield.com`.

CAUTION

If you build your setup utility with the InstallShield SDK that comes with Visual C++, and you upgrade to the Professional version of InstallShield, you have to recreate your setup utility. There is no tool to convert your setup utility from the SDK version to work in the Professional version.

Papers and Articles

The only advice I can give you is read, read, read! The more information you are exposed to, the better developer you will be. The more informed you are, the better able you are to overcome complex development situations and stay at the tip of the spear. Software development is a very dynamic and ever-changing environment. Always expand your knowledge. What's HOT today may NOT be tomorrow. Here are some articles I have found to be very useful:

"Wake Up and Smell the MFC: Using the Visual C++ Classes and Application Framework," Jeff Prosise, *Microsoft Systems Journal*, June 1995, vol. 10, no. 6.

"Programming Windows 95 with MFC, Part II: Working with Display Contexts, Pens, and Brushes," Jeff Prosise, *Microsoft Systems Journal*, July 1995, vol. 10, no. 7.

"Programming Windows 95 with MFC, Part III: Processing Mouse Input," Jeff Prosise, *Microsoft Systems Journal*, August 1995, vol. 10, no. 8.

"Programming Windows 95 with MFC, Part IV: Contending with the Keyboard," Jeff Prosise, *Microsoft Systems Journal*, September 1995, vol. 10, no. 9.

"Programming Windows 95 with MFC, Part V: Menus, Toolbars, and Status Bars," Jeff Prosise, *Microsoft Systems Journal*, November 1995, vol. 10, no. 11.

"Programming Windows 95 with MFC, Part VI: Dialog Boxes, Property Sheets, and Controls," Jeff Prosise, *Microsoft Systems Journal*, December 1995, vol. 10, no. 12.

"Programming Windows 95 with MFC, Part VII: The Document/View Architecture," Jeff Prosise, *Microsoft Systems Journal*, February 1996, vol. 11, no. 2.

"Programming Windows 95 with MFC, Part VIII: Printing and Print Previewing," Jeff Prosise, *Microsoft Systems Journal*, April 1996, vol. 11, no. 4.

"Fun with MFC: 33 Tips to Help You Get the Most out of ...," Paul DiLascia, *Microsoft Systems Journal*, November 1993, vol. 8, no. 11.

"Removing Fatty Deposits from Your Applications Using Our 32-bit Liposuction Tools," Matt Pietrek, *Microsoft Systems Journal*, October 1996, vol. 11, no. 10.

"Build OLE Controls for the Internet that Are Fast, Smart, and Interactive," Michael T. McKeown, *Microsoft Systems Journal*, April 1996, vol. 11, no. 4.

"A Brief History of MFC," *C++ Report*, SIGS Publications.

"Extending MFC," Scott Wingo, *Dr. Dobbs Journal*, January 1996.

"Plunge into MFC's User Interface," Scott Wingo, *Windows Tech Journal*, August 1994.

"Rewriting the MFC Scribble Program Using an OOD Approach," Allen Holub, *Microsoft Systems Journal*, August 1995, vol. 10, no. 8.

"How OLE and COM Solve the Problems of Component Software Design," Kraig Brockschmidt, *Microsoft Systems Journal*, May 1996, vol. 11, no. 5.

"How OLE and COM Solve the Problems of Component Software Design, Part II," Kraig Brockschmidt, *Microsoft Systems Journal*, June 1996, vol. 11, no. 6.

Books on Visual C++, MFC, and Windows Programming

There is a wealth of books on Visual C++, MFC, and Windows programming. A good professional library is a must for every developer. Many of these books have saved my bacon when I needed assistance. I hope you will find them equally useful. I have added a personal endorsement for some of them:

ActiveX Programming Unleashed, Weiing Chen, et al., Sams Publishing, 1997.

I wrote two chapters in *ActiveX Programming Unleashed*. It is an in-depth look into the world of ActiveX and OLE programming. It is a must for software engineers and Webmasters alike.

Beginning Visual C++ 4.0, Ivor Horton, Wrox Press Ltd., 1996.

Beginning Visual C++ Components, Matt Telle, Wrox Press Ltd., 1997.

Building Windows 95 Applications, Kevin J. Goodman, M & T Books, 1995.

Constructing Windows Dialogs, Steve Rimmer, Computing McGraw-Hill, 1994.

Cross-Platform Development Using Visual C++, Chane Cullens and Ken Blackwell, M & T Books, 1995.

Database Developers Guide with Visual C++, Roger Jennings and Peter Hipson, Sams Publishing, 1995.

Essential Visual C++ 4, Mickey Williams, Sams Publishing, 1995.

Heavy Metal Visual C++ Programming, Steve Holzner, Brady Publishing, 1995.

Inside OLE, 3rd Ed., Kraig Brockschmidt, Microsoft Press, 1997.

Inside OLE by Kraig Brockshmidt is a must for any programmer who is doing OLE or ActiveX programming. This book is considered the bible for OLE programming.

Mastering Microsoft Visual C++ Programming, Michael Young, Sybex, 1995.

MFC Internals, Scott Wingo and George Sheppard, Addison Wesley, 1996.

If you really want to dig deep and understand the internals of MFC, this book is for you. It is very well written and helps you understand how MFC works. Scott and George are frequent columnists for several of the Windows software development magazines.

OLE Controls—Inside Out, 3rd Ed., Adam Denning, Microsoft Press, 1997.

Programming Windows 95 with MFC, Jeff Prosise, Microsoft Press, 1996.

Programming Windows 95, Charles Petzold, Microsoft Press, 1996.

Programming the Windows 95 Interface, Nancy Winnick Cluts, Microsoft Press, 1996.

Revolutionary Guide to MFC 4 Programming Using Visual C++, Mike Blaszak, Wrox Press Ltd., 1996.

I cannot say enough about the previous five books: *OLE Controls—Inside Out*, *Programming Windows 95 with MFC*, *Programming Windows 95*, *Programming the Windows 95 Interface*, and *Revolutionary Guide to MFC 4 Programming Using Visual C++*. They have been invaluable sources of information for me. All the authors are current or former Microsoft employees. I actually had the honor of meeting Charles Petzold (revered as the father of Windows) and Jeff Prosise (columnist for *Microsoft Systems Journal*) at Software Development 96 West Conference in San Francisco. Mike Blaszak is also a columnist for *Microsoft Systems Journal*, and his book has an excellent section on OLE with Visual C++.

Revolutionary Guide to Visual C++, Ben Ezzell, Wrox Press, 1996.

Teach Yourself SQL in 14 Days, Jeff Perkins and Bryan Morgan, Sams Publishing, 1995.

Teach Yourself ODBC in 21 Days, Jeff Perkins and Bryan Morgan, Sams Publishing, 1996.

Teach Yourself Visual C++ 4 in 21 Days, Gurewich & Gurewich, Sams Publishing, 1996.

Teach Yourself Visual C++ 4 in 21 Days is a great book for beginners. I was the technical editor for this book during its development and liked it so well I recommended it to my COBOL retreads to learn Visual C++ and MFC. The programmers I have recommended it to have raved about how well organized and easy to follow it is.

Teach Yourself Visual C++ in 21 Days, Namir Clement Shammas, Sams Publishing, 1996.

Teach Yourself Visual C++ in 12 Easy Lessons, Greg Perry, Sams Publishing, 1995.

The Visual Guide to Visual C++, Nancy Nicolaisen, Ventana Communications Group Inc., 1994.

Understanding ActiveX and OLE, David Chappell, Microsoft Press, 1996.

Visual C++ 4.0—Developing Professional Applications in Windows 95 and NT Using MFC, 2nd Ed., Marshall Brain and Lance Lovette, Prentice Hall, 1997.

One of the things I like about *Visual C++ 4.0—Developing Professional Applications in Windows 95 and NT Using MFC* is that it shows you how to do those little extras that make your applications look like a professional shrink-wrapped application. I purchased version 2.0 of this book, and I liked it so much I purchased version 4.0.

Visual C++ 2.0: A Developer's Guide, Alex Leavens, M & T Books, 1995.

Visual C++ Multimedia Adventure Set, Scott Jarol and Peter Aitken, Coriolis Group, 1995.

Visual C++ MasterClass, Wingo, Ramirez, et al., Wrox Press, 1996.

Visual C++ MasterClass is another book from Scott Wingo and others. This book covers several topics I have not seen covered in any other book, such as DirectX programming, MFC Library Extension programming, and Windows Sockets programming. It is a must for any professional library.

Visual C++ Programming, Steven Holzner, Brady Programming Series, 1994.

Visual C++ Unleashed, Viktor Toth, Sams Publishing, 1996.

Windows Interface Guidelines for Software Design, Microsoft Press, 1995.

Windows Interface Guidelines for Software Design is a must for any serious Windows developer. It contains essential guidelines for creating graphical user interfaces for the Windows family of operating systems.

Windows Programmer's Guide to Microsoft Foundation Class Library, Namir Clement Shammas, Sams Publishing, 1996.

Windows 95 Programming in C and C++, Herbert Schildt, Oracle Press, 1994.

Writing Windows Applications with MFC, Bryan Waters, M & T Books, 1994.

Internet

The Internet has brought an information explosion. There are thousands of sites cropping up every day. Here are some Internet sites I have found helpful in my development efforts:

Active Developer Support Program
`http://activex.adsp.or.jp/`

Active Xsite's Shortcuts—ActiveX Resources
`http://www.rapidramp.com/Users/kparker/index.htm`

ActiveX Controls from Alex Spektor
`http://www.voicenet.com/~aspektor/`

ActiveX Resource Center
`http://www.active-x.com/ie.htm`

ActiveX Resources
http://www.gamelan.com/pages/Gamelan.activex.html

ActiveX Source
http://ebola.science.org/ActiveX/

ActiveX Technologies
http://www-math.uni-paderborn.de/~sergiva/activex.html

C++ Virtual Library
http://info.desy.de/user/projects/C++.html

ClubIE Home Page
http://www.clubie.com/

Interface Technologies
http://www.iftech.com/

Manfred Schneider's 700+ Links
http://www.rhein-neckar.de/~cetus/software.htm

Microsoft Site Builder Workshop
http://www.microsoft.com/activex/

MFC FAQ
http://www.stingsoft.com/mfc_faq/

Microsoft Corporation
http://www.microsoft.com/

Poul Costinsky's Class Collection
http://www1.wizsoft.com/~Poul/srs

Stingray Software
http://www.stingsoft.com/

Welcome to ActiveXtra
http://www.activextra.com/

World Wide Web Consortium (W3C)
http://www.w3.org/pub/WWW/

WorldWide Live Activating the Internet
http://207.68.137.35/wwlive/

ZD Net's ActiveXfiles
http://www.zdnet.com/activexfiles/

Newsgroups and FAQs

With newsgroups, you can post questions to fellow developers in the hope that someone out there has the answer. Many times, developers from Microsoft browse the newsgroups and answer questions. Here are a few newsgroups that cover everything from MFC to OLE to C++:

```
comp.os.ms-windows.programmer.tools.mfc

comp.os.ms-windows.programmer.win32

comp.os.ms-windows.programmer.ole

comp.lang.c++

comp.os.ms-windows.programmer.tools

comp.os.ms-windows.programmer.misc

microsoft.public.vc.database

microsoft.public.vc.debugger

microsoft.public.vc.events

microsoft.public.vc.language

microsoft.public.vc.language.macintosh

microsoft.public.vc.mfc

microsoft.public.vc.mfc.docview

microsoft.public.vc.mfc.macintosh

microsoft.public.vc.mfcdatabase

microsoft.public.vc.mfcole

microsoft.public.vc.utilities
```

There are several great Frequently Asked Questions (FAQ) postings. FAQs are powerhouses of collected information.

By far, the best Visual C++/MFC FAQ I have ever seen is the MFC FAQ maintained by Scott Wingo. Scott is the CEO of Stingray Software and coauthor of *MFC Internals*, published by Addison Wesley. Stingray Software Corporation sells Objective Toolkit and Objective Grid MFC Library extensions. Scott's FAQ is such a superb source of information that Microsoft included it in the Microsoft Developer's Network Library. I highly recommend you check out this MFC FAQ.

Listed below are some FAQs that may be helpful in your programming endeavors:

C++ FAQ, Marshall Cline
FTP: `ftp.rtfm.mit.edu/pub/usenet/comp.lang.c`

MFC FAQ, Scott Wingo
Internet: `http://www.stingsoft.com/mfc_faq/`

Portable GUI FAQ, Wade Guthrie
Newsgroup Posting: `comp.windows.misc`

WinHelp FAQ, Pete Davis
Newsgroup Posting: `comp.os.ms-windows.programmer.winhelp`

Windows FAQ, Tom Haapanen
FTP: `ftp.metrics.com:~/faq`

Windows NT FAQ, Adam Hamilton
Newsgroup Posting: `comp.os.ms-windows.nt.misc`

Windows Programming FAQ, Tom Haapanen
FTP: `ftp.metrics.com:~/faq`

Summary

As you can see, there is a lot of information and support to aid you in the development of your Windows-based applications. Gone are the days of cryptic command-line help systems, poor support, and lousy documentation. Available through MSDN, the Internet, books, newsgroups, and FAQs, this type of support is unparalleled in any other development environment. I remember the days of clunking around on a VAX or a UNIX box, and I don't ever want to go back. Although development is still a dynamic and complicated process, the tools and information are available to allow software engineers to concentrate on solving the problem, not on searching for information.

I

Index

X-Y-Z

MACMILLAN COMPUTER PUBLISHING USA

A VIACOM COMPANY

Technical ----- Support:

If you need assistance with the information in this book or with a CD/Disk
accompanying the book, please access the Knowledge Base on our Web
site at **http://www.superlibrary.com/general/support**. Our most
Frequently Asked Questions are answered there. If you do not find the
answer to your questions on our Web site, you may contact Macmillan
Technical Support **(317) 581-3833** or e-mail us at **support@mcp.com**.